THE STRUCTURE OF PROPERTY LAW

In its essence, property law has to provide answers to two very difficult questions: who is entitled to use property, and how are they entitled to use it? Property law is therefore inherently difficult, but not impossibly so. It consists of an ordered and logical system, which aims to take the sting out of fierce disputes.

This book provides a new perspective on property law. By setting out an underlying structure, it allows the reader to understand the fundamental principles of this difficult subject. By providing detailed coverage of individual topics, it shows how those principles apply in practice and provides a comprehensive resource for anyone studying, teaching, researching or practising in property law.

The book is written in an accessible style, with frequent summaries and, in both its pages and companion website (www.hartpub.co.uk/companion/propertylaw.html), it makes use of helpful visual aids. It is ideal reading for law students seeking a rock-solid understanding of how property law and land law work, and contains sufficient detail for use as a course book in:

- Property law
- Land law
- Personal property law

The book also provides detailed analysis of core topics in:

- Equity and Trusts
- Commercial law
- Unjust enrichment and restitution

The Structure
of Property Law

Ben McFarlane

·HART·
PUBLISHING

OXFORD AND PORTLAND, OREGON
2008

Published in North America (US and Canada) by
Hart Publishing
c/o International Specialized Book Services
920 NE 58th Avenue, Suite 300
Portland, OR 97213-3786
USA
Tel: +1 503 287 3093 or toll-free: (1) 800 944 6190
Fax: +1 503 280 8832
E-mail: orders@isbs.com
Website: http://www.isbs.com

Hart Publishing, 16C Worcester Place, OX1 2JW
Telephone: +44 (0)1865 517530 Fax: +44 (0)1865 510710
E-mail: mail@hartpub.co.uk
Website: http://www.hartpub.co.uk

British Library Cataloguing in Publication Data
Data Available

ISBN: 978-1-84113-559-5

Typeset by Forewords Ltd, Oxford
Printed and bound in Great Britain by
TJ International Ltd, Padstow, Cornwall

PREFACE AND ACKNOWLEDGEMENTS

Law, unlike life, must have a structure. Life is messy and throws up impossible problems; law has to be clear and give us workable solutions. To do its job, the law cannot merely replicate reality: it must build its own set of rules. So lawyers, like architects or artists, have to construct something artificial. But artifice, like art or architecture, can have a clarity and coherence rarely seen in the mess of the real world.

Nonetheless, property law can be confusing. The official pronouncements of the legislature and judges may be unclear and incoherent. This book does not merely repeat what the legislature and judges have said; instead, it aims to explain what they have *done*. Just as the law imposes a structure on reality, a practically useful account of the law must uncover a structure to the existing legal rules. To do so, this book sometimes explains conventional rules in unconventional ways: sometimes you have to look a legislator or judge in the eye and have the courage to tell him exactly why he is right.

To the extent that this book attracts disapproval, that disapproval should be directed at me. To the extent that it attracts any credit, that credit should be shared around. I am very grateful to Professor Susan Bright, Professor Andrew Robertson and Dr James Edelman, each of whom provided comments on individual chapters, and to Dr Joshua Getzler who commented on all of Part I as well as Chapter F4. I have learned a great deal by teaching a Personal Property course with Mr William Swadling. I have also benefited from discussions with Professor Robert Stevens, particularly on the subject of persistent rights. I was fortunate to start the book during a term at the Hauser Global Law School of New York University School of Law. The Oxford University Faculty of Law provided funding for research assistance and I was lucky enough to have three excellent assistants: Dervla Kellagher, Adam Al-Attar and Tomas Furlong. Finally, the book has benefited greatly from the expertise, enthusiasm and efficiency of everyone at Hart Publishing.

20 May 2008

CONTENTS: OUTLINE

CONTENTS: DETAIL

TABLE OF CASES

Introductory Note

Cases are presented in alphabetical order without regard to jurisdiction: where a case was decided by a non-English court, the court is specified (ECHR refers to the European Court of Human Rights). A reference such as '409–11ex22' indicates that Example 22 as discussed on pages 409-11 is based on the case in question. Page numbers in red indicate that a section or subsection is principally devoted to discussion of the case, whilst those in **bold** indicate mentions in the body of the text rather than in footnotes alone.

TABLE OF LEGAL INSTRUMENTS

Introductory note

United Kingdom legislation is presented first, followed by other national legislation, international conventions and Roman law sources. Page numbers in red indicate that a section or subsection is principally devoted to the provision(s) in question, whilst those in **bold** indicate references in the body of the text rather than in footnotes alone.

United Kingdom

Statutory instruments

Other countries

Australia

Property Law Act 1958 (Victoria)

Part I

INTRODUCTION

CHAPTER A
THE BASIC TENSION OF PROPERTY LAW

A

THE BASIC TENSION OF PROPERTY LAW

1 THE PROPERTY LAW SYSTEM

Property law is about rights to use things. 'Things' are objects that can be physically located in a particular place: such as land, bikes or the knapsack of the boy on the cover of this book. Property law deals with two very common but impossibly difficult questions: (i) *who* is entitled to use a thing?; and (ii) *how* are they entitled to use it? Property law is therefore difficult, but not impossibly so. It consists of an ordered and logical system that aims to allocate rights to use things in a transparent and predictable way. This book aims to reveal that system and to demonstrate how it can be used to understand and evaluate property law.

It is often said that property law is boring. It is less often said that this is a remarkable compliment to the property law system. It shows how effective the system is in taking the heat out of important and controversial disputes.

EXAMPLE 1

A and B, lovers, move in to a home together. The land on which they live is owned by A. A, without telling B, then borrows money from C Bank. It is a 'mortgage' deal: in return for the loan, A gives C Bank, should A fail to repay the loan as agreed, a power to sell the land and use the proceeds to meet A's debt. A then fails to repay the loan as agreed. A has moved out but B remains in occupation of the land. C Bank wants to: (i) remove B from the land; (ii) sell the land; and (iii) use the proceeds to meet A's debt to C Bank.

C Bank wants to sell the land; but B wants to continue living there. We thus have a dispute about the rights of B and C Bank to use a particular thing: the land. A diagram helps us to understand the dispute; an animated slide assists further and can be viewed on www.hartpub.co.uk/companion/propertylaw.html.

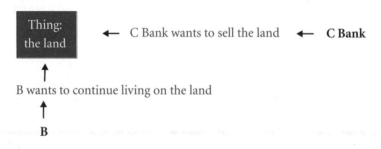

On the face of it, such a dispute should arouse violent passions. Should C Bank be allowed to evict B, in order to sell the land and recover money owed to it by A? Or should B be allowed to remain in his family home? The dilemma is acute enough in its own terms, but it also represents a wider clash between: (i) market forces and commerce; and (ii) social protection and home life.

The personal and political ramifications of the dispute between B and C Bank ought to interest even the most disaffected observer. Yet the property law system softens the sting of such contests. It provides a set of *technical rules* to determine whether B or C Bank is the winner. So the big-hitters of commerce and the home do not slug it out directly: the contest is settled over the chessboard, not in the boxing ring. Less destruction is caused; but fewer spectators are attracted.

Of course, chess can be interesting—but only if you know the rules. And the rules of the property law system are worth knowing. Their genius lies in their ability to deal with *both* very simple and very complex disputes. This means that, whilst the system is bewildering at first, cracking the code allows you to understand even the most difficult cases. And, once the rules are mastered, it is possible to get beyond the technical terms and to see the pervading themes and underlying tensions of property law. After all, no system, no matter how successful, can eliminate the sharp controversies surrounding: (i) *who* gets to use things; and (ii) *how* they get to use them.

2   THE BASIC TENSION OF PROPERTY LAW

The clash between B and C Bank, set out in **Example 1**, is simply an example of a more general dispute that the property law system must resolve.

EXAMPLE 2

B owns a bike. X steals that bike and sells it to C. C, when buying the bike, honestly believes that it belongs to X.

Who should now be permitted to use the bike: B or C? If C is allowed to use the bike, and chooses to do so, should he have to compensate B? It seems there are essentially four options to consider:[1]

	Who is permitted to use the bike: B or C?	Does that person have to pay money to the other party?
Option 1	B	No
Option 2	B	Yes: B must pay C
Option 3	C	Yes: C must pay B
Option 4	C	No

---

[1] Of course, both B and C have a right against X. However, those rights may be of little use in practice: X may be: (i) impossible to trace; or (ii) have no assets from which to pay B or C.

B will hope that the property law system goes for Option 1: (i) B is entitled to use the bike; and (ii) B does not have to pay any money to C. Options 2 and 3 are less attractive to B; and Option 4 is the worst for him.[2]

The structure of this dispute is clearly similar to **Example 1**. B may say that his prior right should be protected: he did not choose to give the bike away, so it should be returned to him. C could argue that commerce is best served if people who buy things in good faith are protected from the hidden claims of former owners.

There are thus important similarities between **Example 1**, involving land, and **Example 2**, involving a bike. In fact, it is possible to set out a general model for such cases:

1. B claims that he has acquired a right to make some use of a particular thing.
2. C claims that, at a later point in time, he too acquired such a right.
3. B and C wish to use that same thing in inconsistent ways, so a dispute arises.

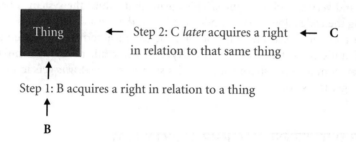

In such a case, there is a clear tension between: (i) protecting a prior user of a thing (B); and (ii) protecting a party who later deals with the thing (C). As a matter of moral reasoning there may well be no right answer to such a dilemma. However, a legal system must give an answer: this **basic tension between B and C**, which runs throughout the property law system, *must* be resolved. And, for the sake of consistency and certainty, a legal system must provide clear, settled rules to resolve the tension. Those rules are based on the **basic structure** of property law (see **Chapter B**).

3 THE BASIC TENSION AND LAND LAW

The **basic structure** of property law is based on core concepts that apply throughout the property law system. We will examine these concepts in the remainder of **Part I** (see **Chapter B and Chapters C1, C2 and C3**). Some parts of the property law system also have their own distinct rules: property law is about rights to use things; and some things are special. Land, for a number of reasons, is one such special thing. As a result, the land law system, whilst it rests on the same basic structure that applies throughout the property law system, forms a distinct part of that system. This is why each of **Parts II and III** is divided into: (i) a set of chapters looking at the general position, applying throughout the property

---

[2] The property law system currently goes for Option 3 (see **D1:3.5.1 and D1:4.3**); and, in rarer cases, Option 1 (see **D1:4.2**). In one of those rarer cases, Option 2 may be used if C, honestly believing the bike was his, has improved the bike and so increased its value (see **D1:4.4**).

law system (see **Chapters D1–D4 and F1–F4**); and (ii) a set of chapters looking at the special position, applying only in the land law system (see **Chapters E1–E6 and G1–G6**). A crucial question crops up throughout this book: is it really necessary to have a special set of rules for land? This must depend on whether, and how, land is different from other things.

3.1 The special features of land

3.1.1 Permanence

Subject to the rarest of exceptions,[3] land is permanent. Whereas other objects that can be physically located (eg bikes) wear out, the usefulness of land endures. This special feature of land is reflected by a special feature of the land law system: ownership of land can be split up over time (see **E1:1**).[4] For example, A, an owner of land, can give B a Lease: B then has ownership of that land for a limited period (see **G1B:1**). In contrast, if A is an owner of a bike, A *cannot* give B ownership of that bike for a limited period (see **D1:1.4.3**).[5]

3.1.2 Uniqueness

'Location, location, location': a crucial feature of any piece of land is its physical location. That physical location can never be shared by another piece of land. In this significant sense, all pieces of land are unique. This special feature of land explains two special rules of land law.

(i) Recovery of the thing itself from X or C?

First, let us say that: (i) B owns a thing, such as a bike; and (ii) X takes physical control of that thing without B's consent or other lawful authority. B can assert his right, as an owner of the thing, against X: by interfering with B's right, X commits a wrong against B. However, there is no guarantee that a court will order X to return the bike to B:[6] rather than getting his thing back, B may well have to settle for receiving money from X (see **D1:4.2**).[7] Similarly, in **Example 2**, the property law system *does* allow B to assert his prior right against C (see **D1:3.5.1**). However, in general, B will *not* be able to force C to return the bike itself: C is permitted to continue using the bike *provided* C pays money to B.

In contrast, if: (i) B has ownership of some land; and (ii) X takes physical control of that land without B's consent or other lawful authority; then (iii) a court *will* make an order (a 'possession order') allowing B to remove X and to take physical control of the land (see **E1:4.2**). This difference between land and other things thus relates to the **remedies question**: the question of how a court will protect B's right. It explains why land is

---

[3] See eg *Holbeck Hall Hotel Ltd v Scarborough BC* [2000] QB 836.

[4] 'E1:1' refers to **Chapter E1, section 1**.

[5] And 'D1:1.4.3' refers to **Chapter D1, section 1.4.3**.

[6] The court has a statutory discretion to make such an order: Torts (Interference with Goods) Act 1977, s 3(2)(a) (see **D1:4.2**).

[7] Instead, B can try to bypass the courts by simply taking his thing back from X. It seems B does have a right to do so where X's *initial* taking of physical control is a wrong against B. However, this form of 'self-help' is very risky: (i) there is no *general* rule that B can use reasonable force to recover a thing that he has wrongfully been deprived of (see *per* Tuckey LJ in *R v Mitchell* [2004] RTR 14 at [18]; *Devoe v Long* [1951] 1 DLR 203 (Court of Appeal of New Brunswick)); and (ii) even if B does have a right to retake control of his thing, he may commit a wrong if he uses excessive force (see eg *Revill v Newbery* [1996] QB 567 where B acted to defend his things from being wrongfully taken by C but used excessive force and thus committed a wrong against C).

sometimes known as 'real property'. 'Real' comes from the Latin for 'thing' (*res*); when used in the phrase 'real property' it indicates that B can recover the *thing itself* if wrongfully deprived of it by X or C.

(ii) Forcing A to transfer the thing itself to B?

Second, let us say A owns a bike and makes a contractual promise to sell his bike to B. A then changes his mind and refuses to go ahead with the promised sale. B can assert his right against A: by breaching his contractual duty to B, A commits a wrong against B. However, it is unlikely that the court will order A to transfer the bike itself to B; B will, almost always, have to settle for receiving money from A. The aim of remedies for breach of contract is to put B in the position he would have been in had A kept his promise: B's right is adequately protected if A gives B any money necessary to allow B to buy a similar bike elsewhere.

However, where A promises to transfer a *unique thing* to B, the position is different. To put B in the position he would have been had A kept his promise, A must give B the *thing itself*. So, in the rare case where A promises to transfer a unique bike to B, A may be ordered to keep his promise.[8] In contrast, if A promises to transfer land to B, the standard position is that a court will order A to keep his promise and to transfer his right to the land to B:[9] after all, each piece of land is unique. Again, this difference between land and other things relates to the **remedies question**: the question of how a court will protect B's right. Where B's contractual right is to acquire a right to land, it is, in general, specifically protected; where B's contractual right is to acquire a right to a thing other than land, B usually has to settle for receiving money.

3.1.3 Capacity for multiple simultaneous use

The same piece of land can be used in many different ways, by many different people, at the same time. For example, let us say:

1. A buys No 32 Acacia Gardens from A0.
2. A0 owns a local shop and makes A promise, when buying No 32, that neither A nor future owners of No 32 will use it as a shop.
3. A acquires No 32 with a 'mortgage' loan: in return for a loan from C Bank, A gives C Bank a security right (see **G4:1**). C Bank thus has a right, if A fails to pay back the loan to: (i) remove A and other occupiers from the land; (ii) sell the land; and (iii) use the proceeds to pay off A's debt.
4. In return for payment from E, a neighbour, A gives E a right to reach E's house by using a path crossing the garden of No 32.
5. A then moves away. He decides to keep the land and use it as an investment by renting it to B. So, in return for paying money to A, B is permitted to occupy the land. B uses the land as his home and allows his lover, D, to live with him.

Each of A0, A, B, C, D and E has a right to make some use (or at least to prevent a

---

[8] So eg if A has promised to transfer to B the very bike ridden by a winner of the Tour de France, B may be able to insist on specific performance of the contract. See eg *Thorn v Public Works Commissioners* (1863) 32 Beav 490. The Sale of Goods Act 1979, s 52 recognises that a court has a discretion to order specific performance of a contract to sell 'specific or ascertained' goods.

[9] There may always be an exception: see eg *Patel v Ali* [1984] Ch 283.

particular use) of the land. Things other than land are also capable of multiple, simultaneous use. If A owns a bike, A can: (i) give B permission to ride the bike; and (ii) offer his bike as security for a loan from C (see F4:1). The difference between land and other things is therefore one of *degree*. However, the difference remains important as it poses a significant question for the land law system: can it reconcile the competing desires of all those who simultaneously want to use the same piece of land? It certainly helps to explain another special feature of the land law system: the longer list of property rights in land (see E1:1).

3.1.4 Social importance

Land is uniquely capable of meeting important social needs. B can only acquire the sense of security and identity that comes with establishing a home[10] *if* he has some sort of right in relation to land. Similarly, it is very difficult to establish business premises without a right to use land. As a result, an interference with B's use of land can have dramatic consequences. For example, eviction from a settled home can cause great stress and disruption; eviction from business premises can cause grave commercial harm.

This special feature of land is reflected in a number of special rules. For example, if: (i) B occupies land as his home; and (ii) C unlawfully prevents B occupying that land *or* with the intention of causing B to leave the land, interferes with the 'peace or comfort' of B or members of B's household, then (iii) C commits a criminal offence.[11] Further, if B has ownership of some land, the rest of the world is under a prima facie duty not to unreasonably interfere with B's use and enjoyment of that land. So, if C's pig farm, next to B's land, produces nauseating smells, C breaches that duty and thus commits the wrong of nuisance against B.[12] However, C commits no such wrong if he interferes, in a similar way, with B's enjoyment of a thing other than land.[13] Further, in some circumstances, A and B's private agreement can be regulated by mandatory rules protecting B's use of land. So, if A gives B a Lease of land for one year, B may have a statutory right to remain even after the year has expired (see G1B:1.2).

This special feature of land also means that certain human rights may be of particular relevance in land law. For example, Article 8 of the European Convention on Human Rights states that: 'Everyone has the right to respect for his private and family life, his home and his correspondence.' So, in **Example 1**, B could argue that C Bank's attempt to force him out of his family home interferes with that human right. As we will see, this right is of course subject to qualifications (see B:8.3.2); but the social importance of land means that the right *may* have a role in shaping the rules of the land law system.

3.1.5 Limited availability

It is impossible to make more land.[14] This special feature of land has a number of conse-

---

10 For a consideration of the importance of the home see eg L. Fox, *Conceptualising Home* (2007), ch 1.

11 Protection from Eviction Act 1977, s 1 (see too E6:3.4.1(vi)). The description set out above is only a summary: for more detail see eg Bright, *Landlord and Tenant Law in Context* (2007) 686–9. See too Criminal Law Act 1977, s 6: C can be guilty of a criminal offence if: (i) B is in occupation of land and objects to C's entry onto the land; and (ii) C knows of B's presence and objection; and (iii) C, without lawful authority, uses or threatens violence in order to gain entry to the land. C does not commit the offence if he himself is a 'displaced residential occupier' (see s 6(3)), ie, if C, not a trespasser, was himself ousted by B (see s 12).

12 *Bone v Seale* [1975] 1 WLR 797.

13 To bring a claim in nuisance, B must have a property right in land: see *Hunter v Canary Wharf* [1997] AC 655.

14 It may, however, be possible to 'reclaim' land currently covered by water.

quences. First, coupled with the many valuable uses to which land can be put, it ensures that land is an *expensive commodity*. For most, acquiring ownership of land is impossible unless a lender, such as C Bank, is willing to provide a substantial loan. In return, C Bank will demand a security right over the land. Second, the limited availability of land intensifies the need for the stock of land to be *freely marketable*. As a result, it is particularly undesirable for an owner to remove land from the market by placing permanent restrictions on its use.

The limited availability of land, coupled with its importance and uniqueness, can lead to special limits being placed on an owner of land. For example, the need to promote the marketability of land has led the land law system to give protection to certain parties, such as C Bank in **Example 1**, who acquire rights relating to land. As we will see, registration rules, particularly prominent in land law, are one means of giving C such protection. Equally, the rules of the land law system have long tried to promote marketability by preventing an owner from limiting the use of land after his death.[15] Further, legislation commonly allows public bodies compulsory purchase powers: powers to acquire land from an owner in order to use it for a specific purpose, such as the building of a motorway.[16]

More startling is the doctrine of *adverse possession*: a means by which an owner of land can lose his right without receiving any compensation. Due to changes in the registered land system,[17] the doctrine of adverse possession now has much less of an impact. However, where it applies, its effect is dramatic. If: (i) X occupies B's land without B's consent;[18] and (ii) B fails, over a long period,[19] to take steps to remove X; then (iii) B's right to the land can be extinguished.[20] The doctrine only applies if X has been acting as an owner of the land: it protects X's claimed ownership, exercised over the long period, by extinguishing B's prior ownership. It can protect X even if X is fully aware that the land initially belongs to B.[21] In this way, the doctrine recognises X's claim (established by his long use) and removes the right of B, who has failed to make use of his land.

The doctrine of adverse possession applies only to land. If: (i) X takes physical control of B's bike without B's consent or other authority; and (ii) B fails, over a long period, to assert his ownership against X; then (iii) there is *no* general rule that the passage of time, by itself, can lead to B losing his ownership of the bike.[22] The limited availability of land supports the

---

[15] For a brief historical account see Birks, ch 18 in *Land Law: Themes and Perspectives* (ed Bright and Dewar, 1998) at 462–7.

[16] The general procedure to be followed where a public body exercises such a power is set out by the Acquisition of Land Act 1981 and the Compulsory Purchase Act 1965. The compensation payable to the party whose land is purchased is regulated by the Land Compensation Act 1961.

[17] In a case where B is registered as owner of the land (and such registration is now the norm) s 83 of the Land Registration Act 2002 replaces the previous rules with those set out in Sched 6 of the 2002 Act. We will discuss the new rules in detail in **E1:3.7.1** and **G1A.3**.

[18] The doctrine can apply where X initially occupies with B's consent, but that consent is then withdrawn: see eg *JA Pye (Oxford) Ltd v Graham* [2003] 1 AC 419 (see **Chapter B, Example 14a**). It can also apply where X has a property right allowing him to occupy the land, but that property right does not bind B: see eg *National Westminster Bank v Ashe* [2008] EWCA Civ 55.

[19] Under s 15 of the Limitation Act 1980, the period is set at 12 years. Under Sched 6 of the 2002 Act, if C adversely possesses for 10 years, he can apply to be registered (in B's place) as a new owner of the land. If B objects to C's application, but then fails (over the next two years) to take steps to remove C, C can then *insist* on being registered in B's place (see **E1:3.7.1**).

[20] Limitation Act 1980, s 17; Land Registration Act 2002, Sched 6.

[21] See eg *JA Pye (Oxford) Ltd v Graham* [2003] 1 AC 419.

[22] If, as in **Example 2**, X steals B's bike and sells it to C, B may lose his ownership of the bike if he does not bring a claim against C within six years from C's purchase of the bike: Limitation Act 1980, ss 3(2) and 4(2) (see **D1.3.7**).

idea that land is too scarce a commodity to remain under the ownership of a party who fails, over a long period, to assert his right. As seen above, it also heightens the need for land to be freely marketable. The doctrine of adverse possession certainly promotes that goal: the extinction of B's right not only protects X, but also anyone later acquiring a right from X (see further **B:8.3.1(iii)**).

3.2   The special features of land and the basic tension

The special features of land have an important effect on the basic tension. We can see this by going back to **Example 1**. In attempting to resolve such a dispute, we could look at the special features of land. However, this only reveals the true extent of the problem.

Special Features Favouring B	Special Features Favouring C Bank
Social importance: B is currently using the land as a home (note Article 8 of the European Convention on Human Rights)	**Limited availability**: High value of land means C Bank may have made a large loan to A and so will suffer a heavy loss if it cannot sell the land
Uniqueness: If B has to move, he may have to change many aspects of his life	**Limited availability**: The need to keep land freely marketable means that C Bank, when acquiring a right from A, should be protected from possible rights of B

On the one hand, B can point to the social importance of land: he is currently using the land as a home and uprooting that home will cause severe disruption. B can also point to the uniqueness of land: even if B is able to find a home elsewhere, it will be in a different location and so B may be forced to change many aspects of his life. So it might seem that the social importance and uniqueness of land should cause the rules of the land law system to lean in favour of someone, such as B, who is currently occupying or otherwise making use of land.

However, C Bank can make a powerful counter-argument. It may well have made a substantial loan to A: the limited availability of land, along with its social importance, ensures that land has a high value. So, if C Bank is unable to sell the land, it is likely to be left substantially out of pocket. It is also important to think about the wider consequences of finding in favour of B. First, whilst it is easy to have sympathy with B rather than with a faceless bank, it should be remembered that if banks have systematic problems in recovering loans, this can have repercussions not just for the bank's customers but for the wider economy.[23] Second, if C Bank is unable to sell the land, we need to consider the effect of such a decision on lenders' future practice. Will lenders have to carry out extensive and

---

However, the six-year period only begins to run *once* a party has bought the bike in good faith and so cannot help X: Limitation Act 1980, s 4(1).

[23] The importance to the wider economy of such banks has been dramatically emphasised by the UK Government's decision to nationalise Northern Rock plc using powers under the Banking (Special Provisions) Act 2008. The problems faced by that bank, a major 'mortgage' lender, were *not* caused by difficulties faced by the bank in recovering loans; but the highly unusual steps taken by the Government nonetheless demonstrate the importance of such banks to the wider economy.

expensive checks to ensure that there are no other users of the home who may later thwart a lender's attempt to sell the land? After all, as land is capable of multiple, simultaneous use, there may be many potential rights that a lender will need to watch out for. The costs incurred by lenders would then be passed on to borrowers. As land is already very expensive, this will make it harder still for would-be homeowners to enter the market. And, given its limited availability, it would be unfortunate if it became very difficult to trade in land. Given that we cannot produce new land, we should be particularly careful to make sure the land we do have does not become permanently burdened and thus difficult to buy or sell.

When first considering **Example 1**, we noted that the dispute between B and C Bank could be characterised as part of a wider clash between commerce and market forces on the one hand and the need for social protection and the maintenance of a home on the other. The fact that the dispute involves land, a special kind of thing, does *not* help us resolve this conflict; instead, it *heightens the tension*. The dispute between market forces and social protection thus draws out the ambivalent nature of land itself. On the one hand, it is of limited availability and constitutes an important financial investment: we therefore do not want the process of buying land to be unduly difficult. Yet on the other hand, it is unique and socially important: we therefore do not want to give insufficient protection to those who use and, in particular, occupy land. Moreover, as land is uniquely susceptible to multiple, simultaneous use, the sort of dispute we have discussed is more likely to arise in relation to land. The special nature of land therefore *affords greater opportunity* for the basic tension underlying property law to arise. It is for these reasons that land law is not only a special form of property law: it is also a form of property law specially worth studying.

4   THE SCOPE OF PROPERTY LAW

Property law is about rights to use things. However, as we will see throughout this book, the principles developed by the property law system can also be applied in other contexts.

EXAMPLE 3

A has an account with Z Bank. A goes into bankruptcy. A's rights, including his bank account, therefore pass to C, A's trustee in bankruptcy. C is under a statutory duty to use A's rights, including A's bank account, to pay off A's creditors. However, B claims that, *before* going bankrupt, A declared a Trust, in B's favour, of A's bank account.

In such a case: (i) C wants to use the value of A's account to pay off A's creditors; but (ii) B wants the value of A's account to be used solely for B's benefit.

In this case, there is no dispute about the use of a thing. A does not have a right to any *thing*: there is no specific bundle of banknotes in a safe at Z Bank that belongs to A. A instead has a *right* to receive from Z Bank, on demand, money equal to the credit in his account. Nor can A's right against Z Bank count as a thing: it certainly exists, but, unlike a plot of land or a bike, it is not an object that can be physically located in a particular place.[24]

---

[24] Gaius stated that 'All the law we use relates to persons, things or actions' (*Institutes* at 1.8: see eg *Institutes of Roman Law*, trans and ed De Zulueta, 1946). In that phrase, 'things' is given a different, *wider* meaning to the

Example 3 is therefore different from **Examples 1 and 2**. It is a dispute about the use of a *right*: B and C want to make inconsistent uses of A's right against Z Bank. There are, however, important similarities between **Example 3** and **Examples 1 and 2**. In particular, the very same model that applied to the first two examples also applies to **Example 3**:

1. B claims that he has acquired a right to make some use of a particular *right held by A*.
2. C claims that, at a later point in time, he too acquired such a right.
3. B and C wish to use that same *right held by A* in inconsistent ways, so a dispute arises.

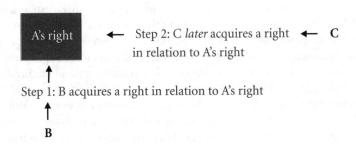

In **Example 3**, there is, again, a clear tension between: (i) protecting B (a prior user of a right held by A); and (ii) protecting C (a party who later deals with the right held by A). So, the **basic tension** can arise not only where there is a dispute about the use of a thing, but also where there is a dispute about the use of a right. As a result, *some parts* of the **basic structure** of property law apply not only to questions about the use of a thing but also to questions about the use of a right (see **B:10**). This means that, to learn about those parts of the basic structure, we will need to consider some cases where the dispute between B and C concerns the use of a right. For example, cases about Trusts of bank accounts (such as **Example 3**) may tell us important things about the general principles of Trusts that also apply to cases involving land or bikes.

Nonetheless, important parts of the basic structure of property law apply *only* to questions about the use of a thing and so *cannot* apply to questions about the use of a right (see eg **B:4.2** and **B:10**). Disputes about the use of a right are, strictly speaking, beyond the scope of the property law system.

meaning adopted in this book: it includes, for example, A's contractual right to receive money from Z Bank. Things in that broad sense can then be divided into: (i) corporeal things; and (ii) incorporeal things (see eg Gaius, *Institutes* at 2.12-2.14). The first category (corporeal things) equates to the meaning of 'things' adopted in this book. So, A's contractual right against Z Bank is, in Gaius's terms, an 'incorporeal thing'; and, in the terms used in this book, not a thing at all (see further **D1:1.1** and note too Pretto-Sakmann, *Boundaries of Personal Property* (2005), Part II).

SUMMARY AND STRUCTURE OF THE BOOK

Property law concerns rights to use things: objects that can be physically located in a particular place. It tells us: (i) *who* is entitled to use a thing; and (ii) *how* they are entitled to use it. Disputes between parties who wish to make inconsistent uses of a thing are inherently difficult and controversial. Such disputes demonstrate the **basic tension** that runs throughout property law between: (i) protecting B (a prior user of a thing); and (ii) protecting C (a party who later acquires a right to use that thing). That basic tension is evident in both Example 1, concerning the use of land, and Example 2, concerning the use of a bike. Due to the special features of land, that basic tension is particularly acute in Example 1.

The basic tension can also arise when B and C wish to make inconsistent uses of a *right initially held by A*. So in Example 3, concerning the use of A's bank account, some of the principles of the property law system may be relevant. However, as such a case does not involve the use of a thing, it is, strictly speaking, beyond the scope of the property law system.

The aim of the property law system is to provide a transparent and predictable means of allocating parties' rights, and hence of settling disputes such as those in Examples 1 and 2. To do so, the property law system relies on a **basic structure**. We will examine this structure in Chapter B. In Chapters C1, C2 and C3 we will look at three essential concepts that form part of that basic structure. The remainder of Part I thus consists of an introduction to the basic structure and basic concepts that apply *throughout* the property law system. In Parts II and III, we will look in more detail at those *general* rules (see Chapters D1–D4 and F1–F4); as well as looking at the *special* rules that make up the land law system (see Chapters E1–E6 and G1–G6).

CHAPTER B
THE BASIC STRUCTURE OF PROPERTY LAW: INTRODUCTION

B

THE BASIC STRUCTURE OF PROPERTY LAW: INTRODUCTION

1 THE BASIC SITUATION

In Chapter A, we looked at the basic tension that underlies property law and is particularly prominent in land law. In this chapter, we will examine the **basic structure** used to resolve this basic tension. To understand this structure, it is useful to concentrate on a particular set of facts: a **basic situation**.

The basic situation builds on the model applied to **A:Examples 1 and 2**.[1] It consists of two separate stages:

1. B claims that he has acquired a right to make some use of a particular thing.
2. C claims that, at a later point in time, he too acquired such a right.
3. B and C wish to use that same thing in inconsistent ways, so a dispute arises.

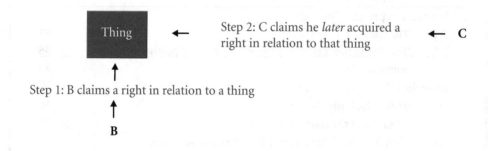

In discussing this basic situation, it will be helpful to use an example. We can use **A:Example 1**. In that case, a dispute arises as B and C want to make mutually inconsistent uses of the land owned by A. The purpose of the basic structure is to resolve the basic tension between B and C by choosing a winner. Of course, although the basic example will thus involve a dispute over land, it is important to remember that the general principles discussed can apply whether the dispute relates to: (i) land; or (ii) to a thing other than land.

---

[1] 'A:Examples 1 and 2' refers to Examples 1 and 2 in Chapter A.

2 ADDRESSING THE BASIC SITUATION: INITIAL POINTS

2.1 The dispute between B and C

EXAMPLE 1

A and B, lovers, move in to a home together. The land on which they live is owned by A. A, without telling B, then borrows money from C Bank. It is a 'mortgage' deal: in return for the loan, A gives C Bank, should A fail to repay the loan as agreed, a power to sell the land and use the proceeds to meet A's debt. A then fails to repay the loan as agreed. A has moved out but B remains in occupation of the land. C Bank wants to: (i) remove B from the land; (ii) sell the land; and (iii) use the proceeds to meet A's debt to C Bank.

The first step in any legal analysis is to ask: *what do the parties want?* The second step is to see *how the parties can get what they want.* That involves moving from the factual position to the legal one by asking what *rights* the parties have. In looking at the parties' rights, we can begin with two questions:

1. The **content question**: this asks if the right claimed by each party allows that party to get what he wants.
2. The **acquisition question**: this asks if that party has, on the facts of the case, acquired the right he claims.

So, in **Example 1**: (i) C Bank wishes to remove B and sell the land; and (ii) B wishes to remain in occupation of the land. Having established what B and C want, we first need to see if each party has a right to use the land as they wish. If only one of those parties has such a right, the dispute between B and C is easily solved. If B has no right to use the thing, and C does have such a right, then C will win; and vice versa. If both claims succeed, but B and C wish to use the thing in mutually consistent ways, there is no dispute: each of B and C can each enjoy his right without getting in the other's way.

The problem of course arises when: (i) *both* B and C have a right to use a thing; and (ii) B and C wish to use that thing in mutually *inconsistent* ways. This is the case in **Example 1**. B clearly has *some* right: at the very least, A has given B permission to share occupation of A's land. And C Bank certainly has acquired a right from A: C Bank has the power to sell A's land if A defaults on the loan repayments. A. As B and C Bank wish to use the land in inconsistent ways, the scene is now set for a dispute. The basic structure of the property law system will be used to resolve that dispute.

To understand the basic structure, it is useful to focus on cases, such as **Example 1**, where a dispute arises between B and C: it is in the heat of such a dispute that the principles of the property law system are forged. However, it would be a mistake to think that the basic structure is *only* relevant when a dispute arises. The property law system aims to allocate rights to use things in a transparent and predictable way. One of the reasons for doing so is to enable parties to *plan their affairs.* So, in **Example 1**, the property law system attempts to make clear to C Bank: (i) what type of right C Bank needs if it wishes to be able to sell the land should A default on the loan repayments (ie, to answer the **content question**); (ii) what C Bank needs to do to acquire that right (ie, to answer the **acquisition question**); and (iii) how and when B may be able to assert a prior right to use the land against C Bank. In this way, the system may allow C Bank to act in such a way as to *avoid* a dispute with B.

2.2   C's position: independent and dependent acquisition

It is useful to distinguish between two basic ways in which a party may acquire a right in relation to a thing.

1. *Dependent acquisition.* This is by far the most common method. It involves a party acquiring a right that derives from, and depends on, the rights of another. So, in **Example 1**, C Bank relies on a dependent acquisition: it claims that A has exercised his power, as an owner of land, to give C Bank a right in relation to that land.
2. *Independent acquisition.* This is a much rarer method. It involves a party acquiring a right through his own *unilateral* conduct.

EXAMPLE 2a

B is an owner of a bike. B loses the bike. It is found by C, who takes physical control of it.

Clearly, C cannot claim to have acquired a right *from* B: he has had no dealings with B. However, by his own action in taking physical control of the bike, C *independently acquires* a right to use the bike (see **D1:1.4.1** and **D1:2.1**). Of course, B still has his ownership of the bike: this means that *each* of B and C has a right to use the bike.[2]

EXAMPLE 2b

B is an owner of a bike. C steals the bike from B and takes physical control of it.

Again, C does not acquire a right from B. Again, by taking physical control of the bike, C independently acquires a right to use the bike. C acquires this right even though, in contrast to **Example 2a**, he has stolen B's bike and so has acted dishonestly. The point is that C independently acquires a right *whenever* he takes physical control of a thing (see **D1:1.4.1** and **D1:2.1**).[3]

2.3   C's position: where C is a creditor of A

C may acquire a right against A that is *unrelated* to the use of a particular thing. However, C's right, although initially unconnected to a particular thing, may ultimately allow C to use that thing. In such a case, a dispute can arise between B and C.

EXAMPLE 3

A and B, lovers, move in to a home together. The land on which they live is owned by A. A also owns a car. A is an electrician and enters a contract with C to rewire C's house. A acts carelessly when carrying out the job, causing a fire that destroys the contents of C's house. By doing so, A has committed a wrong against C and so C will have a right to obtain money from A.[4]

---

[2] Indeed, as we will see in D1:1.4.1, C, like B, is an owner of the bike.

[3] There may be circumstances in which C, because he takes physical control on behalf of his employer or principal, acquires a right for that other party rather than for himself. However, the better view is that, in such a case, C acquires *both* his own right and a right for the other party: see D1:2.1.

[4] The sum payable by A will represent the value to C of the rights A has interfered and compensate C for any relevant loss C has suffered as a consequence of A's wrongful conduct.

C's right against A seems unconnected to any particular thing. It is simply a right that A must act in a particular way: A must pay money to C. But what if A does not have professional liability insurance and cannot afford to pay C? If that is the case, there are two ways in which C may try to use a particular *thing* owned by A.

2.3.1 C is an execution creditor of A

In **Example 3**, if A refuses to pay him, C may go to court and obtain a judgment ordering A to pay C a sum of money. If A still refuses to pay, C can enforce his judgment by obtaining an *execution order*. Such an order permits a Sheriff or a bailiff,[5] acting with the court's authority, to seize particular things of A, such as A's car: if A still fails to pay, those things can be sold and the proceeds used to pay A's judgment debt.[6] However, if B claims that he has a right in relation to A's car, a dispute can arise between B and C: (i) C wants the car to be sold so that the proceeds of sale can be used to satisfy A's duty to pay C; but (ii) B wants to prevent such a sale.[7]

A further method of execution is for C to ask a court for a *charging order* over a right held by A: an order that, if A does not pay the money he has been ordered to pay C, C is allowed to sell A's right and to take the money due to him from the proceeds.[8] In **Example 3**, C is likely to apply for a charging order over A's most valuable right: his ownership of the land.[9] If C obtains such an order, his right is very similar to the right held by C Bank in **Example 1**: C has a power to sell A's land and to use the proceeds to meet a debt due to C.[10] And, as in **Example 1**, a dispute may arise: (i) C wants to sell the land; but (ii) B wants to remain in occupation.[11]

2.3.2 C has a claim in A's insolvency

In **Example 3**, if A is unable to pay the sum due to C, a further possibility is that A may *go into insolvency*.[12] If the extent of A's liabilities (A's duties to others) exceeds the value of his assets (A's rights), an insolvency procedure can be used to divide up the value of A's rights amongst those to whom A owes his duties (A's creditors). If A is an individual or a partnership, his insolvency means that his rights will pass to his *trustee in bankruptcy*.[13] If A

---

5 The Sheriff executes High Court judgments (see Civil Procedure Rules Sched 1, Rules of the Supreme Court Orders 46 and 47); a bailiff executes county court judgments (see Civil Procedure Rules, Sched 2, County Court Rules Order 26).

6 In the High Court, this is authorised by a writ of *fieri facias*; in the county court by a warrant of excecution.

7 See eg *Lock v Heath* (1892) 8 TLR 295; *Ramsay v Margrett* [1894] 2 QB 18.

8 See the Charging Orders Act 1979 and Civil Procedure Rules, Part 73, Section I.

9 Under the Charging Orders Act 1979, s 2(2)(a), a charging order can be made in respect of A's right.

10 Under the Charging Orders Act 1979, s 3(4) a charging order 'shall have the like effect and shall be enforceable in the same courts and in the same manner as an equitable charge created by [A].' C is thus treated as though he has a Purely Equitable Charge. In **Example 1**, C Bank will instead have a Charge: although very similar, those rights are different (see G4:1.4.2).

11 See eg *Pritchard Englefield v Steinberg* [2004] EWHC 1908.

12 If A is an individual or partnership, he will go into bankruptcy; if A Ltd is a company, it will go into insolvency. In this book, we will use 'insolvency' as a general term covering both cases.

13 A's right to his home will return to A if, three years after A becomes bankrupt, A's trustee in bankruptcy has not taken steps to sell the land: see Insolvency Act 1986, s 283A (inserted by the Enterprise Act 2002, s 261(1)). And any attempt by A's trustee in bankruptcy to sell A's land for that purpose will fail if A's land is of low value, so that a sale will bring relatively little benefit for A's creditors: see Insolvency Act 1986, s 313A (inserted by the Enterprise Act 2002, s 261(3)).

Ltd is a company, its insolvency means that an *administrator* or *liquidator* will take charge of A Ltd's rights. In each case, the trustee in bankruptcy or liquidator[14] will be under a duty to: (i) realise the value of A's rights (eg, by selling A's land and car); and (ii) distribute that value amongst A's creditors. In each case, the method of distribution is set out by statute.

In **Example 3**, A's insolvency can therefore lead to a dispute between B and C. C will want A's land and car to be available to A's trustee in bankruptcy so that: (i) A's land and car can be sold; and (ii) the proceeds used to pay A's creditors, including C. B may want to make an inconsistent use of the land and the car. As a result, a dispute may arise. In essence, this is a dispute between B and A's creditors (including C). Formally, however, it will be a dispute between B and A's trustee in bankruptcy: the latter acts on behalf of C and A's other creditors.

SUMMARY of B:2.3

Even if C acquires a right that is *not* related to the use of a thing, it is possible for B and C to find themselves in a dispute as to the use of a thing:

1. To enforce a judgment against A, C may obtain an *execution order* authorising a Sheriff or bailiff to: (i) seize a thing owned by A; (ii) sell that thing; and (iii) use the proceeds to meet A's judgment debt to C.
2. To enforce a judgment against A, C may obtain a *charging order* giving C a power to: (i) sell a thing owned by A; and (ii) use the proceeds to meet A's judgment debt to C.
3. If A goes into insolvency, A's trustee in bankruptcy or liquidator will have a statutory power to: (i) sell a thing owned by A; and (ii) use the proceeds to meet A's debts to C and to other creditors.

---

3   DIRECT RIGHTS

The **basic situation** arises where B and C wish to make mutually inconsistent uses of a specific thing. The property law system has to resolve the **basic tension** between B and C. The key question is whether B—the party who claims to have acquired his right *first*—can assert a right against C.

There are two basic ways in which B can have a right against C. First, B may have a **direct right** against C. A direct right is one that arises against C *because of C's own conduct*. Where B claims such a right, we again need to look at: (i) the **content question** (does the right claimed by B allow him to use the thing as B wishes?); and (ii) the **acquisition question** (has B, on the facts, acquired that right?).

Let us say that, in **Example 1**, C Bank made B a *contractual promise to B* that it would allow B to remain in occupation of the land. By virtue of C Bank's conduct in making that promise, B will acquire a direct right against C Bank; and that right will allow B to occupy the land. This direct right arises as a result of C Bank's conduct and is clearly different from any pre-existing right B may have acquired in his earlier dealings with A.

---

[14] In this book, whenever (as here) a point applies equally to an administrator or liquidator, we will simply refer to a liquidator.

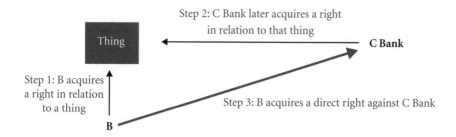

Step 2: C Bank later acquires a right in relation to that thing

Thing

C Bank

Step 1: B acquires a right in relation to a thing

Step 3: B acquires a direct right against C Bank

B

It is worth noting that, in **Example 1**, as in many other cases, the chances of B establishing a direct right against C Bank are very slim. Such a right can only arise from C Bank's conduct. And it has no obvious reason to act in such a way as to give B a direct right. For instance, in **Example 1**, C Bank's aim in acquiring a right from A is to have a power, if A cannot pay back the loan, to sell the land and use the proceeds to meet A's debt. It will be very difficult, if not impossible, for C Bank to sell the land for a decent price if B remains in occupation. So there is no good reason for C Bank to give B a direct right by, for example, making a contractual promise to allow B to continue living in the home.

Nonetheless, as there is always a *chance* that B may have acquired a direct right against C, it is important to keep direct rights in mind. Certainly, some property law disputes are impossible to understand if you overlook the possibility that B may have a direct right against C.[15] However, the relative rarity of such rights focuses attention on the second means by which B can assert a right against C.

4 PRE-EXISTING RIGHTS

If he cannot assert a direct right against C, B will need to show he has a different form of right. This right must be one that: (i) does *not* arise as a result of C's conduct; *but* (ii) can nonetheless bind C. For instance, in **Example 1**, it is very likely that B, in his dealings with A, will have acquired a right to make some use of A's land: at the very least, B will have permission to occupy the land with A. The crucial question is whether B's right, although it was acquired from A, is capable of binding C Bank.

4.1 Personal rights

EXAMPLE 4

A makes a contractual promise to B to mow B's lawn. A then gives his mower to C, as a gift.

B obviously cannot claim that *C* is under a duty to mow B's lawn. Although B's right is a pre-existing one—it arose before C bought the mower—it clearly cannot bind C. A's contractual promise gives B a right against A, and *only* against A. Such a right is known as a *personal right: a right against a person*. It is a right that *A must act in a particular way*.[16] For

---

[15] See eg *Binions v Evans* [1972] Ch 359 and *Ashburn Anstalt v Arnold* [1989] Ch 1 (see E6:3.4.1).

[16] Compare Justinian's Institutes at 3.13: 'An obligation is a legal tie which binds us to the necessity of making some performance in accordance with the laws of our state': see *Justinian's Institutes* (trans and ed Birks and McLeod, 1987).

B to assert such a right, he must find A: the particular person bound it. So, if B acquires a personal right against A, that right can never bind C.

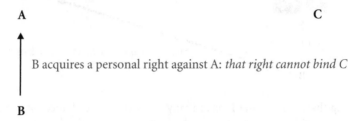

A   **C**

B acquires a personal right against A: *that right cannot bind C*

B

However, fortunately for B, personal rights are not the only type of right. It is possible to acquire a different type of right that, whilst not acquired from C, *is* capable of binding C. There are two types of pre-existing right that have this ability to bind C: *property rights* and *persistent rights.*

4.2   Property rights

A property right is a right that: (i) relates to a thing; *and* (ii) imposes a prima facie duty on the rest of the world (see **D1:1.1**). So, if B has a property right: (i) B has a right to make some use of a particular physical object (eg, land, a bike); *and* (ii) the rest of the world (including C) is under a prima facie duty to B not to interfere with B's use of that thing. So, to assert such a right, B does not need to find a particular person (such as A); rather, he needs to find a particular thing. Once B has found that thing, he can (prima facie) assert his right.

For this reason, property rights are often referred to as *rights in a thing;* or *rights against a thing.* We will use both terms in this book as each provides a useful shorthand way to capture the key attribute of a property right. The latter term draws a useful distinction between a personal right (a right against a person) and a property right (a right against a thing). Strictly speaking, it is misleading: all rights are rights against people.[17] However, if we say that, because he owns a bike, B has a right against that bike, we clearly do *not* mean that B can sue the bike. Rather, we mean that B has a right that imposes a prima facie duty on the rest of the world. Of course, 'prima facie' is important here: it recognises the fact that it may be possible for someone to have a **defence** to B's property right (see **section 5** below).

Despite that possibility, a property right is still tremendously useful to B. If: (i) B has only a personal right against A; then (ii) it is impossible for B to assert that right against C. However, if:

1.   B has a property right in a specific thing; and
2.   C interferes with B's use of that thing; then
3.   C is in breach of a prima facie duty to B; and so

---

[17] See eg Hohfeld (1917) 26 *Yale LJ* 710. Hohfeld prefers to see a property right as a 'multital right': so if B has ownership of a bike, then he has a personal right against each of A, C, D, E, F, etc, as each of them are under a duty not to interfere with his exclusive control of the bike. This raises the question of how property rights differ from other rights good against the rest of the world (eg, each of A, C, D, E, F, etc, is also under a duty not to punch B): this point is discussed in **D1:1.1.1**.

4. If C has no defence to B's property right, C has committed a wrong against B; and so
5. B has a personal right against C, arising as a result of C's commission of the wrong against B (see **D1:4.1.1**).

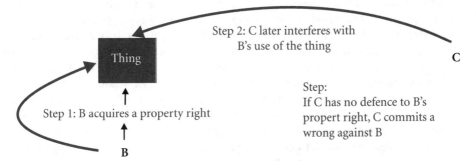

Step 2: C later interferes with B's use of the thing

C

Thing

Step:
If C has no defence to B's propert right, C commits a wrong against B

Step 1: B acquires a property right

B

Ownership is an obvious example of a property right. If B owns land or a bike, the rest of the world is under a prima facie duty to B. It does not matter *who* takes B's bike: whether it is A, C, D, E or X, that party commits a wrong against B *unless* he can show he has a **defence** to B's pre-existing property right. For instance, let us say that, in **Example 1**, B acquired ownership of A's land before C Bank acquired its right from A. B thus has a pre-existing right that counts as a property right. That means C Bank, along with the rest of the world, is under a prima facie duty not to interfere with B's right to exclusive control of the land (see **G1A:4.1**).

Therefore, when considering property rights, there is a crucial dimension to the **content question**. B will need to show that, because of its content, his right *counts as a property right*. As property rights have the special quality of imposing a prima facie duty on the rest of the world, the property law system recognises only a limited list of such rights (see **D1:1.2**). And, as far as the **acquisition question** is concerned, B may also have to satisfy special requirements in order to show that he has acquired a property right. For instance, let us say that, in **Example 1**, A has registered his ownership of the land. If so, to show he has acquired a property right in that land, B will generally need to show that he too has registered his right (see **C2:6** and **E1:2.3**). This registration requirement gives third parties, such as C Bank, a chance to discover the existence of B's property right before deciding whether to deal with the land.

There will thus be many cases in which B is unable to claim a pre-existing property right. It may be that: (i) B fails the content question, as his right is not on the list of permitted property rights; or (ii) B fails the acquisition question, as he cannot show, for example, that he satisfied a registration requirement. In such cases, fortunately for B, there is a second form of pre-existing right that *may* be capable of binding C: a persistent right.

4.3 Persistent rights

If: (i) A is under a duty to B; and (ii) A's duty to B relates to a specific right held by A; and (iii) that specific right is a claim-right or power;[18] then (iv) B has a persistent right. A persistent right is a *right against a specific right held by A*. To assert such a right, B does not

---

[18] For the meaning of this third requirement, see **D2:1.1.3**.

need to find a particular person (such as A); nor does he need to find a particular thing (such as a piece of land or a bike). Instead, B needs to show that C has acquired a right that *depends on the right held by A*. So, in **Example 1**, C Bank acquired a right from A: C Bank's right derives from, and thus depends on, A's ownership of the land. If B can show that he has a pre-existing right against A's ownership of the land, B has a prima facie power to impose a duty on C Bank. The point is that, in such a case, B can draw a link between: (i) the right acquired by C Bank; and (ii) the right against which B has a right (A's ownership of the land). Of course, 'prima facie' is important here: it recognises the fact that it may be possible for someone to have a **defence** to B's persistent right (see **section 5** below).

It is important to emphasise that the *term* 'persistent right', used throughout this book, is a novel one. However, the *concept* is not novel: the term 'persistent right' is used to refer to any right usually called an 'Equitable property right'.[19] That more orthodox term is rejected because it is misleading (see **4.4** below). In particular, it suggests a false analogy between true property rights and persistent rights.

In this book, persistent rights will often be referred to as *rights against a right*. That term draws a useful distinction between such rights and: (i) personal rights (rights against a person); and (ii) property rights (rights against a thing). Strictly speaking, the term 'right against a right' is misleading: all rights are rights against people. However, if we say that B has a right against A's ownership of a bike, we clearly do *not* mean that B can sue A's ownership of the bike. Rather, we mean that if:

1. B has a persistent right against a specific right held by A; and
2. C acquires a right that depends on A's right; then
3. B has a prima facie power to impose a duty on C; and so
4. If C has no defence to B's persistent right; then
5. If B exercises his power (or C is otherwise aware of B's persistent right); then
6. C comes under a duty to B; and so
7. B has a personal right against C (see **D2:4.1.1**).

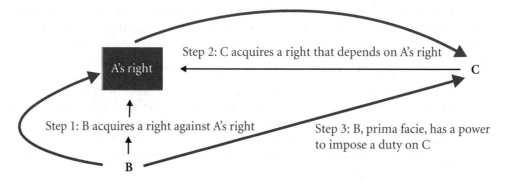

If B claims he has a persistent right, then there is, again, an extra dimension to the **content question**: B needs to show his right counts as a persistent right. However, in contrast to property rights, there is no set list of persistent rights (see **D2:1.4**). Instead, B has a

---

[19] The term 'persistent right' is also used in this book to refer to some rights *not* usually called 'Equitable property rights' (see **4.4.2** below).

persistent right whenever: (i) A is under a duty to B; and (ii) A's duty relates to a specific right held by A; and (iii) that specific right is a claim-right of a power. The content question is thus far easier for B to satisfy. As for the **acquisition question**, B simply needs to show that A has come under such a duty. There are many different means by which A can come under a duty to B (see **D2:2**). The reasons for which A's duty may arise can be classified into six different groups:

1. A's consent to be under such a duty to B;
2. A's entry into a contract with B;
3. A's commission of a wrong against B;
4. A's unjust enrichment at B's expense;
5. A statute imposing a duty on A to B;
6. A residual group of 'other events' that impose a duty on A to B.

If one of those six reasons leads to A being under a duty to B, then B has a *personal right* against A. So, in **Example 4**, A is under a duty to B due to reason 2 above: A's entry into a contract with B.

If A's duty *also* relates to: (i) a specific right held by A; that is (ii) a claim-right or a power; then (iii) B *also* has a *persistent right*. That is *not* the case in **Example 4**: A's duty is simply to act in a particular way (to mow B's lawn); it does *not* relate to a specific claim-right or power held by A.[20]

There will thus be many cases in which: (i) B cannot show he has a pre-existing property right; but (ii) B *can* show that he has a pre-existing persistent right. In **Example 1**, it may be impossible for B to show he has a pre-existing property right in A's land. Certainly, if ownership of the land is registered in A's sole name, B cannot claim that he has ownership of the land. However, a persistent right may come to B's rescue. For example, if: (i) B contributed to the cost of paying for the land; (ii) without making a gift or a loan to A; then (iii) A may well be under a duty to use his ownership of the land, to a certain extent, for B's benefit (see **G3:2.2 and G3:2.4.3(v)**). If so, B will have a persistent right: a right against A's ownership of the land. Crucially, B can acquire such a right without needing to register it (see **C2:6**). If B has a persistent right, then as C Bank acquired a right that depends on A's ownership of the land, B will have a prima facie power to impose a duty on C Bank.

4.4 The differences between property rights and persistent rights

Judges, statutes and commentators do not use the term 'persistent rights'. Instead, they refer to persistent rights as 'Equitable property rights' or, where land is involved, as 'Equitable interests in land'. On this orthodox analysis, persistent rights are seen as a type of a property right. However, to account for the very important differences between true property rights and persistent rights, this orthodox analysis then divides property rights into two categories: (i) Legal property rights; and (ii) Equitable property rights.

---

[20] It could be said that A's duty relates to A's liberty not to mow B's lawn: but a duty relating to a liberty does not give B a persistent right (see **D2:1.1.3**).

Orthodox view	View taken in this book
Legal property rights	**Property rights**
Equitable property rights	**Persistent rights**

On the orthodox view, property rights come in two flavours: (i) Legal; and (ii) Equitable. That distinction depends entirely on history. England once had two separate court systems: Common Law and Equity (see **C1:1**). If a pre-existing right capable of binding third parties was first recognised in a Common Law court, it is called a Legal property right. If it was first recognised in a court of Equity, it is called an Equitable property right.

On the view taken in this book, there are two particular types of pre-existing right that may lead to C being under a duty to B: (i) a right against a thing (a property right); and (ii) a right against a right (a persistent right). So, like the orthodox account, this book identifies two different sorts of pre-existing rights that are capable of binding third parties. The orthodox view divides the rights according to their *historical origin*; this book categorises the rights according to their *nature*. Which view is better?

In defence of the orthodox view, it is certainly true to say that property rights and persistent rights share a very important feature. Unlike a pre-existing personal right against A, a pre-existing property right or persistent right of B is capable of binding C. In particular, consider what happens if A goes into insolvency. If B has: (i) a pre-existing property right; or (ii) a pre-existing persistent right; then (iii) B's right will be prima facie binding on A's trustee in bankruptcy.[21] So if, by 'property right' you mean 'any pre-existing right that is capable of binding A's trustee in bankruptcy', then it makes sense to include a persistent right within your definition of 'property right'.

However, the key problem with the orthodox view is that it hides two vital differences between property rights and persistent rights.

4.4.1 Does B's right relate to a thing?

EXAMPLE 5

A has an account at Z Bank. A declares that he holds that right against Z Bank on Trust for B. A goes into bankruptcy. A's rights, including his bank account, therefore pass to C, A's trustee in bankruptcy.

In such a case, A has a personal right against Z Bank (see **A:Example 3**). A holds that right on Trust for B. As a result of A's consent to holding his right on Trust for B (ie, due to reason 1 set out in **4.3** above), B has a personal right against A. However, B has *more* than a mere personal right against A. A is under a duty to use his bank account for B's benefit: A's duty to B thus relates to a specific claim-right held by A. As a result, B has a persistent right: a right against A's personal right against Z Bank. So, B's right under the Trust is prima facie binding on C: B can thus prevent C withdrawing money from the bank account and distributing it amongst A's creditors.

In **Example 5**, B has a pre-existing right that is capable of binding C. So, on the orthodox view, B has a property right. B's particular property right (the right under a Trust) was first

---

[21] If A is a company (A Co) and goes into liquidation or administrative receivership, A Co's liquidators or receivers will also be bound by any pre-existing property rights and persistent rights in relation to A Co's assets.

recognised by courts of Equity; so, B has an 'Equitable property right'. However, that term is misleading. It seems odd to call B's right a property right when *it does not relate to any specific physical object*. After all, B acquired his right under the Trust from A and, as we saw in **A:Example 3**, A does not have a property right. So, on the orthodox view, we are left with the odd position that:

1. A has only a personal right against Z Bank; *but*
2. By declaring a Trust of that right in B's favour, A can give B an (Equitable) property right.

In **Example 5**, it makes no real sense to say that B has an 'Equitable property right'. B clearly cannot have a property right: a property right is a right against a thing and, in **Example 5**, there is no thing against which B can possibly have a right.

One way to defend the orthodox view would be to say that, in **Example 5**: (i) B's right relates to A's personal right against Z Bank; and (ii) A's personal right against Z Bank counts as a thing; and so (iii) B has a right against a thing. However, there are two responses to that defence.

- *Response 1*: The defence blurs the key distinction between: (a) things; and (b) rights. And you do not need to be a lawyer to see the clear difference between (a) a piece of land, or a bike; and (b) A's right that Z Bank pay him the sum credited to his bank account. In fact, you need to be a lawyer to think that (a) and (b) could *ever* be seen as the same (see further **D1:1.1.1**).
- *Response 2*: In any case, the defence of the orthodox view simply amounts to saying that, in **Example 5**, B has a right against A's right against Z Bank. That is certainly true: but, rather than pretending that A's right against Z Bank is a thing, it is clearer to say that B has a *right against A's right*. That leads us to the view taken in this book. So, in **Example 5**, B has a persistent right: a right against A's right against Z Bank. When C acquires A's right, B has a prima facie power to impose a duty on C: a duty not to use the bank account for any purpose not permitted by B.

4.4.2 Does B have a right against a right?

EXAMPLE 6a

A has a personal right against Z, who owes A £100. A expresses his intention to make an immediate transfer of the benefit of that right to B. A thus makes an 'Equitable assignment' of that right in favour of B. A then goes into insolvency and his personal right against Z passes to C, A's trustee in bankruptcy.

In such a case, as a result of A's consent (ie, due to reason 1 set out in **4.3** above), B has a personal right against A. However, B has *more* than a mere personal right against A. B's right, arising as a result of the Equitable assignment, is prima facie binding on C: B can thus impose a duty on C not to use the right against Z for any purpose other than B's benefit.[22]

In **Example 6a**, B has a right that (i) can bind C; and (ii) was initially recognised by courts of Equity. However, on the orthodox view, B is *not* regarded as having an 'Equitable

---

[22] See eg *Holt v Heatherfield Trust Ltd* [1942] 2 KB 1.

property right'. On the orthodox view, this makes it difficult to explain why B's right is capable of binding C. One possible explanation comes from the term 'Equitable assignment': it could be said that A's right has somehow been *transferred* to B. However, in **Example 6a**, there is *no* transfer of A's right to B. For example, it is clear that B *cannot* bring a direct claim against Z, as B has no right against Z (see **D2:1.2.2**).[23]

Instead, in **Example 6a**: (i) A *keeps* his right against Z; and (ii) A comes under a duty to B in relation to that right. This means that, although B has no direct right against Z, B *can* force A to: (i) bring a claim against Z; and (ii) pay the proceeds of that claim to B.[24] Further, as A's duty to B relates to a specific claim-right held by A, it means that B has a persistent right: a right against A's right. That explains why B has a power to impose a duty on C not to use the right against Z for any purpose other than B's benefit.

EXAMPLE 6b

B Ltd provides shipping insurance to A Co. A Co's ship is then damaged by the carelessness of Z. A Co's policy with B Ltd covers that form of damage; B Ltd therefore pays A Co under the insurance policy. A Co then goes into insolvency; C is appointed as its liquidator.

Z has committed a wrong against A Co by carelessly damaging A Co's ship. A Co therefore has a personal right against Z, arising as a result of Z's wrong (ie, due to reason 3 set out in **4.3** above). However, once it has received the insurance payment from B Ltd, A Co is *not* free to use its personal right against Z for its own benefit. Instead, A Co is under a duty, said to arise under the principle of *subrogation*, to use its personal right against Z for B Ltd's benefit. That duty arises as a result of an express[25] or implied[26] term in A Co's insurance policy: ie, due to reason 2 set out in **4.3** above.[27]

However, B Ltd has *more* than a mere personal right against A. B Ltd's right is prima facie binding on C: B Ltd can thus prevent C claiming money from Z and then distributing that money amongst A's creditors.[28] So, in **Example 6b**, B has a right that: (i) can bind C; and (ii) was recognised by courts of Equity.[29] However, on the orthodox view, B is *not* regarded as having an 'Equitable property right'. On the orthodox view, this makes it

---

[23] See eg *Brandt's Sons & Co v Dunlop Rubber Co* [1905] AC 454.

[24] B can use an expedited procedure to combine in one action (i) his claim against A, and (ii) A's claim against Z. However, that procedure cannot disguise the fact that two *separate* rights are involved and that B has no direct right against Z: see eg *Weddell v JA Pearce & Major* [1988] Ch 26 at 40; *MH Smith (Plant Hire) Ltd v DL Mainwaring* [1986] 2 Lloyds Rep 243 *per* Kerr LJ at 246. Compare **n 30** below.

[25] See Mitchell and Watterson, *Subrogation* (2nd ed, 2007) at 10.166ff.

[26] It seems that in *any* such insurance policy there is an implied contractual promise by A Co to use any right it acquires against a party such as Z for B Ltd's benefit: see eg *per* Lord Goff in *Lord Napier and Ettrick v Hunter* [1993] AC 713 at 744; *per* Lord Hoffmann in *Banque Financière de la Cité v Parc (Battersea) Ltd* [1999] 1 AC 221 at 231.

[27] An alternative analysis is that, in the absence of an express contractual promise by A Co, B Ltd's right arises because of: (i) the need to ensure A Co is not compensated twice over by suing Z and keeping the money; and (ii) the need to ensure Z, rather than B Ltd, bears the cost of the loss caused by Z. See *Somersall v Friedman* [2002] 3 SCR 109 (Supreme Court of Canada) esp *per* Iacobucci J at [50]; See Mitchell and Watterson, *Subrogation* (2nd ed, 2007) at 10.30ff. On that view, A Co's duty arise because of a combination of reasons 4 or 6 set out in **4.3** above (see eg Burrows, *The Law of Restitution* (2nd ed, 2002) at 108–12).

[28] See eg *Holt v Heatherfield Trust Ltd* [1942] 2 KB 1.

[29] In *Yorkshire Insurance Co Ltd v Nisbet Shipping Co Ltd* [1962] 2 QB 330, Diplock J noted at 339 that: 'although often referred to as an 'Equity' [subrogation] is not an exclusively equitable doctrine'. However, his Lordship also acknowledged that Equity's assistance was crucial in allowing B Ltd to force A Co to assert its personal right against Z.

difficult to explain why B Ltd's right is capable of binding C. Certainly, B Ltd does *not* have a direct right against Z: it is impossible for B Ltd to sue Z directly. Instead, as in **Example 6a**, B can force A Co to: (i) bring a claim against Z; and (ii) pay the proceeds of that claim to B.[30]

Therefore, in *both* **Examples 6a and 6b**: (i) A Co *keeps* its right against Z; and (ii) A Co comes under a duty to B Ltd in relation to that right. As A Co's duty to B Ltd relates to a specific claim-right held by A Co, it means that B Ltd has a persistent right: a right against A Co's right. That explains why B Ltd has a power to prevent C making a claim against Z and then using the proceeds to pay A Co's creditors.

The orthodox view thus hides the facts that certain rights, not conventionally thought of as 'Equitable property rights', are in fact persistent rights. The category of persistent rights is thus more useful than the orthodox category: it allows us to see the important similarity between: (i) B's right in **Example 5**; and (ii) B's right in each of **Example 6a** and **Example 6b**.

4.4.3 Is the rest of the word under a prima facie duty to B?

EXAMPLE 7a

A owns a bike and declares that he holds the bike on Trust for B. X then carelessly damages the bike.

EXAMPLE 7b

A owns a bike and declares that he holds the bike on Trust for B. X then steals the bike.

In each case, X does *not* breach any duty to B. B has no right that he can assert against X.[31] In each case, X has interfered with A's right, as an owner, to exclusive control of the bike. X has thereby committed a wrong *against A* and so A has a personal right to sue X. However, B has no such right. It is worth noting that, as A holds his ownership of the bike on Trust for B, A is under a duty to use that right, and its products, for B's benefit. So, if, in **Example 7a or 7b**: (i) A refuses to bring a claim against X, then (ii) B can apply to court to force A to make such a claim.[32] B can use an expedited procedure to combine such an application with A's claim against X.[33] However, that procedural concession cannot hide the key fact that two

---

[30] See eg *Yorkshire Insurance Co Ltd v Nisbet Shipping Co Ltd* [1962] 2 QB 330 at 339 *per* Diplock LJ; *Esso Petroleum Ltd v Hall Russell & Co Ltd, The Esso Bernica* [1989] AC 643 at 663 *per* Lord Goff. B Ltd can again use an expedited procedure to combine in one action (i) his claim against A Co; and (ii) A Co's claim against Z. However, that procedure cannot disguise the fact that two *separate* rights are involved and that B Ltd has no direct right against Z: see eg *MH Smith (Plant Hire) Ltd v DL Mainwaring* [1986] 2 Lloyds Rep 243.

[31] For **Example 7a**, see eg *Leigh and Sillivan Ltd v Aliakmon Shipping Co Ltd (The Aliakmon)* [1986] AC 785. For **Example 7b**, see eg *MCC Proceeds v Shearson Lehmann* [1998] 4 All ER 675; Tettenborn [1996] *CLJ* 36.

[32] It is also worth noting that, in *some* cases where A holds a right on Trust for B, B has a power to force A to transfer that right to B: see **D1:1.4.5(ii)** discussing B's '*Saunders v Vautier* power'. So, *if* the right held on Trust by A is a property right and *if* B has this power, B can acquire a property right by exercising the power. However, even if the right held on Trust by A is a property right, this clearly does not mean that B has a property right in cases where he does not have the power, or has not yet exercised it.

[33] That expedited procedure is commonly referred to as the *Vandepitte* procedure (see eg *Barbados Trust Company Ltd v Bank of Zambia* [2007] EWCA Civ 148 at [30] and [35] *per* Waller LJ) and is named for the case: *Vandepitte v Preferred Accident Insurance Corporation of New York* [1933] AC 70.

separate claims must be made: B has no direct claim against X as X has infringed no right of B.[34]

On the orthodox view, B's right under the Trust counts as an 'Equitable property right' (see **Example 5**). On that view, it is difficult to explain why, in **Examples 7a and 7b**, X does not commit a wrong against B. Certainly, if B's right under the Trust were *really* a property right (a right against a thing), we would expect X's action to count as a wrong against B. After all, in each case: (i) X has interfered with B's use of the bike; and (ii) X has no defence to B's pre-existing right under the Trust. Yet it is absolutely clear, that in **Examples 7a and 7b**, X does *not* commit a wrong against B (see further **D3:2.3.9**).

One response to this is to say that the *entire category* of 'Equitable property rights' should be rejected: **Examples 7a and 7b** can then be explained by saying that a right under a Trust is, in fact, no more than a personal right against A.[35] However, that response cannot be correct.

EXAMPLE 7c

A owns a bike and declares that he holds it on Trust for B. A then goes into bankruptcy and his ownership of the bike passes to C, his trustee in bankruptcy.

EXAMPLE 7d

A owns a bike and declares that he holds it on Trust for B. A then gives the bike to C as a gift. C has no idea that A held the bike on Trust for B; nor could C reasonably have been expected to know about the Trust.

In each case, B has a power to impose a duty on C. If B exercises that power, then, in each case, C is under a duty to B *not* to use the bike for any purpose other than B's benefit. In each case, B can then force C to transfer the bike to T (a party who has agreed to hold the bike on Trust for B).[36]

If B's initial right under the Trust is only a personal right against A, **Examples 7c and 7d** are very hard to explain. It could be said that B's power to impose a duty on C is a *direct right*, arising as a result of C's conduct.[37] On that view, it is *not* B's pre-existing right under the Trust that binds C. However, in **Examples 7c and 7d**, it is very hard to see how C's conduct could justify the recognition of such a direct right: after all, in each case, B can impose a duty on C even if C acted *entirely innocently*.[38] So, it seems we are left with the position that:

---

[34] The distinct nature of the two claims was recently emphasised by Waller LJ in *Barbados Trust Company Ltd v Bank of Zambia* [2007] EWCA Civ 148.

[35] See eg Maitland, *Lectures on Equity* (1929), ch 9 at 117–21; Stone (1917) 17 *Col L Rev* 467.

[36] See eg *per* Lord Wilberforce in *McPhail v Doulton* [1971] AC 424 at 457. In some cases, B will also be able to force C to hand the bike directly over to B: it all depends on the nature of B's initial right under the Trust (see **D1:1.4.5(ii)** and **F3:1.3**).

[37] Such an explanation was given by eg Maitland, *Lectures on Equity* (1909), ch 9 at 117–21; Stone (1917) 17 *Col L Rev* 467, 474ff.

[38] L Smith [2004] *Canadian Business Law Journal* 317 suggests that, originally at least, B's new right against C was based on C's unjust enrichment at B's expense. However, Smith does not suggest that analysis can be used today: in case such as **Examples 7a and 7b**, any enrichment acquired by C comes from A, not from B (see **D4:7**).

1. B's right under the Trust is *not* a property right: it is not a right against the bike (see **Examples 7a and 7b**); and
2. B's right under the Trust is *not* merely a personal right: it is not just a right against A (see **Examples 7c and 7d**).

The best explanation is that B's right under the Trust is a persistent right: a right against A's ownership of the bike. This means that, as a result of declaring a Trust of the bike, A holds a *specific right* (A's ownership of the bike) on Trust for B. This means that: (i) A is under a duty to B; and (ii) B also has a prima facie power to impose a duty on *anyone who acquires a right that depends on A's ownership of the bike*. So:

1. As B has no right against the bike, X does not commit a wrong against B if he simply damages or steals A's bike. And B has no power to impose a duty on a X, as X has not acquired a right from A (see **Examples 7a and 7b**);[39] and
2. B has a right against A's ownership of the bike and so has a prima facie power to impose a duty on C if C acquires A's ownership of the bike (see **Examples 7c and 7d**).

In cases such as **Examples 7c and 7d**, it is tempting to say that C is 'bound by B's pre-existing right under the Trust'. However, that is not quite accurate.[40] Where A holds a right on Trust for B, A may be under a number of different duties to B (see F3:1.3). And, in **Examples 7c and 7d**, many of those duties will *not* bind C.[41] For example, A may be under a duty to B to keep the bike insured against theft or damage. When C acquires the bike, without any knowledge of the pre-existing Trust, C cannot come under such a duty to B: it would be very odd to say that C commits a wrong (a breach of duty) against B by failing to insure the bike. So, it is more accurate to say that B has a power to impose a *more limited* duty on C: a duty not to use his ownership of the bike for his own benefit. That is what we mean when we say that, in **Examples 7c and 7d**, B can assert his pre-existing persistent right against C.

The orthodox view, in calling persistent rights 'Equitable property rights', is clearly misleading. Persistent rights lack one of the key features of a property right: they do not impose a prima facie duty on the rest of the world. Instead, they give B a power to impose a duty on C *if* C acquires a right that depends on the right against which B has a right.

---

[39] This provides an important reason to distinguish between *independent acquisition* and *dependent acquisition* (see 2.2 above). A pre-existing persistent right cannot bind C if (as in **Example 7b**) he *independently* acquires a right. But it can bind C if (as in **Examples 7c and 7d**) C acquires a right *from A*.

[40] See eg L Smith, ch 5 in *Breach of Trust* (ed. Birks and Pretto, 2002); R Nolan (2006) 122 *LQR* 232.

[41] Things are different in the rare case where C, by acting *as though* he holds a right on Trust for B, assumes the duties of A (the initial trustee). In that case, C, by his own conduct, can come under the full range of A's duties to B: see eg *Mara v Browne* [1896] 1 Ch 199. In such a case, C is said to be a 'trustee de son tort' or a 'de facto trustee' (see *per* Lord Millett in *Dubai Aluminium v Salaaam* [2003] 2 AC 366 at [138]).

SUMMARY of B:4.4

The distinction between property rights and persistent rights is more precise than the orthodox divide between 'Legal property rights' and 'Equitable property rights'. It captures the crucial fact that the differences between the two forms of right do *not* simply depend on their historical jurisdictional origin. Rather, each of the two forms of rights has a fundamentally different *nature*. A property right is: (i) a right relating to a thing; that (ii) imposes a prima facie duty on the rest of the world. B has such a right only if his right is on the list of permitted property rights. A persistent right is: (i) a right relating to a claim-right or power held by A; that (ii) imposes a duty on A; and (iii) gives B a prima facie power to impose a duty on anyone acquiring a right that depends on A's right. A persistent right arises *whenever* (i) A is under a duty to B; and (ii) A's duty relates to a specific claim-right or power held by A. So, in this book then, we will continue to use the term persistent right when referring to any of those rights usually called 'Equitable property rights' or 'Equitable interests in land'.

4.5 Pre-existing rights and A's insolvency

If A goes into insolvency, we have seen that a dispute about the use of a thing can arise between: (i) B; and (ii) A's trustee in bankruptcy (or A Ltd's liquidator) acting on behalf of A's creditors (see **2.3.2** above). In such a case, a statutory scheme regulates the distribution of A's rights: different schemes apply where the insolvent party is: (i) an individual or partnership; or (ii) a company. In either case, the fundamental principles of the statutory scheme are based on the **basic structure** of the property law system. In particular, where B wishes to assert a pre-existing right against A's trustee in bankruptcy, or A Ltd's liquidator, it is vital to know if B's right is: (i) a personal right; or (ii) a property right or a persistent right.

4.5.1 Personal right

If A goes into insolvency and B has only a personal right against A, B's position is very weak. In general,[42] B will *not* receive any special protection. B cannot show that he has a right against either: (i) a specific thing formerly owned by A; or (ii) a specific right formerly held by A. So, B has to wait, along with A's other general creditors, for A's trustee in bankruptcy (or A Ltd's liquidator) to realise the value of A's rights and make a payment to B. And of course, as A is insolvent, B will *not* receive the full sum due to him.

EXAMPLE 8a

A owns a bike shop. B orders a particular model of bike from A and pays the £200 price in advance. A then goes into insolvency. A's total liabilities are £100,000: the assets available to A to meet those liabilities are worth only £50,000.

In such a case, B simply has a personal right against A. B does not have a right against a specific thing as A has not given B any *specific* physical object: A has simply promised to give B a particular model of bike (see further **D1:1.1**). Nor does B have a right against a specific

---

[42] Some personal rights of B are singled out for special protection under the statutory insolvency scheme. For example, if B is an employee of A Ltd, his claim for wages will receive extra protection as he is a 'preferential creditor' of A Ltd: see **F4:2.3.4**.

right held by A: A has not promised to give B any specific right (see further **D2:1.1.2**).[43] B can assert his personal right in A's insolvency, but, like other general creditors, he will receive only half of the money due to him.[44] So, although A is under a duty to pay B £200,[45] A's duty to B is discharged if A's trustee in bankruptcy pays £100 to B.

4.5.2 Property right or persistent right

If A goes into insolvency and B has a pre-existing property right or persistent right, B's position is much stronger. In general, B *will* receive special protection.

(i) B has a pre-existing property right

If B has a property right, the rest of the world (including A's trustee in bankruptcy or A Ltd's liquidator) is under a prima facie duty to B not to interfere with B's use of a specific thing. As a result, if he has no defence to B's property right, A's trustee in bankruptcy (or A Ltd's liquidator) commits a wrong[46] against B if he sells that thing and uses the proceeds to pay A's general creditors.[47] B thus is in a privileged position. He does *not* have to wait, along with A's general creditors, for payment. Instead, he can simply assert his pre-existing property right.

> **EXAMPLE 8b**
>
> A has a bike shop. B visits the shop and agrees to buy a specific second-hand bike. B pays the £200 price in advance. B leaves the bike in the shop and plans to collect it later in the week. Before B collects the bike, A goes into insolvency. A's total liabilities are £100,000: the assets available to A to meet those liabilities are worth only £50,000.

In such a case, in contrast to **Example 8a**, B *can* acquire a property right. B has agreed to buy a *specific thing*: the particular bike in the shop. The basic rule in a sale is that B acquires A's ownership whenever A and B intend that B should do so (see **D1:2.2.4(iii)**).[48] In **Example 8b**, it is likely that A and B intended that B would acquire ownership of the bike as soon as B paid for it.[49] As a result, at the moment of A's insolvency, B has a pre-existing property right. A's trustee in bankruptcy is therefore under a prima facie duty not to interfere with B's right to the bike. In **Example 8b**, the same result would occur if B bought his bike from A Ltd: A Ltd's liquidator will be under a prima facie duty not to interfere with B's right to the bike.

If B has a pre-existing property right, he is thus protected if A becomes insolvent. Other creditors of A may complain that the extra protection given to B is unfair. Certainly, as A's

---

[43] For an explanation of whether B can claim a persistent right against A's right to the £200 paid by B, see **D4:4.3.5**.

[44] See eg *re London Wine Co* [1986] PCC 121; *re Goldcorp's Exchange* [1995] 1 AC 74 (discussed in **D1:1.1** and **D2:1.1.2**) and *Carlos Federspiel v Charles Twigg* [1957] 1 Lloyd's Rep 240 (discussed in **D1:2.2.4(iii)(c)**).

[45] This is on the assumption that the bike ordered by B is freely available elsewhere for £200 or less. If that were not the case, A's duty is to pay B the higher cost of acquiring the bike elsewhere.

[46] The wrong of conversion: see **D1:4.1.1** and eg *Stoneleigh Finance Ltd v Phillips* [1965] 2 QB 537.

[47] For the remedies available to B where the trustee in bankruptcy or liquidator commits a wrong against B by interfering with B's property right see **D1:4**.

[48] See Sale of Goods Act 1979, s 17.

[49] In fact, the default rule is that B acquires ownership of the bike as soon as the contract is made with A, even if B has not yet paid for it: see Sale of Goods Act 1979, s 18, Rule 1.

trustee in bankruptcy cannot sell the bike, the money available to pay A's other creditors is reduced. In some situations, B's acquisition of a property right can be set aside to prevent B gaining extra protection in A's insolvency. That will be the case, for example, if A suspected that he would soon become insolvent and sold B a bike at a very low price, simply in order to give B priority over A's general creditors.[50] However, if there is no statutory ground on which A's transaction with B can be set aside, A's general creditors *cannot* complain about the extra protection available to B. After all, in **Example 8b**, as B has ownership of the bike held by A, A would clearly commit a wrong against B if A sold the bike and used the proceeds to pay his creditors. A's insolvency thus makes *no difference* to the position of those creditors: both before and after A's insolvency, the bike cannot be used to pay A's general creditors.

(ii) B has a pre-existing persistent right

EXAMPLE 8c
In his will, A0 transfers £10,000 to A to hold on Trust for B. That money is paid into a special account at Z Bank. Two years later, A goes into insolvency.

EXAMPLE 8d
A Ltd wants to borrow £10,000 from B in order to pay a dividend due to A Ltd's share-holders. B is concerned that A Ltd is close to insolvency. B transfers £10,000 to A Ltd but insists that: (i) A Ltd can use that money *only* for the purpose of paying the dividend; *and* (ii) A Ltd must keep the money in a specific account at Z Bank. Before A Ltd pays the dividend, it goes into insolvency.

In each case, B clearly cannot have a property right: there is no specific thing against which he can claim a right. However, B *can* acquire a persistent right: a right against A's personal right (represented by the bank account) to receive £10,000 from Z Bank. B will acquire such a right if he can show that A is under a duty to B in relation to that specific right. In **Example 8c**, A is clearly under such a duty to B: as a result of agreeing to hold the money on Trust for B, A is under a duty to B not to use that money for his own benefit. A Ltd is also under such a duty in **Example 8d**: although B has given A Ltd a power to spend the money in paying the dividend, A Ltd is under a basic duty not to use the bank account for its own benefit (see **F4:2.4.2**).[51]

In each case, B thus has a persistent right at the moment of A's insolvency. This means that B has a prima facie power to impose a duty on anyone who acquires a right that depends on A's bank account. In **Example 8c**, when A goes into insolvency, his rights, including his account with Z Bank, are transferred to his trustee in bankruptcy. B can then assert his pre-existing persistent right against A's trustee in bankruptcy: like A, A's trustee in bankruptcy is thus under a duty *not* to use that bank account for the purpose of paying A's

---

[50] In such a case, the sale to B can be set aside as a transaction at an undervalue or as an unlawful preference under the Insolvency Act 1986, ss 339–41 (where A is an individual or partnership); ss 238–40 (where A Ltd is a company).

[51] See *Barclays Bank v Quistclose Investments Ltd* [1970] AC 567 (on which **Example 8d** is based), as explained in *Twinsectra v Yardley* [2002] 2 AC 164 (see in particular Lord Millett at [68]–[103] and Lord Hoffmann at [13]).

general creditors.[52] In **Example 8d**, A Ltd's liquidator is under the same duty: the bank account cannot be used to pay A's general creditors.[53]

If B has a pre-existing persistent right, he is thus protected if A goes into insolvency. Other creditors of A may complain that the extra protection given to B is unfair. Certainly, as the account with Z Bank has to be used only for B's benefit, the money available to pay A's other creditors is reduced. In some situations, B's acquisition of a persistent right, like his acquisition of a property right, can be set aside to prevent B gaining extra protection in A's insolvency.[54] However, if there is no statutory ground on which A's transaction with B can be set aside, A's general creditors *cannot* complain about the extra protection available to B. In **Examples 8c and 8d**: (i) A was under a duty to B not to use the bank account for A's own benefit; and (ii) A's trustee in bankruptcy (or A Ltd's liquidator) is under the same duty. A's insolvency thus makes *no difference* to the position of those creditors: both before and after A's insolvency, the value of A's bank account *cannot* be used to pay A's general creditors.

SUMMARY of B:4

In a dispute about rights to use a thing, there are two forms of pre-existing right (ie, of rights *not* acquired as a result of C's conduct) that B may be able to assert against C.

First, if B can show that his right counts as a right against a thing, he will have a property right. Such a right imposes a prima facie duty on the rest of the world, including C. It does not matter whether or not C acquired a right from A: if (i) C interferes with B's use of the thing; and (ii) C has no defence to B's property right; then (iii) C commits a wrong against B. A property right can thus be of great use to B in a dispute about the use of a thing (such as **A:Examples 1 and 2**). However, as a property right is a right against a thing, such rights are irrelevant in a dispute about the use of a right (such as **A:Example 3**).

Second, if B can show that A is under a duty to B in relation to a specific claim-right or power held by A, B will have a persistent right: a right against A's right. Such a right is capable of binding C: if (i) C acquires a right that depends on A's right; and (ii) C has no defence to B's persistent right; then (iii) B has a power to impose a duty on C. A pre-existing persistent right can thus be of great use to B *both*: (i) in a dispute about the use of a thing (such as **A:Examples 1 and 2**); and (ii) in a dispute about the use of a right, such as **A:Example 3**.

---

5 DEFENCES TO PRE-EXISTING RIGHTS

5.1 The concept of a defence

The special feature of a property right (a right against a thing) is that it imposes a prima facie duty on the rest of the world. That qualification—'prima facie'—is very important: it shows that a third party such as C may have a **defence** to B's pre-existing property right. Similarly, the special feature of a persistent right (a right against A's right) is that B has a

---

[52] See Insolvency Act 1986, s 283(3)(a) and (b).

[53] See eg *Barclays Bank v Quistclose Investments Ltd* [1970] AC 567, on which **Example 8d** is based.

[54] For example, the rules relating to transactions at an undervalue and unlawful preferences apply equally to cases where B acquires a property right and those where he acquires a persistent right: Insolvency Act 1986, ss 238–40 and 339–41.

prima facie power to assert that right against C *if* C acquires a right that depends on A's right. Again 'prima facie' is very important: it shows that C, even if he has acquired a right that depends on A's right, may have a **defence** to B's pre-existing persistent right.

It could be said that it is also possible for C to have a defence to a direct right of B. However, the word is used differently in that context. If C has a 'defence' to a claimed direct right of B, this, in general, means that B has *no such right* against C.[55] However, to say C has a defence against a pre-existing right of B does *not* mean that B's right does not exist. For example, if B is an owner of a bike, he has a property right. That right is prima facie binding on the rest of the world. If B permits C to use the bike for an afternoon, clearly C has a defence to B's pre-existing property right: until B revokes that permission, C is entitled to use the bike. However, that does not mean that B's property right ceases to exist: [56] if X steals the bike during that afternoon, X commits a wrong against B.[57]

So, when examining property rights and persistent rights, we need to ask three questions:

1. The **content question**: does the right claimed by B count as a property right or a persistent right?;
2. The **acquisition question**: has B acquired such a right?;
3. The **defences question**: if B has a pre-existing property right or persistent right, does C have a defence to that right?

5.2   The distinction between property rights and persistent rights

The defences question provides further reasons for distinguishing between property rights and persistent rights:

1. There can be a difference between: (i) the *effect* of a defence to a property right; and (ii) the *effect* of a defence to a persistent right.
2. There is a difference between: (i) the *list* of defences available against a property right; and (ii) the *list* of defences available against a persistent right.

5.2.1 The effect of a defence

(i) Property rights

EXAMPLE 9a

B owns a bike. B allows X to borrow that bike for the afternoon.

---

[55] For example, if B claims that he has a direct right against C because C has made a contractual promise to B, C may claim that the contract was procured by a fraudulent misrepresentation made by B. In one sense, that can be seen as a 'defence' to B's claim. However, if C's contention is correct, C has a power to set the contract aside: if C exercises that power, B has no contractual right against C (see eg *Car & Universal Finance Co Ltd v Caldwell* [1965] 1 QB 525: discussed in **D1:1.4.5(i)** and **D1:2.2.2**).

[56] That does not mean that a defence to a property right or a persistent right can *never* have the effect of extinguishing B's pre-existing right. For example, as we saw in **Chapter A**, C can have a defence against B's pre-existing property right if he takes possession, and acts as owner, of B's land over a long period. Where that adverse possession defence applies, B loses his pre-existing property right *completely* and is thus unable to assert it against *anyone* (see further **G1A:3**).

[57] See eg *O'Sullivan v Williams* [1992] 3 All ER 385. X also commits a wrong against C (see eg *The Winkfield* [1902] 1 P 42): C also has a property right, due to his physical control of the bike (see **D1:2.1**).

EXAMPLE 9b

The facts are as in **Example 9a**. X then purports to sell the bike to C.

In **Example 9a**, X has a **defence** to B's pre-existing property right. This means that X's action in using the bike for the afternoon does *not* count as a wrong against B. The presence of a defence thus means that X is *not* under a particular duty to B. We can describe that absence of a duty by saying that X has a *liberty* against B (see **D2:1.1.3**). Of course, the terms of a defence may be limited. So, in **Example 9b**, X commits a wrong against B: by trying to sell the bike to C, X has clearly acted beyond the scope of his liberty.[58] Clearly, the fact that X had a *limited liberty* to use B's bike does not mean that B's property right ceases to exist.

(ii) Persistent rights

EXAMPLE 9c

A owns a bike. A declares that he holds the bike on Trust for B. A, without B's consent or other authority, then sells the bike to C. C, when buying the bike, honestly believes that no one other than A has a right in relation to the bike.

EXAMPLE 9d

The facts are as in **Example 9c**. C then sells the bike to C2, who is fully aware that the bike was initially held by A on Trust for B.

In **Example 9c**, C has a defence against B's pre-existing persistent right (see **5.2.2** below and **D2:3.5**). This means that, although: (i) B had a right against A's ownership of the bike; and (ii) C acquired A's ownership of the bike; (iii) B does *not* have a power to impose a duty on C. As a result, B *cannot* prevent C from using the bike for C's own benefit. The presence of a defence thus means that B has *no power* to impose a duty on C. We can describe that absence of a duty by saying that C has an *immunity* against B (see **D2:1.1.3**).

In **Example 9c**, C's lack of awareness of B's right under the Trust is *one* of the reasons giving C a defence against that right. In contrast, in **Example 9d**, C2 is fully aware of B's initial right. Yet, in **Example 9d**, it is impossible for B to impose a duty on C2.[59] That is because: (i) C2 acquired his right from C; and (ii) B did *not* have a right against C's ownership of the bike. This shows us something important about the effect of C's defence in **Example 9c**: it *destroys B's pre-existing persistent right*.[60]

The *nature* of persistent rights explains this difference between: (i) the effect of a defence to a property right; and (ii) the effect of a defence to a persistent right. A persistent right depends on A being under a duty to B. In **Example 9c**, C's defence means that C is under *no duty* to B. C thus has a *liberty* against B to use his ownership of the bike for his own benefit. As C is under no duty to B, B cannot have a persistent right against C's ownership of the bike. As a result, B has no pre-existing persistent right that he can assert against C2.

---

[58] C also commits a wrong against B by interfering with B's right to exclusive control of the bike: see **5.2.2** below.

[59] See eg *Wilkes v Spooner* [1911] 2 KB 473.

[60] B may, however, have a *new* persistent right. So, in **Example 9c**, if A received £100 from C in exchange for the bike, B will have a persistent right against A's right to that £100. That new persistent right (a right against A's right to

5.2.2 The list of available defences

(i) Property rights

In **Example 9b,** let us say that, when attempting to buy the bike from X, C: (i) pays money to X; and (ii) honestly believes that no one other than X has a right in relation to the bike. In such a case, we can say that C is a 'bona fide purchaser': he acquires a right from X: (i) for value; and (ii) without any 'actual or constructive notice'[61] of B's pre-existing right.

In such a case, the facts are very similar to **A:Example 2.** We saw in Chapter A that the basic tension between B and C is very difficult to resolve: both parties are innocent. The property law system has to resolve the dispute, and it resolves it in B's favour.[62] As B is an owner of the bike, he has a pre-existing property right. And the fact that C is a 'bona fide purchaser' does *not*, by itself, give C a defence to B's pre-existing right.[63] The 'bona fide purchaser defence' is *not* on the list of general defences that can be used against a pre-existing property right.[64]

(ii) Persistent rights

In **Example 9c,** C *does* have a defence to B's pre-existing persistent right. As in **Example 9b,** both parties are innocent: the basic tension is again very difficult to resolve. However, this time, the property law system finds in C's favour.[65] The 'bona fide purchaser defence' *is* on the list of general defences that can be used against a pre-existing *persistent* right.

On the orthodox analysis, this vulnerability to the 'bona fide purchaser' defence is seen as a general feature of 'Equitable property rights'. However, the defence also applies to persistent rights that are not usually regarded as 'Equitable property rights': such as the right acquired by B through an 'Equitable assignment' from A (**Example 6a**); and the right acquired by B Ltd through paying out on A Co's insurance policy (see **Example 6b**).

The 'bona fide purchaser' defence is no longer an important part of the land law system. It has been eliminated from the registered land system and, nowadays, an increasing majority of land in England and Wales is registered land. However, its replacement—the lack of registration defence—has very important similarities with the 'bona fide purchaser' defence (see **E2:3.6.5**). In particular, that lack of registration defence can potentially be used against any pre-existing *persistent* right; but it can almost never be used against a pre-existing *property* right.

---

the £100) is clearly different from B's initial persistent right (a right against A's ownership of the bike): see further D4:4.4.

[61] For more on that term see D2:3.5.1.

[62] C2 will, of course, have a right against C, who has (for example) breached his contractual duty (implied by statute: see s 12 of the Sale of Goods Act 1979) to give C2 a right to the bike free from any pre-existing rights.

[63] In D1:3.3 we will see that, in certain specific situations, C can rely on special defences that are similar, in some respects, to the general 'bona fide purchaser' defence.

[64] We will see in D1:3.5 that if B's pre-existing property right is ownership of money (ie, of specific notes or coins), C can, exceptionally, use the 'bona fide purchaser' defence.

[65] B does have a personal right against A, who has committed the wrong of breach of Trust against B; B can also enforce A's duty to account for the right held on Trust: see F3:4.2. And A also holds the money received from C in return for the bike (and any right that can be identified as a product of that money) on Trust for B: see D4:4.4.

SUMMARY of B:5

If B has a property right, the rest of the world is under a prima facie duty to B not to interfere with B's use of a thing. If C can show he has a defence to B's property right, C can displace that prima facie duty. A defence to a property right thus gives C a *liberty* against B to make some use of the thing. C's liberty may be limited: if C acts beyond the scope of such a liberty, C no longer has a defence to B's property right and commits a wrong against B. Crucially, the existence of C's liberty does not mean that B's property right ceases to exist. The list of general defences to property rights is quite short: in particular, it does not include the 'bona fide purchaser' defence.

If B has a persistent right, he has a prima facie power to impose a duty on C *if* C acquires a right that depends on A's right. If C can show he has a defence to B's persistent right, C can displace that prima facie power. A defence to a property right thus gives C an *immunity*: B does not have a power to impose a duty on C. As a result, C then has a *liberty* against B to use his right for his own benefit. Crucially, the existence of C's liberty means that B does not have a right against C's right. So, if C2 later acquires a right that depends on C's right, B has no pre-existing persistent right that he can assert against C2. As a result, if C has a defence to it, B's pre-existing persistent right may well be destroyed. Further, the list of general defences to persistent rights is longer than the list of defences available against property rights: in particular, it includes the 'bona fide purchaser' defence.

6   REMEDIES

Once we have established what rights B or C have in relation to a thing, we then have to consider the **remedies question**. That question examines how a court will protect the winner's right. At this point, we return to our initial, factual examination of *what the parties want*. So:

1. If B *can* assert either a direct right or a pre-existing right against C, we need to ask how a court will protect B's right; and
2. If B *cannot* assert such a right, and C does have a right to use the thing in question, we need to ask how a court will protect C's right.

When looking at the remedies question, the crucial issue is generally whether the court will: (i) *specifically protect* the right of the winning party; or whether (ii) that party will instead have to settle for receiving money. So, in **Example 9b**: (i) B has a pre-existing property right; and (ii) C has no defence to that right. The crucial practical question is whether the court will specifically protect B's right by ordering C to give physical control of the bike back to B. In general, the court will *not* order C to return the bike to B (see **A:3.1.2(i)**). Instead, B will have to settle for receiving money from C. That sum of money (damages for C's breach of duty to B) will include: (i) a sum representing the value of B's ownership of the bike; and (ii) a sum compensating B for any relevant consequential loss suffered by B as a result of C taking control of the bike (see **D1:4.3**).

In contrast, if B's right relates to land, the opposite is true: in general, B's right *will* be specifically protected (see **A:3.1.2(ii)**). This is the case whether B's right is: (i) a direct right, arising as a result of C's conduct; or (ii) a pre-existing property right or persistent right. So if, in **Example 1**, C Bank makes a contractual promise to B that it will allow B to remain in occupation of the land, B's direct right against C Bank will, in general,[66] be specifically protected.

Even where land is concerned, the remedies available to B may vary. For example, let us say that, in **Example 1**, B can instead assert a pre-existing persistent right against C Bank: a right under a Trust entitling B to 50 per cent of the benefit of A's ownership of the land. In such a case, the remedies question may be crucial. B may wish to remain in occupation of the land; C Bank will instead want to remove B and sell the land, leaving B to receive a half share of the sale proceeds. As we will see, *even though B can assert his pre-existing persistent right against C,* the court is likely to find in C Bank's favour and order that B must consent to a sale of the land (see **G3:4.2**).[67]

7   SUMMARISING THE BASIC STRUCTURE

We are now in a position to summarise the basic structure of the property law system. That structure is applied to cases such as the **basic situation**, in order to resolve the basic tension between B and C. The basic structure can be used to understand and evaluate the vast majority of disputes about the use of a thing. The structure depends on four basic questions:

1. The **content question**;
2. The **acquisition question**;
3. The **defences question**; and
4. The **remedies question**.

The structure as set out below is based on an initial assumption. That assumption is that, if C has a right, C has acquired that right through a *dependent acquisition*: C's right thus depends on A's right. This assumption is important: it means that, if B has a pre-existing persistent right (a right against A's right), B will have a prima facie power to impose a duty on C. In the vast majority of important property law cases, as in **Example 1**, this basic assumption is justified: C does acquire his right from A. This means that, in total, there are three possible ways in which B can assert a right against C: (i) if he has a direct right against C, arising as a result of C's conduct; (ii) if he has a pre-existing persistent right to which C has no defence; or (iii) if he has a pre-existing property right to which C has no defence.

1. Does B have a **direct right** against C that prevents C from making his desired use of the thing in question?
   (i) Content question: does the right B claims prevent C from making his desired use?

---

[66] There are, of course, exceptions: eg, if C's promise is to share occupation with B, a court is unlikely to force B and C to live together by specifically protecting B's right: see eg *Thompson v Park* [1944] KB 408.

[67] See eg *Bank of Ireland v Bell* [2001] 2 FLR 809. It is worth noting that a sale can be ordered even if C initially only has a *personal* right against A. If C obtains a charging order over A's land, C can then ask for A's land to be sold. And, even if B's pre-existing persistent right binds C, such a sale may well be ordered: see eg *Pritchard Englefield v Steinberg* [2004] EWHC 1908.

> (ii) Acquisition question: has B, on the facts, acquired that right?
> **If No to either question: go to 2;**
> **If Yes to both questions, B wins: go to 4**
>
> 2. Did B, immediately before C acquired his right, have a **property right** (a right against a thing) or a **persistent right** (a right against a right) that prevents C from making his desired use of the thing in question?
>   (i) Content question: does the right B claims prevent C from making his desired use? *And* does the right B claims count as a property right or as a persistent right?
>   (ii) Acquisition question: did B, on the facts, acquire that property right or persistent right?
>   **If No to either question, C wins: go to 4;**
>   **If Yes to both questions: go to 3**
>
> 3. Does C have a **defence** to B's pre-existing property right or persistent right?
>   **If No, B wins: go to 4;**
>   **If Yes, C wins: go to 4**
>
> 4. What **remedy** will a court give to protect the winner's right?
>
> In those very rare cases where our initial assumption is not justified, and C has instead acquired his right through an *independent acquisition*, there are only two possible ways in which B can assert a right against C: (i) if he has a direct right against C, arising as a result of C's conduct; or (ii) if he has a pre-existing property right to which C has no defence. In these very rare cases we can still apply the basic structure but, when looking at question 2 above, we will need to remember that, as C has acquired his right independently, a pre-existing persistent right will not assist B.

8 HUMAN RIGHTS AND THE BASIC STRUCTURE

Before beginning to apply the basic structure set out above, we need to consider how human rights fit into it. In particular, does the basic structure have to be modified to take account of the impact of the Human Rights Act 1998?

8.1 How human rights might affect the basic structure

There are two principal ways in which human rights *might* affect the basic structure of property law:

1. Human rights could *introduce a new question* into the basic structure. For example, B or C could be allowed to argue that a human right allows him to make his desired use of a thing. So, B could argue that, even if he has no direct right, property right or persistent right, he can nonetheless assert a human right against C.
2. Human rights could *influence the answers* given to the questions set out above. For example, a judge may need to take such rights into account when deciding: (i) if B has acquired a property right or persistent right; or (ii) if C has a defence to that right.

There is an important contrast between those two methods. In the first, human rights change the structure by requiring us to ask a new question: they could thus be said to operate *directly*. In the second, human rights are accommodated within the existing basic structure: they could thus be said to operate *indirectly*.

8.2   How human rights *do* affect the basic structure

8.2.1 Human rights in English law: where C is a public body

The impact of human rights on English law is chiefly defined by two instruments: (i) the European Convention on Human Rights (the ECHR); and (ii) the Human Rights Act 1998 ('the 1998 Act'). The ECHR provides a set of human rights that states signing the Convention, including the UK, agreed to respect.[68] The 1998 Act defines those rights as the principal source of human rights in English law. This sets the **content** test: if a party claims to have a human right, he will need to show his right is included in the set list of human rights provided by the ECHR.[69]

The focus of the 1998 Act is to ensure that, as far as possible, organs of the state do not breach their duty to respect the rights set out in the ECHR.[70] So, section 6 of the 1998 Act makes clear that it is unlawful for a *public authority* to act in a way which is incompatible with B's ECHR right. Crucially, this means that the 1998 Act does *not* impose a duty on the whole world to respect the rights set out in the ECHR. For example, Article 8 of the ECHR states that 'Everyone has the right to respect for his private and family life, his home and his correspondence.' However, if C sees some of B's letters open on a desk and reads them without B's consent, C does not commit a wrong against B: as C is not a public authority, the 1998 Act does not impose any duty on C to respect B's privacy and correspondence.[71]

This should not be a surprise. After all, the ECHR itself imposes duties on states (the signatories to the ECHR) *not* on individuals: the rights given to B by the ECHR are rights against the state, not against the rest of the world.[72] This has a very important consequence in cases such as **Example 1**. B can try to claim that if C Bank is allowed to sell A's land without B's consent, this will interfere with B's Article 8 right to respect for his home life (see **A:3.1.4**). However, as C Bank is not a public authority, C Bank cannot infringe B's Article 8 right: Article 8 gives B a right against the state, not against C.

---

[68] There are of course other conventions, signed by the UK, that relate to human rights and touch on property law. For example, Art 11(1) of the International Covenant on Economic, Social and Cultural Rights (1996) binds states to take 'appropriate steps to ensure the realization' of 'the right of everyone to an adequate standard of living for himself and his family, including adequate food, clothing and housing, and to the continuous improvement of living conditions.' See further Bright, *Landlord and Tenant Law in Context* (2007) at 293–6.

[69] The **acquisition** test is easily passed: B acquires a human right simply by virtue of existing.

[70] See eg *per* Lord Nicholls in *Aston Cantlow v Wallbank* [2004] 1 AC 546 at [6]: 'the broad purpose sought to be achieved by s 6(1) is not in doubt. The purpose is that those bodies for whose acts the state is answerable before the European Court of Human Rights shall in future be subject to a domestic law obligation not to act incompatibly with Convention rights'; see too *per* Lord Rodger at [160]. This view of the purpose of s 6(1) is also compatible with the view of the majority of the House of Lords in *YL v Birmingham City Council* [2008] 1 AC 95 (see esp *per* Lord Mance at [86] and [87]).

[71] See eg *per* Baroness Hale in *Campbell v MGN Ltd* [2004] 2 AC 457 at [132]: 'The 1998 Act does not create any new cause of action between private persons.' See too *per* Lord Hoffmann at [49]: 'Even now that the equivalent of Article 8 has been enacted as part of English law, it is not directly concerned with the protection of privacy against private persons or corporations. It is, by virtue of section 6 of the 1998 Act, a guarantee of privacy only against public authorities.'

[72] See eg Stevens, *Torts and Rights* (2007) at 236–42.

8.2.2 Human rights and the basic structure: where C is a public body

If C is a public body, the 1998 Act allows B *directly* to assert an ECHR right against C. It may therefore seem that human rights can operate in the first way described in **8.1**: they can *introduce a new question* into the basic structure—does B have a human right that he can assert against C? However, we can be more precise than that. The duty of a public body not to act inconsistently with an ECHR right of B is just an *example* of the wider duty of a public body not to act unlawfully. And this, in turn, is an example of the wider point that, *whatever right* a party (whether a public body or not) may have in relation to a specific thing, that party cannot exercise its right unlawfully.

EXAMPLE 10

A and B own neighbouring plots of land. C buys A's land and wishes to build a nuclear power station on that land. B objects.

In such a case, there is no need for B to go through the basic structure. It does not matter if B can assert a right against C: even though C is an owner of the land, C does *not* have a liberty to build a nuclear power station. To use his land in that way, C needs to get the necessary permission from the relevant public authorities. So we do not get as far as the basic structure: C has no prima facie entitlement to use the land as he wishes. **Example 10** thus demonstrates an important general point: before applying the basic structure, we *always* need to ask if it is *lawful* for each of B and C to make his desired use of the thing.[73]

It seems, then, that we do *not* need to modify the basic structure where C is a public body. If C is a public body, it is subject to special duties, including the duty not to act inconsistently with an ECHR right. If it breaches such a duty, the public body acts unlawfully. And if it is unlawful for C to make a particular use of a thing, C's claim to use the thing in that way will necessarily fail.

8.2.3 Human rights in English law: the general position

Even if C is not itself a public body, the 1998 Act means that an ECHR right of B can still be relevant. It may influence the way in which a judge: (i) interprets a statute; or (ii) applies or develops judge-made law; or (iii) exercises a discretion.

(i) Interpreting a statute

Statutes are passed by Parliament (an organ of the state) and so the state, by passing or enforcing that statute, can be in breach of B's Article 8 right. As a result, section 3 of the 1998 Act instructs courts to interpret legislation 'so far as it is possible to do so' in accordance with the ECHR. This does not mean that a judge *always* has to find that a statute accords with the ECHR. The Act recognises that, in some cases, this will be impossible: in such a case, the court has to apply the statute; but, under section 4 of the Act, it[74] can also

---

[73] For example, if: (i) C (whether a public body or not) is an owner of land; and (ii) decides not to rent his land to B simply on the basis of B's sex, race or disability, C (in general) acts unlawfully (see eg Sex Discrimination Act 1975, ss 1,2 and 30–32; Race Relations Act 1976, ss 1, 3 and 21(1); Disability Discrimination Act 1995, ss 22–4): it does not matter that B has no direct right or pre-existing right that he can assert against C. See Bright, *Landlord and Tenant Law in Context* (2007) at 104.

[74] In England and Wales, such a declaration can only be issued by the High Court, Court of Appeal, or the House of Lords.

issue a 'declaration of incompatibility' alerting Parliament to the problem. Nonetheless, section 3 can have a dramatic effect.

EXAMPLE 11

A has a Freehold. A gives B1 a Lease. B1 dies. At the time of his death, B1 lived with B2, his homosexual partner. B1's Lease is regulated by the Rent Act 1977. Under that Act, a party living with B1 'as his wife or husband' acquires B1's Lease on B1's death. A attempts to remove B2 from the land and B2 claims he has acquired B1's Lease.

In *Ghaidan v Godin-Mendoza*,[75] the House of Lords held that the statutory term 'as his wife or husband' *did* include B2. It was admitted that, before the 1998 Act, the term would not have been interpreted in that way.[76] However, due to section 3 of that Act, the court had to strain to interpret the term in such a way as to ensure that Parliament was *not* in breach of the UK's duty, under Article 14 of the ECHR, not to discriminate on grounds of sexuality when protecting an occupier's Article 8 right to respect for his home.[77] So, the term 'as his wife or husband' was interpreted as including a homosexual lover in a close and stable relationship with B1.

(ii) Applying or developing judge-made law

The ECHR may be relevant even in a case where: (i) C is not a public body; and (ii) no statute is involved. In **Example 1**, B may claim that: (i) if C Bank can remove B from the land; *then* (ii) the state has failed in its *positive* duty to ensure that the legal system respects B's Article 8 right. Certainly, the European Court of Human Rights has found that Article 8 can impose *some* positive duties on a state.[78] So, it may be that, in deciding the dispute arising in **Example 1**, a court has to try to do its best to ensure that the property law system provided by the state adequately protects B's Article 8 right. After all, as made clear by section 6(3)(a) of the 1998 Act, a court itself counts as a public body and so, when deciding the dispute between B and C, it must try to ensure that the state acts compatibly with B's Article 8 right.[79]

However, a number of points need to be remembered:

1. It is clear that Article 8 does not impose a positive duty on a state to ensure that the rest of the world is under a duty to respect B's privacy or home life.[80]
2. The property law system is not the only means employed by a state to protect B's right. For example, even if B has no direct right or pre-existing right that he can assert against C (a public body), B's Article 8 right may be adequately protected by:

---

[75] [2004] 2 AC 557.

[76] See eg *per* Lord Nicholls at [24].

[77] See eg *per* Lord Nicholls at [30]: 'the interpretative obligation decreed by section 3 is of an unusual and far-reaching character'.

[78] See eg *Connors v UK* (2004) 40 EHRR 189 at [84]: Article 8 imposes 'a positive obligation on the Contracting States . . . to facilitate the gypsy way of life'. See generally Mowbray, *The Development of Positive Obligations under the European Convention on Human Rights by the European Court of Human Rights* (2004).

[79] The exact significance of s 6(3)(a) has been hotly debated: see eg *per* Lord Nicholls in *Wilson v First County Trust Ltd (No 2)* [2004] 1 AC 816 at [25]: 'As is well known, the application of section 6(1) to judicial decisions on matters of substantive law is a highly controversial topic.' Wade (2000) 116 *LQR* 217 argues that it allows any ECHR right to bind not only public bodies, but also the rest of the world. That is *not* the prevailing view, however: for persuasive arguments to the contrary, see Hunt [1998] *PL* 423; and Lester and Pannick (2000) 116 *LQR* 380.

[80] See eg *Wainwright v Home Office* [2004] 2 AC 406 esp at [32]; *Campbell v MGN Ltd* [2004] 2 AC 457.

(i) the fact that a watchdog regulates C; and (ii) B's ability to seek judicial review of a decision made by C.[81]

3. There are limits to what a court can do in developing the law; it may be that, on the law as it currently stands, a court has to find in C Bank's favour. If this leaves the state in breach of a positive duty to protect B's right, B can pursue a claim for damages against the state under section 8 of the 1998 Act. [82] Indeed, the possibility of B having such a claim may, in some circumstances, adequately protect B's right.[83]

(iii) Exercising a discretion

The points made in (ii) above also apply where a judge has a discretion. For example, if B rents his home from C (a local authority), the Housing Act 1985 limits the grounds on which C can remove B from the land. Often, C has a power to remove B only if *both*: (i) a particular event has occurred (eg, B has fallen behind in his rent payments); *and* (ii) the court considers it reasonable to make an order that B must leave the land.[84] In deciding if such an order would be reasonable, a court has a fairly wide discretion:[85] in exercising that discretion, it can take into account the need to ensure that C complies with its duty, as a public authority, not to interfere with B's Article 8 right.[86]

8.2.4 Human rights and the basic structure: the general position

If C is not a public body, it seems that human rights can operate only in the second way described in **8.1**: they can *influence the answers* given to the basic questions. For example, it is possible for B or C to use a human right when arguing that a statute should be interpreted in a particular way. This type of argument is perfectly consistent with the basic structure. And, as they did before the 1998 Act, judges may well also take into account human rights when: (i) applying or developing past judicial decisions; and (ii) deciding how best to exercise a discretion. This may be particularly important where the **remedies question** is concerned: a court often has some discretion when deciding what remedy best protects B or C's right.[87] In doing so, it has the freedom to ensure that the remedy awarded is compatible with the parties' human rights.

---

[81] See eg *Marcic v Thames Water Utilities Ltd* [2004] 2 AC 42. B's land was flooded and affected by sewage as a result of the operations of C, a body with statutory powers and duties to manage sewage. B claimed compensation for the damage he had suffered. One of B's arguments was that C had committed the wrong of nuisance. The House of Lords held that: (i) C had not committed such a wrong; and (ii) B's rights under Art 8 and under P1:Art 1 were adequately protected as the Director General of Water Services regulated C *and* any the decisions of the Director General were subject to judicial review (see esp *per* Lord Nicholls at [37]–[47]). Compare *per* Lord Hoffmann in *Wainwright v Home Office* [2004] 2 AC 406 at [33], discussing *Peck v UK* (2003) 36 EHRR 719. In *Peck*, B had been filmed in embarrassing circumstances by a CCTV camera. Lord Hoffmann suggested that one way to protect B's Art 8 right to privacy, rather than by giving B a direct right against C, is to regulate the use of CCTV footage.

[82] S 8 of the 1998 Act gives B this claim for damages. This seems to fulfil the state's duty under Art 13 of the ECHR to provide an 'effective remedy before a national authority' in a case where B's ECHR right is breached.

[83] As suggested by Lord Hoffmann in *Wainwright v Home Office* [2004] 2 AC 406 at [34].

[84] See eg Housing Act 1985, Sched 2, Part I.

[85] See eg *Bell London and Provincial Properties Ltd v Reuben* [1946] 2 All ER 547.

[86] As noted by Lord Bingham and Lord Brown in *Kay v Lambeth LBC* [2006] 2 AC 465 at [34] and [203].

[87] See eg *Thompson v Park* [1944] KB 408; *Patel v Ali* [1984] Ch 283.

SUMMARY of B:8.2

We have seen that, in English law, ECHR rights can be used by the parties in both a *special* way and a *general* way. The special way, applying only where one party is a public body, consists of showing that: (i) it would be unlawful for the public body to use a specific thing in a particular way; as (ii) by doing so, the public body would breach its duty not to interfere with an ECHR right. Human rights can have a direct impact in such a case; but we do not need to modify the basic structure. Rather, we simply need to be aware of the wider and obvious point that C cannot use a thing in a way that is unlawful.

The general way, applying in all cases, consists of using an ECHR right to influence the answers given to the basic questions. This may allow human rights to have an important but indirect impact. Again, it does not mean we need to change the basic structure. Rather, we simply need to be aware that ECHR rights *may* be relevant when applying the basic structure to the facts of a particular case.

8.3   Assessing the impact of human rights

It seems that, without needing to modify the **basic structure**, we can take account of both: (i) the special way in which ECHR rights can be asserted against a public body; and (ii) the general way in which those rights can be asserted. It is also important to ask whether, *in practice*, an ECHR right can make a difference to a dispute concerning the use of a thing. First, we need to consider the particular ECHR rights that may be important in property law.[88]

8.3.1 Article 1 of the First Protocol

(i) The basic right
Article 1 of the First Protocol ('P1:Article 1') begins by stating that 'Every natural or legal person is entitled to the peaceful enjoyment of his possessions.' Clearly, it may be relevant to a dispute about the use of a thing. The crucial issue is whether a particular thing counts as a party's *possession*. The basic structure of property law will be important here: if a party can show he has a property right—a right against a thing—that should mean that the thing counts as his possession. That can be the case even if the party is no longer in physical control of the thing.

EXAMPLE 12

B is an owner of land. C, a Government department, arbitrarily takes over the land.

Whether or not B is in physical control of the land at the time when he loses his right, the land clearly counts as B's 'possession' for the purposes of P1:Article 1. As the Government department (an organ of the state) has deprived B of his land, there is clearly a prima facie interference with B's right under that Article. However, in such a case, there is no need for B to rely on P1:Article 1: he can simply assert his pre-existing property right, as an owner of

---

[88] As well as Art 1 of the First Protocol and Art 8, Art 6 (right to a fair and public hearing) and Art 14 (right not to be discriminated against in enjoyment of a Convention right) may, in rarer cases, be relevant: for consideration of a possible application of Art 14 see **E2:3.4.4**

the land, against C. B's P1:Article 1 right can thus be protected *within* the basic structure of property law.

P1:Article 1 can also be relevant in a dispute about the use of a right. If a party has a personal right, that right can also count as a 'possession' for the purposes of the article.[89] This is the case even though the party's right does not relate to any specific thing. So, if A has a bank account with Z Bank, that personal right can count as A's 'possession'.

(ii) The qualifications to the basic right

There are important qualifications to the right established by P1:Article 1:

1. a party can be deprived of his possessions where the deprivation is: (i) in the public interest; and (ii) 'subject to the conditions provided for by law';[90] and
2. the state has the right to 'enforce such laws as it deems necessary to control the use of property in accordance with the general interest or to secure the payment of taxes or other contributions or penalties.'

An obvious example of the first qualification arises where A goes into insolvency. A's rights (whether property rights; persistent rights; or personal rights) will be transferred to C: A's trustee in bankruptcy. C will be under a statutory duty to use those rights to pay off, as far as possible, A's creditors. As a result of a statute, A thus loses his 'possessions'. This is an interference by the state with A's rights. But it is not a breach of P1:Article 1: it occurs in specific, defined circumstances and is justified by the public interest in protecting creditors.[91] After all, the rights of A's creditors against A are also 'possessions' worthy of protection under P1:Article 1.[92]

An obvious example of the second qualification arises if C wants to build a nuclear power station on his land. C has a general right to the peaceful enjoyment of his land. But, in furtherance of the legitimate aim of protecting the public's safety, the state can impose proportionate restrictions on C's ability to enjoy his land.

(iii) P1:Article 1 and the land law system

When interpreting the P1:Article 1 exceptions, the special features of land may be important (see A:3.1). For example, given its uniqueness and limited availability, as well as the socially important uses to which it can be put, it may be possible to argue that a compulsory purchase of land by the state is 'in the public interest': eg, the special location of B's land may mean he has to give up that land so a new transport link can be built. In such a case, the state's interference with B's land, occurring in specific, defined circumstances and for a clear purpose, is not a breach of P1:Article 1. In some cases, it may even be in the 'public

---

[89] See eg *Wilson v First County Trust Ltd (No 2)* [2004] 1 AC 816, esp *per* Lord Nicholls at [39]; *Back v Finland* (ECHR, 4th Section, 20 July 2004).

[90] If B is not a national of the state in question, the deprivation must be in the public interest and subject to the conditions provided for by 'the general principles of public international law'. Art 1 also makes clear that B's right does not prevent a government enforcing 'such laws as it deems necessary to control the use of property in accordance with the general interest or to secure the payment of taxes or other contributions or penalties'.

[91] It should also be noted that A will be able to retain some rights, such as tools of his trade and items 'necessary for satisfying [A's] basic domestic needs': see Insolvency Act 1986, s 283(2).

[92] A feature of insolvency schemes is that a right of A's creditor may be extinguished even if the trustee in bankruptcy does not fully meet that claim. This is a prima-facie interference with the creditor's right under P1:Art 1 but is justified by the public interest: see the decision of the 4th Section of the European Court of Human Rights in *Back v Finland* (20 July, 2004).

interest' for B's land to be acquired, not by a public authority, but rather by another individual.[93]

EXAMPLE 13

B, an owner of land, grants C a 99-year Lease of B's land. C is in an increasingly awkward position as the 99 years runs out.[94] He may have developed an attachment to the land by his use of it over a long period. He may also have made significant improvements to the land; but it seems that B will get the benefit of these improvements at the end of the 99 years.[95]

In such a case, various statutes have given C, in certain circumstances, the right to buy the land from B, at a price determined by a statutory formula: this process is known as 'enfranchisement'.[96] The state, by means of a statute, forces B to lose his land; and B's land is not directly used for the public good: it instead goes to C. It may thus seem that the state has infringed B's P1:Article 1 right to the peaceful enjoyment of his land. However, the European Court of Human Rights has confirmed that the transfer of B's right to C *can* be in the public interest, if it is a proportionate means of pursuing 'legitimate social, economic or other policies'.[97] Further, the Court recognised that 'modern societies consider housing of the population to be a prime social need, the regulation of which cannot entirely be left to the play of market forces'.[98] In this way, the special social importance of land may be used to *justify* an interference with B's right to the peaceful enjoyment of his possessions.

EXAMPLE 14a

B is registered as the owner of some farmland. B's land includes four fields that adjoin C's farmland. The only vehicular access to those fields is through a gate padlocked by C. From February 1983 until the end of August 1984, C uses those fields with B's permission. From September 1984 onwards, C uses the fields without B's permission. C farms those fields throughout the year and uses them just as an owner would. In 1998, C applies to be registered as the new owner of the fields. In 1999, B applies to court for an order that C must stop using the fields.

EXAMPLE 14b

B is registered as the owner of some land. B lives elsewhere and the land is vacant. In 1996, C, acting without B's consent, moves onto the land and sets up home there. C acts as an owner of the land: for example, he changes the locks and keeps out third parties. In 2006, C applies to be registered as an owner of the land, in place of B. B is contacted but fails to take any action to remove C from the land. In 2008, C is registered as an owner of the land, in place of B.

---

[93] Similarly, the Fifth Amendment to the US Constitution states that private property shall not be taken for public use without just compensation (the 'takings clause'). In its controversial 5–4 decision in *Kelo v City of New London* (2005) 545 US 469, the Supreme Court decided that 'public use' could include the redevelopment of land by a private individual, where that redevelopment would bring economic growth to a community.

[94] Or anyone to whom C has transferred his Lease.

[95] Or anyone to whom B has transferred his right to the land.

[96] See eg Leasehold Reform Act 1967.

[97] *James v UK* (1986) 8 EHRR 123 at [45].

[98] *Ibid* at [47]

In each case, B loses his right to the land as a result of the doctrine of *adverse possession* (see A:3.1.5). The rules relating to adverse possession and registered land were changed by the Land Registration Act 2002 (see E1:3.7 and G1A:2.1 and 3): hence two different examples are set out. Where B is forced to sell his land to a public authority or to a party with a long Lease, B does at least receive money in return for his land. In contrast, in **Examples 14a and 14b**, the doctrine of adverse possession leads to B losing his land *without* any compensation. The doctrine does not result in the state directly taking land from B,[99] but it is based on a statutory provision[100] and so B can argue that, by passing that statute, the state has interfered with his P1:Article 1 right.

There has been an intense debate about the compatibility of the doctrine of adverse possession with P1:Article 1. From B's point of view, it can be argued that the doctrine is an unjustified interference with his ownership of land; from C's point of view, it can be said that the doctrine recognises the need to provide security to a party who has made a long-standing use of land; and is also important in promoting the marketability of land as it protects not only C but also anyone later acquiring a right from C. Further, C can argue that the special features of land, in particular its limited availability, may *justify* the doctrine of adverse possession.

The debate is finely balanced. In *JA Pye (Oxford) Ltd v Graham*,[101] the essential facts of which are identical to **Example 14a**, the House of Lords found that, due to the doctrine of adverse possession, B had lost his right to the land. As a result: (i) B was unable to remove C from the fields; and (ii) C was entitled to be registered as the new owner of those fields.[102] The key facts in that case occurred *before* the 1998 Act came into force. B complained that his P1:Article 1 right had been infringed by the UK and so brought a claim before the European Court of Human Rights. In *JA Pye (Oxford) Ltd v UK*,[103] a Chamber of the Fourth Section decided, by a 4–3 majority, that B's P1:Article 1 right *had* been infringed. Three factors were crucial:

1. The extinction of B's ownership of the land was regarded as a 'deprivation' of B's possession.[104] Such a deprivation, occurring without the payment of compensation to B, can be justified 'only in exceptional circumstances.'[105]
2. B was not given any notification of C's adverse possession, and was therefore not alerted to the risk that, by his failure to remove C, he might lose his rights.[106]
3. B was a registered owner of the land: therefore, there was no risk of a third party believing that C had a better right to the land than B. So the need to protect third parties from that risk did *not* justify extinguishing B's property right.[107]

---

[99] Indeed, the state has lost out through adverse possession: local authorities, owning many pieces of land and with stretched resources have, in the past, lost land by failing to take action against squatters within the prescribed period.

[100] Limitation Act 1980, ss 15 and 17 (in relation to unregistered land); and Land Registration Act 2002, Sched 6 (in relation to registered land).

[101] [2003] 1 AC 419.

[102] See *per* Neuberger J at first instance: [2000] 1 Ch 676 at 709 (Neuberger J's order was reversed by the Court of Appeal but restored by the House of Lords).

[103] Judgment of 15 November 2005: [2005] 3 EGLR 1.

[104] *Ibid* at [61]–[62].

[105] *Ibid* at [72].

[106] *Ibid* at [73].

[107] *Ibid* at [65].

In a case similar to **Example 14a**, an English judge independently reached the same conclusion that the doctrine of adverse possession, as interpreted by the House of Lords in *JA Pye (Oxford) Ltd v Graham*, was incompatible with P1:Article 1. As a result, Nicholas Strauss QC (sitting as a Deputy High Court judge) interpreted the statutory provisions governing adverse possession in such a way as to protect B rather than C.[108]

However, the Grand Chamber of the European Court of Human Rights *reversed* the decision of the Chamber of the Fourth Section.[109] By a 10–7 majority, the Grand Chamber found that B's P1:Article 1 right had *not* been infringed. The majority's finding was based on the view that:

1.   the doctrine's main aim is to 'control the use' of land, by deciding the competing claims of B and C: its purpose is *not* to deprive B of a possession;[110] and

2.   such a control of use can be justified if it is a proportionate response to a legitimate aim. In favouring C when he has occupied for a long period, the doctrine does pursue a legitimate aim: it gives weight to C's 'lengthy, unchallenged possession' and also 'regulates [the] use and transfer' of land by allowing C to transfer his ownership of the land free from B's prior property right;[111] and

3.   although B loses his right without compensation, this can be seen as a proportionate response as the doctrine operates only if B fails, over a long period, to take simple steps to assert his right against C.[112]

As for (3), it is important to note that a state has a 'margin of appreciation': to some extent, it can be given the benefit of the doubt if there is a question as to whether the interference with B's right really is a proportionate response to a legitimate aim.[113]

On this view, the doctrine of adverse possession, as interpreted by the House of Lords in *JA Pye (Oxford) Ltd v Graham*, is within the 'margin of appreciation' given to states when deciding if the interference with B's right is a proportionate response to the legitimate aim of protecting C's long use of land.[114] As a result, B's P1:Article 1 right is *not* breached in a

---

[108] Nicholas Strauss QC (sitting as a Deputy High Court judge) in *Beaulane Properties Ltd v Palmer* [2006] Ch 79: it was held that C's action could not establish *adverse* possession if C's use of the land was not inconsistent with B's planned use of that land. However, that attempt to restrict the operation of adverse possession (earlier championed by eg Lord Denning MR in *Wallis's Cayton Bay Holiday Camp Ltd v Shell-Mex and BP Ltd* [1975] QB 94) was firmly rejected by Lord Browne-Wilkinson in *Pye* [2003] 1 AC 419 at [35]–[38].

[109] [2007] ECHR 44302/02 (30 August 2007).

[110] *Ibid* at [66].The finding of the Grand Chamber casts into doubt an important part of the reasoning in *Beaulane Properties Ltd v Palmer* [2006] Ch 79. As noted by Arden LJ in *Ofulue v Bossert* [2008] EWCA Civ 7 at [49], Nicholas Strauss QC was wrong to hold that the adverse possession doctrine operated to deprive B of a possession rather than to control B's use of land. As a result, the Land Registry's practice of refusing to accept adverse possession claims that do not comply with the *Beaulane* test (noted and criticised by Kerridge and Brierly [2007] *Conv* 552 at 557–8) must end.

[111] *Ibid* at [71] and [74].

[112] *Ibid* at [78]–[80]. It was also stated at [79] that compensation 'sits uneasily' with a limitation provision as one of the purposes of such a provision is to prevent B bringing *any* claim after a certain date. But it is hard to see the relevance of that point in a case where B's registration means that, despite the lapse of time, it can easily be proved B was an owner of the land.

[113] After all, the state, rather than the European Court of Human Rights, is in a better position to judge relevant issues (eg the wider social or economic impact of a rule). The 'margin of appreciation' is also relevant to the determination of an English court: Parliament or the Government, rather than the court, may be in a better position to judge relevant issues (eg, the wider social or economic impact of a rule). See eg *per* Lord Hope in *R v DPP, ex p Kebiline* [2000] 2 AC 326 at 380–81; *per* Lord Woolf in *Poplar Housing Ltd v Donoghue* [2002] QB 48 at [69].

[114] The margin of appreciation was also deemed to be important in *Ofulue v Bossert* [2008] EWCA Civ 7. In that case, the Court of Appeal dismissed B's claim that the loss of his ownership of land, as a result of C's adverse

case such as **Example 14a**: the same conclusion must apply in a case such as **Example 14b**, where B has been warned about the possibility of losing his land.[115]

(iv) Evaluation

The dispute in *JA Pye (Oxford) Ltd v UK* provided an opportunity for European judges to examine the applicability to the English land law system of P1:Article 1. Their deliberations provide a good example of two important points:

1. Human rights reasoning can be relevant in a dispute relating to the use of a thing; *but*
2. Such reasoning cannot, *by itself*, resolve the **basic tension** between B and C.

Certainly, in the *JA Pye* case, recasting the dispute between B and C in terms of human rights did *not* make resolving the **basic tension** any easier. The inherent difficulty of resolving that tension explains why, over the two decisions of the European Court of Human Rights, 11 judges found in B's favour; and 13, in effect,[116] found in C's favour. In fact, in the *JA Pye* case, C can *also* claim the protection of P1:Article 1: under English law, C independently acquires a property right *as soon as* he takes physical control of B's land (see E1:2.1.1).[117] So the human rights analysis simply leads us back to our initial starting point: the basic tension between the needs of B and those of C must be resolved.

8.3.2 Article 8 of the European Convention on Human Rights

(i) The basic right

Article 8 states that: 'Everyone has the right to respect for his private and family life, his home and his correspondence.' That right can be important in a dispute about the use of land. So, in **Example 12**, if the land that is taken by the Government department is B's home, B's Article 8 right is prima facie breached. However, as in **Example 12**, there is no need for B to have recourse to that right: he can simply assert his pre-existing property right, as an owner of the land, against C.

In **Example 1**, B may also claim that his Article 8 right is under threat (see A:3.1.4). After all, if C is allowed to sell A's land, B will have to move out of his home. To consider B's case as its strongest, let us say C is a public body and is thus under a duty not to breach B's Article 8 right. *If* B succeeds in showing that a sale would interfere with B's right to respect for his home, B can bypass the basic structure by showing that it would be unlawful for C to remove B from the land.

Will B's argument succeed? As B has set up home together with A, a forced sale may well

---

possession, was contrary to P1:Art 1. The facts of the case were not identical to those considered by the European Court of Human Rights in *JA Pye*, but the general reasoning of the European Court meant that the application of the doctrine of adverse possession was within the UK's 'margin of appreciation': see *per* Arden LJ at [50]–[57].

[115] The Land Registration Act 2002, Sch 6 changed the law on adverse possession to give greater protection to B, a registered owner of land. After ten years of adverse possession, C must now *apply* to be registered in B's place – B will then be alerted to C's application and, unless special factors apply (see E5:3.2.5), B will have a further two years in which to stake steps to remove C from the land.

[116] Of course C is not a party to the case in the European Court of Human Rights. That court could not disturb the decision of the House of Lords in C's favour (*JA Pye (Oxford) Ltd v Graham* [2003] 1 AC 347). So the European judges finding against B were finding in favour of the UK.

[117] In *JA Pye (Oxford) Ltd v UK* [2007] ECHR 44302/02 (30 August 2007) at [83] there is perhaps a recognition of this point.

seem to interfere with B's right to respect for his home life. However, that is not the end of the matter.

(ii) The qualifications to the basic right

First, B's Article 8 right is not absolute: it is subject to qualifications. Article 8(2) states that the basic right can be interfered with where the interference is both: (i) in accordance with the law; *and* (ii) necessary in a democratic society[118] in the interests of national security, public safety or the economic well-being of the country, for the prevention of disorder or crime, for the protection of health or morals, or for the protection of the rights and freedoms of others.

So, in **Example 1**, C Bank can argue that removing B from B's home is necessary to protect its right to sell A's land should A default in his loan repayments.[119] Indeed, C Bank could even argue that the 'economic well-being of the country' would be threatened if lenders found it difficult to enforce such rights (see **A:3.2**). If C Bank is forced to let B remain on that land and so cannot sell it, C Bank can also argue that this interferes with his right, under P1:Article 1, to the peaceful enjoyment of his possessions: after all, the right given to C Bank by A counts as a 'possession'.

(iii) Article 8 and the land law system

(a) The first view

As we saw when examining adverse possession, the application of human rights reveals the **basic tension** between B and C. It is clear that defining and protecting B's Article 8 right necessarily involves resolving that basic tension. One view is that the basic structure of property law *itself* carries out this balancing of interests and so fully defines and protects B's Article 8 right. On this view, if B wishes to prevent C Bank removing him from the land, B *cannot* bypass the basic structure. Instead, B must show that he can assert against C Bank a direct right, or a pre-existing property right or persistent right. The recognised exceptions to B's Article 8 right and C Bank's competing interests are reflected in the hurdles B has to clear in showing he can assert such a right against C Bank.

EXAMPLE 15

B1 and B2 (a husband and wife) jointly rent a home from C, a local authority. B2 leaves B1 and moves out of the home: she also ends the agreement between B1, B2 and C under which B1 and B2 rented the home. B1 asks C if he can remain as a sole occupier, but C refuses this request as the land is needed to house families rather than individuals. B1 remarries and continues to occupy the home. C brings proceedings to remove B1 from the land.

In such a case, it is clear that, as B2 has ended the agreement under which B1 had a right to occupy the land, B1 no longer has a right against C (see **G1B:Example 21a**). The basic structure thus allows C to remove B1 from the land. However, in *Harrow LBC v Qazi*,[120] the

---

[118] An interference will count as 'necessary in a democratic society' if it: (i) answers a 'pressing social need'; and (ii) is 'proportionate' to the aim pursued: see eg *Connors v UK* (2004) 40 EHRR 189 at [81].

[119] In so doing, C could point to the fact that para 2 of Art 8 allows B's right to be limited where necessary in the interests of 'the economic well-being of the country'.

[120] [2004] 1 AC 983.

essential facts of which are identical to **Example 15,** B1 claimed that, if C removed him from the land, there would nonetheless be a breach of B1's Article 8 right.

The majority of the House of Lords adopted the view set out above. Lord Hope and Lord Scott (with whom Lord Millett agreed) reviewed ECHR cases on the application of Article 8 and held that: (i) if B has no direct right or pre-existing right that he can assert against C; then (ii) *even if C is a public body,* Article 8 does *not* give B an independent means of asserting a right against C.[121] On this view, even in the special case where C is a public body, B *cannot* bypass the basic structure by making an appeal to Article 8: the basic structure itself *wholly* defines and protects B's Article 8 right.

(b) Connors v UK

In *Qazi,* Lord Bingham and Lord Steyn dissented from the confident view taken by the majority, arguing instead that, in 'very highly exceptional cases'[122] it *may* be possible for B to show that the basic structure does *not* fully protect his Article 8 right. That view was later proved correct by the decision of the ECHR in *Connors v UK.*[123]

EXAMPLE 16

B1 and B2 (a husband and wife) are gypsies. From 1984 to 1997 they live in a caravan on a site run by C, a local authority. They briefly move away but return in 1998. C makes a contractual promise that B1 and B2 can occupy a plot on the caravan site. In 2000, C (as it is entitled to do under the terms of the contract) revokes its permission for B1 and B2 to occupy the land and asks B1 and B2 to leave. B1 and B2 apply to the High Court for permission to challenge C's decision by judicial review: that application is refused. C brings summary proceedings to remove B1 and B2 from the land. A court makes an order in C's favour on the basis that, as B1 and B2 no longer have permission to be there, they are wrongfully occupying C's land.

This example is based on the essential facts of *Connors v UK.* It is clear that, as B1 and B2's permission to occupy has been revoked, they have no right against C. As a result, the basic structure gives no protection to B1 and B2. However, B1 and B2 took their case to the European Court of Human Rights, arguing that C (an organ of the state) had breached their Article 8 right. The court found in favour of B1 and B2: this demonstrates that, in some cases at least, the basic structure does *not* fully protect B's Article 8 right.

It is important to note that *Connors* does seem to be a highly unusual case:

1. The court noted that the 'vulnerable position of gypsies as a minority means that some special consideration should be given to their needs and their different lifestyle . . . [t]o this extent, there is thus a positive obligation imposed on the Contracting States under Article 8 to facilitate the gypsy way of life.'[124]

---

[121] *Ibid* at [84] *per* Lord Hope: the Strasbourg jurisprudence has shown that contractual and proprietary rights to possession cannot be defeated by a defence based on article 8'. Lord Scott at [139]: 'I have referred to these Strasbourg decisions in order to try and demonstrate the consistency with which the principle which, to my mind, underlies article 8 has been applied. In no case has article 8 been applied so as to diminish or detract from the contractual and proprietary rights of the person entitled to possession.'
[122] *Per* Lord Bingham at [25].
[123] (2004) 40 EHRR 189.
[124] *Ibid* at [84].

2.   Existing legislation applying in England meant that C's ability to remove B1 and B2 would be limited if: (i) B1 and B2 were renting a house from C rather than a caravan site;[125] or (ii) if B1 and B2 were renting a caravan site from anyone *other* than a local authority.[126]

3.   The court also emphasised the lack of *procedural* protection available to B1 and B2.[127] However, it is hard to see the relevance of this.[128] The key point was that C did not need to show any specific reason for choosing to revoke B1 and B2's permission to occupy: it could simply revoke the permission and then gain a court order to remove B1 and B2. Procedural protection can only assist B1 and B2 if the grounds on which C can end B1 and B2's right to occupy are limited.[129]

The legislation applying at the time of *Connors* thus meant that C's power to revoke its permission and remove B1 and B2 from the land was dependent on the facts that: (i) B1 and B2 were occupying a caravan site provided for gypsies; and (ii) C was a local authority rather than a private landlord. In effect then, the legislation discriminated against gypsies.[130] So, the general rule is that B's Article 8 right should be given *more* protection where B is a gypsy and C is an organ of the state; but, in precisely that situation, English law gave B *less* protection. The UK was therefore found to be in breach of its Article 8 duty to B1 and B2.[131]

(c) The new view

In *Kay v Lambeth LBC*,[132] the House of Lords (sitting in a special panel of seven judges) had the chance to reconsider the relationship between the basic structure and Article 8, in light of the decision of the European Court of Human Rights in *Connors v UK*. The House of Lords held that, in a *very exceptional case*, the basic structure of property law may fail to fully protect B's Article 8 right. So, at least where C is a public body, there must be an opportunity for B to claim that, even though he can assert no direct right or pre-existing right against C, Article 8 means that it would be unlawful for C to prevent B continuing to

---

[125] Housing Act 1985 (see G1B:1.2).

[126] Mobile Homes Act 1983: s 5(1) specifically exempts 'any land occupied by a local authority as a caravan site providing accommodation for gypsies' from the general protection given to B where he is allowed to station a mobile home or caravan on another's land and occupies that mobile home or caravan as his only or main residence.

[127] (2004) 40 EHRR 189, eg at [92].

[128] The analysis here makes it hard to defend the view of Dyson LJ in *Smith (on behalf of the Gypsy Council) v Evans* [2007] EWCA Civ 1318 at [36] at [64] that the key problem in *Connors* was the lack of procedural protection available to B.

[129] As would have been the case if B1 and B2's occupation were protected under the Housing Act 1985 or the Mobile Homes Act 1983.

[130] *Ibid* at [109]: '[B1 and B2's] complaints related in essence to the exemption conferred on local authority gypsy sites.'

[131] As a result, the relevant legislation (s 4 of the Caravans Act 1968) was amended by s 211 of the Housing Act 2004: in a case such as *Connors*, a court hearing C's application to remove B1 and B2 now has a discretion to postpone the removal of B1 and B2 for up to 12 months at a time. This change does *not* put a gypsy occupying a local authority site in *exactly* the same position as a party occupying a home provided by a local authority; nor does it put such an occupier in *exactly* the same position as a party occupying a caravan site provided by a private landlord. However, in *Smith (on behalf of the Gypsy Council) v Evans* [2007] EWCA Civ 1318, the Court of Appeal held that the change meant that English law is now compatible with B's Article 8 right. In any case, cl 301 of the Housing and Regeneration Bill, if passed, will remove the exemption contained in s 5(1) of the Mobile Homes Act 1983 and applying to local authority caravan sites providing accommodation for gypsies.

[132] [2006] 2 AC 465. For a helpful analysis of that decision, see Goymour [2006] *CLJ* 696.

occupy particular land as his home. On this view, simply applying the basic structure would, in some cases, allow C, a public body, to behave unlawfully.

It is important to note that all seven judges agreed that the basic structure will fail to protect B's Article 8 right only in *very exceptional cases*.[133] The majority held that B's personal circumstances are irrelevant in deciding if the basic structure complies with Article 8.[134] Article 8 is therefore relevant *only* if B can show that the legal principles applying to his case are incompatible with his right to respect for his home.[135] So, in a case such as *Connors*, it does not matter that: (i) B1 and B2 had especially strong connections with the caravan site; and (ii) B1 and B2 lived with a baby suffering from a serious illness. Rather, Article 8 is relevant only because of the wider legal principle that singled out gypsies occupying local authority sites for a particularly low level of protection.[136]

So, if C is a public body, it may, very exceptionally, be possible for B to bypass the basic structure and rely on a human right, such as that set out in Article 8. Similarly, when considering the general position that applies when C is not a public body, an appeal to human rights may, again very exceptionally, lead a judge to interpret a statute;[137] apply a past judicial decision; or exercise a discretion in a new and different way.

SUMMARY of B:8

The **basic structure** is the property law's system attempt to resolve the **basic tension** of property law. Arguments based on human rights cannot resolve that tension; instead, they reflect it. When applied to disputes about the use of a thing, Article 1 of the First Protocol and Article 8, like the basic structure, attempt to strike a balance between B and C. In applying the basic structure, it may therefore be useful for judges to draw on human rights: in particular, if a dispute involves a public body, it is important to remember that such a body has a duty not to interfere with ECHR rights.

However, a resort to human rights cannot be used as a way to avoid the basic structure: in almost all cases, that structure will fully define and adequately protect any human right that B or C may claim to have.[138] So, in **Example 1**, there is no need for a judge to 'reinvent the

---

[133] As noted by eg Hughes and Davis [2006] 70 *Conv* 526 at 550–52, this means that the chances of B successfully using Art 8 where he can assert no direct right or pre-existing right against C are very slim. Lord Brown at [211] stated that it would only be in 'infinitely rare' cases such as *Connors* that, despite B's lack of a direct right or pre-existing right, it would be unlawful for a local authority to remove B from its land.

[134] [2006] 2 AC 465 *per* Lord Hope at [110], Lord Scott at [172], Baroness Hale at [192] and Lord Brown at [212].

[135] In contrast, Lord Bingham (with whom Lord Nicholls and Lord Walker agreed) suggested at [27]–[38] that (again in a 'highly exceptional case') the personal circumstances of B *could* be relevant in considering whether B's Art 8 right has been breached. The approach of the majority in *Kay* was confirmed by the Court of Appeal in *Birmingham CC v Doherty* [2006] EWCA Civ 1739 at [22]. The House of Lords heard an appeal from that decision in 2008. The speeches when delivered will be discussed on the companion website.

[136] The 'unusual' and 'discriminatory' nature of that position was noted by Lord Scott at [156]; Baroness Hale at [184]; and Lord Brown at [199]–[200].

[137] For a possible example of this, see *Barca v Mears* [2005] 2 FLR 1 at [39]–[41]. However, as argued in **G2.4** (as well as by Dixon [2005] *Conv* 161) the statute could and should have been interpreted in that way even *without* an appeal to Art 8 of the ECHR.

[138] This explains why, as noted by eg Howell (2007) 123 *LQR* 618, the use of the 1998 Act to rewrite land law would be unwelcome. Note too the concern expressed by Morritt V-C in *National Westminster Bank plc v Malhan* [2004] EWHC 847 at [52] on the use of human rights arguments by B, in a case such as **Example 1**, against C: 'It would create havoc in the mortgage lending field as well as substantial injustice to both borrowers and lenders if priorities clearly settled before the Human Rights Act 1998 came into force could be altered by its application thereafter.'

wheel' by jettisoning the basic structure and attempting, from scratch, to weigh B's Article 8 right to respect for his home against C Bank's right, protected by P1:Article 1, to sell A's land and use the proceeds to meet A's debt. Instead, a judge can take advantage of the **basic structure** that is *already* in place to weigh those competing rights. The House of Lords have therefore made clear that, even if C is a public body, it is only in *very rare* cases that B will be able to bypass the basic structure and directly assert his Article 8 right against C.[139] In *almost every case*, the basic structure will adequately define and protect B's right to respect for his home. Casting disputes between B and C in the language of human rights is a very effective way to reveal the dramatic tensions that lie at the heart of the property law system. However, the human rights analysis, by itself, cannot resolve those tensions: to do that, we need to use the basic structure.

9 DOCTRINE AND PRACTICAL CONVENIENCE

The basic structure aims to provide a set of clear, settled rules and principles that can: (i) resolve the basic tension in a dispute between B and C (see A:1); *and* (ii) allow parties to plan their affairs (see **2.1** above). However, the mere existence of the basic structure does not guarantee such a set of rules. For example, if judges were free to exercise a wide discretion in deciding: (i) if B has a direct right against C; or (ii) if B has a pre-existing persistent right or property right, then (iii) the basic tension would again come to the surface. It would be very difficult for parties to plan their affairs or to predict how disputes might be resolved. So, the basic structure is accompanied by a set of **doctrinal** rules and principles: they are the clear, settled rules that allow the basic structure to function.

However, it must always be remembered that the basic structure is a means to the end of achieving a just result. In A:1, we compared the property law system to chess; but, of course, property law is more than a game.[140] Rather, it has a crucial practical impact on people's lives. As a result, it would be dangerous if, by attributing too much value to the sanctity of the doctrinal rules, judges lost sight entirely of the effect of their decisions. In fact, as we will see at a number of points in this book,[141] both Parliament and judges *have* departed from the doctrinal rules where this is felt to be necessary to achieve a more practically convenient result. The needs of **practical convenience** may thus in some cases conflict with the doctrinal solution.[142]

For example, on a number of occasions, the House of Lords has faced situations where: (i) B wishes to qualify for statutory protection available only to a party with a Lease (a particular property right in land); and (ii) on the standard, doctrinal definition of a Lease, B does *not* have that property right; but (iii) the practically convenient result, furthering the

---

[139] *Kay v Lambeth LBC* [2006] 2 AC 465.

[140] See further Hackney, ch 6 in *The Classification of Obligations* (ed Birks, 1997). Hackney notes at 154 that 'the purity of content of property law may [cause] its predicted results to diverge from contemporary notions of commercial fairness'.

[141] See eg the discussion of the development of the Restrictive Covenant (**E2:1.3.2** and **G6:1.6**).

[142] This contrast between doctrine and practical convenience is based on Harris, ch 8 in *Oxford Essays in Jurisprudence* (3rd Series, ed Eekelaar and Bell, 1987). There, Harris contrasts: (i) 'doctrinal rationality' (an approach focussed on achieving results consistent with doctrine); with (ii) 'utility rationality' (an approach focused on achieving practically convenient results).

underlying purpose of the statute, is to allow B to qualify for the statutory protection.[143] In those cases, it seems that the House of Lords has departed from the doctrinal rules in order to protect B (see **G1B:1.5.2 and 1.5.3**). Conversely, there have been situations where: (i) B wishes to qualify for statutory protection available only to a party with a Lease; and (ii) on the standard, doctrinal definition of a Lease, B *does* have that property right; but (iii) the practically convenient result, furthering the underlying purpose of the statute, is to *deny* B the statutory protection.[144] In at least one such case, it seems that the House of Lords has departed from the doctrinal rules in order to deny B protection (see **G1B:1.5.5**).

It is tempting to dismiss such departures from doctrine as wrong. Certainly, if a judge had a *general* power to depart from doctrine *whenever* he felt that practical convenience demanded a different result, the certainty and consistency provided by the basic structure would be fatally undermined. However, it must be possible for such departures from doctrine to occur *in exceptional cases*. After all, doctrine is not an end in itself: it also aims to achieve a just resolution of the impossibly difficult basic tension. So, where the result demanded by doctrine seems to be out of line with practical convenience, it is important to have a means of modifying it. There is a question about whether such modifications are best made by Parliament rather than by the courts. However, in general, it seems reasonable for a high-level court, such as the House of Lords, to have the power, in exceptional cases, to reconcile doctrine with practical convenience.

There is thus an analogy between: (i) the impact of human rights on the basic structure; and (ii) the impact of practical convenience on the doctrinal rules that develop the basic structure. In each case, each of the two concepts attempts to resolve the basic tension. And, in almost all cases: (i) the results reached by the basic structure are consistent with human rights; and (ii) the results reached by the doctrinal rules are consistent with the needs of practical convenience. In general, then, there is no need to 'reinvent the wheel' by ignoring the basic structure or the doctrinal rules. However, in exceptional cases, it may be appropriate for a judge to depart from the basic structure, or from the doctrinal rules, to ensure that a just result is reached.

10 DISPUTES ABOUT THE USE OF A RIGHT

There is a clear difference between a dispute about the use a thing (eg, a piece of land or a bike) and disputes about the use of a right (eg, A's account at Z Bank): see **A:4**. We noted there that *some, but not all,* parts of the basic structure are relevant to a dispute about the use of a right.

A:EXAMPLE 3

A has an account with Z Bank. A goes into insolvency. A's rights, including his bank account, therefore pass to C, A's trustee in bankruptcy. C is under a statutory duty to use A's rights, including A's bank account, to pay off A's creditors. However, B claims that, *before* going bankrupt, A declared a Trust, in B's favour, of A's bank account.

---

[143] See eg *Antoniades v Villiers* [1990] 1 AC 417; *Bruton v London & Quadrant Housing Trust* [2000] 1 AC 406.
[144] See eg *Burrows v Brent LBC* [1996] 1 WLR 1448.

In such a case, as in the **basic situation**, the basic tension between B and C is evident. Again, B needs to show that he has a right that he can assert against C. The first option, again, is for B to have a *direct right* against C: a right arising as a result of C's conduct. And, again, it is very unlikely that B will have such a right: as in **Example 1**, there is no real reason why C would choose to act in such a way as to give B a direct right.

However, in **A:Example 3**, as in **Example 1**, we need to bear in mind that B may be able to assert a *pre-existing* right against C. However, as there is no *thing* involved, it is impossible for B to have a pre-existing property right. This proves the point made in **A:4**: the basic structure, as set out above, does not apply *in full* to disputes about the use of a right.

Nonetheless, in **A:Example 3**, as in **Example 1**, we need to bear in mind that B may be able to assert a *persistent* right against C. A persistent right is simply a right against a right. It is therefore possible for B to have a pre-existing right against A's right against Z Bank. For example, if B can show that A declared a Trust of his bank account in B's favour, B can acquire a right against A's bank account. As a right under a Trust counts as a persistent right B will, prima facie, have the power to assert that right against C (see **Example 5** above).[145]

This suggests that, in a case such as **A:Example 3**, we need to ask: (i) if B has a direct right against C; and (ii) if B has a pre-existing persistent right against A's right. However, there is an additional question to ask. If A has a right, such as the personal right against Z Bank in **A:Example 3**, it is usually possible for A to *transfer* that right to B. The initial question is whether such a transfer is possible; if it is, B then needs to show that, on the facts, such a transfer has been made. If B can do so, this will generally be decisive: for how can C acquire a right if, *before* C's involvement, A transferred his right to B? For example if, in **A:Example 3**, A transferred his bank account (ie, his personal right against Z Bank) to B before going into bankruptcy, that bank account is no longer held by A and so cannot pass to C.[146]

It is therefore possible to summarise the structure that applies to a dispute about the use of a right initially held by A. It is clear that it is similar to, but also different from, the basic structure applying to disputes about the use of a thing:

1. Did A, before the point at which C claims to have acquired a right, **transfer** the right in question to B?
   (i) Acquisition question: Is the right capable of being transferred to B? If so, has A, on the facts, transferred his right to B?
   If No: go to 2;
   If Yes to both B wins: go to 5
2. Does B have a **direct right** against C that prevents C from making his desired use of the right in question?
   (i) Content question: does the right B claims prevent C from making his desired use?

---

[145] See eg *Barclays Bank v Quistclose Investments Ltd* [1970] AC 567.
[146] B's acquisition of a right can be set aside in A's insolvency if: (i) the transfer of the right to B; or (ii) B's acquisition of a persistent right counts as (for example) a transaction at an undervalue or as an unlawful preference under the Insolvency Act 1986, ss 339–41 (where A is an individual or partnership); ss 238–40 (where A Ltd is a company).

(ii)   Acquisition question: has B, on the facts, acquired that right?
   If No to either question: go to 3;
   If Yes to both questions, B wins: go to 5

3. Did B, immediately before C acquired his right, have a **persistent right** (a right against A's right) that prevents C from making his desired use of the right in question?

   (i)   Content question: does the right B claims prevent C from making his desired use? *And* does the right B claims count as a persistent right?

   (ii)   Acquisition question: has B, on the facts, acquired that right?
      If No to either question, C wins: go to 5
      If Yes to both questions: go to 4

4. Does C have a **defence** to B's pre-existing persistent right?
   If No, B wins: go to 5; If Yes, C wins: go to 5

5. What **remedy** will a court give to protect the winner's right?

11   APPLYING THE BASIC STRUCTURE: AN EXAMPLE

The best way to see the usefulness of the basic structure is to apply it to specific examples. We will, of course, be doing that throughout this book. Here, we will focus on one particular case, *National Provincial Bank v Ainsworth*,[147] that involved a dispute about the use of land. The discussion set out here is accompanied by a set of animated slides available on the companion website. The website also contains examples, again accompanied by slides, of other leading land law cases,[148] as well as to a case involving a thing other than land,[149] and to a case involving a dispute about the use of a right.[150]

11.1 *National Provincial Bank v Ainsworth*: the facts

The basic facts of *National Provincial Bank v Ainsworth* are practically identical to those of **Example 1**. Mr Ainsworth, A, was an owner of land—a home that he occupied with his wife, B, and their children. The marriage hit difficulties and A moved out of the family home. A then borrowed money on a 'mortgage' loan from C, the National Provincial Bank. A's debt was thus secured by giving C a right over A's land, allowing C to sell the land if A defaulted on the loan repayments.[151] C's right is known as a Charge (see **E1:1.1** and **G4:2.1**). A fell behind in his repayments and C wished to enforce its Charge by: (i) removing B from the land; (ii) selling the home; and (iii) using the proceeds of sale to satisfy the outstanding debt owed by A to C.

---

[147] [1965] AC 1175.

[148] *Ashburn Anstalt v Arnold & Co* [1989] Ch 1; *Lloyds Bank plc v Rosset* [1991] 1 AC 107; *City of London Building Society v Flegg* [1988] AC 54.

[149] *Port Line Ltd v Ben Line Steamers Ltd* [1958] 2 QB 146.

[150] *Barclays Bank Ltd v Quistclose Ltd* [1970] AC 567.

[151] These facts are somewhat simplified. After giving C the Charge, A had, with C's consent, transferred his ownership of the home to A's company. This company then gave C a new Charge over the home. When C later tried to remove B and sell the land, B's first step was to get the transfer to A's company set aside: B succeeded but this was held not to invalidate C's Charge. This means that everything was back to the initial situation of C having a Charge over A's land: the transfer to A's company can thus be ignored in analysing the case.

The facts thus fit with the **basic situation**. As it has acquired a Charge over the land, C (National Provincial Bank) has a right to use that land in a particular way. B (Mrs Ainsworth) also has a right to use the land: at the very least, A has given her permission to occupy the land. So, both B and C have a right to use the land. And B and C wish to make inconsistent uses of the land: (i) B wishes to remain in occupation; and (ii) C wishes to remove B and to sell the land. To resolve this basic tension between B and C, we need to apply the basic structure.

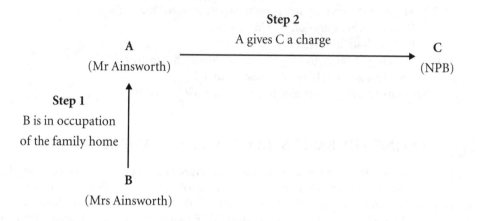

11.2 Applying the basic structure

As this is a case where C acquired its right from A (ie, by a dependent acquisition) we can use the full basic structure as summarised in **section 7** above, including the question of whether B has a pre-existing persistent right she can assert against C.

> **QUESTION 1**
>
> Does B have a direct right against C that prevents C from making its desired use of the thing in question (the land)?   **Answer: No**

This is one of the common cases in which B has no chance of acquiring a direct right against C. For C has done nothing that could lead to B gaining such a right: for example, C has made no promise to give B a right. This is not surprising: as noted in **section 3** above, there is generally no reason for C, having acquired a right over A's land, to act in such a way as to give B a direct right.

> **QUESTION 2**
>
> Did B, immediately before C acquired its right, have a pre-existing property right, or a pre-existing persistent right, that prevents C from making its desired use of the thing in question (the land)?

(i)   Content question: does the right B claims prevent C from making its desired use? *And* does the right B claims count as a property right or persistent right?

       Answer: No

(ii)   Acquisition question: did B, on the facts, acquire that property right or persistent right?

       Answer: N/A

It was clear in *National Provincial Bank v Ainsworth* that B had a pre-existing right against A. In fact, B had two rights. First, A had given B permission to occupy the land: B thus had a *licence* to use the land (see **E6:1**). However, if B merely had a licence, her position would have been very weak: A can simply revoke his permission for B to occupy and B, after a reasonable period, would have to leave the land (see **E6:2.2**).

Second, B had a peculiar right, known as a *'deserted wife's Equity'*.[152] B acquired that right when her relationship with A ended and A moved out of the family home. The 'deserted wife's Equity' no longer exists as a right: it was a product of judges' attempts to regulate the rights of spouses and has now been replaced by a different, statutory right of occupation.[153] However, at the time of *National Provincial Bank v Ainsworth*, that statutory right of occupation did not exist and so B's position depended on the effect of this outdated 'deserted wife's Equity'. It was, essentially, a right that the wife should be looked after by the deserting husband. A large degree of judicial discretion was involved in deciding what was required of a husband in any given case. So, if A had attempted to revoke his permission for B to occupy the home, it is *possible* that B would have been able to use the 'deserted wife's Equity' to prevent A from doing so. But the court would have to consider a wide range of circumstances: such as A and B's conduct towards each other and their relative resources. It might be that A would be prevented from removing B; but, if B had access to suitable alternative accommodation, things might be different.

So, there was a problem even in answering the first part of the content question. If B's licence had been revoked by A, it would no longer allow B to occupy the land. And it was not clear that B's 'deserted wife's Equity' necessarily allowed her to remain in occupation of the land. However, the real difficulty for B lay with the second part of the content question. To show that she had a pre-existing right capable of binding C, B needed to show that her licence or her 'deserted wife's Equity' counted as a property right or as a persistent right.

It was clear that neither of B's rights could count as a property right. The list of property rights in land is longer than the list of property rights in things other than land; but it does not include either the licence or the 'deserted wife's Equity' (see **E1:1**). So, B could not claim a property right.

B therefore had to argue that either the licence or the 'deserted wife's Equity' counted as a persistent right: a right against A's right as owner of the land. To acquire a persistent right, B needs to show that A is under a duty to B in relation to a specific right. B's licence clearly could not count as a persistent right: A could revoke his permission for B to occupy at any point, and so A was under no duty to B. But the Court of Appeal was prepared to say that

---

[152] B also had a property right, arising from her physical control of the land after A left (see **E6:2.3**). However, that right could not bind C as: (i) C acquired its right from A; and (ii) A's property right arose before B's property right.

[153] That right originally arose under the Matrimonial Homes Act 1967 and is now set out by the Family Law Act 1996, ss 30–33.

B's 'deserted wife's Equity' *did* count as a persistent right or, to use the orthodox term employed by the Court of Appeal, as an 'Equitable property right'.[154] The Court of Appeal therefore had to consider **Question 3** of the basic structure: the defences question. The Court of Appeal found that C had no defence to B's pre-existing persistent right. It then considered **Question 4**: the remedies question. As is usual where a right relates to land, the Court of Appeal decided B's right should be specifically protected: it therefore ordered that B could remain in occupation of the land.

The House of Lords, however, reversed the Court of Appeal's decision. It held instead that B's 'deserted wife's Equity' was *not* a persistent right. It was simply a personal right: a right that A must act in a particular way. That is clearly correct. To have a persistent right, B needs to show that A is under a duty to B in relation to a *specific right*. The 'deserted wife's Equity' did not impose such a duty on A. Instead, it obliged A, in a general sense, to look after B. So, for example, even if A was obliged to provide accommodation for B, there was no reason why A had to let B continue to live in *the same house*: A could instead perform his duty by providing B with accommodation elsewhere. So, at most, B could show only that A was under a duty to act in a particular way: to provide B with *somewhere* to live. B's pre-existing right was hence a personal right (a right against A) not a persistent right (a right against A's ownership of the land).

We can understand the *effect* of the House of Lords' decision by applying the basic structure. B cannot satisfy the **content question**: she cannot show that her pre-existing right is either a property right or a persistent right. As a result, there is no need to look at the **acquisition question**.

Further, as B does not have a pre-existing property right or persistent right, **Question 3**—the defences question—is also irrelevant. Instead, we can simply say that: (i) B has no direct right against C; and (ii) B has no pre-existing property right or persistent right; so (iii) B has *no right* she can assert against C. The result then is that C wins: that brings us on to **Question 4**.

QUESTION 4

What **remedy** will a court give to protect the winner's right?

As is usual where C has a right relating to land, C's right was specifically protected. C was therefore free to: (i) remove B from A's land; (ii) sell that land; and (iii) use the proceeds to pay off A's debt.

SUMMARY of B:11.2

The dispute in *National Provincial Bank v Ainsworth* went all the way to the House of Lords as there was some uncertainty about a very important aspect of the **content** question: whether B's right, the 'deserted wife's Equity' counted as a persistent right (or, as the courts put it, an 'Equitable property right'). The Court of Appeal said it did; the House of Lords took the opposite view. This was fatal to B's claim: as (i) she had no direct right against C; and (ii) she had no pre-existing property right in the land; then (iii) B's only chance had been to show that she had a pre-existing persistent right.

---

[154] [1964] Ch 665.

11.3 Human rights

National Provincial Bank v Ainsworth was, of course, decided before the Human Rights Act 1998. It is worth briefly considering whether the result would have been different if that Act had applied. The answer is **no**; and would be **no** even if C were a public body and hence prohibited from interfering with B's ECHR rights.

B could claim that her Article 8 right to respect for her home and family life would be infringed if C were allowed to remove her from the land. However, as noted in **8.3.2** above, that right is not absolute. It can be qualified where necessary for 'the protection of rights and freedoms of others'; and the removal of B is necessary for the protection of C's Charge. Moreover, C could argue that, were B allowed to remain on the land, there would be an interference with its right, protected by P1:Article 1, to the peaceful enjoyment of its possessions. The human rights argument simply reveals the underlying basic tension between B and C. That basic tension is resolved by applying the basic structure. And, as the House of Lords have confirmed, it will only be in very exceptional circumstances that B can bypass that basic structure by relying on a human right (see **8.3.2(iii)(c)** above).[155] And there is nothing very exceptional about the facts of *National Provincial Bank v Ainsworth*.[156]

If the facts of *National Provincial Bank v Ainsworth* arose today, B, instead of having a 'deserted wife's Equity', would have a statutory right to occupy the land owned by A.[157] That right is capable of binding C,[158] but, in a case such as **Example 1**, C will have a defence to B's statutory right if it has not been registered by B.[159] That compromise represents Parliament's attempt to balance the needs of B and of C and thus to protect *both*: (i) B's Article 8 right to respect for her home; and (ii) C's right to use its Charge under P1:Article 1. B does have the chance, by registering her statutory right, to acquire a right that is capable of binding C. But if C checks the register and sees that a statutory right of occupation for B is not recorded there, C can safely acquire its Charge free from any pre-existing statutory right of occupation.

11.4 The basic tension

National Provincial Bank v Ainsworth essentially represents the **basic situation** as set out in both **A:Example 1** and **B:Example 1**. It is thus a case where the claims of commerce are pitted against those of the home (see **A:1**). C wishes to remove B and sell the land so that it can recover the debt owed to it by A. C can argue that the dispute should be resolved in its favour as there are sound commercial reasons for allowing A to raise money by granting a Charge over land. If it becomes very difficult for a party such as C to enforce its Charge, C may be deterred from lending to A; or may only lend at a higher rate. On the other hand, B

---

[155] *Kay v Lambeth LBC* [2006] 2 AC 465.

[156] In *Wood v UK* (1997) 24 EHRR CD 69, the European Court of Human Rights confirmed that there is no breach of Article 8 where C, a party with a Charge, exercises its power to: (i) remove a party from the land; (ii) sell the land; and (iii) use the proceeds to meet a debt owed to C.

[157] See Family Law Act 1996, ss 30–33.

[158] See Family Law Act 1996, s 31(2) and (5).

[159] See Family Law Act 1996, s 31(10) and Land Registration Act 2002, ss 30 and 133. This assumes that A's ownership of the land is registered and that C has registered its Charge. In general, an unregistered right of B *can* bind C if B is in actual occupation of the land (see **C2:6** and **E2:3.6.2**). However, that is *not* the case where B's right is an occupation right arising under the Family Law Act 1996. If the land in **Example 1** is unregistered, the same basic position applies: B's right cannot bind C if it has not been registered.

wishes to continue living, perhaps with her children, in her home. B can argue that the dispute should be resolved in her favour as it is very important to allow parties to be secure in their home. After all, why should B be forced to leave because A has, without the consent of B, given C a later right in the land?

However, as we can see from looking at the decision in *National Provincial Bank v Ainsworth*, the dispute was not simply a contest between commerce and the home. Rather, those general arguments could not be made directly: they have to be filtered through, and constrained by, the **basic structure** of property law. That structure determined the outcome of the case: it stipulates that B can only assert a right against C if B has: (i) a direct right against C; or (ii) a pre-existing property right or persistent right. In the absence of such a right, B was doomed to lose. In the Court of Appeal, B was able to rely indirectly on the argument in favour of the home, by using that argument to convince the judges to regard her right as an 'Equitable property right', ie, as a persistent right. In the House of Lords, however, this argument was rightly rejected: B's right was simply a right that A should act in a particular way: A was not under a duty to B in relation to his specific right as an owner of the land in question. As a result, B's claim to a persistent right failed; and C was able to assert its right to use the land.

SUMMARY of B:11

In Chapter A, we looked at the **basic tension** that underlies property law, and is particularly prominent in land law. In Chapter B, we have seen the **basic structure** the property law system uses to resolve this basic tension. The remainder of the book simply consists of filling in the detail.

The basic structure of property law is evident in even the most complicated cases. Indeed, the only way such cases can be understood is by applying the basic structure and breaking the dispute down into a series of **basic questions**: (i) the **content question**; (ii) the **acquisition question**; (iii) the **defences question**; and (iv) the **remedies question**. This is the way in which the property law system resolves the basic tension and takes the sting out of fierce disputes.

So, when looking at property law, and land law in particular, it is vital to keep the basic structure of property law in mind. That structure is the foundation of the property law system, but of course it is not the only part of the system. To understand the system fully, we need to look in detail at how the basic questions are answered. And, to complete our introduction, we must first examine three **basic concepts**: Equity (which we will examine in **C1**); registration (**C2**); and formality (**C3**).

CHAPTER C1
EQUITY

EQUITY

This chapter aims to provide an overview of the role of Equity within the property law system. Its key point is that, in the property law system, there is no fundamental conflict between: (i) the rules of Common Law; and (ii) the rules of Equity. Rather, those two sets of rules now complement each other and combine to form a coherent whole: the **basic structure**. And those two sets of rules both share the aim of the property law system: to provide a consistent and predictable means of solving the impossibly difficult **basic tension**.

1 AN HISTORICAL INTRODUCTION[1]

Equity is an important but misleading concept. Equity is important because it forms a distinct body of legal rules; it is misleading because it cannot be equated with general notions of fairness or justice. Hence it is vital to distinguish between: (i) Equity with a capital (a distinct body of legal rules); and (ii) equity without a capital (the general notion of fairness or justice).

Equity as a distinct body of legal rules refers simply to the rules developed by judges in a particular English court: the court of Chancery.[2] This court developed its jurisdiction in an unusual way. By the fourteenth century (at the very latest) England had a reasonably well-developed court system. Unlike today, there were numerous local courts, operating independently in their own geographical areas and applying their own local rules. In addition, there were the King's courts, set up to dispense justice on behalf of the monarch. In contrast to the local courts, these could be called 'Common Law' courts: wherever the King's judges happened to be sitting, they would apply a common body of rules. The body of law developed by these courts can therefore be referred to as Common Law. However, litigants were sometimes dissatisfied with the justice dispensed on the King's behalf in his courts. They might then petition the King himself, asking him to intervene and impose a different result. Rather than considering all these cases himself, the King delegated to a particular royal official: the Chancellor. This led to the establishment of a new court: the court of Chancery. And, over time, the Chancellor himself needed to delegate to Chancery judges.

Litigants petitioning the court of Chancery might be motivated by a sense of injustice: a

---

[1] See eg Hohfeld (1913) 11 *Michigan Law Review* 537 esp 546–9; Hackney, *Understanding Equity and Trusts* (1987) ch 1; Hackney, ch 6 and Getzler, ch 7 in *The Classification of Obligations* (ed Birks, 1997); K Mason, ch 3 in *Equity and Commercial Law* (ed Degeling and Edelman, 2005).

[2] 'Court' here is used in a broad sense: the court of Equity came to include both a first instance court and an appeal court, with the establishment in 1851 of the Court of Appeal in Chancery.

feeling that the result the courts of Common Law had imposed, or would impose, was unfair or inadequate. Yet, as courts develop they necessarily build up specific rules that define when they will intervene and give a concrete meaning to the vague notion of injustice. So, just as the Common Law courts built up a specific set of rules,[3] so did the court of Chancery. In this way, the body of law originating in the court of Chancery (Equity with a capital) took on a very different form to equity, the general notion of fairness. As Hackney puts it:

> In the course of the mid seventeenth to early nineteenth centuries, Equity was turned into a systematic body of principles as refined, rigorous and ultimately as unyielding as anything produced by the common law.[4]

The complications of the law and procedure applying in the court of Chancery, satirised in Dickens's *Bleak House* (1852–3), made clear that Equity was not a simple, discretionary gloss on the Common Law.

2 | CONFUSION OR COHERENCE?[5]

As Common Law and Equity developed, each system necessarily influenced the other.[6] As a result, it is important not to over-emphasise the differences between the two sets of rules. Nonetheless, as the court of Chancery developed, the English legal system necessarily found itself in a somewhat bizarre, and certainly illogical, position. Whilst it might just about be sensible to have a layer of local courts alongside national courts, it is surely very strange to have two *competing* sets of national courts. The critical problem is that two sets of national courts can give two sets of answers to the same question. On a particular issue, it might well be the case that the Common Law courts would decide one way, and the courts of Chancery another.

The potential for conflict was limited by the fact that Equity only intervened in certain areas. As a result, Equity could often be seen as a supplementary jurisdiction. A very loose, but potentially useful, analogy can be drawn with the relationship between European Union law and the national law of EU Member States. National law, like the Common Law, has to be general, covering all areas; whereas the impact of European Union law, like Equity, is limited to specific areas. However, in the event of an overlap, it is European Union law that takes priority.[7] The analogous resolution has applied in English law since the seventeenth century: where Common Law and Equity conflict, it is Equity that prevails.[8]

Some progress to a more logical position came in the nineteenth century. In particular,

---

[3] In fact, one reason for taking a case to a Common Law court was the feeling that the result the local courts had imposed, or would impose, was unfair or inadequate. To that extent, the Common Law developed to mitigate the harshness of local courts, just as Equity developed in turn to mitigate the harshness of Common Law courts.

[4] Hackney, *Understanding Equity and Trusts* (1987) ch 1.

[5] See Burrows (2002) 22 *OJLS* 1.

[6] Equity influenced the Common Law: see eg the judgment of Lord Mansfield in *Moses v Macferlan* (1760) 2 Burr 1005. And the Common Law influenced Equity: eg, Hackney has suggested that the duty to account imposed by Common Law on a bailiff, along with the notion of wardship, influenced the development of the Trust: see ch 6 in *The Classification of Obligations* (ed Birks, 1997). For further examples of these cross-jurisdictional influences, see eg Getzler ch 7 in *The Classification of Obligations* (ed Birks, 1997) and K Mason, ch 3 in *Equity and Commercial Law* (ed Degeling and Edelman, 2005).

[7] See eg *Costa v ENEL* [1964] ECR 585; *R v SS Transport, ex p Factortame (No 2)* [1991] 1 AC 603.

[8] This resolution was imposed by King James I after the *Earl of Oxford's Case* (1615) 1 Ch Rep 1.

the Judicature Acts of 1873–5 established a unitary court system.[9] Common Law and Equitable rules could be administered in the same courts by the same judges, with Equity continuing to take priority in case of conflict. However, in those areas where Equity intervenes, English law retains a two-faced quality: rather than being able to say what the law is on a particular point, we often have to say that there is one answer at Common Law, but another in Equity.

Of course, it is possible to explain why, as a matter of history, we are in the position of having two sets of answers to these questions. However, the crucial question is whether we should *continue* to do things this way. If there is a difference between the answer at Common Law and the answer in Equity, we cannot simply say that the systems have different historical origins and leave it at that. Rather, we must ask if the difference can be *justified.*

3 COMMON LAW, EQUITY AND THE BASIC STRUCTURE OF PROPERTY LAW

Equity can provide different answers to the **basic questions** that make up the basic structure of property law. So, in deciding if B has a direct right against C we must look not just at the Common Law but also at Equity. Similarly, in deciding if B has a pre-existing property right or persistent right, it *may* be that we again need to look at both Equity and Common Law.

3.1 Common Law, Equity and direct rights

It is clear that the Common Law recognises means by which B can acquire a direct right against C. For example, B will acquire such a right if C makes a contractual promise to B: in such a case, B's right will arise at Common Law. Equity, however, seems to go further than the Common Law: it recognises means of acquiring direct rights that do not seem to exist, or at least have not been so clearly identified, at Common Law. Two examples of such Equitable principles are: (i) the doctrine of proprietary estoppel (see **C3:Example 3** and **E4**); and (ii) the 'receipt after a promise' principle (see **D3:2.2.2** and **E3:2.2.2**).

Does Equity's recognition of additional means by which B can acquire a direct right cause confusion? It seems not. The Equitable and Common Law principles allowing B to acquire a direct right can be seen as *complementary* rather than conflicting. Together, the principles form a set of means by which B can acquire such a right: individually, each principle can be analysed on its individual merits. Does it matter, then, if a particular means by which B attempts to acquire a direct right is recognised by Equity rather than Common Law?

One suggestion might be that any Equitable means of acquiring such a right is ultimately based on the notion of injustice or 'unconscionability': of preventing C from behaving badly. However, it could, with equal truth, be said that Common Law principles are based on an underlying notion of fairness and preventing injustice. Yet those vague notions must be defined by, and filtered through, specific criteria. Equity, like Common Law, has developed such criteria: it is these rules that determine when rights arise.

---

[9] The Common Law Procedure Acts of 1852 and 1854 also played an important role by, for example, giving Common Law courts a limited power to grant injunctions (a remedy previously associated with courts of Equity).

For example, when looking at proprietary estoppel, we will see that the courts have developed *specific criteria* to determine when that doctrine imposes a duty on A (or C) to B. Those criteria are often said to be based, in a general sense, on 'unconscionability' (see E4:2.3). However, the criteria: (i) set out when B can acquire a right through proprietary estoppel; and (ii) thus define the *specific* meaning of unconscionability in that particular context. If the criteria are satisfied, B will acquire a right: there is no *further* need for B to show that A (or C) has also acted unconscionably. And if the criteria are not satisfied, B will not acquire a right: B cannot escape that result by appealing to a wider notion of 'unconscionability' and showing that A (or C) has, in a general sense, behaved badly.

The same analysis applies to the 'receipt after a promise' principle. For example, in *Ashburn Anstalt v Arnold*,[10] Fox LJ noted that the principle is based, in a general sense, on the need to prevent C behaving 'unconscionably'.[11] However, in that very case, Fox LJ also emphasised that when considering if, in a dispute about the use of land, the 'receipt after a promise' principle gives B a direct right against C, 'certainty is of prime importance'.[12] So, the principle can only apply if *specific criteria* are satisfied; if they are not, B cannot acquire a right by simply showing that C has, in a general sense, behaved badly.

This leads to the question of whether the various Equitable means of acquiring a right have anything in common. Certainly, 'unconscionability' is not a general *test* for when B acquires an Equitable right; rather it is a *conclusion* attached *after* B has satisfied the specific criteria of, for example, proprietary estoppel or the 'receipt after a promise' principle. As L Smith has argued, the way in which 'unconscionability' operates *throughout* Equity depends on this distinction between: (i) a test; and (ii) a conclusion.[13]

In fact, there is no obvious reason why the various means of acquiring an Equitable right *should* have anything in common. After all, we would not expect there to be one overarching principle explaining all the various means by which the Common Law allows B to acquire a right. For example, to find out about Equitable rules applying to the law of contract or the law of unjust enrichment, we tend not to look in books about Equity.[14] Instead, we usually look at books about the law of contract or the law of unjust enrichment, covering *both* Common Law and Equitable rules.[15] Indeed, Maitland, in his *Lectures on Equity*,[16] predicted that:

---

[10] [1989] Ch 1.

[11] *Ibid* at 25: B can only acquire a right against C if C's 'conscience' is affected.

[12] *Ibid* at 26.

[13] L Smith, ch 2 in *Equity and Commercial Law* (ed Degeling and Edelman, 2005) at 24.

[14] As a result, it can be argued that such books on Equity are unnecessary: see Hackney (2001) 177 *LQR* 150.

[15] Pollock, *Principles of Contract at Law and in Equity* (1st ed, 1876) was one of the first books on contract law to bring Common Law and Equitable rules together. Goff and Jones, *The Law of Restitution* (1st ed, 1966) performed the same role for the law of unjust enrichment. No book has fully performed the same role for the law of wrongs. This is because: (i) wrongs tend to be separated into torts (ie, Common Law wrongs) and Equitable wrongs (see eg Winfield, *The Province of the Law of Tort* (1931) ch 6); and (ii) books on wrongs are usually books about torts. For example, McBride and Bagshaw, *Tort Law* (2nd ed, 2005) at 7–8: (i) recognises that the law should treat 'someone who breaches a Common Law duty and someone who breaches an equitable duty in exactly the same way'; but (ii) defines torts as *Common Law* wrongs and so excludes Equitable wrongs from its coverage. That is a reasonable approach: it may be that any book covering all wrongs would be 'unmanageably large to write or read'. *Clerk & Lindsell on Torts* (19th ed, 2007) at 1–6 also defines a tort as a Common Law wrong, whilst including some discussion of Equitable wrongs (at 10–20ff and ch 28). For a different view, supporting the concept of an 'Equitable tort', see eg Edelman (2002) 10 *Torts Law Journal* 64.

[16] *Lectures on Equity* (1909), Lecture 1. As noted by Getzler, ch 10 in *Equity and Commercial Law* (ed Degeling and Edelman, 2005), Maitland's detailed knowledge of the history of Equity did not prevent, and may indeed have allowed, his call to put aside the historical distinction between Equity and Common Law.

the day will come when lawyers will cease to enquire whether a given rule be a rule of equity or a rule of common law: suffice it to say that it is a well-established rule administered by the High Court of Justice.[17]

3.2 Common Law, Equity and property rights

On the orthodox view, Common Law and Equity give different answers to both: (i) the **content question**; and (ii) the **acquisition question** (see **B:4.4**). On that view: (i) Common Law has one list of property rights and Equity has a different, longer list; and (ii) Common Law recognises a number of means by which B can acquire a property right and Equity recognises further ways (see **C3:7.1**). This means we are left with two sets of answers to two fundamental questions. So, if we ask 'Does B have a right against that land?' or 'Does B have a right against that bike?' we may well get one answer at Common Law, and a different answer in Equity.

EXAMPLE 1

A, an owner of a bike, declares that he holds his ownership of the bike on Trust for B.

In such a case, on the orthodox view, the property law system gives two different answers to the fundamental question of 'Who owns the bike?': (i) at Common Law, A has ownership; *but* (ii) in Equity, B has ownership.[18] It seems absurd to think that the property law system could give two different answers to such a fundamental question.[19] On the orthodox view, that absurdity is the product of an historical anomaly: the presence of two competing court systems within one jurisdiction. Whilst that anomaly has now been eliminated, we are left with its legacy. However, that historical analysis can only explain how we have reached the current, paradoxical position; it does not provide us with a reason for maintaining that position.

Despite this, the current position of the property law system *can* be justified. To do so, we need to focus on the *conceptual difference* between a 'Common Law property right' and an 'Equitable property right'. It then becomes clear that Common Law and Equity *do not* give differing answers to the fundamental questions of: (i) what counts as a property right; and (ii) how property rights are acquired.

The key point is that, contrary to the orthodox view, *there is no such thing as an 'Equitable property right'* (see **B:4.4**). So, in **Example 1**, it is *not* the case that: (i) A has a Common Law property right; and (ii) B has an Equitable property right. After all, the rest of the world is *not* under a prima facie duty to B not to interfere with B's use of the bike (see **B:4.4.3**).

---

[17] See too Hackney (2001) 177 *LQR* 150. Macnair (2007) 27 *OJLS* 659 argues that (initially at least) Equitable rules could be seen as depending on the overarching principle of 'conscience' in the *specific* sense of depending on the special *procedural* rules of Equity: those rules allowed the private knowledge of a judge or defendant to have a more prominent role than at Common Law. However, Macnair notes that, by the middle of the 17th century at latest, changes to the Common Law procedural rules rendered this distinction between the two systems 'largely meaningless'.

[18] It is common to refer to B, in a case such as **Example 1**, as an 'Equitable owner': see eg *per* Millett LJ in *MacMillan Inc v Bishopsgate Trust (No 3)* [1995] 1 WLR 978 at 989; Scott (1917) 17 *Columbia Law Review* 269 at 275; Worthington, *Personal Property: Cases and Materials* (2000) at 44; Goode, *Commercial Law* (3rd ed, 2004) at 38.

[19] Hohfeld (1913) 11 *Michigan Law Review* 537 esp at 555–8 adopts a more subtle position: the duties imposed on A to B by Equity necessarily interfere with A's prima facie liberties, as an owner of the bike, to use the bike as he wishes.

The better analysis is that: (i) A has a property right (ownership of the bike); and (ii) A is under a duty to B in relation to that right; so (iii) B has a persistent right: a right against A's ownership of the bike. On this view, the apparent conflict between Common Law and Equity disappears. The two bodies of law do *not* have differing views as to: (i) what rights count as a property right; or (ii) as to how such rights can be acquired. Instead: (i) Common Law deals with the **content** and **acquisition questions** as they apply to property rights; and (ii) Equity deals with the **content** and **acquisition questions** as they apply to persistent rights.

A similar point was made by Maitland, in his *Lectures on Equity*,[20] in relation to a case such as **Example 1**.[21] The extract is worth quoting at length:

> Take the case of a trust. An examiner will sometimes be told that whereas the common law said that [A] was the owner of the [bike], equity said that [B] was the owner. . . . Think what this would mean if it were really true. There are two courts of co-ordinate jurisdiction—one says that A is the owner, the other says that B is the owner [of the bike]. That means civil war and utter anarchy. Of course the statement is an extremely crude one: it is a misleading and dangerous statement. . . . Equity did not say that [B] was the owner of the [bike], it said that [A] was the owner of the [bike], but added that he was bound to hold the [bike] for the benefit of [B]. There was no conflict here.

3.3 Common Law, Equity and persistent rights

Do Common Law and Equity give different answers to the **content question** and the **acquisition question** where persistent rights are concerned? No: there is *no such thing as a Common Law persistent right*. Just as all property rights arise at Common Law, all persistent rights arise in Equity. In fact, the concept of the persistent right is the key contribution of Equity to the property law system.[22]

We can speculate about *why*, as a matter of history, courts of Equity, rather than of Common Law, came to invent the concept of a persistent right. One possibility is that, in operating as a gloss on the Common Law, Equity can often be seen, in a very general sense, as intervening to restrain an unconscionable exercise by A of A's Common Law right. For example, Lord Denning MR used that general idea to explain the basis of both: (i) proprietary estoppel;[23] and (ii) the 'receipt after a promise' principle'.[24] As a result, it may have been easier for Equity to move from: (i) the fact that A's duty to B relates to a specific right held by A; to (ii) recognising that B has a right against A's right; so that (iii) as A's right is subject to that duty, it can also be subject to a duty when it passes to C.

However, whilst that question is—from an historical perspective—an interesting one, it is

---

[20] *Lectures on Equity* (1909), Lecture 1.

[21] Maitland took the view that, in **Example 1**, B has only a personal right against A: *Lectures on Equity* (1909), Lecture 10. However, that view cannot be correct: in **Example 1**, B has more than just a personal right against A: he also has a power to impose a duty on C if C acquires a right that depends on A's ownership of the bike (see **B:Examples 7c and 7d**).

[22] L Smith, ch 2 in *Equity and Commercial Law* (ed Degeling and Edelman, 2005) notes at 33–5 that one of Equity's distinctive features is its willingness to impose duties on third parties: the concept of a persistent right is the mechanism by which that willingness takes effect.

[23] *Crabb v Arun DC* [1976] 1 Ch 179 at 187–8.

[24] *Binions v Evans* [1972] 1 Ch 359 at 367–9. See too *per* Scott LJ in *Bannister v Bannister* [1948] 2 All ER 133 at 135–6.

of limited practical relevance. A related question, of much more importance, is whether it is possible for legal systems not derived from English law, and hence without any tradition of courts of Equity, to adopt the concept of a persistent right.[25] For example, a number of such jurisdictions across the world have made different attempts to introduce concepts based on that classic persistent right: the right under a Trust.[26]

It *is* possible for a system, not based on English law, to import the idea of persistent rights. To do so, such a system simply needs to recognise the distinctive concept of a *right against a right*. The major difficulty for many systems is not the absence of Equity but an acceptance, perhaps because of their Roman law roots, of an exhaustive dichotomy between: (i) rights against a thing (rights *in rem*); and (ii) rights against a person (rights *in personam*). On that view, there is no room for the concept, developed by English law, of a right against a right.[27]

Certainly, it should not be thought that a persistent right, such as a right under a Trust, can only exist in a legal system that has experienced the productive paradox of having two rival court systems within the same jurisdiction. For example, it is possible for B to have a persistent right against an *Equitable right* held by A. In such a case, the same court system gives rise to both: (i) A's right; and (ii) B's right.

EXAMPLE 2

A0 has ownership of a bike and declares that he holds that right on Trust for A. A thus has an Equitable right: a right under a Trust. A then declares he holds that right on Trust for B.

In such a case, A holds his Equitable right (a right under a Trust) on Trust for B. The Trust in B's favour is known as a 'sub-Trust': (i) it is a Trust of A's right; and (ii) A's right itself arises under a Trust. So, whilst: (i) A has a right against A0's ownership of the bike; (ii) B has a right against A's right under that Trust.

It is worth emphasising that, where a sub-Trust arises, A does *not* transfer his right under the initial Trust to B; rather: (i) A *keeps* his right under the initial Trust; and (ii) B acquires a right against A's right under the Trust.[28] B can then, if he wishes, declare a Trust of *his* right: there may be not only a sub-Trust but also a sub-sub-Trust and so on. The creation of each new right against a right forms another link in a chain that can extend indefinitely; and all within the same court system.

The possibility of a chain of sub-Trusts is not merely a conceptual conceit. In fact, it has

---

[25] Gretton (2007) 71 *Rabels Zeitschrift* 802 suggests that the security rights recognised in some civil law systems may be seen as cases where the object of B's right is not a thing but, instead, a right.

[26] See eg in France Law No 2007-211 of 19 February 2007, amending the Code Civil to introduce the concept of a 'fiducie' holding rights separately from his own patrimony; the same term is used in the Quebec Civil Code, see eg Art 1261. For an evaluation of civil law analyses of the Trust, see L Smith, *Trust and Patrimony* in *Revue Generale de Droit* (forthcoming 2008). For a survey of provisions introducing concepts based on the Trust to civil jurisdictions, see eg Lupoi, *Trusts: A Comparative Study* (trans Dix, 2000) and *Trusts Laws of the World: A Collection of Original Texts* (1996).

[27] Hackney, ch 6 in *The Classification of Obligations* (ed Birks, 1997) notes that Equity's 'principal contribution to world legal thought, the trust, cannot be fitted into the Roman scheme (at least not as perceived by the Romans) without serious conscious distortion and lack of technical discipline'. This can be explained by seeing the Trust as an example of a type of right seemingly unrecognised by Roman law: a right against a right.

[28] That distinction is very important when it comes to considering formality rules: in **Example 2**: (i) a *transfer* of a A's pre-existing persistent right must be made in writing signed by A (see **C3:5.2.2**); but (ii) A can orally exercise his power to set up a sub-Trust (see **C3:5.2.1**).

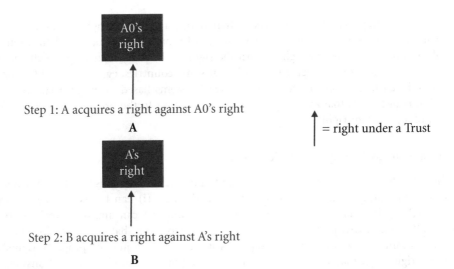

Step 1: A acquires a right against A0's right

A

= right under a Trust

Step 2: B acquires a right against A's right

B

an important commercial use. It is employed in practice in the phenomenon of 'interme-diated security': by the holding of rights (such as shares in a company) through a series of intermediaries.[29] B, an investor in particular shares, may regard himself as the holder of those shares. However, in practice, the shares may be held (or, to use the technical term 'immobilised') by a depository specialising in the clearing and settlement of rights such as shares. That depository, not B, is thus the holder of the shares: so B has no direct right against the company issuing the shares. And B may have no direct relationship with the depository: rather, he may be the last link in a chain of parties (all 'intermediaries') stretching from the depository down to B's agent and finally down to B. From the perspective of English law, the structure depends on: (i) an initial Trust (the depository holding the shares on Trust for A); followed by (ii) a series of sub-Trusts ending with B's agent holding his right on Trust for B.

This chain of 'intermediated security', consisting of a series of persistent rights, has two key advantages. First, each party joining the chain does not need to acquire the actual right (such as shares) held by the depository. That means each link can be added to the chain without the need for repeated transfers of the actual right: so a party joining the chain, such as B, does not need to concern himself with any formal requirements[30] that may be involved in a transfer of the right held by the depository. Second, if one intermediary goes into insol-vency, the chain remains unbroken: that intermediary's right will pass to its trustee in bankruptcy, but the party lower down the chain will be protected as his persistent right will bind the trustee in bankruptcy (see B:4.5.2(ii)). So, even if *all* of the intermediaries between B and the company issuing the shares were to go into insolvency, the chain would not break.

Those two advantages of the 'intermediated security' chain depend on the facts that: (i) B does *not* acquire the actual right held by the depositary (hence B can acquire his right

---

[29] See eg *Citibank v MBIA* [2007] EWCA Civ 11. In 2005, it was estimated that $50,000,000,000,000 was held in intermediated securities: see http://www.imf.org/external/np/seminars/eng/2006/mfl/hk.pdf. The use (or perhaps abuse) of such a mechanism lies behind the problems arising in 2007 for banks such as Northern Rock plc (see A:fn23): the ultimate rights held by the depositary were secured by 'subprime' mortgages and turned out to be of much lower value than assumed.

[30] For example, the transfer of company shares generally requires registration: see C2:3.2 and C3:5.1.2.

without there being a chain of transfers of that right); and (ii) B's right is *not* a personal right (hence it can bind the trustee in bankruptcy of a party higher up the chain). Rather, B's right is a persistent right: a right against the right of the party higher up the chain. The usefulness of 'intermediated security' is such that some countries, eg, France and Germany, have introduced legislation to permit it.[31] In legal systems based on English law, no such legislation is necessary, thanks to Equity's key contribution to the property law system: the concept of a persistent right.

3.4   Common Law, Equity and the defences question

On the orthodox view, Common Law and Equity provide different answers to the **defences question**. For example, the 'bona fide purchaser' defence: (i) can be used, unless statute intervenes,[32] against *any* 'Equitable property right'; but (ii) can almost never[33] be used against a 'Common Law property right' (see **B:5.2.2**). However, that apparent inconsistency between Common Law and Equity disappears if we regard 'Equitable property rights' as persistent rights. On that view, Common Law and Equity do *not* give different answers to the same question: (i) the Common Law rules tell us when C can have a defence to a pre-existing property right; and (ii) the Equitable rules tell us when C can have a defence to a pre-existing persistent right.

3.4.1 The 'bona fide purchaser' defence

> **EXAMPLE 3a**
>
> A owns a bike. A declares that he holds the bike on Trust for B. A, without B's consent or other authority, then sells the bike to C. C, when buying the bike, honestly believes that no one other than A has a right in relation to the bike.

This example is identical to **B:Example 9c**. We saw there that C can use the 'bona fide purchaser' defence against B's pre-existing persistent right.

> **EXAMPLE 3b**
>
> A owns a bike. A holds his ownership of the bike on Trust for B. In return for a loan from C, A, without B's consent or other authority, makes a binding promise to C that, if A defaults on the loan, C will be able to: (i) sell A's right to the bike; and (ii) use the proceeds to meet A's debt. C, when dealing with A, honestly believes that no one other than A has a right in relation to the bike.

In such a case, A does *not* transfer his ownership of the bike to C. Instead, A comes under a duty to C in relation to A's ownership of the bike. As a result, C acquires a persistent right: a

---

[31] A Draft UNIDROIT Convention on Intemediated Securities attempts to harmonise the different rules applying in different jurisdictions. The Law Commission is also undertaking a Project on Property Interests in Intermediated Investment Securities: see http://www.lawcom.gov.uk/investment_securities.htm

[32] The Land Registration Act 2002 has replaced the 'bona fide purchaser' defence, so far as registered land is concerned, with the 'lack of registration defence' established by the Act. However, that defence is, in important ways, modelled on the general bona fide purchaser defence (see **E2:3.6.5**).

[33] C can use the defence against B's ownership of money: eg *Miller v Race* (1758) 1 Burr 452; *Wookey v Pole* (1820) 4 B & Ald (see **D1:3.5.3**).

right against A's ownership of the bike. That form of persistent right can be called a 'Purely Equitable Charge' (see **D2:1.3.1**).[34] C can be described as a 'bona fide purchaser' of that persistent right: (i) he gave value in return for the right; and (ii) when acquiring his right, he did not know, and could not reasonably be expected to know, about B's pre-existing right under the Trust. Nonetheless, in **Example 3b**, C *cannot* use the 'bona fide purchaser' defence against B's right.

Examples 3a and 3b demonstrate an important aspect of the 'bona fide purchaser' defence.

1. C may be able to use the defence if he acquires, from A, the *very right* against which B has a persistent right: see **Example 3a**.
2. However, if C instead acquires a right against A's right, C cannot qualify for the defence: see **Example 3b**.

On the orthodox view the difference between **Example 3a** and **Example 3b** depends on the distinction between: (i) 'Common Law property rights'; and (ii) 'Equitable property rights'. So, in **Example 3a**, C qualifies for the defence because he acquired a 'Common Law property right': A's ownership of the bike. In **Example 3b**, C cannot use the defence as he only acquired an 'Equitable property right': a Purely Equitable Charge. There are said to be two justifications for this difference:[35]

1. If C is a bona fide purchaser of a 'Common Law property right', then Equity cannot touch C—C is thus immune from the effect of B's 'Equitable property right'.
2. Equity intervenes only to prevent bad or unconscionable conduct by C: if C acquired a right without knowing, and without having any reason to know, about B's pre-existing 'Equitable property right', C has not acted unconscionably and is, as a result, immune from the effect of Equity

However, there are a number of problems with these justifications.[36]

1. There are some rare cases in which the 'bona fide purchaser' defence *can* be used against a 'Common Law property right' (see **D1:3.5.3**). As a result, the defence cannot simply be seen as a limit to 'Equitable property rights'.
2. Consider a case where A holds his ownership of a bike on Trust for B, and then transfers that right to C *as a gift*. As C did not give anything in return for A's right, C cannot use the 'bona fide purchaser' defence *even if, when acquiring his right, C had no knowledge of, or reason to know about, B's pre-existing persistent right* (see **B:Example 7d**). So, although C has: (i) acquired a 'Common Law property right'; *and* (ii) C has not acted unconscionably; nonetheless, (iii) B has a power to assert his pre-existing persistent right against C.

---

[34] It arises under a 'fixed charge' transaction: see **F4:1.2.2**.

[35] See eg *per* James LJ in *Pilcher v Rawlins* (1872) LR 7 Ch App 259 at 268–9. His Lordship describes the bona fide purchaser of a property right as having an: 'absolute, unqualified, unanswerable defence, and an unanswerable plea to the jurisdiction of this Court . . . [if C] has satisfied the terms of the plea of purchase for valuable consideration without notice, then, according to my judgment, this Court has no jurisdiction whatever to do anything more than to let him depart in possession of that legal estate, that legal right, that legal advantage which he has obtained, whatever it may be. In such a case a purchaser is entitled to hold that which, without breach of duty, he has had conveyed to him.' See too Hackney, *Understanding Equity and Trusts* (1987), ch 1, s 2(a).

[36] We will consider a further problem with the conventional justifications when examining **D2:Example 19e**.

It seems, then, that the orthodox justifications for the application of the 'bona fide pur-chaser' defence are unconvincing. Instead, we can explain the difference between **Example 3a** and **Example 3b** by focusing on the *nature* of C's right. In **Example 3a**, C acquires *the very right* against which B had a persistent right. In contrast, **Example 3b**, C acquires a *second persistent right*: (i) C acquires a right against A's ownership of the bike; *but* (ii) A is *already* under a duty to B in relation to his ownership of the bike (see further **D2:3.5.3**).

3.5   Common Law, Equity and the remedies question

As a matter of history, Common Law and Equity developed different remedies. Although the differences can again be exaggerated,[37] courts of Equity were more willing to intervene to *specifically protect* a right. In contrast, Common Law courts would generally require a losing party to pay money to the winner.[38] The crucial question is whether confusion is caused by the possibility of there being two different answers to the **remedies question**. And the answer is 'No'. The vital point is that remedies developed by courts of Equity can now be used to give effect to Common Law rights.[39] And remedies developed by the Common Law are available if B has an Equitable right.[40] Equity, through its greater willingness to specifi-cally protect rights, has played an important role in giving judges the tools they need to give practical effect to a party's rights. However, that role is now largely of historical interest.[41] So, just as we did when looking at direct rights in **3.1** above, we can now view remedies, whether provided by Common Law or Equity, as a unified set.

When looking at direct rights, we considered—and rejected—the suggestion that any Equitable principle allowing B to acquire a direct right will be based, in a meaningful sense, on fairness and the need to avoid unconscionable conduct by A or C. A similar suggestion can be made—and should also be rejected—in relation to remedies. Whether a remedy originates in Equity or Common Law, a court will generally have a degree of discretion in awarding it.[42] That discretion, however, does not come from the need to avoid

---

[37] Specific protection at Common Law was also available where eg: (i) C interfered with B's property right in land (see **A:3.2.1**); (ii) A was under a duty to account to B, eg as a bailiff or as a guardian (see eg Hackney, ch 6 in *The Classification of Obligations* (ed Birks, 1997) 142–3); (ii) A was under a duty to pay a specific sum of money to B.

[38] That money would both: (i) serve as a substitute for the right interfered with; and (ii) compensate the winner for any relevant consequential loss caused to him by the loser's interference with his right: see **D1:4.3**.

[39] The Common Law Procedure Acts of 1852 and 1854 gave Common Law courts limited powers to make use of Equitable remedies, such as injunctions. The procedural 'fusion' was completed by the Judicature Act 1873: in the unified court system, a judge has access to *both* Common Law and Equitable remedies, regardless of the historical jurisdictional source of B's right.

[40] Again, this process began before the Judicature Act of 1873: eg, Lord Cairns' Act (the Chancery Amendment Act 1858) gave Equity judges a power, instead of granting an injunction against A, to order A to pay money to B. However, even before that Act, it seems the court of Chancery had a power to order A to pay damages to B: see McDermott (1992) 108 *LQR* 652.

[41] However, in *Harris v Digital Pulse* (2003) 56 *NSWLR* 298 a majority of the New South Wales Court of Appeal held that a particular remedy ('punitive' or 'exemplary' damages: see **D1.4.3.3**) was *not* available where A breached an Equitable duty, even though it may be available where A breaches a Common Law duty to B. That reasoning is hard to understand: (i) the rationale of punitive or exemplary damages is to deter wrongdoing; and (ii) that rationale should apply whether A's duty arises at Common Law or in Equity: see eg the dissent of K Mason P in *Digital Pulse*; Edelman (2003) 119 *LQR* 375; Burrows, ch 15 in *Equity and Commercial Law* (ed Degeling and Edelman, 2005). So any justification of the decision in *Digital Pulse* must depend on one's view of the *general* desir-ability of punitive or exemplary damages: see eg A Mason (former Chief Justice of the High Court of Australia), ch 1 in *Equity and Commercial Law* (ed Degeling and Edelman, 2005) at 13

[42] The same is true of a remedy provided by statute. For example, if: (i) B has ownership of a thing other than

unconscionability; instead, it comes from the fact that, when answering the **remedies question**, a court has to fashion an order that gives the appropriate protection to a right, taking into account the factual circumstances prevailing at the time the order is made. So a court will *always* have to take a wide number of factors into account when deciding what remedy to give: that is true whether the remedy in question was originally provided by courts of Common Law *or* courts of Equity.

Of course, B may have to satisfy additional requirements in order to convince a court to give him a particular remedy (eg, an order specifically protecting his right: see **A:3.1.2**). So, a particular Equitable remedy (such as an injunction) may be awarded more rarely than a particular Common Law remedy (such as a money award). However, this difference depends on: (i) the *nature* of the particular remedy; and (ii) the *nature* of the right it seeks to protect. Such differences should *not* depend on the mere fact that the remedy is a product of Equity rather than Common Law.[43]

4   SUMMARY AND CONCLUSION

4.1   Property rights and persistent rights

It is generally said that the distinction between Common Law and Equity is vital to understanding the property law system. This seems a little surprising, given that the divide depends on a procedural split, between courts of Common Law and courts of Equity, that did not survive into the twentieth century. A central argument of this chapter has been that the contrast between Common Law and Equity is important for only one reason, albeit a very important reason: it serves as a substitute for the distinction between property rights and persistent rights.

Equity's chief, and massively important, contribution to the property law system is thus the invention of persistent rights. Equity did not attempt to reinvent the Common Law wheel, or to enter into a conflict with Common Law courts, by inventing its own, rival list of property rights. So, in a case such as **Example 1**, Equity does not attempt to give B a property right. Rather, Equity's genius consists in holding that: (i) if A has a right (in **Example 1**, ownership of a bike); and (ii) A is under a duty to B in relation to that right (in **Example 1**, that duty arises because of A's exercise of his power to set up a Trust); then (iii) B has more than a personal right against A; B also has a right against *A's right*. To assert his right, B no longer has to find a person (A): rather, he needs to find a right (a right that depends on A's right). So, if B can show that: (i) C now has A's right, or a right that depends on A's right; then (ii) B has a prima facie power to impose a duty on C (see **B:4.3**). Equity

---

land; and (ii) C breaches his duty not to interfere with B's right; and (iii) C still has physical control of B's thing; then (iv) the Torts (Interference with Goods) Act 1977, s 3(2)(b) gives a court the power to specifically enforce B's right by ordering C to return the thing to B (by making an order for 'delivery up'). That remedy is discretionary (see the 1977 Act, s 3(3)(b)) and the court may take into account a wide number of different factors in considering whether to exercise its discretion: see **D1:4.2**.

[43] See eg Burrows, ch 15 in *Equity and Commercial Law* (ed Degeling and Edelman, 2005) esp 381–7, responding to the contrary view taken by *Meagher, Gummow & Lehane's Equity: Doctrine and Remedies* (4th edn, 2002) at [23-020]. See too A Mason (former Chief Justice of the High Court of Australia), ch 1 in *Equity and Commercial Law* (ed Degeling and Edelman, 2005) at 14.

thus operates in a breathtakingly efficient fashion: it does not contradict the Common Law position that A has a particular right; rather it builds on A's right by imposing a duty on A to use that right, in a particular way, for B's benefit. As a result, in **Example 1**: (i) A still has a property right (ownership of the bike); but (ii) A's property right is subjected to a duty owed to B.

4.2   Equity, flexibility and the property law system

By recognising persistent rights, Equity can be said to add important flexibility to the property law system. At Common Law, there was only one type of pre-existing right that B could assert against C: a property right. Thanks to Equity, the property law system now recognises *two* types of pre-existing right that can be asserted against C. This has many advantages, not least to A, an owner of a thing or a holder of a right.

EXAMPLE 4

A has: (i) ownership of a bike; and (ii) a bank account (ie, a personal right against Z Bank). A wants to borrow some money from B. B is reluctant to make the loan without taking security. A could give B such security by: (i) transferring his ownership of the bike to B; or (ii) by transferring to B his personal right against Z Bank.[44] However, in practice, it may be impossible or inconvenient for A to make such a transfer. Instead, A can: (i) keep his ownership of the bike and his bank account; and (ii) make a contractual promise to use those rights as security for his debt to B.

In such a case, as we noted in **Example 3b** above, B acquires a persistent right against A's rights: a Purely Equitable Charge. As a result: (i) if A defaults on the loan, B will have a power to sell A's rights and use the proceeds to meet A's debt to B; *and* (ii) if A goes into insolvency, B has a right that is prima facie binding on A's trustee in bankruptcy. The persistent right thus gives B what he wants: (i) security for his loan to A; and (ii) protection should A go into insolvency.

4.3   The limits of Equity

We started this chapter by noting the fundamental difference between Equity as a body of legal rules and equity as a notion of fairness and justice. That distinction needs to be emphasised. It is true that, through its invention of the concept of a persistent right, Equity has added flexibility to the property law system. However, it should not be assumed that Equitable rights are unregulated.

For example, *specific criteria* dictate when B can acquire a right through: (i) the doctrine of proprietary estoppel (see **E4:3**); or (ii) the 'receipt after a promise' principle (see **D3:2.2.2** and **E3:2.2.2**). Equity does *not* allow B to claim a right by simply appealing to a general notion of fairness, or by merely alleging that A or C has behaved unconscionably.[45] In fact,

---

[44] Either transfer would be a mortgage: B acquires A's right *but* is under a duty to return that right to A if A performs his duty to repay the loan: see **F4:1.2.2**.

[45] So, as noted by L Smith, ch 2 in *Equity and Commercial Law* (ed Degeling and Edelman, 2005), 31: 'a reductionist line, which says that there is not much difference between Common Law and Equity as regards flexibility, is largely accurate'.

as we will see, some of the criteria developed by Equity are criticised for being *too* strict, and for denying a right to a deserving B.[46]

It should be no surprise that Equity carefully regulates the means by which B can acquire: (i) a direct right against C; and (ii) a persistent right. After all, whether it derives from Equity or the Common Law, any principle forming part of the property law system has the same function: to assist in resolving the **basic tension** in property law. That basic tension is too difficult to resolve by general appeals to fairness or justice (see **A:1** and **A:2**). It can only be addressed by a settled set of consistent and predictable rules.

4.4 Confusion or coherence?

It seems that, despite being based on two distinct systems of legal rules, the English property law system is *not* beset by confusion between Common Law and Equity. The basic position is that, within that one system of property law, there is a distinction between two different types of right. Each type of right is capable of binding a third party: it may be asserted against C even if it was not acquired from C.

1. B may have a property right: a right against a thing. If B has such a right: (i) the rest of the world is under a prima facie duty not to interfere with B's use of a thing; and (ii) B's right is almost never vulnerable to the 'bona fide purchaser' defence.
2. B may have a persistent right: a right against A's right. If B has such a right: (i) B has a prima facie power to impose a duty on anyone who acquires a right that depends on A's right; and (ii) B's right will be subject to the 'bona fide purchaser' defence or one of its statutory replacements.[47]

The first type of right is usually called a 'Legal property right'; the second type an 'Equitable property right'. However, it is more accurate to call the first set 'property rights' and the second set 'persistent rights'. It is true that Equity's genius led to the invention of persistent rights: but we can now describe those rights according to their nature rather than their historical origin. And by doing so we can avoid the absurd conclusion that the property law system gives two different answers to questions as fundamental as the **content**, **acquisition** and **defences questions**.

---

[46] See, in particular, the criteria used to decide if B has acquired a right under a Trust of A's ownership of a family home occupied by both A and B: see **G3:2.4.3(v)**. For a case that is accused as being too strict see eg *Burns v Burns* [1984] Ch 317, criticised by Law Com No 179 (2006) at 4.18 to 4.30 and Law Com No 307 (2007), 4.46.

[47] Such as the lack of registration defence applying to registered land under the Land Registration Act, ss 29 and 30 (see **C2:6** and **E2:3.6**)

CHAPTER C2
REGISTRATION

C2

REGISTRATION

1 INTRODUCTION

Registration is a crucial concept in property law, most particularly in land law. In this chapter, we will examine the different roles that registration can play within the basic structure of property law. It is impossible to discuss the land law system without first having a grasp of the general concept of registration. When looking at the English land law system in Parts E and G, we will focus on the rules that apply to registered land. The majority of land in England and Wales is now registered land: (i) the identity of an owner of that land is noted in records kept at the Land Registry; and (ii) dealings with that land are regulated by the Land Registration Act 2002 (see further E5).

Nonetheless, it is important to realise that registration can be relevant even in cases that do *not* involve registered land. For example, registration may be important even where the dispute is about the use of a right, rather than the use of a thing.

EXAMPLE 1

C wishes to acquire shares in a particular company. C plans to buy those shares from A. C wants to be sure that A does indeed hold those shares.

Where C tries to acquire a right to a thing from A, A can often rely on his *physical control* of that thing to persuade C that he does indeed have a right to it. However, shares cannot be physically located in a particular place: (i) they are not things; and so (ii) they cannot be physically controlled.[1] As a result, it will be very helpful to both A and C if C can check A's claim to the shares by looking in a register that records the holders of shares in particular companies. So, one purpose of registration can be to provide *evidence* that A does indeed have a particular right.

EXAMPLE 2

A Co receives a loan from B and, in return, makes a contractual promise that, if it defaults on the loan, B will be able to use whatever rights A Co may hold at that time to meet A Co's debt. So if, when A Co defaults on the loan, A Co has: (i) ownership of a machine; and (ii) personal rights against its customers, then (iii) B will be able to use those rights (eg, by selling off the machine and by collecting the debts from the customers) to pay off the sums due to it from A Co.

---

[1] The holder of company shares therefore does not have a right against a thing (see **D1:1.1.1**) First, shares are not things; second, by acquiring shares in a company, C does not acquire a right against any specific things owned by the company. So, when we talk about a party 'having shares in a company' we mean that he has a set of personal rights against that company. In some cases C, when acquiring shares, may acquire a certificate representing those shares. In such a case, C does acquire a property right: a right to that certificate.

A Co's contractual promise does not give B an immediate persistent right. A Co is still free to use its rights as it wishes and is not yet under a duty to B in relation to any *specific* right. However, B has a *power* to acquire persistent rights: if A Co defaults on the loan, B can impose a duty on A Co in relation to whatever rights A Co may hold at that time. B's power is known as a 'floating charge';[2] like all powers to acquire a persistent right, it is capable of binding a third party (see **D2:1.6**). So, if A Co were to go into insolvency, B could assert its power against A Co's liquidators. This will clearly cause problems for A Co's other creditors: once B has asserted its power, A Co's liquidators may have no, or very few, rights left to use for the benefit of those other creditors.[3]

The deal between A Co and B can thus cause problems for a third party. Let us say C plans to make a loan to A Co. First, C may think there is no need to take security. Although B has a floating charge, A Co is able to deal with its rights as it wishes, without asking for B's consent. So it may appear that A Co has plenty of assets (ie, rights) that it can use to repay C. However, if C makes the loan without taking security, he may be in for a shock. If A Co runs into financial problems, and defaults on its debt to B, B will be able to swoop in and exercise its pre-existing power to acquire a persistent right.[4] So, A Co's rights will first be used to meet the debt it owes to B: it may then be that there are insufficient rights left over to pay C's debt. Second, even if C does take security, he may face the same problem. If A Co gives C the same type of security as B (ie, a second floating charge), C will be prima facie bound by B's pre-existing floating charge. It makes no difference if C is a 'bona fide purchaser' of its floating charge: in such a case, B can still assert its pre-existing power against C (see **D2:3.5.5**).

So, in **Example 2**, the problem for C is that B's power to acquire a persistent right is very difficult to spot. To protect C from this problem, a registration system was introduced by Parliament in 1900.[5] This system allows C, before dealing with A Co, to check if anyone holds a 'floating charge' against the rights of A Co.

2   THE PURPOSE OF REGISTRATION

The central purpose of any register is to provide *publicity*. For example, a register of births, marriages and deaths gives interested parties the opportunity to discover important information about a community. The publicity provided by a register of rights may be useful to a number of different groups: for example, it may provide the Government with information

---

[2] See **F4:2.3**. The key feature of a floating charge is that A Co is not under an immediate duty to hold any specific right as security for B; rather, B has a *power* to acquire such a right: see *re Spectrum Plus Ltd* [2005] 2 AC 680. If B has a 'debenture' he may well have a floating charge (as well as a fixed charge): see Goode, *Commercial Law* (3rd ed, 2004) 588–604 for an example.

[3] As we will see in **F4:2.3.4**, various statutory provisions mean that B's power cannot be asserted against *all* A Co's rights: eg, Insolvency Act 1986, s 176A, introduced by the Enterprise Act 2002, means that a 'prescribed part' (currently approximately 20 per cent) of the benefit of the rights covered by B's floating charge has to be made available to A's unsecured creditors.

[4] See eg *per* Lord Macnaghten in *Salomon v A Salomon & Co Ltd* [1897] AC 22 at 53: B can 'step in and sweep off everything'.

[5] See *re Spectrum Plus Ltd* [2005] 2 AC 680 *per* Lord Scott at [95]–[98] and Lord Walker at [130]–[133]. The registration rules are now set out by the Companies Act 1985, ss 395–9 (see esp s 396(1)(f) for floating charges): those provisions will be replaced by the Companies Act 2006, ss 869–77 (see esp s 860(7)(g) for floating charges) with effect from 1 October 2009.

it can use when making tax assessments. Certainly, such publicity can also be very useful to C: as we have seen, it can allow C to discover: (i) if A indeed has a particular right (as in **Example 1**); and (ii) if B has a pre-existing power or right that may bind C (as in **Example 2**).

Registration can thus be particularly useful to C, both in disputes about the use of a thing and in disputes about the use of a right. A registration system can protect C against the two chief risks he faces when attempting to acquire a right:

1. A, the party C deals with, may in fact lack the power to give C the right. This is the risk from which a register of rights, such as a register of company shareholders, may aim to protect C.
2. Even if A does have the power to give C the right, B may have a pre-existing right that he can assert against C and that will thus reduce the value of C's right. This is the risk from which a register of pre-existing powers or rights, such as a register of floating charges against a company's rights, aims to protect C.

It is important to remember that, in a dispute about the use of a thing or the use of a right, C can be bound not only by a pre-existing right of B but also by a *direct right* of B, arising because of C's conduct (see **B:3**). Registration systems do *not* provide protection against these direct rights. To protect himself against the risk of being bound by such a right, C simply needs to control his own conduct: to make sure he does not act in such a way as to give B a direct right.

3 REGISTRATION AS A LEGAL CONCEPT

The publicity provided by a register of rights can never provide C with full protection: in practice, no such register can ever be completely accurate. In **Example 1**, a register may record A as the holder of some shares, but can C be sure that the register is correct? In **Example 2**, a register may make no mention of a pre-existing floating charge but, again, can C be sure that the register is correct? Of course, if the register is not complete, C may have to make his own inquiries as to whether A is indeed a holder of the shares; or whether there is a floating charge against A Co's assets. The usefulness of having a register will then be reduced: C will have to spend time and money on his own investigations; as a result the possible deal between A and C will be delayed, or perhaps even called off.

Ideally, C would like to have a *guarantee*. In **Example 1**, he wants a guarantee that: (i) if A is recorded as the holder of the shares, then (ii) A does indeed hold those shares. In **Example 2**, he wants a guarantee that: (i) if there is no floating charge recorded on the register; then (ii) no one will be able to assert such a power against him. Such a guarantee can only be provided if *legal consequences* are attached to the fact that a right is, or is not, recorded on a register. Once those legal consequences exist, registration no longer operates neutrally, as a simple record. Rather, registration begins to operate as a legal concept. This introduction of legal consequences allows registration systems to affect the basic structure of property law and hence to have a greater impact on resolving the **basic tension**.

3.1 The positive operation of registration

A registration system can operate both *positively* and *negatively*. When it operates positively, legal consequences are attached to the *fact of registration*. So, in **Example 1**, C wants the register of shareholders to operate positively: he wants the fact of A's registration, by itself, to ensure that A does indeed hold the shares. Registration can thus become part of the **acquisition question**: it enables A to acquire a right simply through being registered as the holder of that right. Unfortunately for C, however, that is *not* how registers of company shareholders operate: the register is not definitive.[6] So, even if A is registered as holding particular shares, it may turn out that, in fact, B is the true holder of those shares.[7]

3.2 The negative operation of registration

When it operates negatively, a registration system attaches legal consequences to a *failure to register*. So, in **Example 2**, C wants the register of floating charges to operate negatively: he wants the fact that B is not registered as holding a floating charge to mean that B cannot assert such a power against C.[8] There are two ways in which a registration system can give C such protection. First, registration could become part of the **acquisition question**: if B has not registered a right, he cannot claim to have acquired it. Second, it could become part of the **defences question**: if B has not registered a right then C, in certain circumstances, will have a defence to it. The register of floating charges works in the second of those two ways: it *may* prevent B from asserting his unregistered floating charge against C.[9] So, a failure to register does *not* prevent B from acquiring his floating charge: B can, for example, assert an unregistered floating charge against A Co (provided it has not gone into insolvency).[10] Nor does B's failure to register give a defence to *all* third parties: B may still be able,[11] for example, to assert an unregistered floating charge against C if C is not a secured creditor or execution creditor of A Co.[12] So, B's failure to register can prevent B from asserting his power against *certain third parties*: in effect, those third parties have a defence to B's pre-existing power.[13] This type of defence is of great importance and deserves its own name: the *lack of registration* defence.

When operating negatively, a registration system can thus protect C in one of two ways.

---

[6] See Companies Act 1985, s 361 (to be replaced on 1 October 2009 by Companies Act 2006, s 127): the register of company members provides only 'prima facie evidence'.

[7] See eg *Taylor v Midland Railway Co* (1860) 28 Beav 287; *Welch v Bank of England* [1955] 1 Ch 508. A company can be compelled by a court to rectify an incorrect register and a court can also order a company to pay damages to C if C loses out as a result of that rectification: see Companies Act 1985, s 359 (to be replaced on 1 October 2009 by Companies Act 2006, s 125).

[8] A register of company shareholders operates negatively (rather than positively): if B attempts to acquire shares from A, a registered shareholder, but fails to register himself as the new shareholder, he cannot acquire those shares. See eg *re Rose* [1949] Ch 78; *MacMillan Inc v Bishopsgate Trust (No 3)* [1995] 1 WLR 978 at 1001.

[9] See Companies Act 1985, ss 395–9 and Companies Act 2006, ss 860–74 (replacing the 1985 provisions from 1 October 2009). S 395(1) of the 1985 Act states that an unregistered floating charge is 'void against the liquidator or any creditor' of A Co; see too s 874 of the 2006 Act: an unregistered floating charge is void against a liquidator, administrator or creditor of A Co.

[10] See Goode, *Commercial Law* (3rd ed, 2004) 667.

[11] Even if the registration system does not protect C, there may be another reason for which B cannot assert his power against C: see **F4:4.3.1**.

[12] See eg *Stroud Architectural Systems Ltd v John Laing Construction Ltd* [1994] BCC 18 (see **F4:n105**).

[13] Technically, C does not need a defence to B's floating charge—as the floating charge gives B only a power to acquire a persistent right, rather than a persistent right itself, that power is not prima facie binding on C: see **D2:1.6** and **D2:3.5.5**. So, B's failure to register a floating charge instead means that B *is not permitted to exercise that power against certain third parties*. In effect, this is identical to the way in which B's failure to register can give C a defence to a pre-existing persistent right or property right.

1. By affecting the **acquisition question**: B's failure to register a right may mean that B has not acquired that right. This has the dramatic consequence that B does not have the right he claims: so B cannot assert that right against *anyone*.
2. By affecting the **defences question**: B's failure to register a right may mean that C, in certain circumstances, can have a defence to B's pre-existing right. It is important to see how this differs from the first method. It means that B *does* have the right he claims; but is prevented from asserting that right against a *limited class* of third parties.

If the second method is used, the crucial question is *in what circumstances* will C have a defence to B's unregistered right. In some registration systems, C may only qualify for the lack of registration defence if he registers his own right. For example, the lack of registration defence operating in registered land is generally available to C only if: (i) B fails to register his right; *and* (ii) if C acquires for value and registers his own right (see **E1:3.6** and **E2:3.6**). The lack of registration defence operating in registered land thus depends on registration operating *both* positively and negatively: (i) positively because the fact of C's registration is one requirement of the defence; (ii) negatively because the absence of B's registration is another requirement of the defence.

The *possible* positive and negative effects of registration can be summarised in the following table:

	Positive operation: *Consequences of registration*	**Negative operation:** *Consequences of a failure to register*
Acquisition question	By registering a right, a party **acquires** that right	By failing to register a right, a party **fails to acquire** that right
Defences question	By registering a right, a party may be able to use the **lack of registration defence** against a pre-existing unregistered right	By failing to register a right, a party allows a later third party to use the **lack of registration defence** against his right

4 THE SCOPE OF REGISTRATION

Whether it operates positively or negatively, the legal concept of registration can be used to protect C. In particular, it can save C the time and money he would otherwise have to invest in checking: (i) if A indeed has the right A claims he has; and (ii) if B has a pre-existing right that may bind C if he acquires a right from A. A registration system potentially offers C a very attractive prospect: a *guarantee* that: (i) C will acquire the right he wishes from A; and (ii) that C will only be bound by a pre-existing right if it is recorded on the register. Whilst it can thus be very advantageous to C, a registration system of course involves certain costs: not only the risk to B of being unable to assert his unregistered right, but also the economic cost of maintaining a public register. We therefore need to ask if the advantages of a registration system[14] can outweigh those costs.

---

[14] As noted above, a registration system, by providing publicity as to rights, can benefit parties other than C: eg, someone considering whether to sell his house may well look at the Land Registry website to see the prices of houses recently sold in his area. Of course, that publicity has its downside, as parties may feel their privacy is infringed by having to put such information in the public domain.

Registration can protect C by limiting the inquiries he needs to make before acquiring a right. However, the need for C to make inquiries is simply a consequence of the facts that: (i) someone other than A may hold the right A claims; and (ii) the property law system recognises that certain pre-existing rights are capable of binding third parties. These facts are a vital part of the basic structure of property law: the existence of property rights and persistent rights, for example, provides prior users of things with an important degree of protection (see **B:4**). We could therefore see C's burden in having to make inquiries as simply the price that has to be paid for that protection.

Moreover, the basic structure of property law already provides some protection for C. As to the first question, of whether A has the right he claims, the property law system provides a set of means by which rights can be acquired: C can ask for evidence that A has acquired his right in one of those ways. As to the second question, of whether a party has a pre-existing property right or persistent right, the property law system protects C in a number of ways. As far as property rights are concerned, the **content question** ensures that there are a very limited number of such rights; the **acquisition question** limits the ways in which such rights can be acquired. As far as persistent rights are concerned, the content and acquisition questions give C less protection, but it will be easier for C to rely on a **defence**: in particular, the 'bona fide purchaser' defence can generally be used against a pre-existing persistent right (see **B:5.2.2(ii)**).

As a result, registration systems are generally deemed to be *unnecessary*. Registration is reserved for circumstances in which it is felt that C is *particularly* in need of protection. A number of factors will be relevant. For example, the lack of registration defence will be particularly important if B's right is otherwise hard for C to discover. This certainly seems to justify the legal consequences that flow from B's failure to register a floating charge over A Co's assets (see **Example 2**). From B's point of view, C's ability to use the lack of registration defence can be more easily justified if it is reasonable to expect B to register his right. Floating charges again provide a good example: B will almost always acquire such a power as part of a commercial transaction. It is therefore very likely that B will have received legal advice and should be aware of the importance of registering his floating charge.

5   REGISTRATION AND LAND LAW

Registration is particularly prominent in land law. We can explain this by looking at the special features of land (see **A:3.1**).

1.   Due to its fixed location, each piece of land is easy to identify. As a result, if a register exists, it is easy to look up a particular piece of land in that register.
2.   Due to its capacity for multiple, simultaneous use, as well as its social importance, the list of property rights and persistent rights relating to land is longer than the list of such rights in things other than land. So, if C acquires a right in land from A, there is an increased risk to C of being bound by a pre-existing right of B.
3.   Due to its permanence, there is an increased risk of a pre-existing property right or persistent right existing in relation to a particular piece of land. So, if C acquires a right in land from A, there is an increased risk to C of being bound by a pre-existing right of B.

4. Due to its limited availability, land is already very expensive. As a result, there is a particularly strong desire to limit the time and cost C must expend in acquiring a right in land. The more expensive the process of buying land becomes, the more difficult it becomes for those of even average wealth to acquire the land they need to set up a home or run a business.

So, the special features of land both: (i) make a registration system possible; and (ii) justify the extra protection such a system can provide to C. However, this leaves open the question of *how* a land registration system should operate. The **basic tension** will govern not only *whether* the concept of registration applies, but also *how* it applies.

6 REGISTRATION, REGISTERED LAND AND THE BASIC TENSION

The impact of the registration concept on the land law system is now largely determined by the Land Registration Act 2002 ('the LRA 2002').[15] While the registered land system governed by that Act does provide important protection for C, it is vital to remember that it does not operate in a vacuum. Even if providing protection for C is the aim of a registration system,[16] it is *not* the aim of property law as a whole. The basic structure of property law attempts to resolve the basic tension by *balancing* the needs of C with those of B. The bare concept of registration is too blunt an instrument to achieve this balance.

6.1 The positive operation of registration

When registration operates *positively*, it can allow B or C to acquire a right simply by the fact of registration. For example, under the LRA 2002, a party can acquire a property right *simply* by virtue of being registered as the holder of that right.[17] The Act has that effect whenever a party **substantively registers** a right. There are limits on substantive registration. Some property rights cannot be substantively registered;[18] and no persistent right can be substantively registered. As a result, a party can *never* acquire a persistent right by the fact of registration. It is true that we sometimes talk about B 'registering' a persistent right: however, that refers to **defensive registration**, not to substantive registration. So, if B has a persistent right, he will usually[19] be able to enter a *notice* on the register, alerting potential third parties, such as C, to the existence of his right. The registration is defensive: its purpose is simply to protect B's right by preventing C from using the lack of registration defence against it. B's registration of his persistent right is not substantive: the fact that B

---

[15] Although the Land Charges Act 1972 also has a role to play (see **section 7** below).

[16] And the Law Commission, in the Report which led to the LRA 2002, does seem to assume that protecting C is the aim of a registration system: see Law Com No 271 at 1.5.

[17] See LRA 2002, s 58.

[18] For example, a Lease of seven years or less, in general, cannot be substantively registered. There is an exception where the Lease is in one of the exceptional categories set out by LRA 2002, s 27(2)(b)(ii)–(v): see **G1B:2.2.1(i)(b)**.

[19] The general rule is that *any* right can be protected by the entry of a notice on the register: see LRA 2002, ss 32–9. However, there are some important exceptions: in particular, a right under a Trust cannot be protected by the entry of a notice: see LRA 2002, s 33(a)(i). If B has a right under a Trust he can enter a restriction on the register (see LRA 2002, ss 40–47) but this restriction will generally fail to give B's right any real protection: it simply alerts C to the possibility of using a different defence (the overreaching defence) against B's right: see **E2:3.4**.

has entered a notice in the register does *not* guarantee that B has acquired that persistent right.

EXAMPLE 3

B is an owner of land but A, forging B's signature on a document, fraudulently purports to transfer B's right to C. C substantively registers his right as an owner of the land.

Under section 58 of the LRA 2002, C will acquire a property right in the land by virtue of his substantive registration. However, a balance must be struck between the interests of B and those of C. So, even where registration does operate positively, the protection it gives to C need not be absolute. In some circumstances, it may be felt that B should have some protection. In **Example 3**, B is an innocent victim of A's fraud: there is hence a strong argument that B should be able to have the register changed, so that C is removed from the register and B is put in C's place. The LRA 2002 recognises this possibility: in certain circumstances, it permits the register to be changed to give effect to an unregistered right of B.[20] In a case such as **Example 3**, that change occurs by a process known as *rectification* as: (i) it involves the correction of a mistake; and (ii) it prejudicially affects the right of a registered owner (see **E5:3.2**).

It would therefore be very surprising if any registration system gave *absolute* protection to C: the registered land system governed by the LRA 2002 certainly does *not* do so. However, it is worth noting that if, in a case such as **Example 3**, B's right is allowed to bind C, C may be allowed to obtain money from the Land Registry. Such a payment, known as an *indemnity*,[21] aims to compensate C for any relevant loss he suffers as a result of the rectification in B's favour (see **E5:3.2.3**) [22]

The payment of compensation by those running the registration system opens up the possibility of a new way to resolve the **basic tension** between B and C. Rather than there being two basic outcomes (B wins or C wins), there is now also the possibility that: (i) B may win and C receives compensation from the Land Registry; or (ii) C may win but B may receive such compensation. This last possibility may be an alternative outcome in a case such as **Example 3**. The outcome suggested above is that: (i) B should be able to assert his pre-existing property right against C; but (ii) C should receive compensation from the Land Registry. An alternative outcome would be to protect C, the new registered owner, but to give B compensation from the Land Registry.

6.2   The negative operation of registration

When registration operates *negatively*, it prevents B from using an unregistered right against C, either by: (i) preventing B from acquiring that right; or (ii) by allowing C to have a defence to that right. However, no registration system goes so far as to say that it is *impossible* for B to assert *any* unregistered property right or persistent right against *all* third parties. First, it may not be true to say that all third parties deserve protection. Where C has

---

[20] LRA 2002, Sch 4.
[21] LRA 2002, Sch 8.
[22] C will of course have a claim against A, arising from A's breach of his contractual promise to transfer a valuable right to C: but, in practice, that claim may provide little help to C as A may be untraceable or bankrupt.

not paid for his right, but rather receives it for free, perhaps C should take that gift subject to B's pre-existing property right or persistent right, even if that pre-existing right is unregistered. For example, the lack of registration defence provided by the LRA 2002 is available to C only if he has acquired a right *for value*.[23] Equally, there may be some circumstances in which C has paid for his right, but nonetheless should not be able to have a defence to B's unregistered right. For example, it can be argued that C should not have a defence if, when he committed to acquiring his right, he was fully aware of, or could easily have discovered, B's unregistered property right or persistent right. We will consider how the LRA 2002 deals with this argument in **E2:3.6**. But one point worth noting here is that if: (i) B has an unregistered persistent right in relation to particular land; but (ii) B is in actual occupation of that land when C commits to acquiring his right from A; then (iii) the general rule is that C will *not* be able to use the lack of registration defence against B's right (see **E2:3.6.2**).[24] In such a case, B's right is said to be an *overriding interest*: it is immune from the lack of registration defence. The point seems to be that, as B was in actual occupation of the registered land, C could easily have discovered B's right:[25] as a result, C does not need the extra protection of the lack of registration defence.[26]

Second, it may be that, in some circumstances, it is simply inappropriate to punish B for his failure to register. For example, it is sometimes possible for B to acquire a property right in land, or a persistent right relating to land, *informally*: without the drawing up of documents or the involvement of professional advisers (see **E1:2** and **E2:2**).[27] In such circumstances, it may seem unreasonable to expect B to register his right; indeed, it would be very harsh to prevent B asserting his right against C simply because of his failure to register. We will consider how the LRA 2002 deals with this argument in **E1:3.6** and **E2:3.6**. One point worth noting here is that, where B is allowed to acquire a Lease (a property right in land) informally (without the use of writing) C cannot use the lack of registration defence against B's right.[28] In such a case, B's right, again, is an *overriding interest*: it is immune from the lack of registration defence. The point seems to be that, as it would be unreasonable to expect B to register his right, B should not lose out through his failure to do so.

---

[23] See LRA 2002, ss 29 and 30.

[24] See LRA 2002, Sched 1 para 2 and Sched 3 para 2.

[25] If: (i) B is in actual occupation of the registered land; but (ii) that occupation is not reasonably discoverable by C; and (iii) C, when he acquired his right, did not know about B's right; then (iv) despite B's actual occupation, B's right does *not* count as an overriding interest: see LRA 2002, Sched 3 para 2(c).

[26] If: (i) C acquires a right in relation to registered land; and (ii) before acquiring his right, C *asks* B if B has a right in relation to that land; and (iii) B does not inform C of B's right; and (iv) if it was reasonable for B to inform C, then (v) despite B's actual occupation, B's right does *not* count as an overriding interest: see LRA 2002, Sched 3 para 2(b).

[27] See esp **E1:2.3.3(iv)**; **E2:2.3.1(iv)**, **2.3.2(iv)** and **2.3.3(iv)**.

[28] See LRA 2002, Sched 1 para 1 and Sch 3 para 1 (see **E5:3.3.3(ii)**).

SUMMARY of C2:6

Whether it operates negatively or positively, the registered land system set up by the LRA 2002 does not operate absolutely. A simple rule that C can *never* be bound by an unregistered right of B will fail properly to balance the needs of C with those of B. In analysing the rules of the land registration system we need to remember that the concept of registration is not an end in itself; it is simply a means of resolving the **basic tension**.

The general impact of the LRA 2002 on the basic structure of land law, sketched out in this section, can be summarised in the following two tables. The tables can be read together and expand on the table set out above in **section 3**. The full combined table is available at the companion website, from where it can be printed out or downloaded.

The first table deals with the effect of the LRA 2002 on the **acquisition question**:

		Positive operation: *Consequences of substantive registration*	**Negative operation:** *Consequences of the absence of substantive registration*
Acquisition question	**Property rights**	By substantively registering his right, a party acquires that right • *but* certain property rights cannot be substantively registered;[29] • *and* a party can lose his right if the register is rectified.[30]	In general, if a party fails to substantively register a right, he fails to acquire that right • *but* certain property rights can be acquired without substantive registration.[31]
	Persistent rights	N/A: no persistent right can be substantively registered.	N/A: substantive registration is never required for the acquisition of a persistent right.

[29] Leases of seven years or less, unless falling within one of the exceptions set out by LRA 2002, s.27(2)(b)(ii)–(v), cannot be substantively registered.

[30] LRA 2002, Sched 4 sets out the rules governing rectification.

[31] There is obviously no need for B substantively to register a right, such as a non-exceptional Lease of seven years or less, that cannot be substantively registered. There is also one type of right (an implied Easement) that *can* be substantively registered, but can nonetheless be acquired without such registration: we will look at the acquisition of implied Easements in **G5:2.4** and **G5:2.6**.

The second table deals with the effect of the LRA 2002 on the **defences question**:

		Positive operation: *Consequences of substantive registration*	**Negative operation:** *Consequences of the absence of defensive registration*
Defences question	**Property rights**	If a party: (i) acquires his right for value;[32] and (ii) substantively registers that right;[33] then (iii) he will be able to use the lack of registration defence against an unregistered property right or persistent right *unless* that pre-existing right counts as an overriding interest.[34]	N/A: If a party has acquired a property right without substantively registering it, that right will almost always be an overriding interest[35] and hence will be immune from the lack of registration defence[36] even if it is not defensively registered.
	Persistent rights	N/A: no persistent right can be substantively registered.	If a party fails to (or cannot)[37] defensively register his persistent right, his right is potentially vulnerable to the lack of registration defence. However, if a party with a persistent right is in actual occupation of the registered land, his right may count as an overriding interest and hence be immune from the lack of registration defence.[38]

The combined effect of the tables on the *lack of registration* defence can be summarised in a flowchart:

---

[32] LRA 2002, ss 29(1) and 30(1) ensure that the lack of registration defence can only be used by a party who acquires his right 'for valuable consideration'.

[33] If C acquires a non-exceptional Lease of seven years or less, C cannot substantively register his right. Nonetheless, C *can* rely on the lack of registration defence: for the purposes of that defence, C is treated *as though* he has substantively registered his Lease: see LRA 2002, s 29(4).

[34] See LRA 2002, ss 29 and 30.

[35] See LRA 2002, Sched 1 paras 1 and 3; Sched 3 paras 1 and 3.

[36] In one very rare situation, B's property right is *not* immune from the lack of registration defence: it is outside the list of overriding interests in registered land. That situation occurs only if B's property right is: (i) an implied Easement; *and* (ii) B has not used that Easement in the year before C acquired his right; *and* (iii) B's Easement was not obvious on a reasonably careful inspection of the land by C; *and* (iv) C, when he acquired his right, did not know about B's Easement: see E5:3.3.3(ii). In contrast, if the land is *not* already registered when C acquires his right, and C registers his ownership of the land, then *all* Easements are overriding: see LRA 2002, Sched 1, para 3.

[37] For example, a right under a Trust cannot be protected by the entry of a notice on the register: LRA 2002, s 33(a)(i).

[38] B needs to show he falls within the LRA 2002, Sched 3 para 2 (or of Sched 1 para 2 where C registers a right in previously unregistered land): the details of that section will be discussed in E2:3.6.

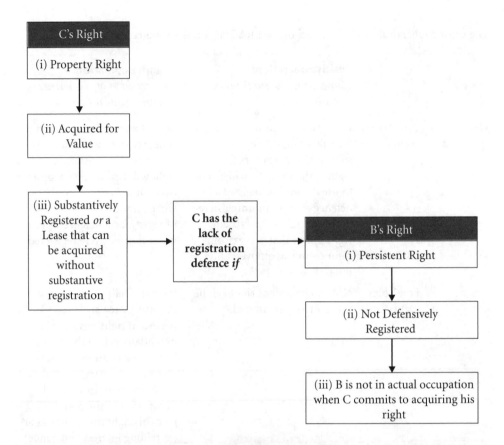

EXAMPLE 4

A, a registered owner of a family home, lives there with B, his wife. In return for a loan from C Bank, A, without the consent of B, gives C Bank a Charge over the land (see **E1:1.1** and **G4:2.1**). A falls behind in his loan repayments and C wishes to enforce its Charge by: (i) removing B from the land; (ii) selling the home; and (iii) using the proceeds of sale to satisfy the outstanding debt owed by A to C. B, as a result of contributing to the costs of buying the land, has a right under a Trust of A's ownership of the land. However: (i) C Bank has substantively registered its Charge; and (ii) B's claimed persistent right is not recorded on the register.[39]

This set of facts is an example of the **basic situation**: its basic facts are identical to: (i) **A:Example 1**; and (ii) **B:Example 1**; and (iii) the facts considered by the House of Lords in its important decision in *Williams & Glyn's Bank Ltd v Boland*.[40] There is a clear difference between **Example 4** and *National Provincial Bank v Ainsworth* (see **B:11**). In the former case, but not the latter, B has a pre-existing persistent right. So, in **Example 4**, B has a

---

[39] As we saw above, under LRA 2002, s 33(a)(i) it is impossible for B to protect a right under a Trust by entering a notice on the register.
[40] [1981] AC 487.

prima facie power to assert her right against C Bank. The crucial question is whether C Bank can use the *lack of registration* defence against B's right.

We can answer that question by examining the flowchart. Starting on the left-hand side, we can see that:

- C Bank acquired a Charge: a property right in land; *and*
- C Bank acquired that right for value: it was given to C Bank in return for the loan made to A; *and*
- C Bank substantively registered its right.

This means it *may* be possible for C Bank to use the lack of registration defence. However, we also need to look at B's pre-existing right:

- B's right is a persistent right; *and*
- B's right was not recorded on the register; *but*
- B was in actual occupation of the registered land when C Bank committed to acquiring its Charge.

So, the final element of the lack of registration defence was missing: as a result, as confirmed by the House of Lords in *Williams & Glyn's Bank v Boland*, B *did* have the power to assert her pre-existing persistent right against C Bank.[41] In *Boland*, the House of Lords considered the provisions of the Land Registration Act 1925; but the LRA 2002 leads to exactly the same result. As we saw in A:1, the facts considered in *Boland* provide a dramatic example of the **basic tension** of property law. In the abstract, that basic tension is impossibly difficult to resolve: it is very hard to know whether: (i) to favour C Bank in order to promote commerce; or (ii) to favour B in order to protect her home. However, in *Boland*, the House of Lords did *not* have to consider that impossibly difficult abstract question. Instead, it simply needed to apply the **basic structure**, including the rules of the registered land system.[42] And, as the result in *Boland* demonstrates, those rules do *not* exist simply to protect C Bank. Rather, they exist as a means to *balance* the needs of C Bank with those of B. Clearly, the introduction of registration does not make the **basic tension** disappear: it is simply one of the tools that can be used in an attempt to resolve that tension.

7 REGISTRATION AND UNREGISTERED LAND

As noted in **section 1** above, the majority of land in England and Wales is now registered land. As a result, we will not examine the special rules that apply to unregistered land.[43]

---

[41] However, this does not mean that, in practice, Mrs Boland would necessarily be able to continue living in her home: it is very likely that, on C Bank's application, a court would order the land to be sold: see G3:4.2.

[42] The *Boland* decision is often analysed in terms of practical convenience and seen as the 'high water-mark' of an approach based on a judicial desire to protect B's home rather than the interests of commerce. However, as shown by the analysis above, the decision was in fact based on applying the doctrinal rules of the land law system: see too Conaglen (2006) 69 *MLR* 583.

[43] Of course, the basic structure of property law applies to unregistered land. As a result, this book covers the basic principles applying to unregistered land; it simply misses out a full examination of the statutory modifications made to those general principles by statutes, such as the LCA 1972, applying only to unregistered land.

However, it is worth noting that registration may be important even where unregistered land is concerned. Indeed, a brief look at a case considering the special rules applying to unregistered land (now set out by the Land Charges Act 1972 ('the LCA 1972')) can illustrate some important points about the general operation of registration.

EXAMPLE 5

A, an owner of unregistered land, makes a contractual promise to sell the land to B, his son. A is thus under a duty to B in relation to a specific right (A's ownership of the land). B thus has a persistent right: a right against A's ownership of the land. The particular form of persistent right acquired by B is often said to arise under an 'Estate Contract'. A then falls out with B and is determined not to transfer the land to B. A therefore transfers his ownership of the land, to C, his wife. The price is only £500, even though the land is worth about £40,000. C does not register her ownership of the land. C knows all about A's prior contractual promise to B. However, C argues that she is not bound by B's pre-existing persistent right as: (i) B had failed to register that right; and (ii) C acquired her right for value.

In *Midland Bank Trust Co Ltd v Green*,[44] the House of Lords considered precisely this situation. It may seem that B should be able to asset his pre-existing persistent right against C. Certainly, as she knew all about B's right, C cannot rely on the general 'bona fide purchaser' defence (see **B:5.2.2(ii)**). However, the problem for B was that he had not registered his persistent right. This meant that, under the LCA 1972, C had a **defence** to B's right: the *lack of registration* defence. That defence applied even though C's ownership of the land, like A's before it, was unregistered.

This may seem a little confusing: as B's right related to land that was unregistered, where could B have registered his right? The answer is that B could, and should, have recorded his right in the Land Charges Register:[45] it is not a register of plots of land, but is rather a register of *names* of landowners. The Land Charges Register thus operates in a similar way to the register of charges over company assets: each register is organised into files based not on particular things, but instead on particular people or companies from whom C might acquire a right. So, in *Midland Bank Trust Co v Green*, B's persistent right could then have been recorded against A's name: a third party, when deciding whether to deal with A's land, could then look at the register, search for A's name, and discover B's right.

In *Green*, the registration concept was applied to dealings with land: as we saw above, the special nature of land may justify the extra protection that the lack of registration defence can offer to C. In *Green*, registration operated *negatively*: it responded to B's failure to enter his right on the Land Charges Register by allowing C to have a defence to that right: the lack of registration defence. The lack of registration defence depended on:

1.   The *nature* of B's right. The LCA 1972[46] does not allow the lack of registration defence to be used against all unregistered rights. Rather, it allows that defence to be used

---

[44] [1981] AC 513.

[45] LPA 1925, s 198 provides that a registered land charge will bind a purchaser irrespective of whether he has notice of B's right. Conversely, LCA 1972, s 4 provides that an unregistered land charge will not affect C, even if he has notice of B's right.

[46] In *Green*, C acquired her right in 1967. The dispute was therefore governed by the Land Charges Act 1925. That Act was replaced by the LCA 1972, and so we will consider the later Act here: none of the changes made by the 1972 Act affect the result or reasoning in *Green*.

against *particular* unregistered rights, including the right acquired by B in **Example 4**.[47]

2. The *nature* of C's right. Even if B's right is vulnerable to the LCA 1972 lack of registration defence, that defence cannot be used by *all* third parties. However, C qualified for the defence because she had acquired ownership of the land.[48]

3. The *circumstances* in which C had acquired her right. To qualify for the LCA 1972 lack of registration defence, C must show she acquired her right *for value.* [49]

These factors may help us to justify C's ability to use the lack of registration defence in **Example 5**. First, it is usually reasonable to expect B to register a persistent right arising as a result of A's contractual promise to transfer his ownership of land to B. Such a contract has to be made in writing signed by both A and B (see **E2:2.3.3**). And such a contract will almost always be drawn up with the assistance of legal advisors: B should therefore be aware of the need to register his right.[50] Second, the defence is not available to all third parties: only to those who acquire a property right in land for 'money or money's worth'.[51] This denies C protection if *either:* (i) he acquires a right for free; *or* (ii) he acquires only a persistent right from A. In those two ways, the lack of registration defence applied in *Green* resembles the general 'bona fide purchaser' defence (see **B:5.2.2(ii)**).

However, **Example 5** is clearly not a straightforward case: if it were, *Green* would not have reached the House of Lords. The complicating factor was that, when acquiring her right, C was *fully aware* of B's unregistered persistent right. As a result, C would clearly *not* have been able to use the general bona fide purchaser defence against that right. Nonetheless, on the facts of **Example 5**, the 1972 Act allows C to use the lack of registration defence. This, as the House of Lords confirmed in *Green*, is the clear meaning of the Act. The dispute went to the House of Lords because the effect of the Act is at odds with the general position that C cannot have a defence to B's pre-existing persistent right if C is aware of that right when choosing to deal with A.

In **Example 5**, if A's ownership of the land is registered, so that the dispute between B and C is governed by the principles set out by the LRA 2002, the result may be different. If: (i) B is in actual occupation of the land when C commits to acquiring a right (as was the case in *Green*); then (ii) B's unregistered persistent right constitutes an overriding interest and so is immune from the lack of registration defence (see **6.2** above). To that extent, and perhaps surprisingly, the lack of registration defence applying in unregistered land gives C *more* protection than the lack of registration defence provided by the registered land system.

Nonetheless, there is an important similarity between both the unregistered land system

---

[47] See LCA 1972, s 2(4)(iv). A right under a Trust is an example of a persistent right to which the lack of registration defence provided by the LCA 1972 does *not* apply: see eg *Kingsnorth Finance v Tizard* [1986] 1 WLR 783. In such a case, C has to try to rely on the general 'bona fide purchaser' defence. In *Tizard*, C was unable to do so as: as B was living in A's home when C acquired its Charge, C could reasonably have been expected to discover B's right.

[48] LCA 1972, s 4(6) gives C a defence against an unregistered Estate Contract only if C acquires 'a legal estate in the land'. 'Legal estate', in that context, includes any property right in the land.

[49] LCA 1972, s 4(6) gives C a defence against an unregistered Estate Contract only if C acquires a legal estate in the land 'for money of money's worth'. So the £500 C paid in return for A's ownership of the land was crucial.

[50] B had received legal advice in *Midland Bank Trust Co v Green*. His solicitors carelessly failed to ensure that B's right was registered. As a result, they committed both: (i) a breach of their contract with B; and (ii) a breach of their non-contractual duty of care to B. So, they were under a duty to pay B money to compensate him for the loss he suffered as a result of the failure to register: see *Midland Bank Trust Co Ltd v Hett, Stubbs & Kemp* [1979] Ch 384.

[51] LCA 1972, s 4(6).

and the registered land system. In each case, C is *never* prevented from using the lack of registration defence *simply* because, when acquiring his right, he knew all about B's unregistered right. Under the LRA 2002, B's actual occupation of registered land may prevent C using the defence; but, if B is *not* in actual occupation, C can qualify for the lack of registration defence *even though* he knows about B's unregistered right. In **E2:3.6.5(i)** we will consider *why* the LRA 2002 adopts that position. For the moment, we simply need to note that, as memorably demonstrated by the decision of the House of Lords in *Midland Bank Trust Co v Green*, the registration concept can have a very dramatic impact on the resolution of the basic tension between B and C.

SUMMARY of C2

In property law, the legal concept of registration involves two things:

1. The existence of a register that records parties' rights; and
2. A set of rules attributing legal consequences to the fact that a party has or has not registered a right.

When those consequences flow from the fact of registration, registration operates *positively* and can affect the **acquisition question**. For example, under section 58 of the LRA 2002, C can acquire a property right simply by substantively registering as a holder of that right. When legal consequences flow from a party's failure to register a right, registration operates *negatively* and can affect both: (i) the **acquisition question**; and (ii) the **defences** question. For example: (i) under sections 4 and 27 of the LRA 2002, B's failure to substantively register a right may prevent him from acquiring that right; and (ii) under sections 29 and 30 of the LRA 2002, B's failure to defensively register a right may allow C to use the lack of registration defence against that right. To qualify for that lack of registration defence, C needs to show that: (i) he acquired a property right; (ii) he acquired that right for value; and (iii) that he substantively registered his right (or acquired a Lease of a type that cannot be substantively registered).[52]

The registration concept protects C against the risk of being bound by a pre-existing right of B. A registration system thus limits the inquiries which C would otherwise have to make before committing himself to a acquiring a right from A. The registration concept can therefore be an important part of the **basic structure** of property law. However, it is not universally applied: it operates only: (i) in relation to things that can be easily identified; and (ii) where C is particularly in need of protection. Where land is concerned, both those conditions are met.

However, even in relation to registered land, it must be remembered that the registration concept is not a be-all and end-all. Whilst registration may provide valuable protection for C, there will be circumstances in which this protection, and in particular the consequences it has for B, cannot be justified. Whether it operates negatively or positively, registration will never operate absolutely. Even in relation to registered land, a simple rule that C can never be bound by an unregistered right of B will fail to balance the needs of third parties such as C with the needs of prior users of the land such as B. So, when considering **Example 4**, we saw that, as confirmed by the House of Lords in *Williams & Glyn's Bank Ltd v Boland*,[53] an

---

[52] LRA 2002, s 29(4).
[53] [1981] AC 487.

unregistered pre-existing persistent right of B may still bind C, *even if* C acquires a property right for value and substantively registers that right. It is thus clear that the concept of registration does *not* allow the basic tension of property law to be ignored in favour of a brutal rule that denies all effect to unregistered rights.

CHAPTER C3
FORMALITY

C3

FORMALITY

1 INTRODUCTION

In **C1**, we saw that principles originally developed by courts of Equity can affect *all* of the basic questions that form part of the property law system. In **C2**, we looked at registration and saw that the concept of registration can affect both the acquisition question and the defences question. In this chapter, our focus is on the **acquisition question**. We will examine the effect of formality on the crucial question of how a party can acquire a right. As we will see, *formality rules* form a prominent part of the property law system and are particularly important in the land law system.

We have already seen one way in which formality can affect the acquisition question. To acquire a property right in registered land, B will, in general, need to substantively register his right (see **C2:6**). If B fails to do so, the registration system governed by the Land Registration Act 2002 ('LRA 2002') operates negatively: it responds to B's failure to register by preventing B from acquiring the right he claims. For example, let us say B claims that A, a registered owner of land, has transferred his registered right to B. If B is not registered as holding that right, B's claim will fail: it will be impossible for B to show that he has acquired A's right. B's failure to take a particular formal step (in this case, substantive registration) may thus prevent him from acquiring a particular right (in this case, A's ownership of the land).

2 FORMALITY AND FORMALITY RULES

Formality concerns the ways in which parties: (i) express their intentions; and (ii) record their intentions, their transactions or their rights. A distinction is often drawn between form and substance.

EXAMPLES 1a–1d

We need to consider four different situations: in each case, A promises to pay B £100:
- (a) A makes the promise orally, in conversation with B;
- (b) A makes the promise orally *and* shakes hands with B when making the promise;
- (c) A makes the promise orally, shakes hands with B *and* later gives B a signed IOU.
- (d) A makes the promise in a written document, signed by A and by a witness; the document is also described, on its face, as a deed.

In each of these four cases, the *substance* of A's promise is the same: he promises to pay B £100. But, in each case, the *form* of A's promise is different: in each case, A expresses or records his intention in a different way.

The forms chosen by parties to express or record their intentions may be of interest to, say, an anthropologist. Those forms only start to interest a lawyer when *legal consequences* depend on the particular form chosen by the parties. In the four cases set out above, the crucial distinction for a lawyer is between the first three cases and the final one. In **Example 1d**, the particular method chosen by A to express his intention means that A is under a legal duty to B to perform his promise. The document used by A to make the promise counts as a deed,[1] and so A's promise is legally enforceable even though it was gratuitous (ie, B gave nothing in return for it). It is sometimes thought that a promise given in a deed imposes a contractual duty on A. However, a promise in a deed is binding: (i) even if B gives nothing in return for it; and (ii) even if it is not part of an agreement between A and B; and (iii) even if B does not know that A has made the promise.[2] Therefore, in **Example 1d** as in **Examples 1a, 1b and 1c**, A's promise does not give B a contractual right. However, in **Example 1d**, in contrast to **Examples 1a, 1b and 1c**, A is under a non-contractual duty to B to perform his promise. Hence, whilst expressing his promise in a deed does not alter the substance of A's promise, it does alter its legal effect.

Rules attaching legal consequences to the parties' choice of form are known as *formality rules*. Our example demonstrates the impact of one such rule: a gratuitous promise to B, if made in a deed, is enforceable by B. Formality rules are often seen as obstacles—annoying hurdles to be cleared before the parties' intentions can be upheld. However, they can sometimes be the price paid to give a *facility* to the parties. For example, the possibility of using a deed gives A the power to make a legally binding gratuitous promise.[3]

EXAMPLES 2a–2d

We need to consider four different situations: in each case, A tells B that, when A dies, all A's rights will go to B:

    (a) A tells B orally, in conversation with B;

    (b) A tells B orally *and* shakes hands with B;

    (c) A tells B orally, shakes hands with B *and* later gives B a signed confirmation;

    (d) A expresses his intention in a document, signed by A and by two witnesses (C and D).

In the four cases set out above, the crucial distinction for a lawyer is between the first three cases and the final one. In **Example 2d**, the particular method chosen by A to express his intention means that, when A dies, B has a prima facie right to acquire all A's rights.[4] The document used by A to express his intention counts as a valid will, as it satisfies the

---

[1] The definition of a deed is given by s 1 of the Law of Property (Miscellaneous Provisions) Act 1989. It is a document that must be: (i) signed not only by the party executing it but also by a witness; and (ii) described, on its face, as a deed. To be properly executed, a deed must also be 'delivered'. In this context, delivery has a technical meaning: it consists of conduct showing that the person executing the deed intends to be bound by it and does not require physical control of the deed to be transferred.

[2] See eg *Macedo v Stroud* [1922] 2 AC 330. See eg Peel, *Treitel's Law of Contract* (12th edn, 2007), 174: 'Consideration is not necessary for the validity of a promise made in a deed. The binding force of such a promise does not depend on contract at all.'

[3] In most jurisdictions in the United States, A has *no* power to make a binding gratuitous promise, even if a deed is used. For problems resulting from this, see Farnsworth (1987) 43 *American Journal of Comparative Law* 359.

[4] B can only acquire those rights of A that: (i) survive A's death; and (ii) are capable of being transferred. Further, in administering the will, A's executors may need to use some of A's right for other purposes (eg, to pay A's creditors). And, under the Inheritance (Provision for Family and Dependants) Act 1975, other parties may apply to court to receive some of A's rights: see **n 8** below.

formality rule imposed by the Wills Act 1837.[5] That Act regulates A's power to make a 'testamentary disposition': to dispose of his rights on his death.[6] A must ensure that his intentions are recorded in a written document signed by A and by two witnesses. A must also avoid a common trap: if A intends to give a right to B on A's death, B should not be one of the two witnesses.[7]

The requirements of the Wills Act, particularly the need for disinterested witnesses, may seem technical—hurdles that have to be cleared before A's intentions can be upheld. We tend to take it for granted that A should have the power to decide what happens to his rights when he dies, but the property law system has not always given A that power. Even today, in many countries, there are still severe limits on that power: for example, 'forced heirship' provisions may mean that certain rights of A are automatically dealt with in a particular way on A's death, whether A likes it or not.[8] So, when considering the formality rules in the Wills Act, it is important to remember that those rules can be seen as the price paid to give a facility to A: the power to decide what happens to his rights when he dies.[9]

Whether a formality rule is seen as an obstacle or as a facility, the crucial question is the same: can we *justify* the legal consequences that flow from the fact the parties have used, or failed to use, a particular form? Before we examine that question, we first need to look at the function of formality rules within the property law system.

3   THE FUNCTION OF FORMALITY RULES

3.1   General position

Within the property law system, the basic function of a formality rule is to *regulate a party's power to give another party a right*. A formality rule achieves that function by requiring that a party's exercise of his power to give another a right *must be expressed or recorded in a particular form*. If B's claim to a right depends on showing that such a power has been exercised, formality rules *may* apply. So, in **Examples 1a–1d**, the need for a deed regulates A's power to make a binding gratuitous promise to B. And in **Examples 2a–2d**, the Wills Act 1837 regulates A's power to transfer rights to B on A's death. But if B's claim does *not* depend on showing that a party has exercised a power to give B a right, formality rules *cannot* apply.

---

[5] See Wills Act 1837, ss 1 and 9.

[6] See Wills Act 1837, s 1. For a consideration of the meaning of 'testamentary disposition', see Critchley (1999) 115 *LQR* 631.

[7] If B is one of the witnesses, the will can still take effect; but B cannot acquire a right as a result of it: Wills Act 1837, ss 14 and 15.

[8] For example, a system may provide that A's property rights in land are automatically acquired, on A's death, by A's children. There are no such provisions in English law. The nearest thing is the Inheritance (Provision for Family and Dependants) Act 1975. That Act gives certain parties (eg, A's spouse/partner/child/someone maintained by A: see s 1) the right to apply to court if they feel A has not made reasonable financial provision for them (whether or not A has made a will). The court has a power under s 2 to order that an applicant should receive a sum of money or specific rights from A's estate. See too **G3:2.4.3(v)(f)**.

[9] A's power is set out by the Wills Act 1837, s 3. This analysis of the Wills Act 1837 is adopted by Hart in *The Concept of Law* (2nd edn, 1994) at 33–8. It has been criticised on historical grounds (the power to transfer rights on death existed before that Act). Nonetheless, Hart's general point is correct: the 1837 Act both: (i) recognises that A has a power to transfer rights on death; *and* (ii) regulates that power by means of a formality rule.

3.2   The acquisition of property rights

There are two general ways in which B can acquire a property right: (i) dependent acquisition; and (ii) independent acquisition (see **B:2.2**). Where B claims to have dependently acquired a property right from A, B must show that A has exercised a power to give B that right. As a result, a formality rule *may* apply to regulate A's power to give B the right (see eg **D1:2.2.4(i)**, **D1:2.2.5** and **E1:2.3**). So, in **Examples 2a–2d**, a formality rule can (and does) apply as, if A has any property rights, B claims that A has exercised a power to transfer those rights, on his death, to B.

In contrast, if B claims to have independently acquired his property right, he relies on his own conduct. As a result, B does not need to show that A has exercised a power to give him a right, and so formality rules are irrelevant (see **D1:2.1** and **E1:2.1.1**).

3.3   The acquisition of persistent rights

To acquire a persistent right, B first needs to show that A is under a duty to B. The reasons for which A may come under a duty to B can be put into six categories (see **B:4.3**). Reasons 1 and 2 (A's consent to be under such a duty to B; and A's entry into a contract with B) *may* be regulated by a formality rule: in each case, A's duty arises as a result of an exercise of a power by A. However, Reasons 3–6 *cannot* be regulated by a formality rule: in each case, A's duty does *not* arise as a result of an exercise of a power by A.

Reason for which A's duty to B arises (see B:4.3)	Can a formality rule regulate B's acquisition of a right against A?
1 A's consent to be under such a duty to B	Yes
2 A's entry into a contract with B	Yes
3 A's commission of a wrong against B	No
4 A's unjust enrichment at B's expense	No
5 A statute imposing a duty on A to B	No
6 Any other event imposing a duty on A to B	No

3.4   The acquisition of personal rights

B can acquire a personal right against Z if: (i) A has a personal right against Z; and (ii) A transfers that right to B. In such a case, B claims that A has exercised a power to transfer a right to B. As a result, a formality rule may be relevant: in fact, A's power *is* regulated by a formality rule (see **5.1** below).

To acquire a personal right against A, B needs to show that A is under a duty to B. So the table set out above applies equally to the acquisition of personal rights. So, in **Examples 1a–1d**, a formality rule can (and does) apply as B claims that A's duty has arisen as a result of Reason 1.

3.5 An example

EXAMPLE 3

A, a registered owner of a family home, lives there with B. A moves out and makes a gratuitous oral promise to transfer his ownership of the land to B. B remains in the home and, relying on A's promise, spends money on the home in the belief that A will honour his promise. A then changes his mind and refuses to transfer his ownership to B.

In such a situation, there are a number of ways in which A *might* have exercised a power to give B a right.

1. A *might* have kept his promise by exercising his power to transfer his ownership to B. Clearly, A did not do so: he changed his mind before making the transfer. Moreover, as we saw in **C2:6**, a formality rule regulates A's power to transfer his ownership to B: B can only acquire A's ownership if B is substantively registered as the new holder of that right.

2. A *might* have exercised his power to enter a contract to transfer his ownership to B. Clearly, A did not do so: he did make a promise to B, but not as part of a bargain in which B provided consideration. Moreover, as we will see, a formality rule means that, to make a contractual promise to transfer his ownership of land to B, A has to use writing, signed by both A and B (see **5.2.1** below and **E2:2.3.3**).

3. A *might* have exercised his power to make a binding gratuitous promise to B. However, A cannot exercise that power orally: he has to use a deed.

So, in **Example 3**, B cannot show that A has exercised a power to give B a right in relation to A's land. This means that B cannot show that he has dependently acquired a property right from A. However, B can still show he has *independently acquired* a property right: once A left, B had physical control of the land and so independently acquired ownership of the land. That property right imposes a prima facie duty on the rest of the world: if X were to come onto the land without B's consent or other authority, X would commit a wrong against B.[10] However, B's independently acquired property right is of no use to B in **Example 3**: it does not bind A, as A has a *pre-existing* property right (see **D1:1.4.1** and **G1A:2.1.3**).

But that is not the end for B. B may be able to claim that A is under a duty to B and that, as a result, B has either: (i) a persistent right; or (ii) a personal right against A. B cannot show that A has exercised a power to give B such a right. However, B may be able to show that he has a right that does *not* depend on A exercising a power to give B a right. To do so, B needs to show that A is under a duty to B for one of Reasons 3–6 above. If B can make such a claim, it will be unaffected by formality rules and so it will not matter that A's promise was oral. We can see this by considering the reasoning of the Court in *Pascoe v Turner*,[11] the essential facts of which are identical to **Example 3**.

In *Pascoe*, the Court of Appeal found that A *was* under a duty to B. B was able to make a claim that did *not* depend on showing that A had exercised a power to give B a right. B acquired a right: as (i) A had made a promise to B; and (ii) B had reasonably relied on A's

---

[10] See *per* Lord Upjohn in *National Provincial Bank v Ainsworth* [1965] AC 1175 at 1232 and **G1A:2.1.2**.
[11] [1979] 1 WLR 431.

promise; and (iii) B would suffer a detriment if A were allowed to go back on that promise. As a result, A was under a duty to ensure that B did not suffer such a detriment. B thus acquired a right against A, under a doctrine known as 'proprietary estoppel' (see **E4**). In fact, the Court of Appeal found that, under that doctrine, A was under a duty to honour his promise and to transfer his ownership of the land to B. As A's duty to B thus related to a specific right held by A (A's ownership of the land) B acquired a persistent right. Formality rules were irrelevant as B's claim did *not* depend on A exercising a power to give B a right. Rather, B's right arose for a different reason: because of the need to protect B from the detriment she would suffer as a result of A's failure to honour his promise.

The result in a case such as *Pascoe v Turner* may seem to depend on an 'exception' to the formality rule we discussed above: the need for a gratuitous promise to be made in a deed. However, it is not an exception to that rule: instead, it shows the true scope of the rule. The rule is *not*: 'A gratuitous promise can never be binding unless made in a deed.' Rather, the rule is that, to exercise his power to make a binding gratuitous promise, A must use a deed. That rule is irrelevant where B acquires a right for some *other reason*, not based on A's exercise of that power. So, in *Pascoe v Turner*, the rule was irrelevant as B's right arose because of the need to protect B from the detriment she would suffer as a result of her reasonable reliance on a commitment that A failed to keep. On the table set out above, B's right arose because of Reason 6, *not* Reasons 1 or 2.

4   JUSTIFYING FORMALITY RULES

Where B's claim *does* depend on showing that A has exercised a power to give B a right, formality rules *may* apply. Of course, a formality rule need not apply *wherever* A has a power to give B a right. For example, if A sells his bike to B, A exercises his power to transfer his ownership of that bike to B. But no formality rule applies: A can transfer his ownership to B even if the sale is not expressed or recorded in writing (see **D1:2.2.4(iii)**). This means that, where A has a power to give B a right, the property law system has to make a choice: should A's power be regulated by a formality rule? In this section, we will look at the considerations that are relevant to that choice.[12]

4.1   Advantages of a formality rule

The basic point of such a rule is to influence A and B's behaviour, by giving them a reason to ensure that A's exercise of a power to give B a right is expressed or recorded in a particular form. So it must be that, in certain situations, the benefits of a particular form are so valuable as to justify a rule that, if the form is *not* used, A's attempt to give B a right will fail.

4.1.1 The provision of evidence

For example, to justify the formality rule applying in **Examples 1a–1d**, we need to ask what benefits come from A's gratuitous promise to B being expressed in a deed. A deed is a

---

[12] See too Critchley, ch 20 in *Land Law Themes and Perspectives* (ed Bright and Dewar, 1998).

written document, signed by a witness as well as A, that is described, on its face, as a deed.[13] The first benefit of A's promise being made in a deed is that the deed will provide useful *evidence.*[14] The written document will provide evidence of: (i) the fact that A made a promise; and (ii) the terms of that promise. Such evidence will be useful to a court if there is a later dispute between A and B; it will also be useful to the parties themselves. The need for evidence is particularly clear if we know that, should any dispute arise, A will no longer be around to explain his intentions to a court: it is hence no surprise that the formality rule applying in **Examples 2a–2d** requires written evidence signed not only by A but also verified by two disinterested witnesses.[15]

Even where no formality rule applies, A and B may well use writing, signed by the parties, to express or record A's exercise of his power to give B a right. For example, if A and B enter a commercial contract, there is no general rule that the contract needs to be written down. However, in practice, A and B will almost always use writing: they recognise that it will be very helpful to have some written evidence that each party agreed to the terms set out in the document.

4.1.2 The promotion of caution

It could be argued that, to ensure there is some solid evidence of A's promise, all we need do is to require that A's promise be made in signed writing. So, in **Examples 1a–1d**, why go further and require that the signed writing must be: (i) signed by a witness; and (ii) described as a deed? These requirements are related to a further benefit: that of promoting *caution.*[16] The concern here is essentially to protect A from exercising his power to give B a right in a rash or ill-considered way. A requirement of signed writing would promote caution as it would prevent A from being bound by a spontaneous oral promise to give B £100. However, the requirement of a deed aims to make doubly sure that A knows what he is doing.

4.1.3 The protection of A from fraudulent claims

From A's point of view, a formality rule can have a further beneficial aspect, linked both to the provision of evidence and the promotion of caution. Such a rule can *protect A from a fraudulent claim* that he has exercised a particular power to give B a right. For example, in the absence of a formality rule requiring a deed, B could try his luck at fabrication and allege that A had orally promised to give him £100. A would no doubt be able to refute such an invented claim, but the time and expense incurred in doing do could cause him inconvenience.[17] In contrast, the rule requiring a deed gives A a cast-iron defence to such a claim:

---

[13] See Law of Property (Miscellaneous Provisions) Act 1989, s 1 and **n 1** above.

[14] See eg Fuller (1941) 41 *Columbia Law Review* 799, 800; Kotz, *European Contract Law,* vol 1 (tr. Weir, 1997) ch 5; Critchley, in *Land Law Themes and Perspectives* (ed Bright and Dewar, 1998) 515–6.

[15] Where wills are concerned, there may be a long time between the signing of the will and a dispute about its meaning. The requirement for two witnesses (a deed needs only one) increases the chances that, if a dispute arises after A's death, there may be a living witness who can be questioned about A's intentions.

[16] See Fuller (1941) 41 *Columbia Law Review* 799 at 800.

[17] *Lalani v Crump* [2007] EWHC 47 provides an excellent example. A had ownership of some land. B claimed that: (i) A had made a promise to transfer that land to B; and (ii) B had relied on that promise. As in **Example 3** above, no formality rule applied: B's claim was *not* based on A's exercise of a power to give B a right. It was eventually held that there was no basis to A's claim that B had made such a promise; however, that decision came almost five years after the dispute between A and B arose and after five separate applications to court had been made.

unless B can produce a document proving A's promise, signed not only by A but also by a witness, B's claim will fail. Of course, no formality rule can give A complete protection: a determined fraudster could fabricate a deed, but he would risk a serious criminal penalty if discovered.[18]

4.1.4 The provision of publicity

A further benefit of using a particular form—again closely linked to the provision of evidence—can be *publicity*. This publicity may be useful to B: for example, if he wants to persuade C to lend him some money by proving A's promise, B may be able to show C the deed. In some situations, publicity will be particularly useful to C. The most obvious case is where, instead of simply making a gratuitous promise to give B £100, A has exercised his power to give B a property right or a persistent right. If B has a property right, that right imposes a prima facie duty on C (see **B:4.2**). And if B has a persistent right against A's right, B will have a prima facie power to assert that right against C if C acquires a right that depends on A's right (see **B:4.3**). A formality rule can protect C by giving him a means to discover B's right *before* deciding to: (i) deal with the thing; or (ii) to acquire a right from A. As far as C is concerned, the best formality rule will be one requiring *registration* of the fact that A has exercised his power to give B a property right or persistent right. In such a case, the registration system operates negatively: B's failure to register a right means that B fails to acquire that right (see **C2:3.2**). In such a case, it is then very easy for C to discover if A has exercised such a power: C simply needs to check the register.[19]

Therefore, the benefits of using a particular form can determine: (i) *if* a particular power of A to give B a right will be regulated by a formality rule; *and* (ii) *what* particular form A must use to exercise that power. If *evidence* (and *protecting A from a fraudulent claim*) is the key concern, signed writing may be enough; although if there is a pressing need for strong evidence, it may also be sensible to require a witness or two. If promoting *caution* is particularly important, further requirements, such as those involved in a deed, may be needed. And if *publicity* is the main goal, registration is the obvious solution.

4.2   Disadvantages of a formality rule

4.2.1 An increase in time and expense

It is clear that formality rules have a downside. First, there is the *time and expense* incurred in complying with a formality rule. For example, to make a promise in a deed, A needs to: (i) set the promise down in signed writing; (ii) ensure that a witness also signs the document; and (iii) ensure that the document is described, on its face, as a deed. This is, in

---

[18] See eg Forgery and Counterfeiting Act 1981, ss 1 and 3 (crimes of making and of using a false instrument). A party fabricating an oral promise from A could be guilty of perjury, if making such a claim in court; but his guilt is much less obvious, as he may well be able to argue that he had simply made an honest error in misinterpreting or misremembering an oral statement by A (see eg *per* Park J in *Lalani v Crump* [2007] EWHC 47 at [46]–[48]).

[19] C can also be protected by having a **defence** against an unregistered property right or persistent right of B (see C2:3.2). In such a case, C's protection does not come from a formality rule, as B can *acquire* his right without registration. A defence may provide less effective protection for third parties: to qualify for a defence, a third party may well need to satisfy particular conditions. For example, the lack of registration defence under the LRA 2002 is only available to C if: (i) he acquires a property right; and (ii) he acquires that right for value; and (iii) he substantively registers that right *or* the right is a Lease that cannot be substantively registered (see C2:6).

fact, a relatively easy thing to do, but A and B may nonetheless feel it is best to use a lawyer to draw up the document. The involvement of a lawyer may well be an advantage, particularly in promoting *caution* and in ensuring the parties understand the consequences of their actions. Nonetheless, the additional expense and delay clearly adds to the cost of A and B's transaction.[20]

4.2.2 The frustration of reasonable expectations

A failure to comply with a formality rule can result in the *frustration of reasonable expectations*. It is clear that there will be situations in which A and B act on the basis that A has given B a right, only to discover that, because a formality rule has not been satisfied, B does not have that right. So, in **Examples 1a–1c**, B may arrange his affairs on the basis that he will soon receive £100 from A. B will then face problems if A changes his mind and decides not to perform his promise. Similarly, in **Examples 2a–2c**, B may rely on his expectation that he will receive A's rights when A dies.

However, a failure to satisfy a formality rule will not necessarily leave B without any right. B will be unable to claim that A exercised his power to give B a particular right; but B may be able to use *some other means* of claiming that he has a right against A. For example, we saw when examining **Example 3** that, in *Pascoe v Turner*,[21] the doctrine of proprietary estoppel ensured that B did not suffer a detriment as a result of his reliance on A's gratuitous promise.[22] A will not always be under a duty to give B the very right he expected; but he will be under a duty to act in such a way as to ensure B suffers no detriment as a result of his reasonable reliance on A's promise (see **E4:4**).[23] In this way, doctrines such as proprietary estoppel can mitigate any problems B may suffer as a result of a formality rule.[24]

4.2.3 An increase in technicality and compexity

Third, formality rules can lead to *technicality and complexity*. For example, a particular formality rule, set out by section 4 of the Statute of Frauds 1677, regulates A's power to make a contractual promise to B to guarantee a duty owed by X to B: if A's promise is not expressed or recorded in writing, B will be unable to enforce it.[25] A may therefore attempt to rely on this formality rule in order to prevent B enforcing A's oral promise to B. A court may then have to deal with the technical and often complex question of whether A's promise counts as a *guarantee*.[26]

---

[20] The view has been taken that many formality rules exist simply to give lawyers more work: see eg Bentham, *Rationale of Judicial Evidence*, vol ii (1827) 553–4. That view, however, overlooks the advantage of formality rules set out in **4.1** above.

[21] [1979] 1 WLR 431.

[22] See too eg *Gillett v Holt* [2001] Ch 210. Where B only discovers that A has failed to keep the promise after A's death, B's right takes effect against A's estate: see eg *re Basham* [1986] 1 WLR 1498; *Jennings v Rice* [2003] 1 P & CR 100; *Ottey v Grundy* [2003] EWCA Civ 1176.

[23] See eg *Jennings v Rice* [2003] 1 P & CR 100.

[24] Secret Trusts, founded on the 'receipt after a promise' principle (see **D3:2.2.2**) provide an example of an alternative means of protection for B where the Wills Act 1837 prevents B showing that A has given him a right: see **F3:2.1.4(iii)(b)**.

[25] See eg *Actionstrength Ltd v International Glass Engineering SpA* [2003] 2 AC 541.

[26] In *Yeoman Credit v Latter* [1961] 1 WLR 828 Harman LJ at 835 graphically stated: 'the question [is] whether this contract was one of guarantee or indemnity. It seems to me a most barren controversy. It dates back, of course, to the Statute of Frauds, and has raised many hair-splitting distinctions of exactly that kind which brings the law into hatred, ridicule and contempt by the public.' For a similar problem, see the debate over the meaning of the word 'disposition' as used in s 53(1)(c) of the Law of Property Act 1925: see **F3:2.2.1**.

4.2.4 A lack of transparency in the law

If a court feels that applying a formality rule may defeat the parties' reasonable expectations, it may be tempting for that court to find a way around that rule. This could be done by finding that the formality rule does not apply: for example, a court could avoid section 4 of the Statute of Frauds 1677 by holding that A's promise is not a guarantee. However, this can then worsen the third problem: the definition of a guarantee will be blurred and it will be harder to state the scope of the formality rule. Alternatively, a court could protect B by admitting that the formality rule applies, and hence that A has failed to exercise a particular power to give B a right, but allowing B to acquire a right by another means. By adopting such a route, a court can protect B without directly challenging the formality rule. However, the law can become less transparent if the different means by which B acquires a right comes to operate *simply* as a means to avoid the formality rule.

For example, in *Pascoe v Turner*,[27] the Court of Appeal allowed B to acquire a right through the doctrine of proprietary estoppel. That decision was justified: B's right did not arise *simply* because of A's oral promise but rather because B, as a result of his reliance on that promise, would suffer a detriment if A failed to keep it. However, the Court of Appeal also decided that A was under a duty to honour the promise and so had to transfer his ownership of the land to B. That conclusion can be questioned. If B's right arose *not* simply because of A's promise but, instead, because of the need to prevent B suffering a detriment as a result of her reliance on that promise, the *extent* of B's right should also depend on the need to prevent B suffering a detriment.[28] B's reliance in *Pascoe* consisted of spending some money on the land: it would seem then that the need to prevent B suffering detriment could have been met by simply ordering A to pay money to B.[29] By finding that A was under a duty to honour his promise and hence to transfer his ownership of the land to B, the Court of Appeal may have acted disproportionately and thus indirectly undermined the rule that, to exercise his power to make a binding gratuitous promise to B, A must use a deed.

4.3   Weighing the advantages and disadvantages

4.3.1 Cases where a formality rule applies: Examples 2a–2d

The advantages and disadvantages of formality rules will have different strengths in different contexts. For example, as noted above, the need for *evidence* is clear when A attempts to exercise his power to direct what will happen to his rights on his death: after all, A will not be around to clarify his intentions. That need for evidence may be sufficiently pressing to justify the requirement of the Wills Act 1837 that A must exercise his power not only in signed writing but also with the acknowledgement of two disinterested witnesses. Promoting *caution* may also be particularly important in this context: it is always tempting for A to make a rash promise as to what will happen to his rights on his death—after all, A will not be around to hear the complaints if he fails to honour such a promise. Protecting A (ie, A's estate) from *fraudulent claims* is also important, as A will not be able to give evidence

---

[27] [1979] 1 WLR 431.
[28] See **E4:4.**
[29] Compare eg *Jennings v Rice* [2003] 1 P & CR 100 (see **E4:4.3**).

as to whether he did intend to give B a right. Finally, *publicity* will also be very useful. When A dies, there may be a number of people hoping to acquire rights from A: a written document provides a simple means for them to discover if they have indeed acquired a right. In fact, this publicity is enhanced by the fact that a will, when A dies, becomes a public document.

In addition, some of the disadvantages of a formality rule are limited by the context in which the Wills Act 1837 operates. Complying with the rule may involve some time and expense but, in any case, disposing of assets on death is usually a somewhat complicated exercise. In fact, the effect of the formality rule in encouraging A to seek legal advice may be valuable in itself: such advice can assist A to dispose of his assets in a legally effective and tax-efficient way.

4.3.2 Cases where a formality rule applies: Examples 1a–1d

The need for A to use a deed to exercise his power to make a binding gratuitous promise also appears to be justified. The basic point is that, as A is receiving nothing in return for his promise, there is a clear need to promote *caution*. In contrast, where A makes a contractual promise, it must be made as part of a bargain in which consideration is provided: A thus receives something in return for his promise. In a contract, the parties' bargain and the provision of consideration can also provide: (i) some external *evidence* of the fact of A's promise; and (ii) some *protection for A against fraudulent claims*. When A makes a gratuitous promise, those factors are missing: a deed may be needed to fill the gap.

One of the main disadvantages of a formality rule may also be reduced: B's expectations may be frustrated if A does not honour an oral promise; but, as B has not given A anything in return for that promise, can B really complain? Of course, if B has relied on A's promise, as in **Example 3**, there is an argument that B should be protected from suffering detriment as a result of that reliance. However, that argument is not inconsistent with the formality rule: as in **Example 3**, it can be addressed by recognising that B has an alternative means of acquiring a right against A.[30] Finally, there may be a special argument in this context about the value of gifts. It could be said that part of the value of a gift lies in the fact that it is freely given. So, if A makes an oral promise to give B £100 and then does honour that promise, B gets more than £100: he gets the money plus the 'warm feeling' of knowing that A was prepared *voluntarily* to give him that money. If instead A's oral promise was legally enforceable by B, then, if A does honour the promise, B may be robbed of the 'warm feeling': he may suspect that A did not honour the promise voluntarily, but did so only because he was legally obliged to do so.[31]

4.3.3 Cases where no formality rule applies

Equally, of course, there are contexts in which the disadvantages of a formality rule outweigh the benefits. For example, let us say A plans to sell his bike to B. As noted above, such a sale involves A exercising his power to transfer his ownership of the bike to B: it

---

[30] See eg *Pascoe v Turner* [1979] 1 WLR 431. The doctrine of proprietary estoppel, discussed above in relation to **Example 3**, currently applies, in English law at least, only where A's promise to B relates to the use of land: it therefore cannot protect B in **Examples 1a–1c**. That restriction on the doctrine is very hard to justify: see **E4:3.1.2**.

[31] For contrasting views as to whether a gratuitous promise should be enforceable, see eg Eisenberg (1979) 47 *University of Chicago Law Review* 1; and Shavell (1991) 20 *Journal of Legal Studies* 401.

could therefore be subject to a formality rule. It could also be said that, as the transaction involves B acquiring a property right, the evidence provided by the use of formality would be useful for C. However, the benefits of using a particular form to make such a sale are limited. As a sale is planned, B must give something in return for the transfer of ownership. This reduces the need to promote *caution*, and to *protect A from a fraudulent claim*. There will also usually be some external evidence of the sale: for example, B may pay money to A and take physical control of the bike. This reduces the need for the extra evidence provided by, for example, signed writing.[32]

The disadvantages of a formality rule are also clear. Most obviously, the time and expense incurred in having to use a particular form may be unwelcome, particularly in everyday transactions. After all, if there were a general formality rule that any sale of a thing had to be made in writing, the queues formed as each customer signs for his purchases could make nipping to the shops for a pint of milk a very different experience.

4.4 The special features of land

Formality rules are particularly prominent in the land law system. To consider if that prominence is justified, we need to see how the possible advantages and disadvantages of a formality rule are affected by the special features of land discussed in A:3.1.

First, *evidence* may be particularly important where land is concerned. Due to its capacity for multiple simultaneous use, as well as its social importance and high financial value, transactions in land can often be complex. For similar reasons, negotiations between A and B as to the possible grant of a right can often be lengthy: a formal requirement helps marks the divide between negotiations and the conclusion of a deal.[33] The evidence provided by a formal document can also be useful to C, in allowing him to discover a pre-existing property right or persistent right. Given its limited availability, there is a particular need to promote the marketability of land by protecting C from the risk of being bound by a hidden property right or persistent right of B.

Second, the need to promote *caution* is particularly relevant in relation to land: given its social importance and high financial value, rash dealings with his rights in land can have a particularly adverse effect on A. For the same reason, the need to *protect A from fraudulent claims* is also increased. Finally, *publicity* can be very important in relation to land. The key point again is the need to promote the marketability of land by allowing C to discover any pre-existing property rights or persistent rights.

Two of the disadvantages of formality rules are less significant in relation to land. In many cases, any added *time and expense* will be hard to notice: the process of acquiring a right relating to land is often inherently lengthy and costly. The *frustration of reasonable expectations* is also less of a risk: given its special features, it is perhaps more likely that a party will realise that a transaction purporting to give him a right relating to land may need to be made in a special form. On the other hand, the final two disadvantages cannot be

---

[32] If: (i) A sells his bike to B; and (ii) B does *not* take physical control of the bike; and (iii) C, relying on A's continued physical control of the bike, then buys the bike from A; then (iv) C may have a **defence** to B's pre-existing property right under the Factors Act 1889, s 8 and the Sale of Goods Act 1979, s 24 (see D1:2.2.4(iii)(f) and D1:3.3.3).

[33] As noted by Robert Walker LJ in *Yaxley v Gotts* [2000] Ch 162 at 175.

avoided: whenever a formality rule applies, there is always a risk of *technicality and complexity*, as well as a *lack of transparency in the law*.

It thus seems that, where land is concerned, formality rules may be easier to justify: the advantages of such a rule are increased; and some of the disadvantages are reduced. The advantages are particularly important in relation to A's power to give B a property right or persistent right. If A instead exercises a power to give B a personal right against A, the need for *evidence* and *publicity* is greatly reduced: B's right is not capable of binding C and so there is no need for C to be able to discover the right.

SUMMARY of C3:4

If A has a power to give B a right, the property law system must decide if A's power should be regulated by a formality rule. There are general advantages and disadvantages to imposing a formality rule:

Advantages	Disadvantages
Provision of evidence	Extra time and expense
Promotion of caution	Frustration of reasonable expectations
Protection of A from fraudulent claims	Technicality and complexity
Provision of publicity	Lack of transparency in the law

In different contexts, these pros and cons will have different weight. So, when considering A's power to direct what happens to his rights on death, the benefits of formality are enhanced and the disadvantages somewhat reduced; the same is true when examining A's power to make a binding gratuitous promise to B. It is therefore no surprise that each of those powers of A is regulated by its own formality rule: see **Examples 1a–1d and 2a–2d**. Where A's power is to give B a property right in land, or a persistent right relating to land, the advantages of formality are again enhanced and its disadvantages reduced. As a result, formality rules play a prominent role in the land law system: see **5.2** and **5.3** below.

In other contexts, the advantages of formality may be reduced and the disadvantages enhanced. It would, for example, be very inconvenient if *every* sale of a thing had to be recorded in writing. Therefore, in each context, it is necessary to weigh up the particular advantages and disadvantages of a formality rule. An analysis of those factors should determine not just *whether* a particular form should be required, but also *what* that form should be. For example, if *publicity* is important, a registration requirement may be justified: see **C2:2**.

5   THE OPERATION OF FORMALITY RULES

Having seen the basic function of formality rules and their possible justifications, we can now sketch out how such rules apply in the property law system.

5.1   Formality rules and personal rights

5.1.1 Acquisition of a new personal right

In a dispute about the use of a thing or the use of a right, it will be important to ask if B has acquired a direct personal right against C. To acquire such a right, B must show that C is under a duty to B. As we saw in **3.4** above, a formality rule *may* be relevant if C's duty arises as a result of: (i) Reason 1 (C's consent to be under such a duty); or (ii) Reason 2 (C's entry into a contract with B). For example, we saw above that if C wishes to make a binding gratuitous promise to B, he must use a deed.

However, such examples are rare. The general position is that C's power to come under a duty to B is *not* regulated by a formality rule. For example, formality rules are usually irrelevant when considering if C has exercised his power to come under a contractual duty to B.[34]

5.1.2. Transfer of an existing personal right

In a dispute between B and C about the use of A's personal right against Z, it will be important to ask if A has transferred that right to B (see **B:10**). As we noted in **3.4** above, A's power to transfer to B a personal right against Z *is* regulated by a formality rule. However, the content of the rule seems to depend on whether A's personal right against Z is: (i) a Common Law right; or (ii) an Equitable right.

> **EXAMPLE 4a**
>
> Z makes a contractual promise to pay A £200 for A's bike. Under the contract, Z must pay within a month of A delivering the bike to Z. A delivers the bike to Z. A then wishes to transfer to B his personal right to receive £200 from Z.

A's personal right against Z arises at Common Law: it arises as a result of Z's contractual duty to A. To transfer a Common Law right to B, A must comply with the formality rule set out by section 136 of the Law of Property Act 1925 ('LPA 1925'). To comply with that rule: (i) A needs to use signed writing to exercise his power to transfer his personal right to B; *and* (ii) Z must be given written notice of the transfer (that notice does not need to come from A and can be given after A expresses, in signed writing, his wish to transfer the right to B).

To transfer an existing Equitable personal right to B, it seems that A must comply with a different formality rule, set out by section 53(1)(c) of the LPA 1925.[35] To comply with that

---

[34] There are of course some exceptions: eg (i) under the Statute of Frauds 1677, s 4 a contract of guarantee cannot be enforced by B against C if it is not evidenced by writing signed by C (see **4.2.3** above); (ii) C's power to make a contractual promise to give B a property right or a persistent right relating to land is regulated by the formality rule imposed by the Law of Property (Miscellaneous Provisions) Act 1989 (see **5.2.1** below).

[35] S 53(1)(c) applies to a 'disposition of an equitable interest or trust'. It is commonly assumed that the section applies where A attempts to transfer an Equitable personal right: see eg Peel, *Treitel's Law of Contract* (12th edn, 2007) 721; M. Smith, *The Law of Assignment* (2007) 6.04, 7.66. Nonetheless, it could be argued that, in the rare case where A's Equitable right is merely a personal right, and not a persistent right, it does not count as an 'equitable *interest*' as it is not capable of binding a third party. If that view were accepted, however, an unwelcome result would follow: as a transfer of an Equitable personal right would not be governed by *any* formality rule, the discrepancy between the rules applying to the transfer of a Common Law and an Equitable personal right would be greater. For that reason alone, 'equitable interest', in the context of s 53(1)(c) at least, should be taken to include an Equitable personal right.

rule: (i) A needs to use signed writing to exercise his power to transfer his personal right to B; *but* (ii) the transfer can be completed *without* Z receiving any notice, written or otherwise.

The formality rule applying to a transfer by A of a personal right thus varies according to whether A's personal right arises at Common Law or in Equity. This difference is usually explained as a matter of the historical divide between the two systems. However, as we saw in **C1**, such an explanation is unconvincing. There seems to be no good reason for the difference between the two formality rules: the law would be more coherent if the same requirement were to apply *whenever* A attempts to transfer to B a personal right against Z (see **6.3** below).

A particular point about section 136 of the LPA 1925 is worth noting here. It is easy to see the formality rule set out by that section as an obstacle—something that can frustrate A's intention to transfer a personal right to B. However, before statute intervened, the traditional position was that, in almost all cases, A simply did *not* have the power to transfer a Common Law personal right to B.[36] Hence, were it not for the statutory rule now set out in section 136, it would almost always be *impossible* for A to transfer a personal right, arising at Common Law, to B. Far from interfering with A's power to transfer such a right to B, section 136 actually *gives* A that power.[37] This can be seen by the fact that section 136 applies only to an 'absolute assignment' of A's right. So, in **Example 4a**, it is impossible for A to transfer to B a right to receive £100 from Z: A must either: (i) transfer his *entire* personal right against Z; *or* (ii) keep that right and give B a different right.[38] So the formality rule set out by section 136, rather than being seen as an obstacle, must be seen as a *facility*.

In some cases, there are additional formality requirements, beyond those set out in section 136. For example, to show that A has transferred shares in Z Co to B (ie, that A has transferred to B his personal rights, as a shareholder, against Z Co) B will generally need to register himself as the holder of those shares. If such a registration requirement applies, and B fails to meet it, A's attempt to transfer the shares to B will fail.[39]

5.2 Formality rules and persistent rights

5.2.1 Acquisition of a new persistent right

A persistent right arises where A is under a duty to B in relation to a specific right. It is useful to break that formula down into two stages: (i) A must be under a duty to B; (ii) A's duty must relate to a specific right held by A. The second stage concerns the **content** of B's right, and so formality rules are clearly irrelevant. The first stage, however, concerns the **acquisition** of B's right, and so formality rules can come into play.

---

[36] There were some limited exceptions: for example, a personal right to receive a specific sum of money, if held by or against the Crown, could be assigned at Common Law: see eg *Miles v Williams* (1714) 1 P Wms 249, 259.

[37] Some personal rights cannot be assigned. For example, it is possible for Z, when entering into a contract with A, to stipulate in the contract that A cannot assign his rights against Z: see *Linden Gardens Trust Ltd v Lenesta Sludge Disposals Ltd* [1994] 1 AC 85 (see **D2:Example 7**). Further, a personal right acquired by A as a result of Z committing a wrong against A cannot, in general, be assigned. This restriction appears to be based on a fear that B should not be allowed to have an interest in, or interfere with, A's claim against Z; but that fear may be overstated: see eg Peel, *Treitel's Law of Contract* (12th edn, 2007) 741–2.

[38] For example, A could set up a Trust of his personal right against Z, by coming under duty to B to use his personal right against Z 50 per cent for B's benefit.

[39] See eg *re Rose* [1949] Ch 78; *MacMillan Inc v Bishopsgate Trust (No 3)* [1995] 1 WLR 978 at 1001.

The first stage consists of showing that A is under a duty to B: by completing that stage, B shows he has a personal right against A. Therefore, the discussion in **5.1.1** above also applies here. A formality rule *may* be relevant if A's duty arises as a result of: (i) Reason 1 (A's consent to be under such a duty); or (ii) Reason 2 (A's entry into a contract with B). However, the general position is that formality rules do *not* affect the means by which B can acquire a new persistent right.

For example, formality rules are usually irrelevant when considering if C is under a contractual duty to B (see **5.1.1**). A further striking example is provided by A's power to give B a persistent right by setting up a Trust in favour of B. If A holds a right he can set up a Trust by simply declaring that he holds that right on Trust for B. A does not need to express or record his declaration in a particular form. Hence, simply by orally announcing 'I hold my bike on Trust for B' A can exercise his power to give B a persistent right: a right against A's ownership of the bike. In fact, A does not even need to use any special words, he simply needs to manifest an intention to be under a duty to B to hold that right for B's benefit.[40]

However, things are different if B claims a persistent right relating to land. *Every* power of A to give B a persistent right relating to land is regulated by a formality rule. Three particular formality rules are relevant: (i) section 53(1)(a) of the LPA 1925; (ii) section 53(1)(b) of the LPA 1925; and (iii) section 2 of the Law of Property (Miscellaneous Provisions) Act 1989 (see **E2:2.3**). Between them, those three rules ensure that, *whenever* B's claim to a persistent right relating to land depends on A exercising a power to give B that right, B must satisfy a formality rule. The three rules have slightly different requirements but, as a minimum, A's exercise of a power to come under a duty to B must be recorded in writing signed by A.

Of course, this does not mean that, to acquire a persistent right relating to land, B must show that a formality rule has been satisfied. B may be able to show that A is under a duty to B *without claiming that A has exercised a power to give B a right*. After all, if A's duty to B arises for any of Reasons 3–6, formality rules are irrelevant (see **3.3** above). B acquires a persistent right if he can show that: (i) A is under a duty to B for such a reason; *and* (ii) A's duty to B relates to a specific right held by A. So, in **Example 3**, A's duty to B arose under the doctrine of proprietary estoppel (an example of Reason 6): as a result, formality rules were irrelevant. In *Pascoe v Turner*,[41] the Court of Appeal held that A's duty was to transfer his ownership of the land to B.[42] As a result, B acquired a persistent right against A's ownership of land *without* needing to satisfy any formality rule.

5.2.2 Transfer of an existing persistent right

If B1 has a persistent right against a right of A, B1 generally has the power to transfer his right to B2. To do so, B1 must comply with the formality rule set out by section 53(1)(c) of the LPA 1925: B1 must exercise his power to transfer the right by using signed writing. Thus, if A holds his ownership of a bike on Trust for B1, and B1 wishes to exercise his power to transfer his right under the Trust to B2, B1 must use signed writing. This rule is *not* specific to land law, or even to disputes about the use of things: it applies to all persistent

---

[40] See eg *Paul v Constance* [1977] 1 WLR 527, discussed in F3:2.1.1.
[41] [1979] 1 WLR 431.
[42] Although, it may be that the Court of Appeal erred when finding that A was under that duty (see 4.2.3 above).

rights. So, if A holds a personal right against Z on Trust for B1, any transfer of B1's right to B2 must be carried out in writing signed by B1.

5.3 Formality rules and property rights

5.3.1 Acquisition of a new property right

The *only* way for B to acquire a new property right in a thing other than land is through an *independent acquisition*: for example, by taking physical control of a thing. In such a case, as we saw in **3.2** above, formality rules are irrelevant.

When we look at land, things are different. The list of property rights in land is longer than the list of property rights in other things (see **E1:1**). For example, if A is an owner of land, he has a power to give B a new property right by giving B a Lease of that land. In general, A's power to give B a new property right in land *is* regulated by a formality rule:

1. Section 52 of the LPA 1925 means that, to exercise his power to give B a property right in land, A generally has to use a deed.
2. Section 27 of the Land Registration Act 2002 means that, to acquire a new property right in registered land, B generally needs to substantively register that right.[43] This is an example of the negative operation of registration: B's failure to register means that he fails to acquire the right (see **C2:6**).

We will examine the formality rules imposed by both sections 52 of the LPA 1925 and section 27 of the LRA 2002 in detail in **E1:2.3**. Although there are exceptions to both rules, the general position is clear: to acquire a new property right in land from A, B must show *both*: (i) that A has used a deed to give B that right; *and* (ii) that B has substantively registered his right.

5.3.2 Transfer of a pre-existing property right

In relation to things other than land, there are three basic methods A can use to transfer a pre-existing property right to B:

1. A can exercise his power to transfer that right in a deed (see **D1:2.2.4(i)**); and
2. A can express his desire to make an immediate transfer *and* ensure that B has physical control of the thing in question (see **D1:2.2.4(ii)**); and
3. A can transfer the right to B by means of a sale (see **D1:2.2.4(iii)**).

The last two methods are by far the most common and do not require A to use any particular form. So, A can give B ownership of a bike as a birthday present without using a deed: he simply needs to hand the bike over to B. And A can sell his bike to B without using a deed. It can therefore be said, as a general rule, that form is irrelevant when considering how B can acquire a pre-existing property right against a thing other than land. However, the exception comes where: (i) A wants to transfer his ownership to B for free; and (ii) it is for some reason impractical for B (or an agent of B) to take physical control of the thing

---

[43] Substantive registration may also be necessary even if the land is not yet registered. For example, if A is an owner of unregistered land and gives B a Lease of more than seven years, B can only acquire that right if he substantively registers it: see LRA 2002, s 4(1)(c)(i).

owned by A. In such a case, if A wants to make an immediate transfer of his right to B, A must use a deed.

Again, a different position applies to land. The two formality rules discussed in **5.3.1** above, imposed by section 52 of the LPA 1925 and section 27 of the LRA 2002, also apply to a transfer of a pre-existing property right in land.[44]

SUMMARY of C3:5

The purpose of this section has been to give an outline of the operation of formality rules in the property law system. This outline can be summarised in a table. The table does not look at the acquisition of a right by B on A's death: in that case, if B claims he has acquired his right as a result of A's exercise of a power to give him that right, the formality rule set out in the Wills Act 1837 must be satisfied (see **Examples 2a–2d** above). The table should be used with some caution: for example, it mentions the principal exceptions to each rule, but it does not give an exhaustive list. If a section number alone is given, the reference is to the Law of Property Act 1925.

| | Does a formality rule apply? | | | |
| | Acquisition of a new right | | Transfer of an existing right | |
	General position	*Exceptions*	General position	*Exceptions*
Personal right	No	Deed required for a gratuitous promise, etc	Yes: s 136 and s 53(1)(c)	–
Persistent right	No	Deed required for a gratuitous promise, etc	Yes: s 53(1)(c)	–
Persistent right relating to land	Yes: s 53(1)(a); s 53(1)(b); s 2 1989 Act[45]	No writing needed where A's duty arises for a reason *other* than A's exercise of a power to give B a right: eg, A's duty arises as a result of proprietary estoppel[46]	Yes: s 53(1)(a) and s 53(1)(c)	–

[44] Note that the rules may apply in a slightly different way according to whether B claims: (i) a new property right in land; or (ii) a transfer of a pre-existing property right in land. For example, LPA 1925, s 54(2) means that, in certain circumstances, A can orally exercise his power to give B a Lease. However, a transfer of such a Lease must be made by means of a deed, as the s 54(2) exception does not apply: see **G1B:2.2.2(i)**.

[45] That is, s 2 of the Law of Property (Miscellaneous Provisions) Act 1989.

[46] See eg **Example 3**.

Property right	No	–	No	Yes: Deed required where B gives nothing in return and does not have physical control of the thing
Property right in land	Yes: s 52 and s 27 LRA 2002	s 54(2);[47] independent acquisition, etc	Yes: s 52 and s 27 LRA 2002	–

This outline reveals some important general points. First, a formality rule simply cannot apply if B's claim to a right does *not* depend on showing that another party has exercised a power to give B a right. Second, where B's claim *does* depend on the exercise of such a power, the property law system has a choice to make: in some situations, it is felt that there is no need for a formal requirement; in others, a formality rule is imposed. The key question is whether the choices made by the property law system can be justified.

6 JUSTIFYING THE OPERATION OF FORMALITY RULES

6.1 Formality rules and land

Formality is felt to be particularly important where B claims: (i) a property right in land; or (ii) a persistent right relating to land. Indeed, with two very limited exceptions,[48] *every* power of A to give B a property right in land, or a persistent right relating to land, is regulated by a formality rule.

Therefore, if B wants to claim such a right and cannot produce (as a minimum) any writing signed by A, his options are severely limited. To acquire a property right in land without satisfying a formality rule, B must show either that: (i) one of the very limited exceptions applies (see **E1:2.3**); *or* (ii) B has *independently acquired* that right. And to acquire a persistent right relating to land without satisfying a formality rule, B must show that A is under a duty to B for some reason *other* than A's exercise of a power to come under a duty to B.

Can we justify the role of formality rules within the land law system? Well, in **4.4** above we saw that, where land is concerned: (i) the advantages of a formality rule are increased; and (ii) the disadvantages are reduced. In particular, it seems that the general need for formality promotes the marketability of land by allowing C to discover pre-existing property rights and persistent rights.[49]

---

[47] S 54(2) sets out an exception for particular Leases of three years or less: see **G1B:2.2.1(i)(a)**.

[48] The first exception is set out in s 54(2) of the LPA 1925; the second arises where B can claim an 'implied periodic tenancy'. In both cases, A can exercise a power to give B a short-term Lease without satisfying any formality rule: see **G1B:2.2.1**.

[49] That need to protect C is also recognised in the requirements of the two exceptions to the general formality rule imposed by s 52 of the LPA 1925: s 54(2) of the LPA 1925 and the 'implied periodic tenancy' (see **G1B:2.2.1**).

6.2   Formality rules and gratuitous exercises of a power to give B a right

Formality also seems to be particularly important where B claims that: (i) A has exercised a power to give B a right; and (ii) B has given nothing in return for A's exercise of that power. As **Examples 1a–1d** demonstrate, A's power to make a binding gratuitous promise to B must be exercised in a deed. And if B claims that: (i) A has transferred his ownership of a thing to B for free; and (ii) B has not taken physical control of that thing; then (iii) B must show that A exercised his power to transfer that right by means of a deed.

The principal justification for such formality rules is to promote *caution* (see **4.1.2** above). However, if A has a property right in a thing other than land, A can transfer that right to B, without receiving anything in return and without using a deed, *provided* B has physical control of the thing. Of course, the chief justification is that it would be inconvenient and inappropriate for all such gifts to be made formally: birthday presents may often be accompanied by a card, but to insist on signed writing or a deed would be ridiculous. But it is also true that the need for B to have physical control of the thing will usually involve A delivering the thing to B, or at least allowing B to take or keep physical control of it. This need for a further step can also promote *caution* by giving A a pause for reflection in which he can change his mind.[50] Perhaps more importantly, B's having physical control of the thing also provides *evidence* of the transfer. That evidence can be very useful in allowing a third party to discover that B has acquired a property right.

There is another very important exception to the general position that, where A receives nothing in return, a formality rule will regulate A's exercise of a power to give B a right. If A has a right that is neither a property right in land nor a persistent right relating to land, A can set up a Trust of that right in B's favour *without* complying with any formality rule (see **5.2.1** above). It must be that, in such a case, the disadvantages of a formality rule are deemed to outweigh the benefits. This does seem somewhat surprising: the need to promote *caution* seems to be important when A exercises his power to hold a right on Trust for B without receiving anything in return.

For example, by simply saying 'I hold my bike on Trust for B' A comes under a duty to use that right *entirely* for B's benefit: the effect of such a declaration on A is similar to the effect of transferring his ownership of the bike to B. It seems strange that A can impose such a significant duty on himself purely by orally expressing his intention to do so. As Hackney has put it: 'No other device in the legal system approaches the massive power of these spoken words in Equity: "I declare myself trustee of this for you".'[51]

The assumption underpinning the current position may well be that the risk of a party rashly setting up a Trust is small. People may often make a gratuitous promise or attempt to make a gift of a thing without thinking through the consequences; yet it is much rarer for someone, in the heat of the moment or without prior thought, to express a desire to be under a duty to B to use a specific right for B's benefit. That sort of more sophisticated intention tends not to pop into one's head.[52]

---

[50] This is not the case if B *already* has physical control of the thing when A exercises his power to make a gratuitous transfer of his property right to B: in such cases, B will acquire A's property right even if no deed is used: see eg *re Stoneham* [1919] 1 Ch 149. The same is true if the thing is lost when A exercises his power and is later found by B: see eg *Thomas v Times Book Co. Ltd* [1966] 1 WLR 911.

[51] See Hackney, *Understanding Equity and Trusts* (1987), 109.

[52] And, in cases where A attempts to transfer a right to B, but fails to do so (eg, because of a failure to comply with

If: (i) A exercises his power to hold a particular right on Trust for B; and (ii) C then acquires that right (or a right that depends on that right) from A; then (iii) B has a prima facie power to impose a duty on C (see **B:4.3**). If A's power were regulated by a formality rule, this could assist C in discovering B's right by providing useful *publicity*. However, the need for publicity is reduced by the fact that, as B has a persistent right, that right is subject to the 'bona fide purchaser' defence (see **B:5.2.2(ii)**). The protection that defence gives to C is important in justifying the fact that B can acquire a persistent right in relation to a thing other than land without satisfying a formality rule. The **acquisition** and **defences questions** can thus combine to resolve the **basic tension** between B and C.

The same two reasons may also explain why A, if he has a personal right against Z, can orally exercise his power to give B a persistent right by means of an 'Equitable Assignment' (see **B:4.4.2**). First, the need to promote caution is reduced by the fact that A is unlikely to give B the benefit of A's personal right against Z without any prior thought. Second, the need for publicity is reduced by the fact that C, if he later acquires A's personal right against Z, may be able to rely on the 'bona fide purchaser' defence.

6.3   Formality rules and the transfer of rights

As the table below shows, if: (i) A has *either* a personal right against Z *or* a persistent right against a right of Z; and (ii) A wishes to transfer that right to B; then (iii) a formality rule *always* applies.

	Formality rule?	Writing signed by A?	Written notice given to Z?
Common Law personal right	Yes: s 136 LPA	Yes	Yes
Equitable personal right or persistent right	Yes: s 53(1)(c) LPA	Yes	No

The justification for the formality rules imposed by sections 136 and 53(1)(c) is that every personal right and persistent right depends on one party (Z) being under a *duty* to another party (A). The transfer of such a right therefore changes the identity of the person to whom Z owes his duty. As a result, it is important to provide Z with *evidence* of that transfer.

EXAMPLE 4b

Z makes a contractual promise to pay A £200 for A's bike. Under the contract, Z must pay within a month of A delivering the bike to Z. A delivers the bike to Z. B then comes to Z and demands payment of £200, claiming that A has exercised his power to transfer his personal right to B.

---

a formality rule) the courts are rightly very careful not to artificially impose a Trust by pretending that, rather than wishing to transfer his right to B, A wished to keep that right and be under a duty to use his right for B's benefit: see esp *Milroy v Lord* (1862) 4 De GF & J 264; *Richards v Delbridge* (1874) LR 18 Eq 11.

In such a case, there is a dilemma for Z: (i) if there *has* been a transfer of A's personal right, Z is under a duty to pay B; but (ii) if there has *not* been such a transfer, Z's duty is to pay A. This dilemma creates a risk for Z: the risk of *performing his duty in favour of the wrong person*. For example, if Z pays £200 to B and it turns out there has *not* been a transfer, Z will still be under a duty to pay £200 to A. A formality rule can help to protect Z from that risk by providing *evidence* of the transfer. The formality rule imposed by section 136 of the LPA 1925 provides particularly good evidence: the transfer to B can only occur if Z has been given written notice of it (see **5.1.2** above).

EXAMPLE 4c

Z holds a bank account on Trust for A and others. Under the Trust, Z is under a duty to pay the annual interest on the account to A. B then comes to Z and demands payment of that interest, claiming that A has exercised his power to transfer his right under the Trust to B.

Z faces the same dilemma as in **Example 4b**: (i) if there *has* been a transfer of A's persistent right, Z is under a duty to pay the interest to B; but (ii) if there has *not* been such a transfer, Z's duty is still to A. Again, a formality rule can provide *evidence* of the transfer and thus assist Z in resolving the dilemma. The rule imposed by section 53(1)(c) of the LPA 1925 means that the transfer to B cannot occur unless it has been made in writing signed by A. Therefore, when B asks for payment, Z can demand to see evidence: writing signed by A. It does seem strange, however, that the transfer to B can take place *without* notice being given to Z. It would seem more consistent if the section 53(1)(c) rule, like that imposed by section 136, required *both*: (i) writing signed by A; and (ii) written notice to Z.

EXAMPLE 4d

The basic facts are as in **Example 4c**. A then: (i) using signed writing, transfers his right under the Trust to B; and (ii) demands that Z make the usual annual interest payment to A.

This situation shows the problem with the current formality rule imposed by section 53(1)(c). As the transfer of A's persistent right to B is complete even without notice being given to Z, Z is exposed to the risk of a fraudulent claim by A, the *original holder of the persistent right*.[53] In **Example 4b**, the notice requirement imposed by section 136 protects Z from that risk: if written notice has not been given to Z, the attempted transfer to B of A's personal right has not succeeded, and so Z is safe in performing his duty to A.

It therefore seems that there is a strong argument for aligning the formality rules imposed by sections 136 and 53(1)(c). This change would have the further advantage of ensuring that the same formality rule would apply to both: (i) a transfer to B of A's Common Law personal right against Z; and (ii) a transfer to B of A's Equitable personal right against Z. If this reform were adopted, the table set out above would be changed: the No in the bottom right corner would be replaced by a **Yes**.

The formality rules set out by sections 136 and 53(1)(c) can thus protect a party subject to a duty from the *risk of performing that duty in favour of the wrong person*. That risk does

---

[53] See eg Trustee Act 1925 s 61: in certain circumstances, the court has a power to relieve a trustee from liability if he breaches a Trust. So if Z acts 'honestly and reasonably' in wrongly paying A rather than B and 'ought fairly to be excused for the breach of Trust' and for failing to ask the court for directions before paying B, the court may reduce or remove Z's liability to B.

not arise where the transfer of a property right is concerned. A property right is unlike a personal right or a persistent right: it does not depend on one party being under a duty to another. Of course, that does not mean there can *never* be a justification for using a formality rule to regulate A's power to transfer a property right to B: for example, such a rule can be justified where: (i) the property right is in land; or (ii) the transfer to B is gratuitous *and* B does not have or take physical control of the thing. However, it does mean that the *particular* need to protect a party from the risk of performing a duty to the wrong person, whilst it may justify applying a formality rule to the transfer of a personal right or a persistent right, cannot justify applying such a rule to the transfer of a property right.

SUMMARY of C3:6

There seem to be three general situations in which A's power to give B a right is regulated by a formality rule:

1. Where A's power is to give B a property right *in land* or a persistent right *relating to land*. This is justified by the special features of land and, in particular, the need for *publicity*. The marketability of land can be promoted by allowing C to discover a pre-existing right of B that may bind him.
2. Where A's power to give B a right is exercised *gratuitously*, ie, without receiving anything in return for B. This is chiefly justified by the need to promote *caution*: to protect A from rashly affecting his legal position.
3. Where A exercises a power to transfer to B: (i) A's existing personal right against Z; or (ii) A's existing persistent right against a right of Z. This is justified by the need for *evidence*. That evidence, or its absence, can then give Z protection against the risk of performing his duty in favour of the wrong person.

---

7 EQUITY AND FORMALITY RULES

Having sketched out the operation of formality rules within the property law system, we can see whether the application of those rules is affected by the distinction between Common Law and Equity.

7.1 The orthodox view

EXAMPLE 5

A, an owner of land, makes a contractual promise to give B a five-year Lease. However, A does not execute a deed granting B that Lease.

B does not have a Lease: the formality rule set out in section 52 of the LPA 1925 has not been satisfied. Nonetheless, as the Court of Appeal confirmed in the classic case of *Walsh v Lonsdale*,[54] B has an Equitable Lease (see **G1B:Example 22a**). On the orthodox view, this creates a clear conflict: according to the Common Law, B does not have a Lease; according

---

[54] (1882) 21 Ch D 9.

to Equity, B does. This means that: (i) there is a fundamental conflict between the application of formality rules at Common Law and in Equity; and (ii) Equity takes a far more relaxed attitude to formality rules than the Common Law.

On the orthodox view, B's acquisition of an Equitable Lease is said to rest on the principle, or 'Equitable maxim' that 'Equity regards as done what ought to be done'. Therefore, because A had made a contractual promise to grant B a Lease, B could be treated, by a court of Equity, *as though* he did have that Lease. There are a number of problems with that orthodox view:

1. Formality requirements, such as the requirement that A must use a deed to exercise his power to give B a Lease, are there for a reason. If the Common Law requires the use of a particular form, why should Equity allow B to bypass that requirement?
2. The orthodox view is that Equity anticipates the Common Law and allows B to acquire the right that A is, in any case, bound to transfer to B. But why should Equity speed things up in that way?
3. The maxim that 'Equity regards as done what ought to be done' is a form of magic spell.[55] Equity cannot *pretend* that A has *already* granted B a Lease when we know, in fact, that A has done no such thing: he has instead *promised* to grant B a Lease.

EXAMPLE 6

A has a personal right against Z. A orally expresses an intention to give B, immediately, the benefit of that personal right.

B does not have A's personal right against Z: the formality rule set out by section 136 of the LPA 1925 has not been satisfied. Nonetheless, an 'Equitable Assignment' has occurred: A can make such an 'assignment' without using any writing and without any notice being given to Z. A simply needs to express his intention to give B, immediately, the benefit of his right.[56] On the orthodox view, this creates a clear conflict: according to the Common Law (as modified by section 136 of the LPA 1925), A's personal right against Z has not been transferred to B; according to Equity, it has been. This means that: (i) there is a fundamental conflict between the application of formality rules at Common Law and in Equity; and (ii) Equity takes a far more relaxed attitude to formality rules than the Common Law (as modified by section 136 of the LPA 1925).

7.2   A different analysis: persistent rights

7.2.1 *No* conflict between Common Law and Equity

The central problem with the orthodox view is that it depends on a fundamental and unexplained inconsistency between Common Law and Equity. On that view, in **Example 5**, Common Law and Equity give different answers to the same question: has B acquired a Lease? And, in **Example 6**, Common Law and Equity give different answers to the same

---

[55] The maxim is persuasively criticised by Swadling in *Equity in Commercial Law* (ed Degeling and Edelman, 2005).

[56] Where, as in **Example 6**, A expresses that intention in relation to a right A *already holds*, there is no need for B to give anything in return for the 'Equitable Assignment'.

question: has B acquired A's personal right against Z? However, this inconsistency can be avoided by focusing on the role of persistent rights within the property law system.

In **Example 5** it is clear that B does *not* have a property right in A's land: A has *not* exercised his power to give B a Lease. That is true whether the situation is analysed through the eyes of Common Law or Equity. Equity does *not* regard A as having given B a Lease. That would be absurd: it is clear that A has *not* exercised his power to do so. However, that does not prevent B acquiring a persistent right. To do so, B needs to show that A is under a duty to B in relation to a specific right. And B *can* show this: as a result of his contractual promise to B, A is under a duty to B in relation to A's power, as an owner of the land, to grant B a Lease of that land (see **E2:1.3.1(i)**).

The right acquired by B in **Example 5** (an 'Equitable Lease') is seen on the orthodox view as an 'Equitable property right'. However, if it is instead seen as a persistent right, the apparent inconsistency between Common Law and Equity disappears. The formality rule requiring a deed regulates A's power to give B a *property* right in land; it does not regulate A's power to give B a persistent right by coming under a contractual duty to B. To come under such a duty, A only needs to satisfy the *different* formality rule imposed by section 2 of the Law of Property (Miscellaneous Provisions) Act 1989; and that rule does not require the use of a deed (see **7.3.1** below).

A similar analysis can be applied to **Example 6**. It is clear that B does *not* have A's personal right against Z: A has *not* exercised his power to transfer that right to B. That is true whether the situation is analysed through the eyes of Common Law or Equity. However, that does not prevent B from acquiring a persistent right. To do so, B needs to show that A is under a duty to B in relation to a specific right. And B *can* show this: as a result of the 'Equitable Assignment', A is under a duty to B in relation to A's personal right against Z (see **B:4.4.2**).

Therefore, in **Example 6**: (i) A *retains* his personal right against Z; and (ii) B acquires a right against that right.[57] The rules about 'Equitable Assignment' are, in fact, rules about when A can come under a duty to B in relation to a specific personal right. If: (i) A has a personal right against Z; and (ii) A expresses an intention that B should immediately acquire the benefit of that right; then (iii) A comes under a duty to B in relation to A's personal right against Z. As a result, the apparent inconsistency between Common Law and Equity disappears.

7.2.2 Equity's approach to formality rules is *not* more relaxed than that of the Common Law

On the orthodox view, Equity's approach to formality rules differs from that of Common Law. However, that apparent inconsistency disappears when we take into account the unique role of Equity in recognising persistent rights. A formality rule regulating A's power to give B a property right in land (like the need for a deed in **Example 5**) *need not* apply to A's power to give B a persistent right. And a formality rule regulating A's power to transfer a personal right to B (like the need for signed writing and written notice to Z in **Example 6**) *need not* apply to A's power to give B a persistent right.

---

[57] This means, for example, that B cannot bring a direct claim against Z: see eg *Brandt's Sons & Co v Dunlop Rubber Co* [1905] AC 454; *MH Smith (Plant Hire) Ltd v DL Mainwaring* [1986] 2 Lloyds Rep 243.

7.3 Justifying Equity's approach to formality rules

It would be very wrong to think that formality rules are irrelevant in Equity. We can see this by looking at each of the three areas, identified in **section 6** above, where formality rules are particularly important.

7.3.1 Formality rules and land law

If A has a property right in land, or a persistent right relating to land, and wishes to exercise a power to give B a right against that right, a formality rule will *always* apply (see **5.2.1** above and **E2:2.3**). So, in **Example 5**, A can only come under a contractual duty to give B a Lease *if* a formality rule has been satisfied. That formality rule is set out by section 2 of the Law of Property (Miscellaneous Provisions) Act 1989 and it is a demanding one: the contract between A and B must be made in a document signed by *both* parties, setting out all the expressly agreed terms of the deal (see **E2:2.3.3**). It is therefore clear that Equity does not simply allow formality rules to be ignored.

It is therefore surprising that Equity, even when operating within the land law system, is often viewed as having a more lenient attitude to formality rules than the Common Law. That view stems from a combination of the facts that: (i) formality rules can only regulate A's exercise of a power to give B a right; and (ii) to acquire a persistent right, A must be under a duty to B. The crucial point is that it may be possible for A to come under a duty to B *without* A exercising a power to come under such a duty to B (see **3.3** above). In such a case, no formality rule will apply.

So, as we saw when looking at **Example 3**, the doctrine of proprietary estoppel may impose a duty on A to B in relation to A's ownership of land. In such a case, B acquires a persistent right. And no formality rule applies as A's duty does *not* arise as a result of A exercising a power to give B a right. That possibility, however, does not depend on Equity somehow being more lenient than the Common Law when it comes to formality rules. Rather, it depends on: (i) the nature of formality rules, which regulate A's exercise of a power to give B a right; (ii) the nature of persistent rights, which arise whenever A is under a duty to B in relation to a specific right; and (iii) the fact that A can be under a duty to B even if A has not exercised a power to come under such a duty (eg, if B's claim is based on any of Reasons 3–6, set out in **3.3** above).

A further reason for viewing Equity as more lenient relates not to the presence or absence of formality rules, but rather to the *requirements* they impose. If B wishes to show that A has exercised a power to give B a property right in registered land, B will, in general, need to show that: (i) a deed has been used; and (ii) that B's right has been substantively registered (see **3.2** above). In contrast, if B wishes to show that A has exercised a power to give B a persistent right relating to registered land, B does *not* need to show that a deed has been used or that his right has been substantively registered (see **E2:2.3**).

This difference does not come from Equity simply adopting a more lenient attitude towards formality rules. Instead, it depends on the different **defences** available against property rights and persistent rights. The chief purpose of requiring a deed or substantive registration is to provide *publicity*: to protect C from the risk of being bound by a hidden pre-existing right. However, where B has a pre-existing persistent right, C's protection from that risk comes not from the **acquisition question** but from the **defences question** (see **6.2** above). For example, if: (i) B's persistent right has not been defensively registered (ie, protected by the entry of a notice on the register); and (ii) B is not in actual occupation of the registered land; then (iii) B's right is vulnerable to the lack of registration defence (see **C2:6**). As a result, the extra publicity provided by a deed or substantive registration is unnecessary: C already has good protection against the risk of being bound by a hidden persistent right of B (see further **E2:Example 13**).

7.3.2 Formality rules and gratuitous exercises of a power to give B a right

A gratuitous exercise by A of his power to give B a right must often be made in a particular form. This can be justified as a way to promote *caution* and to limit the risk of A rashly altering his position without receiving anything in return. However, provided A's right is not a property right in land or a persistent right relating to land, A can gratuitously exercise his power to set up a Trust of that right *without* complying with any formality rule (see **5.2.1** above). Further, if A has a personal right against Z, A can gratuitously exercise his very similar power to make an 'Equitable Assignment' of that right *without* complying with any formality rule.

There is something of an irony here. One of the so-called 'maxims of Equity' is that 'Equity will not assist a volunteer'. However, where A exercises his power to: (i) set up a Trust for B; or (ii) to make an 'Equitable Assignment' in B's favour; then (iii) Equity allows B to acquire a persistent right even though A has orally exercised that power and even though B has given nothing in return. This distinction between property rights and persistent rights, by itself, cannot explain this difference: at Common Law, a gratuitous exercise by A of his power to make a binding promise to B must be made in a deed, even though it results in B acquiring only a personal right against A. Instead, to justify the distinction, we have to rely on the argument made in **6.2** above. Given the relative sophistication involved in setting up a Trust or making an 'Equitable Assignment', the chances of A rashly exercising his power to do so are slim;[58] or at least slim enough *not* to outweigh the general disadvantages that go with any formality rule.

7.3.3 Formality rules and the transfer of rights

There are two different ways in which the distinction between Common Law and Equity may affect the transfer of rights. First, the formality rule regulating A's power to transfer an existing personal right to B differs according to whether A's right arises at Common Law or in Equity (see **6.3** above). At the moment, that is an example of Equity being more lenient in its attitude to formality than the Common Law. There may be an historical explanation for this difference, but there is no current justification for it. Therefore, the current position should be changed: the same formality rule should apply *whenever* A attempts to transfer a personal right to B, whether A's right arises at Common Law or in Equity (see **6.3** above).

The second difference between Common Law and Equity depends on the difference between transferring a right to B and making an 'Equitable Assignment' of that right. As we saw when analysing **Example 6**, A can make an 'Equitable Assignment' without satisfying

---

[58] It is crucial for this analysis that the courts do not reinterpret a failed attempt by A to transfer a right to B as, instead, an attempt by A to set up a Trust of that right or to make an Equitable Assignment of that right. In general, that is precisely the approach taken by the courts: see esp *Milroy v Lord* (1862) 4 De GF & J 264; *Richards v Delbridge* (1874) LR 18 Eq 11 (see too **n 52** above).

any formality rule. This can be justified by the fact that such an 'assignment' does not involve the transfer to B of A's personal right against Z. Instead, it gives B a persistent right against A's personal right (see **7.2.1** above). The crucial point is that, where an 'Equitable Assignment' occurs, Z's duty is still owed to A, not to B. So, B *cannot* bring a claim against Z: instead, B has to force or persuade A to make such a claim (see **B:4.4.2**). The purpose of formality rules relating to the transfer of a personal right or a persistent right is to protect a party such as Z from the risk of performing his duty to the wrong person (see **6.3** above). And, in **Example 6**, there is no such risk for Z: even if an 'Equitable Assignment' has occurred, Z's duty is still owed to A, not to B.

That conclusion is supported by the analogy between A's power to make an 'Equitable Assignment' and A's power to set up a Trust.[59] We know that if A has a personal right against Z, A can give B a persistent right by exercising his power to set up a Trust of his personal right against Z. To do so, A does *not* need to comply with any formality rule. It is therefore no surprise that if A instead gives B a right against A's right by means of an 'Equitable Assignment', no formality rule applies. This analysis shows that, the term 'Equitable Assignment' is very misleading: it does not involve a transfer of A's right to B (see **D2:1.2.2(iii)**).

SUMMARY of C3:7

There are two linked myths about Equity and formality rules. The first is that Equity and Common Law adopt inconsistent approaches to such rules. The second is that Equity's attitude to formality rules is more lenient than that of the Common Law.

However, in general, there is no such conflict between Common Law and Equity. The apparent differences rest instead on the fact that Equity, unlike Common Law, recognises the concept of a persistent right. So, in **Example 5**, Equity does not *pretend* that B has a property right (a Lease); instead, it recognises that, because A is under a duty to B in relation to a specific right, B has a persistent right (an Equitable Lease). And in **Example 6**, when A makes an 'Equitable Assignment' of a personal right, Equity does not *pretend* that A has transferred that right to B; instead, it recognises that, because A is under a duty to B to use his right for B's benefit, B has a persistent right. The one conflict between Common Law and Equity relates to the transfer of personal rights: one formality rule, imposed by section 136 of the LPA 1925, regulates the transfer of a Common Law personal right; a different formality rule, imposed by section 53(1)(c) of the LPA 1925, regulates the transfer of an Equitable personal right. There is no justification for that difference: the current position should be altered so that the section 136 governs both situations (see **6.3** above).

Equally, it is wrong to think that Equity's attitude to formality rules is necessarily more lenient than that of the Common Law. First, formality rules can be very important in Equity: for example, A's power to give B a persistent right relating to land is *always* regulated by a formality rule. Second, differences usually attributed to Equity's lenience in fact depend of the special nature of persistent rights: (i) there is less need for *publicity* of such rights, as C's protection comes from the **defences question** (in particular, from the 'bona fide purchaser' defence); and (ii) there may be less need for *evidence* of such rights: for example, the acquisition by B of a right against A's personal right against Z does *not* create a risk that Z may perform his duty to the wrong person.

---

[59] That analogy is noted by eg M. Smith, *The Law of Assignment* (2007) 6.10.

SUMMARY of C3

Formality rules play an important part in the property law system. They can affect the **acquisition question** by requiring that A's power to give B a right be exercised in a particular form. The rules necessarily have certain disadvantages, such as the time and cost involved in compliance and the frustration of expectations that non-compliance may cause. However, they can also bring important benefits, such as the provision of evidence and publicity of the fact that A has exercised his power to give B a right. Those benefits can be particularly important where B claims that A has exercised a power to give B a property right or a persistent right. Such rights can bind C and a formality rule, particularly one requiring registration, can give C the chance to discover such rights

Formality rules can thus affect the resolution of the **basic tension** between B and C. However, it is important to remember that such rules are only a part of the wider property law system. Their impact is limited in two main ways. First, it may be possible for B to acquire a right *without* relying on an exercise by A of a power to give B a right. In those cases, formality rules cannot affect B's claim. So, if B can acquire a property right through an independent acquisition, formality rules are irrelevant. And they will also be irrelevant if B can acquire a persistent right by showing that A is under a duty to B as a result of A's commission of a wrong against B; A's unjust enrichment at B's expense; a statute imposing a duty on A to B; or for *any* reason (eg, the doctrine of proprietary estoppel) that does not depend on A exercising a power to come under a duty to B. In such a case, if A's duty to B relates to a specific right, B will acquire a persistent right even though no formality rule has been complied with.

Second, formality rules can protect C by affecting the acquisition question. But C can also be protected in other ways: for example, by means of the **defences question**. For example, in cases not involving land, A can exercise his power to set up a Trust in B's favour without complying with any formality rule. C's protection against the risk of being bound by B's hidden right under the Trust comes not from any formality rule but, instead, from the 'bona fide purchaser' defence.

Part II

APPLYING THE BASIC STRUCTURE

CHAPTER D1
PROPERTY RIGHTS

PROPERTY RIGHTS

Property rights are the cornerstone of the property law system. If B has a pre-existing property right, he has a right against a thing. The rest of the world is then under a prima facie duty to B not to interfere with B's use of the thing (see **B:4.2**). As a result, B will be able to assert his property right against *any* third party (C) who interferes with the thing, unless that third party has a defence to B's property right. B asserts his property right by showing that C has committed a *wrong*: that C has breached his duty not to interfere with B's use of the thing (see **B:4.2** and **4.1** below).

In this chapter, our focus is on the general position applying to property rights in *things other than land*. In **E1**, we look specifically at property rights in land. In examining the general position, we will look at each of the basic questions:

Section 1: The **content question**: what rights count as property rights?
Section 2: The **acquisition question**: how can B acquire a property right?
Section 3: The **defences question**: when can C have a defence to B's pre-existing property right?
Section 4: The **remedies question**: if B does have a pre-existing property right to which C has no defence, how will a court protect B's right?

1 THE CONTENT QUESTION

There are two aspects to the content question. The first is relatively trivial: does the right claimed by B allow him to make his desired use of the thing? (See **B:2.1**.) The second, much more significant, aspect is whether the right B claims *counts* as a property right (see **B:4.2**). A property right has two key features:

- it relates to the use of a specific thing; *and*
- it imposes a prima facie duty on the rest of the world (ie, unless he has a defence, anyone else is bound by B's property right).

1.1 B's right relates to the use of a specific thing

A right can only qualify as a property right if it relates to the use of a *thing*: an object that can be physically located.[1] B's Ownership of a bike or of land can thus count as a property

---

[1] See Pretto-Sakmann, *Boundaries of Personal Property: Shares and Sub-Shares* (2005), chs 4 and 5. This model is reflected in the German notion of Ownership (*Eigentum*) as 'indicating the most extensive rights a person may have in land or other tangible (corporeal things)': see Mincke, ch 7 in *Property Problems: From Genes to Pension Funds* (ed Harris, 1993), 78.

right (and so deserves a capital letter): bikes and land are both things. B's right must also relate to a *specific* thing.

B:EXAMPLE 8a

A owns a bike shop. B orders a particular model of bike from A and pays the £200 price in advance. A then goes into insolvency. A's total liabilities are £100,000: the assets available to A to meet those liabilities are worth only £50,000.

As we saw when considering this example in **B:4.5.1**, B clearly has a personal right against A: A is under a contractual duty to provide such a bike for B. However, that personal right may be of little use to B given that A has insufficient assets to meet its duties to its creditors. B would prefer to have a property right: if B has such a right, it will be prima facie binding on A's trustee in bankruptcy. Therefore, if B can identify a specific bike of which he is an owner, B will be able to receive the full value of that bike. However, even though he has paid in advance, B cannot have a property right: A has not given B Ownership of a *specific*, individual bike.[2]

Some rights, often thought of as 'property', do not relate to the use of a thing. This is the case, for example, with: (i) intellectual property rights; and (ii) company shares (see **1.1.1** and **1.1.2** below). Further, there are some rare things that, under the rules of the property law system, *cannot* be the subject of a property right (see **1.1.3** below).

1.1.1 Intellectual property rights and other 'background' rights

(i) The concept of a 'background' right

Some rights are prima facie binding on the rest of the world even though they are not rights against a thing. For example, it does not matter if B is deliberately punched by A, C or X—the rest of the world is under a prima facie duty not to interfere with B's physical integrity.[3] If C interferes with B's right by deliberately or carelessly injuring B, C commits a wrong:[4] as a result, B acquires a direct, personal right against C. So, at an abstract level, there is an analogy between B's right to physical integrity and, say, B's Ownership of a bike: (i) each right is prima facie binding on the rest of the world; so (ii) anyone who interferes with that right, without B's consent or other authority, commits a wrong against B. And, in each case it does not matter whether or not C *knows* he is interfering with B's right: it is no

---

[2] See Sale of Goods Act 1979, s 16. Lord Blackburn explained in *The Effect of the Contract of Sale* (1845) that this result depends on the 'very nature of things': A's promise cannot give B Ownership as it does not identify a specific thing to which such Ownership can relate. In **B:Example 8a**, it is also impossible for B to claim a persistent right (see **D2:1.1.2(ii)**). This means that B has *no* right that gives him priority to A's other creditors: see eg *re London Wine Co* [1986] PCC 121; *re Goldcorp's Exchange* [1995] 1 AC 74. Statute has now intervened where A's promise: (i) does not identify a specific thing; but (ii) does identify a specific bulk of goods from which A is under a duty to give B a thing. In such a case, A and B can become co-holders of A's Ownership of the bulk under the Sale of Goods (Amendment) Act 1995, inserting a new s 20A into the Sale of Goods Act 1979 (see **2.2.4(iii)(d)** below).

[3] It is a prima facie duty because a particular party (eg, C) may have a defence to B's right to physical integrity: for example, if B and C take part in a sanctioned boxing match, C has a *liberty* to deliberately punch B. This (limited) defence to B's right means that C is under no duty not to deliberately punch B (the same analysis applies as in **B:5.2.1(i)**).

[4] B can therefore bring a claim against C in trespass to the person (if C deliberately injures B); or a claim based on C's negligence (if C carelessly injures B).

defence for C to say he deliberately punched B (or took B's bike) in the mistaken belief that B had consented to C doing so (see **4.1.1** below).

However, B's right to physical integrity is a not a right against a thing: it does not relate to a thing *independent* of B himself.[5] In fact, B's right is hard to categorise: it is not a personal right (a right against a specific person); nor it is a persistent right (a right against a right). It can instead be seen as an example of a distinct category: 'background' rights.[6] The existence of B's right to physical integrity explains *why* C commits a wrong when deliberately or carelessly injuring B; but, in general, B's right remains in the background. These background rights are very important to understanding the law of wrongs (including the law of tort):[7] for example, if C defames B, he commits a wrong. C's conduct counts as a wrong as the rest of the world is under a prima facie duty to respect B's right to his reputation.

(ii) Intellectual property rights

If B has a copyright, a trademark or a patent, he may well regard his right as 'property'. Certainly, those rights are prima facie binding on the rest of the world. So, if B has a copyright in a book he has written, the rest of the world is under various duties to B, such as: (i) a duty not to reproduce the book; (ii) a duty not to make a film based on the book; etc.[8] However, strictly speaking, B does not have a right against a *thing*. His copyright does not relate to any physical object that can be located; instead it relates to a form of expression.[9] So, I can have Ownership of *a copy of this book* (a specific thing); *but* (ii) even though I wrote it, I cannot have Ownership of *the book* (the form in which I have expressed a set of ideas).[10]

It is hard to categorise intellectual property rights.[11] For example, if B has a copyright, that right is not a personal right (a right against a specific person); nor it is a persistent

---

[5] See Penner, *The Idea of Property in Law* (1997): (i) B's right to physical integrity is similar to B's Ownership of a bike (Penner at eg 74) as it imposes a prima facie duty on the rest of the world (in Penner's terms, at 26–8, 'a duty *in rem*'); but (ii) the two rights are different as only the latter relates to a thing that can be seen as separate from B (Penner at 111–2).

[6] See Birks in *The Classification of Obligations* (ed Birks, 1997), 11–2. Birks calls a duty not to hit another a primary obligation: 'We accept the existence of primary obligations not to hit and not to defame, and there are many others of the same kind. Plaintiffs never claim those rights as such. They figure only as the superstructure of actions in respect of wrongs.' Pretto-Sakmann, *Boundaries of Personal Property: Shares and Sub-Shares* (2005) adopts that analysis, using the term 'superstructural rights' to refer to what this book calls 'background rights.' See too Rickett, in *Equity and Commercial Law* (ed Degeling and Edelman, 2005), 119–45.

[7] The law of torts being the law of Common Law wrongs (see C1:n 15).

[8] Although as pointed out by Penner, *The Idea of Property in Law* (1997), 120 and Spence, *Intellectual Property* (2007), 13–14, the duties imposed on the rest of the world by B's intellectual property right are more limited than those imposed by, say, B's Ownership of a bike (see eg Copyright, Designs and Patents Act 1988, s 16(1) setting out a specific, *limited* list of the duties imposed on others by B's copyright). For example, C is permitted to read B's book; he is not permitted to ride B's bike.

[9] Spence, *Intellectual Property* (2007), 15–6 argues that intellectual property rights are property rights: property rights in the very right held by B: 'the object of the relevant property right is the legal right itself'. So, if B has a copyright, B has: (i) a right; and (ii) a right in that right. That analysis is very hard to follow. Certainly, B's copyright of a book does not impose a prima facie duty on the rest of the world in relation to B's copyright; rather, it imposes such a duty in relation to the particular ways in which B is allowed to make exclusive use of that protected form of expression (eg, the rest of the world is under a prima facie duty to me not to make a film out of this book).

[10] Due to the more limited nature of the duties owed to B (see n 8 above), both Penner (119) and Spence (13–4) agree that if B has, for example, a copyright, B does *not* have ownership of a form of expression.

[11] For example, the definition of property rights given in this book is based on that developed by Pretto-Sakmann, *Boundaries of Personal Property: Shares and Sub-Shares* (2005). However, Pretto-Sakmann categorises intellectual

right (a right against a right). It can instead be seen as another example of a 'background' right. The existence of B's copyright sits in the background and explains *why* C commits a wrong if, for example, he makes an unauthorised film of B's book. In that way, B's copyright is similar to: (i) B's right to physical integrity; and (ii) B's right to his reputation.

Of course, there are a number of important differences between, for example: (i) B's copyright; and (ii) B's rights to physical integrity or his reputation. Both these differences mean that B's copyright is less likely to be thought of as 'personal' to B:

1. B must act in a particular way (eg, write a book) to acquire a copyright; *but* B does not have to do anything to acquire the latter two rights;
2. B can transfer his copyright to B2; *but* B cannot transfer the latter two rights.

For those reasons, B's right to physical integrity, even though it is prima facie binding on the rest of the world, is rarely thought of as 'property'. In contrast, intellectual property rights, such as a copyright, are generally thought of as 'property'. And if by 'property', we mean that B: (i) has a valuable asset; or (ii) has something he can sell, then it *is* correct to see a copyright as 'property'. However, that cannot mean that it is a *property right*. After all, if A makes a contractual promise to pay B £200, then B has: (i) a valuable asset; and (ii) something he can sell.[12] However, B does not have a *property right*: he does not have a right that is prima facie binding on the rest of the world.[13]

There is of course a difference between: (i) a copyright; and (ii) B's right that A pay him £200: only the first right imposes a prima facie duty on the rest of the world. So if by 'property', we mean that B has such a right, then it *is* correct to think of a copyright as 'property'. However, this does not mean that it is a *property right*. Unlike, say, B's Ownership of a bike, B's copyright does not give B a right in relation to a specific thing. So, in their ability to give B some control of a form of expression (a copyright), an invention (a patent) or a symbol (a trademark), intellectual property rights go beyond the realm of physical objects and thus beyond the scope of property rights. As a result, they are best seen as a special category of 'background rights'.

This distinction may seem pedantic, but it has important consequences. There is a very strong presumption that a physical object can be the subject of a property right.[14] Thus, once such an object exists, B can acquire a right in relation to that thing that is prima facie binding on the rest of the world. There may be a number of justifications for this.

1. Given the physical limits of a thing (eg, a specific bike), it may be impossible for a large number of people to make use of it: allowing a right to exclusive control of the

---

property rights as property rights on the basis that the idea or form of expression to which an intellectual property right relates can count as a thing (104–5). Instead, it is more consistent simply to define a 'thing' as a physical object that can be located in a particular place. For example, under the German system an intellectual property right does not count as Ownership (*Eigentum*) as it does not relate to a physical object: see Mincke, ch 7 in *Property Problems: From Genes to Pension Funds* (ed Harris, 1993), 79.

[12] Assuming that the contract does not contain a term preventing B from transferring his right to B2: see eg *Linden Gardens Trust Ltd v Lenesta Sludge Disposals Ltd* [1994] 1 AC 85.

[13] Mincke, ch 7 in *Property Problems: From Genes to Pension Funds* (ed Harris, 1993) argues that if a right (eg, B's personal right to receive £200 from A) can be transferred, it counts as 'property' and so must relate to an object. He then argues that the object to which B's personal right relates is 'value'. However, that value is created when B's right is created: it is not an external object to which B's right relates. In any case, there is no reason to assume that, if a right can be transferred, it must relate to a specific thing.

[14] Of course there are some exceptions: see 1.1.3 below.

object may therefore be a means of permitting its efficient use without, in practice, losing the chance for wider exploitation of the thing.

2.   The physical existence of the thing provides a warning to third parties: if they interfere with the thing, they may be interfering with another person's property right and thus committing a wrong.

In contrast, a legal system may be more reluctant to give an individual a right, prima facie binding on the rest of the world, in relation to a resource that does *not* exist as a physical thing (eg, a form of expression, an invention, a sign).[15]

1.   As there are no physical limits to that resource, allowing an individual exclusive control of it may deny a wide number of other people the chance to exploit it. For example, we should be very careful before allowing an individual to make exclusive use of a particular word or phrase: the rest of the world will then be under a prima facie duty not to use that word or phrase.[16]

2.   It is much easier for third parties to inadvertently interfere with a right relating to a resource that does not physically exist. For example, how are others to know that, simply by using a certain word or phrase, they are committing a wrong?

Of course, this does not mean that there should *never* be rights that: (i) are prima facie binding on the whole world; and (ii) relate to a non-physical resource that is separate from B. If that were true, there would be no copyrights, patents or trademarks. However, it does demonstrate that, before allowing B to acquire such a right in relation to a non-physical resource, the legal system needs to take into account *additional* concerns. It is therefore very useful to separate the rules relating to property rights from the rules of intellectual property law.

1.1.2 Company shares

If B is a shareholder, he may well talk about 'owning' the company, or at least his own shares in it, and he may well regard those shares as 'property'. If by 'property' B means: (i) a valuable asset; or (ii) something he can sell, B *is* correct to think that his shares are, in that sense, 'property'. However, B does not have a *property right*: he does not have a right against a thing.[17] The company of course may well have property rights: eg, Ownership of land or equipment. However, the company is a distinct, separate legal entity: the company has those property rights; and B instead has a set of personal rights against the company. B's rights as a shareholder thus consist of various rights that the company must act in a particular way. The precise duties of the company will chiefly depend on the company's internal rules but will commonly include, for example: (i) a duty to pay dividends to B; and (ii) a duty to allow B to attend and vote at meetings.

---

[15] See eg Gray [1991] *CLJ* 252.

[16] See Gray's discussion of language as a 'morally non-excludable resource': [1991] CLJ 252 at 284ff, discussing *Davis v Commonwealth of Australia* (1988) 166 *CLR* 79.

[17] This analysis is consistent with that of Pretto-Sakmann, *Boundaries of Personal Property: Shares and Sub-Shares* (2005): in the most exhaustive examination of the question to date, Pretto-Sakmann argues that company shares are not property rights as they are not rights in relation to a specific object that can be located in physical space. For a different view see eg Chambers, *Introduction to Property Law in Australia* (2nd edn, 2008), 199–207.

1.1.3 Objects that cannot be the subject of a property right?

The presumption is that a physical object *can* be the subject of a property right; but, in some rare cases, the particular nature of a physical object may make the idea of B having a right to use that object, prima facie binding on the whole world, distasteful, inappropriate or otherwise unwelcome.[18]

For example, the body of a living person seems to be one of the rare examples, in English law, of a physical object that *cannot* be the subject matter of a property right. B cannot have a property right in his own body: such a right must relate to a thing independent of the right-holder.[19] That limit, however, does not prevent B having a property right in the body of *another* person (eg, X). So, in Roman law, B could have ownership of X, his slave. However, this is clearly not permitted in English law: the bodies of the living form a class of things that cannot be the subject of a property right.

With dead bodies, things are slightly different. First, if the body has been subjected to a preservation process, such as embalming, it seems that, like other things, it can be the subject of a property right.[20] Second, when X dies, his executors[21] have a duty to take care of the body and to deal it with it properly. To enable them to perform those duties, the executors have a right to make a particular, *limited* use of the body. That right may well be prima facie binding on the rest of the world; if so, it counts as a special, limited property right.[22] However, that right clearly does not amount to Ownership: the executors do not have an open-ended set of rights to use X's dead body as they wish.

1.2   Rights prima facie binding on the rest of the world

1.2.1 The 'closed list' principle

Let us say B can show that: (i) he has a right that relates to a particular thing; and (ii) that thing is capable of being the subject-matter of a property right. For B's right to count as a property right, it must also impose a prima facie duty on the rest of the world. There is a very easy way of telling if B's right has that effect: we simply need to: (i) look at the *list of property rights* permitted by the property law system; and (ii) see if B's right is on that list. If B's right is *not* on the list, it will *not* be prima facie binding on the rest of the world.

This basic rule is often referred to as the *numerus clausus* or 'closed list' principle. It has three linked purposes.

1. It provides transparency and predictability. If B claims that his right is a property right, a court can simply check the list: it does not need to 'reinvent the wheel' by

---

[18] See Gray's discussion of 'morally non-excludable resources': [1991] *CLJ* 252 at 280–92.

[19] This point is thoroughly explored by Penner, *The Idea of Property in Law* (1997), esp ch 5, under the heading of the 'separability thesis'. The view taken here fits with Penner's view to the extent that a right can only count as a property right if: (i) it relates to a 'thing'; and (ii) that thing is external to B (see **n 5** above). However, Penner defines a 'thing' as *anything* external to B; not just as an object that can be located in a physical space. Penner therefore takes a wider view of property rights than that taken in this book: including, for example: (i) B's contractual right to receive £200 from A (see eg 129–32); and (ii) B's right under a Trust of a right held by A (see eg 133–8). On Penner's view, those rights *do* relate to a thing: even though, in the case of B's contractual right to receive £200 from A, that relationship is 'indirect' and only takes effect 'through means of a fiction' (see 130).

[20] Eg, the preserved body of Jeremy Bentham, on display at the Law Faculty of University College, London, presumably has an owner.

[21] Or his administrators if X has died without leaving a will.

[22] See Chambers, *Introduction to Property Law in Australia* (2nd edn, 2008), 16.

evaluating that claim and weighing up the pros and cons of allowing B's right to be prima facie binding on the rest of the world.

2. It protects C, a third party dealing with a thing. Like a court, C simply needs to check the list: if the right claimed by B is not there, C will know that he is not under a prima facie duty not to interfere with B's use of the thing.

3. By protecting C, the principle thus promotes the marketability of things: it limits the situations in which a pre-existing right of B, relating to that thing, can bind C.

Although this point has been disputed,[23] it seems the principle may also be economically efficient.[24] For example, by limiting the investigations C needs to take when acquiring a right from A (eg, when buying A's thing), the principle lowers the transaction costs that may be incurred by A and C and thus benefits both A and C.[25] Similarly, the principle may also lower transaction costs between A and B (hence benefiting both A and B): if B wants to acquire a property right from A, there is a list making clear what content B's right must have.

A fundamental point, captured by the 'closed list' principle, is that it is for the property law system, and *not* for individuals, to decide if a right relating to a thing imposes a prima facie duty on the rest of the world. The **basic tension** of property law comes from the conflict between: (i) the need to protect prior users of things (eg, B); and (ii) the need to protect those later acquiring rights in relation to the thing (eg, C) (see A:2). If A and B had the power to conjure up new property rights at will, the balance between these two needs would be decisively upset. C would no longer be able to check for the presence of one or more of a defined set of property rights; instead, C would have to check each of the rights relating to the thing and see if *any* of them had been intended, by A and B, to impose a duty on the rest of the world. As a result, the marketability of things would be severely hampered.

1.2.2 An example

EXAMPLE 1

B Ltd, a manufacturer of bikes, wishes to ensure that those bikes cannot be sold for below a certain price. When B Ltd sells those bikes to A Ltd, a wholesaler, he makes A Ltd promise not to sell any of the bikes for less than £200 (a 'price maintenance clause'). B Ltd also wants to ensure that this condition binds not just A Ltd, but also future purchasers who may wish to sell on the bikes, such as C Ltd, a retailer. So, A Ltd and B Ltd agree that B Ltd's right to stop sales below £200 is prima facie binding on the rest of the world. A Ltd then sells some bikes to C Ltd. C Ltd attempts to sell them to his customers for £150.

If the agreement between A Ltd and B Ltd has given B Ltd a property right, C Ltd is under a prima facie duty to B Ltd not to sell the bikes at a discount. And A Ltd and B Ltd clearly intended that B Ltd should have a property right in the bikes. However, there is no need for

---

[23] See eg Rudden in *Oxford Essays in Jurisprudence: Third Series* (ed Eekelaar and Bell, 1987).

[24] See eg Merrill and Smith (2000) 110 *Yale LJ* 1.

[25] Of course, even if B's pre-existing right is not a property right, it may still be a persistent right. In that case, B does have a prima facie power to impose a duty on C (see B:4.3); *but*, if C is a 'bona fide purchaser', C will have a defence to B's persistent right (see B:5.2.2(ii)).

the property law system automatically to respect the intentions of A Ltd and B Ltd. In fact, the right to stop a thing being sold for below a certain price, whilst it relates to the use of a thing, is *not* on the list of property rights.[26] As a result, B Ltd's right is *not* prima facie binding on the rest of the world.[27]

It is therefore the job of the property law system, and not the parties, to decide if particular rights relating to a thing are prima facie binding on the rest of the world. It is only once the property law system has decided that a particular right counts as a property right that A has the power to give B such a right and thus to regulate the use of a thing, not just between B and himself, but also between B and third parties.

1.2.3 The test for a property right

If B has a right that relates to a thing, then *either:* (i) B's right imposes a prima facie duty on the rest of the world and so counts as a property right; *or* (ii) it does not. The property law system simply has to make a decision as to which rights have that effect. There is thus a unity about the *effect* of property rights: every property right imposes a prima facie duty on the rest of the world. However, there is no conceptual unity to the **content** of such rights: if B has a right relating to a thing, we cannot work out from first principles whether or not it counts as a property right—instead we simply have to look to see if it is on the list of property rights.

There is therefore no principled reason to prevent a particular property law system deciding that, in a case such as **Example 1**, B's right under the 'price maintenance' clause *does* count as a property right. If a property law system chooses to resolve the basic tension between B and C in that way, so be it. The key point is that, given that basic tension is impossibly difficult to resolve (see **A:2**), both judges and parties need a clear way of telling, in advance, if B's particular right does count as a property right. The clarity provided by the 'closed list' principle thus: (i) makes it easier for judges, when hearing disputes about the use of a thing, to make a decision; and (ii) makes it easier for parties, when dealing with a thing, to plan their affairs.

As the 'closed list' principle does not depend on a conceptual link between the content of property rights, it can be criticised as irrational or arbitrary.[28] However, that criticism misses the point. The principle does not necessarily lead to irrational choices: thought can go into the question of whether a right should count as a property right.[29] And the principle is *deliberately* arbitrary. The word 'arbitrary' comes from 'arbiter': a judge.[30] A judge is someone who has to make a decision; and the closed list principle means that, in a case such as **Example 1**, a judge can easily decide if B's right counts as a property right. It means there is no need, in each new case, for a judge to deal with the impossibly difficult question of whether B's right should impose a prima facie duty on the rest of the world.

---

[26] See eg *Taddy & Co v Sterious & Co* [1904] 1 Ch 354.

[27] We will consider whether B's right counts as a persistent right in **D2:1.1.3**.

[28] See eg Gray and Gray, ch 10 in *Rationalizing Property, Equity and Trusts: Essays in Honour of Edward Burn* (ed Getzler, 2003).

[29] In fact, Gray [1991] *CLJ* 252 discusses some of the relevant factors that can sensibly be taken into account when deciding if B's right to a thing should impose a prima facie duty on the rest of the world.

[30] The *Oxford English Dictionary* suggests the source is the Latin 'arbiter': one who goes to see (eg, one who looks into or examines an issue or dispute).

1.3   The list of property rights

The general list of property rights is very short.[31] In fact, it consists of only *one* right: Ownership.

Name	Content	Example
Ownership	B has a right to immediate exclusive control of a thing forever	B owns a bike

In the remainder of this section, we will examine Ownership. It is important to bear in mind that we are *not* trying to come up with a general, abstract definition of the concept of ownership: ownership with a small 'o'. Rather, we are trying to define a specific property right, recognised by the English property law system: Ownership with a capital letter.[32]

1.3.1 Exclusive control

It is very difficult, and generally impossible, to list *all* the rights of use inherent in Ownership. For example, if B has Ownership of a bike, B has the right to ride his bike, but also to paint it, repair it, remove parts of it, use it as part of an artwork, sell it, etc. The sheer number and variety of these rights has always hampered attempts to define 'Ownership'. However, this aspect of Ownership is in fact the key to understanding it.[33] The central feature of Ownership is that, because it gives B the right to exclusive control of a thing, it gives B an 'open-ended'[34] set of rights to make use of that thing.

In **Example 1**, we saw that B's 'price maintenance' clause does *not* give him a property right. Certainly, it cannot count as Ownership: the only duty it purports to impose on A and future purchasers is a duty not to sell the bikes for less than £200. As a result, B cannot claim that the clause gives him a right to exclusive control of the bikes: it gives B only a *limited* right to control the use of the bikes. In understanding Ownership, the essential contrast is between: (i) an open-ended set of rights to use a thing; and (ii) a right to make a limited use of a thing. That distinction can be vitally important in practice (see eg **G1B:1.4** and **G5:1.4**).

Of course, to say that the rights of an owner to use an object are 'open-ended' does not mean that those rights are unlimited. For example, B commits both a crime and a wrong against X if he rides his bike into X with the intention of injuring X; if B owns some bottles of beer he is not allowed to sell them to minors. Clearly, the rights of an owner must be balanced against other important concerns, such as X's right to physical integrity and the need to reduce under-age drinking. However, even if we can list restrictions on the ways in which an owner can use his thing, we can never completely list all the positive ways in which the owner *can* make use of that object: Ownership itself has no inherent limits.

---

[31] A longer list of property rights can exist in relation to land (see **E1:1**). And there are some things that cannot be the subject of property rights (see **1.1.3** above). Dead bodies (not subjected to a process such as stuffing) are an unusual case: they cannot be the subject of Ownership, but *can* be the subject of a particular, limited property right: the right of the executor or administrator of the deceased to have control of the corpse for the purposes of its disposal.

[32] The same distinction between: (i) general concept; and (ii) specific English institution can be made in the same way ((i) lower case; and (ii) upper case) when discussing Equity (see **C1:1**).

[33] See Harris, *Property and Justice* (1996), eg 5, 29–32.

[34] The term comes from Harris: see eg *Property and Justice* (1996), 72 and 73, describing an 'ownership interest' as 'an open-ended set of use-privileges and control powers'.

1.3.2 A right to immediate exclusive control

If A makes a binding promise that he will, in a week's time, transfer his bike to B, then that promise, by itself, cannot give B a property right.[35] B acquires Ownership only when he has a right to *immediate* exclusive control of the bike.[36]

If B has Ownership, B has a right to immediate exclusive control of a thing. B can therefore be described as having an *open-ended set* of rights to use a thing. However, we need to be careful about talking about B's rights in the abstract. As Hohfeld argued, if B has a right, someone must be under a duty to B.

EXAMPLE 1a

B has Ownership of a bike. B leaves it unlocked while he pops into a shop. Z is sitting on a bench near the shop. X1 walks past and sees the unlocked bike. X1 is thinking of buying a similar bike and is keen to take the bike and ride it for five minutes before returning it.

In such a case, X1 has a right *against* Z to take the bike for a spin. Certainly, if X1 were to act in that way, X1 would not be in breach of any duty to Z. This means, to use Hohfeld's terms, X1 has a *liberty*, against Z, to take the bike (see **B:5.2.1(i)** and **D2:1.1.3**). And, against Z, X1 also has a liberty not just to ride the bike, but also to paint it, repair it, remove parts of it, use it as part of an artwork, etc.

The general principle is that, if X1 wants to act in a certain way, he does not have to show a specific legal entitlement to do so: we are all legally free to act in a particular way if we are not under a duty not to do so. This means that X1 has the same liberty not just against Z, but against any passers-by—in fact, against *anyone* in the world who does not have a pre-existing property right in the bike.[37] Similarly, Z has the very same set of liberties against X1. In fact, *anyone* has the same set of liberties against *anyone* who does not have a pre-existing property right in the bike.

This analysis shows that, as far as the bike is concerned, there is a surprising similarity between: (i) the position of B; and (ii) the positions of X1 and Z. Each of the three parties has an open-ended set of liberties, against anyone who does not have a pre-existing property right in the bike, to use the bike.[38] So on this analysis, the 'positive' aspects of Ownership (B's liberty to ride the bike, to paint it, etc) do not seem too important. Yes, B has a liberty against Z to ride the bike; but X1 has the very same liberty against Z; and Z has the very same liberty against X1.

Of course, the crucial difference in B's position is that, if either X1 or Z takes the bike, he commits a wrong against B. Due to B's Ownership, X1 and Z are each under a prima facie *duty* to B not to ride the bike. In contrast, B owes no such duty to X1 or Z. So, to understand the **content** of Ownership, we need to understand the *content of the prima facie duty that the rest of the world owes to B*.[39]

---

[35] See eg *Benjamin's Sale of Goods* (7th edn, 2006) at 1-026.

[36] See eg *per* Chitty LJ in *re Hill* [1897] 1 QB 483 at 493.

[37] X1 will also lose his liberty against a specific person (eg, X3) if, for some reason, X3 has a direct right against X1 preventing X1 from taking the bike (eg, if X1 had made a contractual promise to X3 not to steal any more bikes).

[38] In the English property law system, the fact that B has Ownership of a bike does *not* guarantee that no one else has a pre-existing property right in the bike (see **1.4.1** below).

[39] The rules imposing that duty on the rest of the world are referred to by Harris as 'trespassory rules': see *Property and Justice* (1996), eg 5 and 24–6.

For example, unlike X1 and Z, B has the right to sell the bike.[40] If B sells the bike to B2, B transfers his Ownership of the bike. This means that:

1. B2 is no longer under a duty to B not to ride the bike; and
2. X1 and Z, rather than being under a prima facie duty to B not to ride the bike, now owe that duty to B2.

So, the key aspects of a sale can only be explained by looking at its effect on the duties initially owed to B.[41]

1.3.3 X's duties to B

EXAMPLE 2a

B has Ownership of a bike. B locks the bike up, as he is permitted to do, in a public bike rack. X then attaches a lock to B's bike.

By acting in this way, X has breached his duty not to interfere with B's use of the bike.[42] X thus commits a wrong: the wrong of trespass to goods.[43] That wrong is committed whenever X's breach consists of a deliberate, direct, physical interference with B's thing.[44] It is important to note that X's action is deliberate whenever he knows that he is committing a particular act (eg, X knows he is locking up a bike).[45] It does not matter if X reasonably believes he has a liberty to act in that way (eg, because X reasonably but mistakenly believes, that the bike actually belongs to B2, who has asked X to put a second lock on B2's bike). In that sense, trespass to goods is a 'strict liability' wrong.

EXAMPLE 2b

B has Ownership of a bike. In return for £20 from X, B allows X to borrow the bike for a week. At the end of the week, X refuses to return the bike.

Again, X has breached his duty not to interfere with B's use of the bike. As X initially took physical control of the bike with B's consent, X does not commit the wrong of trespass. Instead, he commits the wrong of conversion.[46] That wrong is committed whenever X's breach consists of a deliberate exclusion of B from the use of B's thing.[47] Again, X's action is deliberate whenever he knows that he is committing a particular act (eg, X knows he is keeping the bike). It does not matter if X reasonably believes he has a liberty to act in that

---

[40] In Hohfeld's terms, the right to sell the bike is a power (see **D2:1.1.3**).

[41] This analysis applies to *any* transfer of B's Ownership of the bike (eg, as when B, in his will, leaves his bike to B2).

[42] If X has a defence to B's Ownership (eg, B consented to X locking the bike) or if X has a property right that binds B (eg, B had earlier stolen the bike from X), then X is under no such duty (see **B:5.2.1(i)** and **1.4.1** below).

[43] See eg *Vine v Waltham Forest LBC* [2000] 1 WLR 2383.

[44] See *Clerk & Lindsell on Torts* (19th edn, 2007), 17-123ff. There is no need for X to have taken away or damaged B's thing: see *per* Butterfield J in *Transco plc v United Utilities Water plc* [2005] EWHC 274 at [20]–[23].

[45] See eg *Wilson v Lombank Ltd* [1963] 1 WLR 1294.

[46] See eg *Howard E Perry v British Railway Board* [1980] 1 WLR 1375. Formerly, X committed the wrong of detinue. That particular wrong was abolished by the Torts (Interference with Goods) Act 1977, s 2(1), but any conduct falling within the scope of detinue now counts as conversion: see s 2(2) of the 1977 Act and Douglas [2008] Conv 30.

[47] See eg *per* Lord Nicholls in *Kuwait Airways Corpn v Iraqi Airways Co (Nos 4 & 5)* [2002] 2 AC 883 at [39]; Douglas [2008] Conv 30.

way (eg, because he is, for whatever reason, confused about the terms of his initial agreement with B).[48] In that sense, conversion is a 'strict liability' wrong.

> **EXAMPLE 2c**
>
> B has Ownership of a bike. B locks his bike up before going for a run. B asks X to look after B's key to the bike lock. X agrees to do so but then throws the key away.

Clearly, X has breached his duty not to interfere with B's use of the key. He has *also* breached his duty not to interfere with B's use of the *bike*. X has again committed the wrong of conversion: he has deliberately excluded B from the use of B's thing.

> **EXAMPLE 2d**
>
> B has Ownership of a bike. B locks his bike up before going for a run. X, driving his car carelessly, skids off the road and smashes into B's bike.

Again, X has breached his duty not to interfere with B's use of the bike. In this case (in contrast to **Examples 2a, 2b and 2c**), X has *not* acted deliberately: he did not intend to commit the act that damaged B's bike. Therefore the protection given to B is more limited: to show X has committed a wrong, B must show that X acted *carelessly*. As a result, the wrong committed by X is generally referred to as the wrong of negligence.[49]

1.3.4 Exclusive control forever

B can have a right to exclusive control of a thing *without* having Ownership. Let us say A has Ownership of a bike and agrees to hire it out to B. A makes a contractual promise to give B exclusive control of the bike for the next six months. That contract, by itself, does not give B Ownership of the bike. If B wants to claim through the contract alone, B must claim through A: B must rely on *dependent acquisition* (see **B:2.2**). However, A has *kept* his Ownership of the bike: he has not transferred that right to B. And, until he takes physical control of the bike, B cannot claim to have *independently* acquired Ownership (see **2.1** below).

  Of course, it is *possible* for a property law system to allow the right B acquires under a hire contract to count as a property right. But to do so, that system would have to recognise an *additional* property right—a property right other than Ownership. And the English property law system does *not* recognise such an additional right (see **1.4.5** below).

1.3.5 Can a right to immediate exclusive control of a thing forever be a personal right against A?

It is important to note that, if B has a right to immediate exclusive control of a thing forever, B *necessarily* has a property right. So, A *cannot*: (i) give B such a right; *and* (ii) stipulate that B has only a personal right against A. This principle has some important consequences (see eg **G1B:1.5.1(i)**). For example, it is important in understanding the

---

[48] See *per* Lord Nicholls in *Kuwait Airways Corpn v Iraqi Airways Co (Nos 4 & 5)* [2002] 2 AC 883 at [78]–[81].

[49] However, as persuasively argued by Stevens, *Torts and Rights* (2007), 291–300, it is misleading to have a wrong known as 'negligence'. That terms simply refers to one of the ways in which a right of B (eg, as in **Example 2d**, a property right) may be infringed by X, even though X has not *deliberately* committed the wrongful act.

acquisition question: if (i) A has Ownership of a thing; and (ii) A comes under a duty to give B a right to immediate exclusive control of that thing forever; then (iii) B acquires more than just a personal right against A—instead, B *immediately* acquires A's Ownership (see **2.2.4(i)** and **2.2.4(iii)** below).

1.4 Property rights other than Ownership?

It is often said that the English property law system's list of property rights extends beyond Ownership. In this section, we will examine some rights that are often referred to as property rights. The argument will be that, in fact, these rights do *not* count as distinct property rights.

1.4.1 Possession

(i) An example

EXAMPLE 3

B has Ownership of a bike. C steals B's bike, by taking physical control of it without B's consent or other lawful authority. C2, acting without the consent of B or C or other lawful authority, takes the bike from C.

When C2 takes the bike, he commits a wrong against *both* C and B. C2's action is a wrong against C because C, by taking physical control of the bike, *independently acquires* a property right (see **B:2.2**). As a result, C2, like the rest of the world, is under a prima facie duty not to interfere with any use C may choose to make of the bike.

It may seem surprising that C, by means of his wrongful conduct in stealing B's bike, can acquire a property right. However, it is beyond doubt. The case of *Costello v Chief Constable of Derbyshire* provides a good example.[50] C had physical control of a car. Police officers, believing the car was stolen, seized the car: they had a statutory authority to do so. However, that authority was only temporary; when it ran out, C brought a claim against the police force, arguing that, by continuing to detain the car, it was committing the wrong of conversion (see **Example 2b**). The Court of Appeal held that, *even if the car had been stolen*, C had a property right he could assert against the police force.[51]

So, in **Example 3**, C acquires a property right simply by taking physical control of the bike. The question is whether C's right is different from Ownership: is it an *additional* type of property right? It is tempting to say 'Yes': it is often said that, whilst B has Ownership of the bike, C has Possession—a different type of property right.[52]

---

[50] [2001] 1 WLR 1437.

[51] It is important to note that, if the police force had been able to identify B (the party from whom the car was stolen) things would have been different. The Torts (Interference with Goods) Act 1977, s 8(1) would then have permitted the police force to show that B had a 'better right than' C. The court could then have taken this into account in determining what order to make: for example, the police force could have been ordered: (i) to return the car to B rather than C; or (ii) to pay damages to B rather than C; or (iii) to pay damages to B as well as to C (although the court cannot impose 'double liability': 1977 Act, s 7).

[52] See eg Bridge, *Personal Property Law* (3rd edn, 2002), ch 2; Goode, *Commercial Law* (3rd edn, 2004), ch 2.

(ii) The nature of C's property right

However, there is a fundamental problem with making this distinction between: (i) B's property right (Ownership); and (ii) C's property right (Possession). It is true that each of B and C has *acquired* his property right in a different way: B, perhaps, by buying the bike from a retailer; C by taking physical control of the bike. Nonetheless, the *content* of the two rights is indistinguishable:

1. The rest of the world is under a prima facie duty to B not to interfere with B's use of the bike. So: (i) when C2 takes the bike, C2 commits a wrong against B; and (ii) when C takes the bike, C commits a wrong against B.
2. The rest of the world is under a prima facie duty to C not to interfere with C's use of the bike. So: (i) when C2 takes the bike, C2 commits a wrong against C.

(iii) Naming C's property right

The name given to a property right should depend on its content. B's right counts as Ownership as B has a right to exclusive control of the bike forever. As C's property right has exactly the same content, it must also count as Ownership.

Therefore, the difference in the positions of B and C does *not* come from the content of their property rights. It comes from the fact that B's property right arose *before* C's property right. This means that, as C has no defence to B's pre-existing property right, C commits a wrong against B when he takes the bike. However, that difference cannot justify giving a different name to C's property right. For example, C2 also acquires a property right when he takes control of the bike. C2's position differs from that of C: C's property right arose *before* C2's property right. However, that surely does not mean that C2 has another, *third* type of property right.[53]

In **Example 3**, therefore, the best approach is to acknowledge that each of B, C and C2 has the *same* property right: each has Ownership of the bike. It may seem wrong to say that C is an owner of the bike, given that B can assert his pre-existing Ownership of the bike against C. However, this does not pose an important problem. It simply shows the need to distinguish between: (i) saying someone is *an* owner of a thing; and (ii) saying that someone is *the owner* of a thing. Certainly, it would not make sense to say that C is *the* owner of the bike. However, we *can* sensibly say that, because C has the property right known as Ownership, C is *an* owner of the bike.

Similarly, it may seem counter-intuitive to say that each of B, C and C2 is an owner of the bike. It means that the bike can have two or more separate owners. However, this does not pose a problem. B, C and C2 each has a right, prima facie binding on the rest of the world, to exclusive control of the bike. All we need is a rule to solve conflicts between each of B, C and C2. And the rule is very clear. In a dispute between any of B, C and C2 we can follow the **basic structure**. So: (i) B can assert his pre-existing property right against both C and C2; and (ii) C can assert his pre-existing property right against C2. Each party's property right has the same effect: (i) it imposes a prima facie duty on the rest of the world; but (ii) it does not impose a duty on a party with a pre-existing property right.

---

[53] Further, there is a danger in calling C's right 'Possession'. In **Example 3**, although C no longer has physical control of the bike, he still has a property right. So, whilst C acquires his right by taking physical control of the bike, he can retain that right even if he loses that physical control.

(iv) Alternative approaches?

We could instead reserve the term 'Ownership' for a party who has the best right to exclusive control of a thing but, as noted above, that would obscure the fact that the content of B's right is exactly the same as the content of C's right. Further, our analysis of **Example 3** would not change even if it turned out that B did *not* have the best right to the bike because, for example, B bought the bike from X, who had stolen it from A.[54]

Or we could ditch the term 'Ownership' completely. For example, we could say that the property right held by each of B, C and C2 is: (i) 'Exclusive Control Forever'; or (ii) 'The Core Property Right'.[55] That would remove the risk of assuming that, because C has Ownership, C is *the* owner of the bike. However, the change would come at a cost: we would no longer be able to refer to *anyone* as an owner of a thing. Instead, we would have to call a party such as B, C or C2: (i) 'a party with a Right to Exclusive Control Forever'; or (ii) 'a party with The Core Property Right'. As a result, this book uses the word 'Ownership' to refer to the core property right, in the confident hope that we can keep sight of the distinction between: (i) being 'an owner'; and (ii) being 'the owner'.

(v) 'Relativity of title'

Example 3 shows that there can be two or more owners of a thing, each making a valid but different claim to Ownership. This possibility is often said to depend on the concept of 'relativity of title'. So, in **Example 3**, we can say, if we want, that C: (i) has 'good title *relative* to C2'; but (ii) does *not* have 'good title *relative* to B'. However, the term 'relativity of title' may not be very helpful. Title (as in 'entitlement') simply means that a party can make a valid claim—in this case, a claim to Ownership. Relativity means that Ownership is not a binary question. It is *not* the case that if B has a valid claim to Ownership, then no one else can have a different, valid claim to Ownership. If, as in **Example 3**, each of B, C and C2 has a valid claim to Ownership, we need a tie-breaker. It is provided by a fundamental rule of the property law system: a pre-existing property right binds everyone who does not have a defence to it.

SUMMARY of D1:1.4.1

We can reject the view that Possession exists as an second property right, additional to Ownership. In **Example 3**, each of C and C2 acquires a property right by taking physical control of B's bike. The **content** of that property right is identical to the content of B's property right:

1. It gives each party a right to exclusive control of the bike forever, as it imposes a prima facie duty on the rest of the world not to interfere with any use each party wishes to make of the bike; but
2. Each party is bound by any pre-existing property right in the bike to which he does not have a defence. So: (i) when C takes the bike, C commits a wrong against B; and (ii) when C2 takes the bike, he commits a wrong against both B and C.

---

[54] The only difference would be that if: (i) B claimed that C or C2 had committed a wrong against B by taking the bike; then (ii) C or C2 could alert the court to the fact that B was bound by A's pre-existing property right: see Torts (Interference with Goods) Act 1977, s 8(1) (see **n 51** above).

[55] Or we could borrow a term from the Sale of Goods Act 1979 (see eg s2) and say that each of B, C and C2 has 'The Property' in the bike.

1.4.2 Security rights

EXAMPLE 4a

A has Ownership of a bike. A wishes to borrow £200 from B. To protect himself against the risk that A may be unable to pay back the money, B insists on a *mortgage* of A's Ownership of the bike. This means that A transfers his Ownership of the bike to B. The deal is that: (i) if A fails to pay B back at the agreed time; then (ii) B has a power to sell the bike; and (iii) to use the proceeds to meet A's debt to B (see **F4:2.1.1**).

EXAMPLE 4b

A has Ownership of a bike. A wishes to borrow £200 from B. To protect himself against the risk that A may be unable to pay back the money, B insists on a *pledge* of the bike. This means that that A allows B to take physical control of the bike: as a result of taking physical control of the thing, B acquires a property right in the bike. The deal is that: (i) if A fails to pay B back at the agreed time; then (ii) B has a power to sell the bike; and (iii) to use the proceeds to meet A's debt to B (see **F4:2.1.2**).

It each case, B acquires his right by way of *security*—to protect B against the risk that A may not perform his duty to B to pay back the £200. It is clearly important that B gains his property right by way of security. For example, it means:

1. If A *does* pay B back as agreed, B will be under a duty either: (i) to transfer his Ownership of the bike back to A (in **Example 4a**); or (ii) to allow A to take back physical control of the bike (in **Example 4b**). The prospect of B being under such a duty must also affect B's position before the agreed time of repayment: B is under a duty to A not to act in such a way as to prevent or impede the possible return of the bike to A (see **F4:1.3 and F4:1.4**).
2. If A *fails* to pay B back as agreed, and B exercises his power to sell the bike, B may receive a sum of money greater than A's outstanding debt to B. In such a case, B is under a duty to transfer that excess to A.[56]

So, special rules apply where B acquires his property right by way of security: we will examine those rules in **F4**. The question here is whether B's right, because it arises by way of security, is different from Ownership: is it an *additional* type of property right? As special rules apply to regulate the relationship of A and B, it is tempting to say 'Yes'. However, those special rules do not change the **content** of B's property right.

In **Example 4a**, B simply acquires Ownership of A's bike: the rest of the world is, prima facie, under a duty not to interfere with any use B may wish to make of the bike. The fact that B acquired his right *by way of security* does impose special duties on B *to A*, but those duties do *not* change the content of B's property right. So, if, before the agreed time of repayment, C interferes with B's Ownership by preventing B from selling the bike, C commits a wrong against B even if, at that point, B is under a duty *to A* not to sell the bike.

In **Example 4b**, although A does not transfer *his* Ownership of the bike to B, B takes

---

[56] Where: (i) A transfers his Ownership of a thing to B; but (ii) B, after selling that thing, is under a duty to pay to A any sum he gains in excess of A's debt to B; then (iii) that duty shows that B acquired his right by way of security: see eg *per* Lord Herschell in *Manchester, Sheffield & Lincolnshire Railway Co v North Central Wagon Co* (1888) 13 App Cas 554 at 560.

physical control of the bike and therefore *independently* acquires Ownership. Given B takes physical control with A's consent, it may seem strange to say that B has *independently* acquired his property right. However, that right arises *not* because of A's permission, but because of B's own conduct in taking physical control of the bike. For example, B does *not* acquire a property right if A simply makes a contractual promise to give B physical control; B's property right arises only when B *actually takes* physical control of the bike.[57] It may be tempting to say that, as A has retained his Ownership of the bike, B only has Possession or 'special property';[58] but, the fact that B's property right arises as a result of his physical control of the bike does *not* affect the content of that right (see **1.4.1** above): A retains his Ownership; and B acquires a new right of Ownership.

1.4.3 The right of a hirer

EXAMPLE 5a

A has Ownership of a bike. A agrees to give B a right to exclusive control of the bike for the next six months. B takes physical control of the bike. One month later, X takes the bike without B's permission.

B cannot claim that A has transferred his Ownership to B: A clearly has not given B a right to exclusive control of the bike *forever*. However, when B takes physical control of the bike, B *independently* acquires a property right. That right is sometimes known as Possession but is better seen as an example of the core property right: Ownership (see **1.4.1** above). Hence, if X takes the bike without the consent of A or B or other authority, X commits a wrong against *both* A and B. B is thus in a strong position: (i) thanks to the hire contract, A is under a duty to B not to interfere with B's use of the bike; and (ii) thanks to his physical control of the bike, B has a property right that ensures the rest of the world is, prima facie, under a duty to B not to interfere with B's use of the bike.

EXAMPLE 5b

A has Ownership of a bike. A agrees to give B a right to exclusive control of the bike for the next six months. After that agreement is made, but before B takes physical control of the bike, X takes the bike without B's permission.

In such a case, in contrast to **Example 5a**, B has not independently acquired Ownership: he has never had physical control of the bike. If B wants to assert a right against X, B may claim that *hire contract itself* gives B a *different* type of property right, perhaps equivalent to 'a right to exclusive control for a fixed period'. If that is the case, then, as soon as the hire contract comes into effect, the rest of the world, including X, is under a prima facie duty to B not to interfere with B's right to use the bike.

However, B's claim will fail: in relation to property other than land, the property law system does *not* recognise a property right equivalent to 'exclusive control for a fixed

---

[57] *Dublin City Distillery Co v Doherty* [1914] AC 823: see eg *per* Lord Atkinson at 843; Lord Parker at 852; Lord Sumner at 865.

[58] The term 'special property' is used by Lord Atkinson in *Dublin City Distillery Co v Doherty* [1914] AC 823 at 843. See too Sale of Goods Act, s 61(1), stating that 'property', as used in the Act, refers to 'the general property in the goods, and not merely a special property'.

period'.[59] This means that it is simply impossible for A to divide his Ownership of a bike into separate, distinct slices of time: A must either transfer his Ownership to B *completely* or not at all.[60]

EXAMPLE 5c

A has Ownership of a bike. A agrees to give B a right to exclusive control of the bike for the next six months and B takes physical control of the bike. Two months later, A transfers his Ownership of the bike to C. C demands that B give physical control of the bike to C; B refuses as his six-month hire period has not run out.

The problem for B is that, if he continues to use the bike, he will interfere with C's Ownership of the bike. If *A* had demanded that B stop using the bike after two months, B could point to the hire contract he entered into with A: that contract gives B a liberty *against* A to use the bike for six months. However, C is under no contractual duty to B. Hence, unless C has acted in such a way as to give B a direct right against C, B will have to argue that his hire contract with A gives B either: (i) a property right in the bike; or (ii) a persistent right against A's Ownership of the bike. The right B acquires under such a contract has never been recognised as a property right; and it cannot count as a persistent right (see **D2:Example 2**).

It is true that, in some cases similar to **Example 5c**, B has been able to assert a right against C. [61] As a result, it is tempting to argue that B's right counts as a property right, or at least as a persistent right.[62] However, in those cases, B relied on a *new* direct right, arising as a result of C's conduct, and not on the pre-existing right he acquired as a result of his contract with A (see **D3:2.3.2**).

It is also true that, in some cases, B's right under a hire contract has been treated *as though* it were a property right. However, none of those cases holds that B's right imposes a prima facie duty on the rest of the world. For example, in *Bristol Airport plc v Powdrill*,[63] the contract of hire between A Co and B Co related to the use of an aircraft. B Co went into insolvency. B Co owed money to Bristol Airport plc; the airport had a statutory right to detain (and eventually sell) aircraft used by B Co.[64] However, the statutory scheme applying on B Co's insolvency specified that the airport could not detain B Co's 'property' unless it had the consent of B Co's administrator or of a court.[65] The airport argued that it did not need such consent as the aircraft were not the 'property' of B Co. The Court of Appeal rejected that argument: for the purpose of applying the statutory insolvency scheme, the aircraft *were* to be regarded as the 'property' of B Co.[66] That result is not particularly surprising: (i) B Co had taken physical control of the aircraft and so, as in **Example 5a**, B Co

---

[59] This point is controversial but for a full discussion reaching the conclusion that no such property right exists, see Swadling, ch 20 in *Interests in Goods* (ed Palmer and McKendrick, 2nd edn, 1998).

[60] This point lies behind the maxim that 'a gift of a [thing] for an hour is a gift of it forever' (see Brooke's *Abridgement, Done et Remainder*, pl 157).

[61] See eg *Lord Strathcona Steamship Co Ltd v Dominion Coal Co Ltd* [1926] AC 108.

[62] See eg Watt [2003] Conv 61.

[63] [1990] Ch 744.

[64] Civil Aviation Act 1982, s 88.

[65] Insolvency Act 1986, s 11(3).

[66] Browne-Wilkinson V-C took the view that B Co's right counted as an 'Equitable property right', ie, as a persistent right: [1990] Ch 744 at 759. That conclusion: (i) was unnecessary for the decision in the case; and (ii) is incorrect (see **D2:Example 2**).

has independently acquired Ownership of the aircraft; (ii) the statutory insolvency scheme lays down a specific, very wide meaning of the term 'property', clearly extending beyond property rights.[67] The result in *Bristol Airport plc v Powdrill* therefore does *not* mean that a hire contract, by itself, gives B a property right.[68]

1.4.4 Other contractual rights to use a thing

Given that a contractual right to make exclusive use of a thing for a fixed period does not give B a property right, it is no surprise that the same is true where B has a more limited contractual right. For example, as we saw in **Example 1**, a 'price maintenance clause'—a contractual promise by A to B not to sell goods at below a certain price—does not give B a property right.

1.4.5 Powers to acquire a property right

(i) A power to rescind the transfer of a property right[69]

EXAMPLE 6a

B has Ownership of a bike. A wants to buy B's bike for £200. B does not want to sell. A tries to persuade B to sell the bike by telling B that A needs the bike for his son, whose bike was recently stolen. A knows that this is untrue. B is taken in by the story and so transfers his Ownership of the bike to A in return for £200.

A's fraudulent misrepresentation does *not* prevent A from acquiring B's Ownership of the bike. After all, B did intend to transfer that right to A (see **2.2.2** below). In that sense, then, the transfer to A is not 'void': it does occur. However, due to A's fraud, the transfer is 'voidable': B has a *power* to unwind the transfer and reclaim his Ownership of the bike.[70] This power is often known as a 'Common Law right to rescind' because:[71] (i) the power was recognised by Common Law courts;[72] and (ii) to rescind means to unwind the transaction between A and B. In this context, it means B regains the right he transferred to A.

---

[67] Insolvency Act 1986, s 436 defines 'property', as used by s 11(3), so as to include, for example, 'things in action' (eg, B's personal right against A that A must pay him £200) and 'obligations . . . arising out of, or incidental to, property'. As Browne-Wilkinson V-C noted ([1990] Ch 744 at 759: '[i]t is hard to think of a wider definition of property.'

[68] Similarly, in *On Demand Information plc v Michael Gerson (Finance) plc* [2001] 1 WLR 1155, the Court of Appeal held that a court can provide relief to B where A attempts to bring the hire period to a premature end by relying on a forfeiture clause in the hire agreement. The possibility of such relief is often regarded as dependent on B having a property right or a persistent right. However, contrary to the view of Bridge, *Personal Property* (3rd edn, 2002), 27–8, the granting of such relief in a hire case does *not* prove that B has such a right as it does not involve allowing B's right under the hire contract to bind a third party.

[69] For detailed discussion of these powers, see Swadling (2005) 121 *LQR* 123; Haecker [2006] *RLR* 20 and 106; *The Law of Rescission* (O'Sullivan et al, 2008).

[70] It seems that B has the same power where his transfer to A is procured by A's duress: see eg *Pao On v Lau Yiu Long* [1980] AC 614 at 634. But note that in *Barton v Armstrong* [1976] AC 104 some deeds entered into by A were said to be *void* for duress.

[71] This term 'Common Law' is used to distinguish this power from an 'Equitable right to rescind' (see **D2:1.6**).

[72] See eg *Load v Green* (1846) 15 M & W 216 (although Swadling (2005) 121 *LQR* 123 challenges the historical analysis in that case).

The facts are as in **Example 6a**. B discovers A's fraud and tells A that he wants the bike back. A then sells the bike to C.

When B tells A that he wants the bike back, B exercises his power to rescind. As a result, B *immediately* regains his Ownership of the bike: that right, previously held by A, passes back to B.[73] There is no need for B to regain physical control of the bike: *as soon as* B exercises his power,[74] B regains his property right. So if, as in **Example 6b**, A transfers the bike to C *after* B has exercised his power to rescind, C will prima facie be bound by B's pre-existing Ownership.[75]

The facts are as in **Example 6a**. *Before* B discovers A's fraud, A transfers the bike, as a gift, to C.

Here, at the moment of the transfer to C, A still has the property right given to him by B. However, even though B's original property right has now passed to C, B is *still* able to exercise his power to rescind: by doing so, B can regain his Ownership and thus take that property right away from C.[76] So, B's power to rescind can be exercised against a third party.

Does that mean that our list of property rights must include *the power to acquire Ownership*? No. A property right imposes a prima facie duty on the rest of the world. If B has the power to acquire Ownership, but has not yet exercised that power, then: (i) whilst A may owe a duty to B (see **D4:3.2.1**); (ii) the rest of the world is *not* under a duty to B.[77] After all, B may decide that, despite the duress or fraud, he is happy to allow the original transaction to stand.[78] So, in **Example 6c**, when C acquires A's Ownership without giving anything in return, C does *not* breach any duty he owes to B. C only breaches a duty if, *after* B has exercised his power to rescind and hence regained his property right, C *then* interferes with B's use of the bike. So, if C transfers Ownership of the bike onto C2 *before* B has exercised his power to rescind, B has no claim against C.

So, whilst it is possible to say, in a loose sense, that B's power to rescind 'can bind a third party' what we really mean is that B may be able to exercise that power even if his original property right has passed to a third party. Crucially, that does not mean that, if B has a power to rescind, the rest of the world is, prima facie, under a duty to B not to interfere with B's right. As a result, we do *not* need to include the power to acquire a property right in our list of property rights. This analysis suggests that Lord Hoffmann was entirely correct when

---

[73] See eg *Car & Universal Finance Ltd v Caldwell* [1965] 1 QB 525.

[74] In some cases, B can exercise his power without informing A: in *Car & Universal Finance Ltd v Caldwell*, B sold his car to A as a result of A's fraud and exercised his power to rescind by informing the police and the AA.

[75] In such a case, A simply transfers the property right A *independently* acquires through his physical control of the bike; that property right is of course subject to B's pre-existing Ownership.

[76] In **3.5.4** below, we will look at examples in which B cannot exercise his power to rescind against C.

[77] As against parties other than A, B has a power and not a claim right (see **D2:1.1.3**). B can change the legal position of a third party; but only if he regains his property right by exercising his power to rescind.

[78] This may be the case if, even in light of the fraud or duress, the transfer of the right remains a good deal for B, eg, because B has sold the right to A for a good price. Of course, things are different if the apparent transfer to B is *void*: in such a case there is no transfer of B's right to A and so B retains his property right throughout: see **2.2.2(i)** below.

making the *obiter* observation, in *Barclays Bank v Boulter*,[79] that, if B transfers his Owner-ship of a thing to A as a result of A's fraud, B 'retains no proprietary interest' in the thing.[80]

EXAMPLE 6d

B has a contractual right against Z: Z is under a duty to pay B £100. As a result of a fraud-ulent misrepresentation from A, B transfers to A his personal right against Z. *Before* B discovers A's fraud, A transfers that personal right, for free, to C.

In such a case, B again has a power to rescind the transfer to A. That power arises *whenever* B transfers a right to A (whether it is a property right, a persistent right or a personal right) as a result of A's duress or fraud. In **Example 6d**, B clearly does *not* have a power to acquire a property right; instead, he has a power to regain his personal right against Z. In **Example 6d**, B *can* exercise that power against C. This demonstrates that, in **Example 6c**, B's ability to exercise his power to rescind against C does *not* depend on the fact that B has a power to acquire a property right. Rather, it is a feature of *all* powers to rescind. This underlines the fact that the result in **Example 6c** does *not* mean that B's power to rescind counts as a property right.

(ii) A power to acquire a property right held by A on Trust for B

EXAMPLE 6e

A has Ownership of a bike. A declares that he holds that right on Trust for B. B is over 18 and of sound mind.

In such a case: (i) A has Ownership of the bike; and (ii) A is under a duty to use that right *entirely* for B's benefit; and (iii) B is an adult and of sound mind. As a result B can, if he chooses, force A to transfer A's Ownership of the bike to B (see **F3:1.3**). This means that, strictly speaking, B does *not* have a power to acquire a property right. Rather, B has a power *to impose a duty on A*—a duty to transfer Ownership of the bike to B. So, if: (i) B exercises that power; and (ii) any formality rules regulating the transfer of A's right to B are complied with; then (iii) B acquires a property right. However, until then, B does *not* have a property right. So, in **Example 6e**, if X were to steal the bike from A, X would commit a wrong against A; but *not* against B (see **B:4.4.3**).

EXAMPLE 6f

A has a personal right against Z; Z is under a duty to pay A £100. A declares that he holds that right on Trust for B. B is over 18 and of sound mind.

Again, B has a power to impose a duty on A to transfer to B his personal right against Z. This shows that, in **Example 6e**, B's power does *not* depend on the fact that A holds a property right on Trust for B. Rather, it depends on the nature of the Trust: (i) A has a duty to use a particular right *entirely* for B's benefit; and (ii) as he is an adult and of sound mind,

---

[79] [1999] 1 WLR 1919 at 1925.
[80] Although, as we will see in **D4:3.2**, B does have a *persistent right* in such a case.

B is the best judge of his own benefit; so (iii) if B wants to acquire the right held on Trust, there is no good reason for A to refuse to transfer that right to B.[81]

1.4.6 'Equitable property rights' to use a thing

It is clear that, even if he does not have Ownership of a thing, B can have an 'Equitable property right' in relation to that thing. So, in **Examples 6e and 6f**, B has an 'Equitable property right' in relation to A's bike. However, B's right is *not* a property right: it does not impose a prima facie duty on the rest of the world (see **B:4.4.3**). In fact, A0 may respond to a limit on the content of property rights by choosing to give B a persistent right.

EXAMPLE 7

A0 has Ownership of a valuable painting. A0 wants to give Ownership of the painting to: (i) B1 for B1's life; then (ii) to B2 for B2's life; then (iii) to the National Gallery.

It is simply not possible for A0 to divide up his Ownership of the painting as he wishes. A0 does want the National Gallery to have a right to exclusive control of the painting forever; but it is not a right to *immediate* control and so cannot count as Ownership (see **1.3.2** above). A0 does want to give B1 a right to immediate exclusive control; but that right is not a right to exclusive control *forever* and so cannot count as Ownership (see **1.3.4** above).

However, by setting up a Trust, A0 can create an arrangement that is very close, and in practice identical, to the one he wants. For example, A0 can transfer his Ownership to A whilst imposing a duty on A to use his Ownership of the painting: (i) for B1's benefit for B1's life; then (ii) for B2's benefit for B2's life; then (iii) for the benefit of the National Gallery. So, although it is impossible for A to divide up Ownership over time, he can, by using a Trust, divide up the *benefit* of Ownership over time.[82] Under that arrangement, B1 and B2 and the National Gallery will each immediately acquire a *persistent right*: a right against A's Ownership of the painting.[83]

SUMMARY of D1:1

B has a property right if his right: (i) relates to a thing; and (ii) imposes a prima facie duty on the rest of the world. So a right that does not relate to a specific thing independent of B (eg, B's right to physical integrity or his reputation; an intellectual property right such as a copyright; a right of a shareholder) cannot be a property right. And there are some rare things (eg, living bodies) that the property law system does not permit to be the subject matter of a property right. However, if B can show his right relates to a thing, it will almost always be the case that the thing in question can be the subject matter of property rights. The crucial question then is whether B's right imposes a prima facie duty on the rest of the world.

---

81 The general position in US jurisdictions is that B does *not* have this power if B's ability to end the Trust would be inconsistent with the intention of the party who set up the Trust (the 'settlor'): see eg *Claflin v Claflin* 20 NE 454 (Mass 1889); Restatement (Second) of Trusts s 337 (1959). In contrast, the view adopted in England and other common law jurisdictions is that, once the Trust is established, the views of the settlor are irrelevant. For a comparison see Matthews (2006) 122 *LQR* 266.

82 There are some cases that appear to suggest A can give B1, B2 and the National Gallery successive property rights. However, those cases are better understood as resting on A's creation of a Trust, so that B1, B2 and the National Gallery each acquire a persistent right: see eg the analysis of Sargant J in *re Swann* [1915] 1 Ch 829.

83 After the deaths of B1 and B2, A is under a duty to use the painting *entirely* for the benefit of the National Gallery. At that point, the Gallery has a power to impose a duty on A to transfer his Ownership of the painting to the Gallery (see **1.4.5(ii)**above).

The property law system provides a very easy answer to that question. Thanks to the 'closed list' (*numerus clausus*) principle, B's right counts as a property right if, *and only if*, it is on the list of permitted property rights. Judges, like bouncers at a nightclub, can thus give a quick answer to B's plea to be admitted to the category of property rights: if it's not on the list, it can't come in. Parliament, like a nightclub owner, can of course alter the list if it wishes; but that almost never happens. Certainly, the list of property rights in relation to property other than land is very short—it includes just one right: Ownership. This gives the property law system important stability and consistency. It also provides protection for third parties dealing with things and thus helps to promote the marketability of things. The 'closed list' principle is thus an important tool in resolving the **basic tension** of property law.

2   THE ACQUISITION QUESTION

There are two basic means by which B can acquire a property right: (i) independent acquisition; and (ii) dependent acquisition (see **B:2.2**). Where B relies on independent acquisition, he acquires a *new* property right, as a result of his own conduct (eg, by taking physical control of a bike, B acquires Ownership of the bike). Where B relies on dependent acquisition, he acquires an *existing* property right as a result of another party exercising a power to give B that right (eg, A transfers his Ownership of a bike to B). As there is only one type of property right to things other than land (Ownership), it is impossible for B to acquire a new property right by means of a dependent acquisition: A cannot both: (i) keep Ownership; and (ii) transfer that Ownership to B.[84]

A's power to give B a right can be regulated by formality rules (see **C3**). If B relies on a dependent acquisition, B needs to show that A has exercised a power to transfer his property right to B. As a result, formality rules *may* be relevant to dependent acquisition: it may be that A's power to transfer a property right to B is regulated, in particular circumstances, by a formality rule (see **C3:5.3.2**). In contrast, where B relies on an independent acquisition, B does *not* claim that A has exercised a power to give B a right. As a result, formality rules are *never* relevant when considering independent acquisition.

2.1   The acquisition of a new property right

The core principle is that B can acquire Ownership by taking physical control of a thing. Even if B commits a wrong by doing so, B's act of taking physical control imposes a prima facie duty on the rest of the world not to interfere with any use B may choose to make of the thing (see **1.4.1** above).[85] This may seem surprising but it is reflected in the maxim that 'Possession is nine-tenths of the law'. In this context, that estimate is an understatement. If B takes physical control of a thing, he acquires a property right that will be effective against much more than 90 per cent of the rest of the world: it will bind *anyone* who has neither: (i) a *defence* to B's property right; nor (ii) a *pre-existing property right* in the thing.

---

[84] A can of course: (i) keep Ownership; and (ii) allow B to take physical control of a thing (see eg **Example 4b** above). In such a case, B acquires his property right independently, by taking physical control.

[85] See eg *Costello v Chief Constable of Derbyshire* [2001] 1 WLR 1437.

For example, in *Armory v Delamirie*,[86] B, a chimney-sweep, found a ring and took to a jeweller's shop to be valued. The jeweller, C, examined the ring and returned it without its jewel. By doing so, C breached his duty not to interfere with B's right to exclusive control of the ring. It made no difference that someone other than B may have had a prior property right to the ring: to protect B and promote stability, C, along with the rest of the world, was under a prima facie duty not to interfere with B's exclusive control of the ring. It is worth emphasising that, once B acquires his right, his right will continue *even if* B ceases to have physical control of the thing.[87] So if, in *Armory v Delamirie*, C2 had stolen the ring from the jeweller, C2 would have committed a wrong against *both C and B*.[88]

The concept of physical control is a simple one.[89] The only difficulties it causes are factual ones, and arise only in unusual situations.[90] Physical control is often referred to as 'possession'.[91] However, that term is best avoided: it is often given a refined, technical definition. For example, it has been said (and often repeated) that, to have possession, B must have *both*: (i) physical control of a thing; *and* (ii) 'a manifest intent, not merely to exclude the world at large from interfering with the thing in question, but to do so on one's own account and in one's own name'.[92] Certainly, it is true to say that, to have physical control of a thing, B must be aware of its existence.[93] Apart from that, however, such technical refinements of the core concept of physical control (derived largely from Roman law)[94] are misleading.[95] In English law, the test is a simple one: B independently acquires a property right *if* and *only if* he takes physical control of a thing. There is no need for B to show he also had an intention, on his own behalf, to exclude others from that thing.[96]

---

[86] (1722) 5 Stra 505.

[87] For example, B can transfer his property right to B2.

[88] In this way, the English property law system varies from Roman law. In Roman law, if: (i) B finds a thing belonging to A; and (ii) C takes that thing from B without B's consent; then (iii) B has an action against C (a 'possessory interdict') as C has directly interfered with B's physical control of the thing. However, if C2 then takes the thing from C, B has no action against C2 (although A does have a 'vindication' action against C2): see Nicholas, *An Introduction to Roman Law* (1962), 108–9.

[89] See eg *Young v Hichens* (1844) 6 QB 606. B was fishing, at sea, for pilchards. He had nearly covered some fish with his net when C interfered by rowing his boat into the net. B claimed: (i) that he had acquired Ownership of the fish; and (ii) by interfering with that property right, C had committed the wrong of trespass. B's claim failed: at the time of C's action, B had *not* taken physical control of the fish.

[90] See eg *Sutton v Buck* (1810) 2 Taunt 302 and *The Tubantia* [1924] P 78, each concerning whether B had physical control of a wrecked ship.

[91] See eg *per* Lord Denman CJ in *Young v Hichens* (1844) 6 QB 606 at 609: 'It does appear almost certain that [B] would have had possession of the fish but for the act of [C]: but it is quite certain that he had not possession.' In other words, a pilchard in the net is worth at least two of the other fish in the sea.

[92] Pollock and Wright, *Possession in the Common Law* (1888), 17. See too eg *per* Sir Henry Duke P in *The Tubantia* [1924] P 78 at 89–90 and Bridge, *Personal Property* (3rd edn, 2002), 17. For the Roman law basis of the requirement, see Nicholas, *An Introduction to Roman Law* (1962), 112.

[93] See eg *Cartwright v Green* (1803) 3 Ves 405.

[94] The quotation set out above from Pollock states that B's intention to exclude others: 'is required in different degrees both by the Roman law and by the Common Law.' That book is an example of both: (i) the widespread use of Roman law by 19th-century legal commentators; and (ii) the distorting effect of those Roman concepts on English law: see Hackney, ch 6 in *The Classification of Obligations* (ed Birks, 1997).

[95] The concept of possession in Roman law had a refined, technical meaning far removed from simple physical control: see Nicholas, *An Introduction to Roman Law* (1962), 110–15. For example, if B borrowed A's bike, with A's permission, B was *not* viewed as having possession of that bike. Such a difference is not surprising, given that possession in Roman law had a very different role to physical control in English law: certainly, it was not a means for B to independently acquire Ownership.

[96] Such an intention *is* relevant when considering the very different question of whether B, as a result of his long use of A's land, can use the *adverse possession* defence against A's pre-existing property right in the land (see G1A:3).

One example of the problems caused by a technical notion of 'possession' occurs in the anomalous case where, even if he has physical control of a thing, B1 is deemed *not* to acquire Ownership. If: (i) B1 is an employee or agent of B2; and (ii) B1 takes physical control of a thing in the course of, and in order to carry out, his duties to B2; then (iii) it seems that B1 is regarded simply as a vehicle for B2. Therefore, whilst B2 acquires Ownership as a result of B1's physical control, B1 himself, the party with actual physical control, does *not* acquire a property right.[97] That view is very difficult to justify: as B1 does have physical control of the thing, *both* B1 and B2 should have a property right. The exception seems to be unprincipled[98] and outdated: it was based on a desire to ensure that an employee could be convicted of larceny if he dishonestly kept goods having initially taken physical control of those goods in discharge of his duties to B2.[99]

It therefore seems that we should be able to state, as a general rule, that B independently acquires Ownership *whenever* he takes physical control of a thing. The question then is whether B can ever do so *without* taking physical control of a thing. We will consider this question by looking first at the independent acquisition of a pre-existing thing; and then at the independent acquisition of a newly created thing. In each, we will see if B2 can independently acquire a property right without taking physical control of a thing.

2.1.1 Independent acquisition without taking physical control? Pre-existing things

(i) B1's physical control also counts as B2's physical control
In some cases, a party is treated as having taken physical control of a thing even if he has not taken control of that thing himself. For example, we have already seen that the physical control of B1, B2's employee or agent, can be attributed to B2 and so allow B2 to acquire Ownership. That principle seems perfectly acceptable: acts of an employee or agent are often attributed to his employer or principal.[100] It may also be possible for B1 to have physical control of a thing both: (i) in his own right; and (ii) *on behalf* of B2. In such a case, B1 and B2 can both be viewed as having physical control of the thing: so B1 and B2 *each* acquires Ownership of the thing.

For example, if B1 has physical control of a thing and 'attorns' to B2 (ie, B1 undertakes to hold the goods for B2), B2 is also viewed as having physical control of the thing. Hence, as: (i) B1 has actual physical control of the thing; and (ii) B2 has deemed physical control of the thing; then (iii) *each* of B1 and B2 has Ownership.[101] It is also possible to transfer

---

[97] See eg *per* Donaldson LJ in *Parker v British Airways Board* [1984] QB 1004 at 1017; Pollock and Wright, *Possession in the Common Law* (1888), 18; Tyler & Palmer, *Crossely Vaines' Personal Property* (5th edn, 1973), 49; Bridge, *Personal Property* (3rd edn, 2002), 20.

[98] A better solution would be that *each* of B and B2 acquires a property right and that B is under a duty, as a result of his contract with B2, to hand the thing over to B2. That duty to hand the thing over is discussed by Donaldson LJ in *Parker v British Airways Board* [1984] QB 1004 at 1014.

[99] See Bridge, *Personal Property* (3rd edn, 2002), 20–21, The definition of larceny, both under the common law and eg s 1 of the Larceny Act 1916 required the defendant to 'take' a thing from the victim: if B were viewed as having a property right through taking physical control of a thing with his employer's authority, then B could argue that his later act in appropriating the thing for his own use was not a 'taking'. Under the Theft Act 1968, no such problem arises: an employee can 'appropriate' a thing within the meaning of s 3(1) even if he initially takes physical control of his employee's thing with authority. The width of the concept of 'appropriation' is made clear by *R v Hinks* [2001] 2 AC 241.

[100] This is one explanation of the doctrine of vicarious liability: see Stevens, *Torts and Rights* (2007), ch 11.

[101] As a result of an attornment, B1 hold the goods as a bailee for B2 and hence owes certain duties to B2: see eg *per* Lord Brandon in *The Aliakmon* [1986] AC 785 at 818.

physical control of goods by means of a special form of document used in international trade: a 'bill of lading'.[102] For example, if B2 has Ownership of goods he may give them to B1, to transport those goods on B1's ship. If B1 gives B2 a bill of lading that document shows that B1 has undertaken to hold the goods for B2. If B2 then transfers the bill of lading to B3, B1 (whether he is aware of the transfer of the bill of lading or not) then holds the goods on behalf of B3 rather than B2.[103] So B2 loses his (deemed) physical control of the goods; and B3 gains that (deemed) physical control. In this way, the bill of lading given by B1 to B2 operates as a 'transferable attornment'.[104] Due to its unique ability to allow another to acquire physical control of goods by means of its transfer, a bill of lading is known as a 'document of title': if B2 chooses to transfer the document to B3, B1 holds those goods on behalf of B3.[105]

(ii) The rights of a landowner to things in or on his land

It has been suggested that: (i) if a thing is in or on B2's land; then (ii) B2 has physical control of that thing *even if* he has not actually taken control of it and *even if* he does not know about its presence in or on his land. Such a suggestion was made in *Waverley BC v Fletcher*.[106] B1, whilst on B2's land, found and took away with him a brooch that had been dropped and submerged by the top level of soil. B1 thus independently acquired Ownership of the brooch. However, the Court of Appeal held that B2 acquired Ownership of the brooch *as soon as* it became submerged by the soil. So, B1, when taking control of the brooch, committed a wrong not just against A (the unidentified party who had dropped the brooch) but also against B2: B1 breached his duty not to interfere with B2's pre-existing property right. The Court of Appeal's reasoning thus depends on the idea that, even though he never had physical control of the brooch, B2 independently acquired Ownership of it.

The Court of Appeal's reasoning in *Waverley BC* is flawed. First, it was said that once the brooch was submerged, it became part and parcel of B2's land, so that B2, as an owner of the land, also had Ownership of the brooch. It is true that if one thing loses its physical identity and becomes subsumed into another thing, the first thing ceases to have an independent existence: this is known as accession (see **2.1.2(iv)** below). However, if this had occurred in *Waverley BC*, then *all* pre-existing property rights in the brooch would have ceased to exist. On that view, the person who originally lost the brooch (A) would lose his Ownership of the brooch and so would be unable to assert a right against either B1 or B2. However, the Court of Appeal's view was that A *retained* Ownership and so, if he came forward, could assert his right against each of B1 or B2.[107] But a court cannot have it both ways: *either:* (i) the brooch lost its identity and became part of the land, so that A's pre-existing property right is destroyed; *or* (ii) the brooch did not lose its identity and A still has

---

[102] See eg *per* Bowen LJ in *Sanders Bros v Maclean & Co* (1883) 11 QBD 327 at 341: 'The law as to the endorsement of bills of lading is as clear as in my opinion the practice of all European merchants is thoroughly understood. A cargo at sea while in the hands of the carrier is necessarily incapable of physical delivery. During this period of transit and voyage, the bill of lading by the law merchant is universally recognised as its symbol, and the indorsement and delivery of the bill of lading operates as a symbolical delivery of the cargo.'

[103] This does not mean that physical control of the bill of lading can always be equated to physical control of the goods. For example, if B4 steals the bill of lading, B4 does not acquire (deemed) physical control of the goods: see *per* Judge Diamond QC in *The Future Express* [1992] 2 Lloyds Rep 79 at 95–6.

[104] *Per* Lord Hobhouse in *The Berge Sisar* [2002] 2 AC 205 at 219.

[105] See further *Benjamin's Sale of Goods* (7th edn, 2006), ch 18, s 2.

[106] [1996] QB 334.

[107] See *per* Auld LJ at 345.

a property right he can assert against each of B1 and B2. On that second view, the brooch does not count as part of B2's land, and so B2's position as an owner of the land does *not* give him Ownership of the brooch.

The puzzling statement of Donaldson LJ in *Parker v British Airways Board*,[108] relied on in *Waverley BC*,[109] that a thing can become an 'integral part of the realty [ie, the land] as against all but the true owner' must be rejected. Either the brooch lost its identity and became part of the land or it did not. The better view must be that it did not. The brooch did not become part of B2's land simply by being submerged by the topsoil. The brooch remained a distinct physical object: after all, once he found the brooch, B1 was easily able to remove it from B2's land.

An alternative way to justify the decision in *Waverley BC* is to say that if B2 has physical control of land, that physical control, as a matter of law rather than a matter of physical fact, extends to all things in or attached to B2's land.[110] However, that cannot be right. If B2 is an owner of land, it is true that B2 has a right to exclusive control not just of the soil itself but also of the vertical space both above and below that soil (within certain limits).[111] However, that right to exclusive control of the space does *not* provide a good reason for deeming that B2 has a right to exclusive control of anything in or on his land. For example, it cannot be the case that, whilst C drives across B2's land, B2 has a right to exclusive control of C's car.

EXAMPLE 8

B2 is an owner of a shop. B1, a customer, finds in the shop, and takes physical control of, a parcel containing banknotes. B1 gives the notes to B2 for safe-keeping. Nobody claims the notes and so B1 asks B2 to return the notes to him. B2 refuses.

In such a case, B2 commits a wrong against B1. B1 acquires a property right in the notes when he takes physical control of them. And B2 does not have a pre-existing property right in the notes: B2 does *not* acquire such a right as soon as the notes are dropped on his land. This is confirmed by the decision of the Divisional Court in *Bridges v Hawkesworth*,[112] the essential facts of which are identical to **Example 8**. Similarly, in *Hannah v Peel*,[113] B1 was in B2's building when he found and took physical control of a brooch. It was held that B2 had no pre-existing property right in the brooch, even though it had been lost in the building on B2's land.

---

[108] [1984] QB 1004 at 1010.

[109] See *per* Auld LJ at 343.

[110] Although note that B2 is viewed as having physical control of any wild animal captured by a trespasser on B2's land, even if that animal is captured by B1 and B2 is unaware of the capture: see eg *Blades v Higgs* (1865) 11 HL Cas 621. However, that principle also seems dubious and may be motivated by an unnecessary desire to prevent the trespasser acquiring Ownership of the wild animal. In *Blades v Higgs*, Lord Chelmsford at 639 doubted an earlier and preferable suggestion (by Holt CJ in *Sutton v Moody* (1697) 1 Ld Raym 250) that if B1 starts a hunt on another's land and captures the wild animal on B2's land, then B2 does *not* acquire physical control of the animal.

[111] See eg *Bernstein v Skyviews Ltd* [1978] QB 479: B2 has no right to exclusive control over the airspace above his land at a height generally used by aircraft.

[112] (1851) 21 LJ (QB) 75. See Goodhart, *Essays in Jurisprudence and the Common Law* (1931), 76–90.

[113] [1945] KB 509. It is true that B2 had not yet moved into the house on his land where the brooch was found. However, as *Moffatt v Kazana* (**Example 9**) suggests, the result should have been the same even if B2 had moved in, provided of course that B2 had not actually taken physical control of the lost brooch.

EXAMPLE 9

B1 is an owner of land. B1 hides a tin full of banknotes in the roof. B1 then transfers his land to B2. B2 discovers the tin and hands it to the police. The police later give the money in the tin back to B2.

In such a case, B1 can assert a right against B2, as confirmed by the decision in *Moffatt v Kazana*, the essential facts of which are identical to **Example 9**.[114] When B1 sold the land to B2, B1 did *not* transfer Ownership of the biscuit tin to B2. Although the tin was hidden in B1's house, there is a clear distinction between: (i) B1's right as an owner of the land (which B1 transferred to B2); and (ii) B's Ownership of the tin (which B1 did *not* transfer to B2).

It thus seems that, in *Waverley BC v Fletcher*, the Court of Appeal was mistaken in thinking that, if a thing is lost in B2's land, B2 immediately acquires Ownership of that thing. It may be that the result in that case was influenced by the fact that B1, when he found the brooch, was trespassing on B2's land: he was in breach of his duty to B2 not to interfere with B2's right to exclusive control of the land.[115] However, B1's independent acquisition of a property right may often involve B1 committing a wrong: for example, a thief taking physical control of a thing acquires a property right (see **1.4.1(i)** above).

In *Parker v British Airways Board*,[116] the Court of Appeal stated that if: (i) a thing is found in or on B2's land; and (ii) before the thing was found, B2 'manifested an intention to exercise control over [the land] and things which may be upon it';[117] then (iii) B2 will deemed to have physical control of that thing. That idea is very hard to support:[118] clearly, having an *intention* to take physical control of a thing is *not* the same as *actually* taking such control.[119] The idea in *Parker* may be that it is possible for B2 to insist that anyone entering his land does so on the basis that, if he takes physical control of any thing found on the land, he does so on behalf of B2. On that view, B1 would effectively become an agent of B2: his actual physical control of the thing can then be attributed to B2. However, it is difficult to see how, as a matter of fact or of law, B2 can unilaterally turn B1 into his agent. The principle suggested in *Parker*, which has not determined the result in any reported case,[120] should therefore be rejected.

(iii) The right of the Crown to treasure
If: (i) B1 finds a thing, whether on his land or on the land of another; and (ii) that thing

---

[114] [1969] 2 QB 152. In that case, B1 asserted his right by bringing an action for 'money had and received': see **D4:6**.

[115] The land was a public park and so B1 had permission to be on the land; however, he did not have permission to use a metal detector, dig up the land and extract things found there.

[116] [1984] QB 1004.

[117] *Per* Donaldson LJ in in *Parker v British Airways Board* [1984] QB 1004 at 1017. His Lordship refers there to B2 manifesting such intention in relation to a building, but the principle presumably extends to any land.

[118] And it was unnecessary for the decision in that case: it was found that B2 had not, on the facts, acquired a property right in the ring. That result in *Parker* is therefore consistent with the view taken in this book.

[119] See eg *Young v Hichens* (1843) 6 QB 606: B did not acquire Ownership of fish by nearly, but not quite, catching them.

[120] In *Parker* itself, it was found that the Board had not manifested such an intention in relation to the 'executive lounge' at Heathrow Airport where the thing in question (a gold bracelet) was found. The fact that the Board controlled entry to the lounge was not by itself enough to manifest an intention to exercise control over things found on the land: see *per* Donaldson LJ at 1019.

counts as 'treasure', as defined by the Treasure Act 1996;[121] then (iii) the Crown[122] acquires a property right in that thing *as soon as* it is found.[123] So, exceptionally, the Crown acquires a property right without having physical control of the thing; and B1 is bound by that pre-existing property right. This exception can be justified by: (i) the desirability of making things of particular historical interest available to the public as a whole;[124] and (ii) the possibility of B1 receiving money (a 'reward') in compensation for being bound by the Crown's pre-existing property right.[125]

SUMMARY of D1:2.1.1

There are two situations where B1's actual physical control of a thing can give B2 Ownership of that thing. In each case, B1 holds *on behalf* of B2: as a result, B1's act in taking or keeping control is *attributed* to B2.

1. If B1 is an employee or agent of B2, and takes or keeps control of the thing so as to perform his duties to B2.
2. If B1 'attorns' to B2 by telling B2 that B1 has control of the thing on B2's behalf. Such an attornment can occur through a bill of lading: in that case, B1 then has control of the thing on behalf of anyone who holds the bill of lading with the consent of its previous holder.

From one perspective, these two cases can be seen as 'exceptions' to the general rule that a party can independently acquire a property right *only* if he takes physical control of that thing. However, neither case should surprise us. Each is simply an example of a wider point, seen in many areas of the legal system: where B1 acts on B2's behalf, B1's action may be attributed to B2.

---

[121] For example, under s 1 of the Act, one type of 'treasure' is a thing (other than a coin) that is at least 300 years old and that has a metallic content of which at least 10 per cent by weight is gold or silver. See too the Treasure (Designation) Order 2002, under which the Secretary of State for Culture, Media and Sport exercised the power under s 2(1) of the 1996 Act to extend the meaning of 'treasure' to include, for example, any object (other than a coin) dating from the Iron Age or earlier containing *any* gold or silver.

[122] If the Crown has given B2 a 'franchise of treasure trove' for the area in which the thing is found, B2 acquires the property right (Treasure Act 1996, ss 4 and 5): so the Prince of Wales acquires a property right in things found as treasure in the Duchy of Cornwall.

[123] B1 is under a statutory duty to report the finding to the local coroner: Treasure Act 1996, s 8.

[124] The assumption being that the Crown will allow such things to be displayed in a public museum: see eg the Mildenhall Treasure (late Roman silver tableware) on display in the British Museum. The Export of Objects of Cultural Interest (Control) Order 2003 has a similar purpose: if B owns an object of cultural interest that is more than 50 years old, B's power to export the thing is limited by the need to obtain an export licence. The export of the thing can then be postponed: this gives museums (and private individuals in the UK) a chance to bid to buy B's thing. For example, in 2007, the Tate used this opportunity to buy Turner's *The Blue Rigi, Lake of Lucerne, Sunrise* (1842). The general rule is that if B turns down a reasonable bid from a public source, B will not be granted an export licence.

[125] Treasure Act 1996, s 10.

2.1.2 Independent acquisition without taking physical control? Newly created things

(i) Manufacture[126]

EXAMPLE 10

B1 has Ownership of some eggs and flour. B2 has Ownership of some milk, butter, sugar and baking powder. B1 uses all these ingredients to make a cake.

The cake is a new thing, distinct from its ingredients. Any claim to Ownership of the cake must therefore be based on an independent acquisition: there is no former owner of the cake who can exercise a power to give Ownership to either B1 or B2. The property law system needs a rule to deal with such a case: the rule is that the party who makes the new thing acquires Ownership of it.[127] So, by virtue of his own conduct in making the cake, B1 acquires Ownership of that newly created thing.[128] It is very hard to think of a situation in which B1 can manufacture a thing without that thing being in the physical control of B1 or someone acting on behalf of B1. As a result, the rule in cases of manufacture seems to be a simple application of the core principle: B1 acquires Ownership of the new thing by taking physical control of it; B2 acquires no property right, even though his ingredients were used, as B2 has never had physical control of the new thing.

If B1 uses B2's things without B2's consent or other authority, then: (i) B1 commits a wrong against B2; and (ii) B1 is unjustly enriched at B2's expense. This means that B2 acquires a personal right against B1. There is a strong argument to say that B2 also acquires a persistent right: a right against B1's Ownership of the newly manufactured thing (see **D4:4.5.1**). However, the fact that B1 has acted without B2's consent or other authority does *not* prevent B1 acquiring Ownership of that thing.

(ii) Mixing

EXAMPLE 11

B1 has a drum filled with 15 gallons of oil; B2 has a drum filled with 10 gallons of oil. B1 takes the drums and pours the contents of each into a container.

The oil in the container is a new thing: it is no longer possible to locate either B1's oil or B2's oil. So, as in any case where two or more things are mixed together in such a way as to lose their distinct identity (see eg **Example 10** above), a new thing is created. Again, the property law system needs a rule to deal with such a case. However, the rule governing **Example 11** differs from that governing **Example 10**. As B1 has not *manufactured* the new thing, but has simply *mixed* two things together, the basic rule here is that Ownership of the

---

[126] The situation arising from the manufacture of a new thing is often referred to as 'specification' (from the Roman law concept of 'specificatio').

[127] Blackstone, *Commentaries on the Law of England* (1756–60), Book 2, 404. That position also seems to have been adopted by Justinian: see Birks, ch 9 in *Interests in Goods* (ed Palmer and McKendrick, 2nd edn, 1998), 228. An alternative, which Birks notes was adopted by the Sabinian school of jurists, is that an owner of the components should have Ownership of the new thing (so, in **Example 10**, B1 and B2 should presumably each have Co-Ownership of the new thing). That position seems to have been rejected by the Court of Appeal in *Borden (UK) Ltd v Scottish Timber Products Ltd* [1981] Ch 25.

[128] This is the case even if B1 commits a wrong: as where B1 takes B2's things without B2's consent or other authority (compare **1.4.1(i)** above).

mixture is held by *both* B1 and B2:[129] B1 and B2 are thus 'co-owners' of the mixture (see
F2.1). Each will have a share of Ownership, with the extent of that share determined by the
proportion each contributed to the mixture. So, in **Example 11**, B1 will have a 60 per cent
share of Ownership; and B2 will have a 40 per cent share.

Even if B1 commits a wrong in taking B2's oil, B1 acquires a property right in the new
mixture.[130] Blackstone recommended a penal rule in such a case, allocating Ownership of
the mixture solely to B2, but that harsh approach has since been rejected.[131] After all, as we
have seen, there are many cases in which B1 can independently acquire Ownership through
a wrongful act. It is true that, if B1 is a deliberate or careless wrongdoer, any evidential
doubt as to the proportion of each party's contribution to the mixture will be decided in
favour of B2. However, that is because of the *general* evidential rule that, where the true
position cannot be established, doubts can be resolved against a wrongdoer; that general
rule is not specific to the **acquisition question**.

It is important to note the contrast between the rules applying to manufacturing and
those applying to mixing. The former rules are consistent with the general principle that B1
acquires a property right through taking physical control of a thing. In contrast, in a mixing
case, B2 acquires a property right in the new thing even though he does *not* have physical
control of that new thing. This leads to a difficult distinction between: (i) manufacturing
cases; and (ii) mixing cases. For example, if B1 mixes his paint with B2's paint to create a
different coloured paint is that a case of: (i) manufacturing (so that *only* B1 has Ownership
of the new paint); or (ii) mixing (so that *each* of B1 and B2 holds Ownership)?

An alternative approach would be to apply the same rule to *both* manufacture and
mixing cases. This would mean that in **Example 11**, as in **Example 10**, B2 would have *no*
property right in the new thing. This would be consistent with the general rule that a party
can independently acquire a property right *only* when: (i) he takes physical control of a
thing; or (ii) when someone takes physical control of a thing on his behalf. If that approach
were adopted, B2's protection, in **Example 11**, would come from having: (i) a personal right
against B1; and (possibly) (ii) a persistent right: a right against B1's Ownership of the
mixture (see **D4:4.5.1**).

This alternative approach would offer greater protection to C, a party buying the new
mixture from B1. C may reasonably believe that B1 has Ownership of the mixture. However,
on the law as it stands, C will be in a nasty shock: even if he is a 'bona fide purchaser' of the
mixture, he will bound by B2's pre-existing property right. If instead B1 were to hold the
mixture on Trust for B1 and B2, B2 would have only a persistent right, rather than a
property right. It would then be possible for C to use the 'bona fide purchaser' defence
against B2's pre-existing right (see **B:5.2.2(ii)**). That may be thought to be a more appropriate resolution of the basic tension between B2 and C.

---

[129] See Blackstone, *Commentaries on the Law of England* (1756–60), Book 2, 405; *Sandeman & Sons v Tyzack and
Branfoot SS Co* [1913] AC 680; *Indian Oil Corpn v Greenstone Shipping* [1988] QB 345. For a full consideration see
Birks, ch 9 in *Interests in Goods* (ed Palmer and McKendrick, 2nd edn, 1998).

[130] *Indian Oil Corpn v Greenstone Shipping* [1988] QB 345.

[131] See *per* Staughton J in *Indian Oil Corpn v Greenstone Shipping* [1988] QB 345 at 369–370. Of course, B1 may
still have to pay money to B2 for breaching his duty not to interfere with B2's right to exclusive control of his
original oil.

(iii) Birth

EXAMPLE 12

B2 is an owner of a sheep. B1 steals the sheep. Whilst it is under the physical control of B1, the sheep gives birth to a lamb.

Any claim to Ownership of the newly born lamb must be based on an independent acquisition: there is no prior owner of that lamb from whom a property right can be acquired. The traditional rule here is that: (i) B1 acquires Ownership of the lamb by taking physical control of it; *but* (ii) B2 acquires a *prior* property right: as B2 is an owner of the sheep, B2 acquires Ownership of the lamb *as soon as* it is born.[132] So, although B1 is the first and as yet only party to have physical control of the lamb, B2 independently acquires a property right *before* B1 acquires his property right.

Like the rule applying to mixing, this is a further exception to the general rule that a party can *only* independently acquire a property right by taking physical control of a thing. And like the rule applying to mixing, this rule can also be questioned.[133] Again, a preferable approach may be to recognise that B2 has a persistent right: a right against B1's Ownership of the lamb, arising as a result of B1's unjust enrichment at B2's expense (see **D4:4.5.1**).

(iv) Combination without mixing or manufacture?[134]

EXAMPLE 13

B1 has Ownership of a bike; B2 has Ownership of a pot of paint. B1 uses B2's paint to paint his bike.

B2's paint has ceased to exist as a distinct thing: it has become part of B1's bike. As a result, B2's property right is destroyed. In contrast, B1's bike, whilst it has been altered, continues to exist as a distinct thing. So, B1's *right* remains the same: he has Ownership of the bike.[135] But the physical state of the bike has changed: it has now been painted.

So, as in **Example 10** and **Example 11**, B2 has *lost* his property right, as the thing he once owned no longer exists. However, in contrast to those cases, *no one acquires a new property right*. A case such as **Example 13** is often described as involving an 'accession': B2's thing (the paint) *accedes to* (ie, becomes part of) B1's thing.

The result in **Example 13** simply depends on the obvious rule that, if B2 has a property right in a particular thing, and that thing ceases to exist as an independent entity, B2's property right must also cease to exist. After all, you cannot both eat your cake and own it. The main difficulties with the principle are simply factual: if the things of B1 and B2 are combined, at what point does either thing lose its identity?[136] For example, if B1 replaces his

---

[132] Blackstone, *Commentaries on the Law of England* (1756–60), Book 2, 390.

[133] The rule was departed from in a case where B1 had physical control of the sheep with B2's consent: *Tucker v Farm and General Investment Trust Ltd* [1966] 2 All ER 508.

[134] The situations discussed here are often referred to as 'accession' (from the Roman law concept of 'accessio').

[135] Blackstone, *Commentaries on the Law of England* (1756–60), Book 2, 404.

[136] If B2's thing is attached to, and becomes part of B1's land, it counts as a 'fixture': see eg *Hobson v Gorringe* [1897] 1 Ch 182; *Melluish (Inspector of Taxes) v BMI (No 3) Ltd* [1996] AC 454. The thing loses its individual identity and becomes part of the land owned by B1. Again, the main difficulty in such case is factual: has B2's thing acceded to B1's land? For discussion see eg Bennett, ch 11 in *Interests in Goods* (ed Palmer and McKendrick, 2nd edn, 1998).

bike's gears, brakes and wheels with those of B2, then: (i) have B2's things acceded to B1's bike; or (ii) has B1's bike acceded to B2's things; or (iii) has B1 manufactured a new thing?[137]

Where B2's thing *does* lose its identity, and becomes part of B1's thing, the outcome is the same even if B1 used B2's paint without B2's consent or other lawful authority.[138] So, even if B1 stole B2's paint, B2 still loses his property right in that paint.[139] In such a case, as in **Example 10**, B2's protection instead comes from having: (i) a personal right against B1; and (possibly) (ii) a persistent right: a right against B1's Ownership of the mixture (see **D4:4.5.2**).

SUMMARY of D1:2.1

The independent acquisition of property rights is based around a core principle: B independently acquires Ownership of a thing *if and only if* he, or someone acting on his behalf, takes physical control of that thing. On the law as it stands, there are some exceptions to that principle; however, each of the exceptions is unjustified.

1. If: (i) B1 *does* take physical control of a thing; but (ii) does so in his capacity as an employee or agent of B2, then (iii) B1 does *not* acquire a property right.
2. If: (i) B2 does *not* take physical control of a thing; but (ii) is an owner of land; and (iii) a thing is *either* found in his land *or* found on his land in a case where B2 has manifested an intention to exercise exclusive control of anything found on his land; then (iv) B2 *does* acquire a property right.
3. If: (i) B2 does *not* take physical control of a thing; but (ii) that thing is a mixture derived in part from B2's thing; then (iii) B2 *does* acquire a property right as a co-owner of the mixture.
4. If: (i) B2 does *not* take physical control of a thing; but (ii) that thing is an animal given birth to by B2's animal; then (iii) B2 *does* acquire a property right as an owner of the newly born animal.

Exception 1 arose for a particular historical reason (to allow B1 to be prosecuted for larceny if he stole the thing after taking control of it as part of his job) and no longer serves any purpose. Exception 2 is very difficult to defend (see **2.1.1** above). Exceptions 3 and 4 are also unnecessary: a better solution in each case is to recognise that: (i) B1 has sole Ownership of the new thing; and (ii) B2 has a persistent right against B1's right.

It thus seems that there is a strong argument for making the moderate reforms needed to allow us to say that B independently acquires a property right if *and only if* he, or someone whose action can be attributed to him, takes physical control of a thing.

---

[137] For consideration of the general principles, see eg Guest (1964) 27 *MLR* 505; Goode, *Hire Purchase Law and Practice* (2nd edn, 1970), 747–58.

[138] Goode, *Hire Purchase Law and Practice* (2nd edn, 1970), 754 adopts a contrary position arguing that, where B1 has acted wrongfully, it may be held that B2 has Ownership of the principal thing (in this case the bike). That result does, as Goode admits, seem 'Draconian' and the US authorities on which it is based should presumably now yield to the less drastic approach favoured by Staughton J in *Indian Oil Corpn v Greenstone Shipping* [1988] QB 345 at 369–70 when considering the related case of a wrongful mixture.

[139] In such a case, as in **Examples 10 and 11** above, B1 should acquire a persistent right against B2's Ownership of the bike (see **D4:4.5.2**). The content of that right should be limited to the extent of B2's enrichment at B1's expense. It is hard to see that B1's paint has contributed to a proportion of the value of the bike so if the paint used by B2 was worth £10, then: (i) B2 should be under a duty to pay B1 £10; and (ii) that duty should be secured by a Purely Equitable Charge against B2's Ownership of the bike (see further **D2:1.2.1** and **D4:4.5.2**).

2.2   The transfer of a pre-existing property right

To dependently acquire Ownership from A, B needs to prove that:

- A had Ownership of a particular thing; *and*
- A intended to exercise his power to transfer his Ownership of that thing to B; *and*
- One of three possible additional factors (deed, delivery or sale) is present.

2.2.1 A's Ownership

It is important to remember that, if B acquires A's Ownership of a thing, this does *not* guarantee that B has the best right to that thing.

> **EXAMPLE 14a**
>
> Z has Ownership of a bike. A steals the bike. A then sells the bike to B.

B, like A and the rest of the world, is under a prima facie duty to Z not to interfere with Z's use of the bike. By taking control of the bike, B therefore commits a wrong against Z. Certainly, B does *not* have a defence to Z's pre-existing property right as a result of the facts that: (i) A has independently acquired Ownership of the bike; and (ii) A has transferred his Ownership to B.

> **EXAMPLE 14b**
>
> Z has Ownership of a bike. A0 steals the bike. A0 then sells the bike to A. A then sells the bike to B.

In this case, A has acquired Ownership dependently. Nonetheless, B is still under a prima facie duty to Z. Certainly, B does not acquire a defence simply because: (i) A0 independently acquired Ownership of the bike; and (ii) A0 then transferred his Ownership to A; and (iii) A then transferred his Ownership to B.[140]

This does *not* mean that B has a problem *whenever* B's property right ultimately depends on an independent acquisition. In fact, ultimately, *all* property rights depend on an independent acquisition. As far as B is concerned, his position is only fully secure when it is impossible for anyone else to show a chain of dependent acquisitions leading back to the *first* independent acquisition of Ownership. In **Examples 14a** and **14b**, B's problem may come from the fact that, for example: (i) Z bought the bike from a friend; (ii) the friend bought it from a shop; (iii) the shop bought it from a wholesaler; and (iv) the wholesaler bought it from the manufacturer. In such a case, Z's property right can be traced back, through a chain of dependent acquisitions, to the manufacturer—the first person to independently acquire Ownership of the bike.

2.2.2 A's intention

If A has Ownership of a particular thing, A has the power to transfer his property right to B.[141] To show that A has intended to exercise that power, B must show that A intended to

---

[140] In such a case, the lapse of time may give B a defence to Z's property right: see **3.7** below.

[141] See eg *Attwater v Attwater* (1853) 18 Beav 330; *re Elliot* [1896] 2 353, esp *per* Chitty J at 356: 'the owner of property has as an incident of his ownership the right to sell and to receive the whole of the proceeds for his own

transfer a *specific right* (A's Ownership) to a *specific person* (B). This rule applies *whenever* A attempts to transfer a right to B, whether that right is a personal right. a persistent right or a property right.

(i) Where a flaw in A's intention prevents the transfer of A's right to B

EXAMPLE 15a

A intends to transfer his Ownership of a £10 note to B. A, by mistake, gives B a £50 note.

EXAMPLE 15b

A intends to transfer his Ownership of a desk to B. A does not realise that he has left a £50 note in the desk. A gives the desk to B.

EXAMPLE 15c

A intends to transfer his Ownership of a £50 note to X. A, by mistake, sends the note to B, who shares the same name as X.

In **Example 15a**, A's Ownership of the £50 note is *not* transferred to B: A did not intend to transfer that *specific right* to B.[142] The same result applies in **Example 15b**: A did intend to transfer his Ownership of the desk; *but* A did not intend to transfer his Ownership of the £50 note.[143] In **Example 15c**, A's Ownership of the £50 note is *not* transferred to B: A did not intend to transfer that right *to B*.[144] In each case, B will *independently* acquire a new property right by taking physical control of the £50 note. However, as A retains his pre-existing Ownership of that note, B, along with the rest of the world, is under a prima facie duty not to interfere with A's right to exclusive control of the note. In such a case it is possible to say that A's attempt to transfer Ownership is 'void': this simply means that there has been no transfer of that right.

---

benefit'. See too **G1B:2.2.2(ii)** and **G1B:5.2**. There may, however, be *statutory* limits on A's power to transfer Ownership. For example, a statute may exclude or limit the power of a national museum to transfer its Ownership of a work of art: see eg Museums and Galleries Act 1992 s 4. And insolvency legislation may give a court the power to set aside particular transfers by A, such as a transfer made at undervalue within a five-year period before A's bankruptcy; or any transfer at an undervalue made with the purpose of prejudicing A's creditors: see Insolvency Act 1986 ss 339 and 423.

[142] See eg *R v Ashwell* (1885) 16 QBD 190. For a contrary view, see Swadling, in *Mapping the Law: Essays in Honour of Peter Birks* (ed Burrows and Rodger, 2006) (questioning both the authority of *R v Ashwell* and the 'notion that there are mistakes so fundamental as to prevent title passing by delivery.')

[143] See eg *Cartwright v Green* (1803) 3 Ves 405; *Merry v Green* (1841) 7 M & W 623. Each case raised the question of whether B, by keeping a hidden thing (eg, the £50 note in **Example 15b**), committed a crime. That question in turn depended on whether B acquired A's Ownership of the hidden thing. In each case, it was found that B's conduct was, potentially, a crime: as a result, it can be inferred that B did *not* acquire A's Ownership of the hidden thing.

[144] See eg *Cundy v Lindsay* (1878) 3 App Cas 459; *Ingram v Little* [1961] 1 QB 31; *Shogun Finance Ltd v Hudson* [2004] 1 AC 919. In some cases (such as *R v Middleton* (1873) LR 2 CCC 38) it can be difficult to establish, as a matter of fact, whether or not A intended to transfer the right to B rather than to another person. Where A deals with B 'face to face', the starting point is that A *does* intend to deal with B: see *Shogun Finance Ltd v Hudson* [2004] 1 AC 919 at [67] and [187].

(ii) Where a flaw in A's intention does not prevent the transfer of A's right to B

EXAMPLE 16a

Y is a customer at A Bank. B forges Y's signature on a cheque for £200 and takes the cheque to A Bank. A Bank, in the mistaken belief that the cheque is genuine, gives B ten £20 notes.

Clearly, A Bank has made a mistake. Nonetheless, A Bank *did* intend to transfer its Ownership of specific notes to B: so, A Bank's Ownership of those notes *does* pass to B. This is confirmed by the decision of Blackburn J in *R v Prince*,[145] the essential facts of which are identical to **Example 16a**.[146]

However, A Bank's mistake was *fraudulently* induced by B. As a result, A Bank has a *power* to acquire a property right: A Bank, when it discovers the fraud, can rescind (ie, unwind) its transfer to B. If A Bank exercises that power to rescind, it *immediately* regains its property right in the notes (see **1.4.5(i)** above). In such a case, the transfer of A's right to B is often said to be 'voidable at Common Law'. That phrase indicates two things: (i) the transfer of the right to B *does* occur—the transaction between A and B is not 'void'; but (ii) A has a power to regain his right.

EXAMPLE 16b

A joins a religious sisterhood. Under the rules of that association, the word of B, the lady superior, is to be treated as the word of God. The rules also forbid members from seeking external advice without the consent of B. A, without receiving anything in return, transfers her car to B.

Again, A's right (Ownership of the car) is transferred to B: A did intend to transfer that right to B. However, there is a flaw in A's intention: it was procured by B's *undue influence* over A. As a result, the transaction between A and B is said to be 'voidable in Equity'. This means that, although A's right has been transferred to B, A has an immediate *power to acquire a persistent right—a right against the right transferred to B*. So, if: (i) A chooses to rescind the transfer to B; *and* (ii) B is, or ought to be, aware of A's exercise of that power; then (iii) B is under a duty to A not to use her Ownership of the car for B's own benefit: in other words, B holds that right on Trust for A. This is confirmed by the decision of the Court of Appeal in *Allcard v Skinner*,[147] on which **Example 16b** is based.

In both **Examples 16a and 16b**, A's power seems to arise because the flaw in A's intention, whilst it does *not* prevent B acquiring A's right, does mean that B would be unjustly enriched at A's expense if B were free to keep that right and use it for his own benefit. We will therefore consider when such powers arise in **D4**. The important point for now is that a flaw in A's intention will *only* prevent B acquiring A's right *if* it means that A has no

---

[145] (1868) LR 1 CCR 150. In *R v Prince*, B had given one of the notes she had received from A Bank to B2. B2 was charged with handling stolen goods. It was found that B2 could not be guilty: A Bank's Ownership of the notes had passed to B.

[146] See too *Car & Universal Finance Co Ltd v Caldwell* [1965] 1 QB 525.

[147] (1887) 36 Ch D 145. The lapse of time meant that A could no longer assert her power to rescind the transfer. Cotton LJ dissented as he held (at 172 and 175) that, as soon as A transferred her rights to B, B held those rights on Trust for B. On that view, instead of acquiring a power to acquire a persistent right, A acquired an immediate persistent right. Cotton LJ's analysis may be correct if B is *immediately aware* of the flaw in A's intention (see **D4:4.2**).

intention to transfer that specific right to B (as in **Examples 15a–15c**). In other cases, the flaw in A's intention may have *an* effect; but it will *not* prevent B acquiring A's right (see **Examples 16a and 16b**).

SUMMARY of D1:2.2.2

To show that A has intended to exercise his power to transfer a pre-existing right to B, B must show that A intended to transfer a *specific right* to a *specific person* (B). If A does not have that intention, the attempted transfer to B is 'void': it simply does not occur (see rows 1 and 2 of the table below). Other flaws in A's intention will *not*, by themselves, prevent B acquiring A's right. However, such flaws may: (i) make the transfer 'voidable at Common Law'—in such a case, A has a power to regain the right he transferred to B (see row 3); or (ii) make the transfer 'voidable in Equity'—in such a case, A has a power to acquire a persistent right against the right he transferred to B (see row 4).

	A's intention	A's position	B's position	Example
1	No intention to transfer *that right*	A retains his right	Does not acquire A's right	*R v Ashwell*
2	No intention to transfer *to* B	A retains his right	Does not acquire A's right	*Cundy v Lindsay*
3	Intention procured by B's fraud (or by B's duress)[148]	A has a power to regain the right transferred to B	Acquires A's right *but* liable to lose that right	*R v Prince*
4	Intention procured by B's undue influence (or caused by any mistake that causes A to transfer a right to B when A is under no duty to do so)[149]	A has a power to acquire a persistent right against the right transferred to B	Acquires A's right *but* liable to come under a duty to A not to use that right for his own benefit	*Allcard v Skinner*

2.2.3 The need for an additional factor

B can *never* acquire a right of A *simply* as a result of A orally expressing his intention to give B that right. So, if A, an owner of a bike, declares that 'I give my bike to B', that statement, by itself, will *not* transfer A's Ownership of the bike to B. A's attempt to transfer his property right to B will succeed only if it is coupled with one of three additional factors: (i) the use of a deed; (ii) B taking physical control of the thing; or (iii) B giving money, or a promise to pay money, in return for A's right. These three factors can be summarised, rather roughly, as: (i) deed; (ii) delivery; and (iii) sale.

---

[148] See **D4:3.2.**
[149] See **D4:4.2.**

2.2.4 The additional factor

(i) Deed

(a) The test

A's statement that 'I give my bike to B' can have the effect of giving B Ownership of the bike if it is made in a particular form: a deed.[150] By using a deed, A can make a binding gratuitous promise to B (see **C3:2**). It is therefore no surprise that A's intention to make an immediate transfer to B of his right to exclusive control of a thing, if expressed in a deed, succeeds in transferring that right to B. After all, if A is under a duty to B to give B a right to immediate exclusive control of a thing forever, B *necessarily* acquires a property right (see **1.3.5** above).

(b) Justification

First, the *evidence* provided by a deed can be particularly useful where B claims a property right. Such evidence can help to protect C from the risk of collusion between A and B. For example, let us say C lends money to A, who then goes into insolvency. A's assets will be sold off and the money will be used to meet, as far as possible, A's debts. C will want A's bike to be sold to increase the funds available to pay A's creditors. However, A may fraudulently claim that, before he went into insolvency, he gave his Ownership of the bike to B. The requirement of a deed will make it more difficult for A and B to concoct such a story.[151]

The *caution* promoted by the need for a deed will help to protect A from rash or poorly considered dealings with his property right (see **C3:6.2**). For example, if A is frustrated after getting a puncture and, in his anger, tells B that B can have the bike, this oral statement cannot, by itself, give B Ownership of the bike. The need for a deed may also *protect A from a fraudulent claim*. For example, B may falsely claim that A exercised his power to give Ownership of the bike to B. Of course, A can simply deny this; but, in the absence of a formality rule, A may have to bear the expense and worry of convincing a court to believe his word rather than B's.

The most important advantage of a deed, however, is *publicity*. The use of a formal document, such as a deed, creates a record of the transaction between A and B and can thus make it easier for C to discover B's property right. When looking at the 'closed list' principle, we saw that discoverability is an important factor in considering the **content** question (see **1.2.1** above). It is also relevant to the acquisition question and can provide a powerful justification for formality rules.

EXAMPLE 17

A has Ownership of a bike. By means of a deed, A transfers that right to B. A keeps physical control of the bike: the plan is for B to pick the bike up in a month's time. A asks C for a loan and offers C a property right in the bike as security for A's duty to repay the loan.

There is a real risk that C may reasonably believe that no one other than A has a property

---

[150] For the definition of a deed, see Law of Property (Miscellaneous Provisions) Act 1989, s 1 (discussed in **C3:n 1**).

[151] Further protection is provided to C by specific rules that limit A's ability to prejudice his creditors. For example, even if A does use a deed to transfer Ownership of the bike to B, that transfer can be set aside if the gift was made by A with the intention of prejudicing his creditors: see Insolvency Act 1986, ss 423–5 (see too **n 141** above).

right in the bike. However, C will be in for a nasty shock if: (i) C accepts a property right in the bike as security; and (ii) A then fails to repay C. C will then want to sell the bike and use the proceeds to meet A's debt. However, C is bound by B's pre-existing property right in the bike: as a result, if C does sell the bike, he commits a wrong against B.

It is thus clear that publicity is particularly important in a case, such as **Example 17**, where: (i) A uses a deed to transfer Ownership of a thing to B; and (ii) A then keeps physical control of that thing. As a result, in such a case, a *further* formality rule applies: the deed used to transfer Ownership to B must be *registered*. The statutory registration requirement, imposed by the Bills of Sale Act of 1878,[152] can apply if: (i) A uses a document to transfer Ownership to B;[153] and (ii) B fails to take physical control of the thing. The deed in **Example 17**, a document by which A transfers Ownership to B, is known as an 'absolute bill of sale'.[154] In such a case, B's failure to register the bill of sale within seven days does *not* prevent B acquiring Ownership but it does prevent B from asserting his Ownership against A's trustee in bankruptcy,[155] or against an execution creditor of A (see **B:2.3.1**).[156]

This means that if, in **Example 17**, the deed giving B Ownership of the bike has not been registered, then C does *not* commit a wrong against B if C applies to court and enforces his power to sell the bike. In this way, the property law system protects C's reasonable expectation that the value of the bike is available to A. The 1878 Act is thus 'designed for the protection of creditors':[157] it aims to protect a third party who might otherwise extend credit to A in the belief that A still has Ownership of the thing in question.[158]

(ii) Delivery

(a) The test

If A declares that 'I give my bike to B' *and* also gives B physical control of the bike (eg, by handing the bike over to B), B will acquire Ownership of the bike *even though no deed has been used*. Situations where B acquires physical control are often said to involve a 'delivery' of the thing by A to B. However, there is no need for *A* to hand the thing to B: all that matters is that B does in fact have physical control of the thing.

---

[152] Bills of Sale Act 1878, ss 4 and 8. In this context, the name of the Act is misleading: a deed can count as a 'bill of sale', even if B is not buying anything from A.

[153] The registration requirement does not apply if B can acquire A's Ownership without relying on the document (eg, as where B takes physical control of the thing), see eg *Ramsay v Margrett* [1894] 2 QB 18. There are also a number of situations where registration is unnecessary, even if the document is crucial in transferring Ownership. For example, the 1878 Act does not apply to: (i) documents used to transfer Ownership 'in the ordinary course of business'; or (ii) documents 'used in the ordinary course of business as proof of possession or control of goods' such as bills of lading (see **2.1.1(i)** above).

[154] 'Absolute' to distinguish it from a 'security' bill of sale: a document used to transfer Ownership to B by way of security. A security bill of sale is governed by the Bills of Sale Act (1878) Amendment Act 1882 as well as by the original 1878 Act: see further **F4:3.1.1(i)**.

[155] B will also be unable to assert his Ownership against an assignee for the benefit of A's creditors.

[156] Bills of Sale Act 1878, s 8.

[157] *Per* Lord Herschell in *Manchester, Sheffield and Lincolnshire Railway Co v North Central Wagon Co* (1888) 13 App Cas 554 at 560: the 1878 Act was 'designed for the protection of creditors, and to prevent their rights being affected by secret assurances of chattels which were permitted to remain in the ostensible possession of a person who had parted with the property in them'.

[158] Registration also protects B by making it clear he does not have Ownership: see eg *per* Lord Blackburn in *Cookson v Swire* (1884) 9 App Cas 653 at 665.

EXAMPLE 18a

A has Ownership of a bike. A lends the bike to B for a week. At the end of the week, B asks A when he should return the bike. A says to B: 'Don't worry, the bike is yours now.'

In such a case, A has not handed the bike to B. However, as B *already* has physical control of the thing, A's oral statement suffices to transfer A's Ownership of the bike to B. This is confirmed by both: (i) the decision of PO Lawrence J in *re Stoneham*;[159] and (ii) part of the decision of the Court of Appeal in *Pascoe v Turner*.[160]

EXAMPLE 18b

A has Ownership of a bike. A has lost the bike. A says to B: 'If you can find the bike, it's yours.' B then finds the bike.

Again, A has not handed the bike to B. However, as soon as B finds and takes physical control of the thing, A's oral statement suffices to transfer A's Ownership of the bike to B. This is confirmed by the decision of Plowman J in *Thomas v Times Book Co Ltd*,[161] on which **Example 18b** is based.

EXAMPLE 18c

A has Ownership of a church organ. A wants to transfer his Ownership to B, the organist. B already has the key to the organ. A tells B: 'The organ is yours'. A also gives B receipts from the builder of the organ and a letter from the vicar of the church recording that the organ belonged to A. A later places B's hand on the organ, again telling B the organ is his.

The concept of physical control is a simple one: the only problem that may arise is factual—whether, in a particular case, B acquired physical control of a thing (see **2.1** above). That problem clearly arises in **Example 18c**. In *Rawlinson v Mort*,[162] the essential facts of which are identical to **Example 18c**, it was held that B *did* have sufficient physical control of the organ: as a result, B acquired A's Ownership of that thing. This result can be explained as depending on: (i) a practical concession based on the difficulty of transferring physical control of large object; and (ii) the significance of B's control of the key—a means to gain exclusive control of that object.

Certainly, the decision in *Rawlinson* does *not* mean that the simple factual concept of physical control should be complicated by introducing a refinement such as 'symbolic delivery'.[163] It is not the case that B has physical control of a thing *whenever* B has physical control of a symbol representing that thing.[164] So, if A: (i) tells B that B now owns A's bike;

---

[159] [1919] 1 Ch 149.

[160] [1979] 1 WLR 431 (see **C3:Example 3**). In *Pascoe*, B occupied a house belonging to A. A told B that the 'house and everything in it are yours'. That oral statement, by itself, could not transfer A's Ownership of the land to B (additional formality rules apply where land is concerned: see **C3:3.5** and **E1:2.2**) *but* it did suffice to transfer A's Ownership of the contents of the house to B: *per* Cumming-Bruce LJ at 435.

[161] [1966] 1 WLR 911.

[162] (1905) 93 LT 555.

[163] Similarly, the notion of 'constructive delivery', discussed by Stoljar (1958) 21 *MLR* 27, also seems to be an unnecessary refinement. It can reasonably be used to refer to the special role of a bill of lading as a document of title (see **2.1.1(i)** above) but otherwise is unhelpful.

[164] See eg *per* Lord Hardwicke in *Ward v Turner* (1752) 2 Ves Sen 431; Barlow (1956) 19 *MLR* 394; Tyler and Palmer, *Crossely Vaines' Personal Property* (5th edn, 1973), 307; Swadling, *English Private Law* (ed Burrows, 2nd edn,

and (ii) gives B the key to the bike lock; then (iii) it *may* be possible to say that B has acquired Ownership as he now has sufficient physical control of the bike.[165] However, if A: (i) tells B that B now owns A's bike; and (ii) gives B a photograph of the bike; then (iii) B clearly does *not* have physical control of the bike and so A's Ownership has *not* been transferred to B.[166] Certainly, it is important to note that 'delivery' cannot be dispensed with simply by showing that A *really did* intend to transfer Ownership: it is an independent and additional factor.[167]

(b) Justification

Why is the need for a deed dispensed with if B has physical control of the thing? Clearly, practical convenience is an important factor: it would be absurd if A needed to use a deed to give B a birthday present. That concern for convenience is reflected in the court's interpretation of the requirement: for example, in the concession made in a case, such as **Example 18c**, where it is difficult for B to unequivocally have physical control of a large object.

B's acquisition of physical control can also bring some of the advantages of a deed. As far as *publicity* is concerned, B's physical control of a thing should alert C to the risk that A may have transferred his Ownership of that thing to B. B's physical control can also provide useful *evidence*, combating possible collusion: A may claim to have given Ownership to B before going bankrupt, but if A kept physical control of the bike, then Ownership, in the absence of a deed or a sale, will remain with A. The need for B to have physical control may also help a court in deciding when B's right arises. Instead of trying to answer the tricky question of when A intended to give B the right, the court can instead test for a hard fact: the point when B took physical control of the bike.

The need for B to take physical control can also *protect A against fraudulent claims* and promote *caution*. It will never be enough for B to claim that A simply said 'I give my bike to B'; instead, in most cases, B will also need to show that A gave him physical control of the bike. The need for that second step will usually give A, if he has made a rash decision to transfer Ownership, a chance to change his mind. The exception occurs in cases such as **Examples 18a and 18b**: in those cases, A's oral statement can transfer A's Ownership to B without any further act from A. The existence of this exception suggests that, in this context, *publicity* (alerting C to the risk that B may have a property right) may be the real justification for 'delivery'.[168]

2007), 4.459. Note that in *re Cole* [1964] Ch 175 a husband showing his wife the contents of their new home and saying 'It's all yours' was held to be insufficient to transfer Ownership, even though some of the items had been touched by the wife. In contrast, in *Lock v Heath* (1892) 8 TLR 295, A's delivery of one chair to B was sufficient to transfer Ownership of a set of furniture represented by the chair.

[165] An alternative view would be that delivery of a key only suffices where, as in *Rawlinson v Mort* (1905) 93 LT 555, the bulky nature of the thing prevents B easily acquiring physical control of the thing itself: see eg *per* Lord Harwicke in *Ward v Turner* (1752) 2 Ves Sen 431 at 433; Barlow (1956) 19 *MLR* 394.

[166] As Diamond (1964) 27 *MLR* 357 puts it at 360: 'only a fool would rely on [symbolic delivery]'.

[167] This point is emphasised by the Court of Appeal in *Cochrane v Moore* (1870) 25 QBD 57.

[168] It can also be said that, in a cases such as **Example 18a and 18b**, it would be 'absurd' for A to regain control of the thing only so as to hand it back over to B (see eg Stoljar (1958) 21 *MLR* 27, 36 and 41). However, even if the results in those cases were different, that absurdity would *not* arise: A could transfer his Ownership to B by using a deed.

(iii) Sale

(a) The basic rule

EXAMPLE 19a

A has Ownership of a bike. On 1 June, A and B make an oral agreement that: (i) B will immediately acquire A's Ownership of the bike; and (ii) B will immediately pay A £200.

In such a case, the basic rule is that B will acquire A's Ownership whenever A and B intend that B should.[169] So, in **Example 19a**, B acquires A's Ownership immediately: there is no need for A to use a deed to transfer that right to B; nor is there any need for B to take physical control of the bike. This is because, in **Example 19a**, a *sale* has occurred. A sale occurs whenever, in return for acquiring Ownership of a thing from A, B: (i) pays money; or (ii) makes a binding promise to pay money.[170] That is the crucial additional factor which, when coupled with A's intention to transfer Ownership, allows B to acquire A's pre-existing property right.

In a sale, B can acquire A's Ownership even though the intentions of A and B have not been recorded in writing. Even if A and B do record those intentions in a document, there is no general need to register that document: the Bills of Sale Act 1878, despite its name, is essentially irrelevant where B acquires A's Ownership by means of a sale.[171]

EXAMPLE 19b

A has Ownership of a car. On 1 June, A and B make an oral agreement that: (i) if B passes his driving test by the end of the month; then (ii) A will transfer his Ownership of the car to B; and (iii) B will pay A £500.

It is clear that, on 1 June, no sale occurs: A has not attempted to transfer his Ownership of the car to B. In the language of the Sale of Goods Act 1979, A and B have instead made an 'agreement to sell'.[172] At that point, therefore, B has only a *personal right* against A: B has not yet acquired a property right. If B does pass his driving test by the end of the month, then a sale will occur:[173] B will acquire A's Ownership of the car whenever A and B, under the terms of their agreement, intend that B should. At that point, without the need for a deed or for B to take physical control of the car, B acquires a *property right*: A's Ownership of the car.

---

[169] See Sale of Goods Act 1979, s 17.

[170] Sale of Goods Act 1979, s 2(1): 'A contract of sale of goods is a contract by which the seller transfers or agrees to transfer the property in goods to the buyer for a money consideration, called the price.'

[171] See *Benjamin's Sale of Goods* (7th edn, 2006), 1-017. The 1878 Act does not apply to 'transfers of goods in the ordinary course of business or any trade or calling' (see s 4). If: (i) one private individual sells goods to another; *and* (ii) that transaction is recorded in a document; *and* (iii) A has kept physical control of the goods; *and* (iv) B has to rely on that document to claim Ownership; then (v) the registration requirement under the Act will apply and so may prevent B asserting his Ownership against A's trustee in bankruptcy or execution creditor. But such cases must be very rare.

[172] Sale of Goods Act 1979, s 2(5).

[173] Sale of Goods Act 1979, s 2(6).

> **EXAMPLE 19c**
>
> A Ltd has Ownership of some steel coil in Korea. A Ltd and B Ltd agree that: (i) B Ltd will acquire A Ltd's Ownership of the coil once it arrives in England; but (ii) whilst it is being shipped to England, B Ltd will bear the risk of any damage to the coil. The coil is then damaged by the carelessness of C Ltd, the owner of the ship carrying the coil to England.

The problem for B Ltd is that, when C Ltd damages the coils, B Ltd does *not* have a property right in those goods. As in **Example 19b**, there is an 'agreement to sell'; *but* A Ltd's property right had not yet passed to B Ltd. Further, B Ltd has not independently acquired a property right: (i) B Ltd has never had physical control of the coil; and (ii) C Ltd does not hold physical control of the coil on behalf of B Ltd. As B Ltd has no property right, C Ltd (along with the rest of the world) is *not* under a duty to B Ltd not to interfere with the coil.[174] This means that, as confirmed by the House of Lords in *The Aliakmon*,[175] C Ltd has committed no wrong against B Ltd.[176]

> **EXAMPLE 19d**
>
> A has Ownership of a bike. B has Ownership of a different bike. On 1 June, A and B make an oral agreement that: (i) B will immediately acquire Ownership of A's bike; and (ii) A will immediately acquire Ownership of B's bike.

If B does not acquire physical control of A's bike, can he nonetheless argue that his agreement with A has given him Ownership of A's bike? The problem for B is that his deal with A does *not* fall within the definition of a sale given by the Sale of Goods Act 1979: B has *not* given money, or a promise to pay money, in return for A's Ownership. This leads to a difficult question: can B acquire A's Ownership *whenever* A makes a contractually binding promise to immediately transfer that right to B? This question can arise not just in a barter case (such as **Example 19d**) but also where, for example, A agrees to immediately transfer his Ownership to B in return for B's agreement to perform a service.

The current position is very unclear.[177] However, in **Example 19d**, a reasonably strong argument can be made in B's favour. It can be argued that there is a general principle that: (i) if A is under a duty to B to make an immediate transfer of his Ownership to B; then (ii) B acquires A's Ownership. After all, if A is under a duty to B to give B a right to immediate exclusive control of a thing forever, B *necessarily* acquires a property right (see **1.3.5** above). This means that B should acquire a property right *both*: (i) when A's duty arises as a result of A's consent (Reason 1 in **B:4.3**) as when A expresses his intention in a deed; and (ii) when A's duty arises as a result of A's entry into a contract with B (Reason 2 in **B:4.3**) as in **Example 19a** *and* **Example 19d**. It could then be said that the Sale of Goods Act 1979 is a code regulating those cases where the contract between A and B imposes a duty on B to pay

---

[174] As A Ltd has kept its Ownership of the coil, C Ltd *does* commit a wrong against A Ltd when carelessly damaging the coil. As a result, C Ltd can be ordered to pay money to A Ltd even though C Ltd's conduct causes A Ltd no loss: see eg *The Sanix Ace* [1987] 1 Lloyd's Rep 465 and section **4.3.2** below.

[175] *Leigh and Sillivan Ltd v Aliakmon Shipping Co Ltd (The Aliakmon)* [1986] AC 785.

[176] As noted by Lord Brandon in *The Aliakmon* at 812, that is the case even if its contract with A Ltd gives B Ltd a persistent right (see **B:4.4.3**).

[177] See *Benjamin's Sale of Goods* (7th edn, 2006), at 1-036: 'Many of the cases are inconclusive; and such dicta as there are are evenly balanced.'

money to A; it does *not* prevent B acquiring Ownership in other cases where A is under a contractual duty to make an immediate transfer of Ownership to B.[178]

(b) The need for specific goods

B:EXAMPLE 8a

A owns a bike shop. B orders a particular model of bike from A and pays the £200 price in advance. A then goes into insolvency. A's total liabilities are £100,000; the assets available to A to meet those liabilities are worth only £50,000.

In such a case, B cannot acquire a property right (see **B:4.5.1**). It is important to realise that this is not the result of a special rule about sales. Even if A were to use a deed, B would not acquire a property right: B can only acquire Ownership once A has exercised his power to give a *particular* property right to B (see **1.1** above).[179] So, if A's trustee in bankruptcy sells off A's whole stock of bikes and uses the money to pay A's general creditors, that trustee in bankruptcy does not commit a wrong against B.[180]

(c) Specifying particular goods

In many sales, as in **B:Example 8a**, A's duty to B does not *initially* relate to any specific thing. In such a case, A can be said to be under a duty in relation to 'unascertained goods'.[181] If everything goes as planned, A's duty will, at some point, relate to specific goods: at that point, B can acquire A's Ownership of those goods. In a case such as **B:Example 8a**, this will clearly occur when A delivers a particular bike to B. However, it may occur at an earlier stage: the question is whether A has made an *irrevocable* choice to transfer his Ownership of a *specific* thing to B so that A's duty now relates to that specific thing. If A has done so, that thing can be said to be 'appropriated to the contract': it is then possible for B to acquire Ownership of that specific thing.[182]

For example, in *Carlos Federspiel & Co v Charles Twigg & Co Ltd*,[183] B Co (a Costa Rican company) ordered a number of bikes from A Ltd (a company based in Wales). At that stage, A Ltd's duty did not relate to any specific bikes. A Ltd, in attempting to fulfil B Co's order, packed the required number of bikes into boxes marked with B Co's address. However, before those boxes left A Ltd's premises, A Ltd hit financial problems. Parties holding pre-existing security rights over A Ltd's assets enforced their rights by appointing C as a receiver—someone to manage A Ltd's rights for the benefit of the secured parties (see **F4:5.2**).

The question was whether, *before* the receiver was appointed, A Ltd had transferred its

---

[178] A contrary argument would be that, in any case where B acquires Ownership as a result of A's contractual duty to B, the set of rules applied by the Sale of Goods Act 1979 are indispensable (especially in governing practical questions such as what happens if the thing sold is damaged; or if B fails to perform his duty to A). However, that view is somewhat dubious: the rules in the 1979 Act are derived in large part from the Sale of Goods Act 1893, which in turn was based largely on judge-made rules: those original judge-made rules could apply to, for example, a barter transaction.

[179] See Sale of Goods Act 1979, ss 16 and 17(1).

[180] See eg *Carlos Federspiel v Charles Twigg* [1957] 1 Lloyd's Rep 240.

[181] 'Unascertained goods' are any goods falling outside the definition of 'specific goods' given by Sale of Goods Act 1979, s 61(1).

[182] The exact time at which B acquires Ownership will of course depend on the parties' intention, as expressed in the contract: see Sale of Goods Act 1979, s 17(1). The default rule, applying if there is no such intention, is that B acquires Ownership when the appropriation occurs: s 18, rule 5(1).

[183] [1957] 1 Lloyd's Rep 240.

Ownership of the specific bikes in the boxes to B Co. If so, B Co had a property right in those bikes and C would therefore commit a wrong if, for example, it sold the bikes and used the proceeds to pay the secured parties. If not, C, as receiver, was free to sell off the bikes; B Co would then be left with a personal claim, for breach of contract, against A Ltd.[184]

Pearson J held that B Co had *not* acquired Ownership of the bikes in the boxes. Although A Ltd clearly intended to deliver those bikes to B Co, A Ltd was not yet under a duty to do so: it was not too late for A Ltd to change its mind.[185] It would have been easy, for example, for A Ltd to write a new address on the boxes and send the bikes to a different customer. As a result, B Co had no pre-existing property right that could bind C. This decision shows that if: (i) A Ltd agrees to sell unascertained goods to B; and (ii) A Ltd has not yet given physical control of any specific goods to B, or to someone deputed to carry those goods to B;[186] then (iii) it can be very difficult for B to acquire Ownership.

(d) Sales from an identified bulk

A tricky problem arises if A has a warehouse that contains 1,000 bikes and makes a contractual promise to sell B 100 bikes *from the stock of 1,000 bikes currently in the warehouse*. Strictly speaking, B cannot acquire Ownership of any particular bikes: A is not under a duty in relation to a specific group of 100 bikes. However, to some extent, particular things have been identified: we know that B's bikes will come from the 1,000 bikes in the warehouse. Parliament has intervened in this situation to allow B, if he has paid for the bikes, to acquire a property right (see **F2:2.2**).[187] B will not acquire Ownership of any particular 100 bikes, but B can become a Co-Owner of *all* 1,000 bikes in the warehouse.[188] This means that A's Ownership of those 1,000 bikes is shared between A and B as tenants in common (see **F2:1.2**)—B with a 10 per cent share, A with a 90 per cent share.

This solution is *not* inconsistent with the fundamental rule that all property rights must relate to a specific thing. The Co-Ownership approach allows B to have a property right that relates to *all* 1,000 bikes in the warehouse. However, the particular statutory solution applies only where there is a sale. So if: (i) A makes a promise in a deed to give B Ownership of 100 of the 1,000 bikes currently in the warehouse; and (ii) B does not pay money or promise to pay money in return; then (iii) B will *not* acquire a property right.[189] The point seems to be that, due to the needs of practical convenience, B deserves extra protection in a sale.

It is important to note the limits on when B can qualify for this extra statutory protection. In particular, A must have promised to give B goods *from a specific set of goods*. So, the statutory rule is of no assistance to B in cases such as **B:Example 8a** or *Carlos Federspiel & Co.*[190] Nor will it always apply where A promises to give B goods from a specific

---

[184] As A Ltd had since gone into liquidation, that personal right was of little value to B.

[185] Pearson J noted that at 256 that A Ltd had not yet performed the 'important and decisive' act of handing the goods over to a carrier for transport to B.

[186] For example, in *Carlos Federspiel*, the result would have been different if A Ltd had delivered the bikes to a carrier to ship to B: see eg Sale of Goods Act 1979, s 18, rule 5(2).

[187] This requirement is set out by the Sale of Goods Act 1979, s 20A, inserted by the Sale of Goods (Amendment) Act 1995.

[188] See the Sale of Goods Act 1979, s 20A.

[189] B acquires such a right if A *expressly* states, in the deed, that A and B are to be Co-Owners of all the bikes in the warehouse; however, in a sale, the s 20A rule applies even if A and B's contract does not express that intention.

[190] For the same reason, the rule does not assist B in cases such as *re Goldcorp's Exchange* [1995] 1 AC 74: at 91, Lord Mustill noted that A did not promise to give B goods from a specific bulk.

warehouse. If the promise does not impose a duty on A to give B goods from the specific set of goods *currently* in the warehouse, but rather means that B's goods will come from whatever goods *happen* to be in the warehouse in the future,[191] A's duty to B does not relate to a specific set of goods.

(e) Justification

Where: (i) A's intention to transfer Ownership is coupled with a deed, or B's physical control of the thing in question; then (ii) *publicity* and *evidence* of B's right is provided; and (iii) to a lesser degree, *caution* is promoted and A is given some *protection from fraudulent claims*. However, things seem to be very different when we turn to a sale. The fact that B is giving money (or a binding promise to pay money) in return allows B to acquire A's Ownership without the need for a deed or for delivery. To explain this, we could note that there is less need to provide *evidence*; to *protect A from fraudulent claims*; and to promote *caution* where a sale is concerned. First, if B claims that A has sold him a bike, a court can test for this by looking for the factors involved in a sale—most obviously, payment or the promise of payment by B. Second, A may need less protection from a fraudulent claim of a sale, or a rash decision to make a sale: A is at least getting something in return.[192]

However, the chief reason for not insisting on a deed or delivery seems instead to be that, in this context, the disadvantages of such a requirement would simply be too great. For reasons of practical commercial convenience, B is allowed to acquire A's property right without a deed or delivery, *if* B pays money or promises to pay money in return for his right. For example, it may be that B wishes to immediately sell his right on to B2. In such a case, delivery to B would create a cumbersome extra stage in the transaction; and the execution of a deed by A would increase the cost and time involved in the transaction.

This leads us back to **Example 19d**. On the one hand, it could be said that: (i) such a case is far rarer than a case where B pays, or promises to pay, money in return for A's Ownership of a thing; so (ii) there is no pressing commercial need to allow B to acquire A's Ownership without a deed or delivery. On the other hand it could be said that the key distinction is between: (i) cases where A makes a promise, or expresses an intention, without receiving anything in return from B; and (ii) cases where B gives something in return, *whether or not it is money*. So, in the first set of cases, a deed must be used: a gratuitous promise by A to B, like a gratuitous attempt to transfer A's Ownership to B unaccompanied by delivery, cannot succeed. But, in the second set of cases, a promise by A to B, like an attempt to transfer A's Ownership to B, *can* succeed. On this view, the needs of practical convenience allowing a sale to transfer A's Ownership are the very same needs that allow a contractual bargain to be made orally. So, on this view, B can acquire A's Ownership *whenever* A is under a duty to immediately transfer that right to B even if, as in **Example 19d**, B has not paid, or promised to pay, money.

(f) The effects of a sale on C

The ability of B to acquire Ownership without a deed or delivery can cause problems. For example, where B acquires Ownership through a sale, a trap is laid for C. B may have acquired Ownership of A's bike even if: (i) no deed has been used; and even if (ii) A still has

---

[191] As may well be the case where A Ltd operates a business and the contents of the warehouse fluctuates over time.

[192] Although of course there is no requirement that B must pay a fair price.

physical control of the bike. There is a clear publicity problem for C: B's property right will be very hard for C to discover.

The problem is not so acute if C simply extends credit to A: after all, although C may be mistaken in his belief that A has Ownership of the bike, A will at least have acquired money, or the right to receive money, as a result of the sale: overall, A's assets may not be too badly depleted. The real problem for C arises if he attempts to acquire A's Ownership, reasonably believing that no one other than A has a property right in the bike. C is then in for a nasty shock if, after paying A or extending credit to A in return for a property right, B then asserts his pre-existing property right against C.

It is therefore important to realise that, in such a situation, the property law system *does* provide some protection to C. This protection does not come from the **acquisition question**: B *will* have Ownership even though no deed was used and A has kept physical control of the bike. Instead, C is given protection through the **defences question**: it is possible for him to have a defence against B's Ownership.

This defence comes from section 8 of the Factors Act 1889 and is confirmed by section 24 of the Sale of Goods Act 1979.[193] It is often known as the 'seller in possession' rule: we will examine it in **3.3.3** below. Section 8 of the Factors Act 1889 is important not only for what it does in this particular context, but also for the broader point it reveals. Rules concerning B's acquisition of a property right, like any rules within the property law system, have to be understood as part of a broader set of rules that aim to resolve the **basic tension** between B and C. So, whilst one part of the system may favour B (eg, the acquisition question, when applied to a sale of goods, allows B to acquire Ownership without the use of a deed or delivery), another part of the system may balance this by favouring C (eg, the defences question, when applied to a right acquired by B in a sale of goods, can give C protection against a hidden property right of B).

2.2.5 Transfer of ownership by way of security: special requirements

EXAMPLE 20

A has Ownership of a bike. A asks B for a loan of £200. B wants to acquire A's Ownership as security for A's duty to repay B; but A does not want to transfer physical control of the bike to B.

In such a case, we might think that A can keep physical control of the bike and transfer Ownership to B by means of a deed. However, in a case like **Example 20**, there is a real *publicity* problem for C. As B has acquired his right by way of security, B will only need to exercise his Ownership if A defaults on the loan. There is also a potential problem for A: he may be exploited by an unscrupulous lender, and lose his Ownership of the bike as a result. The property law system has responded to these two concerns by imposing not only a formality rule (the document used to transfer Ownership must be in a particular form, known as a 'security bill of sale') but also a *registration* requirement: the bill of sale has to be

---

[193] The formulation of the defence in the Sale of Goods Act 1979, s 24 is marginally narrower than that in the Factors Act 1889, s 8: the latter also protects C where he receives goods under 'any agreement for sale, pledge or other disposition thereof.'

registered.[194] If B fails to comply with *either* of those two requirements, he *cannot* acquire A's Ownership. We will examine these additional requirements in **F4:3.1.1(i)**.

SUMMARY of D1:2.2

B can acquire Ownership of a thing through a dependent acquisition:

1. A must have Ownership of a thing.
2. A must intend to transfer his Ownership of that specific thing to B.
3. A's intention must be coupled with one of three additional factors: a deed; delivery (ie, B's physical control of the thing); or sale (ie, B giving money or promising to pay money).

Each of a deed and delivery provides *publicity* and *evidence* as to B's right and, to a lesser degree, promotes *caution* and *protects A from a fraudulent claim*. A sale goes a little way to meeting those needs, but its real justification is to indicate a situation in which the need to facilitate commercial transactions means that a deed or delivery can be dispensed with. The difficulty C may face in discovering that B has acquired Ownership by means of a sale is recognised by the 'seller in possession' defence set out in section 8 of the Factors Act 1889.

Where A wishes to transfer Ownership to B by way of security, B can (in general) only acquire A's Ownership if: (i) his transaction with A is recorded in a particular form ('a security bill of sale'); and (ii) that document is registered. That requirement aims both to protect A from making a bad deal and to protect C from the risk of being bound by a hidden property right of B.

The fact that B can acquire a property right where a deed is used or a sale occurs suggests a wider principle: B acquires A's Ownership *whenever* A is under a duty to give B a right to immediate exclusive control of a specific thing forever. If that principle is correct, B should also acquire a property right where A is under a contractual duty to give B such a right even if, because B has not paid, or promised to pay, money in return, no sale occurs (see **Example 19d** above).

---

3 THE DEFENCES QUESTION

If B can satisfy the **content question** and the **acquisition question** attention then shifts to Question 3 of the **basic structure**: does C have a defence to B's pre-existing property right?

3.1 Introduction: the basic tension

It is often said that property rights 'bind the whole world'. This is simply not true. If B has a property right, the rest of the world is under a prima facie duty not to interfere with B's right to exclusive control of a thing. However, it is possible for C to have a defence to a property right (see **B:5**). If C has such a defence, he has a *liberty*, against B, to make a certain use of a thing owned by B. For example, in certain circumstances, a legal officer has

---

[194] See Bills of Sale Acts 1878 and 1882. The document is registered with a Master of the Queen's Bench Division. Different rules apply where A Co, a company, gives B Ownership by way of security but again B's right will, in practice, have to be registered: this time with the Registrar of Companies (see **3.6** below).

a statutory liberty to take a thing away from B.[195] Whilst B's Ownership is, prima facie, binding on the legal officer, the statute gives that officer a defence to B's right.

The defences question provides a different means of dealing with the **basic tension** between B and C. If B fails to satisfy the content question or the acquisition question, *all* third parties are protected from the risk of being bound by a pre-existing property right of B.[196] If B does satisfy these questions, but his property right is subject to a defence, then a *limited class* of third parties—those third parties who qualify for the defence—will be protected. So, by recognising a particular defence, the property law system can reconcile: (i) the need to give B a right that is prima facie binding on the rest of the world;[197] with (ii) the need to protect *certain* third parties.

A case where: (i) B has a pre-existing property right; and (ii) C has a defence to that right can be seen as the mirror image of a case where C is bound by a new, direct right of B. In the former situation, C is *not* under a duty to B because he is in the class of third parties who qualify for a defence. In the latter situation, C *is* under a duty to B because he is in the class of third parties who, due to their conduct, are subject to such a duty.

In this section, we will examine the principal defences that C can use against a pre-existing property right in a thing other than land. Our focus will be on the **basic situation**: (i) C acquires a right relating to a thing from A; and (ii) B attempts to assert his pre-existing property right against C.

3.2 The consent defence

B's consent to C's conduct can clearly give C a defence to B's pre-existing property right. If B permits C to use B's bike for an afternoon, C has a defence to B's pre-existing property right (see **B:5.1**). B's consent can also be important when considering the **basic situation**. For example, let us say C wishes to acquire Ownership of a bike that is in the physical control of A. B claims to have Ownership of the bike; but A disputes B's claim. One option for C is to: (i) buy the bike from A (thereby acquiring A's Ownership of the bike); and (ii) to persuade B (perhaps by paying B) to consent to C acquiring A's right free from any pre-existing property right of B. If B gives that consent, C has a defence to any such right of B.[198]

---

[195] See eg Police and Criminal Evidence Act 1984, ss 19 and 22.

[196] In such a case, a third party may be bound by a direct right of B: but, of course, such a new, direct right is distinct from B's pre-existing right.

[197] A good example is provided by the 'seller in possession' defence provided by the Factors Act 1889, s 8 and discussed in **2.2.4(iii)(f)** above.

[198] See eg Sale of Goods Act 1979, s 21(1): 'Subject to this Act, where goods are sold by a person who is not their owner, and who does not sell them under the authority or with the consent of the owner, the buyer acquires no better title to the goods than the seller had, unless the owner of the goods is by his conduct precluded from denying the seller's authority to sell.' So, in our example, A transfers his Ownership to C 'under the authority or with the consent of' B and so C has a defence to B's pre-existing property right. The use of the phrase 'the owner' in the statute is very unhelpful: in this context, it simply means a party whose Ownership arose before that of the seller of the goods (B in our example).

3.3 'Apparent power' defences[199]

> ### EXAMPLE 21
>
> B has Ownership of a bike. B lends the bike to A, a friend. B knows that A, who is untrust-worthy and short of money, may well try to raise some money by selling the bike to a third party and keeping the proceeds. A does indeed sell the bike to C, who buys in good faith and without notice of B's right.

A independently acquired Ownership by taking physical control of the bike. A then trans-ferred that right to C. C is prima facie bound by B's pre-existing property right. C cannot use the consent defence as B has not consented to C's use of the bike. However, C can argue that he should have a defence: B has created a situation in which it was reasonable for C to believe that A had a power to transfer Ownership of the bike free from any pre-existing property right. C can argue that, in such a case, the **basic tension** should be resolved in his favour. A similar situation arises where, in contrast to **Example 21**: (i) C *is* aware of B's pre-existing property right; but (ii) C reasonably believes that B has given A a power to give B a property right free from B's pre-existing right (see eg **Example 23** below). In each case, C has relied on A's *apparent power* to give C a property right free from B's pre-existing right. However, in **Example 21**, C will *not* have a defence to B's Ownership of the bike. There is no *general* principle that C has a defence *whenever* C reasonably believes that A has a power to give C a right free from any pre-existing property right. In particular, the fact that B may have acted carelessly in giving physical control of the bike to A is irrelevant: by itself, that carelessness does not give C a defence.[200] Instead, there are certain, *limited* defences that may be available to C *if* specific requirements are satisfied. In each case, the specific requirements of the defence reflect the need to resolve the **basic tension** by balancing the needs of B and C.

3.3.1 Estoppel

(i) Evidential Estoppel

> ### EXAMPLE 22a
>
> B has Ownership of a bike. X, B's son, owes money to C. B owes money to Z. B is worried Z may obtain a court order allowing Z to: (i) take physical control of B's bike; (ii) sell the bike; and (iii) use the proceeds to meet B's debt to Z (see **B:2.3.1**). B therefore tells C that the bike belongs to X, not to B. B does not realise that C already has a court order allowing him to: (i) take physical control of X's bike; (ii) sell it; and (iii) use the proceeds to meet C's debt to X. On the strength of that court order, C takes physical control of the bike and sells it.

The court order in his favour does *not* give C a liberty to take physical control of B's bike. And C cannot rely on the consent defence: B did not give his consent to C's action; he simply told C that the bike belonged to X. However, C *does* have a defence to B's pre-existing

---

[199] See Goode, *Commercial Law* (3rd edn, 2004), ch 16 for a detailed consideration of the defences gathered together in this section. Goode categorises these defences as distinct exceptions to the *nemo dat* rule. That rule is considered in **3.5.1** below.

[200] As confirmed by the House of Lords in *Moorgate Mercantile Co Ltd v Twitchings* [1977] AC 890.

property right. C relied on B's representation by taking physical control of the bike and selling it. As a result, B can be prevented from asserting his property right against C.[201] This means that B *cannot* claim that C, when taking control of the goods, committed a wrong against B. The key points here are: (i) B made a clear representation to C; and (ii) C relied on that representation; and (iii) C would suffer a detriment if B were allowed to deny the truth of that representation. As a result, B is *'estopped'* (ie, stopped or prevented) from denying the truth of his representation that he did not have Ownership of the bike.

This use of estoppel is not unique to the property law system. It is based on a wider concept[202] (often referred to as 'estoppel by representation') [203] that is essentially a rule of evidence (and so can be called *evidential estoppel*).[204] It prevents B from denying a fact if:

- B makes a representation (by words or conduct) about an existing state of affairs; *and*
- C reasonably relies on that representation; *and*
- C would suffer a detriment if B were allowed to deny the truth of his representation.

In **Example 22a**, the fact B is prevented from denying is that he does not have a property right in the bike. Therefore, strictly speaking, evidential estoppel does *not* give C a distinct defence to B's property right. Instead, it can assist if the state of affairs B is prevented from denying means that: (i) B has no property right; or (ii) C has a defence to B's property right. In fact, evidential estoppel can also be used to assist a party in asserting a right—even in asserting a property right.

EXAMPLE 22b

B1 has a warehouse full of bikes. B1 promises to sell 10 bikes to B2. No specific bikes are identified and B2 does not pay B1 in advance. B2 agrees to sell five of those bikes on to C. C pays B2. C asks B1 to confirm that he has physical control of five specific bikes that now belong to C. B1 does so. As a result, C does not press B2 to hand over any bikes to C. B2 then goes bankrupt.

C wants to show he has Ownership of five specific bikes held by B1. On the actual facts of the case, that is impossible: (i) B2 did not acquire Ownership of any *specific* bikes from B1; so (ii) B2 cannot have transferred any such right to C.[205] Nonetheless, evidential estoppel can come to C's rescue:

- B1 made a representation about an existing state of affairs (that he had set aside five *specific* bikes); and
- C relied on that by not taking further steps against B2; and
- C will suffer a detriment if B1 is allowed to deny his representation.

---

[201] See eg the American case of *Horn v Cole* 51 NH 287 (Supreme Court of New Hampshire), on which **Example 22a** is based. For English authority, see eg *Pickard v Sears* (1837) 6 Ad & El 469, esp *per* Lord Denman CJ at 474.

[202] See eg *Pickard v Sears* (1837) 6 Ad & El 469.

[203] This form of estoppel has a variety of (largely unhelpful) names: eg estoppel *in pais*; Common Law estoppel.

[204] See eg *per* Lindley LJ in *Low v Bouverie* [1891] 3 Ch 82 at 101; *per* Viscount Haldane in *London Joint Stock Banking Ltd v Macmillan* [1918] AC 777 at 818: 'It is rather a rule of evidence, capable not the less…of affecting gravely substantive rights.'

[205] Nor can the Sale of Goods Act 1979, s 20A assist C: B2 did not pay for the goods in advance.

As a result, evidential estoppel prevents B1 from denying that he set aside those bikes. That means that C *can* assert a right against B1: *as between B1 and C,* a court does not apply the true facts; instead, it works on the assumption that B1 *did* set aside the bikes. On that assumption, C *does* have Ownership of five specific bikes held by B1. This is confirmed by the decision of the Court of Queen's Bench in *Knights v Wiffen,*[206] the essential facts of which are identical to **Example 22b**. However, this does not mean that C has *really* acquired a property right in any bikes:[207] for example, if X burned down B1's warehouse, he would not commit a wrong against C. The evidential estoppel operates only against B1: it prevents B1 denying a particular fact and, as a result, it prevents B1 denying that C has acquired a property right.

Evidential estoppel can apply even if B does not make a statement to C. For example, if in **Example 22a**: (i) B knew of C's belief that the bike belonged to X; and (ii) B, to C's knowledge, stood by whilst C took control of the bike; then (iii) B's conduct may also prevent him from asserting his property right against C.[208] However, in **Example 21**, C cannot rely on evidential estoppel. In that case, B simply lent the bike to A: it would be implausible to say that, by doing so, B can be taken to represent *to C* that B has no pre-existing property right in the bike.[209]

(ii) Defensive estoppel

The evidential estoppel principle requires B to make a representation about an *existing state of affairs*. If B instead makes a commitment to act in a particular way *in the future*, that particular principle cannot apply. However, a different form of 'estoppel' may apply. There is a general principle that C will have a defence to a right of B if:

- B makes a commitment to C (by his words or conduct) that B will not assert a particular right against C; *and*
- C reasonably relies on that commitment; *and*
- C will suffer a detriment if B does not honour his commitment to C.

This principle can be used only to give C a defence against B's right. It is thus a *defensive estoppel*: it is often referred to as 'promissory estoppel'[210] or 'equitable estoppel'[211] or, from a case famously applying it, '*High Trees*' estoppel.[212] It is not exclusive to the property law system but can also be used, for example, to prevent B (for a time at least) asserting a personal right against C. The logic of the defence is that B cannot assert his right against C until C has had the chance to remove any detriment he may suffer as a result of B asserting that right. This means that C's defence may only be temporary: a court may simply prevent B from asserting his right for a set period.[213]

---

[206] (1879) LR 5 QB 660.

[207] As noted by eg Cooke, *The Modern Law of Estoppel* (2000), 120.

[208] See eg *Pickard v Sears* (1837) 6 Ad & El 469.

[209] See eg *Moorgate Mercantile Co Ltd v Twitchings* [1977] AC 890. For examination of the difficult issue of precisely when B's failure to speak out can give C the estoppel defence see Cooke, *The Modern Law of Estoppel* (2000), 26–32.

[210] One of the best discussions of the principle is in Peel, *Treitel's Law of Contract* (12th edn, 2007), 3.076-3.099. At 3-090 the misleading nature of the name 'promissory estoppel' is pointed out.

[211] That name is also potentially misleading: as we will see in E4, proprietary estoppel, another creation of courts of Equity, is very different from the defensive estoppel we are considering here.

[212] *Central London Property Trust Ltd v High Trees House Ltd* [1947] KB 310.

[213] See eg *Tool Metal Manufacturing Co Ltd v Tungsten Electric Co Ltd* [1955] 1 WLR 761.

3.3.2 The Factors Act 1889, section 2(1)

EXAMPLE 23

B has Ownership of a bike. B gives physical control of his bike to A, a dealer in second-hand bikes. B tells A to sell the bike, but only if he receives an offer of no less than £150. A then sells the bike to C for £100. C knows that B has a pre-existing property right in the bike, but honestly believes that A has the power to give C a right free from B's property right.

As A has physical control of the bike, A also has a property right in the bike. C acquires that right from A but, as C paid less than £150, B has not consented to C taking the bike free from B's pre-existing property right. Nonetheless, as confirmed by section 2(1) of the Factors Act 1889, C has a defence.[214] C's defence is based on A's apparent power to sell the bike to C free from B's pre-existing property right.

The defence applies where:

- A, with B's consent, has physical control of B's goods;[215] *and*
- A is a professional instructed by B to sell goods on B's behalf;[216] *and*
- A allows C to acquire a property right in the goods; *and*
- A does so is in the ordinary course of A's business; *and*
- C acquires his right in good faith, and has no notice that A did not have the necessary power to give C a right free from B's pre-existing property right.

The defence is based, in part, on the need to promote the ease of commercial transactions. However, the defence is carefully limited. For example, if A simply steals B's bike and sells it to C, C will *not* have a defence against B's right, even if he is a 'bona fide purchaser' (see **B:5.2.2(i)**). Similarly, let us say A runs a bike shop. B gives A physical control of B's bike in order to allow A to repair it; but A then sells the bike to C. In such a case, C will not have a defence.[217] A has physical control of the goods with B's consent; but B has *not* allowed A to take physical control of B's bike *for the purpose* of selling that bike.[218]

[214] In the term used by the Sale of Goods Act 1979, s 21(1) B is 'by his conduct precluded from denying' his apparent consent to C's acquisition of a right free from B's pre-existing property right. C's defence was recognised initially at common law: the various Factors Acts of the 19th century confirmed the defence and extended it to cases where A pledges goods to C, ie, where A does not transfer his Ownership to C but A instead allows C, by way of security for a duty owed to C, to take physical control of the goods.

[215] S 2(1) also applies if A, with B's consent, has a 'document of title' to the goods: the point of a document of title, such as a bill of lading, is that it represents the goods and so dealings with it can be used to transfer physical control of the goods: see **2.1.1(i)** above.

[216] The defence set out by the Factors Act 1889, s 2(1) applies only if A is a 'mercantile agent'. So if B had instead given his bike to a friend to sell for not less than £150 and that friend had sold the bike to C for £100, C would *not* have a defence against B's Ownership: see eg *Jerome v Bentley & Co* [1952] 2 All ER 114. A can, however, be a mercantile agent even if he does not run a business dealing in goods, but is instead authorised to sell B's goods on a single occasion: see eg *Lowther v Harris* [1927] 1 KB 393.

[217] That example is given by Goode, *Commercial Law* (3rd edn, 2004), 421.

[218] See *Astley Industrial Trust Ltd v Miller* [1968] 2 All ER 36, considering the meaning of the term 'with the consent of [B]' within the Factors Act 1889, s 2(1) and Goode, *Commercial Law* (3rd edn, 2004), 428 and (considering the common law basis of the requirement) at 420–21.

3.3.3 The Factors Act 1889, section 8

A has Ownership of a bike. On 1 June, A sells that bike to B. B immediately acquires Ownership of the bike but leaves the bike with A, intending to collect it later. On 3 June, A then sells the bike to C. C does not know of, and has no reason to know of, the previous sale to B. C collects the bike from A.

On 1 June, A's initial Ownership of the bike was transferred to B. As A kept physical control of the bike, A then independently acquires a new property right. On 3 June, A transfers that property right to C. B's pre-existing Ownership, acquired on 1 June, is prima facie binding on C. However, to protect C from B's hidden property right, section 8 of the Factors Act 1889 (confirmed by section 24 of the Sale of Goods Act 1979)[219] gives C a defence (as noted in **2.2.4(iii)(f)** above). That defence is often known as the 'seller in possession' defence. The defence applies where:

- A, despite having sold goods to B, has physical control of those goods; *and*
- A allows C to acquire a property right in the goods *or* makes an agreement to do so;[220] *and*
- A delivers the goods to C;[221] *and*
- C receives the goods in good faith and without notice of the sale to B.

There are important differences in the scope of: (i) section 2(1) of the 1889 Act; and (ii) section 8 of that Act. For example, C can rely on the latter defence: (i) even if A does not deal with C in the 'ordinary course of business'; and (ii) even if A is not a professional agent. This raises the possibility that C can rely on the defence even if A transfers his Ownership to C and C gives nothing in return.[222]

3.3.4 The Factors Act 1889, section 9

B has Ownership of a bike. On 1 June, B enters into a contract to sell the bike to A. Under the terms of that contract, A will not acquire B's Ownership until 30 June. However, B allows A to collect the bike immediately. On 3 June, A sells the bike to C. C does not know of, and has no reason to know of, the terms of A's contract with B.

By taking physical control of the bike, A independently acquires a new property right. On 3 June, A transfers that property right to C. B has kept his pre-existing Ownership of the bike: B's property right is prima facie binding on C. However, to protect C from B's hidden

---

[219] We will concentrate on s 8 as it slightly broader than the defence given by s 24 of the 1979 Act.

[220] S 8 refers to a 'sale, pledge or other disposition' or an 'agreement for sale, pledge or other disposition.' The reference to an 'agreement' (not included in Sale of Goods Act 1979, s 24) gives C a defence even if he takes delivery of the goods *before* acquiring his property right from A.

[221] C also has a defence if A delivers to C a 'document of title' to the goods: the point of a document of title, such as a bill of lading, is that it represents the goods and so dealings with it can be used to transfer physical control of the goods: see **2.1.1(i)** above.

[222] The s 24 defence can apply if C acquires his right by means of a 'sale, pledge or other disposition' from A: on the face of it, a gift does count as a disposition. Of course, a judge could find that, in the particular context of s 24, 'disposition' should be limited to transactions in which C gives value.

property right, section 9 of the Factors Act 1889 (confirmed by section 25 of the Sale of Goods Act 1979)[223] gives C a defence. That defence is often known as the 'buyer in possession' defence.

This defence applies where:

- B has sold goods to A or agreed to do so; *and*
- B allowed A to take physical control of those goods *before* A acquired B's Ownership of the goods;[224] *and*
- A allows C to acquire a property right in the goods *or* makes an agreement to do so;[225] *and*
- A delivers the goods to C; [226]
- C receives the goods in good faith and without notice of B's right.

SUMMARY of D1:3.3

In this section, we have considered a number of distinct defences that share important general features. The estoppel defences respond to the fact that, given B's representation or commitment, it is reasonable for C to believe that B has no pre-existing property right; or that B will not assert such a right against C. Each of the three statutory defences applies where B has chosen to allow A to have physical control of a thing. To that extent, B can be said to have created a situation in which it may be reasonable for C to think that, when acquiring his right, C will not be bound by a pre-existing property right of B. Each of the statutory defences also requires that C acts in good faith and without any notice of B's right. Those features, coupled with the general need to promote the ease of commercial transactions, seem to be crucial in resolving the basic tension in C's favour.[227]

However, it is vital to note the limits on these 'apparent power' defences. We can see this by returning to **Example 21**. In that case, C cannot use an estoppel defence: B has not made a representation or commitment to C that B does not have a property right in the bike. Nor can C use any of the Factors Act defences. First, the section 2(1) defence cannot apply: A is not a professional agent and B has not given A physical control for the purpose of allowing A to sell the bike. The section 8 defence cannot apply: A did not sell the bike to B and then keep physical control of it. And the section 9 defence cannot apply: A did not acquire the bike in the course of a sale from B to A. And, if C cannot rely on the specific 'apparent power' defences, C cannot appeal to a more general principle.

---

[223] Again we will concentrate on s 9 as it slightly broader than the defence given by s 25 of the 1979 Act.

[224] S 9 can also apply where B allows A to acquire physical control of a 'document of title' to the goods: this again creates the appearance that B has transferred his property right to A.

[225] The defence as set out in the Sale of Goods Act 1979, s 25 is slightly narrower because it does not apply in a case where A and C have reached only an agreement 'for sale, pledge or other disposition' at the point when C receives the goods.

[226] Delivery can occur as a result of A transferring a document of title to C.

[227] For a similar defence, applying only where C acquires a right in a motor vehicle, see Part III of the Hire-Purchase Act 1964 (see **F4:2.4.1(ii)**), discussed fully by Goode, *Hire-Purchase Law and Practice* (2nd edn, 1970), 617ff and Supplement.

3.4 The overreaching defence

EXAMPLE 26

B wishes to borrow some money from A. A refuses to make the loan unless B provides some security for B's performance of his duty to repay. B gives A security by: (i) allowing A to take physical control of B's bike; and (ii) giving A a power, if B defaults on the loan, to sell the bike and use the proceeds to meet B's debt. B does default on the loan and A sells the bike to C.

In such a case, the form of security given to A can be called a 'pledge' (see **F4:2.1.2**). In such a transaction: (i) B keeps his property right; and (ii) allows A to independently acquire a property right, by taking physical control of B's thing. So, can B assert his pre-existing property right against C?

The answer is 'No'. One analysis is that, when A sells to C, A transfers *B's* property right to C.[228] On that view, C's protection comes from the acquisition question: he has acquired B's pre-existing property right. An alternative view is that: (i) A transfers to C his own property right (arising as a result of A's physical control of B's bike); and (ii) under the terms of the pledge, A has the *power* to transfer A's Ownership to C free from B's pre-existing property right. Even if the terms of the pledge do not expressly give A that power, A must acquire it. A needs the security of knowing that, if B fails to perform his duty, A can raise funds by selling A's Ownership of the bike. In order to get a reasonable price, A needs to be able to sell the bike free from B's pre-existing property right.

On that second view, C's defence in **Example 26** is an example of the *overreaching defence*. This defence is based on A having a power to give C a right free from a pre-existing right of B.[229] Most examples of the defence involve C acquiring a right free from a pre-existing *persistent* right of B (see **D2:3.4** and **E2:3.4**). However, the logic of the defence extends to cases where A has a power to give C a right free from a pre-existing property right of B.[230]

3.5 The 'bona fide purchaser' defence

3.5.1 The general position

A:EXAMPLE 2

B owns a bike. A steals that bike and sells it to C. C, when buying the bike, honestly believes that it belongs to A.

D1:EXAMPLE 21

B has Ownership of a bike. B lends the bike to A, a friend. B knows that A, who is untrustworthy and short of money, may well try to raise some money by selling the bike to a third party and keeping the proceeds. A does indeed sell the bike to C, who buys in good faith and without notice of B's right.

---

[228] See eg *per* Lord Mersey in *The Odessa* [1916] 1 AC 145 at 159.

[229] See Harpum [1990] *CLJ* 277.

[230] A further example occurs where a party dies without making a valid will and his rights pass to A, his personal representative. Even if, under the administration of the estate, B has already acquired a property right, A has the power to give C a property right free from that pre-existing property right of B: see Administration of Estates Act 1925, s 39(1)(i).

In each case, C will acquire A's Ownership, but will have no defence to B's pre-existing property right. It makes no difference that C may be a 'bona fide purchaser' (see **B:5.2.2(i)**). C will *not* have a defence to B's pre-existing property right even if C acquired A's Ownership: (i) for value; and (ii) without any 'actual or constructive notice' of B's right. In such a situation, the **basic tension** is resolved in B's favour: it is C, rather than B, who is left to make a claim against A in an attempt to recover his losses.[231]

So, the general position is that C *cannot* use the 'bona fide purchaser' defence against a pre-existing property right. This solution to the basic tension is often said to depend on the principle of *nemo dat quod non habet*: no one gives what he does not have. However, that principle is not particularly helpful. It relates, if anything, to the **acquisition question** and states an obvious limit on the scope of dependent acquisition: A cannot transfer a right to C if A does not have that right in the first place. But we do not need to use Latin to express that obvious point. In fact, the implied comparison with Roman law may be distinctly unhelpful: in contrast to Roman law, in both **A:Example 2** and **D1:Example 21**, A does have *a* property right in the bike. By taking physical control of it, A independently acquires Ownership of the bike. A can then transfer that property right to C.

The crucial question, to which the *nemo dat* principle is irrelevant, is whether C has a **defence** to B's pre-existing property right. The answer is 'No'. But that conclusion is *not* demanded by logic or by the *nemo dat* principle: it is simply a consequence of the way in which the property law system chooses to resolve the basic tension between B and C.[232]

After all, we have already seen that, in some situations, C *can* have a defence to B's pre-existing property right: see eg **Example 22a** and **Examples 23–26** above. Such cases are often said to constitute exceptions to the *nemo dat* principle.[233] However, that explanation is misleading. The *nemo dat* principle simply means that A cannot give B something that A does not have. Apart from cases where A has a power to transfer B's right to C (eg, where A is B's agent and has B's authority to make such a transfer), there can be no exceptions to that principle. For example, in a case such as **Example 24**, section 8 of the Factors Act 1889 does *not* mean that A transfers B's pre-existing Ownership to C. Instead: (i) A transfers A's property right to C; and (ii) section 8 of the Act gives C a defence against B's pre-existing property right. So, the 'seller in possession' rule contained in section 8 is *not* an exception the *nemo dat* principle.

3.5.2 Justifying the general position

The 'bona fide purchaser' defence is generally available against a pre-existing *persistent* right of B (see **B:5.2.2(ii)**). It offers C valuable protection against the risk of being bound by a hidden persistent right. However, in practice, there is less need for C to have such a defence against a property right. Where B claims a property right, C's protection comes instead from the **content** and **acquisition questions**. The limited list of property rights, and the limited means by which they can be acquired, reduce the risk to C of being bound by a hidden property right of B.

---

[231] See eg *Farquarhson Bros and Co v King and Co* [1902] AC 325.

[232] For example, many other property law systems (eg, the French system and the German system) *do* give C a defence in a case such as **D1:Example 21**, if not in a case such as **A:Example 2.**

[233] See eg Goode, *Commercial Law* (3rd edn, 2004), ch 16.

Further, it may be self-defeating to allow the 'bona fide purchaser' defence to be generally available against a property right. We can see this by considering C's point of view. In **A:Example 2**, the defence would be useful to C. But what if A2 were then to steal C's bike and sell it to C2, a bona fide purchaser? If the defence were permitted, C2 would then have a defence to C's pre-existing Ownership of the bike. In that way, and to that extent, the very security that the 'bona fide purchaser' defence aims to give C would be undermined. C would simply be trading retrospective security (the ability to use the 'bona fide purchaser defence' against a pre-existing property right) for prospective insecurity (the risk that C's own property right could be defeated by a later 'bona fide purchaser' such as C2). In contrast, if C uses the 'bona fide purchaser' defence against a pre-existing *persistent* right of B, C does not face that problem: C's property right will not be vulnerable to a later 'bona fide purchaser'.[234]

Ultimately, a decision as to whether the general 'bona fide purchaser' defence should apply against a property right depends on a view about how best to resolve the **basic tension** between B and C. And this is an impossibly difficult question: as we noted when first looking at **A:Example 2**, there is no morally right answer in such a case. But the property law system must provide an answer. And the answer provided by the English property law system, whilst it is obviously not the only possible solution, has a certain logic. The need to promote the security of property rights means that a pre-existing property right is not, in general, subject to the 'bona fide purchaser' defence. However, the very security and usefulness of property rights is promoted if a bona fide purchaser of such a right is allowed a defence against a pre-existing *persistent* right. That defence allows a hierarchy to develop, with property rights sitting above persistent rights as more powerful. That hierarchy is consistent with the fact that, due to the limited list of property rights and the limited means by such a right can be acquired, a property right is harder to come by than a persistent right.

3.5.3 An exception to the general position: money

EXAMPLE 27

B has Ownership of a £50 note. The note is stolen from B and ends up in the hands of A. A spends a night in C's hotel and gives A the note as payment. When he receives the note, C does not know, and has no reason to suspect, that it has been stolen.

In such a case, C has a defence to B's pre-existing Ownership of the note: this was confirmed by the Court of King's Bench in *Miller v Race*,[235] the essential facts of which are identical to **Example 27**.[236] C has a defence because:

- B's pre-existing property right is Ownership of money;[237] *and*

---

[234] A similar argument may justify why a 'bona fide purchaser' of a *persistent* right has no defence against a pre-existing persistent right (see **D2:3.5.1**).

[235] (1758) 1 Burr 452.

[236] In *Miller v Race*, C delivered the note to the Bank of England and asked for payment but the Bank refused to pay: B had alerted the Bank to the theft and asked them not to pay out on the note. The court held that the Bank was under a duty to pay to C, not to B.

[237] The defence can also apply where C acquires A's Ownership of a document that entitles its holder to receive money from the State or a bank: see *Wookey v Pole* (1820) 4 A & B 1.

- C acquired A's Ownership of the money without any actual or constructive notice[238] of B's right; *and*
- C gave something to A in return for his right.[239]

If B has Ownership of a banknote and that note is stolen by A, B can clearly assert his property right against: (i) A; or (ii) A2, who steals the note from A; or (iii) C2, a third party to whom either thief gives the note as a gift; or (iv) C3, a third party who receives the note from either thief knowing or suspecting it to be stolen.[240] However, in **Example 27**, C, as a 'bona fide purchaser' of the note, has a defence to B's pre-existing property right.

The key point in **Example 27** is that B's property right is Ownership of *money*. In such a case, there are special reasons for resolving the basic tension in C's favour. Money is a universal means of exchange:[241] C, when receiving money from a customer, needs to know that he can accept that money as payment for the services or goods C has given to A. Hence, in this rare case, C can use the 'bona fide purchaser' defence against B's pre-existing property right.

EXAMPLE 27a

The facts are as in **Example 27**. C then uses the £50 note to pay C2 for drinks bought in C2's pub. C2 knows of the theft of B's note. C2 checks the £50 note before accepting it and recognises it as the note stolen from B.

EXAMPLE 27b

The facts are as in **Example 27**. A2 then steals the note from C.

In **Example 27a**, it seems that C2, despite recognising the £50 note before accepting it, also has a defence to B's pre-existing property right. C2 has that defence as C needs to be free to deal with the note without the risk of a later party, to whom C gives his Ownership of the note, being bound by B's pre-existing property right. This makes it tempting to say that the 'bona fide purchaser' defence *destroys* B's pre-existing property right. However, that may not be accurate: in **Example 27b**, there seems to be no good reason to prevent B asserting his pre-existing property right against A2, who has *not* acquired C's Ownership of the note.

3.5.4 Powers to acquire a property right

EXAMPLE 28

As a result of A's fraud, B transfers his Ownership of a bike to A (see eg **Example 6a** above). Before B exercises his power to rescind the transfer, A transfers his Ownership of the bike to C. C: (i) pays A for the bike; and (ii) when he acquires it, he does not know or have any reason to suspect that A acquired his Ownership through fraud.

---

[238] For the meaning of the term 'actual or constructive notice' see **D2:3.5.1**.

[239] C must give 'valuable and bona fide consideration' in return for the money: see *per* Lord Mansfield in *Miller v Race* (1758) 1 Burr 452 at 457.

[240] These examples show that the suggestion of Best J in *Wookey v Pole* (1820) 4 A & B 1 at 7 that 'possession alone must decide to whom [money] belongs' cannot be correct.

[241] See Mann, *The Legal Aspect of Money* (5th edn, 1991), 8: money is 'meant to serve as [a] universal means of exchange in the State of issue'. The current edition, by Proctor, of *Mann on the Legal Aspect of Money* (6th edn, 2005) takes a slightly different definition of money (eg 1.15–1.31); but still notes that 'Money can only serve its required function if it is intended to serve as the universal means of exchange in the State of issue' (1.35).

B's power to rescind the transfer to A gives B a power to acquire a property right: to regain his Ownership of the bike. In general, if A transfers his Ownership of the bike to C *before* B has exercised the power to rescind, B may *still* be able to exercise his power to rescind against C (see **1.4.5(i)** above). There are, however, limits on B's power. One such limit is that B *cannot* exercise his power to rescind against C if C is a 'bona fide purchaser'.[242] In such a case, C has an *immunity*: B cannot exercise his power against C (see **D2:1.1.3**). Therefore, in **Example 28**: (i) C acquires, via A, B's Ownership of the bike; and (ii) B has no power to regain that right from C.

However, **Example 28** is *not* a further exceptional case in which the 'bona fide purchaser' defence can be used against a pre-existing property right: B's power to acquire a property right is not, itself, a property right (see **1.4.5(i)** above). This means that if: (i) B has a power to regain a property right he has transferred to A;[243] and (ii) C then acquires that right from A as a 'bona fide purchaser'; then (iii) it is vital to know whether B exercised his power *before* C acquired C's right. If so, then B has a pre-existing property right; and C, even though he is a 'bona fide purchaser', has no defence to that right (see **3.5.1** above).[244] If not, then C, as he is a 'bona fide purchaser' has an immunity against B: B cannot exercise his power to regain the right against C.

Has B exercised his power *before* C acquires A's right?	Does B have a pre-existing property right when C acquires A's right?	Can B assert his power/right against C if C is a bona fide purchaser of A's right?
Yes	Yes	Yes
No	No	No

3.6 The lack of registration defence

EXAMPLE 29

A Co is a manufacturing company. To secure a loan from B, A Co transfers its Ownership of its manufacturing equipment to B. B allows A Co to retain physical control of that equipment, so A Co can continue to trade. B does not register its property right. C then makes a loan to A Co. A Co fails to repay both B and C and goes into insolvency.

In such a case, a dispute can arise between B and C (see **B:2.3**): (i) B wants to sell the equipment and to have first use of the proceeds to pay off A Co's debt to B; (ii) C may want A Co's liquidator to use the proceeds to pay off *all* A Co's creditors, without allowing B first use of that money. B has a pre-existing property right; but B's failure to register that right

---

[242] See eg *Lewis v Avery* [1972] 1 QB 198. Note that if B can show that he did not intend to transfer his property right to A at all (eg because he intended to transfer his property right to another party, and A pretended to be that party) then B keeps his Ownership *throughout*: B's initial property right never passes to A (see **2.2.2(i)** above). That means B can assert his property right against C even if C is a 'bona fide purchaser': see eg *Cundy v Lindsay* (1878) 3 App Cas 459; *Ingram v Little* [1961] 1 QB 31; *Shogun Finance Ltd v Hudson* [2004] 1 AC 919.

[243] The same analysis applies if B has a power to regain a persistent right or a personal right he transferred to A. If B exercises that power before A deals with C, then B will win against C as A simply has no right to give C. Where property rights are concerned, A, as a result of his physical control of the thing in question, *does* have an independently acquired property right to pass to C: as a result, B's protection comes from the fact that B's *pre-existing* property right is prima facie binding on C.

[244] C does have such a defence if B's property right is in *money* (see **3.5.3** above).

means that C will have a defence to B's pre-existing property right.[245] That defence can be used by a liquidator, administrator or creditor of A Co.[246] It means that, before deciding whether to extend credit to A Co, C can look in the Companies Register and know that he cannot be adversely affected by a security right that is not recorded there.

The extra protection a registration system can give to C is generally deemed to be unnecessary (see **C2:4**). The lack of registration defence is therefore reserved for circumstances in which it is felt that C is *particularly* in need of protection. **Example 29** is such a case: where A Co transfers Ownership of a thing to B by way of security, B's property right may remain hidden unless and until A Co fails to perform its duty to pay B. As the risk to C of being bound by a hidden property right of B is particularly high, the lack of registration defence is used to resolve the basic tension by protecting C.[247]

3.7   The limitation defence[248]

EXAMPLE 30

B has Ownership of a bike. A steals that bike from B and sells it to C. C: (i) pays for the bike; and (ii) does not know, or have any reason to suspect, that A stole the bike. 10 years later, B asserts his property right in the bike against C.

In such a case, C has a defence to B's property right, arising under section 2 of the Limitation Act 1980.[249] That defence arises because of B's failure, over a long period, to assert his right against C. This *limitation defence* is based on the general logic of limitation periods: whenever B has a right—whether it is a personal, persistent or property right—there are sound reasons for limiting the period in which B can assert that right. For example, if C breaches a contract with B, or commits a tort against B, B acquires a direct, personal right against C. The general position is that B has six years in which to assert his right: after that period, the Limitation Act 1980 gives C a defence.[250] The same period applies in our example: when C takes physical control of the bike, he breaches his duty not to interfere with B's right to exclusive control of the bike. C thus commits a tort (the Common Law wrong of conversion) against B, and so B has six years in which to make his claim.[251] If B fails to do so, C acquires a defence and B is prevented from asserting his pre-existing property right against C.

---

[245] Companies Act 1985, s 396(1)(c); replaced by Companies Act 2006, s 860(7)(6) from 1 October 2009.

[246] Companies Act 1985, s 395; replaced by Companies Act 2006, s 874 from 1 October 2009.

[247] Similarly, if A transfers Ownership of a ship or aircraft to B by way of security, C may be able to rely on the lack of registration defence if B fails to register his pre-existing property right: see Merchant Shipping Act 1995, Sch 1, para 7; Mortgaging of Aircraft Order 1972, SI 1972/1268.

[248] If B acquires a property right by way of security, special limitation rules apply under the Limitation Act 1980, s 20. The rules relating to B's ability to claim sums due to him and secured by his property right also apply where B has a Purely Equitable Charge and are discussed in **F4:4.4**. Where A has transferred a property right to B by way of security, A acquires a persistent right: an Equity of Redemption. In some circumstances, B can terminate that persistent right by 'foreclosing' it. Once B's power to foreclose arises, the Limitation Act 1980, s 20(2) gives B 12 years to exercise that power. That period does not begin to run if B has possession of the thing in question.

[249] The limitation period can run in C's favour because C acquired his right in good faith and so, under the Limitation Act 1980, s 4 C's conduct is not regarded as 'related to' A's theft. That section simply states that C needs to 'purchase the stolen chattel in good faith': there seems to be no requirement that C must give value or lack notice of B's right.

[250] See Limitation Act 1980, ss 2 and 5.

[251] Limitation Act 1980, s 2 (general time limited for actions based on a tort).

In fact, when it is used against a property right, the limitation defence has a dramatic effect: it not only gives C a defence, it also extinguishes B's right.[252] This extinction of B's right is very important. First, it means that, once the six-year period is up, C is able to give C2 a right without C2 being subject to a claim from B. Second, it means that, after the six-year period is up, B cannot assert a right against X even if X, for example, steals the bike from C.

If, as in **Example 30**, B's thing is stolen, then the six-year period does *not* begin to run immediately: certainly, A can never rely on the limitation defence.[253] Under section 4 of the Limitation Act 1980, the six-year period only starts to run when someone 'purchases the stolen [bike] in good faith'.[254] So, in **Example 30**, B has six years from the moment C acquires A's Ownership of the bike.[255] This means that if: (i) A steals B's bike in 2008; and (ii) A sells the bike to C, who buys in good faith, in 2009; then (iii) C, or anyone later acquiring a property right in the bike, will have a defence to B's right come 2015. So, if: (i) C keeps the bike for five years; and (ii) sells it to C2 in 2014; then (iii) B only has one year left in which to make a claim against C2.[256]

SUMMARY of D1:3

In the **basic situation**, it is very difficult for C to have a defence to a pre-existing property right. In particular, there is no general 'bona fide purchaser' defence: so if (i) A steals B's bike; and (ii) sells it to C, who acquires A's Ownership for value, and without knowing of or having any reason to suspect the theft; then (iii) C does *not* have a defence to B's pre-existing property right. That is the case no matter how careless B may have been in allowing the bike to be stolen.

However, it is possible for C to have a defence to B's pre-existing property right if:

1. B has given his *consent* to C acquiring a right free from B's property right; *or*
2. B is *estopped* from asserting his property right against C; *or*
3. The circumstances in which C acquired his right fall within the limited cases where a statutory defence is permitted, based on A's *apparent power* to give C a right free from B's pre-existing property right; *or*
4. A *in fact* has such a power, so that C can rely on the *overreaching defence*; *or*
5. C is a 'bona fide purchaser' from A of money in which B has a pre-existing property right; *or*
6. In one of the rare cases where the *lack of registration defence* applies (eg, where A Co

---

[252] Limitation Act 1980, s 3(2). In contrast, a contract claim or a tort claim not based on the assertion of a pre-existing property right is not extinguished by the lapse of time: rather, B is simply prevented from bringing a claim to enforce the right. For example, if X pays money to B more than six years after he was contractually obliged to, X cannot recover that money when he realises that he paid after the limitation period was up: B is not unjustly enriched by the receipt of the money as, at that time, B did still have a right against X: see *per* Lord Mansfield in *Moses v Macferlan* (1760) 2 Burr 1005 at 1012 (see **D4:Example 8a**).

[253] So, in **Example 30**, the fact that C can use the limitation defence and that B's property right, as a result, no longer exists does *not* prevent B bringing a claim against A based on the personal right B acquired against A as a result of A's theft of what was, at the time, B's bike.

[254] Limitation Act 1980, s 4(2).

[255] Limitation Act 1980, s 4.

[256] The same is true even if C2, after five years, stole the bike from C: as far as B is concerned, the limitation clock continues to run so B only has one year in which to bring a claim against C2: see Limitation Act 1980, s 4(1). Of course, the limitation clock does not run on C's claim against C2.

gives B a property right by way of security), and B has failed to register his property right; *or*

7. B has failed to assert his right over a long period, so that C can rely on the *limitation defence.*

The scope of any defence to a pre-existing property right depends ultimately on the resolution of the **basic tension** between B and C. And, as that basic tension is impossibly difficult to resolve, it is impossible to work out, from first principles, when C *should* have a defence. A property law system simply needs to develop a set of workable, internally consistent rules. In English law, and systems based on it, the property law system has made a clear general decision in favour of protecting B's pre-existing property right.

4 THE REMEDIES QUESTION

4.1 Preface: the protection of property rights

4.1.1 Wrongs

(i) The general position

Before looking at the remedies a court may give to protect B's property right, we first need to look at the means by which B can assert such a right. For example, let us say A has stolen B's bike and sold it to C (see eg **A:Example 2**). We know that, even if C is a 'bona fide purchaser', C has no defence to B's pre-existing Ownership of the bike. However, B cannot assert his right by going to court and simply saying 'The bike is mine.' In Roman law, it *was* possible for B to do so: by means of a 'vindicatio' action, B could directly assert his property right. However, the English property law system simply does not include that particular, direct means of asserting a property right. Instead, B has to assert his property right indirectly,[257] by showing that: (i) B has a property right to which C has no defence; so (ii) C is under a duty to B; and (iii) C has breached that duty by interfering with B's thing (see **B:4.2** and **1.3.3** above).

At first glance, this indirect method of protecting property rights may seem strange. However, it is easy to defend. First, there is a sound conceptual reason for the lack of such a direct claim. To directly assert a property right, B would need to go to court and say 'That thing is mine.' However, a property right is a form of background right (see **1.1.1(i)** above). B can no more go to court and only say 'That thing is mine' than he can go to court and only say 'I have a right to physical integrity.'[258]

Second, in practice, the lack of a direct means of asserting his property right causes no problems for B. This is because, assuming C has no defence to B's property right, *any*

---

[257] An alternative for B is to bypass the courts entirely and rely on 'self-help' by retaking physical control of his bike from C. As B has a pre-existing property right to which C has no defence, B is *not* under a duty not to interfere with C's exclusive control of the bike, and so commits no wrong against C if he retakes the bike. However, such self-help is always risky: for example, B still has a duty not to interfere with C's physical integrity and so does commit a wrong if he uses unreasonable force in retaking the bike.

[258] It is possible for B to make a direct claim to a property right as part of an *interpleader* proceeding (see **Example 35** below). However, such a proceeding cannot be initiated by B: it must be initiated by the party controlling the thing (eg, in **Example 35**, the police force that seized the car).

non-trivial interference[259] by C with that right will count as a wrong—as a result, the law of wrongs can provide complete protection for B's right (see **1.3.3** above).[260]

Third, even if the property law system were to allow B to directly assert his property right, there would *still* be a need to protect that right through the law of wrongs. For example, if: (i) A steals B's bike and sells it to C (see eg **A:Example 2**); and (ii) the bike is then destroyed; then (iii) it is no longer possible for B to find the bike and claim 'That's mine.' Instead, B will need to rely on the law of wrongs to assert a right against A or C. So: (i) the law of wrongs *must* be involved in the protection of property rights; and (ii) the law of wrongs can give full protection to B's property right; then (iii) there is simply no need to recognise an action that allows B directly to assert his property right.

(ii) Which wrong?

There is no single wrong that protects B's property right.[261] Instead, B's property right is protected through three distinct, but overlapping, wrongs: trespass, conversion and negligence (see **1.3.3** above). This may not be very rational: it is a product of the peculiar history of the English law of wrongs. However, in practice, this causes no problems for B. If: (i) C has breached his duty not to interfere with B's thing; but (ii) B is unsure precisely which wrong C has committed; then (iii) B, when making a claim against C, can allege that C has committed each of the three wrongs, and then rely on the court to decide which of the specific wrongs C has committed. Further, it is possible to distinguish between the three wrongs:

Wrong	Duty breached by C	Example
Trespass	Not to deliberately and directly interfere with B's exclusive control of a thing	C takes B's bike from B
Conversion	Not to deliberately interfere with B's right to exclusive control of a thing[262]	C buys B's bike from A, who stole the bike from B
Negligence	Not to carelessly damage B's thing	C, driving carelessly, runs over B's bike

---

[259] For example, if C, in taking his bike from a rack, has to move B's bike out of the way, and no damage is caused to B's bike as a result, C certainly does not commit the wrong of conversion (see eg *Fouldes v Willoughby* (1841) 8 M & W 540) and should not be viewed as comitting the wrong of trespass (compare the approach to trespass to the person adopted by Goff LJ in *Collins v Wilcock* [1984] 1 WLR 1172, 1178: see *Clerk and Lindsell on Torts* (19th edn, 2006), 17–123).

[260] In the past, this was not always the case. For example, until the Law Reform (Miscellaneous Provisions) Act 1934, any tort claim against C died with C. As a result, B would sometimes have to try to protect his property right through a different action, such as one possibly based not on C's wrong but rather on C being unjustly enriched at B's expense: see eg *Hambly v Trott* (1776) 1 Cowp 371; *Phillips v Homfray* (1883) 24 Ch D 439.

[261] Torts (Interference with Goods) Act 1977, s 1 uses the term 'wrongful interference with goods' but this does not refer to a single wrong. Rather it is used to cover: (i) conversion; (ii) trespass to goods; (iii) negligent damage to goods; and (iv) 'any other tort so far as it results in damage to goods or to an interest in goods' (including a claim made under the Consumer Protection Act 1987).

[262] See further **(iii)** below. In *Kuwait Airways Corpn v Iraqi Airways Co (Nos 4 & 5)* [2002] 2 AC 883 at [39], Lord Nicholls states that C commits the wrong of conversion against B only if his conduct is 'so extensive an encroachment on the rights of [B] as to exclude from use and possession of the goods'. It is clear that a temporary

So, to determine which particular wrong has been committed, we can ask:

1. Was C's conduct deliberate or accidental?
    —If deliberate, go to 2;
    —If accidental, go to 3.
2. Did C's conduct directly interfere with B's exclusive control?
    —If Yes, C has committed the wrong of trespass;
    —If No, C has committed the wrong of conversion.
3. Did C act carelessly and damage B's thing?
    —If Yes, C has committed the wrong of negligence;
    —If No, C has *not* committed a wrong against B.

In applying these tests, we need to remember that C's conduct is 'deliberate' if C chooses to carry out a particular act, even if C does not realise that, by acting in that way, he is in breach of a duty to B (see **Examples 2a and 2b** above). Therefore, C's action need only be 'deliberate' in the sense that C does intend to use the thing in question; it does not need to be 'deliberate' in the sense of 'done with knowledge of B's property right in that thing'.

In this sense, trespass and conversion are 'strict liability' wrongs.[263] As a result, they are often thought to be anomalous. This view overlooks the fact that trespass and conversion operate in the same way as *all* wrongs committed by C's deliberate interference with a background right of B.[264] For example, if C kisses B, mistakenly believing that B wants him to do so, C interferes with B's background right to physical integrity and hence commits a wrong against B. Similarly, if C interferes with B's background right to B's reputation by making an untrue factual statement about B, C can commit the wrong of defamation even if C honestly believes the fact to be true.[265] So, the 'strict liability' imposed by the wrongs protecting property rights is *not* anomalous.

(iii) The scope of conversion

EXAMPLE 31

B has Ownership of a bike. B makes a contractual promise to A to allow A to have exclusive control of the bike for the next six months. A takes physical control of the bike. C then steals the bike from A.

By taking physical control of the bike, A acquires a property right. By directly interfering with A's exclusive control of the bike, C commits the wrong of trespass against A. On the definition of conversion set out in the table above, C also commits the wrong of conversion against *both* A *and* B.

---

exclusion will count: see eg *Howard E. Perry v British Railways Board* [1980] 1 WLR 1375. The limit noted by Lord Nicholls may well serve simply to ensure that C is not liable for a trivial interference causing no damage to B: see **n 259** above.

[263] The wrong of negligence also imposes a form of strict liability. For example, if C juggles with B's vase and breaks it, C breaches his duty to B *even if* he honestly believed that he (C) was the only person with a property right in the vase.

[264] This argument, and the specific examples it considers, is based on Stevens, *Torts and Rights* (2007): see esp 100–02.

[265] See eg *E Hulton & Co v Jones* [1910] AC 20.

However, on the orthodox definition of conversion, C does *not* commit the wrong of conversion against B.[266] The definition of conversion given here thus differs from the orthodox definition of conversion. On that orthodox view: (i) C only commits conversion against B if he interferes with B's right to immediate control of a thing; and (ii) due to B's contract with A, B does not have such a right to immediate control.

In practice, this difference is irrelevant. It is clear that C *does* commit a wrong against B in **Example 31**.[267] The difference consists simply of how to *define* that wrong: on the view taken here, it is conversion; on the orthodox view, it is a different wrong known as 'reversionary injury'.[268] Hence, there is no disagreement as to the result in a case such as **Example 31**. The view taken in this book is motivated by: (i) the desire to avoid having yet another wrong involved in the protection of property rights;[269] and, more importantly (ii) a rejection of the view that, in **Example 31**, B has no right to immediate control of the bike. That view was taken by the Court of King's Bench in *Gordon v Harper*,[270] a case raising the same question as **Example 31**; but the court's reasoning in that case is flawed.

The key point in **Example 31** is that, when C takes control of the bike, B has Ownership of the bike and so *does* have a right to immediate exclusive control of the bike. B's contract with A does not deprive him of that right: it simply gives A a personal right against B. So: (i) B keeps his Ownership; and (ii) A acquires Ownership by taking physical control of the bike. The wrong of conversion can then protect *each of* A and B because *each* of A and B has Ownership: a right to immediate exclusive control of the bike forever.

EXAMPLE 32

A has Ownership of a bike. A makes a contractual promise to B to allow B to have exclusive control of the bike for the next six months. Before B takes physical control of the bike, C steals the bike from A.

In such a case, on the orthodox view of conversion, it *could* be argued that C commits a wrong against B: when C took the bike, B had a right to exclusive control of the bike. Indeed, in *Iran v Bakarat Galleries Ltd*,[271] the Court of Appeal suggested that, in a case such as **Example 32**, C *does* commit the wrong of conversion against B. However, that statement: (i) played no part in the actual decision in that case; and (ii) is unsupported by authority.[272] We saw when examining **Examples 5b and 5c** that A's contractual promise to B does *not*

---

[266] See eg Tettenborn [1994] CLJ 326; Bridge, *Personal Property* (3rd edn, 2002), 71; *Clerk and Lindsell on Torts* (19th edn, 2006), 17–40.

[267] See eg *Mears v London & South Western Railway Co* (1862) 11 CB (NS) 850; *Tancred v Allgood* (1859) 4 H & N 438.

[268] See eg Bridge, *Personal Property* (3rd edn, 2002), 71; *Clerk and Lindsell on Torts* (19th edn, 2006), 17–138ff.

[269] Bridge, *Personal Property* (3rd edn, 2002), 71 notes that the wrong of 'reversionary injury' is 'close to being swallowed up whole by conversion'.

[270] (1796) 7 TR 9. That case concerned the old wrong of *trover*, now subsumed into conversion. The key question considered by the court was whether B had a right to possession of the things taken by C (ie, whether B had a right to immediate exclusive control of those things).

[271] [2007] EWCA Civ 1374 at [30]: 'Where the owner of goods with an immediate right to possession of them by contract transfers the latter right to another, so that he no longer has an immediate right to possession, but retains ownership, it would seem right in principle that the transferee should be entitled to sue in conversion.'

[272] The Court of Appeal relied on *Jarvis v Williams* [1955] 1 WLR 71: but in that case, the Court of Appeal held *precisely* that A's contractual right against B did *not* impose a duty on C (even though it was a contractual right to allow A to take exclusive control of B's thing) as it did *not* give A a property right: see eg *per* Lord Evershed MR at 74–5.

give B a property right. As a result, B's contract with A merely gives B a personal right against A: it does *not* impose a prima facie duty on the rest of the world. So, by simply taking the bike, C does not commit a wrong against B.[273]

Examples 31 and 32 demonstrate an important point: we need to be precise in determining when C can commit the wrong of conversion against B. The orthodox view is both too narrow and too wide. Too narrow, because it means that, in Example 31, C does *not* commit the wrong of conversion against B. Too wide, because it means that, in Example 32, C *does* commit the wrong of conversion against B. This book adopts a more precise, and simpler view: conversion simply protects Ownership. So, C can commit the wrong of conversion against B *if and only if* B has Ownership: a right to immediate exclusive control of a thing forever.

4.1.2 Unjust enrichment?

It has been argued that B can also use the law of unjust enrichment to assert his property right against C.[274] We will consider this argument in D4:6.1. The conclusion will be that the argument is unsound: the property law system does *not* allow B to assert a property right through the law of unjust enrichment. The basic point is a simple one: in cases such as Example 31, where C steals B's bike, C is *not* enriched at B's expense—after all, B still has his Ownership of the bike.

SUMMARY of D1:4.1

The property law system does not allow B to directly assert his property right against C. B cannot simply go to court and say 'That bike is mine.' Instead, B's property right is protected, like other background rights, through the law of wrongs. Therefore, when looking at the remedies question, we need to ask what remedy a court will give when B succeeds in showing that C has committed one of the wrongs that protects B's property right.

4.2 Specific protection

Whenever we examine the remedies question, the key initial question is whether or not B's right will be specifically protected. So, if A steals B's bike and sells it to C, we know that C commits the wrong of conversion against B. But will a court order C to hand the bike back to B?

The default answer is 'No': C will generally be ordered to pay money to B (see A:3.1.2(i)). In general, money can be seen as an adequate substitute for B's right: for example, if C pays money to B, B can, if he wishes, use that money to buy a replacement bike.[275] However, if B's thing is uniquely different from other similar things (eg, it is the bike ridden by Lance

---

[273] C can commit a wrong against A if he procures a breach by B of B's contract with A (see D3:2.3.5). However: (i) C clearly does not commit that wrong in a case such as Example 31; and (ii) that wrong can be committed *whenever* C procures a breach by B of B's contract with A: it is not a wrong specifically designed to protect A's right to use a thing.

[274] See eg Birks (1997) 11 TLI 2, esp 7–8: 'if I receive money from you but the money remains yours, technically I am no better off, but factually and realistically I am now in control of the buying power represented by the money'. See too Burrows, *The Law of Restitution* (2nd edn, 2002), 185–6. For a possible example see *Holiday v Sigil* (1826) 2 C & P 176.

[275] See eg *per* Megarry V-C in *Howard E. Perry v British Railways Board* [1980] 1 WLR 1375 at 1382–3.

Armstrong when crossing the line to win his first Tour de France) money will not be an adequate substitute for B's right. In such a case, a court does have a discretion to order C to return the thing itself to B.[276] For example, in *Howard E Perry & Co v British Railways Board*,[277] the court ordered C to allow B to take physical control of steel owned by B. It exercised its discretion in B's favour: at that time, substitute steel could be obtained on the open market 'only with great difficulty, if at all'.[278] The decision suggests that B does not need to show his thing is intrinsically unique: it is enough that, due to the prevailing commercial circumstances, money is not an adequate substitute for B's right.

4.3   Money awards

4.3.1 Money as a substitute for B's right

Where, as in most cases, B's property right is not specifically protected, B will have to settle for receiving a sum of money from C (generally known as 'damages').[279] When C pays that money, B's Ownership will cease to exist.[280] In that sense, the money received by B functions as a substitute for B's right. However, it is a substitute for B's right in another sense: if C has interfered with B's right, for example by using B's bike for two months, that interference cannot be undone. But C can be made to pay B money as a substitute for B's right to have had exclusive control of the bike for those two months.

EXAMPLE 33

B has 1,000 shares in Z Co. As a result, B has Ownership of a share certificate.[281] C, acting without B's consent or other authority, transfers that certificate to X. In return, X promises to pay C. As it happens, C does not enforce that promise and so receives no money from X. C then buys 1,000 identical shares in Z Co. As a result, C acquires Ownership of a share certificate: C then transfers the shares and the certificate to B. When C transferred the share certificate to X, B's shares were worth £10 each. When C gives B the new shares, each share is worth £5.

C, by interfering with B's Ownership of the share certificate, commits the wrong of conversion against B. C can argue that, nonetheless, he is not under a duty to pay any money to B: B has suffered no loss because at the end of the story, as at the start, B has a share

---

[276] Torts (Interference with Goods) Act 1977, s 3(2)(a). S 4 confirms that this discretion also exists where B makes an interim request for delivery, ie, where B asks for delivery before bringing his claim against C, or after bringing such a claim but before his claim is heard. The discretion to make an order for delivery also existed before the 1977 Act: see eg *Pusey v Pusey* (1684) 1 Vern 273.

[277] [1980] 1 WLR 1375. The s 4 discretion was used in that case as B made an interim request for delivery.

[278] *Per* Megarry V-C [1980] 1 WLR 1375, 1383. Note too *Costello v Chief Constable of Derbyshire* [2001] 1 WLR 1437: the police force was ordered to return the car itself to C. There was however no discussion of the remedies question in that case.

[279] C can also be ordered to pay money *as well as* being ordered to return a thing to B: 1977 Act, s 3(2)(a). See eg *Costello v Chief Constable of Derbyshire* [2001] 1 WLR 1437: the police force was ordered: (i) to return the car to the claimant; and (ii) to pay money to the claimant as a result of the period in which the police force had wrongfully had physical control of the car.

[280] See Torts (Interference with Goods) Act 1977, s 5.

[281] B cannot have Ownership of shares, as shares are not a thing (see **1.1.2** above). But B can have Ownership of a share certificate: a specific piece of paper. The value of that certificate of course depends on the value of the shares.

certificate for 1,000 shares in Z Co. C can also argue that his conduct has caused B no loss if B, in any case, would not have sold the shares before their drop in value.

However, as confirmed by the Privy Council in *BBMB Finance v Eda Holdings Ltd*,[282] the essential facts of which are identical to **Example 33**, C's argument will fail. Where C commits the wrong of conversion, the basic rule is that C will be ordered to pay a sum equal to the *value of B's right* at the time of C's interference with that right. Of course, B had to give credit for the value of the replacement shares but, as the shares had dropped in value between C's transfer and the replacement, C was liable for that difference in value.

The rule that the damages are set by the value of B's right, not the extent of B's loss, is confirmed by the decision, although not the reasoning, of the House of Lords in *Kuwait Airways Corpn v Iraqi Airways Co (Nos 4 & 5)*.[283] B's aircraft had been seized by the Iraqi Government, which transferred the aircraft to the defendant. The defendant argued that its conversion of the aircraft had caused no loss to B: if the defendant had refused to take the aircraft, the Iraqi Government would simply have made a different use of them and certainly would not have returned them to B. In effect then, the damage to B had already been done by the time of the defendant's involvement. However, the House of Lords rejected this argument: B was allowed to recover substantial damages. That result (if not all the reasoning of the House of Lords) is consistent only with the rule that damages are to be set by the value of B's right, not the extent of the loss caused by the defendant.[284]

This rule is often regarded as anomalous: it is argued that the damages should instead be set by the *extent of B's loss*.[285] However, that view rests on a misunderstanding of the approach to damages in other wrongs. As Stevens has convincingly shown,[286] it is often possible for B to be awarded money *even if* C's wrong causes B no loss. Where C commits a wrong, an important purpose of a money award is to protect and vindicate B's right. That purpose needs to be achieved even if B has suffered no loss. So, in other wrongs as well as in conversion, C can be ordered to pay B money as a substitute for B's right. For example, if C carelessly damages a thing owned by B, C can be ordered to pay money to B, as a substitute for B's right, *even if* C's action caused B no loss.[287] The same analysis applies where C's wrong is based not on his interference with B's property right, but on his interference with a different background right, such as B's right to physical integrity. For example, if a surgeon, against B's wishes, performs an operation that improves B's condition, the surgeon will have to pay money to B for interfering with B's right to physical integrity, *even though* C's wrong has caused B no loss.[288]

---

[282] [1990] 1 WLR 490.

[283] [2002] 2 AC 883.

[284] Lord Nicholls [2002] 2 AC 883, 1090 doubts the rule, stating at [67] that the aim of the damages award is to compensate B's loss. His reasoning is based on the difficult idea that the defendant's conduct did in fact cause B's loss. However, the problems with that reasoning are clear and are pointed out by Stevens, *Torts and Rights* (2007), 63–6.

[285] See eg Tettenborn [1993] CLJ 128; Law Reform Committee 18th Report (1971) Cmnd 4774 at [91].

[286] See Stevens, *Torts and Rights* (2007), ch 4. For a different view, see Edelman, ch 8 in *Mapping the Law: Essays in Memory of Peter Birks* (ed Burrows & Rodger, 2007).

[287] See eg *The Mediana* [1900] AC 113; *The Sanix Ace* [1987] 1 Lloyd's Rep 465; *Burdis v Livsey* [2003] QB 36. See Stevens, *Torts and Rights* (2007), 72–4.

[288] See *B v NHS Hospital Trust* [2002] 2 All ER 449: this example is quoted by Stevens, *Torts and Rights* (2007), 74.

4.3.2 Money as compensation for B's consequential loss

Where C commits a wrong, a money award aims *both*: (i) to serve as a substitute for B's right; *and* (ii) to compensate B for any relevant loss B suffers as a consequence of C's wrong. A loss will not be *relevant* if it is too remote a consequence of C's wrong. In addressing the question of whether a loss is too remote, a court can take into account C's level of fault. For example, let us say A steals B's computer and sells it to C, who is unaware of the theft. B suffers a consequential loss: as he has been deprived of his computer, he is unable to prepare an important document in time to conclude a lucrative contract. Even if the loss of the contract occurs after C's involvement, C cannot be held liable for that consequential loss: it is not a natural result of C's conversion but rather depends on B's special position, unknown to C.[289] However, it can be argued that, due to his dishonesty, A is liable for all loss directly flowing from his taking of the computer.[290]

4.3.3 Money to remove C's gain?

EXAMPLE 34

B owns a bike. A steals that bike and sells it to C. C, when buying the bike, honestly believes that it belongs to A. C then sells the bike to C2 for £200. C invests the £200 in some shares. The shares are now worth £1,000.

In such a case, it seems that B has a power to impose a duty on C to hold his shares on Trust for B.[291] If B exercises that power, he can acquire the full benefit of the shares; and C is thus prevented from making any gain as a result of his interference with B's car. However, that result does *not* depend on a particular remedy given to B as a result of C's wrong against B. Instead, it depends on the **acquisition question**: on a principle allowing B to acquire a *persistent* right where: (i) C has a new right that counts as a product of B's initial right; and (ii) there is no legal basis for C to have the benefit of that new right (see **D4:4.4**). That principle assists B only where C's gain consists in C's acquisition of a *new right that is the product of B's initial right*.

If: (i) C makes a gain as a result of his wrongful interference with B's property right; and (ii) that gain does *not* take the form of a specific right, held by C, that is the product of B's initial right, then (iii) can a court, in order to remedy C's wrong, order C to pay B a sum equal to that gain? This is a hotly disputed issue. A prominent school of thought argues that such 'gain-based' damages are available: even if the courts generally deny the availability of such damages, it is argued that such awards have been made where C's wrong consists of interfering with B's property right.[292] However, some caution is needed. For example, in

---

[289] See eg *Saleslease Ltd v Davis* [1999] 1 WLR 1664.

[290] *Per* Lord Nicholls in *Kuwait Airways Corpn v Iraqi Airways Co (Nos 4 & 5)* [2002] 2 AC 883 at [99]ff. Compare eg *Doyle v Olby* [1969] 2 QB 158, where the Court of Appeal held that, if B suffers loss as a result of C's commission of the wrong of deceit, C is prima facie liable for all losses B suffers as a direct result of C's fraud, even if such losses were not reasonably foreseeable by C.

[291] See *Ryall v Ryall* (1739) 1 Atk 59; *re Kolari* (1981) 36 OR (2d) 473 (Ontario); *per* Millett J in *El Ajou v Dollar Land Holdings* [1993] 3 All ER 717, 734. For discussion see Chambers, *Resulting Trusts* (1997), 116–8. The result also follows from the decision of the Court of Appeal in *Trustee of Jones v Jones* [1997] Ch 159. B's initial right in that case was a personal right: an account with Z Bank. There is no reason for B's right to receive less protection where it is a property right.

[292] See eg Burrows, *Remedies for Torts and Breach of Contract* (3rd edn, 2004), 377–95.

Strand Electric Engineering Co Ltd v Brisford Entertainment Ltd,[293] B Ltd, under a hire contract, allowed C Ltd to use some equipment owned by B Ltd. C Ltd did not return the equipment on time at the end of the hire period and thus committed the wrong of conversion. B Ltd did not suffer any consequential loss as a result of this conversion: for example, it did not lose a chance to hire out the equipment out to another customer. Nonetheless, C Ltd was ordered to pay B Ltd money, based on what B Ltd could reasonably have charged C Ltd for keeping the equipment for the extra period. Denning LJ explained these damages as based on the gain to C Ltd as a result of its conversion.

The difficulty with Denning LJ's explanation is that, as it had no use for the equipment, C Ltd made no profit by keeping it. It may be possible to meet that objection by arguing that the gain to C Ltd can be measured *objectively*: even if C Ltd in fact did not profit, it still made a gain at B Ltd's expense, if only in so far as B Ltd would have charged C Ltd extra to keep the equipment for a longer period. That approach finds a good deal of judicial[294] and academic[295] support and allows a case such as *Strand Electric* to stand for the possibility that a court may award damages to B based on C's gain. However, it would be very odd if such gain-based damages were available *only* where C's wrong consists of breaching a duty not to interfere with B's exclusive control of a thing. After all, it would be odd if B's property rights were protected more keenly than other, presumably more important background rights, such as B's right to physical integrity. On this view, it can then be argued that such gain-based damages should be more widely available.[296]

An alternative explanation is to say that, in *Strand Electric*, C was ordered to pay money to B *not* as a result of C's gain but, instead, as a *substitute for B's right*.[297] After all, part of the value of B's right to exclusive control of a thing is the ability to charge those who wish to hire that thing. On this view, the law's willingness to allow 'gain-based damages' where C interferes with B's property right is easy to understand. B can use such a background right to make money by, for example, hiring out his thing.[298] In contrast, B cannot make money by allowing others to make use of his background right to physical integrity. In fact, on this view, the money award in *Strand Electric*, as well as those given in other similar cases, does not provide *any* evidence of 'gain-based damages': instead, C is simply ordered to pay money as a substitute for B's right.[299]

The crucial point is that the issue of gain-based damages arises *only* if: (i) after paying B money as a substitute for B's right; and (ii) after paying B money as compensation for B's relevant consequential loss; (iii) C *still* retains a gain from his wrong. The difficult question about the availability of gain-based damages therefore arises less often than we might expect. There *are* a number of cases squarely raising the issue. These cases involve C interfering with

---

[293] [1952] 2 QB 246.

[294] See eg *per* Lord Nicholls in *Sempra Metals Ltd v IRC* [2007] 3 WLR 354 at 387.

[295] See eg Edelman, *Gain-Based Damages* (2002), 70–72; Burrows, *Remedies for Torts and Breach of Contract* (3rd edn, 2004), 379–80.

[296] See eg Edelman, *Gain-Based Damages* (2002).

[297] This argument is made by Stevens, *Torts and Rights*,79–84. McInnes, ch 16 in *Equity and Commercial Law* (ed Degeling and Edelman, 2005) takes a similar, but different view, arguing that, in cases such as *Strand Electric*, C's interference with B's right counts as a 'loss' for which B can receive compensation from C.

[298] Similarly, B can use an intellectual property right (another form of background right: see 1.1.1(ii) above) to make money (eg, by licensing others to reproduce part of B's copyrighted book). As a result, 'gain-based damages' are available where C's wrong consists of interfering with B's intellectual property right. However, those damages can again be seen as based on the value of B's underlying right, as expressed in the sum B could reasonably have demanded C in return for giving C a licence to act as C did: see eg *Rickless v United Artists* [1988] QB 40.

[299] As argued by Stevens, *Torts and Rights*, 79–84.

B's property right in land; but there seems to be no reason why different results should be reached if C interferes with B's property right in a thing other than land. For example, in *Bracewell v Appleby*,[300] C committed the wrong of trespass by using a road on B's land to reach C's house. It was estimated that C made a gain of £5,000 as a result of this wrong. However, C was ordered to pay B £2,000: this was judged to be a reasonable sum for B to have asked in return for giving C permission to use the road. In that case there was a clear difference between ordering C to pay money: (i) simply as a substitute for B's right; and (ii) to remove C's gain. And the court opted for option (i): it did not order C to pay 'gain-based damages' to B.[301]

So, it may be that, as the law stands, there is no general rule that, where C makes a gain by interfering with B's property right, C can be ordered to pay B money equal to that gain. However, things may be different in a case where C: (i) acts in a way that C *knows* will interfere with B's right; and (ii) C does so with the intention of making a profit.[302] In order to vindicate B's right, and to deter such wrongdoing, a court may be able to award 'punitive' or 'exemplary' damages:[303] one of the effects of awarding such damages will be to remove any gain C has made.[304] But, in such a case, nothing should turn on the fact that C has interfered with B's *property right*; rather, the availability of such 'exemplary' damages should depend on the nature of C's conduct, not on the nature of B's right.

4.4 An allowance for C?

EXAMPLE 35

B has Ownership of a car. B takes the car to A for repairs. A then sells the car to C. C is entirely innocent: he honestly and reasonably believes that no one other than A has a right in relation to the car. C spends time and money in improving the car. B reports the loss of his car to the police. The local police force finds the car and takes physical control of it. The police force is unsure whether to return that car to B or to C. As a result, it initiates an *inter-pleader* proceeding: this allows a court to hear the claims of both B and C and to decide which of them should be able to take control of the car.

C has no defence to B's pre-existing property right.[305] So, as confirmed by the Court of Appeal in *Greenwood v Bennett*,[306] the basic facts of which are identical to **Example 35**, the starting point is that a court will find that B should be free to take physical control of the car. However, as Lord Denning MR put it:

---

[300] [1975] Ch 408.

[301] See too *Severn Trent Water Authority Ltd v Barnes* [2004] EWCA Civ 570.

[302] For a strong argument in favour of the availability of gain-based damages in such a case see Edelman, *Gain-Based Damages* (2002), esp ch 3. On the analysis given here, such damages would be, in Edelman's terms, 'disgorgement' damages.

[303] See *per* Lord Devlin in *Rookes v Barnard* [1964] AC 1129 at 1221–31, esp 1226–7. For an application of 'exemplary' damages in a case where the defendant committed a wrong by interfering with B's pre-existing property right see *Borders (UK) Ltd v Commissioner of Police of the Metropolis* [2005] EWCA Civ 197, esp [23] and [34].

[304] The courts have made damages awards based on C's gain where C has *knowingly* interfered with an intellectual property right of B: see eg *Slazenger & Sons v Spalding & Bros* [1910] 1 Ch 257. There are now various legislative provisions allowing a court to order C to pay over gains he has made by infringing an intellectual property right of B: see eg Patents Act 1977, s 61(1). However, C can generally avoid such an order by showing that he did not knowingly interfere with B's right: see eg Patents Act 1977, s 62.

[305] Factors Act 1889, s 2(1) cannot apply as B did not give the car to A *for the purpose* of selling it (see **3.3.2** above).

[306] [1973] QB 195.

[i]t would be most unjust if [B] could not only take the car from [C], but also the value of the improvements [C] has done to it—without paying for them . . . [B] should not be allowed unjustly to enrich [himself] at [C's] expense.[307]

So it seems that B should be allowed to take physical control of the car only *if* B pays C a sum of money equal to the increase in value of the car caused by C's work. In effect, C is given an allowance for the improvement he made in the mistaken belief that no one had a pre-existing property right in the car.

The dispute in *Greenwood v Bennett* arose in a slightly strange way, due to the inter-pleader proceedings. But the principle stated by Lord Denning MR is a wider one.[308] For example, imagine a case similar to **Example 35**, but in which the police do not get involved: B asserts his property right against C by claiming that C has committed the wrong of conversion. In such a case, section 6 of the Torts (Interference with Goods) Act 1977 confirms that C can receive an *allowance* as: (i) C worked on the car in the honest belief that no one (other than A) had a pre-existing property right in the car; and (ii) C's work increased the value of the car.[309] This provision can be seen to recognise the fact that, as a result of his honest but mistaken improvements to a thing owned by B, C may have a *direct right* against B, based on the need to prevent B being unjustly enriched at C's expense. The possibility of such a claim provides an innocent C with some limited protection when he is bound by B's pre-existing but hidden property right. However, it is important to note the limits to C's right: if the time and money spent by B does *not* increase the value of B's thing, C will have no direct right against B.[310]

SUMMARY of D1:4

The property law system protects property rights through the law of wrongs: specifically, if B's property right is in a thing other than land, through the wrongs of trespass, conversion and negligence. If C commits such a wrong, the court has a statutory discretion to specifi-cally protect B's right, by ordering C to return the thing in question to B. However, the general position is that B will have to settle for receiving money from C. That money will: (i) serve as a substitute for B's right; *and* (ii) compensate B for any relevant loss he has suffered as a result of C's interference with B's right. And, if C has knowingly committed the wrong, with the intention of making a profit, it may be possible for a court to order C to pay 'exem-plary damages' to B. On this analysis, when a court orders C to pay money to B as a result of C's wrong, nothing turns on the fact that C has interfered with a property right of B: C is treated in exactly the same way *whenever* he commits a wrong against B.

---

[307] [1973] QB 195 at 202.

[308] For discussion see McKendrick, in *Interests in Goods* (ed Palmer and McKendrick, 1st edn, 1993).

[309] Under s 6(2), if: (i) C2 is a 'bona fide purchaser' of the car from C; and (ii) B brings a claim against C2 based on C2's conversion of the car; then (iii) the damages payable to B by C2 can also be reduced as a result of C's improvements. That provision can again be justified by the need to prevent B being unjustly enriched at C2's expense: it avoids the risk that: (i) B can recover the full value of the improved car from C2; and (ii) C2 can then get the full price he paid for the car back from C; (iii) leaving C with no money in return for the improvements he made to the car. It does not however protect C2 where C2 is instead ordered to return the car to B. In such a case, if liable to C2, C may need to bring a direct unjust enrichment claim against B.

[310] Although where C still has physical control of the thing, C's work may be taken into account by a court when considering whether to specifically protect B's right by ordering C to return the thing to B. For example, if, in a case such as **Example 35**, C has spent time and money building a garage to house the car, that may suggest that C should be allowed to keep the car, provided he pays a sum of money to B.

CHAPTER D2
PERSISTENT RIGHTS

PERSISTENT RIGHTS

Persistent rights are a vital part of the property law system. If B has a pre-existing persistent right, he has a right against A's right. If C then acquires a right that depends on A's right, B will have a prima facie power to impose a duty on C (see **B:4.3**). In contrast to property rights, persistent rights can be relevant to *both*: (i) disputes about the use of a thing; *and* (ii) disputes about the use of a right.

In this chapter, our focus is on the general rules relating to persistent rights; we will consider the special rules applying to persistent rights relating to land in **E2**. In examining the general rules, we will look at each of the basic questions:

Section 1: The **content question**: what rights count as persistent rights?
Section 2: The **acquisition question**: how can B acquire a persistent right?
Section 3: The **defences question**: when can C have a defence to B's pre-existing persistent right?
Section 4: The **remedies question**: if B does have a pre-existing persistent right to which C has no defence, how will a court protect B's right?

1 THE CONTENT QUESTION

Where persistent rights are concerned, there are two aspects to the content question. The first is relatively trivial: does the right claimed by B allow him to make his desired use of the thing or the right in question? The second, much more significant, aspect is whether the right B claims *counts* as a persistent right. As we saw in **B:4.3**, the basic rule is that, to have a persistent right, B must show that:

- A is under a duty to B; *and*
- That duty relates to a specific right held by A; *and*
- The specific right held by A is either a claim-right or a power.

1.1 Developing the basic rule

1.1.1 A must be under a duty to B

EXAMPLE 1

A0, in his will, gives £10,000 to A. The will states that the £10,000 is given to A 'in full confidence that A will do what is right as to the disposal of the money between A0's children'.

A0's children may argue that each of them has acquired a persistent right—a right against A's right to the £10,000. However, the will merely states that A0 *hopes* or *believes* that A will use the £10,000 in a particular way: it does not impose a *duty* on A to A0's children. As a result, the will does not give the children a persistent right. This is confirmed by the decision of the Court of Appeal in *re Adams and the Kensington Vestry*,[1] the essential facts of which are identical to **Example 1**.

In some cases, the law simply does not allow A to come under a duty to B in relation to a particular right. For example, A's right to physical integrity is one of the 'background' rights, enjoyed by each of us, that imposes a prima facie duty on the rest of the world (see **D1:1.1.1(i)**). The law does *not* allow us to come under a duty to another in relation to that right. Given its importance, we must each be free to use that right: we cannot bind ourselves not to exercise it.[2]

As a result, B cannot acquire a right against A's right to physical integrity. This inability does *not* depend on the fact that A cannot transfer such a right to B. After all, the creation of a persistent right does not involve the transfer of A's right to B. Rather, it depends on A *keeping* his right and coming under a duty to use that right for B's benefit (see **B:4.4.2** and **C3:7.2**).

1.1.2 A's duty must relate to a specific right held by A

B can have a persistent right against a personal right of A;[3] a property right of A;[4] and even a persistent right of A.[5] However, B can only have a right against the whole of a specific, distinct right currently held by A.[6]

(i) A's duty must relate to the whole of A's right

EXAMPLE 2

A makes a contractual promise to B to allow B to have exclusive control of A's bike for six months.

A's promise does *not* give B a property right in the bike (see **D1:1.4.3**). Nor does it give B a persistent right against A's Ownership of the bike. Although A is under a duty to B, A's duty does not relate to the *whole of A's right*. A has a right to exclusive control of the bike *forever*, but his duty to B is simply to allow B exclusive control of the bike for six months. It is impossible for A to be under a duty to B in relation to *part* of A's right: as rights are indivisible, there is no such thing as a part of a right. Therefore, every persistent right involves A being under a duty in relation to the whole of a specific right (see **1.3** below).

---

[1] [1884] 27 Ch D 394.

[2] See eg *Sunbolf v Alford* (1838) 3 M&W 248; K Tan (1981) 44 *MLR* 166. For example, A could contract with B Ltd to live in a particular house for eight weeks, in order to compete in B Ltd's television show. If A leaves after two weeks, A commits the wrong of breach of contract against B Ltd and may have to pay money to B Ltd as a result. However, B Ltd would itself commit a wrong if it forcibly prevented A from leaving: even though his change of mind involves a breach of contract, A can revoke his consent to remaining in the house.

[3] As when A holds his bank account on Trust for B (see **B:Example 5**).

[4] As when A holds his Ownership of a bike on Trust for B (see **B:Examples 7a–7d**).

[5] As when A has a right under a Trust and holds that right on Trust for B (see **C1:Example 2**).

[6] As rights are generally indivisible, this is just a long-hand way of making the key point that A's duty must relate to a specific right held by A.

(ii) A's duty must relate to a specific right of A

B:EXAMPLE 8a

A owns a bike shop. B orders a particular model of bike from A and pays the £200 price in advance. A then goes into insolvency. A's total liabilities are £100,000: the assets available to A to meet those liabilities are worth only £50,000.

A is under a contractual duty to B. However, B does *not* have a persistent right:[7] A's duty to B does *not* relate to a specific right held by A.[8] A has simply promised to give B a particular type of bike: he has not promised to transfer a *specific* right to B. This means that B's claim to a persistent right fails for exactly the same reason as his claim to a property right (see **D1:2.2.4(iii)(b)**): B's contract with A does not impose a duty on A to transfer his Ownership of any specific bike.[9] Therefore, in **B:Example 8a**, B has to settle for asserting his personal right against A. B will therefore receive, at most, £100 (see **B:4.5.1**).

(iii) A's duty must relate to a distinct right of A

If A has Ownership of a bike, B cannot acquire a persistent right against A's Ownership of the paint on the bike. That paint is part and parcel of the bike itself (see **D1:Example 13**). Hence, as the paint is not a distinct thing, A does not have a specific, *distinct* right to the paint on the bike.

For the same reason, in **Example 2**, B cannot say that he has a right against 'A's Ownership of the bike for the next six months'. A does *not* have a *distinct* right to exclusive control of the bike for the next six months: any such right is simply part and parcel of A's Ownership of the bike. If A's Ownership of the bike could be split into distinct slices of time, it *would* be possible for A to give B a *property right* by transferring his Ownership of the bike to B for six months; but the property law system simply does not allow A to divide up his Ownership in that way (see **D1:1.4.3**).[10]

(iv) A's duty must relate to a right currently held by A

EXAMPLE 3

A has an elderly grandparent. A expects to acquire some rights under the grandparent's will. A declares that he holds any rights he will receive under that will on Trust for B. B gives nothing in return for A's declaration. A acquires £10,000 when the grandparent dies.

A's declaration of a Trust does *not* give B a persistent right against A's right to the £10,000.

---

[7] The question of whether B has a persistent right against A's right to the £200 payment is a different one (see **D4:4.3.5**).

[8] This also explains why B, a party named as a beneficiary of A0's will, does *not* have a persistent right during the period when A0's will is being administered (as confirmed by the Privy Council in *Commission of Stamp Duties v Livingstone* [1965] AC 694). During that period A (A0's administrator or executor) acquires A0's rights and has a duty to use those rights to meet any liabilities of A0; until that is done, we do not know what specific rights of A0 will be available for distribution to the parties named in A0's will. So, during that period, B cannot claim to have a persistent right against the rights held by A: A's duty to B does not yet relate to a specific right held by A.

[9] See eg *re London Wine Co* [1986] PCC 121; *re Goldcorp's Exchange* [1995] 1 AC 74; and the analysis of Worthington [1999] *Journal of Business Law* 1.

[10] Things are different where A is an owner of *land*. In such a case, A can give B a Lease: a right to exclusive control of the land for a limited period that counts as a property right (see **E1:1** and **G1B:1**). To that extent, A's right as an owner of land, unlike other rights, *is* divisible.

When A made that declaration, A did not have that right to the £10,000, and hence A's declaration, by itself, cannot give B a persistent right.[11]

1.1.3 The right held by A must be a claim-right or a power

To understand this limit, we need to examine Hohfeld's seminal analysis of the nature of rights. When we say 'A has a right' we may mean a number of different things. Hohfeld set out four of the different meanings.[12]

1. If we say A, a holder of a bank account, has a right that Z Bank must pay him the £100 credited to A's account, we mean that Z is under a duty to pay A that money. A's right thus correlates to a particular duty of Z: in Hohfeld's terms, A's right is a **claim right** against Z.

2. Let us say that A is employed by Z as a manager of a football club. That deal is due to finish at the end of the year. A has the right, if he chooses, to extend the agreement into a second year. Until A chooses to renew the agreement, his right to renew imposes no duty on Z. So A's right to renew is not a claim right. Instead, it is a **power** against Z: A, by acting in a certain way, can change the legal position of Z. This means that Z is under a liability to A: Z is liable to have his position changed by A's exercise of A's power. So, in this case, A can impose a new contractual duty on Z by choosing to renew the agreement.

3. If we say that A has a right to shop at Tesco's, we may well mean that A is *not* under a duty, whether to Z or anyone else, not to shop there. In such a case, A has a **liberty** against Z. A liberty is, in an important sense, negative: it exists where A is *not* under a duty not to act in a particular way. A liberty can therefore be seen as the negative image of a claim right: A has a claim right against Z where Z is under a duty to A; A has a liberty against Z where A is not under a duty to Z.

4. If we say that A has a right that Z cannot revoke his driving licence, we means that Z does not have a power to change A's legal position in that way. In such a case, A has an **immunity** against Z. Like a liberty, an immunity is essentially negative: it exists where A is *not* under a liability to Z. An immunity can therefore be seen as the negative image of a power: A has a power against Z where Z is under a liability to A; A has an immunity against Z where A is not under a liability to Z.

A's position with regards to Z	Description	Z's position with regards to A	Example
Claim right	Z has a duty to A	**Duty**	A has an account at Z Bank
Power	A can change Z's position	**Liability**	A can renew his contract with Z to manage Z's football team
Liberty	A has no duty to Z	**No claim right**	Z has no right against A to stop A shopping at Tesco's
Immunity	A's position cannot be changed by Z	**No power**	Z has no power to revoke A's driving licence

---

[11] See eg *re Ellenborough* [1903] 1 Ch 697; *In re Parsons* (1980) 45 Ch D 51; *Williams v CIR* [1965] NZLR 395.

[12] See Hohfeld (1913) 23 *Yale LJ* 16. Hohfeld used the term 'privilege' to refer to the type of right that we will call a 'liberty'. However, a 'privilege' is simply a type of liberty—a liberty not enjoyed by everyone.

It is clear that B can have a persistent right against a claim right of A or a power of A. For example, A can hold a bank account on Trust for B.[13] Similarly, A's power to renew an agreement with Z may be held by A on Trust for B.[14]

However, B *cannot* have a persistent right against a liberty of A or an immunity of A. This is because each of a liberty and an immunity is essentially *negative*: there is no positive right of A against which B can have a right. For example, A cannot set up a Trust, in B's favour, of A's liberty against Z to shop at Tesco's. Nor can A set up a Trust, in B's favour, of A's immunity that Z cannot revoke A's driving licence.

D1:EXAMPLE 1

B Ltd, a manufacturer of bikes, wishes to ensure that those bikes cannot be sold for below a certain price. When B Ltd sells those bikes to A Ltd, a wholesaler, he makes A Ltd promise not to sell any of the bikes for less than £200 (a 'price maintenance clause'). B Ltd also wants to ensure that this condition binds not just A Ltd, but also future purchasers who may wish to sell on the bikes, such as C Ltd, a retailer. So, A Ltd and B Ltd agree that B Ltd's right to stop sales below £200 is prima facie binding on the rest of the world. A Ltd then sells some bikes to C Ltd. C Ltd attempts to sell them to his customers for £150.

A Ltd's promise does *not* give B Ltd a property right in the bikes sold to A Ltd (see **D1:1.2.2**). Nor does it give B Ltd a persistent right.[15] A Ltd's duty to B Ltd (not to sell the bikes for less than £200 each) does not relate to the *whole of A Ltd's right*. B Ltd could argue that A Ltd is under a duty in relation to A Ltd's liberty, against B Ltd, to sell any of the bikes for less than £200. However, that argument cannot give B Ltd a persistent right: (i) A Ltd's liberty is part and parcel of A's Ownership of each bike and so is not a *distinct* right; and (ii) in any case, a right in relation to a liberty cannot count as a persistent right.

Similarly, in **Example 2**, B may claim that A is under a contractual duty to B in relation to A's liberty to use A's bike over the next six months. However, B's argument will fail: (i) A's liberty is not a *distinct* right: it is part and parcel of A's Ownership of the bike; and (ii) it is impossible to have a persistent right against a liberty.

In some cases, a liberty or immunity can give rise to a claim right or a power: in such a case, B can have a persistent right against the resulting claim right or power. For example, let us say A holds a milk quota. If we say that the quota gives A a right to produce a certain quantity of milk on his land without having to pay a levy to Z, we mean that A has an *immunity* against Z. So, if A comes under a duty to use that quota for B's benefit, B should *not* acquire a persistent right. However, if *either*: (i) A sells the quota to C and receives money, which A then pays into a new account with Z Bank; *or* (ii) A uses the quota to produce and sell milk and then pays the proceeds into his new account with Z Bank; then (iii) A has used his immunity (the quota) to acquire a claim right (against Z Bank). Hence, at that point, B *can* acquire a persistent right: (i) A was under a duty to B in relation to the quota; and (ii) A's claim right against Z Bank is a product of that quota; so (iii) A is under a duty to B in relation to A's claim right against Z Bank.[16]

---

[13] See eg *Paul v Constance* [1977] 1 WLR 527.
[14] Compare eg *Keech v Sandford* (1726) Sel Cas temp King 61.
[15] See eg *Taddy & Co v Sterious & Co* [1904] 1 Ch 354.
[16] This seems to be the best explanation of the result in *Swift v Dairywise Farms Ltd* [2000] 1 WLR 1177. In that case, Jacobs J held that there could be a Trust of the quota itself. This is true in the sense that, by declaring a Trust of

1.2   Examples of persistent rights

1.2.1 The Purely Equitable Charge

> **EXAMPLE 4a**
>
> A has Ownership of a bike and wants to borrow £200 from B. B demands some security for A's duty to repay the loan. A makes a contractual promise to B that, if A fails to repay the loan as agreed, B can: (i) sell the bike; and (ii) use the proceeds to meet A's debt to B.

In such a case, B acquires a persistent right.[17] This right can be called a Purely Equitable Charge (see **F4:2.2.2**). It gives B a useful form of security: as it is a persistent right, it is protected in A's insolvency (see **B:4.5.2(ii)**). It is possible for A, by means of a mortgage or a pledge, to instead give B a property right by way of security (see **D1:1.4.2**). However, the advantage of a Purely Equitable Charge is that: (i) it gives B a useful security right; and (ii) A can retain both his Ownership of the bike (in contrast to a mortgage) *and* his physical control of the bike (in contrast to a pledge).

A Purely Equitable Charge counts as a persistent right because A is under a duty to B in relation to a specific right held by A. A's duty relates to the *whole* of his right: it is a duty to allow B to sell that right and to use the proceeds to perform a duty owed to B. Of course, this does not mean B will necessarily be able to take *all* the proceeds of sale. In **Example 4a**, it may be that: (i) A is £100 short in repaying B; and (ii) B then sells the bike for £200. In such a case, A can keep the extra £100 realised by the sale. However, this does not alter the fact that, as A's duty is to allow B to sell A's right, A's duty relates to the whole of that right.

> **EXAMPLE 4b**
>
> A Ltd has an account with B Bank. In return for a loan from B Bank, A Ltd makes a contractual promise to B Bank that if A Ltd fails to repay the loan as agreed, B Bank can deduct the extent of A Ltd's unpaid debt from A Ltd's account with B Bank. A Ltd then goes into insolvency.

There has been some controversy as to whether B Bank can acquire a persistent right in such a case. It has been suggested that, if A has a right against B, it is conceptually impossible for A to give B a Purely Equitable Charge over that right.[18] However, the House of Lords, in *re BCCI (No 8)*,[19] confirmed that such a 'charge-back' *does* give B a persistent right: in **Example 4b**, therefore, B Bank does have a persistent right that is capable of binding A Ltd's liquidators. That conclusion must be correct. It *is* conceptually impossible for A to: (i) have a right against B; and (ii) transfer that right to B. In such a case, A's right simply disappears as B's duty to A ceases to exist.[20] However, in **Example 4b**, A Ltd does *not*

---

the quota, A came under a duty to use the quota for B's benefit. However, B should only acquire a persistent right if and when that quota leads to A making a profit: at that point, A acquires a claim right that can be held by A on Trust for B.

[17] See eg *Tailby v Official Receiver* (1888) LR 13 App Cas 523; *re Bond Worth Ltd* [1980] Ch 228 at 250; *re Cosslett (Contractors) Ltd* [1998] Ch 495 at 508.

[18] An argument originally made by Goode, *Legal Problems of Credit and Security* (1st edn, 1982), 86–7 (see now 4th edn, 2008). See too *per* Millett LJ in *re Charge Card Services Ltd* [1987] Ch 150 at 175–6; Goode (1998) 114 *LQR* 178.

[19] [1998] 1 AC 214. See esp *per* Lord Hoffmann at 225–8.

[20] See eg *per* Millett LJ in *re Charge Card Services Ltd* [1987] Ch 150 at 176.

attempt to transfer its bank account to B. There is no conceptual reason why A cannot both: (i) keep his right against B; and (ii) give B a right against that right.[21]

B:EXAMPLE 6b

B Ltd provides shipping insurance to A Co. A Co's ship is then damaged by the carelessness of Z. A Co's policy with B Ltd covers that form of damage; B Ltd therefore pays A Co under the insurance policy. A Co then goes into insolvent liquidation.

In such a case, A Co is under a duty to B Ltd, said to arise under the principle of *subrogation*, in relation to its personal right against Z. As a result, B Ltd has a persistent right: a right against A Co's right against Z (see **B:4.4.2**). B's persistent right can be seen as a Purely Equitable Charge. In particular, A Co will not necessarily need to give B Ltd *all* the money A Co receives from Z. For example, most insurance policies contain an 'excess'. For example, in **B:Example 6b**, A Co may have to bear the first £10,000 of its loss. So, if A Co receives money from Z as compensation for *all* the loss A Co has suffered, A Co will not have to pay *all* that money to B: it can keep £10,000.[22]

The persistent right B acquires under an insurer's subrogation is thus, in its **content**, exactly like a Purely Equitable Charge. However, B's persistent right is usually referred to as an 'Equitable Lien'.[23] The term 'Equitable Lien' is used whenever: (i) B has a Purely Equitable Charge; and (ii) B's right does *not* arise as a result of an express promise by A. However, as B's right has exactly the same **content** as a Purely Equitable Charge, there is really no point in maintaining the separate category of the 'Equitable Lien'. In fact, the term is positively dangerous. It suggests a misleading analogy with a very different type of right: the 'Common Law Lien' (see **F4:2.1.3**).

1.2.2 The right arising under an Equitable Assignment

(i) Equitable Assignment: Type 1

B:EXAMPLE 6a

A has a personal right against Z, who owes A £100. A expresses his intention to make an immediate transfer of the benefit of that right to B. A thus makes an 'Equitable Assignment' of that right in favour of B. A then goes into insolvency and his personal right against Z passes to C, A's trustee in bankruptcy.

In such a case, A is under a duty to B in relation to A's personal right against Z. As a result, B has a persistent right: a right against A's right against Z. This means that B has a power to impose a duty on C (see **B:4.4.2**). B acquires such a persistent right whenever:

- A has a personal right against Z; *and*
- A expresses his intention to give B, immediately, the benefit of that right.

---

[21] Millett LJ in *re Charge Card Services Ltd* [1987] Ch 150 at 176 expressed the fear that a 'charge-back' depends on B having a right to sue himself. However, that is not the case. After all, if: (i) A has a personal right against Z; and (ii) B has a persistent right against A's right; then (iii) B has no right to sue Z (see **B:4.4.2** and **B:4.4.3**).

[22] See eg *Lord Napier & Ettrick v Hunter* [1993] 1 AC 713.

[23] *Ibid.* The House of Lords recognised that, in **B:Example 6b**, B has a persistent right against any damages received by A from Z: that right gives B security for A's duty to repay the money B paid to A under the insurance policy.

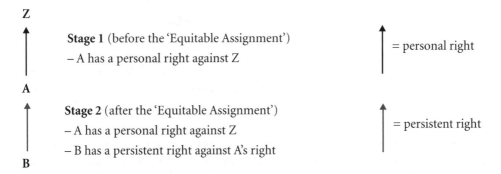

Z

↑

Stage 1 (before the 'Equitable Assignment')
– A has a personal right against Z

A

↑

Stage 2 (after the 'Equitable Assignment')
– A has a personal right against Z
– B has a persistent right against A's right

B

↑ = personal right

↑ = persistent right

This analysis explains why B, after an Equitable Assignment, cannot directly sue Z; instead, B has to force A to assert A's personal right against Z.[24] It also explains why, when making an Equitable Assignment, A does not have to satisfy the formality rule set out by section 136 of the Law of Property Act 1925 (see **C3:5.1.2**). That rule regulates A's power to *transfer* a personal right to B; it does *not* regulate A's power to give B a persistent right by means of an Equitable Assignment (see **C3:7.2**).

(ii) Equitable Assignment: Type 2

> **EXAMPLE 4c**
>
> A has a personal right to receive £200 from Z. As part of a contract with B, A makes a promise to B to transfer that right to B.

> **EXAMPLE 4d**
>
> A expects to receive a personal right against Z, a potential customer. As part of a contract with B, A makes a promise to B to transfer that right, when he receives it, to B.

These cases are clearly different from **B:Example 6a**: A's plan *is* to transfer his right to B. As that transfer has not yet occurred, B does not yet have a personal right against Z: as a result, B cannot bring a direct claim against Z. However, in **Example 4c**, B has an *immediate* persistent right. That right arises because A, is under a *contractual* duty to B in relation to a specific right: his personal right against Z. And in **Example 4d**, B will acquire a persistent right *as soon as* A receives his expected personal right against Z. At that point: (i) A will hold a specific right; and (ii) A will be under a *contractual* duty to B in relation to that right. **Examples 4c and 4d** show that there is a second form of Equitable Assignment arising if:

- A has a personal right against Z; *and*
- A is under a duty to transfer that right to B; *then*
- A is under a duty to use his personal right against Z for B's benefit.

(iii) The need for a new name

The term 'Equitable Assignment' is misleading:

1. It suggests that there is a transfer to B of A's personal right against Z. In fact, as in

---

[24] See eg *Brandt's Sons & Co v Dunlop Rubber Co* [1905] AC 454; *Weddell v JA Pearce & Major* [1988] Ch 26 at 40; *MH Smith (Plant Hire) Ltd v DL Mainwaring* [1986] 2 Lloyds Rep 243 at 246.

B:Example 6a and **Examples 4c and 4d**: (i) A *keeps* his personal right against Z; and (ii) B acquires a right against A's right.

2. It causes confusion with the case where B1 has an existing Equitable right (eg, a right under a Trust) and transfers that right to B2 (see **C3:5.2.2**).[25] As such a case involves a transfer of B1's Equitable right, it can also plausibly be called an 'Equitable Assignment'.

There are thus good reasons to find a new term to describe the persistent right B acquires in **B:Example 6a** and **Examples 4c and 4d**. In each of these cases, the **content** of B's right is identical to the core content of a right under a Trust: A is under a duty to use a right for B's benefit. A simpler approach would therefore be to call B's right a right under a Trust.

1.2.3 The Mortgagor's Right to Redeem

EXAMPLE 5a

B has Ownership of a bike and wants to borrow £200 from A. B transfers his Ownership of the bike to A as security for B's duty to repay the loan. The deal, of course, is that if B *does* succeed in repaying the loan, A will have to transfer his Ownership of the bike back to B.

In such a case, A and B's transaction is a *mortgage* (see **D1:1.4.2**): B is the mortgagor and A the mortgagee. *As soon as* B transfers his right to A, A comes under a duty to B: *if* the loan is repaid, A must transfer the right back to B. A's duty to B relates to a specific right (A's Ownership of the bike) and so B has a persistent right.

B's persistent right is generally known as an 'equity of redemption'. The name comes from the fact that, once the loan is repaid, B can recover (ie, 'redeem') the right he transferred to A as security. However, the term 'equity of redemption' can be confusing (see **F4:1.3 and F4:1.4**). The persistent right B acquires in a case such as **Example 5a** can instead be called a 'Mortgagor's Right to Redeem'.

EXAMPLE 5b

B has a personal right against Z. B transfers that right to A as security for B's duty to repay a loan of £200. The deal, of course, is that if B *does* succeed in repaying the loan, A will have to transfer that personal right back to B.

In such a case, B again has a persistent right: a right against A's personal right against Z. Although a Mortgagor's Right to Redeem is known, on the orthodox view, as an 'Equitable property right', it is thus clear that B can have such a right even though no *thing* is involved. The point is that, *whatever* type of right B transfers by way of security, B acquires a right against that right. The Mortgagor's Right to Redeem therefore provides further support for the view that 'Equitable property rights' are better seen as persistent rights (see **B:4.4**). The Mortgagor's Right to Redeem differs from both a Purely Equitable Charge and a right under a Trust due to the special **content** of A's duty: A is under a duty to transfer a right back to B *if* the duty secured by the transfer of that right is performed.

---

[25] For such a transfer to occur, the formality rule set out by Law of Property Act 1925, s 53(1)(c) must be satisfied (see **F3:2.2**).

1.2.4 The right arising under a Trust

(i) Definition

The right arising under a Trust is the classic example of a persistent right. A Trust arises where two conditions are met:

- A is under a duty to B to use a specific right, in a particular way, for B's benefit; *and*
- A is, overall, under a duty in relation to the whole of that right.

EXAMPLE 6a

A0 has Ownership of a bike. A0 transfers his Ownership of the bike to A subject to a duty: (i) to allow B exclusive control of the bike for the next six months; and then (ii) to use the bike entirely for the benefit of A0.

In such a case, a Trust arises: (i) A is under a duty to B to use his Ownership of the bike, in a particular way, for B's benefit; and (ii) overall, A is under a duty in relation to the whole of his Ownership of the bike. This means that *each* of B and A0 has a persistent right under the Trust: both are 'beneficiaries' of the Trust. It may seem that there is an inconsistency between **Example 6a** and **Example 2**. In each case, the **content** of B's right seems to be the same: A is under a duty to B to allow B exclusive control of the bike for six months. Yet in **Example 6a**, but not in **Example 2**, B has a persistent right.

The explanation is that in **Example 6a**, but not in **Example 2**, A is, *overall*, under a duty in relation to the whole of his right. This means that a Trust arises in **Example 6a**, but not in **Example 2**. This demonstrates the crucial point about a Trust: if A is, *overall*, under a duty in relation to the whole of his right, then B has a persistent right, whatever the nature of A's particular duty to B.[26]

	Content of A's duty to B	Is A, overall, under a duty in relation to the whole of A's Ownership of the bike?	Is there a Trust?	Does B have a persistent right?
Example 2	To allow B exclusive control of A's bike for six months	No	No	No
Example 6a	To allow B exclusive control of A's bike for six months	Yes	Yes	Yes

---

[26] Some limits are imposed. For example, there is a general rule (the 'rule against perpetuities') that can prevent B acquiring a right at too distant a point in the future. When applied to persistent rights, that rule can prevent B acquiring a persistent right where A's duty to B in relation to a specific right may arise at some too distant point in the future. For example, an attempt to set up a Trust under which A has a duty to use a right for the benefit of the first person born in the 25th century will fail. For consideration of the question of what counts as 'a too distant point in the future', see eg *Lewin on Trusts* (ed Mowbray et al, 18th edn, 2008), 5.35ff.

(ii) The core Trust duty

> **EXAMPLE 6b**
>
> The facts are as in **Example 6a**. A then transfers his Ownership of the bike, for free, to C.

Whenever a Trust exists, A is under the **core Trust duty**: a duty not to use a right for his own benefit. In **Examples 6a and 6b**, *each* of B and A0 can enforce that duty against A, and therefore *each* of B and A0 has a persistent right. This means that, in **Example 6b**, each of B and A0 has a power to impose a duty on C: a duty not to use the bike for C's own benefit (see **B:4.3**). If either of B and A0 exercises that power by asserting his pre-existing persistent right against C, C comes under the **core Trust duty**: the duty not to use a right (his Ownership of the bike) for his own benefit. This means that a court can order C to transfer Ownership of the bike to T, a party who has agreed to hold Ownership of the bike subject to the duties imposed by the initial Trust (see further **4.2.2** below).

(iii) The versatility of the Trust: A may be both a trustee and a beneficiary

> **EXAMPLE 6c**
>
> A0 has Ownership of a bike. A0 transfers his Ownership of the bike to A. Under the terms of the transfer, A is: (i) subject to a duty to allow B exclusive control of the bike for the next six months; but then (ii) is free to use the bike entirely for his own benefit.

In such a case, A: (i) holds a right on Trust; and (ii) *is* allowed to use that right for his own benefit. Crucially, however, A is only allowed to use the right for his own benefit *because A also has a right under the Trust*. To take account of this, we can refine the **core Trust duty** by saying that A holds a right on Trust:

- If, and only if, A is under a duty not to use that right for his own benefit, *unless and to the extent that* A has a right under the Trust.

This refinement is important as there are many situations in which A is both: (i) a *trustee* (a party who holds a right on Trust); and (ii) a *beneficiary* (a party who has a persistent right under a Trust). For example, if A and B buy land together, they will hold that right on Trust for themselves (see **G2:1.2.3 and G2:1.2.4**).

> **EXAMPLE 6d**
>
> A has Ownership of a bike. A declares that he holds that right on Trust: (i) subject to a duty to allow B exclusive control of the bike for the next six months; and then (ii) with the freedom to use that right entirely for his own benefit.

This case is obviously very close indeed to **Example 2**. Nonetheless, it may well possible for B to have a persistent right. B can claim that A is not *only* under a duty to B to allow B exclusive control of the bike for the next six months; A is under the core Trust duty. If a court accepts that A did indeed intend to be under that duty,[27] it seems that B must have a persistent right.

---

[27] A court could find that A did not in fact intend to be under the core Trust duty and instead simply intended to make a promise, as part of a bargain with B, to allow B exclusive control of the bike for the next six months. On that interpretation, we are back to **Example 2** and B has no persistent right.

This analysis raises an important question. If: (i) a Trust depends on a trustee being under a duty to a beneficiary; and (ii) the same person (eg, A) can be *both* trustee and beneficiary; then (iii) how can A be under a duty to himself? After all, A cannot enter into a contract with himself or commit a wrong against himself—so how can he be under the core Trust duty *to himself?* The first point to make is that A can never owe the core Trust duty entirely to himself. Therefore, if A has Ownership of a car and declares that he holds the car on Trust entirely for his own benefit, no Trust arises: A simply continues to have Ownership of the car. However, in each of **Examples 6c and 6d**, A owes the core Trust duty to *both* himself and B.

This still leaves the question of how, in **Examples 6c and 6d**, A can have a persistent right against his own right. This possibility is another crucial feature of the Trust. The point is that when becoming a trustee, A takes on a new role. In that role as trustee, A can owe himself, in his role as beneficiary, a duty. An analogy occurs where A is both: (i) a director of a company; and (ii) a holder of shares in that company: in his capacity as a director, A can owe himself a duty in his capacity as a shareholder.[28] So, when a Trust is set up, A takes on a new *office*: the office of trustee.[29] Hence, in **Examples 6c and 6d**, B may complain that A is not properly performing his duty, as trustee, to B. In such a case, one possibility is for a court to remove A as a trustee and to appoint a new trustee (A2) in his place. A will then be forced to transfer his Ownership of the bike to A2. However, A will keep his persistent right under the Trust: A can lose his office as a trustee, but continue in his role as a beneficiary.

SUMMARY of D2:1.2

All persistent rights depend on A being under a duty to B. B's right counts as a persistent right only if A's duty has the correct **content**. The basic test is that A's duty must relate to a specific claim-right or power held by A. There are three situations in which that basic test is satisfied:

1. A has a duty to B to hold a right as security for a duty owed to B. In such a case, B has a Purely Equitable Charge.
2. A has a duty to transfer a right back to B if a duty secured by A's holding of the right (eg, B's duty to pay a loan back to A) is performed. In such a case, B has a Mortgagor's Right to Redeem.
3. A is, overall, under a duty in relation to the whole of his right; and as part of that overall duty, A is under a particular duty to B. In such a case, B has a right under a Trust. Under a Trust, the **content** of B's persistent right can be remarkably varied.

B can also acquire a persistent right as a result of an Equitable Assignment. In such a case, the **content** of B's right can fit into the general definition of a right under a Trust: A is under a duty to use a right (a personal right against Z) for B's benefit. So the possibility of Equitable Assignment does not add anything to the **content** question; it is better seen as a *method* by which B can acquire a persistent right and thus as part of the **acquisition** question.

---

[28] Similarly, A can be both: (i) an executor or administrator of a will; and (ii) a party standing to benefit under that will. In such a case, whilst the estate is being administered, A, in his capacity as an executor or administrator, can owe himself a duty in his capacity as a party entitled under the will.

[29] The concept of a trustee as an office-holder is very prominent in Rudden's analysis of the Trust: see eg (1994) 14 *OJLS* 81 at 88; Lawson and Rudden, *The Law of Property* (3rd edn, 2002), 87.

1.3   Persistent rights and the closed list principle

The content of property rights is limited by the closed list principle (see **D1:1.2.1**). Indeed, as far as things other than land are concerned, there is only one form of property right: Ownership. In contrast, there is a great diversity in the content of persistent rights. The Trust provides the variety. Provided that A is, overall, under a duty in relation to the whole of his right, A can be under almost *any* duty to B, and B will have a persistent right. This means that the closed list principle does *not* apply to persistent rights. For example, in **Examples 6a, 6c and 6d** we saw that, if A0 wants to give B a persistent right to have exclusive control of A0's bike for six months, A0 can do so. A0 simply needs to set up a Trust.

The absence of the closed list principle provides yet another example of the fundamental difference between property rights and persistent rights. The principle makes sense when applied to property rights. That is because there is *no conceptual unity* to the **content** of property rights. If B has a right that relates to a thing, then *either* (i) B's right imposes a prima facie duty on the rest of the world and so counts as a property right; *or* (ii) it does not. The property law system simply has to make a decision as to which rights have that effect (see **D1:1.2.3**): we cannot work out from first principles whether or not a particular right counts as a property right.

In contrast, there *is* a conceptual test to tell us if a right counts as a persistent right. The test is the one set out in **1.1** above: *is A under a duty to B in relation to a specific claim right or power held by A?* If the answer is 'Yes', B has a persistent right. If the answer is 'No', B does not.[30] The Purely Equitable Charge; the Mortgagor's Right to Redeem; and the right under a Trust do *not* count as persistent rights simply because judges or Parliament decided, at some point, that they should be on the list of such rights. Rather, each counts as a persistent right because, in each case, A is under a duty to B in relation to a specific claim right or power held by A.

	Test	**Effect**
Property right	Is it on the list of permitted property rights?	Rest of the world is under a prima facie duty to B
Persistent right	Is A under a duty to B in relation to a specific claim right or power held by A?	B has a power to impose a duty on anyone who acquires a right that depends on A's claim right or power

This point about the conceptual unity of persistent rights has very important practical consequences. If the list of persistent rights, like the list of property rights, were essentially arbitrary, then it would always be possible for B to argue that his particular right should be added to the list. So, in **Example 2** or **D1:Example 1**, B could contend that his right deserves some protection against third parties later acquiring A's Ownership of the bike and so should count as a persistent right.[31] However, that argument is *not* available to B. To show

---

[30] The Restrictive Covenant is an exception (see E2:1.3.2). A's duty to B relates to a liberty of A; but B has a persistent right. However, that exception is very limited: for example, it applies only where A and B each has ownership of neighbouring land (see further G6:1).

[31] Exactly that argument has been made (and occasionally accepted by the courts) when B has a contractual licence: a right to make some use of A's land (see E6:3.4.2).

that his right counts as a persistent right, B *must* show that A is under a duty to B in relation to a specific claim right or power held by A. And, in each of **Example 2** and **D1:Example 1**, B cannot do so.

1.4 The usefulness of persistent rights

Let us say A has a specific right and wants to allow B some or all of the benefit of that right. In a system without persistent rights, A has two main choices: either (i) A can simply transfer the right to B; or (ii) A can make a binding promise to use his right, in a particular way, for B's benefit. It is easy to see that, in some circumstances, neither of those choices will be appropriate.

EXAMPLE 7

A Ltd wants to borrow £10,000 from B Bank. B Bank insists on security for A's duty to repay the loan. A Ltd has a valuable personal right against Z, one of his customers. However, that right arises under a contract and the terms of that contract prevent A Ltd from transferring its personal right against Z.

The 'non-assignment' clause means that A Ltd cannot give B Bank security by simply transferring to B Bank its personal right against Z.[32] A Ltd could make a contractual promise that, if it fails to perform its duty to B Bank, it will make up the shortfall by using the proceeds of its right against Z. However, in a system without persistent rights, that contractual promise will give B Bank only a personal right against A Ltd. That right will be of little use to B Bank if A Ltd goes into insolvency (see **B:4.5.1**). A personal right thus cannot give B Bank the very thing it wants: security against the risk that A Ltd may have insufficient resources to pay back the loan.

Fortunately, because the property law system recognises the concept of a persistent right, A Ltd's problem disappears. A Ltd can give B Bank a valuable security right *without* having to transfer his right to B. To do so, A Ltd simply needs to give B Bank a Purely Equitable Charge, ie, a right against A Ltd's personal right against Z:

1. As A Ltd keeps its personal right against Z, there is no breach of the non-assignment clause; *and*
2. As A Ltd's duty to B Bank relates to that specific right, B Bank has a persistent right, which protects B Bank should A Ltd go into insolvency.

In this section, we will look at just some of the many uses of persistent rights. To do so, we will look at the different **content** of the duties that A may be under to B.

1.4.1 A is under a duty to use a right *entirely* for B's benefit

If A is under a duty to use a right entirely for B's benefit, B clearly has a persistent right: a right against A's right. This will happen if, for example, A has a right and simply declares that he holds that right on Trust for B; or if A has a personal right against Z and expresses his intention to give B, immediately, the benefit of that right. This may all seem

---

[32] See *Linden Gardens Trust Ltd v Lenesta Sludge Disposals Ltd* [1994] 1 AC 85. The point is that, under the terms of Z's contract with A Ltd, Z's contractual duty to A Ltd may cease to exist if A Ltd transfers its right to B Bank.

unnecessary: if A wants B to have the entire benefit of A's right, why doesn't A just transfer that right to B?

(i) Where it is impossible for A to transfer a right to B

In some cases, A is simply unable to transfer his right to B. In these cases, A can give B a persistent right in order to *respond to a restriction on A's power to transfer his right.*

For example, we saw in **Example 7** that if A Ltd has a personal right against Z, that right may arise under a contract containing a 'non-assignment' clause. But a standard non-assignment clause will *not* prevent A Ltd from giving B the entire benefit of that right by setting up a Trust of its contractual right against Z.[33] This is because, if A Ltd declares a Trust of its right, there is no transfer: (i) A Ltd keeps its contractual right against Z; but (ii) A Ltd comes under a duty to use that right for the benefit of B.

It is therefore no surprise that a standard non-assignment clause does not prevent A Ltd from setting up a Trust. The purpose of such a clause is to protect Z by ensuring that only A Ltd can assert a particular right against Z: Z thus knows, for example, that he will be able to rely on particular defences that he can use only against A Ltd.[34] And a declaration of Trust by A Ltd does not interfere with that purpose. If A Ltd holds its personal right against Z on Trust for B, then, as in the case of an Equitable Assignment, B has no direct right against Z (see the diagram in **1.2.2(i)** above). Instead, B simply has a right to force A Ltd to use its personal right against Z for B's benefit.[35] For the same reason, a standard non-assignment clause does not prevent A Ltd from making an Equitable Assignment to B. After all, this involves no transfer to B of A Ltd's personal right against Z (see **1.2.2** above).[36]

If A does *not yet have a right*, it is clearly impossible for A to make an immediate transfer of that right to B. Yet A may want to ensure that, when he does acquire that right, B will immediately get the entire benefit of it. For example, A Ltd may want to give B the entire benefit of a particular right it is very likely to acquire against Z Ltd (one of its customers) when Z Ltd makes its usual annual order. As **Example 4d** shows, one way for A Ltd to do this is to use the second form of Equitable Assignment. A Ltd can thus give B a persistent right in order to *ensure that B will get the benefit of a right A may acquire in the future.*

(ii) Where A does not want to transfer a right to B

EXAMPLE 8

A has £10,000 and wants to use that money to benefit B, his ten-year-old grandson.

It would not be a good idea for A to give the money directly to B. Instead, A can use a Trust to give B the entire benefit of that money. For example, A can give the money to T, a responsible trustee, subject to a duty to use that money for B's benefit. In this case, A gives B a persistent right in order to *protect B from an inability to act in B's own best interests.*

There are many other situations in which it is *possible* for A to give a right directly to B,

---

[33] See eg *Don King Productions Inc v Warren* [2000] Ch 291; *Barbados Trust Company Ltd v Bank of Zambia* [2007] EWCA Civ 148.

[34] See *per* Lord Browne-Wilkinson in *Linden Gardens Trust Ltd v Lenesta Sludge Disposals Ltd* [1994] 1 AC 85 at 105–6.

[35] *Barbados Trust Company Ltd v Bank of Zambia* [2007] EWCA Civ 148.

[36] See eg *Foamcrete Ltd v Thrust Engineering Ltd* [2000] EWCA Civ 351 and the discussion in M Smith, *The Law of Assignment* (2007), 12.141.

but A instead *chooses* to come under a duty to use that right entirely for B's benefit. For example, one attraction to A of an Equitable Assignment may be that A can give B the entire benefit of a right without having to transfer that right to B. This means, for example, that A does not have to comply with the formality rule set out by section 136 of the Law of Property Act 1925 (see **C3:5.1.2**). So, A can give B a persistent right in order to *respond to a formality rule regulating A's power to transfer his right.*[37]

1.4.2 A is under a duty to use a right *partly* for B's benefit

(i) B has a Purely Equitable Charge

In **Example 4a**, B has a Purely Equitable Charge over A's Ownership of the bike. If A is £100 short in repaying B, B can sell A's bike and use the proceeds to meet A's debt. If the bike is sold for £200, A can keep the £100 excess. Hence, A's duty to B relates to the whole of A's right (B can insist on a sale of that right); but A is *not* under a duty to use his right entirely for B's benefit. If A has an existing right, the Purely Equitable Charge is very useful: it allows A *to give B security without transferring his right to B.*[38]

If A Ltd instead wants to give B security over a *future* right, it can do so by making a contractual promise to hold that right as security, *as soon as* it acquires the right. If A Ltd makes such a promise, then, when it does acquire its right, B will acquire an immediate persistent right.[39] This use of the Purely Equitable Charge is *incredibly* important in practice: it allows A Ltd to raise money by giving a lender such as B Bank security not only over the company's existing rights, but also over its *future* rights.

(ii) B has a right under a Trust

EXAMPLE 9

A has £100,000 in his bank account. A wants to ensure that: (i) B2, a charity, eventually gets the benefit of the £100,000; and (ii) that B1, during B1's life, gets the benefit of the income generated by the £100,000.

In such a case, A needs to set up a Trust. For example, A can transfer his right to the £100,000 to T subject to a duty to: (i) invest and manage the £10,000 and its proceeds; (ii) pay the annual interest on the fund to B1, during B1's life; and (iii) on B1's death, pay the capital to B2. In this way, A can use a Trust to divide up the benefits of his right to the £100,000.

Similarly, if A holds shares in a particular company, A may have a number of different rights, such as: (i) a personal right against the company to receive annual dividends; and (ii)

---

[37] By doing so, A does not 'evade' or undermine the formality rule. If a formality rule applies to the *transfer* of a right, this does not mean it should also apply to A's creation of a persistent right against that right. For example, we have seen that the chief purpose of the Law of Property Act 1925, s 136 is to protect Z by allowing him to know to whom he owes his duty (see **C3:6.3**). If A, rather than transferring his right to B, instead: (i) *keeps* his right against Z; and (ii) gives B a persistent right against that right; then (iii) Z's duty is still owed to A. There is hence no need for the s 136 formality rule to apply (see **C3:7.2**).

[38] If A has Ownership of a thing, A can use a pledge to allow B to acquire a property right by way of security (see **D1:1.4.2**). In such a case, A keeps his Ownership of the thing. However, a pledge can be awkward for A as it means allowing B to take physical control of A's thing. And a pledge cannot be used to give B security over a personal right or persistent right of A.

[39] See eg *Tailby v Official Receiver* (1888) 13 App Cas 523.

a power to vote at company meetings. By using a Trust, A can separate out those two benefits. For example, A can transfer the shares to T subject to a duty to: (i) pay the dividends to B1; and (ii) to use the voting powers for the benefit of B2.

A can thus use a Trust in order to *distribute the benefits of a right as A wishes.*[40] This flexibility can be particularly important where A has a property right. For example, we saw in **D1:Example 7** that A can use a Trust to share the benefit of his Ownership of a painting between B1, B2 and the National Gallery. In such a case, A can use a Trust to *respond to a restriction on the content of property rights.*[41]

1.4.3 A's duty to use a right for B's benefit is subject to conditions

EXAMPLE 10a

A has shares in a particular company. A wants to give the benefit of those shares to his grandson, B. B is currently aged 18. A could simply transfer the shares to B. However, A is worried that B, although not a minor, is too young to use the shares prudently.

A could of course hold on to the shares and give them to B only when B is older (eg, when B is 25). However, A may have good reasons for wanting to deal with the shares immediately. For example, in order to avoid being taxed on the shares, A may want to ensure that he no longer has the benefit of them. Alternatively, A may be considering how to leave the shares in his will, in which case, if he dies before B reaches 25, A will need to transfer the shares to T, subject to a duty to give the shares to B *if* B reaches 25.

The solution for A is to set up a Trust.[42] This allows A to *impose conditions on B's enjoyment of a benefit.* For example, A can transfer the shares to T a subject to: (i) a duty to manage the shares and any income they produce (a duty to 'accumulate' the income produced by the shares); (ii) a duty to use the shares entirely for B's benefit if B reaches 25; and (iii) a duty, if B dies before that age, to use the shares for the benefit of B2 (eg, a charity).[43] This ability to impose conditions on B's enjoyment of a benefit makes the Trust a very popular device when A is drawing up a will, as it provides a means for A to exert control over a right even after his death.[44]

---

[40] See eg Worthington, *Equity* (2nd edn, 2006).

[41] By doing so, A does not 'evade' or undermine the limit on the content of property rights. The fact that the property law system does not allow A to give B1 or B2 a property right consisting to exclusive control for a limited period; or to give B2 or the National Gallery a property right consisting of future exclusive control does *not* mean that the same restrictions should apply to persistent rights. For example, one of the chief reasons for restricting the content of property rights is to protect third parties. If B1, B2 and the National Gallery instead acquire persistent rights, a third party buying the painting from a trustee may be able to rely on the 'bona fide purchaser' defence (see **3.5** below) or the overreaching defence (see **3.4** below).

[42] A has to be a little careful. If A simply gives the shares to T, subject to a duty to transfer the shares to B when B reaches 25, B will have a power to *immediately* acquire the shares (see **D1:1.4.5(ii)** and **F3:1.3**). This is often referred to as a '*Saunders v Vautier*' power and is named for the case: (1841) Cr & Ph 240; (1841) 4 Beav 115.

[43] If A fails to make clear what should happen if B dies before reaching 25, T will hold the shares on Trust for *both* B and A: T will be under a duty, if B dies before reaching 25, to hold the shares for A's benefit. The persistent right A thereby acquires (arising under a Resulting Trust: see **D4:4.3**) can cause problems for A. For example it means A still has some of the benefit of the shares and so may be liable for tax on that basis: see eg *Vandervell v IRC* [1967] 2 AC 291.

[44] As can be imagined, parties drawing up wills have been tempted to attach idiosyncratic conditions and courts have sometimes been faced with the difficult task of interpreting how and whether such conditions can apply to particular factual situations: see eg *Clayton v Ramsden* [1943] AC 320; *re Tuck's Settlement Trusts* [1978] Ch 49.

THE CONTENT QUESTION – 1.4   223

EXAMPLE 10b

A has shares in a particular company. A wants to ensure that, after his death, the benefit of those shares will be divided up between his three grandchildren (B1, B2 and B3).

When planning for the future, A has to deal with uncertainty. In his will, A could simply divide the shares into three equal parcels and give one parcel to each grandchild. However, that distribution may turn out to be unwise. Within six months of A's death, B1 may have won the lottery; B2 may have lost his job and be struggling to raise a family; and B3 may have died, leaving his assets to his partner, whom A disliked. If A had known this would happen—or had stayed alive a little longer and so had the chance to alter his will—he would have given *all* the shares to B2. And there are further uncertainties. For example, after his death, A may acquire more grandchildren: if the shares have already been divided up among B1, B2 and B3 there will be no guarantee that the new grandchildren will take *any* of the benefit of those shares.

A can deal with these problems by setting up a particular type of Trust known as a *discretionary Trust*. For example, A can transfer his shares to T, subject to: (i) a duty to manage the shares and the income they produce; (ii) a duty to make sure that, by the end of a fixed period,[45] T has distributed all of the shares and income to at least one of A's grandchildren; (iii) a power to choose *who* among the grandchildren will receive any part of the shares or income *and* to choose *how much* any such recipient will get; and (iv) a duty, if none of A's grandchildren survive him, and if no new grandchildren are born by the end of a fixed period after A's death, to transfer the shares and income to a charity.

The key to a discretionary Trust is that it gives T the *power* to choose how to distribute the benefit of a right. This means that, if the unexpected occurs after A's death, T will be able to react accordingly and to ensure that the benefits of his right are distributed according to the needs or merits of A's grandchildren. Of course, although T has this power, he has a *fiduciary duty* (see **F3:1.2**) to each of A's grandchildren to exercise that power loyally and responsibly, in the best interests of the grandchildren.[46] This means, for example, that T cannot exercise his power perversely or according to his own selfish interests.[47]

A discretionary Trust thus imposes a particular sort of *condition* on B's enjoyment of a right: B only acquires the benefit *if* T chooses to exercise a power in B's favour. A can thus use a discretionary Trust to *allow a trustee to react to unforeseen events*.

SUMMARY of D2:1.4

If A has, or expects to acquire a right, the possibility of giving B a persistent right against A's right may be incredibly useful to A. By giving B such a right, A can:

- respond to a restriction on A's power to transfer his right;
- ensure that B will get some or all of the benefit of a right A may acquire in the future;

---

[45] If A does not fix a period, then one will be supplied by the operation of the rule against 'accumulations'. That rule ensures that there is a limit to the period in which T can hold on to the income produced by a right without distributing that income: see Law of Property Act 1925, ss 164–5 and eg *Lewin on Trusts* (ed Mowbray et al, 18th edn, 2008), 5-99ff.

[46] The essence of a fiduciary duty lies in the special rules that protect and reinforce T's core duty (see **F3:1.2**).

[47] For discussions of the duties of a discretionary trustee, see eg *McPhail v Doulton* [1971] AC 424; *re Hay's Settlement Trusts* [1982] 1 WLR 202.

- respond to a formality rule regulating A's power to transfer his right;
- protect B from an inability to act in his own best interests;
- give B security without transferring his right to B;
- distribute the benefits of a right as A wishes;
- respond to a restriction on the content of property rights;
- impose conditions on B's enjoyment of a benefit; and
- allow a trustee to react to unforeseen events.

Given all the benefits of persistent rights, it is little wonder that many legal systems not based on English law are keen to adopt persistent rights by introducing concepts such as the Trust.[48]

1.5 Powers to regain a right

If B transfers a property right to A as a result of A's fraud or duress, B has a *power* to unwind the transfer and immediately regain that property right. That power does *not* count as a property right: it does not impose a prima facie duty on the rest of the world (see **D1:1.4.5(i)**). However, there is a strong argument that B's right should count as a persistent right: (i) as a result of acquiring B's right through fraud or duress, A owes a duty to B; and (ii) A's duty relates to a specific right, ie, the right B has transferred to A. We will examine this view further in **D4:3.2**. One point worth noting here is that, if B does have a persistent right, this would explain why B cannot exercise his power to rescind against a 'bona fide purchaser' of A's right (see **D1:3.5.4**).

1.6 Powers to acquire a persistent right

1.6.1 An example

EXAMPLE 11a

B joins a religious sisterhood. Under the rules of that association, the word of A, the lady superior, is to be treated as the word of God. The rules also forbid members from seeking external advice without the consent of A. B, without receiving anything in return, transfers her car to A.

This example is essentially identical to **D1:Example 16b**. The only difference is that the names of the parties have been swapped. This is because, in this section, in contrast to **D1:2.2.2(ii)**, we are considering the position not of the party receiving a right, but of the party transferring a right. Of course, the basic principles applying to **D1:Example 16b** also apply here. As it was procured by A's undue influence over B, the transfer of B's right to A is said to be 'voidable in Equity': B is said to have an 'Equitable right to rescind the transfer'.

---

[48] See eg in France, Law No 2007-211 of 19 February 2007, amending the Code Civil to introduce the concept of a 'fiducie' holding rights separately from his own patrimony; the same term is used in the Quebec Civil Code: see eg Art 1261. For a survey of provisions introducing concepts based on the Trust to civil jurisdictions see Lupoi, *Trusts: A Comparative Study* (trans Dix, 2000) and *Trusts Laws of the World: A Collection of Original Texts* (1996). Indeed, Gretton (2007) 71 *Rabels Zeitschrift* 802 suggests that security rights recognised in civil jurisdictions may *already* be based on a concept seemingly identical to that of a right against a right.

This means that, although B's right has been transferred to A, B has an immediate power to acquire a persistent right: a right against the right transferred to A. That power can also arise where B transfers a right to A as a result of a mistake (see **D4:4.2.2**). And it arises whenever B transfers a right to A (whether it is a property right, a persistent right or a personal right) as a result of A's undue influence or B's mistake.

In a case such as **Example 11a**, there are three distinct stages:

Stage 1: Immediately after the transfer to A, B has an 'Equitable right to rescind', ie, a *power to acquire a persistent right.*

Stage 2: After B exercises that power, and A is or ought to be aware of B's exercise of the power, A holds his Ownership of the car on Trust for B.[49]

Stage 3: Once A holds his Ownership of the car on Trust for B, B acquires a *new* power. That new power arises because: (i) A's duty, under the Trust, is to use the right *entirely* for B's benefit; and (ii) B is in the best position to judge his own benefit.[50] By exercising that new power, B can impose a duty on A to transfer Ownership of the car back to B (see **D1:1.4.5(ii)**). As A can be forced to comply with that duty this means that, at the end of the day, B *does* get his right back. But, crucially, B has to exercise *two different powers* to get to that position.

1.6.2 Terminology

In a case such as **Example 11a**, B is generally said to have an 'Equitable right to rescind.' In contrast, if B transfers a right to A as a result of A's duress, or A's fraudulent misrepresentation, B is generally said to have a 'Common Law right to rescind' (see **D1:1.4.5(i)**). However, this terminology is unhelpful:

1. In each case, B does not have a claim right to rescind; instead, B has a *power.*
2. It is better to distinguish these powers according to their nature, not according to the court system in which each was first developed (see **B:4.4.**)
3. Where B has a 'Common Law right to rescind' he has a power to regain the right he transferred to A.
4. Where B has an 'Equitable right to rescind' he has a power to acquire a persistent right against the right he transferred to A.

Orthodox label	B's position	A's position	Triggering circumstances: B's intention is procured by ...
'Common Law right to rescind'	B has a **power** to immediately regain the right he has transferred to A	A has a liability to B to lose the transferred right	−A's duress −A's fraudulent misrepresentation

---

[49] The Trust does not arise as soon as B transfers his right to A; rather, it can arise only once B has exercised his 'Equitable right to rescind'. See eg *per* Millett LJ in *Bristol & West BS v Mothew* [1998] Ch 1 at 22–3. Note too *per* Lord Browne-Wilkinson in *Westdeutsche Landesbank Girozentrale v Islington LBC* [1996] AC 669 at 705: A can only come under the core Trust duty once A has sufficient awareness of the facts giving rise to B's power to rescind (see **D4:4.3**).

[50] See **D1:1.4.5(ii)** and **F3:1.3** for discussion of this power, often called the '*Saunders v Vautier*' power.

| 'Equitable right to rescind' | B has a **power** to acquire a persistent right against the right he has transferred to A | A has a liability to B to come under a duty not to use the transferred right for A's own benefit | −A's undue influence
−A's non-fraudulent misrepresentation
−Any other mistake of A as to a current state of affairs that causes A to transfer a right to B when A is under no duty to do so (see **D4:4.2**) |

1.6.3 'Mere Equities'

In a case such as **Example 11a**, B's 'Equitable right to rescind' is said to give B a 'mere Equity'.[51] This term is used to make clear that, unless and until he exercises his power, B does *not* have an 'Equitable property right'. Certainly, on the analysis taken in this book, it is useful to emphasis that, in a case such as **Example 11a**, B does *not* have a full-blown persistent right. Instead, B has only a power to acquire such a right.

However, it is very unhelpful to call B's power to acquire a persistent right a 'mere Equity'. First, on the orthodox view, the category of 'mere Equities' is notoriously badly defined.[52] Second, the name itself is clearly unsatisfactory: for example, if B has a power to regain a right transferred to A as a result of A's duress or fraud, we do not say that B has a 'mere Common Law'.[53] Both these problems can be avoided if 'mere Equities' are simply understood as *powers to acquire a persistent right.*

Orthodox view		View taken in this book	
Name of B's right	**Test for B's right**	**Name of B's right**	**Test for B's right**
'Equitable property right'	Is B's right on the list of Equitable property rights?	**Persistent right**	**Is A under a duty to B in relation to a specific claim right or power held by A?**
'Mere Equity'	Is B's right on the list of Mere Equities?	**Power to acquire a persistent right**	**Does B have a power to impose a duty on A in relation to a specific claim right or power held by A?**

---

[51] See eg *per* Millett LJ in *Bristol & West BS v Mothew* [1998] Ch 1 at 22; *per* Fry LJ in *Bainbrigge v Browne* (1881) 18 Ch D 188 at eg 196.

[52] See eg *Cheshire and Burn's Modern Law of Real Property* (17th edn, 2006), 812: 'The courts have never found a satisfactory definition of an equity'; *Snell's Equity* (31st edn, 2005, ed McGhee), 2-05: 'It is difficult to define [mere equities] with clarity.' It seems that the category includes, for example, B's power to rectify the terms of a contract under which an extra parcel of land has been transferred to A by virtue of A and B's mutual mistake: *Blacklocks v JB Developments (Godalming) Ltd* [1982] Ch 183. In such a case, B has a power to alter the contract and hence to impose a duty on A to transfer the parcel mistakenly transferred back to B. When A is under such a duty, B has a persistent right: so B's power to rectify gives B a power to acquire a persistent right

[53] Swadling (2005) 121 *LQR* 123 at 133.

The advantage of the view taken in this book is that it emphasises the *conceptual unity* of *both* (i) persistent rights; and (ii) powers to acquire persistent rights. There is no arbitrary list of such rights. B's right counts as a persistent right if A is under a duty to B in relation to a specific claim right or power. And B's power counts as a power to acquire a persistent right if, as in **Example 11a**, B has a power to impose such a duty on A.

1.6.4 Third parties

> **EXAMPLE 11b**
>
> The facts are as in **Example 11a** above. Before B exercises his power to rescind the transfer to A, A gives the car to C as a birthday present.

In such a case, when C acquires his right from A, B has only a 'mere Equity': a power to acquire a persistent right against A's Ownership of the car. As B does not have a pre-existing persistent right, this means that C does *not* need to show that he has a defence to B's power. The question instead is whether *B* can show that, although his original right has now passed to C, B can *still* exercise his power to acquire a persistent right. And, as C has acquired Ownership of the car for free, B *can* exercise his power against C (see **3.5.5** below).[54] By doing so, B can impose the core Trust duty on C and thus acquire a persistent right against C's Ownership of the car. So, it is possible to say that B's power to acquire a persistent right, can, in some cases, be exercised against a third party.

However, this clearly does not mean that our list of persistent rights must also include *the power to acquire a persistent right*. The result in **Example 11b** simply depends on the point we examined in **D1:1.4.5**, namely that, in some cases, it is possible for B to assert a power against a third party. This does *not* mean that B's power is prima facie binding on C. Certainly, it is *not* the case that C needs to show a 'defence' to B's power; rather, *B* must show why C should be under a liability to B.

> **SUMMARY of D2:1**
>
> When asking if B's right counts as a persistent right, we *could* look to see if B's right is on a list of persistent rights. That list, where land is not concerned, would include: (i) the Purely Equitable Charge; (ii) the Mortgagor's Right to Redeem; and (iii) the right arising under a Trust. However, the genius of persistent rights lies precisely in their ability to escape the limits of the 'closed list' principle. There is a vital conceptual unity to persistent rights: they arise *whenever*: (i) A has a claim right or power; and (ii) A is under a duty to B in relation to that claim-right or a power.
>
> The possibility of giving B a persistent right can be immensely useful to A: (i) A can keep his right; *and* (ii) come under a duty to B in relation to that right; and, by so doing (iii) give B a prima facie power to impose a duty on C, a third party (such as A's trustee in bankruptcy) acquiring a right that depends on A's right. And A can do all this *even if* the right acquired by B is not on the closed list of property rights; and *even if* A's initial right is only a personal right or a persistent right.

---

[54] This is assumed in eg *Phillips v Phillips* (1861) 4 De G F &J 208.

2 THE ACQUISITION QUESTION

Property rights can be acquired either by: (i) an *independent acquisition*; or (ii) a *dependent acquisition* (see **D1:2**). In contrast, it is impossible for B to acquire a persistent right by means of an independent acquisition. To acquire a persistent right, B first needs to show that A is under a duty to B; and A cannot come under such a duty simply because of B's unilateral conduct.

Property rights and persistent rights also differ in relation to dependent acquisition. To acquire a property right from A, B needs to show that *A has exercised a power* to give B that right. In contrast, to acquire a right against a right of A, B simply needs to show that *A is under a duty* to B in relation to that right. And that duty can arise as a result of *any* of the six reasons set out in **B:4.3**.

2.1   The acquisition of a new persistent right

To acquire a persistent right, B first needs to show that A is under a duty to B. The reasons for which A's duty may arise can be classified into six different groups (see **B:4.3**):

1. A's consent to be under such a duty to B;
2. A's entry into a contract with B;
3. A's commission of a wrong against B;
4. A's unjust enrichment at B's expense;
5. A statute imposing a duty on A to B;
6. A residual group of 'other events' that impose a duty on A to B.

2.1.1 Consent

(i) Consensual Trusts

If A has a right, A has a power to come under the **core Trust duty** to B. A simply needs to express his intention to be under a duty to B: (i) to use his right, in some way, for B's benefit; *and* (ii) not to use that right for A's own benefit, unless and to the extent that A is also a beneficiary of the Trust. So, if A has Ownership of a bike, A can give B a persistent right by simply declaring that he holds that right on Trust for B. There is no need for A expressly to refer to a Trust: it is enough for A to show that he intends to be under the core Trust duty (see **C3:5.2.1** and **F3:2.1.1**). However, A must intend to *keep* his right and to come under a duty to B in relation to that right: if A instead intends to *transfer* that right to B, and B gives nothing in return, no Trust can arise.[55]

Similarly, if A0 has a right, he can set up a Trust in B's favour by: (i) transferring that right to A; and (ii) attempting to impose the **core Trust duty** on A. So, if A0 has Ownership of a bike, A0 can give B a persistent right by transferring that right to A to hold on Trust for B. Again, there is no need for A0 expressly to refer to a Trust: it is enough for A0 to show that he intends A be under the core Trust duty.

In such a case, A will only be under the core Trust duty if he consents to bear it: if A does not consent, A will *not* hold the right on Trust for B.[56] However, a Trust will not fail for lack

---

[55] See eg *Milroy v Lord* (1862) 4 De G.F. & J 264; *Richards v Delbridge* (1874) LR 18 Eq 11 (see **C3:7.3.2**).
[56] See eg *per* Lord Talbot in *Robinson v Pett* (1734) 3 P Wms 249 at 251.

of a trustee.[57] At B's request, a court can appoint a new trustee:[58] someone who (probably in return for payment) *does* consent to hold the right on Trust for B. A will then be ordered to transfer his right to that new trustee, who will hold it on Trust for B.

Where A exercises his power to come under the core Trust duty to B, there is no need for B to give something in return: the doctrine of consideration is irrelevant as B is not seeking to impose a contractual duty on A. Nor is there is any need for A to express or record his intention in a particular form (see **C3:5.2.1**). It may seem surprising that A's power to give B a persistent right, without receiving anything in return, is not regulated by a formality rule; however, that approach can be justified (see **C3:6.2**).

(ii) Type 1 Equitable Assignments

If A has a personal right against Z, A has a power to make an Equitable Assignment of that right to B. As shown by **B:Example 6a** (see **1.2.2(i)** above), a Type 1 Equitable Assignment occurs simply as a result of A expressing his intention to be under an immediate duty to give B the benefit of A's right. A can thus come under a duty to B even if B gives nothing in return;[59] and even if A orally expresses his intention (see **C3:6.2** and **C3:7.2.1**). For such a Type 1 Equitable Assignment to work: (i) A must *already* have the personal right against Z;[60] and (ii) A must expresses an intention to *immediately* give B the benefit of the right, rather than in the future;[61] and (iii) A must intend to *keep* his personal right against Z: a Type 1 Equitable Assignment cannot occur if A instead intends to transfer that right to B.

Therefore, A can exercise a power to declare a Trust of a right in B's favour, or to make a Type 1 Equitable Assignment. If:

- A has a right; *and*
- A expresses his intention to keep that right and to come under a duty to use the right for B's benefit; *then*
- B acquires a persistent right *even if* A has expressed his intention orally and *even if* B has provided nothing in return for that persistent right.

It is no surprise that the same basic rules apply to: (i) A's power to declare a Trust of a right in B's favour; and (ii) A's power to make a Type 1 Equitable Assignment of that right in B's favour.[62] After all, in each case, A's duty to B arises as a result of A's consent to be under that duty.

---

[57] See eg *per* North J in *re Robinson* [1892] 1 Ch 95 at 100.

[58] See eg Trustee Act 1925, ss 36 and 41.

[59] See eg *re Patrick* [1891] 1 Ch 82; *re McArdle* [1951] Ch 669. A contrary view was taken by the High Court of Australia in *Olsson v Dyson* (1969) 120 CLR 365. That decision seems to assume that A's failure to transfer a right to B (caused by a failure to comply with a formality rule based on the Law of Property Act 1925, s 136) *necessarily* prevents an Equitable Assignment. However, the fact that no *transfer* of A's right occurred should not prevent A keeping his right and B acquiring a persistent right against that right.

[60] *Kekewich v Manning* (1851) 1 De G M & G 176.

[61] *Glegg v Bromley* [1912] 3 KB 474 at 491–2.

[62] See eg *Kekewich v Manning* (1851) 1 De G M & G 176; *Lewin on Trusts* (ed Mowbray et al, 18th edn, 2008), 3.31; M Smith, *The Law of Assignment* (2007), 6.02, arguing that 'informal' non-contractual Equitable assignments (ie, Type 1 Equitable Assignments) 'operate by way of trust'.

(iii) Promises in a deed

EXAMPLE 12a

In June, A expects to acquire a personal right against Z, a potential customer. A makes a promise in a deed that, if he acquires that personal right against Z, he will use it entirely for B's benefit. B provides nothing in return for A's promise. In September, A acquires that right but refuses to use it for B's benefit.

By making his promise, A consented to be under a duty to B. However, in June, A did not have his personal right against Z. So, at that point, A did *not* have a power to set up a Trust of that right, nor to make a Type 1 Equitable Assignment. And, as B provided nothing in return for it, A's promise does not impose a contractual duty on A to B. Nonetheless, B can argue that: (i) as A chose to make his promise in a deed, A is under a duty to B, arising as a result of A's consent (see **C3:2**); and (ii) as A's promise was to use a specific right for B's benefit; then (iii) in September, when A acquires that right, B has a persistent right against A's right.

In principle, B's argument should succeed. Surprisingly, the orthodox view is that a promise made in a deed, by itself, can *never* give B a persistent right. That orthodox view rests on three unconvincing reasons:

1.   A promise in a deed imposes a duty on A at Common Law, but not in Equity. As a result, such a promise, by itself, cannot give B an 'Equitable property right'. However, that reason disappears if we instead see 'Equitable property rights' as persistent rights (see **B:4.4**). All that matters is that A is under a duty to B in relation to a specific right; it does not matter that A's duty was recognised by Common Law rather than Equity.
2.   Where B provides nothing in return for A's promise, B's right will not be specifically protected: B will be denied the remedy of specific performance. This view is incorrect as it confuses the **remedies question** with the **acquisition question** (see **2.1.2(vi)** below). All that matters is that A is under a duty to B in relation to a specific right; it does not matter what remedy may be given to protect that right.
3.   As B has provided nothing in return for A's promise, B is a 'volunteer' and 'Equity will not assist a volunteer'. That view is obviously incorrect. If A exercises his power to set up a Trust in B's favour; or to make a Type 1 Equitable Assignment to B, then B can acquire a persistent right without giving anything in return (see **2.1.1(i) and (ii)** above).

So, in **Example 12a**, contrary to the orthodox view, B *should* acquire a persistent right as soon as A acquires his personal right against Z.[63] In fact, there is no clear authority standing in the way of that conclusion. Cases denying B a persistent right where A's promise is made in a deed differ from **Example 12** in one very important respect. In those cases, A's promise is made to C, *not* to B.[64] In such a case, it is entirely correct to deny B a persistent right: if

---

[63] Similarly, if A makes a promise in a deed to hold a right as security for B, that promise should give B a Purely Equitable Charge. However, in practice, B almost always gives something in return for a Purely Equitable Charge (eg, B makes a loan to A; or B declines to enforce a right he has against A2) so A's promise imposes a contractual duty on A to B and hence falls under **2.1.2(ii)** below.

[64] See eg *re Pryce* [1917] 1 Ch 324; *re Kay's Settlement* [1939] Ch 329; *re Cook's Settlement Trusts* [1965] Ch 902.

A's promise is made to C, then, even if it is made in a deed, it cannot impose a duty on A *to B*.[65] As a result, B cannot acquire a persistent right.

2.1.2 Contract

(i) Promises to come under a duty to B in the future: Trusts and Type 2 Equitable Assignments

EXAMPLE 12bi

In June, A expects to acquire a personal right against Z, a potential customer. A makes a promise that, if he acquires that personal right against Z, he will hold it on Trust for B. B pays A £100 in return for that promise. In September, A acquires that right but refuses to use it for B's benefit.

In contrast to **Example 12a**, B has provided something in return for A's promise: as a result, A is under a contractual duty to B. It is clear that, in such a case, *as soon as* A acquires his right against Z, B acquires a persistent right against A's right. That right arises before, and in the absence of, any action A may take to set up the promised Trust.

EXAMPLE 12bii

In June, A expects to acquire a personal right against Z, a potential customer. A makes a promise that, if he acquires that personal right against Z, he will transfer it to B. B pays A £100 in return for that promise. In September, A acquires that right but refuses to transfer it to B.

Clearly, as no transfer has occurred, B has not acquired A's personal right against Z. However, B can rely on a Type 2 Equitable Assignment. As soon as A acquires his personal right against Z, A is under a contractual duty to transfer his right to B. A is thus under a duty to B in relation to a specific right held by A: as a result, B acquires a persistent right.

EXAMPLE 12ci

A believes he has a personal right against Z. In return for £100 from B, A declares a Trust of that right in B's favour. However, at the time of the declaration, A does not yet have that personal right against Z. A acquires it three months later.

A has not made an *express* promise to hold his right on Trust for B. Instead A tried, and failed, to set up an immediate Trust. However, as: (i) A *attempted* to set up the Trust; *and*

Such cases often involve A making a promise to C that he will transfer a right to C to hold on Trust for B. If A can be seen as intending that C should exercise his right to enforce the promise *on behalf* of B, then: (i) B can force C to exercise that right; (ii) C can acquire substantial damages from A if A fails to perform the promise; and (iii) C will then hold those damages on Trust for B: see eg *Fletcher v Fletcher* (1844) 4 Hare 67. There is no shortage of articles discussing the points raised by these cases: see eg Barton (1975) 91 *LQR* 236; Meagher and Lehane (1976) 92 *LQR* 427; Goddard [1988] Conv 19; McNair (1988) 8 *LS* 172.

[65] S 56 of the Law of Property Act 1925 may assist B (see **D3:2.1.1**), but the Contract (Rights of Third Parties) Act 1999 cannot: if C provides nothing in return for A's promise, A's promise to C is not contractually binding. An exception is made in a limited context: where A's promise is made as part of a 'marriage settlement'. If B is a spouse of A, a child of their marriage, or a descendant of such a child, B is viewed as a party to the deed. A is thus under a duty to B and so B *does* acquire a persistent right as soon as A acquires a right covered by the marriage settlement: see eg *Pullan v Koe* [1913] 1 Ch 9.

(ii) B gave something in return; then (iii) a court will *infer* that A made a contractual promise to set up a Trust in B's favour.[66] So, the result in **Example 12c(i)** matches that in **Example 12b(i)**: *as soon as* A acquires his personal right against Z, B acquires a persistent right against that right. Of course, this result depends on a fiction: A's attempt to set up an *immediate* Trust is seen as a contractual promise to set up a Trust *in the future*. But the fiction can be justified: given that B provided something in return for the attempted Trust, there is no reason why, in **Example 12c(i)**, B should be in a worse position than in Example **12b(i)**.

EXAMPLE 12cii

A believes he has a personal right against Z. In return for £100 from B, A attempts to transfer that right to B. However, at the time of the declaration, A does not yet have that personal right against Z. A acquires it three months later.

Clearly, as no transfer has occurred, B has not acquired A's personal right against Z. However, B can rely on a Type 2 Equitable Assignment. As in **Example 12ci**, because B provided something in return for the attempted transfer, a court will infer that A made a contractual promise to make that transfer. So, as soon as A acquires his personal right against Z, A is under a contractual duty to transfer his right to B: as a result, B acquires a persistent right.

EXAMPLE 12di

In June, A expects to acquire a personal right against Z, a potential customer. A makes a promise that, if he acquires that personal right against Z, he will hold it on Trust for B. A's promise is not made in a deed and B provides nothing in return for it. In September, A acquires that right but refuses to use it for B's benefit.

EXAMPLE 12dii

In June, A expects to acquire a personal right against Z, a potential customer. A makes a promise that, if he acquires that personal right against Z, he will transfer it to B. A's promise is not made in a deed and B provides nothing in return for it. In September, A acquires that right but refuses to transfer it to B.

EXAMPLE 12ei

A believes he has a personal right against Z. A declares a Trust of that right in B's favour. B provides nothing in return. However, at the time of the declaration, A does not yet have that personal right against Z. A acquires that right three months later but refuses to use it for B's benefit.

EXAMPLE 12eii

A believes he has a personal right against Z. A attempts to transfer that right to B. B provides nothing in return. However, at the time of the attempted transfer, A does not yet have that personal right against Z. A acquires it three months later but refuses to transfer it to B.

---

[66] See eg *re Burton's Settlements* [1955] Ch 82 at 103–4. The same principle was applied in a different context in *Parker v Taswell* (1858) 2 De G & J 559.

There is a crucial difference between: (i) **Examples 12b and 12c**; and (ii) **Examples 12d and 12e**. In the latter cases, A's promise to B does *not* impose a duty on A to B: it was not made in a deed, and, as B has provided nothing in return, it cannot impose a contractual duty on A to B. As it does not impose a duty on A to B, A's promise *cannot* give B a persistent right. There is also a crucial difference between: (i) the situations discussed in **2.1.1(i) and (ii)** above; and (ii) **Examples 12d and 12e**. In the former situations, A is dealing with an *existing* right. As a result, an oral expression of A's consent to be under an *immediate* duty to B, even if B gives nothing in return, can impose a duty on A to B and hence give B a persistent right. However where, as in **Examples 12d and 12e**, A deals with a *future* right, an oral expression of consent to be under a duty to B in the *future*, for which B gives nothing in return, *cannot* impose a duty on A to B and so cannot give B a persistent right.[67]

(ii) Promises to come under an immediate or future duty to B: Purely Equitable Charges

1. If A makes a contractual promise to allow B to use a specific right of A as security for a duty owed to B, A comes under an immediate duty to B. As a result, B immediately acquires a persistent right: a Purely Equitable Charge (see **1.2.1** above).
2. If A does not yet have a right, but makes a contractual promise to B that, when A acquires that right, he will hold it as security for B, then B acquires a Purely Equitable Charge as soon as A acquires that right.
3. If A wrongly believes that he already has a right, and makes a contractual promise to hold that right as security for B, B will acquire a Purely Equitable Charge as soon as A acquires that right (by means of the principle applying in **Examples 12ci and 12cii** above).

(iii) Promises to transfer a property right

EXAMPLE 13

A has Ownership of a bike. A and B enter a contract of sale: A promises to transfer his Ownership of the bike to B; B promises to pay £200 in return.

In this situation, persistent rights are irrelevant. The contract of sale can, *by itself*, transfer A's property right to B (see **D1:2.2.4(iii)**). B will acquire A's Ownership of the bike *as soon as A and B intend that B should*. For example, let us say A and B agree that B will acquire Ownership of the bike when he pays the price to A:

1. Before B pays, A is under no duty to transfer his right to B: at that point, B cannot have a persistent right.
2. When B pays, A's property right *immediately* passes to B.

There is thus no point at which A *both* (i) holds Ownership of the bike *and* (ii) is under a duty to B in relation to that right.

---

[67] See eg *re Ellenborough* [1903] 1 Ch 697; *Williams v CIR* [1965] NZLR 395.

> **B:EXAMPLE 8a**
>
> A owns a bike shop. B orders a particular model of bike from A and pays the £200 price in advance. Before A orders a bike for B, A becomes insolvent. A's total liabilities are £100,000; the assets available to A to meet those liabilities are worth only £10,000.

In such a case, A's contractual promise does not impose a duty on A in relation to a *specific* right held by A. As a result, that promise *cannot* give B a persistent right (see **1.1.2(ii)** above).[68]

These examples show that, where sales of goods are concerned, persistent rights have almost no role to play.[69] In contrast, persistent rights will be very important when we look at sales of *land* (see **E2:2.1.1**). If A makes a contractual promise to transfer his ownership of land to B, that promise, by itself, cannot transfer A's right to B. B can only acquire A's ownership of the land if: (i) A's intention to transfer the right is expressed in a deed; and (ii) B substantively registers his right (see **C3:5.3.1**). These formality requirements create a *gap*: a point when (i) A still has his right; *and* (ii) A is under a contractual duty to transfer his right to B. In that gap, B acquires a persistent right against A's ownership of the land.

(iv) Promises to transfer a persistent right

> **EXAMPLE 14**
>
> Z has some shares in a particular company. Z holds those shares on Trust for A. A makes an oral contractual promise to transfer his right under the Trust to B. A then refuses to transfer his persistent right to B.

A's contractual promise to B, by itself, does *not* transfer A's persistent right to B. First, the situation does not involve a sale of goods; second, due to the formality rule imposed by section 53(1)(c) of the Law of Property Act 1925, any such transfer must be made in writing signed by A (see **C3:5.2.2**). However, by making a contractual promise to transfer his persistent right to B, A comes under a duty to B in relation to that right. So: (i) A keeps his persistent right against Z; and (ii) B acquires a persistent right against A's right. As a result, there is a sub-Trust (see **C1:3.3**).

This result was confirmed by the decision of the Court of Appeal in *Neville v Wilson*,[70] on which **Example 14** is based. That decision has been criticised: it has been argued that it allows A and B to evade the formality rule applying to the transfer of a persistent right.[71] However, such criticism is misplaced. The formality rule applies to the *transfer* of A's persistent right. And, in *Neville v Wilson* as in **Example 14**, there is no such transfer: instead A *keeps* his persistent right and B gains a right against A's right (see **C3:7.3.3**).

After all, the section 53(1)(c) formality rule does not apply if: (i) A keeps his persistent right and declares that he holds that right on Trust for B; or if (ii) A keeps his persistent

---

[68] See the reasoning of Lord Hanworth MR in *re Wait* [1927] 1 Ch 606 at 617ff.

[69] 'Almost' no role because A and B could of course structure their contract in such a way as to allow B to acquire a persistent right. For example, the contract of sale could specify that B is to acquire A's Ownership of the bike only when A delivers the bike to B; and also that A is under a duty to deliver the bike when B pays the agreed price. In that case: (i) B can only acquire A's Ownership on delivery; but (ii) B can acquire a persistent right against A's Ownership by paying the price.

[70] [1997] Ch 144.

[71] See Worthington, *Equity* (2nd edn, 2006), 233–5; Gardner, *Introduction to the Law of Trusts* (2nd edn, 2003), 96.

right and makes a Type 1 Equitable Assignment in B's favour. There is therefore no reason why it should apply when B acquires a persistent right as a result of A's contractual promise to B. In all these cases, the risk the formality rule guards against (that Z may not know to whom he owes his duty: see **C3:6.3**) simply does not arise. Both before and after A's contractual promise to B, Z owes his duty to A.

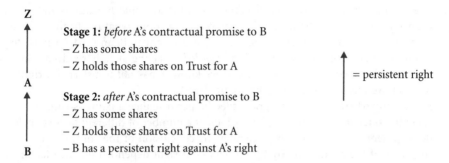

Z

Stage 1: *before* A's contractual promise to B
– Z has some shares
– Z holds those shares on Trust for A

A

= persistent right

Stage 2: *after* A's contractual promise to B
– Z has some shares
– Z holds those shares on Trust for A

B   – B has a persistent right against A's right

(v) Promises to transfer a personal right

We have seen that, if A has a personal right against Z, B can acquire a persistent right as a result of A's contractual promise to transfer that right to B (**Examples 12bii and 12cii**). In these cases, there is a Type 2 Equitable Assignment. It is important to note that these cases do *not* depend on a transfer of A's personal right to B. First, a contractual promise by A to transfer a personal right to B does not involve a sale of goods: the promise itself cannot transfer A's right to B. Second, due to the formality rule imposed by section 136 of the Law of Property Act 1925, any such transfer can occur only if: (i) it is made in writing signed by A; and (ii) written notice is given to Z (see **C3:5.1.2**).

This raises the question of whether a Type 2 Equitable Assignment allows A and B to 'evade' the formality rule imposed by section 136. The answer is 'No': we can apply the same analysis used above when examining a contract to transfer a persistent right. The section 136 formality rule, like the rule imposed by section 53(1)(c), regulates A's power to *transfer* a right; it does not apply if A *keeps* his right and gives B a persistent right against that right (see **C3:7.3.3**).

After all, the formality rule does not apply if: (i) A keeps his personal right against Z and declares that he holds that right on Trust for B; or if (ii) A keeps his personal right against Z and makes a Type 1 Equitable Assignment in B's favour. There is therefore no reason why it should apply to a Type 2 Equitable Assignment. In all these cases, the risk the formality rule guards against (that Z may not know to whom he owes his duty: see **C3:6.3**) simply does not arise. Both before and after A's contractual promise to B, Z owes his duty to A (see the diagram in **1.2.2(i)** above).

(vi) The relevance of specific performance

The discussion in this section has missed out something that, on the orthodox view, is said to be vital to B obtaining a persistent right as a result of A's contractual promise. On the orthodox view, B can only acquire a persistent right if A's contractual promise is *specifically enforceable* (see also **2.2.1(iii)** above).[72] This means that: if (i) A is under a contractual duty

---

[72] See eg Worthington, *Proprietary Interests in Commercial Transactions* (1996), 198–206.

to B in relation to a specific right; but (ii) when considering the **remedies question**, a court would not be willing to specifically protect B's right by ordering A to perform his contractual duty; then (iii) A's contractual promise cannot give B a persistent right.

This orthodox view, whilst widespread, is incorrect: it is contradicted by both principle and authority. As for principle:

1. The need for specific performance comes from the idea that B acquires an 'Equitable property right' due to the maxim 'Equity regards as done what ought to be done'. So, if: (i) A makes a contractual promise to transfer a right to B; and (ii) A can be forced to honour that promise; then (iii) B is *regarded* as having already received that right. However, the maxim makes no sense: if we know A has *not* transferred a right to B, how can we regard B as having that right? (see **C3:7.1**).

2. In deciding whether or not to grant specific performance a court is considering the **remedies question**. In doing so, it may look at a number of different factors, including developments that have taken place after the conclusion of the contract. It would be surprising if the acquisition by B of a persistent right depended on such factors. If it did, the answer to the crucial question of whether or not B has a persistent right could fluctuate according to the circumstances: for example, B might lose his persistent right as a result of A falling ill.[73]

As for authority:

1. If A has a personal right against Z and is under a contractual duty to B to transfer that right to B, B acquires a persistent right. That is the case whether or not A's promise is specifically enforceable.[74] In fact, in most cases, A's promise is *not* specifically enforceable: for example, if A has a personal right to receive £100 from Z, A's failure to transfer that right to B could be protected by ordering A to pay B £100. Nonetheless, B acquires a persistent right.

2. If A makes a contractual promise to transfer a future right to B, or to hold that right as security for B, then, as soon as A acquires that right, B acquires a persistent right. As the House of Lords confirmed in *Tailby v Official Receiver*,[75] that is the case whether or not A's promise is specifically enforceable.

3. The specific performance requirement is said to explain why persistent rights are generally irrelevant when considering a sale of goods: as A's contractual promise to transfer his Ownership of goods to B is not, in general, specifically enforceable, B cannot acquire an 'Equitable property right'. However, as we saw in (**iii**) above, we can explain the current position *without* needing to refer to the absence of specific performance.

---

[73] See *Patel v Ali* [1984] Ch 283. The Court of Appeal decided not to order specific performance of A's contractual promise to transfer a right to B: this was based, in part, on the fact that A had fallen ill. The potential hardship to A of ordering a particular remedy is a sound factor to take into account when deciding the remedies question. However, it cannot make sense for the crucial question of whether B has a persistent right to depend on the state of A's health. For example, consider the position if A went into insolvency: the question of whether B had a right capable of binding A's trustee in bankruptcy would then depend on whether A fell ill before or after going into insolvency.

[74] See M Smith, *The Law of Assignment* (2007), 9.05–9.09.

[75] (1888) 13 App Cas 523: see esp *per* Lord Macnaghten at 547–8.

The better view, therefore, is that, the **acquisition** of a persistent right is unaffected by the availability of the **remedy** of specific performance.[76] The logic of persistent rights is that B acquires such a right *whenever* A is under a duty to B in relation to a specific right. So, as soon as A comes under a contractual duty to transfer a specific right to B, B acquires a persistent right.

2.1.3 Wrongs

A commits a wrong against B if he breaches a duty he owes to B. By committing a wrong, A comes under a second, different duty to B. For example, if A carelessly injures B, A commits a wrong: he has breached his duty to take reasonable care not to interfere with B's physical integrity. As a result of that wrong, A comes under a different duty: a duty to pay B money. That money will serve: (i) as a substitute for the right interfered with; and (ii) as compensation for any relevant loss caused by A's wrong.[77] In such a case, the new right B acquires as a result of A's wrong is clearly a personal right against A. A does not have to use a *specific* right for B's benefit: A simply needs to pay B a sum of money and that money can come from any source.

If, as a result of committing a wrong, A instead comes under a duty to B in relation to a *specific right*, B will acquire a persistent right. However, this occurs only in very rare cases. First, A's commission of a wrong does not generally result in A's acquisition of a specific right: eg, if A carelessly runs B over, A's wrong does not lead to A acquiring a specific right. Second, even if A *does* acquire a specific right as a result of his wrong, the court's focus will usually be on the effect of A's wrong on B, not on any gain made by A as a result of his wrong. So, let us say A carelessly runs B over because A is rushing in order to reach a finishing line in time and win a prize. Even if A wins the prize as a result, it is far from clear that the money A must pay B will be based on the extent of A's gain (see **D1:4.3.3**). Third, *even* if the court does take into account A's gain, the likelihood is that A will simply be ordered to pay B a sum of money *equivalent* in value to A's gain. In our example, therefore, A will *not* be under a duty to transfer the *specific* prize to B.

The courts have, however, recognised some exceptional situations in which A's commission of a wrong *does* give B a persistent right. In these cases: (i) A acquires a specific right as a result of committing a wrong against B; *and* (ii) A is under a duty to transfer that specific right to B.

EXAMPLE 15

A is a government official, responsible for prosecuting criminals. Due to his position, A is under a *fiduciary duty*: a duty to act in the best interests of the government (B). In the hope of receiving lenient treatment from A, X (a criminal) gives A a bribe of £10,000.

In *Attorney-General for Hong Kong v Reid*,[78] the Privy Council decided that, in such a case, A is under a duty to transfer to B the *specific right* given to him as a bribe. So, in **Example 15**, B acquires a persistent right: a right against A's right to the £10,000. That decision has

---

[76] This conclusion is supported by eg Gardner (1987) 7 *OJLS* 60; Meagher et al, *Meagher, Gummow & Lehane's Equity, Doctrines and Remedies* (4th edn, 2002), [6-240]–[6-275].

[77] See eg Stevens, *Torts and Rights* (2007), ch 4; and **D1:4.3**.

[78] [1994] 1 AC 324.

attracted a good deal of disapproval.[79] The crucial question is whether the prosecutor should have been under a duty to transfer a *specific right* (the bribe itself) to the Government. We will examine this question further in **F3:2.4.2**. The justification for imposing such a duty on A depends on the fact that, by accepting the bribe, the prosecutor committed a special form of wrong: a breach of a *fiduciary duty*.[80] In a number of important ways, breaches of such duties are treated differently from other wrongs: the courts are very keen to remove any possible incentives that A might have for breaching a fiduciary duty (see **F3:1.3**). One method is to hold that, if A acquires a right by breaching a fiduciary duty to B, A is under a duty to use that right wholly for B's benefit. Once that duty exists, B necessarily acquires a persistent right.

So it seems that A's commission of a wrong can give B a persistent right *if and only if*:

- A is under a fiduciary duty to B; *and*
- As a result of a breach of that duty, A acquires a specific right.

2.1.4 Unjust enrichment

The key contribution of unjust enrichment to the property law system is its ability to give B a persistent right. B acquires such a right whenever: (i) due to his unjust enrichment at B's expense, A is under a duty to B; and (ii) A's duty to B relates to a specific right held by A. However, this is a very controversial area, and some argue, for example, that A's unjust enrichment at B's expense can *never* give B a persistent right.[81] We will therefore examine it in detail in **D4:4**.

2.1.5 Statute

B acquires a persistent right whenever a statute imposes a duty on A to use a specific right for B's benefit. For example, let us say A0 dies without making a will. Under section 33 of the Administration of Estates Act 1925, A0's rights will pass to his personal representatives (eg, A and A2). Clearly, A and A2 cannot simply use those rights for their own benefit: they are subject to various statutory duties. Once they have used A0's rights to pay off any debts owed by A0, and to meet certain other expenses, A and A2 then have a duty to use the remainder of A0's rights for the benefit of a defined class of people (ie, the close relatives of A0, as defined by the statute). At that point, those relatives acquire persistent rights—rights against the rights held by A and A2.

2.1.6 Other events

In some cases, A's duty to B does not arise as a result of A's consent, a contract, a wrong, an unjust enrichment or a statute. After all, there are many reasons for which A can come under a duty to B, and we cannot expect all those reasons to be exhausted by a classification

---

[79] For arguments contrary to the decision taken in *Reid* see eg Goode (1987) 103 *LQR* 433 and in *Essays on the Law of Restitution* (ed Burrows, 1991), 215–46.

[80] For a different justification of the decision in *Reid* (examined and rejected in **F3:2.1.4(ii)**) see Millett, ch 12 in *Equity and Commercial Law* (ed Degeling and Edelman, 2005), 323–4 and ch 15 in *Mapping the Law: Essays in Memory of Peter Birks* (ed Burrows and Rodger, 2006).

[81] See eg Swadling (1996) 16 *LS* 110; Virgo, *The Law of Restitution* (2nd edn, 2006), ch 20; Grantham and Rickett [2003] CLJ 717.

based on just five categories. As a result, we have the residual but important category of 'other events'.

This category can be very important to the acquisition of persistent rights. For example, A can come under a duty to B as a result of the 'receipt after a promise' principle (see **D3:2.2.2**). If the duty imposed on A is a duty in relation to a specific right, B will acquire a persistent right. For example, in 'secret Trust' cases, the principle imposes a duty on C to hold a specific right on Trust for B: as a result, B acquires a persistent right against the right held by C (see **F3:2.4.3(iii)**).

2.1.7 Formality rules

(i) The general position
The general position is that, except where land is concerned, formality rules are *irrelevant* when deciding if B has acquired a new persistent right (see **C3:5.2.1**).

(ii) The Purely Equitable Charge
The Bills of Sale Act (1878) Amendment Act 1882 regulates the power of A, an individual or partnership[82] with Ownership of a thing, to give B a property right (see **D1:2.2.5**) or a persistent right by way of security. The formality rules imposed by that Act therefore apply if: (i) A has Ownership of a thing; and (ii) A attempts to give B a Purely Equitable Charge over A's Ownership. We will consider those rules in detail in **F4:3.1.1**. One point worth noting here is that, like all formality rules, those rules apply to regulate A's power to give B a right. So, if B acquires a Purely Equitable Charge for some other reason (eg, as in **B:Example 6b**, discussed in **1.2.1** above), formality rules are irrelevant.

SUMMARY OF D2:2.1 AND COMPARISON WITH PROPERTY RIGHTS

In relation to things other than land, there are two basic means by which B can acquire a property right:

- Independent acquisition: B acquires Ownership as a result of his own unilateral conduct in taking physical control of a thing;
- Dependent acquisition: A exercises a power to transfer his Ownership of a thing to B.

In contrast, to acquire a persistent right, B needs to show that A is under a duty to B in relation to a specific claim-right or power held by A. Therefore, when considering the acquisition of persistent rights, *all* the various methods by which A can come under a duty to B are relevant: A's consent; A's entry into a contract with B; A's commission of a wrong; A's unjust enrichment at B's expense; statute; and other events. And, where land is not concerned, formality rules are, in general, irrelevant in deciding if A has come under such a duty to B.

---

[82] If A is a company, the 1882 Act does not apply. However, B's failure to register a Purely Equitable Charge given by A Ltd will mean that B's right will not be protected in A Ltd's insolvency (see **3.6** below and **F4:3.1.2**).

2.2   The transfer of a pre-existing persistent right

EXAMPLE 16

A has Ownership of a bike. A holds that right on Trust for B1. B1 wishes to transfer his right under the Trust to B2.

In such a case, B1 has the power to transfer his pre-existing persistent right to B2. However, that power is regulated by the formality rule set out by section 53(1)(c) of the Law of Property Act 1925 (see **C3:5.2.2**):

> A disposition of an equitable interest or trust subsisting at the time of the disposition, must be in writing signed by the person disposing of the same, or by his agent thereunto lawfully authorised in writing or by will.

Hence, B1's attempt to transfer a pre-existing persistent right will fail if B1 does not exercise that power in signed writing. There are some subtleties to the application of section 53(1)(c): in particular, the word 'disposition' needs to be interpreted carefully. The important cases considering the rule have arisen where B1's pre-existing persistent right is a right under a Trust. As a result, we will examine these cases in **F3:2.2**.

3   THE DEFENCES QUESTION

If B can satisfy the **content question** and the **acquisition question**, he can show he has a persistent right against A's right. Let us say that, as in the **basic situation**, C then acquires a right that depends on A's right. B has a prima facie power to impose a duty on C in relation to that right (see **B:4.3**). However, attention then shifts to **Question 3** of the basic structure: does C have a defence to B's pre-existing persistent right? If so, B will have no power to impose that duty on C: C will have an *immunity* against B (see **B:5.2.1(ii)**).

3.1   Introduction: the basic tension

The defences question provides an important means of dealing with the **basic tension** between B and C (see **D1:3.1**). If B fails to satisfy the **content question** or the **acquisition question**, *all* third parties are protected from the risk of being bound by a pre-existing persistent right of B.[83] If B does satisfy these questions, but his persistent right is subject to a defence, then a *limited class* of third parties—those third parties who qualify for the defence—will be protected from that risk.

Defences are particularly important where persistent rights are concerned. We have seen that the content and acquisition questions may give C little protection against the risk of being bound by a hidden persistent right. For example, if A has a right, there may be little *evidence* of the fact that A holds that right on Trust for B: (i) provided A is, overall, under a duty in relation to the whole of his right, A's duty to B can have any content; and (ii) B can acquire his right as a result of A's oral consent to hold the right on Trust. However, the

---

[83] In such a case, a third party may be bound by a direct right of B: but, of course, such a new, direct right is distinct from B's pre-existing right.

defences question can come to C's rescue: if C acquires A's right for value, and without any actual or constructive notice of B's hidden persistent right, C can use the 'bona fide purchaser' defence (see **B:5.2.2(ii)**). We will examine this defence in detail in **3.5** below; but it is not the only defence that may be used against a persistent right.

3.2   The consent defence

B's consent to C's conduct can clearly give C a defence to B's pre-existing persistent right. For example, let us say C wishes to acquire A's Ownership of a bike. C knows that A holds the bike on Trust for B. One option is for C: (i) to persuade A to transfer A's Ownership to C; and (ii) to persuade B (perhaps by paying B) to consent to C acquiring A's right free from B's pre-existing persistent right. If B gives that consent, C has a defence to B's right under the Trust.[84]

3.3   'Apparent power' defences

D1:EXAMPLE 21

B has Ownership of a bike. B lends the bike to A, a friend. B knows that A, who is untrustworthy and short of money, may well try to raise some money by selling the bike to a third party and keeping the proceeds. A does indeed sell the bike to C, who buys it in good faith and without notice of B's right.

In such a case, C does *not* have a defence to B's pre-existing property right (see **D1:3.3**). However, if A instead held Ownership of the bike *on Trust* for B, C *would* have a defence— the 'bona fide purchaser' defence—to B's pre-existing persistent right. The availability of that defence dramatically reduces the need for C to appeal to an 'apparent power' defence.

EXAMPLE 17

A holds his Ownership of a bike on Trust for B. C is aware of the Trust but A and C both honestly and reasonably believe that, under the terms of the Trust, A has a power to sell the bike for a fair market price. C buys the bike from A at such a price. It turns out that A and C were mistaken: the terms of the Trust do not give A such a power.

Although this point is not entirely clear,[85] C's awareness of B's pre-existing right should *not* prevent C relying on the 'bona fide purchaser' defence. C does have notice of the Trust; but: (i) C made reasonable efforts to ascertain the true position; and (ii) C honestly believed that A *did* have the power to sell the bike; so (iii) C does not have actual or constructive notice of the fact that the sale is a *breach* of the Trust. As far as the 'bona fide purchaser' defence is concerned, the question is *not* whether or not C has notice of B's persistent right. Rather, it

---

[84] See eg *Vandervell v IRC* [1967] 2 AC 291. A held shares on Trust for B1. B1 orally instructed A to transfer A's right to the shares to C. A did so, and C thus acquired the shares. C was not bound by B1's persistent right as B1 had consented to the transfer of the shares (see **F3:2.2**).

[85] In particular, cases relating to Trusts of land (see eg the analysis of Younger J in *re Soden and Alexander's Contract* [1918] 2 Ch 254) suggest that, even if C honestly believes that the Trust gives A the power to transfer a right, C will not be protected. That view seems to rest however on the strict application of the notice test in relation to land: ie, C is taken to have constructive notice of all the actual restrictions on A's power to transfer the right.

is whether or not C has notice of the fact that A does not have the power to give C a right free from B's pre-existing right (see too **F4:4.3.2**).

3.4   The overreaching defence

EXAMPLE 18a

B has Ownership of a bike and wants to borrow £200 from A. B transfers his Ownership of the bike to A as security for B's duty to repay the loan. B fails to repay the loan and A enforces his security by selling the bike to C. C is aware that A held his Ownership of the bike by way of security.

In such a case, B has a pre-existing persistent right: a Mortgagor's Right to Redeem (see **1.2.3** above). However, C has a defence to that right: as B has failed to perform the secured duty, A has the power to sell the bike free from B's pre-existing persistent right. And where A has a power to give C a right free from a pre-existing right of B, C can rely on the over-reaching defence,[86] whether B's right is a property right (see **D1:3.4**) or a persistent right.

EXAMPLE 18b

A0 has some shares and £10,000. A0 transfers the shares and money to A to hold on a discretionary Trust for the benefit of B1, B2 and B3 (see **1.4.3** above). A0 gives A a number of powers including: (i) a power to manage and invest the rights held on Trust; and (ii) a power to raise money for further investments by granting a lender a Purely Equitable Charge over any rights A holds on Trust. A borrows £10,000 from C and uses that money to buy more shares. In return, A gives C a Purely Equitable Charge over the rights that A holds on Trust for B1, B2 and B3.

In such a case, A does not transfer to C any of the rights he holds on Trust; instead: (i) A keeps those rights; and (ii) C acquires a persistent right against those rights. As a result, C *cannot* use the 'bona fide purchaser' defence (see **Examples 19c and 19d** below). However, as A has acted within the powers given to him under the Trust, C can rely on the overreaching defence. As a result, none of B1, B2 and B3 can assert his pre-existing persistent right against C.

In other cases, A's power to deal with a right held on Trust may be more limited. So, in **Example 18b**, A0 might have specified, when setting up the Trust, that A can borrow money *only* if A first obtains the consent of Z, a financial expert. If A0 had imposed that limit on A's power, then, if A were to give C a Purely Equitable Charge without first consulting Z, C would *not* be able to rely on the overreaching defence. In such a case, it would make no difference if A told C that Z *had* given his consent. As far as the overreaching defence is concerned, the question is *not* whether C reasonably believed A acted within his power. Rather, C can only rely on the defence if A *did*, in fact, act within his power.

Equally, if A gives C a right and, in fact, A has a power to do so, then C can rely on the overreaching defence: (i) *even if* C believed A had no such power; and (ii) *even if*, by exercising that power in a particular way, A has acted in breach of his duties, as trustee, to B. For example, let us say that, in **Example 18b**, A exercises his power to borrow money simply

---

[86] See Harpum [1990] *CLJ* 277.

because he wants to run off with the money; or that, in breach of his duty to act in the best interests of B1, B2 and B3, A borrows money at an unnecessarily high rate of interest. In either case, A's exercise of his power to borrow money and give C a Purely Equitable Charge will be a breach of his duties, as trustee, to each of B1, B2 and B3. However, that does *not* change the fact that, as A *does* have the power to give C such a right, C can use the overreaching defence against the pre-existing persistent rights of B1, B2 and B3.

The requirements of the overreaching defence (at least in cases not involving land) can be easily summarised. C can rely on the defence *if and only if*:

- C has acquired a right from A; and
- A has a power to give C such a right free from B's pre-existing property right or persistent right.

3.5 The 'bona fide purchaser' defence

3.5.1 The requirements of the defence

EXAMPLE 19a

A holds his Ownership of a bike on Trust for B. In return for payment from C, A then transfers his Ownership of the bike to C. When C acquires A's right, C does not know about the Trust in B's favour. Nor could C have reasonably been expected to have found out about that Trust.

EXAMPLE 19b

A has a personal right against Z. By means of an Equitable Assignment, A gives B a persistent right against A's right. In return for payment from C, A then transfers that personal right to C.[87] When C acquires A's right, C does not know about the previous Equitable Assignment to B. Nor could C have reasonably been expected to have found out about that Equitable Assignment.

In each case, C can rely on the 'bona fide purchaser' defence. This is because: (i) C acquired his right for value; and (ii) when he acquired his right, C did not know about, and could not reasonably have been expected to discover, B's persistent right. The same analysis applies if: (i) A transfers a right to C, and B has a Purely Equitable Charge over A's right; or (ii) A transfers a right to C, and B has a Mortgagor's Right to Redeem against A's right.

EXAMPLE 19c

A holds his Ownership of a bike on Trust for B. In return for a loan from C, A gives C a Purely Equitable Charge over A's Ownership of the bike. When C acquires A's right, C does not know about the Trust in B's favour. Nor could C have reasonably been expected to have found out about that Trust.

---

[87] For such a transfer to occur, A and C must comply with the formality rule imposed by the Law of Property Act 1925, s 136 (if A's personal right against Z is a Common Law right: see C3:5.1.2). If A's personal right against Z is instead an Equitable right, it seems A and C need only to comply with the formality rule imposed by Law of Property Act 1925, s 53(1)(c) (see C3:5.1.2).

EXAMPLE 19d

A has a personal right against Z. By means of an Equitable Assignment, A gives B a persistent right against A's right. In return for payment from C, A then makes an Equitable Assignment of that same personal right in favour of C. When that Equitable Assignment is made to C, C does not know about the previous Equitable Assignment to B. Nor could C have reasonably been expected to have found out about that previous Equitable Assignment.

In **Example 19c**: (i) B has a pre-existing persistent right against A's right (a right under a Trust); and (ii) C has acquired a right that depends on A's right (a Purely Equitable Charge); so (iii) B has a prima facie power to impose a duty on C. In **Example 19d**: (i) B has a pre-existing persistent right against A's right (arising under an Equitable Assignment); and (ii) C has acquired a right that depends on A's right (again arising under an Equitable Assignment); so (iii) B has a prima facie power to impose a duty on C.

In each case, C *cannot* rely on the 'bona fide purchaser' defence. It is true that: (i) C acquired his right for value; and (ii) when he acquired his right, C did not know about, and could not reasonably have been expected to discover, B's persistent right. However, the problem for C is that he did *not* acquire the *very right* against which B has a persistent right. In **Example 19c**, in contrast to **Example 19a**, C did *not* acquire A's Ownership of the bike; instead, C acquired a Purely Equitable Charge—a right against A's Ownership of the bike. In **Example 19d**, in contrast to **Example 19b**, C did *not* acquire A's personal right against Z; instead, he acquired a right against A's right.

The point is that, in each of **Example 19c** and **Example 19d**, C simply acquired a *further* right against A's right. And A's right was *already* subject to B's right. So, whilst C can show that A is under a duty to C in relation to a specific right, the problem for C is that A is *already* under a duty to B in relation to that very same right.

The requirements of the 'bona fide purchaser' defence thus seem quite clear. C can use that defence if:

- B has a right against A's right; *and*
- A transfers that right to C for value; *and*
- At the time of the transfer,[88] C did not know about,[89] and could not reasonably have been expected to discover,[90] B's persistent right.[91]

---

[88] It seems C is also protected if: (i) he acquires his right by exercising a power against A to acquire that right; and (ii) C acquired that power for value; and (iii) when C acquired that power, C did not know about, and could not reasonably have been expected to discover, B's persistent right: see eg *Wilkes v Bodington* (1707) 2 Vern 599; *per* Millet J in *Macmillan Inc v Bishopsgate Trust (No 3)* [1995] 1 WLR 978 at 1001. That rule is consistent with the analysis taken here: if he acquires a power to acquire A's right, C does not simply acquire a further right against A's right.

[89] If C's *agent* knew about B's pre-existing persistent right, that knowledge can be attributed to C (cf eg D1:2.1.1(i) where we noted that acts of an agent can be attributed to C). In such a case, C is sometimes said to have 'imputed notice' of B's right.

[90] Where land is not concerned, it is only in rare cases that a court will find that C *should* have discovered a pre-existing persistent right of B: see eg Law of Property Act 1925, s 199. In *Manchester Trust v Furness* [1895] 2 QB 539 at 545 Lindley LJ stated that constructive notice has no role to play in 'commercial transactions'. As pointed out in *Snell's Equity* (ed McGhee, 31st edn, 2005), 4–39, that is not correct. The point is rather that, in commercial transactions, C is not generally expected to make particular checks before acquiring a right from A and so a court cannot usually say that C should have discovered a pre-existing persistent right of B.

[91] Strictly speaking, the requirement is that, at the time of the transfer, C did not know about, and could not reasonably have been expected to discover, *the fact that C's acquisition of his right involved A acting in breach of A's duty to B* (see 3:3 above).

The final requirement is something of a mouthful: it can be abbreviated by saying that 'At the time of the transfer, C had no *actual or constructive notice* of B's persistent right.'

3.5.2 The requirements of the defence: the orthodox view

The formulation of the requirements of the 'bona fide purchaser' defence, set out above, is different from the orthodox formulation of those requirements. The orthodox view is that C can use the defence if:

- B has an 'Equitable property right' *and*
- C acquires a 'Legal estate' for value; *and*
- When C acquires that 'Legal estate',[92] C did not know about, and could not reasonably have been expected to discover, B's persistent right.

(i) B must have an 'Equitable property right'
This term does not quite capture the extent of the general 'bona fide purchaser' defence. That defence can be used *whenever* B has a persistent right. It can therefore apply in some cases, such as **Example 19b**, where B's right: (i) is not regarded as an 'Equitable property right'; but (ii) does count as a persistent right (see **B:4.4.2**).

(ii) C must acquire a 'Legal estate'
First, the term 'Legal estate' is confusing. C has a 'Legal estate' if C has a right to exclusive control of land, either forever or for a fixed period (see **E1:1**). Clearly, as **Examples 19a and 19b** show, the 'bona fide purchaser' defence can apply even if C does not acquire such a right.

The orthodox formulation can instead be regarded simply as a way of stating that C needs to acquire a 'Legal property right'. However, that is also misleading. C can use the defence where: (i) B has a persistent right against a personal right of A; and (ii) A transfers that personal right to C (see **Example 19b**).

Again, the orthodox formulation could be amended to say that C instead needs to acquire a 'Legal right'. This would certainly be consistent with the fact that, in **Examples 19c and 19d**, C cannot use the defence. However, there would still be a problem. It would mean that if, in **Example 19b**, A's personal right against Z is an Equitable right, C *cannot* rely on the defence: although C has acquired the very right against which B has a persistent right, he has not acquired a 'Legal right'. It is very difficult to justify why the result, in a case such as **Example 19b**, should depend on whether A's personal right against Z was first recognised by Common Law or Equity.[93]

---

[92] Or when C has a 'better right' (than B) to such a Legal estate: see eg *Snell's Equity* (ed McGhee, 31st edn, 2005), 4–28 (ie, where C has a power to acquire A's right: see **n 88** above).

[93] Cf **C3:6.3**, where it was argued that the formality rule applying to the transfer of a personal right should be the same whether that right is a Common Law personal right or an Equitable personal right.

3.5.3 The requirements of the defence: which view is better?

EXAMPLE 19e

A0 holds a right on Trust for A. A declares a Trust of his persistent right in favour of B. This creates a sub-Trust in B's favour (see **C1:3.3**). In return for payment from C, A then transfers that persistent right to C.[94] When C acquires A's right, C does not know about B's pre-existing right under the Trust. Nor could C have reasonably been expected to have found out about B's right.

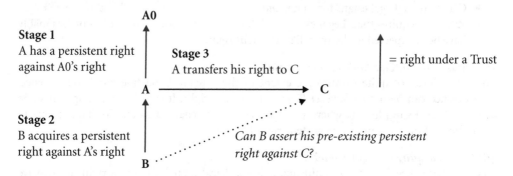

Stage 1
A has a persistent right against A0's right

Stage 3
A transfers his right to C

= right under a Trust

Stage 2
B acquires a persistent right against A's right

Can B assert his pre-existing persistent right against C?

On the orthodox formulation, C *cannot* use the 'bona fide purchaser' defence as he has not acquired a 'Legal right'. Instead, C has acquired an Equitable right: A's persistent right against A0's right. However, that result is very difficult to defend. In **Examples 19a and 19b**, we saw that C *can* use the defence when he acquires the very right against which B has a right. Why should the result be any different in **Example 19e**?

In practice, the difference between the orthodox formulation of the 'bona fide purchaser' defence, and the requirements of that defence as set out in **3.5.1** above, comes down to a key situation, represented by **Example 19e**.[95] That situation arises where: (i) A has an Equitable right; and (ii) B has a persistent right against that right of A; and (iii) A then transfers his Equitable right to C. On the view taken in this book, it *is* possible for C to use the 'bona fide purchaser' defence (assuming he acquires A's Equitable right for value and without any actual or constructive notice of B's right). On the orthodox view, C *cannot* use the defence. The problem with the orthodox view is that: (i) it creates inconsistencies in the property law system; and (ii) it makes the application of the 'bona fide purchaser' defence depend not on the *nature* of C's right (ie, is it the very right against which B has a persistent right?) but instead on the *historical origin* of C's right (ie, was it first recognised in courts of Equity rather than courts of Common Law?).

Judges have made attempts to defend the orthodox view. For example, in *Pilcher v Rawlins*,[96] James LJ stated that

> [if C] has satisfied the terms of the plea of purchase for valuable consideration without notice, then, according to my judgment, this Court has no jurisdiction whatever to do anything more

---

[94] For such a transfer to occur, A must comply with the formality rule imposed by Law of Property Act 1925, s 53(1)(c) (see **C3:5.2.2**).

[95] And also by **Example 19b** (if A's initial personal right against Z is an Equitable right).

[96] (1872) LR 7 Ch App 259 at 268–9.

than to let him depart in possession of that legal estate, that legal right, that legal advantage which he has obtained, whatever it may be.[97]

However, that explanation, based on the idea that a court of Equity does not have 'jurisdiction' to allow B to impose a duty on a 'bona fide purchaser', is unconvincing (see too **C1:3.4.1**). After all, if: (i) A holds his Ownership of a bike on Trust for B; and (ii) A transfers that right, for free, to C; then (iii) C cannot use the 'bona fide purchaser' defence. The mere fact that C has a 'Legal right' does *not* put C beyond the reach of B's persistent right. Rather, that defence, like any defence, protects C simply because the property law system has decided that, in certain cases, the **basic tension** is best resolved in C's favour, rather than in B's favour. Many factors can influence that decision, including, for example: (i) the nature of B's pre-existing right (is it a property right or a persistent right?); (ii) whether C has paid for his right; and (ii) whether C acted innocently (in the sense of having no actual or constructive notice of B's pre-existing right). However, there is no obvious reason why it should matter whether, as a matter of history, C's right was first recognised by courts of Equity rather than courts of Common Law.

In contrast, the view of the 'bona fide purchaser' defence taken in this book *does* relate the application of the defence to a relevant factor. In cases such as **Examples 19c and 19d**, C is not denied the defence simply because he acquires an Equitable right. Rather, C is denied it because: (i) he acquires a right against A's right; and (ii) A's right is *already* subject to B's pre-existing persistent right. So, in **Example 19e**, C *should* be able to rely on the defence. In such a case, C does *not* acquire a second right against A's right; instead, as in **Examples 19a and 19b**, C acquires the *very right* against which B has a persistent right.

On the view taken in this book, there is a clear structure to the 'bona fide purchaser' defence:

1. Let us say B has a pre-existing *property right* in a thing. C later acquires a property right in that same thing. In such a case, C is *not* protected by a general 'bona fide purchaser' defence (see **B:5.2.2(i)** and **D1:3.5**). After all, C has simply acquired a right against a thing that was *already* subject to a right of B.
2. Let us say B has a pre-existing *persistent right* against a right of A. C later acquires a persistent right against that same thing. In such a case, C is *not* protected by a general 'bona fide purchaser' defence. After all, C has simply acquired a right against a right that was *already* subject to a right of B.

3.5.4 An exception to the general position? The rule in *Dearle v Hall*

EXAMPLE 20a

A0 holds a right on Trust for A. In June, A transfers his persistent right under the Trust to B. The transfer is made in writing signed by A, as required by section 53(1)(c) of the Law of Property Act 1925 (see **C3:5.2.2**). Neither A nor B informs A0 of the transfer. In September, in return for payment from C, A then purports to make a second transfer of that same persistent right to C. C has no actual or constructive notice of the earlier transfer to B. C, believing he now has A's persistent right, informs A0 of the transfer. A then goes into insolvency.

---

[97] See too Hackney, *Understanding Equity and Trusts* (1987), ch 1, s 2(a).

In such a case, C seems to face an insurmountable problem. C claims that, in September, A transferred A's persistent right to C; but, at that point, A had *no* persistent right: he had already transferred that right to B. So, as A cannot give what he does not have, C cannot acquire A's persistent right. It seems that C has only a personal right against A,[98] who, like the infamous Victor Lustig,[99] has tricked C into buying something A does not have.

However, that perfectly logical analysis could cause real problems for C. There is no obvious way for C to discover that A has made the first transfer to B. After all, even if C were to ask A0, that gives C no protection: somewhat anomalously, A can transfer his persistent right to B without A0 being informed (see **C3:6.3**, where it is argued that the law should be changed so that notice to A0 *does* become necessary for such a transfer to occur).

As a result, the property law system has departed from the doctrinal position in order to protect C. So, even though A has *already* transferred his persistent right to B, C is permitted to acquire that right. Nonetheless, C still faces a problem: (i) as the first transfer to B is valid, B has a pre-existing persistent right against A0's right; and (ii) the standard 'bona fide purchaser' defence does *not* protect C: C has not acquired A0's right and so has not acquired the *very right* against which B has a persistent right.

However, the property law system *again* steps in to protect C. In **Example 20a**, C *does* have a defence against B's pre-existing persistent right. This is a special application of the 'bona fide purchaser' defence, known as the 'rule in *Dearle v Hall*.[100] That rule says that: (i) *if* C acquires his right from A for value and without actual or constructive notice of the earlier transfer to B; and (ii) A0 is informed of the transfer to C *before* A0 is informed of A's earlier transfer to B, then (ii) C has a defence to B's pre-existing right.

Rules that are named for a case, such as the rule in *Dearle v Hall*, are usually somewhat suspect. If there were a good way of explaining the rule, the rule would have a more illuminating name. Certainly, we need to ask if this special application of the 'bona fide purchaser' defence can be justified. It could be said that, in **Example 20a**, it is particularly hard for C to discover B's pre-existing persistent right. However, that argument is not very convincing. In **Examples 19c and 19d** above, it may be difficult for C to discover B's right; nonetheless, as C does not acquire the very right against which B has a right, C cannot rely on the 'bona fide purchaser' defence.

A more promising approach is to focus on an unusual feature of the rule in *Dearle v Hall*. Unlike most defences, it is not just about protecting C (or parties who later acquire a right from C): it also aims to protect A0. That protection comes from the fact that the rule depends on whether A0 first receives notice of: (i) the transfer to B; or (ii) the transfer to C. In that way, the rule, like the formality rule set out in section 136 of the Law of Property Act 1925, provides useful protection for A0.[101] The key point is that, even in a case where A makes only one transfer of his persistent right, the rule gives B a useful incentive to inform

---

[98] Due to A's insolvency, that personal right may be of limited use to B (see **B:4.5.1**).

[99] See Johnson and Miller, *The Man who Sold the Eiffel Tower* (1961). In 1925, Lustig, posing as a French civil servant, is said to have tricked a scrap metal dealer (one Andre Poisson – the name coincidentally or fishily similar to the French term for 'April Fools' Day') into paying Lustig a bribe in order to win a contract to turn the Eiffel Tower into scrap. Lustig's attempt to repeat the trick later that year was less successful.

[100] (1828) 3 Russ 1. The rule was approved by the House of Lords in *Foster v Cockerell* (1835) 3 Cl & F 456.

[101] In a case such as **Example 20a**, the rule also gives A0 a simple way of knowing whether he should perform his duties as trustee to B or to C. However, that protection is quite limited: for example, the rule does not apply if C, when acquiring his right from A, had actual or constructive notice of the earlier transfer to B. And there is no way for A0 to know whether or not C had such notice.

A0 of the transfer. This goes some way to meeting the current anomaly that A can transfer his persistent right without informing A0 (see **C3:6.3**). In fact, if that anomaly were to be met more directly—by reforming the law to require that a transfer of A's persistent right can occur *only* if A0 is informed of that transfer—then the rule in *Dearle v Hall* would be redundant.

EXAMPLE 20b

A has a personal right against A0: A0 owes A £100. In June, A makes an Equitable Assignment of that right in favour of B. A0 is not given notice of that Equitable Assignment. In September, in return for payment from C, A then makes a further Equitable Assignment of that right in favour of C. C has no actual or constructive notice of the earlier Equitable Assignment in B's favour. C informs A0 of the Equitable Assignment in his favour. A then goes into insolvency.

The first Equitable Assignment can give B a persistent right even though no notice has been given to A0. And C cannot rely on the standard 'bona fide purchaser' defence: he has not acquired the *very right* (A's personal right against A0) against which B has a persistent right. Instead, C has acquired a second persistent right against A's right. However, in **Example 20b** C *does* have a defence against B's right.[102] That defence again comes from the rule in *Dearle v Hall*, which has been extended to deal not just with multiple transfers of the same persistent right, but also with multiple Equitable Assignments.[103]

Can that extension of the rule in *Dearle v Hall* be justified? It seems not. First, in **Example 20b**, in contrast to **Example 20a**, C can acquire a right from A *without* the need for a special rule. This is because, in **Example 20b**, the first Equitable Assignment to B does *not* result in A losing his personal right against A0. As A keeps that right, it is doctrinally possible for A then to give C a second persistent right against that right. Second, in **Example 20b**, in contrast to **Example 20a**, there is *no need to give special protection to A0*. True, the rule in *Dearle v Hall* gives B an incentive to inform A0 of A's initial Equitable Assignment in favour of B. However, that Equitable Assignment has *no effect* on A0. Both before and after the Equitable Assignment, A0 owes his duty to A (see **1.2.2** above, and **C3:7.3.3**). So, in **Example 20a**, *neither* B nor C can bring a direct claim against A0 for £100; instead, he must persuade or force A to bring a claim against A0 (see **B:4.4.2**).

As a result, the extension of the rule in *Dearle v Hall* to cases of a second Equitable Assignment, such as **Example 20b**, serves no purpose and should be reversed.[104] This may seem harsh on C, given that the first Equitable Assignment to B may be very difficult for C

---

[102] See eg *Pfeiffer GmbH v Arbuthnot Factors Ltd* [1988] 1 WLR 150 at 163.

[103] In fact, it has even been suggested (see eg *Pfeiffer GmbH v Arbuthnot Factors Ltd* [1988] 1 WLR 150; Goode, *Commercial Law* (3rd edn, 2004), 56) that the rule can be used in *B*'s favour if: (i) A makes an Equitable Assignment to B; and (ii) A then transfers his personal right against A0 to C who gives value and has no actual or constructive notice of B's right; and (iii) *B* gives notice to A0 before C. That would mean that C, despite acquiring the very right against which B has a right, and acquiring that right for value and without actual or constructive notice, would be unable to rely on the standard 'bona fide purchaser' defence. As Oditah (1989) 9 *OJLS* 513 argues, that suggestion must be rejected.

[104] Goode, *Commercial Law* (3rd edn, 2004), 652 points to practical problems caused by the rule and argues that it is 'high time that the rule in *Dearle v Hall* was abolished'. That suggestion is made in the context of a discussion of multiple Equitable Assignments (eg, **Example 20b**) and need not apply to multiple transfers of persistent rights (eg, **Example 20a**), the original context in which the rule was developed.

to discover. However, that harshness is no greater than in **Examples 19c and 19d**: it flows from the principle that the 'bona fide purchaser' defence is not available to C if he simply acquires a second persistent right against A's right. So, if C wants protection in **Example 20b**, he should insist on a *transfer* of A's personal right, rather than settling for an Equitable Assignment.

The proposal here is therefore that the rule in *Dearle v Hall*, a special adaptation of the general 'bona fide purchaser' defence, is justified by the need to protect C *combined* with the need to protect A0. As a result, the rule can be justified only where: (i) A0 is under a duty to A; and (ii) A's dealings with that right causes a shift in the identity of the party to whom A0 owes that duty, and so creates a risk that A0 may perform his duty in favour of the wrong person. On this view:

1. The rule is justified in a case such as **Example 20a**, involving multiple transfers of A's persistent right; *but*
2. The rule is *not* justified in a case such as **Example 20b**, involving multiple creations of a persistent right against the same right, held throughout by A.

3.5.5 Powers to acquire a persistent right

(i) Powers to acquire a persistent right and third parties

EXAMPLE 21

B has Ownership of a bike. A wants to buy the bike but B is reluctant to sell it. A persuades B to sell by telling him that B's employer now runs a scheme that will allow B to buy a new bike very cheaply. A genuinely believes that statement to be true, but it turns out to be false. On June 1, in reliance on the truth of A's statement, B sells A the bike. On June 2, in return for a loan from C, A then gives C a Purely Equitable Charge over A's Ownership of the bike. When acquiring that Purely Equitable Charge, C does not know, and cannot reasonably have been expected to know, that A obtained his Ownership of the bike as a result of a misrepresentation to B. On June 30, B discovers that his employer does *not* run a scheme allowing him to buy a new bike very cheaply.

In such a case, *as soon as* B transfers his right (Ownership of the bike) to A, B has an 'Equitable right to rescind' the transfer. As a result, B has a 'mere Equity': ie, B has a power to acquire a persistent right against the right he has transferred to A (see **Example 11a** above). In **Example 21**, when C acquires his right on June 2, B has not yet exercised his power to acquire a persistent right. However, in *some* cases, it is possible for B to exercise his power to acquire a persistent right against C (see **Example 11b** above).

However, in **Example 21**, B *cannot* show that he can exercise his power to acquire a persistent right against C. It is reasonably clear that such a power cannot be exercised against C if: (i) C acquires A's right, *or a right against A's right*; and (ii) C acquires that right for value; and (iii) when C acquires his right, he has no actual or constructive notice of B's power.[105] So, in **Example 21**, *even though* C has acquired a persistent right against A's right, C has an immunity against B: B cannot exercise his power against C.

---

[105] See eg *per* Lord Westbury *Phillips v Phillips* (1861) 4 De G F & J 208 at 218. See too *Latec Investments Ltd v Hotel Terrigal Pty Ltd* (1965) 113 CLR 265 (High Court of Australia).

It is important to note that, strictly speaking, **Example 21** is *not* an example of the 'bona fide purchaser' defence:

1. As B has only a *power* to acquire a persistent right, B does *not* have a pre-existing persistent right (see **1.6** above). So, when C acquires his right, B has no right that is prima facie binding on C. As a result, it is not up to C to show he has a defence; rather, it is up to B to show why he should be able to exercise his power against C. Exactly the same point applies where B has a 'Common Law right to rescind': ie, a power to *regain* the right he transferred to A (see **D1:3.5.4**)
2. C has an immunity against B even if, as in **Example 21**, C acquires a *persistent right* against A's right. In contrast, C can use the 'bona fide purchaser' defence *only* if he acquires the very right against which B has a persistent right (see **Examples 19c and 19d**).

This means that if: (i) B has a power to acquire a persistent right against a right held by A; and (ii) C acquires, as a 'bona fide purchaser', a persistent right against A's right; then (iii) it is vital to know whether B exercised his power *before* C acquired C's right.[106]

Did B exercise his power *before* C acquired C's right?	Does B have a pre-existing persistent right when C acquires C's right?	Can B assert his right/power against C if C is a bona fide purchaser of A's right?	Can B assert his right/power against C if C is a bona fide purchaser of a persistent right against A's right?
Yes	Yes	No	Yes
No	No	No	No

(ii) Rights, powers and third parties: the bigger picture

Let us say that: (i) C is a 'bona fide purchaser' of A's right; and (ii) when C acquires that right, B has a pre-existing right. In such a case, there is a crucial difference between cases where B's pre-existing right is: (i) a property right; and (ii) a persistent right against A's right.

B's right	Can B assert his pre-existing right against C: a 'bona fide purchaser' of A's right?
Property right	Yes [107]
Persistent right against A's right	No

Similarly, let us say that: (i) C is a 'bona fide purchaser' of a persistent right against A's right; and (ii) when C acquires that right, B has a pre-existing *power*. In such a case, there is a crucial difference between cases where B's pre-existing power is: (i) a power to acquire a property right; and (ii) a power to acquire a persistent right against A's right.

---

[106] Compare the table in **D1:3.5.4**.
[107] Unless B's property right is a property right in money (see **D1:3.5.3**).

B's power	Can B exercise his power against C: a 'bona fide purchaser' of a *persistent right* against A's right?
Power to regain the right transferred to A	Yes
Power to acquire a persistent right against the right transferred to A	No

3.6 The lack of registration defence

A Co, a manufacturer of bikes, has Ownership of its manufacturing equipment. In return for a loan from B Bank, A Co gives B Bank a Purely Equitable Charge over its Ownership of the equipment. That transaction is recorded in a written document but is not registered with the Companies Registrar. A Co then gives C Bank a second Purely Equitable Charge over its Ownership of its manufacturing equipment.

In such a case, C Bank cannot rely on the 'bona fide purchaser' defence. C Bank has *not* acquired the very right against which B Bank has a right; instead, it has acquired a second persistent right against A Co's right (see **Examples 19c and 19d**). However, B Bank's failure to register its pre-existing persistent right means that C Bank *does* have a defence—the lack of registration defence:[108] B Bank's Purely Equitable Charge is 'void against the liquidator or administrator or any creditor'[109] of A Co, and C Bank is such a creditor.[110]

The lack of registration defence thus means that, before deciding whether to extend credit to A Co, C Bank has an easy means of discovering certain types of pre-existing persistent right.[111] To that extent, the defence performs the same role as when it applies to land (see **C2:6 and C2:7**). And, in one important respect, the defence operates in the same way: C Bank can rely on it even if it *knows* about B Bank's unregistered persistent right.[112] In another way, however, the defence operates differently to the lack of registration defence permitted by the Land Registration Act 2002: C Bank can rely on it even if C Bank has *not* registered its own right.[113] Of course, C Bank, if it is sensible, will register its right; otherwise C2 Bank, when it acquires a later right from A Co, will be able to use the same lack of registration defence against C Bank's right.

---

[108] Companies Act 1985, s 396(1)(c) means that, if not registered, B Bank's Purely Equitable Charge is vulnerable to the lack of registration defence. This provision is to be replaced by Companies Act 2006, s 860(7)(b) with effect from 1 October 2009 (the new rule has exactly the same effect).

[109] Companies Act 1985, s 395(1); to be replaced by Companies Act 2006, s 874(1) with effect from 1 October 2009.

[110] The Companies Act provision, although it refers to 'any creditor' does not protect C unless C is either: (i) a secured creditor (ie, like C Bank in **Example 22**, C has a property right or a persistent right by way of security); or (ii) an execution creditor (see **B:2.3.1**): see *re Ehrmann Bros Ltd* [1906] 2 Ch 697 and **F4:n105**.

[111] Similarly, if A gives B a Purely Equitable Charge over A's Ownership of a ship or aircraft, B's failure to register that persistent right can also allow C to use the lack of registration defence against B's right. See Merchant Shipping Act 1995, Sch 1, para 7; Mortgaging of Aircraft Order 1972, SI 1972/1268.

[112] See eg *re Monolithic Building Company* [1915] 1 Ch 643.

[113] See Goode, *Commercial Law* (3rd edn, 2004), 668. In this way, the lack of registration defence under the Companies Acts operates like the lack of registration defence provided, in unregistered land, by the Land Charges Act 1972 (see **C2:7**). For the position applying to registered land under the Land Registration Act 2002, see **C2:6**.

The extra protection that a registration system can give to C is generally deemed to be unnecessary (see **C2:4**). The lack of registration defence is therefore reserved for rare circumstances, such as **Example 22**, in which it is felt that C is *particularly* in need of protection.

3.7 The limitation defence

In general, limitation rules mean that rights and duties are only enforceable for a limited time. This raises an interesting question as far as persistent rights are concerned: does the expiry of a limitation period applying to the (type of) duty that gave rise to the persistent right *also* prevent B from asserting his persistent right?

EXAMPLE 23

A has shares in a private company. In June 2002, A makes a contractual promise to transfer to B, by the end of the month, those specific shares. A fails to make the promised transfer. Six years pass by. In September 2008, B brings a claim against A.

A's contractual promise, by itself, cannot transfer the shares to B: B can acquire the shares only if B is registered as the new holder of the shares. However, as a result of A's contractual promise, B acquires an immediate persistent right: A is under a duty to B in relation to those shares.[114]

As six years have passed since A's breach of contract, section 5 of the Limitation Act 1980 ('the 1980 Act') prevents B from bringing an action 'founded on' his contract with A. However, in **Example 23**, that does *not* prevent B asserting his persistent right. Once A comes under a duty to B in relation to a specific right, B acquires a persistent right; from that point, the only limitation rules that matter are the *rules that apply to persistent rights*. Those rules operate *whatever* the source of A's duty to B. So, the standard rule applying to contractual claims under the 1980 Act does *not* apply in **Example 23**.

The limitation rules applying to B's persistent right vary according to the nature of that right, and, as a result, we will look at those rules when looking at specific persistent rights in **F3:3.1** and **F4:4.4**.[115] However, one general point about limitation periods and persistent rights is worth noting here. Where B has a persistent right, it may be possible for C to rely on a *non-statutory* limitation defence. This is because courts of Equity developed two special forms of limitation defence.[116] The first allows a statutory limitation period to be applied 'by analogy' to a situation not regulated by the statute. That defence cannot now be relevant in cases where a statute *does* expressly deal with B's attempt to assert a persistent right. For example, if B has a right under a Trust, the 1980 Act regulates when the lapse of time can

---

[114] See eg *Neville v Wilson* [1997] Ch 144. In that case, as in **Example 23**, A's contractual promise related to shares in a *private* company and so was specifically enforceable (as B cannot obtain such shares on the open market). However, on the view taken in this book, there is no need for A's promise to be specifically enforceable: B should acquire a persistent right whenever A's contractual promise is to transfer *specific* shares to B (see **2.1.2(vi)** above).

[115] In **Example 23**, no statutory limitation period applies to B's claim: see Limitation Act 1980, s 21(1)(b). However, if A can show that, due to the lapse of time, it would be unjust to allow B to enforce his right against A, the doctrine of 'laches' may apply to give A a defence: see eg *re Sharpe* [1892] 1 Ch 154; *Nelson v Rye* [1996] 1 WLR 1378 (see **F3:3.1**).

[116] See further Swadling, ch 11 and Watt, ch 12 in *Breach of Trust* (ed Birks and Pretto, 2002)

prevent B asserting his right: as a result, the idea of applying a statutory limitation period 'by analogy' is irrelevant.

Equity also developed the doctrine of 'laches': if B asserts an Equitable right, or asks for an Equitable remedy, that doctrine means that B will be denied a remedy if, due to the lapse of time, injustice would be caused by allowing B to assert his right.[117] In some situations regulated by the 1980 Act, it seems that A or C *may* be able to rely on the 'laches' defence *even if*, under the Act, A or C has no statutory limitation defence (see **F3:3.1**). This is very difficult to justify. As a matter of history, courts of Equity needed to protect defendants in areas unregulated by statutory limitation periods. However, a modern statutory scheme should be comprehensive and thus leave no gaps for the doctrine of laches to fill. After all, the point about the limitation defence is that, at some point, B can be said to have waited too long before asserting his right. The crucial question then is: how long is too long? We need a clear answer to that question: there is a lack of certainty and consistency if the answer depends simply on whether a judge may regard it as 'unjust' for B to assert his right. The question is impossible to answer simply through applying principles (eg, there is no principled distinction between bringing a claim: (i) five years and eleven months after acquiring a right; and (ii) six years after acquiring that right). Therefore, we need a comprehensive *statutory* scheme defining the operation of the limitation defence.

SUMMARY OF D2:3 AND COMPARISON WITH PROPERTY RIGHTS

In **D1:3** we considered the defences that C may be able to use against B's pre-existing property right. In this section, we have examined the same defences and seen that they apply differently where B has a pre-existing *persistent* right.

The two key changes are in relation: to (i) the overreaching defence; and (ii) the 'bona fide purchaser' defence. The former defence, as always, is based on A's power to give C a right free from a pre-existing right of B. The difference is that, where B has a persistent right, it is more likely, *in practice*, that A will have such a power. The 'bona fide purchaser' defence, whilst it can only exceptionally be used against a pre-existing property right, is *always* available where B has a pre-existing persistent right. This is an important difference in *principle*: the defence is crucial in resolving the **basic tension** between B and C. The **content question** and the **acquisition question** give C less protection from the risk of being bound by a pre-existing persistent right of B; but the 'bona fide purchaser' defence can protect C from B's hidden persistent right.

---

4 THE REMEDIES QUESTION

4.1 Preface: the protection of persistent rights

4.1.1 The direct assertion of B's right

(i) The general position

Before looking at the remedies a court may give to protect B's persistent right, we first need

---

[117] See eg *re Sharpe* [1892] 1 Ch 154; *Nelson v Rye* [1996] 1 WLR 1378. The doctrine has a very similar effect to a statutory limitation period: it does not extinguish B's right; it simply prevents B from asserting that right.

to look at the means by which B can assert such a right. If B has a pre-existing *property* right to which A or C has no defence, B *cannot* directly assert that right: B cannot go to court and simply say 'That thing is mine' (see **D1:4.1.1**). However, things are different if B has a pre-existing persistent right to which C has no defence. For example, if A holds his Ownership of a bike on Trust for B, B can *directly* assert his right by asking a court for an order forcing A to comply with the terms of the Trust. If A has transferred his Ownership of the bike to C, and C has no defence to B's right under the Trust, B then has a power to impose the core Trust duty on C. If B does so, he can *directly* enforce that duty by preventing C from using C's Ownership of the bike for C's own benefit.

On the orthodox view, this difference between the means by which property rights and persistent rights can be protected is a difference between Common Law and Equity: (i) 'Common Law property rights' are protected through the law of wrongs; and (ii) 'Equitable property rights' can be asserted directly. The orthodox view assumes that, when asserting his right under a Trust of A's Ownership of a bike, B is in fact saying 'That bike is mine (in Equity).'[118] If that were the case, there would be an inconsistency between Common Law and Equity: we know that B cannot assert a 'Common Law property right' by saying 'That bike is mine.'

However, the difference between the protection of property rights and persistent rights can instead be explained as a result of the *conceptual* difference between property rights and persistent rights. The key feature of a property right is that it is a right, relating to a thing, that imposes a prima facie duty on the rest of the world. A breach of a duty is a wrong; so if C interferes with B's thing, C commits a wrong against B (see **B:4.2**). B's property right is thus a 'background right' protected through the law of wrongs (see **D1:1.1.1** and **D1:4.1.1**).

Persistent rights are different. The key feature of a persistent right is that A is under a duty to B in relation to a specific right held by A. B must assert that right directly, by claiming that A is under a duty to B. If A then transfers his right to C, or gives C a right that depends on A's right, B has a power to impose a duty on C (see **B:4.3**). If B exercises that power, he must then assert his right by claiming that C is under a duty to B. In contrast to a property right, therefore, a persistent right is *not* a background right: it consists simply of A or C being under a duty to B in relation to a specific right.

So, there is no inconsistency between Common Law and Equity. *Neither* system allows B directly to assert a background right; *neither* system allows B to directly claim: 'That bike is mine.' Instead, *each* system allows B to say: 'A is under a duty to me' or 'C is under a duty to me.' That is precisely what B says when using the law of wrongs to assert his property right. And it is also what B says when directly asserting a persistent right. The difference is that, where B has a property right, his pre-existing property right is the *source* of A or C's duty to B. In contrast, where B has a persistent right, that right is the *product* of the fact that A or C is under a duty to B.

It is worth considering precisely what B claims when directly asserting a pre-existing persistent right against a third party (C). In most cases, B simply claims that C is under the same **core duty** as A: a duty in relation to a specific right. It is important to bear in mind that it may well *not* be possible for B to impose *other* duties on C—eg, the additional duties

---

[118] See eg Birks ch 7 in *Breach of Trust* (ed Birks and Pretto, 2002), 216: 'There is no vindication of chattels at common law. However, in equity there is. A claimant can ask a court to declare that the defendant holds the [thing] on trust for him. In effect, he is then directly asserting that the [thing] is his in equity.'

that A owes to B, arising perhaps out of A's agreement to hold a right on Trust for B (see F3:1.3).[119]

Nature of B's pre-existing persistent right	Core duty B can impose on C
Right under a Trust	Core Trust Duty: duty not to use the right for C's own benefit[120]
Purely Equitable Charge	Duty to hold the right as security for a duty owed to B (eg, A's duty to B to repay a loan)
Mortgagor's Right to Redeem	Duty to transfer the right back to B if the duty secured by the mortgage is performed (eg, if B repays a loan to A)

(ii) Rights under a Trust and third parties

EXAMPLE 24a

A holds his Ownership of a bike on Trust entirely for B. In breach of his duties as trustee, A transfers that right, for free, to C. C has no actual or constructive notice of B's pre-existing persistent right. Believing the bike is his to use as he please, C sells the bike to C2 for £200 (C2 also has no actual no actual or constructive notice of B's initial right under the Trust). C then spends the money on a holiday.

EXAMPLE 24b

The facts are as in **Example 24a**. However, *after* acquiring the bike from A, but *before* selling the bike to C2, C is informed by B that: (i) A held his Ownership of the bike on Trust for B; and (ii) A transferred that right to B in breach of his duties as trustee.

In **Example 24a**, B *cannot* assert a persistent right against C. This is *not* because C has a defence to B's pre-existing persistent right. When C acquired Ownership of the bike, B *did* have a power to impose a duty on C in relation to his Ownership of the bike. Although C did not know about, and could not reasonably have been expected to discover, B's persistent right, C acquired the right for free and so was not a 'bona fide purchaser'. The problem for B is that it is now *too late* for him to exercise his power to impose a duty on C: (i) C no longer has Ownership of the bike; and (ii) C does not have a right that counts as a product of C's Ownership of the bike.[121]

In **Example 24b**, things are different: B *can* directly assert a persistent right against C. The point is that, by informing C, B exercised his power to impose a duty on C *whilst C still had Ownership of the bike*. At that point, C came under the core Trust duty to B. As a result, C is under a duty to 'account' to B for the right that C held on Trust for B: C's Ownership of the bike.

---

[119] See too R Nolan (2006) 122 *LQR* 232.

[120] Similarly, if B's right arises under an Equitable Assignment by A of A's personal right against Z, C is under a duty to B: (i) not to use that personal right for C's own benefit.

[121] For B's ability to impose a duty on C in relation to a *product* of C's initial right, see **D4:4.4**.

This duty to account is a very important consequence of the core Trust duty (see **F3:1.1**). The core Trust duty means that: (i) C has a right; and (ii) C is under a duty to B not to use that right for C's own benefit. As a consequence, B can ask C to account for that right. This means that C must produce the right held on Trust. In **Example 24b**, C can no longer produce his Ownership of the bike: he transferred that right to C2. As a result, C must produce a right *of equivalent value*, which can then be held on Trust for B. This means that, in **Example 24b**, C is under a duty to pay £200 that can then be held on Trust for B.

EXAMPLE 24c

The basic facts are as in **Example 24b**. Again, *after* acquiring the bike from A, but *before* selling the bike to C2, C discovers that: (i) A held his Ownership of the bike on Trust for B; and (ii) A transferred that right to B in breach of his duties as trustee. However, C is not told this by B but discovers it from a different source.

Such a case is, in effect, identical to **Example 24b**. Again, once C *knows* the two key facts (facts (i) and (ii)) he is under the core Trust duty to B. Clearly, it makes no difference that B did not inform C. In such a case, B does not need to exercise his power to impose a duty on C: the purpose of exercising that power is to inform C that C is bound by B's pre-existing persistent right and, in **Example 24c**, C already knows the relevant facts.

Example 24c leads on to a difficult point. What if C knows fact (i), but does not *actually* know fact (ii)? It may be that C strongly suspects that the transfer was a breach of A's duties as trustee, but has refrained from checking and simply hopes for the best. In such a case, the courts have made clear that C *is* under the core Trust duty: C cannot escape by his 'wilful blindness' (ie, by simply shutting his eyes to the truth).[122] However, it is easy to think of more tricky examples. There are numerous different points on the path linking a dishonest C (who is fully aware of A's breach of Trust) to an entirely innocent C. And the courts have faced a very difficult job in knowing where to place the barrier between cases where C *is* under the core Trust duty and those where he is not.

At the moment, the courts have decided that C is under the core Trust duty where his knowledge or awareness of A's breach of Trust means that it would be 'unconscionable' for C to be free to use the right obtained from A for his own benefit: in other words, where it would be 'unconscionable' for C *not* to be under the core Trust duty to B.[123] Of course, this test is easy to criticise: it essentially means that C is under the core Trust duty when, given his level of knowledge or awareness, it would be wrong for C *not* to be under the core Trust duty. As so often when the term 'unconscionable' is used, it is used as a conclusion not a test (see **C1:3.1**).

However, we should not be too quick to mock. The tests previously used by the courts, in attempting to be more precise, had become hideously convoluted.[124] And the concept of

---

[122] See eg *per* Peter Gibson J in *Baden v Société Générale pour Favoriser le Développement du Commerce et de l'Industrie en France SA* [1993] 1 WLR 509 at [253]: 'if a person shuts his eyes to the obvious, or if he wilfully and recklessly fails to make obvious inquiries, that person is guilty of unconscionable behaviour such that a court of equity might wish to impute to him the knowledge that he would have gained by opening his eyes or making the obvious inquiries'.

[123] *BCCI v Akindele* [2001] Ch 437.

[124] See the survey of past cases by Nourse LJ in *BCCI v Akindele* [2001] Ch 437. Note esp the discussion of five different types of knowledge in *Baden v Société Générale pour Favoriser le Developpement du Commerce et de l'Industrie en France SA* [1993] 1 WLR 509 at [250].

'unconscionability', when used in this context, does not mean a court can decide for or against C based on its own particular notions of justice; rather, it is used in relation to the *specific* question of C's knowledge or awareness of A's breach of Trust. Further, certainty for C may not be too important here: if C's awareness of A's breach of Trust means that C is 'skating on thin ice', he may deserve little sympathy. And whilst litigation may be necessary to identify whether C's conduct was 'unconscionable', at least the chance of a costly appeal is reduced: it will be difficult for an appeal court to interfere with a trial judge's finding as to unconscionability. In contrast, the previous convoluted test was a recipe for appeals, as it made it easy for a trial judge to err in law by applying the test incorrectly.

The current test is thus that C comes under the core Trust duty to B (and hence under the duty to account) if:

- A holds a right on Trust for B; and
- A transfers that right to C and C has no defence to B's pre-existing persistent right; and
- Whilst C still holds that right (or a right that is a product of that right);
- C has sufficient knowledge or awareness of the fact that he received the right as a result of a breach of Trust by A; so that
- It would be *unconscientious* for C to be free to use that right wholly for his own bene-fit.

If this test is satisfied, the courts say that:

- because of his 'knowing receipt' of a right transferred to him in breach of Trust;
- C is under 'a duty to account to B as a constructive trustee'.[125]

This use of the term 'constructive trustee' has been criticised. It is true that, as in **Examples 24b and 24c**, there is no need for C to be holding a specific right on Trust for B when B makes his claim against C. But that criticism misses the point: B's claim is based on C's duty to account; and that duty arises as a result of the fact that, at one point, C *did* hold a right on Trust for B. And, as that Trust did not arise as a result of C *consenting* to hold on Trust for B, it may be reasonable to say that C is a 'constructive trustee' as opposed to an 'express trustee' (see **F3:2.1.4**).

In contrast, the term 'knowing receipt' *is* unhelpful. As in **Examples 24b and 24c**, C does not need to know about A's breach of Trust *when* he receives his right from A; it is enough if C gains that knowledge at *any* point when C still has that right, or a product of it. So it would be better to say that C's duty to account comes from C's 'knowing holding' of the right.[126]

4.1.2 Wrongs?

The only way for B to assert a pre-existing *property right* against C is to claim that C has committed a wrong against B: the wrongs of trespass, conversion and negligence can each protect B's property right (see **D1:4.1.1**). In contrast, there is *no* wrong that specifically

---

[125] The terminology stems from the judgment of Lord Selborne LC in *Barnes v Addy* (1874) LR 9 Ch App 244 at 251–2. For modern use of the term, see eg *BCCI v Akindele* [2001] Ch 437.

[126] Note the formulation of Nourse LJ in *BCCI v Akindele* [2001] Ch 437 at 455: 'The recipient's state of knowledge must be such as to make it unconscionable for him to retain the benefit of the receipt.' The emphasis is not on C's state of mind when he receives the right, but rather on his state of mind as he holds it.

protects persistent rights from third parties. We can see this by examining **B:Examples 7a and 7b.** If: (i) A holds his Ownership of a bike on Trust for B; and (ii) C carelessly damages or steals the bike; then (iii) C commits a wrong against A; but C does *not* commit a wrong against B. Although B has a persistent right, that right, unlike a property right, does *not* impose a prima facie duty on the rest of the world (see **B:4.4.3**).

In cases such as **Examples 24b and 24c,** it is tempting to say that *both* A and C have committed a wrong against B: (i) by transferring the bike to C, for free, A breached his core Trust duty to B; and (ii) by selling the bike to C2 and spending the proceeds of sale, C breached his core Trust duty to B. However, in those cases, there is simply no need for B to assert a new right against A or C, arising as a result of A or C's commission of a wrong. Instead, B can simply assert his persistent right by enforcing A or C's duty to account for the right held on Trust.[127] B's claim against C, like his claim against A, works in the following way: (i) B asks C to produce the right (Ownership of the bike) that C, at one point, held on Trust for B; (ii) C cannot produce that right or its product; and (iii) C does not have a good excuse his inability to do so; (iv) so C must produce a right of equivalent value to be held on Trust for B. In this way, B avoids any difficulties that may be involved in showing that C (or A) has committed a wrong.[128]

In other cases, however, B's inability to show that a third party has *wrongfully* interfered with B's persistent right can have important practical effects. We can see this by returning to **Example 24a.** In such a case, as C no longer has Ownership of the bike, B can no longer impose the core Trust duty on C. And C has not committed a wrong against B. It is true that C, by his conduct, has interfered with B's enjoyment of B's persistent right. But, when C acted in that way, he had no knowledge of B's pre-existing persistent right.

EXAMPLE 25

B has Ownership of a bike. B lends the bike to A for an afternoon. A gives the bike as a birthday present to C, who honestly and reasonably believes that no one other than A has a right in relation to the bike. C then sells the bike to C2 and spends the proceeds on a holiday.

In such a case, because B's initial right is a *property right,* C *has* committed a wrong against B: the wrong of conversion. It makes no difference that C no longer has the bike; nor does it matter that C acted innocently throughout; nor does it matter that C has spent the money he made when selling the bike. C has committed a wrong against B and so must pay B money as a substitute for B's right and to compensate B for any relevant loss B has suffered as a result (see **D1:4.3**).

Of course, it is possible to disagree with the results in both **Example 24a** and **Example 25.**[129] After all, each case involves resolving the **basic tension;** and there is no perfect way of

---

[127] See eg *re Dawson* [1966] 2 NSWR 211; Elliott (2002) 65 *MLR* 588. It is not entirely clear that the House of Lords appreciated this point in *Target Holdings v Redferns* [1996] AC 421. However, the result in that case is entirely consistent with the view set out here, as explained by Millett (1998) 114 *LQR* 214 at 223–7.

[128] See *Youyang v Minter Ellis Morris Fletcher* (2003) 196 ALR 482 (High Court of Australia); Elliott and Edelman (2003) 119 *LQR* 545.

[129] For example, Birks, ch 7 in *Breach of Trust* (ed Birks and Pretto, 2002) and Lord Nicholls, *Restitution: Past, Present & Future* (ed Cornish et al, 1998), 231–46 argue that the result in **Example 24a** is unduly harsh on B, *if* C used the money to pay for a holiday which C was going to take in any case (see **4.1.3** below). And Tettenborn [1993] *CLJ* 128 and Lord Nicholls in *Kuwait Airways Corpn v Iraqi Airways Co (Nos 4 & 5)* [2002] 2 AC 883 at [79]–[80] suggest that the result in **Example 25** is unduly harsh on C.

doing so. However, it is *not* accurate to say that the results demonstrate an inconsistency in the property law system. On the orthodox view, it is possible to query why B's 'Equitable property right' in **Example 24a** receives less protection that B's 'Common Law property right' in **Example 25**: after all, on that view, B has a property right in each case.[130] However, that view overlooks the fundamental distinction between property rights and persistent rights. In **Example 24a**, B does *not* have a property right. As a result, the rest of the world is *not* under a prima facie duty to B not to interfere with B's pre-existing right. In contrast, in **Example 25**, B *does* have such a right. As C has no defence to it, C *does* commit a wrong by using the bike, even though he acts innocently throughout. That may seem harsh, but it is a product of the property law system's commitment to protect property rights: the approach taken to the **content** and **acquisition questions** ensures that it is very difficult for B to acquire such a right in the first place.

4.1.3 Unjust enrichment?

It has been argued that B can also use the law of unjust enrichment to assert his pre-existing persistent right against C. For example, it has been argued that, in a case such as **Example 24a**, B should have a right against C if the holiday C took was one that C was *in any case* planning to take.[131] The argument is that, by using the proceeds of his Ownership of the bike to pay for the holiday (rather than other money C may have had), C is unjustly enriched at B's expense. We will consider this argument in **D4:7**. The conclusion will be that the argument is unsound: the property law system does *not* allow B to assert a persistent right through the law of unjust enrichment. The basic point is a simple one: in a case such as **Example 24a**, the £200 C receives when selling his Ownership of the bike to C2 does *not* come from B. True, the money is the product of C's Ownership of the bike; but C acquired that right from A, not from B.

SUMMARY of D2:4.1

If B wishes to assert a pre-existing persistent right against C, he must do so by directly asserting that right against C. There is thus no role for the law of wrongs or for the law of unjust enrichment to play when B seeks to assert a pre-existing persistent right.

4.2   Specific protection

4.2.1 The Purely Equitable Charge

EXAMPLE 26

A has Ownership of a bike. In return for a loan of £200 from B, A gives B a Purely Equitable Charge over his Ownership of the bike. A, without B's consent or other authority, then transfers the bike to C. A then fails to make any repayment to B.

If C has no defence, B can assert his Purely Equitable Charge against C. In such a case, there

---

[130] See eg Birks [1989] *LMCLQ* 296 and ch 7 in *Breach of Trust* (ed Birks and Pretto, 2002) and Lord Nicholls, *Restitution: Past, Present & Future* (ed Cornish et al, 1998), 231–246.

[131] For example, Birks, ch 7 in *Breach of Trust* (ed Birks and Pretto, 2002) and Lord Nicholls, *Restitution: Past, Present & Future* (ed Cornish et al, 1998), 231–46.

is no need to consider the distinction between: (i) specific protection; and (ii) receiving a sum of money from C. Specific protection of B's Purely Equitable Charge would consist of allowing B: (i) to sell A's right; and (ii) to use the proceeds of sale to meet A's debt. Therefore, if C offers to pay B a sum of money equal to the value of the bike (or, where it is a lower sum, to A's debt), B's right is fully protected. The same analysis applies where B's persistent right arises under an Equitable Assignment. If C gives B a sum of money equal to A's personal right against Z, then B's right is fully protected.

4.2.2 The Mortgagor's Right to Redeem and rights under a Trust

EXAMPLE 27

B has Ownership of a bike. In return for a loan of £200 from A, B transfers his Ownership of the bike, by way of security, to A. A then transfers his Ownership of the bike to C.

If C has no defence, B can assert his Right to Redeem against C. So, if: (i) B performs the secured duty by repaying A; then (ii) C is under a duty to transfer Ownership of the bike to B. We then need to consider whether a court will make an order: (i) specifically protecting B's right by ordering C to transfer his Ownership of the bike to B; *or* (ii) requiring C to pay a sum of money to B. It seems that C's duty to transfer his right to B *will* be specifically enforced. However, this is a little difficult to understand. The dispute is very similar to that arising where A makes an agreement to sell a specific bike to B: if A refuses to perform, his duty to transfer Ownership will *not*, in general, be specifically enforced (see **A:3.1.2(ii)**).[132] If the specific bike is not unique, B can receive money and use that money to buy a similar bike elsewhere (compare **D1:4.2**). It may be that the Mortgagor's Right to Redeem is treated differently because of the importance the courts have attached to protecting B in a case where he transfers a right by way of security (see **F4:1.3 and F4:1.4**).

EXAMPLE 28

A holds Ownership of a bike on Trust for B. A transfers that right to C.

If C has no defence, B can assert his persistent right against C and thus impose the core Trust duty on C. If this occurs, C is then under a duty not to use his right for his own benefit. If C still has that right, we need to consider whether a court will make an order: (i) specifically protecting B's right by preventing C from use his right for his own benefit; *or* (ii) requiring C to pay a sum of money to B. It is clear that C's duty not to use the right for his own benefit will be specifically enforced. There are a variety of ways in which this may happen. The most usual method is that C will be ordered to transfer Ownership of the bike to C2, a new trustee appointed by the court. C2 will then hold Ownership of the bike subject to *all* the duties imposed on A by the original Trust. Alternatively, if A held the bike on Trust *entirely* for B's benefit, B may require C to transfer the right held on Trust directly to B (see **D1:1.4.5(ii)**).

---

[132] See eg *re Wait* [1927] 1 Ch 606 at 630; *Cohen v Roche* [1927] 1 KB 169.

4.3 Money awards

4.3.1 Money as a substitute for B's right

The starting position is that if: (i) B's pre-existing persistent right binds C, so that C is under a duty to B; then (ii) C's duty to B will be specifically enforced. However, it may be that C *no longer holds* the right against which B has a right. This is the case in **Examples 24b and 24c**. In such a case, it is generally too late for B's right to be specifically protected. As a result, a court will have to do the next best thing and order C to pay a sum of money based on the value of B's right. So, in **Examples 24b and 24c**, we saw that C's duty to account to B for the right initially held on Trust will be enforced by ordering C to pay a sum of money equal to the value of that right. As long as C has failed to comply with his duty to account, there is no need for B to show that C's action has caused B any loss:[133] B is *not* claiming money as compensation for consequential loss; he is claiming money as a substitute for his right.[134]

4.3.2 Money as compensation for B's consequential loss

Where B's pre-existing persistent right binds C, and C is thus under a duty to B, C's delay in performing that duty may cause B consequential loss. In such cases, there is a strong argument that a court should: (i) order C to specifically perform his duty; and (ii) order C to pay B money as compensation for any relevant loss B has suffered as a result of C's delay. It seems clear that, if C's breach of the core Trust duty causes a relevant loss to B, a court can order C to pay B money as compensation for that loss.[135] In other cases, given that C has not committed a specific wrong against B (see **4.2** above), there may be a technical problem about the source of C's duty to compensate B. However, the courts may rely on: (i) a possible inherent jurisdiction, initially arising in Equity, to award money to B;[136] and (ii) the provisions of the Chancery Amendment Act 1858 (Lord Cairns' Act).[137]

4.3.3 Money reflecting C's gain?

EXAMPLE 29a

A holds Ownership of a bike on Trust for B. A transfers that right, for free, to C. C sells the bike for £200 to C2 (a 'bona fide purchaser'). C invests the £200 in some shares now worth £1,000.

---

[133] See **nn 127 and 128** above.

[134] See eg *Underhill & Hayton's Law of Trusts and Trustees* (ed Hayton et al, 17th edn, 2006), 89.7.

[135] See eg *Tang Man Sit v Capacious Investments Ltd* [1996] 1 AC 514 at 526 (re the loss suffered by B as a result of damage to land caused by C's breach of Trust); *Bartlett v Barclays Bank Trust Co Ltd (No 2)* [1980] Ch 515. One explanation of this liability is to see it as part of C's duty to account to B. Another is to see it as based on C's commission of the wrong of breach of Trust. Certainly, where C is in breach of Trust, C is generally in breach of a fiduciary duty to B, and it is clear that C can be ordered to pay money to B to compensate B for relevant loss caused by a breach of a fiduciary duty: see eg *per* Millett LJ in *Bristol & West Building Society v Mothew* [1998] Ch 1 at 18. See Chambers, ch 1 in *Breach of Trust* (ed Birks and Pretto, 2002), 20–23; Hayton, ch 11 in *Equity and Commercial Law* (ed Degeling and Edelman, 2005), 301–4.

[136] See eg *per* Viscount Haldane LC in *Nocton v Lord Ashburton* [1914] AC 932 at 952; Davidson (1982) 13 *Melbourne University Law Review* 349.

[137] See eg *per* Lord Goff in *A-G v Observer Ltd* [1990] 1 AC 109 at 162.

In such a case, B can impose the core Trust duty on C in relation to C's shares. As a result, B, rather than C, gains the benefit of those shares.[138] This result does *not* depend on the remedies question. Rather it depends on the **acquisition question**: on a principle allowing B to acquire a new persistent right, where: (i) C has a new right that counts as a product of B's initial right; and (ii) there is no legal basis for C to have the benefit of that new right (see **D1:4.3.3 and D4:4.4**). That principle assists B only where C's gain consists in C's acquisition of a *new right that is the product of B's initial right*.[139]

EXAMPLE 29b

A holds some shares in Z Co on Trust for B. Under the terms of the Trust, A is not permitted to sell those shares without B's consent. In June, A, without B's consent, sells those shares to C, who knows that the transfer involves a breach of Trust. C pays £900 for the shares. C immediately sells the shares for £1,000 (their true market value at that point) to C2 (a 'bona fide purchaser'). In September, B discovers what has happens. At that point, Z Co shares have doubled in value since June.

C's knowledge of B's pre-existing right means that C held the shares subject to the core Trust duty to B. As a result, C is under a duty to account to B. As C can no longer produce the shares, he must pay B a sum of money equal to their *current* value: £2000.[140] There is no need for B to show that: (i) C committed a wrong against B; and (ii) C made a gain as a result. After all, C has not made a gain. B's protection instead comes from the nature of C's duty to account, which continues even after C has parted with the shares.

In other cases, as we saw in **D1:4.3.3**, it may be possible for B to claim 'punitive' or 'exemplary' damages where C: (i) acts in a way that C *knows* will be in a breach of a duty owed to B; and (ii) does so with the intention of making a profit. There is a difficult question as to whether such damages can ever be available where C (or A) breaches an Equitable duty to B.[141] Discussion of the issue is overshadowed by the technical issue of how such damages could be awarded, given that C (or A) has not committed a specific wrong against B. However, if C has breached a duty owed to B, that technical issue should not obstruct a principled investigation of whether, given the various advantages and disadvantages involved, an award of 'exemplary' damages should be possible.[142] Certainly, it is difficult to see why such an award should be ruled out *just* because C's duty arises in Equity (see **C1:3.5**).[143] As argued in **D1:4.3.3**, the availability of 'exemplary' damages should depend on the nature of C's conduct, not on the nature of B's right.

---

[138] If C, after coming under the core Trust duty, then sold the shares, B can still enforce C's duty to account to B for the value of those shares: see **Example 29b**.

[139] If C's breach of a core Trust duty owed to B counts as a breach of fiduciary duty, C will have to pay B the value of any profits made by C as a result of the breach, whether or not C acquires a specific new right as a result of his breach: see eg *Tang Man Sit v Capacious Investments Ltd* [1996] 1 AC 514.

[140] See eg *re Massingberd's Settlement* (1890) 63 LT 296: that case involved A's duty to account, but the same result should apply where C, due to his 'unconscientious holding' is also subject to a duty to account: that seems to be the best explanation of the decision in *re Bell's Indenture* [1980] 1 WLR 1217.

[141] See eg *Harris v Digital Pulse Pty Ltd* (2003) 56 NSWLR 298 where a 2–1 majority of the Court of Appeal of New South Wales held that exemplary damages should *not* be available as a remedy for a breach of an Equitable duty. For an *obiter dictum* to the contrary see *per* Brett LJ in *Smith v Day* (1882) 21 Ch D 421 at 428.

[142] Hayton ch 11 in *Equity and Commercial Law* (ed Degeling and Edelman, 2005) argues that it should be possible for a court to award exemplary damages against a party breaching a core Trust duty, at least if that party acts 'monstrously' (303).

[143] See Mason ch 3 and Burrows ch 15 in *Equity and Commercial Law* (ed Degeling and Edelman, 2005).

4.4   An allowance for C?

> **EXAMPLE 30**
>
> The facts are as in **Example 29**. B asserts his right against C after C's shares have increased in value. Until that point, C had no actual or constructive notice of B's persistent right. C used his own considerable skill in investing the shares wisely. And C had been planning to buy the shares, using some of his other money, even before he acquired Ownership of the bike from A.

In such a case, it may seem very harsh that C should be deprived of his profit by the accident that he bought the shares with the proceeds of his sale of the bike. There are two possible ways to deal with this apparent unfairness. The first relates to the **content** and **acquisition questions** and was employed by Ungoed-Thomas J in *re Tilley's Will Trusts*.[144] In that case, A held money on Trust for B. A, in breach of trust (but, it seems, with an innocent intention) paid that money into her account with Z Bank. A then used money from that account to buy houses which increased in value. B claimed that A held those houses on Trust for both A and B, with A and B sharing the right under the Trust in proportion to their contributions to the purchase price of the houses.[145]

Ungoed-Thomas J rejected B's argument. His Lordship held instead that A had intended to invest her own money in the houses and could easily have done so, without needing to rely on the money held on Trust for B. As a result, B's initial persistent right could be adequately protected by finding that B had a Purely Equitable Charge over A's rights to the houses. That Purely Equitable Charge gave B security for A's duty to repay the sum of money initially taken from B's Trust. So, if A had taken £2,000 from the Trust, B had a Purely Equitable Charge to secure A's duty to repay £2,000. This meant that A could keep the *whole profit* she had made through her investment in the houses.

Whatever its merits, this method of protecting A, unrelated to the remedies question, was essentially rejected by the House of Lords in *Foskett v McKeown*,[146] a case we will examine in detail in **D4:4.4**. The view taken in that case is that, in a case such as **Example 30**, B can *always* impose the core Trust duty on C in relation to a right, held by C, that is a product of the right initially held on Trust for B.[147]

That leaves us with the second means to address the apparent unfairness to C. This is to give C, in a case such as **Example 30**, a right to a sum of money from B. This *allowance* can recognise the fact that C innocently used his own skill or time in turning B's initial right into a different and more valuable right. It may be reasonable for C to argue that, if an allowance is not given, B will be unjustly enriched at C's expense (see **D1:4.4**): there is no legal basis for B to keep the benefit of C's time and skill without paying anything in return. There are some signs that a court may order B to make such an allowance. For example,

---

[144] [1967] 1 Ch 1179.

[145] So, let us say A held £2,000 on Trust and paid that into an account already credited with £28,000. A then used that money to buy two houses for £30,000 and those houses increased in value to £90,000. On B's argument, A will now hold those houses on Trust for A and B with B having a 1/15th share of the right under the Trust and A having a 14/15th share. B's right would thus be worth £6,000: B initially had a persistent right against A's right to £2,000 and that right has now, like the houses, tripled in value.

[146] [2001] 1 AC 102.

[147] See too *Trustee of Jones v Jones* [1997] Ch 159.

allowances have been given in cases where a defendant has: (i) made a profit whilst innocently breaching a fiduciary duty owed to B; and (ii) has been ordered to pay a sum equal to that profit to B.[148] In a case such as **Example 30**, where C is not even aware that he is under *any* duty to B, C is equally, if not more, deserving of an allowance.[149] Similarly, the courts have an inherent jurisdiction to give remuneration to a trustee in recognition of the effort and skill employed by the trustee.[150] It has been said that one purpose of this remuneration is to prevent a beneficiary being unjustly enriched at the trustee's expense[151] and that purpose also argues in favour of an allowance for C.

SUMMARY OF D2:4 AND COMPARISON WITH PROPERTY RIGHTS

If B wishes to assert a pre-existing property right against C, he must do so by showing that C has committed a wrong (**D1:4.1**). In contrast, if B wishes to assert a pre-existing persistent right against C, he must do so by directly asserting that right against C. There is thus no role for the law of wrongs, or for the law of unjust enrichment, to play when B seeks to assert a pre-existing persistent right.

This clear contrast between property rights and persistent rights is based on the fact that a property right is a background right that imposes a prima facie duty on the rest of the world not to interfere with B's exclusive control of a thing. As that right is a background right, B cannot assert it directly by simply going to court and saying 'That's mine.' A persistent right is a right against a specific right: it depends on A being under a duty to B to use that specific right for B's benefit. A persistent right can therefore be asserted directly: B can go to court and claim that A (or C) is under a duty to B.

When B can assert a pre-existing persistent right against C, the remedies question arises. If C still holds the right against which B has a right (or a product of that right), then C's duty to B will be specifically enforced. If C no longer has such a right, it seems C will be ordered to pay money to B representing the value of B's right and compensating B for any relevant loss he has suffered as a result of any breach of the duty by C.

---

[148] See eg *Boardman v Phipps* [1967] 2 AC 46 at 104, 122; *O'Sullivan v Management Agency & Music Ltd* [1985] 1 QB 428. In *Boardman v Phipps* it was said at 104 and 112 that the defendant's allowance should be on a 'liberal' scale due to the 'work and skill' employed by the defendant in making the gain.

[149] Millett LJ gave the leading judgment in *Trustee of Jones v Jones* [1997] Ch 159, a case raising the same basic problem as **Example 30**. As Peter Millett, in ch 12 in *Equity and Commercial Law* (ed Degeling and Edelman, 2005), 323, he notes there was 'much force' in the argument that C should have received an allowance in *Jones*; however, as C did not ask the court to order such an allowance, the question was not considered.

[150] See eg *Marshall v Holloway* (1820) 2 Swan 432 at 452–4; *Foster v Spencer* [1996] 2 All ER 672.

[151] See *Foster v Spencer* [1996] 2 All ER 672 at 681.

CHAPTER D3
DIRECT RIGHTS

D3

DIRECT RIGHTS

Direct rights provide an important means of dealing with the **basic tension** between B and C. The possibility of acquiring a direct right gives B protection against only a *limited class* of third parties: those who have acted in such a way as to justify B acquiring a right against them (see **B:3**). A direct right can thus protect B if, through failing to satisfy either the **content question** or the **acquisition question**, he has no pre-existing property right or persistent right. It can also protect B where B *does* have such a right, but C has a **defence** to it.

Direct rights are not unique to the property law system: the question of whether C's conduct gives B a right arises throughout the law. For example, almost all of the law of contract and of torts is devoted to answering that question. In theory, then, deciding if B has a direct right against C means knowing *all* the possible means by which a claimant can acquire a right against a defendant. However, as this book focuses on disputes about the use of things and disputes about the use of rights, we will examine the direct rights that are *most likely to arise*, or *can only arise* in the **basic situation** set out in **A:Example 1**.

1 THE CONTENT QUESTION

The first, and straightforward, aspect of the content question is simply whether the new, direct right claimed by B allows B to make his desired use of the thing or right in question. The second aspect is whether B's new direct right counts as a property right, persistent right or personal right. Of course, in the basic situation, B's aim is simply to assert a right *against* C and so B has no need to show that his right is anything more than a simple personal right against C. However, things are different if B wishes to assert a right against C2: a party who *later* acquires a right in relation to the thing or right in question.

> **EXAMPLE 1a**
>
> A has Ownership of a bike. A transfers his Ownership to C. C makes a contractual promise to B that he will allow B to have exclusive control of the bike for the next six months.

As a result of C's contractual promise, B acquires a new, direct right against C. At this stage, it makes no difference whether B's direct right is any more than a personal right against C. If, three months later, C sells the bike to C2, things are different.

To analyse the position between B and C2, we need to go back to the **basic structure**. There are two ways in which B may assert a right against C2: (i) by having a new, direct right against C2, arising because of C2's conduct; *or* (ii) by having a pre-existing right that is capable of binding C2. If, as in **Example 1a**, C2 has done nothing to justify B gaining a new,

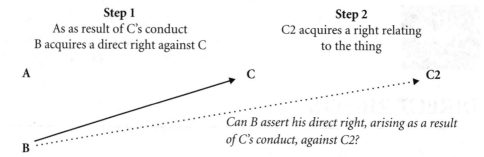

direct right, the **content question** becomes crucial: does the new direct right B acquired as a result of C's conduct count as either a property right or a persistent right? If it does, it will bind C2 unless C2 has a defence to it. If it does not, it is merely a personal right against C and so cannot bind C2.

To discover the nature of B's right, we simply need to examine the principles set out in **D1:1** and **D2:1**. In **Example 1a**, B's right to have exclusive control of the bike for six months does *not* count as a property right (see **D1:1.3.4** and **D1:1.4.3**). Nor does it count as a persistent right (see **D2:Example 2**). So, in **Example 1a**, B can assert a right against C: C's contractual promise to B gives B a direct personal right against C. However, if C then transfers Ownership of the bike to C2, B's only hope is to acquire a *further* direct right against C2, arising as a result of C2's conduct.

2   THE ACQUISITION QUESTION

2.1   Direct and indirect dealings between B and C

The most obvious way for B to acquire a direct right against C is by direct dealings with C. So, in **Example 1a**, B acquired a direct right as a result of C's contractual promise: a promise made to B for which B gave something in return. However, where the **basic situation** arises, it is unlikely that C will deal directly with B: after all, C acquires his right from A, not B. So, throughout this chapter, we will focus on cases where B can acquire a direct right *even though C has not dealt directly with B*.

2.1.1 Deeds and section 56 of the Law of Property Act 1925

On the facts of any particular case, it will usually be easy to tell if C has dealt directly with B. Nonetheless, one twist is worth noting. C can use a deed to give B a direct right (see eg **C3:Example 1d**). If the deed is executed by C alone, it is known as a *deed poll*. C can use such a deed to give B a direct right even if there is no agreement between B and C and even if B is not aware of the deed.[1]

An additional requirement applies to a deed executed not just by C, but by C and another party, such as A. Such a deed is known as an *inter partes* (between parties) deed: the deed itself will record that it is made *between* C and A. Again, C can use such a deed to give

---

[1] See eg *Macedo v Stroud* [1922] 2 AC 330.

B a right. However, the traditional rule is that B can only acquire a right by means of an *inter partes* deed if B is *named* as one of the parties to the deed.[2] Therefore, the deed itself must record that it is made *between* all three parties: A, B and C.

However, where C attempts to give B a right relating to a thing,[3] section 56 of the Law of Property Act 1925 provides an exception. Even if C uses an *inter partes* deed, and fails to name B as a party to the deed, B *can* acquire a right. The section thus means that where C attempts to deal directly with B by means of an *inter partes* deed, C's failure to include B as a party to the deed will *not* prevent B acquiring a direct right against C.

It is important to note the limits of the section 56 exception: it cannot be used *whenever* C makes a promise in a deed that happens to, or is even intended to, benefit B.[4] Instead, C must *purport to deal directly with B*: C must make a promise to B or otherwise attempt to give B a right.[5] As a result, B must be identifiable at the time the deed is executed.[6]

2.2   Cases where B has no pre-existing right

It is possible for B to acquire a direct right against C even if: (i) there are no direct dealings between B and C; *and* (ii) before C acquired his right, B had no right at all—not even a personal right against A.

2.2.1 The Contract (Rights of Third Parties) Act 1999

EXAMPLE 1b

A has Ownership of a bike. A transfers his Ownership to C. The contract of sale between A and C includes a term that C must allow B exclusive control of the bike for the next six months.

It is clear that B cannot acquire a contractual right as a result of C's promise to A: (i) C's promise was made to A, not to B; and (ii) B provided no consideration in return for C's promise. However, B may be able to acquire a *statutory* right against C. The Contract (Rights of Third Parties) Act 1999 ('the 1999 Act') means that, in certain circumstances, a contractual promise made by C to A can give B a direct, statutory right against C. The Act means that if:

- C makes a contractual promise to A; *and*
- B is expressly identified by name, class or description in that contract;[7] *then if either*

---

[2] See eg *Lord Southampton v Brown* (1827) 6 B & C 718; *Chesterfield and Midland Silkstone Colliery Co Ltd v Hawkins* (1865) 3 H & C 677 at 692; *White v Bijou Mansions Ltd* [1938] Ch 351.

[3] S 56 allows B to acquire a right relating to 'land or other property'. The majority of the House of Lords in *Beswick v Beswick* [1968] AC 58 took the strange view that the section can only apply to give B a right relating to land, or to a property right in land. The natural reading of the section, however, is that it can apply whenever C attempts to give B a right relating to the use of a thing.

[4] As was made clear by Neuberger J in *Amsprop Trading Ltd v Harris Distribution Ltd* [1997] 1 WLR 1025.

[5] See too *per* Simonds J in *White v Bijou Mansions Ltd* [1937] Ch 610 at 625: B can only rely on s 56 if 'although not named as a party to the instrument, [B] is yet a person to whom that conveyance or other instrument purports to grant some thing or with which some agreement or covenant is purported to be made'. That view was cited with approval by Lord Upjohn and Lord Pearce in *Beswick v Beswick* [1968] AC 58 at 106 (Lord Upjohn); 92–4 (Lord Pearce) and was also accepted by Neuberger J in *Amsprop Trading Ltd v Harris Distribution Ltd* [1997] 1 WLR 1025.

[6] For example, if C has promised to give a right to 'future owners of A's property', then B, a future owner of that thing, cannot use s 56 as he could not have been specifically identified when C made the promise in the deed.

[7] See s 1(3).

(a)   A and C state in the contract that B can enforce C's promise;[8] *or*

(b)   C's promise purports to confer a benefit on B *and* there is nothing in the contract to show that A and C did not intend the promise to be enforceable by B;[9] *then*

- C is under a duty to B to keep his promise.

So, wherever: (i) C makes a contractual promise to A; and (ii) B is expressly identified by name, class or description in that contract; then (iii) there are two *alternative* routes by which B can enforce C's promise. The first route applies where A and C expressly give B a right to enforce C's promise. The second route applies if two requirements are met: (i) C's promise purports to confer a benefit on B; *and* (ii) there is nothing to show that A and C did not intend, when making the contract, to give B the right to enforce C's promise. In **Example 1b**, the second route will be available to B. As a result, B acquires a direct right against C, arising under the 1999 Act.

2.2.2 The 'receipt after a promise' principle

EXAMPLE 2

A has some shares in Z Co. In his will, A states that the shares should go to C. However, at A's request, C promises A that he, C, will hold the shares on Trust for B. A dies and C acquires A's shares.

It is clear that neither A's estate nor B can acquire a contractual right as a result of C's promise to A: neither A nor B provided any consideration in return for C's promise. Nonetheless, B can acquire a direct right against C: C will hold the right he acquired from A on Trust for B.[10] This may seem surprising. If A wants to exercise his power to set up a Trust arising on his death, A needs to comply with the formality rules set out by the Wills Act 1837 (see **C3:2**). And, in **Example 2**, A has *not* complied with those rules: his intention to set up a Trust in B's favour has not been recorded in a document signed by A and two witnesses.

A's failure to comply with the Wills Act 1837 means that B cannot claim that he has a right under a Trust set up by A. Nonetheless, B can acquire a direct right against C as a result of C's conduct. As C acquired a right from A having promised to use that right for B's benefit, the courts will enforce C's promise. There is much academic debate about whether, and if so why, B should acquire such a direct right against C.[11] However, the courts seem to apply a clear principle, which can be called the 'receipt after a promise' principle. This principle is recognised in a number of different cases: it is not limited to situations where A transfers a right to C in A's will;[12] nor to situations where C promises to hold a right on Trust for B.[13] The principle means that if:

- C makes a promise to come under a duty to B; *and*

---

[8] See Contract (Rights of Third Parties) Act 1999, s 1(1)(a).
[9] See s 1(1)(b).
[10] See eg *Blackwell v Blackwell* [1929] AC 318.
[11] For discussion of the principle applying in **Example 2**, see **F3:2.1.4(iii)(c)**.
[12] See eg *Pallant v Morgan* [1953] Ch 43; *Banner Homes Group plc v Luff Developments Ltd* [2000] Ch 372.
[13] See eg *Lord Strathcona Steamship Co Ltd v Dominion Coal Co* [1926] AC 108. See McFarlane (2004) 118 *LQR* 667 for discussion of the principle and further examples of its application.

- C's promise relates to the use of a particular right; *and*
- C acquires, as a result of that promise, an advantage in relation to the acquisition of that right; *then*
- C is under a duty to B to keep that promise, as far as it relates to the right advantageously acquired by C.

A good example is provided by *Pallant v Morgan*.[14] That case involved land but there is nothing to suggest it would have been decided differently if land had not been involved. B and C both planned to bid for a plot of land (lot 16) that was to be sold at auction. B was prepared to pay up to £2,000; C up to £3,000. B and C teamed up and agreed that: (i) only C would bid; but (ii) if C acquired both lots 15 and 16, C would sell on to B part of lot 15 and part of lot 16. C did succeed in buying both lots and bought lot 16 for under £2,000.

C had thus made a promise regarding the use of lot 16 (to sell part of it on to B); C had acquired an advantage in relation to its acquisition (B had dropped out of the bidding and, as a result, C had got lot 16 for less than £2000); and so the court decided that C was under a duty to B to keep his promise, *as far as it related to lot 16*. C's promise was not binding in relation to lot 15: B had never planned to bid for that lot so, by making the promise to B, C acquired no advantage in relation to lot 15.[15]

The principle thus allows C's promise, even though it was made to A, to be enforced by B, the party who benefits from the promise. It is important to note that B's right does *not* arise as a result of a contract between B and C.[16] Rather, it is based on the principle that, having received a right on a particular basis (that he will allow B to make some use of that right), C is not then allowed to enjoy that right on a different basis. Nor is the principle based on there being a contract between *A* and C. There is thus an important difference between the 'receipt after a promise' principle and the 1999 Act: the former, unlike the latter, can apply even where C does not make a contractual promise. That difference can be very important where land is involved (see E3:2.2.2).

However, in other respects, the 'receipt after a promise' principle may be of more limited use to B than the 1999 Act. The Act can apply *whenever* A makes a contractual promise to B. In contrast, the 'receipt after a promise' principle applies only where: (i) C acquires a right; *and* (ii) C's promise relates to the use of that right; *and* (iii) as a result of his promise, C acquires an advantage in relation to the acquisition of that right.

2.2.3 The 'benefit and burden' principle

The 'benefit and burden' principle, unlike the Contract (Rights of Third Parties) Act 1999 and the 'receipt after a promise' principle, does *not* depend on C making a promise to give B a right. Rather, the 'benefit and burden' principle means that if:

- C chooses to exercise a particular right; *and*

---

[14] [1953] Ch 43.

[15] The decision in *Pallant v Morgan* shows that the 'receipt after a promise' principle can apply not only where C makes a promise to A (as in **Example 2**), but also where C makes a promise directly to B. See too *Banner Homes Group plc v Luff Developments Ltd* [2000] Ch 372.

[16] In *Pallant v Morgan* [1953] Ch 43, the agreement between B and C: (i) was not certain enough to be contractually binding; and (ii) could not be enforced by B as a contract as it was a promise to transfer a property right in land and had not been made in writing.

- C is aware that his exercise of that right is conditional on C coming under a particular duty to B; *then*
- C will be under that duty to B.

The 'benefit and burden' principle can therefore be seen as based on the idea of a *conditional right*.[17] It can be used in a case where, due to an agreement between A and B, C's exercise of a particular right is conditional on C coming under a duty to B.

EXAMPLE 3

A and B make an agreement that A will have the right to lock his bike up on B's land *if* A pays B £50 for each month in which A chooses to use that right. A then transfers his bike to C who is aware of the agreement between A and B and chooses to lock his bike up on B's land.

In such a case, C's conduct in choosing to exercise the right to lock the bike up on B's land (the benefit) brings C under a duty to pay B £50 a month (the burden). Of course, C can choose to stop taking the benefit: he will then avoid any future duty to B.

2.3   Cases where B has a pre-existing personal right against A

If B has a pre-existing personal right against A, there are two ways in which B's chances of acquiring a direct right against C are improved:

(i) The presence of B's personal right may make it *more likely* that B can rely on a means of acquiring a direct right that *can* apply even if B has no pre-existing right against A (see **2.3.1, 2.3.2** and **2.3.3** below).

(ii) The presence of B's personal right may *allow* B to rely on a means of acquiring a direct right that *cannot* apply where B has no pre-existing right against A (see **2.3.4, 2.3.6** and **2.3.7** below).

2.3.1 The Contract (Rights of Third Parties) Act 1999

EXAMPLE 4a

A has Ownership of a bike. A makes a contractual promise to B to allow B exclusive control of the bike for six months. Three months later, A decides to sell the bike to C. The contract of sale between A and C includes a term that C must continue to allow B exclusive control of the bike for the next three months.

As in **Example 1b**, B can use the 1999 Act to acquire a new, direct right against C. B does not *need* a personal right against A in order to rely on the 1999 Act against C. However, in **Example 4a**, in contrast to **Example 1b**, A has a clear financial incentive to insist that C makes a promise to allow B to continue using the bike. If C makes such a promise, A can sell the bike to C *without* exposing himself to a breach of contract claim from B.[18]

---

[17] This point is explored by Davis [1998] *CLJ* 522.

[18] Of course, the reduction in price C is likely to demand in return for making his promise may counterbalance the saving A makes in avoiding liability to B.

EXAMPLE 4b

A makes a contractual promise to B to give B exclusive control of A's bike for the next six months. Three months later, A sells the bike to C. The contract between A and C includes a term that C acquires A's Ownership of the bike 'subject to any rights of B'.

It will be very difficult for B to argue that the inclusion of a 'subject to' term, *by itself*, allows B to acquire a direct right against C under the 1999 Act. In general, such a term merely shows that C is aware of the *risk* of being bound by a pre-existing property right or persistent right of B.[19] If so, the term cannot be said to 'purport to confer a benefit' on B. Therefore, unless the surrounding circumstances show otherwise, C, in **Example 4b**, has *not* promised to come under a duty to B.

2.3.2 The 'receipt after a promise' principle

The controversial decision of the Privy Council in *Lord Strathcona Steamship Co Ltd v Dominion Coal Co Ltd*[20] shows that, long before the 1999 Act was passed, B could acquire a direct right as a result of a promise made by C to A. The basic facts of that case were, in essence, identical to **Example 4a**. A, an owner of a ship, entered a contract with B, allowing B use of the ship for a period.[21] Whilst B was using the ship, A transferred its Ownership to A2. There were a number of further transfers, before A's Ownership ended up with A3, who then sold the ship to C. When C acquired the ship, it promised A3 that it would 'perform and accept' all the duties imposed by B's contract with A; in return, C would receive 'all benefits arising from' that contract, including the right to receive payments from B. C then refused to honour B's contract and attempted to take physical control of the ship.

There was no doubt that B's original contract gave B only a personal right against A: B's right to use the ship for a fixed period does *not* count as a property right or a persistent right (see **Example 1a**).[22] So, if C had simply acquired Ownership of the ship from A3, B would have had no means to resist C's claim for control of the ship. However, the Privy Council held that C was under a duty to B to keep the promise that C made to A3: B thus acquired a direct right against C.

The decision in *Lord Strathcona* may seem surprising.[23] Certainly, both before and after the 1999 Act, C's promise to A cannot give B a contractual right against C. However, C was *not* under a *contractual* duty to B; instead, C's duty to B arose as result of the 'receipt after a promise' principle.[24] For that principle to apply, C must have 'undertaken a new obligation, not otherwise existing'.[25] Certainly, in a case such as **Example 4a**, A has a financial incentive

---

[19] See the analysis of the Court of Appeal in *Ashburn Anstalt v Arnold* [1989] Ch 1 at 25–6.

[20] [1926] AC 108.

[21] This type of contract is known as a time charterparty, or time charter.

[22] See **D1:1.4.3** and **D2:Example 2**.

[23] Indeed, in *Port Line Ltd v Ben Line Steamers Ltd* [1958] QB 146 Diplock J refused to follow the Privy Council's decision, believing that it led to B acquiring a direct right against C even if C simply knew, or ought to have known about B's contract with A. However, the principle in *Lord Strathcona*, as explained here, instead depends on C's having gone further and having *promised* to give B a new right.

[24] See esp *per* Lord Shaw [1926] AC 108 at 116.

[25] *Lloyd v Dugdale* [2002] 2 P & CR 13 at [52]. See also Bright [2000] Conv 398 at 406–7 and 413–4. In deciding if C has made such a promise to give B a new right, it may be useful to look at the price paid by C when acquiring his right from A. If C has paid a lower price than might be expected, this may possibly suggest that C has been given a discount in return for agreeing to give B a new right (see eg *Ashburn Anstalt v Arnold* [1989] Ch 1 at 23F–G, 26E;

to extract such a promise from C: if B does not acquire a right against C, then A will be in breach of his initial contractual duty to B. However, if C simply promises to take his right 'subject to' any rights of B (as in **Example 4b**), that promise, by itself, cannot give B a direct right against C.[26]

2.3.3 The 'benefit and burden' principle

As shown by **Example 3**, the 'benefit and burden' principle can give B a right even if he has no pre-existing right against A.[27] However, in practice, most 'benefit and burden' cases *will* involve B having a right against A. This is because a prior agreement between A and B is necessary in order to show that C's exercise of a right is conditional on C giving B a particular right. The existence of such an agreement means that, in most cases, A will be under a duty to B. In practice, cases involving the 'benefit and burden' principle tend to involve disputes about the use of land (eg, where B and C are neighbours).[28] We will therefore examine the principle in detail in **E3:2.3.3**.

2.3.4 The wrong of procuring a breach by A of A's contractual duty to B

(i) Definition
A's entry into a contract with B clearly gives B a personal right against A. In addition, the rest of the world comes under a duty to B not to *procure a breach by A of A's contract with B*. So if:

- B has a contractual right against A; *and*
- C has actual knowledge of B's contractual right; *and*
- C *either* persuades A to breach his contractual duty to B *or* (perhaps) actively facilitates such a breach; *then*
- C commits a wrong against B and so B acquires a new, direct right against C.

(ii) Problems
The applicability of this wrong to the basic situation has not been fully explored.[29] As a result, it may be difficult in practice for B to argue that C has committed the wrong. There are two reasons for this. First, there is a *general* difficulty with the wrong: its precise require-ments are somewhat unclear.[30] For example, there is a doubt as to whether C can be liable for the wrong in a case where: (i) C knows that his action will cause A to breach his contract with B; but (ii) C has not persuaded A to commit this breach nor used any other unlawful

---

Lloyd v Dugdale [2002] 2 P & CR 13 at [52]). However, care is needed. C may also receive a discount in return for taking the property 'subject to' any possible pre-existing property rights or persistent rights of B. And, provided C has made a promise to give B a new, direct right, the principle can apply even if C has received no discount: see eg the decision of the High Court of Australia in *Bahr v Nicolay (No 2)* (1988) 164 CLR 604.

[26] See *Ashburn Anstalt v Arnold* [1989] Ch 1 at 23F–G and 26E.

[27] In **Example 3**, A is not under a duty to B to lock his bike up on B's land: A simply has a duty to pay B *if* he chooses to lock his bike up there.

[28] This is due to the special features of land: in particular, its fixed location and capacity for multiple simultaneous use (see **A:3.1.2 and A:3.1.3**).

[29] For a judicial consideration of applying the wrong in the basic situation see *Swiss Bank v Lloyds Bank* [1979] Ch 548. The most thorough general examination is by Smith (1977) 41 Conv 318 at 322–3.

[30] Despite the House of Lords' review of the wrong in *OBG Ltd v Allan* [2008] 1 AC 1.

means to cause the breach.[31] Second, there is a *specific* concern about whether the wrong should be applied *at all* to the basic situation.[32] This is due to a fear that the wrong will unduly inhibit A's ability to deal with a thing or a right.[33]

EXAMPLE 5

A has Ownership of a bike and makes a contractual promise to B to allow B exclusive control of the bike for six months. Three months later, C, who knows about A's contract with B, buys the bike from A.

We know that A's promise does not give B a property right or a persistent right. However, B may claim that C, simply by buying the bike with knowledge of B's contract with A, has committed the wrong of procuring a breach by A of A's contract with B. This creates a real problem. We know that if C acquires a right from A, C runs the risk of being bound by a pre-existing *property right* or *persistent right* of B. The property law system protects C from that risk in a number of ways—for example, through the **content question**. The problem is that the resolution of the **basic tension** between B and C will be upset if B, by relying on the wrong of procuring a breach of contract, can bypass the protection given to C by the **content question**. As B's right is only a personal right against A, should B be allowed to use the wrong of procuring a breach of contract as a back-door route to asserting that right against C?

(iii) Application to the basic situation

It has been suggested that the wrong of procuring a breach of contract should *never* be able to apply to the basic situation, at least where land is concerned.[34] However, that view is difficult to support. The purpose of the wrong is to protect B's contractual right against A: it should therefore apply *whenever* B has a contractual right against A. The wrong is based on the need for the rest of the world to respect B's contractual relationship with A. There is no obvious reason why contractual rights relating to the use of things, or even to the use of land, should attract less protection. For example, let us say that A, a cinema owner, makes a contractual promise to allow B to run a confectionary stall in the cinema for five years. That promise only gives B a personal right against A.[35] However, if C, a competitor of B, pays A money to persuade A to breach the contract,[36] C should be liable to B for the wrong of procuring a breach of the contract.

---

[31] See eg *Millar v Bassey* [1994] EMLR 44; McBride and Bagshaw, *Tort Law* (2nd edn, 2005), 393–9; Weir, *Tort Law* (2002), 180–84. For specific consideration of the point in the property context see Smith (1977) 41 *Conv* 318 at 322–3 and Bright [2000] *Conv* 398 at 411–2.

[32] For an argument that the wrong should not be applied to the basic situation (at least where land is concerned) see Smith (1977) 41 *Conv* 318. In *Binions v Evans* [1972] Ch 359 at 371, Megaw LJ suggests that the wrong *could* apply to a case involving land, but notes that further thought is needed as there may be 'special technical considerations in the law relating to land' which prevent the wrong from being applied, or at least modify its application.

[33] This concern is particularly strong where land is concerned: the limited supply of land means that it is particularly important to promote its marketability (see **A:3.1.5**).

[34] See eg Smith (1977) 41 *Conv* 318 at 329: 'where real property principles accord priority to a contract or conveyance over an earlier contract, it should not be open to the earlier contracting party to rely on tort.' However, we now know that B can rely on the tort of conspiracy even if C, a purchaser of land, can use the lack of registration against B's pre-existing persistent right: see *Midland Bank Trust Co Ltd v Green (No 3)* [1982] 1 Ch 529 discussed in **2.4** below.

[35] As it does not give B a right to exclusive control over any land, it is a licence rather than a Lease: see **G1B:1.2**. And a licence does not count as a property right or a persistent right: see **E6:3.4.2**.

[36] B could ask a court for an order specifically protecting B's contractual right against A to use the land. Such orders can be granted, but are unlikely if B's right involves some degree of co-operation with A: see **E6:3.2**.

Indeed, there are cases in which the wrong *has* been applied to the basic situation. For example, in *BMTA v Salvadori*,[37] A, when buying a car, had made a promise, both to the vendor of the car and to B (the British Motor Trade Association) not to sell the car in the next year. C then purchased the car from A before the year was up, knowing of A's promise not to sell. C argued that he had not procured A's breach of the contract with B, as A was willing to sell the car in any case. However, Roxburgh J rejected this argument, holding that the wrong can be committed not only where C *persuades* A to breach his contract, but also where C takes an active step to *facilitate* such a breach.[38]

Does the *Salvadori* decision mean that, in **Example 5**, C commits the wrong of procuring a breach of contract? The answer seems to be 'No'. There is an important difference between *Salvadori* and **Example 5**. In the former case, A was under an explicit contractual duty *not to transfer a right to C* unless certain conditions were met. A therefore breached his contractual duty to B *as soon as* he sold the car to C. C, by participating in a sale that he knew was a breach of A's contract, actively facilitated that breach. In **Example 5**, however, A has simply made a contractual promise to give B exclusive control of A's bike for six months. A has *not* made a contractual promise not to transfer his Ownership of the bike unless certain conditions are met. So the sale to C, *by itself*, does *not* breach A's contractual duty to B.

B could then try to argue that C commits the wrong at a later stage, ie, when C prevents B from using the bike. However, that argument should fail. First, C could argue that his action is justified:[39] C is simply exercising a right he acquired from A; and no breach of contract was involved in C's acquisition of that right. Second, C can point out that, by preventing B from using the bike, C has simply acted in a way that he knows will cause A to be in breach of his contract with B. And this alone cannot be enough to commit a wrong,[40] as a simple example shows.

Let us say I make a contractual promise to my publisher that all the students I teach will buy this book. I inform my students of this promise, but one or two of them do not buy the book.[41] They know that, by acting in this way, they are causing me to breach my contract with my publisher. Yet, disappointingly enough, they do not commit a wrong against me. The point is that I cannot impose a duty on my students by making a promise to my publisher. Similarly A, by promising B exclusive control of the bike for six months, cannot impose a duty on any later owner of the bike, such as C, to honour that promise.

B could then try a different argument: by buying the bike from A, C facilitates an act by A (the sale of the bike) that effectively prevents A from honouring his contract with B. So, although A made no contractual promise not to transfer the bike to C, A is in effect

---

[37] [1949] Ch 556. See too, in relation to land, *Esso Petroleum Co Ltd v Kingswood Motors Ltd* [1974] QB 142, discussed in **E3:2.3.4**

[38] [1949] Ch 566 at 565. This conclusion was buttressed by Roxburgh J's observation that, even if A was willing to sell in breach of contract, he was only willing to sell at a particular price, and C had facilitated the breach by agreeing to meet that price: *ibid*, 566. Note that C does not actively facilitate or procure a breach if he merely allows A to breach a contract by eg, providing A with the tools to do so: see *per* Lord Templeman in *CBS Songs Ltd v Amstrad plc* [1988] AC 1013 at 1058.

[39] As in *Swiss Bank v Lloyds Bank* [1979] Ch 548. For a general consideration of justification in this context see *Edwin Hill & Partners v First National Finance Corpn* [1989] 1 WLR 225.

[40] There are some indications in *Millar v Bassey* [1994] EMLR 44 that C *can* be liable simply for acting in a way that he knows will cause A to breach his contract with B. However, as the example in the text shows, these suggestions must be wrong. The decision of the Court of Appeal in *Millar* was disapproved of by the House of Lords (albeit on other grounds) in *OBG Ltd v Allan* [2008] 1 AC 1.

[41] This may be hard to believe, but it is a purely hypothetical example.

breaching his contract with B by selling the bike to C.[42] As was noted above, there is some confusion about the scope of the wrong of procuring a breach of contract, and so B's argument cannot be rejected out of hand. However, it seems that the better view is that C can never commit the wrong by simply facilitating action by A that leads to, but is not in itself, a breach of contract.[43] And, in any case, there is little chance of a judge allowing B to acquire a direct right against C in such a case (see **2.3.5** below).

SUMMARY of D3:2.3.4

It seems that the dangers of applying the wrong of procuring a breach of contract to the basic situation may be overstated. First, the wrong should, in principle, be capable of applying whenever B has a contractual right against A. Second, there is no need to exclude the wrong in order to protect a third party, such as C, who wishes to acquire a right from A. If, as in **Example 5**, C simply acquires a thing from A with knowledge of B's contractual right against A to use that thing, C does *not* commit the wrong of procuring a breach of contract.

2.3.5 Knowing interference with B's personal right against A?

In *de Mattos v Gibson*,[44] Knight Bruce LJ suggested that if: (i) C acquires a right from A with knowledge of B's pre-existing personal right against A; then (ii) C can be prevented from acting inconsistently with B's right. If that is correct, B *does* have a direct right against C in a case such as **Example 5**. However, later courts have disapproved of Knight Bruce LJ's suggestion.[45] The courts' view seems to be that imposing such a duty on C would *not* be the best way to resolve the **basic tension**: the balance would tilt too far in B's favour if C were bound *whenever* he knew of a pre-existing *personal* right of B. The important lesson, applying across the property law system, is that direct rights must be used sparingly: they cannot unduly undermine the protection afforded to third parties.

There is of course a close link between the so-called '*de Mattos* principle' and the wrong of procuring a breach of contract.[46] It was suggested above that C does *not* commit that wrong where C simply acquires a right from A with the knowledge that A, by giving C that right, is preventing himself from honouring his contract with B. That suggestion gains strong support from the courts' firm rejection of the '*de Mattos* principle'.

---

[42] On this argument, A's sale to C counts as an 'anticipatory breach' either because A is indicating his intention not to perform (see eg *The Hermosa* [1982] 1 Lloyd's Rep 570) or because A is putting the performance of the contract beyond his control (see eg *Universal Cargo Carriers v Citati* [1957] 2 QB 401). However, as those cases demonstrate, proving an anticipatory breach is not straightforward.

[43] See eg Weir, *Economic Torts* (1997), ch 2; and Weir, *Tort Law* (2002), 183; Bright [2000] Conv 398 at 411–2; McBride and Bagshaw, *Tort Law* (2nd edn, 2005), 394–6, esp 396: 'Where neither the making of the contract between [A] and [C] nor the performance of it was in itself a breach of the contract between [A] and [B] and the breach was instead the result of [C] later exercising the rights that she acquired as owner, then it seems correct that [C] should not be liable.'

[44] (1858) 4 D & J 276 at 282. See too *per* Lord Shaw in *Lord Strathcona Steamship Co Ltd v Dominion Coal Co* [1926] AC 108 at 125.

[45] See eg *Port Line Ltd v Ben Line Steamers Ltd* [1958] QB 146; *Swiss Bank v Lloyds Bank* [1979] Ch 548. For the similar treatment of Knight Bruce LJ's suggestion where land is concerned, see **E3:2.3.5**.

[46] Browne-Wilkinson J in *Swiss Bank v Lloyds Bank* [1979] Ch 548 at 573 described the '*de Mattos* principle' as the 'equitable counterpart' of the wrong of procuring a breach of contract. In doing so, Browne-Wilkinson used the limits of the wrong to *restrict* the application of the '*de Mattos* principle'; he did not use the width of the '*de Mattos* principle' to extend the application of the wrong.

2.3.6 The wrong of dishonestly assisting A to breach A's fiduciary duty to B

(i) An example

EXAMPLE 6a

C knows that A holds A's Ownership of a bike on Trust for B. Acting out of spite to B, C persuades A to allow C to destroy the bike.

As A was under the core Trust duty to B, A is under a duty to account to B for the value of the bike (see **D2:4.3.1**). By allowing C to destroy the bike, A also breaches his fiduciary duty, as trustee, to act in B's best interests (see **F3:1.4.3**). C also commits a wrong against B. C has never held a right on Trust for B but C, like the rest of the world, is under a duty to B not to *dishonestly assist* in A's breach of Trust.[47] In **Example 6a**, C breaches that duty to B.

On one view, in **Example 6a**, *each* of A and C is liable for the same wrong: A's breach of Trust.[48] The alternative and, it seems, better view is that B's right arises because C has committed an *independent* wrong: he has breached his duty not to dishonestly assist A in breaching A's fiduciary duty to B.[49] On this view, C's liability is distinct from that of A. The difference between the two views can be crucial when considering the remedies question (see **4:3.1** and **4.3.3** below).

(ii) The scope of the wrong

There seems to be no *general* principle that: (i) if A is under a duty to B; then (ii) C is under a duty to B not to dishonestly assist A in breaching that duty. For example, let us say that C knows A is planning to make a speech containing defamatory comments about B. If C drives B to the venue for the speech, or pays for the hire of the venue, C commits no wrong against B. However, in some situations, a relationship between A and B *can* impose a duty on C. And it seems that one such situation arises where A is under a *fiduciary duty* to B—a duty to act in B's best interests and to subordinate his own wishes to those of B. Fiduciary duties are jealously protected by a number of special rules (see eg **D2:Example 15**). One such rule is that C is under a duty not to dishonestly assist A to breach a fiduciary duty A owes to B.

In **Example 6a**, therefore, B's direct right against C depends on the fact that A was under a fiduciary duty to B and *not* on the fact that A held a right on Trust for B. Indeed, it is possible for A to be under a fiduciary duty to B even if A does *not* hold a right on Trust for B; and even if B has only a personal right against A.[50]

---

[47] C is 'dishonest' if his 'knowledge of the transaction [is] such as to render his participation contrary to normally acceptable standards of honest conduct': *per* Lord Hoffmann, giving the advice of the Privy Council in *Barlow Clowes International Ltd v Eurotrust International Ltd* [2006] 1 WLR 1476 at 1481. For a full discussion of the wrong see Mitchell, ch 6 in *Breach of Trust* (ed Birks & Pretto, 2002).

[48] See Elliott and Mitchell (2004) 67 *MLR* 16; *Underhill and Hayton's Law of Trusts and Trustees* (ed Hayton et al, 17th edn, 2006), 100.19. On that view, A and C are 'jointly and severally' liable for A's wrong. That means B can choose to sue *either* A or C, and can require that party to pay the full sum of money due to B. Of course, B cannot receive more than that sum: for example, he cannot receive the full sum from A and then also sue C. If B recovers the full sum from one of A and C (let's say C), C can then bring a 'contribution' claim against A, so that A has to contribute to the money paid out by C. The extent of A's contribution will depend, essentially, on how blame for the breach of Trust is attributed between A and C.

[49] See eg Stevens, *Torts and Rights* (2007), 281–3.

[50] The mere fact that B has a Purely Equitable Charge; a Mortgagor's Equity of Redemption; or a persistent right

---

EXAMPLE 6b

A is a director of B Co. C, a shareholder in X Co, a rival company, is a newspaper editor. C persuades A, in breach of A's fiduciary duty to B Co, to pass confidential information about B Co to C. C then prints that information in his newspaper. As a result, shares in B Co reduce in value and shares in X Co increase in value.

A is under a fiduciary duty to B Co—a duty, in his role a director, to act in B Co's best interests. A breaches that duty by passing the confidential information to C. And C (motivated by a desire to make more money) dishonestly assists A in this breach. C thus commits a wrong against B Co: he has breached his duty not to dishonestly assist A in his breach of a fiduciary duty owed to B Co. It does not matter that A has never held a right on Trust for B Co.[51]

This important point is obscured by the language the courts traditionally use when recognising that C has committed the wrong. It is often said that:

- because of his dishonest assistance;
- C is under 'a duty to account to B as a constructive trustee'.[52]

A duty to account is a key feature of the Trust: it arises if A holds a right subject to the core Trust duty (see **D2:4.1.1(ii)**). However, such a duty is clearly inappropriate when considering the wrong of dishonest assistance. As **Examples 6a and 6b** show, C can commit that wrong *even if* he has never held a right on Trust for B. The traditional explanation of the dishonest assistant's duty to pay money to B is therefore misleading. Instead, it should be acknowledged that, in both **Examples 6a and 6b**, C is under a duty to pay B money as a result of C's commission of a wrong.[53] So if:

- A is under a fiduciary duty to B; *and*
- C dishonestly assists in a breach by A of that fiduciary duty; *then*
- C commits a wrong against B.

2.3.7 The wrong of conspiring with A to cause harm to B

EXAMPLE 7

A has Ownership of a bike and makes a contractual promise to B to allow B exclusive control of the bike for six months. Three months later, A and B fall out. A and C hatch a plan to harm B: A will sell the bike to C and C will then prevent B from using the bike.

---

arising under an Equitable Assignment does *not*, by itself, mean that A is under a fiduciary duty to B. In fact, in most commercial situations, it would be inappropriate for A to be under such a duty to act in B's best interests. So, in practice, a 'dishonest assistance' claim will be of no use to B if B has a persistent right that does *not* arise under a Trust.

[51] See eg *Statek Corp v Alford* [2008] EWHC 32; *per* Lord Nicholls, giving the advice of the Privy Council in *Royal Brunei Airlines v Tan* [1995] 2 AC 378 at 39: 'A liability in equity to make good resulting loss attaches to a person who dishonestly procures or assists in a breach of trust or fiduciary obligation.' See too the analysis of Potter LJ in the Court of Appeal in *Twinsectra v Yardley* [1999] Lloyd's Rep Bank 438: C can be liable for dishonest assistance even if A does not hold any right on Trust for B. That analysis is supported by Tettenborn [2000] LMCLQ 459 at 465. See too Mitchell, ch 6 in *Breach of Trust* (ed Birks and Pretto, 2002), 160–65.

[52] The terminology stems from the judgment of Lord Selborne LC in *Barnes v Addy* (1874) LR 9 Ch App 244 at 251–2. For modern use of the term see eg *Royal Brunei Airlines v Tan* [1995] 2 AC 378.

[53] See eg L Smith [1999] *CLJ* 294; Edelman, *Gain-Based Damages* (2002), 201–2.

The plan of A and C is based on the fact that A's promise to B does not give B a pre-existing right that is capable of binding C. However, if: (i) A and C plot together to act in a particular way; and (ii) their prime motive in doing so is to cause harm to B (and not, for example, to promote their own commercial interests); then (iii) each of A and C commits a wrong against B: the wrong of conspiracy.[54] It does not matter if A and C only wish to cause *economic* harm to B; or that the way in which they plan to harm B is otherwise perfectly lawful.[55] However, the courts recognise that the wrong of 'lawful act' conspiracy is anomalous.[56] Its scope is reduced by the fact that A and C do not commit the wrong if they act with the prime motive of promoting their own commercial interests.[57]

Despite the limited scope of the wrong, it *does* apply in **Example 7**: B will have a direct right against C, based on C's commission of the wrong of conspiracy.[58] In theory, that wrong can be committed even in a case where B has no initial right against A. However, to show that the action of A and C has caused him harm, B will, in practice, need to show that he had at least a pre-existing personal right against A.[59]

2.3.8 Unjust enrichment?

There seem to be cases, dealing with the **basic situation**, in which B acquires a direct right against C as a result of C's unjust enrichment at B's expense. We will examine these cases in **D4:2.2**. The argument made there is that, apart from the very rare cases in which B deals directly with C, unjust enrichment alone can *never* give B a direct right against C. The key point is that, in the **basic situation**, C acquires his right from A, not from B: as a result, C cannot be unjustly enriched at B's expense.

2.3.9 Knowing receipt of a right transferred to C by A in breach of A's fiduciary duty to B?

In **D2:4.1.1(ii)** we saw that C can come under the core Trust duty to B as a result of C's 'knowing receipt'—or, as it should be called 'knowing holding'—of a right formerly held by A on Trust for B. In such a case, C is under a duty to account to B for the value of the right held by C on Trust for B. From one perspective, it could be said that B has a new, direct right against C: after all, before the transfer to C, C was not under the core Trust duty to B. However, B's claim will fail unless B can show that: (i) B has a pre-existing persistent right (a right under a Trust); and (ii) C has no defence to that right. So, these 'knowing receipt' cases are best seen as based on B's assertion of a pre-existing persistent right.

---

[54] See eg *Crofter Hand Woven Harris Tweed Co v Veitch* [1942] AC 435 esp at 441–2. In *Lonrho Ltd v Shell Petroleum Co Ltd (No 2)* [1982] AC 173 at 188–9, the House of Lords described the wrong as 'highly anomalous' but as 'too well established to be discarded'.

[55] See eg *per* Lord Macnaghten in *Quinn v Leathem* [1901] AC 495 at 510: a 'conspiracy to injure might give rise to civil liability even though the end were brought about by conduct and acts which by themselves, and apart from the element of combination or concerted action, could not be regarded as a legal wrong'. See too *Crofter Hand Woven Harris Tweed Co v Veitch* [1942] AC 435 at 448 and 461.

[56] In *Lonrho Ltd v Shell Petroleum Co Ltd (No 2)* [1982] AC 173 at 188–9, the House of Lords described the wrong as 'highly anomalous' but as 'too well established to be discarded'. For disapproval of the wrong see eg Hohfeld (1913) 23 *Yale Law Journal* 16 at 37 and Stevens, *Torts and Rights* (2007), 251–3.

[57] See eg *Mogul Steamship Co Ltd v McGregor Gow & Co* [1892] AC 25.

[58] For an application of this wrong to the **basic situation** see *Midland Bank Trust Co Ltd v Green (No 3)* [1982] 1 Ch 529. That decision arose from the same facts as *Midland Bank Trust Co Ltd v Green* [1981] AC 513 (see **C2:7**). As the case involved the use of land we will examine it in **E3:2.3.7**.

[59] In *Midland Bank Trust Co Ltd v Green (No 3)* [1982] 1 Ch 529 the wrong applied where A and C had manufactured a situation in which C had a defence to B's pre-existing persistent right.

EXAMPLE 8

B Co has £10,000 in an account with Z Bank. A, a director of B Co, transfers that £10,000 to C. A acts without authority and in breach of the fiduciary duty he owes (as a director) to B Co.

Some courts have assumed that, in such a case, B Co may be able to bring a 'knowing receipt' claim against C.[60] That assumption also has some academic support.[61] However, it must be wrong.[62] A 'knowing receipt' claim depends on C being under a duty to account to B for a right C has held on Trust for B. In **Example 8**, at the start of the story, A holds no right on Trust for B Co. It is B Co, not A, that holds the account with Z Bank.

So, if B Co can show that A had no authority to transfer that right to C,[63] B Co should be able to bring a straightforward unjust enrichment claim against C.[64] The point is that: (i) there has been a direct transfer from B Co to C: £10,000 has been transferred directly to C from B Co's account; and (ii) there is no legal basis for C to have the benefit of that money (see **D4:2.1**). All B Co needs to show is that A had no authority to make the transfer: there is no need for B Co to show that C knew, or should have known, about A's lack of authority.

2.4   Cases where B has a pre-existing persistent right

If, in the **basic situation**: (i) B has a persistent right against a right of A; and (ii) C has no defence to B's right; and (iii) C still holds the right he acquired from A; then (iv) B can directly assert his pre-existing right against C (see **D2:4.1.1**). In such a case, there is generally no need for B to show that he also has a distinct, direct right against C.

However, in other cases, it will not be possible for B to assert his pre-existing persistent right against C: (i) C may no longer hold the right transferred to him by A; or (ii) C may have a defence to B's pre-existing right. In these cases, it may still be possible for B to acquire a new, direct right against C, using one of the means of acquiring such a right set out above. For example, in *Midland Bank Trust Co Ltd v Green*,[65] B had a persistent right against A's ownership of land. A transferred his right to C, who was able to use the lack of registration defence against B's persistent right (see **C2:Example 5**). However, that did not prevent B acquiring a direct right against C, based on C's commission of the wrong of

---

[60] See eg *JJ Harrison (Properties) Ltd v Harrison* [2002] 1 BCLC 162 at [25]; *Ultraframe (UK) Ltd v Fielding* [2005] EWHC 1638 at [1487] *per* Lewison J: 'Although a company is the legal and beneficial owner of its own assets, there is no difficulty in classifying property belonging to a company as trust property for the purpose of knowing receipt, where the company's property has been alienated by its directors in breach of their fiduciary duty.' Yet why should we pretend that the company's right was held on Trust?

[61] See eg Look Chan Ho, ch 8 in *Company Charges: Spectrum and Beyond* (ed Getzler and Payne, 2007), 181; Conaglen and Nolan [2007] *CLJ* 515 at 516–7.

[62] As the High Court of Australia pointed out in *Farah Constructions Pty Ltd v Say-Dee Pty Ltd* [2007] HCA 22 at [114]–[122]. See too *Criterion Properties plc v Stratford UK* [2004] 1 WLR 1846 and Stevens [2004] *LMCLQ* 421.

[63] It is important to note that C will be protected not only if A in fact had authority to transfer the right, but also if A had *apparent* or *ostensible* authority to do so: see eg *Criterion Properties plc v Stratford UK* [2004] 1 WLR 1846 at [29]–[30].

[64] See *per* Lord Nicholls in *Criterion Properties plc v Stratford UK* [2004] 1 WLR 1846 at [4] and *per* Lord Scott at [27]. Lord Nicholls also acknowledges at [4] that if: (i) B Co exercises its power to set aside the transfer to C; and C still has the right transferred to him by A; then (iii) B Co will have a 'proprietary claim'. That claim must involve B Co directly asserting a *persistent right* against the right now held by C: see **D4:4.2** and **D4:4.3**.

[65] [1981] AC 513.

conspiracy (see **2.3.7** above). This demonstrates an important point about direct rights: B may be able to acquire such a right *even if* C has a defence to B's pre-existing persistent right.

2.5   Cases where B has a pre-existing property right

If, in the **basic situation**: (i) B has a pre-existing property right; and (ii) C has no defence to B's right; then (iii) B can assert that right against C. B asserts his right by showing that C has committed a wrong against B (see **D1:4.1.1**). From one perspective, the right B acquires as a result of C's commission of the wrong looks like a new, direct right against C. However, B's claim will fail unless B can show that: (i) B had a pre-existing property right; and (ii) C has no defence to that right. B's claim is therefore clearly based on B's assertion of a pre-existing property right.

However, if C has a defence to B's property right, B will not be able to assert that right against C. In such a case, it may still be possible for B to acquire a new, direct right against C, using one of the means of acquiring such a right set out above.

SUMMARY of D3:2

We have not attempted to set out an exhaustive list of all the means by which B can acquire a direct right against C. For example, if C deals directly with B, there are numerous ways in which C's conduct can lead to B acquiring a right. However, in the **basic situation**, C will generally deal only with A. The question then is whether C's conduct may nonetheless give B a direct right against C.

B may acquire a direct right against C even if B had *no right at all* before C's involvement. If C has made a promise to A to give B a right, the Contract (Rights of Third Parties) Act 1999 and the 'receipt after a promise' principle may allow B to acquire a direct right against C.

If B has a pre-existing personal right against A, then B cannot cannot assert that personal right against C. However, B may acquire a *new*, direct right against C as a result of C's conduct. In practice, the presence of B's personal right against A may it more likely for A to insist on C promising to give B a right. If C makes such a promise to A, B may be able to acquire a right under either the Contract (Rights of Third Parties) Act 1999 or the 'receipt after a promise' principle. It may also be possible for B to rely on the 'benefit and burden' principle to impose on C a duty formerly owed by A to B.

In addition, if B's pre-existing personal right imposes a contractual duty on A, B can acquire a right against C by showing that C has committed the wrong of procuring a breach by A of A's contract with B. And if B's pre-existing personal right imposes a fiduciary duty on A, B can acquire a right against C if he can show that C has committed the wrong of dishonestly assisting A to breach that fiduciary duty. Further, B can acquire a right against C if A and C each committed the wrong of conspiring to harm B. The scope of those three wrongs is very carefully limited. The wrong of procuring a breach of contract applies only where C procures or actively facilitates an act by A that C knows will cause A to breach A's contract with B. The wrong of dishonest assistance requires a high level of fault on C's part and applies only where A is under a fiduciary duty (a duty to act in B's best interests). And the courts are careful to limit the scope of the 'anomalous' wrong of 'lawful act' conspiracy. C is also protected by the fact that, contrary to the suggestion of Knight Bruce LJ in *de Mattos v*

Gibson, B *cannot* acquire a direct right simply by showing that C acquired his right from A with knowledge of B's personal right.

This survey is summarised in the table below: it is assumed throughout that there have been no direct dealings between B and C. The left-hand column shows the principles discussed; the top row shows B's initial position. The table shows whether it is *possible* for the particular principle to apply.

	B has no right against A	B has a personal right against A	B has a persistent right against a right of A	B has a property right[66]
1999 Act	Yes	Yes	Yes	Yes
Receipt after a promise	Yes	Yes	Yes	Yes
Benefit and burden	Yes (although rare in practice)[67]	Yes	Yes	Yes
Procuring a breach of contract	No	Yes —but only if A has a contractual duty to B	Yes —but only if A has a contractual duty to B	No
Dishonest assistance in a breach of fiduciary duty	No	Yes —but only if A has a fiduciary duty to B	Yes —but only if A has a fiduciary duty to B	No
Lawful act conspiracy	No[68]	Yes	Yes	Yes
Unjust enrichment[69]	No	No	No	No

[66] The results assume that B has *only* a property right at the start of the story and so does not also have a separate personal right against A or persistent right against A's right.

[67] The 'benefit and burden' principle can only operate where there is a prior arrangement between A and B; that arrangement is likely to give B a right against A.

[68] If, in the **basic situation**, B has no right against A then there is no need for A to conspire with C to harm B: A can simply prevent B from making his desired use of the thing or right in question.

[69] See **D4:2.**

3 │ THE DEFENCES QUESTION

The defences question arises only if B has a pre-existing property right or persistent right that is prima facie binding on C. It is therefore irrelevant when considering if B has a direct right against C (see **B:5.1**). Of course 'defences', in a general sense, can be relevant when considering a particular means by which B claims to have acquired a direct right against C. For example, if C's action is 'justified', C can show that, despite his prima facie wrongful action, he has not in fact committed the wrong of procuring a breach of contract (see **2.3.4** above). This can be seen as an example of a 'defence', in a general sense, but it is really just part of the test as to whether B has acquired a direct right against C. Certainly, it is very different from the defences question as set out in the **basic structure**: that question arises only where B has a pre-existing property right or persistent right.

4 │ THE REMEDIES QUESTION

4.1 Preface

If B can assert a direct right against C, a court may need to consider what remedy to give to protect B's right. The key issue when looking at the remedies question is whether B's right will be given *specific protection* or whether B will instead have to settle for receiving money from C. If B's direct right against C is a property right, the discussion of the remedies question in **D1:4** will apply. If that right is a persistent right, the principles discussed in **D2:4** will govern the remedies question. We will concentrate here on the position where B's direct right is a personal right against C.

4.2 Specific protection

The general position is that B must settle for receiving money from C: to persuade a court to specifically protect his right, B must show why that standard remedy would be inadequate to protect B's right.[70] So, in **Example 1a**, B acquires a direct right against C under the Contract (Rights of Third Parties) Act 1999. The Act makes clear that the remedies a court may use to protect a contractual right can also be used to protect the statutory right B acquires under the Act.[71] This means that, in theory, a court could order C specifically to perform his promise.

However, the general position is that if C is under a duty to B in relation to a thing other than land, B's right will *not* be specifically protected (see **D1:4.2**). Hence the default position in **Example 1a** is that a court: (i) will not prevent C from taking exclusive control of the bike; but (ii) will order C to pay B money as a substitute for B's right and to compensate B for any relevant loss B suffers as a result of C's wrong (see **D1:4.3**). B's right will only be specifically protected in the rare case when B can say, perhaps because the bike is unique, that money will not adequately protect his right.

---

[70] See eg *Co-Operative Insurance Society Ltd v Argyll Stores (Holdings) Ltd* [1998] AC 1 at 11.
[71] See 1999 Act, s 1(5)

Some of the language used by the courts may suggest that the general position is reversed where B's right arises under the 'receipt after a promise' principle. For example, in *Lord Strathcona Steamship Co Ltd v Dominion Coal Co Ltd*,[72] the 'receipt after a promise' principle was stated in such a way as to suggest that, where it applies, an injunction will *always* be available to specifically protect B's direct right against C. However, that cannot be right. For example, if A makes a direct contractual promise to B to hire out a ship to B, A's contractual promise, in general, will *not* be specifically protected.[73] There seems to be no good reason to give a right arising under the 'receipt after a promise' principle better protection than a contractual right imposing the same duty. The actual result in the *Lord Strathcona* case may be justified: B was said to have a particular 'interest'[74] in continuing to use the ship and so it may be that a money award would have been inadequate to protect B's right. However, it would be dangerous to think that *all* rights arising as a result of the 'receipt after a promise' principle *must* be specifically protected.[75]

In some cases, it may well be too late for B's right to be specifically protected.[76] However, in a case such as *BMTA v Salvadori*,[77] where C procures a breach by A of A's contractual duty not to transfer a right, specific protection is still possible: a court could order C to transfer the right he has acquired back to A.[78] In fact, such an order has been made in a case involving land.[79]

4.3 Money awards

4.3.1 Money as a substitute for B's right

If C breaches a duty he owes to B, then C can be made to pay B money representing the value of B's right (see **D1:4.3.1**). It has also been argued that, where C commits the wrong of dishonestly assisting A to breach a fiduciary duty owed to B: (i) C is under a duty to account to B; and (ii) that duty can be enforced by ordering C to pay B money equal to the value of B's right (see **D2:4.3.1**). That argument depends on the view that: (i) in such a case, C is liable not for his own, independent wrong but for A's wrong (see **2.3.6** above); and so (ii) any remedies available against A can also apply against C.[80] However, the better view is that, in a dishonest assistance case, C is *not* liable for the same wrong as A: instead, he is liable for his own, independent wrong to which specific rules apply.[81] So, if (as in **Examples 6a and 6b**) C does not hold any right on Trust for B, C cannot be under a duty to account to B.

---

[72] [1926] AC 108 at 120.

[73] See *per* Lord Diplock in *The Scaptrade* [1983] 2 AC 694 at 700–01; although there are hints of a different approach in *Lauritzencool AB v Lady Navigation Inc* [2005] 1 WLR 3686 at [12].

[74] [1926] AC 108 at 123.

[75] The same is true of rights arising under the 'benefit and burden' principle.

[76] Of course, the court can order an injunction to prevent C engaging in the same conduct in the future: that was done in *BMTA v Salvadori* [1949] 1 Ch 556.

[77] [1949] 1 Ch 556.

[78] Such an order would not have been possible in *BMTA v Salvadori* itself as C had sold on the cars transferred to him by A.

[79] *Esso Petroleum Co Ltd v Kingswood Motors Ltd* [1974] QB 142.

[80] See eg Elliott and Mitchell (2004) 67 *MLR* 16; *Underhill and Hayton's Law of Trusts and Trustees* (ed Hayton et al, 17th edn, 2006), 100.19.

[81] See eg Stevens, *Torts and Rights* (207), 281–3.

4.3.2 Money as compensation for B's consequential loss

Where C breaches a duty he owes to B, C can be ordered to pay B money not only representing the value of B's right but also compensating B for any relevant loss caused to B by
C's wrong. Remoteness and causation tests tell us which losses of B count as 'relevant' losses.
When considering the wrong of dishonest assistance, it is important to remember that such
tests are usually applied severely against a deceitful or dishonest wrongdoer.[82]

4.3.3 Money representing a gain made by A or C?

It is only in exceptional cases that B is awarded money that: (i) goes beyond the value of B's
right and compensation for relevant loss suffered by B; and (ii) instead extends to the value
of a gain made by C (see **D1:4.3.3**).[83] On one view, however, such an award should generally
be available where C has dishonestly assisted in a breach by A of A's fiduciary duty to B.
That view, as we saw above, is that C is liable for A's breach of fiduciary duty. And, whenever
A is under a fiduciary duty to B, A can be ordered to pay B money equal to any gains A has
made by breaching that duty.[84] On this view, if: (i) A makes such a gain; and (ii) C dishonestly assisted in A's breach of the fiduciary duty; then (iii) C may be made to pay B the value
of the gain *made by A*.[85]

As suggested in **4.3.1** above, a dishonest assister should *not* be liable for A's breach of
fiduciary duty; rather, he commits his own, independent wrong against B. Nonetheless, it
may be possible to treat dishonest assistance as a special form of wrong and to argue that C
should *always* have to pay to B the value of any profit C makes from that wrong. On this
view, in **Example 6b**, a court can order C to pay to B Co a sum equivalent to the increase in
value of C's shares in X Co caused by A's breach of fiduciary duty to B Co. If A commits a
breach of fiduciary duty to B, the courts take the view that, to limit A's incentives to breach
such a duty, A must pay the value of any profits he makes to B.[86] This approach is based on
the perceived need to jealously protect fiduciary duties. That same need explains why the
rest of the world is under a duty not to dishonestly assist A to breach his fiduciary duty to B.
It can be argued that, just as the rules remove any incentive for A to breach his fiduciary
duty to B, so should they remove any incentive for C to dishonestly assist A to breach such a
duty. If that argument is accepted, C *will* always be liable to pay B the value of any profits C
makes from his dishonest assistance.[87] Crucially, however, this argument does *not* depend on

---

[82] Compare the position where the defendant commits the wrong of deceit: see eg *Doyle v Olby (Ironmongers) Ltd*
[1969] 2 QB 158 esp *per* Lord Denning MR at 167: the wrongdoer is 'bound to make reparation for all the actual
damages flowing from the fraudulent inducement.'

[83] Such damages may be awarded, in the guise of 'exemplary' or 'punitive' damages where C deliberately commits
a wrong against A, with the intention of making a profit: see eg *per* Lord Devlin in *Rookes v Barnard* [1964] AC 1129
at 1221–31, esp at 1226–7.

[84] See eg *Attorney General of Hong Kong v Reid* [1994] 1 AC 324. As that case shows, B has a persistent right
against any right acquired by A in breach of A's fiduciary duty to B (see **D2:2.1.3**).

[85] In *Ultraframe (UK) Ltd v Fielding* [2005] EWHC 1638 at [1600]–[1601], Lewison J doubted that such a
surprising result could be correct.

[86] See eg *Regal (Hastings) Ltd v Gulliver* [1967] 2 AC 134; *Boardman v Phipps* [1967] 2 AC 46.

[87] There are cases in which such an approach has been adopted: see eg *Crown Dilmun v Sutton* [2004] EWHC 52
at [204]; *Ultraframe (UK) Ltd v Fielding* [2005] EWHC 1638 at [1595]. The analogy between A's position and C's
position can be pursued further. If A acquires a right in breach of his fiduciary duty to B, A is under a duty to
transfer that right to B and so B acquires a persistent right against A's right: see *Attorney-General of Hong Kong v
Reid* [1994] 1 AC 324, discussed in **D2:2.1.3**. It can be argued that if C acquires a right in breach of his duty not to
dishonestly assist in a breach of fiduciary duty, C should be under a duty to transfer that right to B, so that B again
acquires a persistent right: see eg *Nanus Asia Co Inc v Standard Chartered Bank* [1990] 1 HKLR 396 at 417–9.

saying that C is liable for the same wrong as A. Rather, it: (i) recognises that C's wrong is based on C's distinct duty not to dishonestly assist A to breach a fiduciary duty to B; and (ii) asks what rules can best be applied to that duty. So, whilst C should not be liable for A's gain, it may be that C should be liable for C's own gain.

SUMMARY of D3

Direct rights form a vital part of the property law system. They enable that system to respond to situations in which C's conduct justifies giving B a right against C. They can therefore give B protection against *a limited class of third parties*. It is vital to keep in mind the possibility of such rights. In the course of this book we will come across a number of situations in which direct rights have an important role to play (see eg **E6:3.4.1**, **G5** and **G6**).

However, even if there is a chance of B claiming a direct right against C, B will still prefer to argue that he has a pre-existing property right or persistent right. If B has such a right, it is prima facie binding on C:[88] (i) it will be up to C to show that he has a defence to that right and; (ii) if C cannot do so, B's right will bind C. In contrast, where B claims a direct right against C, the onus is on B to show that C's conduct justifies the recognition of that right. And in practice, it will only be in rare cases that B can convince the court that a direct right should arise. The need to promote the ease of transactions between A and C means that the courts will *not* be quick to find that C's conduct justifies the recognition of a direct right (see eg **2.3.5** above). Once again, a balance must be struck between: (i) protecting prior users of things; and (ii) protecting those who later acquire rights. So, the **basic tension** that runs throughout the property law system shapes the rules governing direct rights.

---

[88] Unless of course C has independently acquired his right, in which case only a pre-existing property right, and not a persistent right, will be prima facie binding on C: see **B:4.4**.

CHAPTER D4
THE IMPACT OF UNJUST ENRICHMENT

THE IMPACT OF UNJUST ENRICHMENT

1 INTRODUCTION

1.1 The general principle

If A is unjustly enriched at B's expense, A comes under a duty to B. The law of unjust enrichment thus provides a means by which B can acquire a right against A (see Reason 4 as set out in **B:4.3**).

> **EXAMPLE 1a**
>
> B wrongly believes that he is under a contractual duty to pay A £100. As a result, B gives A two £50 notes. A spends that money on paying his gas bill.

> **EXAMPLE 1b**
>
> A and B make an agreement under which: (i) B is to give A singing lessons; and (ii) A is to pay B £150 in return. B performs that service. Both parties believe that, as a result of the agreement, A is under a contractual duty to pay B. It turns out that, in fact, the agreement does *not* impose a contractual duty on A or B. A refuses to pay B. The reasonable value of the service performed by B (ie, the market price A would have had to pay to get someone else to give him singing lessons) is £100.

In each case, as soon as A receives the benefit from B, A is under a duty to pay B £100.[1] That duty arises as a result of A's unjust enrichment at B's expense. In each case:

1. A has received a benefit;[2] *and*
2. A's benefit has come from B; *and*
3. It would be unjust for A to retain that benefit.[3]

There are two different ways of explaining why A's enrichment is unjust. The first is to say that A's enrichment is unjust because of a particular 'unjust factor'. So, in **Example 1a**, we can say that the unjust factor is B's *mistake* (B paid A in the mistaken belief that he was under a contractual duty to do so). In **Example 1b**, we can say that the unjust factor is either: (i) B's *mistake* (B performed the service for A in the mistaken belief that A and B had

---

[1] For **Example 1a**, see eg *Kelly v Solari* (1841) 9 M & W 54. For **Example 1b**, see eg *Craven-Ellis v Canons Ltd* [1936] 2 KB 403 (the agreement was not contractually binding as A Co did not have the power to enter into such contracts); *Pavey & Matthews Pty v Paul* (1987) 162 CLR 221 (High Court of Australia: the agreement was not contractually binding as it did not satisfy a formality requirement applying to certain types of building contract).

[2] A performance of a service does not *always* enrich B: but in **Example 1b**, A specifically requested the service and so cannot deny that he has received a benefit.

[3] See eg *per* Lord Steyn in *Banque Financière de la Cité v Parc (Battersea) Ltd* [1999] 1 AC 221 at 227.

made a valid contract); or (ii) a *failure of basis* (as A knew, B performed the service on the basis that A would pay B); or even (iii) A's *free acceptance* (A's acceptance of B's service in the knowledge that B expected payment for it).

The second approach operates at a more general level: A's enrichment is unjust because there is *no legal basis* for A to keep the benefit he has received from B. That approach cannot be wholly divorced from the 'unjust factor' approach: if B properly consents to giving A a benefit for free, then there *is* a legal basis for A to keep that benefit. So, in **Example 1a**, even on the second approach, B's mistake is important: it means B did not properly consent to A receiving B's £100.

The first approach emphasises the *presence* of an 'unjust factor'; the second focuses on the *absence* of a legal basis for A's retention of a benefit. There is an ongoing debate as to which analysis is more convincing.[4] In this book, the second analysis will be adopted. That analysis, unlike the first, provides a general principle that can explain the law of unjust enrichment as a coherent whole.[5] And there is very little practical difference between the two analyses.[6] There is a risk that the second approach may blur the differences between the various reasons that may mean there is no legal basis for A's retention of a benefit.[7] However, the second approach fits the purposes of this book very well as our focus, unlike that of a book on unjust enrichment, is *not* on the detailed reasons that may mean there is no such legal basis. Rather, we are interested in the *consequences* of such an absence: on the impact of unjust enrichment on the property law system.

1.2   An important defence

EXAMPLE 1c

The facts are as in **Example 1a** above, with the difference that A, believing himself to be £100 better off, spends that money on going out for an extravagant dinner.

If, in **Example 1c**: (i) A would not have gone out for such a dinner if he had not received the £100 from B; and (ii) when A spent the money, he did not know of B's mistake in paying the money to him; then (iii) A is no longer unjustly enriched at B's expense. As a result, A is no longer under a duty to B. That result is said to depend on the 'change of position defence':[8] A changed his position in reliance on the honest belief that he was free to

---

[4] Birks, *An Introduction to the Law of Restitution* (1985) takes the first view; Birks, *Unjust Enrichment* (2003) adopts the second. For comparison and discussion, see eg Stevens [2004] *RLR* 270–73; Burrows, ch 2 in *Mapping the Law: Essays in Memory of Peter Birks* (ed Burrows and Rodger, 2006); Barker, ch 4 in *Structure and Justification in Private Law: Essays for Peter Birks* (ed Rickett and Grantham, 2008).

[5] As argued by Baloch (2007) 123 *LQR* 636.

[6] For example, the Limitation Act 1980, s 32(1)(c) applies a special limitation rule where B's claim is for 'relief for the consequences of a mistake' (although note that rule no longer applies where B's mistake relates to the legal effect of tax statutes: see Finance Act 2004, s 320). So, in **Example 1a or 1b**, B may wish to say that he makes such a claim. Adopting the second approach does not prevent that as B's unjust enrichment claim clearly provides relief for B's mistaken payment to A: see eg *per* Lord Hoffmann in *Deutsche Morgan Grenfell Group Plc v Inland Revenue* [2007] 1 AC 558 at [22].

[7] As noted by Burrows, ch 2 in *Mapping the Law: Essays in Memory of Peter Birks* (ed Burrows and Rodger, 2006), 46–7.

[8] See eg *per* Lord Goff in *Lipkin Gorman v Karpnale Ltd* [1991] 2 AC 548 at 580. The defence was also acknowledged by the House of Lords in *Deutsche Morgan Grenfell Group Plc v Inland Revenue* [2007] 1 AC 558. Its requirements are more fully explored by the Privy Council in *Dextra Bank v Bank of Jamaica* [2002] 1 All ER Comm 193 at [34]–[46].

use the right acquired from B for his own benefit. Like all defences to direct rights, it is simply part of the test that tells us if B has acquired a right (see **B:5.1** and **D3:3**): A's change of position means that he is no longer unjustly enriched at B's expense. In contrast, in **Example 1a**, A *cannot* rely on the change of position defence. A did act in reliance on the honest belief that he was free to use the right acquired from B for his own benefit; but A remains unjustly enriched at B's expense, as he retains the benefit of having paid off his gas bill.

The change of position defence is certainly not the *only* defence that can be used against an unjust enrichment claim.[9] However, it is particularly important: if B's claim against A is seen as based on unjust enrichment, then A's change of position may limit or, as in **Example 1c**, entirely block that claim.

1.3 The impact of unjust enrichment

The purpose of this chapter is to set out an overview of the impact of unjust enrichment on the property law system.[10] We will look at the **basic situation** and consider the following questions:

Section 2: Can an unjust enrichment of C give B a direct right against C?

Section 3: Can an unjust enrichment of A (or C) give B a property right?

Section 4: Can an unjust enrichment of A (or C) give B a persistent right against a right held by A (or C)?

Section 5: If B's pre-existing property right or persistent right arises as a result of A's unjust enrichment, what defences can C use against that right?

Section 6: Can B use the law of unjust enrichment to assert a pre-existing property right against C?

Section 7: Can B use the law of unjust enrichment to assert a pre-existing persistent right against C?

2 DIRECT RIGHTS

2.1 Direct transfers from B to C

EXAMPLE 2a

B's bank account with Z Bank is £10,000 in credit. C, a fraudster, goes into a branch of Z Bank and pretends to be B. C tricks Z Bank into paying him £1,000.

In such a case, C is *not* unjustly enriched at B's expense: Z Bank cannot validly debit the

---

[9] For example, in a case such as **Example 1b**, it may be that a particular statute means that *both*: (i) A's agreement with B is not contractually binding on A; *and* (ii) B is not permitted to bring an unjust enrichment claim against A: see eg *Dimond v Lovell* [2002] 1 AC 384; *Wilson v First County Trust Ltd (No 2)* [2004] 1 AC 816 (both cases concerned the effect of the Consumer Credit Act 1974: see **F4:3.1.1(ii)(d)**).

[10] In general, unjust enrichment principles apply in the same way both in relation to land and in relation to other things (although there are some differences: see eg **G3:2.2**): so there is no need for a separate chapter looking at the impact of unjust enrichment on the land law system.

£1,000 from B's account.[11] So, both at the end and at the start of the story, B has a contractual right to receive £10,000 from Z Bank. B therefore has no need for a direct right against C. However, C *is* unjustly enriched at Z Bank's expense and Z Bank does have a direct right against C.[12] Indeed, Z Bank not only has a personal right against C; it also has a *power* to regain its Ownership of the notes it paid out to C (see **D1:Example 16a**).[13]

EXAMPLE 2b

B has a bank account with Z Bank. B, in the mistaken belief that he has a contractual duty to pay C £1,000, instructs Z Bank to transfer £1,000 to C's account at Z2 Bank. Z Bank makes that transfer and B's account with Z Bank is duly debited.

EXAMPLE 2c

B, a firm of solicitors, has an account with Z Bank that is £10,000 in credit. C, one of the partners in the firm, is authorised to make withdrawals from the account. C makes a withdrawal of £1,000 and, in breach of his duties to the other partners, uses the money to gamble in C2's casino.

In these cases, it is almost certain that, under the terms of its contract with B, Z Bank *does* have the power to validly debit B's account. As a result, in contrast to **Example 2a**, the £1,000 received by C *does* come at B's expense. And, in each case, there is no legal basis on which C can keep that benefit. As a result, B has a direct right against C.[14] These cases are straightforward: there is a *direct* transfer of a benefit from B to C.[15]

In **Examples 2b and 2c**, B, at the start of the story, has a personal right against Z Bank. However, even if B does not have such a right, B may still be able to show that C has been unjustly enriched at B's expense: B simply needs to show that C has received a benefit directly from B and that there is no legal basis on which C can retain that benefit (see eg **Example 1b**). So if, in **Examples 2b and 2c**, B's account with Z Bank is overdrawn at the start of the story (so that B in fact has no personal right against Z Bank) B can *still* acquire a direct right against C. The benefit received by C comes at B's expense as B's overdraft (the sum he owes to Z Bank) is increased. The same is true even if, in **Example 2b**, C's account with Z2 Bank is also overdrawn. In such a case, C nonetheless receives a benefit from B: the sum C owes to Z2 Bank is reduced.

Cases in which C is a direct recipient of a benefit from B are cases in which, in effect, C deals directly with B: such cases rarely arise in the **basic situation** (see **D3:2.1**). As far as the

---

[11] B's contract with Z Bank may allow Z Bank, in some circumstances, to debit B's account even if C has acted fraudulently (eg, where B's gross negligence allows C to commit the fraud).

[12] See eg *Banque Belge pour l'Estranger v Hambrouck* [1921] 1 KB 321.

[13] That power is best explained as arising from the fact that C holds his Ownership of those notes on Trust for B (see **2.2.2** below). This analysis is consistent with the result in *Banque Belge pur l'Estranger v Hambrouck* [1921] 1 KB 321: Z Bank was able to assert a pre-existing right against C2 (a party to whom C had given, for free, some of the money Z Bank paid out to C).

[14] For **Example 2b**, see eg *Chase Manhattan v Israel-British Bank* [1981] Ch 105. For **Example 2c**, see eg *Lipkin Gorman v Karpnale Ltd* [1991] 2 AC 548 (although note the claim there was made against the casino that received the money withdrawn by C: see **2.2.2** below).

[15] Technically, of course, C receives its benefit (an increase in the value of its personal right against Z Bank) from Z Bank, not from B. However, Z Bank is simply acting as an agent for B: it is a filter used by B to give C a benefit— see eg *Westminster Bank Ltd v Hilton* (1926) 43 TLR 124 at 126. And, as Z Bank can validly debit the sum it pays from B's account, C's benefit certainly comes from B.

property law system is concerned, the crucial question is whether C can be unjustly enriched at B's expense in a case where C does *not* directly receive a benefit from B.

2.2 No direct transfer from B to C

2.2.1 The general position

EXAMPLE 3

B has a bank account with Z Bank. B, in the mistaken belief that he has a contractual duty to pay A £1,000, instructs Z Bank to transfer £1,000 to A's current account at Z2 Bank. As a result, A's overdraft with Z2 Bank is reduced. Believing himself to be £1000 better off as a result of B's payment, A then withdraws £100 from his savings account (in the form of two £50 notes) and gives that money to C as a birthday present.

When A receives the benefit of the £1000 from B, A is unjustly enriched at B's expense: B therefore has a personal right against A (see **Example 2b**). However, that personal right may be of little value to B if A has gone into insolvency, or is impossible to find. In such a case, B may then claim that *C* is also unjustly enriched at B's expense.

The problem for B is that C received his £100 from A, not from B. Given this lack of a direct transfer of a benefit from B to C, it is very difficult to say that C has been unjustly enriched at B's expense. After all, B had no right in relation to the specific notes that A gave to C.

As a result, it seems that, in the **basic situation**, the law of unjust enrichment will almost *never* allow B to acquire a direct right against C. Any benefit C acquires comes from A and not from B. However, we need to consider an important House of Lords decision that, on its face, contradicts this simple analysis.[16]

2.2.2 *Lipkin Gorman v Karpnale Ltd* [17]

The essential facts of *Lipkin Gorman* are identical to those of **Example 2c** and can be represented in a diagram (see too the animated slides at the companion website):

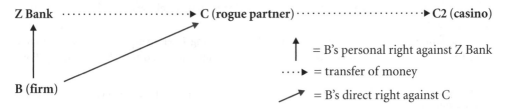

In *Lipkin Gorman*, C2 did not receive a benefit directly from B; rather, C2 received money from C. Nonetheless, the House of Lords: (i) permitted B to assert a right against C2; and (ii) stated that B's right arose as a result of C2's unjust enrichment at B's expense. It has

---

[16] Two Court of Appeal decisions (*Banque Belge pur l'Estranger v Hambrouck* [1921] 1 KB 321 and *Agip (Africa) Ltd v Jackson* [1991] Ch 547) may also seem to allow B a direct right against C, even though C received his benefit from A. The result in each case is correct and can be explained in the same way as the result in *Lipkin Gorman v Karpnale Ltd* [1991] 2 AC 548: for details see the companion website.

[17] [1991] 2 AC 548.

therefore been suggested that, in a case such as **Example 3**, even though C receives a benefit from A rather than from B: (i) C *is* unjustly enriched at B's expense;[18] and so (ii) B has a direct right against C.[19] However, we can explain the result in *Lipkin Gorman* without having to accept the surprising idea that, in **Example 3**, B has a direct right against C.[20]

(i) The reasoning of the House of Lords

In *Lipkin Gorman*, their Lordships did *not* lay down a general principle that C2 is unjustly enriched at B's expense *whenever*: (i) C directly acquires a benefit at B's expense; and (ii) as a result, C then gives a benefit to C2. Instead, in speeches with which the other members of the panel agreed, Lord Templeman and Lord Goff held that, on the facts of *Lipkin Gorman*, B had a *pre-existing property right* in the money that C gave to C2.[21] The reasoning of the House of Lords is thus unrelated to direct rights; instead, it seems that C2's unjust enrichment depends on the fact that B had a pre-existing *property right* in the money received by C2.[22] The reasoning in *Lipkin Gorman* thus does *not* support the proposition that, in **Example 3**, B acquires a direct right against C: in **Example 3**, it is clear that B does *not* have a pre-existing property right in the £100 that A pays to C.

(ii) Difficulties with the reasoning of the House of Lords

There is a different way in which the result (but not the reasoning) in *Lipkin Gorman* could be used to support the idea that, in **Example 3**, B has a direct right against C. The argument runs as follows:

- **Step 1**—The reasoning of the House of Lords in *Lipkin Gorman* cannot be correct: when C2 received the money from B, B did *not* have a pre-existing property right in that money.
- **Step 2**—So the result in *Lipkin Gorman* must be justified in a different way: through the recognition that, although it received nothing directly from B, C2 was unjustly enriched at B's expense.

Of course, it could be said that **Step 2** is flawed: if the reasoning in *Lipkin Gorman* is wrong, it may be that the result is wrong too. However, saying that a result reached by House of Lords is wrong must always be a last resort. And **Step 1** does raise a very important point (at least for a book on property law): in *Lipkin Gorman*, precisely *what* property right did B have in the money given to C2?

Lord Templeman seems to have regarded B as having Ownership of the money that C paid to C2.[23] However, that cannot be right. The money was given to C by Z Bank: Z Bank

---

[18] See eg Birks, *Unjust Enrichment* (2003) ch 4, esp 81–2. In Birks' terms, B's claim against C is based on permissible 'leapfrogging'.

[19] Tettenborn [1997] *RLR* 1 argues that, in a case such as **Example 3**, C is, prima facie, unjustly enriched at B's expense *but* that C should be able to rely on the defence of having lawfully received a right from A. That desirable result can be reached more directly by simply denying that C is unjustly enriched at B's expense.

[20] See eg L Smith (2000) 116 *LQR* 412 making the key distinction between: (i) cases where the defendant is a direct recipient from B (eg, C in **Example 2c**); and (ii) cases where the defendant is a remote recipient (eg, C2 in **Example 2c**). Birks, *Unjust Enrichment* (2003), 82–4 also relies on subrogation cases, such as *Butler v Rice* [1910] 2 Ch 277 to support the view that C can be unjustly enriched at B's expense when receiving a benefit from A. However, those cases, like *Lipkin Gorman*, can be explained in a different way (see n77 below).

[21] See *per* Lord Goff [1991] 2 AC 548 at 573–4; *per* Lord Templeman at 563.

[22] As noted by eg Virgo, *Principles of the Law of Restitution* (2nd edn, 2006), ch 20, esp 570–71; L Smith, (2000) 116 *LQR* 412 and (2001) 79 *Texas Law Review* 2115 at 2159ff.

[23] At one point, his Lordship describes C as holding 'money stolen from [B]': [1991] 2 AC 548 at 563.

had Ownership of the money and then transferred that right to C. There is no point at which B dependently or independently acquired Ownership of that money (see further **4.4.1** below). Lord Goff acknowledged that B did *not* have Ownership of the money paid by C to C2. However, his Lordship went on to hold that, as the money received by C was the product of B's account with Z Bank, B could assert a property right in that money.[24] This suggests that: (i) C had Ownership of the money; but (ii) B had a *different* property right in the same money. However, Ownership is the *only* property right that can exist in relation to things other than land (see **D1:1.4**).

It may be that Lord Goff viewed B as having a *power* to acquire Ownership of the money paid to C. There are two key problems with that view. First, a power to acquire a property right is not, in itself, a property right (see **D1:1.4.5**). Second, why should B have this power? B may have a power to *regain* a property right (eg, where B has a property right and then transfers that right to A due to A's duress or fraud: **D1:1.4.5(i)**). But, in *Lipkin Gorman*, B cannot have had such a power: B had no property right to regain as, at the start of the story, B had only a personal right against Z Bank.

(iii) A different explanation

It may therefore seem that we have only two choices: either (i) the result in *Lipkin Gorman* is wrong; or (ii) C2 can be unjustly enriched at B's expense *even though* C2 has not acquired a benefit from B. However, there is a third way. This third way depends on recognising that, when C received the money from Z Bank:

- C was unjustly enriched at B's expense (as B's account with Z Bank was validly debited); *and*
- C's unjust enrichment consisted in the acquisition of a *specific right* (Ownership of the money paid to C by Z Bank); *so*
- C was under a duty to B in relation to a specific right held by C; *so*
- B had a persistent right against C's Ownership of the money. C held that money on Trust for B as C was under the core Trust duty: a duty to B not to use the money for C's own benefit.

This analysis overcomes the difficulties raised by the reasoning of the House of Lords:

1. No inconsistency is involved in saying that: (i) C has a property right (Ownership of the money);[25] and (ii) B has a *persistent right* against C's right.[26]
2. The analysis does not depend on B having a direct right against C2, arising as a result of C2's unjust enrichment: instead, B asserts his *pre-existing* persistent right against C2.
3. The analysis can explain Lord Goff's view that B had a power to acquire C's Ownership of the money: B can have such a power if C holds his Ownership of the money on Trust entirely for B's benefit (see **D1:1.4.5(ii)**).

On this analysis, there is a crucial difference between the facts in *Lipkin Gorman* and those of **Example 3**. In *Lipkin Gorman*, B had a pre-existing persistent right (a right under a

---

[24] [1991] 2 AC 548 at 573–4.

[25] So, contrary to Lord Templeman, there is no need to say that B had Ownership of the money paid by C to C2.

[26] So, contrary to Lord Goff, there is no need to say that B had a property right other than Ownership in the money paid by C to C2.

Trust) against C's Ownership of the money paid by C to C2. In **Example 3**, in contrast, B has *no* pre-existing right in relation to A's Ownership of the money paid by A to C.

This analysis is controversial: some commentators argue that unjust enrichment can *never* give B a persistent right (see **4.3** below). However, support for the analysis can be found both in cases[27] and in academic writing.[28] Most importantly, the analysis derives some support from the analysis of the House of Lords in *Lipkin Gorman* itself. First, Lord Templeman seems to focus not on C2's *receipt* of money from C (as we would expect if C2's unjust enrichment at B's expense were crucial) but instead on C2's *retention* of that money (as we would expect if B's ability to assert a pre-existing persistent right against C2 were crucial: see **D2:Example 24a**).[29] Second, Lord Goff expressly notes that it would be possible for B to claim: (i) that C held its Ownership of the money on Trust for B; and (ii) that B could assert its right under that Trust against a recipient of that money, such as C2.[30]

Perhaps most importantly, the Trust analysis can explain why, as Lord Goff held, B had a power to acquire C's Ownership of the money. Lord Goff stated that B's power to acquire that property right arose at Common Law, not in Equity: that seems to cause a problem for our Trust analysis. However, Lord Goff based his view on *Taylor v Plumer*.[31] In that case, according to Lord Goff: (i) C held a property right that was the product of B's initial right; and (ii) B had a Common Law power to acquire C's property right. However, it has been conclusively shown that, in *Taylor v Plumer*, the court applied Equitable rules: B in fact had an *Equitable* power to acquire C's property right.[32] So *Taylor*, the decisive authority in *Lipkin Gorman*, in fact depends on: (i) C holding a right on Trust for B; and (ii) B, as a result of that Trust, having a power to acquire C's right (see **D1:1.4.5(ii)**). This should be no surprise. In *Taylor*, as in *Lipkin Gorman*, B's only right at the start of the story was a personal right against Z Bank. In both cases, Z Bank paid money to C. As a result, C acquired Ownership of that money. In such a case, the most B can hope to acquire is a *persistent right* against C's right.

(iv) Applying the new explanation

Of course, it is important to note that the analysis set out here was *not* expressly adopted by the House of Lords in *Lipkin Gorman*.[33] This is largely due to the way the case was presented. B's lawyers argued that B had a Common Law claim against C2: the House of

[27] See eg *per* Millett J in *El Ajou v Dollar Land Holdings* [1993] 3 All ER 717 at 734 (the decision was reversed by the Court of Appeal on a different point: [1994] 2 All ER 685). As the Trust arises as a result of A's unjust enrichment at B's expense, it can be called, as indeed it was by Millet J in *El Ajou*, a 'Resulting Trust' (see **4.3** below).

[28] See esp the analysis of Chambers, *Resulting Trusts* (1997); and L Smith (2001) 79 *Texas Law Review* 2115 at 2159ff.

[29] [1991] 2 AC 548 at 559–60. See too *per* Lord Templeman at 563: 'In the present case money stolen from [B] by [C] has been paid to and is now retained by [C2] and ought to be repaid to [B].' L Smith (2001) 79 *Texas Law Review* 2115 at 2166 also notes this point.

[30] [1991] 2 AC 548 at 572.

[31] (1815) 3 M & S 562. That case was very similar to *Lipkin Gorman*: (i) B had an account with Z Bank; (ii) C had authority to make a withdrawal from that account, but spent the money he received in unauthorised ways, buying US securities and gold; and (iii) C2 (C's assignees in bankruptcy) then acquired those rights from C. B seized the US securities and gold and it was held that, by doing so, B did not commit a wrong against C2.

[32] See *per* Millett LJ in *Trustee of the Property of FC Jones v Jones* [1997] Ch 159 at 169; Khurshid and Matthews (1979) 95 *LQR* 78; Smith [1995] *LMCLQ* 240 and ch 3 in *Landmark Cases in the Law of Restitution* (ed Mitchell and Mitchell, 2006).

[33] Some academic support for the analysis adopted here is provided by L Smith (2001) 79 *Texas Law Review* 2115 at 2159ff.

Lords therefore tried to find a way to support B's claim without relying on the Equitable concept of a persistent right. As a result, Lord Templeman and Lord Goff each stated that the pre-existing right B could assert against C arose at Common Law. However, as we have seen, it is impossible to justify the view that B had either: (i) a property right in the money paid by C to C2; or (ii) a Common Law power to acquire such a property right. A more convincing explanation for the result is to say that: (i) B had a pre-existing *persistent right* against C's Ownership of the money; and (ii) B was able to assert that right against C2.

First, if B had a pre-existing persistent right against C's Ownership of the money, C2 had no defence to that right. In particular, the casino receiving money from a gambler was *not* a 'bona fide purchaser' of that money: in the eyes of the law, as was confirmed by the House of Lords in *Lipkin Gorman*, the casino gave nothing of *value* in return for C's money.[34] Second, if, as in *Lipkin Gorman*, C2 is entirely unaware of B's persistent right, B can only assert that right against C2 if, when B asserts his right, C2 still has *either*: (i) the initial right against which B has a persistent right (in this case, C's money); or (ii) a right that counts as the product of that initial right (see **4.4** below).[35] So if, in *Lipkin Gorman*, C2 had spent all the money received from C *and* had acquired no rights in return (eg, if C2 had used the money to pay for a new advertising campaign), then B would *not* have been able to assert his pre-existing persistent right against C2.

However, once B can show that C2 has received a right against which B has a persistent right, the presumption is that C2 *does* still have that right or its product: the onus is on C2 to show otherwise.[36] In *Lipkin Gorman*, C2 did *not* attempt to show that it no longer had either the money paid to it by C or a right counting as a product of that money.[37] So, in *Lipkin Gorman*, B *was* able to assert its pre-existing persistent right against C2 as: (i) C2 had no defence to B's right; and (ii) C2 still had *either* the very money paid to it by C *or* a right that counted as the product of that money.

In *Lipkin Gorman*, the House of Lords considered whether, as a result of its conduct after receiving the money from C, C2 could use the 'change of position' defence (see **1.2** above). On the analysis set out here, that defence should be irrelevant: B's claim does *not* depend on showing that C2 has been unjustly enriched at B's expense. Instead, it depends on B's assertion of a pre-existing persistent right; and the change of position defence cannot be used in such a case (see **section 5** below).[38]

However, on the facts of *Lipkin Gorman* (at least as presented to the House of Lords) this difference was irrelevant. When gambling at C2's casino C, like most gamblers, made an overall loss. Nonetheless C, like most gamblers, did win *some* of his bets: so C2 paid some winnings to C. As a result, unpicking the transfers from C to C2 and back again is a very complicated process. For example, if C loses four bets and then wins, how much of the winnings from the fifth bet can be seen as the product of the four losing bets? And if C then

---

[34] The law changed on 1 September 2007 when Part 17 of the Gambling Act 2005 came into force.

[35] Strictly speaking, if B imposes a duty on C2 in relation to a right that counts as a product of the initial right against which B has a persistent right, B is *not* directly asserting his pre-existing persistent right. Instead, B exercises his power to acquire a *new* persistent right (see **4.4** below).

[36] See *Madras Official Assignee v Krishnaji Bhat* (1933) 49 TLR 432; *re Tilley's Will Trusts* [1967] Ch 432; *per* Hobhouse J in *Westdeutsche Landesbank Girozentrale v Islington LBC* [1994] 4 All ER 890 at 938. That onus seems sensible: after all, C2 is in a far better position that B to know how C2 has spent its money or otherwise dealt with its rights.

[37] C2 conceded that its use of the money after it was received could *not* prevent B making a claim (unless it allowed C2 to rely on the change of position defence): see *per* Lord Goff [1991] 2 AC 548 at 572.

loses the next four bets, how much of the money staked on those bets can be seen as the product of the winnings made on the fifth bet? To avoid these complications, B and C2 adopted a very sensible position in their litigation: it was agreed that, *overall*, the casino (C2) had profited by almost £175,000 from C's custom. At most, £20,000 of the money C spent at the casino came from sources other than the proceeds of B's bank account. As a result, according to Lord Templeman, C2 was effectively in the position of having received, from the money debited from B's bank account, *one lump sum* of about £155,000.

So, according to the House of Lords, C2 could show that its enrichment at B's expense was limited to £155,000: the sums it received, via C, from B's bank account *minus* the money C2 paid out in winnings to C. However, that result can be explained *without* using the law of unjust enrichment: (i) C received money from B's bank account without B's authority; so (ii) C held that money on Trust for B; and (iii) C2 retained £155,000 of that money; and so (iv) B was able to asset its pre-existing right against C2 by imposing a duty on C2 to hold its right to that £155,000 on Trust for B (see **D2:4.1.1**).

SUMMARY of D4:2

In the **basic situation**, it is very unlikely that C will receive a benefit *directly* from B; instead, C will almost always receive a benefit *from A*. In such cases, the law of unjust enrichment does *not* allow B to acquire a direct right against C. The simple point is that C is not enriched at B's expense: any benefit received by C comes from A and not from B. So, in **Example 3**, C is *not* enriched at B's expense.

The reasoning of the House of Lords in *Lipkin Gorman v Karpnale Ltd* suggests otherwise. However, that reasoning is incorrect and based on a misreading of an important authority: *Taylor v Plumer*. In *Lipkin Gorman*, the defendant casino was *not* enriched at B's expense: the money received by the casino was owned by C, the rogue partner. Nonetheless, the result in *Lipkin Gorman* can be justified. B's claim was successful because: (i) B had a persistent right against the money owned by the rogue partner; and (ii) B was able to assert that pre-existing persistent right against the casino. B's initial persistent right *did* arise as a result of the rogue partner's unjust enrichment (see **4.4** below): the rogue partner *directly* received a benefit from B by taking money from B's bank account without B's authority. However, the defendant casino, like C in **Example 3**, was *not* enriched at B's expense.

---

3   PROPERTY RIGHTS: THE ACQUISITION QUESTION

3.1   Mixing

D1: EXAMPLE 11

B1 has a drum filled with 15 gallons of oil; B2 has a drum filled with 10 gallons of oil. B1 takes the drums and mixes the contents of each in a single container.

In such a case, the mixing destroys the initial property right of each of B1 and B2: neither can identify the thing he initially owned. The courts have held that B1 and B2 are *co-owners* of the mixture: B1 has a 60 per cent share of Ownership of the oil in the container; and B2 has a 40 per cent share of that right (see **D1:2.1.2(ii)**). It is very difficult to explain *why* B2 should acquire *any* property right: (i) that right cannot come from a dependent acquisition (B1 has not given any right to B2); (ii) nor should it come from an independent acquisition (B2 has never had physical control of the mixture).

The only possible explanation for B2's property right is that it comes from B1's unjust enrichment at B2's expense.[39] However, there are two problems with that analysis. First, B2's property right arises as a result of the *fact* that B2's thing contributed to the mixture: there is no need for B2 to show any unjust enrichment of B1. Second, unjust enrichment operates to impose a duty on B1 to B2: in this case, B1 has a duty to B2 not to use the mixture entirely for B1's own benefit. It is very difficult to see why such a duty should give B2 a property right; instead, as argued in **D1:2.1.2(ii)**, B2 should acquire a persistent right against B1's Ownership of the mixture (see **4.5.2** below).

It is worth examining the reasoning of Staughton J in *Indian Oil Corporation v Greenstone Shipping*,[40] the essential facts of which are identical to **D1:Example 11**. His Lordship held that B2 acquired a property right as a co-owner of the new mixture.

The discussion in that case was informed by Roman law:[41] in particular, the Roman solution had an obvious influence on Blackstone's discussion of the issue,[42] which in turn influenced later English decisions. It is not too surprising that, in Roman law, B2 should become a co-owner of the mixture. After all, it is clear that B2 must have some right, and a purely personal right against B1 may seem to offer B2 insufficient protection if B1's Ownership of the mixture passes to a third party.

However, the English property law system has a resource unknown to the Romans: the concept of a persistent right. The best way to protect B2 in a case such as **D1:Example 11** is to recognise that: (i) B1 is unjustly enriched at B2's expense; and (ii) B1's unjust enrichment consists precisely in the acquisition of a specific right (B1's Ownership of the mixture); so (iii) B1's duty to B2 relates to that specific right; so (iii) B2 has a persistent right against B1's Ownership of the mixture. On this approach, B2 *does* have a right that is capable of binding C, a third party later acquiring B1's Ownership of the mixture; and C can rely on the 'bona fide purchaser' defence as protection against B2's hidden persistent right.

3.2   Powers to regain a transferred property right

3.2.1 The source of B's power

D1:EXAMPLE 6a

B has Ownership of a bike. A wants to buy B's bike for £200. B does not want to sell. A tries to persuade B to sell the bike by telling B that A needs the bike for his son, whose bike was recently stolen. A knows that this is untrue. B is taken in by the story and so transfers his Ownership of the bike to A in return for £200.

---

[38] See too *per* Lord Millett in *Foskett v McKeown* [2001] 1 AC 102 at 129.
[39] See Birks, ch 9 in *Interests in Goods* (ed Palmer and McKendrick, 2nd edn, 1998).
[40] [1988] QB 345.
[41] See eg *per* Staughton J [1988] QB 345 at 354 and 364.
[42] See Blackstone, *Commentaries on the Law of England* (1756–60), Book 2, 405.

EXAMPLE 4

B has Ownership of a bike. A threatens to kill B unless B transfers Ownership of the bike to A. B complies with A's demand.

In each of these cases, B has transferred his right to A and has thus lost his initial property right (see **D1:2.2.2**).[43] However, due to A's fraud (**D1:Example 6a**) or duress (**Example 4**), the transfer of B's right to A is said to be 'voidable at Common Law' (see **D1:1.4.5(i)**). As a result, B is said to have a 'right to rescind' the transfer to A: ie, B has a *power* to regain his property right. If B exercises that power, B *immediately* regains his property right: there is no need for A to return physical control of the bike to B.[44] In fact, as long as A still holds Ownership of the bike, B can exercise his power *without informing A*.[45]

The best explanation for B's power is to say that it arises as a result of A's unjust enrichment at B's expense.[46] If B transfers a right to A as a result of A's fraud or duress then: (i) A receives a benefit from B; and (ii) there is no legal basis for A to keep the benefit of that right. So, in **D1:Example 6a** and **Example 4**, A's unjust enrichment at B's expense can lead to B regaining his property right. However, A's unjust enrichment does not *directly* give B a property right; instead, it gives B a *power* to acquire such a right. Therefore, to evaluate the impact of unjust enrichment in these cases, we need to analyse the nature of B's power.

3.2.2 The nature of B's power: the Trust analysis

There are two important features of B's power to regain a right transferred to A:

1. B's power to regain a right arises *whenever* B transfers a right to A as a result of A's fraud or duress: it does not matter whether the right transferred by B is a personal right, persistent right or (as in **D1:Example 6a** and **Example 4**) a property right.
2. If C is not a 'bona fide purchaser' of A's right, it is also possible for B to assert his power to regain the right against C—a party to whom A later transfers his right.[47] So if, in **D1:Example 6a** and **Example 4**, A gives the bike to C as a birthday present, B can still assert his power against C (see **D1:3.5.4**).

B's power to regain a right, arising as a result of A's unjust enrichment at B's expense, thus looks very similar to a *persistent right*. First, it does not need to relate to a thing: instead, it can relate to *any right* held by A. Second, it can bind C if C later acquires A's right. Third, C

---

[43] There have been suggestions that, in **Example 4**, B's right is *not* transferred to A: A's duress makes the purported transfer 'void' (see eg *Barton v Armstrong* [1976] AC 104), at least if B's duress has the effect of turning '[A] into a mere machine' (*per* Holmes J in *Fairbanks v Snow* (1887) 13 NE 595 at 598). If so, B never loses his Ownership of the bike. However, the prevailing view is that the transaction is 'voidable at Common Law': see eg *Pao On v Lau Yiu Long* [1980] AC 614 at 634; *Halpern v Halpern (No 2)* [2007] 1 QB 88 and [2007] 3 WLR 849.

[44] *Car & Universal v Caldwell* [1965] 1 QB 525.

[45] *Ibid per* Sellers LJ at 551, *per* Upjohn LJ at 555 and *per* Davies LJ at 558–9.

[46] An alternative explanation is to say that it arises as a result of A's commission of a wrong. Certainly, where B's transfer occurs as a result of A's fraud, A does commit a wrong against B: the wrong of deceit. However (despite Lord Hoffmann's passing reference to the 'wrong of duress' in *R v A-G for England and Wales* [2003] UKPC 22 at [15]), it is far from clear that all cases of duress involve A committing a wrong against B: see eg McKendrick, ch 10 in *Mapping the Law: Essays in Memory of Peter Birks* (ed Burrows and Rodger, 2006), 196–8.

[47] See eg the analysis of Parke B in *Load v Green* (1846) 15 M & W 216; *Whitehorn Bros v Davison* [1911] 1 KB 463; Sale of Goods Act 1979, s 23 (note the condition that C is protected from B's power *if* C buys the goods in good faith and without notice of the facts giving rise to B's power).

is not bound if he is a 'bona fide purchaser' of A's right.[48] Finally, and, most importantly, it makes sense to say that, in **D1:Example 6a** and **Example 3**, B has a persistent right. This is because: (i) A is under a duty to B (arising as a result of A's unjust enrichment at B's expense); and (ii) A's duty to B relates to a specific right held by A: the right B transferred to A. In such a case, B's persistent right arises under a Trust: A holds a right but is under a duty to B not to use that right for his own benefit.

This analysis may seem surprising. In cases such as **D1:Example 6a** and **Example 4**, as in *Lipkin Gorman v Karpnale Ltd* (see **2.2.2** above),[49] B's power to acquire a property right is regarded as arising at Common Law. However, the Trust analysis provides a far more convincing account of the nature of B's power.[50] For example, it explains why, in **D1:Example 6a** and **Example 4**, B has a power immediately to regain his property right. B has such a power *whenever*: (i) A has a right; and (ii) A is under a duty to B to use that right entirely for B's benefit; and (iii) B is an adult and of sound mind ((see **D1:1.4.5(ii)**).[51] So, when B exercises his 'right to rescind' a transfer procured by A's fraud or duress, B in fact exercises his power, as a beneficiary of a Trust, to impose a duty on A to transfer the right held on Trust directly to B. On this analysis, the power arising in **D1:Example 6a** and **Example 4** arises for exactly the same reason as B's power, in *Lipkin Gorman v Karpnale Ltd*,[52] to acquire Ownership of the money debited from B's bank account (see **2.2.2** above).

A comment of Lord Browne-Wilkinson in *Westdeutsche Landesbank Girozentrale v Islington LBC* provides some support for the analysis adopted here. His Lordship stated that:

> Although it is difficult to find clear authority for the proposition, when property is obtained by fraud equity imposes a constructive trust on the fraudulent recipient: the property is recoverable and traceable in equity.[53]

Similarly, in *Collings v Lee*,[54] the Court of Appeal held that: (i) where B transferred his ownership of land to A as a result of A's fraud; then (ii) A immediately held that right on Trust for B. However, in *Collings*, the Court of Appeal made a distinction between two types of case: (i) those in which A directly acquires B's right as a result of A's fraud; and (ii) those (such as **D1:Example 6a**) in which A's fraud leads to a contractual agreement between A and B and B *then* transfers his right to A as part of that agreement.[55] This distinction was

---

[48] On one view, there is a slight difference between B's right and a true persistent right: in **D1:Example 6a** and **Example 4**, if B tries to assert his right against C, it has been suggested that the burden is on *B* to show that he can do so, not on C to show that he has a defence to B's pre-existing right (see eg *Whitehorn Bros v Davison* [1911] 1 KB 463; *per* Lord Hoffmann in *Barclays Bank plc v Boulter* [1999] 1 WLR 1919 at 1924). However, that suggestion is very hard to support: see eg Swadling (2005) 121 *LQR* 123 at 132–3.

[49] [1991] 2 AC 548.

[50] Swadling (2005) 121 *LQR* 123 notes the insuperable problems that arise from regarding B as having a Common Law power to acquire a property right. His suggestion is that, contrary to the decided cases, B should have *no* power to regain his property right in situations such as **D:Example 6a** and **Example 4**. However, the decisions can be explained by reinterpreting B's power as a consequence of a Trust arising as a result of A's unjust enrichment at B's expense.

[51] The power is often referred to as a '*Saunders v Vautier*' power: named for the case (1841) Cr & Ph 240; (1841) 4 Beav 115.

[52] [1991] 2 AC 548. See too *per* Millett J in *El Ajou v Dollar Land Holdings* [1993] 3 All ER 717 at 734.

[53] [1996] AC 669 at 716. The Trust arising in such a case is better seen as a Resulting Trust, not a Constructive Trust: see *per* Millett J in *El Ajou v Dollar Land Holdings* [1993] 3 All ER 717 at 734 and **4.3** below.

[54] [2001] 2 All ER 332.

[55] See *per* Nourse LJ at 336, building on a comment of Millett LJ in *Lonrho plc v Fayed (No 2)* [1991] 4 All ER 961 at 971.

used in *Shalson v Russo*:[56] there Rimer J held that Lord Browne-Wilkinson's approach could *not* apply if B makes the transfer as part of a contractual agreement with A. On Rimer J's analysis, in such a case, there is *not* an immediate Trust in B's favour. Instead, A *is* entitled to have the benefit of B's right *until* B chooses to exercise his 'right to rescind'.[57]

Certainly, if B decides *not* to exercise his 'right to rescind', B cannot then assert a persistent right. In **D1:Example 6a** it may be that £200 is a good price for the bike, and so B chooses not to reverse his deal with A. In such a case, B may choose to 'affirm' the transfer to A.[58] If B does so: (i) there *is* a legal basis for A to have the benefit of B's right; so (ii) by keeping that right, A is no longer unjustly enriched a B's expense; so (iii) A is no longer under a duty to B in relation to that right; hence (iv) B no longer has a persistent right against A's right.

However, it is very hard to agree with Rimer J that *before* B exercises his 'right to rescind', A is free to use the transferred right as A wishes. It is true that, if B is under a contractual duty to transfer a right to A, there *is* a legal basis for A to keep the benefit of that right (see **4.2.3** below). However, if, due to his duress or fraud, A is fully aware that B has not genuinely consented to the 'agreement' between the parties, then it is very difficult to see why B should be under a contractual duty to A. That conclusion cannot be changed by the fact that, because B has not yet discovered the fraud, B has not yet asked for the return of the right he has transferred to A. So, it seems that Rimer J's analysis is based on a common misunderstanding of the nature, in a case such as **D1:Example 6a**, of B's 'right to rescind'. Contrary to the orthodox view, in such a case, rescission is *not* necessary to remove B's contractual duty to A: due to A's fraud or duress, that duty *never* arises.[59] So, as Lord Browne-Wilkinson has stated, A *immediately* holds the right received from B on Trust for B. In **D1:Example 6a** and **Example 4**, rescission is necessary in order for B to assert his power, as beneficiary of that Trust, to impose a duty on A to transfer the right held on Trust to B.

In **D1:Example 6a** and **Example 4**, B transferred a property right to A as a result of A's fraud or duress. So, when B exercises his power to call for the return of the transferred right, we have a situation in which: (i) A has Ownership of a thing; and (ii) A is under a duty to B to give B immediate exclusive control forever of that thing. In such a situation, B acquires an *immediate* property right: there is no need for B to acquire physical control of A's thing.[60] This is the case where A's duty to give B immediate exclusive control forever arises as a result of: (i) A's promise in a deed (see **D1:2.2.4(i)**); or (ii) A's contractual promise as part of a sale (see **D1:2.2.4(iii)**); or (iii) as in **D1:Example 6a** and **Example 4**, the fact that A holds his property right entirely for B's benefit.[61] The crucial question, it seems, is not the *source* of

---

[56] [2005] Ch 281 at [108]–[120].

[57] *Ibid* at [108].

[58] See eg O'Sullivan et al, *The Law of Rescission* (2008), ch 23. It seems B's conduct cannot amount to an 'affirmation' unless B *knows* not just of the fact entitling him to rescind the transfer (eg, A's fraud) but also of his legal *power* to rescind (see *Habib Bank Ltd v Tufail* [2006] EWCA Civ 374 *per* Lloyd LJ at [20]).

[59] Things are different where the flaw in B's consent does *not* result from A's fraud or duress (but from eg A's undue influence or non-fraudulent misrepresentation: see **4.2.1** below). In those cases, A need not be initially aware of the flaw in B's consent and so B does not immediately acquire a persistent right against the right transferred to A.

[60] See *Car & Universal v Caldwell* [1965] 1 QB 525.

[61] This analysis means B should also acquire an immediate property right where A's duty to give B immediate exclusive control of a thing arises as a result of a contract that is not a sale, such as a barter (see **D1:Example 19d**).

A's duty; rather it is the *content* of that duty: (i) if A has Ownership of a thing; and (ii) A is under a duty to B to give B immediate exclusive control forever of that thing; then (iii) B has an immediate property right in that thing.[62]

SUMMARY of D4:3.2

If B transfers a property right to A as a result of A's fraud or duress, B has a power to regain that right by 'rescinding' the transfer to A. That power arises as a result of A's unjust enrichment at B's expense; if B exercises the power, B *immediately* regains his property right. In such a case, A's unjust enrichment does not *directly* give B a property right. Instead, it gives B an immediate *persistent* right against the right he has transferred to A. B's power to regain the right arises *because* of that persistent right: as A is under a duty use the transferred right entirely for B's benefit, B can impose a duty on A to transfer that right to B. Hence, where A's duty is to transfer Ownership of a specific thing back to B, B *immediately* regains his property right: there is no need for B to take physical control of the thing in question.

3.3 Security rights and 'subrogation'

EXAMPLE 5a

A has Ownership of a yacht. In return for a loan from Z Bank, A gives Z Bank a mortgage of the yacht: A transfers his Ownership of the yacht to Z Bank as security for A's duty to repay the loan (see **D1:Example 4a**). A then steals £10,000 from B and uses that money to pay off his debt to Z Bank. As a result of paying off the loan, A regains its Ownership of the yacht. A then goes into insolvency.

In such a case, A is unjustly enriched at B's expense.[63] At the start of the story, A did have a right in relation to the yacht (a Mortgagor's Right to Redeem: see **D2:1.2.3**); but A's right was subject to Z Bank's security right. At the end of the story, A has regained his Ownership of the yacht *free from* Z Bank's security right. So: (i) A has thus made a gain; (ii) that gain was made by using B's money; and (iii) there is no legal basis for A to retain the benefit he has acquired at B's expense. B therefore clearly has a personal right against A: however, as A has gone into insolvency, that personal right may be of little use to B (see **B:4.5.1**). B may therefore argue that, before A went into insolvency, B had a persistent right against A's Ownership of the yacht: that argument will certainly succeed (see **4.1** below). The question here is whether B can go further and show that he has acquired a *property right*: that may be important in a case where A, rather than going into insolvency, instead transfers his Ownership of the yacht to C, a 'bona fide purchaser'.

In **Example 5a**, B can argue that: (i) A's unjust enrichment at B's expense consists in the gain A has made by the removal of Z Bank's security right; so (ii) that gain consists in A

---

[62] In *Lipkin Gorman*, B could *not* rely on this principle to show that he had Ownership of the money C paid to C2: when C still had Ownership of the money, B was unaware of C's conduct and so had no chance to exercise its power to impose a duty on C to transfer C's Ownership of the money to B. Therefore, when C2 received the money from C, B had only a *persistent right* against C's Ownership of the money.

[63] Note the general analysis of the House of Lords in *Banque Financière de la Cité v Parc (Battersea) Ltd* [1999] 1 AC 221; see too Mitchell and Watterson, *The Law and Practice of Subrogation* (2007), Part II.

regaining Ownership of the yacht free from Z Bank's security right; so (iii) A's duty to pay B money as a result of A's wrongful use of B's £10,000 should also be protected by a security right over A's Ownership of the yacht; and (iv) as Z Bank's security right consisted of Ownership of A's yacht, A is under a duty to give B immediate exclusive control forever of that yacht; and (v) whenever A is under such a duty to B, whatever the source of that duty, B has an *immediate* property right (see **3.2.2** above).

B's argument is correct in principle but it is unclear whether it will succeed in practice. The principle B relies on when making his argument is known as 'subrogation'.[64] That principle was initially recognised by courts of Equity. As a result, in a case such as **Example 5a**, a court may well take the view that subrogation can give B only an '*Equitable* property right': ie, a persistent right against A's Ownership of the yacht.[65] However: (i) *if* (as argued in **3.2.2** above) there is a general principle that B acquires an immediate property right whenever A is under a duty to give B immediate exclusive control of a thing; (ii) then, even if A's duty arises in Equity, or as a result of A's unjust enrichment at B's expense, B should have an *immediate* property right.[66]

We will examine subrogation further in **4.1** below. At this point, it is important to note what subrogation does *not* involve in a case such as **Example 5a**:[67]

1. B does *not* acquire Z Bank's security right. Z Bank's security right secured A's duty to repay the loan made by Z Bank. If B acquires a security right by subrogation, that right will secure a different duty: A's duty to pay B money as a result of A's wrongful taking of B's £10,000.

2. B does *not* acquire a persistent right *against* Z Bank's security right.[68] Z Bank's security right no longer exists: it disappeared when A paid its debt to Z Bank. There is thus a very important difference between the form of 'subrogation' considered here and the insurer's subrogation we considered in **B:Example 6b**.[69]

---

[64] For the application of 'subrogation' to a case similar to **Example 5a**, see eg *Primlake Ltd v Matthews Associates* [2006] EWHC 1227; Mitchell and Watterson, *The Law and Practice of Subrogation* (2007), [6.42]–[6.50].

[65] See eg *per* Neuberger LJ in *Cheltenham & Gloucester Building Society v Appleyard* [2004] EWCA Civ 291 esp at [44]. However, that case involved registered *land*: the general principle that B acquires an immediate property right whenever A is under a duty to give B immediate exclusive control forever of a thing does *not* apply where registered land is concerned.

[66] This may of course cause a problem for C: if B has a property right in a case such as **Example 5a**, B's property right may be very hard for C to discover. In particular, it may be impossible to apply formality or registration rules to B's right: it does not arise as a result of A's exercise of a power to give B such a right but, instead, as a result of A's unjust enrichment at B's expense. Note, however, that the courts do have some flexibility to protect third parties when recognising that B has acquired a security right through subrogation: see eg *Banque Financière de la Cité v Parc (Battersea) Ltd* [1999] 1 AC 221 esp *per* Lord Hoffmann at 236.

[67] See further Mitchell and Watterson, *The Law and Practice of Subrogation* (2007), ch 3.

[68] See eg *per* Lord Hoffmann in *Banque Financière de la Cité v Parc (Battersea) Ltd* [1999] 1 AC 221 at 236; Mitchell and Watterson, *The Law and Practice of Subrogation* (2007), 3.07–3.33.

[69] That distinction is noted by Mitchell and Watterson, *The Law and Practice of Subrogation* (2007): that work refers to the form of subrogation considered here as 'subrogation to an extinguished right'; and to the insurers' subrogation considered in **B:Example 6b** as 'subrogation to a subsisting right'.

SUMMARY of D4:3

Unjust enrichment operates to impose a *duty* on one party (eg, A) to another (eg, B). In general there is no reason why A's unjust enrichment at B's expense should give B a property right: a right prima facie binding on the *rest of the world*. However, there may well be a general principle of the property law system that: (i) if A has Ownership of a thing; and (ii) A is under a duty to B to give B immediate exclusive control forever of that thing; then (iii) B acquires a property right immediately, without needing to take physical control of the thing in question. If that principle is correct, A's unjust enrichment at B's expense can give B a property right *if* it imposes such a duty on A. This seems to be the case where:

1. A's duty to B (arising as a result of A's unjust enrichment at B's expense) is to use A's Ownership of a thing entirely for B's benefit *and* B has exercised his power to impose a duty on A to transfer A's Ownership to B (see **3.2** above).
2. A's duty to B (arising as a result of A's unjust enrichment at B's expense) is to transfer A's Ownership of a thing to B by way of security (see **3.3** above).

4   PERSISTENT RIGHTS: THE ACQUISITION QUESTION

If A is unjustly enriched at B's expense, A is under a duty to B. As a result, B has a personal right against A. To show that he also has a persistent right, B needs to show that A's duty to B relates to *a specific right held by A*.[70] The key question is therefore a simple one: can A's unjust enrichment impose a duty on A in relation to a specific right held by A?

There are some cases where A's unjust enrichment clearly *cannot* give B a persistent right. In **Example 1b**, A's duty to B does not relate to a specific right held by A: A is simply under a duty to pay B a sum of money. However, in many other cases, A's unjust enrichment consists *precisely* in: (i) A's acquisition of a specific new right; *or* (ii) in an increase in the value of a specific right previously held by A. In those cases: (i) A's duty arises because of A's unjust enrichment at B's expense; and (ii) A's enrichment relates to a specific right held by A; so it would be no surprise to find that (iii) A's duty to B relates to a specific right; and therefore that (iv) B has a persistent right against the right held by A.

Where A's enrichment consists in acquiring a specific new right, we would expect B's right to arise under a Trust: to the extent that he is enriched at B's expense, A should be under a duty to B not to use that new right for A's own benefit. Where A's enrichment instead consists in an increase in the value of a specific right previously held by A, we would expect B's right to take the form of a Purely Equitable Charge: A is free to use his right for his own benefit, provided he performs his duty to pay B the value of the gain he has made at B's expense.

EXAMPLE 1a

B wrongly believes that he is under a contractual duty to pay A £100. As a result, B gives A two £50 notes. A spends that money on paying his gas bill.

---

[70] B can only acquire a persistent right if A's duty relates to a specific *claim-right or power* held by A (see **D2:1.1.3**). In the situations considered in this chapter, A's right is always a claim-right or power so, for ease of reference, we can refer simply to A's right.

In such a case, it may well be that, when A receives the notes, A does not know, and could not reasonably be expected to know, that B made a mistake when paying A. If so, it would be very harsh to say that, *as soon as* A acquires Ownership of the notes: (i) A is under a duty to B not to use those notes for A's own benefit; and so (ii) A holds his Ownership of those notes on Trust for B. After all, if A were under such a duty, A would then commit a wrong against B by using the notes to pay his gas bill. And that result seems wholly incorrect, given that: (i) B chose to transfer his Ownership of the notes to A; and (ii) A honestly and reasonably believed that he was free to spend the notes as he wished.[71]

So, in **Example 1a**: if (i) A is unaware of the fact (B's mistake), that means there is no legal basis for A to have the benefit of B's right; then (ii) A cannot be under a duty to B in relation to A's Ownership of those notes; and so (iii) B does not acquire an immediate persistent right. As noted by Lord Browne-Wilkinson in the important case of *Westdeutsche Landesbank Girozentrale v Islington LBC*,[72] if: (i) A honestly and reasonably believes he is entitled to use the right received from B for A's own benefit; then (ii) A *cannot* be under a duty to B in relation to that right.

On this view, where A acquires a right directly from B, A's unjust enrichment at B's expense gives B a persistent right *if and only if*:

- There is no legal basis for A to have the benefit of that right; *and*
- A is aware (or ought to be aware) of the facts meaning that there is no legal basis for A to have the benefit of that right.

In the rest of **section 4**, we will see that, despite some academic opinion to the contrary, the property law system *does* follow the simple model set out here. In fact, the *key* impact of unjust enrichment on the property law system is its ability to give B a persistent right. This analysis certainly fits with the examples we have already considered:

1. In **Example 2c** (as in *Lipkin Gorman v Karpnale*): (i) the party directly acquiring a right from B (C in that example); (ii) *knows* that there is no legal basis for him to have the benefit of B's right; so (iii) he holds that right on Trust for B.
2. In **D1: Example 11**: (i) B1 directly acquires a right (Ownership of the mixture) at B2's expense; and (ii) B1 *knows* of the fact (ie, that B2 has not consented to the mixing) which means there is no legal basis for B1 to take the benefit of B2's right; so (iii) B1 holds his right on Trust for B2, in proportion to B2's contribution to that right.
3. In **D1:Example 6a**: (i) A directly acquires B's right; and (ii) A *knows* of the fact (ie, that A's representation is untrue) which means there is no legal basis for A to have the benefit of B's right; so (iii) A holds that right on Trust for B.
4. In **Example 4**: (i) A directly acquires B's right; and (ii) A *knows* of the fact (ie that B has been coerced) which means there is no legal basis for A to have the benefit of B's right; so (iii) A holds that right on Trust for B.

In those cases, A *knew* of the facts, meaning that there was no legal basis for A to have the benefit of B's right. However, the test set out above is broader: it also applies when A *ought*

---

[71] It would also have the very surprising consequence that, in **Example 1a**, A would be unable to use the change of position defence against B (see **section 5** below).
[72] [1996] AC 669 at 705 and 714–5.

to be aware of those facts. This raises an important question: when can we say that A ought to be aware of those facts? Well, we have already seen how the courts answer an essentially identical question.

D2:EXAMPLE 24a

A holds his Ownership of a bike on Trust entirely for B. In breach of his duties as trustee, A transfers that right, for free, to C. C has no actual or constructive notice of B's pre-existing persistent right. Believing the bike is his to use as he pleases, C sells the bike to C2 for £200 (C2 also has no actual no actual or constructive notice of B's initial right under the Trust). C then spends the money on a holiday.

In **D2:Example 24a**, C is *not* under a duty to B as soon as C receives A's Ownership of the bike: at that point, C is entirely unaware of B's pre-existing persistent right. However, as C has no defence to B's pre-existing persistent right, B has a *power* to impose a duty on C (see **B:4.3**). So, if: (i) *before* C transfers Ownership of the bike to C2; (ii) B tells C that A transferred that right to C in breach of Trust *or* C learns of that fact from a different source; then (iii) C, as a result of his 'knowing receipt' comes under the core Trust duty to B (see **D2:4.1.1(ii) and D2:Examples 24b and 24c**).

The same basic analysis applies in **Example 1a**. The innocent recipient (A in **Example 1a**; C in **D2:Example 24a**) is not under the core Trust duty to B: he is free to use his right for his own benefit. However, B does have a *power* to impose a duty on that innocent recipient. So, in **Example 1a**, if: (i) A still has Ownership of the notes; and (ii) B tells A of his mistake *or* A learns of that fact from other source; then (iii) A comes under the core Trust duty to B.

This analysis is again confirmed by Lord Browne-Wilkinson in *Westdeutsche*.[73] His Lordship stated that, in a case such as **Example 1a**, A comes under the core Trust duty if his awareness of B's mistake means that A's 'conscience' is affected: ie, that it would be unconscionable for A to retain the benefit of the right transferred to him by B. The *very same test* is used in a case such as **D2:Example 24a**,[74] when considering if C's awareness of A's breach of Trust suffices to impose the core Trust duty on C (see **D2:4.1.1(ii)**). This should be no surprise: in each case, the court asks the same question—is the recipient, whilst still holding a particular right, sufficiently aware of the facts giving rise to B's power to acquire a persistent right? If so, then that party (A in **Example 1a**; C in **D2:Example 24a**) is under the core Trust duty to B. If not, no such duty arises.

Of course, this does not mean that **Example 1a** is identical to **D2:Example 24a**. In particular, in **Example 1a**, there is a direct transfer from B to A. As a result, whatever A's awareness of his mistake, B clearly has a direct, personal right against A: A is unjustly enriched at B's expense. It is that enrichment which gives B a power to acquire a persistent right. In contrast, in **D2:Example 24a**, there is no direct transfer from B to C: any benefit C has acquired comes from A, not from B. As a result, C is *not* unjustly enriched at B's expense and so B does *not* have a direct, personal right against C (see **section 7** below). In such a case, B's power to acquire a persistent right does *not* come from C's unjust enrichment; instead, it comes from B's ability to assert his *pre-existing* persistent right against C.

---

[73] [1996] AC 669 at 705.
[74] See *per* Nourse LJ in *BCCI v Akindele* [2001] Ch 437 at 455: 'The recipient's state of knowledge must be such as to make it unconscionable for him to retain the benefit of the receipt.'

4.1   Security rights and 'subrogation'

EXAMPLE 5b

The basic facts are as in **Example 5a** above: the difference is that A's duty to repay Z Bank is secured by a Purely Equitable Charge over A's Ownership of the yacht.

As in **Example 5a,** when A uses B's money to pay off Z Bank's security right: (i) A is unjustly enriched at B's expense; and (ii) A's unjust enrichment consists in the removal of Z Bank's security right. The difference is that Z Bank's security right was a persistent right against A's Ownership of the yacht—*not* a property right. As a result, the need to reverse A's unjust enrichment means that, in **Example 5b,** B must have a persistent right.[75] As a result, B acquires a Purely Equitable Charge against A's Ownership of the yacht,[76] and that Purely Equitable Charge secures A's duty to pay B money as a result of A's wrongful use of B's £10,000. The House of Lords has confirmed that the 'subrogation' principle operating in cases such as **Examples 5a and 5b** depends on A's unjust enrichment at B's expense.[77] As a result, **Example 5b** provides undeniable proof that B can acquire a persistent right as a result of A's unjust enrichment at B's expense.

4.2   Powers to acquire a persistent right against a transferred right

4.2.1 Undue influence and misrepresentation[78]

(i) The source of B's power

EXAMPLE 6a

B has Ownership of a bike. B joins a religious group. Under the rules of that association, the word of A, its leader, is to be treated as the word of God. The rules also forbid members from seeking external advice without the consent of A. B, without receiving anything in return, transfers his bike to A.

---

[75] On the facts of some subrogation cases, A's unjust enrichment can be reversed *without* giving B *exactly* the same right as the right formerly held by Z Bank: see *per* Lord Hoffmann in *Banque Financière de la Cité v Parc (Battersea) Ltd* [1999] 1 AC 221 at 236–7; Mitchell and Watterson, *The Law and Practice of Subrogation* (2007), [8.48]–[8.60].

[76] See eg *Halifax plc v Omar* [2002] 2 P & CR 377. It is worth noting that if A uses B's money to remove Z Bank's personal right against A (eg, to pay off A's overdraft) then the 'subrogation' principle, for the same reason, gives B only a personal right against A (see eg *Filby v Mortgage Express (No 2) Ltd* [2004] EWCA Civ 759).

[77] *Banque Financière de la Cité v Parc (Battersea) Ltd* [1999] 1 AC 221. This means that B can rely on this form of subrogation *only* if B's right is *directly* used to pay off A's debt. For example, if: (i) B gives money to A; and (ii) A then pays off a debt owed by A2 to Z Bank; then (iii) B can rely on subrogation only if it can show that B had a property right or a persistent right in relation to the money used by A to pay off A2's debt: see eg the analysis of May LJ in *Filby v Mortgage Express (No 2) Ltd* [2004] EWCA Civ 759 at [21]–[36]. *Butler v Rice* [1910] 2 Ch 277 (see **n 20** above) is *not* inconsistent with this analysis: in that case B gave money to A for the express purpose of paying off a debt to Z Bank secured by a property right held by Z Bank. In such a case, as B advanced the money to A for a specific, limited purpose, B acquired a persistent right in that money (see the analysis of Lord Millett in *Twinsectra v Yardley* [2002] 2 AC 164 at [68]–[103], discussed in **F4:2.4.2(ii)**). So as that money was then used to allow C to hold a right free from a security right, B acquired a persistent right against C's right.

[78] B may also acquire an 'Equitable right to rescind' a transaction if it has been procured by A's exploitation of a particular weakness of B (see Peel, *Treitel's Law of Contract* (12th edn, 2007), 10-039–10-041: see further **G4:2.1.4(iii)**).

In such a case, A acquires B's Ownership of the bike: B intended to transfer that right to A (see **D1:Example 16b**). And, as B's intention was not procured by any fraud or duress of A, the transfer to A is not 'voidable at Common Law': B therefore has no power to immediately regain his right (see **3.2** above). However, as A's intention has been procured by B's *undue influence*,[79] the transaction between A and B is said to be 'voidable in Equity'. As confirmed by the Court of Appeal in *Allcard v Skinner*,[80] on which **Example 6a** is based, B therefore has an 'Equitable right to rescind' the transfer to A: ie, B has a *power to acquire a persistent right against the right transferred to A*.

EXAMPLE 6b

B has Ownership of a bike. A wants to buy the bike for £200 but B is reluctant to sell it. A persuades B to sell by telling him that B's employer now runs a scheme that will allow B to buy a new bike very cheaply. A genuinely believes that statement to be true, but it turns out to be false. In reliance on the truth of A's statement, B sells A the bike for £200.

Again: (i) B clearly does intend to transfer his Ownership of the bike to A; and (ii) B's intention has not been procured by any fraud or duress of A. However, as B's intention has been procured by B's *misrepresentation*,[81] the transaction between A and B is said to be 'voidable in Equity': B has an 'Equitable right to rescind' the transfer to A. This is the case even though A's misrepresentation was made innocently; and even though it may have been easy for B to check the truth of A's representation before deciding to sell the bike to A.[82] As a result, B has a *power to acquire a persistent right against the right transferred to A*.[83]

In both **Examples 6a and 6b**, B's power arises as a result of A's unjust enrichment at B's expense.[84] If B transfers a right to A as a result of A's undue influence or misrepresentation, then: (i) A receives a benefit from B; and (ii) there is no legal basis for A to have the benefit of that right. However, A's unjust enrichment does not *directly* give B a persistent right; instead, it gives B a *power* to acquire such a right. So, to evaluate the impact of unjust enrichment in these cases, we need to analyse the nature of B's power.

---

[79] For details as to when a transfer can be said to have been procured by undue influence see eg *Royal Bank of Scotland v Etridge (No 2)* [2002] 2 AC 773; Peel, *Treitel's Law of Contract* (12th edn, 2007), 10-008–10-038.

[80] (1887) 36 Ch D 145.

[81] For details as to when a transfer can be said to have been procured by a misrepresentation, see eg Peel, *Treitel's Law of Contract* (12th edn, 2007), ch 9.

[82] See eg *Redgrave v Hurd* (1881) 20 Ch D 1.

[83] See eg *Leaf v International Picture Galleries* [1950] 2 KB 86 (see now Misrepresentation Act 1967, ss 1(1)(b)); *per* Millett LJ in *Bristol & West Building Society v Mothew* [1998] Ch 1 at 22–3; *Twinsectra v Yardley* [1999] Lloyd's Rep Bank 438 at 461–2 (the case went to the House of Lords [2002] 2 AC 164 but this point was not considered). However, academic views differ on this point. At one extreme is O'Sullivan et al, *The Law of Rescission* (2008), 16.38, arguing that, if B's misrepresentation is not fraudulent, A's exercise of his power to rescind should *not* give A an 'Equitable property right'—although the authors admit 'that there is no clear answer as a matter of principle or policy'. At the other extreme is Chambers, *Resulting Trusts* (1997), ch 7, arguing that A acquires an *immediate* 'Equitable property right' *as soon as* his right is transferred to B. The view taken here is closest to that of Worthington: see eg *Proprietary Interests in Commercial Transactions* (1996), 161–8; [2002] *RLR* 28.

[84] Certainly, it cannot arise as a result of a wrong committed by A—as the Court of Appeal emphasised in *Allcard v Skinner* (1887) 36 Ch D 145, the exercise of undue influence is not, in itself, a breach of duty owed by A to B (see too *per* Mummery LJ in *Pesticcio v Huet* [2004] EWCA Civ 372 at [20]; Birks and Chin, in *Good Faith & Fault in Contract Law* (ed Beatson and Friedmann, 1995), ch 3). In *Royal Bank of Scotland v Etridge (No 2)* [2002] 2 AC 773, the House of Lords does refer to undue influence, in a broad sense, as wrongdoing: but it is not suggested there that undue influence involves the commission of a legal wrong (ie, a breach of a duty owed by A to B).

(ii) The nature of B's power

In **Examples 6a and 6b**, it cannot be said that A is under a duty to B *as soon as* A acquires B's right. At that point, it may be the case that A is entirely unaware of the facts meaning that there is no legal basis for A to have the benefit of B's right. For example, in **Example 6b**, each of A and B honestly believes that B's employer runs a bike scheme. This is the key difference between: (i) cases of fraud or duress (eg, **D1:Example 6a** and **Example 4**); and (ii) cases of undue influence or misrepresentation (eg, **Examples 6a and 6b**). In the former cases, A is *necessarily* aware of the flaw in B's intention: A knows that B has acted on the basis of a lie or because of coercion. As a result, A is immediately under the core Trust duty: as soon as B transfers his right to A, B has a persistent right against that right (see **3.2** above). In contrast, in **Examples 6a and 6b**, A need not be aware of the flaw in B's intention; if not, A has no immediate duty to B and so B does *not* acquire an immediate right under a Trust.

In **Examples 6a and 6b**, there is an easy way for B to impose a duty on A: he simply needs to inform A, whilst A still has the right transferred to him by B, of the flaw in B's intention. Once A has that information: (i) A comes under a duty to B in relation to the transferred right; and so (ii) B acquires a persistent right against that right. This is why, in **Examples 6a and 6b**, B has a *power* to acquire a persistent right. For example, in **Example 6b**, B can acquire a persistent right by 'rescinding the contract' with A: by telling A that, as he has discovered his employer does not run a cycle scheme, he now wants A to give the bike back.[85] Of course, if A discovers the flaw in B's intention by another means (eg, if, in **Example 6b**, X tells A that B's employer does not run a bike scheme), then if A still holds the right transferred to him by B, B will again acquire a persistent right against that right.[86] Equally if, in **Example 6a**, A was aware, when receiving B's bike, of B's inability to exercise his own, independent judgment, then A should be under an *immediate* duty to B.[87]

In **Examples 6a and 6b**, A may give C a right in relation to the bike *before* B has exercised his power to acquire a persistent right against A's Ownership of the bike. In such a case, it may be possible for B to assert his *power* to acquire a persistent right against C. However, it will be impossible for B to assert that power if C is a 'bona fide purchaser' *either* of A's Ownership of the bike *or* of a new persistent right depending on A's Ownership of the bike (see **D2:3.5.5**). This demonstrates that, in an important way, the power to acquire a persistent right that B has in **Examples 6a and 6b** is weaker than the actual persistent right that B has in **D1:Example 6a and Example 4**.

---

[85] This 'rescission' works both ways: B will have to repay the £200 he received from A (see eg *per* Bowen LJ in *Newbigging v Adam* (1886) 34 Ch D 582 at 595). If B is unable to do so, B will be unable to exercise his power to 'rescind'. If B claims only a personal right against A, it will suffice if B can pay A the value of any benefits transferred by A under the contract: see eg *O'Sullivan v Management Agency and Music Ltd* [1985] QB 428.

[86] If B discovers the relevant fact, but is happy to allow the sale of the bike to stand (eg, because £200 is a good price for the bike), then B can 'affirm' the transfer. If so, A's duty to B and, with it, B's persistent right, disappears: see **3.2.2** above.

[87] In *Allcard v Skinner* (1887) 36 Ch D 145 itself, on which **Example 6a** is based, Cotton LJ at 175 (in contrast to Lindley and Bowen LJJ) took the view that B acquired a persistent right when B left the sisterhood: any right held by A at that point, earlier transferred by B, was held by A on Trust for B. That view can be defended if it can be said, on the facts, that B's decision to leave the sisterhood in itself gave A sufficient awareness of the previous impairment in B's consent to transfer her right to A.

4.2.2 Mistake

EXAMPLE 7a

B has two children, A1 and A2. B gives A2 £10,000. B wants to make sure he treats A1 and A2 equally, so he also gives A1 £10,000. B then remembers that, six years ago, he gave A1 £5,000.

This case is very similar to **Example 1a**: (i) B's transfer to A1 was caused by B's mistake; and so (ii) there is no legal basis for A1 to retain the benefit of B's right. In the opening paragraphs of this section, it was suggested that, in **Example 1a**, B has a power to acquire a persistent right against the right transferred to B. The same analysis applies in **Example 7a**: B should have a power to acquire a persistent right against the £10,000 transferred to A1.

That analysis is certainly consistent with the decision of Eve J in *Lady Hood of Avalon v Mackinnon*,[88] on which **Example 7a** is based. In that case, B had not yet paid A1; instead, she had executed a deed under which A1 would be paid money in the future. As a result of her mistake, B was allowed to 'rescind' the deed: as in **Example 6a** and **Example 6b**, it can be said that the planned transfer was 'voidable in Equity'. So, if: (i) B had discovered her mistake only *after* paying A1; then (ii) as in a case of undue influence or misrepresentation, B would have had a power to 'rescind' the transfer: ie, a power to acquire a persistent right against the right transferred to A1.[89]

EXAMPLE 7b

B has Ownership of a bike. B mistakenly thinks he is very unwell and will die soon. As a result, B decides to give away all his rights: he gives his Ownership of his bike to A. B then discovers that he is not, and never has been, very unwell.

In such a case, is A unjustly enriched at B's expense if he keeps Ownership of the bike? **Example 7b** reveals a very difficult question that also lurks behind **Example 7a** and **Example 1a**: if: (i) B transfers a right to A as a result of B's mistake; and (ii) A is not responsible for B's mistake; then (iii) does B's mistake, by itself, mean there is no legal basis for A to have the benefit of B's right?

There is no morally correct answer to that question. Certainly, judges have taken different views,[90] and academics also disagree on the best result.[91] There is a tension between: (i) a desire to protect B, who transferred his right as a result of a mistake; and (ii) a desire to protect A and thus to enable A to rely on the transfer from B. This tension, like the **basic tension** of property law itself, is impossible to resolve. However, the law of unjust enrichment has to make a choice. And it seems that, under English law, the current starting point is that: (i) if, when B transfers his right to A; (ii) B is mistaken as to an *existing state of*

---

[88] [1909] 1 Ch 476.

[89] Certainly, A1 should be under a duty to repay the money to B: see eg Jones, *Goff & Jones' Law of Restitution* (7th edn, 2007), 4-022.

[90] Some judges have expressed a very narrow view: B's mistake is only relevant if it caused B to believe he was under a *duty* to transfer his right to A (see eg *per* Bramwell B in *Aiken v Short* (1856) 1 H & N 210). Similarly, it has been said that, in a situation such as **Example 7b**, B's mistake is not relevant as: (i) B did, after all, intend to make a gift to A (see eg *per* Sir Wilfrid Greene MR in *Morgan v Ashcroft* [1938] 1 KB 49 at 66); or (ii) B made no mistake as to the *legal effect* of his transaction with A (see eg *per* Millett LJ in *Gibbon v Mitchell* [1990] 1 WLR 1304 at 1309).

[91] Compare eg Tang (2004) 20 *Journal of Contract Law* 1 (advocating a narrow test in order to protect A) with eg Parker (1959) 58 *Michigan Law Review* 90 and Jones, *Goff & Jones' Law of Restitution* (7th edn, 2007), 4-022 (advocating a wide test in order to protect B).

affairs (eg, in **Example 7b**, the fact that B is very unwell);[92] *and* (iii) B can show that, but for that mistake, B would not have made the transfer; then (iv) A, when he acquires B's right, is unjustly enriched at B's expense.[93]

Wherever the law of unjust enrichment chooses to draw the line, the response of the property law system is the same. *If* there is no legal basis for A to have the benefit of B's right then:

1.   B has an immediate power to acquire a persistent right against the right transferred to A; *and*
2.   If A: (i) still holds the right transferred by B; and (ii) knows or ought to know of B's mistake; then (iii) B has a persistent right against that right: A is under the core Trust duty to B.[94]

4.2.3 An important limit: B has a duty to transfer a right to A

EXAMPLE 8a

In September 2000, B comes under a contractual duty to pay £50 to A. In September 2007, A threatens to sue B for that money. B pays A £50. B then discovers that, as six years had passed since he came under that duty to A, the Limitation Act 1980 prevents A from bringing a claim for that £50.

In such a case, B made a mistake: if he had known that A was unable to enforce his contractual right, B would not have given A the £50. And it does not matter that B's mistake was as to the state of the law: as long as it is a mistake about the *current* state of law, such a mistake can mean there is no legal basis for A to keep the benefit received from B.[95] Nonetheless, A is *not* unjustly enriched at B's expense. The Limitation Act simply prevents A bringing an action to enforce B's duty; it does *not* mean that B's duty no longer exists. So, in **Example 8a**, there *is* a legal basis for A to have the benefit of the £50: B was under a contractual duty to pay that sum to A.[96]

EXAMPLE 8b

B Ltd employs A. B Ltd wants to end that employment. B Ltd and A agree a deal in which: (i) A will leave; and (ii) B Ltd will pay A £100,000. B Ltd makes the payment to A and A leaves his job. B Ltd then discovers that A had earlier breached his employment contract. If B Ltd had known of that breach, it could have sacked A without paying A anything.

---

[92] It seems that B's *unilateral* mistake as to a future event does not mean that A is unjustly enriched: see eg *per* Lord Goff in *Dextra Bank v Bank of Jamaica* [2001] UK PC 50 at [29]; *per* Lewison J in *Ogden v Trustees of the RHS Griffiths 2003 Settlement* [2008] EWHC 118 at [23]. However, if B's mistake is as to a future event, A can be unjustly enriched if: (i) A and B *both* know that B transferred his right to A on a particular basis; and (ii) that basis then fails (see eg **Example 10b** below).

[93] See eg *Barclays Bank Ltd v Simms & Cooke Ltd* [1980] 1 QB 677 esp *per* Goff J at 695; *Ogden v Trustees of the RHS Griffiths 2003 Settlement* [2008] EWHC 118 esp *per* Lewison J at [23]–[25].

[94] See eg *Chase Manhattan Bank v Israel-British Bank Ltd* [1981] Ch 105; *per* Lord Browne-Wilkinson in *Westdeutsche Landesbank Girozentrale v Islington LBC* [1996] AC 669 at 714–5; *per* Judge Chambers QC in *Papamichael v National Westminster Bank* [2003] 1 Lloyds Rep 341 at [223]ff; *per* Lawrence Collins J in *Commerzbank Aktiengesellscshaft v IBM Morgan plc* [2005] 2 All ER (Comm) 564 at [36].

[95] As recognised by the House of Lords in *Kleinwort Benson Ltd v Lincoln City Council* [1999] 2 AC 349. See too *Nurdin & Peacock plc v DB Ramsden & Co Ltd* [1999] 1 WLR 1249.

[96] See eg *per* Lord Mansfield in *Moses v Macferlan* (1760) 2 Burr 1005 at 1012.

In such a case, B Ltd may argue that A is unjustly enriched at B Ltd's expense: A received £100,000 from B Ltd as a result of B Ltd's mistaken assumption that it did not have the power to sack A without payment. However, as confirmed by the House of Lords in *Bell v Lever Brothers*,[97] on which **Example 8b** is based, A is *not* unjustly enriched at B Ltd's expense. There *is* a legal basis for A to have the benefit of the £100,000: B Ltd was under a contractual duty to pay A that money.[98]

It is important to compare **Example 6b** and **Example 8b**. In each case: (i) B transfers a right to A as part of a deal with A; and (ii) B made the deal as a result of a mistake. However, there is a crucial difference between the two cases. In **Example 6b**, in contrast to **Example 8b**, B's mistake was caused by A's misrepresentation to B. As a matter of contract law, such a mistake can prevent B coming under a contractual duty to A: unless B decides to 'affirm' the contract,[99] there is no legal basis for A to have the benefit of B's right. But, as a matter of contract law, the mistake made by B in **Example 8b** *does not* prevent B coming under a contractual duty to A. In contract law, a clear divide is made between: (i) cases where, as a result of fraud, duress, undue influence or misrepresentation,[100] A can be said to be responsible for B's mistake; and (ii) cases where B's mistake has *not* been caused by A's conduct. It seems that in the latter cases, B's mistake does *not* prevent B coming under a contractual duty to A.[101]

This analysis explains why, in considering powers to acquire a persistent right, undue influence and misrepresentation are very prominent. The point is that those factors can prevent B coming under a *contractual duty* to A. However, if B's transfer of a right to A is *not* made as part of an apparent agreement (as in **Examples 1a, 7a and 7b**) there is no reason why *other factors* (eg, B's mistake) cannot give B a persistent right against that right. This analysis thus explains the difference between **Example 1a** and **Example 8b**. In each case: (i) B transfers a right to A; and (ii) B makes the transfer as a result of a mistake. However, there is a crucial difference between the two cases. In **Example 1a**, B is *not* under a contractual duty to A to make the transfer. In **Example 8b**, *despite* his mistake, B is under a contractual duty to A to make the transfer: as a result, there *is* a legal basis for A to keep the benefit of the transferred right.

---

[97] [1932] AC 161.

[98] See Birks, *Unjust Enrichment* (2003), 122–3.

[99] As occurs where B discovers his mistake but nonetheless allows the contract to stand (see eg **3.2.2** above).

[100] If A is under a duty to provide information to B before making a contract with B (eg, as is the case where B provides insurance to A) A's failure to provide that information can: (i) prevent B coming under a contractual duty to A; and (ii) mean that there is no legal basis for A and B to have received benefits under the apparent insurance contract (see eg *Cornhill Insurance Co Ltd v L & B Assenheim* (1937) 58 Lloyds Law Reports 27 at 31). In such a case, A can again be said to be responsible for B's mistake.

[101] For example, a misrepresentation by X will not prevent B coming under a contractual duty to A (see eg *per* Sir John Romilly MR in *Pulsford v Richards* (1853) 17 Beav 87 at 95; but note the special rule applied in *Royal Bank of Scotland v Etridge (No 2)* [2002] 2 AC 773: see **E4:3.1.3**). Of course, if B's mistake means that he does not intend to transfer the specific right in question to A, then the apparent 'transfer' to A will be void and B will retain his right (see **D1:2.2.2(i)**). Of course, in such a case, the nature of B's mistake also means he is under no contractual duty to make the transfer to A: see eg *Cundy v Lindsay* (1878) 3 App Cas 459.

> **SUMMARY of D4:4.2**
>
> If B transfers a right to A as a result of: (i) A's undue influence (see **Example 6a**); or (ii) A's misrepresentation (see **Example 6b**); or (iii) a mistake (see **Example 1a, and Examples 7a and 7b**), that flaw in B's intention may mean that, when A acquires B's right, A is unjustly enriched at B's expense. However, if A is unaware of that flaw, A is *not* under the core Trust duty to B. In such a case, B acquires only a *power to acquire a persistent right*. If: (i) B informs A of the flaw in B's intention; or (ii) A discovers that flaw in a different way; and (iii) at that point, A still holds the right transferred to him by B; then (iv) B has a persistent right against that right: A holds it on Trust for B.
>
> If B makes an agreement to transfer a right to A as a result of (i) A's undue influence; or (ii) A's misrepresentation, that flaw in B's intention can mean that B is *not* under a contractual duty to transfer that right to A (see **Example 6b**). However, if the agreement is simply based on a mistake of B, for which A is *not* responsible, the agreement may still impose a contractual duty on B to transfer a right to A (see **Example 8b**). In such a case, if B makes that transfer, A is *not* unjustly enriched at B's expense: there *is* a legal basis for A to keep the benefit of the transferred right.

4.3 Resulting Trusts

4.3.1 Type 1 Resulting Trusts

> **EXAMPLE 9a**
>
> B has some shares. B transfers those shares to A, subject to a duty to hold those shares on Trust for B1, if B1 reaches the age of 25. Six months later, B1 dies aged 22.

In such a case, it is clear that, when B1 dies, B acquires a persistent right against A's right to the shares: A holds those shares on Trust for B.[102] The Trust in B's favour is known as a Resulting Trust. It has often been referred to as an 'automatic Resulting Trust',[103] but as that label may be misleading, it is best to refer to it as a 'Type 1 Resulting Trust'.[104]

A number of different explanations have been put forward as to *why*, in a case such as **Example 9a**, a Type 1 Resulting Trust arises: it has even been argued that there is *no* convincing explanation for such a Trust.[105] However, the view advocated by Chambers is the most persuasive and is consistent with the analysis taken here: the Trust arises as a result of A's unjust enrichment at B's expense.[106] It is very clear in **Example 9a** that B intended A to be under the core Trust duty: a duty not to use the shares for A's own benefit. B also intended A to be under a duty to use the shares wholly for B1's benefit; but that duty was to arise only if B1 reached the age of 25. So, in **Example 9a**, if A is free to use his shares for his own benefit, A will clearly be unjustly enriched at B's expense. To ensure that does not occur, A now owes the core Trust duty to B. In **Example 9a**, in contrast to the cases

---

[102] See eg *Vandervell v IRC* [1967] 2 AC 291 (see **F3:2.2**).

[103] The term was first used by Megarry V-C in *re Vandervell (No 2)* [1974] 1 Ch 269 at 294.

[104] In *Westdeutsche Landesbank Girozentrale v Islington LBC* [1996] AC 669, Lord Browne-Wilkinson at 708 refers to these Type 1 Resulting Trusts as '(B)' type Resulting Trusts.

[105] See Swadling (2008) 124 *LQR* 72. Swadling's conclusion at 102 is that the Type 1 Resulting Trust 'defies legal analysis.'

[106] See Chambers, *Resulting Trusts* (1997). See too Birks [1996] *RLR* 3.

examined in **4.2** above, we do *not* need to say that B has only a power to acquire a persistent right: A is aware, as soon as he acquires the shares, that he is under a duty not to use the shares for his own benefit.

Of course, in **Example 9a**, it may be that, when transferring his right to A, B intended that: (i) if B1 died before the age of 25; then (ii) A would be free to use the shares for A's own benefit. In such a case, there is no Resulting Trust in B's favour: (i) given B's intention, there *is* a legal basis for A to retain the benefit of the shares, even after B1's premature death; so (ii) A is *not* unjustly enriched if he is free to use the shares for his own benefit. This explains why it is best not to call the Type 1 Resulting Trust an 'automatic' Resulting Trust: as noted by Lord Browne-Wilkinson in *Westdeutsche Landesbank Girozentrale v Islington LBC*,[107] if A can show that B intended A to have the benefit of A's right, there will not be a Resulting Trust in B's favour.

4.3.2 Type 2 Resulting Trusts

EXAMPLE 9b

A0 is a registered owner of some land. B buys A0's right to the land. Without A's knowledge, B registers A as the new holder of A0's right to the land. B does *not* intend to make a gift of the land to A.

In such a case, a Resulting Trust is said to arise in B's favour *as soon as* A acquires his right.[108] The facts giving rise to this form of Resulting Trust seem to differ from those leading to a Type 1 Resulting Trust: B did *not* attempt to set up an immediate Trust in favour of a third party. As a result, this second type of Resulting Trust is often distinguished from the first by being labelled 'presumed' rather than 'automatic',[109] but it is best just to call it a Type 2 Resulting Trust.[110] One reason for avoiding the label 'presumed' is that there is a sharp academic debate about exactly what fact, if any, is 'presumed' in cases such as **Example 9b**.[111]

Again, there is a strong argument that, in a case such as **Example 9b**, the Resulting Trust arises as a result of A's unjust enrichment at B's expense:[112] (i) A obtains a right that B paid for (in whole or in part);[113] and (ii) there is no legal basis for A to have the full benefit of that right (eg, as B did not intend to make a gift to A).

However, there is an important difference between a Type 1 Resulting Trust and a Type 2 Resulting Trust. In the latter case, the Trust *need not* arise as soon as A acquires his right.[114]

---

107 [1996] AC 669 at 708, approving the approach taken in *re West Sussex Constabulary's Trusts* [1971] Ch 1.

108 See eg *In re Vinogradoff; Allen v Jackson* [1935] WN 68 and the other cases cited by Lord Browne-Wilkinson [1996] 2 AC 669 at 705–6.

109 The term was first used by Megarry V-C in *re Vandervell (No 2)* [1974] 1 Ch 269 at 294.

110 In *Westdeutsche Landesbank Girozentrale v Islington LBC* [1996] AC 669, Lord Browne-Wilkinson at 708 refers to these Type 2 Resulting Trusts as '(A)' type Resulting Trusts.

111 See eg Swadling (2004) 124 *LQR* 72 at 74–94.

112 See eg Chambers, *Resulting Trusts* (1997); Birks [1996] *RLR* 3.

113 So if: (i) A and B decide to buy an expensive law book together; and (ii) B gives A a £20 note; and (iii) A uses that note, plus a £20 note of his own, to buy the book; then (iv) A acquires Ownership of the book; and (v) A holds that right on Trust for both himself and B: under that Trust, each of A and B is entitled to 50 per cent of the benefit of A's right.

114 Of course, in some cases, a Type 2 Resulting Trust *can* arise immediately: in the example in the previous footnote, A is immediately aware of the facts meaning that there is no legal basis for him to have the full benefit of Ownership of the book.

For example, in **Example 9b**, we cannot say that A is under the core Trust duty *as soon as* he acquires ownership of the land: at that point, A may be unaware that he even has the right. A can only come under that duty when he has sufficient awareness of the facts meaning that there is no legal basis for him to have the benefit of his right. Until that point, B should have only a *power* to impose the core Trust duty on A: by informing A of those facts, B can impose the core Trust duty on A.

This analysis is a novel one: for example, Chambers argues that Type 2 Resulting Trusts, like their Type 1 counterparts, are: (i) based on A's unjust enrichment and B's expense; and (ii) arise immediately.[115] However, it is consistent with the analysis set out in the opening paragraphs of this section and, more importantly, with the speech of Lord Browne-Wilkinson in *Westdeutsche*.[116] There, his Lordship noted that a Trust should not arise 'unless and until [A] is aware of the factors which give rise to the supposed trust'.[117]

4.3.3 Other cases: fraud and duress

Are there other forms of Resulting Trust, in addition to the two types we have seen so far? The answer depends, of course, on how we define the term 'Resulting Trust'. The best definition, again suggested by Chambers, is that a Resulting Trust is simply *any* Trust that arises as a result of A's unjust enrichment at B's expense. This definition is a good one as it identifies the key feature shared by Type 1 and Type 2 Resulting Trusts. On that definition, the category of Resulting Trusts includes *all* the Trusts that we have seen, and will see, in this chapter. For example, we suggested that, in *Lipkin Gorman v Karpnale Ltd*,[118] C held his Ownership of the money received from B's bank on Trust for B (see **2.2.2** above): as that Trust arose as a result of C's unjust enrichment at B's expense, it is a Resulting Trust (see too **4.4.1** below).

We have also seen that: (i) if B transfers a right to A as a result of A's fraud or duress; then (ii) A holds that right on Trust for B; and (iii) that Trust arises as a result of A's unjust enrichment at B's expense (see **3.2.2** above). Therefore, the Trusts arising in those cases are also examples of Resulting Trusts.[119]

4.3.4 Other cases: B's exercise of a power to acquire a persistent right

If all Trusts arising as a result of A's unjust enrichment at B's expense count as Resulting Trusts, then we can include any Trust arising where: (i) B transfers a right to A; and (ii) because of a flaw in B's intention (eg, A's undue influence or misrepresentation; B's mistake) B has a power to acquire a persistent right against the right transferred to A (see **4.2** above); and (iii) B then exercises that power. When B exercises his power, A holds the transferred

---

[115] Chambers, *Resulting Trusts* (1997), eg 35, 184.

[116] [1996] AC 669 at 705–6. Lord Browne-Wilkinson explains decisions recognising a Resulting Trust in the following way: '[They] are explicable on the ground that, by the time action was brought, [A] or his successors in title have become aware of the facts which gave rise to a resulting trust; his conscience was affected as from the time of such discovery and thereafter he held on a resulting trust under which the property was recovered from him. There is, so far as I am aware, no authority which decides that [A] was a trustee, and therefore accountable for his deeds, at any time before he was aware of the circumstances which gave rise to a resulting trust.'

[117] [1996] 1 AC 669 at 709. See also at 705.

[118] [1991] 2 AC 548.

[119] That label was applied by Millett J in *El Ajou v Dollar Land Holdings* [1993] 3 All ER 717 at 734 when discussing a Trust arising as a result of A's fraud (the decision was reversed by the Court of Appeal on a different point: [1994] 2 All ER 685).

right on Trust for B; and that Trust, like B's power, arises as a result of the need to prevent A's unjust enrichment at B's expense.

4.3.5 Other cases: failure of basis

When looking at unjust enrichment, we can distinguish between: (i) cases of mistake; and (ii) cases of failure of basis (or, as it can also be called, failure of consideration). For example, we saw that, in **Example 1b**, the 'unjust factor' giving rise to B's unjust enrichment claim may be seen as either: (i) B's mistake—B's error about an existing state of affairs; or (ii) a failure of basis—B, as A knew, gave A a benefit in the expectation that a particular event would occur in the future; and that event did not occur.

> **EXAMPLE 10a**
>
> X1 and X2 get married. As a result, B, X1's father, makes a 'marriage settlement': he gives £10,000 to A to hold on Trust for the benefit of X1, X2 and any children they may have. Eighteen years later, on X2's application, the marriage is declared null and void. As a result, A is unsure whether he holds the Trust money: (i) for the benefit of those entitled under the marriage settlement; or (ii) for the benefit of B.

In *re Ames' Settlement*,[120] Vaisey J considered this very set of facts. His Lordship held that it was a 'simple case of money paid on a consideration which failed'.[121] B had transferred his right to the £10,000 to A on a particular basis, known to both B and A: the existence of X1 and X2's marriage. When the marriage was dissolved, that basis failed. As a result, there was no legal basis for A to retain the benefit of his right to the £10,000: A therefore held that right on Trust for B. Vaisey J thus: (i) analysed the case as depending on a failure of basis; and (ii) held that B had acquired a persistent right under a Resulting Trust. That analysis is entirely consistent with the view adopted in this section: (i) at the point when the marriage dissolved, A still had the initial right transferred by B; and (ii) as A was aware, there was no legal basis for A to keep the benefit of that right; and so (iii) A held that right on Trust for B.

The view taken here is, however, very controversial. For example, it is possible to analyse **Example 10a** in a different way. It could be said that B simply made a *mistake*: the marriage was declared to be null and so, strictly speaking, it *never* existed.[122] However, as Vaisey J noted, there may be difficulties with that view: for some purposes, a marriage is considered to have been valid in the period before the annulment.[123] And, even if that alternative analysis is correct, it is vital to note that Vaisey J was prepared to allow B to acquire a persistent right *even if* A's unjust enrichment arose as a result of a failure of basis, and not as a result of B's mistake as to an existing state of affairs.

---

[120] [1946] 1 Ch 217.

[121] *Ibid* at 223.

[122] In *Westdeutsche Landesbank Girozentrale v Islington LBC* [1996] AC 669, Lord Browne-Wilkinson at 715 refers to the analysis in *re Ames* as 'very confused': his Lordship's view is that there is a Type 1 Resulting Trust in such a case.

[123] See *per* Vaisey J at 220: 'I will say at once that the question of a marriage which is not void but voidable is not the least perplexing of the legal principles and hypotheses with which this court is concerned.'

EXAMPLE 10b

B is keen to buy A's bike, worth £200. A and B discuss a sale, but do not reach a final agreement. B pays A £50 as a 'deposit and as part payment'. B then changes his mind and decides not to go ahead with the purchase.

In such a case, provided B's payment was not made as a guarantee that B would not pull out of the planned purchase, A is unjustly enriched at B's expense: there is no legal basis for A to retain the benefit of B's £50 payment. This is confirmed by the decision of the Court of Appeal in *Chillingworth v Esche*,[124] on which **Example 10b** is based. When B transfers his right to A, he is not mistaken about an *existing state of affairs*. Nonetheless, as: (i) A and B both knew that B made the transfer on a particular basis (there would be a sale of the bike to B); and (ii) that basis then failed; then (iii) there is no legal basis for A to retain the benefit of B's right. Therefore, if A still holds that right, A must hold it on a Resulting Trust in favour of B.

B:EXAMPLE 8a

A owns a bike shop. B orders a particular model of bike from A and pays the £200 price in advance. A then goes into insolvency. A's total liabilities are £100,000; the assets available to A to meet those liabilities are worth only £50,000.

In such a case, B certainly has a personal right against A, arising as a result of A's breach of his contractual duty to give B a bike. However, that personal right may be of little use to B, given A's insolvency (see **B:4.5.1**). Further, B does not acquire a property right in any specific bike (see **D1:1.1**); and B does not acquire a persistent right against A's Ownership of any bike (see **D2:1.1.2(ii)**). Can B instead argue that: (i) as A has failed to perform his contractual duty to B, there is no legal basis for A to keep the benefit of the £200 received from B; and (ii) as a result, B has a power to acquire a persistent right against A's right to that £200?

In a case such as **B:Example 8a**, as in **Example 10b**, the key problem for B is a practical one: it is very unlikely that A will still hold the *very £200* B paid to A. After all, A's deal with B did not impose any limits on A's ability to deal with the money, and the chances are that A has spent that money on his day-to-day expenses. However, in the rare case where A does still hold that very right, it seems that A *should* hold that right on Trust for B.[125] Certainly, the courts have recognised that, as a result of A's failure to perform his contractual promise, there is no legal basis for A to retain the benefit of the £200 given to him by B.[126] This means that, even if B made a bad bargain, and could acquire the particular model of bike elsewhere for £150, B can recover *the full £200* from A.[127] It is therefore very hard to resist

---

[124] [1924] 1 Ch 97.

[125] Given the rarity of A retaining the very right transferred to him by B, there is no strong authority on this point: however, the analysis of Bingham J in *Neste Oy v Lloyds Bank plc* [1983] 2 Lloyds Rep 658 provides some support: see too *per* Lord Mustill in *re Goldcorp's Exchange* [1995] AC 74 at 104; and *per* Mann J in *re Farepak Food and Gifts Limited* [2006] EWHC 3272 at [39]–[40].

[126] A contrary argument can be made: there is a legal basis for A to retain the money paid by B *provided* A puts B in the position B would have been in if the contract had been performed (eg, if A pays B whatever it will cost for B to buy the same model of bike elsewhere): see eg McKendrick, ch 8 in *Laundering and Tracing* (ed Birks, 1995), 228–9. However, that argument has *not* been accepted by the courts.

[127] See eg *Rowland v Divall* [1923] 2 KB 500; *Benjamin's Sale of Goods* (7th edn, 2006), 17-090.

the conclusion that A's unjust enrichment, as in the other cases we have examined in this chapter, consists in his acquisition of a specific right: B's £200. As a result, in the rare case where A still has that right at the point when he breaches his contractual promise to B, A should hold that specific right on Trust for B.

This analysis of **Example 10b** and **B:Example 8a** is controversial. For example, even though Birks and Chambers adopt the unjust enrichment analysis of Resulting Trusts, each has argued that a failure of basis can *only* give rise to a Resulting Trust *if* B makes clear, when initially transferring his right to A, that A is not permitted to use that right for his own benefit.[128] On that view, a Resulting Trust *can* arise in **Example 10a**: it was clear from the start that A was not allowed to use the Trust money for his own benefit. In contrast, no Resulting Trust should arise in **Example 10b** and **B:Example 8a**: in those cases, there was no initial restriction on A's use of the right transferred to him by B.

It is hard to see the justification for this suggested limit. Once it is accepted that A is unjustly enriched at B's expense in a case such as **B:Example 8a**, it is impossible to deny that A's unjust enrichment consists in his acquisition of a *specific right* from B. The problem for B is practical, not doctrinal: in practice, it is very unlikely that A will still have the specific right transferred to him by B.[129] However, if A does still hold that right at the point when the basis of the transfer fails, A should hold that right on Resulting Trust for B.

4.3.6 A limit? *Westdeutsche Landesbank Girozentrale v Islington LBC*[130]

(i) The decision in Westdeutsche

EXAMPLE 11

A and B make an agreement that they both believe is contractually binding. Under the agreement, B pays A £2.5 million. A is then under a duty, over a 10-year period, to make regular payments to B: the level of the payments depends on interest rate movements. After two years, A has paid B £1.35 million. A and B then discover that their agreement is *not* contractually binding.

The basic facts of *Westdeutsche Landesbank Girozentrale v Islington LBC* are identical to those of **Example 11**.[131] It is clear that there is no legal basis for A to retain the £1.15 million benefit he has received at B's expense. B therefore clearly has a personal right against A. But is it also possible for B to have a persistent right against a right held by A?[132]

---

[128] Birks, *Unjust Enrichment* (2003), 166–70; Chambers, *Resulting Trusts* (1997), ch 6, 148–53. Burrows adopts a different analysis but arrives at the same conclusion in failure of basis cases: *Law of Restitution* (2nd edn, 2002), 409–11 and (2001) 117 *LQR* 412

[129] This explains why no Resulting Trust arose in: (i) *re Goldcorp's Exchange* [1995] 1 AC 74 (a case essentially similar to **B:Example 8a** where the money received by A had long since been spent when B claimed his persistent right; or (ii) *Westdeutsche Landesbank Girozentrale v Islington LBC* [1996] AC 669 (see **4.3.6** below).

[130] [1996] AC 669.

[131] A was a local authority: its agreement with B was not contractually binding as it was held that local authorities did not have the statutory power to make such agreements (see *Hazell v Hammersmith & Fulham LBC* [1992] 2 AC 1).

[132] The answer to the question will of course be crucial if A becomes insolvent. In *Westdeutsche* itself, the question arose for a different reason: A was a local authority and so there was no risk of insolvency. B claimed a Resulting Trust as, if a Trust existed, A would have to pay B the £1.15m plus *compound interest*. As the House of Lords found there was no such Trust, B had to settle for receiving £1.15m plus only simple interest. However, Lord Goff and Lord Woolf both thought that compound interest *should* be available even if B had only a personal right against A. That

On the analysis set out here, it should be *possible* for a Resulting Trust to arise in a case such as *Westdeutsche*. As soon as A acquired the £2.5 million from B, A was unjustly enriched at B's expense: because the agreement between A and B was not contractually binding, there was no legal basis for A to keep the benefit of that right.[133] At that point, A was not aware of the fact that the agreement was not contractually binding; nor could it be said that A *ought* to have been aware of the fact.[134] So, initially, B simply had a *power to acquire* a persistent right: if B had discovered the agreement was not contractually binding, it could have informed A and thus imposed the core Trust duty on A. This means there was no *immediate* Resulting Trust. Once A discovered the fact that the agreement was not contractually binding, a Resulting Trust could arise: but *only if*, at that point, A still had the initial right received from B.

In *Westdeutsche* itself, A received the £2.5 million from A in June 1987. As Lord Browne-Wilkinson noted, it is then of 'central importance'[135] to see what A did with that money.

1. The money was received by a payment into a particular bank account held by A; within a few months, that bank account was overdrawn. So, from that point, A no longer held the very right transferred by B.
2. The first point at which A might have been aware that the agreement with B was not contractually binding occurred, at the earliest, over two years after A received the payment from B.[136]

So, in *Westdeutsche*, the discovery that the agreement was not contractually binding came *too late for B*: (i) at that point, A no longer held the right transferred by B;[137] and so (ii) it was no longer possible for B to exercise its power to acquire a right under a Resulting Trust. This means that the decision in *Westdeutsche* (that A never held a right on Trust for B) is consistent with the analysis set out here. That is no surprise: the analysis is based in large part on Lord Brown-Wilkinson's statement, in *Westdeutsche*, that a Trust cannot arise 'if and

---

approach was subsequently approved by the House of Lords in *Sempra Metals Ltd v IRC* [2007] 3 WLR 354. So if a case such as *Westdeutsche* arose again today, B could receive compound interest without needing to claim a Resulting Trust.

[133] It could be argued that, if A and B fully performed their deal, then the fact that they had no contract would be irrelevant: the agreement itself could provide a basis for A to keep any benefits received from B. However, that argument is inconsistent with the reasoning of and result reached by the Court of Appeal in *Guinness Mahon & Co Ltd v Kensington and Chelsea Royal London BC* [1999] QB 215 and the House of Lords in *Kleinwort Benson Ltd v Lincoln County Council* [1999] 2 AC 349.

[134] The earliest point when A could have been aware of this point was probably when the first instance decision was made in *Hazell v Hammersmith & Fulham LBC*, holding that A had no statutory authority to make the type of agreement made between A and B: that decision came over two years after A received the £2.5m from B.

[135] [1996] AC 669 at 700.

[136] See **n 134** above.

[137] An important question arises if, at that point, A had a right that counts as the product of the right initially transferred by B: in such a case, can B assert his power to acquire a persistent right against that new right held by A? The answer seems to be 'No': to acquire a persistent right based on 'tracing' (see **4.4** below) B must have, at the start of the story, either a personal right, persistent right, or property right: a *power* to acquire such a right, by itself, does not suffice: see eg *Shalson v Russo* [2005] Ch 281 (see **n 166** below). In *Westdeutsche* itself, the point is irrelevant: there was no evidence that A held a specific right that counted as the product of the initial £2.5m received by A. Hobhouse J at first instance ([1994] 4 All ER 890 at 938–40) and the Court of Appeal ([1994] 1 WLR 938, see esp *per* Dillon LJ at 950), held that A did retain a benefit, but did not identify a *specific right* held by A that counted as the product of the £2.5m.

so long as [A] is ignorant of the facts alleged to affect his conscience' (ie, as long as A is not, nor ought to be, aware of the facts giving rise to the Trust).[138]

(ii) The limit suggested in Westdeutsche

However, in *Westdeutsche*, the House of Lords suggested a specific, stricter limit applying only to the Resulting Trust. It was said that the Type 1 and Type 2 Resulting Trusts are the *only* possible forms of Resulting Trust.[139] That suggestion, as we have seen, is unnecessary for the actual decision in *Westdeutsche*. And it is impossible to reconcile with the evidence: we have seen that a Resulting Trust can arise in many other cases (see **4.2.3, 4.2.4** and **4.2.5** above). In fact, we will see another example of a Resulting Trust, not covered by either the Type 1 or Type 2 Resulting Trust, in **4.4** below.

The limit suggested in *Westdeutsche* is impossible to maintain as it is arbitrary: it separates out two types of cases in which a Trust arises as a result of A's unjust enrichment and states that, in any other case, A's unjust enrichment *cannot* give rise to a Trust. Why did the House of Lords suggest such an unprincipled approach?

It seems that the House of Lords were keen, for two reasons, to limit the situations in which a Trust can arise as a result of A's unjust enrichment at B's expense. First, there is a desire to avoid finding a Trust in cases where A should *not* be under the core Trust duty to B.[140] For example, in *Westdeutsche*, B argued that a Resulting Trust arose *as soon as* A acquired the £2.5 million from B. However, in **Example 11** (as in **Example 1a**) it would be very odd to say that as soon as A acquires the right from B, A is under the core Trust duty to B. So, the House of Lords rightly rejected that part of B's argument. But this does not mean we have to limit the situations in which unjust enrichment can give rise to a Trust. Instead, we simply need to recognise, as we have done throughout **section 4**, that a Resulting Trust arises only if: (i) A still has the right transferred by B; and (ii) A is aware, or ought to be aware, of the facts meaning that there is no legal basis for A to have the benefit of that right.[141]

Second, if B has a persistent right under a Resulting Trust, B then has a pre-existing right that is capable of binding C, a party later acquiring a right that depends on A's right. So if: (i) in **Example 11** or **Example 1a**, A were to transfer to C the money A received from B; then (ii) it may be possible for B to impose a duty on C not to use that right for C's own benefit. The fear is that C, even though he has no means of discovering B's pre-existing power, may be affected by it.[142] The assumption is that, in such a case, the **basic tension** should be resolved in B's favour.

Again, however, we already have a means of dealing with that concern. The property law system provides protection to C against the risk of being bound by a hidden power to acquire a persistent right. That protection does *not* come through the acquisition question; instead, it comes through the **defences question**:

1. If C acquires his right *before* A is or ought to be aware of the facts meaning that there

---

[138] [1996] AC 669 at 705.

[139] See eg *per* Lord Goff at 689 and *per* Lord Browne-Wilkinson at 708.

[140] See *per* Lord Goff at 690 (specifically stating that it would be undesirable for A to be under a duty to account: a key part of the core Trust duty (see **D2:4.1.1(ii)**) and *per* Lord Browne-Wilkinson at 703.

[141] See *per* Lord Browne-Wilkinson [1996] AC 669 at 705.

[142] See eg *per* Lord Browne-Wilkinson [1996] AC 669 at 704 (considering the position, in his Lordship's own example, of the creditors of R1 and R2).

is no legal basis for A to keep the benefit of B's right, then B has only a power to acquire a persistent right. C will have a defence to B's power if C acquires A's right (or a persistent right dependent on that right) for value and without any actual or constructive notice of B's pre-existing power (see **D2:3.5.5**).

2. If C acquires his right *after* A is or ought to be aware of the facts meaning that there is no legal basis for A to keep the benefit of B's right, then B has a persistent right. C will have a defence to B's persistent right if C acquires A's right for value and without any actual or constructive notice of B's pre-existing persistent right (see **D2:3.5**).

It is true that, as Lord Browne-Wilkinson noted in *Westdeutsche*,[143] neither of these defences can protect C if C acquires his right from A *for free*. In such a case, we may have some sympathy for C; but equally we should have sympathy for B. We are confronted again by the impossible problem raised by **A:Example 1**: which of two innocent parties should prevail? There may well be no morally correct way to resolve that **basic tension**. However, the property law system provides an answer. The general position is that: (ia) if A is under a duty to B in relation to a specific right; *or* (ib) if B has a power to impose such a duty on A; and (ii) C then acquires A's right for free; then (iii) B has a power to impose a duty on C not to use that right for C's own benefit. There is no reason why the answer should be different simply because A's duty to B (or B's power to impose a duty on A) arises as a result of unjust enrichment.

It therefore seems that the limit suggested in *Westdeutsche* should be rejected. It is inconsistent with a large number of cases, and is not justified by the fears of the House of Lords. Type 1 and Type 2 Resulting Trusts exemplify a principle: (i) if A acquires a right at B's expense; and (ii) A knows or ought to know that there is no legal basis for A to have the benefit of that right; then (iii) A holds that right on Trust for B. That principle can, and does, apply in situations *not* covered by Type 1 and Type 2 Resulting Trusts.

SUMMARY of D4:4.3

In *Westdeutsche Landesbank Girozentrale v Islington LBC*,[144] the House of Lords recognised two types of Resulting Trust: Type 1 and Type 2. The persistent right B acquires in each case seems to arise as a result of A's unjust enrichment at B's expense. In fact, a Resulting Trust can be defined as a Trust arising as a result of A's unjust enrichment at B's expense. This means that the forms of Resulting Trust *must* extend beyond the two types identified in *Westdeutsche*.

In fact, *all* the Trusts discussed in this Chapter count are Resulting Trusts. Such a Trust arises *whenever*:

*   A acquires a right at B's expense; *and*
*   There is no legal basis for A to have the full benefit of that right; *and*
*   A is aware (or ought to be aware) of the facts meaning that there is no such legal basis.

---

[143] See [1996] AC 669 at 704.
[144] [1996] AC 669.

4.4   Rights against a product of B's initial right

4.4.1 Examples and overview

EXAMPLE 12a

B has Ownership of a bike. A steals B's bike. A then swaps that bike for C's car (ie, in return for giving his Ownership of the bike to C, A receives C's Ownership of the car).

Can B claim that, as soon as C gives the car to A, B has Ownership of the car? The answer is 'No'.[145]

1. B cannot rely on a dependent acquisition: C had Ownership of the car and he exercised his power to transfer his Ownership to A, not to B.
2. B cannot rely on an independent acquisition: B has not taken physical control of the car, and A, when receiving the car, does not act as B's agent.[146]

However, B *can* acquire a *persistent right*: a right against A's Ownership of the car.[147] B's persistent right depends on the fact that, by a process known as *tracing*, B can identify A's Ownership of the car as a *product* of B's initial right: B's Ownership of the bike. A is under a duty not to use his Ownership of his car for his own benefit: A therefore holds his Ownership of the car on Trust for B.

EXAMPLE 12b

A holds his Ownership of a bike on Trust for B. A then swaps that bike for C's car.

Again, B cannot claim that he has Ownership of the car. However, B *can* acquire a new *persistent right*: a right against A's Ownership of the car.[148] B's persistent right depends on the fact that B can identify A's Ownership of the car as a *product* of the right initially held by A on Trust for B: A's Ownership of the bike. And, again, as A is under a duty not to use that right for A's own benefit, A holds his Ownership of the car on Trust for B.

EXAMPLE 12c

B (a firm) has an account with Z Bank. Under the terms of the contract between B and Z Bank, any withdrawal from the account made by A (a partner of the firm) can be validly debited to B's account. A, a partner acting without the authority of the firm, withdraws £5,000 from the account. A uses the money to buy a car.

This case is essentially identical to **Example 2c** and hence to the basic facts of *Lipkin Gorman v Karpnale Ltd* (see **2.2.2** above).[149] First, B can acquire a persistent right against A's

---

[145] The analysis of L Smith, *The Law of Tracing* (1997), 320–32 reaches the same result through different reasoning. Smith points out that there is no justification for the 'expropriation' of the property right in the car acquired by A.

[146] Note that this analysis again shows that, in *Lipkin Gorman v Karpnale Ltd* [1991] 2 AC 548, Lord Templeman's view that B had Ownership of the money received by C must be wrong: Z Bank passed its Ownership of the money directly to C. However, that money was the product of B's initial personal right against Z Bank and so B *can* have a persistent right against C's Ownership of the money (see **2.2.2** above).

[147] See eg *Ryall v Ryall* (1739) 1 Atk 59; *re Kolari* (1981) 36 OR (2d) 473 (Ontario); *per* Millett J in *El Ajou v Dollar Land Holdings* [1993] 3 All ER 717 at 734.

[148] See eg *Foskett v McKeown* [2001] 1 AC 102; *re Hallett's Estate* (1880) 13 Ch D 696; *re Oatway* [1903] 2 Ch 356.

[149] [1991] 2 AC 548.

Ownership of the £5,000 that A receives from Z Bank: A's right counts as a product of B's initial personal right against Z Bank. As A is under a duty not to use that right for A's own benefit, A holds his Ownership of the money on Trust for B.[150] Second, when A uses that money to acquire Ownership of the car, B *can* acquire a new *persistent right*: a right against A's Ownership of the car. In each case, B's persistent right depends on the fact that B can identify A's right as a *product* of B Co's initial right: its personal right against Z Bank.

In each of **Examples 12a, 12b and 12c**, A makes a gain at B's expense: A acquires a right (Ownership of the car) by using B's right. And there is no legal basis for A to have the benefit of B's right. As a result, A is unjustly enriched at B's expense. As A's unjust enrichment consists in acquiring a new specific right, A holds that right on Trust for B. So, in each case, B acquires a right under a Resulting Trust.

This analysis fits with the test for a Resulting Trust set out above in the **Summary of D4:4.3**. The facts of **Examples 12a, 12b and 12c** do vary slightly from those of the cases discussed in that section: B does not transfer a right to A; instead, A acquires a right from C. Nonetheless, the general Resulting Trust principle applies: as A has acquired his right using B's right, A acquires his right *at B's expense*. The general Resulting Trust test, when applied to the particular context of **Examples 12a, 12b and 12c**, produces a specific principle. If A receives a right from C, B can acquire a persistent right against that right if:

- The right that A acquires from C counts as the product of B's right; *and*
- A knows (or ought to know) that there is no legal basis for A to keep the benefit of B's right.

4.4.2 The role of tracing

To apply the principle set out above, we need to know if A's right counts as the product of B's right. In **Examples 12a, 12b and 12c**, that test is very easy to apply: A clearly used B's right in order to acquire Ownership of the car. However, in other cases, things are more difficult.

For example, what happens if, in a case such as **Example 12c**, A: (i) withdraws £5,000 from B's account; and (ii) pays that money into his own account, currently in credit, at Z2 Bank; and (iii) then pays for the car by using money from that account at Z2 Bank. In such a case, has A still acquired Ownership of the car by using the £5,000 taken from B? Is A's Ownership of the car still the *product* of B's initial right against Z Bank; or is it instead, in whole or in part, the product of A's initial right against Z2 Bank?

The rules of *tracing* are used to solve these very difficult evidential problems. We cannot set out those rules in full here,[151] but an overview of the rules is available on the companion

---

[150] See too *Taylor v Plumer* (1815) 3 M & S 562; *Agip (Africa) Ltd v Jackson* [1991] Ch 547. In *Trustee of the Property of FC Jones & Sons v Jones* [1997] Ch 159: (i) A, without authority, received money from B's account with Z Bank; and (ii) A gave some of that money to C; and (iii) C invested that money wisely; and (iv) C then paid the money and profits into an account with Z2 Bank. The Court of Appeal held that Z2 Bank was under a direct duty to pay the money in that account to B. That cannot be right: Z2 Bank's duty must be to C, the account holder. The correct analysis is that: (i) Z2 Bank is under a duty to C; but (ii) B has a persistent right against C's right against Z2 Bank; so B can (iii) force C to withdraw the money in the account and pay it to B. This technical point was glossed over by the Court of Appeal as it made no difference to the result of the case: the point arose in an interpleader proceeding (see **D1:Example 35**): ie, Z2 Bank had already paid the money in the account into court and the court was asked who should be able to collect the money: B or C.

[151] The best account of the process, and the specific rules it entails, is given by L Smith, *The Law of Tracing* (1997).

website. The key point about tracing is that it is simply a *process*:[152] it allows one right to be identified as the product of another. So, if B can 'trace' from his initial right to the right acquired by A, B can satisfy the first part of the test set out above: B can show that A has acquired a right from C by using B's right. However, tracing, *by itself*, does not give B a persistent right.[153] B still has to pass the second part of the test set out above: he must show that A knows (or ought to know) that there is no legal basis for A to keep the benefit of B's right.

EXAMPLE 12d

B has some shares. B sells those shares to A for £800. A uses that £800 to buy a car from C.

In such a case, B can trace from his initial right to A's Ownership of the car: A has used B's initial right to acquire the car. However, B clearly does not have a persistent right against A's Ownership of the car. A, when acquiring that right, is *not* unjustly enriched at B's expense: as B sold the shares to A, there *is* a legal basis for A to have the benefit of B's initial right.

EXAMPLE 12e

The initial facts are as in **Example 12a**. However, after stealing B's bike, A then gives the bike to C as a birthday present. C does not know (nor can reasonably be expected to know) that A stole the bike from B. C then swaps the bike for C2's car.

Again, B can trace from his initial right to C's Ownership of the car. However, the case differs from **Examples 12a, 12b and 12c**. First, as A has not acquired a new right by using B's initial right, there is no point at which A is unjustly enriched at B's expense (see **section 6** below). When he acquires Ownership of the car, C *is* unjustly enriched at B's expense: C has acquired that new right by using B's Ownership of the bike. However, at that point, C does not know (nor can reasonably be expected to know) that there is no legal basis for C to have the benefit of his Ownership of the car.[154] So, the same analysis applies as in, for example, **Example 1a** and **Example 11**: as soon as C acquires Ownership of the car, B has a *power* to acquire a persistent right against C's right. However, B does not have a persistent right unless and until: (i) B exercises that power; or (ii) C discovers, from a different source, that A stole B's bike.[155]

---

[152] See esp *per* Lord Millett in *Foskett v McKeown* [2001] 1 AC 102 at 128.

[153] *Ibid per* Lord Browne-Wilkinson at 109; Lord Steyn at 113; and, especially, Lord Millett at 128.

[154] This distinction may possibly explain the different approaches taken in *Cave v Cave* (1880) 15 Ch D 639 and in re *Ffrench's Estate* (1887) 21 LR Ir 283 (Court of Appeal in Ireland). In *Cave*, A took money he held on Trust for B and used it for his own purposes: as soon as A paid that money into his joint bank account, A held that new right against his bank on Trust for B and so B acquired an immediate right under a Trust (as in **Examples 12a–12c**). In *Ffrench*, A took money he held on Trust for B2 and allowed it to be used in buying land for B1. B1 was also a beneficiary of the Trust and it may well be that A and B1 believed that their transaction was *not* a breach of the Trust. If so, it may be possible to say B1 was not immediately aware that there was no legal basis for him to have the full benefit of his right. The court's conclusion in *Ffrench* (that B2 did not have an immediate persistent right, but instead had only a power to acquire such a right) may therefore be correct. The usual view is that the two cases cannot be reconciled.

[155] There is a debate as to whether the right B acquires after tracing is: (i) an immediate persistent right (the view marginally preferred by L Smith, *The Law of Tracing* (1997), 361: see too *Cave v Cave* above; or (ii) a power to acquire such a right (the view preferred by Birks, *Unjust Enrichment* (2003), 178: see too re *Ffrench's Estate* above). The view taken here is that view (i) is correct where A knows or ought to know of the facts meaning there is no legal basis for him to have the benefit of B's right (as is usually the case); but that view (ii) is correct where A does not have that knowledge.

4.4.3 *Foskett v McKeown*[156]

The analysis set out here is a simple one: *if* B acquires a persistent right (see **Examples 12a, 12b and 12c**) or a power to acquire a persistent right (see **Example 12e**) as a result of tracing, B's right or power arises as a result of A's unjust enrichment at B's expense. That analysis is a controversial one: it has been persuasively proposed by some academics,[157] but opposed by others.[158] More importantly, the unjust enrichment analysis was firmly rejected by the House of Lords in *Foskett v McKeown*. In that case, the House of Lords supported the view that, in cases such as **Examples 12a, 12b and 12c and 12e**, B's right does *not* arise as a result of A's unjust enrichment. The first point to note is that rejection made no difference to the *result* in that case. The second point is that the rejection may be more apparent than real.

(i) The approach in Foskett v McKeown

In *Foskett v McKeown*, the House of Lords considered a case similar to **Example 12b**: (i) A held some money on Trust for B; and (ii) A used some of that money, without B's consent or other authority, to pay some of A's life insurance premiums; then (iii) when A died, the insurer paid out a lump sum to C, a trustee nominated by A to hold that lump sum on Trust for A's wife and children.[159] B argued that C held that money, at least in part, on Trust for B: the money was the product of the insurance premiums and the premiums were paid, at least in part, by the money held on Trust for B.

The first point to note is that, on the facts of *Foskett*, B faced a major problem. A did use some of the Trust money to pay some of the premiums; but, even if A had *not* made those payments, the insurance policy would *not* have lapsed: A's previous payments, by themselves, were enough to keep the policy going until the point when, as it turned out, A died. There was therefore no direct link between the premiums paid using the Trust money and the lump sum received by C. As a result, it should be impossible for B to 'trace' from the money held on Trust to that lump sum: the lump sum is simply *not* a product of B's initial right.[160] In *Foskett*, then, the question we are interested in (do persistent rights depending on tracing arise as a result of: (i) unjust enrichment; or (ii) some other reason?) should simply *not* arise.

However, it was found in *Foskett* that the lump sum payment to C *was* a product of the money initially held on Trust for B:[161] it *was* possible for B to 'trace' into the lump sum payment. So, we are then dealing with a case essentially identical to **Example 12b**. And the

---

[156] [2001] 1 AC 102.

[157] See eg Birks, ch 11 in *Laundering and Tracing* (ed Birks, 1995) and (2001) 54 *CLP* 231; L Smith, *The Law of Tracing* (1997), 303–10; Chambers, *Resulting Trusts* (1997), 116–18; Burrows (2001) 117 *LQR* 412; Tettenborn, ch 11 in *New Perspectives on Property Law, Obligations and Restitution* (ed Hudson, 2004), 230.

[158] See eg Virgo, *The Law of Restitution* (2nd edn, 2006), 572–4; Grantham and Rickett [2003] *CLJ* 717; Rickett, ch 6 in *Equity in Commercial Law* (ed Degeling and Edelman, 2005).

[159] There were in fact two trustees: A's wife and a solicitor. A's wife was not involved in the litigation. Under the terms of the Trust, A's wife was to receive 10 per cent of the policy proceeds, with the remaining 90 per cent shared between A's three children.

[160] In the Court of Appeal, Hobhouse LJ ([1998] Ch 265 at 292) noted that B could not show that B's initial right had been used to acquire any right now held by C. Along with Scott V-C in the Court of Appeal (and the minority in the House of Lords: Lord Hope and Lord Steyn), Hobhouse LJ held that B should be entitled to a Purely Equitable Charge over the policy proceeds, securing C's duty to repay the premiums taken by A from the initial Trust. However, if it is right that the policy proceeds would have been acquired even without the premiums being paid, it is very hard to justify B having *any* right against C.

[161] Lord Millett [2001] 1 AC 102 at 133–4 stated that the policy proceeds should be seen as the product of *all* the premium payments; even if the later payments were not needed to keep the policy valid.

House of Lords did find that B had a persistent right, arising under a Trust, against C's right to the lump-sum payment. Lord Millett (and Lord Browne-Wilkinson and Lord Hoffmann agreed with his Lordship on this point) explicitly rejected the unjust enrichment analysis, stating that:

> The transmission of [B's] property rights from one asset to its traceable proceeds is part of our law of property, not of the law of unjust enrichment.[162]

On that view, in a case such as **Example 12b**, B's persistent right arises because of the need to *protect B's initial property right*.[163] On the terminology used in this book, B's initial right in such a case is not a property right: it is a persistent right. However, the House of Lords naturally used the term 'property right' in its orthodox sense, covering both property rights and persistent rights (see **B:4.4**). So, the principle adopted by the House of Lords is:

- If B has property right or persistent right; *and*
- A acquires a right that can be identified as a product of B's right (ie, if A acquires a right using B's right); *then*
- A is prima facie under a duty to B to use that right for B's benefit: B thus has a right under a Trust.

(ii) Problems with the Foskett approach

The first problem with the *Foskett* approach is that it cannot explain a case such as **Example 12c**. In that case, B's initial right is *not* a property right or a persistent right: it is simply a personal right against Z Bank. Nonetheless, it is clear that, if A acquires a right that is the product of B's right, A may hold that right on Trust for B.[164] It cannot be thought that, in *Foskett*, the House of Lords intended that B should not have a claim in a case like **Example 12c**.[165] The most likely explanation is that B's initial right would be viewed, in this context, as a 'property right'. However, for the sake of clarity (and to preserve the correct definition of a property right: see **B:4.2** and **D1:1.1**), we can modify the first part of the *Foskett* principle:

- If B has *any* right (property right; persistent right; or personal right)[166] . . .

---

[162] *Ibid* at 129. See too Millett's chapters in both *Equity in Commercial Law* (ed Degeling and Edelman, 2005) and *Mapping the Law: Essays in Memory of Peter Birks* (ed Burrows and Rodger, 2006).

[163] *Ibid* per Lord Browne-Wilkinson at 109: 'If, as a result of tracing, it can be said that certain of the policy moneys are what now represent part of the assets subject to the trusts of the purchasers trust deed, then as a matter of English property law the purchasers have an absolute interest in such moneys. . . . This case does not depend on whether it is fair, just and reasonable to give the purchasers an interest as a result of which the court in its discretion provides a remedy. It is a case of hard-nosed property rights'; *per* Lord Millett at 129: 'the plaintiffs seek to vindicate their property rights, not to reverse unjust enrichment'.

[164] See eg *Agip (Africa) Ltd v Jackson* [1991] Ch 547; *Trustee of the Property of FC Jones & Sons v Jones* [1997] Ch 159; and, on the analysis taken in this Chapter, *Lipkin Gorman v Karpnale Ltd* [1991] 2 AC 548.

[165] In fact, Lord Millett (as Millett LJ) allowed such a claim in *Trustee of the Property of FC Jones & Sons v Jones* [1997] Ch 159.

[166] But note that the principle does *not* seem to apply where B initially has only a *power* to acquire a persistent right. So if: (i) B pays two £50 notes to A by mistake; and (ii) A is unaware of that mistake and uses the notes to buy a bike; then (iii) B does *not* have a power to acquire a persistent right against A's Ownership of the bike (see eg Worthington [2002] 10 *RLR* 28 at 59–60; *Shalson v Russo* [2005] Ch 281). O'Sullivan et al, *The Law of Rescission* (2008), 16.40 takes a different view and relies in part on a statement of Millett LJ in *Bristol & West Building Society v Mothew* [1998] Ch 1 at 22–3. However, Millett LJ referred in turn to his own judgment in *El Ajou v Dollar Land Holdings plc* [1993] 3 All ER 717 at 734: in that case, as a result of A's fraud, B acquired an immediate persistent right and so the 'tracing' principles could apply.

The second problem with the *Foskett* approach is that it cannot explain a case such as **Example 12e**. In such a case, it seems B should not have an *immediate* right under a Trust: such a right can arise only when C knows (or ought to know) that his right is the product of B's initial right. After all, in *Westdeutsche Landesbank Girozentrale v Islington LBC*,[167] Lord Browne-Wilkinson made clear that C cannot be under the core Trust duty if he is entirely innocent of the facts giving rise to that duty. It is unlikely that, in *Foskett*, the House of Lords intended to take a different view.[168] So, for the sake of clarity, we can modify the *Foskett* principle by inserting an extra requirement:

- If B has *any* right (property right; persistent right; or personal right); *and*
- A acquires a right that can be identified as a product of B's right; *and*
- A is (or ought to be aware) of the fact that his right is a product of B's right; *then* . . .

The third problem with the *Foskett* approach is a lack of clarity: in the final part of the principle, what does 'prima facie' mean? Clearly, such a qualification is necessary: as shown by **Example 12d**, it cannot be the case that B acquires a right under a Trust *whenever* A holds a right that can be identified as a product of B's initial right. In **Example 12d**, no Trust arises because there is a legal basis for A to have the benefit of B's initial right. We can therefore modify the *Foskett* principle by spelling out that B does *not* acquire a right under a Trust if there is a legal basis for A to have the benefit of B's right.

Putting all those modifications together, the *Foskett* principle reads as follows:

- If B has *any* right (property right, persistent right or personal right); *and*
- A acquires a right that can be identified as a product of B's right; *and*
- A is (or ought to be aware) of the facts meaning that there is no legal basis for A to have the benefit of B's right; *then*
- B has a right under a Trust of A's right.

By this point, the requirements of the *Foskett* principle are *identical* to the principle set out in **4.4.1** above. The only difference between the two formulations relates to their justification. The principle as set out in **4.4.1** is easy to justify: it is simply an application of the wider Resulting Trusts principle discussed in **4.3**—B acquires a persistent right as A's unjust enrichment at B's expense consists precisely of A acquiring a specific right. In *Foskett*, the House of Lords resisted that view: the alternative justification suggested in that case is that B acquires his persistent right *as a consequence* of B's initial right. Of course, that is partly true; but, by itself, it is not very convincing.

First, it states a conclusion, not an explanation: it does not tell us *why*, if B has an initial right, he can also acquire a persistent right against a product of that right.[169] Second, that conclusion may seem obvious in a case like *Foskett* (or **Example 12b**) where B has a persistent right at the start *and* end of the story. However, it is important to note that B does not have the *same* persistent right throughout: in *Foskett*, B's initial right was a right against money held by A; at the end, B's right was against C's right to the lump-sum payment. Moreover, in cases such as **Example 12a** (where B starts with a property right and ends with

---

[167] [1996] AC 669 at 705.

[168] After all, Lord Browne-Wilkinson was also one of the majority in *Foskett*. On the facts of *Foskett*, the question did not arise: it seems B made his claim when C still held the lump sum payment.

[169] A point made by eg Birks, *Unjust Enrichment* (2003), 31–2, 178.

a persistent right) or **Example 12c** (where B starts with a personal right and ends with a persistent right) it is hard to see B's final right as simply a necessary consequence of B's initial right.

So, the apparent conflict between the analysis set out here and the approach in *Foskett* may not, after all, be genuine. Under each approach, the *test* for whether B acquires a persistent right is the same. The analysis set out here has a vital advantage: it explains *why*, if that test is satisfied, B acquires a persistent right. This means we have to ask the same question we asked in **4.3.6(ii)** above, when examining the *Westdeutsche* decision: why did the House of Lords reject the unjust enrichment analysis?

(iii) Problems with the unjust enrichment analysis?

EXAMPLE 13a

A holds some money on Trust for B. A gives £100 of that money, without B's consent or other authority, to C as a birthday present. C uses that money to buy a painting. The painting is now worth £400.

In such a case: (i) C's Ownership of the painting is a product of the right initially held by A on Trust for B; and (ii) there is no legal basis for C to have the benefit of that right; so (iii) B has a power to impose the core Trust duty on C: C can be forced to transfer his Ownership of the painting (or at least £400, ie, the value of the painting) to T to hold on Trust for B.[170] As the majority of the House of Lords emphasised in *Foskett*, it is not possible for C to retain the benefit of his Ownership of the painting by simply paying £100.[171] However, there seems to be a fear that, *if* B's persistent right were seen to arise from unjust enrichment, a court *would* then be limited to ordering C to pay £100.

That concern is misguided: on the unjust enrichment analysis, as set out here, it is *still* the case that, in **Example 13a**, B can acquire the *full benefit* of C's Ownership of the painting. It does not matter that C's right is worth more than the £100 taken by A and given to C. The point is that C's unjust enrichment at B's expense consists precisely in C's acquisition of Ownership of the painting; as a result, C can come under a duty to B not to use that right for C's own benefit. So, in **Example 13a**, the unjust enrichment analysis does *not* prevent the result desired by the majority of the House of Lords.

EXAMPLE 13b

A holds some money on Trust for B. Without B's consent or other authority, A uses £100 of that money to buy a painting. A then gives the painting to C as a birthday present. The painting is now worth £400. To celebrate his acquisition of the painting, C spends £400 on going out for dinner.

In such a case: (i) C's Ownership of the painting is a product of the right initially held by A on Trust for B; and (ii) there is no legal basis for C to have the benefit of that right; so (iii) B has a power to impose the core Trust duty on C. As Lord Millett emphasised in *Foskett*,[172] it

---

[170] If, at the start of the story, A held the money on Trust entirely for B's benefit, B can exercise his power to demand that C transfers his Ownership of the painting to B (see **D1:1.4.5(ii)**).
[171] See eg [2001] 1 AC 102 *per* Lord Browne-Wilkinson at 109–10; *per* Lord Millett at 135.
[172] *Ibid* at 129.

is *not* possible for C to use the change of position defence: B can still acquire a right under a Trust *even though* C spent £400 in the honest and reasonable belief that there was a legal basis for C to have the benefit of the painting. If B's claim against C is directly based on C's unjust enrichment at B's expense, C *can* use that defence (see **1.2** above). So, Lord Millett may have feared that: (i) *if* the unjust enrichment analysis is adopted; then (ii) in a case such as **Example 13b**, C *would* be able to use the change of position defence to prevent B acquiring a right under a Trust.

Again, that concern is misguided: on the unjust enrichment analysis, as set out here, it is *still* the case that, in **Example 13b**, B can acquire the *full benefit* of C's Ownership of the painting. It does not matter that C changed his position in the belief that he was entitled to use his Ownership of the painting for his own benefit. The point is that: (i) *as soon as* A acquired Ownership of the painting, A held that right on Trust for B (see **Example 12b**); and (ii) once B has a persistent right, it does not matter *how* that right arose: the same defences apply against *all* persistent rights (see **D2:3.7**). So, B's persistent right is vulnerable, for example, to the 'bona fide purchaser' defence (in **Example 13b**, C cannot use that defence: he acquired Ownership of the painting for free). However, B's persistent right is *not* vulnerable to the change of position defence: persistent rights are not vulnerable to that defence (see **section 5** below). So, in **Example 13b**, the unjust enrichment analysis does *not* prevent the result desired by Lord Millett: (i) if B acquires a persistent right as a result of A's unjust enrichment; then (ii) when B asserts that right against C, C *cannot* rely on the change of position defence.

The third concern is not expressed in *Foskett v McKeown*, but it does play an important part in Virgo's analysis—which was essentially adopted in *Foskett*.[173] The point is that: (i) if B has a pre-existing persistent right; then (ii) B cannot assert that right against A or C by using the law of unjust enrichment. That point is certainly correct (see **section 6** below). However, it does *not* prevent us adopting the unjust enrichment analysis. In the cases we are examining here, B is *not* relying on unjust enrichment to assert a *pre-existing* persistent right; instead, B relies on unjust enrichment to show he has acquired a *new* persistent right. This is clear in **Examples 12a and 12c**: there, at the start of the story, B does *not* have a persistent right; rather, B relies on A's unjust enrichment to acquire such a right. Once B has that right, B can then assert it directly (see **D2:4.1.1**): so, even though B *acquires* his new persistent right as a result of A's unjust enrichment, B does not need to rely on unjust enrichment when *asserting* that right. The same analysis applies in **Example 12b**—there, at the start, B has a persistent right: a right against A's money. At the end, B acquires a *new* persistent right: a right against A's Ownership of the car. So, again, B relies on unjust enrichment to acquire a new persistent right; not to assert his initial persistent right.

SUMMARY of D4:4.4

Starting with the formulation of the House of Lords in *Foskett v McKeown*, and refining that principle to deal with some obvious problems, we reach the position that:

- If B has *any* right (property right, persistent right or personal right); *and*
- A acquires a right that can be identified (by tracing) as a product of B's right; *then*

---

[173] Virgo, *Principles of the Law of Restitution* (2nd edn, 2006), ch 20, esp 570–74.

- If A is aware (or ought to be aware) that there is no legal basis for A to have the benefit of that right; *then*
- To the extent that A's right is a product of B's right, A is under a duty to B not to use that right for A's own benefit: A thus holds the right on Trust for B.

In such a case, the best explanation for A's duty to B is that it arises to prevent A being unjustly enriched at B's expense. The House of Lords rejected that view in *Foskett*. In doing so, it had valid concerns; but those concerns can be met even if the unjust enrichment analysis is accepted. First, recognising that B's new persistent right arises as a result of unjust enrichment does *not* prevent B benefiting from an increase in value of the new right held by A or C. Second, once B has that new persistent right, even if it arises as a result of unjust enrichment, neither A nor C can use the change of position defence against B's right. Third, allowing B to acquire a *new* persistent right as a result of A's unjust enrichment does not conflict with the principle that B cannot use the law of unjust enrichment to assert a *pre-existing* property right or persistent right. The analysis set out here thus leads to the same results, in practice, as the *Foskett* approach. And it has a crucial advantage: it explains *why* B acquires a new persistent right.

4.5   Persistent rights against B1's Ownership of a newly acquired thing?

4.5.1 Manufacture, mixing and birth

D1:EXAMPLE 10

B1 has Ownership of some eggs and flour. B2 has Ownership of some milk, butter, sugar and baking powder. B1 uses these ingredients to make a cake.

In such a case, B1 acquires Ownership of the newly created thing: the cake (see **D1:2.1.2(i)**). If B1 has used B2's ingredients without B2's consent, there is no legal basis for B1 to have the benefit of those ingredients: B1 would thus be unjustly enriched if he could use his Ownership of the cake entirely for his own benefit. As a result: (i) if B1 is aware (or ought to be aware) of the fact that B2 has not consented to B1's use of the ingredients; then (ii) B1 should be under a duty to B2 not to use the cake entirely for B1's own benefit: ie, B1 should hold his Ownership of the cake on Resulting Trust for B2.

Such a result would: (i) protect B2 by ensuring that B2 has a right that is capable of binding a third party later acquiring Ownership from B1; and (ii) give such a third party the chance to use the 'bona fide purchaser' defence against B2's hidden persistent right. More importantly, it is also consistent with the principle allowing B2 to acquire a persistent right against a right that counts as a product of B2's initial right (see **4.4.1** above).

Exactly the same analysis can apply where B1, without B2's consent or other authority, uses B2's right to acquire a new property right through mixing (see **D1:Example 11**) or birth (**D1:Example 12**). In these cases: (i) B1 is unjustly enriched at B2's expense; and (ii) B1's unjust enrichment consists precisely of B1's acquisition of a new, specific right. As a result, the general Resulting Trust principle discussed in **4.3** must apply. The only difference is the particular context in which the principle applies:

- The principle can apply where A acquires a new, specific right *from B* (see **4.2** and **4.3** above); *and*

- It can also apply where A acquires a new, specific right *from C* by using B's right (see **4.4** above); *and*
- It can also apply where A acquires a new, specific right through an independent acquisition that involves using B's right (see **4.5.1**).

4.5.2 Combinations without mixing or manufacture

D1:EXAMPLE 13

B1 has Ownership of a bike; B2 has Ownership of a pot of paint. B1 uses B2's paint to paint his bike.

In such a case, B2 loses his property right: the thing he formerly owned (the paint) no longer exists as a distinct physical thing (see **D1:2.1.2(iv)**). If: (i) B1 uses B2's paint without B2's consent or other authority; and (ii) B1 increases the value of his bike by painting it; then (iii) B1 is unjustly enriched at B2's expense. B1's unjust enrichment does *not* consist of acquiring a new, specific right; instead, B1's unjust enrichment consists of the *increased value of a right B1 already held*. In this way, there is a link between **D1:Example 13** and the subrogation cases examined in **4.1** above (see eg **Example 5b**). So, in each case, B2's persistent right should not arise under a Trust; instead, it should arise by means of a Purely Equitable Charge.[174] This means that, in **D1:Example 13**, B1 is under a duty to hold his Ownership of the bike as security for his duty to pay B2 money equal to the increased value of the bike.[175]

SUMMARY of D4:4

There is much controversy about the questions of whether and, if so, when B can acquire a persistent right as a result of A's unjust enrichment at B's expense. For example, in both *Westdeutsche Landesbank Girozentrale v Islington LBC*[176] and *Foskett v McKeown*,[177] the House of Lords attempted to limit the ability of unjust enrichment to give rise to a persistent right. Nonetheless, there is an overwhelming weight of evidence in favour of the proposition that B *can* acquire a persistent right as a result of A's unjust enrichment. In fact, the key impact of unjust enrichment on the property law system is its ability to give rise to persistent rights.

First, A's unjust enrichment at B's expense gives B a right under a Trust if:

- A has acquired a right directly from B (see **4.2** and **4.3** above) *or* A has acquired a right from C by using B's right (see **4.4** and **4.5.1** above); *and*
- There is no legal basis for A to have the benefit of that right; *and*
- A is aware (or ought to be aware) of the facts meaning that there is no legal basis for A to have the benefit of that right.

Second, A's unjust enrichment at B's expense gives B a Purely Equitable Charge if:

---

[174] As this Purely Equitable Charge does not arise as a result of B1's consent, it would generally be referred to as an 'Equitable Lien' (see **D2:1.2.1**).
[175] Compare eg *Greenwood v Bennett* [1973] QB 195 (see **D1:Example 35**).
[176] [1996] AC 669 at 714–5.
[177] [2001] 1 AC 102.

- A holds a right; *and*
- At B's expense, the value of A's right is increased (see **4.1** and **4.5.2** above); *and*
- There is no legal basis for A to have that benefit; *and*
- A is aware (or ought to be aware) of the facts, meaning that there is no legal basis for A to have that benefit.

5   PROPERTY RIGHTS AND PERSISTENT RIGHTS: THE DEFENCES QUESTION

If B asserts a direct right against C, based on C's unjust enrichment at B's expense, C may be able to rely on an important defence: the change of position defence (see **1.2** above). This raises an important question: if (i) B instead asserts a *pre-existing* property right or persistent right against C; and (ii) B acquired that pre-existing right by relying on the law of unjust enrichment; then (iii) can C use the change of position defence against B's pre-existing right?

5.1   Where C's change of position occurs *after* B has acquired a property right or persistent right

EXAMPLE 14a

B has Ownership of a bike. A steals the bike and gives it to C (who is not aware of the theft) as a birthday present. C had saved up £150 towards buying a bike. C now spends that money on an extravagant meal.

EXAMPLE 14b

A holds his Ownership of a bike on Trust for B. In breach of Trust, A gives that bike to C (who is not aware of the breach of Trust) as a birthday present. C had saved up £150 towards buying a bike. C now spends that money on an extravagant meal.

In each case, C *cannot* rely on the change of position defence.[178] First, B does not assert a direct right against C, arising as a result of C's unjust enrichment at B's expense. Instead, B simply asserts his pre-existing right against C. Second, the change of position defence is *not* one of the defences available against a pre-existing property right (see **D1:3**) or a pre-existing persistent right (see **D2:3**).

EXAMPLE 13b

A holds some money on Trust for B. Without B's consent or other authority, A uses £100 of that money to buy a painting. A then gives the painting to C as a birthday present. The painting is now worth £400. To celebrate his acquisition of the painting, C spends £400 on going out for dinner.

In such a case, B has a persistent right against A's Ownership of the painting; and B's right arises as a result of A's unjust enrichment at B's expense (see **4.4** above). Nonetheless, as we

---

[178] See eg *Foskett v McKeown* [2001] 1 AC 102.

have seen, C *cannot* rely on the change of position defence.[179] First, B's claim is not based on C's unjust enrichment; instead, B's persistent right arose as a result of A's unjust enrichment. Second, *once* B has a persistent right, the defences available against that right are the same, *however* that right arose (see **D2:3.7**). Therefore, C can rely only on the general defences against a pre-existing persistent right; and, as we have seen, the change of position defence is *not* on the list of such defences.

5.2   Where C's change of position occurs *before* B has acquired a property right or persistent right

EXAMPLE 15a

B has Ownership of a bike worth £200. As a result of a mistake, unknown to A, B transfers his Ownership of the bike, for free, to A. A had saved up £150 towards buying a bike. A now spends that money on an extravagant meal.

EXAMPLE 15b

B has Ownership of a bike. As a result of a mistake, unknown to A, B transfers his Ownership of the bike, for free, to A. A then gives that bike to C as a birthday present. C had saved up £150 towards buying a bike. C now spends that money on an extravagant meal.

Example 15a is very similar to **Example 1a**. If B asserts a direct right against A, arising as a result of A's unjust enrichment at B's expense, A will be able to rely on the change of position defence. In **Example 15a**, B also has a power to acquire a persistent right: as A still has Ownership of the bike, B can impose a duty on A to hold that right on Trust for B (see **4.2.2** above). However, B cannot use that power to avoid the effect of the change of position defence; after all, B's power arises *because* of A's unjust enrichment and so must also be subject to the defence. This means that, in **Example 15a**, B *can* acquire a persistent right against A's Ownership of the bike; *but* only if B pays A £150 to ensure that A, as well as B, is restored to the position he was in before B gave the bike to A.[180]

The same analysis must apply in **Example 15b**. It seems that it is possible for B to assert his power to acquire a persistent right against C. However, that power must remain subject to the change of position defence. So, in **Example 15b**, if B *can* acquire a persistent right against C's Ownership of the bike, B should be able to do so only on the basis that he pays C £150.[181] That result is *not* inconsistent with **Example 13b**: in **Example 13b**, B asserts a

---

[179] See eg *per* Lord Millett in *Foskett v McKeown* [2001] 1 AC 102 at 129.

[180] *Cheese v Thomas* [1994] 1 WLR 129 provides an example of B's power to 'rescind' a transfer being affected by the need to prevent an innocent A from suffering a loss. As Chen-Wishart has noted, the case seems, in effect, to allow A to use the change of position defence: see (1994) 110 *LQR* 173. Certainly, Nicholls V-C emphasised at 136 the need to achieve 'practical justice for both parties' by restoring each of them, as near as possible, to his original position (see too *per* Lord Blackburn in *Erlanger v New Sombrero Phosphate Co* (1878) 3 App Cas 1218 at 1278–9). In *MacKenzie v Royal Bank of Canada* [1934] AC 468 at 476, Lord Atkin suggested that A's subsequent reliance does not 'preclude relief': that is correct but should not rule out the possibility of B's relief being conditional on ensuring that A does not suffer a loss as a result of his change of position: see eg Jones, *Goff & Jones' Law of Restitution* (7th edn, 2007), 40-007; Chen-Wishart (2000) 20 *OJLS* 557 at 572–6 for further analysis of *MacKenzie*.

[181] Worthington [2002] *RLR* 28 at 57–8 argues that C should be able to use the change of position defence, but that the defence, whether used by A or C, is available only in limited cases. However, the courts' reasonably wide discretion to impose conditions on B's exercise of his power contradicts the suggestion that the change of position defence applies only in limited cases: see eg *per* Lord Cottenham LC in *Sturgis v Champneys* (1839) 5 My & Cr 97 at 102.

pre-existing persistent right against C; in **Example 15b**, B attempts to assert a *power* to acquire such a right.

6   PROPERTY RIGHTS: THE REMEDIES QUESTION

6.1   The protection of property rights

EXAMPLE 16

B has Ownership of two £50 notes. B loses those notes. They are found by C.

It has been argued that, in such a case, B can use the law of unjust enrichment to assert his pre-existing property right against C.[182] For example, in *Holiday v Sigil*,[183] the essential facts were identical to **Example 16**. B asserted his right by bringing an action 'for money had and received': the court upheld B's claim and ordered A to pay B £100. B's claim in this case has been analysed as depending on C being unjustly enriched at B's expense.[184]

However, there are problems with that analysis, and it is hotly disputed.[185] The fact that B brought an action 'for money had and received' tells us very little: sometimes, that action is used where B's right arises as a result of C's unjust enrichment; however, it can also be used where C wrongfully takes control of money belonging to B.[186] The central problem with the unjust enrichment analysis is that, as B has retained his Ownership of the note, it is hard to see how C is enriched at B's expense.[187] C does acquire a property right by taking physical control of the note; but C acquires that right independently, not as a result of a transfer from B (see **D1:2.1**). It has been argued that, in order to bring an unjust enrichment claim against C, B could choose to forfeit his property right.[188] However, even if it is possible simply to 'waive' a property right in that way, such a waiver would not transfer any right from B to C; and even if it did, C's enrichment would not be unjust as it would come from B having *chosen* to give up his property right.

An argument in favour of the unjust enrichment analysis runs as follows. If B gives C two £50 notes, in the mistaken belief that he owes C £100, B *can* bring an unjust enrichment claim against C (see **Example 1a**).[189] The case for giving B such a claim seems even stronger in **Example 16**: rather than having an impaired intention to give C the note, B has *no*

---

[182] See eg Birks (1997) 11 *TLI* 2 esp 7–8: 'if I receive money from you but the money remains yours, technically I am no better off, but factually and realistically I am now in control of the buying power represented by the money'. See too Burrows, *The Law of Restitution* (2nd edn, 2002), 185–6.

[183] (1826) 2 C & P 176. B lost a £500 note.

[184] See eg Birks, *Unjust Enrichment* (2003), 53–60, 62.

[185] For alternative views, see eg Virgo, *Principles of the Law of Restitution* (2nd edn, 2006), ch 20; Swadling in *The Limits of Restitutionary Claims: A Comaprative Analysis* (ed Swadling, 1997).

[186] For example, in *Moffatt v Kazana* [1969] 2 QB 152 (see **D1:Example 9**), the precise nature of B's action is not reported: B is said simply to have brought an 'action for the recovery of his money from the defendant'. On the analysis taken in this book, B's claim was based on C's commission of the wrong of conversion.

[187] As noted by Tettenborn, ch 11 in *New Perspectives on Property Law, Obligations and Restitution* (ed Hudson, 2004).

[188] Birks, *Unjust Enrichment* (2003), 56: '[B]'s election to assert that [C] has been unjustly enriched at his expense supposes a renunciation of his title.'

[189] See eg *Kelly v Solari* (1841) 9 M & W 54.

intention to do so.[190] However, the analogy to the mistaken payment case is flawed. In a case such as **Example 1a**, despite the mistake, B does intend to transfer his Ownership of the note to C: as a result, C *does* acquire B's Ownership of the note (see **D1:2.2.2**). C is thus enriched at B's expense as C acquires a right from B. In **Example 16**, by contrast, B does *not* transfer his Ownership of the note to C. As a result, C is not enriched at B's expense.

In a case such as *Holiday v Sigil*, it is therefore far simpler to see B's claim as depending on C's commission of a wrong: property rights in money, like all property rights, are protected through the law of wrongs (see **D1:4.1.1**). So, in **Example 16**: (i) C has no defence to B's pre-existing property right; and thus (ii) by taking the notes, C breaches his duty not to interfere with B's right to exclusive control of the notes; hence (iii) C commits a wrong against B: the wrong of conversion (see **D1:4.1.1**). Crucially, the law of wrongs *fully* protects B's pre-existing property right: there is simply no need for B to have the option of an unjust enrichment claim.[191]

It is true that, in the past, the law of wrongs did *not* always provide full protection for B's property right. For example, certain claims, based on C's commission of a wrong, were said to expire on C's death.[192] So, if C interfered with B's property right and then died, B might then have to find an alternative means of asserting his property right.[193] As a result, there are some judicial statements and decisions that support the availability of an unjust enrichment claim as a means for B to assert his property right.[194] However, nowadays, no useful purpose can be served by such approach: B can now bring a claim based on C's commission of a wrong, even after C's death.[195]

It is important to note that this analysis does not mean that the law of unjust enrichment is entirely irrelevant if, at the start of the story, B has a property right. **Example 12a**, as well as **D1:Examples 10–13**, show that: (i) if B has a property right; and (ii) C acquires a new right that is a product of B's property right; then (iii) B may acquire a persistent right against C's new right, as a result of C's unjust enrichment at B's expense. The crucial point in all these examples is that, in contrast to a case such as **Example 16**: (i) C has acquired a *new right*; and (ii) as that new right counts as a product of B's pre-existing property right, C has acquired that right *at B's expense*. In such a case, B may be able to acquire a persistent right against C's new right, arising as a result of C's unjust enrichment at B's expense. However, that rule is not peculiar to property rights: it can also apply if the right acquired

---

[190] This argument is made by eg Burrows, *The Law of Restitution* (2nd edn, 2002), 182–5. See too Burrows, McKendrick and Edelman, *Cases and Materials on the Law of Restitution* (2nd edn, 2007), 202.

[191] For example, in *Hambly v Trott* (1776) 1 Cowp 371 at 376, Lord Mansfield notes that, if C takes B's horse and uses it without B's consent, C can be ordered to pay B money for the 'use and hire of the horse'. There is no need to see B's ability to claim that money as based on C's unjust enrichment: it can instead be seen to serve as a substitute for the right C interfered with: compare the analysis of *Strand Electric Engineering Co Ltd v Brisford Entertainment Ltd* [1952] 2 QB 246 in **D1:4.3.3**.

[192] In more recent times, B has been permitted to bring a claim based on C's wrong: but only for a very short period after C's death. In *Chesworth v Farrar* [1967] 1 QB 407, C had died after selling B's thing without B's consent. Edmund Davies J, in effect, allowed B to circumvent the short limitation period by analysing B's claim as based on C's unjust enrichment rather than C's wrong. However, the reasoning is very confused: at 417 his Lordship admits that, to bring a claim, B *must* show that C has committed a wrong.

[193] For some of the problems resulting from this rule, see eg *Phillips v Homfray* (1883) 24 Ch D 439, the background to which is considered by Swadling in *The Search for Principle* (ed Swadling and Jones, 1999).

[194] For a famous example, see *per* Lord Mansfield in *Hambly v Trott* (1776) 1 Cowp 371 at 375–7.

[195] See Law Reform (Miscellaneous Provisions) Act 1934, s 1.

by C is a product of B's initial persistent right (see **Example 12b**) or personal right (see **Example 12c**).

7 PERSISTENT RIGHTS: THE REMEDIES QUESTION

7.1 The protection of persistent rights

> **D2:EXAMPLE 24a**
>
> A holds his Ownership of a bike on Trust entirely for B. In breach of his duties as trustee, A transfers that right, for free, to C. C has no actual or constructive notice of B's pre-existing persistent right. Believing the bike is his to use as he pleases, C sells the bike to C2 for £200 (C2 also has no actual no actual or constructive notice of B's initial right under the Trust). C then spends the money on a holiday.

Let us say that C had booked the holiday even before he received the bike from A. So, by spending the money on the holiday, C has *not* changed his position: he is still £200 to the good because he has saved the money he would otherwise have spent on the holiday. Can B then argue that C, by making that saving, has been unjustly enriched at B's expense?

A number of prominent commentators have argued that, in such a case, C *is* unjustly enriched at B's expense.[196] There are usually two strands to that argument: (i) if C interferes with B's pre-existing property right, C is unjustly enriched at B's expense; and so (ii) it must also be possible for C to be unjustly enriched by interfering with B's pre-existing 'Equitable property right' (ie, with B's pre-existing persistent right). Of course, there are two problems with that argument. First, it is *not* true to say that C is unjustly enriched at B's expense when C interferes with B's pre-existing property right (see **section 6** above). Second, *even* if that were true, there is no reason why property rights and persistent rights should be protected in exactly the same way.[197]

More importantly, the courts have consistently[198] rejected the argument that, in a case such as **D2:Example 24a**, C is unjustly enriched at B's expense.[199] The point is that, in such

---

[196] See eg Birks, ch 7 in *Breach of Trust* (ed Birks and Pretto, 2002); Nicholls in *Restitution, Past, Present and Future* (ed Cornish et al, 1998), 231ff; Burrows, *The Law of Restitution* (2nd edn, 2002), 194ff.

[197] See L Smith (2000) 116 *LQR* 412.

[198] It is often said that the difficult case of *re Diplock* [1948] Ch 465, affirmed under the name of *Ministry of Health v Simpson* [1951] AC 251, is an exception. However, in that case, B did *not* have a persistent right. Rather, A was an executor who breached his statutory duty to transfer various rights of the deceased to B, transferring them to C instead. B was allowed to bring a claim against C even though C, during the period in which it held those rights and their product, was not aware of B's claim. That claim was subject to important restrictions: eg, B first had to sue A and could only sue C if, due to A's bankruptcy, he could not recover fully from A. The decision can perhaps be justified on the basis that B had a direct right against C: C was unjustly enriched at B's expense as it had acquired a right that A was under a duty to transfer to B. So, if A owes B £100 and, intending to pay B, gives a £100 note to C by mistake, it may be possible to argue that *B* has a direct right against C as C is unjustly enriched at B's expense. This depends on the contested question of whether such an 'interceptive subtraction' can allow us to say that C's enrichment is at B's expense rather than A's expense: for differing views, see eg Birks, *Unjust Enrichment* (2005), 75–7 and L Smith (1991) 4 *OJLS* 480. Clearly then, as noted by L Smith (2000) 116 *LQR* 412, *re Diplock* does not stand for the idea that if B has a pre-existing persistent right and A simply transfers that right, without authority, to C, C will always be unjustly enriched at B's expense.

[199] See eg *re Montagu's Settlement Trusts* [1987] Ch 264. See too *Farah v Say-Dee* [2007] HCA 22 at [130]–[158] where the High Court of Australia *explicitly* considers, and rejects, the unjust enrichment analysis.

a case, C acquires his right from A: not from B. So any gain made by C is at the expense of A, not of B (see **2.2** above). The unjust enrichment analysis seems to depend on the view that, in a case such as **D2:Example 24a**, A has transferred B's 'property' to C.[200] However, in such a case, C has *not* acquired B's 'property': rather C has acquired a right that was held by A.

Of course, in a case such as **D2:Example 24a**, it may be possible for B to bring a claim against C. If B can show there was a point at which: (i) C held the right transferred to him by A (Ownership of the bike); and (ii) C knew (or ought to have known) that A had transferred that right to C in breach of Trust; then (iii) at that point, C holds the right on Trust for B and so has a duty to account to B for that right (see **D2:Example 24b**). Once C has such a duty to account, B can enforce it by demanding that C produce the right held on Trust. If, C cannot do so, C must then pay money equal to the value of that right so that a new Trust can be established in B's favour. In such a case, B's claim depends on C's 'knowing receipt'—or, more accurately, C's 'knowing holding'—of the right held on Trust for B (see **D2:4.1.1(ii)**). Crucially, B's claim therefore depends on showing that C *knew or ought to have known* about A's breach of Trust.[201]

In contrast, if C *were* unjustly enriched at B's expense in a case such as **D2:Example 24a**, C's knowledge would be irrelevant: B would have a personal right against C, arising as a result of C's unjust enrichment, *even if* C had no idea about B's pre-existing persistent right.[202] The courts' insistence on the relevance of C's knowledge clearly demonstrates that C is *not* unjustly enriched at B's expense simply as a result of receiving a right against which B has a persistent right.[203]

In a case such as **D2:Example 24a**, it may be argued that the property law system gives insufficient protection to B's pre-existing persistent right. For example, if B has a pre-existing *property right* to which C has no defence, C commits a wrong against B even if C innocently interferes with B's thing (see **D1:4.1.1(ii)**). However, it is a mistake to assume that property rights and persistent rights must be protected in exactly the same way: after all, the **content, acquisition** and **defences questions** apply differently to each form of right.[204] The crucial point is that, if B has a property right, he has a right to exclusive control of a thing and the rest of the world is under a prima facie duty to B not to interfere with that thing. In contrast, if B has a persistent right, B has a right against a specific right of A: the rest of the world is *not* under a prima facie duty to B (see **B:4.4.3**). If B has a persistent right against A's right, B does have a prima facie power to impose a duty on anyone who acquires a right that depends on A's right; but if, as in **D2:Example 24a**, C no longer holds the right he received from A, it may be too late for B to assert that power.

This analysis does not mean that the law of unjust enrichment is entirely irrelevant if, at the start of the story, B has a persistent right. **Example 12b** shows that: (i) if B has a

---

[200] For example, Burrows, *The Law of Restitution* (2nd edn, 2002), 194ff discusses this area under the heading 'Standard Three Party Cases: [A] transfers [B]'s property to [C]'.

[201] See eg *BCCI v Akindele* [2001] Ch 437.

[202] See eg *Kelly v Solari* (1841) 9 M & W 54: if B makes a mistaken payment to A, A is under an immediate duty to pay B the value of that payment even if A is unaware of B's mistake.

[203] It also shows that, if B has a pre-existing persistent right, the rest of the world is *not* under a prima facie duty to B (see too **B:4.4.3**). It is therefore misleading to see B's 'knowing receipt' claim as somehow equivalent to a claim based on conversion.

[204] See eg L Smith (2000) 116 *LQR* 412.

persistent right; and (ii) C acquires a new right that is a product of B's persistent right; then (iii) B may acquire a persistent right against C's new right, as a result of C's unjust enrichment at B's expense. The crucial point is that, in contrast to a case such as **D2:Example 24a**, B is not then asserting a *pre-existing* right; instead, he is directly asserting a *new* persistent right.

SUMMARY of D4

It is hard work to assess the impact of unjust enrichment on the property law system. It is only relatively recently that unjust enrichment has been identified as a specific reason to impose a duty on A to B. However, despite the fears expressed by the House of Lords in *Westdeutsche Landesbank Girozentrale v Islington LBC*[205] and *Foskett v McKeown*,[206] unjust enrichment can be fitted into the property law system without undermining the rules of that system. In fact, long before it was fully recognised as a distinct body of law, unjust enrichment played a very important role in that system.

As far as **direct rights** are concerned, the impact of unjust enrichment is minimal. To show that C has been unjustly enriched at B's expense, B must show that C has *directly* acquired a benefit from B. And, in the **basic situation**, this occurs very rarely: C deals with, and acquires any benefit from, A rather than B. As far as the **acquisition of property rights** is concerned, it seems unjust enrichment can play a role, but only in cases where A's unjust enrichment at B's expense leads to A being under a duty to give B immediate exclusive control forever of a thing owned by A. The key impact of unjust enrichment is instead in relation to the **acquisition of persistent rights**: there are many cases where A's unjust enrichment at B's expense consists *either* of (i) A acquiring a new, specific right; or (ii) A acquiring a benefit in relation to a specific right already held by A. In such case, it is only logical that A's duty to B should relate to that specific right held by A: as a result, B may acquire a persistent right against A's right; or at least a power to acquire such a right.

This does not mean, however, that the law of unjust enrichment must have an impact on the **defences question** or the **remedies question**. If B has a property right or a persistent right, the defences available against that right are the same whether or not B acquired the right as a result of A's unjust enrichment. And if B has a pre-existing property right or persistent right (whether or not it arose as a result of A's unjust enrichment), B cannot assert that right by showing that C has been unjustly enriched at B's expense. Rather, a pre-existing property right must be asserted through the law of wrongs; and a pre-existing persistent right must be asserted directly, by imposing a duty on C.

---

[205] [1996] AC 669.
[206] [2001] 1 AC 102.

CHAPTER E1
PROPERTY RIGHTS

E1

PROPERTY RIGHTS

A property right has two key features (see **D1:1.1**):

- it relates to the use of a specific thing; *and*
- it is prima facie binding on the rest of the world (ie, it imposes a prima facie duty on everyone other than B, the holder of the right).

In **D1**, we examined the general position applying to property rights in *things other than land*. In this chapter, we will look specifically at property rights in land, by considering each of the four basic questions:

Section 1   The **content question**: what rights count as property rights in land?

Section 2   The **acquisition question**: how can B acquire a property right in land?

Section 3   The **defences question**: when can C have a defence to B's pre-existing property right in land?

Section 4   The **remedies question**: if B does have a pre-existing property right in land to which C has no defence, how will a court protect B's right?

1   THE CONTENT QUESTION

In relation to things other than land, there is only one general property right: Ownership (see **D1:1.3** and **1.4**). However, as can be seen from the table below, a number of different types of property right can exist in land.[1] This longer list reflects the special features of land: in particular its: (i) permanence; (ii) social importance; and (iii) capacity for multiple simultaneous use (see **A:3.1**).

Name	Content	Example
Freehold	B has a right to immediate exclusive control of land forever	B is a Freehold owner of a plot of land
Lease	B has right to exclusive control of land for a limited period	B has a 10-year Lease of A's land

---

[1] To be fully accurate, the list should also include each of: (i) the Profit; and (ii) the Rentcharge. The former (consisting of a right to take something from A's land) is omitted as it is similar in many ways to an Easement and hence can be treated, to a large extent, as an example of an Easement (see **G5:n1**): see further Law Com No 186 (2008) Part 6. The latter (consisting of a right to receive money from a Freehold owner of land: see eg **G6:n19**) is omitted as, following the Rentcharges Act 1977, it can only be acquired in rare situations.

Name	Content	Example
Easement	B has a Freehold or Lease and has a right to make a *specific, limited* use of some nearby land that is owned by A	B is given a right, intended to bind A and future owners of A's land, to walk across a path on A's land
Charge	B has a right to take exclusive control of land and a power, if a duty owed to B is not performed, to sell A's Freehold or Lease and use the proceeds to meet the duty owed to B	B lends A money to allow A to buy a Freehold and that money is lent as part of a 'mortgage' deal

1.1   Estates in land and interests in land

The table above shows us that, strictly speaking, it is impossible for B to have Ownership of land. If we say that B is an owner of land, we must mean that B has either: (i) a Freehold; or (ii) a Lease. However, it is easy to be too pedantic. First, in the book so far, we have used the term 'owner of land'. That is because, in the contexts where that term has been used, *it makes no difference* whether the party in question has a Freehold or Lease. So, in **A:Example 1**, it is stated that A and B's home is 'owned by A'. When A initially bought that home, he must have bought either a Freehold or a Lease. However, for the purposes of that example, we do not need to know whether A has a Freehold or a Lease: in each case, our analysis of the example would be *exactly the same*.

Second, whilst it is true that B cannot have Ownership of land, there is clearly a very close correspondence between: (i) a Freehold and (ii) Ownership. In fact, in each case, the core **content** of B's right is identical: B has a right to immediate exclusive control of a thing forever. A Freehold is simply the name we give to that right when it relates to land rather than, for example, to a bike.

There is an important difference between Ownership and a Lease: the former is a right to immediate exclusive control *forever*; the latter is a right to exclusive control *for a fixed period* (see **G1B:1.7**).[2] So we *do* need to distinguish between: (i) Ownership; and (ii) a Lease. Nonetheless, the Lease, like both Ownership and a Freehold, is based around the core idea of a *right to exclusive control of a thing*. Therefore, whilst Ownership does not exist as distinct property right in land, the *concept* of ownership is crucial in understanding the content of both the Freehold and the Lease.[3]

This point is recognised by the Law of Property Act 1925 ('the LPA 1925'). Section 1 of that Act draws an important distinction between: (i) *estates in land*; and (ii) *interests in land*. A Freehold and a Lease count as estates: the content of each right depends on the core idea of a right to exclusive control. In contrast, an Easement cannot give B a right to exclusive control of land (see **G5:1.4**); instead, it allows B to make a *specific, limited* use of land: as a result, an Easement counts as an interest and not as an estate (see **G5:1.1**).[4] The Charge is slightly more tricky: technically, it *does* give B an immediate right to exclusive control of

---

[2] In addition, a Lease does not need to give B an *immediate* right to exclusive control (see **G1B:1.6**).
[3] This point is persuasively made by Harris, *Property and Justice* (1996), 68–75: see esp 70: 'The truth is that ownership interests in land, of various magnitudes, are and always have been incidents of legal estates in land.'
[4] See eg Bright, ch 21 in *Land Law Themes and Perspectives* (ed Bright and Dewar, 1998).

land.[5] However, in practice, it does not give B an unconditional right to take exclusive control; rather, B's right is concerned with allowing B access to the financial value of the land (see **G4:5.2** and **G4:5.3**). In practice, then, a Charge operates as an interest in land: it allows B to make a specific, limited use of land.

1.2   The closed list principle

A owns land that includes a canal. A makes a contractual promise to B giving B the exclusive right to put pleasure boats on the canal and to hire those boats to paying customers. C then sets up a rival business hiring out pleasure boats on the same canal.

In such a case, C does *not* commit a wrong against B. This was confirmed by the Exchequer Chamber in *Hill v Tupper*,[6] the facts of which are identical to **Example 1**.

B sued C, claiming that C was wrongfully interfering with B's exclusive right. However, the court held that: (i) B's right was *not* on the list of property rights in land; and so (ii) C was *not* under a duty to B not to hire out pleasure boats on the canal. It may be that A and B *wanted* to give B such a right, but they simply do not have the power to do so: a new form of property right 'cannot be created at the will and pleasure of the owner of property'.[7]

Of course, A can make (almost)[8] any contractual promise he wishes to B: such a promise will: (i) give B a personal right against A; and (ii) impose a duty on the rest of the world not to procure a breach by A of A's contract with B (see **D3:2.3.4**). But it can only give B a property right if the content of B's right matches the content of one of the permitted property rights in land. And, in **Example 1**, B's right fails to do so.[9] C therefore commits a prima facie wrong *against A* if he uses the canal without A's permission;[10] but C commits no wrong against B. **Example 1** thus demonstrates an important point: the closed list (*numerus clausus*) principle (see **D1:1.2.1**) applies to land as much as to other things.

1.3   Extending the list of property rights in land?

1.3.1 The general position

The closed list principle does not mean that the list of property rights in land is closed forever: in theory, new rights could be added to the list. The most recent example of judges making such an addition occurred quite some time ago—certainly no more recently than the end of the 15th century. Then, it was recognised for the first time that: (i) if A has a right to exclusive control of land; and (ii) A gives B a right to exclusive control of that land for a fixed period (a Lease); then (iii) the rest of the world is under a prima facie duty to B not to interfere with B's use of the land during that period. Importantly, section 1 of the

---

[5] The content of a Charge is defined by statute as based on the content of a Lease: LPA 1925, s 87(1) (see **G4:2.1**).

[6] (1863) 2 H & C 122.

[7] *Ibid per* Pollock CB at 127.

[8] For example, A's promise to be B's slave will not be contractually binding on A.

[9] B's right does not give him a Freehold or a Lease as it does not give him exclusive control of the canal (eg, A is also permitted to use the canal: see **G1B:1.4**). And B's right to make a specific, limited use of A's land does not count as an Easement as B does not have a Freehold or Lease of any other land (see **G5:1.2**).

[10] Martin B suggested ((1863) 2 H & C 122 at 128) that, if he secured A's consent, B could bring a claim against C in the name of A. Such a claim would assert A's right against C, not B's right.

LPA 1925 makes clear that any future addition to the list of property rights in land *must* come from Parliament; not from judges.[11] The most recent statutory addition to the list came from that Act, which allowed a Charge to count as a distinct property right in land.[12]

The Law Commission has recently suggested that Parliament should add another right to the list: the Land Obligation.[13] This new property right in land would consist of a duty undertaken by A, in relation to the use of his own land, for the benefit of B's neighbouring land. It would therefore: (i) replace the Restrictive Covenant (currently a persistent right relating to land arising where A's duty is *not* to perform a particular act: see **E2:1.3.2**); and (ii) reform the current law by allowing a *positive* duty agreed to by A to bind third parties (see further **G6:1.1.2**).[14] Given there is no conceptual unity to the content of property rights (see **D1:1.2.3**), the decision as to whether or not to add the Land Obligation to the existing list cannot be determined by applying doctrinal rules. Instead, it essentially comes down to the perceived needs of practical convenience (see **B:9**).

Nonetheless, one point is worth making. The Law Commission has proposed that a *positive* duty of A (eg, a contractual promise by A to B to keep A's roof in good repair), if it satisfies the requirements of a Land Obligation, should give B a property right in A's land. However, it is very difficult to see how such a duty can give B a property right: surely the rest of the world cannot come under a prima facie duty to B to repair A's roof?[15] Of course, that is not the Law Commission's intention; it intends rather that the positive duty should bind only a limited class of third parties (probably those later acquiring a Freehold or a Lease of at least a set minimum length in A's land).[16] So, if Parliament does add the Land Obligation to the list, the positive Land Obligation will be a very unusual form of property right: it will impose a prima facie duty *only* on certain third parties, not on the rest of the world.[17]

1.3.2 An exception?

EXAMPLE 2

A owns some woodland. B Co runs an airport. B Co wants to build a second runway: to do so it needs to ensure that some trees on A's land are cut so that they will not interfere with the aircraft using the runway. C, a protestor opposed to the building of the second runway, goes onto the woodland with fellow protestors, intending to make it impossible for B Co to enter the land and do the necessary work. Three days later, A gives B Co permission to enter the woodland and do the necessary work. B Co is prevented from carrying out the work by the protestors. B applies to court for an order that C and the protestors must leave the land (a 'possession order').

---

[11] S 1(1) and (2) state that only the rights listed there can count as estates or interests in land 'at law': ie, that only the listed rights can count as property rights in land.

[12] See LPA 1925, s 1(2)(c) and (d) and Part III. Prior to the Act, if he wanted to give B a property right in land by way of security, A had to give B either a Freehold or a Lease.

[13] Law Com No 186 (2008): Consultation Paper on Easements, Covenants and Profits a Prendre.

[14] *Ibid* 7.67–7.80.

[15] B's Rentcharge can be used to secure a positive duty of A: however, it does not impose that duty on the rest of the world. Instead, the rest of the world is under a duty not to interfere with B's security right: a right to take exclusive control of the land if the secured duty is not performed.

[16] *Ibid* 9.11–9.21 and 9.37; 10.11–10.27.

[17] The Land Obligation would be anomalous in a further way: it is suggested that it should count as a property right in land *only* if each of A's land and B's land is registered: see Law Com No 186 at 8.31.

Example 2 is very similar to **Example 1**. The problem for B Co is that, to obtain a possession order, it needs to show that: (i) it has a property right in the land; *and* (ii) that property right gives it a right to exclusive control of the land.[18] B Co's agreement with A does *not* give B Co such a right: it gives B Co only a specific, limited right to use A's land and so cannot count as a Freehold or Lease. Further, as B Co has not taken physical control of the land, it cannot show that it has independently acquired a Freehold (see **2.1.1** below). Therefore, whilst C and the protestors are committing a wrong against *A* by remaining on the land without A's permission, *they have not committed any wrong against B Co.*

However, in *Manchester Airport plc v Dutton*,[19] the facts of which are identical to **Example 2**,[20] a majority of the Court of Appeal surprisingly decided to grant B Co a possession order. The principal reason given by the majority was that: (i) B Co had a *contractual* right to go onto the land; and (ii) *if* B Co had exercised that right and gone onto the land, it could have taken physical control of the land; and (iii) *if* B Co had done so, it would have independently acquired a Freehold; and so (iv) C *would* then have committed a wrong against B Co by remaining on the land without B Co's consent.

This analysis overlooks two fundamental points. In **Example 2**, B Co has *not* independently acquired a right as it has not taken physical control of the land: the fact B Co *might have* taken such control is irrelevant. If B nearly catches some fish, that does not give B Ownership of the fish.[21] Second, as A's promise to B only allows B to make a specific, limited use of A's thing, B does not have a right to exclusive control of that thing.

Whether the judges in the majority realised it or not, the decision in *Manchester Airport* depends on saying that A's promise to allow B Co to make a specific, limited use of A's land imposed a prima facie duty to B on the rest of the world. In turn, that depends on an extension of the list of property rights in land. And section 1 of the LPA 1925 makes clear that judges have no power to make such an addition to the list. As a result, from the doctrinal point of view,[22] the decision in *Manchester Airport plc v Dutton* is therefore wrong: the persuasive dissent of Chadwick LJ should be preferred.[23]

2   THE ACQUISITION QUESTION

2.1   The acquisition of a new property right

2.1.1 Independent acquisition

Where B acquires a property right independently, he acquires it as a result of his own,

---

[18] In **Example 2**, B Co could claim that it had acquired an Easement from A. However, the special procedure available to apply for a summary 'possession order' (see **4.1** below) is available only where B has a right to exclusive control of land—an Easement does not give B such a right (see **1.1** above).

[19] [2000] QB 133.

[20] In that case, A was the National Trust: National Trust Act 1939, s 12 prevented it from granting B Co a Lease.

[21] See *Young v Hichens* (1844) 6 QB 606 (**D1:nn 89, 91 and 119**).

[22] It could be said that the decision in *Manchester Airport* can be justified on practical grounds: if B Co's claim had been refused, A would simply have made a claim against C. However: (i) in that case, A was the National Trust: it may have been reluctant to bring a claim against the squatters, as some of its members may sympathise with their concerns; and (ii) it is not obvious that B Co would be able to force A to bring a claim: it may have been limited to receiving money from A as a result of A's breach of its contractual promise to allow B to enter the land.

[23] For further disapproval of the decision, see eg Swadling (2000) 116 *LQR* 354.

unilateral conduct (see **B:2.2** and **D1:2.1**): B does *not* rely on A having exercised a power to give B a property right. It is possible for B to independently acquire: (i) a Freehold; or (ii) an Easement.

If B takes physical control of A's land, B acquires his own Freehold (see **G1A:2.1**). If B: (i) makes a specific, limited use of A's land over a long period; and (ii) makes that use of A's land 'as of right' (eg, not as a result of A's permission); then (iii) the 'doctrine of prescription' may allow B to acquire an Easement over A's land (see **G5:2.8**).[24] In each case, B acquires his right purely as a result of his own conduct.

In contrast, neither a Lease nor a Charge can be acquired independently, as the **content** of each right depends on A having exercised a power to give B a right. The Land Registration Act 2002 ('the LRA 2002') does assume that B can independently acquire a Lease, but that assumption is inconsistent with the very nature of a Lease (see **G1B:2.1**).

2.1.2 Dependent acquisition

In relation to things other than land, there is only one general property right: Ownership. So, if B claims to have acquired a newly created property right in relation to a thing other land, B *must* rely on an independent acquisition. Things are different in relation to land. If A is an owner of land (ie, if A has a Freehold or Lease), A can exercise his power to give B: (i) a Lease;[25] (ii) an Easement; or (iii) a Charge. In such a case, B dependently acquires a *new* property right in A's land. The general position is that A's power cannot be exercised unless the formality rules set out in: (i) section 52 of the LPA 1925 and; (ii) section 27 of the LRA 2002 have been satisfied (see **2.3** below).

2.2   The transfer of a pre-existing property right

If A has a property right in land, A has the power to transfer that right to B. The general rule is that A's power cannot be exercised unless the formality rules set out in: (i) section 52 of the LPA 1925; and (ii) section 27 of the LRA 2002 have been satisfied (see **2.3** below).

2.3   Formality rules and the acquisition of property rights in land

2.3.1 The interaction of section 52 of the LPA 1925 and section 27 of the LRA 2002

Section 52 of the LPA 1925 imposes a basic rule: A must use a deed to exercise his power to give B a property right in land (see **C3:5.3.1**). Section 27 of the LRA 2002 sets out a vital supplementary rule: even if A does use a deed, his attempt to exercise his power to give B a property right will only succeed if B is substantively registered as the holder of that right (see **C2:6.2** and **C3:5.3.1**).

Between them, these two rules create four possibilities.

1. **Neither formality rule applies**: B can then acquire a property right from A *even if* A's exercise of his power to give B such a right has not been put in a deed and B has not

---

[24] The orthodox view of such a case is that B acquires his Easement *dependently*, through an assumed exercise by A (or a former owner of A's land) of his power to give B an Easement. However, that assumed grant is clearly fictional (see **G5:2.8.1**).

[25] So if A has a 10-year Lease, A can give B a 5-year Lease: in such a case, B has a sub-Lease.

been substantively registered as the holder of his right. This occurs in two situations: (i) where B acquires a new[26] Lease of three years or less that meets the requirements of section 54(2) of the LPA 1925 (see **G1B:2.2.1(i)(a)**); *or* (ii) where a court infers, from B's physical control of land and A's acceptance of rent from B, that A has exercised his power to give B a new Lease—such a Lease is known an 'implied periodic tenancy' (see **G1B:2.2.1(ii)**).

2. **Only section 52 applies:** A must use a deed to exercise his power to give B a property right; but there is no need for B to be substantively registered as the holder of his right. This can occur if B claims that A, a holder of an *unregistered* Freehold or Lease, has exercised his power to give B a right—although, even then, substantive registration will be necessary in some cases.[27] However, in the analysis here, as in the rest of the book, we will concentrate on the much more common case where B claims a property right in registered land. There are then just two situations falling within this category: (i) where B acquires a non-exceptional[28] Lease for seven years or less (see **G1B:2.2.1(i)(b)**); *or* (ii) where B acquires an 'implied Easement'—ie, where a court infers from the facts of a case that A has exercised his power to give B an Easement (see **G5:2.4** and **G5:2.6**).[29]

3. **Only section 27 applies:** A does *not* need to use a deed to exercise his power to give B a property right; but B cannot acquire that right unless and until he is substantively registered as its holder. It might be thought that lots of situations fall within this category. However, as we will see below, this possibility is, in practice, irrelevant.

4. **Both section 52 of the LPA 1925 *and* section 27 of the LRA apply:** (i) A must use a deed to exercise his power to give B a property right; and (ii) B cannot acquire that right unless and until he is substantively registered as its holder. This is the default position. All situations not falling into the first three categories fall into this final category.

Why is it that the third possibility never applies in practice? After all, B can acquire a property right simply by virtue of being substantively registered as its holder (see **C2:6.1**). It might therefore seem that, as long as substantive registration occurs, B does not need to worry about section 52 of the LPA 1925. However, if B wishes to be substantively registered as the holder of a property right, he will need to convince the Land Registry that he has indeed acquired that right. And if B claims that he has acquired his right by means of a dependent acquisition from A, section 52 means that B must produce a deed in order to show that A has exercised his power to give B that right.[30] For example, if B wants to be substantively registered as the new holder of A's registered Freehold, B will need to produce

---

[26] A *transfer* of an existing Lease *always* requires a deed: *Crago v Julian* [1992] 1 WLR 372 (see **G1B:2.2.2(i)**).

[27] For example, if A wants to: (i) transfer an unregistered Freehold; or (ii) transfer a Lease with more than seven years to run; or (iii) grant B a Lease for more than seven years to run; then (iv) B will almost always need to substantively register to acquire that right: LRA 2002, s 4.

[28] Some Leases need to be substantively registered even if they are for seven years or less: see LRA 2002, s 27(2)(b)(ii)–(v). Such Leases will be referred to as 'exceptional' throughout this book.

[29] The circumstances in which B can acquire such a right are examined in **G5:2.5** and **G5:2.7**.

[30] B does *not* need to use a deed to show that A has exercised his power to give B: (i) a Lease falling within LPA 1925, s 54(2); or (ii) an implied periodic tenancy. However, neither of those rights can be substantively registered by B: a Lease can only be substantively registered if it is for more than seven years, or is 'exceptional': see LRA 2002, s 3(3).

a Land Registry form signed by A:[31] that form counts as a deed and thus satisfies section 52 of the LPA 1925.

Moreover, the positive operation of substantive registration is not absolute (see **C2:6.1**): whilst B can acquire a property right through substantive registration, he can lose that right if the register is rectified. For example, if B forges A's signature on a Land Registry form, B may trick the Land Registry into registering B as the new holder of A's registered Freehold. A can then apply for the register to be changed. And B will face an obvious problem in trying to resist A's application: as he will not be able to produce a (genuine) deed signed by A, B will not be able to show that A exercised his power to transfer his Freehold to B.

It is therefore clear that B cannot forget about the need for a deed. As a result, it seems clearer to say that, where B relies on a dependent acquisition from A, it is never enough for B to satisfy *only* section 27 of the LRA 2002. This means that there are *no* cases where section 27 of the LRA 2002 applies but section 52 of the LPA 1925 does not.[32]

Property right in registered land dependently acquired by B	Does section 52 of the LPA 1925 apply?	Does section 27 of the LRA 2002 apply?
–Lease falling within section 54(2) –Implied periodic tenancy	No	No
–Non-exceptional Lease of seven years or less –Implied Easement	Yes	No
–**All other property rights**	**Yes**	**Yes**

2.3.2 Analysing formality rules

When looking at section 52 of the LPA 1925 and section 27 of the LRA 2002, we will ask four basic questions that assist in understanding the operation of *any* formality rule:

1. **Scope:** When does the rule apply? Are any exceptions specified?
2. **Satisfaction:** How is the rule satisfied?
3. **Sanctions:** What are the consequences of not satisfying the rule?
4. **Saves:** Can a party acquire a right even if the rule has not been satisfied?

2.3.3 Section 52 of the LPA 1925

(i) Scope

Section 52 states that: 'All conveyances of land or of any interest therein are void for the purpose of conveying or creating a legal estate unless made by deed.'

The effect of this section is to establish the basic rule that, if A wishes to exercise his power to give B a property right in land, he must express his intention in a deed. The term 'a legal estate' usually refers only to a Freehold or a Lease (see **1.1** above). However, in the

---

[31] See eg *per* Baroness Hale in *Stack v Dowden* [2007] 2 AC 432 at [52] discussing Land Registry Form TR1.

[32] Where B acquires a right *independently*, s 52 of the LPA 1925 clearly does not apply. It can be argued that s 27 of the LRA 2002 *does* apply, as B should substantively register his right to be sure of having it. However, that seems to be incorrect: eg, if B takes physical control of registered land and acts as its owner, B immediately, independently acquires a Freehold without the need for substantive registration: (see **G1A:2.1.3**).

special sense used by section 52, 'a legal estate' also includes both an Easement[33] and a Charge.[34] As a result, the starting point is that a deed must be used *whenever* A attempts to give B a property right in land.[35]

As we saw in **2.3.1** above, the scope of the section 52 rule is limited by two exceptions. A can exercise a power to give B a property right in land *without* using a deed if: (i) B acquires a new Lease of three years or less that meets the requirements of section 54(2) of the LPA 1925 (see **G1B:2.2.1(i)(a)**); *or* (ii) where B acquires a new Lease arising under 'an implied periodic tenancy' (see **G1B:2.2.1(ii)**).

(ii) Satisfaction

To satisfy section 52, B needs to show that A used a deed to exercise his power to give B a property right. The requirements of a deed are set out by section 1 of the Law of Property (Miscellaneous Provisions) Act 1989 (see **C3:n1**). The satisfaction question thus seems fairly straightforward. However, complications can arise if A and B deal with each other *electronically*, without using paper documents. Can an electronic document can count as a deed and satisfy section 52?

One argument is that an electronic document including a certified electronic signature will always count, for the purposes of formality rules, as a signed, written document.[36] On this view, such a document *can* count as a deed if it also: (i) describes itself as a deed; and (ii) contains the signature of a witness. However, this argument has not yet been tested in the courts. In general, it is therefore prudent for A and B to draw up a conventional signed document rather than relying on an electronic version.

However, the position is different where registered land is concerned. Section 91 of the LRA 2002 makes clear that an electronic document *can* count as a deed. To do so, the electronic document needs to satisfy certain requirements: in particular it must contain the certified electronic signature of all relevant parties.[37] So, if, for example, A owns a registered Freehold and wishes to give B a five-year Lease, A can do so by using an electronic document complying with the requirements of section 91.[38]

(iii) Sanctions

Where section 52 regulates A's power to give B a property right, the sanction for non-compliance is straightforward. If no deed has been used, B *cannot* show that A has exercised his power to give B a property right.

---

[33] See *Hewlins v Shippam* (1826) B & C 221.
[34] LPA 1925, s 87(1) assumes that a Charge must be made by deed.
[35] The reference in s 52 to a '*legal* estate' makes clear that the formality rule it contains does not apply to persistent rights.
[36] *Electronic Commerce: Formal Requirements in Commercial Transactions: Advice from the Law Commission* (December 2001), ch 3.
[37] See esp s 91(5).
[38] This is on the assumption that the creation of the Lease counts as a 'disposition' by A of his registered estate and hence falls within s 91(2)(a). As the Lease is only for five years, its creation does not fall within s 91(2)(c), as it is not a disposition that 'triggers the requirement of registration'.

(iv) Saves

> ### C3:EXAMPLE 3
>
> A, a registered owner of a family home, lives there with B. A moves out and makes a gratu-itous oral promise to transfer his ownership of the land to B. B remains in the home and, relying on A's promise, spends money on the home in the belief that A will honour his promise. A then changes his mind and refuses to transfer his ownership to B.

In such a case, it does not matter whether A has a Freehold or a Lease: it is clear that A's right has *not* been transferred to B. It seems A was willing to make that transfer at one point; but, as the section 52 formality rule applies and has not been satisfied, A has *not* exercised his power to give B a property right. Nonetheless, as we saw in **C3:3.5**, B can still show that:

1. B has *independently acquired* a property right (see **2.1.1** above). After A left, B had physical control of the land and so independently acquired a Freehold.[39]
2. B has a personal right against A: the doctrine of proprietary estoppel may impose a duty on A, to ensure that B does not suffer a detriment as a result of his reliance on A's promise (see **E4**). And, if that doctrine imposes a duty on A in relation to A's Freehold or Lease (eg, a duty to honour his promise to transfer his right to B), then B will have a *persistent right*.[40]

It is important to note that the possibility of B acquiring a persistent right does *not* undermine the formality rule imposed by section 52 (see **C3:7.2.1**). That rule regulates A's power to give B a property right in land; it does not apply where B instead acquires a persistent right. After all: (i) a persistent right, unlike a property right, does not impose a prima facie duty on the rest of the world; and (ii) if C later acquires a right from A, a number of defences (eg, the lack of registration defence) can protect C against B's pre-existing persistent right (see **E2:3**).

2.3.4 Section 27 of the LRA 2002

(i) Scope
Section 27(1) states that:

> If a disposition of a registered estate or registered charge is required to be completed by regis-tration, it does not operate at law until the relevant registration requirements are met.

The remainder of the section sets out when substantive registration is necessary. The basic rule is that, if B wishes to acquire a property right from A, a party with a registered Freehold or Lease,[41] B *must* substantively register that right.[42] As we saw in **2.3.1** above, the scope of the rule is limited by two exceptions. B can dependently acquire a property right in land

---

[39] See *per* Lord Upjohn in *National Provincial Bank v Ainsworth* [1965] AC 1175 at 1232 (see **G1A:2.1.2**).

[40] See eg *Pascoe v Turner* [1979] 1 WLR 431, the facts of which are identical to **C3:Example 3** (see **C3:3.5**).

[41] The need for substantive registration can also apply in relation to unregistered land as noted at **n 27** above.

[42] S 27(2)(a) and (3)(a) ensure that the *transfer* of a registered Freehold, Lease, Easement or Charge must be substantively registered; s 27(2)(b) sets the basic rule requiring substantive registration for the creation of a Lease; s 27(2)(d) sets the same basic rule for the creation of an express Easement; and s 27(2)(f) requires substantive regis-tration for the creation of a Charge.

without substantively registering that right if: (i) B acquires a non-exceptional Lease for seven years or less (see **G1B:2.2.1(i)(b)**); *or* (ii) B acquires an 'implied Easement' (see **G5:2.4** and **G5:2.6**).

(ii) Satisfaction

To satisfy the section 27 formality rule, B needs to substantively register his right. A Freehold or Lease is registered autonomously, with its own distinct file: if A transfers a registered Freehold to B, B is simply entered in the file as the new holder of that right. If A instead grants B a 10-year Lease, a new file is opened and B is registered as the holder of that right. An Easement[43] or Charge is not registered autonomously, but instead is noted on the file of the Freehold or Lease that it burdens.[44]

At the moment, B can substantively register his right only by applying to the Land Registry and providing copies of the necessary documents. However, the Law Commission and the Land Registry are both keen to develop a system of electronic registration (see **E5:1** and **E5:4**). Once that system is up and running, B will be *required* to substantively register his right by remote, online registration.[45] B will not be able to do this himself; rather, he will have to go to a solicitor or conveyancer who has been authorised by the Land Registry to make a direct online change to the Land Register. The idea is that this form of registration, as it is more direct, will be quicker. It is also intended that it will be a cheaper way for B to register; but this will of course be compromised by the fact that B will have to pay an authorised solicitor or conveyancer to register his right.[46]

(iii) Sanctions

Where section 27 applies, the sanction for non-compliance is straightforward. If B fails substantively to register his right, it will be impossible for B to show that A has exercised his power to give him a property right in A's land.

(iv) Saves

If the section 27 formality rule applies and has not been satisfied, B will not be able to claim that A has exercised his power to give B a property right. So if, in **C3:Example 3**, A's right is a Freehold or a Lease of more than seven years, B's lack of substantive registration provides another reason why B cannot show that he has acquired A's property right. However, B's failure to satisfy the section 27 rule, like a failure to satisfy section 52 of the LPA 1925, does *not* prevent B from: (i) independently acquiring a property right; or (ii) acquiring a personal right against A; or (iii) acquiring a persistent right against a right held by A.

---

[43] Unlike a Freehold, Lease or Charge, an Easement must also benefit a Freehold or Lease held by B (see **G5:1.2**). So, an Easement will also be noted on the file of the Freehold or Lease that it benefits (on the property register).

[44] The file on each registered Freehold or Lease is split into three parts: (i) property register (basic geographical information—eg, location of the land; in the case of a Lease, brief details of the Lease such as its length); (ii) proprietorship register (name and address of the holder of the right; any registered restrictions on the use of the right—eg, any sale must be with the consent of X); and (iii) charges register (any registered burdens on the land eg Easement, Charge or Restrictive Covenant). So B's registered Easement or Charge will be noted on the charges register pertaining to A's Freehold or Lease,

[45] LRA 2002, s 93(2) gives the Lord Chancellor the power to introduce electronic registration requirements (see **E2:2.3.3(ii)**).

[46] In many cases B will already be using a conveyancer to assist in the process of acquiring his right: it is common practice, for example, to employ a conveyancer when buying a house. However, some choose to do their own conveyancing: it seems they will have to go to a District Land Registry to electronically register under supervision.

EXAMPLE 3

A has a Freehold. A makes a contractual promise to transfer that Freehold to B. B pays the agreed purchase price and A executes a deed in B's favour but B fails to substantively register as the new holder of A's Freehold.

In such a case, A retains his Freehold. If B takes physical control of the land, B independently acquires his own, distinct Freehold. And, as a result of A's contractual promise: (i) A has a duty to B to transfer his Freehold to B; and so (ii) B has a persistent right against A's Freehold (see **E2:1.2.4(ii)**).[47]

SUMMARY of E1:2

	Property Rights in Land		
	Independent acquisition	Dependent acquisition from A	
	Can B acquire the right through his own conduct and hence without satisfying any formality rule?	*Is a deed necessary: section 52?*	*Is substantive registration necessary: section 27?*
Freehold	Yes	Yes	Yes
Lease	No	Yes: unless –section 54(2) applies; *or* –implied periodic tenancy	Yes: unless –non-exceptional Lease for seven years or less
Easement	Yes	Yes	Yes: unless –implied Easement
Charge	No	Yes	Yes

3   THE DEFENCES QUESTION

If B can satisfy the **content question** and the **acquisition question** attention then shifts to Question 3 of the **basic structure**: does C have a defence to B's pre-existing property right?

3.1   Introduction and the basic tension

In **D1:3**, we considered general situations in which C may have a defence to B's pre-existing property right. It might seem that, where land is involved, it ought to be easier for C to have such a defence. First, the list of property rights in land is longer than the general list of such rights; a longer list of defences may restore the balance between B and C. Second, given its limited availability, it is particularly important to promote the marketability of land by protecting third parties who wish to acquire a right relating to land.

---

[47] See eg *Lysaght v Edwards* (1876) 2 Ch D 499.

However, these special needs are *already* taken into account through the **acquisition question**. In particular, the general need for substantive registration, imposed by section 27 of the LRA 2002, gives C a good deal of protection from the risk of being bound by a hidden property right of B. If B has substantively registered his pre-existing property right, C can easily discover that right before deciding whether to acquire a right from A. However, B's substantive registration does *not* mean that B's right will always bind C: it may still be possible for C to have a defence to B's right.

In many cases, B's failure to substantively register means that B simply fails to acquire his claimed property right (see **2.3.4** above). In fact, if: (i) A has a registered Freehold or Lease; and (ii) C acquires a right from A in relation to A's land; and (iii) C first checks the register and B is not recorded as having a property right in that land; then (iv) there are only three situations in which B may have a pre-existing property right:

1. If B has *independently acquired* a property right. If B acquired his right *after* A, then C has nothing to worry about: C has acquired his right from A, and so C can base his claim on A's right. This means that, as far as C is concerned, B's right does not count as a *pre-existing* property right: it is not prima facie binding on C. If B acquired his right *before* A, then B's right *is* prima facie binding on C and C *does* need to show he has a defence to B's right.
2. If B has a *non-exceptional Lease of seven years or less*. B can acquire such a property right without needing to substantively register it (see **2.3.4(i)** above and **G1B:2.2.1(i)(b)**). In such a case, C *does* need to show he has a defence to B's right.
3. If B has an *implied Easement*. B can acquire such a property right without needing to substantively register it (see **2.3.4(i)** above and **G5:2.4** and **2.6**). In such a case, C *does* need to show he has a defence to B's right.

3.2 The consent defence

EXAMPLE 4

A has a Freehold. A gives B, his friend, a 15-year Lease at a fairly low rent. A wants to borrow £100,000 from C Bank. C Bank insists: (i) that A must give C Bank a Charge over A's land, to secure A's duty to repay the loan; and (ii) B must consent to C Bank acquiring that Charge free from B's pre-existing Lease. B does sign a form giving the necessary consent, but only because A told B he was borrowing only £50,000 and that signing the consent form was just a 'formality' that would have no effect on B. Two years later, A has failed to repay any of the loan and C Bank wants to enforce its Charge by: (i) removing B from the land; and (ii) selling A's Freehold.

B's consent to C's conduct can clearly give C a defence to B's pre-existing property right in land (see **D1:3.2**).[48] However, complications can arise if B argues that his consent was defective, for example because it was obtained by C's fraud. A particular problem arises in a case such as **Example 4** where B argues that his consent was defective due to A's

---

[48] Compare eg *Woolwich BS v Dickman* [1996] 3 All ER 204. In that case, the special statutory protection available to tenants under the Rent Act 1977 prevented C from relying on B's consent, but the Court of Appeal made clear that, in the absence of such protection, C has a defence to B's pre-existing Lease if B gives his consent to C's acquisition of C's right: *per* Waite LJ at 210 and *per* Morritt LJ at 212.

misconduct:[49] when, if at all, can A's misconduct prevent C relying on the consent defence? This question has arisen most often in cases where A owes money to C; and B agrees to guarantee A's debt in some way. That guarantee can take various forms. For example: (i) B may make a contractual promise to pay A's debt if A fails to do so; or (ii) B may agree to give C a security right over B's property right in land; or (iii) as in **Example 4**, B may consent to C acquiring a security right from A, free from B's pre-existing property right in land.

In such cases, special principles have been developed to deal with the question of whether A's misconduct can affect C.[50] If the relationship between A and B is non-commercial[51] (eg, A and B are married or are co-habitees), C will have to take certain steps to deal with the risk that B's consent may have been induced by A's misconduct.[52] C must take reasonable steps to ensure that B is aware of: [53] (i) the consequences of B's consent; and (ii) the nature and extent of the debt owed by A to C.[54] So if, in **Example 4**, C Bank failed to take such steps, then, as B's consent was procured by A's misrepresentation, C Bank will *not* be able to rely on the consent defence.

3.3   The 'apparent power' defences

A number of different statutory provisions can give C a defence to a pre-existing property right of B where, on the facts, it is reasonable for C to believe that A has a power to give C a right free from B's pre-existing property right (see **D1:3.3.2–3.3.4**). Those provisions do *not* apply where B has a property right in land. However, the general estoppel defences (see **D1:3.3.1**) *can* apply in such a case (see further **E2:3.3**).

3.4   The overreaching defence

EXAMPLE 5

B1 has a Freehold. B1 borrows £100,000 from A Bank: as part of that deal, B1 gives A Bank a Charge. B1 then borrows a further £50,000 from B2, secured by a second Charge. B1 then gives B3 a 21-year Lease. B1 fails to repay his loan from A Bank. A Bank enforces its Charge by selling B1's land to C.

In such a case, C is *not* bound by the property rights of B2[55] or B3.[56] A Bank has a power not only to sell B1's Freehold, but also to sell it to C free from any property rights granted

---

[49] This issue was considered by the House of Lords in *Barclays Bank plc v O'Brien* [1994] 1 AC 180; *Barclays Bank plc v Boulter* [1999] 1 WLR 1919; and *Royal Bank of Scotland v Etridge (No 2)* [2002] 2 AC 773. It arises not only in relation to the consent defence but in any case where B agrees to guarantee a debt owed to C by A.

[50] For detail on these principles see eg Burrows, *Casebook on Contract* (2007), 729–53.

[51] *Royal Bank of Scotland v Etridge (No 2)* [2002] 2 AC 773 at [88].

[52] See eg *per* Lord Nicholls in *Royal Bank of Scotland v Etridge (No 2)* [2002] 2 AC 773 at [87]: 'the creditor [C] must always take reasonable steps to bring home to the individual guarantor [B] the risks he is running by standing as surety'.

[53] C can either: (i) give this information to B itself; or (ii) rely on a statement from B's solicitor that the risks have been explained to B (C can rely on a statement from B's solicitor even if that solicitor is also acting for A): see *Royal Bank of Scotland v Etridge (No 2)* [2002] 2 AC 773 at [95]–[96].

[54] See *Royal Bank of Scotland v Etridge (No 2)* [2002] 2 AC 773 at [54], [55] and [79].

[55] LPA 1925, s 88(1)(b).

[56] See eg *Dudley and District Benefit BS v Emerson* [1949] Ch 707.

by B1, without A Bank's permission,[57] *after* A Bank acquired its Charge. That power ensures that B1, by giving a property right to each of B2 and B3, cannot undermine the value of A Bank's Charge. And, whenever A has a power to give C a right free from a pre-existing right of B, C can rely on the overreaching defence against B's right (see **D1:3.4**).[58]

3.5 The 'bona fide purchaser' defence?

3.5.1 The general position

Unless B's property right is in money, C cannot use the 'bona fide purchaser' defence against a pre-existing property right of B (see **D1:3.5**). This means that C can *never* use the defence against B's property right in land.

3.5.2 Powers to acquire a property right in land

If B transfers a property right to A as a result of A's fraud or duress, B has a power to regain that property right. In **D4:3.2.2**, we suggested that B's power arises because, as soon as A acquires B's right, A holds that right on Trust for B.[59] We will therefore consider B's power to regain a property right in land when looking at persistent rights in relation to land (see **E2:1.5**).

3.6 The lack of registration defence

If C acquires a right in registered land, he may qualify for the lack of registration defence provided by the LRA 2002 (see **C2:6**).[60] To qualify for that defence, C must: (i) acquire a property right for value; and (ii) substantively register that right.[61] However: (i) *if B has a pre-existing property right in land*; then (ii) *C can almost never use the lack of registration defence against B's pre-existing property right.* This is because:

1. If B has a property right this means that, in most cases, B must have substantively registered that right (see **2.3.4** above)—clearly C cannot then use the lack of registration defence.
2. In the rarer cases where B can acquire a property right without substantively registering it, B's right will almost always count as an overriding interest and so will be immune from the lack of registration defence (see **C2:6.2**).

---

[57] Where B1 remains in physical control of the land, LPA 1925, s 99 gives B1 a power to grant certain Leases; but the terms of B1's deal with A Bank generally exclude that power.

[58] A further example occurs where A0, an owner of unregistered land, dies intestate and his rights pass to A, his personal representative. Even if, under the administration of the estate, B has *already* acquired a property right in the land, A has the power to give C a property right free from that pre-existing property right: see Trusts of Land and Appointment of Trustees Act, s 18(1), and Administration of Estates Act 1925, ss 36 and 39(1)(ii). C is protected only if A makes a written statement that he has not given another party a property right in the land; but C can be protected even if that statement is untrue: see eg Burn and Cartwright, *Cheshire and Burn's Modern Law of Real Property* (17th edn, 2006), 989–90.

[59] Indeed, that analysis was adopted by the Court of Appeal in *Collings v Lee* [2001] 2 All ER 332.

[60] If C acquires a right in unregistered land, he may be able to rely on the different lack of registration defence provided by the Land Charges Act 1972 (see **C2:7**).

[61] See LRA 2002, ss 28 and 29. S 29(4) allows C to qualify for the defence if he acquires a non-exceptional Lease of seven years or less (ie, a Lease that cannot be substantively registered).

3.6.1 B's property right was dependently acquired from A

In some cases, B can dependently acquire a property right in land without needing to substantively register that right. This is the case where B acquires: (i) a non-exceptional Lease of seven years or less; or (ii) an implied Easement (see **2.3.4** above). The former type of right *always* counts as an overriding interest (see **E5:3.3.3(ii)** and **G1B:3**);[62] the latter type of right *almost always* counts an overriding interest (see **E5:3.3.3(iii)** and **G5:3.1**).[63]

EXAMPLE 6

A has a Freehold. The following events then take place:

(i)   8 September: A makes a contractual promise to give C a Charge over A's land.
(ii) 15 September: A executes a deed giving C the Charge.
(iii) 20 September: A, by means of a deed, gives B a five-year Lease.
(iv) 30 September: C substantively registers his Charge.

B's Lease counts as an overriding interest: it is therefore impossible for C to rely on the lack of registration defence. True, B's Lease did not exist on 15 September, when C irrevocably committed himself to acquiring his Charge.[64] However, C qualifies for the lack of registration defence only when he substantively registers his property right.[65] And, at that point, B's Lease *did* exist. This result is confirmed by the decision of Sir Richard Scott V-C in *Barclays Bank plc v Zaroovabli*,[66] the essential facts of which are very close to **Example 6**.

Can C instead rely on the *persistent* right he acquired on 8 September, when A made a contractual promise to give C the Charge? Certainly, that persistent right arose *before* B acquired his Lease. Nonetheless, C cannot assert that persistent right against B: when acquiring his Lease, *B* can rely on the lack of registration defence against C's pre-existing persistent right.[67] So: (i) B acquires his Lease free from C's pre-existing persistent right; whereas (ii) C acquires his Charge subject to B's overriding Lease.

Of course, this result can cause problems for C, who is bound by a hidden property right he had no real chance of discovering.[68] However, C will be better protected in the future, if

---

[62] LRA 2002, Sch 3, para 1.

[63] LRA 2002, Sch 3, para 3.

[64] It may seem that C irrevocably commits to acquiring his right on 8 September, when entering his contract with A. However, if C were to discover, *after* the contract but *before* A's execution of the deed, that A had given B a Lease, C could pull out of the contract with A. So C is only *irrevocably* committed when, on 15 September, A executes the deed.

[65] This was confirmed by the House of Lords in *Abbey National BS v Cann* [1991] 1 AC 56: see esp *per* Lord Oliver at 87 and Lord Jauncey at 106. A different rule applies where B claims that his right is overriding by virtue of B's actual occupation of the land (see **E2:3.6.4(i)**). *Cann* considered the position under the Land Registration Act 1925 but the same rules apply under the LRA 2002.

[66] [1997] Ch 321. See esp *per* Scott V-C at 329: 'It is, in my opinion, an inevitable consequence of the ruling in *Abbey National BS v Cann* that overriding interests in existence at the date of registration of a disposition bind [C].' That decision concerned the Land Registration Act 1925, but the result should be the same under the LRA 2002.

[67] B has not substantively registered his Lease (it is impossible to substantively register a non-exceptional Lease of seven years or less); *but* LRA 2002, s 29(4) allows B to qualify for the lack of registration defence.

[68] When C, before committing himself to acquiring a right from A, asks for an official search of the register, C does then acquire protection from the risk of any new *registered* right of B arising in the next 30 days: see LRA 2002, s 72(5) and Land Registration Rules 2003, rule 131. During that 'priority period', the Land Registry will refuse to enter any right of B in the register. C will therefore have time to acquire and substantively register his property right before any entry is made in respect of B's right. However, this method protects C only from new *registered* rights of B; it does not protect C in **Example 6** as B's intervening Lease is unregistered but overriding.

and when the system of electronic registration is up and running (see **E5:4**). For there will then be *no gap* between the points when: (i) C irrevocably commits to acquiring his right (in **Example 6**, 15 September); and when (ii) C substantively registers that right. Those two stages of the transaction will occur *simultaneously*: there will thus be no gap in which B can acquire an overriding Lease (or Easement). However, at the moment, C does face the risk that B may acquire an overriding Lease (or Easement): (i) *after* C commits to acquiring his right; but (ii) *before* C substantively registers that right.[69]

3.6.2 B's property right was independently acquired

EXAMPLE 7a

A has a registered Freehold. B takes physical control of the land and so independently acquires a separate Freehold. A then transfers his Freehold to C.

Here, B's unregistered property right poses no problems for C. A can assert his pre-existing property right against B. As C has acquired a right that depends on A's Freehold, C steps into A's shoes and so is not bound by B's Freehold: as far as C is concerned, B's Freehold does not count as a *pre-existing* property right.

EXAMPLE 7b

A has a registered Freehold. Over a period of 20 years, B walks across A's land to get to his adjoining land. As a result of this long use of A's land, B acquires an Easement over A's land through prescription (see **G5:2.8**). A then transfers his Freehold to C.

In contrast, to **Example 7a**, B's independently acquired property right *does* bind A. In fact, B's Easement is treated as though it were granted by A (see **G5:2.8.1**): it thus arises before C acquires his property right. C may then try to rely on the lack of registration defence. However, B's Easement will almost always be an overriding interest and therefore immune from the lack of registration defence (see **E5:3.3.3(iii)** and **G5:3.1**).[70]

3.7 The limitation defence

The limitation rules applying to B's property right in land vary according to the nature of that right. The same rules apply if B has a Freehold or a Lease (see **G1A:3**); special rules apply to each of an Easement (see **G5:3.4**) and a Charge (**G4:4.1**).

---

[69] *Ruoff & Roper: Registered Conveyancing* (2003, May 2007 update), 15.007 suggests that the LRA 2002 may *already* have reversed the position in a case such as **Example 6**. The suggestion is that C has a defence to B's Lease under s 28 of that Act, which states the basic rule that, if each of B and C has either a property right or a persistent right, the first to acquire his right has priority. The problem with this analysis is that C does not acquire his Charge until 30 September. Until then, C simply has a persistent right. So B, when acquiring his Lease, can rely on the s 29 priority rule (ie, the lack of registration defence) against C's pre-existing persistent right. So, as under the provisions of the Land Registration Act 1925, B will win. Indeed, Harpum and Bignell, *Registered Land* (2004), 9.7 confirms that this 'registration gap' still exists under the LRA 2002 (Harpum was the Law Commissioner who oversaw the work leading to the LRA 2002).

[70] LRA 2002, Sch 3, para 3.

SUMMARY of E1:3

In the **basic situation**, even if C acquires a right in land, it is very difficult for C to have a defence to B's pre-existing property right. C's principal protection against the risk of being bound by a hidden property right comes from the **content question** and the **acquisition question**—*not* from the **defences question**. First, the list of property rights, even in land, is short and carefully controlled. Second, where land is concerned, B will usually have to satisfy a formality rule if he wishes to acquire a property right. Indeed, thanks to section 27 of the LRA 2002, B's failure to substantively register his right will generally ensure that B has no pre-existing property right to assert against C. This formality rule gives C a good deal of protection: it provides *publicity* and thus allows C to discover most pre-existing property rights.

In the rarer cases where B *can* acquire a property right in land without substantive registration, the lack of registration defence generally does *not* protect C. For example, a Lease or Easement acquired by B without substantive registration will almost always be an overriding interest and hence immune from the lack of registration defence. In those cases, it seems that the justifications allowing B to acquire his property right without registration also prevent C relying on the lack of registration defence (see **E5:3.3.3(ii) and (iii)**).

Of course, this does not mean that it is impossible for C to have a defence against B's property right in land. If B consents to C acquiring a right free from B's property right, or if B is estopped from asserting his right, then C will have a defence. The overreaching defence will also protect C if A has the power to give C a right free from B's pre-existing property right. And, in very rare cases, it will also be possible for C to rely on the limitation defence.

---

4   THE REMEDIES QUESTION

4.1   Preface: the protection of property rights in land

Property rights in land, like all property rights, are protected through the law of wrongs. B's Freehold, Lease, Easement or Charge imposes a prima facie duty on the rest of the world. If C has no defence to B's right, and then interferes with B's use of the land, C breaches his duty to B and so commits a wrong. The wrongs protecting B's property right vary according to the nature of that right and so will be examined when we look at each specific right (see **G1A:4.1.1, G1B:4.1, G4:5 and G5:4.1**).

One general point worth noting here is that the wrong of conversion (see **D1:4.1.1**) does *not* apply where C interferes with B's property right in land. In contrast, the wrong of nuisance can apply *only* where C interferes with B's property right in land (see **A:3.1.4**). That wrong can protect B if, for example: (i) C *indirectly* interferes with B's Freehold or Lease (see **G1A:4.1.1 and G1B:1.2**); or (ii) C directly interferes with B's Easement (see **G5:4.1**).[71]

---

[71] See eg *Paine & Co v St Neots Gas & Coke Co* [1939] 3 All ER 812 at 853.

4.2   Specific protection

The starting position adopted by the property law system is clear: a court *will* specifically protect B's property right in land. The general reluctance to grant such remedies is overcome by the special features of land, such as its uniqueness. So, whilst a thing other than land may sometimes (but rarely) be considered unique, a piece of land will always be seen as unique, due to its fixed and distinct location (see **A:3.1.2**). That approach can be questioned:[72] however, any departure from it may cause severe problems.[73] For reasons of simplicity and consistency, it is better to adopt a general rule that each piece of land is unique.

EXAMPLE 8

B is an owner of land. B goes away on holiday for a month and returns to find that C, a squatter, has moved into B's house and has changed the locks.

In such a case, B can assert his pre-existing Freehold or Lease by means of a special, speedy procedure provided by Part 55 of the Civil Procedure Rules.[74] Using that procedure, B can make a summary application for a 'possession order'—an order that C must leave B's land. Usefully for B, and very unusually, there is no need for B to name and identify C: he can simply ask for a possession order, enforceable against anyone who is currently on B's land.[75] The procedure thus recognises that, given the special features of land, a right to exclusive control of land may deserve special protection. It should be emphasised, however, that this special procedure is just that: it is an efficient means for B to apply for a remedy for a wrong committed by C.[76] B should *only* be able to use the procedure where: (i) B has a right to exclusive control of particular land; and (ii) C, by occupying that land, is in breach of his duty to B not to interfere with B's exclusive control.[77]

EXAMPLE 9

B is an owner of land. B is going away and is keen to have a house-sitter. B gives C permission to occupy that land, on condition that C pays B £200 per week. B does not give C a right to exclusive control of the land, but C moves in and sets up home there, occupying the land by himself. B returns from his trip and tells C to move out by the end of the week.

[72] See eg *per* Sopinka J in *Semelhago v Paramadevan* [1996] 2 SCR 415 (Supreme Court of Canada): 'Specific performance should . . . not be granted as a matter of course absent evidence that the property is unique to the extent that its substitute would not be readily available.'

[73] See Chambers, ch 10 in *Equity in Commercial Law* (ed Degeling and Edelman, 2005). Chambers persuasively argues that any departure from the general rule will necessitate judges making impossible value judgments (eg, how great an emotional attachment did B have to his land?) and lead to inconsistent decisions.

[74] It was formerly available under Order 113 of the Rules of the Supreme Court and Order 24 of the County Court Rules.

[75] See eg *McPhail v Persons (Names Unknown)* [1973] Ch 447. In *Kay v Lambeth LBC* [2006] 2 AC 465, it was suggested by Lord Bingham (at [37]) that this aspect of the procedure may be contrary to C's right under Art 8 of the European Convention on Human Rights (see **B:8.3.2**) as it means a court cannot consider any personal circumstances of C (eg, illness) that may justify postponing a possession order. However, the majority of the House of Lords in *Kay* rejected that suggestion (see Lord Hope at [110], Lord Scott at [174], Baroness Hale at [192], and Lord Brown at [206]).

[76] See *per* Chadwick LJ (dissenting) in *Manchester Airport plc v Dutton* [2000] QB 133 at 139H.

[77] For this reason, the majority decision of the Court of Appeal in *Manchester Airport plc v Dutton* [2000] QB 133 (see **1.3.2** above) must be incorrect.

In such a case, the Protection from Eviction Act 1977 limits B's ability to assert his pre-existing Freehold or Lease against C. As C: (i) has set up home on the land; and (ii) is making a regular payment to B; and (iii) does not share occupation with B or any member of B's family; then (iv) B must give C at least *four weeks notice* before taking steps to remove C.[78] The Act recognises, albeit in a very limited way, that the special features of land may justify giving C some special, temporary protection. This demonstrates, once again, the ambivalent nature of land (see **A:3.2**): (i) B's property right is given special protection through the Part 55 procedure; and (ii) C's use of the land as a home may also be given some special protection under the Protection from Eviction Act 1977.

4.3 Money awards

Even if B's property right in land is specifically protected, B may also claim money from C as a result of C's past interference with B's right. A money award will have two purposes: (i) to serve as a substitute for the right C has interfered with; and (ii) to compensate B for any relevant loss he has suffered as a result of C's interference (see **D1:4.3.1 and D1:4.3.2**).[79] In cases involving property rights in land, some judges and commentators have also suggested that a money award may also aim to transfer to B any gain C has made from his wrong.

EXAMPLE 10

B is an owner of land. B grants C a Lease of that land. C's Lease comes to an end but, despite B's demands that C leave the land, C remains in occupation. C does not pay rent to B. C eventually leaves and B claims a money award in relation to C's wrongful occupation after the end of the Lease.

This example is based on *Ministry of Defence v Ashman*.[80] B, the Ministry of Defence, claimed it should be entitled to money representing the market rent it could have obtained for the land during the period of C's wrongful occupation. C pointed out that, given the special nature of the land (accommodation for service personnel and their families) B would only have rented the land out for a reduced rent. The majority of the Court of Appeal stated that C could be ordered to pay a sum to B based on the value *to C* of her wrongful occupation: ie, based on the savings C made through not having to rent alternative accommodation.

However, that approach is very difficult to justify. For example, what if C had a friend who was willing to put C up for free, but C remained in occupation of B's land for the sake of convenience? In such a case, C has made no financial saving through her wrongful occupation. In *Ashman*, Hoffmann and Kennedy LJJ were concerned by the prospect that if a 'gain-based' award was not made, C would only have to pay a small sum to B, based on the small consequential loss suffered by B as a result of C's wrong. However, this overlooks the key point, made by Lloyd LJ in *Ashman*,[81] that B can be awarded money based *not* on C's gain, *nor* on B's consequential loss but, instead, on the value of B's right (see **D1:4.3.1**). The

---

[78] Protection from Eviction Act 1977, s 5.

[79] A money award will also be made in the rare cases where B's pre-existing property right is not specifically protected (see **G1A:4.2**).

[80] (1993) 66 P & CR 195.

[81] *Ibid* at 203.

best way to justify the approach taken by the Court of Appeal in *Ashman* is to say that C can be ordered to pay B money as a substitute for the right C interfered with:[82] B's right to exclusive control of the land for the period of C's wrongful occupation.

On this analysis, *Ashman* is consistent with the approach taken in **D1:4.3.3**, where we analysed other cases involving C's interference with B's property right in land.[83] Those cases are often taken to show that a court can award B money based on C's gain; however, they are in fact better seen as recognising that C can be ordered to pay B money based on the *value of B's right*.[84] So, it can be argued that, whether B's property right is in land or not, B should only receive money based on C's gain if it is permissible to make an award of 'exemplary' or 'punitive' damages against C.[85]

4.4 An allowance for C?

In **D1:4.4**, we considered C's position in a case where C spends time or money as a result of his incorrect belief that B has no pre-existing property right in a particular thing. What happens if it turns out that B *does* have such a right, and C has no defence to it?[86] Where land is concerned, we have seen that B's right will generally be specifically protected. So, C may have spent money in building a house on B's land; but B will then get the benefit of that work. In such a case, if (i) C's work has increased the value of B's right; and (ii) C did that work innocently (ie, C was unaware of the risk that B might have a pre-existing property right); then (iii) C may well have a direct right against B, based on B's unjust enrichment at C's expense (see **D1:4.4**).[87] Where land is concerned, C may also gain some protection from the doctrine of proprietary estoppel (see **E4**). If C's work was done in reliance on B's promise that C had or would acquire a right in relation to the land, B will be under a duty to ensure that C does not suffer a detriment as a result of C's reliance. Proprietary estoppel can impose a duty on B even if C's work does not benefit the land; however, in contrast to unjust enrichment, it does require B to have made a commitment to C.[88]

However, where land is concerned, C's main protection now comes from the land registration system.[89] If land is registered, C should spend time and money *only* if he has acquired a right from a party who is registered as holding a right in that land. In such a case, C's right is not completely secure. For example, let us say that C buys land from A, a registered Freehold owner. It then turns out that A fraudulently registered that right and

---

[82] The Court of Appeal did not make an award in *Ashman*: rather, all three judges agreed that the first instance decision (ordering C to pay money based on the market rent of the land) should be overturned and that the local county court should consider what sum C should pay instead.

[83] See esp *Bracewell v Appleby* [1975] Ch 408.

[84] As argued by Stevens, *Torts and Rights* (2007), 79–84.

[85] For a consideration of when such damages may be available see *per* Lord Devlin in *Rookes v Barnard* [1964] AC 1129 at 1221–31, esp at 1226–7.

[86] If C worked on the land in reliance on a representation made by B to C that B did not have a property right in the land, C may be able to rely on the 'evidential estoppel' defence (see **D1:3.3.1(i)**).

[87] See eg Jones, *Goff & Jones' Law of Restitution* (7th edn, 2007), 6.002–006. For consideration of this point by the Privy Council see *Blue Haven Enterprises Ltd v Tully* [2006] UKPC 17. In that case, there was no unjust enrichment as C, when starting work on the land, knew of the risk that B might have a pre-existing property right: see *per* Lord Scott at [14] and [27].

[88] In *Blue Haven Enterprises Ltd v Tully* [2006] UKPC 17, the Privy Council's analysis of the relationship between unjust enrichment and proprietary estoppel was rather confused: see McFarlane (2006) 1 *Journal of Equity* 156.

[89] The *Blue Haven* case was heard by the Privy Council on appeal from the Court of Appeal of Jamaica and, when C first dealt with the land, it was unregistered.

that B has a pre-existing Freehold in the land. In such a case, B may apply for the register to be rectified, so that B replaces C as the holder of C's registered Freehold (see **C2:6.1**). If B's application is unsuccessful, C's position is secure. But even if B's application succeeds, C will be able to apply to the Land Registry for an *indemnity* payment, compensating C for the loss he suffers as a result of the rectification in B's favour (see **E5:3.2.3**).[90]

---

[90] C cannot qualify for an indemnity payment if B's pre-existing property right is an overriding interest (see **E5:5.2.2** for criticism of this rule).

CHAPTER E2
PERSISTENT RIGHTS

PERSISTENT RIGHTS

A persistent right is a right against a right. B has a persistent right if:

- A has a specific claim-right or a power; *and*
- A is under a duty to B in relation to that claim-right or power (see **D2:1.1**).

In this chapter, we will focus on the situation where B has a persistent right against A's property right in land.[1] In such cases, on the orthodox view, B is said to have an 'Equitable property right in land'. However, B does *not* have a property right: the rest of the world is *not* under a prima facie duty to B (see **B:4.4.3**). And, strictly speaking B does not have a persistent right *in land*; instead, B has a right against A's property right in land (ie, A's Freehold, Lease, Easement or Charge). For the sake of convenience, such persistent rights can be referred to as 'persistent rights relating to land'.

To examine such rights, we will again consider each of the basic questions:

Section 1   The **content question**: what rights count as persistent rights relating to land?
Section 2   The **acquisition question**: how can B acquire such a right?
Section 3   The **defences question**: when can C have a defence to B's pre-existing persistent right relating to land?
Section 4   The **remedies question**: if B does have a pre-existing persistent right relating to land to which C has no defence, how will a court protect B's right?

In **D2**, we saw the general answers given to these questions; here we will focus on how, and why, the answers may be different where land is concerned. In **E1**, we saw that the general rules applying to *property rights* are often displaced where land is concerned. That is not too surprising. After all, property rights are rights against a thing and so may behave differently in relation to land—a thing with special features. In contrast, as a persistent right is a right against a right, it might be thought that persistent rights should operate in the *same way* whether or not they relate to land. However, as we will see, the special features of land do have an impact on the operation of persistent rights.

---

[1] The principles discussed here can, in general, also apply where: (i) A has a persistent right relating to land; and (ii) B claims a right against that right.

1   THE CONTENT QUESTION

1.1   The basic rule

The basic rule we examined in **D2:1.1** also applies where land is concerned. To have a persistent right, B needs to show that:

- A is under a duty to B; *and*
- A's duty to B relates to the whole of a specific, distinct claim-right or power held by A.

A has a Freehold. A makes a contractual promise to allow B to occupy A's land for six months. Two months later, A sells his land to C.

If A has not promised to give B exclusive control of A's land, B's right cannot count as a Lease and so B cannot have a property right (see **G1B:1.4**). And, as A's duty to B does not relate to the whole of a specific, distinct right held by A, B cannot have a persistent right (see **D2:Example 2**). Therefore, A's contractual promise simply gives B a personal right against A.[2] This means that, in **Example 1**, B does *not* have a pre-existing right that he can assert against C.[3]

In a case such as **Example 1**, B's right is often referred to as a 'contractual licence': a *licence* because A has given his permission for B to make a particular use of A's land; and a *contractual* licence as A is under a contractual duty to B not to revoke that permission (see **E6:3**). The land law system's refusal to allow a contractual licence to count as a persistent right has proved controversial: it has been argued that B's contractual licence really ought to be prima facie binding on C (see **E6:3.4.2**). Certainly, from the perspective of practical convenience (see **B:9**), it can be argued that a contractual licence should be prima facie binding on C—after all, such a licence may be the only right B has in his home. However, it is important to note here that the current position is doctrinally correct: it is a product of the principle, applying throughout the property law system, that B can only have a persistent right if A is under a duty to B in relation to a specific claim-right or power held by A.

1.2   General persistent rights

1.2.1 The Purely Equitable Charge

If A has any right (eg, a property right in land), it is possible for B to acquire a Purely Equitable Charge against A's right (see **D2:1.2.1**). For example, let us say A Co gives B a floating charge over all of A Co's current and future assets. When that charge crystallises, B acquires a Purely Equitable Charge over all of the rights held by A Co, including any property rights in land it may have.

---

[2] If B takes physical control of the land (as occurs if B goes into sole occupation of the land), B then *independently* acquires a Freehold (see **E6:2.3**). However, such a property right arises because of B's unilateral conduct, not because of B's agreement with A.

[3] See eg the analysis of the Court of Appeal in *Ashburn Anstalt v Arnold* [1989] Ch 1. Of course, as noted by the Court of Appeal in that case, B may have a *direct right* against C, arising as a result of C's conduct (see **E6:3.4.1**).

However, if A has a Freehold or Lease and B specifically wants to acquire a security right in relation to A's land, B will prefer, if possible, to acquire a Charge. A Charge counts as a property right in land (see **E1:1**) and therefore has a number of advantages over a Purely Equitable Charge. In particular, a Purely Equitable Charge, like all persistent rights relating to land, cannot be substantively registered. In contrast, if B substantively registers his Charge, then B can take advantage of:

- *the positive aspect of registration*—as long as he is registered as holding it, B is guaranteed to have that Charge (see **C2:6.1**); and
- *the negative aspect of registration*—if B has acquired his Charge for value, B may be able to use the lack of registration defence against any pre-existing persistent rights relating to A's land (see **C2:6.2** and **3.6** below).

1.2.2 The right arising under an Equitable Assignment?

In **D2:1.2.2**, we saw that the persistent right arising under an Equitable Assignment is, in its content, identical to a right under a Trust. The term 'Equitable Assignment' is therefore used in this book to refer to a particular means by which B can acquire a right under a Trust. Clearly, as this means of acquiring a persistent right arises only where A has a *personal* right against Z, it is of no use to B if he wants to acquire a persistent right against A's property right in land.

1.2.3 The Mortgagor's Right to Redeem?

If B transfers a right to A by way of security, A holds that right subject to a persistent right of B: a Mortgagor's Right to Redeem (see **D2:1.2.3**). Since 1926, it has been impossible for B to transfer a property right in land by way of security: if B has a Freehold or Lease, B cannot mortgage that right. Instead, to give A a property right by way of security, B must: (i) keep his Freehold or Lease; and (ii) grant A a Charge. B thus *keeps* his property right: there is no possibility of B acquiring a new persistent right; and no need for him to do so. In such a case, B is often said to have an 'equity of redemption', but, as we will see, this is *not* a persistent right and is therefore different from the Mortgagor's Right to Redeem (see **G4:1.4.3**).

1.2.4 The right arising under a Trust

(i) General position

- If A has a property right in land; *and*
- A is under a duty to B in relation to that right; *and*
- A is under a duty, overall, not to use that right for A's own benefit (unless and to the extent that A is also a beneficiary of the Trust); *then*
- A holds his property right in land on Trust for B.

The Trust is an incredibly versatile mechanism (see **D2:1.4**). Its flexibility makes it a very important part of the land law system.

EXAMPLE 2a

A0 has a Freehold. A0 wants to divide his right to exclusive control of the land up so that: (i) B1 has a right to exclusive control for B1's life; then (ii) B2 has a right to exclusive control for B2's life; then (iii) the National Trust has a right to exclusive control of the land forever.

To a certain extent, A0 *can* divide up his right to exclusive control over time: by granting B1 a right to exclusive control of the land for the duration of B1's life, A0 can give B1 a property right (a Lease: see **G1B:1.7.3**).[4] However, A0 *cannot* give B2 a Lease taking effect more than 21 years in the future;[5] and A0 *cannot* give the National Trust a Freehold taking effect in the future (see **G1A:1.4**).

So in **Example 2a**, as in **D1:Example 7**, A0's best option is to set up a Trust. A0 can do so, for example, by transferring his Freehold to A, subject to a duty to use that Freehold: (i) for B1's benefit during B1's life; then (ii) for B2's benefit during B2's life and then (iii) for the benefit of the National Trust. By doing so, A0 can ensure that B1, B2 and the National Trust each has a right to the benefits of the Freehold; *and* that B1, B2 and the National Trust each has a persistent right and so is protected if, for example, A goes into insolvency.[6]

It may seem that, by using a Trust in this way, A0 is somehow evading the restrictions that the Law of Property Act 1925 ('the LPA 1925') places on the content of property rights in land (see **E1:1**). But, crucially, A0 is *not* using the Trust to divide up his Freehold over time; rather, his Freehold simply goes to A. Instead, A0 uses the Trust to divide up the *benefit* of that right over time. The beneficiaries of the Trust (B1, B2 and the National Trust) acquire persistent rights, *not* property rights: the restrictions imposed by the LPA 1925 are *not* undermined.

(ii) Duties to transfer a property right in land

EXAMPLE 2b

A has a Freehold or Lease. A makes a contractual promise to B to transfer that Freehold or Lease to B for a price of £250,000.

A's contractual promise, by itself, cannot transfer his Freehold or Lease to B. That transfer can only occur if a deed is used and (in most cases) if B is substantively registered as the new holder of A's right (see **E1:2.3**). This means that, in **Example 2b**, there is a gap between: (i) A's contractual promise to transfer his right; and (ii) B's acquisition of that right. That gap provides a space in which: (i) A retains his Freehold or Lease; and (ii) A is under a duty to B in relation to that Freehold or Lease; so (iii) B has a persistent right against A's Freehold or Lease. In contrast, if A makes a contractual promise to transfer his Ownership of thing other than land to B, there is usually no such space in which B can acquire a persistent right: A's contractual promise, *by itself*, can transfer Ownership to B (see **D2:Example 13**).[7]

---

[4] A Lease for the duration of B1's life takes effect as a Lease for 90 years determinable on B1's death: see Law of Property Act 1925, s 149(6).

[5] Law of Property Act 1925, s 149(3).

[6] On the death of B1 and B2, the National Trust becomes the sole beneficiary of the Trust and can then insist on A transferring his Freehold directly to the National Trust (see **D1:1.4.5(ii)**).

[7] This difference between the effect of contracts to sell land and contracts to sell goods is generally said to depend on the availability of specific performance in the former case and not the latter: however, we rejected that view in **D2:2.1.2(vi)**.

In such a case, B's persistent right is often referred to as an 'Estate Contract' (see **C2:Example 5**). However, as far as its content is concerned, an Estate Contract is *not* a distinct form of persistent right: as noted by Sir George Jessel MR in *Lysaght v Edwards*,[8] it is simply an example of a Trust.[9] In **Example 2b** B's persistent right arises under a Trust as A is under the core Trust duty to B: a duty not to use his Freehold or Lease for his own benefit.[10] Such a Trust is *not* peculiar to the land law system: it arises *whenever:* (i) A holds a specific right; and (ii) A is under a duty (whether or not is a contractual duty)[11] to transfer that right to B.[12]

Of course, in **Example 2b** the terms of A and B's contract will affect A's duties to B: for example, if the contract fixes a date on which B is to take physical control of the land, A is entitled to occupy the land, or to receive other benefits from the land, until that point.[13] So, A is not in exactly the same position as a party who simply declares that he holds a Freehold or Lease on Trust for B. However, that simply shows the great diversity of the Trust: it does not prevent us saying that, in **Example 2b**, B's persistent right is a right under a Trust.

EXAMPLE 2c

A has a Freehold or Lease. In return for payment from B, A makes a contractual promise to B that, if B chooses to do so, B can buy that Freehold or Lease at any point in the next five years for £250,000.

The key difference with **Example 2b** is that *B* is not under a duty to A: B does not have to go ahead with the purchase of A's Freehold or Lease. However, as A is under a duty to B to transfer his Freehold or Lease to B,[14] B again acquires a persistent right.[15] That persistent right is often referred to as an 'Option to Purchase' but, like an 'Estate Contract', it is best seen as simply an example of a right under a Trust. Again, it is *not* peculiar to the land law system but should arise whenever: (i) A holds a specific right; and (ii) A is under a duty (whether or not is a contractual duty) to transfer that right to B.

---

[8] (1876) 2 Ch D 499 at 506.

[9] That does not mean we can dispense with the term 'Estate Contract': it can still be used to identify a specific example of a right under a Trust. For example, in general, B *cannot* defensively register a right under a Trust by entering a notice on the register (see Land Registration Act 2002, s 33(a)(i)). However, if B's right arises under an Estate Contract (or, as in **Examples 2c and 2d**, under an 'Option to Purchase' or a 'Right of Pre-Emption') it *can* be defensively registered.

[10] The same analysis applies if A comes under a duty to transfer an Easement or a Charge to B.

[11] For a case involving a non-contractual duty to transfer a Freehold to B see *Pascoe v Turner* [1979] 1 WLR 431 (see **C3:Example 3**). If: (i) A tries but fails to directly transfer his property right to B; and (ii) B provides value in return for that attempt; then (iii) A is under a duty to grant B that right and so B acquires a persistent right under the principle discussed at **D2:n66**.

[12] See eg *Neville v Wilson* [1997] Ch 144 (A's duty was to transfer specific shares to B).

[13] See eg *Rayner v Preston* (1881) 18 Ch D 1, see esp *per* Cotton LJ at 6 (A was allowed to keep insurance money received as a result of a fire occurring after the contract of sale was entered but before B was due to take physical control of the land).

[14] It could be said that A's duty arises only when B chooses to go ahead with the purchase (ie, to take up the option). However, that distinction is not convincing: in **Example 2b**, as in any other case where A is under a duty to B, it could be said that B has a choice as to whether or not to enforce A's duty.

[15] See eg *per* Sir George Jessel MR in *London & South Western Railway Co v Gomm* (1882) 20 Ch D 562 at 580–81.

EXAMPLE 2d

A has a Freehold or Lease. In return for payment from B, A makes a contractual promise to B that, *if* A chooses to sell his Freehold or Lease in the next five years, B can buy that Freehold or Lease for £250,000.

In such a case, B is said to have a 'right of pre-emption' or a 'right of first refusal'. The key difference with **Example 2c** is that A is not under an immediate duty to B: if A chooses not to sell his Freehold or Lease, A comes under no duty to B. As a result, as confirmed by the Court of Appeal in *Pritchard v Briggs*,[16] A's contractual promise to B, by itself, cannot give B an immediate persistent right. However, things are different *if A does decide to sell*. As soon as A makes that decision, he is under a duty to B: B is thus in the same position as in **Example 2c**. So, as Templeman and Stephenson LJJ again confirmed in *Pritchard v Briggs*,[17] B *does* acquire a persistent right once A decides to sell. That persistent right is often referred to as a 'Right of Pre-Emption' but, as in **Examples 2b and 2c**, it is better seen as a right under a Trust.

Whatever name we give it, the persistent right B can acquire in **Example 2d** is problematic. As a matter of doctrine, it is correct to say B can only acquire the right *as soon as* A decides to sell. However, as a matter of practical convenience, it is awkward to make A's state of mind the crucial factor in deciding if B has a right that is capable of binding C, a party later acquiring a right from A. For example, in **Example 2d**, what happens if A later gives C a Charge over A's land? B may claim that, when C acquired its Charge, B had a pre-existing persistent right; but that depends on the very difficult factual question of whether A, at that point, had decided to sell the land.

There are two ways to avoid that practical problem. The first is to say that, in a case such as **Example 2d**, A's initial contractual promise to B *can never* give B a persistent right, even if A does then decide to sell the land. That route was chosen by Goff LJ, departing from Templeman and Stephenson LJJ on this point, in *Pritchard v Briggs*.[18] The second is to say that, in a case such as **Example 2d**, A's initial contractual promise to B *immediately* gives B a persistent right, even if A does not then decide to sell the land. That route has, in effect, been chosen by section 115(1) of the Land Registration Act 2002 ('the LRA 2002'). That provision states that:

A right of pre-emption in relation to registered land has effect from the time of creation as an interest capable of binding successors in title (subject to the rules about the effect of dispositions on priority).[19]

So, assuming that A's Freehold or Lease is substantively registered, it is now the case that, in **Example 2d**, B *immediately* acquires a right that is capable of binding C, a party later acquiring a right from A.

---

[16] [1980] Ch 338.
[17] *Ibid* esp *per* Templeman LJ at 418.
[18] *Ibid* at 389 and 394.
[19] The words in brackets simply mean that C may be able to use the lack of registration defence against B's pre-existing Right of Pre-Emption (see **3.6** below).

1.3   Special persistent rights that can exist only in relation to land

1.3.1 The Equitable Lease, Equitable Easement and Equitable Charge

(i) The principle

EXAMPLE 3a

A has Ownership of a bike. A makes a contractual promise to give B exclusive control of the bike for five years. Two months later, A sells his bike to C.

EXAMPLE 3b

A has a Freehold. A makes a contractual promise to give B exclusive control of the land for five years. Two months later, A sells his land to C.

In **Example 3a**, A's promise gives B neither a property right (see **D1:1.4.3**), nor a persistent right (see **D2:Example 2**). However, things are different in **Example 3b**. As a result of his contractual promise to B, A is under a duty to give B exclusive control of the land for a limited period. As a result, it is possible for B to acquire an immediate property right: a Lease (see **G1B:2.2**).

However, in a case such as **Example 3b**, B can only acquire that property right if a deed has been used (see **E1:2.3.3**). If no deed is used, A can still come under a contractual duty to B to give B a right to exclusive control of his land for a limited period.[20] If that duty exists, B acquires an immediate persistent right, known as an Equitable Lease.[21] This seems to create an inconsistency: in **Example 3a**, A's duty to give B exclusive control of a bike for a limited period does *not* give B a persistent right; in **Example 3b**, A's duty to give B exclusive control of land for a limited period *does* give B a persistent right.

This difference can be justified. It is does *not* involve a departure from the basic test for the content of a persistent right. Instead, it is simply a product of the fact that a right to exclusive control of land for a limited period, unlike a right to exclusive control of a bike for a limited period, counts as a property right. This means that in **Example 3b** A, as an owner of land, has a specific, distinct *power*: the power to give B a right, prima facie binding on the rest of the world, to exclusive control of that land for a fixed period. Therefore, if, as in **Example 3b**, A comes under a duty to B in relation to that power, B acquires a persistent right: a right against A's power to grant a Lease. A's power to grant a Lease depends on A's Freehold. So, when A transfers his Freehold to C, C acquires A's power to grant B a Lease. But, as B has a right against that power, B has a prima facie power to impose a duty on C: a duty to use his power to grant B a Lease.

In **Example 3a** things are very different. A, as an owner of a bike, does *not* have a power to give B a property right consisting of the right to exclusive control of that bike for a fixed

---

[20] Although note that a contractual duty can only arise if the agreement between A and B satisfies the formality rule imposed by the Law of Property (Miscellaneous Provisions) Act 1989, s 2 (see **2.3.3** below).

[21] See eg *Walsh v Lonsdale* (1882) 21 Ch D 9. B also acquires a persistent right if A is under a non-contractual duty to give B exclusive control of land for a limited period: see eg *Lloyd v Dugdale* [2002] 2 P & CR 13 (**E4:Example 13**). If: (i) A tries but fails to directly give B a property right in land (eg, a Lease); and (ii) B provides value in return for that attempt; then (iii) A is under a duty to grant B that right and so B acquires a persistent right under the principle discussed at **D2:n66**: see eg *Parker v Taswell* (1858) 2 De G & J 559.

period. So, in **Example 3a,** B *cannot* say that: (i) A has a specific, distinct power; and (ii) A is under a duty to B in relation to that power. As a result, in **Example 3a,** A's contractual promise gives B only a personal right against A.

Examples **3a and 3b** therefore show that, where land is concerned, persistent rights can operate differently. However, that difference flows from the fact that the list of property rights in land is longer than the general list of property rights. That means that A, an owner of land, has specific powers not held by an owner of a bike: powers to grant a Lease, an Easement or a Charge. If A then comes under a duty to B in relation to one of those powers, B acquires a persistent right. If, as in **Example 3b,** A's duty is to grant B a Lease, B acquires an Equitable Lease; if A's duty is to grant B an Easement, B acquires an Equitable Easement;[22] and if A's duty is to grant B a Charge, B acquires an Equitable Charge.[23]

If B has an Equitable Charge, it is very important to distinguish that right from a Purely Equitable Charge (see further **G4:3.4.3**):

1. A Purely Equitable Charge is a form of persistent right that can exist against *any right of A.* So, if A has a personal right against Z Bank, B may have a Purely Equitable Charge over that right.
2. In contrast, an Equitable Charge can exist *only* where A has a property right in land. It is only where A has such a right that A has the power to give B a Charge: a Charge, a distinct form of property right, exists only in relation to land.

(ii) Contractual licences?

In **Example 3b** B acquires a persistent right by showing that: (i) A has a specific power; and (ii) A is under a duty to B in relation to that power. In **Example 1,** B *cannot* rely on that argument to acquire a persistent right: B cannot say he has a right against a specific power held by A. The first, obvious difference is that, in **Example 1,** A is not under a duty to use his power to grant B a specific property right in the land. It is true that A has a power to make a contractual promise to allow B to use the land, but A has already exercised that power. And, in any case, *anyone* can make a contractual promise to allow B to use particular land: for example, A can make a contractual promise to B to allow B to occupy Buckingham Palace for the next six months. In **Example 3b,** in contrast, A's contractual promise relates to a power A has as a result of his own Freehold or Lease: his power to grant B a Lease.

1.3.2 The Restrictive Covenant

EXAMPLE 4

B has a Freehold. B decides to split up his land: he keeps half of it (No 32B) and sells a Freehold of the other half to A (No 32A). At B's insistence A promises, as part of his contractual deal with B, that A and all future owners of all or any part of A's land will *not* use that land for any commercial purpose. A then transfers No 32A to C who wishes to open a shop.

---

[22] See eg *McManus v Cooke* (1887) 35 Ch D 681. Again, B also acquires a persistent right if A is under a non-contractual duty to grant B an Easement: see eg *Crabb v Arun DC* [1976] Ch 179.

[23] See eg *Kinane v Mackie-Conteh* [2005] EWCA Civ 45 (A's duty to grant B a Charge arose as a result of proprietary estoppel).

In such a case, A's contractual promise to B gives B a persistent right: a Restrictive Covenant. As a result, B's right is prima facie binding on C: B has a prima facie power to impose a duty on C not to open a shop on No 32A. This result clearly contrasts with the result in **D1:Example 1**: B's attempt to control the future use of some bikes by means of a 'price maintenance clause' does *not* give B a persistent right (see **D2:1.1.3**). However, where land is involved, things are different: A's binding promise not to make a particular use of his land *can* give B a persistent right if certain requirements are satisfied:

- A has a Freehold or Lease; *and*
- A is under a duty to B *not* to make a particular use of A's land; *and*
- A intends that his duty will bind parties later acquiring A's Freehold or Lease; *and*
- B has a Freehold or Lease that benefits from A's duty.

The Restrictive Covenant, like the Equitable Lease, Equitable Easement and Equitable Charge, is thus a special form of persistent right that can exist only in relation to land. However, unlike those other rights, it *does* depend on a departure from the basic test for the content of a persistent right. In **Example 4**, A's duty to B does *not* relate to a specific claim-right or power held by A. A's duty can be analysed in one of two ways. First, it could be said that A's duty relates to A's liberty to make a commercial use of that land. On that view, the Restrictive Covenant is an exception to the basic rule that a persistent right must relate to a *claim-right or power* held by A. It is that rule which means that, in **D1:Example 1**, B does not have a persistent right (see **D2:1.1.3**).

Second, it could be said (perhaps more accurately) that A's duty relates to A's claim-right that B cannot prevent A making a commercial use of the land. On that view, the Restrictive Covenant is an exception to the basic rule that a persistent right must relate to the *whole* of a specific, distinct right held by A. The point is that A's claim-right against B is simply part and parcel of A's Freehold: along with B, everyone else in the world is under a prima facie duty to A not to intefere with any use A may choose to make of the land. It should not therefore be possible to separate out A's claim-right *against B* and say that B has a persistent right against that particular right;[24] just as, if A has Ownership of a bike, we cannot separate out A's Ownership of the paint on the bike and say that B has a persistent right against that particular right (see **D2:1.1.2(iii)**).

The Restrictive Covenant is thus a clear example of a case in which the land law system departs from a basic *doctrinal* principle in order to meet the perceived needs of *practical convenience* (see **B:9**). The Restrictive Covenant began to be recognised as a persistent right in the second half of the 19th century.[25] It seems that, in a case such as **Example 4**, B might be reluctant to sell part of his land unless he had some means to stop future owners of that land from using it in a way detrimental to B's retained land. For example, B might be a wealthy landowner who wants to invest in a factory; he might want to sell some of his land to make that investment, but be worried that a future owner of that land will use it to build

---

[24] Indeed, if this were possible, B could argue that he has a persistent right in **Example 1**. B could claim that: (i) A has a claim-right against B that B must not occupy A's land; and (ii) as a result of A's contractual promise to B, A is then under a duty to B in relation to that specific claim-right against B. The problem again for B is that he can acquire a persistent right only if A's promise is to give B exclusive control of the land. Otherwise, B cannot show that A's duty to B relates to either the *whole* of A's Freehold or to A's power to grant B a Lease.

[25] See eg *London & South Western Railway Co v Gomm* (1882) 20 Ch D 562 esp *per* Sir George Jessel MR at 583.

a factory himself. And whilst B may be keen to invest in factories, he probably does not want to live next to one.

So, the Restrictive Covenant answered a particular need by allowing B: (i) to sell part of his land to A; and (ii) to impose a duty on A not to use that land in a particular way (eg, not to use it for commercial purposes); and (iii) to acquire a persistent right capable of binding later owners of A's land.[26] The third point is of course crucial: it ensures that B is protected even *after* A transfers his Freehold or Lease to C. In this way, the recognition of the Restrictive Covenant may have played an important practical role: it may have *increased* the marketability and availability of land, by giving parties such as B the security of knowing that he can both (i) sell off part of his land; and (ii) retain some control over the use of that land, for the benefit of his retained land.

As we have seen, the courts have *not* allowed B to acquire a persistent right by (i) selling a thing *other than land* to A; and (ii) imposing a duty on A not to use that thing in a particular way (see eg **D1:Example 1**). Where things other than land are concerned, it may be that there is no need to encourage B to sell such things by giving B a right to control their future use. The Restrictive Covenant may therefore respond to the special features of land: in particular (i) its limited availability, meaning there is a need to increase its market-ability (see **A:3.1.5**); and (ii) its fixed location, meaning that if B owns particular land, he will necessarily be affected by the use made of neighbouring land (see **A:3.1.1 and A:3.1.2**). Those features may have led to the view that, if and only if land is concerned, the needs of practical convenience mean that the Restrictive Covenant must count as a persistent right.

The Law Commission has recently suggested that Parliament should make it impossible for new Restrictive Covenants to arise in relation to registered land.[27] If, in a case such as **Example 4**, B wants to prevent A and future users of A's land from making a particular use of A's land, B would have to ensure that his sale to A included the creation of a Land Obligation—a *property right* based on a duty assumed by A (see **E1:1.3.1**).[28] From a doctrinal perspective, there is something to be said for such a reform. As a persistent right, the Restrictive Covenant is anomalous: it is inconsistent with the basic conceptual test for such rights, as it arises even though A's duty to B does not relate to the whole of a specific claim-right or power held by A. In contrast, there is no conceptual unity to the content of property rights (see **D1:1.2.3**), so allowing B's right, in a case such as **Example 4**, to count as a property right involves *no* doctrinal problem.[29]

1.4   Extending the list of persistent rights relating to land?

The development of the Restrictive Covenant raises an important question. Are there any

---

[26] The importance of Restrictive Covenants is attested to in a comment of Cozens-Hardy LJ in re Nisbet & Potts Contract [1906] 1 Ch 386 at 409: 'The value of estates in the neighbourhood of London and all large towns, and the amenity of those estates, depend almost entirely upon the continuance of the mutual restrictive covenants affecting the user and enjoyment of the land.'

[27] Law Com No 186 (2008): Consultation Paper on Easements, Covenants and Profits a Prendre at 8.98.

[28] Law Com No 186 (2008) Part 8, eg at 8.13. If A instead were to come under a duty to grant B a Land Oblig-ation, B would then acquire a persistent right, arising in the same way as an Equitable Lease, Equitable Easement or Equitable Charge (see **1.3.1(i)** above): Law Com No 186 at 8.45–8.47.

[29] Although, on the Law Commission's proposals a (different) doctrinal problem does arise from the idea that a *positive* duty assumed by A can also count as a Land Obligation and so give B a right prima facie binding the rest of the world (see **E1:1.3.1**).

other situations in which the needs of practical convenience may lead the courts to recognise a new form of persistent right? For example, might those needs trump doctrinal concerns and allow certain forms of contractual licence to count as a persistent right?

Section 1 of the LPA 1925 imposes a statutory limit on the list of property rights in land (see **E1:1.3**). Section 4(1) of the Act appears to do exactly the same in relation to 'Equitable property rights in land'—ie, persistent rights relating to land.[30] Although the section has not been explicitly relied on by the courts (and differing views have been suggested as to its meaning)[31] it seems to have a clear effect: new types of persistent right relating to land can be recognised *only* by Parliament. Any extension to the list of persistent rights relating to land (and any change to the current, doctrinally correct approach to contractual licences) would therefore have to come from Parliament, not the courts.

However, this does *not* mean that persistent rights relating to land, unlike other persistent rights, are subject to the 'closed list' principle. In general, given the conceptual unity to the content of persistent rights, that principle does not apply to persistent rights (see **D2:1.3**). The same is true where land is concerned: for example, almost[32] *any* right of B can count as a persistent right relating to land *if* it arises under a Trust.

EXAMPLE 1a

A0 has a Freehold. A0 transfers his Freehold to A subject to a duty: (i) to allow B to occupy the land for six months; then (ii) to use his Freehold entirely for the benefit of A0. Two months later, acting without B's consent or other authority, A sells his Freehold to C.

In such a case, the content of B's right is identical to the content of his right in **Example 1**. However, as A is, *overall*, under a duty in relation to the whole of his Freehold, A is under the core Trust duty. As a result, B has a persistent right: a right under a Trust. This means that, in contrast to **Example 1**, B has a prima facie power to impose a duty on C. Hence, just as we saw in **D2:Examples 6a, 6b and 6c**, A0 can take advantage of the Trust to ensure that, *whatever* its content, B's right can count as a persistent right.

1.5   Powers to regain a property right in land

EXAMPLE 5

B has a Freehold. A, a fraudster, is paid by B to act as an agent in finding a purchaser for B's Freehold. A tells B that X is willing to buy B's Freehold for £250,000. As a result, B transfers his Freehold to X and X is substantively registered as the holder of that Freehold. It turns out that X is an alias used by A. A does not pay any of the supposed £250,000 purchase price to B.

B has transferred his Freehold to A as a result of A's fraud. As a result, B has a 'Common Law right to rescind the transfer': a power to regain his initial right (see **D1:1.4.5(i)**). That power can be said to arise from the fact that A holds the right received from B on Trust for

---

[30] The section states that: 'After the commencement of this Act (and save as hereinafter expressly enacted), an equitable interest in land shall only be capably of being validly created in any case in which an equivalent equitable interest in property real or personal could have been validly created before such commencement.'

[31] Compare eg Briggs [1983] *Conv* 285 and R Smith, *Property Law* (5th edn, 2005), 43. Briggs's view is the more convincing.

[32] Some limits are imposed: see eg **D2:n26**.

B (see **D4:3.2.2**). That analysis was adopted by the Court of Appeal in *Collings v Lee*,[33] the facts of which are identical to **Example 5**. The Trust is best seen as a Resulting Trust: it arises because: (i) A has acquired a right from B; and (ii) A knows there is no legal basis for A to have the benefit of that right (see **D4:4.3**).

If B transfers his Ownership of a bike to A as a result of A's fraud, B then has a power to regain that right *immediately* (see **D1:Example 6b**). However, in **Example 5**, the rules of the land registration system mean that things are slightly different: the positive operation of registration means that, as long as A is substantively registered, A retains his Freehold (see **C2:6.1**). Therefore, B regains his Freehold only when the register is changed and B is recorded as holding that Freehold.

1.6   Powers to acquire a persistent right relating to land

EXAMPLE 6

B has a Freehold. A wants to buy that Freehold. A persuades B to sell by telling him that B's employer now provides rent-free accommodation to all its employees. A genuinely believes that statement to be true, but it turns out to be false. In reliance on the truth of A's statement, B sells A his Freehold for £250,000.

B has transferred his Freehold to A as a result of A's innocent misrepresentation. As a result, B has an 'Equitable right to rescind the transfer': a power to acquire a persistent right against the right he has transferred to A (see **D2:1.6** and **D4:4.2.1**). In such a case, as soon as A acquires B's Freehold, B is said to have a 'mere Equity'. We have suggested that a 'mere Equity' is best seen as a *power to acquire a persistent right* (see **D2:1.6(iii)**).[34] In contrast to **Example 5**, it is not the case that A is immediately under the core Trust duty to B: when A acquires his right, he does not know that B has transferred it as a result of a misrepresentation. However, as: (i) A has acquired a right from B as a result of A's misrepresentation; so (ii) there is no legal basis for A to have the benefit of that right; (iii) B has a power to acquire a right under a Trust by informing A of the fact meaning that there is no legal basis for A to have the benefit of that right (see **D4:4.2**).

The analysis of **Example 6** is thus identical to the analysis of a case where, as a result of A's innocent misrepresentation, B sells his bike to A (see **D2:Example 21** and **D4:Example 6b**). However, the rules of the land registration system do make a difference when we come to consider what defences C may have against B's pre-existing power to acquire a persistent right relating to registered land (see **3.5.2** below).

---

[33] [2001] 2 All ER 332: see esp *per* Nourse LJ at 336. Nourse LJ does rely on the idea that B 'retained' his initial 'beneficial interest'. That reasoning is incorrect (see esp *per* Lord Browne-Wilkinson in *Westdeutsche Landesbank Girozentrale v Islington LBC* [1996] AC 669 at 706 and 714–5); but the conclusion that A immediately holds his Freehold on Trust for B is valid.

[34] For other examples, see eg *Blacklocks v JB Developments (Godalming) Ltd* [1982] Ch 183. B sold land to A. As a result of the parties' mutual mistake, an extra parcel of land was transferred to A. B had a power to rectify the contract and thus to impose a duty on A to transfer that extra parcel back to B. Once A is under such a duty, B has a persistent right: A's duty relates to his Freehold of that extra parcel. So B's power to rectify gave B a power to acquire a persistent right or, on the orthodox view, a 'mere Equity'.

SUMMARY of E2:1

The special features of land have an impact on the content of persistent rights. First, those special features have led to the recognition of certain *property rights* that can exist only in land—in particular the Lease, Easement and Charge. This means that if A has a Freehold or Lease of land, A has powers unavailable to, say, an owner of a bike, namely powers to give B a Lease, Easement or Charge. If A then comes under a duty to B to exercise such a power in B's favour, B acquires an immediate persistent right. As a result, there are three forms of persistent right that can exist only in relation to land: the Equitable Lease, Equitable Easement and Equitable Charge.

Second, the special features of land mean that, if B has a Freehold or Lease, he has a special interest in the way neighbouring land is used. In particular, the fear that a neighbour may make an unwelcome use of his land might deter B from selling off part of his land. To counter this problem, the courts recognised a new and anomalous persistent right: the Restrictive Covenant. This right is anomalous as B acquires a persistent right even though A's duty does not relate to the whole of a specific claim-right or power held by A. However, as we will see in **G6:1**, there are a number of important limits to the content of the Restrictive Covenant.

2   THE ACQUISITION QUESTION

2.1   The acquisition of a new persistent right

In **D2:2.1**, we looked at six different methods by which A can come under a duty to B: if A's duty relates to a claim-right or power held by A, each of those methods can lead to B acquiring a persistent right. Those same six methods (consent, contract, wrongs, unjust enrichment, statute, other events) can also be used by B to acquire a persistent right relating to land. However, where land is concerned, some special points apply.

2.1.1 Contracts to transfer a right

A contractual promise by A to transfer a right to B can give B a persistent right if two key factors are present: (i) A's promise is to transfer a specific right; and (ii) the contractual promise, by itself, does not operate to transfer that right to B (see **D2:2.1.2(iii)**).

Where A promises to transfer to B a property right or a persistent right relating to land, those factors *will* generally be present. For example, in a standard contract for the sale of a house: (i) A will promise to transfer a *specific* right (his Freehold or Lease); and (ii) the contract, by itself, will not operate to transfer A's right to B (see **Example 2b**). However, to show that A is under such a contractual duty, B will need to show that the formality rule imposed by the Law of Property (Miscellaneous Provisions) Act 1989 has been satisfied (see **2.3.3** below).

2.1.2 Proprietary estoppel

Where land is concerned, there is an important additional means by which A can come under a duty to B: the doctrine of proprietary estoppel. Using the terminology applied in

D2:2.1, proprietary estoppel fits into the 'other events' category: (i) A comes under a duty to B; and (ii) that duty it is not based on A's consent; on a contractual promise of A; on a wrong committed by A; on an unjust enrichment of A at B's expense; or on a statute. If proprietary estoppel imposes a duty on A in relation to specific claim-right or power held by A, B acquires a persistent right.[35]

We will examine the doctrine in detail in **E4**. It operates to impose a duty on A where:

- A makes a commitment to B to use to his land in a certain way; *and*
- B relies on that commitment; *and*
- B has suffered, or will suffer, a detriment as a result of A's refusal to honour his commitment.

Although there are strong arguments for extending the doctrine beyond its traditional scope, it is currently unclear whether, in English law at least, it can apply in a case where A's commitment is entirely unrelated to land (see **E4:3.1.2**).[36] The doctrine is very important in land law. Crucially, its operation is *not* affected by any formality rules (**C3:5.2.1** and **C3:7.3.1**). This is because any right B acquires does *not* depend on A exercising a power to give B that right. Instead, B's right arises as A is under a duty to B to prevent B suffering a detriment as a result of his reasonable reliance on A's commitment (see **E4:2**). The doctrine is therefore regularly relied in cases where B's dealings with A have not been made in, or evidenced by, any signed writing. The decision in *Pascoe v Turner* (see **C3:Example 3**)[37] provides a good example of how B can use the doctrine to acquire a persistent right relating to land even though his dealings with A have been entirely informal.

2.2 The transfer of a pre-existing persistent right

EXAMPLE 7

A has a Freehold. A holds that right on Trust for B1. B1 wishes to transfer his right under the Trust to B2.

If B1 has a pre-existing persistent right, he generally has the power to transfer that right to B2. That power is regulated by two formality rules. First, there is the general rule applying to the transfer of *any* persistent right and set out by section 53(1)(c) of the LPA 1925 (see **C3:5.2.2** and **F3:2.2**). Second, there is a specific formality rule applying where B1's persistent right relates to land. That rule is imposed by section 53(1)(a) of the LPA 1925. However, this overlap causes no problems. The means of satisfying each rule is *exactly the same*: the transfer must be made by in writing, signed either by B1 or his agent.[38] As a result, there is

---

[35] See eg *Pascoe v Turner* [1979] 1 WLR 431: proprietary estoppel imposed a duty on A to transfer his Freehold to B (see **C3:Example 3**); *Crabb v Arun DC* [1976] Ch 179: the doctrine imposed a duty on A to grant B an Easement (see **Example 28** below).

[36] It is important to distinguish proprietary estoppel (which can directly impose a duty on A) from similar but different doctrines such as: (i) *evidential estoppel* (which can prevent A denying the truth of a particular representation: see **D1:3.3.1(i)**); or (ii) *defensive estoppel* (which can limit A's ability to enforce a right against B: see **D1:3.3.1(ii)**). Those two forms of estoppel can apply whether or not land is involved; but they cannot give B an independent personal right against A.

[37] [1979] 1 WLR 431.

[38] S 53(1)(a) stipulates that A's agent can only sign the writing if he has *written* authority to do so. If B claims that A's exercise of that power took effect on A's death, the more onerous formality requirements of the Wills Act 1837 must be satisfied (see **C3:2**). We will focus here on exercise of powers taking effect before A's death.

no need for us to consider separately the transfer of a pre-existing persistent right relating to land: such a transfer is governed by the rules discussed in **F3:2.2**.

If B1 has a persistent right relating to land, that right cannot be substantively registered (see **C2:6.1**). However, B1 will generally be able to defensively register that right by entering a notice on the register.[39] If B1 does so, and then wishes to transfer his right to B2, it makes sense for B2, rather than B1, to be noted on the register as the holder of that right. At the moment, the transfer of the right can take place without the register being changed. However, when electronic registration is up and running (see **E5:4**) it is possible that a rule will be passed meaning that: (i) if B1 has a persistent right protected by a notice on the register; then (ii) B2 can only acquire that right if B2 is electronically registered as its new holder.[40]

2.3   Formality rules and the acquisition of persistent rights relating to land

Formality rules are relevant only where B's acquisition of a right depends on A's exercise of a power to come under a duty to B (see **C3:5.2.1**). Such rules are therefore irrelevant where A's duty arises as Reasons 3–6 set out in **B:4.3**—ie, as a result of:

- A's commission of a wrong against B; *or*
- A's unjust enrichment at B's expense; *or*
- A statute imposing a duty on A; *or*
- Any other event not depending on A exercising a power to come under a duty to B: eg, facts allowing the application of the doctrine of proprietary estoppel (**E4:3**); or of the 'receipt after a promise principle' (**E3:2.3.2**); or of the 'benefit and burden' principle (**E3:2.3.3**).

In contrast, if B's claim to a persistent right relating to land depends on showing that A *has* exercised a power to come under duty to B, B *does* need to show that a formality rule has been satisfied (see **C3:5.2.1**). That is the case where A's duty to B arises as a result of Reasons 1 and 2 set out in **B:4.3**—ie, as a result of:

- A's consent; *or*
- A's contractual promise to B.

In those two cases, the basic formality rule is set out by section 53(1)(a) of the LPA 1925 (see **2.3.1** below). However, if B claims that his persistent right arises as a result of A or C exercising a power to set up a Trust, a different, *more lenient* formality rule applies: it is imposed by section 53(1)(b) of the LPA 1925 (see **2.3.2** below). But if B claims that his persistent right arises as a result of A's contractual promise to give B, in the future, a property right or a persistent right relating to land, a different, *more stringent* formality rule applies: it is imposed by section 2 of the Law of Property (Miscellaneous Provisions) Act 1989 ('the 1989 Act': see **2.3.3** below). In examining these three formality rules, we ask the same four questions set out in **E1:2.3.2** and look at:

1. the *scope* of the rule;
2. at how the rule is *satisfied*;

---

[39] A right arising under a Trust cannot be registered in this way: LRA 2002, s 33(a)(i).
[40] LRA 2002, s 93 gives the Lord Chancellor the power to introduce such a new formality rule.

3. at the *sanction* applying if the rule is not satisfied; and
4. at any *saves* that may apply to allow B to acquire a persistent right despite his failure to comply with the rule.

2.3.1 Section 53(1)(a) of the Law of Property Act 1925

Section 53(1)(a) of the LPA 1925 states that:

> No interest in land can be created or disposed of except by writing signed by the person creating or conveying the same, or by his agent thereunto lawfully authorised in writing, or by will, or by operation of law.

(i) Scope

The term 'interest in land' refers to any right relating to land that is capable of binding a third party (see **B:4.4**): it thus includes persistent rights as well as property rights. However, the rule is irrelevant as far as *property rights* in land are concerned: if B claims that A has given him a property right in land, B will need to satisfy the more stringent formality rules set out by section 52 of the LPA 1925 and section 27 of the Land Registration Act 2002 (see **E1:2.3**).[41] The focus of section 53(1)(a) is therefore on *persistent rights* relating to land.

On its face, the formality rule applies to the acquisition of *any* new persistent right relating to land. However, where a more specific formality rule applies, the basic rule imposed by section 53(1)(a) is displaced. As a result:

- section 53(1)(b) applies to regulate A's power to set up a Trust of a property right or a persistent right relating to land; and
- section 2 of the 1989 Act applies to regulate A's power to make a contractual promise to give B such a right.

Under section 53(1)(a), the need for signed writing does not apply if B's persistent right arises 'by operation of law'. This is a crucial restriction on the scope of the formality rule. It ensures that the rule applies *only* where B claims that A has exercised a power to come under a duty to B. As a result, the rule does *not* apply if A's duty to B arises as a result of any of Reasons 3–6 set out in **B:4.3**. For example, in *Pascoe v Turner* (**C3:Example 3**),[42] B acquired a persistent right as A was under a duty to transfer A's Freehold to B. No signed writing had been used; but this made no difference. A's duty to B did *not* arise as a result of A's exercise of a power to come under a duty to B; instead, it arose under the doctrine of proprietary estoppel. So, the formality rule imposed by section 53(1)(a) did *not* apply: B's persistent right arose 'by operation of law'.

(ii) Satisfaction

EXAMPLE 8a

A Ltd has Ownership of a stock of bikes. A Ltd makes an oral contractual promise to B to hold its Ownership of those bikes as security for a duty A Ltd owes to B.

---

[41] S 54(2) allows certain types of short Lease to be acquired without the use of a deed (see **G1B:2.2.1(i)(a)**). That provision says that the creation of such a Lease cannot be affected by the 'foregoing provisions' of Part II of the LPA 1925: so *neither* s 52 *nor* s 53(1)(a) applies.
[42] [1979] 1 WLR 431.

> **EXAMPLE 8b**
>
> A Ltd has a Freehold. A Ltd makes an oral contractual promise to B to hold his Freehold as security for a duty A Ltd owes to B.

In **Example 8a,** A Ltd's oral promise gives B a persistent right against A's Ownership of the bikes: a Purely Equitable Charge.[43] In **Example 8b,** however, A Ltd's oral promise, by itself, cannot give B a persistent right: section 53(1)(a) has not been satisfied as A Ltd's promise was not made in writing signed by A Ltd or its authorised agent.[44]

Where B claims a persistent right relating to registered land it seems that an electronic document in the appropriate form can count as signed writing.[45] At the moment the use of an electronic document is optional: the formality rule can be satisfied by a signed paper document. In the future, it is possible that a rule could be introduced *requiring* electronic substantive registration of B's persistent right. However, it is unlikely that such a rule will be introduced: under the Land Registration Act 2002, persistent rights cannot be substantively registered, and that approach is likely to continue.

(iii) Sanction

If the section 53(1)(a) formality rule is not satisfied, A's attempt to exercise a power to give B a persistent right will fail. However, B may still have a personal right against A. For example, if A makes an oral contractual promise to B that A will not build on A's land, that promise, by itself, cannot give B a Restrictive Covenant.[46] Nonetheless, A's promise is contractually binding on A: it thus gives B a personal right against A.

(iv) Saves

The signed writing requirement imposed by section 53(1)(a) does *not* apply if B's persistent right arises by 'operation of law'. In such cases, B can acquire a persistent right even though A has not exercised a power to give B such a right. For example, in *Pascoe v Turner* (**C3:Example 3**),[47] B acquired a persistent right by using the doctrine of proprietary estoppel to show that A was under a duty to transfer his Freehold to B.

2.3.2 Section 53(1)(b) of the Law of Property Act 1925

Section 53(1)(b) of the LPA 1925 states that:

> A declaration of trust respecting any land or any interest therein must be manifested and proved by some writing signed by some person who is able to declare such trust or by his will.

---

[43] B will however need to register that right with the Companies Registrar if he wants it to be capable of binding A Ltd's liquidators (see **D2:3.6**).

[44] Similarly, if A wishes to exercise his power to give B a Restrictive Covenant, A's promise not to make a particular use of his land must be made in writing signed by A or A's authorised agent. A 'covenant', strictly speaking, is a promise contained in a deed. But this does not mean that, to acquire the persistent right known as a Restrictive Covenant, B must show that A's promise was made in a deed: to that extent, the term 'Restrictive Covenant' is misleading.

[45] LRA 2002, s 91.

[46] It may be possible for B to acquire such a right by showing it has arisen by 'operation of law', eg, under the doctrine of proprietary estoppel.

[47] [1979] 1 WLR 431.

(i) Scope

If A has a property right in land, or a persistent right relating to land, A may attempt to set up a Trust of that right in B's favour. One way for A to do so is to: (i) keep his right; and (ii) declare that he is under the core Trust duty: a duty not to use his right for his own benefit, unless and to the extent that A too is a beneficiary of the Trust (see **D2:2.1.1(i)**). Similarly, if A0 has a property right in land, or a persistent right relating to land, A0 may attempt to set up a Trust of that right in B's favour by: (i) transferring his right to A; and (ii) imposing the core Trust duty on A.

In each case, the section 53(1)(b) formality rule regulates the power of A or A0 to set up a Trust of his property right in land or persistent right relating to land. The section 53(1)(b) rule applies only to a 'declaration' of Trust: ie, to cases where A or A0 attempts to exercise his power to set up a Trust. So, if B can show that A is under the core Trust duty 'by operation of law' (eg, for a reason *other* than A's consent to be under that duty), then B does *not* rely on a 'declaration' of Trust and so the formality rule is irrelevant. Unlike section 53(1)(a), this section does not explicitly refer to situations where B acquires a right 'by operation of law'. However, it does not need to do so: its scope is already limited by the fact that it applies only to declarations of Trust.

EXAMPLE 9a

A and B move into a home together. A acquires the Freehold but assures B that the house is 'as much yours as mine'. B reasonably relies on that commitment in various ways (eg, by doing work to improve the land). As a result of that reliance, B will suffer a detriment if A goes back on his commitment.

A has made a commitment to share the benefit of his Freehold with B. It may well be that, when he made that commitment, A intended that he would be under the core Trust duty to B (eg, perhaps a duty to use his Freehold 50 per cent for B's benefit and 50 per cent for his own benefit).[48] However, due to section 53(1)(b), the lack of signed writing prevents B from *proving* that A thus exercised his power to set up a Trust. Nonetheless, as confirmed by the Court of Appeal in *Eves v Eves*,[49] the essential facts of which are identical to **Example 9a**, A *can be* under the core Trust duty to B. The Court of Appeal found that, as a result of B's reliance on A's commitment, A held his Freehold on Trust for both himself and B: A was under a duty to use his Freehold one-third for B's benefit and two-thirds for his own benefit. The best explanation for this result is that the doctrine of proprietary estoppel imposed that duty on A.[50] As a result, the section 53(1)(b) formality rule did not apply: B's right did *not* arise as a result of a 'declaration of Trust'; instead, it arose by operation of law.

EXAMPLE 9b

A0 has a Freehold. A0 transfers that Freehold to A. As part of his deal with A0, A orally promises to hold the Freehold on Trust for B.

---

[48] As in *Paul v Constance* [1977] 1 WLR 527 (see **F3:2.1.1**).

[49] [1975] 1 WLR 1338.

[50] In *Eves* itself, the Court of Appeal applied seemingly different reasoning, basing its decision on a 'common intention' Constructive Trust. However, in a case such as *Eves*, that principle seems to be simply an application of proprietary estoppel (see **G3:2.4.5(v)(d)**).

It is clear that A0 intended to impose the core Trust duty on A. However, due to section 53(1)(b), the lack of signed writing prevents B from *proving* that A0 thus exercised his power to set up a Trust. Nonetheless, as confirmed by the Court of Appeal in *Rochefoucauld v Boustead*,[51] the essential facts of which are identical to **Example 9b**, A *is* under the core Trust duty to B. That result can be explained[52] by using the 'receipt after a promise' principle:[53] A, due to the promise he made to A0 when acquiring his Freehold, was under a duty to keep that promise. As a result, A was under a duty to B not to use his Freehold for his own benefit and, as promised, to use his Freehold for B's benefit. As a result, the section 53(1)(b) formality rule did not apply: B's right did *not* arise as a result of a 'declaration of Trust'; instead, it arose by operation of law.

As **Examples 9a and 9b** make clear, a declaration of Trust (ie A or A0's exercise of a power to set up a Trust) is only *one* means by which B can acquire a right under a Trust. If B can show that A is under the core Trust duty *for some other reason*, such as the doctrine of proprietary estoppel (eg, **Example 9a**) or the 'receipt after a promise' principle (eg, **Example 9b**), then B can prove he has a right under a Trust relating to land *without* needing to produce any signed writing.

(ii) Satisfaction

If A0 transfers a right to A to hold on Trust for B, the formality rule can be satisfied by writing signed by *either* A0 or A.[54] The signed writing must enable the court to identify not only the fact that a Trust was intended, but also the specific terms of that Trust: the section 53(1)(b) rule can thus provide evidence as to the content, as well as to the existence, of B's right.[55]

The specific formality rule imposed by section 53(1)(b), applying only to declarations of Trust, is *more lenient* than the general rule imposed by section 53(1)(a). To satisfy the specific rule, A or A0's exercise of his power to set up a Trust must be expressed *or recorded* in signed writing.[56] Unlike section 53(1)(a), and the other formality rules we have seen, section 53(1)(b) does not directly regulate the *acquisition* of B's right; rather, it regulates how B's right is *proved*.

EXAMPLE 10a

A has a Freehold. A makes an oral declaration that he holds his Freehold on Trust for B. A transfers his Freehold to C. A then signs a document recording his earlier declaration of Trust in favour of B.

B can use the later document to prove the existence of the Trust: that Trust will then be acknowledged to have existed *all along*—ie, from the time of A's initial oral declaration.[57]

---

[51] [1897] 1 Ch 196.

[52] In *Rochefoucauld* itself, the Court of Appeal applied different reasoning, allowing B to prove that A0 had declared a Trust in B's favour (see **2.3.2(iv)** below).

[53] See **D3:2.2.2** and **E3:2.2.2**.

[54] See eg *Forster v Hale* (1798) 3 Ves Jr 696; *Gardner v Rowe* (1825) 2 S & S 346, affirmed (1828) 5 Russ 258; *Rochefoucauld v Boustead* [1897] 1 Ch 196. This issue is discussed by Youdan [1984] *CLJ* 306 at 315–20.

[55] See eg *Smith v Matthews* (1860) 3 De GF& J 139. It is, however, enough if the signed writing refers to a closely connected, unsigned document establishing the terms of the Trust: see *Forster v Hale* (1798) 3 Ves Jr 696.

[56] The declaration can also be made in a will. This requires writing not only signed by A but also by two disinterested (so not including A or B) witnesses (see **C3:2**).

[57] *Gardner v Rowe* (1825) 2 S & S 346, affirmed (1828) 5 Russ 258.

Crucially, this means that, when C acquired A's Freehold, B had a pre-*existing* persistent right: B thus has a prima facie power to impose a duty on C. In contrast, if the general section 53(1)(a) rule applied, B's persistent right could only exist, if at all,[58] from the date of the later signed document.

To understand why section 53(1)(b) operates in this unusual way, it is useful to consider the possible justifications for formality rules. The general benefits of a formality rule are: (i) the provision of *evidence*; (ii) the promotion of *caution*; (iii) the *protection of A from fraud*; and (iv) the provision of *publicity* (see C3:4). Despite its unusual effect, section 53(1)(b) still brings the first three benefits: if there is a dispute as to whether or not A declared a Trust in B's favour, B can only prove his persistent right by producing signed writing: (i) this writing will provide the parties and a court with useful *evidence* of the existence and terms of the Trust; (ii) the need for writing also promotes *caution* by preventing B from enforcing a rash oral declaration made by A; and (iii) it also gives A useful *protection from a fraudulent claim* that A declared a Trust in B's favour.[59]

The real difference between section 53(1)(b) and other formality rules therefore relates to the provision of *publicity*. This is clear from **Example 10a**: B's right under the Trust is prima facie binding on C even though the written record of the Trust was made only *after* C acquired his right and so cannot assist C in discovering B's pre-existing persistent right. However, in practice, this lack of publicity causes few problems for C. Crucially, the protection given to C by the **defences question** may justify the special, and more lenient, formality rule.

First, the *lack of registration defence* provides C with particularly strong protection from the risk of being bound by a pre-existing right under a Trust relating to land. Uniquely among persistent rights, a right under a Trust *cannot* be protected by the entry of a notice on the register.[60] As a result, such a right can bind C *only* if B is in actual occupation of the registered land (see **3.6.2** below). Second, where B's pre-existing persistent right arises under a Trust, the *overreaching defence* also gives C particularly strong protection against B's right (see **3.4** below).

It is therefore important not to look at the section 53(1)(b) rule in isolation. As we have seen before (see eg **D1:2.2.4(iii)(f)**), in a case such as **Example 10a**, the **basic tension** between B and C is not resolved simply through the acquisition question. Rather, the defences question is also crucial: so, given the additional protection the defences question gives C against a pre-existing right under a Trust, it may be justifiable to apply a more lenient formality rule when considering the acquisition of such a right.

(iii) Sanction

As shown by **Example 10a**, A's initial failure to comply with section 53(1)(b) does not render A's attempt to set up a Trust invalid. On the contrary, B acquires his persistent right as a result of A's oral declaration. The lack of signed writing then prevents B from *proving* he has acquired that right. In the absence of any writing, B is thus in a frustrating position: he

---

[58] In the absence of s 53(1)(b), it could be argued that A's later signed writing cannot give rise to a Trust as it does not consist of an attempt by A to set up a Trust, but only of an attempt to confirm something that does not in fact exist.

[59] S 53(1)(b) derives from s 7 of the Statute of Frauds 1677, the purpose of which was to protect A from fraudulent claims by B.

[60] LRA 2002, s 33(a)(i).

may know his right exists, but he cannot prove it. And, for most practical purposes, it is proof that counts.

EXAMPLE 10b

A has a Freehold. A rents the land out and receives £1,000 a month from the occupiers. A makes an oral declaration that he holds his Freehold on Trust for B. For the first month, A pays the rental income from the land to B. A and B then fall out. A decides to use his Freehold entirely for his own benefit and stops paying the rental income to B.

As A holds his Freehold on Trust for B, A has a duty to pay the rental income from the land to B. However, in the absence of any writing signed by A, B cannot prove that A is under that duty. Nonetheless, A cannot claim back the initial £1,000 he paid to B. A may have paid that money to B in the mistaken belief that B was able to prove a Trust; but that makes no difference. If B keeps the money, he is *not* unjustly enriched at A's expense: as A is under a valid, albeit unprovable, duty to pay that money to B, there *is* a legal basis on which B can keep the money (see **D4:4.2.3**).

(iv) Saves

Examples 9a and 9b show that, even if B cannot prove that a Trust has been declared in his favour, B may nonetheless be able to show that A is under the core Trust duty to B. However, it is worth noting that there are two other ways of explaining the results in **Examples 9a and 9b**. The first depends on the wording of section 53(2) of the LPA 1925:

> [Section 53(1)(b)] does not affect the creation or operation of resulting, implied or construct-ive trusts.

Therefore, if each of the Trusts arising in **Examples 9a and 9b** counts as either a Resulting Trust or a Constructive Trust,[61] the formality rule set out by section 53(1)(b) does not apply. So, what is the definition of each type of Trust? Courts have often been unclear about the division between the Resulting Trust and the Constructive Trust. Nonetheless, one point is reasonably clear: Resulting Trusts and Constructive Trusts are different from Express Trusts. And an Express Trust arises when A or A0 exercises a power to set up a Trust. A Trust can therefore count as a Resulting Trust or a Constructive Trust *only* if it does not depend on A or A0 having exercised a power to set up a Trust.

This means that, if B's right arises under a Resulting Trust or a Constructive Trust, B's right does *not* depend on showing that A or A0 has declared a Trust. Section 53(2) is therefore irrelevant. Even without that provision, section 53(1)(b) does not apply: the formality rule applies only to a 'declaration of Trust'. So, section 53(2), by itself, cannot explain why a Trust arises in **Examples 9a and 9b**. Instead, in each case, we have to ask *if* B can acquire a right under a Trust *without* relying on A or A0's exercise of a power to set up that Trust.

The second alternative explanation of **Examples 9a and 9b** depends on the assumption

---

[61] The term 'implied' seems to add nothing to s 53(2). For example, the Trust arising in *Paul v Constance* [1977] 1 WLR 527 could be described as implied as A was found to have intended to set up a Trust even though he did not expressly state his intention to do so. However, it is clear that such a Trust, if arising in relation to land, would *not* fall within s 53(2): as it is based on a 'declaration' of Trust (ie, on A's exercise of a power to set up a Trust), the formality rule set out in s 53(1)(b) must apply.

that a 'statute cannot be used as an instrument of fraud': a court is permitted to ignore section 53(1)(b) if, by doing so, it can prevent A from *acting fraudulently*. That view was adopted by the Court of Appeal in the case on which **Example 9b** is based: *Rochefoucald v Boustead*.[62] The court held that: (i) if it applied section 53(1)(b) A would get away with a fraud; so (ii) it could ignore that formality rule and instead allow B, despite the lack of signed writing, to prove that A0 had declared a Trust in B's favour.[63]

This fraud analysis has been relied on in a number of other cases—some considering section 53(1)(b),[64] others dealing with different formality rules.[65] Further, the exception has some academic support.[66] On this analysis, the crucial question is: what counts as fraud? In **Example 9b**, A has not acted fraudulently in the specific sense of committing the wrong of deceit: he did not deliberately or recklessly make a misrepresentation of an existing fact to B.[67] Instead, A's fraud seems to be established by the facts that: (i) A promised A0, as part of the deal in which he acquired his Freehold, that he would hold that Freehold on Trust for B; and (ii) A0 transferred his Freehold to A as a result of A's promise. However, given those facts, there is no need to rely on the fraud analysis: the 'receipt after a promise' principle can apply to impose a duty on A, owed to B, to keep his promise to hold his Freehold on Trust for B (see E3:2.2.2).

Similarly, it has been suggested that the result in *Eves v Eves*, on which **Example 9a** is based, can also be explained on the fraud analysis (even though that analysis was not adopted by the Court of Appeal in *Eves*).[68] Again, A did not act fraudulently in the specific sense of committing the wrong of deceit. Instead, A's fraud must come from: (i) A's commitment to B that B would have a share of the benefit of A's Freehold; and (ii) A's wish to go back on that commitment, even though such action would cause detriment to B, who had reasonably relied on A's commitment. However, given those facts, there is no need to rely on the fraud analysis: the doctrine of proprietary estoppel can apply to impose a duty on A to give B a share of the benefit of A's Freehold (see E4:3).

It seems, then, that we have a choice in **Examples 9a and 9b**. We can explain the results by saying *either*: (i) A comes under the core Trust duty for a reason other than A or A0's declaration of Trust; *or* (ii) A comes under the core Trust duty because of A or A0's declaration of Trust *and* B is allowed to prove that declaration because section 53(1)(b) cannot be used as an instrument of fraud. The first explanation is clearly the better one.

First, it is more transparent: in **Examples 9a and 9b**, a judge cannot simply invoke the

---

[62] [1897] 1 Ch 196.

[63] *Ibid* at 206 to 207 *per* Lindley LJ: 'It is further established by a series of cases, the propriety of which cannot now be questioned, that the Statute of Frauds does not prevent the proof of a fraud; and that it is a fraud on the part of a person to whom land is conveyed as a trustee, and who knows it was so conveyed, to deny the trust and claim the land himself.'

[64] See eg *per* Ungoed-Thomas J at first instance in *Hodgson v Marks* [1971] Ch 892 at 906 and 908. See too the decision of the New South Wales Court of Appeal in *Allen v Snyder* [1977] 2 NSWLR 685 *per* Glass JA at 693: 'The trust is enforced, because it is unconscionable of the legal owner to rely on the statute to defeat the beneficial interest. It could justifiably be called an express trust, as it was in *Rochefoucauld v Boustead*.'

[65] In relation to the Wills Act 1837, see eg *per* Lord Westbury in *McCormick v Grogan* (1869) LR 4 HL 82 at 86 and 97.

[66] See eg Swadling, in *Restitution and Equity*, vol 1: *Resulting Trusts and Equitable Compensation* (ed Birks and Rose, 2000), 63: 'The trust which [A0] had intended to create was enforceable under the principle laid down by the Court of Appeal in *Rochefoucauld v Boustead*, that equity will not allow a statute designed to prevent fraud to be used as an instrument of fraud.'

[67] For the definition of the wrong of deceit see eg *Derry v Peek* (1889) LR 14 App Cas 337.

[68] See eg Swadling, *English Private Law* (ed Burrows, 2nd edn, 2007), 4.208.

ill-defined notion of 'fraud'. B can only acquire a right under a Trust if he can show that a specific principle (eg, proprietary estoppel; the 'receipt after a promise' principle) imposes the core Trust duty on A. Second, it is constitutionally justified: on its express wording, section 53(1)(b) applies only to a 'declaration' of Trust and so does not apply if B acquires a right under a Trust through some other means. In contrast, the section makes *no* reference to fraud—certainly, there is *no* statutory provision to the effect that the rule does not apply in cases of fraud. The assumption that 'a statute cannot be used as an instrument of fraud' is constitutionally dubious:[69] after all, a statute can be whatever it wants to be. A good example is provided by the Land Charges Act 1925, which was considered by the House of Lords in *Midland Bank Trust Co v Green* (see **C2:Example 5**).[70] As we saw in **C2:7**, A and C behaved very badly in that case,[71] yet the House of Lords did *not* say that C's fraud meant she was unable to rely on the statutory lack of registration defence provided by the Land Charges Act 1925.

2.3.3 Section 2 of the Law of Property (Miscellaneous Provisions) Act 1989

Section 2 of the Law of Property (Miscellaneous Provisions) Act 1989 states that:

> (1) A contract for the sale or other disposition of an interest in land can only be made in writing and only by incorporating all the terms which the parties have expressly agreed in one document or, where the contracts are exchanged, in each.
>
> (2) The terms may be incorporated in a document either by being set out in it or by reference to some other document.
>
> (3) The document incorporating the terms or, where the contracts are exchanged, one of the documents incorporating them (but not necessarily the same one) must be signed by or on behalf of each party to the contract . . .

(i) Scope

EXAMPLE 11a

A has a Freehold. A makes a promise to B that, if B lends A £100,000, A will give B a Charge over A's land. A's promise is made in writing signed by A. In reliance on A's promise, B lends A £100,000.

If A's promise imposes a duty on A to grant B a Charge, B acquires an immediate persistent right: an Equitable Charge (see **1.3.1(i)** above). Although A's promise was made as part of a bargain with B, it does *not* impose a contractual duty on A.[72] As it is a promise to give B a property right in land, it can only be contractually binding if the section 2 formality rule has been satisfied. And that rule has not been satisfied: A's promise has not been made in a written document signed by *both* A and B. A's promise does satisfy the basic formality rule

---

[69] See eg the concern raised by Critchley (1999) 115 *LQR* 631 at 653–4: 'It should be noted that merely because the fraud maxim may render informality justifiable as a matter of policy does not mean that it is constitutionally justifiable for the courts to create an exception to an apparently clear and mandatory statutory provision.'

[70] [1981] AC 513.

[71] Indeed, they committed the wrong of conspiracy (see **E3:2.3.7**): see *Midland Bank Trust Co Ltd v Green (No 3)* [1982] 1 Ch 529.

[72] As confirmed by the Court of Appeal in *Kinane v Mackie-Conteh* [2005] EWCA Civ 45, on which **Example 11a** is based.

set out by section 53(1)(a) of the LPA 1925: it is in writing signed by A. However, section 2 of the 1989 Act displaces that basic rule with a *stricter* one.

A has a Freehold. A makes a promise to B that, if B lends A £100,000, A will hold his Freehold as security for his duty to repay the loan to B. A's promise is made in writing signed by A. In reliance on A's promise, B lends A £100,000.

In this case: (i) A's promise *does* impose a contractual duty on A; and (ii) as the basic section 53(1)(a) rule has been satisfied, that promise *does* give B a persistent right: a Purely Equitable Charge. The stricter section 2 rule is irrelevant: once B lends the money to A, A is not promising to give B a right *in the future*; instead, A has given B an *immediate* persistent right.[73] Similarly, in **Example 4**, B can acquire a Restrictive Covenant even if A's promise not to make a particular use of his land is not made in writing signed by both A and B: as A's promise gives B an immediate persistent right, the general section 53(1)(a) rule applies, *not* the stricter section 2 rule.

Section 2(5) sets out a number of exceptions to the section 2 rule. Three particular types of contract are exempted from its requirements: (i) a contract to grant a Lease that meets the requirements of section 54(2) of the LPA 1925; (ii) a contract made in the course of a public auction; and (iii) a contract, other than a regulated mortgage contract, regulated by the Financial Services and Markets Act 2000. In those three cases, A's promise can be contractually binding even if it does not meet the requirements of section 2.

The first exception is no surprise: if the requirements of section 54(2) are satisfied, A can orally grant B a Lease (see **G1B:2.2.1(i)(a)**); so it is only logical that A can also make a contract to grant B such a Lease without using writing. The second exception is simply to allow the practice of selling land by public auction to continue in its existing form;[74] and the third similarly allows the sale of particular investments to go ahead as usual even if the investment includes land.[75]

Section 2(5) goes on to state that:

> nothing in this section [ie, in section 2] affects the creation or operation of resulting, implied or constructive trusts.

A makes an oral promise to sell his Freehold to B for £250,000.

A's promise to transfer his Freehold to B is clearly within the scope of section 2: as a result, it does not impose a contractual duty on A. However, relying on section 2(5), B can try to argue that the section 2 rule does not apply: where A makes a contractual promise to give B a Freehold, B acquires an immediate persistent right under a Trust (see **1.2.4(ii)** above). This right can be said to arise under a 'resulting, implied or constructive trust': (i) there is a Trust, as A is under the core Trust duty;[76] and (ii) the Trust is 'resulting, implied or

---

[73] This distinction reflects that suggested by Arden LJ in *Kinane v Mackie-Conteh* [2005] EWCA Civ 45 at [35].
[74] See Law Com No 164, para 4.11.
[75] *Ibid* para 4.12. The sale will, however, be regulated by the Financial Services and Mortgages Act 2000.
[76] See eg *per* Sir George Jessel MR in *Lysaght v Edwards* (1876) 2 Ch D 499 at 506.

constructive' as it does not arise as a result of A exercising a power to set up a Trust (see
2.3.2(iv) above).

Of course, B's argument must be wrong. For the purported Trust to arise, A has to be
under a duty to transfer his Freehold to B; and, as A's promise was oral, it cannot be contractually binding. Yet if the 'operation of resulting, implied and constructive trusts' really
were an exception to the section 2 formality rule, B's argument would be correct. The
problem is that the 'resulting, implied or constructive trust' exception is redundant:

1. To show he has a right under a Trust relating to land, B needs to show A is under a
   duty to B.
2. A's duty to B must be either contractual or non-contractual. If it is a contractual
   duty, section 2 may apply. If it is not contractual, section 2 cannot apply.
3. So the crucial question is *not* whether B's right arises under a 'resulting, implied or
   constructive trust'. It is whether or not A's duty to B is a contractual duty.

The section 2(5) 'exception' is thus a clumsy and unnecessary addition to section 2. It does
not appear in the draft Bill attached to the Law Commission Report that led to the Act. [77] It
seems that section 2(5) may have been inserted simply in order to duplicate the section
53(2) 'exception' to the section 53(1)(b) formality rule (see **2.3.2(iv)** above). However, that
'exception' is also redundant. When considering the scope of section 53(1)(b) the key
question is simply whether A's duty to B arises as a result of a declaration of a Trust: ie, as a
result of A or A0 exercising a power to set up a Trust. And when considering the scope of
section 2, the key question is simply whether A's duty to B arises as a result of a contractual
promise to give B, in the future, a property right in land or a persistent right relating to
land.

(ii) Satisfaction

To satisfy section 2, A and B must ensure that all the expressly agreed terms of their contract
are incorporated into a single document signed by, or on behalf of, *both* parties.[78] This
requirement, more onerous than that imposed by section 53(1)(a), may be justified by the
purpose of the section 2 formality rule. One of the chief goals of the section is to provide
evidence of the terms of A and B's contract.[79] Such evidence can easily be found if there is a
single document, signed by both A and B, setting out all the expressly agreed terms of their
deal.[80]

No general formality rule applies if A makes a contractual promise to give B a property
right in, or persistent right relating to, a thing other than land. For example, A and B can
make an oral contract for the sale of A's bike to B. However, the special features of land (see

---

[77] See Law Com No 164. Nor was there such any such exception in the previous formality rule regulating
contracts for the creation or transfer of property rights in land or persistent rights relating to land: Law of Property
Act 1925, s 40.

[78] If a term omitted from the written document can be seen as part of a separate or 'collateral' contract, then the
failure to include it in the written document will *not* prevent that written document from satisfying s 2: see eg
Record v Bell [1991] 1 WLR 853. However, the courts are careful not to allow the concept of a collateral contract to
undermine the s 2 formality rule: see eg *per* Morritt C in *Business Environment Bow Lane Ltd v Deanwater Estates Ltd*
[2007] EWCA Civ 622 at [42]–[44].

[79] See *per* Robert Walker LJ in *Yaxley v Gotts* [2000] Ch 162 at 175.

[80] If the document were signed only by A, it would be easier for B to deny that the terms of the document actually
reflected the terms of the parties' deal.

A:3.1) mean that transactions in land can often be very complex: in this context, the provision of evidence may be particularly important (see **C3:4.4**). Further, negotiations between A and B as to the possible grant of a right can often be lengthy: the section 2 formality rule helps mark the divide between negotiations and the conclusion of a deal.

A very important change to the method of satisfying section 2 will occur if and when electronic registration comes into full operation (see **E5:4**). Under section 93 of the Land Registration Act 2002, the Lord Chancellor is authorised to make new formality rules. In particular, section 93(2) (with italics added) states that a rule could be introduced with the effect that:

> A disposition to which this section applies, *or a contract to make such a disposition*, only has effect if it is made by means of a document in electronic form and if, when the document purports to take effect
> (a) it is electronically communicated to the registrar, and
> (b) the relevant registration requirements are met.

The crucial importance of section 93(2) lies in the words italicised above: the reference to 'a contract to make such a disposition'. 'Disposition' here refers to the exercise by A of a power to give B a property right. This means that: (i) if A promises B that he will give B a property right in registered land; then (ii) B will only acquire a contractual right against A if an electronic document is used *and* if the contract is electronically registered. To that extent, section 2 will be replaced:[81] to show that A is under a contractual duty to B, it will no longer be enough for B to show that his agreement with A was made in writing, signed by both parties, containing all the expressly agreed terms of the contract. Instead, B will also have to show that: (i) the contract was made in an electronic document; and crucially (ii) that the fact of the contract was communicated to the registrar for inclusion on the register.

EXAMPLE 13

A has a Freehold. A makes a promise to sell his Freehold to B for £250,000. The promise is in a written document, signed by both A and B, containing all the expressly agreed terms of the deal between A and B.

1. B pays the purchase price and goes into occupation of the land but does not apply to be registered as the new holder of A's Freehold.
2. A, taking advantage of the fact that he remains registered as the holder of the Freehold, then sells that Freehold to C.
3. C is registered as the new holder of A's Freehold.

B cannot acquire A's Freehold until he substantively registers himself as the new holder of that right (see **E1:2.3.4**). However, as section 2 has been satisfied, A is under a contractual duty to transfer his Freehold to B. B therefore has a persistent right against A's Freehold. That persistent right existed before C acquired his Freehold from A. So, B's persistent right is prima facie binding on C. C can try to rely on the lack of registration defence, but as B was in actual occupation of A's land when C committed to acquiring his right, B's persistent right is immune from the lack of registration defence: it is an overriding interest (see **C2:6**

---

[81] S 2 would still apply where A's contractual promise is to give B a new *persistent right*; or to transfer to B an existing persistent right that has not been protected by the entry of a notice on the register. The creation of a new persistent right or the transfer of such a right does not count as a 'disposition' for the purposes of s 93(2).

and **3.6.2** below). Therefore, despite his failure to register, B *can* assert his pre-existing persistent right against C.

Things will be very different if and when the new formality rule is introduced under section 93(2) of the Land Registration Act 2002. In **Example 13**, B's failure to apply to have his contract with A registered will mean that A is *not* under a contractual duty to B. As a result, unless B can say that A is under a *non-contractual* duty to B, B will not have a persistent right, and so will not have no pre-existing right he can assert against C.[82]

We need to consider if it is possible to justify such a change. The chief purpose of a registration requirement is to provide *publicity*: to make it easier for C to discover B's pre-existing right (see **C2:2**). The argument in favour of the new electronic registration requirement is that it will make it easier for C to discover the persistent right B acquires as a result of A's contractual promise to give B a property right in land. However, the benefit of publicity can be exaggerated where persistent rights are concerned (see **2.3.2(ii)** above). In general, the **defences question** adequately protects C against the risk of being bound by a pre-existing persistent right relating to land. Under the current law, in **Example 13**, B can only assert his persistent right against C because he is in actual occupation of the land when C commits to acquiring his Freehold. That occupation provides publicity: it alerts C to the risk that B may have a persistent right in relation to the land (see **3.6.3** below). As a result, it seems unnecessary to insist on the further publicity provided by registration of B's contract with A.

(iii) Sanction

If the section 2 formality rule is not satisfied, neither A nor B will be under a contractual duty to the other. This means that B will have *neither*: (i) a persistent right arising as a result of A's contractual promise; *nor* (ii) a personal right against A arising as a result of A's contractual promise.[83] After rules are passed under section 93(2) of the LRA 2002, B's failure to electronically register a contract in which A promises to give B a property right will mean that B has neither a persistent right nor a personal right against A. That result seems disproportionate: given that the purpose of registration is to provide publicity for C, it is very hard to see why B's failure to register should also prevent B from having a personal contractual right against A.

(iv) Saves

If section 2 has not been satisfied, B will be unable to argue that A is under a contractual duty to B. However, section 2 does not prevent B from showing that A is under a *non-contractual* duty to B. And, if A's non-contractual duty is to exercise his power to give B a property right or persistent right, B will acquire an immediate persistent right (see **1.3.1(i)** above). Strictly speaking, this is not a save. Rather, it is a consequence of the *scope* of section 2: the formality rule imposed by the section is simply irrelevant where B claims A is under a *non-contractual* duty.

We can see this by going to back to **Example 11a**. The Court of Appeal considered a set of essentially identical facts in *Kinane v Mackie-Conteh*.[84] A refused to give B the promised

---

[82] B will independently acquire a Freehold by taking physical control of the land, but that right cannot bind C: C acquires A's Freehold, which arose *before* B's independently acquired Freehold.

[83] Compare the effect of s 53(1)(a). If the formality rule set out in that section is not satisfied, B can still acquire a personal right against A: see **2.3.1(iii)** above.

[84] [2005] EWCA Civ 45.

Charge. Certainly, A can use section 2 to show that he was not under a *contractual* duty to give B the Charge. However, as acknowledged by the Court of Appeal, B can instead use the doctrine of proprietary estoppel to impose such a duty on A: (i) A had made a commitment to give B the Charge; and (ii) by making the loan to A, B had reasonably relied on that commitment; and (iii) B would clearly suffer a detriment if A were allowed to renege on the commitment: B would then have no security for A's duty to repay the loan and would be at risk if, for example, A went into insolvency (see **B:4.5.1**). The doctrine of proprietary estoppel thus operates to impose a *non-contractual* duty on A to grant B the Charge. As a result of that duty, B acquires a persistent right: an Equitable Charge (see **1.3.1(i)** above).

In *Kinane*, the Court of relied on the section 2(5) 'exception' to explain why A's promise to B, even though it did not satisfy the section 2 formality rule, gave B a persistent right. However, that use of section 2(5) is *unnecessary*: the section 2 formality rule is irrelevant if, instead of claiming A is under a *contractual* duty, B instead relies on the doctrine of proprietary estoppel (see **C3:7.3.1** and **E4:7**). The use of section 2(5) is also *incorrect*. In *Kinane*, the Court of Appeal held that, in a case such as **Example 11a**, B acquires a right under a Constructive Trust. However, A is *not* under the core Trust duty to B: A's only duty to B is to grant B the promised Charge. Therefore, B does *not* have a right under a Trust: he has an Equitable Charge (see **G3:2.4.3(iv)**).

Given the Court of Appeal's reasoning in *Kinane*, it is worth emphasising that section 2 does not regulate A's ability to come under a *promissory* duty to B; rather, it operates on A's ability to come under a *contractual* duty to B. For example, in *Crabb v Arun District Council*,[85] A's conduct led B reasonably to believe that A would grant B an Easement. As A had not made a promise in writing, B could not enforce any contractual duty of A.[86] Nonetheless, as: (i) B had relied on A's commitment; and (ii) B would suffer a detriment if A were allowed to go back on that commitment; (iii) the doctrine of proprietary estoppel imposed a duty on A—as the Court of Appeal held, a duty to grant B the promised Easement. In *Crabb*, there was no discussion of Constructive Trusts: there was no need to show an exception to the formality rule as that rule only regulated A's power to come under a contractual duty to B (ie, it applied only to Reason 2 in **B:4.3**).

The 'receipt after a promise' principle can also apply to impose a non-contractual duty on A. For example, in *Pallant v Morgan*[87] C made an oral promise to transfer a Freehold of particular land to B (see **D3:2.2.2**). That promise did not give B an enforceable contractual right. However, as a result of C's promise: (i) C acquired a Freehold of that particular land; and (ii) C acquired an advantage in relation to his acquisition of that right; so (iii) the 'receipt after a promise' principle applied to impose a duty on C to keep his promise to B. As a result, B acquired a persistent right: C was under a duty to transfer the Freehold to B.[88]

It seems, therefore, that proprietary estoppel and the 'receipt after a promise' principle may provide important 'saves' for B: each allows B to acquire a persistent right relating to land, based on a promise made by A or C, without complying with any formality rule. Of course, this does raise the question of whether a formality rule *ought* to apply either to

---

[85] [1976] Ch 179.

[86] See LPA 1925, s 40 (a predecessor of s 2 with different requirements and effect, which applied in *Crabb v Arun DC*: for discussion of its effect in that case see Millett (1976) 92 *LQR* 342).

[87] [1953] Ch 43.

[88] For another example, see *Rochefoucauld v Boustead* [1897] Ch 196 (see **2.3.2(i)** and **2.3.2(iv)** above).

proprietary estoppel or to the 'receipt after a promise' principle. Extending the section 2 formality rule to *all* promises to give B a property right or persistent right relating to land would bring the usual benefits. In particular, the use of formality would provide *evidence* and promote *caution* by protecting A from the consequences of making a rash oral promise. Courts and parties would be spared time-consuming litigation about whether or not A made an oral promise to B.[89]

However, it seems that, as far as non-contractual duties are concerned, those benefits are trumped by other needs. For example, where B's claim is based on proprietary estoppel, the need to protect B's detrimental reliance on A can justify B's informal acquisition of a right (see **E4:7**). It is also important to note that, from B's point of view, a proprietary estoppel claim is not 'as good as' a contractual claim: in particular, there is no guarantee that A will be under a duty to keep his promise to B (see **E4:4**). Similarly, where the 'receipt after a promise' principle operates, the benefits of formality are outweighed by the need to prevent C from unjustly benefiting by keeping the right he acquired as a result of his promise without also keeping that promise (see **D3:2.2.2**).

SUMMARY of E2:2

Three special formality rules, applying only where land is concerned, regulate A's power to give B a persistent right. The basic rule, requiring writing signed by A, is set out by section 53(1)(a) of the LPA 1925. That rule is displaced by a more lenient rule applying only to declarations of Trust by A or A0 (section 53(1)(b) of the LPA 1925). And it is displaced by a stricter rule applying only to contractual promises by A to give B, in the future, a property right in land or a persistent right relating to land (section 2 of the 1989 Act).

Each of these three rules is satisfied in a different way; however, none of the rules requires B to substantively register his persistent right. This marks an important difference between: (i) the acquisition of property rights in land (see **E1:2.3.4**); and (ii) the acquisition of persistent rights relating to land. That difference can be justified by the fact that, if B has a pre-existing persistent right, the **defences question** provides C with a good deal of protection from the risk of being bound by that right. In contrast, if B has a pre-existing *property* right, the **defences question** gives C very little protection from that risk (see **E1:3**). So, the *publicity* provided by a substantive registration requirement is generally essential where property rights are concerned; but is redundant where persistent rights are in issue.

The three rules have an important feature in common: they apply only where B claims that A's duty to B arises as a result of: (i) A's consent; or (ii) A's contractual promise to B (ie, Reasons 1 and 2 set out in **B:4.3**). The rules do *not* apply if B instead claims that A's duty arises as a result of: (i) A's commission of a wrong; or (ii) A's unjust enrichment at B's expense; or (iii) a statute imposing a duty on A; or (iv) any other event (ie, Reasons 3–6 set out in **B:4.3**). In those cases, B can acquire a persistent right relating to land *without* satisfying any formality rule.

---

[89] For an example of such litigation, see eg *Lalani v Crump* [2007] EWHC 47 (see **C3:n17**)

3 THE DEFENCES QUESTION

If B can satisfy the **content question** and the **acquisition question**, attention then shifts to **Question 3** of the basic structure: does C have a defence to B's pre-existing persistent right?

3.1 Introduction and the basic tension

If B claims to have a pre-existing *property right* in land, C's chief protection comes from the **content question** (see **E1:1**) and the **acquisition question** (see **E1:2**). However, we have seen that, where B claims to have a pre-existing *persistent right* in relation to land, those questions are answered differently. First, it is easier for B to show that his right counts as a persistent right (the closed list principle does not apply to such rights: see **1.4** above). Second, it is easier for B to acquire such a right (eg, B never needs to substantively register in order to acquire such a right). This does not mean that, where persistent rights are concerned, the **basic tension** is simply resolved in B's favour. Rather, it means that the bulk of C's protection comes from the **defences question**. In practice, the most important defences for C are: (i) the *overreaching defence* (see **3.4** below); and (ii) the *lack of registration defence* (see **3.6** below). Each of those defences can be used where B has a pre-existing persistent right in relation to a thing other than land (see **D2:3.4** and **D2:3.6**); however, where land is concerned, each defence gives C *extra* protection.

3.2 The consent defence

EXAMPLE 14

A has a Freehold. A holds that Freehold on Trust for both A and B. In return for a loan from C Bank, A plans to give C Bank a Charge over the land. B signs a document consenting to C Bank's acquisition of the Charge.

It is clear that B's consent gives C Bank a defence to B's pre-existing persistent right.[90] However, complications can arise if B argues that his consent was defective, for example because it was obtained by fraud, duress, undue influence or misrepresentation. A particular problem arises if B argues that his consent was defective due to some misconduct by A: can A's misconduct prevent C Bank from relying on the consent defence? In such a case, A's misconduct *can* prevent C Bank from relying on the consent defence; but only if the special conditions set out by the House of Lords in *Royal Bank of Scotland v Etridge (No 2)*[91] are met (see **E1:3.2**).

---

[90] See eg *Royal Bank of Scotland v Etridge (No 2)* [2002] 2 AC 773.
[91] [2002] 2 AC 773. For further details, see Burrows, *Casebook on Contract* (2007), 729–53.

3.3 The 'apparent power' defences

A buys a Freehold of some empty land. A buys that Freehold with the help of money provided by B. As B does not intend a gift of that money, and there is no other legal basis for A to have its benefit, A holds that Freehold on Trust for both A and B (see eg **D4:4.3**). A plans to borrow money to build a home for A and B on the land. C Bank lends A that money and, in return, A grants C Bank a Charge over A's Freehold.

In **Example 15**, B has not explicitly given his consent to C Bank's acquisition of the Charge. However, it may nonetheless be reasonable for C Bank to believe that such consent has been given. For example, if B *knew* that A would have to borrow money to build on the land, B can also be taken to know that any lender would want security over the land. It may then be unreasonable for B to assert his pre-existing persistent right against C Bank. So, it may be possible for C to rely on the general *defensive estoppel* principle: (i) if B acts in such a way as to lead C reasonably to believe that B will not assert a right against C; and (ii) C then relies on that belief; then (iii) B may be prevented (for a time at least) from asserting his right against C (see **D1:3.1.1(i)**).

However, things should be different if B did *not* know that A needed to borrow money to build on the land. For example, it may be that A and B have enough money to pay for the building, but A, without B's consent, decides to borrow money from C Bank for his own purposes. In such a case, the defensive estoppel principle should not apply: it cannot be said that B has acted in such a way as to lead C Bank to believe that B will not assert his pre-existing persistent right. Yet, in a number of cases, C Bank *has* been allowed a defence.[92] Those decisions seem to depend on the need to give a party acquiring a security right special protection; we will examine them in detail in **G4:4.2.2(ii)**.

3.4 The overreaching defence

The overreaching defence is based on A having a power to give C a right free from a pre-existing right of B.[93] The defence is particularly important where B has a persistent right (see **D2:3.4**). In general, it applies in the same basic way where B's persistent right relates to land.

B1 has a Freehold. B1 borrows £100,000 from A Bank. As part of that deal, B1 gives A Bank a Charge. B1 then makes a contractual promise giving B2 an option to buy the land for £150,000 at any time in the next five years. B1 then fails to repay the loan to A Bank. A Bank exercises its power to: (i) sell B1's Freehold to C; and (ii) use the proceeds of sale to meet B1's debt to A Bank.

B1's contractual promise to B2 gives B2 an immediate persistent right (see **Example 2c**). However, C is *not* bound by B2's pre-existing persistent right. A Bank has a power not only

---

[92] See eg *Abbey National v Cann* [1991] 1 AC 56; *Bristol & West BS v Henning* [1985] 1 WLR 778; *Paddington BC v Mendelsohn* (1985) 50 P & CR 244; *Equity & Law Home Loans Ltd v Prestige* [1992] 1 WLR 137.
[93] See Harpum [1990] *CLJ* 277.

to sell B1's Freehold, but also to sell it to C free from any property rights (see **E1:3.4**) *or* persistent rights created by B1 without A Bank's permission. C can use the overreaching defence even if he knows all about B2's pre-existing right. And C can use the defence even if, when selling to C, A Bank breached its duty to B to sell the land in good faith (ie, to honestly try to get a reasonable price for the land).[94] A Bank's breach of duty means that it has committed a wrong against B; but it does *not* prevent C using the overreaching defence: it cannot change the fact that A Bank has the *power* to sell B's Freehold to C.[95]

3.4.1 The basic scope of the defence

In examining the overreaching defence, the crucial question is always: does A have a power to give C a right free from B's pre-existing right? As we have seen, one example occurs where A has a Charge, as A then has a power to sell the land free from a pre-existing persistent right created by B1 without A's permission. Another, very important example occurs where A holds a property right in land, or a persistent right relating to land, on Trust for B.

EXAMPLE 17a

A has a Freehold. A buys that Freehold with the help of money provided by B. As B does not intend a gift of that money, and there is no other legal basis for A to have its benefit, A holds that Freehold on Trust for both A and B. A, in return for a loan from C Bank and without B's consent or other authority, gives C Bank a Charge over the land.

B has a pre-existing persistent right: due to B's contribution to the purchase price, A holds his Freehold on Trust for both A and B (see **D4:4.3**). Does C have a defence to that right? Section 6(1) of the Trusts of Land and Appointment of Trustees Act 1996 (the 1996 Act) states that:

> For the purpose of exercising their functions as trustees, the trustees of land have in relation to the land subject to the trust all the powers of an absolute owner.

So, if, as in **Example 17a**: (i) A holds a property right in land, or a persistent right relating to land, on Trust for B; then (ii) section 6(1) gives A all the powers of an absolute owner; so (iii) A necessarily has a power to give any third party a right free from B's right under the Trust. Therefore, as a result of section 6(1),[96] if A holds a property right in land, or a persistent right relating to land, on Trust for B, A *always* has the power to give C a right free from B's pre-existing persistent right. This means that, on the face of it, C will *always* be able to use the overreaching defence against a pre-existing persistent right arising under a Trust of land.[97] If that is the case, then in **Example 17a**, C Bank has a defence to B's right

---

[94] A Bank's duties to B in relation to such a sale are rather limited (see **F4:5.1.3(ii)**).

[95] C should therefore be able to use the defence even if he *knows* that A Bank has breached its duty to B: the suggestion to the contrary, made by Crossman J in *Waring v London & Manchester Assurance Co Ltd* [1935] Ch 311 at 318, should be rejected (see **F4:5.1.4(i)**).

[96] It has been argued (see eg Harpum [1990] *CLJ* 277, eg at 309; Jackson (2006) 69 *MLR* 214 and [2007] *Conv* 120) that provisions such as ss 18 and 20 of the Land Registration Act 1925 (and now ss 23 and 26 of the LRA 2002) also give a trustee of land such powers. But the courts have never suggested that overreaching operates differently in registered as opposed to unregistered land. And if ss 23 and 26 of the LRA 2002 did confer such wide powers, C could rely on overreaching as a defence against *any* persistent right relating to registered land, even if did not acquire a right from a trustee of land. However, ss 23 and 26 of the LRA 2002 may play a role in support of the basic powers given by section 6 of the 1996 Act: see **3.4.2(i)** below.

[97] Prior to the 1996 Act, A had a statutory power to give C a right *if* B's right arose: (i) under a statutory 'Trust for

under the Trust *even if:* (i) C Bank knows all about B's pre-existing right; and (ii) A, when giving C Bank its right, has acted in breach of his duties, as trustee, to B;[98] and (iii) C Bank knows that A has acted in breach of those duties. Thanks to section 6(1), it seems that the only relevant question (ie, does A have a power to give C Bank a right?) must be answered in C Bank's favour.

Section 6(1) thus creates a crucial distinction between: (i) Trusts relating to land; and (ii) all other Trusts. In other Trusts, C will only be able to use the overreaching defence if the terms of the Trust (or of a specific statute) give A the necessary power to give C a right. In contrast, where A holds a property right in land or a persistent right relating to land on Trust, then A will *always* have the powers of an 'absolute owner' and so will have a power to give C a right.

However, section 6(1) in fact simply gives C the *chance* of relying on the overreaching defence. Where land is concerned, there are some limits to the operation of the defence, and those limits mean that, in **Example 17a**, C Bank *cannot* use the overreaching defence.

3.4.2 The limits to the defence

(i) Section 8 of the 1996 Act

Section 8 of the 1996 Act allows A0, when setting up a Trust of a Freehold or Lease to be held by A, to expressly limit A's powers.[99] Section 8 thus gives a party setting up a Trust relating to land an important (and somewhat surprising) power to restrict the future use of that land.[100] Similarly, even without expressly avoiding section 6(1), A0 can impose a requirement that A must get the consent of X before exercising a particular power.[101]

In such a case, a *restriction* can be entered on the register recording the limit on A's powers.[102] This restriction: (i) informs C of that limit; and (ii) instructs the Land Registry *not* to permit C to be registered as a holder of a right if the limit has not been complied with. If no such restriction is entered, C may face a problem. Consider a case where: (i) A1

---

sale' governed by the LPA 1925, ss 34 and 36; or (ii) under a settlement governed by the Settled Land Act 1925 (see s 28'(1) of the LPA 1925, buttressed by s 17 of the Trustee Act 1925). In a case such as **Example 17a**, A did have such a statutory power, as B's right was regarded as arising under a statutory 'Trust for sale': see eg *Bull v Bull* [1955] 1 QB 234 (see **G3:1A.1**).

[98] It is true that s 6(6) of the 1996 Act states that: 'the powers conferred [by s 6(1)] shall not be exercised in contravention of, or of an order made in pursuance of, any other enactment or any rules of law or equity'. However, s 6(6) does not remove A's power to sell to C; it simply spells out the obvious point that A's exercise of the power may nonetheless involve a breach of A's duty to B. In a series of articles, Ferris and Battersby argued for the opposite conclusion: [1998] *Conv* 168; [2001] *Conv* 221; (2002) 118 *LQR* 270. On their view, s 6(6), by removing A's power to act in breach of Trust, dramatically reduced the scope of overreaching. However, that would be a very surprising result: certainly it was not intended by Law Com No 181, the report that led to the 1996 Act. The better view, set out by Dixon [2000] *Conv* 267, is that s 6(6) does *not* limit C's ability to use the overreaching defence: it just ensures that s 6(1) cannot be used by A as a defence to B's claim that A has breached a duty to B.

[99] For example, A0 can transfer his Freehold to A to hold on Trust for B and state *expressly* that he does not wish s 6(1) of the 1996 Act to apply to that Trust.

[100] For methods which may be used to escape such limits see Watt [1997] *Conv* 263. Contrast Settled Land Act 1925, s 106 making clear that a party setting up a particular type of Trust relating to land (a settlement) could not restrict the powers of the party able to deal with the Freehold or Lease of that land.

[101] 1996 Act, s 10 provides that if the consent of more than two persons is required for the exercise of A's power, then the consent of *any two* of those persons 'is sufficient in favour of the purchaser'. This means that, even though A breaches his duties as Trustee by exercising his power without all the required consents, C may still be able to rely on the overreaching defence as A will be deemed to have acted within his powers.

[102] LRA 2002, ss 40–42.

and A2 hold a Freehold on Trust for B, who is in actual occupation of the land; (ii) the terms of that Trust prevent A1 and A2 from selling the Freehold without X's consent; (iii) there is no restriction on the register so C is unaware of the limit; (iv) C then proceeds to buy the Freehold from A1 and A2, assuming that he can rely on the overreaching defence; but (v) it turns out that X has not given such consent.

On the face of it, in such a case, C *cannot* rely on the overreaching defence: A1 and A2 have acted beyond the scope of their powers. Nor can C rely on the lack of registration defence: B was in actual occupation of the land when C acquired his right (see **3.6.2** below). On one view, this could be said to be a perfectly reasonable result. On the other hand, it could be said that C should not have to take the risk of there being a hidden limit on the powers of A1 and A2.[103] In fact, it is generally assumed that, in such a case, C *can* rely on the overreaching defence, thanks to sections 23 and 26 of the LRA 2002.[104] Certainly, section 23 means that, as holders of a registered Freehold or Lease, A1 and A2 have a power to transfer that right to C. And section 26 means that, as there is no restriction on the register recording the limit on A1 and A2's power, that power is 'taken to be free from any limitation affecting the validity of a disposition'. So, C can argue that *despite* the express limit on A1 and A2's power, sections 23 and 26 of the LRA 2002 restore the general position, applying under section 6(1) of the 1996 Act:[105] as far as C is concerned, the hidden limit on the power of A1 and A2 can be ignored.[106]

Of course, in **Example 17a**, this tricky analysis is irrelevant: section 8 provides no assistance to B. In such a case, where the Trust has not been expressly set up, there is nothing to restrict the powers given to A by section 6(1): A therefore has all the powers of an 'absolute owner'. However, the second limit on overreaching may help B.

(ii) Section 2(1) of the LPA 1925

Section 2(1) of the LPA 1925 imposes limits on the operation of the overreaching defence in the land law system.[107] First, C must show he is a 'purchaser of a legal estate in land'. This means the defence is only available if C *both*: (i) acquires a property right from A;[108] *and* (ii) gives something in return for that right.[109] So, if C acquires only a persistent right from A,

---

[103] See eg *per* Morritt V-C in *National Westminster Bank plc v Malhan* [2004] EWHC 847 at [43] expressing the general view that C should not have to concern himself with the precise terms of any pre-existing Trust relating to A1 and A2's Freehold or Lease. That view is often referred to, for no very convincing reason, as the 'curtain principle'.

[104] See eg Law Com No 271 4.8–4.11; R Smith, *Plural Ownership* (2005), 194–5. Where an unregistered Freehold or Lease is held on Trust, C may instead be able to rely on the 1996 Act, s 16(3).

[105] See eg Ferris and Battersby (2003) 119 *LQR* 94 at 121–2. For further consideration of section 26 see Ferris, ch 6 in *Modern Studies in Property Law*, vol 2 (ed Cooke, 2003).

[106] B could attempt to rely on the fact that the LRA 2002, s 26(3) states that s 26 'has effect only for the purpose of preventing the title of a disponee [ie C] being questioned'. So B could point out that he is *not* disputing that C has validly acquired a Freehold; instead, he is claiming that C holds that Freehold on Trust for B. However, C's argument is that: (i) if C has acquired a Freehold from A1 and A2; then (ii) A1 and A2 must be deemed to have the power to give C that Freehold; and so (iii) the overreaching defence must be capable of applying.

[107] In *National Westminster Bank plc v Malhan* [2004] EWHC 847 Morritt V-C at [41]–[42] took the *obiter* view that the section *permits* overreaching and that overreaching is therefore *not* based on A's exercise of a power to give C a right. However, that view is very difficult to defend given the general nature of the overreaching defence as set out by, for example, the analysis of Harpum [1990] *CLJ* 277 (approved by Peter Gibson LJ in *State Bank of India v Sood* [1997] Ch 276 at 281).

[108] As used in s 2(1), 'legal estate in land' refers to any property right in land: as it does when used in s 52 of the same Act (see **E1:2.3.3(i)**).

[109] S 205(1)(xxi) of the LPA 1925 states that a 'purchaser' means a purchaser 'for valuable consideration'.

or acquires his right for free, he *cannot* use the overreaching defence.[110] However, section 2(1) does make clear that if C acquires a property right from A, and gives something in return, C can use the overreaching defence *even if he knows all about B's pre-existing persistent right.*[111]

Section 2(1)(ii) of the LPA 1925 imposes a crucial further restriction. That section says that C can use the overreaching defence only if:

> the requirements of section 27 of this Act respecting the payment of capital money arising on such a conveyance are complied with.

The 'conveyance' is A's grant or transfer of a property right to C. So, if C has paid money to A in return for that right, C can only use the overreaching defence if the section 27 requirement is met. This means that C must pay the money *either:* (i) to a trust corporation; *or* (ii) to at least two trustees.

So, thanks to section 2(1) of the LPA 1925, *even if* A has the power, under section 6(1) of the 1996 Act, to give C a right, C can only use the overreaching defence if:

- C acquires a property right from A; *and*
- C gives something in return for that right; *and*
- *If* C pays any money in return for the right, C must pay that money either to a trust corporation or to at least two trustees.

As a result, in **Example 17a**, C Bank *cannot* rely on the overreaching defence. It has acquired a property right in land (a Charge); and it did give something in return for that right (it made the loan to A). However, C Bank's problem is that it has not met the section 27 requirement: (i) it did pay money in return for its property right; *but* (ii) it only paid that money to A, and did not pay it to a trust corporation or to at least two trustees. This is confirmed by the House of Lords decision in *Williams & Glyn's Bank v Boland,*[112] the essential facts of which are identical to **Example 17a.**

EXAMPLE 17b

A1 and A2 have a Freehold. They bought that Freehold with the help of money provided by B. As B does not intend a gift of that money, and there is no other legal basis for A1 and A2 to have its benefit, A1 and A2 hold their Freehold on Trust for A1, A2 and B. Without B's consent or other authority, and in return for a loan of £100,000 from C Bank, A1 and A2 give C Bank a Charge over the land.

In such a case, C Bank *can* use the overreaching defence against the right of B. First, as A1 and A2 are 'trustees of land', section 6(1) of the 1996 Act gives them all the powers of an absolute owner, including the power to give C Bank a Charge. As in **Example 17a**, C Bank paid money in return for its right. However, in contrast to **Example 17a**, C Bank *has*

---

[110] That result is *not* changed by ss 23 and 26 of the LRA 2002: see Ferris and Battersby (2003) 119 *LQR* 94 at 121–2.

[111] S 2(1) states that: 'A conveyance to a purchaser of a legal estate in land shall overreach any equitable power or interest affecting that estate, *whether or not he has notice thereof,* if . . .'. This ensures that, although the general definition given to 'purchaser' by s 205(xxi) of the Act includes a requirement of 'good faith', C's knowledge of B's right does not prevent C from relying on the overreaching defence.

[112] [1981] AC 487.

complied with the extra requirement imposed by sections 2 and 27 of the LPA 1925: C Bank paid that money to at least two trustees—to both A1 and A2.

This is confirmed by the decision of the House of Lords in *City of London Building Society v Flegg*,[113] the essential facts of which are identical to **Example 17b**.[114] The result in that case has been criticised and we will consider it further (see **3.4.4** below). As a matter of doctrine, however, it cannot be faulted. The main argument of B was that he was in actual occupation of the land when C Bank acquired its Charge. As we have seen, such actual occupation means that the pre-existing persistent right of B is an *overriding interest*: it is immune to the lack of registration defence (see **C2:6.2**). However, C Bank did not need to use that defence; it could instead rely on the overreaching defence. And B's actual occupation makes no difference to the overreaching defence.[115]

B's actual occupation is relevant to the lack of registration defence: registration is important as it provides publicity and thus allows C to discover B's right. Actual occupation can serve as a substitute for defensive registration: B's presence on the land also allows C Bank to discover B's right (see **3.6.3** below). However, publicity is irrelevant as far as overreaching is concerned: C can rely on that defence *even if C knows all about B's pre-existing right*. The key to overreaching is simply the power of A to give C a right; and that power exists whether or not B is in actual occupation of A's land.

EXAMPLE 17c

The initial facts are as in **Example 17b**. A1 and A2 already owe a large sum of money to C Bank. C Bank is pressing for payment; but A1 and A2 persuade C Bank to wait by granting C Bank a Charge over their Freehold to secure A1 and A2's past and future debts to C Bank.

As in **Example 17b**, C Bank *can* use the overreaching defence against B's pre-existing persistent right. It makes no difference that C Bank has not paid any money to A1 and A2. Section 2(1) of the LPA 1925 does *not* impose a requirement that C must make such a payment. Rather, it states that *if* such a payment is made, C must pay the money to a trust corporation or at least two trustees. Section 2(1) does impose a requirement that C must give value for his property right. But, as **Example 17c** shows, it is possible to give value without directly paying any money. This analysis is confirmed by the decision of the Court of Appeal in *State Bank of India v Sood*,[116] the essential facts of which are identical to **Example 17c**.

---

[113] [1988] AC 54.

[114] In *Flegg*, B1 and B2 had both contributed to the purchase price, and so A1 and A2 held the Freehold on Trust for A1, A2, B1 and B2 rather than on Trust for A1, A2 and B. That difference between *Flegg* and **Example 17b** is irrelevant. *Flegg* occurred before the 1996 Act: the power of A1 and A2 to give C Bank a Charge came instead from the fact that the rights of B1 and B2 arose under a statutory Trust for sale: see *per* Lord Oliver [1988] AC 54 at 78 and 90; and *per* Lord Templeman at 71 (see too **n 97** above).

[115] In *Flegg*, an argument was made that LPA 1925, s 14 prevents C from relying on the overreaching defence if B is in actual occupation. It states that: '[Part 1 of the LPA 1925] shall not prejudicially affect the interest of any person in possession or in actual occupation of land to which he may be entitled in right of such possession or occupation.' That interpretation of s 14 was rejected by the House of Lords in *Flegg*; but on a ground that no longer applies, as it is based on the statutory Trust for sale replaced by the 1996 Act (see **G3:1A.1**). The conclusion that s 14 is irrelevant can, however, be justified: (i) Part 1 of the LPA 1925 does contain ss 2 and 27, but they *limit* overreaching rather than permitting it; and (ii) if B is in actual occupation of land, he does not acquire his persistent right *as a result* of that occupation. S 14 seems instead to deal with the independent Freehold a party acquires by taking physical control of land, rather than with a party who has a right under a Trust and also happens to be in actual occupation.

[116] [1997] Ch 276. Like *Flegg*, *Sood* occurred before the passing of s 6(1) of the 1996 Act. A1 and A2 nevertheless had the same power to give C a Charge under s 28(1) of the LPA 1925, buttressed by s 17 of the Trustee Act 1925.

EXAMPLE 17d

A has a Freehold. A buys that Freehold with the help of money provided by B. As B does not intend a gift of that money, and there is no other legal basis for A to have its benefit, A holds that Freehold on Trust for both A and B. A already owes a large sum of money to C Bank. C Bank is pressing for payment; but A persuades C Bank to wait by granting C Bank a Charge over their Freehold to secure A's past and future debts to C Bank.

The initial facts are identical to **Example 17a**; but there is a crucial difference. As in **Example 17c**, C Bank has not paid any money in return for its right. As a result, there is *no need* for C Bank to deal with a trust corporation or at least two trustees. So, in contrast to **Example 17a**, the fact that A is a sole trustee does *not* prevent C Bank from relying on the overreaching defence. First, A is a trustee of land and so has a power under section 6(1) of the 1996 Act to give C Bank a Charge. Second, as in **Example 17c**, C Bank has acquired a property right for value. And, as shown by the decision in *Sood*, as C Bank has paid no money in return for his right, there is no need for C Bank to pay anything to a trust corporation or at least two trustees. There is no actual decision dealing with a case such as **Example 17d**. So it may be that, in such a case, a court could deny C Bank the overreaching defence, perhaps as a result of a view that, from the perspective of practical convenience, B deserves protection. However, the doctrinal result is clear: the logic of the overreaching defence means that it *must* be available to C Bank in **Example 17d**. From one perspective, that result may seem harsh on B. However, in the abstract, the **basic tension** between B and C is impossibly difficult to resolve; we simply have to apply the specific rules of the property law system. And, in **Example 17d**, those rules allow C Bank to use the overreaching defence against B's pre-existing right under a Trust.

Examples 17c and 17d thus reveal an important point about the application of the overreaching defence where B has a right under a Trust of land. B is vulnerable to the defence even if there is only one trustee: A. If: (i) C acquires a property right for value; and (ii) C acquires that right without paying any money; then (iii) C can rely on the overreaching defence even if he acquires his right from A, the sole trustee.

	Two or more trustees?	Capital money paid by C?	Overreaching defence applies?	Authority
Example 17a	No	Yes	No	*Boland*
Example 17b	Yes	Yes	Yes	*Flegg*
Example 17c	Yes	No	Yes	*Sood*
Example 17d	No	No	Yes	–

3.4.3 The effect of the defence

(i) Overreaching does not give B a new persistent right

It is often assumed that overreaching has *two* counterbalancing effects: (i) it gives C a defence against B's pre-existing persistent right; but (ii) it allows B to claim a persistent right against any money C pays in return for his right. It is certainly true that, in cases such as

Example 17b (see eg *City of London Building Society v Flegg*),[117] A1 and A2 hold the loan money advanced by C Bank on Trust for A1, A2 and B. However, we do *not* need to use overreaching to explain that Trust. Instead, it arises because: (i) A1 and A2 have acquired that money by using a right held on Trust for B; so (ii) there is no legal basis for A1 and A2 to have the full benefit of that money; and (iii) A1 and A2 are aware of the fact meaning that there is no such legal basis; so (iv) A1 and A2 hold that money on Trust for B (see **D4:4.4**).[118] B thus acquires a new persistent right (a right against A1 and A2's right to the £100,000) as, by tracing, B can identify that new right as the product of the right initially held on Trust for B.

The same Trust of the loan money arises in **Example 17a**, even though, in that case, C Bank *cannot* rely on the overreaching defence. Even if overreaching did not exist, it would still be possible for B, in a case such as **Example 17b**, to acquire a persistent right against the loan money paid to A1 and A2. It is therefore a mistake to think that overreaching both: (i) takes from B with one hand (by giving C a defence against B's pre-existing persistent right); and (ii) gives to B with the other (by giving B a new persistent right against any money paid by C in return for C's right). Instead, overreaching simply *takes* from B. This is made very clear by **Example 17c**. As C Bank did not give any money in return for its right, C Bank's acquisition of its Charge did not lead to B acquiring a new persistent right. Nonetheless, as confirmed by the Court of Appeal in *State Bank of India v Sood*,[119] the overreaching defence still applied and prevented B asserting his pre-existing persistent right against C Bank.

(ii) The impact of section 2(2) of the LPA 1925

Section 2(1) of the LPA 1925 limits the scope of overreaching where A is a trustee of land. However, if the requirements of that section are met, and overreaching does occur, section 2(2) will, in certain very limited cases, *amplify* the effect of overreaching.

EXAMPLE 18

A0 has a Freehold. A0 makes a contractual promise to give B1 a Charge over that Freehold. As a result, B1 acquires an immediate Equitable Charge against A0's Freehold (see **1.3.1(i)** above). A0 then transfers his Freehold to A, a trust corporation, to hold on Trust for B2. A then gives C Bank a Charge over the land to secure existing and future debts of A to C Bank.

It is clear that C Bank can use the overreaching defence against B2's pre-existing persistent right (see **Example 17c**). And, due to section 2(2) of the LPA 1925, C Bank can *also* use the overreaching defence against *B1*'s pre-existing persistent right, even though: (i) B1's persistent right does *not* arise under a Trust of land; and (ii) B1's persistent right arose before the Trust of A's Freehold. That section states that: (i) if a property right in land, or a persistent right relating to land, is held on Trust by a trust corporation, or by trustees appointed by a court; then (ii) C, when acquiring a property right from such trustees, can use the overreaching defence against a persistent right 'having priority' to the Trust.

---

117 [1988] AC 54.

118 If B initially had a 50 per cent share of the right under the Trust of the Freehold, with A1 and A2 having the same share, then there *is* a legal basis on which A1 and A2 can use 50 per cent of the loan money for their own benefit. So A1 and A2 do not hold the loan money entirely for B's benefit: instead they hold it 50 per cent for B's benefit and 50 per cent for their own.

119 [1997] Ch 276.

The scope of section 2(2) is very limited. First, it can only assist C in the rare case where he acquires a right from a trust corporation or from trustees appointed by a court. Second, section 2(3) states that many important persistent rights cannot be overreached under section 2(2). In practice, section 2(2) only really assists C where the pre-existing right of B1, arising before the Trust, is either: (i) an Equitable Charge (as in **Example 18**); or (ii) a Purely Equitable Charge.

3.4.4 Justifying the defence?

(i) Arguments against the defence

As a matter of doctrine, authorities on the scope of overreaching, such as *City of London BS v Flegg*[120] and *State Bank of India v Sood*,[121] make perfect sense. However, from the point of view of practical convenience, such decisions have attracted criticism. For example, the Law Commission, when considering the scope of overreaching, expressed the view (*not* acted on by Parliament when passing the 1996 Act) that, in a case like *Flegg* (ie, **Example 17b**), overreaching operates too harshly. The Law Commission proposed that C should be unable to use the overreaching defence against B's pre-existing persistent right under a Trust if, when C committed to acquiring his right, B was an adult in actual occupation of the land.[122] The argument seems to be that, in such a case, the **basic tension** between B and C is should be resolved in B's favour.[123]

Certainly, thanks to section 6(1) of the 1996 Act, the overreaching defence operates in a special way where Trusts relating to land are concerned. The usual position is that, if A holds a right on Trust for B, A does *not* have a general power to give C a right free from B's right under the Trust. Yet, unless the terms of the Trust make clear that it is not to apply, section 6(1) means that a trustee of land will *always* have that power. That difference cannot be justified simply by pointing to the special features of land: a right under a Trust is also treated very differently from other forms of persistent right relating to land. For example, if: (i) A has a Freehold; and (ii) B has an Equitable Lease, an Equitable Easement or an Equitable Charge; then (iii) A does *not* have a general power to give C a right free from B's pre-existing persistent right. So, why should things be different where B's pre-existing right arises under a Trust?

Further, it has also been suggested that the current operation of overreaching may be inconsistent with the European Convention on Human Rights (ECHR). First, in a case such as **Example 17b**, it can be argued that C Bank's use of the defence may be contrary to B's right, under Article 8, to respect for his home.[124] Second, it can also be argued that the operation of overreaching may be contrary to B's right, under Article 14, not to be

---

[120] [1988] AC 54.

[121] [1997] Ch 276.

[122] Law Com No 188 at 4.3.

[123] In fact, even in *Sood* itself Peter Gibson LJ suggested that 'even when [money] is received by two trustees [eg, as in **Example 17b**] . . . it might be though that the beneficiaries in occupation are insufficiently protected': [1997] Ch 276 at 290.

[124] This argument was raised by B in both *Birmingham Midshires Mortgage Services Ltd v Sabherwal* (2000) 80 P & CR 256 and *National Westminster Bank plc v Malhan* [2004] EWHC 847 at [45]. It did not directly apply to the facts of either case, as the overreaching defence operated before the coming into force of the Human Rights Act 1998. Moreover, in each case C was not a public body and hence B could not argue that it was unlawful for C to act in a way contrary to B's right under Art 8.

discriminated against in his enjoyment of a right under the ECHR.[125] After all, in a case such as **Example 17a**, C cannot use the overreaching defence: why should B's right receive less protection in **Example 17b**? What justification is there for treating Mr and Mrs Flegg differently from Mrs Boland?

(ii) Responding to the arguments

The first argument against the current scope of overreaching is simply that, in a case such as **Example 17b**, B should be protected because of his actual occupation. That argument makes no sense from a doctrinal point of view (see **3.4.2** above). From the point of view of practical convenience, the argument may be that B's actual occupation makes a difference because it proves the importance to B of his right under the Trust. If so, the argument needs to be refined: it seems to be that C should not be able to rely on the overreaching defence *if* B occupies land as his home.

There is a profound difficulty with evaluating such an argument: it is impossible in the abstract to identify a 'correct' answer to resolving the **basic tension** between B and C (see A:3). Of course, there is much to be said for protecting B where he occupies land as his home; but there is also much to be said for protecting C and facilitating transactions in land. To deal with the dispute between B and C, we have come up with the land law system. In any particular case, all we can really hope to do is to provide an answer that is consistent with the current land law system. And there is *no* principle within the current system that B should always be protected where he occupies land as his home. Occupation of a home, by itself, gives B no protection against C—as shown by, for example, *National Provincial Bank v Ainsworth* (see B:11).[126]

The second argument against the current scope of overreaching is that B's persistent right under a Trust should not be treated differently from other forms of persistent right relating to land. In general, C's chief protection against such rights comes from the lack of registration defence (see **3.6** below). Under the Land Registration Act 2002, that defence provides C with quite strong protection. If C acquires a property right in the land for value (as in **Example 17b**), B's pre-existing persistent right can bind C only if: (i) it has been defensively registered; or (ii) B is in actual occupation of the land when C commits to acquiring his right. In fact, the lack of registration defence already gives C *special* protection against rights under a Trust. Unlike all other persistent rights relating to registered land, such a right *cannot* be defensively registered: B cannot protect his pre-existing right under a Trust by entering a notice on the register.

The argument is that, as the lack of registration defence *already* gives C good protection against the risk of being bound by B's pre-existing right under a Trust, there is no need for C to get the *further* protection of overreaching. Again, evaluating that argument depends on working out the best way to resolve the **basic tension**. It is impossible to give a 'correct' answer. However, it is worth noting that it may be justifiable to give C special protection against rights arising under a Trust. That extra protection, provided through the **defences question**, can be seen as balancing out the more lenient treatment B receives when it comes

---

[125] This argument was raised by B in *National Westminster Bank plc v Malhan* [2004] EWHC 847 at [45]. Under Art 1 of Protocol 12, Art 14 applies not only to the enjoyment of rights under the ECHR but also to rights arising under national law; however, the UK has not yet ratified Protocol 12. For a consideration of Art 14, see eg *R v Secretary of State for Work and Pensions, exp Carson* [2005] UKHL 37.

[126] [1965] AC 1175.

to the **content question** and the **acquisition question**. As to the content question, as long as, *overall,* A is under a duty in relation to the whole of a right, *any* duty of A to B, no matter what its content, can give B a right under a Trust (see **1.2.4** above). As to the acquisition question, section 53(1)(b) of the LPA 1925 means that A can exercise a power to give B a right under a Trust relating to land without using any signed writing (see **2.3.2(ii)** above and **Example 10a**).

The human rights arguments can be more easily dealt with. First, in a case such as **Example 17b**, C Bank can argue that the interference with B's Article 8 right is necessary in order to properly protect C Bank's Charge (see **B:8.3.2(ii)**). In its attempt to provide rules resolving the basic tension, the State has to take account of both B's rights and C's rights; it is allowed a 'margin of appreciation' in making its decision.[127] It is very hard to say that the overreaching defence, in itself, is not a permissible tool for the State to use in resolving the basic tension.[128] The argument based on Article 14 is quite weak. First, even if it is accepted, it need not be used to limit overreaching; it could instead be used to extend it so that it also applies in *both* **Examples 17a and 17b**. Indeed, C (rather than B) could argue that the current law is discriminatory: why should C be in a worse position where he pays to one trustee rather than two? Second, it may be possible to justify the current position. We need to remember that the section 27 requirement of payment to a trust corporation or at least two trustees applies *only* where C pays money in return for his right (see **Example 17c**). The requirement aims to reduce the chances of the money disappearing: a single trustee is more likely to succumb to the temptation to run off with the money. Of course, as shown by a case such as *City of London Building Society v Flegg,*[129] the requirement does not always provide useful protection to B: A1 and A2 defaulted on the loan repayments to C Bank and had presumably spent the money they had received from C Bank, rather than giving a share of it to B. Nonetheless, any 'discrimination' between **Example 17a and 17b** may in fact depend on an intelligible distinction.[130]

3.5 The 'bona fide purchaser' defence?

3.5.1 The general position

In general, the 'bona fide purchaser' defence plays a crucial role in protecting C against the risk of being bound by a hidden persistent right of B (see **B:5.2.2(ii)** and **D2:3.5**). However, where land is concerned, the 'bona fide purchaser' defence has been deemed unfit for its purpose of protecting C. The problem is that C cannot rely on the defence if he has 'constructive notice' of B's pre-existing persistent right: ie, if C, when he acquired his right, *ought* to have known of B's right (see **D2:3.5.1**). This can cause a problem for C: how much checking does C need to do to keep a judge happy? The risk for C is that if a judge later

---

[127] See eg *Ofulue v Bossert* [2008] EWCA Civ 7 esp *per* Arden LJ at [33]–[37].

[128] Compare eg the Grand Chamber of the ECHR in *JA Pye (Oxford) Ltd v UK* [2007] ECHR 44302/02 (30 August 2007), analysing the doctrine of adverse possession as a legitimate way for the State to control the use of land.

[129] [1988] AC 54.

[130] Compare eg *R v Secretary of State for Work and Pensions, ex p Carson* [2005] UKHL 37 *per* Lord Hoffmann at [41]: his Lordship held that a rule giving a person under 25 a lower rate of Jobseeker's Allowance and Income Support could be justified given the need for 'legal certainty and a workable rule'. Similarly, the need for payment to a trust corporation or two trustees is no guarantee that the recipient will not disappear with the money, but it aims to limit that risk through a clear and workable rule.

decides that: (i) C did not make sufficient inquiries; and (ii) if C *had* made sufficient inquiries he would have discovered B's persistent right; then (iii) C will be found to have 'constructive notice' of B's right and so will be unable to rely on the 'bona fide purchaser' defence.

Where things other than land are concerned, this risk to C is not too great: in practice, there is very little C can do to attempt to discover pre-existing persistent rights in relation to things other than land.[131] However, where land is concerned, the picture is very different. First, unlike other things, land is permanent and capable of multiple, simultaneous use (see **A:3.2**). So, when acquiring a right relating to land, C should be aware that someone other than A *may* have a right in relation to that land. Second, C can be expected to examine any documents setting out how A acquired his right in the land and recording past dealings with the land. Given that dealings with land are generally well documented, there may be a lot of material for C to sift through. Further, C can be expected to examine the land itself, and to ask anyone other than A occupying or using the land if he claims a right relating to that land. Specific facts may also be said to ring alarm bells and so demand further checks to see if, for example, an occupier of the land is paying rent to someone other than A.[132]

The 'bona fide purchaser' defence, when applied to land, thus caused C an acute dilemma. Should he try to save time and expense by limiting his inquiries and so take the risk that a judge would later view those inquiries as insufficient? Or should he play safe and devote time and money in making extra inquiries, thereby increasing the costs he incurs in acquiring his right? A similar dilemma can arise if a police officer investigating a crime is under a duty of care to future victims of the criminal. Should he devote the resources he considers appropriate to the case, thereby giving himself more time to perform his other duties? The risk then is that a judge may later view his efforts as unreasonably brief and hence a breach of his duty of care to those future victims. Or should he instead spend extra time on the case, making sure he discharges that duty of care, but also jeopardising his ability to perform his other duties?

The English courts have decided that it is a bad thing for a police officer to be under such a dilemma: as a result, a police officer has no general duty of care, when investigating a crime, to future victims of the criminal.[133] Similarly, Parliament decided that it is a bad thing for C, when acquiring a right in land, to be subject to the uncertain standard of 'constructive notice'. It led to third parties spending too much time and money before acquiring a right in land and so interfered with the marketability of land. So, Parliament has effectively eliminated the 'bona fide purchaser' defence from the English land law system.[134] C's protection from a hidden persistent right of B now comes from the lack of registration defence: that defence dispenses with the slippery notion of 'constructive notice' and attempts to replace it with a simple factual test (see **3.6.4** below).

---

[131] Of course, if C is warned that B may have such a right, then some further inquiry will be necessary: see *Jones v Smith* (1841) 1 Hare 43; affirmed (1843) 1 Ph 244.

[132] *Hunt v Luck* [1902] 1 Ch 428.

[133] See eg *Hill v CC West Yorkshire* [1989] AC 53: see esp *per* Lord Keith at 63–4.

[134] It can still apply where unregistered land is concerned, if B's right is not one of those rights which needs to be noted on the Land Charges Register: see eg *Kingsnorth Finance v Tizard* [1986] 1 WLR 783.

3.5.2 Powers to acquire a persistent right relating to land

If B has a power to acquire a persistent right against a right held by A (often known as a 'mere Equity': see **D2:1.6(iii)**), it may be possible for B to asset that power against C. However, C will be protected if he is: (i) a 'bona fide purchaser' of A's right; *or* (ii) a 'bona fide purchaser' of a persistent right against A's right (see **D2:3.5.5**).[135] So, if B has such a power, C can rely on: (i) the standard 'bona fide purchaser' defence; and (ii) an extra defence, based on C's acquisition of a persistent right for value and without actual or constructive notice of B's power. However, where B has a power to acquire a persistent right relating to land, things are different.

EXAMPLE 19

B has a Freehold. A wants to buy that Freehold. A persuades B to sell by telling him that B's employer now provides rent-free accommodation to all its employees. A genuinely believes that statement to be true, but it is false. In reliance on the truth of A's statement, B sells A his Freehold for £250,000. In return for a loan from C, A then gives C a Purely Equitable Charge over A's Freehold. B then discovers that A's representation was false.

In such a case, as soon as A acquires B's Freehold, B has a *power to acquire a persistent right* (see **Example 6**). By informing A that his representation was false (and hence that there is no legal basis for A to have the benefit of the transferred Freehold), B can impose the core Trust duty on A. If B asserts that power, can he acquire a right free from C's Purely Equitable Charge? Applying general principles, the answer is 'No'. Although C acquired only a persistent right from A, C acquired that right for value and without any actual or constructive notice of B's power: as a result, C can rely on the special defence applying against powers to acquire a persistent right.[136]

However, where registered land is concerned, things are different. In a case such as **Example 19**, it seems that C does *not* have a defence to B's pre-existing power. This is due to two factors. First, section 116(b) of the Land Registration Act 2002 states that a 'mere Equity' (ie, a power to acquire a persistent right) is an 'interest capable of binding successors in title'. Second, section 28 of that Act states the general rule that, in a dispute between B's right and C's right, whichever right arose *first* will prevail. That basic rule is of course subject to the lack of registration defence set out in sections 29 and 30. However, to qualify for that defence, C needs to show he has acquired and substantively registered a *property right in land*. And, in **Example 19**, C has acquired only a persistent right.

This result is surprising. The chief purpose of the Land Registration Act 2002 is to make it easier for C to acquire a right in relation to land by giving *extra* protection to C. Yet in **Example 19**, C has *less* protection than he would receive if acquiring a persistent right unrelated to land (see eg **D2:Example 21**). A possible justification may be that the 2002 Act does not aim to protect *all* third parties; instead, it seeks to protect those third parties who acquire for value, and substantively register, a property right in land (see too **E5:3.2.3(ii)**). It can also be said that, by entirely eliminating any defence based on 'bona fide purchase', the 2002 Act makes the law simpler. However, the problem with the general 'bona fide purchaser' defence is not its complexity, but its failure to provide adequate protection to C (see **3.5.1** above). There is no good reason to give C *less* protection against B's pre-existing

---

[135] See eg *Phillips v Phillips* (1861) 4 De GF & J 208 *per* Lord Westbury at 218.
[136] See eg *re Ffrench's Estate* (1887) 21 LR Ir 283 (Court of Appeal in Ireland).

power by: (i) removing the special form of the 'bona fide purchaser' defence; and (ii) replacing it with nothing.

3.6 The lack of registration defence

In this section we will examine the most important example of the lack of registration defence: the defence provided by the Land Registration Act 2002 ('the LRA 2002') where C acquires a right in relation to registered land. We examined the general requirements of that defence in C2:6: see the flowchart set out in the **Summary of C2:6**. The LRA 2002 also provides a similar, but slightly different, lack of registration defence where C registers a Freehold or Lease for the first time.[137] The Land Charges Act 1972 also provides a similar, but different lack of registration defence where C acquires a right in relation to unregistered land (see C2:7). However, we will focus here on what is overwhelmingly the most common situation: where C acquires a right in relation to land that is already registered.

3.6.1 The requirements of the defence

The defence is largely irrelevant when considering property rights in land: (i) in order to acquire a property right in the first place, B will generally need to substantively register that right (see E1:2.3.4); and (ii) if B can acquire a property right without substantive registration, his property right almost always counts as an overriding interest and so is immune from the lack of registration defence (see E1:3.6). However, things are very different when considering persistent rights relating to land: (i) B *never* needs to substantively register to acquire a persistent right;[138] and (ii) B's persistent right, *by itself*, can *never* count as an overriding interest:[139] it can only count as such an interest if B is *also* in actual occupation of the land when C commits to acquiring his right. This means that, in practice, the defence may be crucial in giving C protection against a pre-existing persistent right.

C can use the defence against B's pre-existing persistent right if:

- C acquires for value, and substantively registers,[140] a property right; *and*
- when C acquired his right,[141] B's persistent right was *not* defensively registered by means of an entry of a notice on the register; *and*
- when C committed to acquiring his right, B was not in actual occupation of the land.

The defence is particularly important where B's persistent right arises under a Trust: in general, it is *impossible* for B to defensively register such a right.[142] As a result, C will be able

---

[137] In such a case, a wider range of pre-existing but unregistered rights are capable of binding C: compare LRA 2002, ss 11 and 12 and Sch 1 (applying in the case of first registration) with ss 29 and 30 and Sch 3 (applying where C acquires a property right in registered land).

[138] Things may change if rules requiring electronic registration are implemented under s 93(2) of the LRA 2002 (see 2.3.3 above).

[139] For example, if B has a Lease (a property right in land) he has an overriding interest whether or not he occupies the land (see LRA 2002, Sch 3 para(1) and E1:Example 6). If B instead has an Equitable Lease (a persistent right relating to land) his right counts as an overriding interest *only* if B is in actual occupation of the land when C commits to acquiring his right.

[140] See LRA 2002, ss 29 and 30. S 29(4) allows C to qualify for the defence if he acquires a non-exceptional Lease of seven years or less (ie, a Lease that cannot be substantively registered: see G1B:2.2.1(i)(b)).

[141] Before committing himself to acquiring a right from A, C will ask for an official search of the register. C then acquires protection from the risk of any new *registered* right of B arising in the next 30 days (see E1:n68). However, C may be bound by a new *overriding* interest of B arising before C is substantively registered (see E1:Example 6).

[142] LRA 2002, s 33(a)(i). If B's right can be called an Estate Contract (see **Example 2b**), an Option to Purchase (see

to use the defence unless B is in actual occupation of the land at the relevant time. If the Trust imposes any specific limits on A's ability to give B a right, B can enter a *restriction* on the register, alerting C to that limit. The effect of the restriction is that, if the specific limit is breached, C should *not* be substantively registered as the holder of a right acquired from A. However, a restriction may give B very little protection: for example, it may simply alert C to the fact that, in order to use the overreaching defence against B's right, C needs to ensure that any money paid when acquiring his right goes to at least two trustees (see **3.4.2(ii)** above).

3.6.2 The effect of actual occupation

EXAMPLE 20

A has a Freehold. B, A's partner, occupies the land along with A. B has no property right in the land or persistent right against A's Freehold. A then gives C Bank a Charge over the land.

This case is essentially identical to *National Provincial Bank v Ainsworth*:[143] B has no right that he can assert against C (see **B:11**). B's actual occupation is irrelevant as he has no pre-existing property right or persistent right that he can assert against C Bank. Actual occupation comes in when considering the **defences question**: it can allow B to prevent C using the lack of registration defence. However, in **Example 20**, as in *National Provincial Bank v Ainsworth*, B does not get as far as the defences question: he has no pre-existing right that is prima facie binding on C.

It is therefore crucial to remember that the LRA 2002 does not protect *people* in actual occupation of registered land; it protects *persistent rights* belonging to those people.[144] And the LRA 2002 protects those persistent rights in a particular way: it makes them immune from the lack of registration defence. So, even if B has a persistent right and is in actual occupation, C may still be able to use a *different* defence against B's right. For example, in **Example 17b**, as confirmed by the House of Lords in *City of London Building Society v Flegg*,[145] B's actual occupation does *not* prevent C Bank using the overreaching defence against B's persistent right.

3.6.3 Justifying the effect of actual occupation

EXAMPLE 21

A and B have neighbouring Freeholds. A makes a contractual promise to give B a right of way over A's land. B thus acquires an immediate persistent right: an Equitable Easement. B fails to defensively register that right. A then takes up a job in a different town and moves out of his house. To prevent the house standing vacant, A allows B to occupy it. A then sells his Freehold to C.

Example 2c), or a Right of Pre-Emption (see **Example 2d**), then it *can* be protected by the entry of a notice—even though, as argued in **1.2.4(ii)** above, the content of B's right in such cases is identical to that of a right under a Trust.

[143] [1965] AC 1175.

[144] Of course, a *property right* of B also counts as an overriding interest if accompanied by actual occupation. But in any case, B's property right, by itself and without any actual occupation, will almost always be an overriding interest (see **E1:3.6**). So the practical importance of actual occupation lies in its protection of persistent rights.

[145] [1988] AC 54.

Purely as a matter of chance, B is in actual occupation of A's land when C commits to acquiring his right. As a result, C will *not* be able to use the lack of registration defence against B's pre-existing Equitable Easement. Of course, that persistent right does not allow B to occupy the land; so C will be able to remove B from the house. Nonetheless, C will be unable to prevent B from exercising a right of way over C's land.

Example 21 shows that B's actual occupation can protect *any* persistent right of B, even if that right does not allow B to occupy the land.[146] Indeed, even if B had moved into A's vacant house *without* A's permission, B's Equitable Easement would still be an overriding interest. This shows that we *cannot* justify the effect of actual occupation by saying that it is very important to protect rights to occupy land: actual occupation can protect B even if he has *no right to occupy the land.*

The importance of B's actual occupation, as suggested in **C2:6.2**, is that it permits C to easily discover B's right. In that way, it makes up for B's failure to defensively register his right: it provides the *publicity* that such registration would provide.[147] As we will see in the next section, that explanation fits with the detailed definition of actual occupation.

3.6.4 Testing for actual occupation

(i) Timing

> **EXAMPLE 22**
>
> A has a Freehold of a house. A holds that Freehold on Trust for A and B. A and B have not moved into the house. The following events then take place:
>
> (i)   8 September: A, without B's consent or other authority, makes a contractual promise to give C Bank a Charge over A's land.
> (ii) 15 September: A executes a deed giving C Bank the Charge.
> (iii) 20 September: A and B move into the house.
> (iv) 30 September: C Bank substantively registers its Charge.

In such a case, timing is crucial: when do we test for actual occupation? There are two main options:

Option 1   30 September: C Bank did not acquire its property right until then, when it substantively registered its Charge. At that point, B was in actual occupation.

Option 2   15 September: At that point, C Bank irrevocably committed itself to acquiring its Charge.[148] At that point, B was not in actual occupation.

---

[146] See eg *Webb v Pollmount* [1966] Ch 584.

[147] See eg Jackson (2003) 119 *LQR* 660 at 677: 'The first principle of title registration is to ensure that purchasers take a clear title to the extent that they could not acquire information concerning adverse encumbrances either from an inspection of the land register or by inspection of the land itself.'

[148] See eg *per* Lord Oliver in *Abbey National BS v Cann* [1991] 1 AC 56 at 84: the relevant time is 'completion' (when A executes the deed) *not* 'contract' (when A agrees to give C Bank the Charge). In **Example 22**, if B were to go into occupation on September 10th (after the parties contracted, but before execution) C could discover that occupation and then pull out of the contract with A: the existence of B's adverse right is a breach of A's core contractual duty to give C a Charge free from any pre-existing rights and that breach allows C to terminate his contract with A (see **E1:n64**).

In *Abbey National v Cann*,[149] on which **Example 22** is based, the House of Lords went for **Option 2. Option 1** may seem to make more technical sense: certainly, as far as *other* overriding interests are concerned, the question is whether B's right exists when C substantively registers his right (see **E1:Example 6**).[150] However, when considering the particular case of actual occupation, **Option 2** makes more sense: it fits with the justification for the effect of actual occupation. For B's actual occupation can only provide C with a means of discovering B's right if that actual occupation exists *before* C commits to acquiring his right.

When electronic registration is up and running, things will change, as there will be no need to apply a different timing test to actual occupation. There will then be no gap between the points when: (i) C commits to acquiring his property right; and (ii) the point when C substantively registers that right (see **E1:3.6.1**). So, in **Example 22**, C Bank would be electronically registered as holding its Charge on 15th September. As a result, *all* overriding interests can then be tested for at the moment of C's substantive registration.[151]

(ii) Basic definition

To define the scope of any concept used in a legal rule, we need to know the purpose of that rule. As far as the definition of actual occupation is concerned, there is a tension between two aspects of the rule's purpose. First, the chief aim of the lack of registration defence is to avoid the uncertainty of the former 'bona fide purchaser' defence, with its slippery notion of 'constructive notice' (see **3.5.1** above). To avoid these problems creeping into the lack of registration defence, there is a strong argument that the actual occupation test should be a simple, *factual* one, lacking the subtleties of constructive notice. However, on the other hand, the justification for the effect of actual occupation is that it allows C easily to discover B's right. As a result, there is an argument for defining actual occupation not by a simple factual test, but by reference to the question of whether, in a particular case, the extent of B's presence on the land means that C can reasonably be expected to discover B's right relating to the land.

The tension between these two approaches certainly shaped the definition given to actual occupation under the Land Registration Act 1925. The first ('factual') view clearly influenced the decision of the House of Lords in *Williams and Glyn's Bank v Boland* (see **C2:Example 4**).[152] C Bank argued that, although B lived on the registered land, B should not be considered to be in 'actual occupation'. The argument was based on the second, 'notice' view: (i) B occupied with her husband, A; so (ii) her presence on the land could not be said to alert C Bank to the possibility that B had her own, independent right: it was reasonable for C Bank to assume that B (like Mrs Ainsworth in *NPB v Ainsworth*) was simply occupying the land with permission of her husband. In *Boland*, the House of Lords rejected that argument: Lord Wilberforce emphasised that a simple, factual test should be used to define actual occupation and declared that those words are 'ordinary words of plain English, and should, in my opinion, be interpreted as such'.[153]

---

[149] [1991] 1 AC 56. See esp *per* Lord Oliver at 83–7 and *per* Lord Jauncey at 103–6.

[150] See eg *per* Lord Oliver at 87 and *per* Lord Jauncey at 106.

[151] Equally, C will then also be protected from the risk of B acquiring an overriding *property right* in the gap between committing to acquiring his right and being registered as the holder of that right: see eg *Barclays Bank plc v Zaroovabli* [1997] Ch 321 (**E1:Example 6**).

[152] [1981] AC 487.

[153] *Ibid* at 504.

EXAMPLE 23

A has a Freehold. A holds that Freehold on Trust for A and B. A and B do not immediately move into the house, as it needs to be renovated. B supervises the builders and is often present on the land. Acting without B's consent or other authority, A grants C Bank a Charge over the land in return for a loan from C Bank.

In a simple, factual sense, it may be difficult to say that B is in actual occupation. However, if, on the facts, C should have known, or even did know, about B's right, it will be very tempting for a judge to say that B was in actual occupation and hence had an overriding interest. For example, the facts of *Lloyds Bank v Rosset*[154] are very similar to those in **Example 23**. The Court of Appeal emphasised that, in deciding if B is in actual occupation, the nature of the land in question has to be taken into account.[155] If the buildings on the land are being renovated, we cannot expect B to live there: the test for 'actual occupation' is therefore set at a lower standard. The point seems to be that, in such a case, C Bank cannot reasonably use the fact that no one currently lives on the land to infer that no one other than A has a right in relation to that land. As we have seen, the second ('notice') view also influenced the House of Lords in *Abbey National Building Society v Cann*,[156] when considering the timing question.

Further, in defining 'actual occupation' for the purposes of the Land Registration Act 1925, the courts developed some specific rules that seem to favour the 'notice' view rather than the 'factual' view. For example:

- Actual occupation involves 'some degree of permanence and continuity' and requires more than a 'fleeting presence'—eg, acts preparatory to moving in, such as fitting curtains, will not suffice.[157]
- As we have seen, the nature of the land should be taken into account—eg, actions that would not usually count as actual occupation may qualify where a building on the land is being renovated.[158]
- B can be in actual occupation without being personally present on the land—a temporary absence from an established home does not prevent B being in actual occupation[159]—and, it seems, B can be in actual occupation if his agent or employee, acting as B's representative, is in actual occupation.[160]

Equally, B can be personally present and *not* be in actual occupation. For example, if B is a company director working from company offices, he may occupy these as a representative of the company and not in his own right.[161] In addition, it seems that it is impossible for someone under the age of 18[162] (and perhaps anyone unable to respond to an inquiry from

---

154 The Court of Appeal's decision, considering actual occupation, is [1989] Ch 350. The House of Lords [1991] 1 AC 107 held that B did not in fact have a pre-existing persistent right and so the lack of registration defence was irrelevant.

155 [1989] Ch 350 esp at 375–9, 393–9, 403–7.

156 [1991] 1 AC 56.

157 *Abbey National v Cann* [1991] 1 AC 56: see *per* Lord Oliver at 93.

158 *Lloyds Bank v Rosset* [1989] Ch 350 (CA).

159 *Chhokar v Chhokar* [1984] FLR 313.

160 *Strand Securities Ltd v Caswell* [1965] Ch 958.

161 *Lloyd v Dugdale* [2002] 2 P & CR 167.

162 *Hypo-Mortgage Services Ltd v Robinson* [1997] 2 FLR 71.

C as to whether they have a right in the land) to be in actual occupation in his own right, even if physically present.[163]

It is clear that some of these rules are based on the need to ensure that C is bound only where, due to B's presence on the land, C could reasonably be expected to discover B's right. However, it is important to bear in mind that these rules were developed before the passing of the LRA 2002. That Act specifies that, in some cases where C cannot reasonably be expected to discover B's right, B's right will *not* be overriding *even if* B is in actual occupation. These exceptions will perhaps allow the courts, in defining 'actual occupation' itself, to give more effect to the first view and go for a simple, factual test, safe in the knowledge that, even if B is in actual occupation, his right will not be overriding if C could not reasonably have discovered it.

(iii) Exceptions

It may just be possible to think of a case in which B is in actual occupation, but his right is not easily discoverable by C. Allowing B an overriding interest in such a case would be inconsistent with the justification for the effect of actual occupation: it would allow a hidden right of B to bind C. It is therefore no surprise that, in such a case, the LRA 2002 makes an exception to the basic rule: (i) *even though* B is in actual occupation; (ii) B does *not* have an overriding interest; and so (iii) B's persistent right is vulnerable to the lack of registration defence. C can rely on that exception if two factors are present: (i) B's actual occupation 'would not have been obvious on a reasonably careful inspection of the land';[164] *and* (ii) C had no actual knowledge of B's *right*.[165]

The LRA 2002 provides a further exception if three factors are present: (i) C asks B if he has a right in relation to the registered land; and (ii) B fails to disclose his right;[166] and (iii) B could reasonably have been expected to have disclosed his right.[167] This exception again aims to protect C from the risk of being bound by a hidden persistent right. Technically, C may be unable to rely on the lack of registration defence even if he has asked B and B has not disclosed his right; but only in a case where it is not reasonable to expect B to make such a disclosure. Such cases must presumably be rare: if B *thinks* he may have a right, it is presumably reasonable for him to tell C.[168]

3.6.5 Comparing the lack of registration and 'bona fide purchaser' defences

The 'bona fide purchaser' defence no longer applies to persistent rights relating to registered

---

[163] If a child under the age of 18 is seen as a representative of an adult parent or guardian, then his presence could, however, allow the parent or guardian to be in actual occupation.

[164] Sch 3, para 2(c)(i).

[165] Sch 3, para 2(c)(ii). Technically, it is only such knowledge of B's *right* that prevents C from relying on para 2(c)(i): this means that C could know of B's *occupation* but still attempt to argue that B's right is not overriding as that occupation would not have been obvious on a reasonably careful inspection of the land at the time of the disposition to C. However, it would be possible for a court to say that, since C knew of B's occupation, that occupation must have been obvious on a reasonably careful inspection of the land *by C.*

[166] Sch 3, para 2(b).

[167] *Ibid.*

[168] An obvious example occurs where, because of his age or incapacity, B cannot understand or answer C's inquiry. In such a case, C could try to rely on cases applying the Land Registration Act 1925 and suggesting that a minor cannot be in actual occupation of land (see eg *Hypo-Mortgage Services Ltd v Robinson* [1997] 2 FLR 71). However, that may be difficult for C given the LRA 2002, Sch 3, para 2(b) *expressly* protects B in a case where it is not reasonable to expect him to disclose his right.

land: it has been replaced by the lack of registration defence, now set out by the LRA 2002. However, there are close similarities between the 'bona fide purchaser' defence, as it used to apply in land law, and its replacement.

	Defence	
	'Bona fide purchaser'	**Lack of registration**
B's right	Persistent right	Persistent right[169]
C's right	Property right	Property right
C acquires his right …	For value	For value[170]
Defence does not apply if …	C has actual or constructive notice of B's right	B's right has been defensively registered *or* B is in actual occupation

Given these similarities, it would be a mistake to see the lack of registration defence as a complete break from the 'bona fide purchaser' defence. The two defences have the same basic aim: to protect C from a hidden persistent right of B. And, where land is concerned, the two defences share important features: (i) in practice, each is used against a pre-existing persistent right; (ii) each defence applies only if C acquires a property right for value; and (iii) in practice, neither defence applies if B is in actual occupation of the land when C commits to acquiring his right.[171] As a result, the lack of registration defence is best seen not as a *replacement* of the 'bona fide purchaser' defence, but rather as a *modification* of that defence. Due to the special features of land, that modification is necessary in order to provide extra protection to C, a party acquiring a property right in land (see **C2:5**).

(i) Advantages to C of the lack of registration defence
From C's perspective, the lack of registration defence has two key advantages when compared to the 'bona fide purchaser' defence:

- It can protect C even if B claims C *ought* to have discovered B's pre-existing persistent right: C's constructive notice does not prevent C using the defence.
- It can protect C even if C *actually* knows about B's pre-existing persistent right: C's actual notice does not prevent C using the defence.

That first advantage is no surprise: the purpose of replacing the 'bona fide purchaser' defence with the lack of registration defence is to avoid the problems caused to C by the concept of constructive notice (see **3.5.1** above). The lack of registration defence is much more helpful to C as it focuses instead on simple, factual questions: (i) did B defensively

---

[169] In practice, the lack of registration defence can almost never be used against a pre-existing property right in land (see **E1:3.6**).

[170] In general, C must also substantively register his right. However, in practice, that does not operate as an additional requirement: (i) in general, such substantive registration is necessary simply in order for C to acquire a property right (see **E1:2.3.4**); and (ii) if C acquires a Lease that cannot be substantively registered, C can still rely on the lack of registration defence: see LRA 2002, s 29(4) and (iii) if C acquires an implied Easement, then he does not need to substantively register that Easement; but he must also have acquired a Freehold or Lease and so can use the lack of registration defence as a result of acquiring that Freehold or Lease.

[171] B's actual occupation would almost always give C constructive notice of B's pre-existing persistent right: see eg *Kingsnorth Finance v Tizard* [1986] 1 WLR 783.

register his right? And, if not: (ii) was B in actual occupation of the land when C committed to acquiring his right?

The second advantage is more controversial. It means that C may be able to use the lack of registration defence even if he *is fully aware* of B's right. There is certainly a strong argument that: (i) if C is fully aware of B's right; but (ii) C nonetheless chooses to go ahead and acquire a right in the land; then (iii) C ought to take the consequences and be bound by B's persistent right.[172] After all, the chief purpose of registration is to provide publicity so that C can easily discover B's pre-existing right. So, if that publicity is unnecessary, because C is *in any case* aware of B's right, why should B's failure to register give C a defence?

This argument led to *Midland Bank Trust Co Ltd v Green* (**C2:Example 5**)[173] going all the way to the House of Lords. That case did not concern registered land; rather, it dealt with unregistered land and the lack of registration defence provided by the Land Charges Act 1925. As we saw in **C2:7**, the House of Lords allowed C to use that lack of registration defence even though C, before deciding to acquire her right, knew about B's pre-existing persistent right. As a matter of statutory interpretation, that decision was clearly correct. The Land Charges Act 1925, like the LRA 2002,[174] contains no provision stating that C's knowledge of an unregistered right prevents him from using the lack of registration defence. However, the crucial question for us is whether either Act is *justified* in allowing C to use the defence in such circumstances.

There may be a good *practical* reason for allowing C to use a lack of registration defence even if he is fully aware of B's right. Let us imagine that the LRA 2002 contained a rule that, if C has actual notice of B's pre-existing persistent right, C cannot rely on the lack of registration defence. It would then be open for B to claim, in any particular case, that C *did* know about B's right. So, instead of merely asking reasonably simple questions—ie, (i) was B's right defensively registered?; if not (ii) was B in actual occupation?—a court would then have to inquire into C's state of mind. The process of trying to prove or disprove C's knowledge may well be lengthy and expensive. Furthermore, such a rule would give C an incentive for bad behaviour. B is likely to point to objective factors (such as documents disclosing his right) that may lead a court to infer that C did in fact know about B's right, As a result, C will have an incentive, when dealing with A, to make minimal inquiries, so that it cannot be said that he had actual notice of B's right. If C makes only limited inquiries, it will be tempting for a court to look not just at what C knew, but also at what he *ought* to have known or *ought* to have done. This brings us back to the difficult concept of constructive notice.[175] And the chief aim of the lack of registration defence is to *avoid* the problems of constructive notice.

Therefore, it may be that allowing C to use the lack of registration defence even where C is fully aware of B's right is the price that we have to pay for the key advantage of the lack of registration defence: its ability to protect C from having to engage in either: (i) time-consuming and expensive checks before acquiring his right; or (ii) time-consuming and

---

[172] See eg Battersby (1995) 58 *MLR* 637 esp at 655–6; Howell [1996] *Conv* 34 esp at 42.

[173] [1981] AC 513.

[174] And the current Act governing unregistered land: the Land Charges Act 1972.

[175] Law Com No 254 (the Consultation Paper leading up to the LRA 2002) at 3.46 noted the problem of preventing an actual knowledge test from becoming closer to a constructive notice test: this was given as one of the reasons for rejecting such a test.

expensive litigation after acquiring his right. An analogy can be drawn with the concept of absolute privilege in the law of defamation. When it applies (as, for example, to proceedings in Parliament[176] or judicial proceedings[177]) absolute privilege allows the defendant to have a defence to a defamation action even where he has maliciously made an untrue statement damaging the claimant's reputation. In principle, this seems excessive: what possible reason can there be for protecting malicious statements? However, the purpose of absolute privilege is not to protect those who make malicious statements: it is to give the party making the statement the security of knowing that the statement cannot possibly give rise to a defamation action. That party does not need to worry about defending an allegation that he made the statement maliciously; just as C, when using the lack of registration defence, does not need to worry about the risk of rebutting B's claim that he knew about B's pre-existing persistent right.

Of course, it is worth noting that, if the actual facts of *Midland Bank Trust Co Ltd v Green* (**C2:Example 5**)[178] were to occur in registered land, C would *not* be able to rely on the lack of registration defence: in that case, B *was* in actual occupation of the land when C committed to acquiring her right. As a result, it may be argued that the scheme of the LRA 2002 is inconsistent: (i) B's actual occupation can prevent C relying on the lack of registration defence because C *ought* to be aware of B's right; but (ii) if B is not in actual occupation, C can use the defence even if he *is* aware of B's right.

As a matter of principle, there is certainly an inconsistency. However, it has a practical explanation. Like any other part of the land law system, the LRA 2002 and the lack of registration defence it provides attempt to resolve the **basic tension**: to strike a compromise between the interests of B and of C. Under the Act, the complex question of what C *ought* to have known is limited to a simple, factual question: was B in actual occupation? A test based on actual occupation is thus a *substitute* for a test based on C's knowledge: it is a very rough equivalent of the test but has the crucial advantage of focusing the inquiry on a simple, factual question. In this way, as so often in land law, the very difficult and controversial task of resolving the **basic tension** is transformed into a matter of applying a particular, technical rule. But that rule is certainly not irrational: it attempts to balance the needs of B and C whilst promoting the marketability of land, a unique and limited resource.

(ii) Advantages to B of the lack of registration defence?

In comparing the two defences, it is important to note that the very existence of a register capable of recording persistent rights relating to land would have radically changed the operation of the 'bona fide purchaser' defence. Once such a register exists, B has an obvious way of preventing C from relying on the 'bona fide purchaser' defence: B simply needs to have his persistent right noted on the register, so that C then has, at the very least, constructive notice of B's right.[179] The existence of a register can thus provide an important *facility* to B: it allows B to protect himself against the 'bona fide purchaser' defence by ensuring that *all* potential third parties have notice of his right. However, that advantage to

---

[176] Parliamentary Papers Act 1840.
[177] Defamation Act 1996, s 15.
[178] [1981] AC 513.
[179] Compare LPA 1925, s 199 stating that (in unregistered land) C is deemed to have notice of any right noted on the Land Charges Register.

B depends on the simple *existence* of a register: it does not depend on the particular rules of the registration system.[180]

3.7 The limitation defence

The general points made about the application of the limitation defence to persistent rights, set out in **D2:3.7**, also apply to persistent rights relating to land. In particular, once B has a persistent right, the limitation period applying to that right does *not* depend on the reason for which B acquired that right. So, if B acquires a right under a Trust of A's Freehold as a result of A's contractual promise to B, the limitation period applying to contractual claims does *not* apply to a claim by B to assert his persistent right. The limitation rules vary according to the nature of B's particular persistent right: as a result, we will look at those rules when looking at specific persistent rights in eg **G4:4.1** and **G6:3.4**.

SUMMARY of E2:3

As the **content question** and the **acquisition question** provide C with relatively little protection against the risk of being bound by a pre-existing persistent right, the **defences question** is crucial. The same is true where land is concerned. C's principal protection against the risk of being bound by a *property* right in land comes from the content question and the acquisition question, not the defences question. However, things are different where persistent rights are concerned. First, the content of such rights is not limited by the closed list principle. Second, there is no general rule that B needs to substantively register in order to acquire a persistent right relating to registered land. It may therefore be difficult for C to discover a pre-existing persistent right of B. As a result, the defences question performs a crucial role in protecting C.

It seems that, where land is concerned, there is a particular need to protect C. For example, the overreaching defence and the lack of registration defence can both be used, in limited circumstances, against a persistent right unrelated to land (see **D2:3.4** and **D2:3.6**). However, those defences apply much more widely where land is concerned.

First, if A holds a property right in land or a persistent right relating to land on Trust for B, section 6(1) of the Trusts of Land and Appointment of Trustees Act 1996 gives A all the powers of an absolute owner. As a result, the overreaching defence is much more prominent where land is concerned: there is no similar power for A in cases not involving land. Second, registration systems are rare in relation to things other than land. However, the system now regulated by the LRA 2002 covers the vast majority of land in England and Wales. By providing a lack of registration defence, it performs the role formerly reserved to the 'bona fide purchaser' defence: it protects C from the risk of being bound by a hidden persistent right of B. In doing so, it provides C with *extra* protection: in particular, C may be able to rely on the lack of registration defence even if he has actual or constructive notice of B's right.

---

[180] There is one very rare case in which the lack of registration defence may give B better protection than the 'bona fide purchaser' defence: where (i) B is in actual occupation but cannot reasonably be expected to disclose his right; and (ii) the reason for which B cannot disclose his right (eg, some incapacity of B) is not obvious to C. In such a case, C can be said to be a 'bona fide purchaser'; but it seems he may not be able to rely on the lack of registration defence: see LRA 2002, Sch 3, para 2(b).

It is therefore clear that, where land is concerned, the **defences question** gives C special protection against the risk of being bound by B's pre-existing persistent right. It may be possible to justify this difference by pointing to the special features of land—in particular, its limited availability and the need to promote its marketability (see **A:3.1.5**). However, B can also argue that, due to the special features of land (in particular its uniqueness and social importance: see **A:3.1.2** and **A:3.1.4**), his persistent right should receive *greater*, not less, protection than a persistent right unrelated to land. Certainly, we have seen that, particularly where the overreaching defence and the lack of registration defence are concerned, there is some disquiet about the ease with which C, when acquiring a property right in land for value, may have a defence against B's persistent right. This illustrates the point made in **A:3.2**: the special features of land *heighten* the basic tension between B and C.

4   THE REMEDIES QUESTION

4.1   Preface: the protection of persistent rights in land

4.1.1 The general position

EXAMPLE 24

A has a Freehold. A makes a contractual promise to give B a Lease. B moves into actual occupation of the land. A then sells his Freehold to C.

In such a case: (i) A's contractual promise gives B an Equitable Lease (see **1.3.1(i)** above); and (ii) C has no defence to B's right (see esp **3.6.2** above); so (iii) B has a pre-existing persistent right that binds C. As a result, B has a power to impose a duty on C (see **B:4.3**): in this case, a duty to grant B the promised Lease. Persistent rights relating to land, like all persistent rights, are asserted by imposing a duty on C and then enforcing that duty (see **D2:4.1.1**).

4.1.2 Rights under a Trust and third parties

EXAMPLE 25a

A has a Freehold worth £250,000. A holds that right on Trust entirely for B's benefit. B is in actual occupation of the land. Without B's consent or other authority, A then sells his Freehold to C for £150,000. C forces B to move out of the land. C then sells that Freehold to C2 for £250,000.

The first point is that B's pre-existing persistent right cannot bind C2: as B was not in actual occupation of the land when C2 acquired his Freehold, C2 can use the lack of registration defence. And it is now too late for B to impose a duty on C to hold his Freehold on Trust for B: C no longer has that Freehold. However, as shown by **D2:Example 24b**, it may still be possible for B to show that, *whilst C still had that Freehold*, C was under the core Trust duty to B. To do so, B needs to show that, at a point when C still had the Freehold, C had sufficient awareness of the fact that A had transferred the Freehold to C in breach of A's duties, as trustee, to B. In such a case, C is a 'knowing recipient'—or, more accurately, a knowing holder—of that Freehold and is under the core Trust duty to B (see **D2:4.1.1(ii)**).[181] As a result, C is then under a duty to account to B for that Freehold. In **Example 25**, C can no longer perform that duty: he cannot produce the Freehold or a product of that Freehold acquired with B's consent or other authority. So, C can be ordered to pay B money equal to the value of the Freehold: in this case, it seems, £250,000.[182]

EXAMPLE 25b

A has a Freehold. A holds that right on Trust entirely for B's benefit. B is *not* in actual occupation of the land. Without B's consent or other authority, A then sells his Freehold to C for £150,000. C is fully aware that A's transfer of the Freehold involves a breach by A of his duties, as trustee, to B.

EXAMPLE 25c

A1 and A2 have a Freehold worth £250,000. They hold that right on Trust entirely for B's benefit. B is in actual occupation of the land. Without B's consent or other authority, A1 and A2 sells their Freehold to C for £150,000. C is fully aware that A's transfer of the Freehold involves a breach by A of his duties, as trustee, to B.

In each case, B *cannot* assert his pre-existing persistent right against C. In **Example 25b**, C can rely on the lack of registration defence (see **3.6** above); in **Example 25c**, C can rely on the overreaching defence (see **3.4** above). In each case, C's awareness of the breach of Trust does *not* prevent C relying on the defence in question.

It has been suggested that, in such cases, B can nonetheless acquire a right against C based on C's 'knowing receipt' of the Freehold held on Trust for B.[183] However, as confirmed by the High Court of Australia in *Farah v Say-Dee*,[184] that suggestion must be wrong. A claim based on 'knowing receipt'—or, more accurately, knowing holding—is a way to enforce C's duty to account for a right he holds, or did hold, on Trust for B. In **Examples 25b and 25c**, there is no point at which C holds a right on Trust for B: as he has a defence to B's pre-existing persistent right, C is *not* bound by B's initial right under the Trust. It is possible that, in **Examples 25b and 25c**, B may be able to show he has a new, direct right against C arising, for example, because C has dishonestly assisted in A's breach of his fiduciary duty to act in B's best interests (see **E3:2.3.6**). But B certainly *cannot* assert

---

[181] The mere fact that B was in actual occupation may not be enough to say that C has sufficient awareness of the fact that A transferred the Freehold in breach of his duties to C. As emphasised by Megarry V-C in *re Montagu's Settlement Trusts* [1987] Ch 264, it is important to distinguish between two separate questions: (i) whether the facts would give C constructive notice so as to prevent C relying on the 'bona fide purchaser' defence; and (ii) whether the facts go further and give C sufficient awareness so as to impose the core Trust duty on C. That crucial distinction was overlooked by Vinelott J in an *obiter dictum* in *Eagle Trust plc v SBC Securities Ltd* [1993] 1 WLR 484 at 503–4.

[182] In addition, if: (i) C still holds either that very right (his right to the £250,000) or a right that can be identified, through tracing, as a product of that right; then (ii) as C is aware that there is no legal basis for C to have the benefit of that right; (iii) C holds that right on Trust for B (see **D4:4.4**).

[183] See eg Law Com No 254 at 3.48; Law Com No 271 at 4.11. Cooke and O'Connor (2004) 120 *LQR* 640 at 661–2 say that the possibility of bringing a knowing receipt claim when C can rely on the lack of registration defence 'remains open' in English law. Ferris and Battersby (2003) 119 *LQR* 94 at 122 assume such a claim can be made even if C can rely on the overreaching defence. *Obiter dicta* in support of the possibility can be found: eg *per* Graham J in *Peffer v Rigg* [1977] 1 WLR 285 at 294.

[184] [2007] HCA 22 at [190]–[198] esp at [193].

his pre-existing right against C and so cannot claim that C is under a duty to account for a right he held on Trust for B.

4.2   Specific protection

4.2.1 The general position

If B can directly assert a persistent right against C it seems that, where possible, a court will specifically protect B's right by ordering C to perform his duty to B (see **D2:4.2**). And, given the uniqueness of each piece of land (see **A:3.1.2**) specific protection is also more likely where B has a right relating to land (whether it is a property right, persistent right or personal right). As a result, it is no surprise to see that persistent rights relating to land are, in general, specifically protected. So, in **Example 24**, the starting point is that C will be ordered to perform his duty to grant B a Lease; special factors would have to apply for a court instead to order C simply to pay money to B.[185] However, this does not mean that persistent rights relating to land are *always* specifically protected.

EXAMPLE 26

A and B have neighbouring Freeholds. As a result of A's contractual promise to B that neither A nor future owners will build more than 60 houses on A's land, B has a Restrictive Covenant. B defensively registers his right by entering a notice on the register. A then sells his Freehold to C Ltd. C Ltd builds and sells 90 houses on the land.

In such a case, specific protection of B's Restrictive Covenant would require a court to make an order that the additional 30 homes be pulled down. Given the wastefulness of such an order and the harm it would cause to third parties, it is very unlikely that a court will specifically protect B's right. This is confirmed by the decision of Brightman J in *Wrotham Park Estate Co Ltd v Parkside Homes Ltd*,[186] on which **Example 26** is based.

4.2.2 Rights under a Trust and third parties

EXAMPLE 27

A has a Freehold. A buys that Freehold with the help of money provided by B. As B does not intend a gift of that money, and there is no other legal basis for A to have its benefit, A holds that Freehold on Trust for both A and B. A, in return for a loan from C Bank and without B's consent or other authority, gives C Bank a Charge over the land. A then fails to repay the loan as agreed. C Bank wants to: (i) remove A and B from the land; and (ii) sell the land; and (iii) use the proceeds of sale to meet A's debt.

The facts are essentially identical to those of *Williams & Glyn's Bank v Boland*.[187] B's pre-existing right under the Trust binds C Bank: C Bank cannot rely on the overreaching

---

[185] As we noted in **E1:4.2**, the general assumption that rights relating to land merit specific protection can be questioned (see eg *per* Sopinka J in *Semelhago v Paramadevan* [1996] 2 SCR 415 (Supreme Court of Canada)). However, a different approach could cause real problems of inconsistency: see Chambers, ch 10 in *Equity in Commercial Law* (ed Degeling and Edelman, 2005).
[186] [1974] 1 WLR 798.
[187] [1981] AC 413.

defence (see **Example 17a**); and, due to B's actual occupation, C Bank cannot rely on the lack of registration defence (see **C2:Example 4**). This means that B can impose the core Trust duty on C Bank (see **D2:4.1.1**). B may then claim that he is entitled to remain in occupation of the land, by arguing that:

Step 1   As C Bank is under the core Trust duty to B, C Bank must allow B to occupy the land; and

Step 2   B's right against C Bank to occupy the land should be specifically protected.

However, B faces a problem. A did not hold his Freehold on Trust *entirely* for B's benefit; A, like B, had a right under the Trust. For example, if A and B each paid half of the purchase price of the Freehold, they may each have a right to a 50 per cent share of the benefit of that Freehold. In such a case: (i) even though B can impose the core Trust duty on C Bank; (ii) the nature of the Trust means that C Bank, like A, is permitted to use 50 per cent of the value of the Freehold for its own benefit. This means that B may not be able to establish **Step 1** of his argument.[188] If C Bank were under an absolute duty to allow B to occupy the land, that would interfere with C Bank's own right, derived from A, to use 50 per cent of the value of the Freehold for its own benefit.

In fact, in a case such as **Example 27**, the general rule is that C Bank *will* be permitted to remove A and B from the land and to sell the land (see **G3:4.2**).[189] However, that is not because the court gives a particular answer to the **remedies question**; rather it is because the Trust in B's favour does not give B an absolute right to occupy the land. This does not mean that B's ability to assert his persistent right against C Bank is pointless: it ensures that B will receive some of the proceeds of sale of the land.[190] In contrast, in a case such as **Example 17b**, where C Bank has a defence to B's persistent right, B will have no direct right in relation to the proceeds of sale.[191]

4.3 Money awards

4.3.1 Money as a substitute for B's right

In some cases, it will be too late for B's persistent right to be specifically protected. In such a case, a court will have to do the next best thing and order C to pay a sum of money based on the value of B's right. For example, in **Example 25a**, C no longer has the Freehold he received from A and so cannot perform his duty to B to produce that right; C will therefore be ordered to pay B the value of that Freehold (see **D2:4.3.1**).

Similarly, in **Example 26** it is, in practice, too late for B's Restrictive Covenant to be

---

[188] If A or C holds a Freehold or Lease on Trust for B, the question of whether B has a right to occupy that land is governed by ss 12 and 13 of the Trusts of Land and Appointment of Trustees Act 1996 (see **G3:1.2.2(ii)**).

[189] See eg *Bank of Ireland v Bell* [2001] 2 FLR 809; *First National Bank v Achampong* [2004] 1 FCR 18. C Bank's application to remove B and sell the land will usually be made under s 14 of the Trusts of Land and Appointment of Trustees Act 1996 and a court will apply the principles set out in s 15 of that Act. If A has gone into insolvency, the question of sale will instead be governed by the Insolvency Act 1986 (see **G2:4.2**).

[190] So if the initial Trust gave B a 50 per cent share of the benefit of A's Freehold, the starting point is that B will receive 50 per cent of the proceeds of the sale.

[191] In a case like **Example 17b**: if (i) C Bank sells the land; and (ii) the proceeds of the sale exceed the debt A owes to C Bank; then (iii) C Bank must pay the excess to A1 and A2. A1 and A2 will then hold that excess subject to the terms of the initial Trust in favour of A1, A2 and B: the excess proceeds of the sale are a product of the Freehold initially held on Trust for B (see **D4:4.4**).

specifically protected; B will therefore have to settle for receiving money from C. C's duty to pay money to B arises as a result of C's commission of a wrong: his breach of his duty to B not to build more than 60 houses. In *Wrotham Park Estate Co Ltd v Parkside Homes Ltd*,[192] on which **Example 26** is based, C Ltd argued that: (i) the money he should pay B should be based on the loss B suffered as a result of C Ltd's wrong; and (ii) B had suffered no real loss by having an extra 30 houses on the land next to his. That argument overlooks the fact that, when C breaches a duty to B, C can be ordered to pay B money based on the value of B's right.

How can we value B's right in a case such as **Example 26**? The method adopted by Brightman J in *Wrotham Park* was to ask what sum B would have accepted in order to allow C Ltd to build the extra 30 houses. In that case, it was found that, if asked by C Ltd for such permission, B would *not* have given it to C Ltd. However, that does not mean that a court cannot put a financial value on B's right.[193] That value can be judged objectively by asking how much money a hypothetical holder of the same right could have extracted for its release. For example, if X carelessly destroys B's car, X cannot argue that the car is worth less *to B* than its objective value because B never uses it and never intended to sell it; or because B is rich and has lots of other cars. Those subjective considerations may be relevant when asking what *consequential loss* B suffers as a result of C's wrong; but they cannot affect the sum given to B as a substitute for B's right.

In *Wrotham Park*, it was decided that C Ltd should pay B 5 per cent of the profit C made by building the extra houses. That decision can be justified if, on the facts, that figure can be seen as a reasonable estimate of the objective value of B's right. However, in reaching that figure, Brightman J looked at a number of factors that ought to be irrelevant, as they are unrelated to the objective value of B's right. For example, the relatively small 5 per cent figure was based, in part, on B's failure to object more promptly to C Ltd's building of the extra houses.[194] It is difficult to see how this failure helps us to measure the value of B's right: it is not directly related to the question of how much money a hypothetical claimant, if he was prepared to release the right, could have extracted from C.[195]

4.3.2 Money as compensation for B's consequential loss

EXAMPLE 28

A and B are neighbouring landowners. A makes a non-contractual promise to give B a right of way over A's land, allowing B to get to his land from a nearby road. B relies on that promise by selling off part of his land without reserving a right of way over the sold land to get to his retained land from the road. A then refuses to give B the promised right of way over A's land. As a result, B is unable to get to his retained land from the road and so cannot use that land.

---

[192] [1974] 1 WLR 798.

[193] For example, if X offers me payment for permission to cut off my big toe, I will refuse. But if X then cuts it off anyway, a court has to put a financial value on my right when ordering X to pay money to me.

[194] [1974] 1 WLR 798 at 815–6.

[195] It may be *indirectly* related: it could be said that the value of such a right depends in part on the benefit it gives to the holder of the right; and, in *Wrotham Park*, that benefit could not have been great as otherwise B would have objected more promptly to the breach of his right.

In *Crabb v Arun DC*,[196] the Court of Appeal considered an essentially identical set of facts. It held that the doctrine of proprietary estoppel imposed a duty on A to grant B the promised right of way. On the analysis set out in this book, B therefore has a persistent right: an Equitable Easement (see **1.3.1** above). The plan had been that B would pay A for the right of way: a price of £3,000 had been suggested. However, the Court of Appeal held that B did *not* have to pay for the Easement. B was able to acquire the Easement for free because, as a result of A's delay in keeping his promise, B had been unable to use his retained land for over a year. So, in effect, A was ordered to pay money to B as a result of the consequential loss B had suffered through A's interference with B's persistent right.

4.3.3 Money reflecting C's gain?

The decision of Brightman J in *Wrotham Park Estate Co Ltd v Parkside Homes Ltd* (**Example 26**),[197] from one perspective, can be seen as evidence of the court's willingness to order C to pay B money based on the gain C has made as a result of breaching his duty to B. However, as we have seen, that decision can best be explained as depending on the general principle that, in such a case, C can be ordered to pay money based on the value of B's right. In that way, *Wrotham Park* can be analysed in the same way as *Ministry of Defence v Ashman* (**E1:Example 10**)[198] and *Strand Electric Engineering Co Ltd v Brisford Entertainment Ltd* (see **D1:4.3.3**).[199]

Of course, this analysis does not preclude the possibility that B may be able to claim 'punitive' or 'exemplary' damages where C: (i) acts in a way that C *knows* will be in breach of a duty owed to B; and (ii) does so with the intention of making a profit (see **D2:4.3.3**).

4.4   An allowance for C?

The general principles set out in **D2:4.4** apply equally where B's pre-existing persistent right relates to land. In such a case, if B has made a promise to C, it may also be possible for C to acquire a right against B arising under the doctrine of proprietary estoppel (see **E1:4.4**).

One situation worth noting can arise where: (i) A holds a Freehold or Lease on Trust for A and B; and (ii) A transfers that Freehold or Lease to C; and (iii) C then, in the honest belief that no one else has a right in relation to the land, spends money on improving or maintaining the land (eg, on making mortgage payments to pay off a Charge secured on the land). In such a case, if B's pre-existing persistent right binds C, C's expenditure will benefit *both* B and C.[200] So, C can argue that: (i) B has received a benefit at C's expense (the increased or maintained value of B's right under the Trust); and (ii) there is no legal basis for B to keep that benefit.[201] On the principles set out in **D4:4.4**, therefore, we would expect that:

---

[196] [1976] Ch 179. See too **E4:1**.

[197] [1974] 1 WLR 798.

[198] (1993) 66 P & CR 195.

[199] [1952] 2 QB 246.

[200] Of course, not all work or expenditure by C will benefit B: if C spends two weeks decorating a room in the house very badly, B acquires no benefit.

[201] Where C spends time or money on the land *knowing* that B has, or may have, a right in relation to that land, it is more difficult for C to show there is no legal basis for B to keep the benefit *chose* to confer on B: see eg *Leigh v v Dickeson* (1884) 15 QBD 60 *per* Brett MR at 64 and Cotton LJ at 66. Things are different if C's work consists of performing a duty owed by both B and C (eg, a duty, under a Lease, to make repairs): in such a case, C cannot be said to have *chosen* to give B the benefit.

(i) B has a duty to pay C the value of the benefit received by C; and (ii) B's duty is secured by a Purely Equitable Charge, held by C, over B's right under the Trust. That does indeed seem to be the result reached by the courts, although it is often applied through the somewhat opaque process of 'Equitable accounting', taking place when the land is sold.[202] Those principles can also apply where C is bound by a hidden *property right* of B. They may also apply where land is not involved, but, in practice, they are particularly prominent when considering the use of land.[203]

---

[202] See eg *Leigh v v Dickeson* (1884) 15 QBD 60 *per* Brett MR at 65. The process can also occur if the land is partitioned (ie physically divided between B and C) see eg *re Jones, Farrington v Foster* [1893] 2 Ch 461.

[203] In cases involving Trusts of land, the accounting process must now be carried out in a way compatible with the Trusts of Land and Appointment of Trustees Act: see eg *Murphy v Gooch* [2007] EWCA Civ 603. As noted there, if C has had sole occupation of the land for a period, C may also be under a duty to pay 'occupation rent' to B: see **G2:1.4.2(i)**.

CHAPTER E3
DIRECT RIGHTS

DIRECT RIGHTS

OVERVIEW

Direct rights provide an important means of dealing with the **basic tension** between B and C. The possibility of acquiring a direct right gives B protection against only a *limited class* of third parties: those who have acted in such a way as to justify B acquiring a right against them (see **B:3**). A direct right can thus protect B if, through failing to satisfy either the **content question** or the **acquisition question**, he has no pre-existing property right or persistent right. It can also protect B where B *does* have such a right, but C has a **defence** to it.

Direct rights can therefore be particularly important where land is concerned. First, the registration system provided by the Land Registration Act 2002 ('the LRA 2002') gives C a good deal of protection against the risk of being bound by a pre-existing property right or persistent right of B. For example, B's failure to substantively register a claimed property right may mean that B fails to acquire that right (see **E1:2.3.4**). And B's failure to defensively register a persistent right may allow C to use the lack of registration defence against that right (see **E2:3.6**). However, registration systems do *not* aim to protect C from the risk of being bound by a direct right of B (see **C2.2**). This means that, even if he has failed to register a pre-existing right, B may nonetheless be able to assert a direct right against C. This point is particularly topical: the LRA 2002 seeks to make it increasingly[1] hard for B to assert an unregistered pre-existing right against C. As a result, B will more frequently be forced to claim a direct right against C.[2] And if a court feels that, on the facts of the case, the **basic tension** ought to be resolved in B's favour, it may be willing to accept B's claim and find that, as a result of C's conduct, B has acquired a direct right against C.

Second, the permanence and fixed location of land means that direct rights may be particularly important when considering the position of *neighbours*.

---

[1] Increasingly harder as, once e-conveyancing is up and running, rules passed under s 93(2) of the Land Registration Act 2002 will make it still more difficult for B to assert an unregistered pre-existing right (see **E2:2.3.3(ii)**).

[2] Law Com No 271, on which the Land Registration Act 2002 is based, makes clear that the registration system set up by the Act does nothing to prevent B from asserting a direct right against C: see paras 3.48–3.49, 4.11 and 7.7. R Smith, ch 2 in *Land Law: Issues, Debates, Policy* (ed Tee, 2002), 47 follows the Privy Council's statement in *Gardener v Lewis* [1998] 1 WLR 1535 by describing the principle as preventing C from relying on B's lack of registration to escape a *personal* liability to B. However, it is important to emphasise that B's direct right, arising as a result of C's conduct, may be a persistent right or even a property right: see eg *per* Wilson and Toohey JJ in *Bahr v Nicholay (No 2)* (1988) 164 CLR 604 at 637–8 and *per* Brennan J *ibid* at 653; *per* Isaacs J in *Barry v Heider* (1914) 19 CLR 197 at 213–6; and *per* Dillon J in *Lyus v Prowsa* [1982] 2 All ER 953 at 962g.

EXAMPLE 1a

B has a Freehold. B decides to split up his land: he keeps half of it (No 32B) and sells a Freehold of the other half to A (No 32A). At B's insistence A promises, as part of his contractual deal with B, that: (a) A and all future owners of all or any part of A's land will ensure that the buildings on A's land are properly maintained; and (b) A, when selling the land, will insist that the purchaser also makes promises (a) and (b).

As long as A and B continue to hold the neighbouring Freeholds, the position is straight-forward: B can assert his direct, contractual right against A. However, complications arise if: (i) B transfers his Freehold to B2; *or* (ii) A transfers his Freehold to C. If the transfer to B2 occurs first, we will need to consider the following questions:

- Can B2 assert a right against A? And, after A's sale to C:
- Can B2 assert a right against C?

And if the transfer to C occurs first, we will need to ask:

- Can B assert a right against C? And, after B's sale to B2:
- Can B2 assert a right against C?

When considering any claims against C, it is important to note that A's promises *cannot* give B a property right or a persistent right. In **E2:Example 4**, we considered a similar set of facts. In that case, A's promise did give B a persistent right: a Restrictive Covenant. However, in **Example 1a**, A's promises are *positive*: he is promising to perform particular acts, not simply to refrain from making a particular use of his land. However, it may still be possible for B (or B2) to have a new, direct right against C (see **section 2** below). Crucially, as far as the acquisition of a *direct* right is concerned, it makes no difference whether A's duty (or C's duty) is positive or negative.

SUMMARY of E3:OVERVIEW

It is clear that where land is concerned, direct rights can be particularly important in two situations:

1. Where B's failure to register means that B cannot assert a pre-existing property right or persistent right against C.
2. Where A (a neighbouring landowner) has made a promise to B in relation to A's land, but that promise cannot give B a persistent right as it imposes a *positive* duty on A.

1   THE CONTENT QUESTION

The first, and straightforward, aspect of the content question is simply whether the new, direct right claimed by B allows B to make his desired use of the thing or right in question. The second aspect is whether B's new direct right counts as a property right, a persistent right or a personal right (see **D3:1**).

EXAMPLE 2

A has a Freehold. A transfers his Freehold to C. C makes a contractual promise to B that he will allow B to occupy that land for the next six months. Two months later, C sells his Freehold to C2.

As a result of C's contractual promise to B, B clearly has a new, direct right against C. That direct right can count as a property right (a Lease: see **E1:1.1**) or as a persistent right (an Equitable Lease: see **E2:1.3.1(i)**) *only* if it imposes a duty on C to give B exclusive control of C's land for a limited period. So, if C's promise does *not* impose such a duty on C, then: (i) B simply has a personal right against C, ie, a contractual licence (see **E2:1.3.1(ii)**); and so (ii) B has no pre-existing right he can assert against C2. In such a case, B's only hope is to show that he has acquired a *further* direct right against C2, arising as a result of C2's conduct.

2 THE ACQUISITION QUESTION

2.1 Direct and indirect dealings between B and C

The most obvious way for B to acquire a direct right against C is by direct dealings with C. So, in **Example 2**, B acquired a direct right as a result of C's contractual promise: a promise made to B for which B gave something in return. However, where the **basic situation** arises, it is unlikely that C will deal directly with B: after all, C acquires his right from A, not B. Throughout this chapter, as in **D3**, we will therefore focus on cases where B can acquire a direct right *even though C has not dealt directly with B*. The basic principles governing these cases are set out in **D3**. Here, we need only to examine the *special* features arising when the basic principles are applied by the land law system.

2.1.1 Deeds and section 56 of the Law of Property Act 1925

If the conditions of section 56 of the LPA 1925 are met, B can acquire a direct right against C as a result of a deed made between A and C (see **D3:2.1.1**). Section 56 is particularly important where land is concerned: a deed must be used when A transfers a Freehold or Lease to C (see **E1:2.3.3**). In fact, almost all of the cases cited in **D3:2.1.1** involved disputes about the use of land.[3] And most of those disputes involved the rights of *neighbours*.

EXAMPLE 1b

The facts are as in **Example 1a**. When buying A's Freehold, C *does* make promises (a) and (b) to A. C then fails to maintain the buildings on his land.

If: (i) C makes those promises in a deed executed by A and C; and (ii) C purports to make those promises *to* B; then (iii) section 56 can apply; and so (iv) C is under a duty to B to keep his promise to maintain the buildings on C's land. As C's promise is a positive one, it

---

[3] See eg *White v Bijou Mansions Ltd* [1937] Ch 610; *Amsprop Trading Ltd v Harris Distribution Ltd* [1997] 1 WLR 1025. The majority of the House of Lords in *Beswick v Beswick* [1968] AC 58 took the strange view that the section can apply *only* where land is concerned. The natural reading of the section, however, is that it can apply whenever C attempts to give B a right relating to the use of a thing.

cannot give B a persistent right. Hence, if C were later to sell his Freehold to C2, B would *not* have a pre-existing right that he can assert against C2.

EXAMPLE 1c

The facts are as in **Example 1b**. B then sells his Freehold to B2. C then fails to maintain the buildings on his land.

In such a case, B2 *cannot* acquire a direct right against C by relying on section 56: C purported to make promises to B, not to B2. Even if C made his promise 'to B and future owners of B's land', B2 *cannot* rely on section 56: C's promise must be made to B2 *specifically*, not as an unidentified member of a general class.[4]

2.1.2 Assignment of a direct right from B to B2

(i) The effect of an assignment

EXAMPLE 1d

The facts are as in **Example 1a**. B then sells his Freehold to B2. A then fails to maintain the buildings on his land.

In such a case, one method for B2 to acquire a direct right against A is through *assignment*: by the transfer from B to B2 of B's direct right against A.[5] Similarly, assignment may be able to assist B2 in **Example 1c**: B2 may be able to show that he has received B's direct right against C. Certainly, it is possible for B to transfer to B2 *not only* B's Freehold *but also* B's direct right against C. Assignment depends on the fact that: (i) if B has a right against A or C then; (ii) B, in general, has a *power* to transfer that right to B2.[6] This means that, although B2 may not have dealt directly with A or C, B2 can take advantage of the right that B acquired through his direct dealings with A or C.

Assignment is particularly important when considering the rights of neighbours:

1. The permanence and fixed location of land means that B2, when buying B's Freehold, may well be keen to have some control of C's use of the neighbouring land; so
2. B2 may well ask B to assign to B2 any rights that B has against C; and
3. If B is moving away, there is no reason for B to hold on to those rights.

Crucially, B's power to assign arises whether C's duty to B is positive or negative: it can

---

[4] See too *per* Simonds J in *White v Bijou Mansions Ltd* [1937] Ch 610 at 625: B can only rely on s 56 if 'although not named as a party to the instrument, [B] is yet a person to whom that conveyance or other instrument purports to grant some thing or with which some agreement or covenant is purported to be made'. That view was cited with approval by Lord Upjohn and Lord Pearce in *Beswick v Beswick* [1968] AC 58 at 106 (Lord Upjohn) and at 92–4 (Lord Pearce), and was also accepted by Neuberger J in *Amsprop Trading Ltd v Harris Distribution Ltd* [1997] 1 WLR 1025.

[5] 'Assignment' here thus means a true transfer of B's right to B2. It must therefore be distinguished from an 'Equitable Assignment': that instead involves (i) B keeping his right; and (ii) B giving B2 a persistent right against B's right (see **D2:1.2.2**).

[6] Some rights, however, cannot be assigned. For example, it may be that, when A or C makes a promise to B, the parties intend that only B should have a right to enforce that promise (eg, because the promisor's willingness to perform depends on his personal relationship with B): see eg Peel, *Treitel's Law of Contract* (12th edn, 2007), 738–40. A promisor can also stipulate, when making his promise, that it will cease to bind him if B attempts to assign his right to B2: see eg *Linden Gardens Trust Ltd v Lenesta Sludge Disposals Ltd* [1994] 1 AC 85 and **D2:1.4.1(i)**.

therefore assist B2 in **Example 1c**. However, in such a case, as C's duty to B is positive, B has only a personal right against C. So, B's assignment of that right can give B2 a right against C; but it cannot give B2 a right against C2, a party later acquiring C's land.

Of course, in **Example 1a**, B can also assign his initial personal right against A, arising as a result of A's contractual promise to A. Such an assignment will be useful to B2 if B sells to B2 whilst A is still the neighbouring Freehold owner. However, B's assignment of his personal right *against A* clearly cannot give B2 a direct right against C.

(ii) The requirements for an assignment

In **Example 1a**, B has a personal right against A, arising as a result of A's contractual promise to B. In **Example 1c**, B has a personal right against C, arising as a result of C's promise to B, made in a deed. In general, if B wants to transfer a personal right to B2, he must: (i) express his intention to transfer that right; and (ii) satisfy the formality rule set out by section 136 of the Law of Property Act 1925 (the LPA 1925) (see **C3:5.1.2**).

(iii) Problems with assignment

From the perspective of future owners of B's land, assignment may present some problems:

1. Assignment may be of limited use if B's land changes hands a number of times. If: (i) B sells his Freehold to B2; and (ii) B2 then sells on to B3; then (iii) B3 can rely on assignment only if he can show *both* that B assigned the right to B2 *and* that B2 then assigned the right to B3. Proving such a 'chain of assignments' can be awkward and time-consuming: the claimant needs to prove each link in the chain.[7]

2. A transfer of B's personal right against A or C must be absolute.[8] This means that, if B sells *part* of his land to B2, B *cannot* both: (i) assign his right against A or C to B2; *and* (ii) keep that right for himself. So assignment can be used to transfer a right, but not to duplicate it. This is obviously an important restriction on the usefulness of assignment in the context of promises between neighbouring landowners.

3. If B2 relies on an assignment, any money he may receive from A or C as a result of a breach of his duty will be limited by the rule that A or C cannot be made to pay any more to B2 than he could have been made to pay to B.[9] The rule is a sensible one: it protects the position of A or C by ensuring that B's assignment of his right does not expose A or C to the risk of paying out a bigger sum of money as a result of breaching his duty. However, where: (i) B2 suffers consequential loss as a result of that breach; and (ii) that loss would *not* have been suffered by B; then (iii) the rule prevents B2 from recovering compensation for that loss from A or C.

---

[7] B3 could attempt to claim that an assignment can be *implied* into each transfer as a result of s 62 of the LPA 1925. Under that section if: (i) B transfers his Freehold or Lease to B2; then (ii) if there is no evidence of a contrary intention of B and B2; (iii) B also conveys to B2 any 'rights and advantages whatsoever, appertaining or reputed to appertain to [B's land]'. However, that section *cannot* be used to imply a transfer to B2 of B's direct personal right against A or C. First, it may be difficult to say that B's right appertains or is reputed to appertain to B's land: the right may support B's use of the land but can exist independently of it. Second, more importantly, s 62 says that the transfer to B2 shall 'operate to convey' rights to B2; and it is difficult to say that an assignment of a personal right counts as a conveyance as that term is generally applied only to the transfer of a property right (see too **G6:2.3.1(iii)**).

[8] LPA 1925, s 136(1).

[9] See eg *Dawson v GN & City Railway* [1905] 1 KB 620: a case involving an assignment of a direct right on a sale of land by B to B2.

These limits on assignment diminish its usefulness to a future owner of B's land. These problems are no surprise. Assignment is a *general* mechanism for transferring a right from one party to another: it is not designed specifically for the particular context in which B's right benefits his land. The property law system reacted to this practical inconvenience by recognising a special concept, known as *annexation*. This is a different means by which B's right against A or C can pass to B2; and it applies *only* where B's right relates to land owned by B.[10]

2.1.3 Annexation: B's direct right becomes part and parcel of B's Freehold or Lease

(i) The effect of an annexation

If B2 can show that B's direct right against A or C has been 'annexed' to B's Freehold or Lease, B2 acquires that right *simply* as a result of acquiring a Freehold or Lease from B. So, in **Example 1a**, B's rights against A, arising as a result of A's promises (a) and (b), may be annexed to B's land. Whereas assignment occurs (if at all) when B transfers his Freehold or Lease to B2, annexation occurs (if at all) *as soon as* A (or C) makes his promise to B. Its effect is to make B's direct right, arising as a result of that promise, part and parcel of B's Freehold or Lease. This means that, if B2 acquires a Freehold or Lease of all or part of B's land, B2 *automatically* acquires the benefit of B's direct right. Annexation, like assignment, thus allows B2 to take advantage of the right that B acquired through his direct dealings with A or C. And, like assignment, it can also impose a positive duty on A or C to B2.

> **EXAMPLE 3**
>
> B has a Freehold. B enters into a contract with A. Under that contract, A promises, in return for payment, to repair and 'maintain for all time' the river bank adjoining the land of B. B then sells her land to B2; and B2 gives a Lease of the land to B3. A then breaches the promise to maintain the river banks. As a result, the river floods and ruins the crops on B3's land. B2 and B3 both claim money from A as a result of the loss caused by A's breach of its duty to repair and maintain the river bank.

B2 and B3 need to show that A is under a duty to each of them to repair and maintain the river bank. B2 may be able to show that B assigned her direct right against A to B2. However, assignment is of little use to B3: (i) given that B2 kept his Freehold when granting B3 a Lease, B2 is unlikely to assign any personal right against A; and (ii) B3 has suffered special loss as a result of the damage to his crops and, when assignment applies, A cannot be made to pay more than he would have had to pay to B.

However, in *Smith & Snipes Hall Farm Ltd v River Douglas Catchment Board*,[11] the essential facts of which are identical to **Example 3**, the Court of Appeal confirmed that B3 could recover full compensation from A by relying on annexation. It was found that: (i) B's direct right against A had been annexed to B's land; and so (ii) the benefit of that right

---

[10] This special rule seems to date from at least the 14th century: see eg *The Prior's Case* (1368) YB 42 Edw 3, Hil, pl 14.

[11] [1949] 2 KB 500.

automatically passed to anyone later acquiring a Freehold or Lease that depended on B's initial Freehold.[12]

(ii) The requirements for an annexation

Annexation occurs where:

- A is under a duty to B; *and*
- A's duty benefits B's land;[13] *and*
- A and B intend, when creating A's duty, that future owners of B's land will automatically acquire B's right;[14] *and*
- The land to which B's right is annexed can be ascertained by looking at the agreement between A and B.[15]

Where annexation occurs, it never happens in the abstract: B's right must be annexed to B's Freehold or Lease of a *particular* piece of land. It is important to note that B's right need not be annexed to all of B's Freehold: it may be that the right instead becomes part and parcel of only a particular part of B's land. In that case, the right will pass automatically only to future owners of all or part of that particular part of B's land.[16] So we always need ask *to which particular land* B's right is annexed (see **G6:2.3.2(iv)**).

In *Smith & Snipes*, the Court of Appeal held that the four requirements set out above had been satisfied. First, A clearly made a binding promise to B. Second, A's promise did benefit B's land, rather than just B: its purpose was to protect land adjoining the river. Third, A had promised to maintain the river banks 'for all time': this indicated an intention that future owners of B's land should also have a right to enforce A's promise.[17] In any case, section 78 of the LPA 1925 states that if A's promise 'relates to land' of B, it is deemed to be made not just with B, but also with future owners of B's land. That provision is very important: it means that, if A's promise benefits B's land, it is very easy for B3 to show that the third requirement is satisfied.[18] Finally, the original contract did contain a general description of the land benefiting from A's promise and, by using other evidence and looking at the surrounding circumstances, the court could therefore identify the land benefiting from the promise. The purpose of the fourth requirement is to ensure that A can establish if a future owner of a particular part of B's land has, by acquiring that land, also acquired a right against A. And, given A's knowledge of the surrounding circumstances, that purpose was satisfied in *Smith & Snipes*. In that case, as each of B2 and B3 has acquired a right in relation to the whole of B's land, there was no point to A trying to argue that B's right had been annexed only to a particular part of B's land.

It is important to note that, in *Smith and Snipes*, B3 did not acquire exactly the same

---

[12] So if B4 independently acquired a Freehold, by taking physical control of B2's land, it seems that B4 will *not* acquire the direct right annexed to B's Freehold.

[13] The promise must, in itself, increase the value of B's land, or affect the way in which B occupies the land. This requirement is often expressed by the idea that A's promise must 'touch and concern' B's land. The same requirement applies as part of the content of an Easement (see **G5:1.2**) and of a Restrictive Covenant (see **G6:1.2**). As in those cases, the requirement is satisfied if A's promise benefits a business run from B's land.

[14] The promise thus cannot be one that is intended to be purely personal to B.

[15] See eg *Smith & Snipes Hall Farm Ltd v River Douglas Catchment Board* [1949] 2 KB 500 at 511–2.

[16] It is possible for a right to be annexed to the *entirety* of all or part of B's land, so that a future owner of only a part of that land will not acquire the right (see **G6:2.3.2(v):Option 2**).

[17] See esp *per* Somervell LJ [1949] 2 KB 500 at 511.

[18] See eg *Federated Homes Ltd v Mill Lodge Properties Ltd* [1980] 1 WLR 594 (discussed in **G6:2.3.2(iii)**).

right as B. B had a Freehold; B3 acquired a Lease. It seems there was once a rule that annexation could be used only by a party who had the very same estate as B. However, the Court of Appeal held that this supposed limit was removed by section 78, which indicates that B3 can acquire B's right if he is a 'successor in title [of B]' or a person 'deriving title under [B]'. As B3's Lease was based on the Freehold given by B to B2, it was clear that B3 did count as a person 'deriving title under B'.

(iii) Advantages of annexation

As **Example 3** demonstrates, annexation is a very useful concept to future owners of B's land. It has three particular advantages over assignment:

1. There is no need for a chain of assignments. B's right automatically passes with B's land (or the relevant part of it) to B2, B3 and so on.
2. B's right against A can be *multiplied*. If B sells part of his land to B2 then: (i) B can keep his right against A; and (ii) B2 can also acquire a matching direct right against A.
3. If B2 suffers a loss as a result of A's breach of his duty, the money that A can be ordered to pay B2 is not limited to the sum A might have had to pay to B.

Annexation is unique to the land law system: a direct right against A can *never* become part and parcel of B's Ownership of a thing other than land. It seems that annexation meets a particular need existing only in relation to land. That need arises from the special features of land: in particular its permanence and fixed location (see **A:3.1.1**). Those features mean that a direct right against A may be of value to B not just in his personal capacity, but also in his capacity as an owner, for the time being, of a piece of land. Annexation recognises this by giving B the opportunity, when acquiring a direct right against A, to act not just on his own behalf, but also on behalf of future owners of B's land. By recognising annexation, the land law system thus imposes an additional burden on A. However, if A has chosen to make a promise that relates to B's land and is intended to be enforceable by future owners of B's land, it seems reasonable that A should bear that burden. After all, it can be argued that, in a case such as **Example 3**, A should not be able to escape from the full consequence of his binding promise just because B has sold his land on to B2.

2.2   Cases where B has no pre-existing right

It is possible for B to acquire a direct right against C even if: (i) there are no direct dealings between B and C; and (ii) before C acquired his right, B had no right at all.

2.2.1 The Contract (Rights of Third Parties) Act 1999

EXAMPLE 4

A has a Freehold. A transfers his Freehold to C. The contract between A and C includes a term that C must allow B to occupy the land for the next three months.

The Contract (Rights of Third Parties) Act 1999 ('the 1999 Act') means that, in certain circumstances, a contractual promise made by C to A can give B a direct, statutory right against C (see **D3:2.2.1**). In **Example 4**, C's promise to A is made as part of a contract in which A transfers his Freehold to B. As a result, that promise can only impose a *contractual* duty on C if the formality rule imposed by section 2 of the Law of Property (Miscellaneous Provisions) Act 1989 is satisfied (see **E2:2.3.3**). If it is not, C's promise to give B a direct right is not a *contractual* promise,[19] and so the 1999 Act cannot apply.

2.2.2 The 'receipt after a promise' principle

EXAMPLE 5

A has a Freehold. C makes an oral promise to A that he will hold that Freehold on Trust for B. A transfers his Freehold to C.

If, in **Example 5** A instead transferred to C: (i) A's personal right against Z; or (ii) A's Ownership of a bike, it would be very simple for B to acquire a direct right against C. B could simply point to C's oral promise to show that, when transferring his right to C, A exercised his power to set up a Trust of that right in B's favour (see **D2:2.1.1(i)**). However, things are different in **Example 5**. The special formality rule imposed by section 53(1)(b) of the Law of Property Act 1925 means that, to prove that A or C has declared a Trust in B's favour, B needs to produce written evidence signed by A or C (see **E2:2.3.2**).

So, in **Example 5**, B cannot prove that A or C has exercised a power to set up a Trust in B's favour. But B *can* rely on the 'receipt after a promise' principle (see **D3:2.2.2**). In doing so, B does *not* need to prove that anyone has exercised a power to set up a Trust. Instead, B's claim depends on showing that, due to his conduct, C is under a duty to B to keep his promise and hence hold his Freehold on Trust for B. As we saw when examining *Rochefoucauld v Boustead* (**E2:Example 9b**),[20] the section 53(1)(b) formality rule has no effect on that claim: B's right is *not* based on any 'declaration' of Trust; rather, it depends on the 'receipt after a promise' principle.

2.2.3 The 'benefit and burden' principle

As it depends on a prior agreement between A and B, the 'benefit and burden' principle is most likely to apply in cases where B, at the start of the story, has a personal right against A. We will therefore consider the principle in detail in **2.3.3** below.

2.3   Cases where B has a pre-existing personal right against A

2.3.1 The Contract (Rights of Third Parties) Act 1999

EXAMPLE 1e

The facts are as in **Example 1a**. When buying A's Freehold, C *does* make promises (a) and (b) to A. C then fails to maintain the buildings on his land. B then sells his Freehold to B2. C continues to fail to maintain these buildings.

---

[19] B may argue that C's promise did not form part of the contract of sale between A and C but was rather part of a separate 'collateral' bargain which does not need to comply with the formal requirements of s 2 of the 1989 Act. However, the courts are often reluctant to find such a collateral contract: see eg *Business Environment Bow Lane Ltd v Deanwater Estates Ltd* [2007] EWCA Civ 622 at [42]–[44] and **E2:n78**.

[20] [1897] 1 Ch 196. See too *Pallant v Morgan* [1933] Ch 43 (discussed in **D3:2.2.2**).

B2 cannot rely on section 56 of the LPA 1925 to acquire a direct right against C (see **2.1.1** above). However, B2 *can* acquire such a right under the Contract (Rights of Third Parties) Act 1999 ('the 1999 Act'). Under the 1999 Act, C's promise does not need to be a promise *to* B2. It is enough for that promise: (i) to purport to confer a benefit on B2; and (ii) for B2 to be identified by 'name, class or description'. So if C's promise to A is made for the 'benefit of B and future owners of B's land' it can give B2 a direct right against C under the 1999 Act. As a result, the 1999 Act can be very important when considering the rights of neighbours.

2.3.2 The 'receipt after a promise' principle

(i) General position and the 'Constructive Trust' problem

> **EXAMPLE 6**
>
> A has a Freehold. A makes a contractual promise to allow B to occupy, for the rest of his life, a cottage on A's land. That promise does not give B a right to exclusive control of the land. A then sells his Freehold to C. C makes an oral promise to A that he will allow B to remain in occupation of the cottage. As a result, C pays a reduced price for A's Freehold.

As C's promise is oral, it does not satisfy the formality rule imposed by section 2 of the Law of Property (Miscellaneous Provisions) Act and so does not impose a contractual duty on C to A. As a result, B cannot rely on the 1999 Act to acquire a direct right against C. However, B may be able to rely on the 'receipt after a promise' principle. For example, in *Binions v Evans*,[21] on which **Example 6** is based, Lord Denning MR stated that it would be 'utterly inequitable for [C] to turn [B] out contrary to the stipulation subject to which [C] took the premises'.[22] The decision can be seen as an application of the 'receipt after a promise' principle: (i) C made a promise relating to the use of his Freehold (a promise to allow B to occupy the cottage); and (ii) as a result, C acquired an advantage in relation to the acquisition of his Freehold (he paid a lower price); so (iii) C is under a duty to B to keep his promise.

In *Binions v Evans*, Lord Denning MR took the view that B's direct right arose under a 'Constructive Trust'.[23] This suggests that B has a persistent right. So, if C were then to transfer his Freehold to C2, B would have a prima facie power to assert his right under the Constructive Trust against C2. However, that cannot be right.[24] In *Binions v Evans*, C simply promised to allow B to occupy the land: such a promise does not give B a persistent right (see **E2:1.3.1(ii)**). First:

1. A made a promise to B to allow B to occupy A's land. Even if B gave something in return for that promise, it gives B only a personal right against A—a contractual licence.[25]
2. C's identical promise is given to A not to B; and B gives nothing in return for it. It

---

[21] [1972] Ch 359.

[22] *Ibid* at 368.

[23] *Ibid*.

[24] For disapproval of the idea that B's right in *Binions v Evans* arose under a Constructive Trust, see eg Bright [2000] *Conv* 398, 404–5; Swadling, in *English Private Law* (ed Burrows, 2nd edn, 2007), 4.125; Gardner *Introduction to the Law of Trusts* (2nd edn, 2003), 161–2; McFarlane [2003] *Conv* 473.

[25] See eg *Ashburn Anstalt v Arnold* [1989] Ch 1.

would therefore be absurd if C's promise could give B anything other than a personal right against C.

Second, there is clearly no Trust in *Binions v Evans*. C is not under the core Trust duty: he does not hold a specific right subject to a duty not to use that right for his own benefit. After all, provided C complies with his promise to allow B to occupy the land, C can use his Freehold as he wishes.

In *Ashburn Anstalt v Arnold*, the Court of Appeal continued to refer to the right B can acquire, in a case such as **Example 6**, as a right under a 'Constructive Trust'.[26] The confusion stems from cases such as *Bannister v Bannister*.[27] In that case: (i) A transferred a Freehold to C; and (ii) C made an oral promise to hold that Freehold on Trust for B. The 'receipt after a promise' principle applied and C was thus under a duty to keep his promise. As a result, C was under the core Trust duty: the direct right acquired by B was properly described as a right under a Trust.[28] However, this does not mean that *all* applications of the 'receipt after a promise' principle involve a Constructive Trust. The crucial factor is the *content of C's promise*. If, as in *Bannister v Bannister*, C has promised to hold a specific right for B's benefit *or* to transfer a specific right to B (see **D2:2.1.2**), a Trust will arise. If, as in **Example 6**, C has made a different promise, there can be no Trust.

2.3.3 The 'benefit and burden' principle

This principle, unlike the Contract (Rights of Third Parties) Act 1999 and the 'receipt after a promise' principle, does *not* depend on C making a promise to A. Rather, the 'benefit and burden' principle means that if:

- C chooses to exercise a particular right; *and*
- C is aware that his exercise of that right is conditional on C coming under a particular duty to B; *then*
- C will be under that duty to B.

The principle can be important when considering the rights of neighbours. Like the 1999 Act and the 'receipt after a promise' principle, it can be used to impose a positive duty on C.

EXAMPLE 7a

B has a Freehold of a large park. B divides up the park and sells plots to a large number of purchasers, including A. B retains a Freehold of the roads through the park and a seaside path skirting it. B and the purchasers of the plots, including A, sign a deed. The deed: (i) gives the purchasers the right to use the roads and seaside path retained by B; and (ii) imposes a duty on the purchasers to pay an annual contribution towards the costs of maintaining the road and the path. A then transfers his Freehold to C. C uses the roads and seaside path but refuses to pay the annual contribution.

C has made no promise, whether to A or to B, to contribute to the costs. Further, A's promise to B cannot give B a property right or persistent right as it imposes a positive duty.

---

[26] [1989] Ch 1 at 22–6.

[27] [1948] 2 All ER 133. See too *Rochefoucauld v Boustead* [1897] 1 Ch 196.

[28] And that right, because it arose under the 'receipt after a promise' principle, is properly described as a Constructive Trust: see **G3:2.4.3(ii)**.

Nonetheless, in *Halsall v Brizell*,[29] the essential facts of which are identical to **Example 7a**, Upjohn J held that C was under a duty to B to pay an annual contribution. B acquired a direct right against C as a result of C's conduct in exercising his right to use the roads and seaside path. C had chosen to exercise that right and, according to the deed entered into by B and A, the right was conditional on the payment of the annual contribution.[30] It was simply not possible for C to choose to enjoy the benefit of that right without also being subject to the correlative burden.

Upjohn J based his decision on the principle that C 'cannot take [a] benefit under a deed without subscribing to the obligations thereunder'.[31] However, we need to treat this statement very carefully. First, the 'benefit and burden' principle can apply even where no deed is used.[32] Second, there are many cases that *do* involve deeds, but where the principle does *not* apply.

EXAMPLE 7b

B has a Freehold. B divides up his land, selling a part to A and keeping the rest. There is a cottage on A's land that shares its roof with a house on B's land. As part of the sale, A promises B that A and future owners of his land will keep the roof of the cottage in good repair. A then transfers his Freehold to C. C refuses to repair the cottage roof.

As long as A keeps his Freehold, B is protected: he can simply assert his contractual right against A. However, does B have any right against C? As in *Halsall*, A's promise imposes a positive duty: it cannot give B a property right or a persistent right. In *Rhone v Stephens*,[33] the essential facts of which are identical to **Example 7b**, B instead claimed that he had a direct right against C, arising under the 'benefit and burden' principle. The deed of transfer, signed by A and B, had given A and B certain rights over each other's land: for example, A had acquired a right of support which meant that B's house had to continue to give physical support to A's cottage. B argued that C could not choose to enjoy the benefit of this right of support without also accepting the burden, set out in the same deed between A and B, of keeping the roof in good repair.

In *Rhone v Stephens*, the House of Lords rejected B's argument. Lord Templeman approved of the decision in *Halsall*, but pointed out that the 'benefit and burden' principle could *not* apply to **Example 7b**. The mere presence of a benefit to C (the right to support) in the same deed as the supposed burden (the duty to maintain the roof) was *not* enough to trigger the operation of the principle. Rather, the principle depends on C's conduct in *choosing* to exercise a right that is *conditional* on accepting a particular burden. In *Rhone*, there was nothing in the arrangement between A and B to indicate that an owner of A's land could exercise that right *only if* he also kept the roof in good repair. Further, it could not be said that C had made a choice to exercise the right to support: C's cottage benefited from the physical support of B's adjoining house whether C liked it or not.

---

[29] [1957] Ch 169.

[30] It was important, as Upjohn J noted at 182, that C's only right to use the roads and seaside path came from the deed, and was hence conditional on making the annual payment set out in that deed.

[31] *Ibid* at 182.

[32] For example, in *ER Ives v High* [1967] 2 QB 379, both Lord Denning MR and Danckwerts LJ held that the principle could apply where A and B, neighbouring landowners, made an oral agreement.

[33] [1994] 2 AC 310.

In *Halsall* there was also an objective link between the benefit and the burden: the burden was linked to the cost to B of providing the benefit to C. However, this does not seem to be a requirement of the principle. For example, let us say A and B, neighbouring landowners, strike a deal that, in return for allowing A to park a car on B's land, A will allow B to use a path across A's land. If A sells his land to C, and C later exercises the right to park on B's land, it would seem that B will acquire a direct right against C, allowing him to walk across C's land.[34] It should make no difference that there is no objective link between the burden (allowing B to walk across C's land) and the benefit (parking a car on B's land).

It seems, therefore, that the 'benefit and burden' principle is essentially a principle about *conditional rights*.[35] An arrangement between A and B may give A a right *provided that* A bears a particular burden. If C, who later acquires a right from A, chooses to exercise that right, then it seems B will be able to force C to comply with the burden: B will thus acquire a direct right against C. This principle does not require C to deal directly with B; but it does seem to require that C must at least be *aware* of the arrangement between A and B. For if C is unaware of the arrangement, it is impossible to say that, by choosing to exercise the right, C has in any sense accepted the burden attached to that right.

2.3.4 The wrong of procuring a breach by A of A's contractual duty to B

There is a concern that the wrong of procuring a breach of contract may *too easily* give B a direct right against C (see **D3:2.3.4**). It has been argued that there are particular problems where *land* is concerned: the wrong should *not* be applied as it has the potential to undermine the protection given to C by the **content question**, the **acquisition question** and the **defences question**.[36]

EXAMPLE 8

A has a Freehold. A makes a contractual promise to B to allow B to occupy A's land for six months. That promise does not give B a right to exclusive control of the land. Three months later, C plans to buy A's Freehold. C knows about A's contract with B.

A's promise to B does not give a property right or persistent right: B has only a contractual licence. The **content question** thus protects C against the risk of being bound by B's pre-existing right. Nonetheless, C faces a clear risk: (i) if he buys A's Freehold; and (ii) refuses to allow B to occupy the land for a further three months; then (iii) C may commit the wrong of procuring a breach of A's contract with B (compare **D3:Example 5**).

The fear is that B may be able to use the wrong of procuring a breach of contract as a back-door route to asserting a pre-existing *personal* right against C. This concern is particularly acute where land is concerned. In particular, the need to protect C has led to the

---

[34] For example, in *ER Ives v High* [1967] 2 QB 379, both Lord Denning MR and Danckwerts LJ held that the principle could apply where A and B, neighbouring landowners, orally agreed that A should have the right for the foundations of a building on A's land to encroach onto B's land, provided that B had the right to go across A's land to get from B's house to a road. However, it is difficult to see how C, a later owner of A's land, could be said to have *chosen* to exercise the right for the foundations to encroach onto B's land, and so it may well be that, for that reason only, the principle should *not* have applied in that case.

[35] This point is explored by Davis [1998] *CLJ* 522.

[36] See eg R Smith (1977) 41 *Conv* 318 at 329: 'where real property principles accord priority to a contract or conveyance over an earlier contract, it should not be open to the earlier contracting party to rely on tort'.

existence of a registration system. However, such a system does *not* protect C against the risk of being bound by a direct right (see **C2:2**). So, it seems that the protection given to C could be bypassed if B were able to use the wrong of procuring a breach of contract to acquire a direct right against C.

However, the courts *are* willing to apply the wrong even where land is concerned. This is demonstrated by *Esso Petroleum Co Ltd v Kingswood Motors Ltd*.[37] A had a Freehold and operated a petrol station on his land. B supplied petrol to A. A was under a contractual duty to B: (i) to notify B before selling his Freehold; and (ii) to ensure that any purchaser also entered into an agreement to use fuel supplied by B. A breached this duty by selling to C without taking those steps. It was held that, as C knew about B's contract with A, C had committed the wrong of procuring a breach of contract. This willingness to apply the wrong even where land is concerned seems correct. It seems that the wrong is based on the need for the rest of the world to respect B's contractual relationship with A.[38] There is no obvious reason why contractual rights relating to the use of land should attract less protection (see **D3:2.3.4(iii)**).

However, this does *not* mean that C will necessarily commit the wrong if, in **Example 8**, he goes ahead and buys A's Freehold and then seeks to remove B from the land. There is an important difference between **Example 8** and the situation in *Kingswood Motors*. In the latter case, A was under an explicit contractual duty *not to transfer his Freehold to C* unless certain conditions were met. A therefore breached his contractual duty to B *as soon as* he, A, sold the land to C. C, by participating in a sale that he knew to breach those conditions, was actively facilitating A's breach of contract. In **Example 8**, however, A has simply made a contractual promise to allow B to occupy A's land for six months. A has *not* made a contractual promise not to transfer his Freehold unless certain conditions are met. As a result, the sale to C, *by itself*, does *not* breach A's contractual duty to B: that duty is breached only at a later stage—when C asserts his right and prevents B from using the land. So, just as the facts in **D3:Example 5** can be distinguished from those in *BMTA v Salvadori*,[39] so can the facts in **Example 8** be distinguished from those in *Esso Petroleum Co Ltd v Kingswood Motors Ltd*.[40]

B can make other arguments in an attempt to show that, in **Example 8**, C has committed the wrong of procuring a breach of contract. However, in **D3:2.3.4**, we saw that those arguments should fail. It thus seems that the dangers of applying the wrong of procuring a breach of contract to the **basic situation**, even where land is involved, may be overstated.

2.3.5 Knowing interference with B's personal right against A?

In **D3:2.3.5** we noted the suggestion, made most famously by Knight Bruce LJ in *de Mattos v Gibson*,[41] that B can acquire a direct right against C whenever C knowingly interferes with a pre-existing *personal* right of B. That suggestion was, in fact, based on an earlier case

---

[37] [1974] QB 142.
[38] See eg Stevens, *Torts and Rights* (2007), 281.
[39] [1949] Ch 556.
[40] [1974] QB 142.
[41] (1858) 4 D&J 276 at 282. See too *per* Lord Shaw in *Lord Strathcona Steamship Co Ltd v Dominion Coal Co Ltd* [1926] AC 108 at 125.

involving land: *Tulk v Moxhay*.[42] However, the courts' general resistance to the suggestion, noted in **D3:2.3.5**, is also apparent in cases involving land.[43]

It is certainly true that, in *Tulk v Moxhay*, the Court of Appeal *did* allow B to acquire a direct right against C as a result of C's knowing interference with B's contractual right against A (see **G6:1.7**). However, later cases reinterpreted the decision in *Tulk*: it was seen as a case in which B was able to assert a pre-existing *persistent* right (a Restrictive Covenant) against C. This reinterpretation of *Tulk* allowed the courts to accept the result in that case, whilst also rejecting the idea that B acquires a direct right *whenever* C knowingly interferes with B's personal right against A. In particular, the new analysis protects C: B's right can only count as a Restrictive Covenant if it meets certain requirements. For example, if A is under a *positive* duty to B, *or* if A's duty does not benefit any land held by B, B's right cannot count as a Restrictive Covenant. In such cases: (i) B does not acquire a persistent right as a result of A's promise; and (ii) B cannot acquire a direct right against C *simply* because of C's knowing interference with B's personal right against A.

For example in *London County Council v Allen*,[44] A, when buying a Freehold from B, had made a promise to B not to make a particular use of that land. A then transferred that Freehold to C. C proceeded to use the land in the way A had promised not to. The Court of Appeal held that A's promise to B did not count as a Restrictive Covenant as it did not benefit any land held by B. And B could *not* acquire a direct right against C simply as a result of C's knowing interference with B's personal right against A.

2.3.6 The wrong of dishonestly assisting A to breach a fiduciary duty owed to B

B will acquire a direct right against C if C commits the wrong of 'dishonest assistance' (**D3:2.3.6**): the account given there applies in just the same way where land is concerned.

2.3.7 The wrong of conspiring with A to cause harm to B

C2:EXAMPLE 5

A has an unregistered Freehold. A makes a contractual promise to sell the land to B, his son. A then falls out with B and is determined not to transfer the land to B. A transfers his ownership of the land, to C, his wife. The price is only £500, even though the land is worth about £40,000.

A's contractual promise to B gives B a persistent right (see **E2:1.3.1(i)**). However, in *Midland Bank Trust Co Ltd v Green*,[45] on which **C2:Example 5** is based, the House of Lords confirmed that, as a result of B's failure to register that right as a land charge, C had a defence to it.[46] However, registration systems do *not* aim to protect C against the risk of being bound by a direct right. And, in **C2:Example 5**, B can acquire a direct right against C. Although A and C have each acted in a way that is otherwise lawful, as A and C have acted with the prime motive of causing harm to B, each has committed the wrong of 'lawful act'

---

[42] (1848) 2 Ph 774.

[43] See eg *London County Council v Allen* [1914] 3 KB 642.

[44] [1914] 3 KB 642.

[45] [1981] AC 513.

[46] See now Land Charges Act 1972, ss 2 and 4.

conspiracy against B: this was confirmed by the Court of Appeal in *Midland Bank Trust Co Ltd v Green (No 3)*.[47]

2.3.8 Other means of acquiring a direct right?

In **D3:2.8** and **D3:2.9**, we saw that, where C acquires a right from A, B *cannot* acquire a direct right against C by relying on either: (i) C's unjust enrichment at B's expense; or (ii) C's 'knowing receipt' of a right held by A on Trust for B. The latter point, considered in detail in **E2:4.1.2** is worth repeating as it has sometimes been incorrectly assumed, where land is involved, that B can bring a claim based on C's 'knowing receipt' *even if* C has a defence to B's pre-existing right under a Trust.[48]

SUMMARY of E3:2

In **D3:2**, we examined the general principles that tell us when B can acquire a direct right against C. Those general principles also apply in the land law system. At certain points, however, the special features of land have an impact. For example, the permanence and fixed location of land have led to an *additional* means by which B2 can acquire a direct right against A or C. If (i) A or C makes a binding promise to B; then (ii) if certain requirements are met, the benefit of that promise can become *annexed* to all or part of B's Freehold or Lease; so that (iii) if B2 acquires a Freehold or Lease of all or part of that land; then (iv) B2 also acquires a right against A or C. Annexation provides a particularly useful means for B2 to acquire the benefit of B's right.

In other cases, the special features of land have *increased the relevance* of a general means by which B can acquire a direct right. For example, the permanence and fixed location of land increase the chances that: (i) *if* B has a direct right against A or C, then (ii) B may exercise his power to transfer (to 'assign') that right to B2. Those special features of land also make it more likely that A and B, neighbours, may make an arrangement under which A acquires a conditional right. B may then be able to rely on that arrangement to acquire a direct right against C under the 'benefit and burden' principle. The uniqueness of each piece of land also means that if B has a right to make some use of A's land, that right will generally be specifically protected by a court. So A, if he wishes to prevent B enjoying a right to use A's land, may have to concoct a plan to transfer his land to C. This means we need to be aware of the possibility of B acquiring a direct right against C by showing that A and C have committed the wrong of conspiracy.

It is important to note that, particularly when considering the position of neighbours, all these means of acquiring a direct right can be used *both*: (i) to impose a negative duty on A or C; *and* (ii) to impose a positive duty on A or C. It is impossible for A's positive duty to give B (or B2) a property right or a persistent right; but that does *not* prevent B (or B2) acquiring a direct right against C as a result of C's conduct. Of course, as it imposes a positive duty, that direct right will only be a personal right and so will not be capable of binding C2.

---

[47] [1982] 1 Ch 529. The court rejected the argument that it is impossible for a husband and wife to conspire together.
[48] See eg Law Com No 254 at 3.48; Law Com No 271 at 4.11.

Conversely, the special features of land may sometimes make it *more difficult* for B to acquire a direct right against C. For example, they may justify the extra formality rules that apply where land is involved. If B wishes to rely on the Contract (Rights of Third Parties) Act 1999, B needs to show that C has made a contractual promise to A: in some cases, this can only happen if C's promise is in the form required by section 2 of the Law of Property (Miscellaneous Provisions) Act 1989. Similarly, if A transfers a property right in land to C, and C orally promises to hold that right on Trust for B, section 53(1)(b) of the Law of Property Act 1925 will prevent B from showing that either A or C has exercised a power to set up a Trust in B's favour. In such a case, B will therefore need to turn to the 'receipt after a promise' principle to show that C is under a duty to hold the right on Trust for B.

The table below summarises the conclusions of this section and includes the special points that arise where land is concerned. It is assumed throughout that there have been no direct dealings between B and C.

	B has no pre-existing right	B has a personal right against A
1999 Act		Yes—but note that, to show C's promise to A imposes a contractual duty on C, B may need to show that the formality rule set out by section 2 of the Law of Property (Miscellaneous Provisions) Act 1989 has been satisfied
Receipt after a promise		Yes—may be particularly important where C makes an *oral* promise to hold a property right in land/a persistent right relating to land on Trust for B (as section 53(1)(b) of the Law of Property Act 1925 will prevent B proving that A or C exercised a power to set up a Trust)
Benefit and burden	Yes (in theory)	Yes—may be particularly relevant where A and B are neighbours
Procuring a Breach of Contract	No	Yes—but only if A has a contractual duty to B
Dishonest Assistance	No	Yes—but only if A has a fiduciary duty to B
Lawful Act Conspiracy	Yes (in theory)	Yes—B's right is likely to be specifically protected if A tries to interfere with it, and so A may be tempted to conspire with C to defeat B's right

3 THE REMEDIES QUESTION

In **D3:4** we considered the general principles governing the remedy a court may give to protect B's direct right against C. Here we will consider how things may be different where land is concerned. If a court does not specifically protect B's right, but instead orders C to pay money to B, the principles set out in **D3:4.3** apply: the fact that land is involved makes no difference. However, things can be different when considering whether B's right will be given specific protection.[49]

If B has a right to make a particular use of land, the starting point is that B's right deserves specific protection: due to the uniqueness of each piece of land, money will be inadequate to protect B's right (see **A:3.1.2**). So, in **Examples 2, 4 and 6**, B acquires a right against C as a result of C's promise to allow B to occupy land. In general, that right will be specifically protected:[50] (i) if C tries to remove B from the land, a court will order an injunction to prevent C from doing so; and (ii) if C tries to prevent B going into occupation, a court will order C specifically to perform his promise to allow B to occupy.[51]

In *Esso Petroleum Co Ltd v Kingswood Motors Ltd*,[52] C committed the wrong of procuring A to breach his contractual duty to B not to sell his petrol station without first meeting certain conditions. The court specifically protected B's right by ordering C to transfer the petrol station back to A. It seems that this dramatic form of protection for B's right should also be available in a case such as **C2:Example 5** where A and C commit the wrong of conspiracy. If the chief purpose of the transfer of A's Freehold to C is to harm B, it seems that the best way to protect B is to order C to transfer that right back to A.[53]

SUMMARY of E3

Direct rights form a vital part of the property law system. They enable that system to respond to situations in which C's conduct justifies giving B a right against C. They can therefore give B protection against *a limited class of third parties*. In the land law system, direct rights may be particularly important. First, as the land registration system makes it increasingly difficult for B to assert a pre-existing property right or persistent right against C, B may be forced to claim he has acquired a direct right against C. Second, direct rights can be very prominent when considering the rights of neighbours. The concept of annexation, applying only in the land law system, also gives B2 a means of acquiring a direct right held by B, a former owner of B2's land.

Nonetheless, in practice, it will only be in rare cases that B can convince the court that he has acquired a direct right against C. The need to promote the ease of transactions in land means that the courts will not be quick to find that C's conduct justifies the recognition of direct right. Once again, a balance must be struck between: (i) protecting prior users of land; and (ii) protecting those who later acquire a right to use that land. Thus, the **basic tension** that runs throughout the land law system also shapes the rules governing direct rights.

---

[49] As in **D3:4**, we will concentrate on cases where B's direct right is a personal right against C: if B's direct right is a property right, the remedies question will be governed by the principles set out in **E1:4**; if it is a persistent right, that question will be governed by the principles set out in **E2:4**.

[50] The remedies available where C breaches or threatens to breach a contractual right also apply where, as in **Example 4**, C breaches or threatens to breach a duty to B arising under the Act: see 1999 Act, s 1(5).

[51] See further **E6:3.2**. Of course, B's right will not always be specifically protected. For example, if a promise (made by A or C) involves some degree of co-operation between the promising party and B, and such co-operation is no longer possible, B will have to settle for receiving money: see eg *Thompson v Park* [1944] KB 408 esp *per* Goddard LJ at 409: 'the court cannot specifically enforce an agreement for two people to live peaceably under the same roof'.

[52] [1974] QB 142.

[53] It seems that, in *Midland Bank Trust Co Ltd v Green (No 3)* [1982] 1 Ch 529, B (or B's estate as B had died) was content to receive money from C and so did not ask for an order that C transfer her Freehold back to A.

CHAPTER E4
PROPRIETARY ESTOPPEL

E4

PROPRIETARY ESTOPPEL

1 THE NATURE OF PROPRIETARY ESTOPPEL

Proprietary estoppel is a doctrine identifying a reason for which A can come under a duty to B. In English law, it is generally assumed to apply *only* where land is concerned.[1] The doctrine establishes that A comes under a duty to B if:

- A makes a commitment to B to use his land in a certain way; *and*
- B reasonably relies on that commitment; *and*
- B will suffer a detriment as a result of A's failure to honour that commitment.

In this formulation, the word 'commitment' is synonymous with 'promise'. If B's proprietary estoppel claim succeeds, A will be under a duty to B. For example, in *Jennings v Rice*,[2] A assured B that she would leave him her house and its contents (worth over £400,000 in total) when she died. B relied on that commitment by looking after A without payment. B suffered a detriment when A died without leaving her Freehold and furniture to B. As a result, B acquired a personal right against A: A was under a duty to pay B £200,000.[3]

In some cases, however, B can use proprietary estoppel to impose a duty on A in relation to a specific right. For example, A may be under a duty to transfer a Freehold to B; or to grant B a property right in A's land. In such a case, B acquires a persistent right. For example, in *Pascoe v Turner* (**C3:Example 3**),[4] the Court of Appeal held that, due to the doctrine of proprietary estoppel, A was under a duty to transfer his Freehold to B. As a result, B had an immediate persistent right: a right under a Trust (see **E2:1.4.2(ii)**). In *Crabb v Arun District Council*,[5] A and B had entered into negotiations about A granting B a right of way (an Easement) over A's land. An agreement in principle had been reached and A, by its conduct, led B to believe that the Easement would be granted. B relied on that belief by selling off part of his own land without reserving a right of access to his remaining land: B thought that he would be able to get to his remaining land by using the right of way he expected to acquire over A's land. A then refused to grant B the Easement. As a result, B suffered a detriment: he now had no means to get to his land. Proprietary estoppel therefore operated to impose a duty on A to give B his expected Easement. B thus acquired an immediate persistent right: an Equitable Easement (see **E2:1.3.1(i)**).

---

[1] See eg Peel, *Treitel's Law of Contract* (12th edn, 2007), 3–127.
[2] [2003] 1 P & CR 100.
[3] A personal right against A can be asserted, on A's death, against A's executors who then have to meet the claim from A's assets.
[4] [1979] 1 WLR 431.
[5] [1976] Ch 179.

2 THE PURPOSE OF PROPRIETARY ESTOPPEL

There is no consensus as to the purpose of proprietary estoppel. Judges have failed to identify a clear role for the doctrine, and academics disagree as to its aims.[6] Despite this, the view taken in this book is that proprietary estoppel has a distinct and important goal: to protect B from suffering a detriment as a result of his reasonable reliance on A's commitment.[7] Crucially, this purpose seems to fit with both: (i) the *requirements* of proprietary estoppel (see **section 3** below); and (ii) with the *extent of a right* arising through proprietary estoppel (see **section 4** below).

Proprietary estoppel allows B to acquire a right even if A has not exercised a power to give B a right; even if A has made no contractual promise to B; and even if A has not been unjustly enriched at B's expense. For example, in *Crabb v Arun DC*, it was clear that A had *not* exercised its power to give B an Easement. Nor had A made a contractual promise to give B such a right:[8] (i) the parties had not reached a final agreement; (ii) B had not provided any consideration in return for A's commitment; and (iii) the relevant formality rule had not been satisfied.[9] And A was not unjustly enriched by B's action in selling off part of his land without reserving a right of way. Nonetheless, proprietary estoppel operated to protect B. On this analysis, in a case such as *Crabb v Arun DC*, B acquires his right because of Reason 6 (see **B:4.3**): the 'other reason' in question being the need to protect B from suffering a detriment as a result of his reasonable reliance on A's commitment.

Given the debate about its purpose, we do need to consider some alternative views as to the purpose of proprietary estoppel. It will be seen that these views have a common flaw: they confuse one of the many possible *effects* of the doctrine with its wider *purpose*.

2.1 Avoiding formality rules

On one view, proprietary estoppel is simply a response to the strict formality rules of the land law system: it gives B a means to acquire a persistent right even though A's commitment has not been made in writing.[10] It is certainly true that, in some cases, the doctrine does have that *effect*.

EXAMPLE 1

A and B live in a house together. A has a Freehold and owns almost all the contents of the house (furniture, etc). The relationship between A and B breaks down. A moves out and tells B that the house and everything in it are hers. Over two years, B relies on A's commitment by spending money on decorating and improving the house.

---

[6] Compare eg Moriarty (1984) 100 *LQR* 376 (proprietary estoppel as a mechanism for the informal creation of property rights in land); Birks (1996) 26 *University of Western Australia Law Review* 1 at 60 (proprietary estoppel as a means to enforce A's commitment); Goff and Jones, *The Law of Restitution* (7th edn, 2006), 230–35 (proprietary estoppel as a means to reverse an unjust enrichment of A); Spence, *Protecting Reliance: The Emerging Doctrine of Equitable Estoppel* (1999) (proprietary estoppel as a means to respond to a wrong committed by A).

[7] For more detail, see Bright & McFarlane [2005] *CLJ* 449.

[8] See Millett (1976) 92 *LQR* 342.

[9] That formality rule, since replaced by s 2 of the Law of Property (Miscellaneous Provisions) Act 1989, was s 40 of the Law of Property Act 1925.

[10] See Moriarty (1984) 100 *LQR* 376. Note too Cartwright, ch 3 in *Rationalizing Property, Equity and Trusts: Essays in Honour of Edward Burn* (ed Getzler, 2003), 46, 49.

In *Pascoe v Turner*,[11] the essential facts of which are identical to **Example 1**, the Court of Appeal held that A was under a duty to transfer his Freehold to B. A's Ownership of the contents of the house had already been transferred to B as A had exercised his power to transfer his Ownership of the contents to B: there was no need for A to use a deed as B already had physical control of the contents of the house (see **D1:Example 18a**).[12] However, A's oral commitment could not give B the Freehold: A's intention had not been expressed in a deed and the Freehold had not been substantively registered in B's name (see **E1:2.3**). Hence, as the relevant formality rules had not been satisfied, A kept his Freehold. The doctrine of proprietary estoppel then operated, according to the Court of Appeal, to impose a duty on A to transfer that Freehold to B (see too **C3:Example 3**).

So, one *effect* of the decision in *Pascoe* is to protect B from a failure to comply with a formality rule regulating the transfer of A's Freehold. However, it should not be assumed that this is the *purpose* of proprietary estoppel. For example, in *Crabb v Arun DC*,[13] formality rules were not the only thing preventing B from claiming that he had acquired an Easement, or that A had made a contractual promise to give B such a right. First, A had not attempted to exercise his power to give B an Easement. Second, the basic elements of a contract were missing: there was no certain, finalised agreement between A and B; nor had B provided any consideration in return for a promise from A. So, even if there were *no* relevant formality rules, it would *still* have been impossible (in the absence of proprietary estoppel) for B to acquire a right.[14] So, whilst proprietary estoppel can have the *effect* of protecting B from a failure to comply with a formality rule, that is not its *purpose*.

2.2   Enforcing commitments

On another view, proprietary estoppel aims to keep A to the commitments he makes about the use of his land.[15] It is certainly true that, in some cases, the doctrine does have the *effect* of enforcing such a commitment. So in both *Pascoe v Turner* and *Crabb v Arun DC*, A was under a duty to keep his commitment to B.

However, it should not be assumed that the *purpose* of proprietary estoppel is to enforce A's commitment. In *Jennings v Rice*, for example, A's commitment was to give B her Freehold and the contents of her house (together worth £435,000);[16] but the Court of Appeal upheld the judge's order that A was under a duty to pay B £200,000. The Court of Appeal made clear that a successful proprietary estoppel claim will *not* automatically lead to A having to honour his commitment (see further **section 4** below).[17]

---

[11] [1979] 1 WLR 431.

[12] As noted by Cumming-Bruce LJ: [1979] 1 WLR 431 at 435.

[13] [1976] Ch 179.

[14] For more on why B had no contractual claim in *Crabb*, see the note by Millett (counsel for B in that case): (1976) 92 *LQR* 342.

[15] See eg Birks (1996) 26 *University of Western Australia Law Review* 1 at 60; Cooke (1997) 17 *LS* 258.

[16] B claimed that A had made a commitment to leave *all* her assets to B, but this was rejected: see Aldous LJ [2003] 1 P & CR 100 at [17].

[17] See too *Ottey v Grundy* [2003] EWCA Civ 1176 and *per* Dyson LJ in *Cobbe v Yeomans Row Management Ltd* [2006] 1 WLR 2964 at [125].

EXAMPLE 2

A promises B that she will leave her Freehold to B. B relies on this by looking after A but, a month later, A dies.[18]

In such a case, it would make no sense for A's estate to be under a duty to give B the Freehold. A's promise is not binding on A as it was not made in a deed or as part of a contract. As a result, B has no entitlement to have his expectation protected. As demonstrated by *Jennings v Rice*, the role of proprietary estoppel is to protect B from suffering a detriment through his reliance on A's commitment. In *some* cases, B can only be properly protected if A is under a duty to keep to his commitment. For example, in *Crabb v Arun DC*, B's reliance consisted in failing to ensure a right of access to his land. When A refused to honour his commitment and denied B an Easement, B suffered a very heavy detriment: he was unable properly to use his land. The only way to prevent B continuing to suffer such a detriment was to force A to give B the expected Easement. However, it seems that proprietary estoppel need only have the *effect* of enforcing A's commitment where such a result is necessary to achieve the underlying *purpose* of the doctrine: to prevent B suffering a detriment as a result of his reliance on A's commitment.

2.3 Preventing unconscionable conduct

On a further, surprisingly popular view, proprietary estoppel aims to prevent A from acting unconscionably.[19] For example, it could be said that in *Crabb v Arun DC*, given A's conduct in encouraging B to believe that an Easement would be granted, the only decent or reasonable thing for A to do was to give B that Easement.

However, this view is either trite or dangerously misleading. It is trite in the sense that *any* means of acquiring rights is, to some extent, designed to prevent or respond to unconscionable conduct by A. So, contract law can be said to prevent A acting unconscionably by failing to honour a bargain with B; the law of unjust enrichment can be said to prevent A acting unconscionably by retaining a benefit he has acquired at B's expense when there is no legal basis for A to do so; and so on.

The point is that each particular means of acquiring a right deals with a particular form of conduct by A and has specific, detailed requirements that look beyond the simple label of unconscionable conduct. So, if we say that A's action is unconscionable, that is not a *test* for seeing if A is under a duty to B; it is rather a *conclusion* that applies because, for some more specific reason, A has come under a duty to B (see **C1:3.1**). So, if B wants to claim he has a contractual right against A, B cannot go to court and simply claim that A has acted unconscionably: B has to show that he and A reached a certain agreement; that the agreement was intended to be legally binding; that B provided consideration; and so on. Similarly, if B wants to acquire a right through proprietary estoppel, he must satisfy particular requirements, as discussed above. To suggest that B can go to court and acquire a right by simply suggesting that A has acted unconscionably would be dangerously misleading.

---

[18] A similar case is posited by Aldous LJ in *Jennings v Rice* [2003] 1 P & CR 100 at [37].

[19] See eg Halliwell (1994) 14 *LS* 15; *Snell's Equity* (ed McGhee, 31st edn, 2005), 10–15. For judicial references to unconscionability, see eg *per* Oliver J in *Taylor Fashions Ltd v Liverpool Victoria Trustees Ltd* [1982] QB 133 at 151; *per* Robert Walker LJ in *Gillett v Holt* [2001] Ch 210 at 225.

SUMMARY of E4:2

Proprietary estoppel is a means by which B can acquire a right against A. Where the doctrine applies, B will always acquire a personal right against A; in some cases, A's duty to B will relate to a specific right and so B will also acquire a persistent right. The doctrine aims to prevent B suffering detriment as a result of his reliance on A's commitment, made to B, to use A's land in a certain way.

3 THE REQUIREMENTS OF PROPRIETARY ESTOPPEL

Proprietary estoppel has three basic elements: (i) a commitment from A; (ii) reasonable reliance on that commitment by B; and (iii) actual or potential detriment to B if A fails to honour his commitment.

3.1 A's commitment to B

3.1.1 Has A made a commitment to B?

As can be seen in many areas of the law, in particular contract law, the test for commitment is an objective one: is it reasonable for B to believe that A has committed himself to acting in a particular way? Of course, it is not enough for B to *hope* that A will act in a particular way, or even to think that A *ought* to do so.[20]

EXAMPLE 3

A has a Freehold. B regularly visits and cares for A, an elderly neighbour who has no relatives. B assumes that, because of his kindness, A will or even ought to leave B his Freehold when A dies.

In such a case, the doctrine of proprietary estoppel does not impose a duty on A: A has not acted in such a way as to make it reasonable for B to believe that A is committed to leaving him the Freehold.

It is worth noting that A can make a commitment by leading B to believe that B *already has* a right in relation to A's land. The point is that, if B has such a right, A will be under a duty to B to act in a particular way in the future. For example, in *Pascoe v Turner*, A assured B that the house and everything in it were hers. By doing so, A made a commitment not only to allow B to remain in the house but also to transfer the Freehold to B.

EXAMPLE 4

A has a Freehold. B has a Lease of A's land. A assures B that B has a right to renew the Lease. A genuinely believes B has such a right; but A is mistaken.

In such a case, A has led B reasonably to believe that A is committed to allowing B to renew a Lease. A has thus made a commitment to B and so, as confirmed by the influential decision of Oliver J in *Taylor Fashions Ltd v Liverpool Victoria Trustees*,[21] the doctrine of

---

[20] See eg *per* Lord Templeman in *Attorney General for Hong Kong v Humphreys Estate Ltd* [1987] AC 114 at 127–8.
[21] [1982] QB 133.

proprietary estoppel may apply. It does not matter that A mistakenly believed he was already under a duty to allow B to renew the Lease.[22] Nor does it matter that A's mistake was a honest one: the doctrine of proprietary estoppel does *not* require B to show that A has behaved badly, or knowingly led B on.[23]

The obvious way for A to make a commitment is by *expressly* committing himself to act in a certain way. For example, as in *Jennings v Rice*, A can make an explicit promise to B that he will leave his house to B.[24] An express promise can thus count as a commitment. However, A can also make a commitment without making an express promise: such a commitment can instead be implied from A's conduct.

EXAMPLE 5

A and B have neighbouring Freeholds. A and B enter negotiations about A possibly giving B an Easement over A's land. The negotiations have not led to a final contract, but A and B reach an agreement in principle as to the route B would take over A's land. A then builds a fence, separating its land from B's land. A leaves a gap in the fence to allow B access to A's land; A later builds a gate in that gap. In reliance on his expectation that A will grant B the planned Easement, B sells off part of his land without reserving a right of way over that land to his retained land.

Example 5 is identical to the essential facts of *Crabb v Arun DC*. As confirmed by the Court of Appeal, the doctrine of proprietary estoppel applies: A has made a commitment to B even without making an express promise. A has both: (i) reached an agreement in principle with B; and (ii) led B to think that the agreement in principle would be honoured. As a result, A has led B reasonably to believe that A has committed itself to giving B an Easement.[25]

Indeed, in some cases, the fact that A has *failed to act* can, coupled with other conduct of A, lead B reasonably to believe that A has committed himself to act in a particular way.

EXAMPLE 6

A has a Freehold. A and B come to a general agreement that, if B succeeds in obtaining planning permission for A's land, A will sell that land to B at a particular price. Both parties know that this general agreement is not contractually binding. Nonetheless, B continues to prepare the planning application. A allows B to do this, even after A decides that she is not going to honour the agreement.

In such a case, it may be possible to say that A has made a commitment to B. Of course, everything depends on the specific facts of the case but, as confirmed by the decision of the Court of Appeal in *Cobbe v Yeoman's Row Management Ltd*,[26] on which **Example 6** is based,

---

[22] Of course, things would be different if A assures B that A will renew the Lease *if* B has a right to renew: A's commitment would then be conditional on the fact of B having such a right; so if B has no such right, A can refuse to renew the Lease without breaching his commitment.

[23] This provides a good example of why it is misleading to assume that proprietary estoppel is based on the need to respond to 'unconscionable' conduct of A (see **3.4** below).

[24] See too *Lloyd v Dugdale* [2002] 2 P & CR 13: A made an express commitment to grant B a Lease of business premises.

[25] See McFarlane [2005] *Conv* 501.

[26] [2006] 1 WLR 2964. That decision is currently on appeal to the House of Lords. It would not be a great surprise

it may be possible to say that: (i) if A and B make an agreement in principle; and (ii) B acts in a particular way in the expectation that A will honour that agreement; and (iii) A knows that B is acting in that way; then (iii) A's failure to disabuse B, if known to B, may mean that it is reasonable for B to believe that A is committed to honouring the agreement in principle.

EXAMPLE 7

A has a Freehold of land that is currently vacant. B goes onto the land and begins to build a house. A knows that B is building the house but fails to intervene.

This case is clearly different from **Example 6**: there has been no prior dealing between A and B and there is certainly no agreement in principle between the parties. If B is not aware that A: (i) knows about B's work; *and* (ii) is choosing not to intervene, it is very difficult to see how B can have a proprietary estoppel claim.[27] The point is that, in such a case, B cannot reasonably believe that A has committed himself to act in a particular way. After all, B is not even aware of A. In such a case, the best B can hope for, it seems, is to bring a claim against A based not on proprietary estoppel but, instead, on unjust enrichment.[28]

Finally, it is always possible for A to make clear that he is *not* committing himself to act in a particular way. For example, let us say A and B enter into negotiations for the grant by A of a Lease to B. A can make it clear that, unless and until he signs a binding contract, he is not committing himself to granting the Lease. In such a case, any general agreement A and B may reach is said to be 'subject to contract'. This makes clear that, in the absence of a contract, B cannot reasonably believe that A has committed himself to act in a particular way.[29]

3.1.2 Has A made the right sort of commitment to B?

The traditional view is that, for proprietary estoppel to apply, A must have made a commitment to use his *land* in a particular way.[30] The commitment can be to give B a property right in land, or a persistent right relating to land. Or it may simply be that A will use his land in some other way for B's benefit, for example by giving B permission to make some use of A's land.[31]

Where A has made a commitment relating to the use of land, it seems that proprietary estoppel can also be used to give B a right in relation to *other* things. So, if A promises B that he will leave B everything, including his Freehold and other rights, it is possible for

---

if the House of Lords found that, on the specific facts of the case, A had *not* made a commitment to honour her agreement in principle with B. For discussion of the House of Lords' decision, see the companion website.

[27] However, there are some important judicial statements to the effect that, in such a case, B *will* have a proprietary estoppel claim: see eg *per* Lord Cranworth LC in *Ramsden v Dyson* (1866) LR 1 HL 129 at 140–41. But, if B is not aware of A's failure to intervene, it is very difficult to say that B has *relied* on A.

[28] See **E1:4.4** and McFarlane (2006) 1 *Journal of Equity* 156, discussing *Blue Haven Enterprises Ltd v Tully* [2006] UKPC 17. Such a claim should be possible where B has conferred a benefit on A as a result of a mistaken belief about B's *current* rights; but if B has instead acted under a mistaken belief as to how A would act in the future, he needs to show that A knew of and shared his expectation: see *Dextra Bank and Trust Co Ltd v Bank of Jamaica* [2002] 1 All ER (Comm) 193 at 202–3 and **D4:4.3.5**.

[29] See eg *Attorney General for Hong Kong v Humphreys Estate Ltd* [1987] AC 114.

[30] See eg Peel, *Treitel's Law of Contract* (12th edn, 2007), 3–127.

[31] See eg *Pennine Raceways v Kirklees MBC* [1983] QB 382; *Parker v Parker* [2003] EWHC (Ch) 846.

proprietary estoppel to impose a duty on A in relation to *all* of A's rights, not just his Free-hold.[32] In addition, there have been some *obiter* suggestions that proprietary estoppel can apply even where A's commitment relates solely to a thing other than land,[33] or to a personal right.[34] Furthermore, there is a High Court decision in which proprietary estoppel was applied where A had made a commitment to use a personal right against Z (a life assurance policy and its proceeds) for B's benefit.[35]

So, it may be that English law is moving slowly towards the position taken in some other jurisdictions:[36] A can come under a duty to B *whenever* B would suffer a detriment as a result of his reasonable reliance on a commitment made by A, even if A's commitment does not relate to land. Certainly, the traditional restriction is very hard to justify.

EXAMPLE 8

A and B have neighbouring Freeholds. They reach an agreement in principle that A will give B an Easement and that B will pay A £3,000 in return. A needs to knock down a building on his land that blocks B's planned right of way. B assures A that he will go ahead with the deal and so A knocks down the building. B then decides to pull out of the deal.

We have seen that, in *Crabb v Arun DC*, B acquired a right against A as a result of his reliance on A's commitment to grant him an Easement. Here the question is whether A can acquire a right against B. A has reasonably relied on B's commitment and has suffered a detriment in doing so. And yet, in English law at least,[37] A has no right against B: there is no contract between the parties; and proprietary estoppel does not apply as B's commitment does not relate to B's land, or, indeed, to *any* specific right held by B.

Of course, we have seen throughout this book that special rules often apply to land. However, the special features of land do *not* seem to explain why the law should impose a duty on A to prevent B suffering a detriment only where B relies on a commitment relating to land. It is true that, in some cases, the special features of land, in particular its financial

---

[32] See eg *re Basham* [1986] 1 WLR 1498.

[33] See eg *per* Megaw LJ in *Western Fish Products v Penrith DC* [1981] 2 All ER 204 at 218.

[34] See *per* Lord Hoffmann in *Yeda Research & Development Co Ltd v Rhone-Poulenc Rorer International Holdings Inc* [2008] 1 All ER 425 at [22]: 'there is no reason why the equitable rules of proprietary estoppel should not apply to a patent in the same way as to other property'. On the view taken in this book, a patent is a form of personal right (see **D1:1.1.1**) but it can be described as 'property' if that term is used in a general sense to include any right. See too *per* Mummery LJ in *Brooker v Fisher* [2008] EWCA Civ 287 at [34]: proprietary estoppel is an 'equitable defence' available in a copyright claim.

[35] *Strover v Strover* [2005] EWHC 860. It may also be that the otherwise puzzling decision of the Court of Appeal in *Brewer Street Investments Ltd v Barclays Woollen Co Ltd* [1954] 1 QB 258 can best be explained as an example of proprietary estoppel being applied to a promise by A (a prospective tenant) to take a Lease from B: see eg Beatson, *The Use and Abuse of Unjust Enrichment* (1991), 34–5.

[36] See eg *Waltons Stores (Interstate Ltd) v Maher* (1988) 164 CLR 387 (High Court of Australia); s 90 of the Restatement of Contracts (Second) (setting out the principle applying in many of the jurisdictions within the United States). For further consideration of those jurisdictions see D Nolan (2000) *KCLJ* 202; McFarlane, Hauser Global Law Program Working Paper Series 2006: http://www.nyulawglobal.org/workingpapers/glwp_1206.htm. The Australian rule, unlike that in the United States, *may* be limited to situations where A makes a promise to give B a right—it would hence exclude the case where A simply promises to perform a service for B, such as mowing B's lawn: see eg *per* Brennan J in *Walton Stores (Interstate Ltd) v Maher* (1988) 164 CLR 387 at 428; Roberston [2000] *MULR* 7.

[37] B could acquire a right against A under Australian law: see the very similar case of *Waltons Stores (Interstate Ltd) v Maher* (1988) 164 CLR 387; and in the vast majority of jurisdictions in the United States: see eg s 90 of the Restatement of Contracts (Second).

value and social importance, do mean that B's reliance will be of a particularly significant character: it may consist, for example, of building a house or setting up a home on A's land. Yet this is not true in all proprietary estoppel cases;[38] and, as **Example 8** shows, a party can also rely in substantial ways on a commitment that does not relate to another party's land.

It is true that the proprietary estoppel is bound to be more prominent where land is concerned: the special formality rules applying to land increase the chances that B will have to turn to proprietary estoppel for protection. Nonetheless, proprietary estoppel does much more than simply protect B from a failure to comply with a formality rule (see **2.1** above). Its purpose is wider: to prevent B suffering a detriment through his reasonable reliance on A's commitment. And it is very hard to explain why that aim does not also apply where B relies on a commitment unrelated to land.

There seem to be three main reasons why English law has not yet fully embraced a wider version of proprietary estoppel. First, neither the Court of Appeal[39] nor the House of Lords has been presented with a strong case exposing the unprincipled basis of the current limit.[40] Second, there is a fear that extending the doctrine could undermine contract law, by allowing B to acquire a right against A as a result of A's non-contractual commitment.[41] On the view taken here, that fear can be easily addressed—proprietary estoppel, unlike contract, does not always aim to enforce commitments: it does not compete with, but rather complements, contract law. However, as noted above, there is no consensus about the purpose of proprietary estoppel; so the fear is difficult to allay. Finally, there is a fear that extending the doctrine could undermine the certainty of commercial transactions, by allowing B to acquire a right based on ill-defined notions of 'unconscionability'. On the view taken here, that fear can be easily addressed—proprietary estoppel, like contract or unjust enrichment, is *not* based on a general notion of justice or unconscionability: it has its own specific and detailed requirements.

3.2   B's reasonable reliance

3.2.1 B must rely on A's commitment

B must reasonably rely on his belief that A will act in a particular way. For example, let us say that A makes an explicit promise that, when he dies, his land will go to B. If this promise has no effect on B, who simply carries on as normal, B can have no proprietary estoppel claim.

In theory, proving reliance can be tricky if A and B are family members or lovers. For example, consider the situation where A promises B, his grandson, that he will leave B his Freehold when he dies. B claims to have relied on this by looking after A. In theory, to prove

---

[38] See eg *Yaxley v Gotts* [2000] Ch 162: B's reliance consisted in doing building work for A.

[39] As noted above, it may well be that, in *Brewer Street Investments Ltd v Barclays Woollen Co Ltd* [1954] 1 QB 258, the Court of Appeal, without realising it, extended the scope of proprietary estoppel. The facts of that case revealed the arbitrariness of the orthodox view of the doctrine. B, a landowner, had made changes to his land in reliance on A's promise that A would take a Lease of B's land. The arbitrariness of limiting proprietary estoppel was clear—on the orthodox view, A could have a claim against B if A relied on B's commitment to grant a Lease; but B could not claim against A if he relied on A's commitment to take a Lease.

[40] An attempt was made to persuade the Court of Appeal to expand the doctrine in *Baird Textile Holdings Ltd v Marks & Spencer plc* [2001] EWCA Civ 274, [2002] 1 All ER (Comm) 737. However, on the facts, B's case was very weak: A had made no commitment to act in a particular way in the future.

[41] See eg *per* Denning LJ in *Combe v Combe* [1951] 2 KB 215 at 220.

reliance, B needs to show: (i) that A's promise was *a* reason why B looked after A; *and* (ii) that, if the promise had not been made, B would *not* have acted in that way. Therefore, B does not need to show that A's promise was the *only* thing leading him to care for A; but he does need to show that his natural affection for A, or sense of family duty would not, by itself, have given him sufficient motivation to look after A.[42] This places B in a slightly awkward position: it would seem that his chances of acquiring a right are increased by showing he is not a naturally caring person.

In practice, the approach of the courts reduces this problem. The general rule, applying not just to proprietary estoppel but also in other areas of the law, is that: (i) if A makes a statement that is likely, objectively speaking, to cause B to act in a particular way; and (ii) B has acted in that way; then (iii) it will be presumed that B did act in reliance on A's statement.[43] Objectively, a promise by A to leave B land does provide a reason why B might look after A without payment: so if B acts in that way, A will then face the very difficult job of showing that B would have cared for A *even if* A had not made the promise. In addition, the courts seem to have developed a special rule, applying only to proprietary estoppel, which makes things even easier for B.

That special rule was adopted in *Wayling v Jones*.[44] A owned a hotel and promised to leave it to B on his death. B claimed to have relied on that promise by working for A in return for very low pay. A died without honouring his commitment to leave the hotel to B. A's estate argued that, even if no promise had been made, B would still have acted as he did: A and B were lovers and their relationship, by itself, would have given B sufficient motivation to work for A for very low pay. The Court of Appeal rejected this argument by adopting a highly unusual test: it was said that B's proprietary estoppel claim would fail only if B would have continued working for very low pay even if *A had told B that he was going to break his promise.* Of course, it is very unlikely B would do so: the breach of trust involved in going back on the commitment would necessarily affect B's relationship with A—indeed, it could be that B would not only stop helping out with A's business but would also end his relationship with A.

As a matter of legal doctrine, the test adopted in *Wayling v Jones* is clearly wrong. To show B has relied on A's promise, we need to compare how B acted after A's promise with how B would have acted if no promise had been made. The problem in *Wayling* was that, when cross-examined in court, B seemed to suggest that he would have acted in the same way even if A had made no promise. If that was true then, as a matter of doctrine, B's proprietary estoppel claim should fail. Yet, as a matter of practical convenience, it seems the Court of Appeal were keen to find in B's favour: A and B had lived together for over 15 years and still did so at the time of A's death. And A's will *did* leave *a* hotel to B—it just left the *wrong* hotel to B: A's will gave B the hotel A had previously owned and it seems that, after selling that hotel and buying a new one, A had simply forgotten to amend his will. It is

---

[42] This caused an insurmountable problem for B in *Coombes v Smith* [1986] 1 WLR 808. It was held that B would have acted in the same way (looking after A and B's children, giving up a job, decorating, etc) even if A had made no commitment to her, as her action was motivated by her relationship with A and the children. It seems *Coombes v Smith* [1986] 1 WLR 808 would now be decided differently: either through proprietary estoppel, using the later decision in *Wayling v Jones* (1993) 69 P & CR 170; or through a 'common intention' Constructive Trust as used in, for example, *Grant v Edwards* [1986] Ch 638 and approved by the House of Lords in *Lloyds Bank v Rosset* [1991] 1 AC 107 (see **G3:2.4.5(v)**).

[43] See eg *Smith v Chadwick* (1884) 9 App Cas 187 at 196; applied to proprietary estoppel in eg *Greasley v Cooke* [1980] 1 WLR 1306.

[44] (1993) 69 P & CR 170.

therefore no surprise that the Court of Appeal wished to prevent B losing out simply because he had suggested when cross-examined that he would have been generous enough to work for A for very low pay even if A had made no promise.[45]

However, there was no need in *Wayling v Jones* for the Court of Appeal to adopt a special test for reliance. In cross-examination, B had simply said that he would have 'stayed with' A even if A had not made the promise to leave him the hotel. This can be taken to mean that B would have remained in a relationship with A: it does not necessarily mean that B would have worked for A for very low pay. Indeed, it was when B queried his pay that A made the promise to B: this does suggest that the promise provided an important reason for B to continue to accept such low pay. Therefore, the conventional test seems to have been satisfied: (i) A made a promise that was likely, objectively speaking, to cause B to act in a particular way; and (ii) B did act in that way; and (iii) A's executors could not show that B would have acted in that same way even if the promise had not been made.

3.2.2 B's reliance on A's commitment must be reasonable

EXAMPLE 9

A has a Freehold. B has been saving money towards a deposit on a first house. A, an elderly relative of B, promises B that he will leave his land to B. As a result, B withdraws his savings and uses them to gamble in a casino, losing everything.

B has no proprietary estoppel claim: his reliance is not a reasonable response to A's commitment. B cannot expect A to be under a duty to protect B from suffering a detriment caused by B's decision to gamble with his savings. That decision was made by B and, even if B made it as a result of A's commitment, it cannot be seen as reasonable reliance on A's commitment. The detriment B suffers is the result of B's own unreasonable choice, not of A's failure to honour his commitment.

3.3   B's detriment

EXAMPLE 10

A has a Freehold. A makes a commitment to leave his house to B. In reliance, B sells his own house and moves into rented accommodation. Two years later A changes his mind and tells B he will not leave his house to B. During those two years, there has been a crash in the housing market. As a result, even taking into account moving costs and the rent he paid during those two years, B can easily afford to buy back his former house, or at least a similar house.[46]

---

[45] If the facts of *Wayling v Jones* were to occur today, then even if he had no proprietary estoppel claim, B could try to rely on the Inheritance (Provision for Family and Dependants) Act 1975: that Act gives the court a power to give B some of A's assets, even if A did not leave those assets to B in his will. However, at the time of *Wayling*, there was a difficulty with applying that Act on the death of someone like A: B's long-term homosexual partner. Under s 2 of the Law Reform (Succession) Act 1995, a new provision was inserted in the 1975 Act to deal with the position of B where he had lived in the same household as A 'as the husband or wife [of A]'. Following *Ghaidan v Godin-Mendoza* [2004] 2 AC 557 (see **B:8.2.3(i)**) it seems that, due to the Human Rights Act 1998, that term should now be interpreted so as to include a long-term homosexual partner. As that option was clearly not open to the Court of Appeal in *Wayling v Jones* it is perhaps understandable that it avoided the problem by extending the scope of proprietary estoppel.

[46] B could argue that he has suffered a detriment if cannot buy back the *very same* house he originally had. The

B has no proprietary estoppel claim: B has relied on A's commitment, but A's failure to honour that commitment has not caused B any detriment. Detriment must be tested at the moment when A refuses or fails to honour his commitment:[47] in **Example 10**, when A tells B he will not leave B his house. In **Example 10**, B does not get the benefit of A's Freehold and so B is certainly in a worse position that he would have been had A kept to his commitment. However, that does not mean B has suffered a detriment. To judge that, we need to compare B's position when A fails to honour his commitment with B's position *before* he reasonably relied on that commitment. If B's position is no worse than his position before he relied, B can have no proprietary estoppel claim. So, in **Example 10**, B has no claim: he is no worse position than he was before relying on A's promise.[48]

B can suffer a detriment even if his reliance on A has not made him financially worse off. In *Gillett v Holt*,[49] for example, B had worked on A's farm for almost 40 years. During that period, A had made a number of promises that, when he died, he would leave B the farm. The first of those promises was made eight years after B had begun to work for A. B clearly relied on those promises: (i) he continued to work at the farm; (ii) he improved the farmhouse he lived in; and (iii) he sold his own house and took no steps to get on the property ladder. It was thus clear that B had based his future plans on the assumption that he would indeed inherit A's farm. However, before his death, A made clear that he would *not* honour that commitment. When B brought a proprietary estoppel claim, A argued that B's current position was no worse than the position B was in, over 30 years ago, before A first made the commitment. A contended that B had: (i) received an adequate wage in return for his work on the farm; (ii) had been allowed to live in A's farmhouse; and (iii) had benefited from any improvements he made to that accommodation.

In *Gillett v Holt*, the Court of Appeal firmly rejected A's argument. Even if it were true that B would suffer no *financial* detriment as a result of A's failure to honour his commitment, A would still be under a duty to B. A purely financial analysis of detriment fails to capture the fact that B had structured his future plans on the assumption of inheriting A's farm and that A's change of heart would clearly disrupt those plans. In particular, B had, throughout a period of over 30 years, let opportunities pass by (eg, to keep his own land; to seek employment elsewhere) and had subordinated his wishes[50] to those of A. B had done so on the basis that A would honour his commitment and so clearly suffered a detriment when A changed his mind.

The two requirements of reliance and detriment are often run together. However, that can lead to confusion. In particular, proprietary estoppel can still apply even if B's reliance, in itself, is *beneficial* to B. For example, in *Crabb v Arun DC*,[51] B's reliance consisted of selling off part of his land without reserving an Easement. By virtue of not reserving an

---

courts do take the uniqueness of land into account when answering the remedies question; but it is unlikely that, in **Example 10**, a court would use that uniqueness to allow B to acquire a right against A.

[47] See the seminal judgment of Dixon J in a decision of the High Court of Australia: *Grundt v Great Boulder Proprietary Gold Mines Ltd* (1938) 59 CLR 641 eg at 674–5: '[T]he real detriment or harm from which the law seeks to give protection is that which *would* flow from the change of position if the assumption were deserted that led to it' (italics added).

[48] In contrast, if the housing market had boomed, B would have a claim, as his decision to sell his house would have caused him a detriment.

[49] [2001] Ch 210.

[50] *Ibid* at 234.

[51] [1976] Ch 179.

Easement, B almost certainly got a better price for the land he sold off: in that sense, his reliance could be seen as beneficial. However, when A refused to honour his commitment to give B an Easement over A's land, B nonetheless suffered a detriment: he was unable to get to his remaining land. This underlines the crucial fact that proprietary estoppel is not about B 'detrimentally relying'; rather, it is about protecting B from the detriment that he has suffered or will suffer due to A's failure to honour his commitment.[52]

3.4   Unconscionable conduct by A?

In **2.3** above, we considered and dismissed the view that the purpose of proprietary estoppel is to prevent unconscionable conduct by A. Nonetheless, it could be argued that, whilst unconscionable conduct by A is not *sufficient* for a proprietary estoppel claim it is *necessary*. On this view, even if B would suffer a detriment as a result of his reasonable reliance on A's commitment, A can resist B's proprietary estoppel claim by showing that A has not acted unconscionably. However, there is simply no evidence to support that view. Whilst judges often comment that proprietary estoppel has the *abstract* aim of preventing unconscionable conduct,[53] there is no case in which: (i) B has satisfied the three basic requirements of proprietary estoppel; but (ii) B has failed to acquire a right simply because A has not acted unconscionably. The point is that the requirements themselves *define* when B can acquire a right: in this context, the only way for A to show he has not acted unconscionably is for A to show that the specific requirements of proprietary estoppel have not been met.[54]

So, does unconscionability have *any* role to play in relation to the requirements of proprietary estoppel? Well, the courts have used the concept exactly as we would expect: as an abstract idea that does not replace, but can help to define, the three specific requirements of the doctrine. So, in *Taylor Fashions Ltd v Liverpool Victoria Trustees Ltd*,[55] Oliver J had to consider a case where the essential facts were identical to **Example 4**. A argued that the requirements of proprietary estoppel had not been met as, when encouraging B to believe that B had a right to renew a Lease of A's land, A genuinely believed that B did have such a right. A 19th-century decision[56] appeared to support A, suggesting that A's lack of knowledge of the true position is fatal to B's proprietary estoppel claim. Oliver J rejected A's argument: by encouraging B's belief, A had made a commitment to B, even though A was not aware of the true position (see **3.1.1** above). B had then relied on that belief, and would suffer a detriment if A did not honour its commitment. The three basic requirements of proprietary estoppel were thus satisfied.

In reaching that decision, Oliver J referred to unconscionability. His Lordship stated that the 19th-century decision, requiring A to know the true position, was inconsistent with the more modern trend for a 'broad test of whether in the circumstances the conduct complained of is unconscionable'.[57] But it is vital to note that the 'broad test' does not

---

[52] See *per* Dixon J in *Grundt v Great Boulder Proprietary Gold Mines Ltd* (1938) 59 CLR 641 at 674–5.

[53] See eg *per* Oliver J in *Taylor Fashions Ltd v Liverpool Victoria Trustees Ltd* [1982] QB 133 at 151; *per* Robert Walker LJ in *Gillett v Holt* [2001] Ch 210 at 225.

[54] Handley, *Estoppel by Conduct & Election* (2007) argues persuasively that unconscionability is not a distinct requirement of other forms of estoppel; his analysis can also be applied to proprietary estoppel.

[55] [1982] QB 133.

[56] *Wilmott v Barber* (1880) 15 Ch D 96.

[57] [1982] QB 133 at 154.

replace the specific requirements of the doctrine; it is instead used to help *refine* those requirements. And so, the concept of unconscionability was used for a limited purpose: to decide that A can be held to have made a commitment to act in a particular way even if A acts on the basis of a honest but mistaken belief that he is *already* under a duty to act in that way.

In fact, Oliver J could very easily have made the same decision *without* referring to unconscionability. Instead, his Lordship could simply have pointed out that an objective test is used to establish whether A has made a commitment to B. A's knowledge of the true position is therefore irrelevant as it does not change the effect of A's conduct of B (see **3.1.1** above). Indeed, the decision in *Taylor Fashions* shows the real danger of overemphasising the importance of unconscionability. For it was *A*, not B, who had placed most reliance on the concept. A had strenuously argued that, as it had simply made an honest mistake in encouraging B to believe B had a pre-existing right to renew the Lease, it had not acted unconscionably.[58] Oliver J's decision, in rejecting this argument, shows that bad or unconscionable conduct by A is *not* required for a proprietary estoppel claim.

SUMMARY of E4:3

There are three specific requirements of proprietary estoppel: (i) a commitment by A to B; (ii) reasonable reliance by B; and (iii) actual or potential detriment to B as a result of A's failure to honour his commitment. Those requirements reflect the specific purpose of the doctrine: to prevent B suffering a detriment as a result of his reliance on A. The specific requirements make clear that proprietary estoppel is not simply a magic wand that a court can wave *whenever* it wishes to protect B. Indeed, it would be a grave mistake to view proprietary estoppel in that way. We have seen throughout this book that the property law system attempts to resolve the **basic tension** through a set of certain, well-defined rules. There is no room within that system for a judge to have an unregulated, general discretion to impose a duty on A whenever, in his view, justice demands.

At the moment, proprietary estoppel, in English law at least, applies only if A makes a commitment to his land in a particular way. However, there seems to be no good reason for limiting the doctrine in this way: properly understood, the doctrine could play a useful wider role in preventing B from suffering a detriment *whenever* he relies on a commitment, made by A, that A then refuses to honour.

---

4 THE EXTENT OF A'S DUTY TO B

4.1 The problem

If B can meet the three requirements for a proprietary estoppel claim, A will be under a duty to B. We then need to look at the *extent* of B's right: to ask what particular duty is imposed on A. For example, in both *Jennings v Rice*[59] and *Crabb v Arun DC*,[60] B suffered

---

[58] See [1982] QB 133 at 144, where Oliver J summarises the argument of Millett QC, counsel for *A*, that B cannot have acquired a right through proprietary estoppel as A has not acted unconscionably.

[59] [2003] 1 P & CR 100.

[60] [1976] Ch 179.

detriment as a result of A's failure to honour a commitment, relating to A's land, on which B had relied. In *Jennings v Rice*, A was *not* under a duty to honour his commitment to give B the Freehold; instead, A was under a duty to pay B £200,000. In contrast, in *Crabb v Arun DC*, A *was* under a duty to keep his commitment to give B an Easement.

So, in *Crabb v Arun DC*, the extent of B's right was set by A's commitment; in *Jennings v Rice*, it was not. Are the courts acting inconsistently, or are the different results simply the product of the same test being applied to different facts? To answer this, we need to see what test the courts use when deciding on the extent of B's right.

However, there is no consensus as to how the courts determine the extent of a right acquired through proprietary estoppel. Judges have failed to identify a clear test;[61] and academics disagree as to what the test should be.[62] This is no surprise. There is no consensus as to the *purpose* of proprietary estoppel (see **section 2** above). And the test for the extent of B's right must depend on that purpose.

Purpose of proprietary estoppel	Extent of B's right
To avoid formality rules	B gets the right A intended to give B[63]
To enforce commitments	B gets the right A intended to give B[64]
To prevent A's unconscionable conduct	B gets whatever right is necessary to prevent A acting unconscionably[65]
To prevent B suffering a detriment	B gets whatever right is necessary to prevent B suffering a detriment as a result of his reasonable reliance on A

Of course, this confusion has unfortunate effects. As the results of a proprietary estoppel claim are hard to predict, the land law system is less transparent; as it is difficult for lawyers to give advice on the probable outcome of such a claim, parties may therefore have to resort to litigation to determine their rights. This uncertainty is particularly unwelcome as proprietary estoppel can give B a persistent right: a right capable of binding C.[66] And, as we have seen throughout this book, the general stance of the land law system is that, if B's pre-existing right is capable of binding him, C ought to be able to discover that right.

4.2   The solution?

To come up with a clear test to determine the extent of a right arising through proprietary estoppel, we need to define the purpose of the doctrine. It was suggested in **section 2** above that its purpose is to protect B from suffering a detriment where he has reasonably relied on

---

[61] See eg *Cobbe v Yeomans Row Management Ltd* [2006] 1 WLR 2964: note esp Dyson LJ at [121] and Mummery LJ at [95], reaching the depressing finding that the award made by the judge in that case was the 'least unsatisfactory' way to decide on the extent of B's right.

[62] For some views differing from those set out here, see eg Cooke (1997) 17 *LS* 258; Gardner (1999) 115 *LQR* 438 and (2006) 122 *LQR* 492; Edelman (1999) 15 *Journal of Contract Law* 179.

[63] See eg Moriarty (1984) 100 *LQR* 376.

[64] See eg Birks (1996) 26 *University of Western Australia Law Review* 1 at 60; Edelman (1999) 15 *Journal of Contract Law* 179.

[65] See eg Halliwell (1994) 14 *LS* 15.

[66] See LRA 2002, s 116(a).

a commitment made by A. That purpose certainly seems to be reflected in the requirements of the doctrine; it should also govern the extent of B's right. So the test suggested here is that the doctrine imposes a *duty on A to act in such a way as to ensure that B does not suffer a detriment as a result of B's reasonable reliance on A's commitment.*

This suggested test means there is no guarantee that B's expectation will be protected: it may be the case, as in **Example 2** and *Jennings v Rice*, that B's detriment can be reversed or prevented *without* A honouring his commitment to B. So, in **Example 2**, B's detriment consists of the fact that he has cared for A, for a month, for free. That detriment can be reversed by imposing a duty on A to pay B a sum of money, perhaps equal to the market value of the care provided by B.[67] After all, B's proprietary estoppel claim would not arise *at all* if B had suffered no detriment in the first place; hence, if A's duty is sufficient to reverse that detriment, B can have no complaint.[68]

Importantly, the suggested test underlines the difference between: (i) a duty arising under proprietary estoppel; and (ii) a contractual duty. In the latter case, B, by virtue of satisfying the requirements of a contractual claim, *is* entitled to have his expectation protected: the extent of B's right will be set by the need to enforce A's commitment. However, in the former case, as B has *not* satisfied the requirements of a contractual claim, he has no such entitlement. Instead, he will acquire only the right necessary to ensure he suffers no detriment as a result of A's failure to keep his commitment.

The suggested test also differs from the 'unconscionability' test. That test is essentially meaningless: it provides no useful guidance as to what right B will acquire. It is also based on a misunderstanding of the nature of proprietary estoppel. The doctrine allows B to acquire a right in defined circumstances: where the three requirements have been satisfied. It should not be used by a court as an excuse for readjusting the parties' rights as a court sees fit.[69]

The dangers of the 'unconscionability' test can be seen in the Court of Appeal's decision in *Sledmore v Dalby*.[70] (i) A had made a commitment to allow B to remain in A's house for the rest of B's life; (ii) B had relied on this by doing some work and spending money on that house over a three-year period; and (iii) B would have suffered a detriment if A had removed B from the house immediately after B had done that work. However, B remained in occupation of the house, rent-free, for a further 15 years. A then attempted to remove B. B claimed that, due to proprietary estoppel, A was under a duty to honour his commitment to allow B to remain in A's house for the rest of B's life.

In *Sledmore*, the Court of Appeal held that A was under no duty to B. That decision must be correct. Following his reliance on A's commitment, B would have suffered a detriment if A had immediately sought to remove B. However, as B had since enjoyed 15 years rent-free accommodation, any detriment had long since disappeared: as a result, any right B had initially acquired through proprietary estoppel had long since been exhausted.[71] The *decision*

---

[67] This, it seems, was the basis of the decision in *Jennings v Rice* [2003] 1 P & CR 100.

[68] See eg *per* Dyson LJ in *Cobbe v Yeomans Row Management Ltd* [2006] 1 WLR 2964 at [125]: 'if an award of what the claimant expected to receive if the assurances had been met is disproportionate to the detriment suffered by him in reliance on those assurances, then it is unlikely to be just to make an award on that basis'.

[69] For an argument to the contrary, see Rotherham, *Proprietary Remedies in Context* (2002), 33–42 and 296–7.

[70] (1996) 72 P & CR 196.

[71] See *per* Roch LJ at 204–5: 'the minimum equity to do justice to [B] on the facts of this case was an equity which has now expired'.

of the Court of Appeal is thus consistent with the test suggested here: the extent of B's right is set by the need to prevent B suffering a detriment. Indeed, this point comes across strongly in the reasoning of Hobhouse LJ, who, quoting from an Australian judgment, stressed the need for proportionality between 'the remedy and the detriment which is its purpose to avoid'.[72]

However, the *reasoning* of Roch LJ is inconsistent with the test suggested here. His Lordship pointed to a number of factors that seem to be wholly irrelevant. In particular, the relative needs of A and B were compared: it was found that A, vulnerable and in financial difficulties, had a greater need to occupy the house than B, who was in employment and had somewhere else to live.[73] Such factors may be relevant to some abstract notion that rights relating to land should be distributed according to people's needs, but they can have *no* relevance to the extent of the right B acquires through proprietary estoppel. When a court adjudicates such a claim, it has the power to define the rights of A and B for a specific reason: B has relied on a commitment of A to use A's land in a certain way, and B has suffered or will suffer a detriment as a result of A's failure to honour that commitment. Any decision the court makes as to the extent of B's right must be limited by that specific reason: the court cannot take advantage of A and B's presence before it to adjust their rights according to some wider and different question of their respective needs. After all, we do not have a land law system in which judges can simply order A, a wealthy owner of two homes, to let B, who has nowhere to live, occupy A's second home. Issues of relative hardship *can* be relevant when we move to the **remedies question** (see **section 5** below); but such wider issues should not affect the the extent of B's right. For that reason, the 'unconscionability' test must be rejected.

4.3 The suggested test

The concept of *proportionality* is central to the suggested test. The test can be said to depend on achieving *proportionality* between: (i) the extent of the right acquired by B; and (ii) the degree of detriment B has suffered or will suffer.[74] It is for this reason that, as noted by Aldous LJ in *Jennings v Rice*, the extent of B's right can change according to the degree of B's reasonable reliance on A: it makes a difference whether B relies on A's commitment for 'one month, one year, or twenty years'[75] as the longer B relies, the greater B's detriment will be if A does not honour his commitment.

The suggested test seems to have influenced the Court of Appeal in *Jennings v Rice*.[76] As a result of A's commitment to leave B her Freehold and furniture, B, originally A's gardener, had run errands, done odd jobs and cared for A, for free, for at least seven years. For at least two years before A's death, B had spent nearly every night at her house, to provide A with some security. The first instance judge had found that A (and hence A's executors on her

---

[72] The words quoted are taken directly from the judgment of Mason CJ in *Commonwealth of Australia v Verwayen* (1990) 170 CLR 394, quoted by Hobhouse LJ in *Sledmore* at 209.

[73] See *per* Roch LJ (1996) 72 P & CR 196 at 204.

[74] See eg *per* Hobhouse LJ in *Sledmore v Dalby* (1996) 72 P & CR 196 at 209; *per* Robert Walker LJ in *Jennings v Rice* [2003] 1 P & CR 100 at [50] and [56]; *per* Dyson LJ in *Cobbe v Yeomans Row Management Ltd* [2006] 1 WLR 2964 at [125].

[75] See *per* Aldous LJ in *Jennings v Rice* [2003] 1 P & CR 100 at [37].

[76] [2003] 1 P & CR 100. See too *Ottey v Grundy* [2003] EWCA Civ 1176.

death) was under a duty to pay B £200,000. That sum seems to have been based on the value of the full-time nursing care that B had, in effect, provided for at least two years before A's death. B appealed against that decision, arguing that A's executors should be bound to honour her commitment and to give him the Freehold and furniture, valued at £435,000. The Court of Appeal rejected that appeal, making clear that there was no rule that B's right must be set by A's commitment. It also upheld the judge's award, suggesting that the extent of B's right should be determined by the need to prevent B suffering a detriment as a result of the unpaid services he provided in reliance on A's commitment.

Of course, in practice, it may be difficult precisely to measure the degree of detriment B has suffered or will suffer.[77] To that extent, a court must possess some discretion to exercise a judgment, according to the facts of the case, as to the degree of B's detriment. The presence of such discretion is not unusual. For example, if A commits a wrong against B, a court has to gauge the value of B's right; and must also put a financial value on any relevant consequential loss suffered by B (see D1:4.3). Such a process can never be entirely precise, particularly when abstract rights (eg, B's right to reputation or physical integrity) are translated into sums of money. However, as Robert Walker LJ (now Lord Walker) emphasised in *Jennings v Rice*, this does *not* mean that a court is permitted to 'exercise a completely unfettered discretion according to the individual judge's notion of what is fair in any particular case'.[78]

However, despite that warning, Robert Walker LJ himself, in *Jennings v Rice*, went beyond the test suggested here. In that case, his Lordship stated that the extent of B's right can depend on a long list of factors, many unrelated to the extent of B's detriment:[79]

- misconduct of B;
- particularly oppressive conduct by A;
- the need for a clean break—eg, the fact that parties who have fallen out cannot be forced to live with each other;
- alterations in A's assets and circumstances, especially where B's reliance occurred over a long period;
- the likely effect of taxation;
- (to a limited extent) the other legal or moral claims on A.

A number of these factors are relevant to the **remedies question** (see **section 5** below). However, it is difficult to see their relevance to the different and prior question of the *extent* of B's right. Indeed, some of the factors, such as those based on the conduct of the parties, or on A's circumstances, come close to allowing a court to set B's right by reference to a general view of the moral quality of the parties' conduct; or of their general financial needs. Again, it needs to be emphasised that a court should not have such a wide discretion: its job is simply to give effect to B's proprietary estoppel claim.

---

[77] As noted by Robert Walker LJ in *Jennings v Rice* [2003] 1 P & CR 100 at [51].
[78] [2003] 1 P & CR 100 at [43]. Robert Walker LJ's comment therefore casts grave doubt on the approach adopted by Roch LJ in *Sledmore v Dalby* (1996) 72 P & CR 196.
[79] [2003] 1 P & CR 100 at [52].

4.4 Enforcing A's commitment

If the extent of B's right is set by the extent of B's detriment, how can we explain cases, such as *Crabb v Arun DC*,[80] in which A came under a duty to honour his commitment to B? Quite easily. In some cases, the need to prevent B suffering a detriment can be met *only* by enforcing A's commitment.[81] *Crabb* is a good example. B's particular reliance consisted in selling off part of his land without reserving a means of access to his remaining land. By refusing to honour its commitment to give B an Easement, A made B's remaining land inaccessible and, in effect, worthless. There were only two ways A could reverse this detriment: (i) by paying B the difference between the current value of his land and the value of that land with a right of access; or (ii) by giving B the promised Easement. Faced with such a choice, A would clearly opt for the much less expensive second option. And this is reflected by the Court of Appeal's decision that A was under a duty to grant B the Easement.

Of course, in general, it is always possible for A to prevent B suffering a detriment by simply honouring his commitment to B. This point is often stated in the form of a rule that the extent of B's right can never *exceed* his 'expectation'.[82] However, where, as in *Crabb*, A is *late* in honouring that commitment, A may be obliged not only to do what he originally promised but also to compensate B for the detriment B suffered as a result of A's delay (see too **E2:4.3.2**).[83]

Crabb is just one example of a case in which enforcing A's commitment is the only way to prevent B suffering a detriment. In *Jennings v Rice*, Robert Walker LJ identified a further set of cases in which B's expectation will generally be enforced.[84] In these cases, A has made a commitment to B *in return for* particular, clearly defined action from B. However, this bargain is, for some reason, not contractually binding: perhaps because a relevant formality rule, such as that set out by section 2 of the Law of Property (Miscellaneous Provisions) Act 1989, has not been complied with;[85] perhaps because the agreement has not yet been finalised. Nonetheless, if B then relies on A's commitment by completing his side of the bargain, A will generally be under a duty to honour his commitment. In such a case, the *parties themselves* have allocated a particular value to B's action: their bargain thus defines what is necessary to prevent B suffering a detriment.

EXAMPLE 11

A has a Freehold. A wants to convert his house into flats. A reaches an unwritten agreement with B that, if B does the necessary building work, A will give B a 99-year Lease of the ground floor flat. B completes his side of the bargain, but A refuses to honour his commitment.

---

[80] [1976] Ch 179.

[81] See too *Gillett v Holt* [2001] Ch 210; *Thorner v Curtis* [2007] EWHC 2422. See further Bright and McFarlane [2005] *CLJ* 449 at 456–465.

[82] See eg *Burrows & Burrows v Sharp* (1989) 23 *HLR* 82 at 92 'In general [the court] would, if possible, want to avoid giving the claimant more than he was ever intended to have.'

[83] This explains why, in *Crabb*, A was under a duty to grant B an Easement for free.

[84] [2003] 1 P & CR 100 at [45]. It seems that in these cases, the factors identified by Robert Walker LJ in *Jennings* and discussed above, will *not* be relevant.

[85] See **E2:2.3.3**.

In such a case, A is not under a *contractual* duty to B: his promise to give B a 99-year Lease has not been made in writing and so does not satisfy the formality rule laid down by section 2 of the 1989 Act. However, as the Court of Appeal confirmed in *Yaxley v Gotts*,[86] the essential facts of which are identical to **Example 11**, proprietary estoppel imposes a duty on A: (i) A made a commitment to B; (ii) B reasonably relied on that commitment; and (iii) B would suffer a detriment as a result of A's failure to honour the commitment. In such a case, in order to prevent B suffering a detriment, the court could look at the work done by B and, as in *Jennings v Rice*, attempt to calculate its market value: A's duty could then be to pay B that sum. However, in **Example 11**, there is no need for the court to do this: the *parties themselves* have already placed a value on B's work. So, as confirmed by the Court of Appeal in *Yaxley v Gotts*, the best solution is for A to be under a duty to honour his commitment to B.

It might seem that, in these bargain cases, proprietary estoppel is undermining the requirements of contract law. As in contract law, B's expectation is protected; but the usual requirements of a contract are absent. However, there are important differences between the bargain cases and contract law:

- if A makes a contractual promise to B, A is under an immediate duty to keep that promise;[87] whereas
- if A makes a non-contractual promise to B, and B then relies on that promise, A can refuse to perform that promise *as long as* he prevents B from suffering a detriment as a result of B's reliance up to the point of A's refusal.

So, in **Example 11**, *if* A had pulled out of his informal bargain with B *before* B had completed the agreed work, A would *not* necessarily have been under a duty to give B the agreed Lease of the ground floor flat. Moreover, in some cases, it may be that, even if B does complete his side of the bargain, proprietary estoppel will not impose a duty on A to honour his commitment to B. This may be the case where the bargain involves B's doing work over an uncertain period and that period ends sooner than the parties expected (or wished).

EXAMPLE 12

A has a Freehold. A makes a promise to leave his Freehold to B if B looks after A for the rest of A's life. A dies a month later.

B has completed his side of the bargain and so, if A's promise were contractually binding, B's expectation of the Freehold would be protected. However, as A's promise is not contractually binding, B has to rely on proprietary estoppel. It is very unlikely that A's estate will be under a duty to honour A's commitment.[88] Technically, B has completed his side of the bargain, but the parties themselves cannot be said to have allocated a particular value to the

---

[86] [2000] Ch 162.

[87] A proprietary estoppel bargain case is very close to a unilateral contract. Where there is a unilateral contract, if A withdraws a promise as B is attempting to perform the condition necessary to enforce that promise, A will be in breach of contact. The standard view (set out but queried by Peel, *Treitel's Law of Contract* (12th edn, 2007), 2-057) is that B can then claim money reflecting his expectation. On some facts, both an estoppel and a unilateral contract analysis may be possible: see eg *Errington v Errington* [1952] 1 KB 290.

[88] See eg Aldous LJ in *Jennings v Rice* [2003] 1 P & CR 100 at [37]; compare **Example 2**.

detriment B *actually* suffered: when the bargain was made, the parties did not envisage that B would care for A for so short a time.

4.5   The cases

It seems that the suggested test is, generally speaking, in line with the *results* reached by the Court of Appeal in cases such as *Crabb v Arun DC*,[89] *Sledmore v Dalby*,[90] *Yaxley v Gotts*,[91] *Jennings v Rice*,[92] *Cobbe v Yeoman's Row Management Ltd*[93] and *Powell v Benny*.[94] As Robertson has noted, the general trend in England, as well as Australia, is consistent with the suggestion that the doctrine aims to prevent B suffering a detriment as a result of A's failure to honour his commitment.[95] Of course, it is not possible to come up with a meaningful test that fits all the *reasoning* used in these cases. As noted above, there is a lot of confusion about the proper test and, as a result, judicial reasoning in this area is usually vague and often inconsistent.[96]

Equally, it is not possible to come up with a meaningful test that explains *all* past results. For example, after the emphasis placed on proportionality in *Jennings v Rice*, the decision in *Pascoe v Turner* (**Example 1** and **C3:Example 3**)[97] is open to question. B had relied on A's statement that the house belonged to her by spending her own time and money on redecoration, improvements and repairs to the house. When A went back on his commitment and sought to remove B, the Court of Appeal held that A was under a duty to transfer the Freehold of the house to B. When A refused to honour his commitment, B suffered a detriment through her expenditure on the house; she had also arranged her affairs on the basis that the house belonged to her. Nonetheless, it is highly debatable that the *only* way to reverse that detriment was to order A to transfer the Freehold to her. A duty to pay B money to compensate her for her expenditure and to enable her to find temporary alternative accommodation would surely have sufficed.[98] Unfortunately, that possibility was not considered by the Court of Appeal.[99]

It is no surprise that the test suggested here cannot explain every decided case. No meaningful test can: judges have failed to adopt a consistent view as to the purpose of proprietary estoppel and hence as to the test to use when determining the extent of B's right. Of course, a test based on 'unconscionability' or an unfettered discretion *could* explain every decision; but it would be empty of content and no use as a guide in future cases. It seems that, for the sake of transparency and certainty, the courts need to grasp the nettle

---

[89] [1976] Ch 179.

[90] (1996) 72 P & CR 196.

[91] [2000] Ch 162.

[92] [2003] 1 P & CR 100.

[93] [2006] 1 WLR 2964. That decision is currently on appeal to the House of Lords. For discussion of the House of Lords' decision, see the companion website.

[94] [2007] EWCA Civ 1283.

[95] Robertson, 'The Reliance Basis of Proprietary Estoppel Remedies' [2008] *Conv* forthcoming.

[96] See eg the despairing comment of Dyson LJ in *Cobbe v Yeomans Row Management Ltd* [2006] 1 WLR 2964 at [121].

[97] [1979] 1 WLR 431.

[98] The Court of Appeal was concerned that B should not acquire a right (such as a licence or a Lease) that would involve a continuing relationship with A that A might abuse. However, a clean break could have been achieved by ordering A to pay a sum of money to B.

[99] Problems with the Court of Appeal's decision were also noted in **C3:4.2.3**.

and fix on a specific test. The test suggested here has the twin advantages of: (i) consistency in principle (it fits with the requirements of proprietary estoppel and helps to distinguish the doctrine from contract law); and (ii) consistency with the results in the vast majority of decided cases.

SUMMARY of E4:4
At the moment, there is no consensus as to how to determine the extent of a right acquired by B through proprietary estoppel. As a result, the law in this area is inconsistent and uncertain. We need a test that, like the requirements for proprietary estoppel, reflects the purpose of the doctrine. The best suggestion seems to be that the extent of B's right should be set by the need to ensure B suffers no detriment as a result of A's failure to honour the commitment, made by A, on which B has reasonably relied. This test explains why, in cases such as *Jennings v Rice*, proprietary estoppel does not impose a duty on A to honour his commitment to B. It can also explain why in other cases, such as *Crabb v Arun DC*, A *is* under a duty to honour his commitment. It also meets the need, identified by the Court of Appeal in *Jennings v Rice*, to provide a clear test and to ensure that B's right is proportionate to his detriment. Most importantly, it makes the extent of B's right depend on the reason for which the right arises in the first place: the need to prevent B suffering a detriment as a result of his reliance on A's commitment.

5 THE REMEDIES QUESTION

Once a court has decided on the extent of B's right, it also needs to decide what remedy to give to protect that right. The **remedies question**, of course, arises *whenever* B seeks to assert a right. Where, as in *Jennings v Rice*, A's duty is simply to pay money to B, the remedies question is straightforward: A is simply ordered to pay that sum. However, if A is under a duty to perform a particular act, for example to allow B to use his land, or to give B a property right, the court has to make an important choice: should B's right be specifically protected?

In general, if B's right relates to land, we would expect that right to be specifically protected (see E1:4.2, E2:4.2 and E3:4). For example, in *Crabb v Arun DC*[100] A was under a duty to give B an Easement; and the Court of Appeal specifically protected B's right by ordering A to grant B that Easement. Specific protection was particularly important in that case, as it allowed B to acquire a right necessary to support his own land.[101] Similarly, it may be that B, by his occupation of A's land, has developed a specific connection to that land, so that his removal from that land would cause him a particular detriment. For example, in *Gillett v Holt*,[102] B had been living in A's farmhouse for over 25 years: as B had established a home there, it was no surprise that the Court of Appeal ordered A specifically to perform his duty to give B the Freehold of that farmhouse.[103]

---

[100] [1976] Ch 179.
[101] See too *Ward v Kirkland* [1967] Ch 194 and *ER Ives Investments Ltd v High* [1967] 2 QB 379.
[102] [2001] Ch 210.
[103] See too *Dillwyn v Llewellyn* (1862) 4 De GF & J 517. Occupation can also be important where business premises are concerned. In *JT Developments v Quinn* (1991) 62 P & CR 33, B had been running his business from A's land for five years and A's duty to give B a new Lease was specifically enforced: see too *Lloyd v Dugdale* [2002] 2 P & CR 13.

In contrast, in *Yaxley v Gotts*,[104] the Court of Appeal did *not* specifically enforce A's duty to grant B a Lease. Instead, the court gave A the option of paying B money equivalent to the value of the promised Lease. That result *may* have been based on the fact that, in *Yaxley*, B did not need the Lease to support any land of his own or to provide him with a home or business premises: B had instead planned to use the Lease to make money, by renting out the flat.[105] As a result, it is possible to argue that payment by A of a sum of money could adequately protect B's right.[106]

It should be emphasised that, whether B's right arises through proprietary estoppel *or* some other means, a wide range of factors are relevant at the remedy stage. In fact, it is here that the list of factors given by Robert Walker LJ in *Jennings v Rice*, and set out in **4.3** above, can play a role—not because B's right has arisen through proprietary estoppel but because those factors are *always* relevant when considering the remedies question. For example, the need for a 'clean break' can be taken into account to prevent specific enforcement of A's duty to allow B to share occupation of A's house.[107] This is true even if A's duty is a contractual one: no matter how A's duty arises, it does not make sense for a court to force A and B to live together.[108] Similarly, an 'alteration in A's circumstances' is relevant, at the remedy stage, even if A's duty is based on a contract: so, in *Patel v Ali*,[109] a court declined to order specific performance of A's contractual duty to transfer a Freehold to B, as, since making the contract, A had endured severe personal difficulties.

The crucial point, then, is that the general discretion the court possesses when looking at the remedies question *does not depend on the fact that B's right arose through proprietary estoppel*. Rather, it is simply the consequence of the fact that a court has to do the best it can, taking into account all the prevailing circumstances, to give practical effect to B's right.

6   THE EFFECT OF B'S RIGHT ON C

6.1   The suggested analysis

Where B acquires a right through proprietary estoppel, it should be easy to establish the effect of that right on C. If A is simply under a duty to act in a particular way (eg, to pay B money; to allow B to occupy A's land) B has a purely *personal right* against A. *Jennings v Rice*[110] is an example of such a case: A was under a duty to pay B money and hence B had only a personal right against A. In such a case, B has no pre-existing right that can bind C.

However, if A is under a duty in relation to a specific claim right or power held by A (eg, A is under a duty to transfer his Freehold to B; A is under a duty to give B an Easement), B has a *persistent right*. This right will arise *as soon as*, due to B's reliance on A's commitment,

---

[104] [2000] Ch 162.

[105] Indeed, after completing the conversion, B did rent out the flat and receive the income for a period before A and B fell out and A reneged on his commitment to B.

[106] Although note there is a risk of inconsistency if a court asks, in every case, whether B's connection with and plans for the land really justify specific protection (see **E1:4.2 esp at n 73**).

[107] For a proprietary estoppel example, see eg *Baker v Baker & Baker* [1993] 2 FLR 247.

[108] For a contractual example, see *Thompson v Park* [1944] KB 408: Goddard LJ at 409 noted that: 'the court cannot specifically enforce an agreement for two people to live peaceably under the same roof'.

[109] [1984] Ch 283.

[110] [2003] 1 P & CR 100.

A comes under such a duty to B. *Crabb v Arun DC*[111] is an example of such a case: as soon as B sold off part of his land without reserving a right of access, A was under a duty to give B an Easement. As a result, B acquired an immediate Equitable Easement. So if, after that point, C had acquired a right from A, B would have had a prima facie power to assert his right against C. [112]

The crucial question, therefore, is whether A is under a duty to B in relation to a specific right. That will be the case if: (i) A is under a duty to transfer his right to B (as was the case in *Pascoe v Turner*);[113] or (ii) A is under a duty to exercise his power to give B a new property right (as was the case in *Crabb v Arun DC*).[114] To see if A is under such a duty, we need to apply the test set out in **4.3** above: A will only be under such a duty to B if, to prevent B suffering a detriment as a result of his reliance on A, it is necessary for A to: (i) transfer his right to B; or (ii) grant B a new property right. On this view, proprietary estoppel operates like *any other reason* (eg, contract, wrongs, unjust enrichment) by which A can come under a duty to B: B acquires a persistent right if and only if A is under a duty in relation to a specific right. This view does, in general, fit the results reached in the relevant cases.[115]

EXAMPLE 13

A has a Freehold of business premises. A makes a promise to give B a Lease of that land. As a result, B moves into the premises and improves them. A then refuses to grant B the promised Lease. A sells his Freehold to C, who is registered as the new holder of the Freehold.

The crucial question is whether A has a duty to grant B the promised Lease. If this is necessary to ensure that B suffers no detriment, B acquires a persistent right: an Equitable Lease (see **E2:1.3.1(i)**). For example, in *Lloyd v Dugdale*,[116] the basic facts of which were essentially identical to **Example 13**, B incurred costs in moving into the premises and had begun to establish his business there: the first instance judge therefore found, and the Court of Appeal confirmed, that A was under a duty to grant B the promised Lease. This meant that, as the first instance judge and Court of Appeal also confirmed, B had a prima facie power to assert his Equitable Lease against C. However, the problem for B was that C was able to use the lack of registration defence: B's right had not been defensively registered and B was not in actual occupation of A's land when C committed to acquiring its right (see **E2:3.6**).[117]

---

[111] [1976] Ch 179.

[112] In *Crabb* itself, no third party was involved. However, A's failure to allow B access over A's land, following B's reliance on A's commitment, was described by Scarman LJ at 199 as an 'infringement of an equitable right possessed by [B]': that right can be seen as an Equitable Easement.

[113] [1979] 1 WLR 431 (**Example 1** and **C3:Example 3**).

[114] See too *Yaxley v Gotts* [2000] Ch 162.

[115] See further McFarlane [2003] *CLJ* 661.

[116] [2002] 2 P & CR 13.

[117] The first instance judge had found that B *was* in actual occupation, and hence that his right bound C, but the Court of Appeal held instead that B had not personally been in actual occupation of the land, as he was present only as a representative of his company (see **E2:3.6.4(ii)**). This meant that the company was in actual occupation of the land, but had no persistent right; whereas B, who had the persistent right, was not in actual occupation. Hence there was no pre-existing right that bound C.

EXAMPLE 14

A has a Freehold and makes a commitment to leave that Freehold to B. As a result, B spends his weekends caring for A. Two years later, A changes his mind and transfers his Freehold to C.

In such a case, B should have no persistent right. As shown by the decision of the Court of Appeal in *Jennings v Rice*, A will not be under a duty to honour his commitment to transfer his Freehold to B. Instead, A's duty to ensure B suffers no detriment can be met if A pays B a sum of money. As a result, A's duty does *not* relate to a specific right: he can use *any* sum of money to pay B.

EXAMPLE 15

A has a Freehold and makes a commitment to allow B to run a monthly motor racing event on that land. B gives nothing in return for A's commitment, but relies on it by making modifications to A's land. A then transfers his Freehold to C.

Again, B should have no persistent right. At most, A will be under a duty to honour his commitment to B: this means A will be under a duty to allow B to make a limited use of A's land. A is under the same duty where B has a contractual licence: in such a case, A's duty does not relate to a specific claim-right or power of A and so B has only a personal right against A (see **E2:1.3.1(ii)** and **E6:4.4.2**).[118]

6.2   The orthodox view

Unfortunately, the seemingly straightforward analysis set out above differs markedly from the judicial and academic consensus as to the effect of a right arising through proprietary estoppel on C. That orthodox view treats such a right very differently from a right arising through other means. It takes a *two-stage* approach to the acquisition of a right through proprietary estoppel. The first stage is complete once all the requirements of the doctrine have been met: B has relied on A's commitment, and has suffered, or would suffer, a detriment if A fails to honour that commitment. At that stage, we would expect B already to have a right against A: after all, the requirements of the doctrine have been met. However, on the orthodox view, B does not yet have a right against A. B has only an 'equity by estoppel' or 'inchoate equity':[119] a right to go to court and 'bend the ear of the court of conscience to listen sympathetically to his plea for a restraint upon the landowner's exercise of his rights'.[120] B only acquires an actual right at the second, later stage: when the court chooses to award B a right by ordering A to act in a particular way.

We can see this two-stage approach in action by applying it to the facts of *Crabb v Arun DC*:

---

[118] In *Pennine Raceways Ltd v Kirklees MBC* [1983] QB 382, the basic facts of which are identical to **Example 15**, the Court of Appeal held that B was a 'person interested in land' for the purposes of a particular statute imposing a duty on a local authority to pay compensation to B when revoking its permission for the motor racing events. However, as Eveleigh LJ noted at 391, that conclusion does not mean that B's right is 'an interest in land in a strict conveyancing sense' (ie, a right capable of binding a third party).

[119] 'Inchoate' means 'just beginning' or 'imperfect'.

[120] Gray and Gray, *Elements of Land Law* (4th edn, 2005), 10.212.

	Begins when	B's right
Stage 1	B sells off his land without reserving an Easement	'Equity by estoppel'
Stage 2	The court orders A to grant B an Easement	Equitable Easement

Stage 1 begins after B reasonably relies on A's commitment by selling off some of his land without reserving an Easement. At that point, the three requirements of proprietary estoppel are present and so B acquires an 'equity by estoppel'. Stage 2 begins once a judge has held that A is under a duty to give B an Easement: at that point B acquires an Equitable Easement.

So, in a case such as *Crabb v Arun DC*, if C acquires a right in relation to A's land *after* Stage 2 has begun, things are fairly clear. Due to the court order, A is under a duty to give B an Easement: A is thus under a duty in relation to a specific right and so C *is prima facie* bound by B's pre-existing Equitable Easement. However, if C instead acquires his right during Stage 1 (ie, *before* the court has made its order, but after B has relied on A's commitment) everything depends on the status of B's mysterious 'equity by estoppel'. C can be bound by B's proprietary estoppel claim if, and only if, the 'equity by estoppel' counts as a persistent right.

	Point when C acquires a right from A	Can B assert a pre-existing right v C?
Stage 1	After B's reliance	Depends on the effect of an 'equity by estoppel'
Stage 2	After the court order in B's favour	Yes

So, on the orthodox view, a choice has to be made: is an 'equity by estoppel' capable of binding a third party or not? The consensus answer is 'Yes': and so that was the position adopted by the Law Commission, when preparing the draft provision that is now section 116(a) of the Land Registration Act 2002 ('the LRA 2002'). That section provides—'for the avoidance of doubt'—that, where registered land is concerned, an 'equity by estoppel' counts as a right that is prima facie binding on C, a party later acquiring a right from A.

6.3 Comparing the two views

The orthodox view treats proprietary estoppel in an odd way and therefore leads to odd results. First, as a matter of principle, it is strange to say that the doctrine works in two separate stages, and that B has no actual right until a court makes an order. Certainly, we do not talk of 'inchoate' contracts, wrongs or unjust enrichments: the rule is that B's right arises as soon as all the relevant requirements for the acquisition of the right have been met. Therefore, if A commits a wrong by carelessly running B over, B acquires a right against A immediately: there is no need to wait for a court order.[121] Indeed, we do not usually think of courts as awarding rights to the parties: unless they have a special statutory jurisdiction, the job of the courts is not to confer new rights but to *recognise* rights the parties have already

---

[121] This is why, if a court finds A has a duty to pay money to B as a result of A's commission of a wrong, A can be ordered to pay interest on that money for the period between the commission of the wrong and the court order: see Supreme Court Act 1981, s 35A. For consideration of a court's non-statutory jurisdiction to make interest awards see *Westdeutsche Landesbank v Islington LBC* [1996] AC 669 and *Sempra Metals Ltd v IRC* [2007] 3 WLR 354.

acquired.[122] To say that, even after the requirements of proprietary estoppel have been met, B only has an 'equity by estoppel' (a right to go to court) gives insufficient weight to the fact that B has relied on A's commitment and would suffer a detriment if that commitment were not honoured: after all, vexatious litigants aside, *everyone* has the right to go to court. In fact, there are a number of cases in which the courts have recognised that B has a definite right *before* any court order has been made in his favour.[123]

The special, two-stage view of proprietary estoppel *would* be defensible if the doctrine gave the courts an unfettered discretion to vary the rights of A and B. In such a world, it would be very difficult to say that B has a right before the court had exercised its discretion and awarded B a right.[124] However, as we have seen, proprietary estoppel does *not* operate in that way: like contract, wrongs and unjust enrichment, it is a means of acquiring a right that has its own specific requirements. Indeed, the two-stage model seems to be based on an out-dated, seemingly medieval model of the law, where parties go cap in hand to an all-powerful representative of the monarch and hope that he will exercise his unregulated largesse in their favour.

The two-stage model, and the special treatment it accords proprietary estoppel, is thus overcomplicated and unnecessary. There is simply no need for the 'equity by estoppel':[125] if B acquires a right through proprietary estoppel that right should arise immediately. Moreover, the two-stage model leads to problems in practice: once we have the redundant 'equity by estoppel' we need to decide what to do with it—in particular, is it capable of binding a third party? However, as soon as we even ask that question, we are doomed to get the wrong answer. If we say that the 'equity by estoppel' is only a personal right, we cannot explain cases such as **Example 13**, in which it is clear that B's right is capable of binding C, even though C acquired his right before any court order had been made in B's favour. Conversely, if we say that the 'equity by estoppel' *is* capable of binding a third party, we are left with the very odd result that, in cases such as **Examples 14 and 15**, B's pre-existing right *can* bind C even though A's duty is simply to pay B a sum of money (**Example 14**) or to allow B to make a particular use of A's land (**Example 15**).

So, the Law Commission, when drafting a provision about the effect of an 'equity by estoppel' was bound to make a mistake. It opted for the view that an 'equity by estoppel' *is* capable of binding C. This leads to the absurd result that, in cases such as **Examples 14 and**

---

[122] See eg *per* Nourse LJ in *re Polly Peck (No 2)* [1998] 3 All ER 812 at 831.

[123] See eg *Voyce v Voyce* (1991) 62 P & CR 290, esp *per* Dillon LJ at 294. See further McFarlane [2003] *CLJ* 667. Note too a number of Australian decisions confirming that B's right exists before any court order and so constitutes a limit on A's rights that must be taken into account when considering A's pension entitlements: eg *Repatriation Commission v Tsourounakis* [2004] FCAFC 332; *Kintominas v Secretary, Department of Social Security* (1991) 30 FCR 475; *Sarkis v Deputy Commissioner of Taxation* [2005] VSCA 67; *Secretary, Department of Family and Community Services v Wall* [2006] FCA 863; *Young v Lalic* [2006] NSWSC 18; but compare *Repatriation Commission v Tsourounakis* [2007] FCAFC 29. I am grateful to Professor Andrew Robertson for pointing out these cases to me.

[124] See eg Hayton [1990] *Conv* 370; (1993) 109 *LQR* 485; Rotherham *Proprietary Remedies in Context* (2002), ch 13.

[125] It is worth noting how the 'inchoate equity' concept was introduced. In the Court of Appeal's decision in *National Provincial Bank v Ainsworth* [1964] Ch 665 (see **B:11**) Lord Denning MR held that Mrs Ainsworth's licence could bind a third party (the bank) as it was coupled with 'an equity'. That decision was of course overturned by the House of Lords [1965] AC 1175, who firmly rejected the fictional 'equity'. However, in the interim, Lord Denning MR had again used the 'equity' concept, this time in an estoppel case: *Inwards v Baker* [1965] 2 QB 29. That case did *not* go to the House of Lords, and as the decision of the House in *NPB* did not concern proprietary estoppel, the heresy of the 'estoppel equity' was allowed to survive.

15, B can assert a pre-existing right against C if C acquires a right *before* a court order is made in B's favour. However, if C acquires his right *after* such a court order, B's pre-existing right cannot bind C: at that stage, B no longer has an 'estoppel equity' but simply has a personal right against A. This seems ludicrous: after all, B's right is harder to discover before a court order and so should be *less* likely to bind C at that stage.

It seems, then, from the point of view of both principle and practice, the orthodox view should be rejected.[126] Proprietary estoppel, like any other means by which B can acquire a right, should give B a pre-existing right capable of binding C *only* if A is under a duty to B in relation to a specific right.

6.4 The impact of section 116(a) of the Land Registration Act 2002

This leaves us with the tricky question of what to do about section 116(a) of the LRA 2002. The section reads as follows:

> It is hereby declared for the avoidance of doubt that, in relation to registered land, each of the following:
> (a) an equity by estoppel, and
> (b) a mere equity
> has effect from the time the equity arises as an interest capable of binding successors in title (subject to the rules about the effect of dispositions on priority).

The section thus assumes that *whenever* B has a proprietary estoppel claim, he has, at least until a court order is made in his favour, a right that is prima facie binding on C. This is unfortunate, as it seems to be a statutory entrenchment of the orthodox, but mistaken view. As a repeal of the provision is unlikely, the best we can hope for is that judges will interpret the provision in a creative way, to avoid the absurdities that would result from giving it a literal effect.

One possible solution is to interpret the term 'equity by estoppel', as used in section 116(a), to refer *only* to cases (eg, **Example 13**) in which B's proprietary estoppel claim imposes a duty on A to B in relation to a specific right. This would ensure that B cannot rely on section 116(a) in cases (eg, **Examples 14 and 15**) where A is simply under a duty to pay B money or to allow B to use A's land. Such an interpretation can be justified by the fact that section 116(a) is expressly stated to be 'for the avoidance of doubt': as a result, it should not be given the effect of changing the law by allowing B, in cases such as **Examples 14 and 15**, to have a right capable of binding C. It can also be supported by the point that section 116(b) allows a 'mere equity' to bind C: clearly 'equity' as used in section 116(b) cannot refer to *every* situation where B has a right, arising in Equity, against A. Rather, 'mere equity' has a more limited, technical meaning: it refers to situations where B has a power to acquire a persistent right (see **D2:1.6(iii)**). So it is, perhaps, not too big a stretch for 'equity by estoppel', in section 116(a), to be given a similarly limited meaning.

Of course, the interpretation suggested here is somewhat strained. However, the alternative is far worse. If section 116(a) is given the effect the Law Commission intended, we are left with the absurd position that *whenever* B has a proprietary estoppel claim, he acquires a

---

[126] See further Battersby in *Land Law: Themes and Perspectives* (ed Bright and Dewar, 1998), 503–4 and McFarlane [2003] *CLJ* 661. Doubts about the Law Commission's view of section 116(a) are also expressed by *Snell's Equity* (ed McGhee, 31st edn, 2005), 10-28.

right capable of binding C. That is inconsistent with a fundamental principle of the property law system: B's pre-existing right should be capable of binding C only if it is either: (i) a property right; or (ii) a persistent right (ie, A is under a duty to B in relation to a specific claim right or power held by A).[127] Certainly, it would be very strange if a provision of the LRA 2002, a piece of legislation primarily designed to protect C, were to make it so much easier for B to acquire a right that is capable of binding C.

SUMMARY of E4:6

Proprietary estoppel, like contract, wrongs or unjust enrichment, is simply a reason for which A can come under a duty to B. It should give B a persistent right only if it imposes a duty on A in relation to a specific claim right or power held by A. So, in cases where A's duty is: (i) to give B a sum of money (see **Example 14**); or (ii) to allow B to make a particular use of land (see **Example 15**); then (iii) B should *not* have a persistent right. In contrast, if A's duty is: (i) to transfer a right to B (see eg *Pascoe v Turner*);[128] or (ii) to give B a new property right (see **Example 13**); then (iii) B should have a persistent right.

However, the orthodox view is different. On that view, proprietary estoppel, unlike contract, wrongs or unjust enrichment, can only give B a right *after* a court has made an order in B's favour. Until then, B has only an 'equity by estoppel': a right to go to court. Remarkably, however, this imperfect, uncertain right, as confirmed by section 116(a) of the LRA 2002, is capable of binding C. Therefore, even where A's duty is simply to give B money (**Example 14**) or to allow B to make a limited use of A's land (**Example 15**), B will acquire (at least until a court makes an order in his favour) a right capable of binding C. That is a very surprising result. There is no reason why rights arising through proprietary estoppel should be treated differently from rights arising through other means: after all, proprietary estoppel is simply a means by which B can impose a duty on A.

7   FORMALITY RULES AND PROPRIETARY ESTOPPEL

It is worth reiterating that, as we saw in C3:7.3.1, proprietary estoppel is not regulated by any formality rules. This means that A's commitment to B does *not* have to be made or recorded in writing. This is because, to acquire a right through proprietary estoppel, B does *not* need to show that A has exercised a power to come under a duty to B. Rather, A's duty comes from the need to prevent B suffering a detriment as a result of his reliance on A's commitment.

It would be possible to change the current position and to introduce a formality rule. Such a rule would regulate the operation of proprietary estoppel by requiring that any commitment made by A to B would have to be made or recorded in a particular form, eg, signed writing. However, such a rule will never be introduced: it would interfere with the

---

[127] There are, of course, exceptions to that principle: for example, we have seen that a personal right to occupy land arising under the Family Law Act 1996 may be capable of binding C if it is registered (see **B:11.3**). That exception can be justified by the particular need to protect those occupying land owned by their partner. However, there can be no policy concern justifying the conferral of special protection to *all* parties with a right arising through proprietary estoppel: after all, commercial parties can acquire such rights (see eg *Cobbe v Yeomans Row Management Ltd* [2006] 1 WLR 2964).

[128] [1979] 1 WLR 431.

doctrine's key aim of preventing B suffering a detriment through his reliance on A. For the current position acknowledges a crucial practical point: B does frequently rely on A's informal commitment about how A will use his land. And where B would suffer detriment as a result of A's failure to honour such a commitment, B deserves protection. The need to protect B outweighs the benefits of imposing a formality rule (see **E2:2.3.3(iv)**).

8 PROPRIETARY ESTOPPEL AND THE LAW OF OBLIGATIONS

Before we leave proprietary estoppel, it is worth thinking about its place within the wider law of obligations. Given the general confusion surrounding the doctrine, it is no surprise to learn that there is no consensus about its relationship with other means of acquiring rights. For example, the doctrine has been seen, like contract, as a means of enforcing a commitment made by A.[129] And it has been seen, like wrongs, as reacting to a breach by A of a duty owed to B.[130] It has also been argued that the doctrine is simply one means of identifying when A has been unjustly enriched at B's expense.[131] Yet another view is that the doctrine has no unifying role and that so-called proprietary estoppel cases can instead be broken down into decisions enforcing commitments, identifying wrongs or reversing unjust enrichments.[132]

This confusion is, of course, linked to the uncertainty about the purpose of proprietary estoppel. The view taken here is that the doctrine aims to ensure that B suffers no detriment as a result of his reasonable reliance on a commitment made by A to B. On this view, the doctrine, unlike contract law, is *not* about enforcing commitments. This explains why A's commitment does not have to pass all the usual contractual tests (eg, there is no need for a definite agreement; for B to provide consideration; to satisfy the formality rule imposed by section 2 of the Law of Property (Miscellaneous Provisions Act) 1989). It also explains why, as in *Jennings v Rice*,[133] A is not always obliged to honour his commitment.

The doctrine does not, strictly speaking, define when A's conduct counts as a wrong: as A's commitment is not binding on him, A does not commit a wrong by refusing to honour it. A's action *would* be wrongful if: (i) A breached his commitment; *and* (ii) A did not reverse any detriment B suffers as a result. So, in that sense proprietary estoppel steps in to ensure A does not act wrongfully.[134] However, A's initial duty to B does not arise as a result of a wrong: B's right can arise as soon as he relies on A's commitment and, at that point, it cannot be said that A has breached any duty to B: after all, A may be fully intending to honour his commitment.[135] Nor is the doctrine simply part of the law of unjust enrichment: B can acquire a right even if, as in *Crabb v Arun DC*,[136] his reliance does not confer a benefit

---

[129] See eg Birks (1996) 26 *University of Western Australia Law Review* 1 at 60.
[130] See eg Spence, *Protecting Reliance: The Emerging Doctrine of Equitable Estoppel* (1999).
[131] See eg Goff and Jones, *The Law of Restitution* (6th edn, 2002), 230–35.
[132] See Worthington, *Equity* (2nd edn, 2006), 246–54.
[133] [2003] 1 P & CR 100.
[134] In the elegant phrase used by John Gardner in relation to a different form of liability, proprietary estoppel corrects not a wrong, but what would be a wrong apart from the act of correcting it: (1996) 46 *University of Toronto Law Journal* 459 at n 21.
[135] Similarly, once A makes a contractual promise to B, A comes under a duty to B and so commits a wrong if he breaches his promise: but A's initial duty to keep his promise does not arise as a result of a wrong—it arises as a result of A's entry into the contract.
[136] [1976] Ch 179.

on A.[137] It seems that proprietary estoppel is concerned with B's detriment, not A's enrichment. It is that aim—of ensuring B suffers no detriment—that unifies cases of proprietary estoppel and so refutes the view that the doctrine is simply an amalgamation of cases based on contract, wrongs and unjust enrichment.

Therefore, on the view taken in this book, proprietary estoppel, like the 'receipt after a promise' principle, fits in the 'other events' category (Reason 6 as set out in **B:4.3**). If the doctrine's *purpose* is to ensure B suffers no detriment as a result of his reasonable reliance on A's commitment, we have to ask important questions about its current *scope*. It is very hard to defend the restriction of the doctrine to commitments relating to land; or even to commitments relating to things. There is a strong argument that the doctrine should be capable of applying *whenever* A makes a commitment as to his own future action on which B relies (see **3.1.2** above).

If this is true, and the doctrine can apply even where A's commitment does not relate to a thing, the doctrine should not be known as *proprietary* estoppel. Equally, even on the law as it currently stands, we should remove the confusing reference to *estoppel*. That word gives the potentially misleading suggestion of a link between: (i) proprietary estoppel; and (ii) evidential estoppel (see **D1:3.3.1(i)**); and (iii) defensive estoppel (see **D1:3.3.1(ii)**). Evidential estoppel[138] can properly be called 'estoppel' as it results in A being prevented (ie, stopped) from denying the truth of a statement. Defensive estoppel[139] can properly be called 'estoppel' as it results in A being prevented (ie, stopped) from asserting a right against B.[140] Further, neither principle, by itself, constitutes a reason for imposing a duty on A to B.[141] In contrast:

- proprietary estoppel is not simply about preventing A from acting in a particular way: it imposes a positive duty on A to ensure that B suffers no detriment as a result of A's failure to honour a commitment; and
- proprietary estoppel is an independent means by which A can come under a duty to B.

This leaves us in the amusing, but somewhat disconcerting, position that 'proprietary estoppel' is: (i) *not* a form of estoppel; and (ii) should *not* be limited to property (ie, objects that can be physically located). Perhaps much of the confusion that plagues the doctrine could be avoided by giving it a more accurate name, emphasising its role in ensuring B suffers no detriment as a result of his reasonable reliance on a commitment, made by A to B, that A has refused to honour. Any suggestions as to such a new name are welcome.

SUMMARY of E4

Proprietary estoppel is a means by which B can impose a duty on A. It applies if three conditions are met:

---

[137] See further McFarlane (2006) 1 *Journal of Equity* 156.

[138] Generally known as 'estoppel by representation' or 'Common Law estoppel'.

[139] Generally known as 'promissory estoppel' or 'Equitable estoppel'.

[140] Although it is important to note that A may only be *temporarily* stopped from asserting his right: see eg *Tool Metal Manufacturing Co Ltd v Tungsten Electric Co Ltd* [1955] 1 WLR 761.

[141] Evidential estoppel may be used to prevent A denying a particular fact that is essential in allowing B to acquire a right; however, in such a case, B's right arises because of an independent reason allowing B to acquire that right (eg, a contract): see too **D1:Example 22b**.

- A makes a commitment to B to use to his land in a certain way; *and*
- B reasonably relies on that commitment; *and*
- B has suffered, or will suffer, a detriment as a result of A's refusal to honour his commitment.

Whilst there is no current consensus about the purpose of the doctrine, its requirements suggest that its aim is to ensure B suffers no detriment as a result of his reasonable reliance on A's commitment. As a result, the extent of A's duty should be set by that goal. This means, as the courts have recognised, that proprietary estoppel does not demand the enforcement of A's commitment.

Like any other means by which B can acquire a right, proprietary estoppel can give B a persistent right—but only in limited circumstances. In particular, B will have a persistent right if A is under a duty: (i) to transfer a right to B; or (ii) to use his power as a holder of a Freehold or Lease to give B a property right in A's land. In all other cases, as, for example, when A's duty is: (i) to pay a sum of money to B; or (ii) to allow B to make a limited use of A's land, B should have only a personal right against A. Unfortunately, that simple model has been blurred by the enactment of section 116(a) of the LRA 2002. That section suggests that, *whenever* proprietary estoppel imposes a duty on A, B acquires an 'equity by estoppel': a right that is capable of binding C (although that right will cease to exist once B's proprietary estoppel claim gets to court and an order is made in B's favour). It is hoped, however, that judges will interpret section 116(a) in such a way as to avoid that absurd result.

CHAPTER E5
THE LAND REGISTRATION ACT 2002

THE LAND REGISTRATION ACT 2002

The majority of land in England and Wales is registered land: someone is recorded by the Land Registry as having a Freehold or Lease of that land. As a result, when looking at the land law system we have assumed that the land in question is registered. In **C2, E1 and E2** we considered many of the rules imposed by the Land Registration Act 2002 ('the Act') to govern dealings with registered land. The purpose of this chapter is to evaluate the Act by examining its impact on the land law system.

1 THE AIMS OF THE ACT

Like any piece of legislation, the Act was designed to achieve a number of goals. For example, one of its purposes was to remedy some poor drafting in the Land Registration Act 1925,[1] and to reverse the effect of some judicial decisions interpreting that statute.[2] However, whilst these technical changes were of concern to land lawyers they would never, by themselves, have persuaded Parliament to pass the Act: a busy legislature needs some convincing before taking the time to consider a Bill.

The political catalyst to the Act was the recurring complaint of those buying and, to a lesser extent, selling houses in England and Wales. Exasperation at the slow and costly process of buying a house was a long-standing, albeit very boring, feature of middle-class conversation. The difficulties of the conveyancing process seemed particularly out of date against the backdrop of a booming property market. This created the political will to tackle the problem by making changes to the land law system.

The chief purpose of the Act is, therefore, to make conveyancing simpler. Or, put in the terms of the **basic situation**, it is *to reduce the delays and expense to C in acquiring a property right in land*. By 1998, over 80 per cent of the estimated titles to land were registered so, not surprisingly, the reforms focused on the registered land system. There are two ways in which conveyancing can be made simpler. First, the *process* of buying land can be streamlined. Second, the *legal rules* affecting that process can be changed to give greater protection to a purchaser. The Act adopts both these strategies; the introduction of electronic conveyancing plays a crucial role in each of them.

---

[1] For example, the grounds for rectification set out in s 82 of the Land Registration Act 1925 were needlessly complex and are set out more succinctly in Schedule 4 of the Act.

[2] Such as the holding in *Celsteel Ltd v Alton House Holdings Ltd* [1985] 1 WLR 204 that an Equitable Easement could count as an overriding interest in its own right, and could thus be immune from the lack of registration defence even if B was not in actual occupation. This decision created an anomaly as the general rule is that persistent rights, such as an Equitable Easement, can only be overriding if accompanied by actual occupation: **E2:3.6**.

As to *process*, the Act paves the way for a system of electronic conveyancing. Such a system will make life easier for C, a party acquiring a right in registered land. First, C can check the register online. Second, when dealing with A, a registered owner, C can use electronic documents rather than paper contracts or deeds.[3] Finally, C's own right can be registered electronically. In these purely technical ways, the introduction of electronic conveyancing, like the advent of the telephone or the typewriter, can offer some savings of time and, perhaps, expense.[4]

The Law Commission plans to capitalise on the introduction of electronic conveyancing by making a further change to the conveyancing process. The Commission envisages a 'chain manager' who can monitor, electronically, the progress of each link in a chain of house sales.[5] This is an attempt to deal with a common problem, arising where A intends to sell his house to C, but A first has to buy his new house from X. Any delay in the negotiations between A and X will also delay the sale from A to C. It is a common complaint that a problem further down the chain, which he cannot attempt to solve, can cause significant delays to C. The 'chain manager' will be able to electronically survey the progress of each link in a chain, attempting to prevent problems from arising and encouraging their resolution when they do arise. Again, however, this is simply a change to the *process* of conveyancing: it is not contemplated that the chain manager will have any legal powers to impose solutions to the problems he spots.

As to the *legal rules*, the following statement of the Law Commission shows us the basic aim of the Act:

> The fundamental objective of the Bill is that, under the system of electronic dealing with land that it seeks to create, the register should be a complete and accurate reflection of the state of the title of the land at any given time, so that it is possible to investigate title to land on line, with the absolute minimum of additional enquiries and inspections.[6]

The key aim of the Act is to provide *certainty* for C, by protecting C against the risk of being bound by a pre-existing but unregistered right of B. The Act therefore makes a number of changes to the legal rules governing both the **acquisition** of property rights, and the **defences** available against persistent rights. Many of these changes had immediate effect and were considered in E1:2.3.4 and E2:3.6. However, other important changes will occur only when the electronic conveyancing system is up and running. As we saw in E1:2.3.4(ii) and E2:2.3.3(ii), rules will then be introduced, under section 93(2) of the Act, to impose a system of compulsory electronic registration. These rules will have an important effect on resolving the **basic tension** between B and C.

First, when acquiring a right from A, C will have the opportunity to ensure that his right is electronically registered *as soon as* C is committed to acquiring it. This will mean the end of the 'registration gap' that currently exists in the period between: (i) A executing a deed to

---

[3] This is permitted by s 91 of the Act (as we noted in E1:2.3.3(ii)).

[4] The need for electronic registration to be carried out by a licensed party may *increase* the costs for C if C would otherwise have done his own conveyancing. Sch 3 para 7(1) of the Act imposes a duty on the Land Registry to provide 'such assistance as [it] thinks appropriate' to a such a 'do it yourself' conveyancer. However, the Law Commission envisaged that the Land Registry will charge for this service: see Law Com No 271 at 13.73 (see too E1:2.3.4(ii).

[5] See Law Com No 271 at 2.52 and 13.65. The Land Registry have developed a 'Chain Matrix' service to allow progress to be monitored online.

[6] Law Com No 271 at 1.5.

give C a property right; and (ii) C acquiring that right by being substantively registered as its holder. We have seen that C currently faces a problem where B acquires a property right, counting as an overriding interest, during that period (see **E1:Example 6**). Under the electronic system, that problem will disappear: B's pre-existing but unregistered property right will only be able to bind C if it exists at the moment when C commits to acquiring his right.[7]

Second, electronic registration will become part of the test not just for the acquisition of certain property rights, but also for the existence of a *contract* by A to give B such a right (see **E2:2.3.3(ii)**). As a result, B's failure to electronically register may not only prevent him from acquiring a property right, but it will also prevent him from showing that A is under a contractual duty to give B such a right. As a result, in order to show he has a persistent right, B will need to show that A is under a *non-contractual* duty to give him such a right (see **E2:2.3.3(i) and (iv)**). The risk to C of being bound by a pre-existing but unregistered persistent right will thus be reduced (see **E2:Example 13**).

Whilst the Act came into effect in October 2003, the electronic conveyancing system is yet to become fully operational. It was always expected that, due to the need to resolve technical issues, the electronic system would be introduced over a number of years. At the moment, then, there is no system of 'chain managers'; nor have general rules been made under section 93(2) to make electronic registration compulsory.

This means that the Act can be viewed in two distinct stages. First, we need to look at the *immediate changes* introduced by the Act, analysing the ways in which, within the existing non-electronic system, greater protection is given to C (see **sections 2 and 3** below). Second, we will look at the effect the electronic system will have when it is fully operational (see **section 4** below). However, it is important to remember that both strands of the Act do need to be seen together: certainly, this is how we will proceed when analysing the overall effect of the Act (see **section 5** below).

2   THE AIMS OF THE ACT AND THE BASIC TENSION

Before looking at the detail of the Act, it worth pausing to reflect on its basic aim: to provide certainty for C and hence to reduce the delays and expense to C in acquiring a property right in land. A trap is created by the fact that registration systems can provide important protection to C. It is easy to assume that: (i) because a key purpose of such a system is to protect C; then (ii) the merit of such a system consists entirely in how far it protects C. On this view, a registration system that offers lots of protection to C is good; one that offers less protection is bad.

However, this reasoning is seriously flawed. The registered land system is merely a part of the wider land law system. Such a system aims to resolve the impossibly difficult **basic tension**. That tension cannot be adequately resolved by simply preferring the interests of C to those of B. Registration is no more than a tool used in an attempt to resolve the basic tension: it is not a concept which allows that basic tension to be ignored (see **C2:6.2**). It is therefore important to remember that a registered land system should be evaluated not by

---

[7] That is already the test that applies to persistent rights, as B must be in actual occupation when C commits to acquiring his right (see **E2:Example 22**).

seeing how well it protects C, but rather by seeing how well it balances the competing interests of B and of C.

The Law Commission's statement as to the 'fundamental objective' of its reforms suggests that it may have fallen into the error of assuming that the more protection it provides to C, the better a land registration system becomes. However, when we examine the actual provisions of the Act, a different picture emerges. Despite the rhetoric of the Law Commission, the draft Bill it produced, and the resulting Act, *do* strike a balance between B and C. Indeed, the need for such a compromise can be seen even in the Commission's seemingly one-sided statement as to the 'fundamental objective' of the Act. That statement refers to the need to have the 'absolute minimum of additional enquiries and inspections'. If the register *were* complete and accurate, then, in order to see if land was affected by any pre-existing rights, C could simply look on the register: there would be no need for C to make *any* additional enquiries and inspections. In wishing to *minimise*, rather than *eliminate*, the need for such enquiries, the Law Commission is recognising, as does the Act, that, in certain circumstances, C can be bound by an unregistered right of B.

3   THE IMPACT OF THE ACT: THE CURRENT POSITION

In this section, we will concentrate on the three key 'gaps' in C's protection: situations in which B, despite his failure to register a pre-existing right, may be able to assert a right against C.

3.1   Direct rights

Registration systems do not aim to protect C against the risk of being bound by a direct right of B (see **C2:2** and **E3:Overview**). As a result, the Act has no effect on B's ability to assert a direct right against C.[8] So, if a court wishes to protect B despite his failure to register, one way to do so is to find that B has a direct right against C. However, if the courts are too hasty in finding that C's conduct has led to B acquiring a direct right, the certainty provided to C by the Act would be undermined. The courts should therefore be careful to ensure that B only acquires a direct right if one of the tests for acquiring such a right, set out in **E3:2**, has been satisfied.

3.2   Rectification of the register

3.2.1 Introduction

EXAMPLE 1

B has a Freehold. A, by forging B's signature, purports to transfer B's Freehold to C1. C1 is unaware of A's fraud and is substantively registered as the new holder of B's Freehold. C1 grants C2 a 10-year Lease and C2 substantively registers that Lease.

[8] This important principle is not stated explicitly in the Act, but is accepted in Law Com No 271, on which the Act is based: see 3.48, 3.49, 4.11 and 7.7. See further **E3:n2**.

By virtue of his substantive registration, each of C1 and C2 has a property right in the land (see **C2:6.1**).[9] However, the protection given to C1 and C2 is not absolute. Each will have a valid property right for as long as he is registered as having one; but B may apply to have the register *rectified*. Rectification consists of a change to the register causing loss to a registered party:[10] it can be used as a means of giving effect to B's pre-existing but unregistered property right. As a result, rectification can undermine the certainty provided to C1 and C2 by the positive operation of registration. However, where the register is rectified, C1 and C2 will have the chance of claiming an *indemnity*: money, provided by the Land Registry, to compensate C1 and C2 for loss suffered as a result of the change to the register. Whilst rectification thus gives a means to balance the needs of B with those of C, indemnity allows a more subtle resolution of the basic tension, and can be used to ensure that neither B nor C is left empty-handed.

3.2.2 The basic test: rectification

(i) An initial ground

The grounds on which rectification can be made are set out in Schedule 4 of the Act. The most important of these allows for the 'correction of mistakes'.[11] In **Example 1**, it seems fairly clear that, in registering C1 as holding a Freehold, the Land Registry has been taken in by A's fraud and has made a mistake.[12] However, is C2's registration 'a mistake'? After all, C2 dealt with C1, who as a registered Freehold owner, had a statutory power to grant C2 a Lease.[13] The prevailing view, therefore, is that C2's registration is *not* a 'mistake'.[14]

It is, however, possible to argue against that prevailing view and to say that, in **Example 1**, C2's registration is indeed a 'mistake'. First, the starting point, under the general principles of the property law system, is that B cannot be bound by a right, such as C2's Lease, that depends on another's fraudulent attempt to acquire B's property right. Second, the Act allows B to receive an indemnity if his application for rectification is unsuccessful; however, this indemnity is only available if B suffers loss by reason of a 'mistake whose correction would involve rectification of the register'.[15] This is a useful provision: it provides a means to uphold C's right whilst giving B some financial protection. However, it applies only if the court can say that a 'mistake' has occurred: if there is no mistake, the power to make an indemnity payment to B will not arise. As a result, courts have a reason to take a reasonably broad view of what counts as a 'mistake' under the Act.

Third, in interpreting the term 'mistake' it is reasonable to take into account the position under the Land Registration Act 1925: the Law Commission stated that the new Act was *not* intended to make significant changes to previous practice; rather, the aim was to make the

---

[9] LRA 2002, s 58.

[10] LRA 2002, Sch 4 para 1. If a change to the register does not cause loss to a registered party but simply, for example, updates the register (eg, by noting on the register an overriding interest that is any case binding on C) the change is known as an alteration rather than as a rectification: see Law Com No 271 at 10.6 and 10.7.

[11] LRA 2002, Sch 4 para 2(1)(a).

[12] See eg *Ruoff & Roper: Registered Conveyancing* (2003, 2006 release), 46.028.

[13] LRA 2002, ss 23 and 24.

[14] See eg *Ruoff & Roper: Registered Conveyancing* (2003, 2006 release), 46.030.

[15] Sch 8, para 1(1)(b). There are other provisions allowing an indemnity, but none is relevant in **Example 1**.

law more transparent.[16] Under the 1925 Act, the grounds for rectification were quite wide. For example, under section 82(1)(g), rectification could occur

> where a [Freehold or Lease] has been registered in the name of a person who if the land had not been registered would not have been [entitled to the Freehold or Lease].[17]

In **Example 1**, this provision allows for the possibility of *both* C1 and C2 being removed from the register.[18]

(ii) A further requirement

However, even if the registration of C2, like that of C1, can be seen as a 'mistake', that is not enough to allow rectification. The Act limits rectification against a party in 'possession' of registered land.[19] In such a case, rectification cannot occur unless:

- the registered party in possession has 'by fraud or lack of proper care caused or sub-stantially contributed to the mistake'[20] *or*
- 'it would for any other reason be unjust'[21] for the rectification not to be made.

In **Example 1**, C2 is clearly in physical control of the land; and under section 131(2) of the Act, C1 is *also* treated as being in 'possession': the physical control of a tenant means that his landlord is also in 'possession' of the registered land. Again, however, the conditions for rectification are somewhat unclear: in **Example 1**, would it be unjust for C1 to retain a Freehold and for C2 to retain a Lease?

B would certainly argue that, as he gave no consent to either the transfer to C1 or the grant of the Lease to C2, it would be unjust if B were forced either to lose his Freehold entirely or to wait 10 years before taking physical control of his land. Certainly, as C1 is simply receiving rent from C2, it could be said that rectification should be allowed against C1: he will be adequately protected by receiving an indemnity payment. The term 'unjust not to rectify' was also used in the 1925 Act, and the courts often interpreted that term in a way favourable to B.[22] However, things may be different where C2 is concerned. If C2 has set up a home or business premises on the land, it may be hard for B to show that it would be unjust if B, rather than C2, were forced to accept an indemnity payment.[23]

---

[16] See Law Com No 254 at 8.1: 'We conclude that the existing law and practice in relation to rectification are largely sound, and that the main deficiencies lie in the way in which the legislation is drafted. In light of this we make recommendations for reform which are primarily clarificatory rather than substantive.' See too Law Com Rep 271 at 2.38 and 10.4.

[17] LRA 1925, s 82(1)(g).

[18] The reasoning in *Argyle BS v Hammond* (1984) 49 P & CR 148 is certainly consistent with that view.

[19] LRA 2002, Sch 4 para 3(2).

[20] LRA 2002, Sch 4 para 3(2)(a).

[21] LRA 2002, Sch 4 para 3(2)(b).

[22] *Norwich & Peterborough Building Society v Steed* [1993] Ch 16; *Malory Enterprises Ltd v Cheshire Homes (UK) Ltd* [2002] Ch 216. For criticism of the *Malory* decision by the Law Commissioner who oversaw the project leading to the LRA 2002, see Harpum, ch 9 in *Rationalizing Property, Equity and Trusts: Essays in Honour of Edward Burn* (ed Getzler, 2003).

[23] See eg *Pinto v Lim* [2005] EWHC 630. In that case, the fact that C had occupied the registered land for four years as his home was important in Blackburne J's decision not to order rectification. In that case, B was a co-owner a Freehold with B2; B2 then forged B's signature on a transfer of the Freehold to B2; B2 then sold the Freehold to C. B was not seeking to move back into the land; and even if B had wished to do so, it is in general unlikely that, even if his right were binding C, B would be able to insist on occupying the land (see **G2:4**). It is therefore unsurprising that, in *Pinto*, the court considered that an indemnity payment would adequately protect B. In *Epps v Esso Petroleum Co Ltd* [1973] 1 WLR 1071, it was held that, even though B would otherwise have been entitled to the land, it would

3.2.3 The basic test: indemnity

(i) An initial ground

The grounds on which a party can receive an indemnity from the Land Registry are set out in Schedule 8 to the Act: the first two are the most important. The first arises where C suffers loss by reason of a rectification of the register.[24] So if, in **Example 1**, C1 or C2 is removed from the register, an indemnity may be payable. 'Rectification', as used in the Act, refers only to situations where both: (i) the register is changed in a way that involves the correction of a mistake; *and* (ii) the change prejudicially affects C's registered right. Thus, if the register is changed simply in order to update the register, or to include an overriding interest of B that is, in any case, *already* binding on C, no indemnity is payable. In such a case, the change to the register simply records the existing situation and is referred to as an 'alteration'. In **Example 1**, however, an indemnity may be payable to C1 or C2 as if either is removed from the register, he will lose a right he currently holds. If an indemnity is payable, the sum payable will depend, in part,[25] on the value of the right lost by C1 or C2. The value of that right is assessed *at the time of the rectification*: after all, that is the point when C1 or C2 loses his right.[26]

Second, an indemnity may be payable if a party suffers loss by reason of 'a mistake whose correction would involve rectification of the register'.[27] So if, in **Example 1**, B fails in his attempt to remove either C1 or C2 from the register, B can qualify for an indemnity payment *if* he shows that the registration of C1 or C2 is a 'mistake'. If an indemnity is payable, the sum payable will depend, in part,[28] on the value of the right lost by B. In this case, the value of B's right is assessed *at the time of the mistake*: in **Example 1**, at the time when C1 or C2 registered his right.[29] This approach seems correct: after all, it is the fact of C1 or C2's initial registration that causes B's loss.[30] However, it has important consequences in practice. For example, if the value of the land in question has increased in the period between C1 or C2's initial registration and the decision to deny B rectification, B has to settle for receiving the lower sum (plus interest).

(ii) A further requirement

Even if one of the two grounds applies, this means only that an indemnity *may* be payable. For example, a party cannot receive an indemnity in respect of any loss suffered wholly or partly as a result of that party's own fraud.[31] So, in **Example 1**, if A were to forge B's signature and register himself as the new holder of B's Freehold, A clearly cannot receive an indemnity if the register is then rectified in B's favour. The same rule applies if A transfers

---

not be 'unjust not to rectify': however, in that case, B had contributed to the problem by building a boundary wall along the wrong line. In *Kingalton Ltd v Thames Water Development Ltd* [2002] 1 P & CR 15, C's possession of land was also taken into account by the Court of Appeal in deciding not to order rectification; although in that case B had in any case made an offer to C in relation to the use by C of the disputed strip of land.

[24] LRA 2002, Sch 8 para 1(1)(a).

[25] C1 or C2 may also be able to recover compensation for consequential loss suffered as a result of the rectification eg moving expenses.

[26] LRA 2002, Sch 8 para 6(a).

[27] LRA 2002, Sch 8 para 1(1)(b).

[28] B may also be able to recover compensation for consequential loss suffered as a result of the refusal to rectify.

[29] LRA 2002, Sch 8 para 6(b).

[30] See Law Com No 271 at 10.43.

[31] LRA 2002, Sch 8 para 5(1)(a).

his Freehold *for free* to C: in such a case, A's fraud is held against C and C can receive no indemnity.[32] That is a little harsh: after all, even though he acquired his right for free, C may have suffered loss by, for example, giving up accommodation elsewhere or making improvements to the land.[33] However, it seems the purpose of the Act is not to protect *everyone* who relies on the register; rather it is to protect C if he acquires for value, and registers, a right relating to the registered land (cf **E2:Example 19**).[34]

Further, a party cannot receive an indemnity in respect of any loss suffered wholly as a result of his own lack of proper care.[35] And if a loss is caused *in part* by a party's lack of such care, the indemnity payable will be reduced 'to such extent as is fair having regard to his share in the responsibility for the loss'. As the Law Commission noted, the Land Registry should not have to provide compensation for a party who is, in whole or in part, 'the author of his or her own misfortune'.[36] However, this concept of lack of proper care does imply that, in some circumstances at least, C cannot *simply* rely on the register when acquiring a right in registered land. It may be that, due perhaps to suspicious circumstances surrounding the acquisition of his right, C must undertake further investigations; if C fails to do so, and the register is rectified, C's own lack of proper care may be seen as a cause of his loss. This demonstrates again that, despite the rhetoric of the Law Commission, C cannot assume that the register provides a 'complete and accurate' record of all rights relating to the land.

3.2.4 Insurance or guarantee?

When interpreting the rectification and indemnity provision of the Act, the courts must apply inherently vague terms such as 'mistake' and 'unjust'. In doing so, the courts face an important question about the philosophy of the Act. Should it be seen: (i) primarily as a means to protect C, in which case those terms should be interpreted narrowly, to limit the availability of rectification; or (ii) as a means to balance the interests of B and C: an aim best served by a wider interpretation of those terms, based perhaps on the position under the 1925 Act? In making this decision, it will be useful for a court to bear in mind the general point that the test of a registration system is not how far it protects a registered C, but rather how well it balances the interests of B and C.

In particular, in a case such as **Example 1**, there is more than one way in which a registration system may protect a party such as C1 or C2. For example, under the 1925 Act, provisions such as section 82(1)(g) seem to mean that such a party is still subject to the risk of losing the land if B has an unregistered but pre-existing property right. We might then ask what advantage there was for C, under the 1925 Act, in being a registered, rather than an unregistered, owner. The answer is that, if C lost his registered right, he could receive an indemnity from the Land Registry. In **Example 1**, it is almost certain that C1 and C2 would receive an indemnity following rectification in B's favour. In contrast, if the land in question

---

[32] LRA 2002, Sch 8 para 5(3).

[33] C could, of course, try to seek redress against A (although that may be difficult if A is under no contractual duty to C) or against B (in the law of unjust enrichment) if C's mistaken improvements to the land have conferred a benefit on B: see **E1:4.4**.

[34] To escape the consequences of A's fraud, C must acquire his right 'for valuable consideration' and must either substantively register his right *or* protect it by entering a notice on the register: LRA 2002, Sch 8 para 5(3).

[35] LRA 2002, Sch 8 para 5(1)(b).

[36] Law Com No 271 at 10.47.

had been unregistered, C1's only remedy would be to bring a claim for money against A, the fraudster, who may well be untraceable or bankrupt.[37] In this way, the registration system under the 1925 Act could be seen to operate as a form of *insurance*: it did not eliminate the risk that C might lose his registered right; it rather gave C financial protection against that risk.

On that view, the registration fee paid by C when registering his right operates as a form of premium: C buys financial protection against the risk that he might lose out to a pre-existing right of B. In this way, the 1925 Act could be seen not as a means to protect registered parties *at all costs*, but rather as an attempt to balance the interests of B and C. Indeed, as the registration system grew and it became a requirement for C to register his ownership of land, the system could be seen to operate as a form of *compulsory insurance*. The advantage of a compulsory insurance system, of course, is that premiums are kept low: everyone is forced to insure, even if the risk in his particular case is very small.[38]

Judging from the general rhetoric of the Law Commission Report that led to it, we would expect the Act to reject this insurance philosophy in favour of giving greater protection to C. For example, the Act might have *guaranteed* C's registered property right by eliminating rectification. Clearly, the Act did not attempt to do that. As noted above, the Law Commission stated that the Act was *not* intended to change the law established under the 1925 Act.[39] A judge interpreting the 2002 Act could take this statement as evidence that the grounds of rectification available under that Act are just as wide as under the 1925 Act, and interpret the terms 'mistake' and 'unjust' accordingly.[40]

3.2.5 Adverse possession

A further, specific ground on which the register can be changed is set out in Schedule 6, which allows a party to apply for registration if he has been in adverse possession of registered land for 10 years (see too **B:8.1.3(iii)**). We will examine those rules in more detail in **G1A:3**. They are a departure from the previous rules and, in general, protect a registered holder of a Freehold or Lease from losing his right without warning. However, it is worth noting that B can be registered as the new holder of C's right, even if C objects, where:

- B has a Freehold or Lease of land neighbouring C's land; *and*
- B has had physical control of part of C's land, adjoining B's land, for 10 years; *and*
- B has acted in the reasonable belief that that part of C's land is in fact part of the land covered by his own Freehold or Lease.[41]

---

[37] C2 may have a contractual claim against C1 as C1 will have has breached his promise to give C2 a right to exclusive control of the land for 10 years.

[38] In contrast, if insurance is not compulsory, it may be that C will opt for insurance only where there is a reasonable risk that B has a better right: in such a case, the premium will be high.

[39] Law Com No 254 at 8.1.

[40] Harpum, ch 9 in *Rationalizing Property, Equity and Trusts: Essays in Honour of Edward Burn* (ed Getzler, 2003) takes a very different view, arguing that it is important to see the LRA 2002 as a break from the previous law. That view is important as Harpum was the Law Commissioner overseeing the project that led to the 2002 Act. However, the wording of the Act itself does not force a court to adopt that view.

[41] LRA 2002, Sch 6 para 5. B cannot rely on this provision if the boundary between his land and C's has been specifically determined by means of a special procedure under s 60 of the Act; nor if C's Freehold or Lease was registered less than a year before B's application for rectification.

This rule again shows that providing certainty for C is not the only aim of the Act: the Act also recognises the value of allowing legal rights to reflect settled expectations, such as those established by the unchallenged position of a fence separating B's land from C's land.

SUMMARY of E5:3.2

Under the Act, the positive operation of the registration system provides important protection for C: C acquires his property right simply by being registered as the holder of that right. However, C's protection is not absolute. The **basic tension** and the need to balance C's needs with those of B are recognised by the possibility of rectification. As a result, values other than certainty for C come into play. First, *security for B* is promoted by giving B, a holder of a right, some protection against the risk of fraudulent or unjustified registration. Second, *settled expectations* can be protected: if B has had, for 10 years, physical control of land registered to his neighbour in the reasonable belief that the land in fact belongs to B, B can have his assumed right to exclusive control of that land confirmed through a change to the register. It is clear, then, that the Act, like the land law system as a whole, does not just aim for certainty for C; rather, it seeks to balance the needs of B and C.

Indeed, striking a balance between B and C is made easier by the possibility of giving an indemnity to B or C when either is caused loss by the granting or refusal of rectification. As a result, the registered land system has four ways of dealing with a dispute between B and C:

	Rectification in favour of B?	C retains his right?	Indemnity for B?	Indemnity for C?
Option 1	Yes	No	–	No
Option 2	Yes	No	–	Yes
Option 3	No	Yes	Yes	–
Option 4	No	Yes	No	–

We can compare these four options with those set out in A:2. The difference here is that any money received by B or C comes *not* from the other party but instead from the Land Registry. In this way, far from ignoring the **basic tension** by always protecting the registered C against the unregistered B, the registered land system can in fact offer more subtle solutions to the basic tension, by offering extra ways of resolving a dispute between B and C.

3.3 Overriding interests

3.3.1 Introduction

An overriding interest is a property right or persistent right of B that is immune from the lack of registration defence (see C2:6.2, E1:3.6 and E2:3.6). Such a right can bind C even if: (i) it has not been defensively registered; and (ii) C has acquired a property right for value.[42] Given their power to bind C even if unregistered, overriding interests are an inherently controversial part of any land registration system. The Law Commission expressed its attitude to overriding interests as follows:

---

[42] It should be remembered that an overriding interest will not *always* bind C. Whilst C cannot rely on the lack of registration defence, he may be able to rely on a different defence (eg, the overreaching defence): see *City of London Building Society v Flegg* [1988] AC 54 (**E2:Example 17b**).

It is the fact that overriding interests do not appear on the register, yet bind any person who acquires an interest in registered land, that makes them such an unsatisfactory feature of the system of registered conveyancing.[43]

It is no surprise that the Law Commission took this line: it is consistent with its view of the fundamental objective of the registration system (see **section 1** above). However, the purpose of such a system is not simply to provide security for C; it is rather to balance the interests of C with those of B. Overriding interests form a vital part of that balance. No registration system would go so far as to say that B, a party with a pre-existing but unregistered property right or persistent right, should *never* be able to assert that right against C. As a result, it is possible to take the opposite view to that of the Law Commission. It is the *very fact* that overriding interests give B the chance, in some circumstances, to assert his unregistered right against C that makes these interests a *crucial part* of the system of registered conveyancing.

The real question, therefore, is not whether there should be such a thing as an overriding interest. Rather, the question is *when* should B have such a right? It is important to note that, if C is bound by an overriding interest, *no* indemnity is payable to C. Even if a change to the register is made as a result of B's overriding interest, that change does *not* count as a rectification: it does not 'prejudicially affect' C's right as C was *already* bound by B's right, even before the change was made.[44] We saw when considering rectification—the second gap in C's protection—that, in many situations, C will at least receive some monetary compensation in return for being bound by B's unregistered right. However, this is not the case where C is bound by an overriding interest. Similarly, if C can use the lack of registration defence against a pre-existing property right or persistent right of B, no indemnity is payable to B.

Therefore, where their dispute concerns an overriding interest, the registered land system has fewer means to resolve the basic tension between B and C. Instead of the four possible resolutions set out in the **Summary of 3.2** above there are only two potential outcomes:

	Can C use the lack of registration defence?	Indemnity for B?	Indemnity for C?
Option 1: B's right is overriding	No	–	No
Option 2: B's right is not overriding	Yes	No	–

3.3.2 Rationale: the Law Commission's view

The Law Commission regarded the very *concept* of overriding interests as an 'unsatisfactory' part of a land registration system. Nonetheless, it conceded that these interests would have a *limited* role to play under the Act:

---

[43] Law Com No 271 at 8.6.
[44] Such a change to the register is therefore not a rectification: see LRA 2002, Sch 4 para 1.

> The Bill seeks to restrict such interests as far as possible. The guiding principle on which it proceeds is that interests should be overriding only where it is unreasonable to expect them to be protected in the register.[45]

This approach focuses on B's position: (i) the general rule is that, if C acquires a property right for value, B's unregistered right cannot bind C; and (ii) this rule is relaxed *only* where B cannot reasonably be expected to register his right. The idea is that the negative operation of registration (when the system responds to B's failure to register: see **C2:3.2**) is a form of punishment for B. Thus, if B cannot reasonably be expected to register his right, it would be unfair for him to suffer the punishment of being exposed to the lack of registration defence.

The first question to ask is whether the Law Commission's justification for overriding interests can account for the law *as it is*: (i) can it explain the list of overriding interests established by the Act; and (ii) can it explain why other rights do not count as overriding interests? In answering this question, we will concentrate on the situation where C acquires a right in relation to land that is already registered. In such a case, Schedule 3 of the Act sets out the list of overriding interests.[46]

3.3.3 Examples of overriding interests

(i) A property right or persistent right of a party in actual occupation

EXAMPLE 2

A has a Freehold. A and B enter a contract under which A is to transfer the Freehold to B. B, a land law expert, is well aware of the need to register the transfer. However, as a symbolic protest against what he sees as the failings of the Act, B fails to do so. B pays the purchase price and moves into the house. A, taking advantage of the fact that he retains his Freehold, transfers it to C.

B's failure to substantively register means that he has no property right (see **E1:2.3.4**). However, as A is under a contractual duty to transfer his Freehold to B, B does have a persistent right (see **E2:1.2.4(ii)**). And, as B is in actual occupation of the land when C commits to acquiring his right from A, B's persistent right counts, under paragraph 2 of Schedule 3 to the Act, as an overriding interest (see **E2:3.6.2**). This is the case even though it is clearly reasonable to expect B to register his right. As **Example 2** shows, the presence or absence of actual occupation is *irrelevant* to the question of whether B can be expected to register his right.

To explain why B's right is overriding in **Example 2** we need to look beyond the Law Commission's justification for overriding interests. The importance of actual occupation lies in the fact that *C can reasonably be expected to discover B's right* (**E2:3.6.3**). B's physical presence on the land can be said to be equivalent to B's protecting his right through defensive registration: it is simply another way to provide publicity and to allow C easily to discover B's right.

---

[45] Law Com 271, para 2.25. See also para 8.6: 'Our conclusion was that interests should only have overriding status where protection against buyers was needed, but where it was neither reasonable to expect nor sensible to require any entry on the register.'

[46] In the less common case of 'first registration' (where C registers a property right in relation to land and no Freehold or Lease of that land is recorded on the register), a different and slightly longer list of overriding interests applies under Sch 1.

(ii) Leases

EXAMPLE 3a

A has a Freehold. A, by means of a deed, gives B a five-year Lease. B does not defensively register the Lease. A transfers his Freehold to C. When C commits to acquiring his right, B is not in actual occupation of the land.

Again, it does not seem unreasonable to ask B to register his right. As a deed has been used, the transaction between A and B may well have involved lawyers: B should be made aware of the possibility of protecting his right by entering a notice on the register. Nonetheless, B's Lease counts, under paragraph 1 of Schedule 3 to the Act, as an overriding interest: if B can acquire a Lease without substantively registering it, that Lease is overriding (see **E1:3.6.1**).

   To explain why B's right is overriding in **Example 3a** we again need to look beyond the Law Commission's justification for overriding interests. First, there is the need to *protect B's property right* (see **E1:3.6.1**). The Act can be seen to adopt the general position applying throughout property law: if B has a property right, it is very difficult for C to have a defence to that right. C's protection against the risk of being bound by a property right comes *not* from the **defences question** but instead from the **content question** and the **acquisition question**. Second, it may be that, where B acquires a Lease by means of a deed, *C can reasonably be expected to discover B's right*: the paper trail left by a deed increases the chances of C discovering B's Lease.

EXAMPLE 3b

A has a Freehold. A orally gives B a three-year Lease of the land. B does not defensively register this Lease. A transfers his Freehold to C.

In such a case, B's Lease is an overriding interest. Although no deed has been used, B can acquire a Lease if his right meets the test set out by section 54(2) of the LPA 1925 (see **G1B:2.2.1(i)(a)**). So, even if B is not in actual occupation of the land when C commits to acquiring his right, C will be unable to use the lack of registration defence. Here it seems the Law Commission's rationale *does* apply: it would be unreasonable to expect B to register his Lease, given it was informally created. This may seem harsh to C: if B is not in actual occupation, it may be impossible for him to discover B's Lease. However, the requirements of section 54(2) do give C some protection. That section applies only if:

(i)   B's Lease is for three years or less; *and*
(ii) it is at the 'best rent reasonably obtainable without taking a fine';[47] *and*
(iii) B has an immediate right to physical control of A's land.

The rent condition is worth noting. It means that, even if C is bound by B's Lease, C will at least receive a reasonable rent in return.

---

[47] A 'fine' is a one-off payment made as a premium at the start of a Lease.

(iii) Easements

EXAMPLE 4

A has a Freehold. A transfers part of his land to B. The grant by A to B of an Easement over A's remaining land is implied into the transfer to B: B thus acquires an Easement over A's land (see G5:2.4). B is substantively registered as holding the Freehold he receives from A but does not apply to be substantively registered as holding an Easement over A's land. A then transfers his Freehold of the remaining land to C.

In such a case, B's Easement can be overriding. First, B can acquire an Easement without needing to substantively register his right: B can acquire an implied Easement without substantive registration of that right (see **E1:2.3.4(i)**). It could be that, in such a case, the Law Commission's rationale applies: if A has not expressly given B an Easement, it may not be reasonable to expect B to register. However, in **Example 4**, an implied Easement can arise only if it is reasonable for B to believe, when acquiring his right from A, that A also intended to exercise his power to give B an Easement. The very facts giving rise to an implied Easement will therefore often alert C to the risk that B has such a right. For example, if the land sold to B is entirely surrounded by A's remaining land, there will be an implied Easement giving B a right of way over A's land. It may therefore be that such an Easement can count as an overriding interest because *C can reasonably be expected to discover B's right*: when acquiring his land from A, C should realise that, even if he has no registered right, B may well have an Easement over A's land.

An Easement can only be overriding, under paragraph 3 of Schedule 3 to the Act, if one or more of the following three factors is present. B's Easement must:

(i)   be known to C when C acquires his right; *or*
(ii) be obvious to C on a reasonably careful inspection of A's land; *or*
(iii) have been used by B at some point in the year before C acquired his right.

Clearly, these factors are entirely unrelated to the question of whether it is reasonable to expect B to register his Easement. Instead, the first two factors support the notion that C can be bound by an unregistered right if he can reasonably be expected to discover it. The third factor is different: if B has used his Easement within the past year, C can be bound by it even if C could *not* reasonably be expected to discover that Easement. In such a case, it may be that B's Easement is overriding because of the need to acknowledge the *importance of the right to B*. The fact that B has recently been using the right may be taken to demonstrate that the right is of some significance to B in enabling him to get full use of his own land. It is worth noting that Easements can be of tremendous value to B: for example, a right of access over A's land may be essential in allowing B to get to and make use of his land.[48] This may well be a relevant factor to take into account in resolving the **basic tension** between B and C. Again, it shows that certainty for C is not the only value reflected in the Act. Indeed, the *importance of the right to B* seems to be the justification for allowing many of the diverse overriding interests set out in paragraphs 4–14 of Schedule 3 to the Act.[49]

---

[48] See eg *Crabb v Arun DC* [1976] Ch 179 (**E4:Example 5**): B's land had been 'sterilised' (*per* Lord Denning MR at 187 and 189; *per* Scarman LJ at 199) and rendered unusable by A's denial of a promised right of way.

[49] The rights set out in those paragraphs include, for example, local land charges and public rights. Under the

3.3.4 Rights that do not count as overriding interests

EXAMPLE 5

A has a Freehold of a house. A wants to convert his house into flats. A reaches an unwritten agreement with B that, if B does the necessary building work, A will give B a 99-year Lease of the ground floor flat. B completes his side of the bargain, but A does not grant B the promised Lease and instead transfers his Freehold to C. B is not in actual occupation of the flat when C commits to acquiring his right.

In such a case, as we saw in **E4:Example 11**, A is under a duty to grant B the agreed Lease.[50] That duty arises as soon as B completes the agreed building work. So, when C acquires his right, B has a pre-existing persistent right: an Equitable Lease (see **E4:6.1**).[51] However, as B is *not* in actual occupation, his Equitable Lease does *not* count as an overriding interest. This is the case even though, as B's right arose informally, it is not reasonable to expect B to register it.

Example 5 forms a clear contrast with **Example 3a**. In **Example 3a**, B's right was overriding even though B could easily have registered his right; in **Example 5** B's right is not overriding even though B could not reasonably be expected to register it. It therefore seems that the Law Commission's suggested rationale for overriding interests is, again, misleading. Instead, there are two possible justifications for the difference between **Example 5** and **Example 3a**. First, the *importance of property rights*. A Lease is overriding in its own right; an Equitable Lease is not. Similarly an Easement is almost always overriding; an Equitable Easement is not. This distinction reflects the basic stance of the property law system: it is easier for C to have a defence against a persistent right than against a property right. The lack of registration defence under the Act can be seen, in some respects, as a modification of the bona fide purchaser defence, and this defence, in general, applies against persistent rights not property rights (see **E2:3.6.5**). Second, the *chances of C discovering B's right* are usually increased if B's right if a property right rather than a persistent right.[52] For example, if the requirements of section 54(2) of the LPA 1925 do not apply, A will need to have executed a deed in order for B to acquire a Lease; in contrast, as **Example 5** shows, B may be able to acquire an Equitable Lease, even for a long period, without the need for any writing.

Local Land Charges Act 1975, there are various local registers that record local land charges—burdens imposed on land by public bodies using statutory powers. If a local land charge is not recorded on the appropriate register, then it will still bind C; however, C will be able to claim compensation from the public authority which failed to register the charge. The point is that, like public rights, these local land charges exist for the wider public benefit and hence are immune from any lack of registration defence.

[50] See *Yaxley v Gotts* [2000] Ch 162.

[51] On the orthodox view set out in **E4:6.2**, B also has a right capable of binding C: an 'equity by estoppel' covered by the LRA 2002, s 116(a).

[52] A Lease for three years or less, arising orally under s 54(2), provides a counterexample. In such a case, the Law Commission's justification that B's right is overriding because it would be unreasonable to expect registration can be applied.

SUMMARY of E5:3.3

The lack of registration defence is crucial to the Act's professed aim of providing certainty for C. However, like all defences, it is not a means to protect *all* third parties. First, it can only protect C if he acquires a property right for value. This immediately tells us that certainty for C is not the only aim of the Act: the Act does acknowledge, for example, that the **basic tension** between B and C should be resolved differently where C has acquired his right for free.

More significantly, the immunity of overriding interests to the lack of registration defence creates an important gap in the protection available to C. That immunity makes overriding interests a vital tool in allowing the registration system to balance the needs of B and C. The Law Commission's stated view is that B's right should only be overriding where it is unreasonable to expect B to ensure that his right is recorded on the register. This is a very narrow view and is not reflected in the provisions of the Act.

The Law Commission's rationale may explain, in part, some of the overriding interests allowed under the Act. For example, it is certainly unreasonable to expect B to register a short Lease acquired orally under section 54(2) of the LPA (see **Example 3b**). However, it may be equally unreasonable to expect B to register a persistent right arising through proprietary estoppel and such a right is *not* in itself, an overriding interest (see **Example 5**). Further, the Act allows a right to be overriding even where it is not unreasonable to expect B to register that right (see **Examples 2 and 3a**).

Overriding interests reflect a number of different values. A's right may be overriding because *C can reasonably be expected to discover B's right*. This explains why actual occupation can turn a pre-existing persistent right into an overriding interest (see **Example 2**). It may also explain why a Lease created by a deed (see **Example 3a**) and an implied Easement (see **Example 4**) may count as overriding interests. In these cases, the publicity provided by registration is unnecessary: C can discover B's right by other means. If a property right can be acquired without substantive registration it will, in almost all cases, count as an overriding interest (see **Examples 3a, 3b and 4**). The Act thus also recognises the general importance of *protecting property rights.*

3.4   Extra protection for B

The chief purpose of the Act is to protect C: (i) direct rights; (ii) rectification; and (iii) overriding interests are three gaps in C's protection that allow the registered land system to reflect other values. Surprisingly, there are also ways in which the Act has *increased the protection available to B.*

First, there are a number of situations where: (i) before the Act, it was unclear whether B's pre-existing right was capable of binding a third party acquiring a right from A; but (ii) as a result of the Act, it is clear that B's right *is* prima facie binding on such a third party. That is the case with regards to: (i) Rights of Pre-Emption (due to section 115 of the Act: see **E2:Example 2d**); and (ii) 'Equities by Estoppel' (due to section 116(a) of the Act: see **E4:6.4** although note the doubts expressed there about the effect of section 116(a)).

Second, where B has a pre-existing power to acquire a persistent right—a 'mere Equity'—section 116(b) of the Act, coupled with section 28, means that C cannot use the general 'bona fide purchaser' defence to show that B cannot assert his power against C.

Instead, C has to attempt to rely on the lack of registration defence, with its requirement that C must have acquired a property right in the registered land (see **E2:Example 19**).

SUMMARY of E5:3

One useful way of summarising the current effect of the Act is to ask when, in the **basic situation**, B may be able to assert a right against C despite having no pre-existing right noted on the register.

First, B may be able to assert a new, *direct right* against C. If C's conduct suffices to give B such a right, B's lack of registration is irrelevant. Second, B may be able to have the register *rectified*: changed to include an unregistered right of B that would not otherwise bind C. If such rectification is allowed, C may receive an indemnity: financial compensation for loss caused to C by the rectification. If rectification is not permitted, but B has suffered loss as a result of a 'mistake' in the register, B may receive an indemnity: financial compensation for loss caused to B by the fact of C's registration. Third, if C did not acquire his property right for value, he will not be able to use the lack of registration defence provided by the Act: an unregistered property right or persistent right of B will therefore bind C, unless C can rely on a different defence to that right. Fourth, even if C did acquire his registered right for value, he will not be able to use the lack of registration defence against an *overriding interest* of B.

As a result, it is clear that protecting C is not the only goal pursued by the Act. Even if B has no registered right, there are situations in which B still has the chance to assert a right against C. Indeed, it is worth noting that, as a result of sections 115 and 116, the protection available to C in some situations is even *reduced*. It is clear, then, that despite the rhetoric of the Law Commission's Report, the registered land system, like the land law system as a whole, attempts to resolve the **basic tension** by striking a balance between the needs of B and of C.

---

4 THE POSITION AFTER THE INTRODUCTION OF ELECTRONIC REGISTRATION

4.1 Introduction

The introduction of electronic conveyancing is an essential part of the reform of the registered land system. The promise of a simple, cheap, electronic means of acquiring rights in land was the basis on which the Law Commission's proposals found their way into Parliament's packed legislative timetable and resulted in the Act.

We noted in **section 1** that, in purely technical ways, the introduction of electronic conveyancing can affect the *process* by which rights are registered. However, the Law Commission aims to go further and, when electronic conveyancing is up and running, to introduce changes to the *legal rules* in order to give extra protection to C.

4.2 Compulsory electronic registration

The crucial section in assessing the impact of electronic conveyancing on the registration system is section 93 of the Act. It does not make any immediate changes; rather it authorises the Lord Chancellor to make new rules once satisfied that the electronic conveyancing system can work satisfactorily. These rules will impose a *new formality requirement to dealings with registered land.* The crucial point is that an electronic registration requirement may be applied to *contracts* to give B a property right or a persistent right (see **E2:2.3.3(ii)**).

The dramatic consequences of this change can be seen by going back to **Example 2.** Currently, B has an overriding interest: (i) B acquires a persistent right as a result of his contract with A; and (ii) B's actual occupation turns that persistent right into an overriding interest. In the future, if B fails to electronically register his *contract* with A, A will be under no contractual duty to B. So, unless B can rely on some other, non-contractual means of showing A is under a duty to transfer his Freehold to B (eg, proprietary estoppel), B will *not* acquire a persistent right. Therefore, *even if B is in actual occupation of the registered land,* C will be protected.[53]

4.3 Justifying compulsory electronic registration

As shown by its potential impact in a case such as **Example 2,** an electronic registration requirement can increase C's protection, by limiting the chances that B can acquire an overriding interest. As a result, the introduction of electronic conveyancing can be used to promote the main aim of the Act. However, the mere fact that registration can be carried out electronically does not, by itself, justify giving greater protection to C: the **basic tension** between B and C is unaltered by the fact that transactions in land can be carried out or recorded in a new way. And, when examining **E2:Example 13**, we saw the argument that, in a case such as **Example 2,** there is no need to insist on the registration of B's contract with A: B's actual occupation of the land performs the role of registration by giving C publicity of B's pre-existing right.

Nonetheless, one of the concerns in designing a registration system is to ensure that, where it would be unreasonable to expect B to register his right on the register, B does not suffer from his failure to do so. A new electronic process *can* then be relevant: if a cheap and simple means of entering his right on the register is available, there are more situations in which it is reasonable to expect B to register. As a result, electronic registration can lead to C having more protection against unregistered rights.

This analysis is made all the more important by the Law Commission's view as to the justification for overriding interests. As we saw in **3.3.2** above, its argument is that B's right should be overriding *only* where it is unreasonable to expect B to register. Therefore, the easier it becomes for B to register, the fewer overriding interests there should be. On this view, it is perfectly logical to make a link between electronic conveyancing and protecting C by limiting B's chances of establishing an overriding interest.

However, as we saw in **3.3.3**, the problem with the Law Commission's analysis is that it overlooks other good reasons for allowing B's right to be overriding. In particular, it ignores the equally forceful argument that B's right should be overriding where C should reasonably be able to discover it. Therefore, in **Example 2,** B's actual occupation is important as it gives C every chance of discovering B's claim to the land. And B's presence on the land has this effect whether the registration system is electronic or not. It seems then that the point made

---

[53] As demonstrated by *National Provincial Bank v Ainsworth* [1965] AC 1175 (see **B:11**), B's actual occupation merely prevents C relying on the lack of registration defence; if B has no pre-existing right that is prima facie binding on C, C has no need to rely on that defence. B's only hope in such a case is to show he has a new, direct right against C.

when considering **E2:Example 13** remains valid: rules made under section 93(2) may have an overly severe effect on B.

4.4 The likely scope of compulsory electronic registration

Whilst section 93(2) allows the Lord Chancellor to make rules requiring certain dealings with registered land to be recorded on the register, it does not state which particular transactions will be brought into this scheme of compulsory electronic registration. However, it is fairly easy to predict the scope of the new rules. First, if substantive registration is currently necessary for B to acquire a property right, rules are likely to be passed to require that such a right must be registered electronically (see **E1:2.3.4(i)**). So, if A, a registered owner, attempts to give B either a Freehold, a Lease for more than seven years,[54] an Easement or a Charge, B will not acquire that right unless and until he electronically registers it. As a result, all *contracts* to grant or transfer such a right will also have to be electronically registered to be valid. Second, there are plans to extend the scope of compulsory registration so that if A grants B a Lease of more than three years, that Lease must be registered.[55] The justification is that the introduction of electronic conveyancing will make it easier both for B to register such a right and for the Land Registry to administer a register including more of these shorter Leases.

Leases which can arise orally under section 54(2) of the LPA (see **G1B:2.2.1(i)(a)**) and as implied periodic Leases (see **G1B:2.2.1(ii)**) will presumably be unaffected by any rules passed under section 93(2). As they can currently take effect as property rights without the need for any writing (see **E1:2.3.3(i)**) it would be odd to impose the more stringent formality requirement of compulsory registration. Such Leases will therefore continue to arise without the need for registration, and also to be overriding interests. Similarly, it is likely that implied Easements will not need to be electronically registered in their own right and will also continue to be capable of being overriding interests. However, B can only acquire such an Easement if it is implied into a transaction by which B acquires a Freehold or Lease and this underlying transaction will, in general, have to be electronically registered.

As we have seen, as section 93(2) contemplates that *contracts* to give B a property right will need to be electronically registered, registration will for the first time have an impact on the acquisition of persistent rights. However, it is unlikely that a requirement of compulsory electronic registration will apply where B relies on a non-contractual means of acquiring a persistent right. For example, it is very likely that B will continue to be able to acquire a persistent right through proprietary estoppel without needing to electronically register either A's commitment or his right (see **E2:2.3.3(iv)**).

Indeed, such informal means of acquiring a persistent right will become all the more prominent after the enactment of rules under section 93(2).[56]

---

[54] Or one of the exceptional shorter Leases currently requiring registration under the LRA 2002 (see **G1B:2.2.1(i)(b)**).

[55] See Law Com No 271 at 3.17, 3.30, 4.20 and 6.11.

[56] As noted by eg Dixon in *Modern Studies in Property Law* vol 2 (ed Cooke, 2003) and [2003] *Conv* 136.

SUMMARY of E5:4

Section 93(2) of the Act is an important provision, both in practical and theoretical terms. Its effect is to allow rules to be passed imposing a new formality requirement of electronic registration, applying not only to situations where A attempts to give B a property right, but also where A attempts to *enter a contract* to give B such a right. This means B's failure to register will prevent B claiming that A is under a contractual duty to B. Therefore, if B is unable to rely on a different means of acquiring a persistent right, he will have no pre-existing right to assert against C.

The theoretical importance of section 93(2) lies in its linking of the fact of registration to the existence of B's right. However, rules passed under the section will simply impose new formality requirements and such requirements are never comprehensive (see **C3:3**). For example, it is likely that, if the conditions of section 54(2) of the LPA 1925 are met, B will still be able to acquire a Lease without electronic registration. Moreover, as formality requirements regulate an exercise by A of his power to give B a right, rights arising though other means will continue to arise informally. As a result, persistent rights arising by proprietary estoppel will escape the system of compulsory electronic registration. Therefore, if B has such a right, and is in actual occupation of the registered land when C electronically registers his right, B's unregistered right will be capable of binding C. This demonstrates that, even in a world of electronic registration, the register will never be 'complete and accurate': C will always have to make further inquiries, chiefly by inspecting the land itself.

Even in the brave new world of electronic registration, gaps in the protection given to C will therefore remain. B will still be able, in certain circumstances: (i) to assert a direct right against C; (ii) to have the register rectified; and (iii) to have an overriding interest. After all, the major change brought about by the introduction of electronic registration—the application of a registration requirement to contracts to grant a property right—is not a novelty: section 2(1) of the Law of Property (Miscellaneous Provisions) Act 1989 already imposes a particular formality requirement to such contracts (see **E2:2.3.3**). So, once again, the registration system will be a reflection of, rather than a complete break from, the general principles of the land law system.

5   CONCLUSION: EVALUATING THE ACT

5.1   The practical impact

The basic aim of the Act is to simplify conveyancing; its chief tool for achieving this is the introduction of an electronic system. This means that the Act can only be fully evaluated by an empirical study, carried out once electronic conveyancing is fully operational, assessing the efficiency of the system.[57] However, it is overwhelmingly likely that the Act will not succeed in silencing those who complain about the time and cost involved in buying a house. The chief cause of annoyance to purchasers does *not* come from the risk of being bound by a pre-existing right of B; rather, it is the *process* of buying a house that causes problems.

First, there is the problem that, before committing to a contract, a buyer needs to pay for

---

[57] An full empirical assessment would involve the monitoring of middle-class conversations: see **section 1** above.

a survey to check the condition of the vendor's land: that is the case even if another potential buyer has already paid for such a survey. The survey may be expensive and may in fact deter the buyer from proceeding with the sale. One solution to this would be to place responsibility on the vendor to carry out a survey and to include it in a 'Home Information Pack'; however, that idea has now been rejected.[58] Second, there is the practice of offers to buy being accepted 'subject to contract'. This means that, whilst the potential buyer may feel reasonably secure once his offered price has been accepted, no binding agreement has been concluded and the vendor is free to impose further conditions or to pull out of the sale entirely. Equally, in a falling market, a vendor may face the risk that the potential buyer may demand a discount at the last moment.[59] In fact, the current system encourages such brinksmanship: for example, if the buyer knows that his vendor is part of a 'chain' (ie, is already committed to his own purchase), then it may be difficult for the vendor to refuse a last-minute reduction in price. Unless some mechanism is introduced to deal with this uncertain period between acceptance of an offer and conclusion of a binding contract (such as, perhaps, a deposit system),[60] buying a house in England and Wales[61] will continue, for those who can afford it, to be a fraught process.

5.2   The legal impact

5.2.1 The values of the Act

As an ancillary means towards the goal of simplifying conveyancing, the Act changes the legal rules that balance the claims of B and C. The Act thus tackles the **basic tension** in land law and alters the answers to some of the **basic questions** used to resolve that tension. These changes can be evaluated immediately and by a conceptual rather than an empirical analysis.

The starting point for the Act is the need to protect C, a party acquiring a registered right for value, from any property rights and persistent right that are not recorded on the register. The main aim of the Act is thus to provide *protection for C*. However, that protection is not absolute: the Act acknowledges other values. First, it may be possible for B to assert a direct right against C: the Act gives C no protection against such rights. Second, B may be able to assert an unregistered pre-existing right against C by having the register rectified. The possibility of rectification recognises the value of *security for B*: B's pre-existing right can be protected, for example against a fraudulent transfer, even if C himself is innocent. Where the register is changed due to B's adverse possession of land that is registered in C's name,

---

[58] It has been compulsory, since December 2007, for a vendor of a home in England or Wales to provide a 'Home Information Pack'. However, whilst a 'Home Condition Report' can be included as an optional document, a vendor has no duty to provide a survey of his land: see www.homeinformationpacks.gov.uk.

[59] A tactic as unattractive as its name ('gazundering'), it is apparently recommended by certain websites (see eg Brignall, 'Is there a gazunderer in you?', *The Guardian*, 12 April 2008).

[60] In 1987 the Conveyancing Standing Committee issued a Practice Direction on 'Pre-Contract Deposits'. As discussed in [1988] *Conv* at 80, the plan was that, on acceptance of an offer to purchase, both vendor and purchaser should pay a deposit equal to half of one per cent of the purchase price to a neutral third party. If the parties proceeded to reach a binding contract within four weeks, the deposits would be repaid; if one party withdrew for a reason not permitted by the deposit agreement, the other party would receive both deposits.

[61] The system is different in Scotland, as in most other European jurisdictions. In Scotland, sales are often conducted through a sealed-bid system: once a bid is accepted, then both vendor and purchaser are bound: see eg the Scottish Executive's Guide to House Purchase, available from its website.

but which B reasonably and honestly believes he owns, the need to protect *B's settled expec-tations* is upheld. If rectification occurs, C may well be able to receive an indemnity payment, compensating him for the loss of his registered right. The possibility of an indemnity is a very important aspect of the registered system, as it allows certainty for C to be promoted not by eliminating all other claims, but rather by recognising some claims and, where they arise, giving C compensation. And, if rectification is refused, but B suffers loss by reason of a mistake in the register, B may also be able to obtain an indemnity.

Third, if B's pre-existing property right or persistent right is unregistered, it may still bind C if it counts as an overriding interest. For example, B's persistent right can be over-riding if B is in actual occupation of the registered land when C commits to acquiring his right. C's security is therefore undermined, and the value of protecting B's right recognised, but only to the extent that *C can reasonably be expected to discover B's right.* Where B, despite his failure to register, has nonetheless acquired a property right, such as a non-exceptional Lease of seven years or less or an implied Easement, B's right will be overriding whether B was in actual occupation or not. In some circumstances, it may be that C ought to have discovered such a right; in other cases, it is the need to *protect B's property right* that leads to B's right being overriding. Similarly, the assorted rights set out in paragraphs 4–14 of Schedule 3 are given overriding status, independently of actual occupation, simply because of the need to *protect an important right of B.*

5.2.2 Missed possibilities?

It is clear that there is a gap between the rhetoric of the Law Commission and the reality of the Act. The Commission saw the promotion of certainty for C as the controlling aim of the registered land system; but that security is undermined in order to recognise other values. It may then be thought that the Law Commission's rhetoric is irrelevant; the provisions of the Act are all that matter. However, the Commission's assumptions about the aims of a regis-tration system necessarily shaped the proposals it made. If the inescapable need to balance the claims of B and C had been explicitly recognised, a different Act might have been pro-duced.

For example, we have seen that the possibility of an indemnity may provide a useful way to balance the needs of B. However, under the Act, an indemnity can be paid to C only if rectification is made against him; and to B only if there is a mistake in the register and his claim for rectification is denied. The Law Commission did not fully explore using indemnity payments in relation to overriding interests. Hence the Act maintains the position that, if C is bound by an unregistered but overriding right, he *cannot* claim an indemnity. Where C ought reasonably to have discovered B's overriding right (as, for example, when B is in actual occupation), it makes sense that no indemnity is payable. However, C may be bound by an overriding right that he could *not* reasonably have discovered: as, for example, when C is bound by an oral Lease (see **Example 3b**) or where C is bound by an implied Easement that was not reasonably discoverable by C but was used by B in the previous year (see eg **Example 4**). In those cases, there may be a good argument for C to receive an indemnity. Similarly, there may be cases where B cannot reasonably have been expected to register his right, yet that right is not overriding (see **Example 5**). Here too there is perhaps a case that B should receive an indemnity if C can rely on the lack of registration defence.

On this view, there would be four, rather that two options, available when considering C's claim to rely on the lack of registration defence:

Possible reformed system:

	Can C use the lack of registration defence?	Indemnity for B?	Indemnity for C?	Possible Example
Option 1: B's right is overriding	No	–	No	Example 2
Option 2: B's right is overriding	No	–	Yes	Example 3b
Option 3: B's right is not overriding	Yes	Yes	–	Example 5
Option 3: B's right is not overriding	Yes	No	–	Example 2 if B is not in actual occupation

Of course, arguments can be made against such a system. It would be more expensive to operate—both to the Land Registry (which would have to make more indemnity payments)[62] and to parties and the courts (there will be costs in determining which of the four categories applies in a given case). However, for the purposes of this analysis, the crucial point is that the rhetoric of the Law Commission, in refusing explicitly to acknowledge the undeniable fact that a registration system must balance the needs of B and C, seems to have prevented a proper *consideration* of the argument.

5.2.3 The interpretation and effect of the Act

Finally, when examining the provisions of the Act, it must be remembered that these provisions will be interpreted and applied by the courts: the approach they adopt in doing so will have a crucial impact on the operation of the Act. Here again, the Law Commission's rhetoric is relevant: it argues for the Act to be interpreted so as to favour the needs of C.[63] Yet it seems unlikely that the courts will take such a one-sided approach: they are far more likely to appreciate that the registration system is a tool attempting to resolve the **basic tension** and to balance the needs of B and C.[64] Moreover, even if the provisions of the Act itself are interpreted in C's favour, it will still be possible for courts to develop ways around those provisions. For example, we have seen that, even when electronic registration is up

---

[62] However, the Land Registry currently operates with a healthy annual surplus: the operating surplus for the financial year 2005–6 was £30.75m and indemnity payments totalled £14.12m; for 2006–7 the surplus was £96.3m and £5.25m was paid out by way of indemnity: Land Registry, *Annual Report and Accounts 2005–6* at 83 and *Annual Report and Accounts 2006–7* at 38 and 64. The Law Commission's view that extending indemnity payments to overriding interests would cause financial problems is dubious: see Law Com No 254 at 4.19.

[63] See eg Harpum, ch 9 in *Rationalizing Property, Equity and Trusts: Essays in Honour of Edward Burn* (ed Getzler, 2003), arguing that the rectification provisions of the Act should be interpreted narrowly in order to serve the purpose of the Act in providing certainty for C.

[64] Certainly, when interpreting the Land Registration Act 1925, the courts often went to surprising lengths to protect an unregistered B: see eg Graham J's reasoning in *Peffer v Rigg* [1977] 1 WLR 285; *Celsteel v Alton House Holdings Ltd* [1985] 1 WLR 204.

and running, it is very likely that B's failure to register will not prevent him from acquiring a persistent right through proprietary estoppel. A court could therefore protect an unregistered party, in actual occupation at the time C commits to acquiring his right, by expanding the scope of proprietary estoppel. Similarly, the courts could also provide protection for an unregistered B, whether in actual occupation or not, by extending the means by which B can acquire a direct right against C.

CHAPTER E6
LICENCES

LICENCES

1 DEFINITION

A licence is simply a permission. In the context of the property law system, it refers to a permission to make a particular use of a thing belonging to another.

EXAMPLE 1a

A is an owner of a bike. A allows B to borrow that bike for an afternoon.

EXAMPLE 1b

A is a Freehold owner of land. A invites B to dinner at A's house.

In each case, B is under a prima facie duty not to interfere with A's right to exclusive control of a particular thing. However, A has given B permission to act in a way that would otherwise be a breach of B's duty to A. We might say that B therefore has a right to make a particular use of A's thing. But we may mean a number of different things when we say that B has a 'right' (see D2:1.1.3). In particular, in **Examples 1a and 1b**, A is *not* under a duty to B to allow B to use A's thing. So, in **Example 1b**, A does not commit a wrong if he changes his mind and revokes B's invitation to dinner. In Hohfeld's terms, B does not have a claim right against A.[1] Instead, B has a *liberty* to make a particular use of A's thing: at least until A revokes his permission, B is *not under a duty to A not to make a particular use of A's thing.*[2]

EXAMPLE 2

A and B are Freehold owners of neighbouring land. A grants B an Easement allowing B to walk across a path on A's land.

In **Example 2**, A's grant of the Easement gives B a liberty: it means that B is no longer under a duty to A not to walk on A's path. However, in such a case, B is *not* described as having a licence. B's liberty arises as part of a property right held by B (an Easement): that property right means that A, along with the rest of the world, is under a prima facie duty not to interfere with B's right to walk across A's path. Therefore, B has more than a simple liberty against A: he has a claim right that is prima facie binding on the rest of the world.

Similarly, if B has a persistent right in relation to A's land, such as a right under a Trust, A

---

[1] See eg *per* Vaughan CJ in *Thomas v Sorrell* (1667) Vaugh 330 at 351: 'A dispensation or licence properly passeth no interest, nor alters or transfers property in any thing, but only makes an action lawful which, without it, had been unlawful. As a licence to go beyond the seas, to hunt in a man's park, to come into his house, are only actions, which without licence, had been unlawful.'

[2] For an examination of the licence by Hohfeld, see (1917) *Yale Law Journal* 66 esp at 94.

may well be under a duty to B to allow B to make a particular use of A's land. Again, in such a case, B is not described as having a licence: B's liberty to use A's land instead arises as part of B's persistent right. This means that B has more than a simple liberty: (i) he has a claim right against A; and (ii) he also has a prima facie power to assert that right against C, a party who later acquires a right from A (see **E2:Example 1a**).

This means that, in the context of the property law system, B is described as having a licence if:

- B has a liberty to make a particular use of A's thing; *and*
- B's liberty does not arise as part of a property right or persistent right held by B.

On this definition, B can have a licence to use A's bike (as in **Example 1a**) as well as a licence to use A's land (as in **Example 1b**). However, in this chapter, we will focus on the case where B's licence relates to land: it is in this context that the status of B's licence has proved controversial. We will look at a number of different types of licence. In each case, we need to look at:

- B's rights against A; and
- B's rights against X: a stranger who interferes with B's use of A's land; and
- B's rights against C: a third party who acquires a right in relation to A's land from A and then interferes with B's use of the land.

2 THE BARE LICENCE

2.1 Definition

A bare licence is the simplest form of licence. It arises in a case, such as **Example 1b**, where B has a licence and A has *no* duty to B not to revoke that licence.

2.2 B's rights against A

If A invites B over for dinner, A can choose to revoke the licence at any time. If: (i) A revokes the licence before B arrives; and (ii) B insists on coming in any case; then (iii) B breaches his duty not to interfere with A's exclusive control of the land and so commits the wrong of trespass. If B is already on the land when A revokes the licence, B will have a 'packing up period':[3] a reasonable period in which to leave A's land. As soon as that period ends, B's liberty to be on A's land ceases and B, if he remains on A's land, is a trespasser. And, whenever B is a trespasser on A's land, A has a liberty to use reasonable force, if necessary, to remove B from A's land. Therefore, if B refuses to leave and A uses such force, A does not commit a wrong against B.

---

[3] See eg *Winter Garden Theatres Ltd v Millennium Productions Ltd* [1948] AC 173 *per* Viscount Simon at 188–9 and *per* Lord Macdermott at 206. See Hill [2001] *CLJ* 89 for further discussion.

2.3 B's rights against X

If B has a licence, this simply means that B is not under a duty to A not to make a particular use of A's land. B's bare licence, by itself, certainly does not impose any duty on strangers such as X.

EXAMPLE 3

A has a Freehold and goes away for a week. A gives B permission, if B wishes, to occupy the land as a 'house-sitter' for A. B goes into occupation of the land.

If B takes physical control of A's land, B independently acquires a property right in A's land (see E1:2.1.1). This means that, in **Example 3**, the rest of the world is under a prima facie duty not to interfere with B's right to exclusive control of that land. So if X, a stranger, comes onto the land, he commits a wrong against B.[4] It is important to note that X's duty does *not* arise as a result of B's licence; instead, it arises as a result of the property right B acquires by taking physical control of A's land. B acquires such a property right even if he has no permission from A to occupy the land: this makes clear that B's property right does not depend on his licence from A.

2.4 B's rights against C

2.4.1 Direct right

There are many different ways in which B can acquire a direct right against C (see E3:2). However, those means all focus on the conduct of C. If B simply has a bare licence there is no incentive for C, when acquiring a right from A, to act in such a way as to give B a direct right.

2.4.2 Pre-existing right

First, B cannot argue that his bare licence counts as a property right: that liberty is not on the current list of recognised property rights in land. Second, B does not have a persistent right: A is not under a duty to B in relation to a specific right.[5]

3 THE CONTRACTUAL LICENCE

3.1 Definition

EXAMPLE 4

A has a Freehold. A makes a contractual promise to allow B to share occupation of A's land with A and A's family for six months, in return for a weekly payment of £50 from B.

---

[4] See eg *National Provincial Bank v Ainsworth* [1965] AC 1175 at 1232 *per* Lord Upjohn: 'in truth and in fact the wife [B] at all material times was and is in exclusive occupation of the home. Until her husband [A] returns she has the dominion over the house and she could clearly bring proceedings against trespassers.'

[5] See eg *per* Lord Wilberforce in *National Provincial Bank v Ainsworth* [1965] AC 1175 at 1248: B's right lacks the 'degree of permanence and stability' required of a persistent right.

If the contract imposes a duty on A to give B a right to exclusive control of the land, or part of the land, for a limited period, B acquires a property right: a Lease (see E1:1.1). That is the case even if the agreement between A and B is described by the parties as a 'licence agreement' (see G1B:1.5.1). However, in **Example 4**, the contract clearly does *not* give B that right: B must instead share occupation of A's land. B therefore has a liberty to make a particular use of A's land; and that liberty does not arise as part of a property right or persistent right. B therefore has a licence.

3.2 B's rights against A

In **Example 4**, in contrast to **Example 3**, B has more than a simple liberty to use A's land. In addition, A is under a *contractual duty* to B not to revoke B's licence. This means that, under the contract, B does have a claim right against A: so if A revokes B's licence before the end of the six-month period, this *may* be a breach of A's contractual promise to B. Everything turns on the precise terms of the contract between A and B. For example, the parties may have expressly agreed that A can revoke the licence if B fails to pay his weekly £50. Certain terms can also be implied into A and B's agreement: for example, even if A does not make this clear, A will clearly have an implied power to revoke the licence if B is discovered to be stealing from A.[6]

In **Example 4**, if A revokes B's licence after two months simply because he takes a dislike to B, it is very likely that A's revocation of B's licence is a breach of contract. Two questions then arise. First, does A's revocation, after a 'packing up period', remove B's liberty to use A's land and hence turn B into a trespasser? If so, A can then, if necessary, use reasonable force to remove B from the land even though, under the terms of the contract, A is still under a duty to B not to revoke the licence. The answer is that, even though A has revoked the licence, B *cannot* be a trespasser if A is still under a contractual duty to B not to revoke the licence. So, if: (i) A asks B to leave after two months; but (ii) A is under a contractual duty to allow B to remain for a further four months; then (iii) if B refuses to leave, A is *not* permitted to use reasonable force to remove B.[7] B's liberty to use A's land is regulated by the terms of his contract with A and can survive any action by A that is a breach of that contract.

Second, what remedy will a court give to respond to A's breach of contract? For example, if A has removed B from the land, or threatens to do so, will a court specifically protect B's right against A by means of an order forcing A to continue to allow B to use the land? This is of course part of the **remedies question**: where land is concerned, the courts will, in general, specifically protect B's right (see eg A:3.1.2). That general position also applies here: even if B has not yet begun to use A's land, the default position is that a court will specifically protect B's contractual licence.[8]

However, this specific protection is not automatic. In a case such as **Example 4**, it is in fact quite likely that, if A succeeded in removing B from the land, a court would not order A to allow B back into occupation. After all, it would be odd for the court to force two parties

---

[6] For an example of an implied contractual power to revoke a contractual licence, arising in a commercial context, see *Winter Garden Theatres Ltd v Millennium Productions Ltd* [1948] AC 173.

[7] See *Hurst v Picture Theatres* [1915] 1 KB 1, reversing the position adopted in *Wood v Leadbitter* (1845) 13 M & W 838.

[8] See eg *Verall v Great Yarmouth BC* [1981] 1 QB 202.

who have fallen out to share occupation: 'the court cannot specifically enforce an agreement for two people to live peaceably under the same roof'.[9] In such a case, B will have to settle for receiving money from A based on the value of B's right under the licence and compensating B for any relevant loss he has suffered as a result of A's breach.

The two questions discussed here need to be treated separately. So, in **Example 4**, the fact that a court will not specifically protect B's contractual licence does *not* mean that, if A revokes that licence in breach of contract, B will become a trespasser if he remains on A's land.[10] It also does not mean that a court will necessarily find in A's favour, if A revokes B's licence and then applies to court for an order forcing B to leave. It is open for a judge to decline to give an order assisting A to breach his contractual promise to B, even if, were B applying to court, that judge would not order A specifically to perform that contractual promise.[11]

3.3   B's rights against X

The difference between a bare licence and a contractual licence is simply that A is under a contractual duty to B not to use his power to revoke B's licence. It is therefore very difficult to see why a contractual licence, by itself, should give B any right against X.

However, when considering **E1:Example 2**, we saw that the majority of the Court of Appeal, in *Manchester Airport plc v Dutton*,[12] allowed B (a party with only a contractual licence) to assert a right against X. The principal reason[13] given was that: (i) *if* B had gone onto A's land, it would have been able to assert a right against X; and (ii) given B had a contractual right to go onto the land, it would be odd if B were unable to bring a claim against X simply because B had not *yet* gone onto the land.[14] Yet this devalues the importance of B's entry onto the land: it overlooks the crucial fact that if B enters the land and takes physical control of it, B independently acquires a property right that he can assert against X.[15] If B has not yet gone onto the land, he has no such right and so X commits no wrong *against* B by trespassing on the land. It seems then that the powerful dissent of

---

[9] *Per* Goddard LJ in *Thompson v Park* [1944] KB 408, considering a case where A had made a contractual promise to share occupation of a school with B, another teacher, and the relationship between the two had broken down. The approach of the Court of Appeal in *Thompson* was doubted by Lord Denning MR in *Verall v Great Yarmouth BC* [1981] 1 QB 202 at 216 but it seems correct and was approved by Megarry V-C in *Hounslow LBC v Twickenham GD Ltd* [1971] Ch 233 at 250.

[10] This point is noted by Megarry V-C in *Hounslow LBC v Twickenham GD Ltd* [1971] 1 Ch 233 at 254–5: 'All that I need say, in order to avoid possible misunderstanding, is that in light of the *Winter Garden* case I find it difficult to see how a contractual licensee can be treated as a trespasser so long as his contract entitles him to be on the land; and this is so whether or not his contract is specifically enforceable.'

[11] See *Hounslow LBC v Twickenham GD Ltd* [1971] 1 Ch 233. The council [A] applied for an order that B, contractors working on A's land, had to leave that land. B argued that A was under a contractual duty to allow B to remain. Megarry V-C refused A's application and noted at 251: 'On the view that I take, in the present case it does not matter whether the contract is or is not specifically enforceable: the court will not assist [A] in a breach of contract.'

[12] [2000] QB 133.

[13] There is also a suggestion that the summary possession procedure has its own special rules and can be used by B even if he does not have a right that he can assert against X: see *per* Kennedy LJ at 151. That reasoning is flawed however as any procedure is simply a means for B to assert a right: see *per* Chadwick LJ (dissenting) at 141.

[14] See eg *per* Laws LJ at 149–50.

[15] In this way, the majority in *Dutton* made the same error present in the *obiter dictum* of the Court of Appeal in *Iran v Bakarat Galleries Ltd* [2007] EWCA Civ 1374 at [30] (see **D1:Example 32**).

Chadwick LJ in *Dutton* is to be preferred:[16] B's contractual licence should *not* impose a prima facie duty on X to B (see **E1:1.3.2**).

3.4   B's rights against C

3.4.1 Direct rights

If A is under a contractual duty to B in relation to A's power to revoke B's licence, B's chances of acquiring a direct right against C are increased. In particular, three means of acquiring such a right may be relevant.

(i) The wrong of procuring a breach by A of A's contract with B

> **EXAMPLE 5**
>
> A has a Freehold. A makes a contractual promise to B to allow B to occupy A's land for six months. That promise does not give B a right to exclusive control of the land. Three months later, C plans to buy A's Freehold. C knows about A's contract with B.

A's entry into a contract with B imposes a duty on the rest of the world not to knowingly procure a breach by A of A's duty (see **E3:2.3.4**).[17] However, when examining an identical example (**E3:Example 8**), we saw that C does not commit a wrong against B if he simply acquires a right from A with knowledge that, if C prevents B using the land, A will then be in breach of his contractual duty to B.[18] So if, in **Example 5**, A were to sell his Freehold to C, who then refused to allow B to continue using the land, C would *not* commit the wrong of procuring a breach of contract, even if he acquired the land with knowledge of B's contractual licence.

(ii) The Contract (Rights of Third Parties) Act 1999

> **EXAMPLE 6**
>
> A has a Freehold. In return for a one-off payment from B, A makes a contractual promise to allow B, over the next five years, to fix posters on the wall of a building on A's land. Two years later, A decides to sell his land to C.

A knows that if he sells the land to C, and C then stops B from putting his posters up, A will be in breach of his contractual duty to B. The prospect of having to pay money to B as a result of such a breach gives A an incentive, when selling the land to C, to make C promise to honour B's licence. If C makes such a promise to A when acquiring A's Freehold, B can acquire a direct right against C under the Contract (Rights of Third Parties) Act 1999 (see **E3:2.3.1**). It is worth repeating that, if C makes his promise to A as part of the purchase of A's Freehold, C's promise will only impose a contractual duty if it satisfies the formality rule imposed by section 2 of the Law of Property (Miscellaneous Provisions) Act 1989 (see

---

[16] See esp [2000] QB 133 at 146–7. See too Swadling (2000) 116 *LQR* 358.

[17] See eg *Esso Petroleum Co Ltd v Kingswood Motors Ltd* [1974] QB 142.

[18] In *Binions v Evans* [1973] Ch 359 at 371, Megaw LJ suggested in passing that C *could* commit the wrong in such a case; however, that view was only tentatively expressed. For further consideration of the issue, see R Smith (1977) 41 *Conv* 318.

E2:2.3.3). If C's promise does *not* satisfy that rule, for example because it is made orally, B may, however, be able to acquire a direct right against C by turning to the 'receipt after a promise' principle.

(iii) The 'receipt after a promise' principle

If: (i) C makes a promise to A to respect B's licence; and (ii) as a result of making that promise, C acquires an advantage in relation to the acquisition of his A's Freehold or Lease; then (iii) B can acquire a direct right against C under the 'receipt after a promise' principle (see E3:2.3.2). For example, in *Binions v Evans*,[19] Lord Denning MR took the view that B's initial agreement with A gave B only a contractual licence. Nonetheless, his Lordship also found that C had acquired A's land on the basis that C would honour B's licence; as a result it would be 'utterly inequitable for [C] to turn [B] out contrary to the stipulation subject to which [C] took the premises'.[20] The 'receipt after a promise' principle is independent of the 1999 Act and so can apply even if C's promise to A is not contractually binding. The principle is similar to the Act in that it can only give B a direct right if C makes a promise to give B a right: C must have 'undertaken a new obligation, not otherwise existing'.[21] If C simply acquires his right 'subject to' any pre-existing right B *may* have in the land, it may be impossible for B to show that C has promised to come under a duty to B: the 'subject to' term may instead simply alert C to the risk that he may be bound, willy-nilly, by a pre-existing property right or persistent right of B.[22] If so, *neither* the 1999 Act nor the 'receipt after a promise' principle can operate to give B a new, direct right against C (see **D3:2.3.1** and **D3:2.3.2**).[23]

3.4.2 Pre-existing rights

B cannot argue that his contractual licence counts as a property right: such a right is not on the current list of recognised property rights in land. Further, as A is not under a duty to B in relation to a specific claim right or power held by A, B does not have a persistent right (see **E1:1.3.1(ii)**). Certainly, A is not under a duty to B in relation to the whole of A's Freehold; A simply has to allow B to make a particular use of A's land.

In any of **Examples 4–6**, B could try to argue instead that A is under a duty to B in relation to A's *power* to revoke B's licence: ie in relation to A's power to remove B's liberty to use A's land. B could argue that: (i) as A has a contractual duty to B not to use his power to revoke B's licence; then (ii) B has a persistent right against A's power to revoke that liberty. However, such an argument gives B no protection if A then transfers his Freehold to C. When C acquires A's Freehold, C can assert that property right against B: B, like the rest of the world, is under a prima facie duty not to interfere with C's right to exclusive control of the land. B was not under such a duty to A as A had given B a liberty to make a particular use of the land. However, C has given B no such liberty. B can try to claim that he has a persistent right against A's power to revoke B's liberty; *but that makes no difference to C. C*

---

[19] [1972] Ch 359.

[20] *Ibid* at 368.

[21] *Per* Sir Christopher Slade LJ in *Lloyd v Dugdale* [2002] 2 P & CR 13 at [52]. See also Bright [2000] *Conv* 398, 406–7 and 413–4.

[22] Just as, if C buys a car from A 'subject to any defects in the engine', neither A nor C is promising there will be such defects. Instead, A is simply alerting C to the risk that such defects may exist.

[23] See esp *per* Fox LJ in *Ashburn Anstalt v Arnold* [1989] Ch 1 at 25–6.

does *not* need a power to revoke a liberty: C has not given B any such liberty to use the land. As a result, C can simply assert his right to exclusive control of the land against B.

Despite this, a number of arguments have been made in favour of allowing at least some contractual licences to count as persistent rights. However, it is important to note that section 4(1) of the Law of Property Act 1925 ('the LPA 1925') lays down a clear rule that the list of persistent rights relating to land is fixed (see **E2:1.4**). This means that any addition to the list can come only from Parliament; it is not open to the judges to extend the list.

(i) The specific protection argument

In *Errington v Errington & Woods*,[24] Denning LJ put forward a deceptively simple argument, building on the fact that a court will, in general, specifically protect B's contractual licence if A revokes it in breach of contract (see **3.2** above). The argument is that: (i) A can be prevented from revoking the licence; so (ii) B has a right to use the land for the duration of the licence; so (iii) B has a right relating to land that is capable of binding C, a later owner of that land.[25]

Denning LJ's argument, whilst it has found some academic and judicial support,[26] is based on a *non sequitur*. The availability of a particular remedy as a means of enforcing A's contractual duty to B does not give B a *general* right to use the land. Rather, such a remedy protects B's right *against A*, arising as a result of A's contractual promise to B. As Lord Wilberforce pointed out in a later case, a personal right against A is not capable of binding third parties simply because a court will specifically protect it.[27] The argument made by Denning LJ thus confuses two sets of very different cases: (i) where A is under a contractual duty to exercise his power to give B a property right in land, and so B acquires an immediate persistent right against A's power to do so (see **E2:1.3.1(i)**); and (ii) where A is under a contractual duty not to revoke B's licence and so B has a contractual right *against A* (see **E2:1.3.1(ii)**).

(ii) The 'Constructive Trust' argument

Lord Denning MR recognised, in *Binions v Evans*,[28] that B may acquire a new, direct right against C if C makes a promise to A that he will respect B's licence. This can be justified as an application of the 'receipt after a promise' principle: B acquires a new direct right against C (see **3.4.1(iii)**). In *Binions*, B's right was said to arise under a 'Constructive Trust'.[29] However, as we saw in **E3:2.3.2**, that analysis is incorrect. If C has simply promised to respect B's licence, C is not under the core Trust duty: C does not have to use a specific right for B's benefit. And, given that A's initial promise to B (for which B gives something in return) gives B only a personal right against A, there is no reason why C's promise to A to respect that licence (for which B gives nothing in return) should give B a persistent right.

In *DHN Food Distributors Ltd v London Borough of Tower Hamlets*,[30] Lord Denning went

---

[24] [1952] 1 KB 290.

[25] *Ibid* at 296–8.

[26] See eg Watt [2003] *Conv* 61 and *per* Browne-Wilkinson V-C in *Bristol Airport v Powdrill* [1990] Ch 744 at 759.

[27] See Lord Wilberforce in *NPB v Ainsworth* [1965] AC 1175 at 1253: 'The fact that a contractual right can be specifically performed, or its breach prevented by injunction, does not mean that the right is any the less of a personal character or that a purchaser with notice is bound by it: what is relevant is the nature of the right, not the remedy which exists for its enforcement.' See too McFarlane [2003] *Conv* 473.

[28] [1972] Ch 359.

[29] The same assumption was made in *Ashburn Anstalt v Arnold* [1989] Ch 1.

[30] [1976] 1 WLR 852

further still and stated that this 'Constructive Trust' arises *as soon as*[31] A gives B a contractual licence; and so, as soon as B has a contractual licence, B has an immediate persistent right. Again, that analysis is incorrect.[32] It overlooks the fact that, where the receipt after a promise principle applies, B's right against C is a new, direct right, arising because of C's conduct. The right is entirely independent of B's initial contractual licence with A. This shows the importance of using the **basic structure** to distinguish the two very different questions of: (i) whether B has a new, direct right against C (the question in *Binions*); and (ii) whether B has a pre-existing persistent right (the question considered in *DHN*). This error was pointed out in *Ashburn Anstalt v Arnold*.[33] There, the Court of Appeal confirmed that B may be able to acquire a new, direct right against C if C makes a promise to honour B's licence; but that a Constructive Trust does *not* arise whenever B initially acquires a contractual licence.[34] To avoid that error, it is important to remember that, in a case such as *Binions v Evans*, it is *not* B's initial contractual licence that binds C; rather, it is a new, direct right B acquires against C as a result of C's conduct.

(iii) The exclusive control argument

Lord Denning made his arguments that a contractual licence should be capable of binding third parties from the 1950s and into the 1980s. During this same period, the Court of Appeal, again led by Lord Denning, adopted a particularly narrow approach to the definition of a Lease.

EXAMPLE 7

A has a Freehold. A makes a contractual agreement giving B a right to exclusive control of A's land for one year; in return, B pays A £100 per week. The agreement makes clear that A does not intend to grant B a Lease.

Nowadays, in such a case, B is viewed as having a Lease.[35] It does not matter that A did not intend to grant B such a right; B's right can count as a Lease as A has given B a right to exclusive control, for a limited period, of A's land (see **G1B:1.5.1**). However, from the 1950s to the 1980s, the Court of Appeal took a different view, holding that if A did not intend to give B a Lease, no Lease would arise.[36] As Denning LJ put it in *Errington v Errington & Woods*:

---

[31] *Ibid* at 859.

[32] The actual result in *DHN* is correct, however. The question to be decided was whether the defendant local authority was under a statutory duty to provide compensation to B as a result of a compulsory purchase of land occupied by B and owned by A (a subsidiary company of B). Goff and Shaw LJJ found that A held its right to the land on Resulting Trust for B and so B thus had a sufficient 'interest' in the land. It is also possible to find that B has a sufficient 'interest' to receive statutory compensation even if B has only a personal right against A: see eg *Pennine Raceways v Kirklees MBC* [1983] QB 382 *per* Everleigh LJ at 391 (see **E4:fn118**).

[33] [1989] Ch 1.

[34] *Ibid* at 24 *per* Fox LJ: 'For the reasons which we have already indicated, we prefer the line of authorities which determine that a contractual licence does not create a property interest. We do not think that the argument is assisted by the bare assertion that the interest arises under a constructive trust.'

[35] See eg *Street v Mountford* [1985] AC 809.

[36] See eg *Marcroft Wagons v Smith* [1951] 2 KB 496; *Cobb v Lane* [1952] 1 All ER 1199; *Murray Bull & Co v Murray* [1953] 1 QB 211; *Marchant v Charters* [1977] 1 WLR 1181; *Somma v Hazelhurst* [1978] 1 WLR 1014.

The result of all these cases is that, although a person who is let into exclusive possession is, prima facie, to be considered to be a tenant, nevertheless he will not be held to be so if the circumstances negative any intention to create a tenancy.[37]

The chief reason for that unorthodox[38] view was that, if B had a Lease, B would also acquire various forms of statutory protection: in some circumstances, for example, B would have a right to remain in occupation of A's land even after the end of the agreed contractual period (see **G1B:1.2**). The Court of Appeal therefore altered the definition of a Lease to make it easier for A to avoid being caught by those statutory rules.[39] The Court of Appeal's approach during that period is now of historical interest only: first, in 1985, the House of Lords rejected that approach and thus restored the orthodox position that, in **Example 7**, B has a Lease.[40] Second, during the 1980s, the statutory protection available to most parties with Leases was, in any case, dramatically reduced.

However, the Court of Appeal's approach is important in helping us to understand a source of the pressure to turn at least some contractual licences into persistent rights. Under that approach, in a case such as **Example 7**, B has only a contractual licence. However, as B has a right to exclusive control of A's land, it seems strange that B has only a personal right against A. It was therefore argued that a contractual licence, *if it gave B a right to exclusive control*, should be capable of binding C.[41] However that argument is now irrelevant. It has been accepted that, in a case such as **Example 7**, B *does* have a right that is capable of binding C; but that comes from a recognition that B has a Lease, not from any change in the status of contractual licences. The return to an orthodox definition of a Lease thus removes much of the pressure, to which Lord Denning was no doubt reacting in cases such as *Errington v Errington & Woods*,[42] to allow at least some contractual licences to be capable of binding C.

(iv) The analogy with the Restrictive Covenant

Some commentators reacted with surprise to Denning LJ's attempt, in *Errington v Errington & Woods*, to turn a contractual licence into a right capable of binding C. For example, Wade pointed out that it would be 'revolutionary' to recognise a new form of persistent right.[43] However, in defending Denning LJ's decision, Cheshire noted that,[44] in the past, the courts had done just that: in the second half of the 19th century, the Restrictive Covenant had been added to the list of persistent rights relating to land (see **E2:1.3.2**). Cheshire took this as evidence that a further new right, such as a contractual licence, could also be added to the list. As noted above, that argument does seem to overlook the effect of section 4(1) of the 1925 Act; whereas the Restrictive Covenant was developed by judges as a new persistent right *before* 1926, it should be impossible for judges, after 1925, to perform the same process with the contractual licence.

---

[37] [1952] 1 KB 290 at 298.

[38] It was inconsistent with prior authority: see eg *Allan v Liverpool Overseers* (1874) LR 9 QB 180; *Lynes v Snaith* [1899] 1 QB 486

[39] See eg *Cobb v Lane* [1952] 1 TLR 1037 at 1041; *Marchant v Charters* [1977] 1 WLR 1181 at 1185.

[40] See *Street v Mountford* [1985] AC 809.

[41] See eg Maudsley (1956) 20 *Conv* 281.

[42] [1952] 1 KB 290.

[43] (1952) 68 *LQR* 337 at 338–9.

[44] (1953) 16 *MLR* 1 at 9–10.

Nonetheless, Cheshire's argument raises two interesting points.[45] First, the journey of the Restrictive Covenant from a personal right to a persistent right was a gradual one, and direct rights played a very important part (see **G6:1.7**). For example, Cheshire gives *Tulk v Moxhay*[46] as a case in which the Restrictive Covenant was recognised as a persistent right. However, the court's reasoning in that case was rather that B had a new, direct right against C—*not* that B's initial agreement with A gave him a right that was capable of binding C.[47] It is not impossible that the contractual licence could follow a similar path. For example, if the courts relaxed the tests for when B, a party with a contractual licence, acquires a direct right against C, we might come very close to the point where B's initial contractual licence is prima facie binding on C. At that point, Parliament could step in to take the final step and confirm the contractual licence as a persistent right.

However, it must be emphasised that there is no current evidence that any form of contractual licence is evolving in this way. In *Ashburn Anstalt v Arnold*,[48] the Court of Appeal made clear that there must be good grounds for allowing B to acquire a direct right against C; B cannot acquire such a right, for example, simply because C knew about B's contractual licence (see **E3:2.3.5**). And in any case, the development of the Restrictive Covenant demonstrates that it is very unlikely that *all* contractual licences would become persistent rights. As the Restrictive Covenant came to be recognised as a persistent right, limits were placed on it. For example, B's right can count as a Restrictive Covenant only if it benefits some land owned by B;[49] and only if it imposes a negative, rather than a positive duty, on A.[50] These limits are no surprise: if B's initial right comes to be recognised as a persistent right, the courts will naturally examine the precise nature of B's right. So, at most, the analogy with the Restrictive Covenant tells us that only *particular forms* of contractual licence could become persistent rights.

There may be particular significance to the fact that, to count as a persistent right, a Restrictive Covenant must benefit some land of B. If B's right counts as a persistent right relating to A's land, this has the effect of potentially limiting the usefulness and market-ability of A's land: that is a particular problem, given the limited availability of land (see **A:3.1.5**). Where B's right is a Restrictive Covenant, the burden to A's land is offset by a corresponding benefit to B's land. In some cases, that benefit can be very significant: it may ensure, for example, that future owners of B's land do not have to live next door to a factory or to business premises. And the possibility of obtaining a Restrictive Covenant may even increase the marketability of land by allowing an owner of land: (i) to sell part of it; and (ii) to retain some control over the use of that part. As a result, the needs of practical convenience may have justified allowing the Restrictive Covenant to count as a persistent right despite the doctrinal objections (see **E2:1.3.2**).

However, if even some contractual licences were to become persistent rights, then: (i) the

---

[45] See further McFarlane [2003] *Conv* 473.

[46] (1848) 2 Ph 774.

[47] See **G6:1.7** and note esp *per* Lord Cottenham LC in *Tulk v Moxhay* (1848) 2 Ph 774 at 777–8: 'the question is, not whether the covenant runs with the land, but whether a party shall be permitted to use the land in a manner inconsistent with the contract entered into by his vendor, and with notice of which he purchased'.

[48] [1989] Ch 1 at 26: 'In matters relating to the title to land, certainty is of prime importance. We do not think it desirable that constructive trusts of land should be imposed in reliance on inferences from slender materials.'

[49] See eg *London County Council v Allen* [1914] 3 KB 642.

[50] See eg *Haywood v Brunswick Permanent Benefit Building Society* (1881) 8 QBD 403; *Austerberry v Oldham Corpn* (1885) 29 Ch D 750.

value of A's land would be limited by B's right; and (ii) there would be no such correspond-ing benefit to another piece of land.

(v) The analogy with the 'estoppel licence'

There are some cases in which the courts have held, or assumed, that an 'estoppel licence' is capable of binding C (see **4.4.2** below). Commentators have pointed out that, in some cases at least, there is a close link between an estoppel licence and a contractual licence; that (correct) observation has then been used as an argument that the contractual licence should also be capable of binding C.[51] However, the argument for parity of treatment can be accepted without arguing that *both* estoppel licences and contractual licences should count as persistent rights. It could equally be argued that *neither* type of right should be capable of binding C. And it is possible to explain the cases in which 'estoppel licences' appear to bind third parties *without* admitting that B acquires a persistent right whenever his licence arises by estoppel (ie, where the doctrine of proprietary estoppel imposes a duty on A not to revoke B's permission to make a particular use of A's land: see **4.4.2** below).

(vi) The effect of Article 8 of the European Convention on Human Rights

B's only right to his 'home' may come from a contractual licence with A. If A then transfers his Freehold to C, B may try to argue that his Article 8 right to respect for his home would be interfered with if C were allowed to remove B from the land before the end of B's licence period. It is very unlikely that such an appeal to the Human Rights Act 1998 will work. B faces two particular problems. First, Article 8(2) makes clear that B's right must be balanced against C's right as an owner of the land. Indeed, the House of Lords, when considering the position of a licensee, held that, in all but the most exceptional cases, there will be *no* breach of B's Article 8 right if C removes B in a situation where the current land law rules allow C to do so (see **B:8.3.2(iii)(c)**).[52]

In any case, B's right to his home may be respected even if C is allowed to remove B from the land before the end of B's licence period (see **B:8.2.3(ii)**). If that occurs, B will be able to claim money from A, as A will be in breach of his contractual duty to B: this right to receive money provides some protection for B's Article 8 right. Further, statute may limit C's freedom to remove B: even though B has no right he can assert against C, C may well have to give B four weeks' written notice before insisting that B move out of B's home.[53] It therefore seems clear that B's Article 8 right can be adequately respected without allowing a contractual licence to occupy a home to count as a persistent right.

(vii) The effect of section 116(b) of the Land Registration Act 2002

Section 116(b) of the LRA 2002 states that, in registered land, a 'mere Equity' is prima facie binding on C (see **E2:3.5.2** and **E5:3.4**). If he has a contractual licence, B may try to argue that he has such a 'mere Equity'. Certainly, B has an 'Equity' in the sense that a court may well protect B's contract with A through the Equitable remedies of specific performance or

---

[51] See eg Thompson [1983] *Conv* 57; Moriarty (1984) 100 *LQR* 376.

[52] *Kay v Lambeth London Borough Council* [2006] 2 AC 465.

[53] Protection from Eviction Act 1977, s 5(1A) applies where B has a 'periodic licence to occupy premises as a dwelling'. Some contractual licences are excluded from the 1977 Act: see s 3A. The Act does not apply, for example, if the licence involves B sharing accommodation with A or a member of A's family; or if, immediately before giving B the licence, A occupied the land as his only or principal home. Where it applies, the Act gives B strong protection: C commits a criminal offence if he attempts to remove B contrary to the terms of the Act: see s 1(2) (see **A:3.1.4**).

an injunction. However, it is clear that, when proposing the clause that became section 116(b), the Law Commission did *not* intend to change the status of a contractual licence.[54] Instead, a 'mere Equity' is better understood as referring only to situations in which B has a power to acquire a persistent right (see **D2:1.6(iii)**); it cannot be used to cover situations where B has only a personal right against A.

SUMMARY of E6:3

The only difference between a bare licence and a contractual licence is that, in the latter case, A has a contractual duty to B not to exercise his power to revoke B's licence. A's contractual duty has an important effect on B's rights against A. First, if A revokes B's licence in breach of contract, A commits a wrong against B. B's right against A will, in general, be specifically protected; even if not, A will have to pay money to B as a result of his wrongful revocation of the licence. Second, if A revokes the licence in breach of contract, B does *not* become a trespasser: B continues to have a liberty to make the agreed use of A's land and so A cannot use force to remove B from the land.

A's contractual duty to B can also have an effect on C, a party who later acquires a right from A. First, C, like the rest of the world, is under a duty not to knowingly procure a breach by A of A's contractual duty to B. Second, in order to protect himself from breaching his contractual duty and hence having to pay money to B, A may insist that C, when acquiring his right, promises to honour B's licence. If C makes such a promise to A, B may be able to use either the Contract (Rights of Third Parties) Act 1999 or the 'receipt after a promise' principle to acquire a new, direct right against C.

However, A's contractual duty to B does not have the effect of turning B's licence into a property right or a persistent right. A number of arguments have been made in favour of allowing at least some contractual licences to be capable of binding C; but, as we have seen, none of those arguments is convincing. In particular, if A is under a contractual duty to give B exclusive control of A's land for a limited period, it is now recognised that B has a right capable of binding C. But this did not occur as a result of allowing such a contractual licence to count as a persistent right; instead, it came from the courts' return to the orthodox position that, in such a case, B has a Lease: a property right in A's land.

---

4   THE ESTOPPEL LICENCE

4.1   Definition

We have to be careful when defining 'estoppel licence'. The term can be used in two very different ways. The first, popular amongst judges and commentators, refers to a situation where: (i) B has a liberty to make some use of A's land; *and* (ii) A is also under a duty to B, arising under the doctrine of proprietary estoppel. However, that usage causes confusion.

---

[54] See Law Com No 271 at 5.32–5.37.

EXAMPLE 8

A has a Freehold. A invites B, his son, to build a bungalow on the land. B does so and lives in the bungalow as his home for 20 years.

EXAMPLE 9

A has a Freehold. A promises B, his father, that, if B pays for building work necessary to add an extra room to A's house, A will allow B to move into A's house and share occupation of that house with A and A's family for the rest of B's life, or until A sells the land.

On the first usage of 'estoppel licence', B has an estoppel licence in both **Examples 8 and 9**. However, it is clear that B's rights in each case are very different. In **Example 8** the doctrine of proprietary estoppel is very likely to impose a duty on A give B a property right: for example, A may have to transfer part of his Freehold to B; or, at least, give B a Lease of the bungalow for the remainder of B's life. In such a case, A is under a duty to B in relation to a specific right and so B has an immediate persistent right (see **E4:6.1**). This means that, if C later acquires a right from A, B will have a prima facie power to assert his persistent right against C. For example, in *Inwards v Baker*,[55] the essential facts of which are identical to **Example 8**, Lord Denning MR took the view that B did indeed have a right that was capable of binding a party later buying A's Freehold. If B is described, in such a case, as having an 'estoppel licence' it may therefore seem that his licence is capable of binding C. However, in such a case, it is *not* B's liberty to occupy A's land that binds C. Instead, it is the *separate* persistent right B acquires as a result of A's duty, arising through proprietary estoppel, to give B a property right in A's land.[56] So, if A's duty is to allow B exclusive control of the land for a limited period, B has an Equitable Lease. If A is instead under a duty to transfer his Freehold to B; or to give B the benefit of that Freehold for a period, B has a right under a Trust. It is that Equitable Lease or right under a Trust that can bind C, *not* B's licence.

This first usage of 'estoppel licence' is thus a potent source of confusion. In particular, it has led to the view that: (i) as an 'estoppel licence' is seen as capable of binding C in a case such as **Example 8**; then (ii) a standard contractual licence should also have that effect (see **3.4.2(v)** above). But of course there is a clear difference between the two cases: in a standard contractual licence case, A is *not* under any duty to B to give B a property right.[57] A number of cases in which an 'estoppel licence' has been seen as capable of binding C are in fact cases where: (i) A was under a duty, arising because of proprietary estoppel, to give B a property right; and so (ii) B therefore acquired a persistent right (see **E2:1.3.1(i)**).[58] Those

---

[55] [1965] 2 QB 29.

[56] See McFarlane [2003] *CLJ* 661 at 678–9.

[57] Moriarty (1984) 100 *LQR* 376 views contractual licence cases as cases in which B is allowed to acquire an 'Equitable property right' by informal means. In that way, he equates such cases with 'estoppel licence' cases such as **Example 8**, where A is under a duty to give B a property right in A's land. However, it is clear that, in a standard contractual licence case, A is under no such duty to B.

[58] See eg *ER Ives Investments Ltd v High* [1967] 2 QB 379. In that case, C should have been able to use the lack of registration defence against the persistent right B acquired through proprietary estoppel. An alternative explanation for the decision of the Court of Appeal is that B had a direct right against C, arising under the 'benefit and burden' principle: see eg Battersby [1995] *MLR* 637. But, on the facts of the case, there are problems with that alternative explanation (see **E3:n34**).

cases *cannot* provide a useful analogy to simple contractual licence cases:[59] the **content** of B's right is very different.

The second usage of 'estoppel licence' is the one we will use. It is more limited and refers only to the situation where: (i) B has a liberty to make some use of A's land; *and* (ii) A's duty to B does not arise as part of a property right or a persistent right held by B; and (iii) A is under a duty to B, arising as the result of the doctrine of proprietary estoppel, not to revoke B's liberty. On this definition, an estoppel licence has exactly the same **content** as a contractual licence: the only difference is the source of A's duty not to revoke B's liberty.

On this view, B does *not* have an estoppel licence in **Example 8**; but he does have such a right in **Example 9**. In the latter case, as B has relied on A's commitment by completing his side of a bargain, proprietary estoppel imposes a duty on A to honour his commitment to B (see **E4:Example 11**). As a result, A is simply under a duty not to revoke B's permission to share occupation of A's land.

4.2 B's rights against A

In a case such as **Example 9**, B's rights against A should be identical to those B acquires under a contractual licence (see **3.2** above). Of course, just like a contractual licence, an estoppel licence will be regulated by its own terms: so if the appropriate response to B's estoppel claim is to recognise that B has a licence to occupy A's land for five years, then A can obviously remove B from the land at the end of that period. However, if A revokes B's licence during that period, B should not become a trespasser. And, in general, a court should specifically protect B's right by ordering A to continue to allow B to use A's land. Of course, just as with a contractual licence, specific protection is not guaranteed: for example if, in **Example 9**, A and B fall out, a court should not force them to continue living together. Instead, A will be ordered to pay B money as a substitute for B's right to occupy the land and to compensate B for any relevant consequential loss B suffers as a result of A's breach of his duty not to revoke B's licence. Certainly, in *Baker v Baker*,[60] on which **Example 9** is based, A was ordered to pay money to B when their relationship broke down and A ordered B to leave the home.[61]

4.3 B's rights against X

Again, in a case such as **Example 9**, B's position should be identical to that of a contractual licensee (see **3.3** above).

---

[59] *Errington v Errington & Woods* [1952] 1 KB 290 is an interesting example. Denning LJ treated B's right as arising under a contractual licence. However, B had relied on A's commitment to transfer a Freehold to B if B made mortgage payments. It seems, then, that the doctrine of proprietary estoppel may have imposed a duty on A to honour that commitment. On that view, B acquired a persistent right through proprietary estoppel. So the decision in *Errington* may be correct even though a contractual licence does not count as a persistent right: see further *per* Fox LJ in *Ashburn Anstalt v Arnold* [1989] Ch 1 at 17.

[60] [1993] 2 FLR 247.

[61] In *Baker*, B moved into rent-free local authority accommodation. Dillon LJ (dissenting on this point) held that, as a result, the money that A had to pay B should be reduced. Certainly, the provision of rent-free accommodation reduced the consequential loss B suffered as a result of A's breach of his duty to B; but, as the majority of the Court of Appeal pointed out, it cannot affect the value of B's right (see eg *per* Beldam LJ at 254–5 and *per* Roch LJ at 258).

4.4 B's rights against C

4.4.1 Direct rights

Again, in a case such as **Example 9**, B's position, as regards both direct rights and pre-existing rights, should be identical to that of a contractual licensee. A again has an incentive to extract a promise from C to honour B's licence: if C were to buy the land and then remove B before the end of the licence period, A would again have to pay money to B. The difference is that the wrong committed by A would be a breach of a duty arising as a result of proprietary estoppel, rather than a breach of a duty arising as a result of A's contractual promise.

4.4.2 Pre-existing rights

In some cases, it has been held or assumed that B's 'estoppel licence' is capable of binding C. The first point to make is that, in many of these cases, 'estoppel licence' is used in the first sense discussed above: in such cases, as in **Example 8**, it is not B's licence that binds C; rather it is a separate persistent right B acquires as a result of proprietary estoppel. In true estoppel licence cases, such as **Example 9**, B has no such right.

However, there are some decisions in which even a true estoppel licence has been assumed to be capable of binding C.[62] The key point about those decisions is that they were made during the period in which the Court of Appeal, led by Lord Denning, took the view that a simple contractual licence was also a persistent right. Given the identical content of true estoppel licences and contractual licences, it is no surprise that the Court of Appeal treated the two types of right in the same way. However, given the decision of the Court of Appeal in *Ashburn Anstalt v Arnold*,[63] it is now clear that a contractual licence does *not* count as a persistent right. So, the very consistency of treatment that once led the estoppel licence to be seen as a capable of binding C now demands that the estoppel licence, like the contractual licence, is *not* a persistent right.[64]

The status of an estoppel licence in a case such as **Example 9** has, however, been confused by the passing of section 116(a) of the LRA 2002. That section appears to allow *all* rights arising by proprietary estoppel to function as persistent rights—at least if C acquires his right before any court order made in B's favour (see **E4:6.4**). If section 116(a) has that effect, the impact of B's right on C no longer depends on the **content** of B's right; instead, it depends on the means by which B's right was **acquired**. So B's right may have exactly the same content as a contractual licence but, because it happens to arise through proprietary estoppel, it will be capable of binding C. In particular, as the 'equity by estoppel' ceases if a court order is made in B's favour, the land law system would be in a very odd position: C could be bound by B's estoppel licence but *only* if C acquired his right before a court order recognising B's licence. Yet it is in just such a situation that B's right may be particularly difficult to discover. Therefore, if section 116(a) is given its natural interpretation, an absurd position would arise:

---

[62] See eg *Williams v Staite* [1979] Ch 291.
[63] [1989] Ch 1.
[64] This point is made by Battersby, ch 19 in *Land Law—Themes and Perspectives* (ed Bright and Dewar, 1998), 503–4; McFarlane [2003] *CLJ* 661 at 664–5; and Swadling, *English Private Law* (ed Burrows, 2nd edn, 2007), 4.128.

Name of B's right	Content of B's right	Is B's right capable of binding C?
Contractual licence	B has a liberty to use A's land; A is under a duty to B not to revoke that liberty	No: B has only a personal right against A
Estoppel licence (after court order recognising the licence)	B has a liberty to use A's land; A is under a duty to B not to revoke that liberty	No: B has only a personal right against A
Estoppel licence (before court order)	B has a liberty to use A's land; A is under a duty to B not to revoke that liberty	Yes: see LRA 2002, section 116(a)

To avoid that absurdity, section 116(a) should be interpreted in a narrow way: B should be regarded as having an 'equity by estoppel' *only* if B's proprietary estoppel claim gives rise to a recognised persistent right (see **E4:6.4**). Therefore, in a case such as **Example 9**, where A's only duty is not to revoke B's licence, section 116(a) should not apply. However, this narrow interpretation is not the one favoured by the Law Commission,[65] which first proposed the section, and so we may be left with the absurd position set out in the table above.

SUMMARY of E6:4

It is vital to distinguish between two uses of the term 'estoppel licence'. First, the term can be used *whenever* B has a liberty to use A's land *and* A is under a duty to B, arising as a result of proprietary estoppel. It is dangerous to use the term in that way as the **content** of B's right may be very different to that of a standard licence. For example, if A's duty to B is to give B a property right in A's land, B will have a persistent right and that right will be prima facie binding on C.

The term 'estoppel licence' should therefore be confined to the case where B has a liberty to use A's land and A is under a duty, arising as a result of proprietary estoppel, not to revoke that liberty. In such a case, the **content** of B's right is identical to that of a contractual licence; the only difference is that B has acquired his right through proprietary estoppel rather than a contract. B's right should therefore be treated in exactly the same way as a contractual licence. In particular, as it is now clear that contractual licences are merely personal rights, the same must be true of estoppel licences. However, unless it is given a narrow interpretation, section 116(a) of the LRA 2002 may cause a problem: it seems to mean that, *whenever* proprietary estoppel imposes a duty on A, B acquires a right that is capable of binding C—an 'equity by estoppel'.

---

5   OTHER FORMS OF LICENCE

5.1   Statutory licences

A statutory licence arises when: (i) B has a liberty to make a particular use of A's land; *and*

---

[65] See Law Com No 271 at 5.30.

(ii) that liberty does not arise as part of a property right or persistent right held by B; and (iii) A is under a statutory duty to B not to revoke that liberty. The **content** of such a licence is identical to a contractual licence and an estoppel licence; the difference lies in the source of A's duty to B and thus in the means by which B acquires his right against A. As we would expect, the rights of a statutory licensee against A, X or C will generally be regulated by the particular statute that imposes A's duty.

One statutory licence of particular note is the licence enjoyed by B to occupy a dwelling-house which his spouse or civil partner[66] (A) has a right to occupy (eg, because A has a Freehold or Lease of the land). A's duty to allow B to occupy A's land arises under section 30 of the Family Law Act 1996 ('the FLA 1996': see **B:11.3**). That Act is a successor to the Matrimonial Homes Act 1967, which was passed after the House of Lords decision in *National Provincial Bank v Ainsworth*.[67] Mrs Ainsworth's 'deserted wife's equity' was the only source of her claim that her husband was under a duty to allow her to occupy the home he owned (see **B:11.2**). That very uncertain right, essentially improvised by the courts, was replaced by the statutory right to occupy first set out in the 1967 Act.

Of course, B's right is still subject to a number of qualifications: so, if A has a Freehold, A has no absolute duty to allow B, her husband, to occupy that land. Instead, section 33 of the FLA 1996 lays down a number of different factors a court should take into account in deciding if B has such a right:[68] the risk of A, B or a 'relevant child' suffering 'significant harm' is a particularly important factor.[69] Indeed, a court has the power not only to regulate B's right to occupy but also to regulate *A's* right:[70] for example, if A's continued occupation would present a risk to B, a court may make an order preventing A from occupying the home.

The statutory right to occupy that B can acquire under the Family Law Act is also capable of binding C.[71] However, if C acquires a property right from A for value, B's statutory right can bind C *only* if it is defensively registered.[72] Even if B is in actual occupation of A's registered land when C commits to acquiring his right, B's statutory right to occupy does *not* count as an overriding interest.[73]

5.2   Licences coupled with an interest

A licence coupled with an interest arises where: (i) B has a liberty to make some use of A's land; *and* (ii) that liberty protects a property right held by B. It is doubtful whether it is worth identifying such licences as a separate category. After all, a licence was defined above

---

[66] Civil Partnership Act 2004, s 82 and Sch 9 para 1 amends the 1996 Act to make it applicable to civil partners as well as to spouses. Unless a court orders otherwise, the statutory right ends on divorce, dissolution of the civil partnership, or the death of either A or B: FLA 1996, ss 30(8) and 33(5).

[67] [1965] AC 1175.

[68] See esp s 33(6).

[69] FLA 1996, s 33(7).

[70] FLA 1996, s 33(3)(c).

[71] FLA 1996, s 31(2): the right counts as a 'charge on the estate or interest' of A.

[72] Even in such a case, C can apply under FLA 1996, s 33 to have B's right to occupy terminated. In considering such an application, a court will take into account all the circumstances in deciding what order is 'just and reasonable': see *Kaur v Gill* [1988] Fam 110 for an example showing that there is no guarantee B will be permitted to remain in occupation.

[73] FLA 1996, s 31(10)(b).

so as to exclude a liberty arising as part of a property right or a persistent right held by B (see **section 1** above).

A has a Freehold. A, by means of a deed, grants B a right to go onto A's land and cut down timber growing there.

In such a case, B could be said to have a 'licence coupled with an interest'. B has a liberty to go onto A's land; and that liberty arises as part of the property right (known as a 'Profit': see **E1:n1**) that A has given to B. In **Example 10**, B's liberty is clearly part and parcel of his property right in A's land. So, if X were to interfere with B's liberty to go onto A's land, X would, prima facie, commit a wrong against B. And if A were to transfer his Freehold to C, B's liberty to go onto the land will be prima facie binding on C. However, this does not mean that B's liberty counts as a distinct property right. In each case it is the Profit, a recognised form of property right, that B asserts against X or C. It therefore adds nothing to our analysis of **Example 10** to say that B has a 'licence coupled with an interest'; it is far simpler to say that B has only a Profit: a property right that entitles B not just to cut down timber on A's land but also to enter A's land for that purpose.

A has a Freehold. In return for payment from B, A makes a contractual promise to allow B: (i) to go onto A's land; (ii) to cut down timber growing on the land; and (iii) to set up a sawmill on A's land.

The essential facts of **Example 11** are identical to those in *James Jones and Sons Ltd v Earl of Tankerville*.[74] In that case, A revoked B's licence and attempted to stop B's employees from using A's land. Parker J specifically protected B's contractual right against A by making an order preventing A from interfering with B's timber-cutting operation. That result is no surprise: the courts, in general, will specifically protect B's contractual right that A must not revoke B's liberty to use A's land (see **3.2** above). However, in 1909, when judgment was given in *James Jones*, there was some doubt that the courts would grant such a remedy in a case where B has only a contractual licence. As a result, Parker J sought to distinguish *James Jones* from such a case by finding that B had more than a contractual licence: he had, instead, a licence 'coupled with or granted in aid of a legal interest conferred on [B]'.[75] Nowadays, such an analysis is unnecessary: B can be adequately protected against A even if B has only a contractual licence.

A more important question in a case such as **Example 11** is whether B has a right that he can assert against X or C. If B's right is simply a contractual licence, it does not count as a property right or persistent right in A's land.[76] However, as noted by Parker J in *James Jones*, the contract between A and B can suffice to transfer A's Ownership of the timber on A's land to B.[77] This means that, if either X or C interferes with B's right to exclusive control of that

---

[74] [1909] 2 Ch D 440.

[75] *Ibid* at 442.

[76] Although as we have seen if B is in physical control of A's land he will thereby acquire a property right that he can assert against X (see **2.3** above).

[77] Timber growing on A's land and to be cut down can count as 'goods' for the purposes of the Sale of Goods Act 1979: see s 61(1) of that Act.

timber, each will commit a wrong against B (see **D1:4.1.1**). What if, instead of directly interfering with the timber, C prevents B from having access to the land, now owned by C, where the timber is found?[78] There are then two possibilities. First, B could argue that, as A is under a contractual duty to allow B a right amounting to a Profit, B has a persistent right: an Equitable Profit. That possibility was not explored in *James Jones*; but, if B has such a persistent right, he will be able to assert it against C. Second, B could argue that, by denying B access to the timber, C is interfering with B's property right in that timber and so commits the wrong of conversion.[79] Crucially, neither of those two possibilities depends on B having a 'licence coupled with an interest': instead, B relies either on a persistent right against A's Freehold (an Equitable Profit) or on a property right in the timber on A's land. It therefore seems that there is no good reason for preserving the distinct category of a 'licence coupled with an interest'.

SUMMARY of E6

The current position

If B has a licence, he has a liberty to make a particular use of A's land. In some cases, A is also under a duty to B not to use his power to revoke B's liberty. If A's duty arises as a result of a contract, B has a contractual licence; if it arises as a result of proprietary estoppel, B has an estoppel licence; if it arises as a result of statute, B has a statutory licence. In each case, B has a personal right against A; when it comes to the **remedies question**, B's right will, in general, be specifically protected. If C later acquires a right from A, B may acquire a direct right against C. In particular, to avoid breaching his duty to B, A may insist that C promises to honour B's licence: if C makes such a promise to A, B may be able to acquire a direct right against C under the Contract (Rights of Third Parties) Act 1999 or the 'receipt after a promise' principle.

However, A's duty not to revoke B's licence does *not* give B either a property right or a persistent right. For example, if A transfers his Freehold to C, and B has no direct right against C, C is free to prevent B from using the land even if, by doing so, C causes A to be in breach of his duty to B. There have been some cases in which the Court of Appeal, led by Lord Denning, held or assumed that a contractual licence[80] or an estoppel licence[81] *does* give B a persistent right. However, that reasoning is inconsistent with clear House of Lords authority[82] and was rejected by the Court of Appeal in *Ashburn Anstalt v Arnold*.[83] There have also been cases in which the term 'estoppel licence' is used to refer to a case where the doctrine of proprietary estoppel imposes a duty on A to give B a property right in A's land. In such cases, B *does* have a persistent right, but that persistent right is separate from any licence B may have.

---

[78] If X physically prevents B from going onto C's land, X clearly commits the wrong of trespass to the person. C can however argue that he has a liberty to prevent trespassers, such as B, from entering his land.

[79] See eg *Howard E Perry v British Railway Board* [1980] 1 WLR 1375. Formerly, X committed the wrong of detinue. That particular wrong was abolished by the Torts (Interference with Goods) Act 1977, s 2(1), but any conduct falling within the scope of detinue now counts as conversion: see s 2(2) of the 1977 Act and Douglas [2008] *Conv* 30.

[80] See eg *Errington v Errington & Woods* [1952] 1 KB 290; *DHN Food Distributors Ltd v Tower Hamlets* [1976] 1 WLR 852.

[81] See eg *Williams v Staite* [1979] Ch 291.

[82] *King v David Allen & Sons, Billposting Ltd* [1936] 3 All ER 483; *NPB v Ainsworth* [1965] AC 1175.

[83] [1989] Ch 1.

Future reforms?

Various arguments that have been made in favour of allowing at least some contractual licences to count as persistent rights (see **3.4.2** above). None of those arguments is persuasive. Certainly, from a doctrinal point of view, B should not acquire a persistent right against A's Freehold or Lease simply because A is under a duty to B not to revoke B's licence. First, A's duty does not relate to the whole of A's Freehold or Lease. Second, A may be under a duty in relation to A's liberty to make a particular use of his land; but a right against a liberty does not count as a persistent right. Third, A may be under a duty in relation to his power to revoke B's licence; but that fact cannot give B a right he can assert against C: C needs no power to revoke B's permission to occupy as C did not give B that permission. C can prevent B from continuing to use the land by simply enforcing B's duty not to interfere with C's exclusive control of the land.

The Restrictive Covenant has been recognised as a persistent right in relation to land even though it does not impose a duty on A in relation to a specific claim right or power (**E2:1.3.2**). This demonstrates that the doctrinally correct position is sometimes overturned, in the interests of practical convenience. So, it is not impossible that the needs of practical convenience may one day lead to certain types of licence being recognised as persistent rights. Everything comes down to the **basic tension** between: (i) protecting a prior user of the land, such as B; and (ii) on the other, protecting those later acquiring rights in the land, such as C. Section 4(1) of the LPA 1925 makes clear that any decision to change the current law and allow a licence to bind a third party must be made by Parliament.

If such a reform were made, a number of points would need to be borne in mind. First, there is little prospect of a reform under which B acquires a persistent right *whenever* A is under a duty not to revoke B's licence. Rather, the precise **content** of B's right would have to be examined and situations in which B is particularly in need of protection would have to be isolated. For example, cases where B's licence enables him to occupy land as his home may be seen as especially worthy of protection; although, as we have seen, the pressure for reform has been reduced by the fact that B will in any case acquire a property right (a Lease) if A is under a duty to allow B exclusive control of A's land for a limited period.

Second, if certain forms of licence were to count as persistent rights, a number of subsidiary questions would have to be answered. In particular, what *formality rules* would apply to B's **acquisition** of such a right? For example, the default rule under section 53(1)(a) of the LPA 1925 is that A's power to give B a persistent right can only be exercised in writing signed by A (see **E2:2.3.1**). Further, what **defences** might C have to B's persistent right? The default position is that, if C acquires a property right from A for value, C takes this free from any persistent right that has not been defensively regisered; unless of course B is in actual occupation of A's land when C commits to acquiring his right. It is therefore vital to remember that, in considering any particular reform to the land law system, the whole of the **basic structure** must be kept in mind.

PART III

SPECIFIC RIGHTS

CHAPTER F1
OWNERSHIP

OWNERSHIP

In **D1**, we looked in detail at Ownership: the *only* property right that can exist in things other than land. This chapter is essentially a very brief reminder of the points made in **D1**.

A makes a contractual promise to B to mow B's lawn.

It would be inaccurate to say that B has Ownership of a personal right against A. That personal right is not a physical object and so cannot be the subject matter of a property right (see **D1:1.1**). We should simply say that B has a personal right against A. Similarly, if B has an account at A Bank, B simply has a personal right against A Bank: B does not have Ownership of any money held by A Bank; nor does B have Ownership of his bank account.

As it is a property right, Ownership can *only* be important when we look at disputes about the use of things (such as bikes); it has no role to play in disputes about the use of rights (such as B's account with A Bank).

1 THE CONTENT QUESTION

Ownership consists of B having:

- an immediate, unconditional right to exclusive control of a thing;
- forever.

As Ownership is the only form of property right in things other than land, this means A0 *cannot* give B a property right that gives B:

- a right to exclusive control of a thing to take effect only in the future (eg, A0 attempts to give B a property right allowing B exclusive control of A0's bike from the end of the next month); or
- a conditional right to exclusive control of a thing (eg, A0 attempts to give B a property right allowing B exclusive control of A0's bike *if* B's bike is stolen within the next six months); or
- a right to exclusive control of a thing for a limited time only (eg, A0 attempts to give B a property right allowing B exclusive control of A0's bike for six months: see **D1:1.4.3**).

In such cases, A0 can of course make a contractual promise to B to allow exclusive control of the bike on those terms, but that will give B only a personal right against A0. If A0 wants to give B more than a personal right (eg, because B wishes to have a right capable of binding

A0's trustee in bankruptcy) A0 needs to give B a *persistent right*. A0's best option is to set up a Trust. For example, A0 can transfer his Ownership to A subject to a duty to use that right for B's benefit: (i) at some point in the future; or (ii) if a particular condition is satisfied; or (iii) for a limited period (see eg **D1:Example 7**).

In such cases B does *not* acquire a property right: the rest of the world is *not* under a duty to B not to interfere with B's use of the thing (see **B:4.3**). However, B's persistent right under the Trust will give him the *benefit* (subject to the limits set by the Trust) of A's right to exclusive control of the thing. Crucially, B can also assert his right against a third party later acquiring a right from A, such as A's trustee in bankruptcy (see **B:4.5.2(ii)**).

2   THE ACQUISITION QUESTION

Ownership can be acquired either independently or dependently. Where B acquires it independently, B acquires a *new* property right as a result of his own, unilateral action. For example, if B takes physical control of A's bike—even if he simply steals it from A—B acquires Ownership of the bike. The rest of the world is under a prima facie duty not to interfere with any use B may choose to make of the bike (see **D1:2.1**). Of course, this does not mean that A loses his pre-existing Ownership. Rather, it means that *both* A and B have Ownership of the bike. In any dispute between A and B, A will prevail: (i) A has a pre-existing property right; and (ii) B has no defence to it (see **D1:1.4.1**).

Where B acquires Ownership dependently, he acquires a pre-existing property right. If A has Ownership, he has the power to transfer his right to B (see **D1:2.2.2**). It seems to be impossible, for example, for A0 both to: (i) give A an immediate right to exclusive control of a thing forever; *and* (ii) to restrict A's power to transfer that right.[1] So, unless statute intervenes,[2] or either or A or B suffers from some personal incapacity, it seems A *always* has the power to transfer his Ownership to B.[3]

3   THE DEFENCES QUESTION

It is very difficult for C to have a defence to B's pre-existing Ownership. For example, if A steals B's bike and sells it to C, C will not have a defence as a result of the mere fact that he acquired A's Ownership of the bike: (i) for value; and (ii) without any actual or constructive notice of B's pre-existing right. The 'bona fide purchaser' defence thus cannot be used against B's Ownership of the bike. However, there are some, limited situations in which C can have a defence to B's property right (see **D1:3**).

[1] Of course, it may be that A, by transferring his right to B, breaches a duty owed to A0; however, this does not prevent B acquiring A's Ownership (see eg **D1:Example 1**, where A Ltd breaches its contractual duty to B Ltd but C nonetheless acquires A Ltd's Ownership of the bikes).

[2] For example, a statute may exclude or limit the power of a national museum to transfer its Ownership of a work of art: see eg Museums and Galleries Act 1992, s 4. And insolvency legislation may give a court the power to set aside particular transfers by A, such as a transfer made at undervalue within a five-year period before A's bankruptcy; or any transfer at an undervalue made with the purpose of prejudicing A's creditors: see Insolvency Act 1986, ss 339 and 423.

[3] See eg *Attwater v Attwater* (1853) 18 Beav 330; *re Elliot* [1896] 2 353, esp *per* Chitty J at 356: 'the owner of property has as an incident of his ownership the right to sell and to receive the whole of the proceeds for his own benefit.' See too **G1B:2.2.2(ii)** and **G1B:5.2**.

4   THE REMEDIES QUESTION

If B has Ownership of a thing, B cannot directly assert that right by simply going to court and saying 'That thing is mine!' Rather, B asserts his property right by showing that C has committed a wrong: C has breached his duty not to interfere with B's exclusive control of the thing. So, when looking at the **remedies question**, we look at how a court responds to C's commission of a wrong (see **D1:4.1**). In some cases, a court may specifically protect B's property right: for example by ordering C to return B's bike to B (see **D1.4.2**). However, in general, B has to settle for receiving money from C (see **D1:4.3**).

CHAPTER F2
CO-OWNERSHIP

CO-OWNERSHIP

It is possible for the same right to be held by two or more people at the same time. This is true of all rights whether they are personal rights, persistent rights or property rights.

Each of B1 and B2 holds the *same right at the same time*. It would be a mistake to think B1 and B2 each have a separate right against A: there is only one right and it is held jointly by B1 and B2. Similarly, if B1 and B2 open a joint account with A Bank, B1 and B2 each holds the same personal right against A Bank.

In such a case, it is often said that B1 and B2 are 'co-owners': they are co-owners of the personal right against A. However, in **Example 1**, it is clear that B1 and B2 do not each hold Ownership: they each hold a personal right, not a property right. To avoid confusion, it would be better to say that B1 and B2 are *co-holders* of a personal right against A. If we say instead that B1 and B2 are 'co-owners' of that right, this can cause confusion. After all, it is inaccurate to say that B has Ownership of a personal right against A (see **F1:Example 1**). It is therefore misleading to say that B1 and B2 can have Co-Ownership of such a right.

In this chapter, we will focus on situations where the right that B1 and B2 each hold, at the same time, is Ownership. In such a case: (i) B1 and B2 are co-holders of that right; thus (ii) they have Co-Ownership in the proper sense of the term: each holds, at the same time, the property right known as Ownership. In that sense, Co-Ownership can be relevant *only* when looking at disputes involving the use of a thing. Co-Ownership is thus a specific example of co-holding. So, many of the principles we will discuss in this chapter are of more general application: they apply whenever B1 and B2 co-hold a right. As a result, those principles can also be important in a case such as **Example 1**.

1 THE CONTENT QUESTION

If B1 and B2 have Co-Ownership, then B1 and B2, acting together, have the rights of an owner: an immediate, unconditional right to exclusive control of a thing forever. Co-Ownership can take effect only in one of two forms: (i) joint tenancy; and (ii) tenancy in common.

1.1   The joint tenancy

1.1.1 The general position

It is possible for two or more parties to hold the same right at the same time *as a team*. This form of co-holding is known as a *joint tenancy*; B1 and B2 can be said to be joint tenants of the right. So, in **Example 1**, A's contractual promise is made to B1 and B2 jointly: the team comprised of B1 and B2 thus has a right against A. This means, for example, that B1 *cannot* sue A by himself: B1 and B2 need to sue A together.[1] It also means that if B1 dies, the co-holding ends: B2 becomes the sole holder of the personal right against A. B1 has no independent right that he can deal with in his will: the right against A is *not* held by B1 and B2 separately; rather, it is held by them as a team. Before B1's death, the team consists of B1 and B2; after B1's death, the team consists of B2 alone. This feature of the joint tenancy is often known as 'survivorship'.

1.1.2 The joint tenancy and co-ownership

EXAMPLE 2

A has Ownership of a bike. A sells the bike jointly to B1 and B2.

In **Example 2**, as in **Example 1**, B1 and B2 each hold the same right at the same time *as a team*. In **Example 2**, that right is Ownership and so B1 and B2, as well as being co-holders of a right, also have Co-Ownership. B1 and B2 are also joint tenants. This means, for example, that if B1 wishes to transfer Ownership of the bike to C, B1 cannot do so by himself: he must act together with B2.[2] It also means that if B1 dies, the Co-Ownership ends: B2 becomes the sole holder of the property right.

B1 and B2's holding of Ownership as joint tenants is often said to involve 'four unities': (i) unity of possession; (ii) unity of title; (iii) unity of time; and (iv) unity of interest. 'Unity of possession' simply means that, together, B1 and B2 have a right to exclusive control of the thing.

EXAMPLE 3

A has a motorhome with two storeys. A sells the bottom storey to B1 and the top storey to B2.

In such a case, B1 and B2 are *not* Co-Owners of the motorhome. They do not hold the same right at the same time. B1 has Ownership of the bottom storey; and B2 has Ownership of the top storey. One way of explaining this is to say that B1 and B2 do not have 'unity of possession'. It is not the case that B1 and B2 are both members of a team that has a right to exclusive control of the whole of the motorhome. In fact, B2 is under a duty to B1 not to interfere with B1's use of the bottom storey; and B1 is under a duty to B2 not to interfere with B2's use of the top storey.

---

[1] If B2 refuses to sue, even after B1 has offered to pay any costs involved in the action, B1 can join B2 as a co-defendant and thus ask a court to force B2 to join in the claim against A: see eg *Cullen v Knowles* [1898] 2 QB 380 (compare the *Vandepitte* procedure available to a beneficiary when a trustee refuses to assert a right against a third party: see **B:n33**).

[2] Or obtain a court order forcing B2 to consent to the sale.

The other three unities (title, time, interest) are simply ways of expressing the point that, if B1 and B2 are joint tenants, they do not have independent rights, but rather hold the same right as part of a team. Unity of title means that the right of each joint tenant arises in *the same way*; unity of time means that the right of each joint tenant arises at *the same time*; and unity of interest means that each joint tenant has *the same right*.

So, the four unities are *not* a set of purely technical requirements: they simply restate the fundamental point that each joint tenant holds the same right at the same time. This is because each joint tenant acts as part of a team, and that team holds a single right.

The nature of the joint tenancy was well captured, over 700 years ago, by Bracton. He said that a joint tenant 'holds everything and nothing':[3]

- Each joint tenant, in his capacity as a member of the team, has a right to exclusive control over the whole thing; *but*
- Each joint tenant, individually, has no right he can assert against X; no individual share of Ownership to call his own; and nothing to pass on when he dies. His rights come entirely from his membership of the team.

1.2   The tenancy in common

1.2.1 The general position

Is it possible for B1 and B2 to co-hold a right *without* being joint tenants: ie, can B1 and B2 co-hold a right without holding it solely as members of a team? The general answer is No. In **Example 1**, B1 and B2 co-hold the same personal right against A. The right is held by a team comprised of B1 and B2. It is impossible to see how B1 and B2 could co-hold that personal right in any other way.[4] So, the general rule is that, if B1 and B2 are to co-hold a right, they *must* do so as joint tenants.[5]

This may seem somewhat inflexible. What if B1 and B2 want to co-hold the personal right against A in a different way? For example, let us say the personal right is an account with A Bank. B1 and B2 each pay money into the account. B1 wants to ensure that, when he dies, he has an individual right to a share of the bank account that he can give to his children in his will. If B1 and B2 co-hold the account as joint tenants, B1 has *no* individual right: when B1 dies, B2 will become the sole holder of the account and will thus get the benefit of money paid in by B1. The solution is for B1 and B2 to set up a Trust.[6]

---

[3] *Bracton de Legibus et Consuetudinibus Angliae* (ed Woodbine and Thorne, 1968–77), vol 4, 336: each joint tenant '*totum tenet et nihil tenet*'. See too Coke, *Commentaries on Littleton*, 188b: joint tenants hold 'by one joint title and in one right.'

[4] It should be noted that it is possible for A to make a promise to B1 and B2 jointly *and* to make separate promises to B1 and B2. If A does so, B1 and B2 are joint tenants of a personal right against A *and* have separate, individual rights against A. So, B1 and B2 do then have individual rights to sue A that they can deal with as they please. Where A makes a promise *in a deed* to B1 and B2 jointly, s 81 of the Law of Property Act 1925 stipulates that A's promise shall 'be construed as being also made with each of [B1 and B2]' unless a contrary intention is expressed: so the default rule in such a case is that A does also make separate promises to B1 and B2.

[5] See eg Coke, *Commentaries on Littleton*, 198a; *re McKerrell* [1912] 2 Ch 648; R Smith, *Plural Ownership* (2005), 209–10 (although Smith seems to be a little doubtful as to whether the rule is justified).

[6] Of course, such a Trust can only be set up if both B1 and B2 agree. However, a court may be prepared to infer from the evidence that, even if a Trust was not expressly set up, B1 and B2 both intended to be under a duty to hold the account for the benefit of B1 and B2 in specific proportions: see eg R Smith, *Plural Ownership* (2005), 210–11. Further, if B1 pays money into the account and does not intend the benefit of the ensuing credit to be held jointly

B1 and B2 open an account with A Bank. B1 and B2 agree that each is under a duty to the other to share the benefit of the account between them in specific proportions: 75 per cent to B1; 25 per cent to B2.

The beauty of this solution is that B1 and B2 can continue to hold the account, as the law insists, as joint tenants. But B1 and B2 can hold that right on Trust for each other. It is even possible to set up a Trust where the duty of B1 and B2 is to share the benefit of the account between B1 and B2 in proportion to their overall contributions to the account. Once this Trust is set up, B1 *does* have his own, individual right that he can deal with as he pleases (eg, by passing it to his children in his will). B1's individual right is *not* the account itself; rather, it is a persistent right under the Trust: a right against B1 and B2's jointly held right against A Bank.

1.2.2 The tenancy in common and co-ownership

Is it possible for B1 and B2 to co-hold Ownership of a thing *without* being joint tenants? The answer is 'Yes'. It is possible for: (i) B1 and B2 together to have a right to exclusive control of a thing; and, *at the same time*, for (ii) each of B1 and B2 to have an individual, *separate* right.

B1 owns 100 tonnes of grain in a warehouse. B1 gives B2 a 25 per cent share of that stock of grain.

B1 and B2 together have a right to exclusive control of the stock of grain. As in **Example 2**, there is 'unity of possession': each of B1 and B2 is entitled, as a member of a team, to exclusive control of *all* of the 100 tonnes of grain. B2 does not have a distinct right to a specific 25 tonnes of grain: B1 does not intend to give B2 such a right and has not identified any specific portion of grain. Rather, B1 has given B2 an '*undivided* share' of the total 100 tonnes. However, it is important that B2 has an undivided *share*: this means that B1 and B2 do each have a *separate* right. Their rights arose in *different ways* and at *different times*. And B1 has an undivided share of 75 per cent, whereas B2's undivided share is 25 per cent. The case is thus different from **Example 2**: the four unities are *not* present as B1 and B2, as well as holding as a member of a team, each has his own, distinct right.

Therefore, in **Example 5** (as in **D1:Example 11**), B1 and B2 *are* co-holders of Ownership of the total 100 tonnes, *without* being joint tenants. This shows us that, in contrast to a personal right against A, Ownership does not have to be co-held under a joint tenancy. This second form of Co-Ownership is known as a *tenancy in common*. As it is a form of Co-Ownership, it shares a key feature with the joint tenancy: B1 and B2 are each entitled, as a member of a team, to exclusive control of a thing. But, as it is a separate form of Co-Ownership, it is crucially different from the joint tenancy: *as well as* his entitlement, as a member of a team, to exclusive control, B1 and B2 each has an individual 'undivided share'

---

by B1 and B2, B1 and B2 may come under a duty to use the account for the benefit of B1 and B2 in specific proportions in order to prevent B2 being unjustly enriched at B1's expense: see eg *Marshal v Crutwell* (1875) LR 20 Eq 328; *Heseltine v Heseltine* [1971] 1 All ER 952 (see **D4:4.3.2**).

of Ownership. So, B1 *does* have his own, independent right that he can deal with as he pleases, for example by leaving it to his children in his will. This means that when B1 dies, B2 does *not* become the sole holder of Ownership: both before and after B1's death, B2 keeps his individual 75 per cent share of Ownership.

1.3   The rights of co-owners against the rest of the world

If B1 and B2 are co-owners—whether as joint tenants or tenants in common—then, by acting together, they have a right to exclusive control of a thing. The team, comprised of B1 and B2, thus has exactly the same right as a sole owner. This means that the rest of the world is under a prima facie duty not to interfere with any use the team of B1 and B2 may wish to make of the thing. Hence, if: (i) X steals or carelessly damages a bike co-owned by B1 and B2; then (ii) X thus breaches a duty, owed to the team of B1 and B2; so (iii) X thus commits a wrong against the team of B1 and B2. Strictly speaking, neither B1 nor B2 can sue X individually. This means that, in the past, if B1 were to sue X by himself, without joining B2 as a co-defendant,[7] X could object and have the action halted.[8] However, nowadays, a court has a procedural power to allow a claim to proceed even if such an objection is made.[9]

1.4   The rights of one co-owner against another co-owner

What if B1 and B2 are co-owners of a bike and B2, without B1's consent or other authority, destroys or carelessly damages the bike? In such a case, B2 commits a wrong against B1.[10] This shows that B1, in his capacity as a member of the co-owning team, *does* have a limited, independent right: B2 is under a duty not to interfere with B1's right, as a member of the team, to have exclusive control of the bike. Conversely, of course, B1 is under the same duty to B2.

B2 does not commit a wrong against B1 *whenever* B2 asserts a right over the whole of the co-owned thing. Co-Ownership necessarily involves 'unity of possession': as far as each co-owner is concerned, unity of possession has both a positive and negative aspect. Positively, B1, in his capacity as a team member, can make use of the whole of the thing. Negatively, B1 cannot prevent B2 from asserting the very same right.[11] The crucial point is

---

[7] By joining B2 as a co-defendant, B1 gives the court a chance to force B2 to join in the claim against X so that B1 and B2 make that claim as a team.

[8] See eg *Addison v Overend* (1796) 6 TR 766. In *Bloxham v Hubbard* (1804) 5 East 407, Lord Ellenborough CJ stated that X had to raise this point in a specific way: by a plea of abatement. As X had not done so in that case, B1 was allowed to bring a claim against X.

[9] See eg *per* Devlin J in *Baker v Barclays Bank Ltd* [1955] 1 WLR 822 at 830, relying on RSC Ord 116, r 11 (see now CPR 19).

[10] See eg *Farrar v Beswick* (1836) 1 M & W 682; *per* Devlin J in *Baker v Barclays Bank Ltd* [1955] 1 WLR 822 at 827. Depending on B2's precise act, he will commit the wrong of conversion; trespass; or negligence (see **D1:4.1.1(ii)**). The fact that B2 is a co-owner does not give B2 any defence: in a case where B2 destroys the co-owned thing, this is confirmed by s 10(1)(a) of the Torts (Interference with Goods) Act 1977.

[11] *Fennings v Lord Grenville* (1808) 1 Taunt 241 provides a memorable but unpleasant example. The combined efforts of B1 and B2 had led to the capture and killing of a whale in water around the Galapagos Islands. As a result, B1 and B2 became tenants in common of the whale. B1, acting unilaterally, turned all the whale's fat and blubber into oil. B2 objected but could not show that B1's action was wrongful. As Lord Hatherley LC explained in the later case of *Jacobs v Seward* (1872) 5 LR (HL) 464 at 472: 'the very purpose of capturing a whale was to turn it into oil'. The resulting oil, and any proceeds from its sale, would also be held by B1 and B2 as tenants in common, so B1 could not profit at B2's expense by his actions.

that B2 commits a wrong if he goes further and uses the thing as though he were a sole owner (eg, by destroying it, or selling it and taking all the proceeds for himself):[12] at that point, B2 acts inconsistently with B1's right, as a team member, to exclusive control of the thing.

Clearly, problems will arise if B1 and B2 disagree as to how to use the co-owned thing. For example, what if B1 wishes to sell a co-owned bike but B2 instead wishes to keep it? B1 cannot go ahead and sell the bike without B2's consent. First, B1, acting alone, cannot transfer Ownership to C; Ownership of the bike is held by B1 and B2 so *both* of them have to consent if Ownership is to be transferred to C. Second, if B1 attempts to transfer Ownership by himself, he will be in breach of his duty to B2 not to interfere with B2's right to use the bike.[13]

If B1 does attempt to sell the bike to C without B2's consent, and receives £200 from C as a result, it is important to note that B2 has a choice:

1. B2 can assert his right, as a co-owner of the bike, against C;[14] *or*
2. B2 can acquire a right in relation to the £200 received by B1: (i) that right is clearly a product of a right co-held by B1 and B2 (Ownership of the bike); and (ii) B1 is aware of the facts meaning that there is no legal basis on which B1 can keep the full benefit of that right to the £200; so (iii) B1 holds his right to the £200 on Trust for both B1 and B2 (see **D4:4.4**).

Of course, B2 cannot assert *both* rights: he needs to make a choice.[15] If he chooses the second option (eg, because £200 is a good price for the bike and B1 still holds his right to the £200), then the terms of the Trust will depend on how B1 and B2 originally held Ownership of the bike. If B1 and B2 were joint tenants, they will be joint tenants of the right under the Trust of B1's right to the £200. If they were instead tenants in common, each will have an individual right under the Trust: eg, if B2 had a 75 per cent share of Ownership of the bike, B1 will be under a duty to use his right to the £200 75 per cent for B2's benefit.

It is therefore clear that if he wishes to sell the bike to C, B1 first needs to get the consent of B2. What if B2 refuses and B1 thinks this refusal is unreasonable? One would imagine that the property law system would provide a set of specific rules to regulate such disputes. B1 could apply to a court to ask for an order forcing B2 to agree to the proposed sale; the court could then apply those rules in deciding whether or not to make such an order. Such rules do exist where B1 and B2 have Co-Ownership of land (ie, where the right co-held by B1 and B2 is a Freehold or a Lease: see **G2:1.4**). Surprisingly, in other cases of

---

[12] See *per* Devlin J in *Baker v Barclays Bank Ltd* [1955] 1 WLR 822 at 527: 'the mere fact that [B2] takes possession of [the thing] will not be sufficient to amount to a conversion, because he is entitled to possession of it. Neither party, however, is entitled to exclusive possession and, if one of the two carries out an act which can be justified only by the right to exclusive possession, then he [commits the wrong of conversion].'

[13] See s 10(1)(b) of the Torts (Interference with Goods) Act 1977. That provision reverses the doctrinally correct position previously taken by the courts: ie, that as an attempt by B1 to transfer Ownership to C has no effect on B2's right, it therefore does not interfere with B2's right to make use of the thing and so does not count as a wrong: *Mayhew v Herrick* (1849) 7 CB 229.

[14] B2 and C will in fact each be tenants in common of Ownership of the bike: see **Example 12** below. Therefore, B2 will certainly be able to prevent C treating the bike as though C were a sole owner of it: see eg *per* Devlin J at n 12 above.

[15] Often called an 'election': see eg L Smith, *The Law of Tracing* (1997), 358–61.

Co-Ownership, there is no such set of rules.[16] In fact, one limited statutory provision aside,[17] there are *no* special rules to regulate Co-Ownership of things other than land.

So, if B1 wants to sell and B2 refuses, a court has to resolve the dispute between B1 and B2 on first principles. The most obvious course for a court is to order a sale of the co-owned thing, with the proceeds to be divided between B1 and B2: (i) 50–50 if they are joint tenants; (ii) according to the size of their undivided shares if they are tenants in common. If B2 objects to such a sale, he should be invited to become solely entitled to Ownership by buying out B1's share. If B2 cannot afford to do so, there seems to be no good reason (in the absence, for example, of some prior agreement between B1 and B2) to allow B2 to resist a sale and thus to prevent B1 from realising the financial value of his actual or potential share of Ownership.

1.5 Equitable co-holding

1.5.1 The general position: co-holding an Equitable right

EXAMPLE 6

A has a personal right against Z. A makes an Equitable Assignment of that right to B1 and B2 jointly.

In general, the effect of an Equitable Assignment is that: (i) A keeps his right; and (ii) A comes under a duty to B in relation to that right; so (iii) B acquires a persistent right against A's right (see **D2:1.2.2**). In **Example 6**, A's duty is owed to B1 and B2 jointly: so B1 and B2 are joint tenants of the persistent right against A's right.

EXAMPLE 7

A0 has a personal right against Z. A0 transfers that right to A subject to a duty to use that right for the benefit of B1 and B2, in shares of 75 per cent and 25 per cent.

In such a case, A is under the core Trust duty: each of B1 and B2 has a *separate* right under the Trust. Strictly speaking, B1 and B2 do *not* co-hold any right: B1 has his right to a 75 per cent share of the benefit; and B2 has his separate right to a 25 per cent share. So, whilst the effect of the Trust is to ensure that, together, B1 and B2 have the entire benefit of A's right, B1 and B2 each hold a separate right under the Trust.

1.5.2 Equitable Co-Ownership?

EXAMPLE 8

A has Ownership of a bike. A is under a duty, owed jointly to B1 and B2, to use his Ownership for the joint benefit of B1 and B2.

In this case, B1 and B2 do co-hold, as joint tenants, a right under a Trust. However, there is

---

[16] In a monograph dealing with co-ownership (R Smith, *Plural Ownership*, 2005) the discussion of the rules governing a simple case of co-ownership of things other than land takes up less than a page (217–8): there are almost no rules to discuss.

[17] S 188(1) of the Law of Property Act 1925: see **1.6.2** below.

no Co-Ownership: the right co-held by B1 and B2 is *not* Ownership. Rather, A has Owner-ship, and B1 and B2, as a team, hold a persistent right against A's Ownership. That persistent right should not be called 'Equitable Ownership': Ownership is a property right; and there are no Equitable property rights. So, as there is no such thing as 'Equitable Ownership' (see **C1:3.2**), there is no such thing as 'Equitable Co-Ownership'. If, in **Example 8**, X destroys or damages the bike, B1 and B2 are *not* able to make a claim directly against X. X commits no wrong against B1 and B2 as they do not have a property right (see **B:4.4.3**).[18]

1.6   Ending co-holding

1.6.1 The general position

If B1 and B2 hold the same right as a team, that co-holding can end. This will be the case if the right itself ceases to exist. So, if A makes a contractual promise jointly to B1 and B2 to mow a lawn weekly for six months, the right of B1 and B2 ends after six months. B1 and B2 can also agree to terminate their co-holding: for example, if B1 and B2 co-hold a bank account they can agree to close the account *and* split the proceeds between them. However, the co-holding will not end *simply* because B1 and B2 decide to close the account: the default position is that B1 and B2 will then co-hold the money they acquire when closing it. Similarly, if B1 and B2 choose to realise the value of a bike by, for example, selling it to C, the sale, by itself, will not end their co-holding: the default position is that B1 and B2 will co-hold the proceeds of sale. Therefore, if either party claims that the co-holding has ended, he needs to show not just that B1 and B2 intended to close the account or sell the bike; but also that B1 and B2 intended to have separate rights to the proceeds.[19]

If B1 and B2 are joint tenants, co-holding will also end when either party dies: the survivor will be solely entitled to the right. It is also possible for B1 unilaterally to terminate a co-holding by making a 'release' to B2: ie, by dropping out of the team that co-holds the right.[20]

1.6.2 Ending co-ownership

The general principles set out above also apply where B1 and B2 have Co-Ownership. In addition, Co-Ownership will cease whenever its key feature, unity of possession, disappears. So, if B1 and B2 have Co-Ownership of a motorhome and decide that, as in **Example 3**, B1 will have a right to exclusive control of the bottom storey, and B2 a right to exclusive control of the top one, their Co-Ownership of the motorhome will end.

Under section 188(1) of the Law of Property Act 1925 ('the LPA 1925') a special rule applies where B1 and B2 have Co-Ownership of a number of things (other than land) as

---

[18] X does commit a wrong against A; and A is under a duty to use his right to sue X for the benefit of B1 and B2 (see **B:4.4.3**).

[19] On the facts of a particular case, it may of course be possible to infer that B1 and B2 had such an intention from the decision to close the account or sell the bike.

[20] In such a case, B1 is *not* transferring any share to B2, as he has no share to give. A release is thus different from a transfer or assignment: see eg *per* Sir John Vinelott in the Court of Appeal in *Burton v Camden LBC* [1998] 1 FLR 681 at 684. However, it seems that, for reasons of practical convenience, the term 'assignment', when used in a particular statute, can be given a special meaning that covers a release: see the House of Lords in *Burton v Camden LBC* [2000] 2 WLR 427.

tenants in common. A party whose undivided share is 50 per cent or more can apply to a court for an order for 'division of the [things] or any of them' co-owned by B1 and B2.[21] The court may make 'such order and give any consequential directions as it think fit'. This section gives the court only a very limited power. In particular, it seems from its wording that the court cannot order that something unrelated to division (eg, a sale) should occur.[22]

SUMMARY of F2:1

In general, there is only one way for B1 and B2 to co-hold a right: they must hold that right together, as a team. In such a case, B1 and B2 are joint tenants. Where B1 and B2 hold Ownership as joint tenants, the 'four unities' are present. Unity of possession simply means that B1 and B2, acting as a team, have a right to exclusive control of a thing. The three unities of title, time and interest simply mean that, as B1 and B2 are acting only as a team, they have the same right, acquired in the same way.

Ownership, however, can also be co-held by B1 and B2 as tenants in common. In such a case, there is unity of possession: again, B1 and B2, acting as a team, have a right to exclusive control of a thing. However, *in addition*, each of B1 and B2 has his own, individual right: an undivided share of Ownership. There is hence no need for unity of title, time or interest: B1 and B2 have different rights, acquired in different ways.

When looking at Co-Ownership, therefore, we need to ask if B1 and B2 are joint tenants or tenants in common. The most dramatic difference between the two possibilities operates when one of the Co-Owners dies. If B1 dies as a joint tenant, he has no individual right to pass on in his will. The team had Ownership before B1's death and the team continues to have Ownership afterwards; the difference of course is that the team now consists only of B2, who becomes solely entitled to Ownership. If B1 dies as a tenant in common, he *does* have an individual right, an undivided share of Ownership, which he can pass on in his will. So, again, B2's position is unaffected by B1's death: before B1's death, B2 had his own, individual share; after B1's death, B2 still has that share.

When B1 dies as a joint tenant, it is often said that the 'doctrine of survivorship' leads to the result that B2 becomes solely entitled to Ownership. That doctrine can then be attacked as unfair to B1: after all, B1 may have contributed to the price paid to acquire Ownership— why should he have no individual right to pass on his will? However, it is a mistake to see survivorship as some sort of technical, independent doctrine. It simply flows from the nature of a joint tenancy. In fact, nothing changes with B1's death: the team has Ownership before the death; the team has Ownership after it.

---

2   THE ACQUISITION QUESTION

2.1   Independent acquisition

It is possible for B1 and B2 to acquire Ownership jointly and independently. For example, if B1 and B2 jointly take physical control of a thing, as a team, they should jointly acquire Ownership of that thing. Similarly, if B1 and B2 jointly manufacture a new thing, they

---

[21] The provision of course also applies where there are more than two tenants in common.
[22] See R Smith, *Plural Ownership* (2005), 218.

should jointly acquire Ownership of it. And if B1 creates a mixture of B1's thing and B2's thing, the law currently allows B2 to acquire a share of that mixture (see **D1:Example 11**).[23] So, to see if B1 and B2 have independently acquired Ownership, we simply need to look at the means of acquiring Ownership examined in **D1:2.1**. If B1 and B2 have jointly satisfied one of those tests, they will be joint tenants of a new property right.[24]

2.2 Dependent acquisition

In looking at dependent acquisition, we simply need to go through the tests stated in **D1:2.2** to see if B1 and B2 have together acquired A's pre-existing Ownership. A has a power to transfer his property right to B1 and B2, either as joint tenants or as tenants in common, and can exercise that power by means: of (i) a deed; (ii) by delivery;[25] or (iii) by a sale. So, in **Example 2**, A sells his bike jointly to B1 and B2, and so B1 and B2 acquire the same right as a team: neither acquires an individual undivided share. As a result, B1 and B2 are joint tenants.

If B1 has Ownership, then, as we saw in **Example 5**, B1 can exercise a power to give B2 an undivided share of that right. It may well be that such a transfer has to occur by a deed or by sale: it is hard to see how B1 can deliver an undivided share to B2.[26]

EXAMPLE 9

B1 has Ownership of 100 tonnes of grain in a warehouse. B1 makes a contractual promise to B2 to sell 25 tonnes of that grain to B2. B2 pays B1 the agreed price. However, B1 does not set aside any specific 25 tonnes of grain. B1 goes into insolvency.

The basic doctrinal rule is that B2 cannot acquire a property right: (i) a property right is a right relating to the use of a specific thing; and (ii) B2 cannot identify any specific grain that has become his (see **D1:n2** and **D1:2.2.4(iii)(b)**). The very same problem prevents B2 acquiring a persistent right: B2 cannot identify any specific right in relation to which B1 is under a duty to B2 (see **D2:1.1.2(ii)**). So, it might seem that, even though he has paid B1, B2 will have no pre-existing property right or persistent right that he can assert against C, B1's trustee in bankruptcy.

However, in **Example 9**, the Sale of Goods (Amendment) Act 1995 comes to B2's rescue. That Act inserted a new section 20A in the Sale of Goods Act 1979.[27] That section provides that *if*:

---

[23] Although it was argued in **D4:3.1** that, instead: (i) B1 should have sole Ownership of the mixture; and (ii) B1 should hold that right on Trust for B1 and B2.

[24] It is difficult to see how B1 and B2 can become tenants in common by virtue of an independent acquisition: but *Fennings v Lord Grenville* (1808) 1 Taunt 241 provides an example, based on the local custom of the Galapagos Islands. By capturing and killing a whale, B1 and B2 took physical control of it and hence independently acquired Ownership. The local custom was that B1 and B2 became tenants in common of the whale.

[25] In such a case, there is a question as to whether A has to allow *both* B1 and B2 jointly to acquire physical control, or whether it is enough for A to allow *either* B1 or B2 to take physical control on behalf of B1 and B2 jointly.

[26] See eg *Cochrane v Moore* (1870) 25 QBD 57. It may be that by allowing B2 to take physical control of the whole thing, even for a brief period, B1 can make a form of 'ceremonial' delivery of B2's undivided share.

[27] The section is discussed in detail by McKendrick, ch 16 in *Interests in Goods* (ed Palmer and McKendrick, 2nd edn, 1998).

- B1 makes a contractual promise to B2 to transfer Ownership of a specified quantity of goods, from an identified bulk, to B2; *and*
- B2 has paid the agreed price for some or all of the goods covered by the contract; *then*
- B1 and B2 become Co-Owners of that identified bulk: each has an undivided share and B2's share is based on the quantity of goods paid for by him and due to him under the contract.

In **Example 9**: (i) B1's promise is to transfer Ownership of a specific quantity of goods (25 tonnes of grain); (ii) those goods are to come from an identified bulk (the 100 tonnes in the warehouse); and (iii) B2 has paid in full. B1 and B2 are thus co-owners of the 100 tonnes: B1 has an undivided share of 75 per cent; B2 of 25 per cent. Of course, in **Example 9**, B1 and B2 never contemplated becoming co-owners. Instead, that solution is imposed by statute as a means of giving B2 a right capable of binding C *without* altering the fundamental rule that B2 cannot acquire a property right in an unidentified thing; or a persistent right against an unidentified right. The section 20A solution works only because B1 has identified a 'bulk' from which B2's goods are to come: it is therefore possible to give B2 a share of B1's Ownership of that bulk. The rule thus cannot help B in a case, such as **B:Example 8a**, where A has not promised to give B goods from any specific bulk (see **D1:2.2.4(iii)(d)**).[28]

2.2.1 Joint tenancy or tenancy in common?

When looking at dependent acquisition, it is crucial to ask whether B1 and B2 have acquired Ownership as joint tenants or tenants in common. The basic rules are very simple. The default rule is that B1 and B2 acquire their right as joint tenants; a tenancy in common exists only if A, when transferring Ownership to B1 and B2, exercises his power to give each of B1 and B2 an undivided share of Ownership.

(i) Proving a tenancy in common: express words in the transfer to B1 and B2

A does not need to explicitly state that he intends B1 and B2 to acquire Ownership as tenants in common. Any express reference to shares, or individual entitlements, leads to a tenancy in common. For example, if A gives Ownership to B1 and B2 'in equal shares' he has exercised his power to transfer Ownership to B1 and B2 as tenants in common.[29] However, in the absence of any such 'words of severance', it seems B1 and B2 must be joint tenants.

If A instead gives a *personal right* to B1 and B2 'in equal shares', B1 and B2 will still hold that right as joint tenants: it is impossible to hold a personal right as tenants in common (see **1.2.1** above). However, as in **Example 4**, a Trust can come to the rescue. A's intention can be given effect to by recognising a Trust: A can be regarded as having imposed a duty on each of B1 and B2 to hold the personal right on Trust for each other in equal shares.

---

[28] For that reason s 20A offers B no consolation in a case such as *re London Wine Co* [1986] PCC 121 or *re Goldcorp's Exchange* [1995] 1 AC 74. In each case, A did not promise to provide B's goods from a specific bulk: see eg *per* Lord Mustill in *re Goldcorp* at 91.

[29] See eg *per* Lord Hatherley LC in *Robertson v Fraser* (1871) LR 6 Ch App 696 at 699: 'I cannot doubt, having regard to the authorities respecting the effect of such words as 'amongst' and 'respectively', that anything which in the slightest degree indicates an intention to divide the property must be held to abrogate the idea of a joint tenancy, and to create a tenancy in common.'

(ii) Other cases? Circumstances surrounding the transfer to B1 and B2

If A has not transferred Ownership to B1 and B2 as tenants in common, B1 and B2 *must be* joint tenants. Nonetheless, if: (i) the circumstances surrounding the acquisition of Ownership by B1 and B2 show that B1 and B2 intended that each would acquire his own individual right; then (ii) a Trust will arise; and (iii) under that Trust, each of B1 and B2 will have his have his own individual right. So, as in **Example 4**, B1 and B2 hold a right jointly and, *in addition*, each is under a duty to use that right for the benefit of the other. Crucially, this means that each of B1 and B2 has a separate right that he can, for example, pass on when he dies. In such cases, it is often said that: (i) B1 and B2 are 'joint tenants at Common Law'; but (ii) 'tenants in common in Equity'.[30] On that orthodox view, Common Law and Equity give different answers to the same question of whether B1 and B2 each has an individual share of Ownership: (i) Common Law says 'No'; but (ii) Equity says 'Yes'.

However, that orthodox view is not accurate (see too **C1:3.2**). Whilst B1 and B2 do each acquire an individual right, that right is *not* a share of Ownership; instead, each of B1 and B2 has a persistent right under a Trust. Therefore, in such cases, Common Law and Equity are *not* inconsistent: (i) as no 'words of severance' were used, B1 and B2 hold Ownership as joint tenants; but (ii) as the surrounding circumstances show that B1 and B2 intended that each would have his own individual right, B1 and B2 each has an individual right under a Trust.

When will the surrounding circumstances show that B1 and B2 intended that each would have his own individual right? Prominent examples include: (i) where B1 and B2 make unequal contributions to the price paid when acquiring Ownership from A;[31] (ii) where B1 and B2 acquire Ownership from A as security (ie, as part of a mortgage transaction: see **D1:Example 4a**);[32] and (iii) where B1 and B2 acquire Ownership together to use it for their separate business purposes.[33] However, this does not mean that, in such cases, a Trust will necessarily arise: everything depends on whether, in the particular case, B1 and B2 intended that each would acquire his own individual right. Similarly, it is a mistake to think that there is a set list of such circumstances in which B1 and B2 can be found to have such an intention.[34]

These cases raise an interesting question that has not been properly addressed by the courts: *why* does a Trust arise? Put another way, what is the specific reason for which B1 and B2 each come under a duty to use their Ownership for the benefit of the other? In the case of unequal contributions to the purchase price, such a Trust can perhaps be seen as a Type 2 Resulting Trust (see **D4:4.3.2**).[35] For example, if: (i) B1 pays 65 per cent of the purchase price; and (ii) B1 does not intend that he and B2 will *only* hold Ownership as part of a team; then (iii) there is no legal basis for B2 to have the benefit of B1's contribution; and so (iv) B2 would be unjustly enriched at B1's expense if B1 and B2 simply held Ownership as

---

[30] See eg *Lake v Craddock* (1732) 3 P Wms 158; *Morley v Bird* (1798) 3 Ves 628.

[31] See eg *Robinson v Preston* (1858) 4 K & J 505.

[32] See eg *Morley v Bird* (1798) 3 Ves 628. So even if: (i) B1 and B2 lend exactly the same sum to A; and (ii) A transfers Ownership to B1 and B2 to secure his duty to repay that loan; then (iii) the starting point is that each of B1 and B2 has his own individual right under a Trust.

[33] See eg *Lake v Craddock* (1732) 3 P Wms 158; *per* Lord Brightman in *Malayan Credit Ltd v Jack Chia-MPH Ltd* [1986] AC 549 at 560.

[34] This was emphasised by Lord Brightman in *Malayan Credit Ltd v Jack Chia-MPH Ltd* [1986] AC 549 at 560.

[35] The Resulting Trust analysis was applied by Lord Neuberger in *Stack v Dowden* [2007] 2 AC 432 at [111]–[115]. It is also adopted by R Smith, *Plural Ownership* (2005), 37.

joint tenants. However, in other cases, the source of the Trust is harder to find. It seems that the shared intention of B1 and B2 that each is to have his own individual right, *by itself*, imposes a duty on each of B1 and B2. That is unusual: the general rule is that an unexpressed intention, by itself, cannot impose such a duty and so cannot give rise to a Trust.

Three possible explanations can be put forward for the Trust arising in these cases:

Option 1:   Although no express statement has been made, B1 and B2 have exercised their power to set up a Trust and so have each consented to be under a duty to the other. On that view, the Trust arises because of Reason 1 set out in **B:4.3**; *or*

Option 2:   B1 and B2 have each made an implied promise to the other that each will have an individual share of Ownership. The 'receipt after a promise' principle then applies to impose a duty on B1 and B2. On that view, the Trust arises because of Reason 6 set out in **B:4.3**; *or*

Option 3:   A special principle, applying only where B1 and B2 acquire a right as joint tenants, means that the shared intention of B1 and B2 *by itself* imposes a duty on B1 and B2. On that view, the Trust arises because of Reason 6 set out in **B:4.3**.

Option 3 fits most closely with the courts' approach.[36] However, it is not entirely satisfactory. In particular, when B1 and B2 acquire Ownership, the Trust device is unnecessary: a simpler solution would be to find that, due to the circumstances surrounding the transfer to B1 and B2, they simply acquired Ownership as tenants in common. This would mean rejecting the orthodox view that such a tenancy in common can arise only where A, by using 'words of severance', exercises his power to create it. However, in effect, the courts have *already* rejected that view: they have just done it through the back door, by conveniently finding a Trust.

(iii) Other cases? The needs of practical convenience?

Let us say that B1 and B2 dependently acquire Ownership from A, each paying half of the purchase price. B1 then dies. There are no words of severance in the transfer from A, and so B1 and B2 hold Ownership as joint tenants. If there is no Trust under which each of B1 and B2 has an individual right, then, at the time of B1's death, B2 will be free to take the full benefit of Ownership. In a case where B1 and B2 have not deliberately chosen that result, this may seem harsh: particularly if B1 believed he had an individual share of Ownership and made his will on that basis. Indeed, judges have often commented, sometimes in dramatic terms, on the severity of survivorship.[37] The perceived needs of practical convenience may therefore influence a judge to find, in a case where there is no clear evidence in favour

---

[36] **Option 1** is problematic as, whilst the surrounding circumstances can be taken into account when deciding if a party has exercised his power to set up a Trust (see eg *Paul v Constance* [1977] 1 WLR 527), it seems to be necessary for that party to at least make *some* express statement (eg, in *Paul v Constance*, A had told B a bank account was 'as much yours as mine'). It is also causes problems where B1 and B2 acquire a Freehold or Lease: a Trust can arise in such a case even if no writing has been used (see **G2:2.2.1(ii)**); but if that Trust is seen as depending on the parties' exercise of a power to set up a Trust, it would have to be proved in writing due to s 53(1)(b) of the LPA 1925 (see **E2:2.3.2**).

[37] Survivorship is described by the court in *R v Williams* (1735) Bunb 342 at 343 as 'looked upon as odious in equity'; see too Lord Denning MR during argument in *Burgess v Rawnsley* [1975] 1 Ch 429 at 432 referring to the effect of survivorship as 'like the worst technicality of the common law'.

of either a joint tenancy or a tenancy in common, that the surrounding circumstances justify a finding that B1 and B2 impliedly intended that each would have his own individual share of Ownership: in such a case, a Trust can then arise.

Alternatively, even if B1 and B2 are initially joint tenants, it is still possible for them to become tenants in common, and hence for B2 to have a share he can pass on when he dies. This process of converting a joint tenancy into a tenancy in common is known as *severance*.

2.3   Severance: the acquisition of an individual right

Severance is the process by which a joint tenancy is turned into a tenancy in common. It is part of the **acquisition question** as it is a means by which a joint tenant, who has no individual right, can acquire an undivided share of Ownership. It can apply whether the initial joint tenancy of B1 and B2 was acquired independently or dependently.

Before we examine how severance occurs, we need to examine its effect. If B1 and B2's joint tenancy is severed, the parties will become tenants in common, each holding a half share of Ownership. Similarly, if a joint tenancy of B1, B2 and B3 is severed, each will hold a third share of Ownership. It is important to note that severance operates in this way even if the joint tenants, when initially acquiring Ownership, contributed differing proportions of the purchase price. For example, it may be that B1 paid 80 per cent of the price and B2 only 20 per cent. Nonetheless, if B1 and B2 expressly chose to be joint tenants then, if that joint tenancy is severed, each will hold a 50 per cent share of Ownership. This can create something of a trap for a party who makes the bigger contribution but chooses to become a joint tenant.

Where there are three or more joint tenants, it is possible for B3 to sever without ending the joint tenancy of B1 and B2. In such a case, severance gives B3 an individual share; but it does *not* give B1 and B2 such a share.

EXAMPLE 10

B1, B2 and B3 hold Ownership of a bike as joint tenants. B3 transfers his 'share' of Ownership to C. B1 then dies.

This act by B3 causes a severance of the joint tenancy between B1, B2 and B3 (see **2.3.1** below). C thus gains an undivided one-third share of Ownership and so will be a tenant in common along with B1 and B2. However, there is no need for B1 and B2, *as between themselves*, to cease being joint tenants: they will, as a team, hold the remaining two-thirds share of Ownership. So: (i) C is a tenant in common with a one-third share; and (ii) the team of B1 and B2, with a two-thirds share, is the other tenant in common. This means that, when B1 dies, B2 is solely entitled to the two-thirds share.

Stage 1: before severance	Stage 2: after severance	Stage 3: after B1's death	
B1+B2+B3	B1+B2 2/3 C 1/3	B2 2/3 C 1/3	=ownership

2.3.1 'An act operating on a joint tenant's own share'

If B1 and B2 are joint tenants, each can, by his own, unilateral action, give C either: (i) an undivided share of Ownership; or (ii) a right relating to such a share. B1 thus has the power to acquire and deal with an undivided share *without* having to obtain any consent from B2.

EXAMPLE 11

B1 and B2 hold Ownership of a bike as joint tenants. B1 transfers a half share of Ownership to C.

By this 'act operating on his own share', B1 exercises his power to acquire and deal with an undivided share of Ownership. The severance means that B1 acquires, and transfers to C, a 50 per cent share of Ownership. Even though B2 may have no knowledge of the transfer, B2 and C now hold Ownership of the bike as tenants in common.

EXAMPLE 12

B1 and B2 hold Ownership of a bike as joint tenants. B1 attempts to transfer Ownership of the bike to C.

Such a case may arise if B1, in order to receive more money from C, tricks C into thinking that B1 is the sole holder of Ownership of the bike. Of course, a transfer of Ownership can only occur if both B1 and B2 consent. Nonetheless, as in **Example 11**, B1 has exercised his power to acquire and deal with a 50 per cent share of Ownership. So, as in **Example 11**, B2 and C now hold Ownership of the bike as tenants in common.

There is, of course, a technical hitch with this method of severance. In both **Examples 11 and 12**, when B1 attempts to give C a right, B1 is still a joint tenant and hence has no individual share to give to C. Strictly speaking, B1 should sever first and *then* transfer his undivided share to C. However, this technically correct approach would cause two problems. First, a trap would be created for C: he may reasonably believe he is getting a share of Ownership from B1, only to find that B1 has no individual share to give. The desire to protect C, an important consideration when resolving the **basic tension**, has therefore led the courts to reject the technical view. Second, it seems to be unnecessarily complicated to insist on B1's first severing and then giving C a right. As a result, the technical view has never taken hold: an act by B1 giving C a right in relation to a distinct share is allowed to have the effect of simultaneously: (i) causing a severance (thus giving B his own share); *and* (ii) giving C a right in relation to that distinct share.

EXAMPLE 13

B1 and B2 hold Ownership of a bike as joint tenants. B1 makes a contractual promise to C to allow C to have exclusive control of the bike for six months.

It seems that severance should not occur. Even if B1 were solely entitled to Ownership, B1's contractual promise would give C only a personal right against B1. And C can acquire such a personal right even if B1 and B2 continue to hold Ownership as joint tenants. The desire to protect C therefore does *not* require that B1 must have an undivided share of Ownership and so there is no need for severance.

EXAMPLE 14

B1 and B2 hold Ownership of a bike as joint tenants. In return for a loan from C, B1 makes a contractual promise to C to use his right to the bike as security for his duty to repay the loan.

Severance should occur here. The plan is for C to acquire a persistent right: a Purely Equitable Charge (see **D2:1.2.1**). C can only acquire such a right if B1 holds a *specific right* with a duty to hold that right as security (see **D2:1.1.2**). The desire to protect C therefore requires that B1 must have an individual right—an undivided share of Ownership–that he can hold as security for C; so severance must occur. The same analysis applies if B1 declares a Trust in C's favour.[38]

It is therefore clear that the desire to protect C is the key to this form of severance. However, the ability to sever by an act operating on his own share also provides B1 with an important facility. It means he can unilaterally choose to end the joint tenancy, and to realise the monetary value of his right as a joint tenant by, for example, selling a distinct share to C; or using that share as security for a loan made by C.

2.3.2 Agreement between B1 and B2[39]

B1 and B2 can simply agree that they are to hold Ownership as tenants in common. This form of severance provides another facility to B1 and B2: it allows B1 and B2 to sever without getting C involved; but only if each of them agrees. The agreement between B1 and B2 does *not* need to be legally binding. Rather, there simply needs to be evidence that the parties mutually intended that each would acquire his own individual right.[40] As the agreement does not to be legally binding, its terms do not need to be as precisely defined as a contract; and moreover the parties do not need to satisfy any formality rules.[41]

However, B1 and B2 do need to have a common intention to sever. Negotiations between them about a possible severance, such as on offer by B1 to buy B2's share for a set price and a counter-offer by B2 to sell it to B1 at a higher price, will *not* suffice unless an agreement has been reached.[42] And if a *conditional* agreement has been reached, and that condition has not yet been satisfied, no severance can occur.[43] So, if the deal is that B1 and B2 will acquire undivided shares when they get divorced, and they are not yet divorced at the time of B1's death, no severance has occurred.

The agreement between B1 and B2 must necessarily involve the acquisition of an individual right by each of B1 and B2. Therefore, a simple agreement by B1 and B2 to sell a co-owned thing will *not* effect a severance: a sale will not necessarily end a joint tenancy, as the default position is that B1 and B2 will simply become joint tenants of the proceeds of

---

[38] If B1: (i) holds a specific right; and (ii) comes under a contractual duty to set up a Trust of that right in C's favour or to transfer that right to C; then the usual result is that C acquires a persistent right: a right under a Trust (see **D2:2.1.2**). So, to protect C, severance must also occur where B1 comes under such a duty: see eg *re Hewett* [1894] 1 Ch 362.

[39] A number of the cases cited here involve disputes relating to land; however, the relevant principles apply equally where B1 and B2 have Co-Ownership of a thing other than land.

[40] See eg *Burgess v Rawnsley* [1975] Ch 429 *per* Sir John Pennycuick at 446: 'The significance of an agreement is not that it binds the parties; but that it serves as an indication of common intention to sever'. We will see an important consequence of this in **G2:Example 29**.

[41] That latter point is very important where land is concerned (see **G2:2.4.3**).

[42] As emphasised by Sir John Pennycuick in *Burgess v Rawnsley* [1975] Ch 429 at 447.

[43] See eg *Gore & Snell v Carpenter* (1990) 60 P & CR 456.

sale (see **1.6.1** above).[44] Equally, an agreement that B1 will become solely entitled to Ownership will *not* effect a severance. Whilst the agreement does contemplate the end of the joint tenancy, it does not involve giving *each of* B1 and B2 his own individual right. It is important to remember that severance does not *just* involve the termination of a joint tenancy: it involves: (i) termination of a joint tenancy; *and* (ii) the creation of a tenancy in common. It is thus a process by which a party acquires his own individual right.[45]

Mutual agreement is generally regarded as a method of severance developed by Equity.[46] On that view, a mutual agreement means that: (i) B1 and B2 continue to hold Ownership as joint tenants; but (ii) each of B1 and B2 acquires an individual right under a Trust. This means that, technically speaking, severance does not occur: B1 and B2 do not hold Ownership as tenants in common. Rather, as in **Example 4**, the individual right acquired by each of B1 and B2 is a right under a Trust.

In practice, this makes little difference: the key point is that the mutual agreement gives each of B1 and B2 an individual right that he can, for example, pass on when he dies. So, even if the orthodox view is correct and mutual agreement does not turn B1 and B2 into tenants in common, it may still be reasonable to call it severance: it has the key feature of giving each of B1 and B2 an individual right. Doctrinally, however, viewing severance by mutual agreement as giving rise to a Trust may cause a problem: *why* should a Trust arise as a result of a non-binding agreement between B1 and B2? As suggested in **2.2.1(ii)** above when considering the initial question of whether B1 and B2 hold Ownership as tenants in common, the best approach may be to permit mutual agreement to effect a *true* severance.[47] On that view, it would lead to each of B1 and B2 acquiring an undivided share of Ownership, rather than a right under a Trust.

2.3.2 Mutual course of dealing[48]

The third form of severance does not provide a facility to joint tenants; instead, it protects them from a particular danger.

EXAMPLE 15

B1 and B2 hold Ownership of a yacht as joint tenants. B1 and B2 both behave as though each has his own undivided share of Ownership and so B1 reasonably believes he has such a share. B1 draws up his will on the basis that he has a share of Ownership to pass on to his children. B1 dies.

The danger is clear. B1 believes he has an undivided share of Ownership, and has made his will on that basis. Yet when B1 dies the truth may be revealed allowing B2 to become solely entitled to Ownership of the yacht. In that case, the children to whom B1 has left his 'share' of Ownership will get nothing.

To protect B1 and his children from this danger, the decision of Page-Wood V-C in

---

[44] See eg *Nielson-Jones v Fedden* [1975] Ch 222.

[45] *Ibid* at 229.

[46] See eg R Smith, *Plural Ownership* (2005), 67; *Snell's Equity* (ed McGhee, 31st edn, 2005), 5–22.

[47] It is perhaps worth noting that when discussing methods of severance in *Williams v Hensman* (1861) 1 J & H 546 at 557, Page-Wood V-C does not distinguish between Common Law and Equitable methods.

[48] Again, a number of the cases cited here involve disputes relating to land; however the relevant principles apply equally where B1 and B2 have Co-Ownership of a thing other than land.

Williams v Hensman[49] confirmed a third method of severance. It occurs when each joint tenant, to the knowledge of the other joint tenants, conducts himself on the assumption that he has his own individual share of Ownership. This form of severance is often known as 'severance by a mutual course of dealing'.

It is important to emphasise that this method of severance depends on particular action by *all* of the joint tenants who are to acquire an undivided share.[50] If B1 simply has the mistaken belief that he has such a share and acts on that basis by, for example, leaving his 'share' in his will, there is no severance: there has been no *mutual* course of dealing by both B1 and B2. The crucial point is that B2 needs to be responsible, to some extent, for B1's mistaken belief. The logic of this method of severance is therefore closely linked to the principle behind estoppel doctrines, such as proprietary estoppel (see **D1:3.3.1** and **E4**): B1 should not suffer a detriment as a result of his reasonable reliance on a belief for which B2 was, in part at least, responsible.[51]

Certainly, despite the occasional indication to the contrary by some judges,[52] this method of severance should *not* be used as a last resort that can be used to mop up situations not falling into either of the previous two methods. For example, if negotiations between B1 and B2 have not led to an agreement, it is very unlikely that there will be severance by a mutual course of conduct: the parties will lack the necessary shared assumption that they are *already* tenants in common.[53]

2.3.4 Situations where severance is imposed

There are certain events that lead to the property law system giving B1 and B2 an undivided share and thus turning their joint tenancy into a tenancy in common. For example, if B1 goes into insolvency, his rights pass to C, his trustee in bankruptcy (see **B:2.3.2**). However, strictly speaking, B1 has no individual right that can pass to C. As a result, B1's insolvency itself is deemed to sever any joint tenancy under which B1 co-holds a right with B2: C thus acquires an undivided share of that right and can use it for the benefit of B1's creditors. Further, if B2 unlawfully kills B1, it is clear that B2 cannot become solely entitled to the right jointly held by B1 and B2. One way to prevent this is to regard the unlawful killing as an act of severance, ending the joint tenancy as well as the unfortunate joint tenant.[54]

---

[49] (1861) 1 J & H 546.

[50] See eg *Hunter v Babbage* [1994] 2 FLR 806 *per* McDonnell QC sitting as a Deputy High Court judge at 813: 'The course of dealing must be sufficient . . . to intimate that the interests of all were *mutually* treated as constituting a tenancy in common.' It seems that the mutual course of dealing need not be joined in by all the joint tenants. If B1, B2, B3 and B4 hold Ownership as joint tenants, a mutual course of dealing between B1 and B2 could lead to B1 and B2 acquiring undivided quarter shares, but B3 and B4 holding a half share as joint tenants.

[51] As with mutual agreement, mutual course of dealing is generally regarded as an Equitable method of severance. However, as suggested above in relation to mutual agreement, it may be better to see it as true method of severance, by which B1 and B2 each acquire an undivided share of Ownership, rather than a right under a Trust.

[52] See eg *per* Lord Denning MR in *Burgess v Rawnsley* [1975] Ch 429 at 439.

[53] See eg *per* John McDonnell QC sitting as a Deputy High Court judge in *Hunter v Babbage* [1994] 2 FLR 806 at 818.

[54] See eg *per* Vinelott J in *re K* [1985] Ch 85 at 100. The Forfeiture Act 1982 may allow a court to vary the result. A different way to prevent B2 benefiting is by saying, as some courts in Australia, New Zealand and Canada have done, that: (i) B2 becomes solely entitled to the jointly held right; but (ii) as he acquired that right by committing a wrong against B1, then (iii) B2 holds the right subject to a duty to use it 50 per cent for the benefit of B1's estate and 50 per cent for his own benefit: B1's estate thus acquires a persistent right under a Trust: see eg *re Stone* [1989] 1 Qd R 351 at 352.

2.3.5 Acts which do *not* sever

EXAMPLE 16

B1 and B2 hold Ownership of a bike as joint tenants. B1 declares to B2 that he wishes to end the joint tenancy immediately and acquire an undivided share of Ownership.

Severance does not occur.[55] B1's declaration certainly does not count as an 'act operating on his own share': there is clearly no need to give B1 an undivided share in order to protect a third party. Nor is there an agreement or mutual course of conduct: B1 has simply expressed his own, unilateral wish.

EXAMPLE 17

B1 and B2 hold Ownership of a bike as joint tenants. B1 makes a will leaving his 'share' of Ownership of the bike to C.

Again, severance does not occur. The making of the will is not an 'act operating on B1's own share' as it has no immediate effect: B1 is free to revoke the will whenever he pleases, as it takes effect only on his death. And, again, this unilateral act by B1 does not, by itself,[56] amount to an agreement with B2 or a mutual course of conduct carried out by both B1 and B2.

However, as noted above, it is often regarded as unfair that a joint tenant is unable to pass on a share on his death. This has had two effects: (i) there have been suggestions that severance should be reformed: eg, to allow severance by will so that B1's attempt to leave his 'share' to C on his death will succeed; (ii) on occasion, judges have taken a creative approach to severance in order to find, in a particular case, that a joint tenancy has been severed. The calls for reform and judicial creativity are both particularly prominent where land is involved.[57] This seems to be a consequence of the special features of land (see **A:3.1**): its social importance and financial value make the perceived harshness of the doctrine of survivorship all the more dramatic. We will therefore consider the possibilities of reform in **G2:2.4.6** when focusing on Co-Ownership of land.

SUMMARY of F2:2.3

Severance is a process by which B1 and B2, who hold Ownership as joint tenants, can acquire an undivided share of that Ownership, and thus hold that Ownership as tenants in common. Where B1 and B2 hold Ownership as joint tenants, there are three principal methods of severance:

- An act by B1 giving his undivided 'share' of Ownership to C; or giving C a persistent right against B1's undivided 'share' of Ownership;

---

[55] Lord Denning MR in *Burgess v Rawnsley* [1975] Ch 429 at 439 argued that severance does occur in such a situation. That suggestion is unsupported by authority and has been roundly rejected: most thoroughly by the High Court of Australia in *Corin v Patton* (1990) 169 CLR 540 but see too *Hunter v Babbage* [1994] 2 FLR 806.

[56] If, for example, both B1 and B2 make wills because of a shared assumption that they are already tenants in common, then this can provide evidence of a severance by a mutual course of dealing.

[57] As to the judicial creativity, see eg Lord Denning MR in *Burgess v Rawnsley* [1975] Ch 429. The other two Court of Appeal judges relied on more orthodox principles, but surprisingly held that the trial judge's decision (very hard to justify when applying those orthodox principles) should not be disturbed.

- An agreement by B1 and B2 to acquire undivided shares of Ownership;
- Action by B1 and B2, to the knowledge of the other, on the assumption that each has an undivided share of Ownership.

In addition, there are certain circumstances, such as the insolvency of B1 or the unlawful killing by B1 of B2, that automatically lead to B1 and B2 acquiring a undivided share of Ownership. However, B1 does not acquire such a share simply by telling B2 that he wishes to acquire one; or by virtue of making a will leaving his 'share' to C.

3 THE DEFENCES QUESTION

If B is solely entitled to Ownership of a thing, it is very difficult for C to have a defence against B's pre-existing property right (see **D1:3**). If Ownership of a thing is held by the team made up of B1 and B2, rather than by B alone, C's position is *exactly the same*. C can rely on the limited defences discussed in **D1:3**; but there are no extra defences[58] he can rely on due to the fact that Ownership is held by the team of B1 and B2 rather than by B alone.[59]

4 THE REMEDIES QUESTION

If B1 and B2, acting as a team, can assert their pre-existing Ownership against C, then C is in *exactly the same* position as where B, who is solely entitled to Ownership, asserts his pre-existing right against C. Therefore, the discussion of remedies in **D1:4** applies here. The principles examined there will govern the position if, for example, A steals a thing co-owned by B1 and B2 and sells it to C.[60]

Things are slightly different if C acquires his right from B1 (as in **Example 12**). If C has no defence, C will be bound by B2's pre-existing property right and C and B2 will hold Ownership as tenants in common, each with his own undivided share. If, as is likely, C and B2 have inconsistent desires as to how to use the co-owned thing, a court may have to decide what remedy to give to protect B2's right. In doing so, the court is deciding a dispute between co-owners and so the discussion in **1.4** above applies.

---

[58] One special point applies where Co-Ownership rights arise under s 20A of the Sale of Goods Act 1995. If A sells an unspecific part of a bulk to B1 and then to B2, we have seen that B1 and B2 can each become co-owners of that bulk. If A then delivers a specific part of the bulk to B1, technically A and B1 may commit the wrong of conversion against B2 (by excluding B2 from control of the part of the bulk given to B1): s 20B prevents that by ensuring that B2 is deemed to have consented to the delivery to B1. So the section allows A and B1 to rely on the consent defence (see **D1:3.2**).

[59] In a case such as **Example 12**, where B1 sells a co-owned bike to C without the consent of B2, C does acquire B1's share of Ownership. B2 and C are thus tenants in common and so C does not commit the wrong of conversion against B2 simply by using the bike; however, he does commit that wrong if he uses the bike in a way inconsistent with B2's right, as a co-owner, to exclusive control of the bike (see **fn14** above).

[60] It may seem there is a risk to C if: (i) B1 asserts a right against C and C is ordered to pay money to B1; and (ii) B2 then also asserts a right against C. The correct way to deal with this risk, as noted in **1.3** above, is through insisting that, as B1 and B2 hold Ownership as a team then, whether they are joint tenants or tenants in common, neither B1 nor B2 should be able to sue C individually. The Torts (Interference with Goods) Act 1977, s 8 may also seem to give C some protection against such double liability, but it seems instead to be focused on a case where B1 and B2 are not co-owners but instead each have a *separate* pre-existing property right: as where (i) B1 acquires Ownership of a bike from a shop; (ii) B2 then also acquires Ownership by stealing the bike; and (iii) C then takes the bike and thus commits two separate wrongs against B1 and B2.

CHAPTER F3
THE TRUST

F3

THE TRUST

The right under a Trust is the classic example of a persistent right. Trusts can be important not only in disputes about the use of things, but also in disputes about the use of rights. B can claim not only that A holds A's Ownership of a bike on Trust for B; but also that A holds his bank account (a personal right against Z Bank) on Trust for B. In fact, the practical importance of Trusts lies precisely in their ability to give B a persistent right against a personal right of A (such as A's bank account; or A's shares in Z Co).

1 THE CONTENT QUESTION

1.1 The core Trust duty

B's right counts as a right under a Trust if two conditions are met:

- A is under a duty to B to use a specific right, in a particular way, for B's benefit; *and*
- A is, overall, under a duty in relation to the whole of that right.

In such a case, A is under the core Trust duty: the duty not to use a right for his own benefit, unless and to the extent that A is also a beneficiary of the Trust (see **D2:1.2.4(ii)**). Provided A is, *overall*, under that core Trust duty, the nature of A's particular duty to B is irrelevant (see **D2:1.2.4**). As long as A's duty to B relates to the right held on Trust by A, B has a persistent right.[1] This explains the incredible *versatility* of the Trust: as we saw in **D2:1.4**, the Trust can be used for a wide number of different purposes.

Whenever A is under the core Trust duty, A is also under a *duty to account to B for the right held on Trust* (see **D2:4.1.1(ii)**). That duty is an integral part of the core Trust duty and is very important in practice: it means that A, at B's request, must be able to produce *either*: (i) the right initially held on Trust for B; or (ii) a permitted product of that right.[2] If A is unable to do so, and has no legitimate excuse for his failure, A can be ordered to pay a sum

---

[1] If A simply has a *power* to use a right for B's benefit, but has no duty to do so, then B does not have a persistent right, even if A is under a duty to B to exercise that power carefully and without self-interest. In such a case, B benefits from a *fiduciary power*; he does not have a persistent right under a Trust. A discretionary Trust (see **D2:1.4.3**) differs from the case where B simply benefits from a fiduciary power: in a discretionary Trust, A has the same power to use a right for B's benefit; but he also has a *duty* to use a particular right for the benefit of at least one of a class of people including B: see eg *per* Lord Eldon in *Brown v Higgs* (1803) 8 Ves Jr 561 at 570; *re Saxone Shoe Co Ltd* [1962] 1 WLR 943.

[2] For example, if A holds shares on Trust for B, the terms of the Trust may permit A to sell those particular shares and invest the proceeds of sale in other shares. In such a case, A can perform his duty to account by producing those new shares: they are a permitted product of the right initially held on Trust.

of money equal to the value of the right that should be held on Trust. B's claim is based simply on the fact that A has failed to perform his duty to account: B does *not* need to show that A has breached any of his other duties as trustee (eg, that A has managed the right held on Trust carelessly or dishonestly); *nor* does B need to show that any specific act of A has caused B a loss (see **D2:4.1.2**).[3]

The duty to account also means that A can, for example, be ordered to pay the value the right initially held on Trust *would* have had *if* A had acted properly and complied with his duties as trustee. So, if A held shares on Trust for B but: (i) sold those shares, in breach of his duties as trustee, when they were worth £1,000; and (ii) those shares are now worth £2,000; then (iii) as A cannot perform his duty to account by producing the shares, he can be made to pay a sum equal to the value of those shares: £2,000 (see **D2:Example 29b**).[4]

1.2   Duties arising from the core Trust duty

If A is under the core Trust duty, certain other duties are imposed on A, even if he did not expressly consent to them. For example, A comes under a duty to B: (i) not to put himself in a position where his own personal interests may conflict with his duties to B; and (ii) not to make a personal gain out of his position as trustee.[5] These duties are said to come, respectively, from the 'no conflict' and 'no profit' rules. They are both regarded as core examples of *fiduciary duties*.[6] The duties can be seen to protect, and reinforce, the core Trust duty: for example, the 'no conflict' rule aims to ensure that A does not use the right held on Trust for his own benefit.[7]

Further, once A is under the core Trust duty, he also comes under a duty to B to take care in exercising his power to manage the right held on Trust. So, if A holds shares on Trust for B, he has a duty to take care when deciding how to invest the shares and the income they produce. The basic standard of care developed by the courts is that A 'ought to conduct the business of the trust in the same manner that an ordinary prudent man of business would conduct his own'.[8] That duty has now been replaced, in particular circumstances, by the essentially identical duty imposed by the Trustee Act 2000.[9]

These additional duties all arise as a consequence of the core Trust duty. However, in

---

[3] See eg *re Dawson* [1966] 2 NSWR 211; *Youyang v Minter Ellis Morris Fletcher* (2003) 196 ALR 482 (High Court of Australia); Elliott (2002) 65 *MLR* 588; Elliott and Edelman (2003) 119 *LQR* 545. The result in *Target Holdings v Redferns* [1996] AC 421 is consistent with the view set out here (as explained by Millett (1998) 114 *LQR* 214 at 223–7). In *Redferns* A initially held money on Trust and was permitted to pay out that money *if* B were given a Charge over X's land. As B did receive that Charge, there was no longer any need for A to produce the money initially held on Trust.

[4] See eg *re Massingberd's Settlement* (1890) 63 LT 296.

[5] See eg *per* Lord Upjohn in *Boardman v Phipps* [1967] 2 AC 46 at 123. For an example of a fiduciary duty applying to a party not initially holding a right on Trust: see *Attorney-General for Hong Kong v Reid* [1994] 1 AC 324.

[6] There is much debate about the precise meaning of the term 'fiduciary duty' (see eg Getzler, ch 31 in *Mapping the Law* (ed Burrows and Rodger, 2007); Conaglen (2005) 121 *LQR* 452; L Smith, ch 4 in *Rationalizing Property, Equity and Trusts: Essays in Honour of Edward Burn* (ed Getzler, 2003); Birks (2002) *TLI* 34). On any view, the duties arising out of the 'no conflict' and 'no-profit' rules are regarded as fiduciary duties.

[7] See eg *per* Lord Brougham in *Hamilton v Wright* (1842) 9 Cl & Fin 111; Congalen (2005) 121 *LQR* 452 at 460–72.

[8] *Per* Jessel MR in *Speight v Gaunt* (1882) 22 Ch D 727 at 739.

[9] Activities regulated by the Trustee Act 2000 (such as making investments of a right held on Trust) are subject to a duty of care imposed by s 1 of the Act.

contrast to the duty to account, they are *not* an integral part of that core Trust duty. This means that B can have a right under a Trust even if the terms of the Trust make clear that A is *not* under these additional duties.[10] As long as A is under the core Trust duty, B will have the important benefit of a persistent right: a right under a Trust. That right, of course, gives B protection if A goes into insolvency (see **B:4.5.2(ii)**). However, B can have a right under a Trust *even if* A is *not* under the duties discussed in this section (**1.2**).

This point is very important in practice. For example, commercial financing transactions, such as securitisations, may be carried out by using a Trust (see **C1:3.3**). If A0 Bank has some rights (eg, against borrowers from the bank), it may wish to raise money immediately by offering investors, such as B, the chance to take some of the benefit of those rights. One method is for: (i) A0 Bank to set up a Trust of those rights in favour of A; and then (ii) for A to hold those rights on Trust with a duty to use those rights, to a certain proportion, for B's benefit. In such a scheme: (i) A0 Bank and B avoid the difficulties that may be entailed in a transfer of A0 Bank's right to B (see **D2:1.4.1**); *and* (ii) B gets the benefit of a persistent right: he is not exposed to the risk of A0 Bank or A going into insolvency.[11] However, for commercial reasons, A0 Bank and A may wish to ensure that A is relatively free to deal with its rights and is not under onerous duties to investors such as B. The parties' aim may therefore be: (i) to give B a persistent right; but (ii) at the same time, to ensure A is free from additional duties to B. It seems this can be done—provided, of course, that A is under the core Trust duty and is *not* free to use the rights it holds for its own benefit (unless and to the extent that A is also a beneficiary of the Trust).[12]

1.3 Further duties

If: (i) A0 transfers a right to A to hold on Trust for B; *or* (ii) A declares that he holds a right on Trust for B; then (iii) A may also agree to be under further duties to B, going beyond the duties examined in **1.1** and **1.2** above. For example, A may come under a duty not to use a right for B's benefit unless certain conditions are met (see **D2:1.4.3**); or to consult with X on how to manage the right held on Trust (see **D2:3.4**); or not to invest a right held on Trust in particular ways (eg, not to invest in particular companies). These additional duties may be very important in practice; but they are not necessary for the existence of a Trust: B can acquire a persistent right under a Trust even if such additional duties are absent.

EXAMPLE 1a

A0 transfers some shares to A to hold on Trust for B. The terms of the Trust state that: (i) A must transfer the shares to B when B reaches the age of 25, but not before then; and (ii) until then, A must pay the annual share dividends to B. B turns 18 and demands that A must transfer the shares to him immediately.

---

[10] In *Armitage v Nurse* [1998] Ch 241 at 253–4 Millett LJ stated that, to set up a Trust, A0 must ensure that A is under a minimum duty to 'perform the trusts honestly and in good faith for the benefit of B'. This correctly suggests that a Trust can be stripped down to the bare essentials: the core Trust duty. The test of 'honesty' and 'good faith' may amount to asking: (i) is A genuinely under a *duty* to use a right, in a particular way, for B's benefit?; and (ii) is A genuinely under a *duty* not to use that right for his own benefit (unless and to the extent that A is also a beneficiary of the Trust)?

[11] See eg *per* Arden LJ in *Citibank NA v MBIA Assurance SA* [2007] EWCA Civ 11 at [1]–[4].

[12] For an example see *Citibank NA v MBIA Assurance SA* [2007] EWCA Civ 11.

EXAMPLE 1b

A0 transfers some shares to A to hold on Trust. The terms of the Trust state that: (i) A must transfer the shares to B when B reaches the age of 25, but not before then; and (ii) until then, A must pay the annual share dividends to B; and (iii) if B does not reach the age of 25, the shares should be transferred to Oxfam. B turns 18 and demands that A must transfer the shares to him immediately.

In each case, B attempts to assert the power we examined in **D1:1.4.5(ii)**. If: (i) A holds a right on Trust entirely for B's benefit; and (ii) B is an adult and of sound mind; then (iii) B has the power to impose a duty on A to transfer that right directly to B. The problem seems to be that A has consented to an additional duty: a duty not to transfer the shares to B until B turns 25. However, in **Example 1a**, as B is the only beneficiary of the Trust, that duty is owed *to* B. So, B can simply waive that duty: just as, if someone owes you £100, you can choose to release them from that duty to pay you. Once B waives that additional duty, B *can* then impose a duty on A to transfer the shares directly to B: this is confirmed by the decision in *Saunders v Vautier*.[13] This may seem surprising,[14] but it is a consequence of the fact that any duties imposed by the Trust are owed to the beneficiaries of that Trust.[15] Therefore, if the beneficiaries consent, those duties can be waived.

In **Example 1b**, things are clearly different. B is *not* the only party with a persistent right under the Trust: Oxfam is also a beneficiary. Unless *both* B and Oxfam agree, A's duty not to transfer the shares to B until B reaches 25 *cannot* be waived. This shows that it is perfectly possible for A0 to set up a Trust that achieves his aim of ensuring that B cannot receive the shares before turning 25 (see **D2:1.4.3**).

1.4 The core Trust duty and C

EXAMPLE 2

A0 transfers shares to A to hold on Trust for B. The terms of the Trust impose a number of duties on A, in addition to the core Trust duty. A, a professional trustee who receives payment in return for acting as a trustee, consents to those additional duties. Acting without B's consent or other authority, A transfers the shares, for free, to C.

As C has no defence to B's pre-existing persistent right, B has a power to impose the core Trust duty on C (see **B:4.3**). If B exercises that power, then C comes under the core Trust duty to B. C then holds the shares on Trust for B and so is also subject to the additional duties set out in **1.2** above. However, C is *not* subject to any of the further duties that the terms of the initial Trust may have imposed on A: after all, unlike A, C has not consented to those duties. The same analysis applies in a case where, before B asserts his pre-existing right

---

[13] (1841) Cr & Ph 240; (1841) 4 Beav 115. B's power to impose a duty on A to transfer to B a right held on Trust entirely for B's benefit is often referred to as a *Saunders v Vautier* power.

[14] For further justifications of this result, see Matthews (2006) 122 *LQR* 266.

[15] The general position in United States jurisdictions is that, if it would be inconsistent with the intention of A0, B *cannot* waive a duty imposed by the terms of the Trust: see eg *Claflin v Claflin* 20 NE 454 (Mass 1889); Restatement (Second) of Trusts s 337 (1959). That may be seen as a practically convenient result, but it raises a doctrinal problem, in a case such as **Example 1a** to whom does A0 owe his duty not to transfer the shares to B until B reaches 25?

under the Trust, C discovers B's right through some other means. C's awareness of B's right imposes only the core Trust duty on C (and so allows B to enforce C's duty to account through a 'knowing receipt' claim: see D2:4.1.1(ii)).

Hence, when we say the pre-existing Trust binds C, we need to be careful: (i) C is bound by B's pre-existing persistent right; and (ii) that persistent right arises because A is under the core Trust duty; so (iii) the additional duties imposed on A by the terms of the Trust are *not* part of B's persistent right under the Trust; and so (iv) those additional duties do not bind C.[16] As a result, as Nolan has observed, it is a mistake to think that C must be subject to *all* the same duties as A.[17]

SUMMARY of F3:1

A Trust arises whenever A has a right and is under a duty *both* to use that right for B's benefit *and* not to use that right for A's own benefit—unless and to the extent that A also has a right under the Trust. Trusts are therefore incredibly diverse. Whenever A is under the core Trust duty, A also has a duty to account to B for the right held on Trust. In practice, A is also likely to be under a range of other duties, arising either as a consequence of the fact that A holds a right on Trust for B or a result of A's express consent. However, unlike the core Trust duty, those other duties are not *necessary* for the existence of a Trust.

If A transfers a right held on Trust to C, B's pre-existing persistent right under the Trust is prima facie binding on C. This means that B has a power to impose the core Trust duty on C. However, if B exercises that power, C does *not* come under all the duties imposed on A by the terms of the initial Trust. It is the core Trust duty that makes B's right a persistent right; and it is that core Trust duty to which C is subject.

2   THE ACQUISITION QUESTION

2.1   The acquisition of a new right under a Trust

To acquire a persistent right under a Trust, B first needs to show that A is under a duty to B: the core Trust duty. To see if A has come under that duty, we need to bear in mind all the possible means by which A can come under a duty to B (see B:4.3 and D2:2.1).

If the core Trust duty arises as a result of A's consent to be under that duty (ie, because of A or A0 exercising his power to set up a Trust), the Trust can be called an *Express Trust*. If the core Trust duty instead arises because of A's unjust enrichment at B's expense, the Trust can be called a *Resulting Trust* (see D4:4.3). If the core Trust duty arises because of a statute, it can be called a *Statutory Trust*. And if that core Trust duty arise for any other reason (eg, A's contractual promise; A's commission of a wrong; the 'receipt after a promise' principle, etc); the Trust can be called a *Constructive Trust*.

---

[16] Things are different in the very rare case where C is a 'trustee de son tort' (as Lord Millett noted in *Dubai Aluminium v Salaam* [2003] 2 AC 366 at [138], 'de facto trustees' is a better term). In such a case, B acquires a new, direct right against C arising as a result of C's apparent consent to take on A's duties as trustee. See eg *Mara v Browne* [1896] 1 Ch 199. Even in such a case, C should only be under the duty to account if he acquired the right held on Trust or at least had the means of acquiring it: see eg *re Barney* [1892] 2 Ch 265.

[17] See R Nolan (2006) 122 *LQR* 232.

Reason for which the core Trust duty arises (see B:4.3)	Type of Trust
1 A's consent to be under that duty	Express
2 A's entry into a contract with B	Constructive
3 A's commission of a wrong against B	Constructive
4 A's unjust enrichment at B's expense	Resulting
5 A statute imposing a duty on A to B	Constructive
6 A residual group of 'other events' that impose a duty on A to B	Constructive

Whenever B claims that A is under the core Trust duty to B, it is crucial to know which of the six reasons B is relying on to make his claim. However, in any particular case, *once* a court has decided that A is under the core Trust duty to B, the practical outcome of that case will be generally be the same no matter what label (Express, Resulting or Constructive) the court attaches to the Trust. This means that a court may be untroubled by the question of how to label the Trust that has arisen;[18] as a result, there are some cases in which the label used by the court is not consistent with the scheme set out here.[19] In fact, it is impossible to have a principled scheme that accounts for the labels used by the courts in *every case*. However, as the terms Express, Resulting and Constructive can be, and often are, used to distinguish Trusts according to how the Trust arose, we do need to have a scheme, such as the one set out above, that is both: (i) principled; and (ii) accounts for the standard usage of the terms Express, Resulting and Constructive.

2.1.1 Consent: Express Trusts

To acquire a right under an Express Trust, B simply needs to show that: (i) A holds a right; and (ii) A has consented to being under the core Trust duty to B. Such a Trust can arise if A0 transfers a right to A subject to the core Trust duty; or if A imposes that duty on himself by declaring a Trust, in B's favour, of a right A already holds. [20] There is no need for A's consent to be expressed or recorded in any particular form: no formality rule applies (see **C3:6.2**).[21]

EXAMPLE 3a

A has a bank account (a personal right against Z Bank). A authorises B to make withdrawals from the account. Money won by A and B when playing bingo together is paid into the account. A tells B that the 'money' in the account is 'as much yours as mine'.

---

[18] See eg *per* Lord Denning MR in *Hussey v Palmer* [1972] 1 WLR 1286 at 1289–90: 'Although the [B] alleged that there was a resulting trust, I should have thought that the trust in this case, if there was one, was more in the nature of a constructive trust: but this is more a matter of words than anything else.'

[19] See eg *per* Lord Browne-Wilkinson in *Westdeutsche v Islington LBC* [1996] AC 669 at 715 using the Constructive Trust label to refer to the Trust arising where A is aware that money he retains was paid to him by B due to a mistake; on the scheme set out here such a Trust is a Resulting Trust (see **D4:4.3.2**).

[20] As a result, an attempt by A to declare himself a trustee of a future right cannot give B an immediate persistent right (see **D2:1.1.2(iv)**). If B provided something in return for the declaration, it will give B a persistent right *if and when* A acquires the right in question; strictly speaking that is not an Express Trust as it arises as a result of A being regarded as having made a binding promise to B to set up a Trust (see **D2:n66**).

[21] It is worth noting that if: (i) A holds Ownership of a thing (eg, a bike) on Trust; and (ii) A's consent *is* recorded in writing; and (iii) A retains physical control of the thing; then (iv) the Bills of Sale Act 1878 may prevent B asserting his right under the Trust if A goes into insolvency, if the document setting up the Trust has not been registered as a bill of sale (see **D1:2.2.4(i)(b)**).

A's statements to B, given the wider context, reveal an intention of A that he should be under a duty to B to use the bank account for the benefit of *both* A and B. This is confirmed by the Court of Appeal's decision in *Paul v Constance*.[22] As a result of his consent, A is under the core Trust duty: he has exercised a power to set up a Trust in B's favour.[23] It is thus clear that A0 or A can exercise a power to set up a Trust without expressly using the word 'Trust'.

EXAMPLE 3b

A has a Freehold. A is concerned that, if he goes bankrupt, his Freehold will be sold off and the proceeds used to pay off his creditors. A therefore signs a document declaring that he holds his Freehold on Trust for B1 and B2 (his wife and daughter). B1 also signs the document but is unaware of its supposed effect. There is no change in the way in which the land is used. C later obtains a judgment against A and seeks to enforce the judgment by obtaining a charging order over A's Freehold. A claims that such an order cannot be granted as he holds his Freehold on Trust for B1 and B2.

In such a case, A *has* expressly used the word 'Trust'. However, as confirmed by the decision in *Midland Bank v Wyatt*,[24] A has *not* succeeded in setting up a Trust. This is because there is no evidence that A *genuinely* intended to be under the core Trust duty: instead, A planned to rely on the document 'declaring' the Trust only as part of a plan to defeat his creditors.[25] In such a case, the supposed Trust can be said to be a 'sham'.[26] However, we need to be careful. For example, there *can* be cases where: (i) A genuinely intends to be under the core Trust duty; (ii) so that a Trust does arise; but (iii) on A's insolvency, the insolvency rules mean that B's right under that Trust is not permitted to bind A's trustee in bankruptcy because A acted with the *motive* (the 'substantial purpose')[27] of prejudicing his current or future creditors.[28]

However, a 'sham Trust' as in **Example 3b** is different: it is *not* an initially valid Trust that fails because of A's intention to deceive or to cheat creditors. Rather, in a case such as **Example 3b**, there is no Trust at all: for the simple reason that A did not intend to be under the core Trust duty. Hence although the term 'sham' may be useful in understanding *evidential* rules (eg, a court may be permitted to look at additional evidence to see if a signed document does genuinely record A's intention),[29] it does not otherwise affect the acquisition question (see too **G1A:1.2** and **G1B:1.5.2(i)**).

---

[22] [1977] 1 WLR 527.

[23] In *Paul v Constance*, the trial judge's finding, upheld by the Court of Appeal, was that A and B each had an individual right to 50 per cent of the benefit of the bank account. An alternative interpretation, seemingly equally consistent with A's statements to B, is that A and B held the right under the Trust as joint tenants. As A then died, this would have resulted in B having 100 per cent of the benefit of the bank account; instead, B acquired only 50 per cent of the benefit of that right.

[24] [1995] 1 FLR 696. See further McFarlane and Simpson, ch 8 in *Rationalizing Property, Equity and Trusts: Essays in Honour of Edward Burn* (ed Getzler, 2003).

[25] *Per* DEM Young QC (sitting as a Deputy High Court judge) [1995] 1 FLR 696 at 707: 'It follows that even if the deed was entered into without any dishonest or fraudulent motive but was entered into on the basis of mistaken advice, in my judgment such a transaction will still be void and therefore an unenforceable transaction if it was not intended to be acted upon but was entered into for some different or ulterior motive.'

[26] Compare **G1A:Example 1**.

[27] See eg *Royscot Spa Leasing Ltd v Lovett* [1995] BCC 502.

[28] Insolvency Act 1986, ss 339 and 432.

[29] See Conaglen [2008] *CLJ* 176.

To set up a Trust, A also needs to satisfy *certainty requirements*. There are said to be three such requirements. Each of them depends on the fundamental nature of persistent rights; none of them derives from the special character of the Trust:

1. *Certainty of intention:* This simply means that A must intend to impose a *duty* on the holder of the right (see **D2:1.1.1**).[30]
2. *Certainty of subject matter:* This simply means that it must be possible to identify the *right* to be held on Trust (see **D2:1.1.2** and **B:Example 8b**).[31]
3. *Certainty of objects:* This requires that the *duty* imposed on A is certain enough to be enforced by the courts.[32]

The certainty of objects test deserves further attention. For example, A0 may try to set up a Trust under which A is under a duty to distribute a sum of money equally amongst A0's grandchildren. In such a case, it is clear that A can comply with his duty only if we can tell *how many* grandchildren A0 has. Even if A knows that B1 is clearly a grandchild of A0, A cannot distribute any money to B1: unless he knows how many grandchildren A0 has in total, A cannot tell what share B should receive.

Things are different if A0 sets up a Trust under which A holds £100,000 with a duty to distribute £1,000 to each grandchild of A0, and to give any money remaining after 21 years to Oxfam. B1 can claim his money immediately because A's duty to B1 is clear, irrespective of how many grandchildren A0 has. The way in which certainty of objects requirement operates where A0 attempts to set up a *discretionary* Trust is slightly complicated, and is discussed further on the companion website. However, the rules are based on the fundamental aim of ensuring that the duty imposed on A must be certain enough to be enforced by a court.

2.1.2 Unjust enrichment: Resulting Trusts

To acquire a right under a Resulting Trust, B needs to show that: (i) A holds a right; and (ii) A acquired that right at B's expense; and (iii) A is aware of the facts meaning there is no legal basis for A to retain the full benefit of that right. In such a case, A is unjustly enriched at B's expense *and* A's duty to B relates to the specific right that A acquired at B's expense. This analysis is controversial and was discussed in full in **D4:4.3 and D4:4.4.**

2.1.3 Statute: Statutory Trusts

To acquire a right under a Statutory Trust, B needs to show that: (i) A holds a right; and (ii) a statute imposes the core Trust duty on A in relation to that right. For example, if A0 goes into insolvency, his rights are automatically transferred to his trustee in bankruptcy. The trustee in bankruptcy has a statutory duty to use those rights for the benefit of A0's creditors; clearly he is not free to use those rights for his own benefit. The Trust is thus imposed as a mechanism to allow the benefits of A0's rights to be allocated, according to a system laid down by Parliament and the courts, amongst A0's creditors. Similarly, if A0 dies

---

[30] See eg *re Adams and the Kensington Vestry* [1884] 27 Ch D 394.
[31] See eg *re London Wine Co* [1986] PCC 121; *re Goldcorp's Exchange* [1995] 1 AC 74.
[32] The requirement thus has the same purpose as the certainty test in contract law. An agreement can only impose a contractual duty on A if that duty is certain enough to be enforced by a court: see eg *Walford v Miles* [1992] 2 AC 128. Similarly, a Trust cannot exist if the duty which A0 attempts to impose on A is too uncertain to be enforced.

without making a will, A0's rights will pass to his personal representative (A) who, after meeting any claims against A0, will hold any remaining rights subject to a Trust imposed by section 33 of the Administration of Estates Act 1925.

2.1.4 Contract, wrongs and other events: Constructive Trusts

(i) Contract

To acquire a right under a Constructive Trust arising as a result of A's entry into a contract, B needs to show that: (i) A holds a right; and (ii) A is under a contractual duty to B; and *either* (iiia) A's duty is to set up a Trust of that right in B's favour (see **D2:2.1.2(i)**); *or* (iiib) A's duty is to transfer that right to B (see **D2:2.1.2(iii)(iv) and (v)**).

If A comes under such a contractual duty to B *before* A acquires the right in question, the Constructive Trust arises *as soon as* A acquires that right.[33] If A's contractual duty arises as part of a contract of sale of goods, there is generally no point at which the Constructive Trust can arise: the existence of A's duty to allow B immediate exclusive control of the goods forever, *by itself*, transfers A's Ownership to B and so there is no point when A both: (i) holds Ownership; and (ii) is under a duty to transfer that right to B (see **D2:2.1.2(iii)**).

These Constructive Trusts clearly share a feature with Express Trusts: A has consented to come under a duty to B. However, the *reason* for which the Trust arises is different. In an Express Trust, A's consent, by itself, gives rise to the Trust. Here, however, B needs to show A is under a contractual duty to B. An example can demonstrate this difference.

D2:EXAMPLE 12ei

A believes he has a personal right against Z. A declares a Trust of that right in B's favour. B provides nothing in return. However, at the time of the declaration, A does not yet have that personal right against Z. A acquires that right three months later but refuses to use it for B's benefit.

In such a case, no Trust arises. A has consented to holding a right on Trust for B. However, A's initial declaration did not create an Express Trust: at that point A did not hold the right in question.[34] And, as B provided nothing in return for A's attempt to set up the Trust, A is under no contractual duty to B: so no Constructive Trust can arise. Therefore, when A acquires his right, he is free to use it for his own benefit.

Constructive Trusts arising as a result of A's contractual duty to B have been criticised.[35] It may seem unfair for B to acquire a persistent right simply as a result of his contract with A. For example, we can compare B's position with that of V, someone who A carelessly runs over. As A has committed a wrong against V, V has a personal right against A: a right to

---

[33] See eg *Pullan v Koe* [1913] 1 Ch 9.

[34] See eg *re Ellenborough* [1903] 1 Ch 697; *Williams v CIR* [1965] NZLR 395.

[35] See eg Swadling in *Equity in Commercial Law* (ed Degeling and Edelman, 2005). He concludes (at 487): that 'the vendor–purchaser constructive trust cannot be justified. It rests on a fiction and has no rational basis. It gives protection in insolvency where no priority is deserved.' As we saw in **D2:2.1.2**, it is true that the orthodox explanation of these Constructive Trusts (depending on the idea that 'Equity regards as done what ought to be done') is unsatisfactory. However, the Constructive Trusts can nonetheless be justified. B's protection in insolvency comes from the fact that he has a persistent right. If A has carelessly injured V, then, unlike B, V does *not* have a persistent right and so has no protection in insolvency. But the difference between the positions of B and V can be justified: A's duty to B, but not to V, relates to a specific right held by A.

receive money from A. However, if A goes into insolvency before V has received payment, V will face a problem (see **B:4.5.1**). In contrast, as B has a persistent right, B has greater protection in A's insolvency (see **B:4.5.2(ii)**). Why should B be better protected?

The answer is clear. B acquires a persistent right as A is under a duty to B in relation to a *specific right*. And, due to the nature of his contractual promise, A is under the core Trust duty: A is not permitted to use his right for his own benefit. In contrast, V has only a personal right as A's duty to V is to pay a sum of money: that duty does not relate to any specific right held by A (see **D2:2.1.3**). B's persistent right, as it is a right against a specific right held by A, is then prima facie binding on a third party who later acquires A's right, such as A's trustee in bankruptcy (see **B:4.5.2(ii)**). That is the sound doctrinal reason why B is protected in A's insolvency.

Of course, the different treatment of V and B, whilst doctrinally justified, may still seem unfair from the perspective of practical convenience (see **B:9**). It all depends what your view of fairness is; but any such concern is best addressed by changing the statutory insolvency regime so as to give greater protection to victims of a wrong, such as V.

(ii) Wrongs

In **D2:2.1.3** we saw that: (i) in general, A's commission of a wrong against B does *not* give B a persistent right: B has only a personal right against A; but that (ii) where A acquires a right by acting in breach of a fiduciary duty to B, A is under a duty to B in relation to that specific right and so B acquires a persistent right. As confirmed by the Privy Council in *Attorney-General for Hong Kong v Reid*,[36] B's right arises under a Constructive Trust.

There is a question as to whether, in such a case, A's duty to B really should relate to the *specific* right acquired by A. It can be argued that if, say: (i) A receives a bribe of £100,000 in breach of his fiduciary duty to B; then (ii) A's duty to B should simply be to pay B a sum of money equal to the gain A has made by taking the bribe. So if, as in *Reid*, A invests the bribe wisely and makes, say, a further £100,000, then A should be under a duty to pay B £200,000. On that view, B has only a personal right against A: A's duty does not relate to a specific right held by A but is simply a duty to pay B a sum of money. It seems the courts have rejected that approach as it does not do enough to deter A from breaching his fiduciary duty.

For example, in *Reid* itself, A had invested the bribe in land. In such a case, if A's duty is simply to pay B a sum of money, it may be possible for A: (i) to keep his land; and (ii) to borrow money from C to pay B; and (iii) to give C a Charge over the land to secure his duty to repay B. It may thus be that if A is simply under a duty to pay a sum of money to B (even a sum based on the current value of the land) that will *not* sufficiently deter A from breaching his fiduciary duty to B. After all, we have seen that the property law system recognises the special features and desirability of land by, for example, giving specific protection to rights related to land (see eg **A:3.1.2**).

Certainly, deterrence is a particular concern when considering fiduciary duties: on one view, the fiduciary duty A breached in *Reid* (a duty not to let his personal interests conflict with his duties to B) exists precisely to protect those other duties A owes to B.[37] So it may be

---

[36] [1994] 1 AC 324. See too *Daraydan Holdings Ltd v Solland International Ltd* [2005] Ch 119. For further examples of a Constructive Trust arising as a result of A's breach of fiduciary duty to B see *Keech v Sandford* (1726) 2 Eq Cas Abr 741 (where A was a trustee); and *Soulos v Korkontzilas* (1997) 146 DLR (4th) 214 (Supreme Court of Canada).

[37] See esp Conaglen (2005) 122 *LQR* 452.

that the needs of deterrence are *so strong* that A must come under a duty to B in relation to the *specific right* he acquires in breach of his fiduciary duty to B. That of course is a question of how we should best respond to breaches of fiduciary duty. However, *once* it is decided that A's duty to B relates to the specific right acquired by A, it must follow that B has a persistent right.

The Constructive Trust arising from A's breach of fiduciary duty has been criticised.[38] Again, it is said that it is unfair for B to be better protected, in the event of A's insolvency, than parties such as V—someone carelessly run over by A. However, it can be justified in exactly the same way as the Constructive Trusts arising as a result of A's contractual promise to B. *Once* it is decided that A's duty to B relates to a specific right, B must have a persistent right. Perhaps the rules on fiduciary duties should change so that A's duty is simply to pay a sum of money to B; but, until then, B must have a persistent right.

(iii) Other events

(a) Rights against a product of B's initial right?

In **D4:4**, we saw that a Trust can arise where: (i) A holds a right; and (ii) that right can be identified, by 'tracing', as a product of a right initially held by B or (of a right initially held on Trust for B); and (iii) A is aware of the facts meaning there is no legal basis A to retain the full benefit of that right. In *Foskett v McKeown*,[39] the House of Lords took the view that such a Trust arises because of the need to protect B's initial 'property' (see **D4:4.4.3**). On that view, the Trust must be a Constructive Trust arising because of an 'other event' (eg, because of an event falling within Reason 6 set out in **B:4.3**). However, although this analysis is again controversial, the Trust is best seen as a Resulting Trust, arising as a result of A's unjust enrichment at B's expense (see **D4:4.4**).

(b) Secret Trusts: the 'receipt after a promise' principle

D3:EXAMPLE 2
A has some shares in Z Co. In his will, A states that the shares should go to C. However, at A's request, C promises A that C he will hold the shares on Trust for B. A dies and C acquires A's shares.

In such a case, C holds the shares on Trust for B.[40] This form of Trust is often known as a 'secret Trust': (i) it is secret as the terms of the Trust are *not* recorded in A's will; but (ii) nonetheless a Trust arises. There is some controversy as to the *reason* for which this Trust arises. On one view, it is best seen as an Express Trust. The problem with this view is that, whilst A does have the power to set up a Trust on his death, it is a power to make a 'testamentary disposition' and so is regulated by the formality rules set out by the Wills Act 1837 (see **C3:2**). And, in **D3:Example 2**, A has *not* complied with those rules: his intention to set up a Trust in B's favour has not been recorded in a document signed by A and two witnesses.

One response is to say that the Trust is an Express Trust 'arising outside the will'.[41]

---

[38] See esp Goode (1987) 103 *LQR* 433 and in *Essays on the Law of Restitution* (ed Burrows, 1991).
[39] [2001] 1 AC 102.
[40] See eg *Blackwell v Blackwell* [1929] AC 318.
[41] See eg *per* Megarry V-C in *re Snowden* [1979] Ch 528 at 535; *Parker & Mellows' Modern Law of Trusts* (ed Oakley, 8th edn, 2003), 118–22.

However, as noted by Critchley,[42] that cannot be right. The fact that the terms of the Trust are not set out in a written document signed by A and two witnesses is *the very reason* why the Trust cannot be an Express Trust. A different response is to say that the Trust is an Express Trust that arises because a court will prevent C from relying on the formality rules set out by the Wills Act 1837: a court must not permit that statute to be used as 'an instrument of fraud'.[43] However, there are real problems with that explanation (see E2:2.3.2(iv)).

The better view is that, in **D3:Example 2**, the secret Trust is *not* an Express Trust: A's failure to satisfy the relevant formality rules means that A has *not* exercised his power to set up a Trust. Nonetheless, C is under the core Trust duty: the 'receipt after a promise' principle' imposes that duty as: (i) C holds a right; and (ii) C made a promise to hold that right on Trust for B; and (iii) C acquired that right as a result of that promise (see D3:2.2.2). On this view, the Trust is a Constructive Trust.

It is important to emphasise that the 'receipt after a promise' principle does not always lead to a Trust. For example, if the promise made by C does not relate to any specific right held by C, it cannot lead to C coming under the core Trust duty to B (see esp E3:2.3.2). However, if: (i) C holds a right; and *either* (iia) C made a promise to hold that right on Trust for B[44] *or* (iib) C promised to transfer that right to B;[45] then (iii) if the 'receipt after a promise' principle applies, C is under the core Trust duty to B.

The Trust arising in a case such as **D3:Example 2** has attracted some disapproval.[46] From the perspective of practical convenience 'secret Trusts' may seem to cause a problem: they allow A to circumvent the formality rule imposed by the Wills Act 1837.[47] However, from a doctrinal point of view, such Trusts are perfectly legitimate. The 'receipt after a promise' principle imposes a duty on C to B to keep his promise; as a result, C is under the core Trust duty to B. C's promise does not need to comply with the formality rule imposed by the Wills Act: B's right arises on A's death, not on C's death, and so C is not making a 'testamentary disposition'.

(c) Mutual wills: the Contract (Rights of Third Parties) Act 1999?

EXAMPLE 4

A1 and A2 make an agreement under which each promises to leave any rights he has at his death to B. A2 dies first, leaving his rights to B as promised. A1 then decides not to honour the agreement. A1 dies and leaves his rights to C.

As a result of his agreement with A2, A1 comes under a contractual duty to A2. Nowadays, B can rely on the Contract (Rights of Third Parties) Act 1999 to show that A1 is under a statutory duty to B to ensure that specific rights (the rights held by A1 at the time of his

---

[42] Critchley (1999) 115 *LQR* 631.

[43] See eg *per* Lord Hatherley LC in *McCormick v Grogan* (1869) LR 4 HL 82 at 88–9 and *per* Lord Westbury *ibid* at 97.

[44] As in eg *Rochefoucuald v Boustead* [1897] 1 Ch 196; *Neale v Willis* (1968) 19 P & CR 836; *Banner Homes Group plc v Luff Developments Ltd* [2000] Ch 372.

[45] As in eg *Pallant v Morgan* [1953] Ch 43.

[46] See eg Challinor [2005] *Conv* 492.

[47] From the point of view of practical convenience, this could conversely be said to be a *strength* of the secret Trust: as wills become public on A's death, A may have good reason for hiding B's identity. Certainly, it seems parties may still be keen to use secret Trusts: see Meager [2003] *Conv* 203.

death) are transferred to B. This means that, at least at the moment of his death, A1 holds his rights on Trust for B. So, since the coming into force of the 1999 Act, it seems that a Trust can arise as a result of A's *statutory* duty to B.

However, even before the 1999 Act, the courts held that A1's promise to A2 could give rise to a Constructive Trust, arising under the doctrine of 'mutual wills'. For that doctrine to apply, A1's promise must be contractually binding.[48] However, A1 cannot be under a contractual duty *to B* as: (i) A1 made no promise to B; and (ii) B provided nothing in return for A1's promise. So the doctrine of mutual wills seems to depend an 'other event' (eg, a principle falling into Reason 6 as set out in **B:4.3**). As it depends on A1's promise to A2, it is close to the 'receipt after a promise' principle. However, there is an important difference: in **Example 4**, A1's duty to B relates to *any* rights A1 has at his death, whether or not he acquired those rights as a result of his promise to A2.

The Constructive Trust arising under the 'mutual wills' doctrine is an unusual one. It certainly exists at the time of A1's death, but in fact arises before then. When A2 dies and complies with his side of the bargain by leaving his rights to B, A1 then comes under a definite duty to B: it is too late for A1 and A2 to vary their initial agreement. So, when A2 dies, A1 is under the core Trust duty in relation to *all his rights*. However, this does not mean that A1 is unable to use those rights for his own benefit: A1's duty comes from his agreement with A2. Under that agreement, A1 is clearly free to take the benefit of his rights during his life:[49] A1's promise is simply to give B whatever rights A1 has on his death. This means that, although A1 is subject to the core Trust duty, A1 also has a *power* to deal with his rights as he wishes during his life (eg, to spend his money on a holiday) *provided* that A1 does not deal with those rights contrary to the express or implied terms of his agreement with A2.[50] For example, it seems that A1's power does not allow him simply to give away all his rights, during his life, to Oxfam:[51] unless that was expressly permitted in his contract with A2, it would clearly be contrary to an implied term of his promise to A2.

Can this form of Constructive Trust be justified? It may well be that, even though the 'mutual wills' doctrine was recognised long before the Contract (Rights of Third Parties) Act 1999, it applies one of the key principles behind that Act. A1 is under a duty to B as: (i) A1 made a contractual promise to A2; and (ii) the promise expressly identifies B and purports to confer a benefit on him; and (iii) there is nothing to suggest A1 and A2 do not intend B to acquire a right to enforce A1's promise. So, if that principle is justified (and Parliament, by means of the 1999 Act, has now told us that it is), then A1 is under the core Trust duty to B.

---

[48] See *re Dale* [1994] Ch 31 at 38; *re Goodchild* [1997] 1 WLR 1216 at 1224. But note that if A1's promise is to leave to B rights that A1 has acquired under A2's will, the 'receipt after a promise' principle can apply to impose a duty on A1 to leave those rights to B even if A1's promise to A2 is *not* contractual. The difference is that the doctrine of mutual wills, as in *re Dale* [1994] Ch 31, can also impose a duty on A1 in relation to rights A1 has *not* acquired under A2's will. This is noted by Leggatt LJ in *re Goodchild* [1997] 1 WLR 1216 at 1224 when drawing a distinction between mutual wills and secret trusts: as discussed in **D3:2.2.2** the latter depend on the "receipt after a promise" principle.

[49] See eg *re Newey* [1994] 2 NZLR 590 (High Court of New Zealand).

[50] For this reason, Carnwath J in *re Goodchild* [1996] 1 WLR 694 at 700 described the Trust as 'an unusual form of trust, since it does not prevent [A1] using the assets during his lifetime.'

[51] See eg *per* Dixon J in *Birmingham v Renfrew* (1937) 57 CLR 666 at 689 (High Court of Australia).

(d) A's attempt to transfer a right to B?

A plans to transfer some shares to B. A signs a transfer form and delivers it to B in March. B is registered as the new holder of the shares in June. A dies less than four years later. In calculating the tax due on A's death, it is crucial to know whether A was free to use the shares for his own benefit in April.

The essential facts of *re Rose*[52] are identical to those in **Example 5**. In that case, the Court of Appeal held that A was *not* free to use the shares for his own benefit in April, and so his estate could not be taxed on those shares. Clearly, A was still the holder of the shares in April: B only acquired the shares when he was registered as their new holder in June. However, the Court of Appeal found that A held those shares on Trust for B from March: at that point, A had done everything he could to transfer the shares to B.

This form of Trust, whilst it has been approved in other cases,[53] is very difficult to explain:[54] why A should be under any duty to B? It has been suggested that A's duty arises because: (i) A has attempted to transfer a right to B; *and* (ii) A has done everything he can to effect such a transfer. But it is very difficult to say why A should be under a duty to B simply because A did his best to give B a right. Certainly, A intended to transfer the right to B, not to give B a persistent right against A's right: so A has *not* exercised his power to set up a Trust or to make a Type 1 Equitable Assignment (see **D2:1.2.2(i)**). And A has made no contractual promise to transfer the right; nor has B provided anything in return for the right: so there can be no Type 2 Equitable Assignment (see **D2:1.2.2(ii)**).

In fact, there is a significant weakness in the Court of Appeal's approach in *re Rose*. It depends on the mistaken assumption that A's attempt to transfer the shares can be 'valid in Equity' even if it is not 'valid at Common Law'.[55] A's attempt to transfer the shares either succeeds or it does not. In *re Rose*, it had not succeeded by April as B had not registered as the new holder of the shares. It is nonsensical to say that, by April, the transfer had succeeded in Equity but not at Common Law. No legal system can have two separate and competing rules sets of rules about how a right is transferred (see **C3:7.3.3** and **D2:1.2.2(iii)**). English law has just one set of rules about how B can acquire A's right; and a different set of rules about when B can acquire a right against A's right. To acquire a right against A's right, B needs to show that A is under a duty to B in relation to that right. In *re Rose*, there is no reason for A to be under such a duty; the decision of the Court of Appeal must therefore be incorrect.[56]

This analysis also casts doubt on the judgment of Arden LJ in *Pennington v Waine*.[57] That

---

[52] [1952] Ch 499.

[53] See eg *Mascall v Mascall* (1984) 50 P & CR 119 at 126; *Pennington v Waine* [2002] 1 WLR 2075 at [59].

[54] See too Chambers (1999) 37 *Alberta Law Review* 173 at 196–7.

[55] See esp *per* Lord Evershed MR at 510–11 and *per* Jenkings LJ at 518–9. See too *per* Arden LJ in *Pennington v Waine* [2002] 1 WLR 2075 at [59].

[56] It could be argued that, once B had the completed transfer form, B had a *power* to acquire the shares by registering as their new holder. However, in *re Rose*, Article 33 of the company's articles of association gave the directors a power in their 'absolute and uncontrolled discretion' to refuse to register a proposed transfer of the shares.

[57] [2002] 1 WLR 2075. In his judgment, Clarke LJ provided an alternative reason for finding that B had a persistent right. His Lordship argued that A had made an Equitable Assignment of the shares to B. That analysis may work on the facts of *Pennington*; but it cannot apply to *re Rose* as an Equitable Assignment involves A keeping a right and giving B the benefit of that right: in *re Rose* A's intention was instead to transfer the shares to B.

case was similar to *re Rose* and **Example 5**: the difference was that A had signed the share transfer form but had not yet delivered it to B. Arden LJ stated that A held the shares on Constructive Trust for B as it would be 'unconscionable' for A to object to B registering as the new holder of the shares.[58] However, no clear reason was given for that conclusion. One possibility is that A came under a duty to transfer the shares to B because: (i) A had made a commitment to transfer the shares to B; and (ii) B had relied on that commitment (in *Pennington*, B had become a director of the company on the understanding that he would acquire the shares); and (iii) B would suffer a detriment if that commitment were not honoured. That argument depends on the doctrine of proprietary estoppel; there are two problems with it.

1. On the orthodox view of the current law, that doctrine can only apply if A's commitment relates in some way to land. However, there is a strong argument that the doctrine should be extended to cover other commitments by A (see **E4:3.1.2**). It may just be that the result in *Pennington v Waine* provides some evidence of such an extension.
2. Proprietary estoppel does not always lead to A being under a duty to honour his commitment to B (see **E4:4**). In *Pennington*, the need to ensure that B suffers no detriment as a result of his reliance could most likely have been met by imposing a duty on A to pay B a sum of money: in such a case, no Constructive Trust should arise.

(e) Unjust enrichment?

In some cases, judges have referred to a Trust arising from unjust enrichment as a Constructive Trust.[59] However, on the approach adopted in this book, any Trust arising from A's unjust enrichment at B's expense counts as a Resulting Trust. In the United States, the orthodox view is that *all* Constructive Trusts respond to unjust enrichment. That view, as Chambers has convincingly shown,[60] is impossible to defend. For example, the Constructive Trusts we examined in section **2.1.4(i)** cannot possibly be seen as based on A's unjust enrichment: they are based instead on A's contractual duty to B.

(f) Unconscionability?

Constructive Trusts are sometimes said to depend on unconscionability. The idea seems to be that a Constructive Trust will arise if, and only if, A can be said to have acted in an 'unconscionable' fashion. However, that idea is misleading.

1. It is *over-inclusive*: there are many situations in which A acts unconscionably and there is no Constructive Trust. For example, let us say A deliberately runs B over. That is a poor way to behave, a crime, and a breach of A's duty not to interfere with B's right to physical integrity; but it does not give rise to a Trust (see **2.1.4(ii)** above).
2. It is also *under-inclusive*: A can be subject to the core Trust duty even if he has not acted unconscionably. For example, if A makes a contractual promise to transfer a specific right to B, a Constructive Trust arises *as soon as* A acquires the right in

---

[58] [2002] 1 WLR 2075 at [64].
[59] See eg Lord Browne-Wilkinson's analysis, in *Westdeutsche v Islington LBC* [1996] AC 669 at 715, of *Chase Manhattan Bank v Israel-British Bank* [1981] Ch 105. For analysis of the Trust arising in *Chase Manhattan*, see **D4:Example 2b.**
[60] See (1997) 37 *Alberta Law Review* 173.

question (see **2.1.4(i)** above). However, at that point, A has not acted unconscionably: he may fully intend to transfer the right.

This is not to deny that judges often talk of 'unconscionability' when considering if a Constructive Trust has arisen. Equally, when considering if A has committed a wrong, judges may often talk about 'fairness'. However, as we noted in **C1:3.1**, this is simply an example of the way in which such abstract concepts are used throughout the law: not as a test, but as a conclusion.[61]

(g) Remedial Constructive Trusts?

The Constructive Trusts we have looked at all arise as soon as A comes under the core Trust duty to B. For example, if A accepts a bribe contrary to his fiduciary duty to B, a Constructive Trust arises *as soon as* A accepts that bribe: at that point, A comes under a duty not to use that bribe for his own benefit. Any later court decision *recognises* that Trust; it does not create the Trust. This is no surprise. Constructive Trusts, like all persistent rights, are based on the fact that A is under a particular duty to B. And duties arise as soon as all the relevant facts have occurred, even before the parties have gone to court.

'Remedial Constructive Trusts' are different. A 'remedial Constructive Trust' arises only *after* a court has made an order creating that Trust. The Trust is thus a remedy given by the court: from B's point of view, a remedial Constructive Trust is therefore less attractive than a standard Constructive Trust.

EXAMPLE 6

X pays £10,000 to A. A then goes into insolvency. B goes to court and proves that A accepted the £10,000 as a bribe, contrary to his fiduciary duty to B.

	Analysis	Binds A's trustee in bankruptcy?
Constructive Trust	B's persistent right arose as soon as A accepted the bribe.	Yes: B acquires his persistent right *before* A goes into insolvency
Remedial Constructive Trust	B's persistent right arises only *after* the court makes an order creating such a Trust.	No: B gains no advantage over other creditors who have a personal right against A.

This example demonstrates that the 'remedial Constructive Trust' approach would be preferred by both: (i) other creditors of A; and (ii) C, a third party later acquiring a right that depends on the bribe received by A. However, it must be emphasised that the remedial Constructive Trust *forms no part of English law*. It has been conclusively rejected by the English courts.[62] Unless it is expressly given to them by a statute, judges simply do not have the power to *create* new rights; instead, they can only recognise rights that have already arisen. If the persistent right arises *because* of a particular fact (A's acceptance of the bribe)

---

[61] See eg L Smith, ch 2 in *Equity and Commercial Law* (ed Degeling and Edelman, 2005), 24.
[62] See esp *Re Polly Peck (No 2)* [1998] 3 All ER 812 and *per* Lord Browne-Wilkinson in *Westdeutsche v Islington LBC* [1996] AC 669 at 714–5 (describing a standard Constructive Trust as an 'institutional' Constructive Trust).

it must arise *at the time* that the fact occurred. This analysis supports the argument made in
E4:6 that, if B acquires a right through proprietary estoppel, that right arises *at the time* that
the relevant facts occur and before any court order in B's favour.

SUMMARY of F3:2.1.4

Constructive Trusts form a residual category: A is under the core Trust duty and that duty
has *not* arisen because A or A0 exercised his power to set up a Trust; nor because of A's unjust
enrichment at B's expense; nor because of a statute. There are hence a wide variety of means
by which B can acquire a right under a Constructive Trust. Those means can be broken down
into three distinct categories: (i) where A has made a contractual promise to B; (ii) where A
has committed a wrong against B; and (iii) other reasons, such as the doctrine of 'mutual
wills' and the 'receipt after a promise' principle.

Of course, in each category, further requirements have to be met before A can be under
the core Trust duty. A contract, like the 'receipt after a promise' principle, will only give rise
to a Constructive Trust if: (i) A is under a duty to set up a Trust in B's favour; or (ii) if A is
under a duty to transfer a right to B. A wrong will only give rise to a Constructive Trust if it is
a breach of fiduciary duty and if A acquires a right as a result of that breach.

Constructive Trusts, like Resulting Trusts, are inherently controversial. A third party, such
as a creditor who only has a personal right against A, may ask if it is really necessary for B to
have a persistent right. It could be argued that the **basic tension** between B and third parties
would be better resolved by giving B only a personal right against A. But the logic of
persistent rights demands that, if A's duty to B relates to a specific right, B has a persistent
right. So, *if* we can justify the fact that A is under such a duty, we can also justify any
advantage B acquires as a result of a Constructive Trust: such an advantage comes not from
an arbitrary decision to favour B, but, instead, from the underlying source of A's duty and the
very logic of persistent rights.

SUMMARY of F3:2.1

To acquire a persistent right under a Trust, B first needs to show that A is under a duty to B:
the core Trust duty. If a Trust arises as a result of A's consent to be under the core Trust duty,
the Trust is an *Express Trust*. Express Trusts are easy to justify: B acquires a persistent right
because A or A0 has exercised a power to give B such a right. If a Trust arises because of a
statute, it is a *Statutory Trust*. Such Trusts are also easy to justify: B acquires a persistent right
because Parliament has decided he should.

If a Trust arises because of A's unjust enrichment at B's expense, the Trust is a *Resulting
Trust*. These Trusts are harder to justify: their basis and scope are controversial matters. It was
argued in D4:4.3 that such a Trust should arise whenever:

- A acquires a right from B or at B's expense; *and*
- There is no legal basis on which A can have the benefit of that right; *and*
- A is aware that there is no such legal basis.

If a Trust arises as result of A's contractual promise to B; as a result of A's commission of a
wrong against B; or as result of any other reason not already mentioned, it is a *Constructive
Trust*. Like Resulting Trusts, Constructive Trusts are tricky to justify: their basis and scope are
controversial matters. It has been argued here that such a Trust should arise whenever:

- A makes a contractual promise to B to set up a Trust in B's favour; *or*
- A makes a contractual promise to B to transfer a right to B; *or*
- A acquires a right in breach of a fiduciary duty to B; *or*
- The doctrine of mutual wills applies: *or*
- The 'receipt after a promise' principle applies to a promise made by A to set up a Trust in B's favour or to transfer a right to B.

2.2   The transfer of a pre-existing right under a Trust

If A holds a right on Trust for B1, B1 has a power to transfer that right to B2. B1's power is subject to the formality rule imposed by section 53(1)(c) of the Law of Property Act 1925 (see **C3:5.2.2** and **D2:2.2**):

> A disposition of an equitable interest or trust subsisting at the time of the disposition, must be in writing signed by the person disposing of the same, or by his agent thereunto lawfully authorised in writing or by will.

2.2.1 Scope

The rule is not specific to Trusts: it applies *whenever* B1 attempts to transfer a persistent right to B2.[63] However, we will examine the rule here as cases considering it have tended to concern dealings with a right under a Trust. Unlike the other formality rules imposed by section 53 of the LPA 1925 (see **E2:2.3.1** and **E2.2.3.2**) the rule applies *whether or not* B1's persistent right relates to land. The justification for the rule is identical to the justification for the rule imposed by section 136 of the LPA 1925 (see **C3:5.1.2**): it lies in the *evidence* provided by signed writing. If B1 has a persistent right, A must be under a duty to B1. The transfer of B1's persistent right therefore changes A's position: A now owes his duty to B2 rather than to B1. A requirement of signed writing gives A a chance of discovering that such a shift has occurred (see **C3:6.3**). In particular, it means that: (i) if A is under the core Trust duty to B1; and (ii) B2 claims that, as B1 has transferred his right under the Trust to B2, A now owes that duty to B2; then (iii) if B2 does not produce writing signed by B1 as evidence of the supposed transfer, A can refuse to perform his duty to B2.

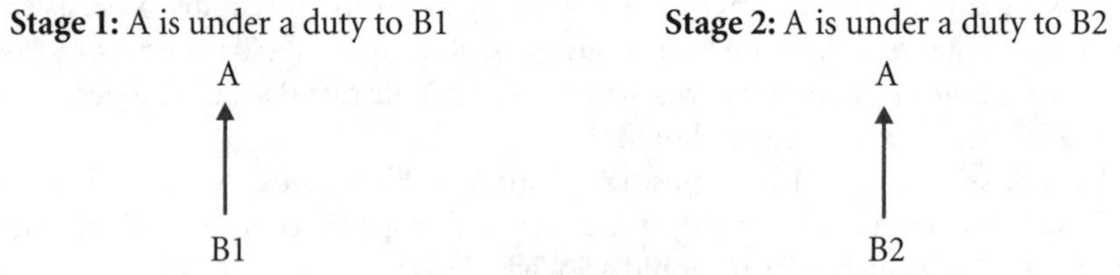

Stage 1: A is under a duty to B1   **Stage 2:** A is under a duty to B2

A   A

↑   ↑

B1   B2

Diagram I. A disposition of a persistent right

The concept of a 'disposition' seems simple enough: section 53(1)(c) aims to regulate B1's power to transfer his persistent right to B2. However, the precise meaning of 'disposition'

---

[63] The term 'equitable interest or trust' is rather clumsy. 'Equitable interest' refers to any Equitable right that is capable of binding a third party (ie, to persistent rights). 'Trust' refers to a right under a Trust (ie something already covered by the term 'equitable interest').

has been the subject of some fierce disputes often arising out of B1's desire to resist a tax demand by showing that he managed to rid himself of a persistent right.[64] In interpreting 'disposition' the courts have taken a purposive approach: they have tried to apply section 53(1)(c) in a way that best furthers its aims. As a result, we have to be very careful in setting out the meaning of a 'disposition'. First, we will consider the purpose of section 53(1)(c); second we will see how the courts have applied the section in practice.

(i) The concept of a 'disposition': defining the purpose of section 53(1)(c)

In *Vandervell v IRC*,[65] Lord Upjohn stated that the purpose of the section is:

> to prevent hidden oral transactions in equitable interests in fraud of those truly entitled, and making it difficult, if not impossible, for the trustees to ascertain who are in truth his beneficiaries.[66]

This statement could be interpreted as meaning that there are two, separate purposes to the section: (i) to protect B1 from fraud; and (ii) to provide evidence so as to protect A from the risk of performing his duty to the wrong person.

(a) To protect B1 from fraud

The evidence provided by the formality rule can certainly help B1. The requirement of writing signed by B1 makes it much harder for B2 to fraudulently claim that B1 has transferred his persistent right to B2 (see **C3:4.1.3**). However, it is clear that the section cannot *just* be about protecting B1 from the risk of fraud.

EXAMPLE 7

A holds some shares on Trust for B1. B2 claims that B1 orally declared a Trust of his persistent right in favour of B2.

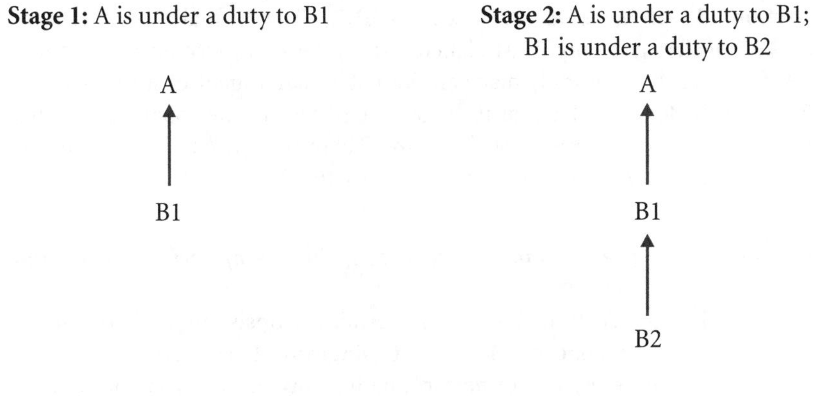

Stage 1: A is under a duty to B1

A

B1

Stage 2: A is under a duty to B1;
B1 is under a duty to B2

A

B1

B2

Diagram II. B2 claims that a sub-Trust has arisen (see **C3:3.3**)

---

[64] See eg *Grey v IRC* [1960] AC 1; *Vandervell v IRC* [1967] 2 AC 291.
[65] [1967] 2 AC 291
[66] *Ibid* at 311.

If B2's claim is accepted by a court, B1 will be under a duty to use his persistent right for the benefit of B2. So, if: (i) A were to pay any dividends from the shares to B1; then (ii) B1 would be under a duty to pay that money on to B2. B2 therefore certainly has a reason to make a fraudulent claim that B1 orally declared a Trust of his persistent right. And section 53(1)(c) gives B1 *no protection* against such a fraudulent claim. The formality rule does not apply: B2 is *not* claiming that B1 disposed of his persistent right. Instead, B2 is claiming that: (i) B1 has kept this right; and (ii) B1 has come under a duty to use that right for B2's benefit. And, provided B1's persistent right is not a right against a property right in land, or a persistent right relating to land (in which case section 53(1)(b) of the LPA 1925 applies: see **E2:2.3.2**), B2 can prove such a declaration without producing any writing signed by B1.

If: (i) section 53(1)(c) had the independent purpose of protecting B1 from the risk of fraud; then (ii) it would also require signed writing in a case such as **Diagram II**. However, writing is *not* required in such a case. The explanation is that *A still owes his duty to B1*. So, if: (i) B2 approaches A1 and ask A1 to pay any dividends from the shares directly to B2; and (ii) B2 bases this demand on an alleged oral declaration of Trust by B1; then (iii) A1 can simply refuse to pay B2: *even if* B1 has declared such a Trust, A still owes his duty to B1, not to B2.

It is important to recognise that if B1 declares a sub-Trust in favour of B2, B1 does not simply drop out of the picture so that A owes a duty directly to B2. After all, such a sub-Trust depends on B1 having a persistent right in the first place; and B1 must keep that right for the sub-Trust to exist. So, although A may *choose* to deal directly with B2, he has no duty to do so. Although this analysis has been questioned,[67] it was confirmed by the Court of Appeal in *Nelson v Greening & Sykes*.[68]

The difference between **Diagram I** and **Diagram II** is also reflected in the different formality rules applying to: (i) the transfer of a personal right; and (ii) an Equitable Assignment or declaration of Trust of a personal right. If B1 has a personal right against A, B1 generally has the power to transfer that right to B2: that power is regulated by the formality rule set out by section 136 of the LPA 1925 (see **C3:5.1.2**). The formality rule ensures that A discovers the transfer: not only must signed writing be used, written notice must also be given to A. However, B1 can orally make an Equitable Assignment of his personal right (see **D2:1.2.2**), or orally declare a Trust of it. If so: (i) B1 keeps his personal right against A; and (ii) B2 gains a persistent right against that right. There is no need for the formality rule to apply in such a case as, throughout, A owes his duty to B1.

(b) To provide evidence so as to protect A from the risk of performing his duty to the wrong person

This justification for section 53(1)(c) is certainly consistent with the fact that the formality rule applies in **Diagram I** but not **Diagram II**. However, the rule does not currently protect A from *every* risk of performing his duty to the wrong person.

---

[67] See eg Battersby [1979] *Conv* 17 at 28 arguing that if the sub-Trust is 'passive' (eg, one where B1 is simply under a duty to transfer his right to B2) then B1 drops out of the picture and A owes a duty directly to B2.

[68] [2007] EWCA Civ 1358: see *per* Lawrence Collins LJ at [47]–[57].

EXAMPLE 8

A holds some shares on Trust for B1. B1, by using signed writing, transfers his right under the Trust to B2. B1 then asks A to comply with his duty, under the terms of the Trust, to pay the annual dividends to B1.

A cannot demand to see any writing from B1: B1 is simply asserting his original persistent right. And there may be no means for A to discover the written transfer to B2. Nonetheless, if A pays out the money to B1, A will be in breach of his duty to B2. As it stands, section 53(1)(c) does not protect A against this risk. There is a strong argument for reforming the rule so that, like section 136 of the LPA 1925, a transfer of B1's right can be made only by: (i) the use of signed writing; *and* (ii) the giving of written notice to A. After all, there is no reason why A should have less protection simply because the duty he owes to B happens to be the core Trust duty, or to relate to a specific right held by A (see **C3:6.3**).

(ii) The concept of a 'disposition': judicial decisions

In looking at the scope of the section 53(1)(c) formality rule, we need to consider three important decisions. The facts of each will be simplified somewhat, so that we can concentrate on their essential features. The transactions in each case are also represented in a set of slides, available on the companion website. Each of the three cases involves sophisticated commercial parties; it may therefore seem strange that formality rules caused a problem. However, in each of the cases, the tax system gave B1 an incentive to attempt to transfer his initial persistent right *without* using signed writing.

(a) Grey v IRC

In *Grey v IRC*,[69] shares were held by A on Trust for B1. B1 instructed A to hold these shares on Trust for B2. This transaction was later recorded in writing but B1's initial instruction was purely oral. If the writing was simply a record of a transaction that had *already* occurred, it could not give rise to a tax liability. However, if the transaction was made *as a result* of the writing, it did expose B1 to tax. The Inland Revenue argued for the latter interpretation and claimed that B1's initial oral instruction, by itself, could not be effective to transfer B1's right under the Trust to B2: such a transfer was within the scope of section 53(1)(c) and so could only be made by using signed writing.

This argument was accepted by the House of Lords. B1 had simply attempted to exercise his power to transfer his persistent right to B2. The facts of *Grey* fit within **Diagram I**: if such a transaction could occur without signed writing, then: (i) B2 could claim that A now owes his duty to B2; and (ii) A could not insist on seeing signed writing before performing his duty to B2.

The only twist in *Grey* was that, on the facts of the case, B1 had orally informed A of the transfer: A knew about the transfer and hence the risk of A's wrongly performing his duty did not arise. This raises the question of whether there should be an exception to the formality rule in a case which: (i) falls within **Diagram I**; but (ii) where A *does* happen to know about the transfer of B1's persistent right.

Allowing such an exception would greatly undermine the usefulness of the formality rule. In *any* case where no signed writing is used, B1 or B2 could then attempt to convince a

---

[69] [1960] AC 1. For a detailed discussion of the facts see Battersby [1979] *Conv* 17 and Green (1984) 47 *MLR* 385.

court that the exception applies because, on the facts of the case, A nonetheless knew about the transfer. The certainty and simplicity provided by the formality rule would thus be undermined: A would no longer be safe in saying that, as there is no signed writing, he is not under a duty to B2. And a court could no longer rely on the absence of signed writing as a simple way to determine that B1 has not transferred his persistent right to B2. Instead, in any case, time and money might have to be spent in investigating if, on the facts, A happened to know about the transfer of B1's persistent right. So, it seems correct that, as held in *Grey v IRC*, signed writing is still necessary *even if* A has been orally informed by B1 of the transfer to B2.

(b) Vandervell v IRC

In *Vandervell v IRC*,[70] shares were again held by A on Trust for B1. B1 orally instructed A to transfer the shares to C. A did so, and C thus acquired the shares. Unlike in *Grey*, C did *not* acquire the persistent right initially held by B1. Instead, C acquired the right held on Trust by A: the shares themselves.

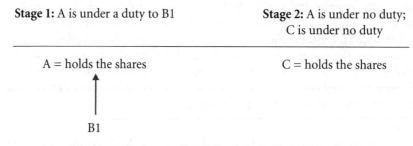

Stage 1: A is under a duty to B1   **Stage 2:** A is under no duty; C is under no duty

A = holds the shares   C = holds the shares

B1

Diagram III. A transfer of the right held on Trust by A

The Inland Revenue wanted to tax B1 on the basis that B1 still had his persistent right to the shares. Its argument was that, despite the apparent transfer of the shares to C, B1 had retained his persistent right as his oral instruction to A did not satisfy section 53(1)(c). The Revenue argued that the transfer of the shares to C fell within the scope of the formality rule as it counted as a 'disposition' of B1's persistent right. On that argument **Diagram III** is explained as follows: (i) at Stage 1, B1 has a persistent right; and (ii) at Stage 2, B1 has no such right; thus (iii) B1 claims to have disposed of that right; and so (iv) B1 must show that he has used signed writing.

The Revenue's argument as to the effect of section 53(1)(c) was rejected by the House of Lords. B1 had *not* attempted to transfer his persistent right. Instead, A had transferred the shares themselves to C. There was no risk that A might wrongly perform his duty to someone other than B1:

1. The transaction put an end to A's duty to B.
2. A was *necessarily* involved in the transaction—it depended on A exercising his power to transfer the shares to C.

This reasoning reveals the key differences between **Diagram I** (*Grey v IRC*) and **Diagram III**

---

[70] [1967] 2 AC 291.

(*Vandervell v IRC*). In **Diagram I**, the transaction can be carried out by B1 without the co-operation of A. As there is hence a risk of such a transfer happening behind the back of A, signed writing is needed to provide A with evidence of the transfer. In contrast, in **Diagram III**, the transaction cannot occur behind the back of A, as only A can transfer the right held on Trust to C.[71]

Therefore, although B1 rids himself of his persistent right in **Diagram III**, that does not mean there is a 'disposition' in the sense intended by section 53(1)(c). The formality rule has to be interpreted according to its purpose; and its purpose of protecting A simply does not apply in **Diagram III**.

(c) re Vandervell (No 2)

In *Vandervell v IRC*, the Revenue got their man in the end. For when C acquired the shares, it also entered into an agreement with A2: the Vandervell Trustee Company. Under this agreement, A2 had an 'option': the right to buy the shares from C at a fixed price within a particular period. The Revenue argued that this option was held by A2 on Trust for B1, and therefore that B1 could still be taxed on the shares—although he had got rid of his initial persistent right, he had a *new* persistent right: a right against A2's right to buy the shares.

The House of Lords, in *Vandervell v IRC*, accepted this argument (which, of course, has nothing to do with formality rules). It was held that, as A2 was a trustee company, and hence employed to hold rights for the benefit of others, A2 did not hold the option for its own benefit. A2 must therefore be holding the option on Trust for *someone*. And who might that someone be? B1 seemed to be the only viable candidate: (i) at the start of the story, B1 had the benefit of the shares; and (ii) it was B1 who instructed A1 to transfer the shares to C; and (iii) it was B1 who had ensured that C would agree to give A2 the option.

The House of Lords thus held that a Type 1 Resulting Trust had arisen in B1's favour (see **D4:4.3.1**). On their Lordships' view of the facts: (i) A2 had acquired a right (the option); and (ii) A2 had acquired that right at the expense of B1; and (iii) as it was intended that A2 should be under the core Trust duty, there was no legal basis for A2 to keep the benefit of that right.

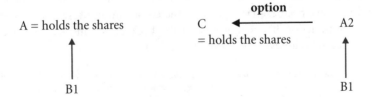

Stage 1: A is under a duty to B1

Stage 2: C has a duty to allow A2 to buy the shares if A2 wishes; A2 holds its right against C on Trust for B1

option

A = holds the shares

C ← A2
= holds the shares

B1   B1

Diagram IV. C gives an option to A2 to purchase the right formerly held by A on Trust for B1

---

[71] For the same reason, without any writing being used, it is possible for: (i) B1 to give up his right under the

The third case, *re Vandervell (No 2)*,[72] considered B1's attempt to get rid of his new persistent right: the right under the Trust of A2's option. B1 orally instructed A2 to exercise the option: to buy the shares from C by paying the agreed price. To do this, A2 made use of a fund of money that it held on Trust for B2. It seems clear that B1 assumed that, as result of this manoeuvre, A2 now held the shares on Trust for B2.

However, after B1's death, B1's estate argued that, in fact, the shares were held on Trust for B1.[73] The estate's argument can be put in the following way: (i) A2 had held the option on Trust for B1; and (ii) the shares were the product of that option; and (iii) there was no legal basis for A2 to have the benefit of the shares; so (iv) A2 held the shares on Trust for B1. The only way to avoid that result would be through a transfer by B1 to B2 of his persistent right (in either the option or the shares): but there was no writing signed by B1 making such a transfer.

Stage 1: A2 is under a duty to B1   **Stage 2:** A2 is under a duty to B2

Diagram V. A2 uses money held on Trust for B2 to exercise its option to acquire the right held by C

The Court of Appeal rejected the estate's argument. It held instead that, as B1 had intended, the shares were held by A2 on Trust for B2 *even though* no signed writing had been used. This decision has proved controversial.[74] Certainly, the three members of the Court of Appeal gave a host of different reasons for their decision, none of which is very convincing. The key problem is that the facts seem very close to those in **Diagram I** (*Grey v IRC*), where, as we have seen, the House of Lords held that section 53(1)(c) *did* apply.

However, there is one key difference between **Diagram I** and **Diagram V**. In the latter case: (i) **Stage 1** involves A2 holding a right on Trust for B1 (the option); and (ii) **Stage 2** involves A2 holding a *different right* (the shares) on Trust for B2. By going back to the purpose of section 53(1)(c), we can see how that seemingly small difference may be crucial. As in **Diagram III** (*Vandervell v IRC*), A2 was necessarily involved in the transaction. The option could not have been exercised without the co-operation of A2. As a result, there was no risk of the transaction happening behind the back of A2 and so no need for signed writing to provide A2 with evidence of the transaction.

Trust, by releasing A from the core Trust duty (see eg *re Paradise Motor Co* [1968] 1 WLR 1125); and (ii) A to declare a Trust of his right in favour of B2. That process achieves a result similar to **Diagram I** (A now holds on Trust for B2); but it has to involve the co-operation of A and so does not raise the risk of A performing his duty to the wrong person.

[72] [1974] Ch 269.

[73] B1's estate made this argument as it feared that it would be taxed by the Revenue on the basis that it did indeed have a persistent right under a Trust of the shares.

[74] See eg Green (1984) 47 *MLR* 385 at 413–21. Green concludes that the decision is 'addressed to, and hence likely to be confined to, its particular facts.'

Further, we can ask *how* B2 acquired his right under the Trust of the shares. It can be argued that B2's right did *not* arise simply because of B1's intention. Rather: (i) A2 holds the shares; and (ii) A2 acquired those shares by using money held on Trust for B2; and (iii) there is no legal basis for A2 to keep the benefit of those shares; so (iv) A2 holds those shares on Resulting Trust for B2 (see **D4:4.4**). On this view, section 53(1)(c) does not apply: B2's persistent right arises because of the need to prevent A2's unjust enrichment, *not* because of an exercise by B1 of his power to transfer his persistent right to B2.

The difficulty in *re Vandervell (No 2)* perhaps stems from a conflict between two possible Resulting Trust arguments. On any view, there is no legal basis for A2 to keep the benefit of the shares.

1. According to the estate: (i) the shares are the product of the *option* that A2 held on Trust for B1; so (ii) A2 must hold the shares on Trust for B1.
2. According to B2: (i) the shares are the product of the *money* that A2 held on Trust for B2 and used to exercise the option; so (ii) A2 must hold the shares on Trust for B2.

To resolve this conflict, we need to think about the *purpose* of the Trust arising in such a case: to avoid unjust enrichment (see **D4:4**). It is then clear that the shares should be held on Trust for B2, not B1.

1. B1 *intended* that the shares should be held for the benefit of B2. So B1 gave A2 the power to exercise the option, *provided* it would then hold the shares on Trust for B2. So, if A2 does hold the shares in that way, there *is* a legal basis for B1's loss of his initial persistent right.
2. B2 did *not* consent to A2 buying the shares with the money A2 held on Trust for B2. If A2 holds the shares on Trust for B1, then B1 would be unjustly enriched at B2's expense.

It is true that B1's intention to benefit B2 was not expressed in signed writing and so could not, by itself, transfer any persistent right from B1 to B2. But B1's intention can be used in a different way:[75] his intention to benefit B2 shows that, *if* A2 holds the shares on Trust for B2 (as found by the Court of Appeal in *re Vandevell (No 2)*), then neither A2 nor B2 is unjustly enriched at B1's expense.

(iii) An exception? Section 53(2)
As applied to section 53(1)(c), section 53(2) states that:

> [Section 53(1)(c)] does not affect the creation or operation of resulting, implied or constructive trusts.

This exception may seem to restrict the scope of the section 53(1)(c) formality rule. However, it is difficult to see how it can sensibly apply to that rule. First, the Resulting Trust or Constructive Trust referred to could be *B1's* initial persistent right.[76] However, it *cannot*

---

[75] This is consistent with the argument of Chambers (1999) 37 *Alberta Law Review* 173 that, in a Constructive Trust, B1's intention (even if not expressed in the form necessary to create a Trust by itself) can be relevant, *when coupled with other factors*, in justifying a Constructive Trust. See too Chambers's analysis of *Hodgson v Marks* [1971] 1 Ch 892 in *Resulting Trusts* (1997), 34: 'The intention to create a trust, though ineffective for that purpose, proves that the transfer "was not intended as a gift". *re Vandervell (No 2)* is the converse: B1's intention to transfer his right, whilst not effective for that purpose, proves that B1 *did* intend a gift (ie he was willing to lose his persistent right in order to benefit B2).

be the case that: (i) if B1's initial persistent right arises under such a Resulting Trust or a Constructive Trust; then (ii) B1 can transfer that right to B2 without using any signed writing.[77] The purpose of the writing requirement—the need to protect A from the risk of wrongly performing his duty in favour of someone other than B1—applies no matter how A's initial duty to B1 arises.

Second, the Resulting Trust or Constructive Trust referred to could be *B2's* persistent right. Section 53(2) would then refer to a case where B2 acquires a right against B1's initial persistent right by means of a Resulting Trust or a Constructive Trust. However, in such a case, there is no need for an exception to section 53(1)(c). If: (i) B1 keeps his initial persistent right; and (ii) B2 acquires a right against that right; then (iii) *in any case*, the section 53(1)(c) formality rule does not apply as A still owes his duty to B1, not to B2 (see **Diagram II**). That is not a special rule about Resulting Trusts or Constructive Trusts: equally, B1 can: (i) keep his initial persistent right; and (ii) orally set up an Express Trust of that right in favour of B2.

It therefore seems that, as is the case when it applies to the section 53(1)(a) formality rule *and* to the section 53(1)(b) rule, section 53(2) is redundant. When analysing the scope of section 53(1)(c), it is therefore best to forget about section 53(2). In some cases, the courts have relied on the 'exception';[78] but the results can be explained without needing to invoke section 53(2) (see **2.2.4** below).

SUMMARY of F3:2.2.1

The formality rule set out by section 53(1)(c) regulates B1's power to transfer an existing persistent right to B2. The rule applies to *all* persistent rights, even those that do not relate to land. It is based on a feature shared by all persistent rights: the existence of a duty owed by A to B1. An exercise by B1 of his power to transfer his persistent right to B2 necessarily involves a shift in A's duty from B1 to B2. The possibility of such a shift creates a risk for A: the risk that A may wrongly perform his duty to someone other than B1. The need for signed writing, imposed by section 53(1)(c), protects A, by providing evidence that A can demand to see before performing his duty in favour of B2 rather than B1. However, the current rule does not go far enough: A still faces the risk that B1 may transfer his right to B2 and then demand that A performs his duty to B1. In such a case, there is no means for A to discover the earlier transfer. A better approach would be to align the section 53(1)(c) rule with that imposed by section 136 of the LPA 1925 and to require *both*: (i) writing signed by B1; and (ii) written notice given to A.

The scope of the section 53(1)(c) formality rule is determined by its purpose. The rule does not apply where B2 acquires a new persistent right: in such a case, A's existing duty to B1 is not altered (see **Diagram II**). Nor does it apply where A is necessarily involved in a transaction that shifts A's duty to B2: in such a case, there is no risk of A's duty being altered behind his back (see **Diagram III**). Nor does it apply where B2 acquires a persistent right *not* because of a transfer from B1, but rather for some other reason (see **Diagram V**). That final point is confirmed by the strictly unnecessary section 53(2).

---

[76] The term 'implied trust' seems to add nothing to s 53(2): see **E2:n61**.

[77] In *re Vandervell (No 2)* [1974] Ch 269 at 320, Lord Denning MR seems to suggest that this is indeed the effect of s 53(2).

[78] See eg *Neville v Wilson* [1997] Ch 144.

2.2.2 Satisfaction

To satisfy section 53(1)(c), B1 must ensure he uses writing, signed either by himself or his agent,[79] to exercise his power to transfer his right to B2.[80] There is no need for B1 or B2 to notify A of the transfer.[81] However, as we have seen, there is a strong argument that the rule should be changed to require the giving of written notice to A.

2.2.3 Sanction

The sanction is a simple one: if B1 fails to exercise his power to transfer his persistent right in signed writing, the attempted transfer will be ineffective. B2 will fail to acquire B1's persistent right; B1, whether he wants to or not,[82] will retain his right.

2.2.4 Saves

If section 53(1)(c) has not been satisfied, B2's claim to have acquired B1's persistent right *must* fail. However, it is still possible for B2 to show that: (i) B1 has kept his initial persistent right; and (ii) B2 has acquired a new right against B1's right. In such cases, there is no shift in A's duty: he owes it to B1 throughout. As a result, no signed writing is required. For example, we have seen that B1 can orally declare a Trust of his persistent right in B2's favour (see **Diagram II**).[83] Similarly, if B1 either: (ia) makes an oral contractual promise to transfer his persistent right to B2 (see **D2:2.1.2(iv)**); or (ib) in return for some value given by B2 (eg, money) orally attempts to transfer his persistent right to B2 (see **D2:2.1.2(i)**); then (ii) B1 will hold his persistent right on Constructive Trust for B2.[84]

   This analysis is confirmed by the decision of the Court of Appeal in *Neville v Wilson*.[85] In that case, B1's oral contractual promise to transfer a persistent right to B2 gave B2 a new persistent right. Yet the decision in *Neville v Wilson* has attracted disapproval.[86] The supposed problem is that B2 acquires his persistent right without anything having been put in writing: the decision is said to undermine the formality rule in section 53(1)(c). However, this disapproval is misplaced. There is no need for signed writing in such a case as B2's acquisition of a persistent right does *not* affect A, who continues to owe his duty to B1. It is therefore perfectly coherent to have a formality rule that: (i) applies to a *transfer* of a persistent right from B1 to B2; but (ii) does *not* apply to a contract to make such a transfer. After all, the formality rule imposed by section 136 of the LPA 1925 applies to a transfer of a

---

[79] The agent must have written authority to sign on B1's behalf.

[80] If B1 wishes to transfer his persistent right on his death, he will of course have to satisfy the additional requirements of the Wills Act 1837: see **C3:2.**

[81] The rule in *Dearle v Hall* (1828) 3 Russ 1 (see **D2:3.5.4**) does give B2 an incentive to notify A: if he fails to do so, he faces the risk that: (i) B1 may make a second transfer of the right under the Trust to B3; and (ii) B3 may be a 'bona fide purchaser' of that right; so (iii) if B3 then informs A of the second transfer before B2 informs A of the first transfer, B3 has a defence to B2's pre-existing persistent right.

[82] By virtue of retaining the right, B1 may be subject to an unwelcome tax demand, as in *Grey v IRC* [1960] AC 1.

[83] If B1's initial persistent right relates to land, s 53(1)(b) of the LPA 1925 will apply and so B2 will be unable to prove the Trust unless he can produce some writing signed by B1 (see **E2:2.3.2**).

[84] Similarly, if B1, in return for value provided by B2, attempts to make an *immediate* transfer of his persistent right to B2 and, because of a failure to use signed writing, that attempt fails, B2 should acquire a right against B1's persistent right (see **D2:n66**).

[85] [1997] Ch 144.

[86] Worthington, *Equity* (2nd edn, 2006), 233–5 and Gardner, *Introduction to the Law of Trusts* (2nd edn, 2003), 96.

personal right from B1 to B2, but not to a contract to make such a transfer (see D2:1.2.2(ii)).

In *Neville v Wilson*, the Court of Appeal based its decision on the section 53(2) 'exception'. It is certainly true that B2's persistent right arose under a Constructive Trust: it depended on B1's contractual promise to B2 (see **2.1.4(i)** above). However, there was no need for the court to have relied on section 53(2). The facts were *in any case* outside the scope of section 53(1)(c): B2 was not claiming that B1 had transferred his existing persistent right to B2; there was no 'disposition' by B1 of his persistent right.

3   THE DEFENCES QUESTION

In D2:3 we examined the general defences that C may be able to use against a persistent right. Where B's right arises under a Trust, C may use *any* of those defences. The most important defences in practice are the overreaching defence and the 'bona fide purchaser' defence. The application of those defences to a right under a Trust was examined fully in D2:3.4 and D2:3.5.

3.1   The limitation defence: the Limitation Act 1980

The defence made available by the Limitation Act 1980 varies according to the nature of B's initial persistent right. If B tries to assert his pre-existing right under a Trust by making a claim against C, the basic rule is set out by section 21(3): B has six years from the time that claim arises.[87] However, there are two important situations in which that statutory time limit does *not* apply:

- If B makes a claim 'to recover from the trustee trust property or the proceeds of trust property in the possession of the trustee, or previously received by the trustee and converted to his use' (see section 21(1)(b)).
- If B makes a claim is 'in respect of any fraud or fraudulent breach of trust to which the trustee was a party or privy' (see section 21(1)(a)).

EXAMPLE 9

A holds shares on Trust for B. A, in breach of his duties as trustee, transfers those shares, for free, to C. C is entirely unaware that A held those shares on Trust for B. Ten years later, when C still has those shares, B attempts to assert his pre-existing right under the Trust by imposing the core Trust duty on C.

B's first chance to bring a claim against C arose ten years ago, when C first acquired the shares. B therefore needs to show that the statutory six-year limit does not apply. First, B may argue that he is making a claim that falls within section 21(1)(b): he is trying to recover the very right that was initially held on Trust for B. However, that exception applies

---

[87] The section applies to 'an action by a beneficiary to recover trust property or in respect of any breach of trust'. It therefore applies to any claim B may bring against A for the breach of A's duties as trustee: not only for A's breach of the core Trust duty but also for A's breach of any additional duties imposed by the particular terms of the Trust (see 1.2 and 1.3 above).

only where B brings a claim against a 'trustee'. And it seems that, in a case such as **Example 9**, C does *not* count as a 'trustee' for the purpose of the exception.[88] First, C certainly did not consent to be under the core Trust duty to B.[89] Second, during the six years immediately following his acquisition of the shares, C remained entirely innocent of B's initial persistent right. It seems that, to show the section 21(1)(b) exception applies, B needs to show that, during those first six years, C became a 'trustee' by gaining *sufficient awareness* of the fact that A had transferred the shares to B in breach of his duties as trustee.[90]

The test for this sufficient awareness should be exactly the same test that applies if B brings a 'knowing receipt' claim against C (see **D2:4.1.1(ii)**): does C's awareness of the facts allowing B to impose the core Trust duty on C make it unconscionable for C to be free to use the shares for his own benefit?[91] This fits with the general principle stated by Lord Browne-Wilkinson in *Westdeutsche Landesbank Girozentrale v Islington LBC*:[92] C can only come under the core Trust duty if C has sufficient awareness of the facts giving rise to that duty. This means that if: (i) during the six years immediately following C's acquisition of the shares, C does not gain knowledge of B's pre-existing right such as to make it 'unconscionable' for C to be free to use the shares for his own benefit; then (ii) B cannot rely on the section 21(1)(b) exception; and so (iii) C can rely on the limitation defence.

In such a case, the section 21(1)(a) exception may assist B. Of course, C has not acted fraudulently. Surprisingly, it seems that: (i) if A acted fraudulently in transferring the shares, in breach of his duties as trustee, to C; then (ii) B's assertion of his right against C can be seen as a claim 'in respect of' A's fraudulent breach.[93] This means that C *cannot* rely on the statutory six-year limitation period. Instead, his only protection will come from the general Equitable principle of laches (see **D2:3.7**).

That reasoning is very hard to follow. In one sense, B's claim against C depends on A's breach of his duties as trustee: if there had been no transfer of the shares, there would be no need for B to bring a claim against C. However, in a more important sense, B's claim against C is independent of A's breach: it consists simply of B asserting his pre-existing persistent right against C. That claim is independent of any other claim B may have against A in

---

[88] The cases on this question are far from straightforward. For an important survey, see Millett LJ in *Paragon Finance plc v DB Thakerar & Co* [1999] 1 All ER 400. For discussion, see eg Swadling, ch 11 in *Breach of Trust* (ed Birks and Pretto, 2002).

[89] In *Rochefoucauld v Boustead* [1897] 1 Ch 196, B acquired a right under a Trust as a result of C's promise to hold on Trust for B (see **E2:Example 9b**). As C had thus consented to the core Trust duty, C counted as a 'trustee' and so could *not* rely on the statutory limitation period when B asserted his right under the Trust against C. However, contrary to the view taken by the Court of Appeal in *Rochefoucauld*, in that case, C's consent did *not* mean that the right enforced by B arose under an Express Trust (this point is noted by Millett LJ in *Paragon Finance plc v DB Thakerar & Co* [1999] 1 All ER 400 at 409–10). As C's consent was not recorded in writing, B could not prove that a Trust had been declared in his favour. Instead, B's right arose under a Constructive Trust, based on the 'receipt after a promise' principle (see **E2:2.3.2(i) and (iv)**).

[90] Swadling, ch 11 in *Breach of Trust* (ed Birks and Pretto, 2002) takes a different view: if C still has the right initially held on Trust for B, no statutory limitation period applies. However, as Swadling notes at 343, that view entails finding that s 21(3) 'cannot mean what it says'. And the general reasons in favour of a limitation period (eg, protecting C's settled expectation) can be used to justify protecting C in such a case.

[91] See *BCCI v Akindele* [2001] Ch 437.

[92] [1996] AC 669 at 705.

[93] *GL Baker Ltd v Medway Building and Supplies Ltd* [1958] 1 WLR 1216. If: (i) B acquires a right under a Trust because of A's fraudulent conduct; and (ii) A commits a non-fraudulent breach of his core Trust duty; then (iii) the section 21(1)(a) exception does *not* apply. That seems to be the best explanation of the result in *Paragon Finance plc v DB Thakerar & Co* [1999] 1 All ER 400.

respect of the breach of his duties as trustee (eg, for compensation for loss caused to B as a result of A's breach). Certainly, B's claim against C is the same whether or not A acted fraudulently; there is no good reason why A's fraud should cause C to have less protection.[94]

4   THE REMEDIES QUESTION

If A consents to hold a right on Trust for B, A will generally be under: (i) the core Trust duty; and (ii) a number of additional duties. Where possible, a court will specifically protect B's rights by ensuring that A's duties are performed: a court may even: (i) remove A and appoint a new trustee; or (ii) execute the Trust itself, by performing a particular duty of A. If A has already committed a breach, it may be too late for B's right to be specifically protected. As A has breached a duty to B, A has committed a wrong against B and so A can be ordered to pay money to B based on: (i) the value of B's right; and (ii) any relevant loss B has suffered as a result of A's wrong.[95] B may even claim that A should be made to pay exemplary or punitive damages as a result of his wrong.[96] However, in many cases, it is far simpler for B simply to enforce A's duty to account (see **1.1** above). There is then no need for B to show: (i) that A has committed a specific breach of any of his other duties as trustee; *or* (ii) that A's breach has caused B any loss.[97] Here we will focus on how B's pre-existing right under a Trust is protected if he can assert it against C.

4.1   Where C still has the right initially held on Trust for B (or its product)

EXAMPLE 10a

A holds shares on Trust for B. Acting without B's consent or other authority, A transfers those shares, for free, to C.

EXAMPLE 10b

The facts are as in **Example 10a**. After receiving the shares from A, C sells those shares and invests the proceeds in a painting.

In each case, C has no defence to B's pre-existing right under the Trust. B asserts that pre-existing right *directly*: by imposing the core Trust duty on C. In **Example 10a**, C thus comes under a duty, owed to B, not to use the shares for his own benefit. In **Example 10b**, C's duty

---

[94] There is an analogy here with the indemnity provisions under the LRA 2002: if a rectification of the register causes loss to A, but that rectification responded to a mistake caused by A's fraud, A can receive no indemnity. If: (i) A then gives C a right for free; and (ii) C is entirely innocent of A's initial fraud (as in **Example 9**); then (iii) C can also be regarded as having acted fraudulently and can thus be denied an indemnity (see **E5:3.2.3(ii)**). However, that position may be defended on the basis that the registration system aims principally to protect parties who acquire registered rights *for value*. Whereas the limitation defence, in protecting settled expectations, ought to be available even if C has acquired his right for free.

[95] In *Target Holdings Ltd v Redferns* [1996] AC 421, the House of Lords recognises that such a claim is possible (see esp *per* Lord Browne-Wilkinson at 434–5. See too Chambers, ch 1 in *Breach of Trust* (ed Birks and Pretto, 2002), 20–3; Edelman & Elliott (2004) 18 *Trust Law International* 116 at 118–22; Hayton, ch 11 in *Equity and Commercial Law* (ed Degeling and Edelman, 2005), 301–4.

[96] Hayton *ibid* argues that it should be possible for a court to award exemplary damages against a party breaching a core Trust duty, at least if that party acts 'monstrously' (at 303).

[97] See eg *re Dawson* [1966] 2 NSWR 211; *Youyang v Minter Ellis Morris Fletcher* (2003) 196 ALR 482 (High Court of Australia); Elliott (2002) 65 *MLR* 588; Elliott and Edelman (2003) 119 *LQR* 545.

instead relates to his Ownership of the painting: a right that counts as a product of the right initially held on Trust for B (see **D4:4.4**). Once C is under the core Trust duty to B, B's right is specifically protected.

The precise method in which B's right is specifically protected depends on the nature of the initial Trust. First, it may be that A initially held the shares on Trust not just for B1 but also for B2, B3, etc. If so, the general rule is that C must transfer his right to A2, a new trustee appointed by the court (see **D2:4.2.2**). A2 will then hold that right subject to *all* the duties imposed on A by the original Trust. Alternatively, if A held the shares on Trust *entirely* for B's benefit, B may require C to transfer the right held on Trust directly to B (see **D1:1.4.5(ii)**).

4.2   Where C no longer has the right initially held on Trust for B (or its product)

EXAMPLE 10c

The facts are as in **Example 10b**. C sells the painting and spends the money on a holiday.

In such a case, C has *neither*: (i) the right initially held on Trust for B; *nor* (ii) a right that counts as the product of that right. As a result, it is too late for B to impose the core Trust duty on C for the future. However, it is possible that C was under that duty *even if* B has not imposed that duty on C. As we have seen, C can come under the core Trust duty if: (i) *whilst* C still had the shares or Ownership of the painting; (ii) C had sufficient awareness of the fact A had transferred those shares to C in breach of A's duties as trustee. If B can show that C had that awareness, B can bring a claim against C based on C's 'knowing receipt' (or—as it should be called—knowing holding). That claim enforces C's duty to account to B for the right he held on Trust for B (ie, the shares or Ownership of the painting). Of course, as C no longer has either right, it is too late for C's duty to account to be specifically enforced. However, C can be made to pay money equal to the value of the right held on Trust (see **D2:Examples 24b and 24c**).

In such a case, the precise method in which B's right is protected again depends on the nature of the initial Trust. First, it may be that A initially held the shares on Trust not just for B1 but also for B2, B3, etc. If so, the general rule is that C must pay the money to A2, a new trustee appointed by the court (see **D2:4.2.2**).[98] A2 will then hold that right subject to *all* the duties imposed on A by the original Trust. Alternatively, if A held the shares on Trust *entirely* for B's benefit, B may require C to pay the money directly to B (see **D1:1.4.5(ii)**).[99]

---

[98] See eg *per* Knox J in *Hillsdown plc v Pensions Ombudsman* [1997] 1 All ER 862 at 897.
[99] See eg *per* Lord Browne-Wilkinson in *Target Holdings v Redferns* [1996] AC 421 at 435.

CHAPTER F4
SECURITY

F4

SECURITY

1 INTRODUCTION[1]

1.1 Security and the basic tension

EXAMPLE 1

A wishes to borrow £200 from B. If B makes the loan, B will have a personal right against A: A will be under a duty to repay the £200, plus agreed interest. However, B is worried that A will be unable to repay the loan. In particular, B knows that if A fails to repay and goes into insolvency, B will be unable to recover the full sum owed to him by A.

In such a case, B wants to have more than a simple personal right against A. If A does fail to repay, B wants the *protection* of being able to rely on *another* right as a means to ensure that he receives the money due to him from A. This protection can take a number of different forms. For example, A2 may make a contractual promise to B that, if A fails to repay the loan as agreed, A2 will make up any shortfall. This *guarantee* gives B the security of being able to rely on another right: a personal right against A2.[2] However, B again faces a risk: it may be that *each* of A and A2 will be unable to pay and that *each* will go into insolvency.

B may therefore want the *security* of a right that is capable of binding a third party, such as A's trustee in bankruptcy. In such a case, the rules of the property law system have a vital role to play. Those rules tell us that B needs to acquire: (i) a property right; or (ii) a persistent right; or (iii) a power to acquire a persistent right. In this chapter, we will look at how those rules apply to the special case where B's *purpose* in acquiring such a right is to have security for a duty owed to B. It will not be possible to cover all the nuances of the law on security.[3] Rather, the aim of this chapter is to show how the **basic structure** can be used to understand: (i) the nature of security rights; and (ii) the differences between particular types of security right.

A number of important concerns affect the way in which the basic structure applies to

---

[1] In writing this chapter, I found the analysis set out by L Smith in ch 5 of *English Private Law* (ed Burrows, 2nd edn, 2007) very helpful. The Law Commission completed a project on security rights given by companies in 2005 (see Law Com Consultation Papers No 164 (2002) and 176 (2004); Law Com No 296 (2005): for discussion see eg Beale (2004) 4 *Journal of International Banking and Finance Law* 117; Bridge ch 12 in *Company Charges* (ed Getzler and Payne, 2006). Some of the points made in that project are noted here, but the detail of the proposed reforms are not examined: although it seems the proposals are being considered by the Government, there seems to be no current prospect of those detailed reforms being enacted by Parliament.

[2] B's ability to enforce a contract of guarantee is regulated by a formality rule: under the Statute of Frauds 1677, s 4, B can only enforce A2's contractual duty if he can produce written evidence of the contract, signed by A2: see eg *Actionstrength Ltd* v *International Glass Engineering SpA* [2003] 2 AC 541

[3] For further detail see eg *The Law of Personal Property Security* (ed Beale *et al*, 2007).

security rights. First, there is the *need to protect A*, the party giving security to B. In many cases, B takes security when extending credit to A. In such situations there is a risk that B will exploit A's need for money by imposing harsh terms on A. That risk can of course arise even if B does not take security: statutory rules applying to consumer credit agreements[4] protect A whether or not A gives B a security right. However, where A gives B security, the consequences to A of failing to perform his duty to B can be particularly severe.

Second, there is the *need to protect B*. The possibility of acquiring a security right may be an important factor in B's decision to extend credit to A. Without that credit, A may struggle to have the goods he wishes, or to develop his business. If the property law system makes it difficult for B to acquire such security, there is a risk that the flow of credit will be impeded.[5]

Finally, there is the *need to protect C*. If B acquires by way of security a property right, persistent right or power to acquire a persistent right, B's right or power may be hard for C to discover. For example, B may acquire a security right in relation to a thing even though A keeps both physical control and his Ownership of that thing. There is thus a clear risk to C of being bound by a hidden security right of B. In particular, if B has a security right in relation to a thing or right held by A, and A goes into insolvency, that thing or right *cannot* be used to pay off A's other creditors: this can cause problems for C (see **C2:Example 2**). For example, if C plans to supply goods or services to A, C may think that there is no need to insist on advance payment, or to acquire a security right himself. After all, A appears to have plenty of rights that A can use to pay C. However, if C extends credit to A, he may be in for a shock. If A goes into insolvency, B will be able to assert his security right and A's general creditors, such as C, are left to fight over A's remaining rights. Further, even if C does take security, he may face the same problem: if B's property right or persistent right arose before C's right, it will take priority should A become insolvent.

Of course, these needs to protect A, B and C will often conflict. When examining security rights, we thus need to be aware not only of the **basic tension** between the needs of B and C, but also of the tension between protecting a borrower (A) and a lender (B).

1.2   Defining security

1.2.1 The definition

We can define a security right as:

- a property right; persistent right; or power to acquire a persistent right
- that arises as a means to protect B if a duty owed to B is not performed.

1.2.2 Transactions giving B a security right

It is important to distinguish between: (i) the type of *transaction* in which A gives B a

---

[4] See eg Consumer Credit Act 1974 (as amended by the Consumer Credit Act 2006).

[5] The 'credit crunch' experienced in the second half of 2007 is evidence of the wider economic problems that can be caused where the flow of credit is impeded. There is a difficult question as to whether a legal system that does not recognise secured credit would be less efficient than our current system: see eg Schwartz (1981) 10 *Journal of Legal Studies* 1; White (1984) 37 *Vanderbilt Law Review* 473; Mokal (2002) 22 *OJLS* 687; Getzler, ch 10 in *Company Charges* (ed Getzler and Payne, 2006) esp 231–4.

security right; and (ii) the content of the *right* B acquires. We have already seen some examples of transactions by which B can acquire a security right (see eg **D1:1.4.2**). In **Example 1**:

- a *mortgage* would consist of A transferring his Ownership of a bike to B: if A then fails to repay the loan, B has the power to sell the bike and use the proceeds to meet A's debt.
- a *pledge* would consist of A allowing B to take physical control of A's bike: if A then fails to repay the loan, B again has the power to sell the bike and use the proceeds to meet A's debt.
- a *consensual lien* is another means by which A can give B a security right. It can be used only in cases where B *already* has physical control of a thing belonging to A (eg, A's bike). It consists of A allowing B to retain physical control of the bike if A does not repay the loan.

A fourth type of transaction by which A can give B a security right is the *charge*. A charge transaction can take two forms so, in **Example 1**:

- a *fixed charge* would consist of A making a binding promise to allow B, if A fails to repay the loan, to sell A's bike and to use the proceeds to meet A's debt; and
- a *floating charge* would consist of A making a binding promise that *if* a certain event occurs (eg, A fails to repay the loan by an agreed date), A will *then* be under a duty to allow B to use a particular right held by A at that point to meet A's debt.

This means that, as Millett LJ noted in *re Coslett (Contractors Ltd)*,[6] there are four types of transaction by which A can choose to give B a security right:

(i)   mortgage;
(ii) pledge;
(iii) consensual lien;
(iv) charge.

In each of the first three cases, as applied to **Example 1**, B acquires a property right. In the case of a fixed charge transaction, B acquires a persistent right: a Purely Equitable Charge (see **D2:1.2.1**). In the case of a floating charge transaction, B acquires a power to acquire a persistent right: that power is itself known as a floating charge (see **C2:Example 2**). Where the transaction is a pledge or a consensual lien, B necessarily has physical control of a thing. B's physical control is important as it may allow C to discover B's pre-existing property right. In contrast, B can acquire a property right or persistent right under a mortgage or a charge *without* ever needing to have physical control of a thing. This means that the risk to C of being bound by a hidden right of B is particularly high where B acquires a right under a mortgage or charge.

As a result, if B's security right arises under a mortgage or a charge, it is almost always the case that *registration rules* will apply: B's ability to assert his right against C will depend on whether B has registered either the transaction with A, or the right B acquired as a result. For example, if A Ltd gives B a right under a charge, B's failure to register that right generally means that B will not be able to assert it against a liquidator, administrator or

---

[6] [1998] Ch 495 at 508: 'There are only four kinds of consensual security known to English law: (i) pledge (ii) contractual lien; (iii) equitable charge; and (iv) mortgage.'

creditor of A Ltd (see **C2:3.2** and **4.2.2** below). Registration thus operates *negatively*—it responds to B's failure to register by depriving him of the key advantage of a security right: a right that protects him if A Ltd goes into insolvency. The impact of registration provides a crucial practical reason for distinguishing security rights arising under a mortgage or charge from the rights we will discuss in **2.4** below: rights that may protect B, but are not true security rights.

1.3 Security and the protection of A

In this chapter, we will focus on B's position, by examining the **content** and **acquisition** of a security right; the **defences** that C may be able to use against such a right; and the **remedies** which may be available to B when enforcing his security. However, it is important to note the special protection given to A in a security transaction.

1.3.1 A's power to remove B's security right

EXAMPLE 1a

A has Ownership of a bike. A wishes to borrow £200 from B. In return for making the loan, B wants to acquire a security right either against A's bike; or against A's Ownership of the bike.

In such a case, there are four transactions by which A can give B such a security right. A fundamental feature of all four transactions is that A will have a power to remove B's security right: to exercise that power, A simply needs to perform the secured duty (in **Example 1a**, to repay the loan as agreed). This is an essential feature of a security right: it exists for the purpose of protecting B from the risk that a secured duty will not be performed. So, if that duty *is* performed, B's security right disappears. The removal of B's security right is often known as *redemption*: so, in **Example 1a**, if A repays the loan, A is said to redeem the thing or the right over which he has given B a security right.

EXAMPLE 1b

A has Ownership of a bike. In return for a loan of £200 from B, A promises B that: (i) A will repay the loan at a 6 per cent annual rate of interest; and (ii) if A fails to repay the loan within six months, B can sell the bike and use the proceeds to meet A's debt.

In such a case, A is under a duty to B in relation to a specific right held by A: A's Ownership of the bike. As a result, B acquires a persistent right: a Purely Equitable Charge (see **D2:1.2.1**). Under the terms of the deal, A has a contractual power to 'redeem' his Ownership of the bike: ie, to remove B's Purely Equitable Charge. However, A's contractual power lasts only six months.

EXAMPLE 1c

The facts are as in **Example 1b**. Six months pass and A has not repaid any of the loan. Two weeks later, B has not yet exercised his power to sell the bike. At that point, A offers to pay B: (i) the original £200 plus interest at the agreed rate (the interest also covering the further two weeks); and (ii) any extra costs incurred by B as a result of the delay in repayment.

In such a case, can B refuse to accept A's money and insist on selling A's bike? Clearly not:

there is no good reason for B to act in that way. As we have seen, an essential feature of a security right is that it exists for the purpose of protecting B from the risk that a secured duty will not be performed. In **Example 1c**, A *is*, to all practical purposes, willing and able to perform the secured duty. The courts have recognised that, in such a case, A *does* have a power to remove B's security right *even though* A's contractual power to redeem has lapsed.[7] As this point was first recognised by courts of Equity, A's power is often referred to as an 'equity of redemption'. However, the jurisdictional origin of the power that A has in **Example 1c** is not important. Rather, the key point is to distinguish between: (i) A's *contractual* power to redeem (ie, to remove B's security right) *and* (ii) A's *non-contractual* power to redeem.

1.3.2 Protecting A's non-contractual power to remove B's security right

> **EXAMPLE 1d**
>
> The facts are as in **Example 1c**. The contract between A and B also states that, if A does not repay the loan within six months, A must pay B a penalty of £2,000 in order to remove B's security right.

In such a case, the additional term attempts to limit A's non-contractual power to remove B's security right. Such a term will *not* impose a duty on A: in security transactions, the courts protect A's power to redeem by ensuring that such significant obstacles cannot interfere with A's exercise of the power.[8] As this principle has been particularly prominent in the land law system, we will examine it in detail in **G4:2.1.5**.

1.4   The Mortgagor's Right to Redeem: a persistent right

> **EXAMPLE 1e**
>
> A has Ownership of a bike. In return for a loan of £200 from B, A transfers his Ownership of the bike to B. A promises B that: (i) A will repay the loan at a 6 per cent annual rate of interest; and (ii) if A fails to repay the loan within six months, B can sell the bike and use the proceeds to meet A's debt.

This is an example of a mortgage transaction: a transfer of A's right *by way of security*. This means that, as in **Example 1c**, A has *both* (i) a contractual right to regain Ownership by paying off the debt within six months; *and* (ii) a non-contractual right to regain Ownership by paying off the debt (including additional interest and costs) after that point. In such a case: (i) B has an immediate (conditional) duty: he must return A's Ownership of the bike if A pays off the loan; and (ii) B's duty thus relates to a specific right held by B: Ownership of the bike. As a result, A has a persistent right against B's Ownership of the bike: a Mortgagor's Right to Redeem (see **D2:1.2.3**).

---

[7] See eg *per* Lord Eldon in *Seton v Slade* (1802) 7 Ves 265; *per* Jessel MR in *Campbell v Holyland* (1877) 7 Ch D 166 at 171; the survey of Lord Parker in *Kreglinger v New Patagonia Meat and Cold Storage Co Ltd* [1914] 1 AC 25; *per* Scott V-C in *Medforth v Blake* [2000] Ch 86 at 101. For discussion of the historical development of this Equitable right to redeem, see eg Sugarman and Warrington in *Property Problems: From Genes to Pension Funds* (ed Harris, 1997).

[8] See eg *per* Lord Parker in *Kreglinger v New Patagonia Meat and Cold Storage Co Ltd* [1914] 1 AC 25 at 61.

The persistent right A acquires in **Example 1e** is more usually referred to as an 'equity of redemption'. However, that term is potentially misleading. It is also used to refer to A's Equitable right, arising *after* the contractual payment period has passed, to remove B's security right by performing the secured duty. However, A's persistent right arises *as soon as* the mortgage occurs:[9] A has that right even when A has a contractual right to redeem. So, on the orthodox terminology, A's persistent right (the 'equity of redemption') is easy to confuse with A's non-contractual right to regain the mortgaged right (the 'equitable right to redeem').

Further, *whenever* B has a security right, A has an Equitable right to remove B's security right by performing the secured duty. However, A's persistent right arises *only* in a mortgage: it is only in such a case that A's performance of the secured duty means that B must transfer a specific right back to A. For example, if: (i) A gives B a Purely Equitable Charge as security for a loan; and (ii) A then pays off the loan; then (iii) B does not hold any right subject to a duty to A: A's payment simply removes B's security right. So, it is possible for A to have an Equitable right to redeem without having a Mortgagor's Right to Redeem.

2   THE CONTENT QUESTION

In looking at the content question, we need to ask if the right acquired by B as security counts as (i) a property right; or (ii) a persistent right; or (iii) a power to acquire such a right. We therefore need to distinguish between: (i) the type of *transaction* under which B acquires his right (mortgage, pledge, consensual lien or charge); and (ii) the type of *right* B acquires as a result of that transaction.

2.1   Property rights

2.1.1 Mortgages

EXAMPLE 2

A has Ownership of a bike. As security for his duty to repay a loan of £200 to B, A transfers his Ownership of that bike to B.

In such a case, the right acquired by B clearly counts as a property right. A has given B that right for the purpose of security but that does not change the fact that, due to its content, B's right counts as Ownership (see **D1:1.4.2**). This means that the rest of the world, including A, is under a prima facie duty to B not to interfere with B's right to exclusive control of the bike.

The fact that B has acquired his property right for the purpose of security does have important consequences. First, although A has transferred his Ownership to B, the agreement between A and B may well allow A to continue using the mortgaged thing. In **Example 2**, A may need to use his bike in order to get to work and hence earn the money he needs to repay B. It is therefore in the interests of both A and B that B should allow A to continue using the bike.

---

[9] See eg *Brown v Cole* (1845) 14 Sim 427; *Twentieth Century Banking Corpn Ltd v Wilkinson* [1977] Ch 99.

Second, if A *does* pay B back as agreed, B will be under a duty to transfer his Ownership of the bike back to A. As a result, A has a persistent right: a Mortgagor's Right to Redeem. This must affect B's position before the agreed time of repayment: B is under a duty to A not to act in such a way as to prevent or impede the possible return of the bike to A. So if, in **Example 2**, A is due to repay B in two months' time and B destroys the bike before then, B commits a wrong against A.

EXAMPLE 2a

The facts are as in **Example 2**. A is under a duty to pay B £210 six months after the making of the loan. Six months pass and A fails to repay. B then sells the bike to C for £300.

First, we can consider C's position. C has acquired B's Ownership of the bike. A has a pre-existing persistent right (his Mortgagor's Right to Redeem) against B's Ownership. However, A cannot assert that right against C. The key point is that, if A *fails* to repay the loan as agreed, the terms of the mortgage transaction give B an important basic power: the power to sell the bike and to use the proceeds to meet any shortfall in A's repayments.[10] If B exercises that power by selling to C, C can then use the overreaching defence against A's pre-existing right (see **D2:3.4**)

Second, we can consider B's position. B has received £300 in return for transferring his Ownership of the bike to C. But, as B acquired his Ownership by way of security for the performance of A's duty to pay £210 to B, B is under a duty to A to transfer the excess £90 to A. As B's duty to A thus relates to a specific right, B holds his right to that £90 on Trust for A.

It is important to be careful in using the term 'mortgage'. A mortgage occurs whenever *A transfers a right to B as security for a duty owed to B.*[11] This has a number of consequences.

(i)   There can be mortgages in which the right acquired by B does *not count as a property right*. For example, let us say A has a personal right against Z; or a persistent right against a right of Z. If A transfers that right to B by way of security, a mortgage has taken place. But the right acquired by B is clearly not a property right.

(ii) There can be mortgages in which A transfers a right to B in order to secure a duty owed to B by *someone other than A*. For example, if A2 is under a duty to B, that duty can be secured by A transferring a right to B.

(iii) B may acquire security *without there being a mortgage*. As we will see, there are many situations in which B can acquire a right (even a property right) as security *without* A transferring any right to B.

(iv) If a mortgage does occur, A will *always acquire a Mortgagor's Right to Redeem*. As A has transferred a right to B as security for the performance of a duty owed to B, B is under a duty to transfer the right back to A if the duty owed to B is performed.

---

[10] That power can come from a number of sources. It may be an express term of A and B's agreement and, in the absence of such a term, it will be implied: see eg *Deverges v Sandeman, Clark & Co* [1902] 1 Ch 579. If a mortgage is made by deed, B has a statutory power of sale under the Law of Property Act 1925 s 101. However, that power, unlike an express or implied power, is subject to restrictions set out by s 103 (see **5.1.3(i)** below).

[11] See eg *per* Lindley LJ in *Santley v Wilde* [1899] 2 Ch 474 at 474: 'A mortgage is a conveyance of land or an assignment of chattels as security for the payment of a debt or the discharge of some other obligation for which it is given.' It is of course also possible to mortgage a personal right: see eg *per* Buckley LJ in *Swiss Bank Corpn v Lloyds Bank Ltd* [1982] AC 584 at 595 discussing a possible mortgage of shares and other personal rights.

2.1.2 Pledges

EXAMPLE 3

A has Ownership of a bike. As security for his duty to repay a loan of £200 to B, A allows B to take physical control of A's bike.

In such a case, B acquires Ownership through an *independent acquisition.* In contrast to **Example 2,** A has *not* transferred a property right to B. Instead, B's property right arises as a result of his physical control of the bike. This means that the rest of the world, including A, is under a prima facie duty to B not to interfere with B's right to exclusive control of the bike. Further, as A has allowed B to take physical control of the bike, B has a right against A to have such control. This means that, by keeping the bike, B does not commit a wrong against A.[12] Crucially, as B's right to have such control arose as part of a pledge, it binds not only A but also anyone who later acquires A's Ownership of the thing, including A's trustee in bankruptcy.

As in a mortgage, the fact that B has acquired his property right for the purpose of security has important consequences. We saw that, in a mortgage, B may allow A to continue using the mortgaged thing. For a pledge to arise, B must first take physical control of the pledged thing. However, it is possible for B to return physical control of the pledged thing to A without losing his security.[13] Therefore, if B returns the pledged thing to A for a specific purpose (eg, to allow A to sell the thing),[14] B continues to have both a property right *and* a right to have physical control of the thing until the duty secured by the pledge is performed.

Second, if A *does* pay B back as agreed, A's consent to B's physical control of the pledged thing will end. So if, in **Example 3:** (i) A repays B as agreed; and (ii) B retains physical control of the bike; then (iii) B commits a wrong against A. As in a mortgage, B is also under a duty to A not to act in such a way as to prevent or impede the possible return of the bike to A. And, as in a mortgage, B also has an important basic power: the power to sell the bike and to use the proceeds to meet any shortfall in A's repayments. In fact, the discussion of **Example 2** above applies in exactly the same way where B's security arises under a pledge rather than a mortgage.[15] The only difference is that, in the cases of a pledge, the overreaching defence protects C against A's pre-existing *property right* (Ownership of the bike: see **D1:3.4**) rather than A's pre-existing persistent right (a Mortgagor's Right to Redeem).

A pledge thus occurs whenever *A allows B to take physical control of a thing as security for a duty owed to B.* There are thus a number of important differences between a mortgage and a pledge.

---

[12] To that extent, B's position is similar to that of a licensee who has taken physical control of land with the consent of A, an owner of the land: see **E6:2.3.**

[13] See eg *Reeves v Capper* (1838) 5 Bing NC 136.

[14] In international sales, B may lend money to A to enable A to purchase goods. That loan is often secured by a pledge of the goods purchased: B acquires physical control by receipt of a bill of lading (see **D1:2.1.1(i)**). B will often release the bill of lading to A to allow A to sell the goods. This release generally occurs under a 'trust receipt': A promises to hold his property right in the goods on Trust for B (at least to the extent of A's debt to B). See eg *Benjamin's Sale of Goods* (7th edn, 2007), 7-033, 18-235 and 23-133.

[15] See eg *Deverges v Sandeman, Clark & Co* [1902] 1 Ch 579. On the question of B's power of sale, see eg *per* Lord Mersey in *The Odessa* [1916] 1 AC 145 at 159. On the question of B holding any excess realised by sale on Trust for A, see *Mathew v TM Sutton Ltd* [1994] 1 WLR 1455.

(i)   In a pledge, unlike a mortgage, B *always* acquires a property right. A pledge, unlike a mortgage, can therefore exist only in relation to a specific *thing*: there can be no pledge of a personal right or a persistent right.[16]

(ii)   In a pledge, unlike a mortgage, B must take physical control of the thing in question.[17]

(iii) In a pledge, unlike a mortgage, A does not transfer a right to B. A thus retains his Ownership of the pledged thing. There is thus no need for A to acquire a persistent right as result of the pledge.

2.1.3 Consensual liens

EXAMPLE 4

A has Ownership of a painting. He is going away on holiday and leaves it with B for safe-keeping. A and B enter a contract in which A is to pay B £200 for looking after the painting. The contract provides that B can retain control of the painting until A pays the £200. A returns from holiday and demands the painting back before paying the £200.

In such a case, B has a property right: by taking physical control of the painting, he independently acquired Ownership. A did not allow B to take physical control for the *purpose* of giving B security: after all, when A handed the painting over to B, A was under no duty to pay B. There has thus been no pledge of the painting. By refusing to return the painting to A, B seems to commit a breach of his duty not to interfere with A's right to exclusive control. However, A is under a contractual duty to B to allow B to keep control of the painting until A performs his duty to pay B £200. This duty of A to allow B to retain physical control until a secured duty is performed is the essence of the lien: it means B does *not* commit a wrong when he refuses to return the painting to A. Crucially, as B's right to have such control arose with A's consent, it binds not only A but also anyone who later acquires A's Ownership of the thing, including A's trustee in bankruptcy.

In a case such as **Example 4**, B's right is often said to arise under a 'Common Law' lien. This term is used to distinguish such a lien from an 'Equitable' lien. However, the term 'Equitable' lien is redundant and should be rejected (see **D2:1.2.1**). In fact, it is actively misleading: as we will see in **3.2.3** below there are significant differences between 'Common Law' and 'Equitable' liens. As a result, in **Example 4**, there is no need to refer to the transaction as involving a 'Common Law' lien: it simply involves a lien.

A lien depends on B independently acquiring Ownership *and* on B having a right against A to keep physical control of the thing. A lien thus has some similarities to a pledge.

(i)   In a lien, as in a pledge, B *always* acquires a property right. A lien, like a pledge, can

---

[16] In *MCC Proceeds Inc v Shearson Lehmann* [1998] 4 All ER 675, company share *certificates* (ie, things) were pledged by A to B; however there can be no pledge of the shares themselves (ie, personal rights against a company). It seems that in *MCC* the pledge of the share certificates may have been accompanied by a mortgage of the shares themselves: Mummery LJ at 687 stated that A had 'validly transferred legal title in the shares' to B. Certainly, the deal between A and B gave B the power to sell the shares themselves when the secured duty was not performed.

[17] See *Dublin City Distillery Co v Doherty* [1914] AC 823. B does not acquire a security right simply by having a contractual right to take physical control of a thing; he must have such control, either on his own account or via a party who has physical control on his behalf.

therefore exist only in relation to a specific *thing*: there can be no lien of a personal right or a persistent right.

(iii) In a lien, like a pledge, B must have physical control of the thing in question.

(iv) In a lien, like a pledge, A does not transfer a right to B. A thus retains his Ownership of the thing over which B has a lien. There is thus no need for A to acquire a persistent right as result of the lien.

However, there are significant differences between a lien and a pledge.

(i) In a lien, unlike a pledge, B does not *acquire* physical control as security for a duty owed to B.[18]

(ii) In a lien, unlike a pledge, B only has a power against A to sell the thing if A expressly gives B that power.

(iii) In a lien, unlike a pledge, if B voluntarily gives up physical control of the thing, B loses his right against A to have physical control of the thing.

EXAMPLE 4a

The facts are as in **Example 4**. A continues to fail to pay the £200 due to B and, a month after A's return from holiday, B sells the painting to C for £400.

First, we can consider B's position. A did not expressly give B a power to sell the painting. And such a power is not automatically implied into a lien. Therefore, as B has no power against A to sell the painting, B commits a wrong against A by selling to C. A thus has a personal right against B and B will be ordered to pay A money representing the value of A's Ownership of the painting and compensating A for any relevant loss A has suffered as a consequence of the sale.[19] Of course, A still owes B £200: that sum can be set-off by B against the money he must pay A as a result of his wrongful sale.[20] Further, as the £400 received by B is a product of A's Ownership of the painting and there is no legal basis for B to have the benefit of that £400, B holds his right to the £400 on Trust for A (see **D4:4.4**).

Second, we can consider C's position. As a result of his physical control of the painting, B independently acquired Ownership of the painting. B transferred that right to C. However, as B had no power against A to sell the painting, C *cannot* rely on the overreaching defence against A's pre-existing Ownership of the painting.

The third difference between a lien and a pledge can also be seen by considering **Example 4a**. C may try to argue that, when selling the painting to him, B transferred not only B's Ownership of the painting but also B's right, as against A, to retain physical control of the painting. On that analysis, *C* now has a right against A to keep the painting: at least until A pays the £200 he owes to B. If that argument is correct, then C, even though he has interfered with A's right to exclusive control, has not committed a wrong against A. However, C's argument has *not* been accepted.[21] B's right against A to keep control of the

---

[18] See eg *per* Millett LJ in *re Cosslett (Contractors) Ltd* [1998] Ch 495 at 508: 'A pledge and a contractual lien both depend on the delivery of possession to the creditor. The difference between them is that in the case of a pledge the owner delivers possession to the creditor as security, whereas in the case of a lien the creditor retains possession of goods previously delivered to him for some other purpose.'

[19] See eg *Mulliner v Florence* (1878) 3 QBD 485.

[20] No set-off was allowed in *Mulliner* as the debt secured by the lien was owed to B by someone other than A.

[21] See eg *Wilkins v Carmichael* (1779) 1 Doug 101. A, an owner of a ship claimed that the captain, C, had committed a wrong by keeping control of A's ship. One of C's arguments was that he had a right to retain physical

painting cannot be transferred: B loses that right when he chooses to give up physical control of the painting.[22]

Liens are sometimes described as 'particular' or 'general'. In a particular lien, there is a link between the thing against which B has a property right and the secured duty. So, in **Example 4**, there is a particular lien: the lien gives B a right to retain the painting; and A's duty to B arises as a result of B's care of that painting. In a general lien, there is no such link. In a case such as **Example 4**, therefore, B's lien is a general lien if it secures *all* A's duties to B, including, for example, A's duty to pay B for previous occasions on which B looked after A's artwork.

SUMMARY of F4:2.1

There are three types of transaction that allow B to acquire a property right by way of security. In each case, B acquires Ownership of a thing. A mortgage consists of B dependently acquiring Ownership: (i) A transfers his Ownership to B as security *and* (ii) B can retain Ownership until the duty owed to B (ie, the secured duty) is performed. A pledge consists of B independently acquiring Ownership: (i) A allows B to take physical control of a thing as security; *and* (ii) B has a right to retain control until the secured duty is performed. A lien also consists of B independently acquiring Ownership. Although A has not chosen to allow B to take physical control as security: (i) B already has physical control of a thing; *and* (ii) B has a right to retain such control until the secured duty is performed.

A mortgage and a pledge differ from a lien as B has a power against A to sell the thing if the secured duty is not performed. If B exercises that power by selling to C, C will be able to use the overreaching defence against A's pre-existing persistent right (in the case of a mortgage) or against A's pre-existing property right (in the case of a pledge). B can then use the proceeds of sale to meet the secured duty. Any money left over will be held by B on Trust for A.

A pledge and a lien differ from a mortgage as B does *not* acquire A's Ownership. Instead, B independently acquires Ownership by taking physical control of the thing. And, in each case, B also has a right to keep the thing until the secured duty is performed. Crucially, that right, as it arises as part of a pledge or a lien, binds not only A but also anyone acquiring a right from A.

The table below considers the position where A's property right is used as security for a duty owed to B.

	B's right	A's right	Does B always have a power of sale?
Mortgage	Ownership	Mortgagor's Right to Redeem	Yes
Pledge	Ownership	Ownership	Yes
Lien	Ownership	Ownership	No

control of the ship as he had paid B, a carpenter who had done repairs to the ship. As a result, C argued, B's repairing lien had been transferred to C. Lord Mansfield at 105 rejected that argument: B's right to retain physical control ceased when he gave up control of the ship and so could not be transferred to C.

[22] If B loses physical control *without* choosing to give it up (eg, where X steals the bike from C), B does not lose his right to retain physical control: see eg *Wallace v Woodgate* (1824) Ry & Mood 193.

2.2 Persistent rights

If the right B acquires by way of security is a persistent right, rather than a property right, B's protection is slightly reduced. First, the rest of the world will *not* be under a duty to B. Second, if C acquires a right from A, C may be able to use one of the additional defences available against a persistent right, such as the 'bona fide purchaser' defence. Nonetheless, a persistent right shares a key feature with a property right: it is capable of binding a third party, such as A's trustee in bankruptcy (see **B:4.5.2(ii)**).

2.2.1 Mortgages

EXAMPLE 5

Z holds some shares on Trust for A. As security for his duty to repay a loan of £2000 to B, A transfers his right under the Trust to B.

A mortgage occurs whenever A transfers a right to B as security. B can therefore acquire a persistent right by means of a mortgage. So, in **Example 5**, if *each* of A and Z goes into insolvency, B will be protected: if A fails to repay the loan, B can use the security of his persistent right against Z's shares. As we saw in **1.2.1** above, important consequences flow from the fact that B has acquired his persistent right for the purpose of security.

First, if A *does* pay B back as agreed, B will be under a duty to transfer his persistent right back to A. The prospect of such a transfer means that, as soon as he acquires his right from A, B is under a duty to A in relation to that right. This means that A has a persistent right: a Mortgagor's Right to Redeem. In **Example 5**, A's persistent right is a right against B's persistent right. So, if A mortgages a persistent right to B, a chain of persistent rights arises: in **Example 5**, B has a persistent right against a right held by Z; and A in turn has a right against B's persistent right.

Second, B will have a power of sale if the duty secured by the mortgage is not performed. Any excess received by B will again be held by B on Trust for A. It is therefore clear that certain basic rules apply whenever a mortgage occurs, whether the right transferred by way of security is a property right, a persistent right or a personal right.

EXAMPLE 6

A has Ownership of a bike. As security for his duty to repay £200 to B1, A transfers his Ownership of that bike to B1. B1 allows A to retain physical control of the bike. A then wishes to borrow a further £500 from B2. A assures B2 that no one else has a property right in the bike. B2 makes the loan to A in return for a mortgage of the bike.

In such a case, B2 has been tricked: as a result of the first mortgage, B1 now has A's initial Ownership of the bike. A does, however, have a persistent right against B1's Ownership of the bike: a Mortgagor's Right to Redeem. A's second mortgage to B2 can thus operate as a transfer of A's Right to Redeem to B2: a Mortgagor's Right to Redeem can itself be mortgaged.

Of course, unless B2 has a defence to B1's pre-existing property right, the Right to Redeem acquired by B2 is of less value than the property right B2 hoped to acquire from A. Nonetheless, that Right to Redeem may be of some use to B2. For example, let us say A fails to pay any of the sums due to B1 and B2; and that A's bike is particularly valuable and worth £1,000. In that case, once B1 sells the bike and takes his £200, B1 will hold the extra £800 on Trust for A. B2 will then have a persistent right against A's right under the Trust: that persistent right will give B2 security for A's duty to repay B2.

2.2.2 Charges

EXAMPLE 7

A has Ownership of a bike. In return for receiving a loan of £200 from B, A makes a contractual promise to B that, if he fails to repay the loan, he will allow B to sell the bike and to use the proceeds to meet the debt.

B acquires a persistent right: a Purely Equitable Charge (see **D2:1.2.1**). A has come under a duty to B and that duty relates to a specific right held by A: A's Ownership of the bike. It is important to note that A has *not* mortgaged his Ownership of the bike. Rather than transferring his property right to B, A has: (i) retained that right; and (ii) given B a persistent right against it. Nor has A given B a pledge or a lien: B has not taken physical control of the bike. Nor has A transferred a pre-existing persistent right to B. Instead, A has given B a *new* persistent right by way of security.

The opportunity of giving B a Purely Equitable Charge can be very valuable to A. It allows A to give B security, and thus to persuade B to extend credit to A, *without* having to transfer any right to B. This means that the creation of a Purely Equitable Charge has three key advantages over a mortgage: these benefits are further examples of the usefulness of persistent rights (see **D2:Example 7**).

(i)   If A does not have the power to transfer a right to B, A may still be able to give B a Purely Equitable Charge over that right (see **D2:1.4.1(i)**).

(ii) If A does not yet have a right, A can still make a binding promise to hold that right, when he acquires it, as security for a duty owed to B. B will then acquire a Purely Equitable Charge *as soon as* A acquires that right: there is no need for a later transfer of the right to B (see **D2:1.4.1(i)**).

(iii) If formality rules regulate A's power to transfer a right to B, those rules will not regulate A's power to give B a Purely Equitable Charge over that right (see **D2:1.4.1(ii)**).

EXAMPLE 8

A Ltd is an international company. It wants to borrow a large sum from B Bank. A Ltd has a large number of rights. Those rights are governed by the laws of a number of different countries. It is not clear whether all the rights can be transferred; nor is it clear what formality rules might apply to regulate transfers of any of the rights. B Bank also wants to receive security over future rights A Ltd will acquire against its customers.

In such a case, it may well be impossible, in practice, to arrange a mortgage of A Ltd's current rights to B Bank. And it is impossible, as a matter of doctrine, for A Ltd to mortgage rights it does not yet have. However, A Ltd can give B Bank a Purely Equitable Charge over particular rights it currently has; and over particular rights it expects to acquire. As we will see when examining **Examples 10a, 10b and 10c**, there is then no need to check whether A Ltd has the power to transfer those rights to B Bank; or to see what formality rules may regulate such a power; or to see whether A Ltd actually has those rights at the moment when it gives B Bank the Purely Equitable Charge.

EXAMPLE 9

A Ltd has an account at B Bank. In return for a loan from B Bank, A Ltd makes a binding promise to allow B Bank to use any credit in A Ltd's account with B's Bank as security for the loan.

It is clear that A cannot give B Bank security by a mortgage of his account with B Bank. A bank account is simply a personal right against B Bank; it is impossible for A to transfer such a right to B Bank. A can make a binding promise to waive its right against B Bank; but the effect of that promise will be to end A's right against B Bank, not to transfer that right.

However, A *can* give B Bank security by a charge of his account with B Bank. In **Example 9**, A Ltd's promise gives B a Purely Equitable Charge: a right against A Ltd's right against B Bank. The transaction is often referred to as a 'charge-back': A has a personal right against B and then charges that right to B. The possibility of giving B such a right has been doubted;[23] but it was confirmed by the House of Lords in *In re BCCI (No 8)*.[24] And the view of the House of Lords is correct: A can retain his personal right against B Bank whilst also giving B Bank a persistent right against A's right. Therefore, in **Example 9**, if A Ltd goes into insolvency owing B Bank £2000 under the loan; and A Ltd has £3000 in its account with B Bank, B Bank can deduct the £2000 owed and pay only the excess £1000 to A Ltd's liquidators. In fact, this is one of the cases where the general registration requirement does *not* apply: B Bank can assert its Purely Equitable Charge against A Ltd's liquidators even if it did not register its right.[25]

2.2.3 Equitable Assignments?

B can acquire a persistent right as a result of an Equitable Assignment by A (see **D2:1.2.2**). If A has a personal right against Z, two forms of Equitable Assignment are possible:

Type 1 A expresses an intention to give B, immediately, the benefit of that right; *or*
Type 2 A comes under a duty to transfer that right to B.

It is therefore possible for A to make an Equitable Assignment by way of security. However, an Equitable Assignment does *not* count as an additional form of transaction by which B can acquire a security right. If an Equitable Assignment is made by way of security, its effect is that: (i) B has a persistent right against a personal right of A; and (ii) if the secured duty is not performed, B has the power to use that right to meet that duty. In such a case, the Equitable Assignment is effectively identical to a charge. Indeed, given its content, B's

---

[23] See eg the decision of Millett J in *re Charge Card Services Ltd* [1987] 1 Ch 150. Goode had also expressed the view that charge-backs are conceptually impossible: see eg *Legal Problems of Credit and Security* (2nd edn, 1988), 124–9.

[24] [1998] AC 214. The facts of **Example 9** are a simplified version of that case.

[25] See eg *per* Lord Hoffmann in *re BCCI (No 8)* [1998] AC 214 at 227. The proposals set out in Law Com No 296 will extend the registration ('filing' under the new scheme) requirements to cases where B's security right relates to a bank account. However, under those proposals, filing is unnecessary if B has 'control' of A Ltd's bank account: see Law Com No 296 at 5.19–5.20. That is clearly the case in **Example 9**.

persistent right is best seen as a Purely Equitable Charge. As a result, the general registration requirement will apply if A goes into insolvency and B wishes to assert his right.

It is worth noting two particular ways in which a **Type 2** Equitable Assignment can give B a Purely Equitable Charge. The first occurs where A has an existing personal right against Z and attempts, but fails, to transfer that right to B by way of a mortgage.

(i) Failed mortgages of an existing personal right

EXAMPLE 10a

A Ltd has a personal right against Z, a customer who has not yet paid A Ltd for goods supplied. In return for a loan from B, A Ltd attempts to transfer to B its personal right against Z. However, A Ltd's contract with Z is on Z's standard terms of business, and includes a 'non-assignment' clause—a term preventing A Ltd from transferring any of its contractual rights against Z. A Ltd then goes into insolvency.

EXAMPLE 10b

The basic facts are as in **Example 10a**. This time there is no 'non-assignment' clause. However, A Ltd goes into insolvency before written notice of the attempted transfer to B is given to Z.

In each case, A Ltd has attempted to mortgage its personal right against Z: to transfer that right to Z by way of security. In each case, A Ltd failed. In **Example 10a**, it simply has no power to make such a transfer. In **Example 10b**, A Ltd does have that power.[26] However, section 136 of the Law of Property Act 1925 ('the LPA 1925') imposes a formality rule that regulates A Ltd's power (see **C3:5.1.2**). And in **Example 10b**, that formality rule was *not* complied with before A Ltd's insolvency: at that point, Z had not received written notice of the transfer to B. As a result, in each of **Examples 10a and 10b**, A Ltd, when it went into insolvency, still had its personal right against Z.

Nonetheless, in each of **Examples 10a and 10b**, a **Type 2** Equitable Assignment occurs: because B gave A the loan in return for the attempted mortgage, A is under a duty to transfer his right to B (see **D2:Example 12cii**). As a result, B acquires a persistent right: a right against A's personal right against Z. As noted above, that persistent right is best seen as a Purely Equitable Charge.

B may have preferred to have acquired, instead, A Ltd's *actual* personal right against Z. For example, as A Ltd has retained that right, B cannot sue Z directly: he must rely on, or force, A Ltd to do so (see **B:4.4.2**).[27] However, a persistent right still provides valuable security for B. If B registers its right and A Ltd goes into insolvency, B's persistent right is capable of binding A Ltd's liquidators. So, if those liquidators enforce A Ltd's personal right

---

[26] See eg *Tancred v Delagoa Bay and East Africa Railway* (1889) 23 QBD 239. Under the Law of Property Act 1925, s 136, A Ltd can only transfer a personal right by means of an 'absolute assignment'. Although B has to transfer the right back to A Ltd if the secured duty is performed, a transfer by way of mortgage counts as an absolute assignment: see eg *per* Mance LJ in *Raiffeisen Zentralbank Osterreich AG v Five Star Trading LLC* [2001] QB 285 at [74].

[27] B will have a problem if A Ltd has been wound up and so is unable to sue Z. B will then need to have A Ltd restored to the Companies Register: see *per* Kerr LJ in *MH Smith (Plant Hire) Ltd v DL Mainwaring* [1986] 2 Lloyds Rep 243 at 246.

against Z, they will not be free to distribute that money to A Ltd's general creditors but will instead have to hold the money received as security for A Ltd's duty to repay B.

(ii) Mortgages of future personal rights

> **EXAMPLE 10c**
>
> A Ltd knows that, in the future, it will acquire personal rights against its customers. In return for a loan from B, A Ltd makes a binding promise to B that it will transfer to B any such rights that it acquires in the next six months. The plan is that B is to have those rights as security for A Ltd's duty to repay the loan. Three months later, A Ltd has acquired a number of new personal rights against its customers. However, A Ltd has not repaid B and goes into insolvency.

When receiving the loan from B, it is impossible for A Ltd *immediately* to transfer rights it will only acquire in the future. However, by making a binding promise to B, A Ltd does come under an immediate duty to B. When A Ltd then acquires a new personal right against a customer, B acquires an *immediate* persistent right against that right (see **D2:Example 12bii**).[28] So, even if A Ltd goes into insolvency before performing its duty to transfer those rights to B, B is still protected: it has a persistent right against the new personal rights acquired by A Ltd. Again, B's right is best seen as a Purely Equitable Charge and so can only bind A Ltd's liquidators if it was properly registered.

2.2.4 The creation of a Trust?

If A has a *pre-existing* persistent right under a Trust, A can transfer that right to B by way of security (see **2.2.1** above). If A attempts to give B a security right through the *creation* of a Trust, the transaction will be viewed as a charge. As a result, the creation of a Trust does *not* count as an additional transaction by which A can give B a security right. In fact, the right B acquires is better seen as a Purely Equitable Charge rather than a right under a Trust. The key point is that: (i) if A has a right; and (ii) A attempts to give B a security right in relation to that right; then (iii) A does *not* come under the core Trust duty to B: A is free to use his right for his own benefit, *provided* the secured duty is performed. This means that the persistent right acquired by B as a result of A's attempt to set up a Trust should count as a Purely Equitable Charge and hence be subject to any registration rules applying to such rights.

> **SUMMARY of F4:2.2**
>
> There are essentially two types of transaction that allow B to acquire a persistent right by way of security. A mortgage consists of a transfer of a right by A to B by way of security. If A has a pre-existing persistent right against a right of Z, A can transfer that right to B by way of a mortgage. In such a case, B's security consists of a persistent right against Z's right: if the secured duty is not performed, B can sell that right and use the proceeds to meet the secured duty. The *type* of persistent right acquired by B will depend on the right mortgaged by A. For example, if the pre-existing right mortgaged by A is a right under a Trust, that is the right B will acquire.

---

[28] See *Tailby v Official Receiver* (1888) 13 App Cas 523, on which **Example 10c** is based.

A charge consists of A retaining a right and giving B a new persistent right against that right. In such a case, B's security consists of a persistent right against A's right. The *type* of persistent right acquired by B is always the same: a Purely Equitable Charge. If the secured duty is not performed, B can use the proceeds of A's right to meet the secured duty. The charge is particularly useful in practice: (i) in contrast to a mortgage, it allows A to give B security without having to transfer a right to B; and (ii) in contrast to a pledge or a lien, it allows A to give B security without having to give B physical control of a thing. A charge, unlike a mortgage, can also be used to give B security over a future right: as soon as A acquires that right, B will have a persistent right against it. And a charge, unlike a mortgage, can be used to give B security over A's personal right against B.

Whether B's persistent right arises under a mortgage or a charge, it is subject to the general registration requirement. Unlike a pledge or a lien, a mortgage or charge can be used to give B a security right that: (i) gives B protection on A's insolvency; *and* (ii) can arise without B having physical control of a thing. As a result, registration is generally necessary to protect C from the risk of losing out due to a hidden persistent right of B.

2.3   Powers to acquire a persistent right: the floating charge

A power to acquire a persistent right can give B valuable security. If: (i) B has a power to acquire a Purely Equitable Charge; and (ii) the secured duty is not performed; then (iii) B can exercise that power and thus acquire a power to use a particular right of A to meet the duty owed to B. The basic position is that, if B has a power to acquire a persistent right against a right of A, B can exercise his power against C if C acquires, for free, a right that depends on A's right (see **D2:Example 11b**). As a result, B can assert his power to acquire a persistent right against A's trustee in bankruptcy; or against A Ltd's liquidators.

There is a particularly important transaction by which B can acquire a power to acquire a persistent right by way of security. It is an example of a charge: both the transaction and the power arising under it are known as a *floating charge*.

2.3.1 Definition

EXAMPLE 11

A Ltd is a bike manufacturer. Its rights include: (i) Ownership of finished but unsold bikes; and (ii) contractual rights against various wholesalers who order bikes from A Ltd. To persuade B Bank to make a substantial loan, A Ltd wants to give B Bank security over: (i) its current and future stock of finished but unsold bikes; and (ii) its current and future contractual rights against the wholesalers. But A Ltd needs to be free to continue to use those rights, and their proceeds, in its usual course of business. For example, it needs to be free to sell finished bikes and to collect sums due from the wholesalers; and it needs to be free to use the proceeds obtained to buy new parts and to pay wages.

In such a case, a mortgage, pledge or consensual lien will not do the trick. As A Ltd wishes to give B Bank security over future as well as current rights, a charge is the only suitable transaction. But A Ltd does not want to come under an immediate duty to hold *specific rights* as security for B Bank. Instead, A Ltd wants to have the freedom to use its rights in the ordinary course of business. The solution is to use a charge to give B Bank a *power to acquire persistent rights*.

Where a charge gives B a power to acquire a persistent right, it is known as a *floating charge*. A charge that instead gives B an immediate persistent right is known as a *fixed charge*. So, in **Examples 9, 10a, 10b and 10c** the transaction between A Ltd and B is a fixed charge. In such cases *either*:

(i) B acquires an immediate persistent right (a Purely Equitable Charge) in relation to a right held by A Ltd at the time of the transaction (as in **Examples 9, 10a and 10b**); *or*

(ii) B does not acquire an immediate persistent right as A Ltd does not have the right in question at the time of the transaction; *but* B acquires an immediate persistent right (a Purely Equitable Charge) *as soon as* A Ltd acquires that right (as in **Example 10c**).

Instead, in **Example 11**, A Ltd will give B Bank a power to acquire a persistent right. So, A Ltd is not under a duty to hold any *specific* rights as security until B Bank exercises its power. When B Bank exercises that power, his floating charge (a power to acquire a persistent right) will turn into a fixed charge (a persistent right).[29] At that point, B Bank's floating charge is said to *crystallise*.[30] The agreement between A Ltd and B Bank is also very likely to prescribe that, if certain events occur, B Bank's power is automatically exercised: those events can be known as crystallising events.[31]

2.3.2 The distinction between a floating charge and a fixed charge

The conceptual distinction between a floating charge and a fixed charge is clear:

Name of right	Nature of right
Floating charge	Power to acquire a persistent right
Fixed charge	Persistent right

This analysis is based on that of the House of Lords in *re Spectrum Plus Ltd*.[32] In that case, it was held that B Bank's right was a floating charge, not a fixed charge. That conclusion was based on the fact that, under the terms of the charge, A Ltd was *not* under a duty to hold any specific rights as security for its debt to B Bank.[33] Although the terms of the charge did impose some immediate restrictions on A Ltd's use of its charged rights, A Ltd had the power, as against B Bank, to use those rights for purposes other than as security for the debt owed to B Bank.

It is important to note that the distinction between a floating charge and a fixed charge does *not* depend on whether the charge relates to current or future rights.

EXAMPLE 12

A Ltd has a personal right against Z, a customer. A Ltd charges that right to B Bank. Under the terms of the charge, A Ltd is free to collect the money due to it from Z and to spend that money on A Ltd's ordinary business purposes. Under the terms of the charge, B Bank has the power, by giving notice to A Ltd, to revoke A Ltd's power to use the right in that way.

---

[29] See eg *per* Kay LJ in *Biggerstaff v Rowatt's Wharf Ltd* [1896] 2 Ch 93 at 106.
[30] See eg *per* Buckley LJ in *Evans v Rival Granite Quarries Ltd* [1910] 2 KB 979 at 999.
[31] *Re Brightlife Ltd* [1987] Ch 200 confirms the validity of such clauses.
[32] [2005] 2 AC 680. See too Worthington, ch 3 in *Company Charges: Spectrum and Beyond* (ed Getzler and Payne, 2006) and *Proprietary Interests in Commercial Transactions* (1996), ch 4.
[33] See *re Spectrum Plus Ltd* [2005] 2 AC 680 *per* Lord Scott at [107]; Lord Walker at [138]–[139].

In such a case, although the charge relates to a right currently held by A Ltd, it is a floating charge.[34] A Ltd has the power to use the right for purposes other than holding it as security for B Bank: so B Bank has only a power to acquire a persistent right. **Example 12** thus also shows that the distinction between a floating charge and a fixed charge does *not* depend on whether the charge relates to a specific right. In **Example 12**, B Bank can identify a specific right to which its charge relates; but, as A Ltd is not yet under a duty to hold that right as security for its duty to repay B Bank, B Bank does not yet have a persistent right.

The courts' approach to drawing the distinction between a floating charge and a fixed charge can be usefully compared to their approach when distinguishing between a Lease of land and a licence to use land. As we will see in **2.3.4**, there are a number of reasons why B Bank may wish to argue that its security right is a fixed rather than a floating charge. And as we will see in **G1B:1.2**, there are similarly a number of reasons why A, an owner of land, may wish to argue that he has given B a license rather than a Lease. The courts therefore have to deal with situations in which parties wish to give the impression that B's right is one type (a fixed charge or a licence) whereas the **content** of B's right means that B's right is of a different type (a floating charge or a Lease).

First, in each area, the *label* used by the parties is not definitive: A and B may describe B's right as a fixed charge or as a licence; but if the right acquired by B does not meet the test laid down by the courts, it will instead be a floating charge or a Lease. Second, the *intentions* of the parties are only relevant to the extent that they affect the nature of the right acquired by B. For example, if A and B fully intend that B's right counts as a fixed charge or as a licence, that intention is irrelevant if the right in fact given to B counts as a floating charge or as a Lease (see **G1B:1.5.1**). Third, in practice, there may be borderline cases in which the distinction is difficult to draw. For example, in the land law system, B's right can count as a Lease if it gives B a right to exclusive control of land for a limited period. If the agreement between A and B imposes some limits on B's right to occupy A's land, that agreement may still give B a Lease: it may be that B has a basic right to exclusive control of the land and has simply made contractual promises to A limiting that right. Equally, even if the agreement between A Ltd and B Bank imposes some limits on how A Ltd is to deal with particular rights, that agreement may still give B Bank a floating charge: it may be that, despite those limits, A Ltd is still free to use its rights for a purpose other than as security for a duty owed to B Bank.

2.3.3 The advantages of a floating charge

The essential advantage of a floating charge is that it gives B Bank security but also allows A Ltd to get on with its business.[35] This can be of benefit not only to A Ltd but also to B Bank: in **Example 11**, if A Ltd can trade as usual, it is more likely to make the money it needs to repay B Bank. In particular, if: (i) A Ltd, acting within the powers given to it by the floating

---

[34] *Ibid per* Lord Scott at [107].

[35] See eg Goode, ch 2 in *Company Charges: Spectrum and Beyond* (ed Getzler and Payne, 2006), 11: 'The floating charge is one of equity's most brilliant creations. It has enabled financiers to advance large sums of money on the security of a company's inventory and receivables while leaving the debtor company free, within the limits set by the charge, to dispose of such assets in the ordinary course of business free from the security interest.' Receivables are debts due to A Ltd—eg, in **Example 11**, A Ltd's contractual rights against its wholesalers. It is worth noting, however, that Goode's chapter goes on to argue for the abolition of the floating charge, but only by altering the definition of a fixed charge to allow it to fulfil the vital role of a floating charge.

charge, gives C a right; then (ii) B Bank cannot assert its power against C; as (iii) C can rely on the overreaching defence (see **D2:3.4**).[36]

Due to the freedom it gives A Ltd, the floating charge can also be used to give B Bank security over a large proportion of A Ltd's total assets.[37] Before the Enterprise Act 2002, this meant that B Bank could qualify for an important advantage: the right, if A Ltd ran into financial problems, to appoint an administrative receiver. That receiver could essentially run A Ltd's business for the benefit of B Bank:[38] if B Bank's charge related to the 'whole or (substantially the whole) of' A Ltd's assets, the receiver also had the power to sell off A Ltd's business as a going concern.[39] However, the position is now different. Instead of appointing an administrative receiver to run A Ltd's business for it, B Bank can instead appoint an administrator. An administrator, unlike an administrative receiver, is under a duty to 'perform his functions in the interest of the company's creditors as a whole'.[40] However, a floating charge over a substantial proportion of A Ltd's assets still gives B Bank the advantage of being able to choose the particular administrator.[41]

2.3.4 The disadvantages to B of a floating charge

In practice, the distinction between a floating charge and a fixed charge has important consequences. One such consequence concerns B Bank's ability to assert its right against C1, a party who acquires a right from A Ltd *before* A Ltd's insolvency. We will consider that point in **4.3** below. However, B Bank's chief concern is the effect of its right *after* A Ltd's insolvency. After all, the key advantage of a security right is that it can be asserted against A Ltd's liquidators. However, whilst a floating charge does give B Bank that security, the insolvency legislation treats floating charges differently from fixed charges.

Under that legislation, there are four particular disadvantages to B Bank of holding a floating charge rather than a fixed charge.

(i)   If the general assets of A Ltd (ie, those rights that A Ltd is free to use for its own benefit) do not suffice to fully meet the claims of A Ltd's preferential creditors,[42] any rights of A Ltd subject to a floating charge *can* be used to meet those claims.[43]

(ii)   If the general assets of A Ltd do not suffice to meet the costs of A Ltd's liquidation (eg, liquidators' fees), any rights of A Ltd subject to a floating charge *can* be used to meet those claims.[44]

---

[36] See eg R Nolan (2004) 120 *LQR* 108. There is a question as to whether overreaching operates here as a true *defence* or instead as a reason preventing B exercising his power against C.

[37] B Bank could of course acquire a fixed charge over the same proportion, but A Ltd's duty to hold those assets as security would prevent A Ltd running its business effectively.

[38] The duties owed by an administrative receiver to A Ltd are quite limited: see eg *Downsview Nominees Ltd v First City Corp Ltd* [1993] AC 295.

[39] Insolvency Act 1986, s 29(2).

[40] Insolvency Act 1986, Sch B1, para 3(2). See Armour and Mokal [2004] *LMCLQ* 28.

[41] Insolvency Act 1986, Sch B1, para 16. The administrator can be appointed without a court order.

[42] Preferential creditors include, in particular, any employees of A Ltd who are owed wages. But each employee can only claim up to £800 as a preferential creditor. The class of preferential creditors used to include the Crown, claiming unpaid taxes: but the Enterprise Act 2002 has changed that.

[43] Insolvency Act 1986, ss 40, 175, 386 and Sch 6, Sch B1, para 99(5). This provision caused the dispute in *re Spectrum Plus Ltd* [2005] 2 AC 680.

[44] Insolvency Act 1986, s 175ZA as introduced by Companies Act 2006, s 1282. This provision reverses the effct of *Buchler v Talbot* [2004] 2 AC 298. For discussion see Mokal [2004] *LMCLQ* 387 and (taking a different view) Armour and Walters (2006) 122 *LQR* 295.

(iii)   A proportion of any rights held by A Ltd subject to a floating charge (the 'pre-scribed part') cannot be used for the sole benefit of B Bank but instead must be available for distribution amongst A Ltd's unsecured creditors.[45]

(iv)   If A Ltd gave B Bank a floating charge shortly before A Ltd's insolvency,[46] B Bank acquires a security right only to the extent of the value provided by B Bank in return for the charge *and* at the same time as, or after, the creation of the charge.[47]

These four consequences do *not* apply if B Bank has a fixed charge rather than a floating charge.[48] The usefulness of these provisions, each of which aims to give some protection to unsecured creditors of A Ltd, has been challenged.[49] Nonetheless, there is at least a conceptual justification for treating a floating charge differently from a fixed charge.[50] If A Ltd has a floating charge, it has only a power to acquire a persistent right. In contrast, if B has a persistent right under a fixed charge, A Ltd is *already* under a duty to hold a specific right as security. Just as the defences available to C against a power to acquire a persistent right differ from, and are more extensive than, those available against a persistent right (see D2:3.5.5), so it can be argued that insolvency rules should distinguish between a floating and a fixed charge. As the former is only a power to acquire a persistent right, B needs to show why that right should be capable of adversely affecting A Ltd's unsecured creditors: statute can then impose limits on B's ability to do so. In contrast, those same limits may be inappropriate where B has a pre-existing persistent right.[51]

SUMMARY of F4:2.3

B can acquire a security right through a transaction known as a charge. There are two forms of that transaction. A fixed charge transaction gives B an immediate persistent right: a Purely Equitable Charge. A floating charge transaction instead gives B a *power* to acquire a persistent right: a power to acquire a Purely Equitable Charge. The difference between the two transaction depends on A's freedom to use the rights over which B acquires security. If A is under an immediate duty to hold those rights as security for a duty owed to B, it is a fixed charge transaction and B has a Purely Equitable Charge. If A is instead free to use those rights for purposes other than as security for a duty owed to B (eg, as when A Ltd is free to use those rights in its ordinary course of business), it is a floating charge transaction and B instead has a power to acquire a Purely Equitable Charge.

---

[45] Insolvency Act 1976, s 176A as introduced by Enterprise Act 2002.

[46] The relevant period is two years prior to insolvency if B Bank is connected to A Ltd; and one year in other cases.

[47] Insolvency Act 1986, s 245.

[48] Like any right acquired shortly before A Ltd's insolvency, a fixed charge can be set aside as an unlawful preference if it was given to B shortly before A Ltd's insolvency and with the aim of preferring B to other creditors: see eg Insolvency Act 1986, ss 239(5) and 240(1)(a); but the additional rule in the Insolvency Act 1986, s 245 applies *only* to floating charges.

[49] See eg Armour, ch 9 in *Company Charges: Spectrum and Beyond* (ed Getzler and Payne, 2006).

[50] See too Mokal [2004] *LMCLQ* 387.

[51] This does not mean that, if B has a persistent right, he is *always* protected in A Ltd's insolvency. For example, B's persistent right, like any security right, may set aside as an unlawful preference; as an undervalue transaction; or as a fraudulent transfer: see eg Insolvency Act 1986, ss 239(5) and 240(1)(a); s 238; and s 423.

The floating charge is very important in practice. It can be used to allow A Ltd the freedom to run its business whilst, at the same time, giving B valuable security over a substantial proportion of A Ltd's rights. Its usefulness to A Ltd depends on the freedom it allows A Ltd. Its usefulness to B depends on the fact that B, even *before* he exercises his power to acquire a Purely Equitable Charge, has a valuable security right: crucially, an unexercised power to acquire a persistent right is capable of binding a third party and, as a result, B is protected if A Ltd goes into insolvency. However, a power to acquire a persistent right deserves less protection than an actual persistent right: this is reflected in the fact that, if B has a floating rather than a fixed charge, his protection in the event of A Ltd's insolvency is subject to certain conditions: (i) B must first allow A Ltd's liquidators, if necessary, to use any rights covered by the floating charge to pay A Ltd's preferential creditors and to meet the expenses of A Ltd's liquidators; and (ii) a 'prescribed part' of the rights covered by the floating charge can be used to meet the claims of creditors other than B.

2.4   The distinction between protection and security

We have defined a security right as a property right, persistent right or power to acquire a persistent right that arises to *secure* the performance of a duty owed to B. That definition excludes particular rights that B may have as *protection* against the risk of a party failing to perform a duty owed to B. First, it excludes the situation, discussed in **1.1** above, where A2 guarantees a duty owed by A to B. In such a case, B acquires a personal right against A2. That right gives him some extra protection but it does not provide security: B is still exposed to the risk that *each* of A and A2 will go into insolvency.

Second, our definition also excludes situations where B does have a property right or a persistent right, but that right does not arise as a means to protect B if a party fails to perform a duty owed to B. In such cases, B's right may provide *protection* in the event of A's insolvency, but it does not count as a *security* right.

2.4.1 The retention of a right by B

(i) Hire purchase, conditional sales and retention of title clauses

EXAMPLE 13

B has Ownership of a car. A wishes to buy the car but cannot afford to pay the full price as a lump sum. A and B reach an agreement whereby: (i) B gives A physical control of the car in return for regular monthly payments; and (ii) at the end of a set period, A can pay a small sum to B and acquire Ownership of the car.

In such a case, B could choose to *immediately* transfer his Ownership of the car to A. B would then have no security for A's duty to pay B the agreed sums and so would be taking the risk that A may be unable to keep up the payments. Instead, in **Example 13**, B makes clear that A is to acquire B's Ownership of the car *only* when A has made all the payments. So, until that point, B retains Ownership and thus has some protection: if A fails to pay as arranged, B can revoke his permission for A to have control of the car.

B's retention of Ownership until he is fully paid is thus the central feature of hire-purchase and conditional sale agreements. However, in such cases, B's property right does not count, on our definition, as a security right. This is because B's property right does not *arise as a means to protect B if A's duty is not performed*. After all, B had his property right even *before* he dealt with A. This means that B's property right escapes the general registration rules that can apply to true security rights.

EXAMPLE 14

B supplies yarn to A Ltd, a fabric manufacturer. The contract between A Ltd and B stipulates that A Ltd is to pay £4,000 for the yarn; and that sum is due two months after receipt of the yarn. The contract also contains a clause that B retains his Ownership of the yarn until it is paid for by A Ltd. The contract gives A Ltd the power to use that yarn and to sell any fabric produced from the yarn. A Ltd runs into financial problems and does not pay for the yarn. C is appointed as its receiver. B tells C that he intends to retake physical control of any yarn that A Ltd has not paid for. However, C allows A Ltd to use some of the unpaid for yarn to continue its manufacturing.

In such a case, B sells goods to A Ltd with a 'retention of title' clause. Under a sale, the basic rule is B's Ownership passes to A when it is intended to pass (see **D1:2.2.4(iii)(a)**). As a result, B can stipulate that, even though he has allowed A to take physical control of the thing sold, A is not to acquire B's Ownership until he has paid the full price.[52] In **Example 14**, B had a pre-existing property right in the yarn when C allowed A Ltd to use that yarn. As C had no permission from B to do so, C committed a wrong: he breached his duty not to interfere with B's right to exclusive control of the yarn. This is confirmed by the decision of the Court of Appeal in *Clough Mill Ltd v Martin*,[53] the essential facts of which are identical to **Example 14**.

Again, B's retention of Ownership until he is fully paid provides B with important protection. However, B's property right does not count, on our definition, as a security right. Again, B had that property right even *before* he dealt with A. This means that B's property right escapes the general registration rules that can apply to true security rights.

(ii) Problems arising from the retention of rights

B's retention of a property right by way of protection can clearly give rise to problems. First, a hire-purchase deal amounts to B, a finance company, extending credit to A, the hire-purchaser. In the consumer context, such credit transactions are regulated by statute in an attempt to promote transparency and to protect the borrower (A) from exploitation. Such a deal can also cause problems for C. B retains Ownership and allows A to have physical control of the thing. C may then acquire a right from A in the reasonable belief that no one other than A has a property right in the thing. As a result, a statutory defence, provided by Part III of the Hire-Purchase Act 1964 may apply to protect C against B's Ownership.[54] That defence is similar to the statutory defences discussed in **D1:3.3**.[55] The defence applies only if:

---

[52] Sale of Goods Act 1979, s 19(1).

[53] [1985] 1 WLR 111.

[54] For further details see Goode, *Hire-Purchase Law and Practice* (2nd edn, 1970), 617ff and Supplement.

[55] In particular, it is similar to the defence given by s 9 of the Factors Act 1889 (see **D1:3.3.4**). One of the aims of the hire-purchase transaction, as initially designed, was precisely to avoid that s 9 defence: as A is only 'renting' the car, he is not a 'buyer in possession' and so C cannot use the s 9 defence against B's pre-existing property right if he buys the car from A.

- B has Ownership of a motor vehicle and allows A to take physical control of it under a hire-purchase or conditional sale deal;
- C, a 'private purchaser',[56] acquires a right from A[57] in relation to the motor vehicle;
- C acquires his right in good faith and without notice of B's right.

'Retention of title' clauses can also cause problems for C. If, in **Example 14**, C2 acquires a right from A in relation to the yarn, in the reasonable belief that no one other than A has a property right in that yarn, C2 may well be able to rely on the 'buyer in possession' defence provided by section 9 of the Factors Act 1889 (see **D1:3.3.4**). However, that defence is limited. It did not assist C in *Clough Mill Ltd* as C did not acquire a right through a 'sale, pledge or other disposition' from A Ltd: C was simply appointed as receiver of A Ltd. Nor would it assist C2, a party who lends money to A Ltd in the reasonable belief that no one other than A Ltd has a property right in the yarn in A Ltd's factory.

In *Clough Mill Ltd v Martin*, C argued that he was not bound by B's pre-existing Ownership as B had failed to register it. However, the Court of Appeal rejected that argument. Whilst a security right acquired by B under a mortgage or a charge would need to be registered to bind A Ltd's receiver, there is no need for B to register the fact that he has sold a thing to A Ltd with a 'retention of title' clause. In such a case, B is not asserting a true security right: he is simply relying on his pre-existing Ownership. The property law system is therefore perfectly consistent in: (i) allowing C to use the lack of registration defence against a unregistered mortgage or charge; whilst (ii) not allowing C to use that defence against a property right retained by B under a 'retention of title' clause. Of course, it can always be argued that the **basic tension** between B and C should be resolved differently: there is certainly a risk that C may lose out as a result of a hidden 'retention of title' clause.[58] In its 2005 report on Company Security Interests, the Law Commission felt there was an argument for such a reform; but did not propose any immediate changes, feeling that further study was required.[59]

EXAMPLE 14b

The basic facts are as in **Example 14a**. The contract between A Ltd and B also stipulates that, until A Ltd pays B for the yarn supplied, B is to have Ownership of any fabric produced by A Ltd with that yarn;[60] *and* that A Ltd is to hold the proceeds of sale of any of that fabric on Trust for B.[61] A Ltd does manufacture some fabric using the yarn. It sells the fabric to C1 for £5,000 before running into financial problems. C2 is appointed as A Ltd's receiver. B claims the £5,000 received by A Ltd from C1 is held on Trust for B and so cannot be used by C2 to pay other creditors of A Ltd.

---

[56] A 'private purchaser' is one who is not a 'trade or finance purchaser': ie, one who is not in business to sell cars outright or under hire purchase or conditional sale agreements: see Hire Purchase Act 1964, s 29(2).

[57] C is protected whether he acquires A's Ownership directly from A or via a 'trade or finance purchaser' acting on A's behalf.

[58] See eg Law Com Consultation Paper No 164 at 4.185. See too Diamond, *A Review of Security Interests in Property* (1989). The approach taken by the United States Uniform Commercial Code (Article 9) is different and provides protection for C. Under 9-102, the property right of a party who has employed a 'retention of title' clause is treated as a security right and must be registered if it is to bind C

[59] See Law Com No 296 at 1.14 and 1.60–1.66. The question may be revisited as part of the Law Commission's project on the 'transfer of title by non-owners'.

[60] Such a clause is often known as a 'products' clause.

[61] Such a clause is often known as a 'proceeds' clause.

We noted above that the contract between A Ltd and B gives A Ltd a power to sell fabric produced with the yarn even if A Ltd has not yet paid B. Such a term may be necessary to allow A Ltd to carry on its business and to raise the money needed to repay B. However, it means that B cannot assert any pre-existing property right or persistent right against C1: C1 can rely on the overreaching defence. B can claim instead that A Ltd holds the proceeds of sale received from C1 on Trust for B. However, C2 can argue that, if B has a persistent right in relation to the £5000 received by A Ltd, B's right arises under a charge: B's failure to register that right thus prevents B from asserting his right against C2.

We saw that, on the facts of **Example 14**, a similar argument by C2 failed. In that case, B relied on his pre-existing Ownership of the yarn, not on a new right acquired as security. However, in **Example 14b**, things are different. B is *not* claiming a right he had *before* his dealings with A Ltd. Instead, he is claiming a new persistent right. The question then is whether B has acquired that right under a charge: if so, C2 can rely on the lack of registration defence. And it is clear that B's right *is* a true security right: his persistent right under the Trust will disappear if and when A Ltd pays B for the yarn it bought. In fact, B's persistent right is better seen as a Purely Equitable Charge rather than a right under a Trust. After all, A Ltd is not under the core Trust duty to B: A Ltd can use the £5,000 received from C1 for its own benefit *provided* A Ltd pays B the £4,000 it owes to B. In fact, A Ltd does not even need to use the money received from C1 to pay B: A Ltd can discharge its duty to B by paying B £4,000 from *any* source. So, in **Example 14b**, C2's argument succeeds. B's persistent right *is* subject to the lack of registration defence:[62] B has crossed the line from *retaining* a right by way of protection to *acquiring* a right by way of security.[63]

2.4.2 The *Quistclose* Trust

(i) Definition

> **EXAMPLE 15**
>
> A Ltd wants to borrow money from B in order to pay a dividend due to A Ltd's shareholders. B is concerned that A Ltd is close to insolvency. B transfers the money to A Ltd but insists that: (i) A Ltd can use that money *only* for the purpose of paying the dividend; *and* (ii) that A Ltd must keep the money in a specific account at Z Bank.

B has lost its right to the money it transferred it to A Ltd; and A Ltd clearly has a personal right against Z Bank. However, A Ltd is not free to use that right as it wishes; instead, A Ltd is under a duty to B *not* to use that money for its own benefit. A Ltd is thus under the core Trust duty and so A Ltd holds the account on Trust for B. This gives B valuable protection;

---

[62] See eg *Pfeiffer Weinkellerei-Weinkauf GmbH & Co v Arbuthnot Factors Ltd* [1988] 1 WLR 150. For a 'products' clause see eg *re Peachdart Ltd* [1984] 1 Ch 131.

[63] If C2 was appointed as a receiver *after* A Ltd manufactured the fabric from B's yarn and *before* A Ltd sold that fabric, B may try to claim a persistent right in relation to that fabric. As noted in **D1:2.1.2(i)**, in such a manufacture case, B's initial property right simply disappears. This means that, again, B's claim is to a *new* right arising by way of security and so registration is necessary: see eg *re Peachdart Ltd* [1984] 1 Ch 131. B may try to assert his pre-existing Ownership by claiming that A Ltd has *not* manufactured a new thing: that the fabric is in fact just an improved version of the yarn. In that case, we are back to **Example 14**: B's property right does not need to be registered. However, in a case where A Ltd's efforts have substantially increased the value of the thing, such a claim is unlikely to be accepted: the product of the manufacturing process will be seen as a new thing, separate from the thing supplied by B: see eg *re Peachdart Ltd* [1984] 1 Ch 131.

if A Ltd goes into insolvency before paying the dividend, B will have a power to assert its pre-existing right under the Trust against A Ltd's liquidators and so will be able to reclaim *all* the money in the account. This result was confirmed by the House of Lords in *Barclays Bank v Quistclose Investments Ltd* itself,[64] on which **Example 15** is based.

Again B's persistent right does *not* count as a security right: it is not used as a means to protect B if A Ltd fails to perform a duty owed to B. For example, if A Ltd goes into insolvency *before* paying the dividend, A Ltd's duty to repay the loan simply does not arise; but B still has his persistent right. The general registration requirement thus does *not* apply: B's right under the Trust can bind A Ltd's liquidators even if B did not register it. A Ltd's duty to repay the loan arises only *after* A Ltd pays the dividend. And at that point, B has no security for A Ltd's duty to repay: A Ltd no longer holds the right against which B had a persistent right. So, if A Ltd goes into insolvency after paying the dividend, B has no security. B cannot assert its pre-existing persistent right against the shareholders receiving the dividend: they can rely on the overreaching defence as B gave A Ltd a power to pay the dividend. And A Ltd no longer holds any right against which B has a persistent right.

In **Example 15**, as in **Examples 13 and 14**, B's right is *not* a security right. In all three cases, B's right does *not* arise as security for a duty owed by A: B's right exists *before* A comes under a duty to pay B. However, there are important differences between **Example 15** and **Examples 13 and 14**. First, in **Examples 13 and 14**, B is protected by *retaining* a property right he had *before* his dealings with A. In **Example 15**, B is protected by acquiring a *new* persistent right *as a result* of his dealings with A. Second, in **Examples 13 and 14**, B's right is similar to a security right: it ceases to exist if the secured duty is performed (eg, if A pays B the price of goods sold under a 'retention of title' clause). In **Example 15**, the existence of B's right does *not* depend on whether or not A has yet performed his duty (eg, in **Example 15** itself, A's duty to repay B's loan): in fact, if A uses the right received from B for the agreed purpose, A's duty to B arises at precisely the moment that B's right under the Trust ceases to exist. It is therefore worth noting that whilst the Law Commission has viewed cases where B retains a right as very similar to cases of true security (and hence considered extending registration requirements to those cases), it has (correctly) *not* taken the same view of *Quistclose* Trusts.[65]

(ii) Problems arising from the Quistclose Trust

The *Quistclose* Trust gives rise to both conceptual and practical problems. The conceptual problems flow from the reasoning of the House of Lords in *Barclays Bank v Quistclose Investments Ltd* itself.[66] Lord Wilberforce's reasoning in that case is flawed as it depends on two doctrinally dubious assumptions. The first is that, as soon as A Ltd received the money, it held it on Trust for the *purpose* of paying the dividend. However, a Trust does not arise where A holds a right subject to a duty to use that right for a non-charitable purpose; a

---

[64] [1970] AC 567.

[65] See eg Law Com Consultation Paper No 164 at 7.53 and 7.54. See too Law Com Consultation Paper No 176 at 3.61. The suggestion in No 164 is that such Trusts should be outside even an extended registration requirement for one of two reasons: because no security arises *or* because they arise by operation of law. On the view taken here, the first reason applies; so there is no need to examine the (potentially difficult) question of whether or not the *Quistclose* Trust arises by operation of law. For consideration of that issue, see eg Penner, ch 3 in *The Quistclose Trust* (ed Swadling, 2004).

[66] [1970] AC 567.

Trust, like any persistent right, can arise only where A is under a duty to a *specific person*.[67] The second assumption is that B's persistent right arose when A Ltd went into insolvency and paying the dividend thus became impossible or, at least, pointless. However, on that analysis, B's persistent right, which protects him in A Ltd's insolvency, did not exist before that insolvency. That analysis is inconsistent with fundamental rules of insolvency law: those rules are based on the notion that B can assert only a *pre-existing* property right or persistent right against A Ltd's liquidators.[68]

In *Twinsectra Ltd v Yardley*,[69] the House of Lords took the opportunity to solve those conceptual problems by justifying the *Quistclose* decision on different grounds. As Lord Millett emphasised, there is no purpose Trust in a case such as **Example 15**. Rather, A Ltd holds the money on Trust for B, but with a *power* to spend the money on the purpose agreed with B. That analysis seems to be correct.[70] After all, A Ltd is under the core Trust duty to B as soon as it receives the money from B: A Ltd has a duty to B not to use that money for its own benefit.

The practical problems arising from the *Quistclose* Trust are similar to those arising where, as in **Examples 13 and 14**, B protects himself by retaining a property right. There is a risk that C, a third party dealing with A Ltd, may reasonably believe that A Ltd is free to use the money received from B as it wishes: B's pre-existing persistent right may thus be hidden to B. However, those practical problems can be overstated. First, the general registration requirement does *not* apply where A Ltd gives B a charge over a bank account held by A Ltd.[71] So, in *Quistclose* itself, B did not avoid a registration requirement: even if A Ltd had simply given B a Purely Equitable Charge over A Ltd's bank account, B would not have needed to register his right. Second, a *Quistclose* Trust can only arise if A Ltd and B intend that A Ltd is not free to use its right as it wishes; this may give C some indication of the Trust.[72] In *Quistclose*, for example, the money paid to A Ltd was held in a special account. Finally, it seems that, due to the conceptual doubts surrounding it, the *Quistclose* Trust is not a popular choice for a lender seeking protection.[73]

SUMMARY of F4:2.4

B has a security right if he has:
- a property right; a persistent right; or a power to acquire a persistent right; *and*
- that right arises as a means to protect B if a duty owed to B is not performed.

---

[67] See eg *re Shaw* [1957] 1 WLR 729.

[68] See eg Stevens, ch 8 in *The Quistclose Trust* (ed Swadling, 2004).

[69] [2002] 2 AC 164. See in particular *per* Lord Millett at [68]–[103] and Lord Hoffmann at [13]. Lord Hutton at [25] agrees with their analysis of the Trust.

[70] Although for doubts, see eg Swadling, ch 2 and Chambers ch 5 in *The Quistclose Trust* (ed Swadling, 2004).

[71] See eg *per* Lord Hoffmann in *re BCCI (No 8)* [1998] AC 214 at 227. The proposals set out in Law Com No 296 will extend the registration ('filing' under the new scheme) requirement but such filing is not required if B has 'control' of A Ltd's bank account: see Law Com No 296 at 5.19–5.20. In *Quistclose* itself it seems that, under those proposals, B would *not* need to file its right under the Trust as it was in control of A Ltd's account: the bank had been told of the purpose of the loan and that it could only be used for paying A Ltd's dividend.

[72] Although if B can give A Ltd a very wide power to use the money lent by B, this point loses all force. Chambers, ch 5 in *The Quistclose Trust* (ed Swadling, 2004) argues that the *Quistclose* Trust can only arise where B advances money for a specific purpose, but Lord Millett's analysis in *Twinsectra v Yardley* is not so limited.

[73] See eg McKendrick, ch 7 in *The Quistclose Trust* (ed Swadling, 2004). 151–2: 'there are simply too many uncertainties surrounding the scope and basis of the decision [in *Quistclose*] for it to be invoked by practitioners on a regular basis with any degree of confidence'.

If A wishes to give B a security right, then, as noted by Millett LJ in *re Cosslett (Contractors) Ltd*, there are four methods available to B: mortgage, pledge, consensual lien and charge. To acquire a security right by means of a pledge or consensual lien, B needs to take physical control of a thing: this requirement provides some protection to C against the risk of being bound by a hidden security right of B. If B instead acquires his security right by means of a mortgage or charge, then, in general, B must register that right: if he fails to do so, B will *not* be protected should A go into insolvency and so will lose the main benefit of a security right.

It is important to distinguish true security rights from situations where B uses a property right or a persistent right *not* to secure A's duty to B but instead as a different form of protection. If B retains a property right when dealing with A, for example under a hire-purchase deal or through a 'retention of title' clause, B does not acquire a new right by way of security. As a result, the general registration requirement does *not* apply: B can assert his right in A's insolvency even if he has not registered it. And if B acquires a persistent right under a *Quistclose* Trust, the new persistent right acquired by B arises before, and so does *not* secure, A's duty to repay a loan to B. In such a case, B can again assert his right in A's insolvency even if he has not registered it.

SUMMARY of F4:2

A security right is a property right or a persistent right acquired by B for the purpose of protecting B if a duty owed to B is not performed. There are four types of *transaction* by which A can give B a security right: mortgage, pledge, consensual lien and charge. In a pledge or a consensual lien, B always has a property right: Ownership. In a mortgage, A transfers a right to B: that right may be a property right or a persistent right. In a fixed charge, A gives B a persistent right: a Purely Equitable Charge. In a floating charge, A gives B a power to acquire a Purely Equitable Charge. This means there are three types of *right* that B can acquire as security: Ownership; a Purely Equitable Charge; or a power to acquire a Purely Equitable Charge.

Nature of B's Security Right	Name of B's Security Right	Transaction by which B's Security Right is Acquired
Property Right	Ownership	Mortgage (of A's Ownership); Pledge; Consensual lien
Persistent Right	Purely Equitable Charge	Fixed Charge
Power to Acquire a Persistent Right	Power to Acquire a Purely Equitable Charge	Floating Charge

3 THE ACQUISITION QUESTION

3.1 Property rights

3.1.1 Mortgages where A is an individual or partnership

(i) The Bills of Sale Act (1878) Amendment Act 1882 ('the 1882 Act')

> **EXAMPLE 16**
>
> A has Ownership of a bike. A asks B for a loan of £200. B wishes to acquire A's Ownership as security for A's duty to repay B.

A mortgage can only be created as a result of A's consent: it requires A to exercise his power to transfer Ownership to B. Special formality rules regulate A's power to transfer his property right to B by way of security (see **D1:2.2.5**). These rules are imposed by the Bills of Sale Act (1878) Amendment Act 1882. It is very important to distinguish the 1882 Act from the Bills of Sale Act 1878. The 1878 Act imposes a registration requirement where A keeps physical control of a thing after transferring his Ownership to B by means of a document (the document is known as a 'bill of sale': see **D1:2.2.4(i)(b)**). If B fails to register the document, he will be unable to assert his Ownership in A's insolvency; or against an execution creditor of A. The 1878 Act is thus 'designed for the protection of creditors':[74] it aims to protect a third party who might otherwise extend credit to A in the belief that A still has Ownership of the thing in question. The formality rule imposed by the 1878 Act is *not* limited to cases where B attempts to acquire Ownership by way of security.

In contrast, the 1882 Act imposes more stringent formality requirements that apply *only* where B attempts to acquire a property right or a persistent right by way of security.[75] The Act imposes two rules, each with its own purpose. The first rule is that A and B's transaction must be recorded in a particular written form. The purpose of that rule is to protect A from exploitation by an unscrupulous lender.[76] If it is not satisfied, B will *not* acquire A's Ownership. Further, any underlying loan agreement is invalid: as a result, B will *not* even acquire a contractual right against A.

The second rule imposed by the 1882 Act is that the written document recording the agreement must be registered. The chief purpose of that rule, like the formality rule imposed by the 1878 Act, is to protect third parties who might otherwise extend credit to A. If B fails to register, he can still acquire a *personal* right against A: any underlying loan agreement, set out as required by the first formality rule, will be valid. However, B's failure to register means that he does *not* acquire a property right or a persistent right from A. The

---

[74] Per Lord Herschell in *Manchester, Sheffield and Lincolnshire Railway Co v North Central Wagon Co* (1888) 13 App Cas 554 at 560: the 1878 Act was 'designed for the protection of creditors, and to prevent their rights being affected by secret assurances of chattels which were permitted to remain in the ostensible possession of a person who had parted with the property in them'.

[75] 1882 Act, s 3.

[76] See eg *per* Lord Herschell in *Manchester, Sheffield and Lincolnshire Railway Co v North Central Wagon Co* (1888) 13 App Cas 554 at 560: the purpose of the 1882 Act was 'to prevent needy persons being entrapped into signing complicated documents which they might often be unable to comprehend, and so being subjected by their creditors to the enforcement of harsh and unreasonable provisions'.

two formality rules imposed by the 1882 Act are limited to cases where B attempts to acquire a security right.

(a) Scope

The 1882 Act ('the Act' in this section) does *not* apply to mortgages entered into by companies. And there are certain types of mortgage that are outside the scope of the Act[77]—eg, where the right mortgaged by A is his Ownership of a ship or an aircraft.[78] A key purpose of the formality rules imposed by the Act is to protect A from exploitation by an unscrupulous lender. It seems that companies do not need this protection; nor, perhaps, does a party rich enough to own a ship or aircraft.

The Act does *not* apply to mortgages of personal rights.[79] For example, if A wants to transfer company shares to B, formality rules apply: B needs to be registered as the new holder of the shares (see **C2:3.2**). But if A wants to transfer such shares to B by way of security, no additional formality rules are imposed by the Act. The Act thus seems to recognise that the need to protect A from losing his Ownership of a thing may be greater than the need to protect A from losing a personal right. Equally, the need to protect third parties is greater where mortgages of a thing are concerned: A's physical control of a thing may lead C to believe that no one other than A has a property right in that thing.

The wording of the 1882 Act suggests that, like the 1878 Act, it applies only *if* A and B's transaction is recorded in a written document. This raises the possibility that if, in a case such as **Example 16**, A and B deal with each other orally, the Act does not apply.[80] In **Example 16**, B could insist that A deliver his bike to B. That act of delivery to B would allow B to acquire Ownership, by way of security, without the need for any document. B could then return physical control of the bike to A, to allow A to continue to use it. If it is true that the 1882 Act does not apply, as A and B have dealt with each other without using a document, the purpose of the Act seems to be undermined. First, whether or not a document is used, A needs protection from an unscrupulous lender. Second, whether or not a document is used, third parties need protection from B's hidden property right or persistent right. It seems then that the 1882 Act must apply *even if* A and B do not use a written document.[81]

(b) Satisfaction

In a case such as **Example 16**, the Act imposes *two* formality rules. First, the agreement between A and B, including both the underlying loan by B and the mortgage by A, must be made in writing signed by both A and B and by at least one witness.[82] That agreement must also contain particular information—eg, it must list all the rights mortgaged by A. In this way, this first formality rule provides *evidence* of the parties' agreement; promotes *caution*; and *protects A from fraudulent claims*. In addition, as the Act prescribes the form of

---

[77] Agricultural mortgages are not covered by the Acts but by specific legislation: Agricultural Credits Act 1928. S 1 of the Bills of Sale Act 1890 also excepts security on imported goods that are in transit.

[78] A mortgage of A's Ownership of a ship or aircraft may, however, need to be registered in a specific register: see (c) below.

[79] S 4 of the Bills of Sale Act 1878 limits the Acts to 'personal chattels'.

[80] This possibility is noted by Goode, *Commercial Law* (3rd edn, 2004), 647.

[81] The position may, however, be different under the 1878 Act: that Act does not have the same aim of protecting A.

[82] 1882 Act, ss 9 and 10.

document used, it deals with the problem that, prior to the Act, 'certain forms of document were in use by moneylenders as a means of puzzling ignorant borrowers'.[83]

Second, the document describing the agreement must be registered within seven days of the agreement.[84] This is done by registering the document with a particular judicial official: a Master of the Queen's Bench Division of the High Court.[85] In this way, this second formality rule provides *publicity*: if the mortgage is registered, an interested third party (in **Example 16**, someone thinking of lending to A, or taking a mortgage of A's bike) can easily discover B's property right.

(c) Sanctions

In a case such as **Example 16**, each of the formality rules imposed by the Act has a different sanction.

First, if the agreement between A and B is not made in the correct form, it is of no legal effect: so B does *not* acquire A's Ownership; and the agreement does *not* give B a personal right against A.[86] In this way, the requirement for a particular written document protects A. It promotes *caution* by ensuring both that: (i) a rash decision by A to give B security does not result in A losing Ownership; and (ii) such a decision does not impose a contractual duty on A to repay the loan to B.

Second, even if there is a written document in the correct form, B's failure to register that document within seven days means that B cannot acquire a property right or a persistent right from A. So, in **Example 16**, B's failure to register means that B does *not* acquire A's Ownership.[87] In this way, the registration requirement promotes *publicity*: it protects C from the risk of being bound by a hidden property right of B. In particular, the rule protects third parties who may have lent money to A, or given A other forms of credit, in the reasonable belief that A had Ownership of the bike. For example, after his first agreement with B, A may have mortgaged his bike to *C* to secure a loan from C. If C checks and discovers there is no registered mortgage of that bike, C can then proceed in the knowledge that any earlier lender does not have Ownership of the bike.

If the written document is in the required form, and B fails to register it, the underlying agreement between A and B can still give B a personal right against A.[88] That seems reasonable: the chief purpose of registration is to provide publicity, rather than to protect A. Indeed, it is a little surprising that B's failure to register, rather than giving a **defence** to third parties (such as A's trustee in bankruptcy) instead prevents B from acquiring A's Ownership.[89] In fact, in two cases where A is presumably less in need of protection—when

---

[83] *Per* Lord Esher in *re Townsend* (1886) 16 QBD 532 at 545. The Consumer Credit Act 1974 adopts the same policy.

[84] 1882 Act, s 8.

[85] 1882 Act, s 13.

[86] 1882 Act, ss 4, 5, 8 and 9. Under s 12, even if the formality requirements are complied with, B cannot acquire Ownership if the mortgage is made or given in return for a sum of £30 or less.

[87] 1882 Act, ss 8.

[88] However, A may be able to rely on some other means of showing that he is not under a contractual duty to B: for example, the provisions of the Consumer Credit Act 1974, which apply to unsecured loans and secured loans, may protect A.

[89] There is thus a distinction between 'security' bills of sale and other bills of sale. As we saw in **D1:2.2.4(i)(b)**, a failure to register a non-security bill of sale does not prevent B acquiring A's Ownership but instead protects third parties: ss 4 and 8 of the Bills of Sale Act 1878.

B acquires Ownership of a ship[90] or an aircraft[91] by way of security—B's failure to register his right in the special register for ship or aircraft mortgages does not prevent B from acquiring Ownership *but* may instead lead to C having a **defence** against B's right.

(d) Saves

EXAMPLE 16a

The facts are as in **Example 16**. A and B agree that B will lend A £200; that A will pay B £230 in six months' time; and that A's duty will be secured by a transfer of A's Ownership of the bike to B. The agreement is not recorded in signed writing. B lends A £200 and A fails to repay as agreed.

In such a case, the formality rules of the Act have *not* been satisfied. In the absence of the required written document, B does *not* acquire Ownership of A's bike: this means that B has no power to sell the bike and to use the proceeds to meet A's debt. Further, the absence of such a document means that A is *not* under a duty to pay B the agreed £230. However, as B has given £200 on the basis that the agreement between A and B was binding, A would be unjustly enriched if he were able to keep the benefit of that money. As a result, B has a personal right against A:[92] A must pay B £200. However, as B has no security right, B has no protection if A goes into insolvency.

An interesting question arises if, at the point when it becomes clear to A that his agreement with B is not binding, A still has either the £200 B transferred to A, or a new right that counts as a product of that right. In such a case, B could try to rely on the principles discussed in **D4:4.3** to claim that A holds either the £200 or the new right on Resulting Trust for B. If that argument is accepted, B has a persistent right that is capable of binding third parties and is protected in A's insolvency. The particular question to be considered here is whether B's acquisition of such a right would be contrary to the policy of the Act. There is an argument that it would *not* be. Those Acts prevent B acquiring Ownership of A's bike as security; they should not affect B's ability to assert a persistent right under a Resulting Trust. After all, such a right is not a security right: it does not exist to protect any duty of A to B but responds instead to the fact that A, due to his unjust enrichment at B's expense, is under the core Trust duty to B.

(ii) The Consumer Credit Act 1974 (as amended by the Consumer Credit Act 2006)

(a) Scope

The Consumer Credit Act 1974 (CCA) is *not* limited to cases where B acquires a security right. However, it can apply in such cases. As a result, there can be cases in which, to acquire an enforceable security right, B needs to comply with *both* the 1882 Act and the CCA. In general, the CCA applies whenever: (i) A is a consumer; and (ii) B extends credit to A.[93]

(b) Satisfaction

The CCA imposes a number of formality rules. A consumer credit agreement is only

---

[90] Merchant Shipping Act 1995, Sch 1, para 7.
[91] Mortgaging of Aircraft Order 1972, SI 1972/1268.
[92] See eg *North Central Wagon Finance Co Ltd v Brailsford* [1962] 1 WLR 1288.
[93] The Act thus applies to conditional sale and hire-purchase agreements (see eg s 9).

'properly executed' if both A and B sign a written document. The contents of that document are carefully regulated:[94] for example, it must contain all the expressly agreed terms of the contract; and it must set out the sum of credit given to A by B.[95] The document must also set out any security right given to B.[96]

(c) Sanctions

If the agreement is not properly executed, it is impossible for B to enforce his rights under that agreement without first obtaining a court order.[97] This means that, unless he obtains such a order, B cannot enforce *either* (i) his personal right against A to repay the loan on the agreed terms; *or* (ii) any security rights given to B under the agreement.[98] In deciding whether to make an order, the court has a reasonably wide discretion. It can, for example, allow B to enforce a right only on specific terms; or allow B to recover less than the agreed sum from A.[99]

(d) Saves

If a court does *not* allow B to enforce his agreement with A, no saves are available to B. Indeed, B is not even allowed to argue that A would be unjustly enriched at B's expense if A were allowed to retain any benefit given to him by B under the unenforceable agreement.[100]

3.1.2 Mortgages where A is a company

EXAMPLE 17

A Ltd has Ownership of manufacturing equipment. A Ltd asks B Bank for a loan of £20,000. B Bank wishes to acquire A's Ownership of that equipment as security for A Ltd's duty to repay B Bank.

As we have seen, as A Ltd is a company, the 1882 Act does not apply. This means that the agreement between A Ltd and B Bank does not have to be made in the form required by those Acts. Nor does any document need to be registered with a Master of the Queen's Bench Division. However, a separate registration requirement is imposed by the Companies Act:[101] information about the mortgage,[102] and any document creating or recording it, must be sent to the Registrar of Companies for inclusion in the register of charges.[103] The

---

[94] CCA 1974, s 61 means that the document must contain any 'prescribed terms'—ie, terms which, under regulations made by the Secretary of State under s 60(1), must be included in such a document.

[95] See eg *Wilson v First County Trust Ltd (No 2)* [2004] 1 AC 816. In that case, B's failure to correctly state the level of credit meant that, under s 127(3) of the 1974 Act, the court had *no* power to allow B to enforce the terms. That provision has been repealed by the 2006 Act, s 15: the court now *always* has the power to allow enforcement by B.

[96] CCA 1974, s 105(1).

[97] CCA 1974, s 65(1).

[98] CCA 1974, s 113(1) and (2) ensure that, if the formal requirements of the Act are not complied with, B can only enforce a security right if he obtains a court order.

[99] CCA 1974, s 127(1)(ii) and (2).

[100] See eg *Dimond v Lovell* [2002] 1 AC 384; *Wilson v First County Trust Ltd (No 2)* [2004] 1 AC 816. The view is that, if B were allowed to recover, for example, money advanced to A under the unenforceable agreement, the policy of the CCA would be undermined.

[101] The position is currently governed by the Companies Act 1985. The Companies Act 2006 is being gradually phased in: the provisions relating to company charges are due to take effect from 1 October 2009.

[102] The 'prescribed' information includes eg the date of creation of B's right; the sum secured by the mortgage; and the identity of B.

[103] The Acts list types of security rights requiring registration, rather than setting out a general requirement: see Companies Act 1985, s 395(1) and Companies Act 2006, s 860(7). The effect of the list, however, is that, in practice, the registration requirement applies to all mortgages.

legislation refers to 'charges' entered into by a company but that term includes mortgages.[104] If B does not register his right within 21 days, he cannot assert that right against a 'liquidator or administrator or any creditor' of A Ltd.[105] So, in **Example 17**, if B Bank fails to register: (i) it does acquire Ownership of the equipment; but (ii) it does *not* acquire a useful security right as it will not be protected if A Ltd goes into insolvency.[106]

The requirements applying to a mortgage by A Ltd thus resemble the requirements applying to a mortgage by A. However, there is an essential difference. In the former case, the emphasis is on providing *publicity* to protect third parties who may deal with A Ltd. As a result, the registration requirement applies not only to mortgages of property rights but also to mortgages of personal rights formerly held by A Ltd. Such personal rights may form a very important part of the assets of A Ltd and a third party thus needs a means of discovering whether those rights are freely available to A Ltd. Where companies are concerned, the need to protect the party granting the mortgage, by promoting *caution*, disappears: unlike the 1882 Act, the Companies Acts therefore do *not* impose formality requirements in relation to the **acquisition question**.

3.1.3 Pledge

(i) Basic position

Like, a mortgage, a pledge can only be created by A's consent: it consists of A allowing B to take physical control, by way of security, of a thing owned by A. However, in a pledge, B does not acquire his property right by means of a transfer from A. Instead, B acquires a new property right through an independent acquisition. To acquire a property right by means of a pledge, B therefore needs to show that he has physical control of a thing (see **D1:2.1.1**). Three points are worth noting.

First, B can acquire physical control if A has physical control of a thing and 'attorns' to B. An attornment consists of A indicating that he holds the goods for B: that his physical control counts as B's physical control. This means that A can create a pledge without giving up his physical control of a thing: he can simply indicate to B that he holds that thing on B's behalf.[107]

Second, B can acquire physical control of goods held by another through a document of title, such as a bill of lading. The use of a document of title to give B physical control of goods held by another is simply an example of attornment.[108]

---

[104] Companies Act 1985, s 296(4); Companies Act 2006, s 861(5).

[105] Companies Act 1985, s 295; Companies Act 2006, s 874(1). In effect, C is protected only if he is a secured creditor (ie, if C also has a security right) or an execution creditor (see **B:2.3.1**). If C is simply a general creditor of A Ltd, and A Ltd has not gone into administration or liquidation, no dispute can arise between B Bank and C about specific rights held by A Ltd: certainly C cannot complain about A Ltd charging any such rights to B Bank: see Goode, *Commercial Law* (3rd edn, 2004), 667.

[106] The special registration requirements applying to mortgages of ships and aircraft, discussed in 3.1.1(i)(c) above, apply to mortgages by a company as well as to mortgages by an individual or partnership.

[107] See eg *Dublin City Distillery Co v Doherty* [1914] AC 823.

[108] See eg *per* Lord Hobhouse in *The Berge Sisar* [2002] 2 AC 205 at 219.

EXAMPLE 18

A0, a manufacturer based in the United States, has Ownership of 1,000 bikes. A0 sells those bikes to A Ltd, a wholesaler based in England. The bikes are shipped on a vessel operated by X Co. X Co takes physical control of the goods and issues a bill of lading to A0. A0 endorses the bill of lading to A Ltd and transfers it to A Ltd. A Ltd wishes to borrow money from B Bank. As security for the loan, A Ltd endorses the bill of lading to B Bank and transfers it to B Bank.

In such a case, the dealings between A Ltd and B Bank can occur whilst the bikes are still at sea and hence under the physical control of X Co. Through holding the bill of lading, endorsed by A0, A Ltd acquired physical control of the bikes: X Co's physical control then counted as A Ltd's physical control. By transferring the bill of lading to B Bank, A Ltd gives B Bank physical control: X Co's physical control now counts as B Bank's physical control. A Ltd can thus pledge the bikes to B Bank without B Bank needing to take physical control of the bikes themselves: such is the magic of a document of title.

Third, if A creates a pledge by allowing B to take physical control of a thing, the pledge continues even if B later gives up physical control. Therefore, B can also allow A to retake physical control of the thing without destroying his pledge. In **Example 18**, B Bank can allow A Ltd to take physical control of the bikes without losing its security right. For example, A Ltd may well need to sell those bikes in order to repay B Bank. B Bank can then allow A Ltd to take and sell the bikes. This is usually done through a 'trust receipt': a document specifying that: (i) A Ltd can take and sell the bikes; but (ii) that B Bank's security right remains and can also be asserted against any proceeds of sale obtained by A Ltd. If C buys those bikes, he cannot be bound by B Bank's security right: he can rely on the overreaching defence as B Bank has given A Ltd the power to sell the bikes. However, if A Ltd goes into insolvency before selling the bikes, B Bank can assert its security right in those bikes against A Ltd's liquidator. And if: (i) A Ltd sells the bikes; and (ii) receives the proceeds from C; and then (iii) A Ltd goes into insolvency; (iv) B Bank can assert its security right against those proceeds (a Purely Equitable Charge) against A Ltd's liquidators.[109]

(ii) Formalities?

The general position is that *no formality rule regulates A's power to create a pledge.* The 1882 Act does not apply as B's property right comes from his physical control of the thing in question: there is no need for B to rely on any document.[110] And, for the same reason, a pledge does not fall within the registration requirements of the Companies Acts.[111]

This position may seem surprising. The first formality rule imposed by the 1882 Act aims to protect A from the risk of rashly giving B security and of being exploited by a lender. It might be thought that A faces that risk in a pledge as much as a mortgage. Two points are worth noting. In a pledge, the need for A to allow B to have physical control may promote caution: it is a more significant step than entering a mortgage under which A retains control of a thing. However, that point is weakened by the fact A may be able to keep physical control even after a pledge: the pledge may arise by attornment, or B may allow A to take

---

[109] See eg *re David Allester* [1922] 2 Ch 211 (see too **n 14** above).
[110] *Re Hardwicke, ex p Hubbard* (1886) 17 QBD 690.
[111] See eg *per* Astbury J in *In re David Allester* [1922] 2 Ch 211 at 216.

back physical control. Second, A is given some protection if B is a pawnbroker—ie, someone who, in the course of his business, takes pledges from individuals. In such a case, the Consumer Credit Act 1974 applies: the pawnbroker must be licensed and must give A a document containing prescribed information about the deal.[112] The 1974 Act also regulates A's power to give B a contractual right and can thus give A important protection against the risk of exploitation by B.[113]

The registration requirement imposed by the 1882 Act, like that arising under the Companies Acts, aims to give C a chance to discover B's property right. In a pledge, such requirement might seem unnecessary: as B has physical control of the thing, his property right should be obvious. However, a pledge can still cause problems for C. First, if A 'attorns' to B, a pledge can arise even if A retains physical control. If that attornment is made in, or later confirmed by, a written document, that document *is* caught by the registration requirement.[114] That seems correct as, in such a case, B's property right depends on the document rather than his *actual* control of the thing. However, C faces a problem if the attornment is purely oral: there is an argument for saying that, in such a case, the oral attornment is ineffective as all attornments must be put in writing and registered.[115]

Second, a pledge can continue even if B allows A to regain physical control. In such cases, it may again be very difficult to discover B's security right. When considering **Example 18**, we saw that B Bank may release goods to A Ltd under a 'trust receipt'. Such a document does *not* need to be registered as it does not create B Bank's security right.[116] The pledge arose earlier when the bill of lading was transferred to B Bank;[117] the trust receipt merely regulates A Ltd's control of the goods. However, if A Ltd does sell the goods, B Bank then claims a *new* security right over the proceeds. From a doctrinal perspective, it seems that B Bank's security right over the proceeds (a Purely Equitable Charge) *should* be subject to the registration requirement. That right is a new one and is *not* a continuation of the original pledge: after all: (i) B Bank's pledge comes from its physical control of the goods; and (ii) its new security right in relation to the money comes from its agreement with A Ltd, made as a condition of B Bank's decision to release the goods to A Ltd. Despite this, it has been held, seemingly for reasons of practical convenience,[118] that B Bank can acquire a security right over the proceeds of sale, binding on A Ltd's liquidators, *without* registration.[119]

3.1.4 Consensual lien

As with a pledge, the general position is that *no formality rule regulates A's power to create a lien*.[120] However, as with a pledge, formality rules such as those set out in the CCA 1974 may

---

[112] CCA 1974, ss 39–40 and 115. The pawnbroker commits an offence if those provisions are breached.

[113] See eg *Wilson v First County Trust Ltd (No 2)* [2004] 1 AC 816.

[114] *Dublin City Distillery Ltd v Doherty* [1914] AC 923.

[115] This argument is the same as the one made in **3.1.1(i)(a)** above to the effect that B cannot avoid the 1882 Act by means of a purely oral mortgage.

[116] *Re David Allester Ltd* [1922] 2 Ch 211.

[117] The bill of lading does not need to be registered as it is specifically excluded from the definition of a 'bill of sale': see Bills of Sale Act 1878, s 4.

[118] Essentially to make B Bank more willing to release goods to A Ltd and so to facilitate A Ltd's sale of the goods and use of the proceeds to meet its debt to B Bank.

[119] *Re David Allester Ltd* [1922] 2 Ch 211. For criticism of this aspect of the decision, see eg Beale *et al*, *The Law of Personal Property Security* (2007), 3.22–3.24.

[120] That is the case even if A, when agreeing to the lien, also gives B a power to sell the thing: see eg *Great Eastern Rwy Co Ltd v Lord's Trustee* [1909] AC 109.

regulate A's power to make a binding agreement to receive credit from B and, under that agreement, to allow B to keep physical control of a thing owned by A. The problems caused to third parties by a lien are less severe than those caused by a pledge: in particular, as we saw in **2.1.3** above, a lien, unlike a pledge, ceases if B gives up physical control.

3.1.5 Non-consensual lien

A lien differs from a mortgage and a pledge as B has Ownership *before* A decides to give B a security right. B's Ownership comes from his pre-existing physical control of the thing. In a lien, B crucially also has a right, against A and anyone acquiring a right from A, to retain physical control of the thing until the secured duty is performed. In a 'non-consensual lien', the source of B's right to retain control is *not* a contractual promise by A, but is rather some other event.

> **EXAMPLE 19a**
>
> A has Ownership of a bike. It is damaged and A takes it to B's bike shop for repairs. B repairs the bike but A fails to pay the sum agreed for B's work. B refuses to give A physical control of the bike until A pays the sum due.

In such a case, it might seem that B is breaching his duty not to interfere with A's right to exclusive control of the bike. Certainly, A has not given his consent to B's retention of the bike as security for A's debt to B. However, in **Example 19a**, B does *not* commit a wrong. The property law system imposes a duty on A to allow B to retain control of the bike as security for A's duty to pay B: a non-consensual lien arises. B's property right comes from his physical control of the bike; and B acquired that control with A's consent. However, B's right against A to retain control until paid, the essence of a lien, does not arise as result of A's consent.

It is difficult to identify the precise source of A's duty to allow B to retain control of the bike as security. Unjust enrichment may be one possibility: in a case such as **Example 19a**, B's lien arises only if his work has *improved* A's bike.[121] It may thus be that if A were allowed to retake control of the bike, with B having only his personal right to sue A, A could be regarded as unjustly enriched at B's expense.

> **EXAMPLE 19b**
>
> A has Ownership of a car. X agrees to repair the car and A gives physical control of the car to X for that purpose. X then sells the car to B. B reasonably believes that no one other than X has a property right in the car. B spends time and money in improving the car. A then asserts his pre-existing Ownership of the car against B.

In such a case, B has no defence to A's pre-existing property right.[122] However, in *Greenwood v Bennett* (**D1:Example 35**)[123] the Court of Appeal assumed[124] that, in such a case, a court

---

[121] See eg *Hatton v Car Maintenance Ltd* [1915] 1 Ch 621. *Jacobs v Latour* (1828) 5 Bing 130 confirms that a trainer of a racehorse has a lien: he is not merely keeping the horse, but is improving it.

[122] For example, B cannot rely on the defence provided by the Factors Act 1889, s 2(1) as A simply gave the car to X for repairs: he did not give X any power to sell his Ownership of the car (see **D1:3.3.2**).

[123] [1973] QB 195.

[124] The facts of *Greenwood* varied slightly from those of **Example 19b**. The car had come into the physical control

would not order B to return the car to A *unless* A paid a sum of money to B equal to the increase in the value of the car caused by B's work. As Lord Denning MR put it:

> It would be most unjust if [A] could not only take the car from [B], but also the value of the improvements [B] has done to it—without paying for them . . . [A] should not be allowed unjustly to enrich [himself] at [B's] expense.[125]

This can be seen as an aspect of the **remedies question**: a court will not specifically protect A's right unless A pays a sum of money to B. However, the Court of Appeal's approach goes further: it suggests that, if A took physical control of the car, without a court order, he would commit a wrong against B. It seems that there are two results of B's work on the car:

(i) A is under a duty, arising in the law of unjust enrichment, to pay a sum of money to B; *and*

(ii) B has a non-contractual lien to retain physical control of the car until that sum is paid by A.

It is hard to find a consistent policy behind the recognition of non-consensual liens. Some common examples (such as the lien of an innkeeper over the goods of a guest to secure his duty to pay for food and board) are related to the fact that B, in providing a service to A, exercised a 'common calling'.[126] If B carries on such an activity, he is under a general duty not to turn away customers. This makes it impossible for B to refuse customers he regards as unlikely to pay; a security right over those customers' goods may reduce the harm B suffers as a result.

Liens can also be imposed by statute. The 'unpaid vendor's lien' is an important example. If B transfers his Ownership of a thing to A by means of a sale and A does not perform his duty to pay the price, B can retain physical control as security for A's duty.[127] In such a case, B also has a limited statutory power to sell the goods:[128] for example, B can exercise that power if he gives A notice of his intention to do so and thus gives A a chance to perform his duty to pay the price to B.[129] That power does *not* exist as security for A's duty: if B exercises that power, he can keep *all* the proceeds of sale rather than just the money needed to meet A's duty. So if B sells to A for £100 and then exercises his power of sale by selling to C for £150, B can keep the whole £150.[130]

---

of the police who had been ordered by the first instance judge to hand the car over to A, who had sold it. B's claim was simply that A should pay a sum of money to B: there was no question of B having a lien as he had already lost physical control of the car.

[125] [1973] QB 195 at 202.

[126] Other examples include the non-consensual liens of a sea carrier over cargo for freight charges and of a lawyer over clients' papers. The latter has a general lien and so can retain control of papers even if the debt due by the client does not relate to those papers. The reasons why some non-consensual liens are general and others particular are not clear and originally depended on custom: see eg *Plaice v Allcock* (1866) 4 F & F 1074.

[127] Sale of Goods Act 1979, ss 38–43.

[128] Sale of Goods Act 1979, s 48.

[129] If B exercises that power by selling to C, C can then use the overreaching defence against A's pre-existing property right (see D1:3.4).

[130] *RV Ward v Bignall* [1967] 1 QB 534. This result is based on the idea that, by exercising his power of sale, B terminates the contract of sale with A and so exercises a power to regain the property right he transferred to A under that contract.

SUMMARY of F4:3.1

To acquire a property right by way of security, B needs *both* to satisfy the general rules applying to the acquisition of Ownership (discussed in **D1:2**) *and* to satisfy any additional rules that may apply to the acquisition of Ownership by way of security. In a mortgage, B acquires his property right by means of a dependent acquisition from A. B therefore has to satisfy the general principles set out in **D1:2.2**. In addition, if A is an individual or partnership, B has to satisfy the formality rules imposed by the 1882 Act. A failure to draw up a written document of the prescribed form will prevent B from acquiring A's Ownership *and* from acquiring a contractual right against A. A failure to register that document will prevent B from acquiring A's Ownership. The 1882 Act does not apply where a company grants a mortgage. However, in such a case, a failure to register the mortgage with the Registrar of Companies will deprive B of a useful security right, by preventing him from asserting his right in A Ltd's insolvency, or against a secured or execution creditor of A Ltd.

In a pledge and a lien, B instead acquires Ownership by an independent acquisition: by having physical control of a thing owned by A. B therefore has to satisfy the general principles set out in **D2:2.1.1**. In general, no additional formality rules apply to a pledge or a lien. However there is an argument that, if B acquires physical control through an attornment by A, that attornment should be put in writing and registered. In a lien, B's security comes from his right against A to retain physical control until the secured duty is performed. That right can come *either* from A's binding promise or a different source. In some cases, B acquires a lien through his conduct in providing a particular service to A.

3.2   Persistent rights

3.2.1 Mortgages

If A has a pre-existing persistent right against a right of Z (eg, where Z holds a right on Trust for A), A may be able to give B security by mortgaging that right to B. A must satisfy the general rules applying to the transfer of a pre-existing persistent right (see **F3:2.2**). In particular, A must satisfy the formality rule imposed by section 53(1)(c) of the LPA 1925 by exercising his power to transfer his persistent right in signed writing. The two formality rules imposed by the Bills of Sale Act (1878) Amendment Act 1882 ('the 1882 Act') also apply if A's persistent right relates to a thing (eg, where Z holds his Ownership of a car on Trust for A);[131] but not if A's persistent right relates only to a right (eg, where Z holds a bank account on Trust for A).

Where A Ltd transfers a pre-existing persistent right relating to a thing: (i) the section 53(1)(c) formality rule must be satisfied if B is to acquire A Ltd's persistent right; *and* (ii) B must register that right to ensure that it will be protected in A Ltd's insolvency.[132]

---

[131] The definition of bills of sale given by s 4 of the 1878 Act (which applies to the 1882 Act) includes 'any agreement . . . by which a right in equity to chattels, or to any charge or security thereon, . . . shall be conferred'.

[132] Under the Companies Act 2006, s 860(7)(b); the Companies Act 1985, s 396(1)(c) the registration requirement applies to any security created by A Ltd that would require registration as a bill of sale if executed by an individual.

3.2.2 Charges

In a fixed or floating charge transaction, B acquires a security right as a result of A coming under a duty (or a potential duty) to hold a particular right as security for a duty owed to B. As far as acquisition is concerned, the initial question is whether A has come under a duty to B: usually, that duty is a contractual one. In addition, if A is an individual, the formality rules imposed by the 1882 Act apply. The discussion of those rules in **3.1.1** above therefore also applies where, rather than transferring his Ownership to B by way of a mortgage, A instead chooses to give B a Purely Equitable Charge. Similarly, the general registration requirement under the Companies Act also applies to a charge: the discussion in **3.1.2** thus applies where A Ltd gives B a Purely Equitable Charge.

There is an important consequence of the application of the 1882 Act where A is an individual or partnership. One of the formality requirements under that Act is that the written document must specify the rights of A over which B is to have security. This makes it very difficult for A to give B a security right over a right A does not yet have: it will be impossible to specify such a right in the written document.[133] It is important to remember that the 1882 Act does not apply where A gives B security over personal rights of A. Thus A *can* give B a Purely Equitable Charge over future personal rights A may acquire against his customers.[134]

3.2.3 Other situations where B acquires a Purely Equitable Charge

B acquires a Purely Equitable Charge *whenever* A is under a duty to hold a particular right as security for a duty owed to B. A's duty need not arise as a result of a contractual promise by A. As a result, even if the transaction between A and B does not count as a charge, B may still acquire a Purely Equitable Charge. The right B acquires in such a case is often referred to as an 'Equitable Lien'. However, the **content** of that right is identical to that of a Purely Equitable Charge: the term 'Equitable Lien' simply tells us that the Purely Equitable Charge arose for some reason other than A's contractual promise to hold a right as security (see **D2:1.2.1**).

In fact, the term 'Equitable Lien' is actively unhelpful. It suggests a similarity with the right B acquires under a lien transaction. However, such a case is clearly very different from the situation where B has a non-consensual Purely Equitable Charge.

'Common Law' Lien (Lien Transaction)	**'Equitable Lien'** (Non-Consensual Purely Equitable Charge)
B has a property right	B has a persistent right
B's security right depends on his physical control of a thing	B's security right depends on A's duty to B
B does not have a power to sell the thing (unless A has expressly given B that power)	B does have a power to sell A's right

---

[133] See eg *Thomas v Kelly and Baker* (1888) 13 App Cas 506.

[134] See eg *Tailby v The Official Receiver* (1888) 13 App Cas 523. But note that if A gives B a security right over a set of A's rights against customers, this may count as a 'general assignment [by way of security or charge] to another person of his existing or future book debts'. If so, under s 344 of the Insolvency Act 1986, B must register his right if he wants to be able to assert it against A's trustee in bankruptcy in respect of any debts not paid by A's customers at the point of A's insolvency.

It is therefore clear that the orthodox term ('Equitable Lien') should be rejected: B's right is best described as a non-consensual Purely Equitable Charge. One example of such a Purely Equitable Charge is provided by the right B (an insurer who has paid A compensation for loss suffered by A) acquires in relation to money paid to A by Z (a party who wrongfully caused that damage: see **B:Example 6b** and **D2:1.2.1**).[135] So, if: (i) Z wrongfully destroys A's bike; and (ii) B pays A £150 in respect of that loss under A's insurance policy; and (iii) A then recovers £200 (the full value of the bike) from Z; then (iv) A holds that £200 as security for his duty to pay B £150.

EXAMPLE 20a

A has Ownership of a bike. A makes a contractual promise to B to hold that right as security for A's duty to pay B £200. Acting without B's authority, A exchanges his bike for a new bike.

In such a case, A is under a duty to hold his Ownership of the new bike as security for his duty to pay B £200. A has made no contractual promise to do so, but the duty arises as a result of the principles discussed in **D4:4.4**: (i) B can identify A's Ownership of the new bike as a product of the right initially held by A as security for B; and (ii) there is no legal basis for A to have the benefit of holding that right free from a security right in B's favour.

EXAMPLE 20b

A holds his Ownership of a bike (worth £200) on Trust for B. Acting without B's consent or other authority, A sells the bike. A uses the proceeds of sale to buy some shares.

Again, the principles discussed in **D4:4.4** apply: B can identify A's shares as the product of the right initially held on Trust. In such a case, B can impose a duty on A to hold the new right on Trust for B. That will be a particularly attractive option for B if A's shares have increased in value. It seems that B has the alternative option of acquiring a Purely Equitable Charge.[136] Instead of asserting a right under a Trust of the shares, B can impose a duty on A to hold those shares as security for A's duty to pay B money as a result of A's breach of Trust. However, it is difficult to see why B might choose that option. Even if A's shares decrease in value, choosing the Trust does not cause B any problems. For example, if the shares are worth £100, B can claim their value under a Trust and, by enforcing A's duty to account, require A to pay B a further £100. There is thus no reason for B to choose a Purely Equitable Charge rather than a Trust.

It seems then that, at a general level, it may be possible to draw a link between at least some non-consensual liens and some non-consensual charges. In **3.1.5** above, we saw that some non-consensual liens can be explained as arising to prevent A being unjustly enriched at B's expense: B is allowed to retain physical control of a thing he has improved as security for A's duty to pay B for those improvements. Some non-consensual charges can also be explained in the same way: B has a persistent right against a right held by A as, if A were free to use that right wholly for his own benefit, A would be unjustly enriched at B's expense. However, just as it is difficult to explain all non-consensual liens as arising as a result of unjust enrichment, the same is true of non-consensual charges. For example, if B has a personal right against A, a court may make a *charging order*: an order imposing a duty

---

[135] See *Lord Napier & Ettrick v Hunter* [1993] 1 AC 713.
[136] See *per* Lord Millett in *Foskett v McKeown* [2001] 1 AC 102 at 130.

on A to hold a specific right as security for his duty to pay B (see **B:2.3.1**).[137] There need be no specific link between the source of A's duty to B and the right that A is ordered to hold as security for B.

3.3 Powers to acquire a persistent right: floating charges

To acquire a power to acquire a persistent right by way of security, B has to show that A is under a duty to allow B, in certain circumstances, to acquire a Purely Equitable Charge. In a floating charge transaction, A's promise will almost always be contractually binding, as B gives something in return for it (eg, money advanced under a loan). However, if A is an individual, A's promise may need to satisfy the first formality rule imposed by the 1882 Act. This means that a written document must specify any things in relation to which B is to acquire a security right. This does not prevent A from giving B a floating charge: first, a floating charge can exist over a specific right, such as A's Ownership of a bike (see **2.3.2** above); second, the 1882 Act does not apply where A gives B security over a personal right held by A, such as a bank account. However, it does mean that A cannot give B security over a fluctuating set of rights including future *property rights* A may acquire.

In contrast, the 1882 Act does not apply to security rights given by companies. It is therefore possible for A Ltd to give B a floating charge that relates to future property rights A Ltd may acquire. If B then registers that charge, it will be protected in A Ltd's insolvency and thus will give B a useful security right.

4 THE DEFENCES QUESTION

To acquire a useful security right, B needs to ensure that his right will be protected in A's insolvency. As we have seen, B will often need to *register* his right. If A is an individual, B's failure to comply with the registration requirement imposed by the 1882 Act means that he simply does not acquire a property right or a persistent right from A. If A Ltd gives B a security right, B's failure to register does not prevent B acquiring a property right or a persistent right from A. Instead, it means that B will not have a useful security right: he will not be able to assert his right against A Ltd's administrators or liquidators; or against a creditor of A Ltd.[138.]

4.1 Property rights

4.1.1 Mortgage

> **EXAMPLE 21a**
>
> A has Ownership of a bike worth £200. In return for a loan of £100 from B, A transfers that right to B by way of security. The transaction is recorded in a written document that meets the requirements of the 1882 Act and is registered by B. B allows A to retain physical control of the bike. A then sells the bike to C.

---

[137] See the Charging Orders Act 1979.
[138] See **n 105** above.

In such a case, B has a pre-existing property right: Ownership of the bike. And C has no defence to that right. This is *not* because of the fact that B registered the mortgage. It is not reasonable to expect anyone buying a bike to check the register of bills of sale. Rather, it is because, as we saw in **D1:3**, it is very difficult for C to have a defence to a property right. In particular, C cannot argue that, by allowing A to retain physical control of the bike, B created the appearance that no one other than A had a property right in the bike. Nor can C rely on any of the limited statutory defences set out in **D1:3.3**.

It might seem them that, in **Example 21a**, C should be able to rely on the defence set out in section 8 of the Factors Act 1889 (see **D1:3.3.3**). Certainly, the *principle* behind that defence seems to apply: (i) B has acquired Ownership from A; but (ii) by allowing A to retain physical control, B has led C reasonably to believe that no one other than A has a property right in the bike. However, the statutory defence applies only where B acquires his right from A by means of a *sale*. As section 62(4) of the Sale of Goods Act 1979 confirms, **Example 21a** is therefore beyond the scope of the defence: B acquired his right by means of a mortgage, not a sale. This position, whilst it emphasises the limited nature of the statutory defence set out in **D1:3.3**, is difficult to defend.[139] As far as C is concerned, the fact that B acquired his right by means of a mortgage rather than a sale makes little difference: it certainly does not make B's right, in practice, easier to discover. C's only consolation is that as B's right arises under a mortgage, C can defeat B's property right by performing the duty secured by B's mortgage. So, in **Example 21a**, C can retain control of the bike by paying B the sum due from A under the loan agreement (£100 plus any agreed interest).[140]

EXAMPLE 21b

A Ltd has Ownership of a stock of bikes worth £20,000. In return for a loan of £10,000 from B, A Ltd transfers that right to B by way of a mortgage. B *fails* to register the transaction as required by the Companies Act. A Ltd then sells the bikes to C.

It is worth noting here that, despite B's failure to register the mortgage, C has *no* defence to B's pre-existing property right. B's failure to register under the Companies Act does *not* prevent B acquiring a property right. It simply prevents B asserting that right against an administrator, liquidator or creditor of A Ltd.[141] As C falls into none of those categories, he can still be bound by B's property right.[142] However, if section 8 of the Factors Act 1889 were extended to cover **Example 21a**, C would also be able to use that extended defence in **Example 21b**.[143]

---

[139] Bridge, *The Sale of Goods* (1997), 453 argues that s 62(4) could be given a narrow interpretation so as to allow C to rely on the s 8 defence.

[140] Of course, if the sum secured is greater than or close to the value of the thing, the opportunity of paying B off provides little comfort for C.

[141] See **n 105** above.

[142] See eg *Stroud Architectural Systems Ltd v John Laing Construction Ltd* [1994] 2 BCLC 276.

[143] Under the Companies Act 1989, s 95, C *was to* have a defence in **Example 21b**: that section stated that B's failure to comply with a registration requirement prevented B asserting his right against an administrator, liquidator or 'any person who for value acquires an interest in or right over the property subject to the charge'. However, that Act never came into force and was repealed by the Companies Act 2006.

4.1.2 Pledge

EXAMPLE 22a

A has Ownership of a bike worth £200. In return for a loan of £100 from B, A pledges that bike to B. A then sells the bike to C.

C can argue that, in a pledge, A retains his Ownership of the bike. A thus has a property right that arose *before* B's property right. However, the problem for C is that, as A *consented* to B acquiring physical control of the bike, C is also bound by that consent. So, as in **Examples 21a and 21b**, C can only retain control of the bike if he pays the sum due from A to B.[144]

If B retains physical control of the bike, **Example 22a** is unlikely to arise: why would C buy a bike from A if A did not have physical control of it? The real problem for C occurs if B allows A to retake physical control of the bike and A then sells the bike to C. In such a case, we need to ask *why* B allowed A to take control of the bike. If B did so with the purpose of allowing A to sell the bike, B has given A a *power* to sell the bike free from B's pre-existing property right. As a result, if A acts within the boundaries of that power, C then has a defence against B's right: the overreaching defence (see **D1:3.4**). C can also use that defence if B allows A to sell pledged goods after releasing those goods to A by means of a 'trust receipt' (see **3.1.3(i)** above).

EXAMPLE 22b

The facts are as in **Example 18** above. B Bank, using a 'trust receipt' allows A Ltd to sell the pledged bikes. However, A Ltd instead pledges the bikes to C Bank.

In such a case, C Bank *cannot* rely on the overreaching defence. A Ltd had the power to *sell* the bikes free from B Bank's property right; it did not have a power to *pledge* those bikes to C Bank. However, C Bank can rely on the defence provided by section 2(1) of the Factors Act 1889 and discussed in **D1:3.3.2**. B Bank gave A Ltd (a professional agent) control of the bikes for the purpose of allowing A Ltd to dispose of those bikes; A Ltd, acting in the ordinary course of its business, then allowed C Bank to acquire a property right in the bikes. As C Bank acquired its right in good faith and without notice of B Bank's right, C has a defence to B's Bank pre-existing property right.[145]

4.1.3 Lien

EXAMPLE 23a

The facts are as in **Example 4**: A has Ownership of a painting. He is going away on holiday and leaves it with B for safe-keeping. A and B enter a contract under which A is to pay B £200 for looking after the painting. The contract provides that B can retain control of the painting until A pays the £200. Whilst the painting is still in B's physical control, A transfers his Ownership of the painting to C. A's debt remains unpaid but C demands the painting from B.

---

[144] See eg *Franklin v Neate* (1844) LR 1 QB 585.
[145] See eg *Lloyds Bank Ltd v Bank of America National Trust and Saving Association* [1938] 2 KB 147.

In a lien, as in a pledge, A retains his Ownership: A is thus free to sell the painting to C. However, as in a pledge, B does not commit a wrong against A if B retains physical control of the painting. B's right to retain physical control binds not only A but also a party later acquiring A's Ownership. B's right continues until *either* (i) B chooses to give up physical control of the panting *or* (ii) the duty secured by the lien is performed. So, if B refuses to hand over the painting to C, C's only option is to perform the secured duty by paying B £200.

EXAMPLE 23b

The facts are as in **Example 4**. Although B has not yet been paid by A, B allows A to retake physical control of the painting. A then sells the painting to C.

In such a case, there is an important difference between a lien and a pledge. In a pledge, B's security right continues even if he allows A to retake physical control of the thing. So, C needs to show he has a defence against B's pre-existing property right by relying on, for example, the overreaching defence or section 2(1) of the Factors Act 1889. In contrast, in a lien, B's security right ends if he chooses to give up physical control by allowing A to retake the thing.[146] Therefore, in **Example 23b**, B has no pre-existing property right he can assert against C. B did acquire a property right through his initial physical control of the property. However, C acquires his property right from A; and A's property right arose before B's property right. And crucially, in contrast to **Example 23a**, B has no right against C to physical control of the painting: that right ended when B allowed A to retake the painting.[147]

4.2 Persistent rights

4.2.1 Mortgages

EXAMPLE 24a

Z holds Ownership of a bike on Trust for A. As security for his duty to repay a loan of £2,000 to B, A transfers his right under the Trust to B. B registers, as a bill of sale, the document by which A made that transfer. Before A repays B, Z sells to C the shares he holds on Trust for B. Z acts without B's consent or other authority. C has no actual or constructive notice of the fact that Z held the shares on Trust.

These facts demonstrates the potential weakness of the security right B acquires in a case such as **Example 5**. As B has a persistent right (a right against Z's right), B is necessarily vulnerable to the 'bona fide purchaser' defence. This means C acquires the shares free from B's security right. Of course, B still has a right to receive £2,000 plus interest from A, but B has no protection if A goes into insolvency. In contrast, if A had instead held some shares in his own name, and transferred those shares to B as security, B would not have been exposed to the risk of the 'bona fide purchaser' defence.

---

[146] See eg *Wilkins v Carmichael* (1779) 1 Doug 101.
[147] This analysis also applies to cases of non-consensual liens (eg, **Example 19a**).

EXAMPLE 24b

The facts are as in **Example 5**. Before A repays B, A borrows money from C. In return, A attempts to mortgage his right under the Trust to C.

In such a case, the general position is that the 'rule in *Dearle v Hall*'[148] determines whether B or C acquires A's right under the Trust (see **D2:3.5.4**). Therefore, if C gives notice to Z (the party initially holding the shares on Trust for A) *before* B gives such notice to Z, C *may* be able to acquire A's right under the Trust, free from any claim of B. However, the rule in *Dearle v Hall* protects C only where he is a 'bona fide purchaser': C must acquire his right from A for value and without actual or constructive notice of B's right. And in **Example 24b**, it is hard to say that C has no *constructive* notice of B's right: B registered the document creating that right. It is true that if C simply buys a bike from A, C cannot reasonably be expected to check the register of bills of sale. However, things are different where, as in **Example 24b**, C instead acquires his right by way of security and so also has to register a bill of sale. The 1882 Act thus adopts the sensible solution that, in a dispute between B and C, the winner is the first to register the document by which A gave him a security right.[149]

4.2.2 Charges

EXAMPLE 25a

The facts are as in **Example 7**: A has Ownership of a bike. In return for receiving a loan of £200 from B, A makes a contractual promise to B that, if he fails to repay the loan, he will allow B to sell the bike and to use the proceeds to meet the debt. B registers the document creating the charge as a bill of sale. Before A repays B, A sells the bike to C. C buys the bike without any actual or constructive notice of B's Purely Equitable Charge.

Again, C has a defence to B's pre-existing persistent right: C can thus acquire A's Ownership of the bike free from B's Purely Equitable Charge. It makes no difference that B has registered the document creating the charge as a bill of sale. Certainly, we cannot say that such registration gives C constructive notice of B's right.[150] Things may be different if, instead of buying the bike, C acquires A's Ownership of the bike by way of security. As A has thus mortgaged his bike to C, it *is* reasonable for C to check the register of bills of sale: after all, C will need to register the mortgage if he wants to acquire a useful security right. In such a case, then, it may be possible to argue that B's registration *does* give C constructive notice of B's right so that C cannot rely on the 'bona fide purchaser' defence.

EXAMPLE 25b

The facts are as in **Example 7**. B registers the document creating the charge as a bill of sale. Before A repays B, A borrows money from C and in return, gives C a Purely Equitable Charge over A's Ownership of the bike.

---

[148] (1828) 3 Russ 1. The rule was approved by the House of Lords in *Foster v Cockerell* (1835) 3 Cl & F 456.

[149] See 1882 Act, s 5 and 1878 Act, s 10.

[150] See eg *per* Cotton LJ in *Joseph v Lyons* (1884) 15 QBD 280 at 286: it is not reasonable to expect C to check the register (see **4.1.1** above).

In this case, B *can* assert his security right against C. As in **Example 25a**, B has a pre-existing persistent right. And, in contrast to **Example 25a**, C *cannot* use the 'bona fide purchaser' defence. The point is that C has not acquired the very right of A against which B has a right; instead, C has acquired a second right against that right (see **D2:3.5.1**).

EXAMPLE 26a

A Ltd makes a contractual promise to B Bank to hold a specific stock of bikes as security for a debt owed to B Bank. B Bank fails to register the charge with the Registrar of Companies . A then sells part of that stock of bikes to C. C is aware of A Ltd's promise to B Bank.

In this case, B Bank *can* assert its security right against C. C cannot rely on the 'bona fide purchaser' defence as it is aware of B Bank's right. And B Bank's failure to register the charge does *not* give C a defence:[151] under the Companies Act, a failure to register simply prevents B Bank from asserting its Purely Equitable Charge against a liquidator or administrator and against a creditor of A Ltd.[152]

EXAMPLE 26b

A Ltd makes a contractual promise to B Bank to hold a specific stock of bikes as security for a debt owed to B Bank. B Bank fails to register the charge with the Registrar of Companies . A Ltd then borrows more money from C Bank. In return, A Ltd makes a contractual promise to C Bank to hold that same stock of bikes as security for its debt to C Bank. C Bank is aware of A Ltd's earlier promise to B Bank. C Bank *does* register its charge. A Ltd fails to pay its debts to B Bank and C Bank and goes into insolvency.

In this case, B Bank *cannot* assert its security right against C Bank. In contrast to **Example 26a**, C Bank *is* a (secured) creditor of A Ltd and so the Companies Act prevents B Bank from asserting its Purely Equitable Charge against C Bank. That means that A Ltd's liquidator will first use the value of the stock of bikes to pay off the debt to C Bank: any money left will then be distributed amongst A Ltd's general creditors, including B Bank. So C Bank, unlike B Bank, is protected in A Ltd's insolvency. It is irrelevant that C Bank only acquired a persistent right rather than a property right; it is also irrelevant that C Bank was aware of B's pre-existing persistent right.[153] The point is that C Bank does not need to rely on the 'bona fide purchaser' defence: the Companies Act makes clear that B's unregistered Purely Equitable Charge cannot bind C Bank.[154]

---

[151] See eg *Stroud Architectural Systems Ltd v John Laing Construction Ltd* [1994] 2 BCLC 276.

[152] See **n 105** above.

[153] B Bank could try to claim that, as C Bank knew about A Ltd's earlier contractual promise to B Bank, C Bank has committed the wrong of procuring a breach by A Ltd of its contract with B Bank. The analysis of **D3:Example 5** in **D3:2.3.4** suggests that B Bank's claim is a difficult one to make. And even if it succeeds, it simply gives B Bank a direct personal right against C Bank: it does not alter the fact that only C Bank is protected in A Ltd's insolvency.

[154] The case can thus be compared with *Midland Bank Trust Co Ltd v Green* [1981] AC 513 (**C3:Example 5**): C's knowledge of B's pre-existing persistent right does not prevent C relying on a statute making B's right 'void' as against C (see too **E2:3.6.5**).

4.3   Powers to acquire a persistent right

4.3.1 The general position

EXAMPLE 27a

A Ltd is a bike manufacturer. In return for a loan from B Bank, A Ltd gives B Bank a charge over its stock of finished but unsold bikes and over its current and future contractual rights against its wholesalers. Under the terms of that charge, A Ltd is free to continue to use those rights, and their proceeds, in the usual course of business—at least until the occurrence of particular 'crystallising' events such as A Ltd ceasing to trade, or A Ltd failing to make a loan repayment to B Bank on the due date. B Bank registers its charge with the Registrar of Companies. A Ltd then sells part of its stock of bikes to C, a wholesaler.

In such a case, the transaction between A Ltd and B Bank is a *floating charge*: B Bank thus has a power to acquire a persistent right against the rights covered by the charge. Clearly, B Bank cannot assert that power against C. Whilst C has acquired some of the rights covered by the charge, the terms of the charge give A the power to transfer Ownership of part of its stock, in the normal course of business, to C. Indeed, as we saw in 2.3.1 above, when considering **Example 11**, the key feature of a floating charge is that it gives A Ltd the freedom to deal with its rights. As A Ltd has the power to transfer Ownership to C free from B Bank's power to acquire a persistent right, we can say that B Bank's power has been *overreached*.[155] It does not matter whether or not C was aware of B Bank's power: even if it had notice of that power, C is protected as A Ltd acted within the scope of the authority given to it by the floating charge (see **D2:3.4**).

4.3.2 The effect of a 'negative pledge clause'

EXAMPLE 27b

The facts are as in **Example 27a**. A term in the deal between A Ltd and B Bank expressly prevents A Ltd from using any of its stock of its bikes as security for anyone other than B Bank. In return for a loan from C Bank, A Ltd then gives C Bank a Purely Equitable Charge over particular bikes. A Ltd goes into insolvency, having failed to pay back either the loan to B Bank or the loan to C Bank.

In such a case, B Bank needs to show why it should be able to assert its pre-existing power to acquire a persistent right against C Bank. However, the obstacle B Bank faced in **Example 27a** has disappeared. C Bank cannot claim that B Bank's power has been overreached as, when giving C Bank its Purely Equitable Charge, A Ltd did not act within the scope of its authority. Here, the deal between A Ltd and B Bank expressly prevents A Ltd from giving C Bank such a right in relation to its stock of bikes. That restriction on A Ltd's power is often referred to as 'negative pledge'.

However, C Bank may still be protected in **Example 27b**. In **D2:3.5.5**, we noted an important principle, which we can call the *Phillips* principle:[156]

---

[155] See eg R Nolan (2004) 120 *LQR* 108.
[156] See *per* Lord Westbury in *Phillips v Phillips* (1861) 4 De GF & J 208 at 218.

- If B has a power to acquire a persistent right against a right of A; *and*
- C then acquires a persistent right against that right of A; *and*
- C acquires his right for value and without notice of B's pre-existing power; *then*
- B cannot assert his power to acquire a persistent right against C.

The first two points are clearly present in **Example 27b**. The crucial question is whether C Bank acquired its right without actual or constructive notice of B Bank's pre-existing power. We have to be careful here. First, B Bank has registered its charge. We have seen that such registration does not necessarily give a third party notice of the registered right. However, as C Bank itself acquired a charge (something requiring registration) it is reasonable to expect C Bank to check the register. Therefore, it looks like B Bank's registration may give C Bank constructive notice and hence prevent C Bank relying on the *Phillips* principle.

But there is a further twist. C Bank can argue that B Bank's registration simply gives it notice of the *existence* of the charge to B Bank; it does not give C notice of the *terms* of that charge. C Bank can therefore say that it assumed that (as in **Example 27a**) the charge in B Bank's favour gave A Ltd the power to give C Bank a security right *free from* B Bank's floating charge. The important point here, as we noted in D2:3.3, is that C can be a 'bona fide purchaser' even if he knows of the existence of B's pre-existing power. The crucial question is not simply whether C had notice of that power; but, more precisely, whether C had notice that A's action in giving C a right was contrary to the terms of B's power. So, if C Bank's argument is correct, C Bank *can* rely on the *Phillips* principle, and hence be protected from B Bank's power *even though* C Bank knew of the existence of that power.

The courts have sided with C Bank on this issue.[157] First, the registration of B Bank's charge is *not* taken to give C Bank constructive notice of the *terms* of the charge. Second, it seems that C Bank is entitled to presume that, in general, B Bank's charge will *not* contain a term preventing A Ltd from giving C Bank a later security right.[158] This second point can, however, be challenged. It raises an empirical question: are such terms ('negative pledge clauses') such a common feature of floating charges that C Bank *should* assume that such a clause will exist *whenever* A Ltd gives B Bank a floating charge? It has been persuasively argued that such clauses are now so common that C Bank should make that assumption.[159] The very existence of a floating charge should therefore mean that, if C Bank takes a later security right from A Ltd, it takes the risk that A Ltd does not have the power to give C Bank that right free from B Bank's power to acquire a persistent right. However, that view has not yet been accepted by the courts.

The result of all this is that, in **Example 27b**, C Bank will be able to rely on the *Phillips* principle and so B Bank will be unable to assert its power to acquire a persistent right against C Bank. This means that the value of the stock of bikes in relation to which C Bank has a Purely Equitable Charge will first be used to meet A Ltd's debt to C Bank. If any money remains, it will then be used to meet A Ltd's debt to B Bank.[160] If any further money remains, it will then be used to meet the claims of A Ltd's general creditors.

---

[157] See eg *English & Scottish Mercantile Investment Co v Brunton* [1892] 2 QB 700; *Siebe Gorman & Co Ltd v Barclays Bank Ltd* [1979] 2 Lloyd's Rep 142.

[158] See eg *per* Lord Jessel MR in *re Colonial Trusts, ex p Bradshaw* (1879) 15 Ch D 465 at 472.

[159] See eg Farrar (1974) 38 *Conv* 315; for counter-arguments, see Goode, *Commercial Law* (3rd edn, 2004), 665.

[160] Although this is subject to the points noted in 2.3.4 above: as B Bank's right arises under a floating charge, the statutory insolvency rules subordinate B Bank's right to, for example, preferential creditors of A Ltd.

EXAMPLE 27c

The facts are as in **Example 27b**. However, in this case, C Bank, when it acquires its Purely Equitable Charge from A Ltd, has actual knowledge of the term of B Bank's charge and thus knows that the terms of that charge prevent A Ltd from using its stock of bikes as security for anyone other than B Bank.

In such a case, it should be possible for B Bank to assert its power to acquire a persistent right against C Bank.[161] Certainly, due to its knowledge of the restriction on A Ltd's power, C cannot rely on the *Phillips* principle. In practice, this means that the value of the stock of bikes will first be used to meet A Ltd's debt to B Bank.[162] If any money remains, it will then be used to meet A Ltd's debt to C Bank. If any further money remains, it will then be used to meet the claims of A Ltd's general creditors.

In **Example 27c**, B Bank can also argue that it has a new, *direct right* against C Bank as C Bank has committed a wrong against B Bank: the wrong of procuring a breach by A Ltd of A Ltd's contract with B Bank (see **D3:2.3.4**). Crucially, as in *BMTA v Salvadori*,[163] A Ltd commits a breach of contract *as soon as* it gives C Bank the Purely Equitable Charge. By acquiring that right from A Ltd, C Bank thus actively facilitates A Ltd's breach of contract. C Bank can thus be ordered to pay B Bank money representing the value of B Bank's contractual right with A Ltd and compensating B Bank for any consequential loss it has suffered as a result of that breach. However, the problem for B Bank with this route is that if C Bank is insolvent, B Bank's personal right against C Bank may be of little value. B Bank will therefore prefer to assert its power to acquire a persistent right; and thus take first bite of the money realised when A Ltd's liquidator sells the stock of bikes.

SUMMARY of F4:4.3

If B Bank acquires a right under a floating charge, it has a power to acquire a persistent right. A Ltd is given an initial freedom to deal with the rights covered by the floating charge. If A Ltd then gives C a right that relates to the rights covered by the floating charge, we need to ask:

1. Did A Ltd act within the authority given to it by the floating charge agreement? If **Yes**, B Bank cannot assert its power to acquire a persistent right against C. If **No**, go to 2.
2. Did C acquire a property right or persistent right from A Ltd, for value and without notice of the restriction on A Ltd's authority? If **Yes**, B Bank cannot assert is power to acquire a persistent right against C. If **No**, B Bank should be able to assert that power against C.

---

[161] See eg *per* Chadwick LJ in *re Portbase Clothing Ltd* [1993] Ch 388 at 401. In *Griffiths v Yorkshire Bank Ltd* [1994] 1 WLR 1427, Morritt J took a different view. That view has however attracted criticism: see eg Goode, *Commercial Law* (3rd edn, 2004), 687; Beale *et al, The Law of Personal Property Security* (2007), 13.44.

[162] Although this is subject to the points noted in 2.3.4 above: as B Bank's right arises under a floating charge, the statutory insolvency rules subordinate B Bank's right to, for example, preferential creditors of A Ltd.

[163] [1949] Ch 556 (see **D3:2.3.4(iii)**).

In applying question 2, it is important to note that B Bank's registration of its charge, although it creates a public record of the restriction on A Ltd's power to give C a right, is *not* currently viewed as giving C constructive notice of the that restriction. In practice, therefore, B Bank faces the difficult job of showing that C in fact knew about that restriction, or ought to have known about it for some other reason.

4.4 The limitation defence

The lapse of time may give A or C a defence if B attempts to assert his security right. Special limitation rules, imposed by section 20 of the Limitation Act 1980, apply in such a case. For example, if B's right secures A's duty to pay a sum of money to B, B has 12 years, from the point when the money is due, to bring an action to recover that sum. So, even if A's duty to pay that money arises from a contract (in which case the standard limitation rule is that B has six years from A's breach of contract to bring a claim), B has the benefit of a 12-year limitation period. However, the standard six-year period applies to B's claim to recover arrears of interest.[164]

5 THE REMEDIES QUESTION: ENFORCEMENT OF B'S SECURITY RIGHT

If B's property right or persistent right secures a duty owed by A to B, the **remedies question** arises when A fails to perform that duty: how can B use his security right to meet A's duty? It is important to remember that, even after the contractual time for performance of A's secured duty has passed, A will nonetheless have a power to remove B's security right by exercising his power to 'redeem' (see **1.3.1** above). Hence the methods of enforcement considered here are all subject to the proviso that, if A exercises his power to redeem, B will no longer have a security right to enforce. Further, (i) if B acquires his security right by means of a bill of sale, the Bills of Sale Act (1878) Amendment Act 1882 regulates B's enforcement of his right; and (ii) if B acquires his security right under an agreement regulated by the Consumer Credit Act 1974, that Act regulates B's enforcement of his right. We will briefly consider the effect of those Acts in **5.3.1** below.

5.1 Sale

Under the LPA 1925, section 91(2) a court has a discretion, on an application from B, to order a sale of any thing or right of A in relation to which B has a security right.[165] The court can direct a sale 'on such terms as it thinks fit' and need not allow A any further time to 'redeem' by performing the secured duty. B can thus apply for a sale even if he has no power of sale; but the disadvantage, of course, is that B has to make an application to court.

---

[164] See s 20(5). There are exceptions where a prior party with a Charge has been in possession of A's thing; and also where the rights over which B has security include a future interest or life insurance policy: see ss 20(6) and (7).

[165] Or an application from 'any person interested either in the mortgage money or in the right of redemption'. For example, in *Palk v Mortgage Services Funding plc* [1993] Ch 330, a sale was ordered at A's request: A feared that a delay in selling would simply increase A's debt to B.

Things are clearly simpler for B if he can show he has a power to sell: B can then sell without needing a court order.

5.1.1 Powers of sale

(i) Express powers
If B has a security right, his principal protection comes from his ability to (i) sell A's right; and (ii) use the proceeds to meeting the duty owed to B. So, when acquiring a security right from A, B will normally ensure that he is given an express power to sell A's right, should the secured duty not be performed. That power is a fundamental feature of mortgages, charges and pledges. It is possible for B to have a lien without having a power of sale; however, in a consensually created lien, A may expressly give B that power (see **2.1.3** above).

(ii) Implied powers
Even if A has not expressly given B a power of sale, it may be possible for the courts to infer that the parties intended, as part of their deal, that B should have such a power. For example, if (i) A mortgages his Ownership of a bike to B; and (ii) B then takes physical control of the bike; and (iii) the secured duty has not been performed within the agreed time;[166] then (iv) B has an implied power to sell the bike.[167]

(iii) A statutory power of sale
In addition to any power of sale B acquires under the express or implied terms of his deal with A, B may also acquire a statutory power of sale. That power is set out by section 101(1)(i) of the LPA 1925. It can arise only where B acquires his security right by means of a *deed*.[168] If the secured duty is not performed, it is convenient for B to rely on this statutory power of sale: in particular, the provisions of the LPA 1925 give C useful protection if he acquires a right as a result of B's exercise of the statutory power of sale.[169]

Under section 101(1)(i), B has the statutory power of sale when 'the mortgage money has become due'.[170] Although section 101(1)(i) refers to the 'mortgage money' it is worth noting that the term includes 'money's worth'[171] and so could be applied where the duty secured by B's security right is *not* a duty to pay money. Presumably, in such a case, B's statutory power of sale will arise when the time for performing the secured duty passes. In cases where B lends a large sum to A, and A agrees to repay the sum in instalments, A's default will consist in missing a repayment instalment. So, in those cases, B can ensure he has a statutory power of sale on A's default by including a provision in the security trans-action that, for the purposes of section 101(1)(i), A's duty to repay the entire sum arises a very short time (eg, one month) after B lends A the money.[172]

---

[166] If the parties did not agree a specific time for the performance of the secured duty, B must (i) give A notice that he intends to enforce his security right; and (ii) give A a reasonable time to perform the secured duty: see eg *per* Cozens-Hardy MR in *Stubbs v Slater* [1910] 1 Ch 632 at 639.

[167] See eg *Deverges v Sandeman, Clark & Co* [1902] 1 Ch 579; *Stubbs v Slater* [1910] 1 Ch 632.

[168] For the definition of a deed see C3:2.

[169] See s 104. Under s 104(3), when B sells to C, it is presumed that, if the statutory power is applicable, the sale is made under that power.

[170] 'Mortgage' here is not used in the technical sense of a transfer of a right by way of security: instead it includes a charge or a lien (see LPA 1925, s 205(xvi)) and so s 101(1)(i) can also apply if B has acquired, by means of a deed, a Purely Equitable Charge.

[171] LPA 1925, s 205(1)(xvi).

[172] Such clauses are common where B advances a large sum to A and receives a security right over A's land in

5.1.2 The effect of a sale where B has a power to sell

EXAMPLE 1b

A has Ownership of a bike. In return for a loan of £200 from B, A promises B that: (i) A will repay the loan at a 6 per cent annual rate of interest; and (ii) if A fails to repay the loan within six months, B can sell the bike and use the proceeds to meet A's debt.

In such a case, B has an express power of sale. If B exercises that power by selling the bike to C, C will receive A's Ownership of the bike: A cannot assert his pre-existing property right against C as C can rely on the overreaching defence (see **D1:3.4**). If the proceeds of sale exceed A's liability to B, B is under a duty to pay that excess to A: A thus has a persistent right against B's right to the excess.[173]

We noted above that B's enforcement of his security right is subject to A's power to 'redeem' by performing the secured duty. However, A's power to redeem ends (i) if B exercises his power of sale by transferring A's right to C; *and* (ii) if B exercises his power of sale by making a *contract* to transfer A's right to C.[174]

5.1.3 B's duties to A in relation to sale

(i) Special duties in relation to the statutory power of sale

The statutory power of sale provided by the LPA 1925, section 101 is regulated by section 103 of that Act. B's exercise of that power will be a breach of a duty to A *unless* one of the following conditions has been met:

1. B has served a notice on A requiring payment and A has failed to pay within three months from service of the notice; *or*
2. Interest is due and A has failed to pay that interest within two months; *or*
3. A has breached a non-payment duty imposed by the deed creating B's security right or by the LPA 1925.

It is important to remember that if B relies instead on a power of sale arising from the express or implied terms of his deal with A, these statutory conditions do *not* apply.

It is often said that, if none of those conditions is met, B's statutory power of sale has *arisen*; but is not *exercisable*. However, that terminology is unhelpful. If B has a statutory power of sale under section 101(1)(i) and then sells before one of the section 103 conditions has been met, this does *not* mean B has no power to sell. In particular, as we will see in **5.1.4** below, it does *not* prevent C acquiring A's right.

(ii) General duties relating to sale

B's general duties to A apply *whenever* B exercises a power of sale: whether that power is statutory or instead arises under the express or implied terms of B's deal with A. The source

---

return: see *West Bromwich BS v Wilkinson* [2005] 1 WLR 2303 at [25] for an example of such a clause. Alternatively, those terms can provide that *if* A misses an instalment payment, the whole sum is due.

[173] See eg *per* Salmon LJ in *Cuckmere Brick Co v Mutual Finance Ltd* [1971] 1 Ch 949 at 966; *per* Kay J in *Banner v Berridge* (1880) LR 18 Ch D 254 at 269.

[174] See *Waring v London and Manchester Assurance Co Ltd* [1935] Ch 310.

of these duties is the fact that, when B exercises his power of sale, A's economic position is *dependent* on B.

EXAMPLE 1b

A has Ownership of a bike. In return for a loan of £200 from B, A promises B that: (i) A will repay the loan at a 6 per cent annual rate of interest; and (ii) if A fails to repay the loan within six months, B can sell the bike and use the proceeds to meet A's debt. After six months, A still owes B £150. The market value of A's bike is £500.

If B exercises his power of sale and receives £500, B can keep £150 of that money but is under a duty to transfer the £350 excess to A. However, as B is in control of the sale, B may be tempted to accept the first offer he receives for the bike, even if that offer is only £400. Receiving £100 less makes no difference to B: either way, he will get his £150. But taking that low offer will adversely affect A, who will receive only £250. As A is thus dependent on B, B is under certain duties to A.

First, B is under a duty to exercise his power of sale in good faith:[175] without the motive of harming A's interests. Therefore if B's decision to accept the £400 offer is based on a desire for A to receive less money, B is under a duty to pay a further £100 to A. Second, B is under further duties to take reasonable care in achieving a reasonable price. However, the courts have not clearly stated the extent of these additional duties. The usual approach is to say: (i) B is under a duty to take reasonable care to get the true market value of A's right at the moment B choose to sell it; but that (ii) B is free to choose when to sell; and (iii) B is not under a duty to take steps or invest money in order to make A's right more attractive to buyers.

So, if B decides to sell A's right but fails to advertise the sale, or to inform potential buyers of a particularly attractive aspect of A's right (eg, if A's right is a Freehold, that there is planning permission to develop the land),[176] then B is in breach of a duty: having decided to sell, B ought to take obvious steps to ensure he receives the market value for A's right. But if B decides to sell quickly as he does not want to wait to receive money owed to him by A, A *cannot* complain that B would have got a higher price by waiting for the market to pick up, or by taking steps to make A's right more attractive (eg, if A's right is a Freehold, by taking steps to get planning permission).[177]

The current position may seem a little unclear but the essential point is that B's action, even if it results in a lower price when A's right is sold, *cannot* be a breach of duty if B *acted in pursuit of his own reasonable interest*. The crucial point is that B is *not* subject to the core Trust duty: he does not have a duty to use his power of sale only in A's best interests.[178] Therefore, if B decides to sell sooner rather than later as he wants his money as soon as possible, A cannot complain. And if B decides he does not want to incur the delay or expense involved in making A's right more attractive to buyers, A cannot complain. However, if B's decision is not taken in pursuance of his own reasonable interest, A *can* complain. After all, if B has decided to sell, he has no reasonable interest in selling without informing potential purchasers of the true merits of A's right. And if B has decided to sell,

---

[175] See eg *per* Lord Templeman in *Tse Kwong Lam v Wong Chit Sen* [1983] 1 WLR 1349 at 1355.
[176] That was the case in *Cuckmere Brick Co v Mutual Finance Ltd* [1971] 1 Ch 949.
[177] See *Silven Properties Ltd v Royal Bank of Scotland plc* [2004] 1 WLR 997.
[178] See eg *per* Lightman J in *Silven Properties Ltd v Royal Bank of Scotland plc* [2004] 1 WLR 997 at [14].

he has no reasonable interest in taking a first, low offer when, by waiting for only a short period, he can obtain the true market price.

Some confusion has been caused by viewing B as being under a duty to take reasonable care not to harm A's economic interests.[179] In the 1960s, the law of negligence developed to recognise that, in exceptional case, B can be under such a duty of care.[180] However, as noted by the Privy Council in *Downsview Nominees Ltd v First City Corporation Ltd*,[181] such a duty is entirely inappropriate when B has a security right and exercises his power of sale. Such a duty cannot be imposed if it is likely to lead to a conflict between legitimate interests;[182] and B clearly does have a legitimate interest in enforcing his security right. Further, it seems that B's duties to A do not depend on the law of negligence. If B fails to perform one of his duties to A, A does *not* claim money for the value of his right and the relevant loss he has suffered as a result of B's breach.[183] Rather, the relationship between A and B is an accounting relationship: B is under a duty to account to A for the money he *should* receive by properly exercising his power of sale.[184]

5.1.4 The effect of a breach by B of B's duties to A in relation to sale

(i) The effect on C

If: (i) B has a power of sale and (ii) B exercise that power by selling to C, then (iii) C acquires his right free from any pre-existing right of A. The fact that B may have breached one of his duties to A makes *no difference* to C's position. Exactly the same position applies as when a trustee has a power of sale: if the trustee exercises that power and gives C a right, C can use the overreaching defence against any pre-existing rights under the Trust *even if* the trustee acted in breach of his duties as trustee (see **D2:3.4**).

There are, however, some cases in which it is suggested that, if C *knows* about B's breach of duty before the sale, then that sale does *not* operate to pass A's right to C.[185] This suggestion is very difficult to support. It may be possible, in rare cases, for A to argue that he has a new, direct right against C, arising as a result of C's conduct (see eg **D3:2**);[186] but if B does have a power of sale, C's knowledge that B is exercising that power in breach of a duty to A should *not* prevent C acquiring A's right.

(ii) The effect on B

If A learns that B is planning a sale in breach of one of B's duties to A, A can intervene and prevent the sale. If A discovers the breach too late, A is left to bring a claim against B. Such a claim is best seen as enforcing B's duty to account to A for the sum B *should* have received

---

179 See eg the analysis of Lord Denning MR in *Standard Chartered Bank Ltd v Walker* [1982] 1 WLR 1410.

180 See eg *Hedley Byrne & Co Ltd v Heller & Partners Ltd* [1964] AC 465.

181 See *per* Lord Templeman [1993] AC 295 at 315.

182 See eg *per* Lord Browne-Wilkinson in *White v Jones* [1995] 2 AC 207 at 276.

183 As noted by the Court of Appeal in *Silven Properties Ltd v Royal Bank of Scotland plc* [2004] 1 WLR 997 at [19].

184 See eg *per* Lord Templeman in *Downsview Nominees* [1993] AC 295 at 311–2. The discussion there is a little ambiguous as Lord Templeman describes the money B must pay A as 'damages'. However, his Lordship also notes that the sum due can be taken into account not just by A but also by later parties who also have security rights in relation to the same right as B.

185 See eg *per* Crossman J in *Waring v London & Manchester Assurance Co Ltd* [1935] Ch 311 at 318.

186 But note that C's knowledge that A is breaching a duty to B by transferring a right to C is not, in itself, enough to give B a direct right against C (see **D3:2.3.5**).

had he complied with his duties to A. There should thus be no need for A to show that B's breach of duty caused A any consequential loss.[187]

5.2 Appointment of a receiver

A sale gives B access to the capital value of A's right. B may instead wish to have access to the income generated by A's right. B can achieve this by appointing a *receiver*: a party who manages A's right in order to produce income from that right. This method of enforcement may be useful where A's right is, for example, a Freehold or Lease; or where A's rights consist of business assets. That income can then be used to meet the secured duty—eg, to pay off a debt owed by A to B. B can apply to court and ask for a receiver to be appointed;[188] but things are simpler if B can rely directly on a power to make such an appointment.

The power to appoint a receiver was *formerly* particularly important in cases where B's security related to the whole (or substantially the whole) of a company's business. In such a case, the security transaction could give B a power to appoint an 'administrative receiver':[189] a party who takes over the running of A Ltd's *entire business* and also has the power to sell that business as a going concern.[190] That administrative receiver could essentially run A Ltd's business for the benefit of B Bank.[191] However, the position is now different: if the initial security transaction between A Ltd and B Bank occurred after 15 September 2003, the circumstances in which B Bank can appoint an administrative receiver are very limited.[192] Instead of appointing such a receiver to run A Ltd's business for it, B Bank can instead appoint an administrator. An administrator, unlike an administrative receiver, is under a duty (like that of a liquidator) to 'perform his functions in the interest of the company's creditors as a whole'.[193] However, if B Bank has a security right over a substantial proportion of A Ltd's assets, B Bank does still have the advantage of being able to choose the administrator and to appoint that administrator without needing the approval of a court.[194]

5.2.1 Powers to appoint a receiver

(i) Express and implied powers
In their deal, A and B can give B an express power to appoint a receiver. Like an express power of sale, that power will also be subject to A's ability to 'redeem'. It seems that, in the absence of an express power, the courts will not generally infer that the parties intended B to have such a power.

(ii) A statutory power
In 5.1.1(iii) above, we examined section 101(1)(i) of the LPA 1925. If the conditions of that provision are met, section 101(1)(iii) means that B has not only a power of sale but also a power to appoint a receiver.

---

[187] On this general point about the duty to account, see eg Elliott (2002) 65 *MLR* 588 (see D2:4.1.1(ii)).

[188] See eg *Berney v Sewell* (1820) 1 Jac & W 647. Beale *et al*, *The Law of Personal Property Security* (2007), 17.57 reports that 'this jurisdiction is rarely used now'.

[189] See eg *Carlos Federspiel & Co v Charles Twigg & Co Ltd* [1957] 1 Lloyd's Rep 240 (see D1:2.2.4(iii)(c)).

[190] Insolvency Act 1986, s 29(2).

[191] See eg *Downsview Nominees Ltd v First City Corporation Ltd* [1993] AC 295.

[192] See Insolvency Act 1986, ss 72B–72G (as inserted by the Enterprise Act 2002, s 250).

[193] Insolvency Act 1986, Sch B1, para 3(2). See Armour and Mokal [2004] *LMCLQ* 28.

[194] Insolvency Act 1986, Sch B1, para 14 (inserted by the Enterprise Act 2002, s 248).

5.2.2 The effect of appointing a receiver

As far as B is concerned, the key advantages of a receiver are that: (i) the receiver can manage A's right for B's benefit; (ii) the income produced by A's right (after the receiver's expenses)[195] will go to meeting the secured duty (eg, A's duty to repay a loan to B); *and* (iii) the receiver is *not* an agent of B. The last point is important. If A is unhappy with the receiver's management of A's right (eg, A feels more income could be produced, so that his debt to B could be paid off more quickly), A cannot complain to B.

As we saw above, if B exercises a power of sale, B is under certain duties to A. The very same duties apply where a receiver is appointed; but those duties are owed to A by the receiver, *not* by B.[196] This point is confirmed, in relation to B's statutory power to appoint a receiver, by section 109(2) of the LPA 1925: under that section, the receiver is an agent of A, not of B. This may seem surprising but, if a receiver manages A's right so as to reduce the debt owed by A, then the receiver is acting on A's behalf.[197] As a result, if B has a power of sale, B may use a receiver to make that sale: any complaint by A as to the conduct of the sale must then be addressed to the receiver, not to B.

Section 103 of the LPA 1925 regulates B's statutory power to appoint a receiver, just as it regulates B's power of sale. So, if B appoints a receiver where one of the conditions set out in section 103 (see **5.1.3(i)** above) has not been met, B is in breach of a duty to A. However, once the receiver is appointed, B cannot be liable for the receiver's actions.[198]

5.2.3 The receiver's duties to A

When exercising his duties, a receiver may be affected by the same conflict of interest that affects B when exercising a power of sale. On the one hand, a receiver owes a duty to B to manage the right in B's interest; however, that duty may conflict with A's economic interests. The conflict is regulated by the principles set out in **5.1.3** above. As a result, the receiver's duties to A are very limited. A receiver is *not* under a general duty to take reasonable care to protect A's interests;[199] and is instead entitled to pursue B's reasonable interests, even if they conflict with the interest of A.[200]

5.2.4 The effect of a breach by a receiver of his duties to A

If a receiver breaches a duty owed to A (eg, by failing to take a simple step to increase the income generated by A's right), A can bring a claim against the receiver. This claim, like a claim brought against B when he breaches a duty in relation to sale, is *not* based on the wrong of negligence but on principles developed in Equity.[201] It seems also to arise as a result of the receiver being under a duty to account to A. After all, a receiver is under a duty

---

[195] Where a receiver is appointed under the statutory power, s 109(6) regulates the receiver's power to deduct expenses.

[196] See eg *Gaskell v Gosling* [1896] 1 QB 669; *Medforth v Blake* [2000] Ch 86.

[197] That analysis does not apply where A gives B a security right to secure a debt owed by X to B. In such a case, s 109(2) still means that the receiver is A's agent. This may be justified by the fact that, in giving B such a security right, A has already shown a willingness to act for X's benefit.

[198] Although if the receiver acts in a particular way on the express instructions of B, B may be liable: *per* Scott V-C in *Medforth v Blake* [2000] Ch 86 at 95. It is hard to explain the basis of this liability, however.

[199] See eg *Downsview Nominees Ltd v First City Corporation Ltd* [1993] AC 295; *Medforth v Blake* [2000] Ch 86.

[200] The receiver's duties to A can also be limited by the terms of A and B's initial security transaction.

[201] See *Medforth v Blake* [2000] Ch 86.

to account *both* to A and to B. Therefore, if a receiver's breach consists in an act that reduces the income generated by A's right, the receiver may have to pay money to both A and B.

5.3 Taking physical control of A's thing

Where B's security right relates to a thing owned by A, B may be able to enforce his right by taking physical control of A's thing. In a lien, and usually in a pledge, B will already have physical control of A's thing at the point when the secured duty is not performed. If A has mortgaged his Ownership of a thing to B, then B already has a right to exclusive control of that thing: that right exists *as soon as* the mortgage is concluded and does not depend on the failure to perform the secured duty.[202] However, the express or implied terms of the mortgage will often give A a right to keep physical control until a failure to perform the secured duty.[203] In a charge transaction, B's persistent right, by itself, does not give B a right to physical control of A's thing.[204] However, the terms of the charge transaction may well give B such a right, arising on a failure to perform the secured duty.

5.3.1 Taking physical control prior to a sale

B's usual reason for wishing to take physical control of A's thing is to facilitate a sale of that thing. In those cases, B will only act if he has a power of sale (see **5.1** above). Where B takes physical control for the purpose of a sale, his duties to A are very limited (see **5.1.3** above).

If the Bills of Sale Act (1878) Amendment Act 1882 applies, B's right to take physical control is regulated by the particular terms that *must* be present if the document used by the parties is to give B a security right. Under those terms, B is given a right to take physical control of A's thing if, for example, A fails to perform his secured duty to pay B, or where the thing held by A is at risk from another party.[205] In such a case, B also has a power to sell A's thing, *unless* A applies to court within five days of B's taking the thing and shows that the reason justifying B's taking is no longer applicable[206] (eg, because A has now performed his duty to pay an instalment to B).

Further, if B's security right arises as part of an agreement regulated by the Consumer Credit Act 1974, B cannot enforce his security right unless he first serves a 'default notice' on A.[207] That notice must: (i) specify A's breach; (ii) specify what remedial action is required by A (eg, paying an instalment); and (iii) allow A at least 14 days to take that remedial action.[208]

---

[202] See eg *per* Harman J in *Four-Maids Ltd v Dudley Marshall (Properties) Ltd* [1957] Ch 317 at 320: B has his right to exclusive control 'before the ink is dry on the mortgage.'

[203] The courts may be able to infer the existence of an implied term where the secured duty is a duty of A to repay a debt in instalments: in such a case, it can generally be inferred that A is entitled to physical control of the thing until he fails to pay an instalment.

[204] See eg *per* Atkin LJ in *National Provincial and Union Bank v Charnley* [1924] 1 KB 431 at 450.

[205] See the 1882 Act, s 7; *Johnson v Diprose* [1893] 1 QB 512. The risk from a third party may arise if, for example, an execution creditor has an order allowing him to sell A's thing to meet A's judgment debt.

[206] See *per* Lopes LJ in *re Morritt* (1886) 18 QBD 222 at 241.

[207] Consumer Credit Act 1974, s 87(1)(c) and (e).

[208] Consumer Credit Act 1974, s 88 as modified by Consumer Credit Act 2006, s 14.

5.3.2 Taking physical control for purposes other than sale

If B's security right arises under a lien, and B has no power of sale, B's only method of enforcing his security right is to keep physical control of A's thing until the secured duty is performed. In theory, B could adopt the same method to enforce security rights arising in other transactions. However, this is a very risky way of proceeding.[209] The problem for B is that, once he exercises his right to physical control of A's thing, B is (i) under a duty to take reasonable care of A's thing; and (ii) under a strict duty to account to A for the income that *should* be generated by that thing.[210] B thus faces a risk that a court will find that he could have done more to maximise the income produced by the thing.[211] So, if B wants to benefit from the income produced by the thing, he is best advised to appoint a receiver instead of taking physical control himself.

5.4   Foreclosure: terminating A's right to redeem

In a mortgage transaction, and *only* in that transaction, there is a dramatic means by which B can enforce his security right. It is known as 'foreclosure' and consists of the termination of A's right to redeem. It allows B to keep the mortgaged right (ie, the right transferred to him by A) free from any duty to return that right to A.[212] Foreclosure can thus give B a windfall.

EXAMPLE 1b

A has Ownership of a bike. In return for a loan of £200 from B, A transfers his Ownership of the bike to B and promises B that: (i) A will repay the loan at a 6 per cent annual rate of interest; and (ii) if A fails to repay the loan within six months, B can sell the bike and use the proceeds to meet A's debt. After six months, A still owes B £150. The market value of A's bike is £500.

If foreclosure occurs, B is free to sell the bike and keep the full £500. Such a result seems harsh on A: after all, the purpose of the mortgage is to secure A's duty to repay the loan and A only owes B a further £150. Further, foreclosure can harm other parties, who have a right in relation to A's Right to Redeem (eg, B2, a party to whom A mortgaged his Right to Redeem).[213] Thus, there are procedures in place to protect A and those whose rights depend on A.

First, foreclosure can occur only by means of a court order. If B applies for such an order, A and other interested parties must be informed. It is then possible to ask the court to use its power, under section 91 of the LPA 1925, to order a sale of the bike. In a case such as **Example 1b**, a sale is almost certain to be ordered: as it will occur whilst A's Right to

---

[209] It promotes the 'hostage function' of security rights: see Clarke and Kohler, *Property Law: Commentary and Materials* (2005), 18.1.2.4.

[210] Of course B is not expected to act contrary to his own interests or to take undue risks: but actions maximising the income from A's thing will generally be in the best interests of *both* A and B.

[211] See eg *White v City of London Brewery* (1889) 42 Ch D 237; *Silven Properties Ltd v Royal Bank of Scotland plc* [2004] 1 WLR 997 at 1004.

[212] See eg *Carter v Wake* (1877) LR 4 Ch D 605.

[213] A Right to Redeem, like any other persistent right, can be transferred to B2 by way of security. This may occur, for example, if B2 is unaware of the first mortgage and enters into a mortgage transaction believing he will receive A's Ownership of the bike.

Redeem is intact, A will receive £350 of the proceeds of sale.[214] Further, even if the court grants a provisional foreclosure order, that order will give A and others a further period in which to redeem. Indeed, even a final foreclosure order may be reversed.[215] As a result, foreclosure is, in practice, irrelevant:[216] B is much better advised to enforce his security right by means of a sale or the appointment of a receiver.

---

[214] See eg *Union Bank of London v Ingram* (1882) 20 Ch D 463.
[215] Foreclosure can thus be 'reopened': this can occur even after B has sold the mortgaged right: see eg *Campbell v Holyland* (1877) 7 Ch D 166.
[216] As noted by Beale *et al*, *The Law of Personal Property Security* (2007), 17.24.

CHAPTER G1A
OWNERSHIP: THE FREEHOLD

OWNERSHIP: THE FREEHOLD

From a purely technical perspective, it is true to say that no one has Ownership of land. Instead, if B has a right to exclusive control of land, he must have either: (i) a Freehold; or (ii) a Lease. This is made clear by section 1 of the Law of Property Act 1925 ('the LPA 1925'), which refers to the Freehold and Lease by their technical names: the 'fee simple absolute in possession' and the 'term of years'. However, contrary to some views,[1] this does *not* mean that Ownership is irrelevant in land law. On the contrary, we will see that the **content** of each of the Freehold and the Lease depends on the right at the heart of Ownership: a right to exclusive control of a thing.[2]

1 THE CONTENT QUESTION

1.1 Definition

B has a Freehold if he has:

- an immediate, unconditional right to exclusive control of land;
- forever.

The Freehold is thus no more and no less than Ownership of land (see **E1:1**). In the terminology of the LPA 1925 the Freehold is one of only two 'estates' in land.

1.2 A right to exclusive control

EXAMPLE 1

A1 has a Freehold. A1 occupies the house with A2, his wife. A1 is under a statutory duty not to remove A2 from the land (see **E6:5.1**). A1 has not protected her statutory right by entering a notice on the register. A1 purports to transfer his Freehold to B: a token sum is stated as the price and B is substantively registered as the new holder of A1's Freehold. B attempts to remove A2 from the land.

In such a case, due to section 58 of the Land Registration Act 2002 ('the LRA 2002'), B acquires a Freehold simply as a result of his substantive registration (see **C2:6.1**). Further, as A2's statutory right was not noted on the register, it cannot bind B—even if A2 was in

---

[1] See eg Hargreaves (1956) 19 *MLR* 14.

[2] This point is persuasively made by Harris: see eg *Property and Justice* (1996), 68–74. See too Pollock and Maitland, *History of English Law* (1911), vol ii, 2–6; *per* Lord Hoffmann in *Hunter v Canary Wharf* [1997] AC 655 at 703: 'Exclusive possession, de jure or de facto, now or in the future, is the bedrock of English land law.'

actual occupation of the land when B acquired his right.[3] However, in **Example 1**, A2 can apply for the register to be changed: she can argue that, in fact, A1 did *not* exercise his power to transfer his Freehold to B. A2's argument is that the purported transfer is a *sham*: A1 and B simply wish to create the impression that A1 has transferred his Freehold to B, whereas, in fact, A1 has retained his Freehold. A2's argument does not depend on a special doctrine that allows the transfer to B to be set aside.[4] Rather it consists of showing that, because A1 did not in fact intend B to have the rights that make up a Freehold, there has in fact been no transfer of A1's Freehold to B.

In *Ferris v Weaven*,[5] the essential facts of which were identical to **Example 1**,[6] A2's argument was accepted. Jones J held that, despite the documents signed by A1 and B, A1 had *not* exercised his power to transfer his Freehold to B. That conclusion was based on the fact that A1 never genuinely intended to transfer to B his right to exclusive control of the land. As B did not acquire that right to exclusive control, B did not acquire a Freehold. As a result, B had no right to remove A2 from the land.[7]

The mere fact that A1 transfers a Freehold to B with the *motive* of harming A2 does *not* make that transaction a 'sham': a transfer occurs as A1 and B do genuinely intend that B is to acquire a right to exclusive control of the land.[8] However, in *Ferris*, B did not acquire a Freehold as: 'although in outward show the ownership was vested in the purchaser, in substance and reality it was still vested in the husband'.[9] As Harris persuasively argued, to see if B genuinely acquired a Freehold, we need to decide if B was genuinely intended to acquire the right at the core of Ownership: the right to exclusive control of a thing.[10]

1.3   An unconditional right to exclusive control

The technical term for a Freehold, used by section 1 of the LPA 1925, is a 'fee simple absolute in possession'. 'Fee simple absolute' means that B has an *unconditional* right to exclusive control.

EXAMPLE 2

A0 has a Freehold. A0 (i) wants to leave his land to B on A0's death; but (ii) does not want B to get the land if, (a) within 10 years of A's death, B has not yet gained a university degree; *or* if (b) B has ceased to make an annual £1,000 contribution to Oxfam.

In his will, A0 might try to grant B a right to exclusive control of A0's land forever that (a) will arise only if B, within 10 years of A's death, has a university degree; and (b) will

---

[3] Family Law Act 1996, s 31(10)(b) (see **B:11.3**).

[4] In that sense, there is no special 'sham' doctrine: see McFarlane and Simpson, ch 8 in *Rationalizing Property, Equity and Trusts: Essays in Honour of Edward Burn* (ed Getzler, 2003). However, the notion of a 'sham' can be invoked to explain why, as a matter of *evidence*, a court can look beyond the written transfer in order to ascertain the intentions of A1 and B: see Conaglen [2008] *CLJ* 176 (see too **F3:2.1.1**).

[5] [1952] 2 All ER 233.

[6] No registration occurred in *Ferris*, so A2 did not have to ask for a change to the register. However, the principles should be the same: if the apparent transfer to B is a sham, then (i) B's registration must be a 'mistake'; and (ii) even if B has taken physical control of the land, it would be unjust for change not to be made (see LRA 2002, Sch 4, discussed in **E5:3.2**).

[7] See eg Lord Wilberforce's analysis of *Ferris* in *NPB v Ainsworth* [1965] AC 1175 at 1257.

[8] See eg *Midland Bank Trust Co v Green* [1981] AC 513 (see **C2:Example 5** and **E3:2.3.7**).

[9] *Per* Megarry V-C, analysing *Ferris* in the later case of *Miles v Bull* [1969] 1 QB 258.

[10] *Property and Justice* (1996), 68–74.

terminate if B fails to make the annual contribution to Oxfam. However, A0 has *no* power to give B such a right: a *conditional* right to exclusive control does *not* count as a property right in land.[11]

If A0 wants to give B such a conditional benefit, A0 must instead set up a Trust (see D2:1.4.3). So, in **Example 2**, A0 can leave his Freehold to A, subject to a duty to use that Freehold entirely for B's benefit, *if* (a) B, within 10 years of A's death, has a university degree and (b) *for so long as* B makes the charitable contribution.[12] In such a case, B does *not* acquire a property right in the land; instead he acquires a persistent right against A's Freehold.

1.4   An immediate right to exclusive control

The technical term for a Freehold, used by section 1 of the LPA 1925, is a 'fee simple absolute in possession'. 'In possession' simply means that B has an immediate right to exclusive control.

EXAMPLE 3

A0 has a Freehold. A0: (i) wants to raise some money by selling his land to B; but (ii) does not want to vacate that land immediately.

A0 might try to grant B a right to exclusive control of A0's land forever that will only take effect in two years' time. However, A0 has *no* power to give B such a right: a *future* right to exclusive control does *not* count as a property right in land.[13] If A0 wants to give B such a future benefit, A0 must instead set up a Trust (see E2:Example 2a).

1.5   A right to exclusive control forever

The key distinction between a Freehold and a Lease is that the former gives B a right to exclusive control *forever*. So, if B has a Freehold of land he is, in practice, in an identical position to a party with Ownership of a bike: he has an immediate, unconditional right to exclusive control of a specific thing that is unlimited in time.

SUMMARY of G1A:1

One of the special features of land is its permanence. A, an owner of land, may wish to divide up his right to exclusive control of that land in subtle and complicated ways. For as far back as we know, there has been a question as to how much freedom the land law system should give A.[14] The desire to limit A's powers has come from: (i) the need to protect C from the risk of being bound by a hidden, future property right of B; and (ii) the need to keep land marketable by preventing A imposing future limits on the use of land.

---

[11] The position was different before the LPA 1925. It was then possible for A to give B a 'future estate': a right to exclusive control of land taking effect at some point in the future, eg, on the death of a party with a 'life estate' (ie, a right to exclusive control of land for his life).

[12] When setting up a Trust, A0 must make sure the conditions imposed are sufficiently certain so that they can be enforced by a court: see eg *Clayton v Ramsden* [1943] AC 320.

[13] Again, the position was different before the LPA 1925.

[14] For a very brief historical summary, see Birks, ch 18 in *Land Law: Themes and Perspectives* (ed Bright and Dewar, 1998). For some of the complications produced by the pre-1926 law, see *Cheshire & Burn's Modern Law of Real Property* (ed Burn and Cartwright, 17th edn, 2006), chs 14–7.

So, here, as everywhere, the **basic tension** is apparent. The resolution provided by the LPA 1925 is simple and elegant. If A wants to give B a right to exclusive control of land that imposes a prima facie duty on the rest of the world, A has only two choices. First, he can transfer his Freehold to B, and thus give B an immediate, unconditional right to exclusive control of the land forever. Second, he can give B a Lease: a right to exclusive control of the land for a limited period. A cannot give B a property right consisting of a conditional or future right to exclusive control of land. If A wants to give B an immediate right entitling B to the conditional or future *benefit* of a right to exclusive control, A must use a Trust. In such a case, B does *not* have a property right; instead, he has a persistent right against the Freehold or Lease held on Trust for his benefit.

2 THE ACQUISITION QUESTION

2.1 Independent acquisition

2.1.1 General principles

B can independently acquire a thing by taking physical control of that thing (see D2:2.1). Exactly the same principle applies where land is concerned. Therefore, if B takes physical control of land, even if A has a pre-existing Freehold of that land, B independently acquires his own Freehold. That is the case whether B acts: (i) with A's consent or other authority;[15] or (ii) without A's consent or other authority.[16] As a result, the rest of the world is under a prima facie duty to B not to interfere with B's right to exclusive control of that land. However, if he takes physical control of A's land without A's consent, B of course commits a wrong against A. Unless and until B has a defence against A's pre-existing Freehold, B is under a duty to A not to interfere with A's prior right to exclusive control of the land.

It is important to note that, if he takes physical control of land, B *immediately* acquires a Freehold. The adverse possession rules (see A:3.1.5 and B:8.3.1(iii)) mean that, in some circumstances, the lapse of time may give B a **defence** to A's pre-existing Freehold (see **section 3** below). However, B acquires his property right *as soon as* he takes physical control of the land: it is at that point that the rest of the world comes under a prima facie duty to B.

EXAMPLE 4a

A has a Freehold. A sets off on a year-long holiday and leaves his land unoccupied. Two months later, B, acting without A's consent or other authority, moves into A's house and changes the locks. B then goes away for a week. During that week, C (who also acts without A's consent or other authority) moves into the house and changes the locks.

In such a case, each of B and C commits a wrong against A: each of them has breached his duty not to interfere with A's right to exclusive control of the land. And C also commits a wrong against B: he has breached his duty not to interfere with B's right to exclusive control

---

[15] See eg *National Provincial Bank v Ainsworth* [1965] AC 1175 esp *per* Lord Upjohn at 1232.
[16] See eg *Asher v Whitlock* [1865] 1 QB 1.

of the land.[17] The general principles we examined in **D1:1.4.1** (see **D1:Example 3**) thus apply in *exactly the same way* in the land law system.

2.1.2 The special features of land

The special features of land do *not* mean that special principles apply to the independent acquisition of a Freehold. However, they do mean that, in practice, special considerations may affect the *application* of the general principles. In particular, the special features of land mean that it may be more difficult for B to show he has physical control. First, due to its fixed location, a piece of land, unlike a bike, cannot simply be picked up and taken away by B. So, to establish physical control of land, B may need to (for example): (i) put up a fence around that land; or (ii) put up, and then, enforce a notice keeping others off the land.[18] However, it is impossible to state a more precise test: the acts necessary to establish physical control vary according to the nature of the land in question.[19] In practice, it may be useful to ask whether B used the land as a Freehold owner might use it.[20]

Second, due to its capacity for multiple simultaneous use, it may be possible for B to make use of land *without* taking physical control of it. For example, if B: (i) grazes a cow on some land; and (ii) cuts and takes hay from that land; then (iii) those acts may *not* amount to physical control. Instead of using the land as a Freehold owner might, B has simply made a particular, limited use of the land.[21]

To independently acquire a property right in any thing, B needs to show he has *exclusive* physical control of that thing. This general principle has an important consequence where land is concerned. It means that if B simply *shares* occupation of land with A, then it is impossible for *either* A and B, acting individually, to have physical control of the land. At any one time, there can only be one party with physical control of a thing.[22] If A and B are acting as a team, so that they *jointly* have physical control of the land, then the team of A and B can be the one party with physical control. In such a case, A and B *jointly* acquire a property right: they will co-hold a Freehold as joint tenants (see **G2:2.1**).

EXAMPLE 4b

A has a Freehold. B shares occupation of the land with A. A then moves out but B, with A's consent, remains in occupation of the land.

When B shares occupation with A, B does not have physical control of the land and so does not have an independently acquired property right. So, when A and B occupy together, if C

---

[17] See eg *Asher v Whitlock* [1865] 1 QB 1; *per* Lord Hoffmann in *Hunter v Canary Wharf* [1997] AC 655 at 703.

[18] See *per* Slade J in *Powell v McFarlane* (1977) 38 P & CR 452 at 477.

[19] See *per* Slade J, *ibid* at 470–71: a passage approved by Lord Browne-Wilkinson in *JA Pye (Oxford) Ltd v Graham* [2003] 1 AC 419 at [41].

[20] See eg *per* Lord Macnaghten in *Perry v Clissold* [1907] AC 73 at 79: 'It cannot be disputed that a person in possession of land in the assumed character of owner and exercising peaceably the ordinary rights of ownership has a perfectly good title against all the world but the rightful owner.' See too *Allen v Roughley* [1955] 94 CLR 98. Note too *JA Pye (Oxford) Ltd v Graham* [2003] 1 AC 419 at [19] and [75].

[21] See *Powell v McFarlane* (1977) 38 P & CR 452.

[22] See eg *per* Lord Hope in *JA Pye (Oxford) Ltd v Graham* [2003] 1 AC 419 at [70]: 'The general rule, which English law has derived from Roman law, is that only one person can be in possession at any one time. Exclusivity is the essence of possession.' There is no need to derive this rule from Roman law: it comes instead from the fact that it is impossible to say that two people can each, separately, have physical control of the same thing at the same time.

were to: (i) come onto the land without the permission of A or other authority; or if (ii) C's neighbouring pig farm were to produce nauseating smells, then (iii) C would commit a wrong against A, but not against B. For example, in *Hunter v Canary Wharf*,[23] the House of Lords held that: (i) if B shares occupation of land with A and B simply has a liberty to occupy that land (a licence: see **E6:1**); then (ii) C cannot commit the wrong of nuisance against B. As Lord Hoffmann explained, the key point is that B has no property right as he does not have 'exclusive possession' (ie, physical control) of the land.[24]

However, when A moves out, B *does* have physical control of the land: at that point, even if he occupies with A's permission, B can independently acquire a Freehold. So if C were *then* to: (i) come onto the land without the permission of A or B or other authority; or if (ii) C's neighbouring pig farm were *then* to produce nauseating smells; (iii) C would commit a wrong against *both* A (who still has his initial Freehold) *and* B (who now has his own, independent Freehold). For example, in *National Provincial Bank Ltd v Ainsworth*, Lord Upjohn considered a case identical to **Example 4b** and stated that:

> in truth and in fact [B] at all material times was and is in exclusive occupation of the home. Until [A] returns she has the dominion over the house and she could clearly bring proceedings against trespassers.[25]

2.1.3 The impact of the Land Registration Act 2002?

On the face of it, the independent acquisition of a Freehold may seem to conflict with registered land principles. For example, the Law Commission—in the Report (Law Com No 271) that led to the LRA 2002—took the view that we should aim for a system in which registration is the *only* means by which B can acquire a Freehold. The Law Commission's expressed aim was for a system in which 'it will be the fact of registration, and registration alone, that confers title'.[26] On that view, B's physical control of land, by itself, cannot give B a Freehold.

However, no provision in the LRA 2002 explicitly changes the general position set out above. The Law Commission stated that the reforms it proposed 'abandon[s] the notion that a squatter acquires title once he or she has been in adverse possession for twelve years'. Certainly, the LRA 2002 means that B no longer has an automatic defence against A's pre-existing property right if B has adversely possessed A's land for 12 years (see **section 3** below). However, that Act does *nothing* to change the fundamental principle that, *as soon as* he takes physical control of land, B acquires a Freehold of that land. So for this reason as well as others (see eg **E5:3.2**), the LRA 2002 has *not* implemented the Law Commission's ambition to have a system of 'title by registration' in which registration is the only means by which B can acquire a Freehold.

It is also important to remember that, under the LRA 2002, it is not land itself that is substantively registered; rather it is property rights in land. A's registration as a Freehold

---

[23] [1997] AC 655.

[24] *Ibid* at 703. Lord Hoffmann at 708 also made the *obiter* suggestion that if B has a right under a Trust of A's Freehold or Lease of the land, C can then commit the wrong of nuisance against B. However, there is no authority for that proposition and it seems to be incorrect: crucially, a persistent right under a Trust does not impose a prima facie duty on the rest of the world (see **B:4.4.3**).

[25] [1965] AC 1175 at 1232. See too *per* Lord Hoffmann in *Hunter v Canary Wharf* [1997] AC 655 at 703.

[26] Law Com No 271 at 1.10.

owner does *not* prevent B acquiring a separate, unregistered Freehold of that same land. After all, it is possible for each of A and B to each have separate Ownership of a thing other than land (see **D1:1.4.1**); that same principle of 'relativity of title' can also apply in the registered land system.

In any case, despite the rhetoric in Law Com No 271, it is no surprise that the LRA 2002 did not alter the principle that B independently acquires a Freehold as soon as he takes physical control of land. That principle gives B protection against a third party (eg, C in **Example 4a**) who later interferes with B's use of the land. However, it does nothing to undermine the chief goal of the LRA 2002: to provide greater protection to a party with a registered right. So, in **Example 4a**, A can clearly remove B from the land: *A's* position is not affected by B's independent acquisition of a Freehold. Moreover, if A were to transfer his registered Freehold to A2, A2 could also remove B from the land. The security given to a registered Freehold owner is *not* undermined by the ability of B to independently acquire a Freehold.

2.2 Dependent acquisition

If A has a Freehold, he has a power to transfer that right to B. Such a transfer can occur only if the parties satisfy the formality rules imposed by: (i) section 52 of the LPA 1925; and (ii) section 27 of the LRA 2002 (see **E1:2.3**). It is worth noting that limits can be placed on A's power to transfer a Freehold to B (eg, if A holds his Freehold on Trust, the terms of the Trust may impose limits on that power). If such a limit is noted on the register, through the entry of a *restriction*, then B should only be registered as the new holder of A's Freehold if that limit is observed.[27]

3 THE DEFENCES QUESTION

If B has a pre-existing property right in land, it is very difficult for C to have a defence against that right (see **E1:3**). This is certainly the case if B has a Freehold. If B independently acquires a Freehold, it is important to note that B may acquire a defence against A's pre-existing Freehold. If A's Freehold is unregistered, the Limitation Act 1980[28] can give B a defence if A's land has been adversely possessed for 12 years.[29] However, the position is different where A has a registered Freehold: (i) the lapse of time *alone* can never give B a

---

[27] See LRA 2002, ss 40–44. See too **E2:3.4.2(i)**.

[28] See s 15. Under s 17, if the limitation period has run, A's pre-existing property right ceases to exist. This prevents A from asserting a pre-existing property right against a party later acquiring a right in B's land. The compatability of these provisions with the Human Rights Act 1998 was considered in **B:8.3.1**.

[29] See eg *JA Pye (Oxford) Ltd v Graham* [2003] 1 AC 419. B himself does not need to have been in physical control of the land for the full 12 years: for example, if B1 has been in adverse possession for six years and then transfers his Freehold to B2, who remains in possession for a further six years, A cannot remove B2: see eg *Mount Carmel Investments Ltd v Peter Thurlow Ltd* [1988] 1 WLR 1078. The 12-year period runs only if A has a right to remove the adverse possessor. So if A gives A1 a 21-year Lease, and B adversely possesses the land for 12 years during that Lease, the limitation clock can run against A1 (and thus give B a defence to A1's pre-existing Lease); but it cannot run against A (see eg *Fairweather v St Marleybone Property Co Ltd* [1963] AC 510). The point is that, during the Lease, A does not have a right to remove B from the land.

defence;[30] (ii) but if B has adversely possessed A's land for 10 years, B can apply to be registered as the new holder of A's Freehold (see **E5:3.2.5**).[31]

The concept of 'adverse possession' is thus crucial when asking if B has a defence to A's pre-existing Freehold. In considering it, we need to distinguish between two questions:

1. Has B taken physical control of the land, and thus independently acquired a Freehold? (see **2.1** above).
2. Has B *adversely possessed* the land so that the lapse of time allows B to gain a defence to A's pre-existing property right?

The two questions must be distinguished as it is clear that B can be in physical control of land *without* adversely possessing it. So, in **Example 4b**, B is in physical control and thus has a Freehold. However, as B is in control of the land with A's consent, B is *not* adversely possessing the land:[32] so even if B remains in occupation for a further 10 years, B cannot apply for the register to be changed under Schedule 6 of the LRA 2002. Further, it is clear that adverse possession consists of *both*: (i) B's physical control of the land (often referred to as 'factual possession'); *and* (ii) B's intention, as evidenced from his conduct, to assert a right to exclusive control of that land (often referred to as 'intention to possess' or 'animus possidendi').[33] Therefore, the 10-year period under Schedule 6 of the LRA 2002 cannot begin to run unless *both*: (i) and (ii) are present. Yet there seems to be no reason why, if *only* (i) is present, B should not independently acquire a Freehold: B should acquire such a right *whenever* he has physical control of land.[34]

4   THE REMEDIES QUESTION

4.1 Preface: the protection of B's Freehold

4.1.1 General position

A Freehold of land, like Ownership of a bike, is protected through the law of wrongs (see **E1:4.1**). These wrongs recognise B's basic negative duty not to interfere with B's right to exclusive control of land.

---

[30] See LRA 2002, s 96 (ensuring that the provisions of the Limitation Act 1980, ss 15 and 17 no longer apply where A has a registered Freehold or Lease).

[31] LRA 2002, Sch 6, para 1(1). 'Adverse possession' as used in the 2002 Act has the same meaning as applied to the 1980 Act: see LRA 2002, Sch 6, para 11(1).

[32] See eg *per* Slade J in *Powell v McFarlane* (1977) 38 P & CR 452 at 469: 'time can never run in favour of [B if B] occupies or uses land by licence of [A] and [that] licence has not been duly determined, because no right of action to recover the land has ever accrued against [B]; consequently [B] has no 'adverse possession' however long his occupation or use may have lasted.'

[33] See eg *JA Pye (Oxford) Ltd v Graham* [2003] 1 AC 419.

[34] See **D1:2.1**, **text at nn 89–96**, arguing that 'intention to possess' is *not* required in order for B to independently acquire a property right.

Wrong	Duty breached by A	Example
Trespass	Not to directly interfere with B's exclusive control of land	C comes onto B's land without B's consent or other authority
Negligence	Not to carelessly damage B's land	C carelessly starts a fire that destroys B's house
Nuisance	Not to unreasonably[35] interfere with B's use and enjoyment of his land	C runs a pig farm next to B's land that produces nauseating smells[36]

4.1.2 Positive duties of C

EXAMPLE 5

B and C are neighbours; each has a Freehold. Lightning strikes a tree on C's land and a fire starts. C could easily put out the fire, but fails to do so. The fire spreads and causes damage to B's land.

In such a case, if: (i) X, a passer-by, saw the fire and could easily have put it out; then (ii) X does *not* commit a wrong against B if he fails to take any action. Although B has a Freehold, the rest of the world is not under a general *positive* duty to take steps to protect B's land. However, in *Goldman v Hargrave*,[37] the essential facts of which are identical to **Example 5**, the Privy Council recognised that C has a special *positive* duty, arising from the fact that he is B's neighbour.[38] The content of this duty is limited: C does not have to take any objectively reasonable steps to protect B's land. Instead, C only needs to do the *best he can*, given his skills and resources.[39] If C breaches that duty, he commits the wrong of nuisance.[40]

It is very unusual for C to be under such a positive duty to B. However, it may be justified on grounds of mutuality: if C (or an occupier of C's land) is under such a duty to B, then C also has the benefit of B (or an occupier of B's land) being under the same duty to C.[41] Further, one of the special features of land is its fixed location: this means B is to some extent dependent on the conduct of his neighbours.

---

[35] 'Unreasonably' here does not mean that C has failed to take reasonable care. Rather, it means that C's activity is unreasonable. For example, if the alleged nuisance consists of C making a particular use of C's land, the reasonableness of that use will depend on factors such as the location and nature of C's land: an activity that is reasonable in an industrial estate may not be reasonable in a residential area (see eg *per* Byles J (during argument) in *Hole v Barlow* (1858) 4 CB NS 334 at 340; *per* Lord Westbury LC in *St Helen's Smelting Co v Tipping* (1865) 11 HL Cas 642 at 650–51).

[36] *Bone v Seale* [1975] 1 WLR 797.

[37] [1967] 1 AC 645.

[38] See too *Leakey v National Trust* [1980] QB 485 and *Holbeck Hall Hotel Ltd v Scarborough Borough Council* [2000] QB 836 confirming that the duty applies to a *natural* cause of danger arising from the condition of C's land (the duty was not breached in *Holbeck Hall*).

[39] *Per* Lord Wilberforce in *Goldman* at 663: 'the standard ought to be to require of [C] what it is reasonable to expect of him in his individual circumstances'. The duty is thus different from the general *objective* duty to take reasonable care *not* to harm another: see eg *Nettleship v Weston* [1971] 2 QB 691.

[40] In *Goldman* itself, B successfully argued that C had committed the wrong of *negligence*; but later claims (eg *Leakey v National Trust* [1980] QB 485 and *Holbeck Hall Hotel Ltd v Scarborough Borough Council* [2000] QB 836) have made use of the wrong of nuisance. It should not matter which form is used; nuisance may be more accurate as B's claim depends on B having a property right in land.

[41] Alternatively, C's duty may be seen as a burden imposed as a corollary of his Freehold: see eg Stevens, *Torts and Rights* (2007), 15–6.

4.1.3 Further rights of B

B's dependency on his neighbours is recognised in other ways. For example, if B's land is physically supported by C's land, C is under a duty to B not to interfere with that support. C's duty arises simply from the location of his land: it is thus said to depend on a 'natural right' of B. Again, the duty is very limited: C is *not* under a duty not to withdraw support from any *buildings* on B's land: his duty only relates to support of B's *land*.[42] Further, B also has a 'natural right' to receive water flowing across C's land to B's land[43] *if* it flows in a defined channel.[44] If C interferes with either of these natural rights, C commits the wrong of nuisance.

4.2 Specific protection

The general principles set out in **E1:4.2** apply where B has a Freehold: in general, his right will be specifically protected.[45] Certainly, B's core right to have physical control of the land will almost always be specifically protected. In particular, if a third party is in physical control of B's land, B will be able to use the speedy possession procedure made available by Part 55 of the Civil Procedure Rules.

However, where B instead seeks to enforce one of the duties imposed on his neighbours (eg, C's duty, recognised by the law of nuisance, not to unreasonably interfere with B's use and enjoyment of B's land), there may be some cases in which B has to settle for money. For example, a court can decline to grant an injunction ordering C to comply with a duty if: (i) such an injunction would be oppressive to C; and (ii) the loss suffered by B can be properly compensated by a small award of damages.[46] In rare cases, the wider public interest may also be used as a reason to refuse an injunction, even where C's continued conduct causes a significant loss to B. In such a case, due to the continuing interference with B's right, C will be ordered to pay a substantial sum of money to B.[47]

In some cases, potential hardship to C is taken into account by suspending the introduction of an injunction. For example, if C is committing the wrong of nuisance by running a commercial activity on his land, a suspension can give C time to reorganise that activity so as to avoid interfering with B's Freehold.[48] Hardship can be a key issue in the rare case

---

[42] Further, it is a duty not to remove the support given by C's *land* to B's land: so C does not commit a wrong if he removes water that supports B's land: see *Popplewell v Hodkinson* (1869) LR 4 Ex Ch 248; *Stephens v Anglian Water Authority* [1987] 1 WLR 1381.

[43] Subject to C's liberty to make an ordinary and reasonable use of that water when it flows through C's land: see *per* Lord Macnaghten in *John Young & Co v The Bankier Distillery Co* [1893] AC 691 at 698.

[44] See eg *Swindon Waterworks Co Ltd v Wilts & Berks Canal Navigation Co* (1875) LR 7 HL 697. B does *not* have a natural right to water that does *not* flow in a definite channel: C has a liberty to take such water for his own use. Even if C acts maliciously in doing so, he commits no wrong against B: *Bradford Corpn v Pickles* [1895] AC 587.

[45] See eg *per* Lord Evershed MR in *Pride of Derby v Celanese* [1953] Ch 149 at 181: 'It is, I think, well settled that if A proves that his proprietary rights are being wrongfully interfered with by B, and that B intends to continue his wrong, then A is prima facie entitled to an injunction, and he will be deprived of that remedy only if special circumstances exist, including the circumstance that damages are an adequate remedy for the wrong that he has suffered.'

[46] See eg *Shelfer v City of London Electric Lighting Co* [1895] 1 Ch 287.

[47] See eg *Dennis v Ministry of Defence* [2003] EWHC 793: the court refused to make a declaration (an order that would have had the same effect as an injunction) that the Royal Air Force [C] could not fly jets in such a way as to interfere with the B's enjoyment of his land. This meant C could continue to commit the wrong of nuisance. However, B did receive damages of £950,000 to compensate him for loss both caused and to be caused by the flying (on the basis that the RAF would in any case stop the flights in 2012).

[48] See eg *Pride of Derby v British Celanese* [1953] Ch 149 esp at 181–2.

where B is seeking an injunction to force C to take *positive steps*.[49] For example, *Redland Bricks v Morris*[50] concerned B's 'natural right' to have his land supported by C's land. C's land had slipped, causing damage to B's land. C was ordered to pay B money as compensation for that damage; but B also wanted the court to compel C to reinforce C's land: it was very likely that, if C did not do so, further slippages would occur. The House of Lords held that such an injunction would *not* be appropriate. An important factor seems to have been that the cost to C of carrying out such work (£30,000–35,000) would impose a disproportionate hardship on C: the part of B's land at risk from further slippages was valued at just £1,500–1,600.[51] As a result, B's right to support was not specifically protected: B instead had to wait and claim compensation for any further loss he might suffer as a result of future slippages.[52]

4.3 Money awards

If C has *already* interfered with B's Freehold, it may be too late to specifically protect B's right. In such a case, B must settle for receiving money from C. Any money payable by C will serve as: (i) a substitute for the right C has interfered with; and (ii) compensation for any relevant consequential loss suffered by B (see D1:4.3). For example, if C commits the wrong of nuisance by running a pig farm producing nauseating smells, then B can recover money even if C's wrong has not caused any consequential loss to B (eg, because B cannot show that C's action reduced the price B could have asked for if selling his Freehold). The point is that: 'the value of the right to occupy a house which smells of pigs must be less than the value of the occupation of an equivalent house which does not'.[53] It thus seems that, in such a case, B can receive money as a substitute for the right C has interfered with: the right, as part of B's Freehold, to live in a house that does not smell of pigs.[54] In D1:4.3.3 and E1:4.3, we examined a number of cases where: (i) C wrongfully interferes with B's Freehold; and (ii) on one view, C is ordered to pay B money based on the gain C has made through his wrong.[55] However, it was argued there that many of those decisions can instead be explained as based on the need for C to pay B money based on the value of B's right.

---

[49] In most cases, of course, B will simply be seeking an order to stop the defendant from acting in a particular way.

[50] [1970] AC 652.

[51] See eg *per* Lord Upjohn at 667, referring to the 'unreasonable' cost to the defendant of reinforcing his land.

[52] One possibility for B, in a case such as *Redland Bricks v Morris*, is to offer to pay a third party to carry out the necessary works on A's land; or to carry out such works himself. The problem is that A may simply refuse to allow anyone on to his land to do the work. However, B can then turn to the Access to Neighbouring Land Act 1992. That Act allows a court to make an 'access order' to B where he wants to enter neighbouring land to 'carry out works'. If B can show the work is 'reasonably necessary for the preservation' of all or part of his land, and the work would be 'substantially more difficult to carry out' without a right to go on to A's land, the court will make an access order. However, no order can be made if it would be unreasonable to do so, given the interference, disturbance or hardship the order might cause to A.

[53] *Per* Lord Hoffmann in *Hunter v Canary Wharf Ltd* [1997] AC 665 at 706.

[54] Lord Hoffmann characterises such money as *compensation*; but it is perhaps better seen as a substitute for the value of B's right: see Stevens, *Torts and Rights* (2007), 63.

[55] See eg *Bracewell v Appleby* [1975] Ch 408; *Ministry of Defence v Ashman* (1993) 66 P & CR 195.

CHAPTER G1B
OWNERSHIP: THE LEASE

OWNERSHIP: THE LEASE

1 THE CONTENT QUESTION

1.1 Definition

B has a Lease if he has:

- a right to exclusive control of land;
- for a limited period.

A Lease thus consists of Ownership of land *for a limited period*. In the terminology of the Law of Property Act 1925 (the LPA 1925) the Lease is one of only two 'estates' in land. The Freehold and the Lease are the *only* two rights that give B exclusive control of land.

So, if A has a Freehold and makes a binding promise to B1 to allow B1 exclusive control of the land for the next 21 years, B1 acquires a Lease. If B1 then makes a binding promise to B2 to allow B2 exclusive control of the land for the next five years, B2 also acquires a Lease. B2, if he wishes, can then transfer his five-year Lease to B3.[1]

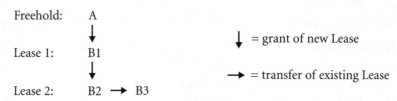

In such a case, A and B1 are in a *landlord–tenant* relationship: A is the landlord and B1 is the tenant. B1 and B2 were also in such a relationship: as the result of B2's transfer of the Lease, B3 has now stepped into the shoes of B2. So, there is now a landlord–tenant relationship between: (i) A and B1; and (ii) B1 and B3.

1.2 The distinction between a Lease and a licence

EXAMPLE 1

A has a Freehold. A makes a contractual promise to allow B to occupy A's land for six months. Three months later, A transfers his Freehold to C.

---

[1] B2's transfer of the Lease to B3 may be a breach of a duty imposed on B2 by his agreement with B1. If so, B3 still acquires B2's Lease (*Old Grovebury Manor Farm Ltd v W Seymour Plant Sales and Hire Ltd (No 2)* [1979] 1 WLR 1397); but B2's breach may have serious consequences for B3: see **2.2.2(ii)** below.

If the contractual agreement gives B a right to exclusive control of A's land for six months, B has a Lease. If it does not give B such a right, he has a contractual licence: B has a liberty to make use of A's land and A is under a contractual duty to B not to revoke that liberty (see E6:1).

The distinction between a Lease and a licence is fundamental. A licence, even a contractual licence, does *not* count as a property right or a persistent right (see E6:3.4.2). In **Example 1**, if B's agreement with A gives him a licence, B will thus have no pre-existing right that he can assert against C. However, if that agreement gives him a right to exclusive control of A's land, B will have a Lease: a pre-existing property right that imposes a prima facie duty on C. In fact, if B has a Lease, the rest of the world is under a prima facie duty not to interfere with B's use of the land. For example, if X runs a nearby pig farm that produces nauseating smells, X commits the wrong of nuisance against B (see **G1A:4.1.1**).[2]

Even if no third parties are involved, there are still advantages to B in having a Lease rather than a licence.

1. Particular statutes may give B certain rights against A if, but only if, B has a Lease.[3]
2. Judges have developed basic duties of A (and also of B) that are implied by law into all Leases, whether the parties expressly agreed to those duties or not.

The second point is of less importance than the first. English judges have been cautious in implying duties into Leases and so the implied duties of A and B are very limited.[4] B has a duty not to alter permanently the physical character of the land;[5] A has a duty not to interfere with B's expected use of the land and not to allow a substantial interference with B's physical control of the land.[6] In fact, it may even be possible to argue that these duties are not dependent on B having a Lease: similar duties could be implied into a contractual licence allowing B to occupy land as a home.

The first point can be important in practice. For example, section 11 of the Landlord and Tenant Act 1985 applies where A grants B a Lease, for less than seven years, of a home.[7] It imposes certain basic duties on A to keep the house in a reasonable condition: for example, where repairs to the structure and exterior of the house are necessary, A must pay for those repairs. A cannot avoid this duty by simply specifying in the agreement that he is not liable for repairs: the duty is mandatory and A has to get the permission of a court to contract out of it. In contrast, if A gives B a contractual licence of a house, no such duties are implied: A is free to stipulate that he has no duty to repair the house B occupies.

In the past, the first point was of even greater practical relevance. Under now-repealed

---

[2] In contrast, if B has *only* a licence (eg, as where B shares occupation of land with A), X is under no such duty to B and thus cannot commit the wrong of nuisance against B: see *Hunter v Canary Wharf* [1997] AC 655.

[3] The exact nature of the right B needs to acquire statutory protection, as well as the term used to describe that right, varies from statute to statute. For example, s 11 of the Landlord and Tenant Act 1985 applies only to 'leases'; the Rent Act 1977 applies to 'tenancies' but that was taken to require that B has a Lease. As we will see below, the term 'lease', when used in the context of a statute, may have a different meaning to the usual meaning of 'Lease' as a property right.

[4] Judges in other jurisdictions have displayed less reluctance: see eg *Javins v First National Realty* (1970) 428 F 2d 1071 (District of Columbia Court of Appeals). For a comparison between the English and US approaches see Bright, *Landlord and Tenant Law in Context* (2007) 30–5.

[5] See eg *Marsden v Edward Heyes* [1927] 2 KB 1, applying *Horsefall v Mather* (1815) Holt NP 7.

[6] See eg *Markham v Paget* [1908] 1 Ch 697.

[7] The term used in the Act is a 'dwelling-house'.

legislation, such as the Rent Acts,[8] a good deal of statutory protection was available to B *if* he had a Lease. For example, B had the right, subject to certain conditions, to remain in occupation of his home even *after* the end of the period agreed with A. This 'security of tenure' ensured that B's right to exclusive control of the land endured even if A wished to use the land for a different purpose. B could also argue that the rent agreed with A was unfairly high and should be changed: these 'rent control' provisions also gave B valuable security.

The degree of statutory protection available to B varied with changes of government: on one view, securing B's occupation is vital to protecting the vulnerable; on another view, statutory intervention is an unwarranted interference with A's freedom to enter into private agreements relating to his own land. Current legislation generally reflects the view that if A gives B a Lease, the parties' agreement will determine both: (i) the length of B's occupation; and (ii) the rent payable by B. In general, then, B receives little statutory protection. For example, if A gives B a standard residential Lease, the default position is that B acquires an 'assured shorthold tenancy'.[9] When the initially agreed period ends, A can remove B from the land as long as: (i) A gives B at least 2 months' notice; and (ii) at least 6 months have passed since the grant of the Lease.[10] And A is free to set whatever rent he chooses.[11] However, in other cases, B can acquire some statutory protection:

1. Significant protection is still given to B where he has a Lease of a home and A is a *social landlord* such as, in particular, a local authority.[12] For example, A's power to terminate the Lease, even at the end of the initially agreed period, is limited. In those cases, it seems, less value is attached to A's freedom to use its land as it wishes.

2. If B has a Lease of a home and A, a private landlord, has *chosen* to give B an *assured tenancy*, B receives some important statutory protection. For example, A's power to terminate the Lease, even at the end of the initially agreed period, is limited. However, B acquires such protection only if A decides to give B such an assured tenancy.[13]

3. If B has a Lease of *business premises*, statute may limit A's ability to end the Lease. In particular, B may have a statutory right to continue using the land at the end of the

---

[8] Ie, the Rent Act 1977 and its predecessors. Some Leases, entered into before 15 January 1989, are still governed by the Rent Acts. These are known as 'regulated tenancies' but now represent only a very small proportion of private rented accommodation: see Bright, *Landlord and Tenant Law in Context* (2007) 203.

[9] Housing Act 1988, s 19A.

[10] The Law Commission's latest proposals on the protection of residential occupiers do not change that basic position. Those proposals include the sensible suggestion that the limited statutory protection available to B against A should be the same whether B has a Lease or a contractual licence: see Law Commission Report No 297 (2006) eg 1.5.

[11] The Unfair Terms in Consumer Contract Regulations 1999 can apply where B, a consumer, acquires a Lease from A. For detail of the impact of those terms on Leases see the Office of Fair Trading's *Guidance on Unfair Terms in Tenancy Agreements* (OFT 356, 2005). However the Regulations do not apply to 'core terms' (such as rent) provided such terms are set out by A in plain and intelligible language.

[12] The protection available to B takes two forms, First, where A is a local authority (or one of the other bodies falling under s 80(1) of the Housing Act 1985), B may have a 'secure tenancy' under the Housing Act 1985. Second, where A is a registered housing association, A will be encouraged to give B an 'assured tenancy' under the Housing Act 1988: such a tenancy, in practice, gives B similar protection to that provided by a secure tenancy.

[13] Prior to 1997, the default position was that B had an 'assured tenancy'. So if A did not choose to give B an 'assured shorthold tenancy' B could acquire statutory protection: as claimed, eg, in *Gray v Taylor* [1998] 1 WLR 1093 (see Example 9b below).

agreed period.[14] In those cases, it seems, more value is attached to B's need to continue using A's land.

4. If B has a *very long residential Lease*, he may have a statutory right to buy A's Freehold. In those cases, it seems that the long connection B may have with the land, and the improvements he may have made to it, justify B having the chance to make his right to exclusive control permanent (see **B:8.3.1**).[15]

5. If B has as an *agricultural business Lease*, he may have some statutory protection if: (i) he has made improvements to the land; provided that (ii) A give written consent to those improvements.[16] This limited protection is justified by the need to give B an incentive to make improvements that may increase the productivity of the land.

1.3 Doctrine v practical convenience

In the past, the Rent Acts gave an occupier of a home a strong incentive to claim a Lease. Equally, they meant that A was often very keen to avoid granting B a Lease. This led to a sharp battle between the parties and to a dilemma for the courts. For example, if a court felt that: (i) B's rights did, strictly speaking, amount to a Lease; but (ii) on the facts, B did not deserve to have all the protection of the Rent Acts; then (iii) it would be tempting for the court to *restrict* the true definition of a Lease and find that B had only a licence.[17] For example, from the 1950s to the 1980s, the Court of Appeal, led by Lord Denning, adopted a deliberately narrow definition of a Lease precisely because of this desire to limit the impact of the Rent Acts (see **E6:3.4.2(iii)**).[18] The converse was also true: if B's case seemed deserving, a court might be tempted to *expand* the true definition of a Lease in order to protect B.[19]

There may thus be an important tension between: (i) the demands of *doctrine*; and (ii) the perceived needs of *practical convenience* (see **B:9**).[20] The doctrinal definition of a Lease provided by the land law system may clash with what a judge perceives as the practically convenient result. We need to be aware of this tension when looking at decisions about the content of a Lease. We must always be alert to the possibility that a judge's view as to whether B's rights amounted to a Lease may have been guided by the desirability or otherwise of allowing B to rely on a particular statute; and *not* by a desire to reach the doctrinally correct conclusion.

---

[14] Landlord and Tenant Act 1954, Part II. See *per* Lord Nicholls in *Graysim Ltd v P & O Property Holdings Ltd* [1996] AC 329 at 334.

[15] The exercise of such a right is known as 'enfranchisement': see eg Leasehold Reform Act 1967. In addition, if B has a Lease of any length from a local authority, he may have a 'right to buy' his landlord's Freehold under the Housing Act 1985.

[16] B acquires this protection if he has a 'farm business tenancy' under the Agricultural Tenancies Act 1995. Agricultural Leases entered into before 1 September 1995 are regulated instead by the Agricultural Holdings Act 1986: if B has an 'agricultural holding' under that Act or its predecessors he has, in very general terms, a right to continue in occupation as long as he farms the land properly. Many of these agricultural holdings, which can pass to B's successor, remain in force today: see Bright, *Landlord and Tenant Law in Context* (2007) 264.

[17] See eg *Marchant v Charters* [1977] 1 WLR 1181.

[18] As explained by Lord Denning MR in *Cobb v Lane* [1952] 1 TLR 1037.

[19] The decision of the House of Lords in *Bruton v London & Quadrant Housing Trust* [2000] 1 AC 406 provides a modern example (see **1.5.3** below).

[20] For a general theoretical discussion of the clash between doctrine and practical convenience in property law (from which the terms as used here are derived), see Harris in *Oxford Essays on Jurisprudence* (3rd series, 1987, eds, Eekelaar and Bell).

1.4   A right to exclusive control: general position

1.4.1   Doctrine

The doctrinal test for a Lease depends on whether B has a right to exclusive control of land for a limited period. The current test for a Lease is based on that doctrinal position. In a case such as **Example 1**, the courts test for a Lease by asking if B has a right to *exclusive possession* of the land. That term is synonymous with a *right to exclusive control*. As Lord Templeman put it in the leading case of *Street v Mountford*,[21] if B has exclusive possession he has 'the rights of an owner of land, which is in the real sense his land albeit temporarily and subject to certain restrictions'.[22]

For example, if B's agreement with A gives A the power to: (i) allow other people into occupation of the land; or (ii) move B into different accommodation,[23] B clearly does *not* have a Lease: he does not have a right to exclusive control. And if the agreement merely permits B to use the land for a specific, limited purpose, B clearly does *not* have a Lease: he does not have a right to exclusive control.[24]

In theory, it should be relatively easy to see if the agreement gives B a right to exclusive control. As Lord Templeman suggested in *Street v Mountford*, we need to ask 'who is the owner for the time being?': during the period of the agreement, is Ownership vested in A or in B? Where A does grant B a Lease, A transfers his right to exclusive control to B for the period of the Lease. If A does not grant B a Lease, A retains his right to exclusive control and comes under a duty to allow B to make a limited use of land. At any given time, the right to exclusive control must be vested *either* in A or in B. So, if A has retained open-ended powers to use the land, such as a power to come onto the land at any time to provide B with services such as cooking or cleaning,[25] B *cannot* have a Lease: A, rather than B, has a right to exclusive control of the land.

	B's Right	A's Right
B has a Lease	Right to exclusive control	Right to make a limited use of the land
B has a Licence	Right to make a limited use of the land	Right to exclusive control

Of course, in practice, things may be more complicated. Certainly, B can have a Lease even if A imposes some restrictions on B's use of the land: for example, a term that B may not keep pets on the land does not prevent B having a Lease. And if A gives B permission to use land for a particular purpose, but the nature of that land means it can only really be used for that purpose, B may still have a Lease.[26] In such a case, the limits on B's use of the

---

[21] [1985] AC 809.

[22] *Ibid* at 816.

[23] See eg *Westminster CC v Clarke* [1992] AC 288.

[24] In *Hunts Refuse v Norfolk* [1997] 1 EGLR 16, A had a Freehold of a quarry and gave B an 'exclusive licence and full liberty to use the Site for depositing waste without restriction as to amount for the period of 21 years'. A thus allowed B to use the land only for a specific purpose: the depositing of waste. As B could not claim to have a right to exclusive control of the land, the Court of Appeal decided that B had no Lease.

[25] See eg *Huwyler v Ruddy* (1995) 28 HLR 550.

[26] See eg *Addiscombe Estates v Crabbe* [1958] 1 QB 513: the land in question was to be used as a tennis club.

land come from the nature of the land rather than the nature of B's right.[27] However, in practice, in can be hard to distinguish between:

1. a case where A gives B a right to exclusive control for a limited period, whilst also reserving certain rights to use and control the land; *and*
2. a case where A retains his right to exclusive control, but gives B a number of contractual rights to use the land.

So, if the agreement between A and B gives *both* A and B a set of rights to use and control the land, it may be difficult to decide in practice whether: (i) the right to exclusive control is held by A (hence B has a licence); *or* (ii) that right has instead been transferred, for a limited period to B (hence B has a Lease). The crucial difference between the two cases is that in the latter, but not the former, B has a property right in the land: the rest of the world is thus under a prima facie duty not to interfere with B's use of the land.

1.4.2 Practical convenience

The basic test for a Lease, set out in *Street v Mountford*, is squarely consistent with doctrine. However, the perceived needs of practical convenience have had an important impact on the courts' *application* of that test. We can see this by considering five specific questions that may arise when applying the test.

1.5   A right to exclusive control: specific questions

1.5.1 What if A does not intend to give B a Lease?

(i) Doctrine

If the rights given by A to B entitle B to exclusive control of the land for a limited period, then, providing he satisfies the acquisition question, B will have a Lease. This is the case *even if A did not intend to give B a Lease.* A's intention is of course crucial when we ask the first question: what rights does the agreement give to B? However, A's intention is irrelevant when we ask the second question: do the rights given to B amount to a Lease? There are two points here. First, it is for the land law system, not A, to define a Lease. That point is not specific to property law. For example, let us say A makes an oral promise to give B £100 in two weeks' time. A and B both call the promise 'a contract' and intend it to be binding. However, it does *not* give B a contractual right against A: no consideration has been provided by B. As the law's test for a contract has not been satisfied, A and B's intention to have a contract is irrelevant.

The second point is that it is simply not possible for A *both* to: (i) give B a right to exclusive control of a thing; and (ii) to deny that B has a property right. This point is specific to property law. It shows that: (i) *if* A gives B a right to exclusive control of a thing; *then* (ii) A's intention to give B only a personal right is irrelevant.[28] Of course, this does not mean A is trapped into giving B a Lease. If A is keen to ensure that B does not acquire a

---

[27] See eg Morritt LJ's analysis of *Addiscombe Estates v Crabbe* in *Hunts Refuse v Norfolk* [1997] 1 EGLR 16.

[28] This point is specific to cases where A gives B a right to exclusive control. So, for example, A's intention to give B only a personal right *can* prevent B acquiring: (i) an Easement (see **G5:1.6**); or (ii) a Restrictive Covenant (see **G6:1.3**).

Lease, A simply needs to ensure that the rights he gives B under agreement do not amount to a right to exclusive control.

We can draw an analogy with cooking. A can choose his own ingredients when cooking: his intention is therefore crucial to what he produces. But if A chooses to: (i) mix together flour, eggs, sugar, butter and baking powder; and (ii) put the mixture in a tin and heat it in the oven; then (iii) whether he likes it or not, A makes a cake. It does not matter that A intended to make a casserole: he is judged by what he produces and he has produced a cake. If A wants to make a casserole, the solution is simple: he needs to choose the right ingredients.

EXAMPLE 2

The facts are as in **Example 1**. The written agreement between A and B makes clear that A does not intend to grant B a Lease: for example, B is referred to throughout as 'the licensee'. The agreement does however give B a right to exclusive control of the land for a limited period.

In such a case, A's intention does *not* prevent B's right counting as a Lease. This was confirmed by the House of Lords, in *Street v Mountford*,[29] on which **Example 2** is based. This might seem to be an example of a court bending the rules to thwart A's unscrupulous attempt to avoid giving B the statutory protection available under the Rent Acts. However, the decision is perfectly correct as a matter of doctrine: it is conceptually impossible for A to give B a right to exclusive control for a limited period and then to claim that B has only a licence.

(ii) Practical Convenience

Prior to the decision in *Street*, a number of Court of Appeal decisions had held that: (i) *if* A gave B a right to exclusive control for a limited period; but (ii) A did not intend to grant B a Lease; then (ii) B did *not* have a Lease.[30] That view seems to have been motivated by practical convenience: in some cases, judges may have felt that B did not deserve the statutory protection available to a party with a Lease.[31]

EXAMPLE 3

A has a Freehold of a cottage. A gives B1 a Lease of the cottage determinable on B1's death. When B1 dies, A gives a similar Lease to B2 (B1's wife). B2 occupies the land with B3 (her daughter). When B2 dies, A does not wish to grant B3 a Lease: A would prefer to make the cottage available to A2. However, out of kindness to B3, A allows B3 to remain in occupation, paying rent, for six months. A now wants to remove B3 and allow A2 to occupy the cottage.

In *Marcroft Wagons Ltd v Smith*,[32] on which **Example 3** is based, B3 claimed that: (i) A's acceptance of rent from B3 created a new Lease in favour of B3; and so (ii) B3 had a

---

[29] [1985] AC 809.

[30] See eg *Marcroft Wagons v Smith* [1951] 2 KB 496; *Marchant v Charters* [1977] 1 WLR 1181; *Somma v Hazelhurst* [1978] 1 WLR 1014.

[31] As explicitly stated by Lord Denning MR in *Cobb v Lane* [1952] 1 TLR 1037 at 1041.

[32] [1951] 2 KB 496. In that case, B2 had acquired a Lease because a statute (the Increase of Rent and Mortgage (Interest) Restrictions Act 1920) had given B2 a right to such a Lease. So, to that extent, A's use of the land had already been curtailed by statute.

statutory right (under the now repealed Rent Restriction Acts) to remain in occupation of the land. B's claim, as a matter of doctrine, seems to be valid: A had given B a right to exclusive control of the land for a limited period (see **2.1.2(ii)** below) . However, the Court of Appeal clearly thought it would be unsatisfactory for A to be bound by the statutory protection that a Lease would give B3: as a result of his generosity in allowing B3 to remain temporarily, A might then be unable to use the cottage for any other purpose for a very long time. The Court of Appeal therefore made clear that the traditional, doctrinal test for a Lease should be varied.[33]

In this way, a court could depart from doctrine to reach what it perceived to be a practically convenient result. However, in *Street v Mountford*,[34] the traditional,[35] doctrinal position was restored. Of course, that return to doctrine can in itself be seen to give effect to a different view of practical convenience: this time the emphasis is on protecting B, rather than protecting A. So, just as the statutes regulating Leases have changed with different governments, so can the definition of a Lease vary according to judges' differing views of the demands of practical convenience.

1.5.2 What if A does not intend to give B a right to exclusive control?

(i) Doctrine

There seems to be an obvious way for A to ensure that B does not acquire a Lease: A simply needs to ensure that the rights acquired by B under the agreement do *not* amount to a right to exclusive control.

EXAMPLE 4

The facts are as in **Example 1**. The signed, written agreement between A and B makes clear that A has the right to allow other parties onto the land to share occupation with B.

In such a case, that term clearly means that B does *not* have a right to exclusive control of the land. If B wants to claim a Lease, he will therefore need to show that this term is, for some reason, not binding.

The basic test is that B is bound if it is reasonable for A to believe that B has agreed to a particular term.[36] The test is thus an 'objective one': even if B may inwardly have had no intention to be bound by the term, his apparent willingness suffices. If B has signed a document, it is almost always reasonable for A to believe that B has agreed to be bound by the terms of that document.[37] However, if the term is, on the facts, wholly implausible, this may allow B to say that, despite his signature, it was *not* reasonable for A to believe that B was agreeing to the term. So, in **Example 4**, a term that A is free to insert other occupiers may be wholly implausible *if* the premises are too small to be reasonably occupied by another person alongside B. Similarly, if there were to be a term in an agreement denying B the right to occupy between 10.30 am and noon each day, that term may be so

---

[33] See esp *per* Denning LJ at 505–6.
[34] [1985] AC 809
[35] See eg *Lynes v Snaith* [1899] 1 QB 486; *Allan v Liverpool Overseers* (1874) LR 9 QB 180.
[36] See eg *Smith v Hughes* (1871) LR 6 QB 597 at 607.
[37] An exception occurs where A has misrepresented the meaning of the term to B: see eg *Curtis v Chemical Cleaning & Dyeing Co* [1951] 1 KB 805.

'astonishingly extreme' that, even if B signs the agreement, A cannot reasonably believe that B is agreeing to be bound by such a term.[38] As a result, a court *may* be doctrinally justified in ignoring that term when deciding if the agreement gives B a right to exclusive control of the land.

An apparent term will also fail to be contractually binding if it is a 'sham'. The sham concept is, however, very limited. It is simply an application of the general rule that a term is only contractually binding if it is reasonable for A to believe that B has agreed to it.[39] For example, let us say A sells a right to B for £10,000; but, in the written contract of sale, the parties record the price as £15,000. They do so in an attempt to minimise B's tax bill. It is not reasonable for A to believe that B has agreed to pay £15,000: the parties have agreed otherwise, and they intend to use the document simply to trick the tax authorities. The promise to pay £15,000 can thus be described as a 'sham'—although it is debatable whether calling it a 'sham' adds anything to our analysis. The promise does not give A a right simply because of the *general rule* that A can only acquire a contractual right against B if it is reasonable for A to believe that B has agreed to be bound.

In theory then, there are two chief ways in which B could argue that the term allowing A to insert other occupiers is not contractually binding:

1. As it is factually very unlikely that anyone else could occupy along with B, it is wholly implausible for A to believe B is agreeing to such a term; *or*
2. A and B did not intend the term to be binding (i.e. it is a 'sham' inserted to trick third parties).

However, it is very hard to see how that second method could ever apply in a case such as **Example 4**. Certainly, A and B are not conspiring to hide their true intentions: A genuinely *does* intend the term to be binding.[40] After all, the whole point of the term is to prevent B gaining the right to exclusive control necessary for B to have a Lease.

Nonetheless, in *Antoniades v Villiers*,[41] the House of Lords held that a term such as that used in **Example 4** could be ignored in deciding if B had a right to exclusive control. One doctrinal means of justifying that decision is to say that, on the facts of the case, the term was wholly implausible: as the premises were too small for another occupier to be inserted, it was unreasonable for A to believe that B was agreeing to be bound by the term.[42] However, in an important speech, Lord Templeman adopted more expansive reasoning,

---

[38] See *per* Ralph Gibson LJ in *Crancour Ltd v da Silvaesa* (1986) 18 HLR 265 at 274–6; *per* Lord Donaldson MR in *Aslan v Murphy* [1990] 1 WLR 766 at 772.

[39] See McFarlane & Simpson, ch 8 in *Rationalizing Property, Equity and Trusts: Essays in Honour of Edward Burn* (ed Getzler, 2003). The 'sham' concept may have an independent role to play when deciding what *evidence* a court can take into account when determiing the parties' intentions: see Conaglen (2008) *CLJ* 176. For 'sham' Trusts see **F3:2.1.1**.

[40] See eg Bingham LJ in the Court of Appeal in *Antoniades v Villiers* [1988] 3 WLR 139 at 149: 'If the written agreements are to be discarded as a sham, it must be shown not only that the occupants intended to enjoy a right to exclusive possession but also that the landlord shared that intention. In my view he plainly did not. He was determined that they should not enjoy that right. Doubtless his determination was conditioned by his desire that the relationship between himself and the occupants should not be governed by the Rent Acts, but that consideration must be understood as fortifying rather than undermining his intention that the occupants should have no right to exclusive possession.'

[41] [1990] 1 AC 417.

[42] This seems to be the view of the facts taken by Lord Oliver in *Antoniades v Villiers* [1990] 1 AC 417 at 469 and (perhaps) by Lord Jauncey at 477.

holding that the term could be rejected as a sham *or* a 'pretence'. This suggests there is a third means by which B can show a term is not binding: by showing it is a 'pretence'.

In his speech, Lord Templeman gave no clear definition of a 'pretence'. His Lordship did however suggest that a term might be disregarded if:[43]

1. the term was inserted by A *with the purpose* of giving B a licence rather than a Lease;[44] *or*

2. if A did not *in practice* attempt to rely on the term. [45]

The first suggestion cannot be correct. If A chooses not to give B a right to exclusive control, he is free to do so: he is under no duty to give B a Lease. In the same way, if A puts money in a tax-exempt savings account, A acts with the *purpose* of avoiding tax: but that does not mean A's action needs to be set aside and tax levied on that money.[46]

The second suggestion means that if, in **Example 4**, A does not *in fact* try to insert another occupier, the term giving him a right to do so can be disregarded. Yet this is also very dubious: in determining whether B has a right to exclusive control, we need to look at the *rights* of the parties. And those rights are determined by the intention of the parties when making their agreement. The mere fact that A has not yet tried to insert another occupier does not, by itself, demonstrate that A and B did not *intend* A to have the right to do so.

The best attempt to reconcile the concept of a 'pretence' with the need to uphold doctrinal rules consists of saying that a term can be disregarded if A *never intended to enforce the term in practice*.[47] However, this is a very difficult test to apply: it all depends on what we mean by 'enforcement'. For example, A may not plan to insert another occupier but if A intends to rely on the term to show that B does not have a right to exclusive control, then, in a sense, he does intend to enforce that term. More importantly, it seems to be inconsistent with the general doctrinal rules applying to contractual rights. Under those rules, the crucial question is not whether A intended to enforce a term; but simply whether the term was *intended to give A a right*.[48]

(ii) Practical convenience

In dealing with cases where A does not intend to give B a right to exclusive control, the courts have thus gone beyond the limits of doctrine: they have sometimes disregarded terms that, according to the usual rules, ought to bind B. In particular, it seems that the courts' willingness to disregard terms as 'pretences' cannot be doctrinally justified. Nonetheless, the

---

[43] Lord Templeman at 462 also suggested that a term can be disregarded if it would have the effect of depriving B of the statutory protection given by the Rent Act 1977. However, that cannot be right: the statutory protection applies only if B has a Lease; and B cannot have a Lease if he has no right to exclusive control.

[44] [1990] 1 AC 417 at 462.

[45] [1990] 1 AC 417 at 462. See too *Aslan v Murphy* [1990] 1 WLR 766.

[46] Tax cases make very clear that A's action cannot be disregarded simply because A acted with the *purpose* of avoiding tax: see eg *IRC v Duke of Westminster* [1936] AC 1. See esp. *per* Lord Tomlin at 19–20: 'Every man is entitled to arrange his own affairs so the tax attaching under the appropriate Acts is less than it otherwise would be.'

[47] This analysis is developed by Bright [2002] CLJ 146.

[48] See eg *Burdis v Livsey* [2003] QB 36 esp at [44]: 'Commercial parties may, and often do, choose not to enforce their strict legal rights without intending to create or demonstrate some different state of affairs.' This view is developed further by McFarlane and Simpson, ch 8, in *Rationalizing Property, Equity and Trusts: Essays in Honour of Edward Burn* (ed Getzler, 2003) 172–8.

line taken by the courts is readily understandable: as a matter of practical convenience it may seem harsh to deny B the statutory protection available to those with Leases *if*, in substance,[49] B is occupying land as his home. Indeed, it is interesting to note that the Law Commission's current plans for improving the relevant statutes include a proposal that they should apply *whenever* B is occupying a home and paying rent: not just when B has a Lease.[50] On this view, B could qualify for statutory protection even if he had no right to exclusive control. This proposal is based on the eminently sensible view that, as the statutory protection gives B particular rights *against* A, rather than against third parties, that protection should be available even if B does not have a property right.

It can therefore be argued that, in cases such as *Antoniades v Villiers*, the courts were, in effect, *anticipating* the Law Commission's proposal: they extended statutory protection to B although, strictly speaking, B did not have a Lease.[51] As a matter of practical convenience this approach can be commended. Certainly, the protection formerly available to occupiers under the Rent Acts could easily have been undermined if A simply needed to make clear his intention not to give B a right to exclusive control. The problem, however, is that the courts' approach has had two effects: (i) it has allowed B to qualify for statutory protection against A; *and* (ii) it has allowed B to acquire a property right. This second consequence may have unwelcome consequences for third parties: they are then prima facie bound by B's right *even though*, strictly speaking, B has no right to exclusive control of the land.

A more transparent approach would have involved the courts admitting that the word 'Lease', when used to define the scope of statutory protection, has a *special, non-doctrinal* meaning and so covers cases in which B does not have a property right. So, it could be said that, in a case like *Antoniades v Villiers*, B did *not* have a true Lease: B had no right to exclusive control as A had a right to insert other occupiers. However, as A had not used this right, B, in substance, exclusively occupied the premises as his home. And such occupation may be enough to give B a 'Lease', in the *special, non-doctrinal sense intended by the Rent Act 1977*. If that approach were adopted, the courts could reconcile: (i) the need to give B statutory protection against A; with (ii) the need to protect third parties who may later deal with the land. This would seem to a better way to resolve the **basic tension** between B and C and, indeed, is reflected in the Law Commission's current proposals.

---

[49] This preference for 'substance over form' is reflected in an extra-judicial article by Lord Templeman in *Rationalizing Property, Equity and Trusts: Essays in Honour of Edward Burn* (ed Getzler, 2003) 130–34.

[50] See Law Commission Report No 297 (2006) eg at 1.5: '[W]e recommend a new 'consumer protection' approach which focuses on the contract between the landlord and the occupier . . . our recommended scheme does not depend on technical legal issues of whether or not there is a tenancy as opposed to a licence'.

[51] This view is developed further by McFarlane and Simpson, ch 8, in *Rationalizing Property, Equity and Trusts: Essays in Honour of Edward Burn* (ed Getzler, 2003).

1.5.3 What if A is unable to give B a right to exclusive control?

(i) Doctrine

> **EXAMPLE 5a**
>
> A0 has a Freehold. A0 makes a contractual agreement to allow A to make a limited use of the land. Under the terms of that agreement, A takes physical control of the land. A then enters into a contractual agreement with B under which B has a right to exclusive control of the land for six months.

> **EXAMPLE 5b**
>
> The facts are as in **Example 5a**: with the difference that, before entering into the contract with B, A does *not* take physical control of the land.

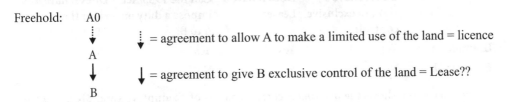

Freehold: A0

A

B

⋮ = agreement to allow A to make a limited use of the land = licence

↓ = agreement to give B exclusive control of the land = Lease??

In such a case, can B have a Lease? This depends on the rights of A: A clearly cannot give B a right to exclusive control of the land if A has no such right. In **Example 5a**, A has *two* distinct rights. First, A has a personal right against A0—a contractual licence—arising as a result of his agreement with A0. Second, by taking physical control of the land, A independently acquires a Freehold of that land (see **G1A:2.1**). So, A *does* have a right to exclusive control of the land.[52] This means that A *can* give B a right to exclusive control: B *can* thus acquire a Lease.

In contrast, in **Example 5b**, A has only *one* right: a personal right against A0 arising as a result of his contractual licence. A thus has *no* right to exclusive control of the land and so should *not* be able to give B a Lease. If B takes physical control of the land, B then independently acquires a Freehold; but B does not have a Lease and A and B are *not* in a landlord–tenant relationship.

When considering B's position against A0 or a party acquiring a right from A0, there is no real difference between **Example 5a** and **Example 5b**.[53] It is true that, in the first example, B does have a Lease. As a result, the rest of the world is under a prima facie duty to B. However, B's Lease does *not* impose a duty on A0, or anyone acquiring a right from A0: B has no defence to A0's pre-existing Freehold. So if, under the terms of A's licence, A0 can remove A from the land, A0 will also be able to remove B.[54] Similarly, if A0 transfers his

---

[52] See eg *National Provincial Bank v Ainsworth* [1965] AC 1175 at 1232 *per* Lord Upjohn, discussing the position of Mrs Ainsworth (a licensee) after her husband left the home: 'in truth and in fact the wife [B] at all material times was and is in exclusive occupation of the home. Until her husband [A] returns she has the dominion over the house and she could clearly bring proceedings against trespassers.'

[53] There is, however, a difference if C acquires a right from A rather than from A0. In the first example, but not the second, B's pre-existing property right (acquired from A) will be prima facie binding on C.

[54] As confirmed by the House of Lords in *Kay v Lambeth LBC* [2006] 2 AC 465, esp *per* Lord Scott at [138]–[148].

Freehold to C, *neither* A nor B has a pre-existing right that can bind C. So, in **Example 5a**, B's Lease is rather weak: it depends on A's *independently acquired* Freehold, which is itself vulnerable to A0's pre-existing Freehold. Similarly, in **Example 5b**, the rest of the world is under a prima facie duty to B: B has a Freehold as a result of his physical control of the land. But, again, B has no defence to A0's pre-existing Freehold.

Nonetheless, the difference between **Example 5a** and **Example 5b** may be crucial when considering B's rights *against* A. For example, it may well be that the contract between A and B does not impose a duty on A to repair the premises. However, if B has a Lease, for seven years or less, of a home, section 11 of the Landlord and Tenant Act 1985 (the 1985 Act) imposes a statutory duty on A to carry out certain repairs. So, in **Example 5b**, but *not* in **Example 5a**, A may be under a statutory duty to B, arising under the 1985 Act, to carry out certain repairs.

	Does A have a right to exclusive control?	Does B have a Lease?	Can the 1985 Act impose a duty on A to B?	Does B have a right that binds A0?
Example 5a	Yes	Yes	Yes	No
Example 5b	No	No	No	No

The table above shows the *doctrinally* correct analysis of **Examples 5a** and **5b**. In *Bruton v London & Quadrant Housing Trust*,[55] the House of Lords considered facts essentially identical to **Example 5a**. It was held that: (i) B *did* acquire a Lease from A; and so (ii) the 1985 Act did apply to impose a duty on A. That *result* is consistent with the reasoning set out here. However, the *reasoning* of the House of Lords goes further. On that reasoning, A can grant B a Lease *even if A has no right to exclusive control of the land*: B can therefore acquire a Lease in *both* **Example 5a** *and* **Example 5b**.

EXAMPLE 6

A makes a contractual promise to B to give B exclusive control of Buckingham Palace for six months.

According to the House of Lords in *Bruton*, B *does* acquire a Lease. It does not matter that A has no right to exclusive control of the Palace; nor even that A has no liberty to make any use of it. The House of Lords took the view that B can have a Lease *whenever* A makes a contractual promise to give B exclusive control of some land. From a doctrinal point of view, that reasoning is impossible to defend.[56]

(ii) Practical convenience

The *Bruton* decision, quite deliberately, allows B to have a 'Lease' *without* having a property right.[57] It extends the term 'Lease' to a particular type of contractual duty: a duty to allow B

---

[55] [2000] 1 AC 406.

[56] See eg Bright (2000) 116 *LQR* 7; Dixon (2000) 59 *CLJ* 25.

[57] The analysis of the House of Lords means there is no room for a so-called 'tenancy by estoppel': see *per* Lord Hoffmann at 416. A tenancy by estoppel used to arise if: (i) A is under a duty to give B exclusive control of land for a limited period; but (ii) A has no property right. The effect of a tenancy by estoppel is that the duties of A and B, against each other, are the same *as if* A and B were landlord and tenant. Such a tenancy is now unnecessary:

exclusive control of land for a limited period. So, in **Example 6**, the contractual agreement between A and B, although it only gives B a personal right against A, can count as a 'Lease'.

Of course, in most cases where A makes a contractual promise to give B exclusive control of land, A *does* have a right to exclusive control of that land. In such cases, B will have a property right: a Lease. But, in the rarer case, such as **Example 6**, where A does *not* have such a right, A's contractual promise, according to the House of Lords, can still give B a 'Lease'. The view of the House of the Lords is thus that if B has a Lease, then he will *usually*, but *not always*, have a property right.[58] This view is inconsistent with the fundamental doctrinal principle that a Lease is a property right in land.

However, from the perspective of practical convenience, it may be possible to justify the reasoning of the House of Lords. It is very important to realise that *Bruton* itself did *not* involve any third parties. B claimed a Lease solely in order to show that A was under a statutory duty, under the 1985 Act, to make repairs. So, like *Antoniades v Villiers*,[59] *Bruton* was a dispute between A and B. Given this, A's argument (that B cannot have a Lease as A does not have a right to exclusive control of the land) looks very unattractive. After all, it is not B's fault that A is just a licensee. B can argue that if the agreement would otherwise suffice to give B a right to exclusive control, why should A wriggle out of the duty to repair simply because of the nature of A's agreement with A0? Certainly, B could say that the purpose of section 11 of the 1985 Act is to ensure that B, a short-term occupier, is not saddled with the cost of repairs that will confer benefits lasting beyond the end of B's occupation. That purpose is furthered by protecting *all* parties occupying a home for less than seven years, whether they have a property right or not.

It may therefore be possible to explain the reasoning in *Bruton* by adopting the same approach we applied to the 'pretence' cases, such as *Antoniades v Villiers*, in **1.5.2** above. The reasoning depends *not* on B having a Lease in the standard sense of a property right; but instead on B having a 'Lease' in the broader sense of that term intended by a particular statute.

1.5.4 What if B1 and B2 occupy land together?

EXAMPLE 7

A has a Freehold. A enters into two separate agreements with B1 and B2, giving each party the right, for a limited period, to occupy the land.

Clearly neither B1 nor B2 can *individually* claim to have a Lease: as each must share with the other, neither has a right to exclusive control. However, it is possible for two parties to combine to form a team, and for that team to hold a right *together* (see **F2:1.1**). So B1 and

---

according to the House of Lords, A's lack of a property right does not prevent B acquiring a Lease: so A and B are *actually* landlord and tenant. For an argument that the tenancy by estoppel analysis *might* nonetheless have been applied to the facts of *Bruton* see Routley [2000] 63 *MLR* 424 and the dissenting judgment of Sir Brian Neill in the Court of Appeal: [1998] QB 834.

[58] See *per* Lord Hoffmann [2000] 1 AC 406 at 415. The analysis of the House of Lords in *Kay v Lambeth LBC* [2006] 2 AC 465 (see *per* Lord Scott at [138]–[148]) confirms that B does *not* have a Lease in the sense of a property right that derives from A0's right to exclusive control of the land. Rather, as noted by Lord Scott at [144], B is in the same position as if he acquired a Lease from a squatter on A0's land.

[59] [1990] 1 AC 417.

B2 can claim that they form a team that has a single right to exclusive control of the land. If that is the case, B1 and B2 will be *co-holders* of a Lease and, as a result, *co-owners* of the land. In **G2:1.2.5**, we will examine the special considerations that apply in a case such as **Example 7**.

1.5.5 Is a right to exclusive control for a limited period always a Lease?

It is often said that there are exceptions to the basic test: situations in which B has a right to exclusive control for a limited period *but* does not have a Lease. In *Street v Mountford*,[60] Lord Templeman suggests three basic exceptions:

- A and B have no intention to create legal relations;
- A has no power to give B a Lease;
- B's right arises from some other legal relationship: eg, B has a Freehold; B is a service occupier.

(i) Doctrine

As was pointed out by Millett LJ in the Court of Appeal in *Bruton v London & Quadrant Housing Trust*,[61] the first two categories are *not* genuine exceptions. First, if the parties have no intention to create legal relations, it is impossible for B to say that he has acquired, through an agreement with A, any *right* to exclusive control. An intention to create legal relations must be present before an agreement can give rise to rights. However, as we will see below, practical convenience can play an important role when a court decides the factual question of whether, in a particular case, the parties did intend to create legal relations.

Second, if A simply has no power to give B a Lease, then A cannot give B a right to exclusive control. So, in a case such as **Example 6**, A's lack of a right to exclusive control means that A cannot give B a property right. A may be able to give B a 'Lease' in the wider sense intended by the Landlord and Tenant Act 1985 but, as the House of Lords made clear in *Bruton*, B cannot have a property right.

This leaves the final category. In *Street v Mountford*, Lord Templeman said that:

> an occupier who enjoys exclusive possession is not necessarily a tenant. He may be owner in fee simple, a trespasser, a mortgagee in possession, an object of charity or a service occupier.[62]

The first three examples are simply situations in which B does not have a right to exclusive control *for a limited period* and so are not true exceptions to the basic test. The latter two are more difficult. First, if B is an 'object of charity', this simply tells us about A's motives in giving B a right to exclusive control for a limited period. Those motives may tell us why A gave B a particular right, but should not change the **content** of that right. After all, if A is moved to give his Freehold away to B because B is homeless, A is free to do so: B still acquires the Freehold even though he is an 'object of charity'. There is no reason why it should be impossible for A to give an 'object of charity' a Lease: certainly, B can acquire a Lease even if he is under no duty to pay rent to A.[63]

---

[60] [1985] AC 809 at 818.
[61] [1998] QB 834 at 843, referring to his earlier comments in *Camden London Borough v Shortlife Community Housing* (1992) 25 HLR 330.
[62] [1985] AC 809 at 826H–827B.
[63] See LPA 1925, s 205(1)(xxvii) and *Ashburn Anstalt v Arnold* [1989] Ch 1 at 9–10.

There may be a doctrinal explanation, albeit a rather unsatisfactory one, for the service occupier case. If B acquires physical control of a thing in the course of his duties as an employee of A, B, exceptionally, does *not* acquire a property right (see **D1:2.1**). Similarly, it could be argued that it is impossible for A to *transfer* a right to exclusive control of land to an employee: at least if A attempts to give B that right as part of the terms of B's employment, so as to enable B to better perform his duties as an employer... So if A, a local authority, makes a contractual promise to give B, a school caretaker, exclusive control for a limited period of a house on the school grounds, B cannot have a Lease. However, this argument depends on extending the proposition that an employee does not acquire a property right when taking physical control of a thing in the course of his appointment. And that proposition is already doctrinally dubious (see **D1:2.1**).

(ii) Practical convenience

(a) The 'tolerated trespasser'

> **EXAMPLE 9a**
>
> A, a local authority, has a Freehold. A grants B a Lease of land B is to use as his home. B runs up serious rent arrears. A obtains a court order allowing it to remove B from the land (a possession order). A then makes an agreement with B that B can stay on the land, provided B complies with certain conditions. B remains in occupation for a further two years, but then breaches one of those conditions. A, relying on its earlier possession order, seeks to remove B from the land.

B's initial Lease is a 'secure tenancy': B thus receives some statutory protection under Part IV of the Housing Act 1985 (see **1.2** above). In particular, A can only end the Lease by obtaining a court order: the statute specifies when a court may grant such an order.[64] To obtain its possession order, A convinced a court that it was permitted to end B's initial Lease. B's initial Lease then ended on the date set out in the order.[65] However, B can claim that A's agreement to allow B to remain in occupation then gave B a second, *new* Lease. If that is correct, B's new Lease will also be protected by statute: A can then only end that Lease by following the statutory procedure. B's argument is thus that A must start from scratch and cannot rely on the order it obtained to end B's initial Lease.

From a doctrinal perspective, B's argument seems convincing: as in **Example 3** above, the new agreement between A and B gives B a right to exclusive control for a limited period. However, in *Burrows v Brent LBC*,[66] on which **Example 9a** is based, the House of Lords rejected B's argument. It found that the new agreement between A and B did *not* give B a right to exclusive control of the land as A and B had *not* intended that agreement to create legal relations.[67] B therefore did not have a Lease and was described instead as a 'tolerated trespasser': someone who had no right to be on the land, but whom A, for a period of two years, had chosen not to remove.[68]

---

[64] For further detail see Bright, *Landlord and Tenant Law in Context* (2007) 613–39.

[65] Housing Act 1985, s 82(2).

[66] [1996] 1 WLR 1448.

[67] See *per* Lord Browne-Wilkinson [1996] 1 WLR 1448 at 1454–5. See too the analysis of Arden LJ in *Lambeth London Borough Council v O'Kane* [2005] EWCA Civ 1010.

[68] The concept of a 'tolerated trespasser' is a difficult one: see Loveland (2007) 123 *LQR* 455; Bright (2003) 119 *LQR* 495.

This reasoning is very difficult to support.[69] It seems odd to say that A did not intend the new agreement with B to create legal rights; after all, that agreement contained carefully defined conditions on which B was allowed to occupy A's land.[70] The decision in *Burrows* is thus similar to *Marcroft Wagons v Smith* (see **1.5.1(ii)** above).[71] In that case, the Court of Appeal held that B had no Lease because A had not intended to grant B a Lease. Of course, following its decision in *Street v Mountford*,[72] the House of Lords could not adopt that reasoning in *Burrows*: instead, it adopted the different tactic of finding, as a matter of fact, that A did not intend to give B *any* legal right.

As a matter of practical convenience, the decision in *Burrows* may be defensible. As a later court noted, there may be 'reasons of policy' for denying B a new Lease.[73] If B is recognised as having a new Lease in **Example 9a**, then B gains the statutory protection afforded by the Housing Act 1985. However, in practice, that protection will only be temporary: if, for example, B is again in arrears of rent, A will be able to use the statutory procedure to end the new Lease. Yet A will be put to the time and expense of having to apply for a possession order from scratch. So, in **Example 9a**, the only immediate effect of recognising that B has a Lease is to increase the time and expense incurred by A. Further, there might be a wider consequence of finding such a Lease. Let us say B2, occupying under a Lease from A (a local authority), is in arrears of rent. A obtains a possession order. B2 suggests a new arrangement under which he can continue in occupation. If A knows that such a new deal will give B2 a new Lease, and hence new statutory rights, A may well reject it and proceed to remove B2 from the land. This is of no benefit to B2 and also of little benefit to A: it is unlikely that, in practice, A will be able to recover the rent arrears, and A's statutory duty to deal with homelessness may even mean that, if A chooses to enforce the possession order by removing B2, A will have a duty to find some alternative accommodation for B2 and anyone who had been occupying the land with B2.[74]

So it seems that, in a case such as **Example 9a**, *each* of A and B needs a way to reach a new agreement that does not have the effect of giving B a new Lease.[75] The tolerated trespasser concept, based on the fiction that the new arrangement between the parties is not

---

[69] An alternative explanation for the 'tolerated trespasser' is that no new Lease arises as B continues to occupy under the *original* Lease which is in 'limbo' as it may revive under s 85(2) of the Housing Act 1988. However, in *Leadenhall Residential 2 Ltd v Stirling* [2002] 1 WLR 499, the 1985 Act did not apply: A was a private landlord and B's original Lease was an assured tenancy protected under the Housing Act 1988. Nonetheless, the Court of Appeal held that, an agreement entered into by A and B after a possession order was granted did not (initially at least) lead to a new Lease as A and B (initially at least) had no intention to create legal relations. So, as the 'tolerated trespasser' concept can apply outside the Housing Act 1985, it cannot be based simply on that Act: see too *Knowsley Housing Trust v White* [2007] 1 WLR 2897 (although note that permission to appeal to the House of Lords has been granted in that case).

[70] See eg Bright (2003) 119 *LQR* 495.

[71] [1951] 2 KB 496.

[72] [1985] AC 809.

[73] *Per* Roch LJ in *Pemberton v Southwark LBC* [2000] 1 WLR 1672 at 1677: 'There are reasons of policy why a former secure tenant who has been allowed to remain in occupation of premises upon terms . . . does not [have] a new tenancy or a licence.' See too *Leadenhall Residential 2 Ltd v Stirling Ltd* [2002] 1 WLR 499.

[74] In some cases where B2 defaults on rent, it can be said that B2 is *intentionally* homeless, and so A's statutory duty to B2 is more limited (see Housing Act 1996, ss 190–91). However, it may not always be possible to say that B2's failure to keep up the rent was intentional; and it will certainly be very difficult to say that the homelessness of any members of B2's family, previously occupying the land leased to B2, is intentional.

[75] In *Knowsley Housing Trust v White* [2007] 1 WLR 2897 at [18], Buxton LJ described the 'tolerated trespasser' concept as 'humane . . . in avoiding immediate expulsions of socially deprived tenants from their accommodation.'

intended to create legal rights, serves that role. The fiction is emphasised by a later case that dealt with the question of whether B, a so-called tolerated trespasser, could bring a claim in nuisance against A.[76] It was held that, as B had a right against A to exclusive control of the land,[77] A was under a duty to B not to unreasonably interfere with B's enjoyment of the land.

So, if B is a tolerated trespasser: (i) he may have a Lease for one purpose: he is allowed to bring a claim in nuisance against A; *but* (ii) not for another purpose: he does not qualify for protection under the Housing Act 1985. In other words, B does have a Lease in the sense of a property right; but not in the sense in which that word is used in the Housing Act 1985. As a result, it seems that the decision in *Burrows v Brent LBC* achieves the exact opposite of *Antoniades v Villiers* and *Bruton v London & Quadrant Housing Trust*. In that pair of cases: (i) B does *not* have a Lease, in the sense of a property right; *but* (ii) B has a 'Lease' in the special, *wider* sense of that term used by a particular statute. In contrast, in *Burrows*: (i) B *does* have a Lease, in the sense of a property right; *but* (ii) B does *not* have a 'Lease' in the special, *narrower* sense of that term used by a particular statute.

Possible explanation of three House of Lords' decisions:

	Does B have a Lease (ie, a property right in land)?	**Does B have a 'Lease' in the sense intended by a statute?**
Antoniades	No[78]	Yes[79]
Bruton	No[80]	Yes[81]
Burrows	Yes[82]	No[83]

Whilst it does fulfil its practical purpose of denying B, in a case such as **Example 9a**, a new Lease with statutory protection, the 'tolerated trespasser' concept also causes some practical problems.[84] As a result, the courts have tried to find different practical solutions in a case such as **Example 9a**. In particular, when A initially applies for physical control of the land, a

---

[76] *Pemberton v Southwark LBC* [2000] 1 WLR 1672. By having physical control of the land, B independently acquired a Freehold and so could bring a nuisance claim against X without needing to show his agreement with A gave him a Lease. However, to bring such a claim against A, B had to show that he had acquired a right to exclusive control *from A*.

[77] As Roch LJ put it at 1682 B had 'exclusive occupation and possession' of the land and hence had a 'sufficient interest' in the land to sue in nuisance. Sir Christopher Slade at 1685–6 also notes that B had 'the right to exclusive possession'.

[78] Under the approach to the 'pretence' question adopted by the House of Lords in *Antoniades*, B *does* have a right to exclusive control of the land for a limited period and so has a property right. However, on the view taken in this book, the 'pretence' doctrine does not justify ignoring a term that prevents B acquiring a right to exclusive control of the land and so, in such a case, B should *not* have a property right.

[79] The statute in question was the Rent Act 1977.

[80] As discussed in **1.5.3(i)** above, B *does* have a property right if A was in physical control of the land when entering the agreement with B. However, the reasoning of the House of Lords in *Bruton* does not depend on A having physical control of the land and so can apply when B has no property right: see eg *per* Lord Hoffmann [2000] 1 AC 406 at 415.

[81] The statute in question was the Landlord and Tenant Act 1985.

[82] As shown by the fact that a 'tolerated trespasser' can sue A in nuisance: *Pemberton v Southwark LBC* [2000] 1 WLR 1672.

[83] The statute in question was the Housing Act 1985.

[84] See *Bristol CC v Hassan* [2006] 1 WLR 2582 at [34] and [35]. As a result of those problems, the Department for Communities and Local Government are investigating what reforms might be made: see Tolerated Trespassers: Consultation (August 2007).

court will now give A a *postponed possession order*: that order will *not* set a specific date on which B must give up physical control of the land.[85] This means that B's initial Lease continues:[86] there is no need to use the 'tolerated trespasser' concept to prevent B acquiring a second, new Lease. The postponed possession order will stipulate that B must comply with particular conditions (eg, B makes up the rent arrears and continues to pay rent). If B fails to comply with any of the conditions, A can apply to court for an order fixing a specific date on which B must leave the land and therefore bringing B's Lease to an end.[87]

(b) The 'object of charity'

A1 and A2, trustees of a charity, have a Freehold. A1 and A2 have a duty to use that land only for the charitable purpose of providing accommodation to elderly people in need. B occupies one of the flats on that land. B's agreement with A1 and A2 gives B a right to exclusive control of the land in return for B paying a small monthly sum to pay for maintenance and some essential services.

In such a case, there are no doctrinal grounds for denying B a Lease: B has a right to exclusive control of the land for a limited period. However, in *Gray v Taylor*,[88] on which **Example 9b** is based, the Court of Appeal found that, as B was an 'object of charity', he did not have a Lease. No third party was involved: B claimed a Lease in order to qualify for statutory protection that would make it more difficult for A to remove B from the land.[89] The decision to deny B a Lease seems to have been based purely on the needs of practical convenience. First, there is a desire not to 'punish' A1 and A2 for their generosity.[90] Second, there is a desire to give A1 and A2 the flexibility to respond if B's position changes. For example, if B wins the lottery, the trustees may wish to remove B so that, in accordance with their charitable duty, they can make the accommodation available to a needier party. Yet if B has a Lease, the statutory rights he thereby acquires could make it difficult for the trustees to remove B.[91]

It thus seems that the 'object of charity' exception, like the 'tolerated trespasser' concept, has been used to *narrow* the scope of statutory protection by giving a special meaning to the term 'Lease' as used in a particular statute. However, this should not mean that B can never acquire a Lease, in the sense of a property right in land, if he is an 'object of charity'. B, like anyone else, should have such a property right if he has a right to exclusive control of land for a limited period.[92]

---

[85] Such an order was advocated by the Court of Appeal in *Bristol CC v Hassan* [2006] 1 WLR 2582: see now s IV of the Practice Direction supplementing Part 55 of the Civil Procedure Rules.

[86] Similarly, under the Law Commission's proposals, B's initial Lease will continue (even after a possession order with a specific date is granted) until B actually gives up physical control of the land: Law Com No 297 (2006) at 4.54–4.56.

[87] This new form of possession order was advocated by the Court of Appeal only in May 2006 so there will still be parties falling into the 'tolerated trespasser' category. Further, the new form of order applied only to cases where B has a 'secure tenancy' from a local authority, whereas it seems the 'tolerated trespasser' category can also apply where B initially has an 'assured tenancy' from a private landlord: see *Knowsley Housing Trust v White* [2007] 1 WLR 2897 (although note that permission to appeal to the House of Lords has been granted).

[88] [1998] 1 WLR 1093.

[89] B would have been an 'assured tenant' under the Housing Act 1988.

[90] That desire is clear in *Marcroft Wagons v Smith* [1951] 2 KB 496 (see 1.5.1(ii) above).

[91] See esp *per* Nourse LJ at 1099.

[92] Barr, in *Modern Studies in Property Law* (ed Cooke, 2001) 247–9 points out that there is no reason why a charity cannot make a contractual agreement to give B a right to exclusive control of land.

As it is based on practical convenience rather than doctrine, the scope of the 'object of charity' exception is unclear. For example, in *Bruton v London & Quadrant Housing Trust*,[93] the essential facts were as in **Example 5a** above. A0, a local authority, had a Freehold. It planned to develop the land at some point but, until then, it decided to make the land available as short-term accommodation for those in need of housing. It therefore gave A, a housing association, a licence of the land. When B claimed he had a Lease, one of A's arguments was that, as it was acting out of charitable motives, it should not be burdened by the statutory rights B would acquire as a result of having a Lease. However, this argument was firmly rejected by the House of Lords. Lord Hoffmann stated that the fact that A was a 'responsible landlord performing socially valuable functions' was irrelevant.[94] The **content** of B's right cannot depend on the motives for which A gave B that right.

(c) The 'service occupier'

Practical convenience has also influenced the courts in holding that a 'service occupier', even if he has a right to exclusive control of land for a limited period, does not have a Lease. The point seems to be that, if A gives B a right to exclusive control of land so as to enable B better to perform his duties as A's employee, A needs to have the freedom to end B's right when B's employment ends. As a result, the statutory security of tenure potentially available to a party with a Lease is clearly inappropriate. Of course, Parliament could deal with this problem directly by giving A the right to remove B in such a situation. However, it may be that, given the traditional rule that a service occupier cannot have a Lease, Parliament did not feel the need to provide such an exception. As a result, even if that traditional rule were to change so that a service occupier can have a Lease, it may be correct to interpret the term 'Lease', when used in a particular statute conferring security of tenure, as *not* including the Lease held by a service occupier.

SUMMARY of G1B:1.5

The basic test for a Lease is clear: B has such a right if he has a right to exclusive control of land for a limited period. It seems that, *whenever* B claims he has a Lease in order to show that he has a property right in land (and therefore that the rest of the world is under a prima facie duty to B), the courts have applied this standard definition. However, in many cases, B claims he has a 'Lease' but is *not* interested in showing he has a property right. Instead, B simply wishes to rely on a particular *statute* that gives protection only to parties who have a 'Lease'. For example, under the Rent Acts, a residential occupier could claim security of tenure and the right to a fair rent if he had a 'Lease': that is why B claimed a 'Lease' in *Marcroft Wagons v Smith*,[95] *Street v Mountford*[96] and *Antoniades v Villiers*.[97] Similarly, in *Gray v Taylor*,[98] B claimed a 'Lease' in order to qualify for the protection provided to an 'assured tenant' by the Housing Act 1988. The statutory protection available to residential occupiers is now very much reduced. However, if B has a 'Lease' of seven years or less of a

---

[93] [2000] 1 AC 406.
[94] [2000] 1 AC 406 at 414.
[95] [1951] 2 KB 496
[96] [1985] AC 809.
[97] [1990] 1 AC 417.
[98] [1998] 1 WLR 1093.

home, section 11 of the Landlord and Tenant Act 1985 imposes a duty to repair on A: that is why B claimed a 'Lease' in *Bruton v London & Quadrant Housing Trust*.[99] And if A is a local authority, B may claim a 'Lease' in order to acquire security of tenure under the Housing Act 1985: that was why B claimed a Lease in *Burrows v Brent LBC*.[100]

In such cases, where B's *only* reason in claiming a 'Lease' is to claim statutory protection, the determining factor may simply be whether a court believes that B *deserves* the statutory protection in question. Thus B may be given that protection even if he does not truly have a right to exclusive control of the land and so cannot have a Lease in the standard sense of a property right in land. The House of Lords expressly admitted this in *Bruton*; and may have impliedly acknowledged it in their decision in *Antoniades v Villiers*. Equally, B may be denied statutory protection even if he does in fact have a right to exclusive control of land for a limited period and thus has a Lease in the standard sense of a property right in land: this seems to be the effect of *Burrows v Brent LBC* and *Gray v Taylor*.

On this view, it is crucial to distinguish between: (i) the courts' approach to defining what counts as a Lease in the standard sense of a property right in land; and (ii) the courts' approach to defining what counts as a 'Lease' when applying a statute. In cases such as *Antoniades*, *Bruton* and *Burrows*, the House of Lords did *not* change the answer to the content question: it did not address the test for when B's right counts as a property right. Instead, it interpreted particular statutes in such a way as to ensure that B acquired statutory protection if, and only if, it made practical sense for B to receive that protection.

On the view put forward here, the battle between doctrine and practical convenience has not compromised the content of a Lease, in the standard sense of a property right in land. Rather, that battle has influenced the *different* question of how courts interpret the term 'Lease' when it is used to set the scope of statutory protection available to an occupier of land. On one view, which seems to be adopted by the House of Lords in *Street v Mountford*,[101] the term 'Lease', when used in a statute, should be given its standard, doctrinal meaning. On a different view, explicitly adopted by the House of Lords *Bruton* and implicit in *Antoniades* and *Burrows*, the term 'Lease' can, in a particular statutory context, be given a special, non-standard meaning. The clash between these two views has nothing to do with the question of whether B has a property right; it is rather a dispute about the proper role of judges when interpreting legislation. This is of course an interesting issue, but its resolution will not affect the basic point that B has a Lease (a property right in land) if, and only if, he has a right to exclusive control of land for a limited period.

1.6   An unconditional (but not necessarily immediate) right to exclusive control

Section 1 of the LPA 1925 defines a Freehold as a 'fee simple absolute in possession'. This means that B's right to exclusive control must be unconditional (see **G1A:1.3**) and immediate (see **G1A:1.4**). The same section defines a Lease as a 'term of years absolute'. 'Absolute' again means B's right to exclusive control must be unconditional. However, there is no requirement that a Lease must be 'in possession'. This means that A can give B a Lease under which B's right to exclusive control will take effect only in the *future*. For example, if,

---

[99] [2000] 1 AC 406.
[100] [1996] 1 WLR 1448.
[101] [1985] AC 809.

in September 2008, A makes a contractual promise to give B exclusive control of land for five years from 1 January 2009, B *immediately* acquires a Lease. So, if A then transfers his Freehold to C in December 2008, C is prima facie bound by B's pre-existing property right.

There are some limits on such future (or 'reversionary') Leases. If, in September 2008, A makes a contractual promise to give B exclusive control of land for five years from 1 January 2030, B does *not* acquire a Lease: section 149(3) of the LPA 1925 states that such a future Lease has to take effect in possession within 21 years of its creation.[102]

1.7   A right to exclusive control for a limited period

1.7.1   The basic rule

A Lease consists of a right to exclusive control of land for a limited period. So, if A gives B a right to exclusive control of land 'until England win the football World Cup' that right does not count as a Lease. The problem is *not* that the parties will be unable to tell if the specified event has happened:[103] if and when England win the football World Cup, they (and everyone else) will know about it. The problem is rather that it is impossible for A to know *if and when* he can regain his right to exclusive control of the land. And that uncertainty is simply incompatible with a Lease. A Lease arises where A retains his property right in the land and grants B a new property right. So, if A grants B a Lease, A does *not* lose his property right in the land. But if it were possible to have a Lease in which A does not know if and when he will again have a right to exclusive control of the land, A's property right will, in effect, be meaningless.[104]

EXAMPLE 10a

A, a local authority, has a Freehold. A grants B a right to exclusive control of a strip of that land adjoining a road. B is to have that right 'until the strip of land is needed for road-widening'.

In such a case, A's agreement with B cannot give B a Lease: B's right to exclusive control for that uncertain period is inconsistent with A's Freehold. This result was confirmed by the House of Lords in *Prudential Assurance Ltd v London Residuary Board*,[105] the basic facts of which are identical to **Example 10a**. In that case, Lord Browne-Wilkinson expressed frustration that the rationale for the rule was unclear, stating that 'No one has produced any satisfactory for the genesis of the rule' that 'the maximum duration of a [Lease must be] ascertainable from the outset'.[106] However, the problem may lie with his Lordship's formulation of the rule. It is *not* the case that the maximum length of the Lease must be known at the outset:[107] the important point is that A must be able to tell if and when he will be able

---

[102] Section 149(3) applies where A attempts to give B a right to exclusive control 'at a rent' or 'in consideration of a fine'.

[103] As was confirmed by the House of Lords in *Prudential Assurance v London Residuary Board* [1992] 2 AC 386, the analysis of the Court of Appeal on this point in *Ashburn Anstalt v Arnold* [1989] Ch 1 is thus incorrect.

[104] For alternative analyses of the possible purposes of the need for a limited period, see eg Bright (1993) 13 *LS* 38; Sparkes (1993) 109 *LQR* 93.

[105] [1992] 2 AC 386.

[106] *Ibid* at 396: his Lordship also described the rule as 'ancient and technical' and serving no useful purpose.

[107] The total duration of a periodic tenancy need not be known at the outset: see **1.7.2(i)** below.

to assert his right to exclusive control of the land. The rule therefore has a valid doctrinal purpose. So, in **Example 10a**, as A does not know if and when the land may be needed for road-widening, A does not know if and when he will be able to exercise his right to exclusive control of the land: A's Freehold could thus become meaningless if B's right were allowed to count as a Lease.

1.7.2 The effect of the basic rule

In **Example 10a**, B does *not* have a property right entitling him to exclusive control of the land until it is needed for road-widening. So what right does B have?

(i) A periodic tenancy

EXAMPLE 10b
The facts are as in **Example 10a**. A and B agree that B is to pay A an annual rent of £500.

In such a case, B *does* acquire a Lease. Of course, that Lease cannot give him a right to exclusive control until the land is needed for road-widening. In fact, the Lease does *not* arise as a result of A and B's express agreement. Instead, it arises as a result of: (i) B's conduct in paying rent; *and* (ii) A's conduct in accepting that rent. As a result of that conduct, a court can infer that A has exercised his power to grant B a Lease. In such a case, B's right arises under an *implied periodic tenancy*. We will examine this means of acquiring a Lease in **2.2.1(ii)** below.

A periodic tenancy is formed by a succession of Leases for a period (eg, a week, a month or a year) that continue to arise from one period to the next *unless* either A or B gives notice to the other that he will not renew the Lease. For example, if A gives B a yearly periodic tenancy on 1 January 2008, B's right to exclusive control will automatically continue from one year to the next: each year, B will acquire a new yearly Lease. If either A or B decides not to renew the Lease, he needs to give the other party six months' notice.[108] So, if A decides in October 2008 that he wishes to end the Lease, B's right to exclusive control will end on 1 January 2010: (i) B's current yearly Lease runs until 31 December 2008; (ii) A is too late to give B six months' notice of his intention not to renew the Lease on 1 January 2009; (iii) so, on 1 January 2009, A has to renew the Lease for another year. Of course, if A had decided not to renew in *May* 2008, he would be bound only until 1 January 2009: by acting in May 2008, he can give B six months' notice of his intention not to renew the Lease on 1 January 2009.

A periodic tenancy is sometimes said to be an exception to the need for a limited period: at the start of the Lease, neither A nor B can be sure how long the Lease will last. However, even if A and B do continue to renew the Lease (as will occur in **Example 10b** as B continues to pay rent and A continues to accept that rent) they simply create a succession of one-year Leases, each of which has a limited period.[109] Second, and more importantly, the

---

[108] If B instead has a monthly periodic tenancy, either side can give one month's notice of a refusal to renew the Lease. And if B has a weekly periodic tenancy, the notice period is one week.

[109] The courts, however, treat a succession of periodic tenancies, for some purposes, as one single Lease: see eg *Legg v Strudwick* (1709) 2 Salk 414 and the discussion in *Bowen v Anderson* [1894] 1 QB 164. However, for most important purposes, that is not the case. So, even if a yearly periodic tenancy ends up lasting for 10 years, it is not caught by any of the formality rules applying to a 10-year Lease: see eg *re Knight, ex p Voisey* (1882) 21 Ch D 442: see too **5.3.4** below.

periodic tenancy is not inconsistent with the *rationale* of the limited period rule. For A, from the outset, has a definite right to regain exclusive control of the land: by giving B sufficient notice, he can simply refuse to renew B's periodic tenancy.[110] So, in **Example 10b**, A can simply give B notice that he does not intend to renew B's implied periodic tenancy. If A does so within six months of the end of the current yearly tenancy, A will be bound to grant B a new yearly tenancy, and so will have to wait until the end of that year before regaining exclusive control of the land. However, it is *certain* that A can regain that control. The periodic tenancy is thus *not* an exception to the need for a limited period. Rather, it nicely demonstrates the rationale of that rule: to ensure that A has a guaranteed right to regain exclusive control of his land.

(ii) A tenancy at will

EXAMPLE 10c

The facts are as in **Example 10a**. A and B agreed that B would not have to pay A rent: instead, B paid a single up-front fee of £5000.

In such a case, B *cannot* acquire a Lease by means of an implied periodic tenancy. No rent has been paid by B and accepted by A. So, the conduct of the parties *cannot* lead a court to infer that A exercised his power to grant B a Lease. It seems that B has only a *tenancy at will.* This type of Lease arises where: (i) B has a right to exclusive control of A's land; and (ii) A can end that right *at any time, without giving notice.*[111] B is thus in a very weak position: there is no guaranteed minimum period for which B can use the land.[112] Nonetheless, a tenancy at will *does* count as Lease. The rationale of the limited period rule is met: as A can end B's Lease whenever he wishes, there is a definite future point at which A can regain exclusive control of the land.

As a tenancy at will counts as a Lease, B can qualify for some statutory protection against A.[113] Moreover, as B has a right to exclusive control for a limited period, he has a property right. However, B's right cannot bind C if C acquires a right from A: A's decision to give C that right will be taken as a decision to terminate B's tenancy at will.[114] Moreover, the death of either A or B will also end B's right to exclusive control: for that reason the tenancy at will is sometimes said to involve a purely 'personal relation' between A and B.[115]

---

[110] This point is noted by Lord Templeman in *Prudential Assurance v London Residuary Body* [1992] 2 AC 386 at 394: 'A tenancy from year to year is saved from being uncertain because each party has power by notice to determine at the end of any year.'

[111] The standard position in a tenancy at will is that B also has the right to end the tenancy at any time. B may wish to use this right in a case where the tenancy at will includes a duty to pay rent.

[112] If A does end B's tenancy at will before the land is needed for road-widening, B can argue that A will be unjustly enriched if he is allowed to retain the benefit of the £5000 paid by B to A. B can argue that money was paid under a mistake of law: B wrongly believed he had a legal right to exclusive control of the land until the land was needed for road-widening. Compare eg *Nurdin & Peacock Plc v DB Ramsden & Co Ltd* [1999] 1 WLR 1249.

[113] Eg, a tenant at will had statutory protection under the Rent Acts.

[114] The same is true of the 'tenancy by sufferance'. This appears to be a form of tenancy by will, arising when B, after the expiry of a Lease, remains in physical control of the land without the consent of A. The tenancy at sufferance is basically a holding device that prevents any limitation period from running against A whilst he decides what to do about B. If A decides to object to B's possession, the tenancy by sufferance ends and B becomes a trespasser; if A decides to consent, the tenancy by sufferance ends and B becomes a tenant at will or, if he pays rent, a tenant with an implied periodic tenancy.

[115] *Per* Viscount Simonds in *Wheeler v Mercer* [1957] AC 416 at 427

(iii) A contractual right?

In **Examples 10b** and **10c**, can B instead rely on a simple contractual right against A? After all, it seems that B has a contractual licence: (i) A has given B liberty to occupy the land; and (ii) A is under a contractual duty to B not to revoke that liberty until the land is needed for road-widening. So, if A were to seek to remove B before that point, B could ask a court to specifically protect his right (see **E6:3.2**); even if no such order is made, B could then claim money from A as a result of A's breach of contract.

The courts seem to have rejected this possibility.[116] In *Prudential Assurance*, for example, Lord Browne-Wilkinson expressed some concern that, as a result of B having only a periodic tenancy, A was free to end B's right even if the land was not needed for road-widening. That was seen as the inevitable result of a finding that the planned Lease had not arisen; no consideration was given to the possibility that B might instead be able to assert a contractual licence against A. The assumption is that the parties' rights are governed *wholly* by the periodic tenancy or, in **Example 10c**, the tenancy at will.[117] This has the paradoxical consequence that, in **Examples 10b** and **10c**, B is *worse* off (in relation to A at least) as a result of the fact that his agreement with A gives him a right to exclusive control. If it did not give B such a right, B would simply have a contractual licence: A would be under a contractual duty to allow B to use the land until it was needed for road-widening and so could simply enforce that right against B.

1.7.3 A Lease for life?

A may attempt to give B a right to exclusive control of land until B's death; or until the death of someone other than B. In such a case, B should acquire a Lease: it is clear that, at some point in the future, A will regain his right to exclusive control of the land. Under the LPA 1925, B *does* acquire a Lease: but, under section 149(6), the Lease is recharacterised as a Lease for 90 years determinable on the death of the relevant person.[118] That provision puts a maximum duration on B's Lease: but it should not be thought that all Leases need to have such a limit. After all, in a periodic tenancy or tenancy at will it may not be clear, at the outset, how long B's right to exclusive control will last. But such Leases, like a Lease for life, are valid: it is certain that A will regain his right to exclusive control of the land.

SUMMARY of G1B:1.7

A Lease arises where A keeps his property right in land and gives B a right to exclusive control, for a limited period, of that land. A Lease for an unlimited period is a conceptual impossibility. Such a Lease would be inconsistent with A's property right: there must be a *guaranteed point at which A can again exercise his right to exclusive control of the land*. This requirement for a limited period is entirely consistent with the periodic tenancy and the tenancy at will. In each case, there is a definite point at which A can, if he wishes, regain exclusive control of the land.

---

[116] It was explicitly rejected by Lord Greene MR in *Lace v Chantler* [1944] KB 368 at 372.

[117] As noted by Bright, *Landlord and Tenant Law in Context* (2007) 75–6, there is no 'convincing reason' for this assumption.

[118] After that death, A has to give one month's written notice to end the Lease: s 149(6).

1.8   Covenants in Leases

1.8.1   Introduction

If A makes a contractual agreement giving B a right to exclusive control of land for a limited period, B has a Lease. In practice, the contract between them also imposes duties on B owed to A (eg, a duty to pay rent); and further duties on A owed to B (eg, to carry out major repairs). As a result, each of A and B will have rights against the other. Certain duties are implied *whenever* B has a Lease: B has a duty to A not to alter permanently the physical character of the land;[119] A has a duty to B not to interfere with B's expected use of the land and not to allow a substantial interference with B's physical control of the land (see **1.2** above).[120] And statutes may also impose duties when B has a Lease: for example, section 11 of the Landlord and Tenant Act 1985 imposes a duty on A to carry out particular repairs whenever B has a Lease, for seven years or less, of a home (see **1.2** above).

Some of the express, implied or statutory rights that B acquires against A may bind not only A but also A2, a party to whom A transfers his property right. And some of the express, implied or statutory rights that A acquires against B may bind not only B but also B2, a party to whom B transfers his Lease. Rights with this effect can be known as 'leasehold covenants'. They form part of A and B's initial landlord–tenant relationship and regulate that relationship even if A2 and B2 have now stepped into the shoes of A and B.

1.8.2   The effect of leasehold covenants

EXAMPLE 11a

A Ltd has a Freehold of business premises. A Ltd makes a contractual agreement with B Co under which B Co has a right to exclusive control of the land for 21 years. B Co promises to pay a rent of £1000 a month; A Ltd promises to undertake major repairs that may be required. A Ltd is a paper manufacturing business and so makes B Co promise that: (i) it will not run a paper manufacturing business on the land; and (ii) for the duration of the Lease, it will buy paper from A Ltd. In return, A Ltd promises to provide any paper ordered by B Co for its own use at a 15 per cent discount. B Co is substantively registered as holding a 21-year Lease. Two years later, A Ltd transfers its Freehold to A2; a further year later, B Co transfers its Lease to B2.

Freehold: A → A2   ↓ = grant of new Lease

Lease 1:   B → B2   → = transfer of existing Lease or Freehold

Initially, a landlord–tenant relationship existed between A and B. Such a relationship now exists between A2 and B2.

1.   A2 is under a duty to B2: (i) not to interfere with B2's right to exclusive control of the land; *and* (ii) to observe any landlord's 'leasehold covenants' contained in the

---

[119] See eg *Marsden v Edward Heyes* [1927] 2 KB 1, applying *Horsefall v Mather* (1815) Holt NP 7.
[120] See eg *Markham v Paget* [1908] 1 Ch 697.

agreement between A and B (such as the duty to carry out any major repairs that may be required).
2.   B2 is under a duty to A2 to observe any tenant's 'leasehold covenants' (such as the duty to pay a rent of £1000 a month).

This enforcement of 'leasehold covenants' is often said to depend on 'privity of estate': it arises because A2 has acquired A Ltd's estate (in this case, a Freehold)[121] and B2 has acquired B Co's estate (a Lease).

Whilst leasehold covenants can thus bind third parties, it would be a mistake to think of these covenants as independent property rights or persistent rights. They do *not* impose duties on the rest of the world; nor are they prima facie binding on any third party who acquires a right from A or B. Rather, they can only bind those third parties who step into the shoes of A or B by acquiring the *very property right* initially held by A (A's Freehold) or by B (B's Lease).

EXAMPLE 11b

The facts are as in **Example 11a**. B2 grants B3 a two-year Lease of the land. A2 then declares a Trust of its Freehold in favour of C.

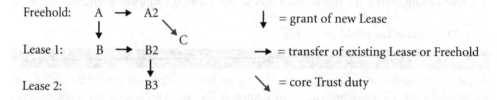

In such a case, B3 is *not* bound by any leasehold covenants in A and B's original Lease. Unlike B2, B3 has not stepped into the shoes of B: he has not acquired the very Lease B held. Instead, B2 has kept that property right and has given B3 a *new* property right. So, if B2 fails to perform his duty to pay £1000 a month rent to A2, A2 *cannot* sue B3 for that rent.

Similarly, C is *not* bound by any leasehold covenants in A and B's original Lease. Unlike A2, C has not stepped into the shoes of A: he has not acquired the very Freehold A held. Instead, A has kept that property right and has given C a *new* persistent right. So, if A2 fails to perform his duty to carry out repairs, B2 *cannot* sue C.

Leasehold covenants therefore need to be carefully distinguished from the Restrictive Covenant (see **E2:1.3.2** and **G6**). In **Examples 11a** and **11b**, B Co's promise not to run a paper manufacturing business on the land gives A Ltd a Restrictive Covenant. That right counts as a persistent right and so can bind not just B Co but also *anyone* who acquires a right that depends on B Co's right. So, in **Example 11b**, A Ltd has a prima facie power to assert its Restrictive Covenant against B3 and thus to impose a duty on B3 not to run a paper manufacturing business on the land. Of course, there is an important difference in the content of a Restrictive Covenant and a leasehold covenant. To count as a Restrictive

---

[121] The principle applies in the same way if the initial landlord–tenant relationship arises when A, a party with a Lease, grants B a sub-Lease.

Covenant (a persistent right) B Co's promise must be *negative*: it must be a promise *not* to make a particular use of the land.[122] In contrast, a positive duty, such as duty to pay rent, *can* count as a leasehold covenant.

1.8.3 The content of leasehold covenants

Not all rights arising in a Lease agreement count as leasehold covenants. In **Examples 11a** and **11b**, B Co's duty to pay rent binds B2; and A Ltd's duty to undertake major repairs bind A2. In contrast, B Co's promise to buy paper exclusively from A Ltd does *not* count as a leasehold covenant: it will not bind B2. And A Ltd's promise to provide any paper ordered by B Co for its own use at a 15 per cent discount does *not* count as a leasehold covenant: it will not bind A2.

This result was formerly reached by applying the rule that a duty imposed in a Lease counts as a leasehold covenant only if the content of the duty 'touches and concerns the land'.[123] However, the Landlord and Tenant (Covenants) Act 1995 adopts a different test. Under the Act, *any* promise in the original Lease will bind A2 and B2 *unless* it is apparent that the promise is personal to one or both of A and B.[124] It is by applying this new test that: (i) B Co's duty to buy paper from A Ltd will be held not to bind B2; and (ii) A Ltd's duty to sell paper to B Co at a discount will be held not to bind A2.

1.8.4 The Landlord and Tenant (Covenants) Act 1995

The Act sets out a code that: (i) applies to any Lease created on or after 1 January 1996;[125] and (ii) regulates how and when rights arising in a Lease can be enforced by, or against, parties other than A and B. The Act cannot be discussed in detail here.[126] However, one reform is worth noting.

The Act ensures that if B makes a promise to A in a Lease, B's contractual duty to A ends when B transfers the Lease to B2. Before this reform, B could remain under a contractual duty to A even after transferring his Lease.[127] Under the Act, B can only be held liable for B2's breach of a promise made by B *if* A and B have entered into an 'authorised guarantee arrangement' (AGA). Under such an arrangement, B guarantees that B2 will perform the promise originally made by B. B will then be liable for a breach by B2; but not for a breach by any later holder of the Lease, such as B3 or B4. On the face of it, there is not much incentive for B to enter into an AGA: however, as we will see in **2.2.2** below, the original

---

[122] See eg *Rhone v Stephens* [1994] 2 AC 310.

[123] Examples of promises not touching and concerning the land include a promise by B to repair tools (*Williams v Earle* (1868) LR 3 QB 739); and a promise by A to pay B money at the end of the Lease if the Lease is not renewed (*re Hunter's Lease* [1942] Ch 124).

[124] It is, in theory, possible to have a covenant that is personal to A but not to B (or vice versa). If a promise made by B is personal to B but not to A then: (i) it can be enforced by A2 against B; but (ii) it cannot be enforced by A or A2 against B2.

[125] The Act also affects the way in which, in a pre-1996 Lease, a landlord (eg, A, A2, A3, etc) can enforce B's duty to pay a fixed sum (eg, rent) after B has assigned his Lease to B2: see ss 17–19.

[126] For detailed discussion see eg Bright, *Landlord and Tenant Law in Context* (2007), ch 18.

[127] Similarly, B could assert his contractual right against A even after A transferred his Freehold to A2. Even after the Act, B can still bring a contractual claim in such a case. However, ss 6–8 allow A to avoid this liability if A gives notice of the transfer to B and B does not object; or if A gives notice to B and a court finds that it is reasonable for A to be released from his contractual duty to B.

Lease will often state that B must get A's consent to a transfer of the Lease. As a condition of giving such consent, A may require that B enter into an AGA.

2 THE ACQUISITION QUESTION

2.1 Independent acquisition?

It is impossible for B to acquire a Lease by means of an independent acquisition. If B takes physical control of land, he acquires a Freehold: there is no time limit to his right to exclusive control.

EXAMPLE 12

A has a Freehold owner. He gives B1 a 99-year Lease of his land. Whilst B1 is absent, B2 takes physical control of the land.

In such a case B2 independently acquires a Freehold: he does not acquire B1's Lease. This is confirmed by the decision of the Court of Appeal in *Tichborne v Weir*.[128] In that case, it was held that a leasehold covenant entered into by B1 did not bind B2. As we have seen, a leasehold covenant can bind B2 only if B2 steps into B1's shoes by acquiring B1's Lease (see **1.8.2** above). And, in **Example 12**, B2 does *not* acquire B1's Lease; instead he independently acquires a Freehold. If, as occurred in *Tichborne*, B2 remains in physical control of the land for a long period and a statutory limitation period extinguishes B1's Lease,[129] the position does not change. The limitation statute does *not* transfer B1's Lease to B2: it simply extinguishes B1's Lease.[130]

It seems, however, that the Land Registration Act 2002 departs from this basic position. Let us say that, in **Example 12**, B2 retains physical control of the land for 10 years. Under Schedule 6 of the 2002 Act, B2 can then apply to be registered: not, it seems, as the holder of his own, independent Freehold; but rather as the new holder of B1's registered Lease.[131] There is no principled justification for this approach. By taking physical control of the land, B2 acquires a Freehold rather than a Lease.[132] And if B2 is registered as the new holder of B1's Lease, B2 then acquires a set of rights against, and duties to, A.[133] Yet there is no doctrinal reason why B2 should acquire the rights or duties arising under A and B1's initial Lease agreement.

There is simply no need for the approach adopted in the 2002 Act: the transfer of B1's

---

[128] See eg *Tichborne v Weir* (1892) 67 LT 735.

[129] See Limitation Act 1980, s 17 (see **G1A:3**).

[130] As Lord Esher MR noted in *Tichborne v Weir* (1892) 67 LT 73, the limitation statute does not effect a 'statutory conveyance' of B1's Lease to B2.

[131] This is the assumption made by the Law Commission: see Law Com No 271 at eg 14.69. The odd wording of para 1 of Sch 6 of the 2002 Act states that B2 may apply to be registered as holding a 'registered estate in land if he has been in adverse possession of the *estate* [emphasis added] for the period of ten years ending on the date of the application'. Of course, it is the land itself, not B1's estate, that B2 adversely possesses.

[132] This is acknowledged in Law Com No 271 at eg 14.68 and also by para 9(1) of Sch 6 of the LRA 2002: where B is registered following his adverse possession 'the title by virtue of adverse possession which he had at the time of the application is extinguished'. So, in **Example 12**, B2's Freehold thus disappears, to be replaced by the registered Lease. It is of course bizarre that the B2's registration should extinguish *B2's right* as well as B1's right.

[133] See the discussion of leasehold covenants in **1.8** above.

Lease to B2 is both unprincipled and unnecessary. The lapse of time should simply lead (as it does in unregistered land)[134] to the extinction of B1's pre-existing Lease.[135] A better solution, if B2 satisfies the criteria laid down by Schedule 6 of the 2002 Act, is to rectify the register so as to: (i) remove B1's Lease; and (ii) register B2 as holding a new Freehold. B2's Freehold would of course be qualified by the fact that it is subject to A's pre-existing registered Freehold. This would mean there would be *two* separate registered Freeholds: one held by A, the other by B. That prospect seems to have deterred the drafters of both the Land Registration Act 1925[136] and the 2002 Act. However, the simultaneous existence of two Freeholds is nothing to fear (see **G1A:2.1.3**): we have a clear rule that says that A's Freehold, as it arose first, can be asserted against B2.

2.2 Dependent acquisition

B can only acquire a Lease if A has validly exercised his power to give B a Lease. If A has a Freehold or Lease, A can grant B a new Lease. Alternatively, if A already has a Lease, he can transfer that pre-existing property right to B.

2.2.1 Creation of a New Lease

(i) Express grant

A's power to give B a Lease can be regulated by the formality rules imposed by section 52 of the LPA 1925 and section 27 of the LRA 2002 (see **E1:2.3**).

	Section 52 LPA: is a deed necessary?	Section 27 LRA: is substantive registration necessary?
Lease of three years or less	Yes *unless* section 54(2) LPA applies	No *unless* the Lease is 'exceptional'
Lease of more than three years but no more than seven years	Yes	No *unless* the Lease is 'exceptional'
Lease of more than seven years	Yes	Yes

It is clear from the table that we need to know: (i) the scope of section 54(2) of the LPA 1925; and (ii) the definition of an 'exceptional' Lease.

(a) Section 54(2) of the LPA 1925

The first exception, set out in section 54(2) of the LPA 1925, applies only if three conditions are met:

- A grants B a Lease of three years or less; *and*

---

[134] Limitation Act 1980, s 17.

[135] In fact, the Law Commission's original plan (Law Com No 254 at 10.70 to 10.76, 10.78) *was* to allow B to register as holding his own, independent Freehold. However, the Commission changed its mind following the decision in *Central London Commercial Estates Ltd v Kato Kagaku Ltd* [1998] 4 All ER 948. That decision was based on the odd provisions of s 75 of the 1925 Act: it is unfortunate that its effect lives on.

[136] Under s 75 of the LRA 1925, the very odd response was to impose a statutory Trust: in **Example 12**, the expiry of the limitation period would lead to B1 holding his registered Lease on Trust for B2.

- B has an immediate right to exclusive control of the land; *and*
- B is under a duty to pay the 'best rent that is reasonably obtainable without taking a fine'.

If those conditions are met, B can acquire a Lease without the need for a deed and without there being *any writing at all*. Section 54(2) is thus an exception to section 52 as it allows short Leases to be created orally. However, it is important to note that *not all short Leases are covered by the exception.*

EXAMPLE 13a

A has a Freehold. On 1 March, A and B sign a document stating that B will have a right to exclusive control of the land for three years from 1 April. B is under a duty to pay £1000 a month as rent.

In such a case, B *cannot* rely on section 54(2). B's claimed Lease does not 'take effect in possession' as there is a gap between A and B's agreement and the start of B's right to exclusive control.[137] As a result, the basic section 52 formality rule applies: as no deed has been used, A has not exercised his power to give B the intended three-year Lease.

EXAMPLE 13b

A has a Freehold. On 1 March, A and B sign a document stating that B has a three-year Lease. A reasonable market rent would be £1000 a month but, as A and B are friends, B is under a duty to pay only £500 a month. B moves into the premises immediately.

Again, B *cannot* rely on section 54(2). His claimed Lease is not 'at the best rent which can be reasonably obtained without taking a fine'. So, as no deed has been used, A has not exercised his power to give B the intended three-year Lease.

There does seem to be logic to the requirements of section 54(2). Formality rules can have disadvantages (see **C3:4.2**). In particular, the time and possible expense involved in using a deed may be inappropriate where A plans to give B only a short Lease. Further, where the Lease is for three years or less, the advantages of a formality rule may be less important. For example, the need for *caution* and to *protect A from a fraudulent claim* is reduced: B's right will be of relatively short effect and, in return for temporarily losing his right to exclusive control of the land, A will at least receive a reasonable rent from B.

If A can give a short Lease orally, the absence of a deed or writing can make B's Lease difficult for C to discover.[138] The conditions of section 54(2) therefore give C some protection. First, the requirement for B's right to exclusive control to arise immediately *reduces the risk* to C of being bound by a hidden Lease. If there were no such requirement then, in **Example 13a**, C could be bound by B's oral Lease even if C acquired A's Freehold on 15 March: at that point, it would be very difficult for C to discover B's Lease. It should be noted, however, that the test is whether the agreement between A and B gives B an immediate *right* to exclusive control of the land, not whether B immediately exercises that right. So, if in **Example 13a**, B's right to exclusive control began on 1 March, section 54(2)

---

[137] *Long v Tower Hamlets LBC* [1998] Ch 197: see Bright [1998] *Conv* 229.

[138] It is worth noting that C will not be able to rely on the lack of registration defence as a Lease counts as an overriding interest: see para 1 of Sch 3 of the LRA 2002, discussed in **E1:3.6**.

would apply even if, in fact, B did not move into until 1 April. Second, the 'best rent' requirement *softens the blow* to C of being bound by B's Lease. Even if C is under a duty to allow B exclusive control of the land for the remainder of the Lease, C will at least receive the rent due from B.[139]

(b) 'Exceptional' Leases under section 27 of the LRA 2002

The general rule imposed by section 27 of the LRA 2002 is that A cannot exercise his power to grant B a property right if B does not substantively register his right (see **E1:2.3.4**). However, in general, that registration requirement does *not* apply if A grants B a Lease of seven years or less. The registration requirement is likely to be extended to all Leases of more than 3 years when electronic registration is up and running (see **E5:4.4**):[140] it will then be easier both for B to register his right and for the Land Registry to deal with the additional information such registration will bring. However, even if that change is introduced, there will still be unregistered Leases that may bind C. The justification is that the disadvantages of a formality requirement (eg, increased time and expense) outweigh the advantages that go with registration (ie, the publicity that makes it easier for C to discover B's right). In particular, even if B's Lease is not registered, it may still be possible for C to discover that right: either by discovering the deed used to create B's Lease (if it does not fall within section 54(2)); or by observing that B is in occupation of the land, or is taking rent from the occupier.

However, there are some exceptional Leases that are *particularly* hard for C to discover. These Leases,[141] which must be registered even if they are granted for a period of seven years or less, are:

1. Leases where the gap between A and B's agreement and the start of B's right to exclusive control is more than three months ('future Leases');[142]
2. Leases where, during the period of the Lease, B does not have a continuous right to exclusive control: eg, where B has a right to exclusive control only in July and August of each year ('time-share Leases').[143]

In both cases, the publicity provided by registration is particularly important: C may acquire a right from A at a point when B has a Lease *but* does not have a right to exclusive control of the land. In case 1, as we noted above when examining **Example 13a**, C may acquire a right from A in the gap between A's agreement with B and the start of B's right to exclusive control. In case 2, C may acquire a right from A in the period of the year when B does not have his right to exclusive control.

---

[139] This element also helps to protect A: the cautionary function of the formality requirement is less important when, in returning for giving B a Lease, A acquires a reasonable rent.

[140] See Law Com No 271 at 3.17, 3.30, 4.20, 6.11.

[141] Under s 27(2)(b)(iv) and (v) of the LRA 2002, two other forms of Lease also require substantive registration even if they are granted for seven years or less. These Leases arise under the Housing Act 1985: under that Act, one of the conditions applying to such Leases was that they had to be registered (see s 154 and Sch 9A para 2(1) of the Housing Act 1985). So the 2002 Act simply confirmed that position.

[142] LRA 2002, s 27(2)(b)(ii).

[143] LRA 2002, s 27(2)(b)(iii).

(ii) Inferred grant: the implied periodic tenancy

(a) Definition

If A has not expressly exercised his power to give B a Lease, it may still be possible for a court to *infer*, from the conduct of A and B, that A has exercised that power.

That inference arises only if: (i) B has offered payments of rent; and (ii) A has accepted those payments. In such a case, B's Lease is referred to as an *implied periodic tenancy*. So, when examining **Example 10b**, we saw that A's continued acceptance of rent can lead a court to infer that A has given B a succession of yearly Leases. As demonstrated by **Example 10b**, that inference can be made even where A tried and failed to give B a Lease of a different length. Similarly, in **Examples 13a and 13b**, A's acceptance of a monthly rent can lead a court to infer that A has given B a succession of monthly Leases.

It is often said that, for the inference to arise, B also needs to be in physical control of A's land.[144] That may, of course, be very helpful in making clear that a payment made to A by B was a rent payment and was not made for some other reason. Technically, however, it does not seem to be necessary for B to be in physical control of A's land.[145] An implied periodic tenancy can arise as long as a court is confident that B's money was offered and accepted as rent: as a payment in return for a right to exclusive control of A's land for a limited period.[146]

Where B's Lease arises under an implied periodic tenancy, the period of the Lease will depend on the basis on which B's rent was calculated. If it was calculated on a weekly basis, B will have a succession of weekly Leases; if on a monthly basis, B will have a succession of monthly Leases; if on a yearly or part-yearly basis (eg, quarterly or six-monthly), B will have a succession of yearly Leases.

Of course, if rent is paid by B and accepted by A, there will usually be an express agreement between the parties. However, in such cases, there may be a reason why that express agreement does not give rise to a Lease.

1. A and B's express agreement may not amount to a valid exercise by A of his power to give B a Lease. As shown by **Example 10b**, that agreement may not give B a right to exclusive control *for a limited period*; and as shown by **Examples 13a and 13b**, A may not have complied with a *formality rule* regulating his power to give B a Lease.

2. A and B's express agreement may have expired: for example, as in **Examples 3 and 9a**, B may remain in physical control of the land and continue paying rent after the end of an expressly agreed Lease.

3. Where A and B are negotiating for, but have not yet reached, an express agreement, A may nonetheless allow B to take control of the land and begin paying rent.

In some ways, B's acquisition of a Lease by means of an implied periodic tenancy appears to

---

[144] See eg *per* Kelly CB in *Martin v Smith* (1874) LR 9 EX 50 at 52.

[145] See eg *Huffell v Armistead* (1865) 7 C&P 56. B did in fact take physical control of the land, but the implied periodic tenancy was found to arise *before* B did so.

[146] There may be cases in which B pays money in return for permission from A to occupy A's land and that payment does *not* count as rent. In *Leadenhall Residential 2 Ltd v Stirling* [2002] 1 WLR 499, A obtained a possession order but declined to enforce it as long as B paid A rent arrears due under a previous Lease and 'mesne profits', ie, a monthly sum payable by B as a result of his wrongful occupation of A's land. There was no implied periodic tenancy as the money paid by B was *not* rent under a new Lease. Instead, that money was the price paid by B in return for A not enforcing the possession order. Whilst that arrangement was in place B was thus, in effect, a 'tolerated trespasser' (see **1.5.5(ii)(a)** above): see eg *per* Lloyd J at [30].

be an example of independent acquisition. However, B does *not* gain his right simply as a result of his own conduct: rather B's right arises because the court infers that A exercised his power to give B a Lease. B's right comes from an inference made about the intentions of *both* A and B, derived from *both* parties' conduct. In particular, as we will see in (c) below, it is important to remember that payment and acceptance of money does not *guarantee* B a Lease. If A can show he nonetheless did *not* intend to give B a right to exclusive control of the land for a fixed term, but rather accepted B's money for some other reason, the court will not infer that A granted B a Lease.

(b) Formalities

An implied periodic tenancy is based on an assumption that A has exercised his power to give B a Lease. This raises the question of how formality rules apply to the acquisition of such a Lease. First, there can be no need for B substantively to register: the inferred Lease will have a term, at the longest, of a year. Second, in some cases, B can rely on section 54(2) to escape the need for a deed. However, section 54(2) only applies where B's Lease is 'at the best rent that is reasonably obtainable without taking a fine' and there is no guarantee that B's claimed periodic tenancy will satisfy this requirement: to acquire such a Lease, B must be paying *some* rent, but he need not be paying the *best* rent reasonably obtainable.

So, if section 54(2) does not apply, then A could argue that, as no deed has been used, B does not have a Lease. In practice, however, this argument will not succeed. As in **Examples 10b, 13a and 13b**, an implied periodic tenancy can arise even if no deed has been used. One technical reason is that an implied periodic tenancy is covered by section 52(2)(d) of the LPA 1925, which exempts 'leases or tenancies or other assurances not required by law to be made in writing'. Further, the facts giving rise to the implied periodic tenancy may: (i) provide the necessary *evidence* of A and B's intentions; *and* (ii) provide *publicity* by alerting C to the existence of B's Lease.

(c) Doctrine and practical convenience

If an implied periodic tenancy arises, B will have a Lease and thus may gain statutory protection. As a result, in deciding whether to infer that A has exercised his power to grant B a Lease, a court may be influenced by the desirability or otherwise of allowing B such protection. As we saw in **1.5** above, the perceived needs of practical convenience may affect a court's willingness to find that B has a Lease. The tension between doctrine and practical convenience is particularly acute in this context: if an implied periodic tenancy arises, A may be burdened by statutory duties to B even though A has not *expressly* given B any rights.

EXAMPLE 14

A has a Freehold of business premises. A and B begin negotiating about the possible grant by A of a 10-year Lease to B. B pays £2500 to A as 'rent for three months in advance' and takes physical control of the land. The negotiations then break down and A attempts to remove B from the land.

In such a case, B can argue that: (i) as a result of A's acceptance of rent, B has a Lease (arising under an implied periodic tenancy); *and* (ii) as B has a Lease of business premises, he has a statutory right (under Part II of the Landlord and Tenant Act 1954) to renew that Lease and hence to remain in occupation of the land. However, in *Javad v Mohammed*

Aqil,[147] on which the facts of **Example 14** are based, the Court of Appeal rejected B's argument. The court's approach was expressly influenced by the statutory background. Noting the 'extent to which statute has intervened in landlord–tenant relationships',[148] Nicholls LJ held that the courts should be cautious in inferring that A has exercised his power to give B a Lease.

The perceived needs of practical convenience can thus influence a court's willingness to find an implied periodic tenancy. In **Example 14**, it may seem undesirable for B to have any statutory protection. It is clear that A wanted to be free to remove B if the negotiations for an expressly agreed Lease failed. And if B does acquire statutory protection in such a case, the wider commercial effects could be harmful: in future cases, A would be reluctant to allow B into occupation of the premises during the parties' negotiations. A would thus lose the chance of receiving rent from B during that period; and B would lose the chance to get his business up and running as soon as possible.

Nonetheless, the approach taken in *Javad* can be easily reconciled with doctrine.[149] The statutory protection available to those with Leases makes A *less likely* to intend to give B a right to exclusive control for a limited period. As a matter of *fact*, the courts must then be more careful about inferring that A has exercised his power to give B a Lease. And in *Javad* itself, as A and B were involved in ongoing and uncertain negotiations, it was in any case very unlikely that A would wish to give B a right to exclusive control *for a set period* such as a week, a month or a year. After all, A wants to retain the right to remove B from the land if the negotiations come to nothing. So, in a case such as **Example 14**, the correct inference to draw, as in *Javad*, is that A intends to give B a right to exclusive control of the land that A can terminate *whenever A wishes*. As a result, B does not acquire a weekly, monthly or yearly Lease under an implied periodic tenancy: instead, B acquires a tenancy at will.[150] And, under Part II of the Landlord and Tenant Act 1954, a tenant at will of business premises does *not* have a right to renew his Lease. So, in a case such as **Example 14**, a court does not need to depart from doctrine in order to find that B has no statutory protection.[151]

(iii) What if B1 grants B2 a Lease in breach of the terms of B1's Lease?

EXAMPLE 15

A has a Freehold. A grants B1 a 21-year Lease. A's agreement with B1 contains a term preventing B1 from transferring the Lease or from granting a sub-Lease without A's consent. The agreement also states that, if B1 breaches that promise, A can terminate B1's Lease. One year later, B1 grants B2 a 10-year Lease without obtaining A's consent.

---

[147] [1999] 1 WLR 1007.

[148] *Ibid* at 1012.

[149] See too Bright, ch 2 in *Landlord and Tenant Law: Past, Present and Future* (ed Bright, 2006).

[150] See too *Cardiothoracic Institute v Shrewdcrest Ltd* [1986] 1 WLR 368: there B remained in occupation after the expiry of a Lease while A and B negotiated about the grant of a new Lease. Knox J found that there was no implied periodic tenancy and that B instead was a tenant at will.

[151] Similarly, if A is a local authority, the security of tenure given by Part IV of the Housing Act 1985 does *not* apply if B has only a tenancy at will: *Banjo v Brent London Borough Council* [2005] 1 WLR 2520. A tenancy at will can, however, qualify for protection, where A is a private landlord, as an assured tenancy under the Housing Act 1988. In *Leadenhall Residential 2 Ltd v Stirling* [2002] 1 WLR 499, the Court of Appeal effectively allowed the 'tolerated trespasser' concept to be used to find that, even though A allowed B to retain physical control of land in return for payment, there was neither a tenancy at will nor an implied periodic tenancy and hence that B did not have statutory protection as an assured tenant. In such a case, the needs of practical convenience, discussed in 1.5.5(ii)(a) above, seem to dictate the result.

In such a case, B2 *does* acquire a 10-year Lease.[152] When B1 deals with B2, B1 has a right to exclusive control of the land for the next 20 years: B1 therefore has the power to give B2 such a right for the next 10 years. However, by granting B2 that Lease, B1 is in breach of his contractual duty to A and A has a power to *terminate* B1's Lease. If a court allows A to exercise that power and end B1's Lease,[153] B1's right to exclusive control will end. As a result, B2's Lease, derived from and dependent on B1's right to exclusive control, will also end. B1's breach can thus have an important effect on B2 (see further **2.2.2(ii)** below).

2.2.2 Transfer of a pre-existing Lease

If B2 claims that he has acquired a Lease as a result of B1's transfer to B2 of a pre-existing Lease, B2 needs to show that: (i) B1 had a Lease; and (ii) that B1 exercised his power to transfer that Lease to B2.

(i) Formality rules

Formality rules can regulate B1's power to transfer a Lease. For example, if B1's Lease is substantively registered, section 27 of the LRA 2002 applies: B1's Lease can only be transferred to B2 if B2 is substantively registered as the new holder of the Lease. If B1's Lease is not substantively registered, section 52 of the LPA 1925 applies: A's Lease can only be transferred to B by means of a deed.

EXAMPLE 16a

A has a Freehold. A orally gives B1 a right to exclusive control of the land for three years. B1's right to exclusive control arises immediately and is given in return for a market rent. B1 wishes to transfer that Lease to B2.

B1's Lease can arise even though no deed has been used: it meets the requirements of section 54(2) of the LPA 1925 (see **2.2.1(i)(a)** above). Nonetheless, B1 *cannot* orally transfer that Lease to B2. A deed must be used as the general section 52 formality rule applies. As confirmed by the Court of Appeal in *Crago v Julian*,[154] the section 54(2) exception applies only to the *creation* of Leases, not to their transfer.

(ii) What if B1's transfer to B2 is a breach of the terms of B1's Lease?

EXAMPLE 16b

The facts are as in **Example 15** above: with the difference that, one year after acquiring his Lease from A, B1 transfers that Lease to B2.

---

[152] See *per* Lord Russell in *Old Grovebury Manor Farm Ltd v W Seymour Plant Sales and Hire Ltd (No 2)* [1979] 1 WLR 1397 at 1398 (that case involved a transfer of B1's Lease in breach of a duty to A, but the reasoning applies equally to the grant of a sub-Lease by B1).

[153] As we will see in **4.3** below, the courts have a discretion to prevent A exercising his power to terminate (or 'forfeit') B1's Lease.

[154] [1992] 1 WLR 372. If B1 attempts to transfer the Lease using writing that satisfies the Law of Property (Miscellaneous Provisions) Act 1989, s 2(1) (see **E2:2.2.3**) then, although B1 keeps his Lease, B2 may acquire an Equitable Lease (see eg *per* Lord Chelmsford LC in *Parker v Taswell* (1858) 2 De G & J 559 at 570–1 and **D2:2.1.2**).

In such a case, B2 *does* acquire B1's Lease.[155] It is simply not possible for A, in his agreement with B1, to deny B1 the power to transfer his Lease. The same rule applies where B1 has a Freehold: A cannot transfer a Freehold to B1 and deny B1 the power to transfer that Freehold to B2.[156] Across the property law system, there is a clear rule that if B1 has a right to exclusive control of a thing (eg, ownership of a thing other than land; a Freehold of land; or a Lease of land) then B1 *does* have the power to transfer that property right to B2. So, A cannot both: (i) transfer his right to exclusive control to B1 (even for a limited period); *and* (ii) prevent B1 from transferring that right to B2.[157]

However, in **Example 16b**, B1 is clearly in breach of his contractual duty to A. This can have an effect on B2. If A is allowed to exercise his power to terminate B1's Lease, B2's right to exclusive control, derived from and dependent on B1's Lease, will also end. As a result, A will be able to remove B2 from the land. So, in **Example 16b**, A can serve a notice on B2[158] and apply for a court order for possession of the land.

Although the court always has the discretion not to permit the termination of B1's Lease,[159] it is clear that B2's position can be affected by B1's duty to A not to transfer the Lease.[160] In fact, such terms are quite common.[161] For example, A may specify in his initial agreement with B1 that B1 can transfer the Lease to B2 only if B1 enters into an 'authorised guarantee arrangement' (AGA) (see **1.8.4** above).[162] That agreement will allow A to pursue a claim against B1 if B2 fails to perform a guaranteed duty, such as the duty to pay rent.

The initial agreement between A and B1 may provide that a transfer is allowed *if* the current landlord consents. In those cases, when B1 asks for permission to transfer his Lease, the Landlord and Tenant Act 1987, section 19, and the Landlord and Tenant Act 1988 impose various statutory duties on A (or any party, such as A2, who has since acquired A's initial Freehold or Lease). In particular: (i) A must respond to the request within a reasonable time; (ii) A must give consent, unless A can show that it is reasonable not to do so; (iii) A cannot impose conditions on that consent, unless A can show such conditions are

---

[155] *Old Grovebury Manor Farm Ltd v W Seymour Plant Sales and Hire Ltd (No 2)* [1979] 1 WLR 1397.

[156] See eg *Attwater v Attwater* (1853) 18 Beav 330; *re Elliot* [1896] 2 353, esp *per* Chitty J at 356: 'the owner of property has as an incident of his ownership the right to sell and to receive the whole of the proceeds for his own benefit.' *In re Macleay* (1875) LR 20 Eq 186 suggests a restriction on sales 'outside the family' can limit B's power to transfer a Freehold; however that decision has been questioned (see eg *re Rosher* (1884) 26 Ch D 801) and was not followed in *re Brown* [1954] 1 Ch 39.

[157] It may, however, be possible to impose such conditions where he gives B a right under a Trust: in such a case, B acquires only a persistent right.

[158] As B1's breach does not relate to non-payment of rent, s 146 of the LPA 1925 provides that A must serve a notice. In a case such as **Example 15**, the notice must be served on B2, not B1: see *Old Grovebury Manor Farm Ltd v W Seymour Plant Sales and Hire Ltd (No 2)* [1979] 1 WLR 1397.

[159] See s 146(2) of the LPA 1925 and eg *Hyman v Rose* [1912] AC 623.

[160] Under the Law Commission's proposed scheme for dealing with tenant defaults, a breach by B1 of a duty not to transfer the Lease is to be treated as a breach by B2: see Law Com No 303 (2006) at 3.60. This allows the scheme to apply where, in a case such as **Example 15**, A seeks to terminate B2's Lease.

[161] For further detail on such clauses and their interpretation see Bright, *Landlord and Tenant Law in Context* (2007) 530–34.

[162] Similarly, A could stipulate that B1 can grant a sub-Lease to B2 only if B2 makes a particular contractual promise to A. By that means, A can have greater control over B2's use of the land than would otherwise be possible. If he acquires a sub-Lease, B2 is not in a landlord–tenant relationship with A and so is not bound by leasehold covenants: see **1.8.2** above.

reasonable; and (iv) A must give B1 written notice of his decision, specifying any reasons for which A has denied the request.[163]

A's failure to comply with these statutory duties can count as a wrong against B1: in such a case, A will be under a duty to pay B1 money representing the value of B1's right and compensating B1 for any relevant loss suffered by B1.[164] Indeed, it may even be possible for punitive damages to be awarded if A's conduct is particularly outrageous.[165] As a result, if A enters a Lease with B1 and wants to have control over any transfer of the Lease, the safest option for A is simply to impose an absolute duty on B1 not to transfer the Lease. After all, if B1 then suggests a transfer that A is happy with, A can waive B1's duty. However, the problem for A may be that a Lease with such a prohibition on transfer may be a less attractive product: for example, B1 may expect to pay a lower rent in return for accepting such a prohibition.

In addition to any prohibitions that A may impose in his agreement with B1, statute can also impose duties on B1 in relation to the transfer of a Lease. For example,[166] the general rule is that, if B1 is a secure tenant under Part IV of the Housing Act 1985, he *cannot* assign that tenancy.[167] After all, if a local authority, in discharge of its statutory duties to provide housing, has chosen to give accommodation to B1, B1 cannot undermine that decision by transferring his Lease to B2.

SUMMARY of G1B:2

B can only acquire a Lease if A has validly exercised his power to give B a Lease. Where A attempts expressly to give B a new Lease, B will have to show: (i) that A intended to give him a right to exclusive control of the land for a limited period; and (ii) that any relevant formality rules have been complied with. If B is unable to do this, he may argue that, due to A's acceptance of rent paid by B, a court can *infer* that A exercised his power to grant B a Lease. If such an inference is made, B's Lease arises under an implied periodic tenancy. In such a case, the length of B's Lease will *not* be set by A and B's express agreement. Instead, it will depend on the period in relation to which B paid rent.

Where B1 has a Lease, he may transfer that Lease to B2. B2 will need to show: (i) that B1 intended to transfer his pre-existing Lease to B2; and (ii) that any relevant formality rules have been complied with. Even if B1's Lease arose orally under section 54(2) of the LPA 1925, B1's power to transfer that Lease to B2 *must* be exercised in a deed.

---

[163] See Landlord and Tenant Act 1988, ss 1 and 5(3). A cannot later rely on a particular reason for refusing consent if he does not notify B of that reason in writing within a reasonable time of B's request: see eg *Go West Ltd v Spigarolo* [2003] QB 1140 at [22]. For discussion of how these 'reasonableness' tests are applied see Bright, *Landlord and Tenant Law in Context* (2007) 524–30.

[164] See eg *Blockbuster Entertainment Ltd v Barnsdale Properties Ltd* [2003] EWHC 2912.

[165] See *Design Progression Ltd v Thurloe Properties Ltd* [2004] EWHC 324.

[166] For consideration of other statutory rules applying to residential Leases and the reforms proposed by the Law Commission in Report No 297 (2006) see Bright, *Landlord and Tenant Law in Context* (2007) at pp.534-542.

[167] Housing Act 1985, s 91(1): see eg *City of London Corp v Brown* (1989) 22 HLR 32. For discussion of the general rule and its exceptions see Bright, *Landlord and Tenant Law in Context* (2007) 535–7.

If B1 has a Lease, B1's conduct in transferring his Lease to B2, or giving B2 a new sub-Lease, may be a breach of the terms of B1's Lease with A. In such a case, B1's breach can cause problems for B2. It may be that B1's breach gives A a power to terminate B1's right to exclusive control. If A has that right, and is able to exercise it by terminating B1's Lease, B2's Lease will also end.

3 THE DEFENCES QUESTION

If B has a Lease, he has a property right in land. As a result, the rest of the world is under a prima facie duty to B, for the period of the Lease, not to interfere with B's right to exclusive control of that land. It is very difficult for C to have a defence to a pre-existing property right in land (see **E1:3**).[168]

In particular, if B has a Lease, it will be *impossible* for C to use the lack of registration defence against B's Lease. First, in order for B to acquire a Lease of more than seven years,[169] B will need to substantively register that Lease. In such a case, C will obviously be unable to rely on the lack of registration defence. Second, if B has managed to acquire a Lease without substantive registration, his Lease counts as an overriding interest: as a result, it is immune from the lack of registration defence.[170]

4 THE REMEDIES QUESTION

4.1 B's right to exclusive control

The core of a Lease is B's right to exclusive control of land for a limited period. The rest of the world is therefore under a prima facie duty to B, during the period of the Lease, not to interfere with B's exclusive control of the land. If a third party does not have a defence to B's Lease, and breaches that duty, that third party commits a wrong against B (see **E1:4.1.1**). B can then bring a claim against that third party based on the wrongs of trespass, nuisance or negligence: those wrongs apply in the way set out in **G1A:4.1.1**. A court will almost always grant a remedy that specifically protects B's right to exclusive control of the land.[171] In fact, if a third party is in physical control of the land, B will be able to use the speedy possession procedure made available by Part 55 of the Civil Procedure Rules.

---

[168] E1:3.7.1 examines when the lapse of time, in combination with other factors, may prevent B from resisting an application by C to have the register rectified and B's registered Lease removed.

[169] Or one of the exceptional Leases of seven years or less set out in s 27(2)(b)(ii)–(v) of the LRA 2002.

[170] LRA 2002, Sch 3 para 1.

[171] When Leases were first recognised as property rights, the rule was not a Lease (unlike a Freehold) would *not* be specifically protected. However, by the end of the 15th century at the latest, B's Lease was specifically protected (in the action of ejectment) and this distinction with the Freehold disappeared. See eg Simpson, *A History of the Land Law* (2nd edn, 1986) 144. Nonetheless, Leases were for long afterwards still seen 'personal property': see eg *Belaney v Belaney* (1866) LR 2 Eq 210 (if B1 has a Lease and, in his will, leaves his personal property and personal estate to B2, then B2 acquires the Lease).

4.2 B's rights under leasehold covenants

As well as his core right to exclusive control, B is likely to have other rights as a result of his agreement with A: for example, A may have a duty to carry out particular repairs. If those rights count as 'leasehold covenants', they will bind not only A but also any third party, such as A2, who steps into A's shoes and thus enters into the landlord–tenant relationship with B (see **1.8.2** above). The general position is that such rights, like other rights relating to land, are specifically protected. So if A breaches his duty to repair, B can: (i) claim money as compensation for any relevant loss that failure has caused him;[172] *and* (ii) get an order forcing A to ensure that the repairs are carried out.[173] An additional remedy is also available to B: it may be appropriate if, for example, A cannot be traced or A is refusing to comply with his duty to repair. That remedy is for the court to appoint a *receiver* or *manager:* a party who can take on some of the functions of a landlord and who can thus receive B's rent on A's behalf and use that money to fulfil A's duty to repair.[174]

If A or A2 commits a particularly serious breach of a leasehold covenant, B may try to use that as a reason to terminate his Lease. It is rare for his agreement with A to give B that power to terminate the Lease. However, there is a general contractual doctrine that allows one party to terminate a contract if the other party commits a fundamental breach of his contractual duties.[175] If A's breach deprives B of 'substantially the whole benefit'[176] B is due to receive under the contract, B can terminate that contract.

EXAMPLE 17

A has a Freehold of a house. A grants B a five-year Lease with a £300 monthly rent. A fails to carry out any repairs even though the ceiling of one bedroom has collapsed; water pipes have burst; part of the roof is leaking; and there is damp in the hall. B wants to terminate the Lease so that he is free to move out and no longer has to pay rent.

In such a case, even if A has not made a contractual promise to undertake repairs, section 11 of the Landlord and Tenant Act 1985 imposes such a duty on A. As A is in serious breach of that duty, B is entitled to terminate the Lease. By doing so, B releases himself from his duty to pay rent for the remainder of the five-year term. This analysis was adopted by Stephen Sedley QC, sitting in the County Court, when deciding *Hussein v Mehlman*,[177] on which **Example 17** is based. At the time, his decision was a novel one;[178] but the general principle it applies is surely correct and has since been confirmed by the Court of Appeal.[179]

---

[172] See eg *Wallace v Manchester CC* [1998] 3 EGLR 38.

[173] See eg *Jeune v Queen's Cross Ltd* [1974] Ch 97. See too Landlord and Tenant Act 1985, s 17. The surprising traditional rule, examined and disapproved of by Lawrence Collins QC in *Rainbow Estates Ltd v Tokenhold Ltd* [1999] Ch 64 was that any leasehold covenant imposing a duty to repair could not be specifically enforced.

[174] Supreme Court Act 1981, s 37(1). See eg *Hart v Emelkirk Ltd* [1983] 1 WLR 1289; *Caws and Fort Management Co Ltd v Stafford* [2007] EWCA Civ 1187.

[175] See eg Peel, *Treitel's Law of Contract* (12th ed, 2007), ch 18.

[176] *Per* Lord Diplock in *Afovos Shipping Co SA v R Pagnan ('The Afovos')* [1983] 1 WLR 195 at 202.

[177] [1992] 2 EGLR 87.

[178] See eg Bright [1993] Conv 71; Harpum (1993) 52 CLJ 212.

[179] See eg *Chartered Trust plc v Davies* (1998) 76 P & CR 396. That case did not concern a breach of a duty to repair, but the principle must apply whenever A's breach of duty deprives B of substantially the whole benefit he is due to receive under the agreement.

4.3   A's right to regain exclusive control

In a Lease, A, as well as B, has a property right in the land. The requirement that a Lease must be for a limited period ensures that, at some definite point in the future A can, if he wishes, regain exclusive control of the land (see **1.7.1** above). When the agreed period of B's Lease ends, then, if B has no statutory right to: (i) remain in occupation;[180] or (ii) to renew the Lease;[181] or (iii) to extend the Lease;[182] or (iv) to buy A's property right,[183] A's right to regain exclusive control will be specifically protected.[184]

If A wishes to terminate the Lease *before* the end of the agreed period, things are more difficult. A may well insert an express term in his agreement with B giving him the power to end the Lease early in certain circumstances: eg, if B fails to perform a leasehold covenant such as the duty to pay rent; or if, as in **Examples 15 and 16b**, B grants a sub-Lease or transfers his Lease to B2 without A's consent. Such a clause is said to give A the power to 'forfeit' B's Lease. However, A is not permitted to immediately remove B from the land by relying on such a clause. Instead, courts of Equity developed means of protecting B from the penal effects of such a clause; and legislation now provides B with further protection. Of course, there is a need to balance protection for B with A's legitimate interest in regaining control of the land. As a result, the law relating to the forfeiture of Leases is notoriously complex; simplifying reforms have been proposed in the Law Commission's 2006 Report.[185]

The Law Commission's proposals are based around: (i) one sensible idea that is *not* part of the present law; and (ii) two sensible ideas that form the basis of the present law. The first general principle is that A cannot bring an early end to B's Lease without a court order. Under the current law, B's Lease technically ends *before* a court order (even though A usually needs such an order to remove B): the court order is a response to the forfeiture that occurs when A exercises his power to terminate the Lease following B's breach.[186] This creates problems: it means B's occupation of the land in the period *after* a claim is brought is not fully regulated by the Lease agreement. For example, in that period, B is no longer under the contractual duty to pay rent to A.[187]

The second general principle behind the Law Commission's proposals is that, if B objects to being removed from the land, A must get a court order if A wants to obtain possession.[188] That principle is present in the current law; even though B's Lease ends before that

---

[180] As may be the case under Part IV of the Housing Act 1985 if A is a local authority.

[181] As may be the case under Part II of the Landlord and Tenant Act 1954 if B has a business Lease.

[182] As may be the case under the Leasehold Reform, Housing and Urban Development Act 1993 if B has a long lease (ie, a Lease granted for a term over 21 years) of a flat.

[183] As may be the case under, eg, the Leasehold Reform Act 1967 if B has a long Lease (ie, a Lease granted for a term over 21 years).

[184] Of course, in regaining exclusive control, A must be careful not to breach the Protection from Eviction Act 1977 (see **E6:3.4.2(vi)**). So if B refuses to leave, A should apply to court for a possession order.

[185] Law Com No 303 (2006).

[186] Under the current law, forfeiture can also occur by 'peaceable re-entry': by A entering the land. That method of forfeiture is 'dubious and dangerous' (*per* Lord Templeman in *Billson v Residential Apartments Ltd* [1992] 1 AC 494 at 536) and tends to be used only where B has abandoned business premises.

[187] See eg *Moore v Assignment Courier Ltd* [1977] 1 WLR 638. B instead has to pay 'mesne rent': a reasonable rent that can be seen based on the need either: (i) to prevent B being unjustly enriched at A's expense by occupying for free; or (ii) to compensate A for B's wrongful occupation of the land: see the discussion in *Ministry of Defence v Ashman* (1993) 66 P & CR 195 and **E1:4.3**.

[188] The proposals allow a 'summary termination' procedure: termination can then occur without a court order, but only if B fails, within one month, to object to a summary termination notice served by A.

point, A almost always needs to obtain a court order to remove B.[189] The third general principle is that the courts can give B protection in a case where, even though a forfeiture clause applies, B can remedy his breach. For example, courts of Equity were careful to protect B from a clause allowing forfeiture for non-payment of rent. Such a clause was seen, essentially, as a means for A to have *security* for B's duty to pay rent. Where one party *transfers* a right to another as security for a debt, the courts developed the notion of an 'Equitable right to redeem': even if the debtor did not pay the debt exactly as agreed, he could still regain the right transferred to the creditor if he made up the arrears (see **F4:1.3**). The same principle was applied to forfeiture cases: even if B breaches his duty to pay rent, a court has the discretion *not* to grant a possession order to A *if* B makes up the arrears.[190] That principle will also apply under the Law Commission's proposals.[191]

5   THE NATURE OF A LEASE: CONTRACT OR PROPERTY?

5.1   A false opposition

It is often said that there is a tension between two different views of the Lease. On the first view, the Lease is seen as primarily a *property right*; on the second, it is seen as chiefly a *contractual right*. The characterisation of the Lease as either primarily proprietary or chiefly contractual is said to have a practical effect in the contexts discussed in **5.3** below.

However, this tension is an illusion. There is *no* conflict between property rights on the one hand and contractual rights on the other. The classification of a right as a property right depends on the **content question**: does B's right impose a prima facie duty on the rest of the world not to interfere with B's use of a thing? The classification of a right as a contractual right depends on the **acquisition question**: does B's right arise as a result of a promise which, because it was made in an agreement for which consideration was provided, binds A? It is therefore perfectly possible for B to have a right that is *both*: (i) a property right; *and* (ii) a contractual right. An example occurs where A, by means of a sale, transfers his ownership of a bike to B. B acquires a property right; and that right arises as a result of the contractual bargain between A and B (see **D1:2.2.4(iii)**).

Indeed, in almost all cases where he has a Lease, B's right to exclusive control of land for a fixed period is *both*: (i) a property right; *and* (ii) a contractual right. It is a property right because it is a right, relating to a thing, that imposes a prima facie duty on the rest of the world (see **D1:1.1**). It is a contractual right as B acquires that right as a result of a promise made to B in return for which B provided consideration. In fact, B usually acquires a number of different contractual rights: (i) a right to exclusive control of the land for a limited period; (ii) the benefit of contractually agreed leasehold covenants (rights that can

---

[189] A may be able to bypass the need for a court order by exercising his right to peaceable re-entry, but that route is rarely available, see n 186 above.

[190] See eg *Howard v Fanshawe* [1895] 2 Ch 581. The analogy with security means that Equity's protection is limited to cases where B's breach consists of a failure to pay a sum of money due to A. A wider principle is enforced by statute: see eg LPA 1925, s 146.

[191] See eg cl 9(3)(c) of the Law Commission's draft Landlord and Tenant (Termination of Tenancies) Bill. A court can also make a 'remedial order' (see cl 13) denying A exclusive control of the land but specifying how B is to remedy his breach.

be enforced against parties later acquiring A's estate); and (iii) personal rights against A.[192] All those rights are **acquired** in the same way; but their **content** differs.

This analysis does not mean that a Lease *must* arise as a result of a contract. It is possible for a Lease to arise purely by consent: A can exercise his power to grant B a Lease *without* coming under any contractual duties to B.[193] However, it does mean that it is misleading to say that there is a tension between the proprietary view of the Lease and the contractual view of the Lease. A Lease is simply a property right that can, and almost always does, arise through a contract. Indeed, when analysing the practical problems that are often said to depend on a choice between the 'proprietary' and 'contractual' views, that false opposition only obscures the solution to the problems.

5.2   Leases as property rights

EXAMPLE 18

A has a Freehold. A makes an oral agreement to give B an immediate right to exclusive control of the land for three years, at a market rent. Before B takes physical control of the land, X moves in.

In such a case, X commits a wrong against B. Even though B has not taken physical control of the land, his agreement with A gives him a property right. The rest of the world is under a prima facie duty to B not to interfere with B's right, for the next three years, to exclusive control of the land. It is thus clear that B's right to exclusive control of the land is not *only* a contractual right: it is also a property right.

EXAMPLE 19

A makes a contractual promise to pay B1 £100. In his agreement with B1, A stipulates that B1 cannot transfer his contractual right against A. B1 then attempts to transfer his right to B2.

In such a case, B2 does *not* acquire B1's personal right against A. A has stipulated, in effect, that A's duty to pay £100 will end if B1 attempts to transfer his right against A. As B1's attempted transfer thus releases A from his duty to B1, B2 has no right he can assert against A.[194]

In contrast, we saw when examining **Examples 15 and 16b** above that if B1 transfers a Lease to B2 (or grants B2 a new Lease) in breach of his agreement with A, B2 *does* acquire a Lease. The problem for B2 is that A may be able to terminate that Lease but, nonetheless, B2 does acquire a property right. A Lease is thus treated in the same way as other Ownership rights (see **2.2.2(ii)** above): the usual rule applying to contractual rights, such as that in **Example 19**, does not apply. Again, it is clear that B's right to exclusive control of the land is

---

[192] So, in **Example 11a**, B Co's contractual rights include: (i) a right to exclusive control of the land for a limited period; (ii) a right that A Ltd and later owners of A's Ltd Freehold carry out major repairs; and (iii) a personal right against A Ltd that A Ltd must sell paper to B Co at a discount.

[193] See *per* Millett LJ (dissenting) in *Ingram v IRC* [1997] 4 All ER 395 at 421–2: 'There is no doubt that a lease is property. It is a legal estate in land. It may be created by grant or attornment as well as by contract and need not contain any covenants at all.' There was a successful appeal against the decision of the majority of the Court of Appeal ([2000] 1 AC 293) and Lord Hutton at 310 expressly agreed with Millett LJ's analysis of the nature of a Lease.

[194] See *Linden Gardens Trust Ltd v Lenesta Sludge Disposals Ltd* [1994] 1 AC 85.

not *only* a contractual right: it is also a property right giving B Ownership of land (for a limited period).

5.3   Leases as contractual rights

5.3.1 *Bruton v London & Quadrant Housing Trust*

We considered the House of Lords decision in *Bruton* in 1.5.3 above. We saw that its effect is to allow B to have a 'Lease', at least in the sense in which that term is used in the Landlord and Tenant Act 1985, even if B's agreement with A does not in fact give B a property right. According to the House of Lords, B can also have a 'Lease' if A is under a contractual duty to give B a right to exclusive control of land for a limited period. The decision can be analysed as favouring a 'contractual' rather than a 'proprietary' view of the Lease. However, such an analysis must be treated with a great deal of caution.

First, the *decision* in *Bruton* can be easily explained. As A had taken physical control of the land, A had its own independently acquired Freehold and was thus in a position to give B a Lease, in the standard sense of a property right in land (see **Example 5a** above). So, in *Bruton*, as in many other cases, B's Lease is *both* a property right and a contractual right. Second, the *reasoning* in *Bruton* can also be explained. The term 'Lease', at least when used in the Landlord and Tenant Act 1985, may be given an extending meaning including: (i) cases where B has a property right; and (ii) cases B has a personal right against A to exclusive control of land for a limited period. The point is simply that B's right can count as a 'Lease' (for the purposes of a particular statute) even if it gives B only a personal right against A. The *Bruton* reasoning thus has no effect at all on the vast majority of cases, in which B's Lease is *both* a property right and a contractual right.

5.3.2 The doctrine of termination for breach

If A commits a particularly serious breach of a leasehold covenant, it may be possible for B, under general contractual principles, to terminate his Lease agreement with A (see **4.2** above). This is an application of a doctrine that allows one party to terminate a contract if the other party commits a fundamental breach of his contractual duties. The application of that doctrine to the Lease can be analysed as favouring a 'contractual' rather than a 'proprietary' view of the Lease. However, that analysis, again, must be treated with caution.

First, the application of a contractual doctrine to Leases is no surprise: as we have seen, if B has a Lease, he almost always has *both* a property right *and* a contractual right. The possibility of termination for breach thus proves only that a Lease may depend on a contract; it does *not* show that a Lease is not a property right.

The real issue in a case such as **Example 17**, where B attempts to terminate a Lease as a result of A's breach, is the *characterisation of the parties' bargain*. B acquires a power to terminate a contract if A's breach deprives B of 'substantially the whole benefit'[195] of his bargain with A. If, in **Example 17**, we say that B has essentially bargained for *only* a right to exclusive control of land for five years, A's failure to carry out repairs cannot give B a power to terminate: it does not affect B's right to exclusive control. If, instead, we say that B has

---

[195] *Per* Lord Diplock in *Afovos Shipping Co SA v R Pagnan* ('*The Afovos*') [1983] 1 WLR 195 at 202. See further Peel, *Treitel's Law of Contract* (12th ed, 2007) ch 18.

essentially bargained for accommodation of a certain minimum standard for five years, A's failure to carry out repairs *can* give B a power to terminate: it may affect the quality of B's accommodation. The real question, unrelated to the supposed 'property' v 'contract' debate, is therefore *how we view B's bargain*.[196] In decisions such a *Hussein v Mehlman*[197] the courts have moved to the eminently sensible view that, in a residential Lease, B *can* lose substantially the whole benefit of his bargain even if he still has the right to exclusive control of land. As a result, the doctrine of termination for breach gains a new prominence. However, this does not mean that the Lease is now seen as more 'contractual' as opposed to 'proprietary'. Instead, it simply means that the essence of A and B's bargain is now characterised in a different, more realistic way: it is not enough for A to give B a property right in land; B is interested in having somewhere habitable to live.

Second, it is vital to note that the doctrine of termination for breach forms part of a wider principle that can operate *even in the absence of a contract*.[198] For example, let us say B is keen to purchase A's house. A and B make a preliminary, non-binding agreement and B pays A £1000 'subject to contract' to demonstrate his keenness. If B later decides not to proceed with the purchase, then there will be no contract between the parties. Nonetheless, B has (at least) a personal right against A:[199] A is under a duty to pay B £1000. B's right arises because the reason for which B paid A (the contemplated purchase) no longer exists. As a result, A would be unjustly enriched at B's expense if A were not under a duty to pay B £1000.[200]

The same principle underlies cases of termination for breach of contract. B is allowed to end the contract because he is no longer receiving substantially the whole benefit of his bargain: the basis on which he entered the contract has failed. The contractual doctrine is thus an example of a *wider* principle that, as shown by the example of the £1000 payment, is *not* limited to contracts. The wider principle can apply whenever one party *chooses* to give another a right.[201] Its application to Leases, therefore, does not prove that Leases are chiefly contractual. Instead, it reflects the obvious point that a Lease arises as a result of the consent of A and B.

5.3.3 The doctrine of frustration

EXAMPLE 20

A has a Freehold of business premises. A grants B Ltd, a logistics company, a 21-year Lease at a rent of £10,000 per month. A knows that B Ltd intends to use the premises as a distribution warehouse. A year later, to both parties' surprise, the road leading to the premises is permanently shut, making it impossible for B Ltd to make his intended use of A's land.

---

[196] See Bright, *Landlord and Tenant Law in Context* (2007) 30–33.

[197] [1992] 2 EGLR 87.

[198] See eg Birks, *An Introduction to the Law of Restitution* (1985) 223–6.

[199] B should also have a power to acquire a persistent right against A's right to the £1000 (see **D4:4.2**).

[200] *Chillingworth v Esche* [1924] 1 Ch 97. The payment there was made as a 'deposit and in part payment of the purchase price'. It was found that the payment was not made as a guarantee by B that he would complete the purchase (see eg *per* Pollock MR at 107): hence A was under a duty to return the deposit to B. Note that even if the payment had been made as such a guarantee, the court now has a discretion to order its return: LPA 1925, s 49(2).

[201] See McFarlane and Stevens (2002) 118 *LQR* 569, and the works cited therein, for a fuller discussion of 'failure of basis' and the different senses in which the phrase has been used.

In such a case, is B Ltd still under a duty to pay A £10,000 a month rent for the next 20 years? B will argue that the dramatic change of circumstances means that his agreement with A has been *frustrated* and that the contractual duties of A and B are thus at an end.

Prior to 1981, it seems that the courts would not accept B Ltd's argument. It was assumed that a Lease could never be frustrated as, no matter how circumstances might change, B Ltd would still have the right to exclusive control of the land for a limited period. As long as B's acquisition of that right is seen as the defining feature of his agreement with A, that agreement can never be frustrated. However, in *National Carriers Ltd v Panalpina (Northern) Ltd*,[202] the House of Lords adopted a different approach, holding that it is possible, in extreme circumstances, for an agreement giving B a Lease to be frustrated. The application of the doctrine of frustration to the Lease can be analysed as supporting a 'contractual' rather than a 'proprietary' view of the Lease. However, that analysis, again, must be treated with caution. In fact, we can make exactly the same points as are made in **5.3.2** above.

First, the application of a contractual doctrine to Leases is no surprise: as we have seen, if B has a Lease, his property right is almost always a contractual right. The possibility of a Lease being frustrated thus proves only that a Lease may depend on a contract; it does *not* show that a Lease is not a property right.

The novelty of the House of Lords' reasoning in *Panalpina* does not consist in seeing the Lease as based on a contract. Again, it depends on the *characterisation of the parties' bargain*. The basic test for frustration is whether the new circumstances deprive one or both of the parties of 'substantially the whole benefit'[203] of their bargain. The test is thus very similar to that applying to B's power to terminate for breach. So, in **Example 20**, if we say that, in essence, B Ltd has bargained *only* for a right to exclusive control of land for 21 years, the closure of the road cannot frustrate the Lease, as it does not affect B's right to exclusive control. If, instead, we say that, in essence, B has bargained for control of a distribution warehouse for 21 years, the closure of the road *can* frustrate the contract. The real question, unrelated to the supposed 'property' v 'contract' debate, is therefore how we view B's bargain. In the *Panalpina* decision, the House of Lords took the eminently sensible view that, in a commercial Lease, B *can* lose substantially the whole benefit of his bargain even if he still has the right to exclusive control of land.[204] As a result, the doctrine of frustration gains a new prominence. However, this does not mean the Lease is now seen as more 'contractual' as opposed to 'proprietary': it simply means that the essence of A and B's bargain is now characterised in a different, more realistic way.

Second, the doctrine of frustration is, in any case, not a purely contractual principle. Like the doctrine of termination for breach, examined in **5.3.2** above, it rests on the wider 'failure of basis' principle. The possibility of a Lease being frustrated thus proves only that a Lease arises as a result of the consent of A and B.

---

[202] [1981] AC 675.

[203] See eg *Davis Contractors Ltd v Fareham Urban DC* [1956] AC 696. See further Peel, *Treitel's Law of Contract* (12th ed, 2007) ch 19.

[204] In *Panalpina* itself, the court declined to find frustration on the facts because B was only deprived of use of the land for 20 months of his 10-year Lease. As a result, the change of circumstance did not deprive B of substantially the whole benefit of his bargain with A. However, in **Example 20**, there is a stronger case for finding frustration.

5.3.4 The renewal of a co-held periodic tenancy

A has a Freehold. In January 2000, A grants a yearly periodic tenancy to B1 and B2. All of the parties are happy for the arrangement to continue, and so B1 and B2 gain a succession of one-year Leases. In May 2007, B1 gives notice to A that he does not intend to renew the Lease in January 2008. B2, however, wishes to remain in occupation.

In January 2008, does the Lease of B1 and B2 end, allowing A to remove B2 and to regain exclusive control of the land? The House of Lords considered that question in *Hammersmith & Fulham LBC v Monk*,[205] on which **Example 21a** is based. According to Lord Browne-Wilkinson, the question could be seen to depend on differing views of the nature of a Lease. B2 could emphasise the 'proprietary' nature of the Lease by arguing that B1's unilateral decision not to renew should not be able to deprive B2 of his property right.[206] A instead could focus on the 'contractual' nature of the Lease.[207] A's argument is that: (i) B2's right to be on the land depends on an agreement between A, B1 and B2; and (ii) the consent of *all* the parties is necessary for that agreement to continue. In *Monk*, the House of Lords found in favour of A.[208] That conclusion can be analysed as supporting a 'contractual' rather than a 'proprietary' view of the Lease.[209] However, that analysis, again, must be treated with caution.

A has a Freehold. A gives B1 and B2 a 10-year Lease. At the end of that 10-year period, A asks B1 and B2 if they wish to enter another 10-year Lease. B1 does not want to; but B2 is keen to renew the Lease.

During the initial 10-year period, it is impossible for B1 unilaterally to terminate the Lease. During that time, B1 and B2, acting together, have a property right. Like all co-holders of a right, their dealings with that right have to be governed by their mutual consent or, where they disagree, by a court order. However, once the 10 years are up, things are different. B1 is free to choose what agreements, if any, he wishes to enter. B1 can then unilaterally refuse to renew the Lease. B2 can take a new Lease on by himself (if A consents) but B2 clearly cannot force B1 to enter a new Lease against B1's wishes.

Example 21b shows that the real question in *Monk* relates to the nature of a periodic tenancy. On one view, a periodic tenancy, no matter how long it lasts, can be seen as just one, continuous Lease. On that view, in **Example 21a**, B1 should *not* be able to unilaterally end the periodic tenancy: after all, in **Example 21b**, B1 cannot unilaterally end the Lease during its 10-year term. It is true that a periodic tenancy is seen, for some purposes, as one,

---

[205] [1992] 1 AC 478.

[206] See eg *per* Lord Browne-Wilkinson at 492 noting a case in which '[t]he contractual, as opposed to the property, approach was adopted'.

[207] See eg *per* Lord Bridge at 483: 'As a a matter of principle I see no reason why this question should receive any different answer in the context of the contractual relationship of landlord and tenant than that which it would receive in any other contractual context.'

[208] For an unsuccessful attempt to argue that B2's loss of his Lease is a breach of B2's human right under Art 8 of the ECHR, see *Harrow LBC v Qazi* [2004] 1 AC 983 (see **B:Example 15**).

[209] *Hussein v Mehlman* [1992] EGLR 87.

continuous Lease. However, a periodic tenancy in fact consists of a number of individual Leases (see **1.7.2(i)** above). So in **Example 21a**, B1 and B2 have a succession of yearly Leases. A periodic tenancy will be renewed automatically if not ended by the parties; but that cannot hide the fact that, like any Lease, a periodic tenancy must be renewed if it is to continue from one term to the next. So, in **Example 21a**, B1 should have the freedom unilaterally to refuse to renew the periodic tenancy: after all, in **Example 21b**, B1 can refuse to renew the Lease once the 10-year period is up.

So, it is no surprise that, in *Monk*, the House of Lords found in A's favour: B1 *was* able to unilaterally to refuse to renew the periodic tenancy. However, there is no need to see the decision as preferring a 'contractual' view of the Lease; instead, it depends on the *characterisation of a periodic tenancy*. In *Monk*, such a tenancy is correctly seen to consist of a series of individual Leases; each of which needs to be renewed, with the parties' consent, at the end of its term.

SUMMARY of G1B:5

A Lease, in the standard sense, is always a property right: that property right almost always arises under a contract between A and B. In such cases, there is no conflict between 'contract' (the means by which B **acquires** his right); and 'property' (the **content** of B's right: the fact that B has a right in relation to a thing that imposes a prima facie duty on the rest of the world). It seems from the House of Lords' decision in *Bruton* that it is possible for B to have a 'Lease', in the particular sense in which a statute may use that word, even if B does not have a property right. However, this purely personal 'Lease' does not affect our definition of a Lease: in its standard sense it is always a property right.

Where B has a standard Lease, it may be possible for that Lease to be terminated as a result of a breach of contract; or for it to be frustrated as result of a dramatic change in circumstances. The courts' recognition of these possibilities is *not* based on a 'contractualisation' of the Lease. Instead, it is based on a characterisation of the bargain entered into by A and B. It is not based on seeing a Lease as 'contract' rather than 'property'. Indeed, the doctrines of termination for breach and frustration are based on a wider principle that applies not only to contracts but *whenever* rights arise as a result of the consent of A and B. Similarly, the fact that a standard Lease is a property right is not altered by one co-holder's ability to refuse to renew a periodic tenancy. The courts' recognition of that ability is *not* based on a 'contractualisation' of the Lease. Instead, it is based on the characterisation of a periodic tenancy: to continue from one limited period to the next, a periodic tenancy must be renewed; and it can only be renewed with the consent of all the parties.

6 THE EQUITABLE LEASE

If B has an Equitable Lease he does not have a property right in land. Instead he has a persistent right: a right against A's Freehold or Lease. Nonetheless, it is worth briefly considering the Equitable Lease here, in order to compare it with the Lease.

6.1 The content question

B has an Equitable Lease if: (i) A has a Freehold or a Lease; and (ii) A is under a duty to give B a right to exclusive control of that land for a limited period. The content of an Equitable Lease is thus governed by the content of the Lease, discussed in **section 1** above. So, if A makes a contractual promise to give B exclusive control of land until England win the football World Cup, B does *not* acquire an Equitable Lease: A is not under a duty to give B a right to exclusive control of land *for a limited period*. If B has a Lease, in the sense in which a particular statute uses that word, B may acquire important statutory rights. In general, the term 'Lease', when used in such statutes, *is* taken to include an Equitable Lease.[210]

Where A grants B a Lease, it will almost always be the case that A and B acquire additional rights against each other, some of which may count as leasehold covenants and hence be binding on A2 and B2 (see **1.8.2** above). Similarly, where A is under a duty to grant B a Lease, it will almost always be the case that each of A and B has additional rights against the other.

EXAMPLE 22a

A has a Freehold. A and B enter negotiations for the grant by A of Lease to B. A and B make a written agreement, signed by each party and recording all the expressly agreed terms of the deal, that: (i) B will have a right to exclusive control of the land for five years; and (ii) that each of A and B will be under various duties (eg, B will be under a duty to A to pay an annual rent of £10,000; A will be under a duty to B to carry out any major repairs). One term of the agreement is that A may ask B for a year's rent in advance.

In such a case, B does *not* acquire a property right from A:[211] as no deed has been used, the formality rule set out by section 52 of the LPA 1925 has not been satisfied. However, the formality rule set out by section 2 of the Law of Property (Miscellaneous Provisions) Act 1989 has been satisfied and so A has exercised his power to make a contractual promise to give B a Lease (see **E2:2.3.3**). As a result, A is under a duty to grant B a Lease: B thus has an Equitable Lease. Equally, B is under a duty to A to pay A, on request, a year's rent in advance.[212]

Equitable Leases are also covered by the Landlord and Tenant (Covenant) Act 1995 (see **1.8.4** above).[213] So if, in **Example 22a**: (i) A were to transfer his Freehold to A2; and (ii) B

---

[210] This is made clear in some statutes (eg s 28(1) of the Landlord and Tenant (Covenants) Act 1995) and is assumed to be the position in relation to others.

[211] B will *independently* acquire a Freehold if he takes physical control of the land.

[212] See *Walsh v Lonsdale* (1882) 21 Ch D 9.

[213] For Equitable Leases acquired *before* 1996, to which the Act does not apply, the position is different. The original rule was that the burden of promises contained in an Equitable Lease would *not* pass on a transfer of the Equitable Lease; however, the Court of Appeal in *Boyer v Warbey* [1953] 1 QB 234 advocated an approach closer to that applying to promises in Leases. As a result, the rules relating to such Equitable Leases are quite complicated: for more, see R Smith [1978] *CLJ* 98.

were to transfer his Equitable Lease to B2; then (iii) A2 could ask B2 for a year's rent in advance.

6.2 The acquisition question

6.2.1 General position

We examined the acquisition of persistent rights relating to land in **E2:2**. B can acquire an Equitable Lease without needing to substantively register that Lease; and without the use of a deed. If B claims that A is under a *contractual* duty to grant B a Lease, then, as in **Example 22a**, B needs to show that the formality rule set out by section 2 of the 1989 Act has been satisfied. If B claims instead that A is under a *non-contractual* duty to grant B a Lease, *no* formality rule applies. For example, in **E4:Example 11**, we saw that B will acquire an Equitable Lease if the doctrine of proprietary estoppel imposes a duty on A to grant B a Lease.[214]

6.2.2 The relevance of specific performance?

In **D2:2.1.2(ii)**, we examined, and rejected, the conventional view that B can only acquire an 'Equitable property right' if A's contractual promise to give B a property right is specifically enforceable. That view has been expressed in a number of cases involving Equitable Leases.[215] It is therefore worth repeating that authority[216] and principle both dictate that B acquires a persistent right *whenever* A is under a *duty* to give B a property right; it does not matter what remedy a court might give to enforce that duty. In fact, Gardner's thorough analysis of the authorities relating to Equitable Leases makes clear that there is no sound foundation for the supposed requirement of specific performance.[217]

6.2.3 An overlap with the implied periodic tenancy?

EXAMPLE 22b

The facts are as in **Example 22a**. After reaching his agreement with A, B takes physical control of A's land and pays a quarterly rent to A. One year later, B moves out of the land; but B continues paying rent to A. A sells his Freehold to C, who is registered as the new holder of A's Freehold.

In such a case, C will be able to use the lack of registration defence against B's pre-existing Equitable Lease. As B was not in actual occupation of the land when C committed to acquiring his right, B's right cannot count as an overriding interest.[218] However, B may

---

[214] See eg *JT Developments v Quinn* (1991) 62 P & CR 33; *Lloyd v Dugdale* [2002] 2 P & CR 13.

[215] See eg *Coatsworth v Johnson* (1886) 55 LJQB 220 (the decision can perhaps be explained on the basis that, due to B's breach of his agreement with A, A had a power to terminate the contract and hence end his duty to grant B a Lease); *Warmington v Miller* [1973] QB 877 (the decision can perhaps be explained on the basis that, as A's agreement was in breach of a term of a Lease held by A from A0, A0 could terminate A's Lease, thus meaning that A had no right against which B could have a persistent right).

[216] See esp *Holroyd v Marshall* (1862) 10 HLC 191; *Tailby v Official Receiver* (1888) 13 App Cas 523.

[217] (1987) 7 *OJLS* 60.

[218] That is the case even if B gave a sub-Lease to B2 who occupied the land and paid rent to B. The receipt of such rent from an occupier of land *did* give B an overriding interest under LRA 1925, s 70(1)(g); but that rule no longer applies under the LRA 2002.

argue that, in addition to his Equitable Lease, he also acquired a Lease by means of an *implied periodic tenancy* as A accepted rent from B (see **1.7.2(i)** above). Crucially, a Lease arising under an implied periodic tenancy is immune from the lack of registration defence (see **section 3** above) and so can bind C. So, in **Example 22b**, does B have *both*: (i) an Equitable Lease (as A is under a duty to grant B a Lease); *and* (ii) a Lease, arising under an implied periodic tenancy (as A has accepted rent from B)?

In *Walsh v Lonsdale*,[219] the facts considered by the Court of Appeal were essentially identical to those in **Example 22a**. In that case, A attempted to rely on the term in the planned Lease giving A the right to request a year's rent in advance. B instead wished to rely on the implied periodic tenancy, which contained no such term. A was successful, and some of the comments of the judges suggest that the Equitable Lease is to be preferred to the implied periodic tenancy; or even, more generally, that 'Equity prevails over the Common Law'.[220] On this view, B has *only* an Equitable Lease and so does not have a Lease arising under an implied periodic tenancy. However, the *result* in *Walsh* can be explained without using such reasoning. That case did not involve any third party: and, whether or not an implied periodic tenancy arose, B was clearly under a contractual duty to A to pay a year's rent in advance if requested.

The decision in *Walsh* thus does *not* rule out B's argument in **Example 22b**. Nonetheless, we *can* support the proposition that, if B has an Equitable Lease, it is impossible for an implied periodic tenancy to arise. This does not depend on an assertion that 'Equity prevails over the Common Law.' Rather, it depends on the fact that, where he acquires a Lease under an implied periodic tenancy, B's Lease arises as result of an inference about A and B's intentions. And the inference that A intended to give B a yearly periodic tenancy seems inappropriate if we know that A is in fact under a duty to give B a different form of Lease. The Equitable Lease should be preferred to the implied periodic tenancy *not* because 'Equity prevails over Common Law' but rather because it better reflects the intentions of the parties.

6.3   The defences question

Under the LRA 2002, B can defensively register an Equitable Lease by entering a notice on the register.[221] Such a notice will prevent C, if he later acquires a right in the land, from relying on the lack of registration defence. If B does not defensively register, his Equitable Lease is vulnerable to the lack of registration defence (see **E2:3.6**). It does not qualify as an overriding interest in its own right: paragraph 1 of Schedule 3 applies only to Leases.[222] So, if C has acquired for value and substantively registered a property right in the land, he will have a defence to B's unregistered Equitable Lease *unless* B was in actual occupation of the land when C committed to acquiring his right.

---

[219] (1882) 21 Ch D 9.

[220] See eg *per* Jessel MR at 14.

[221] LRA 2002, s 32.

[222] It refers to 'a leasehold estate in land granted for a term not exceeding seven years': granted refers only to the creation of a property right (ie, a 'legal lease' or, in the terminology of this book, a Lease): see *City Permanent Building Society v Miller* [1952] Ch 840.

6.4   The remedies question

The discussion in **section 4** above also applies where B has an Equitable Lease. One point to bear in mind is that if B has an Equitable Lease and has not taken physical control of the land, B has no right that he can assert against X, a stranger who does not acquire a right from A but who comes onto or otherwise interferes with the land. In such a case, B will have to rely on the terms of any agreement he has with A in order to persuade or force A to take action against X.

SUMMARY of G1B:6

As it is a persistent right rather than a property right, an Equitable Lease clearly differs from a Lease. However, in practice, an Equitable Lease may be just as useful to B as a Lease. For example, if B is in actual occupation of A's land *or* has defensively registered his Equitable Lease by entering a notice on the register, B will not be vulnerable to the lack of registration defence. B will also have the benefit of any rights (and the burden of any duties) agreed in the planned Lease. Such rights, are also capable of counting as leasehold covenants and thus binding and benefiting parties later acquiring A's estate or B's Equitable Lease. Finally, B will not miss out any statutory protection by virtue of having an Equitable Lease rather than a Lease.[223]

---

[223] One disadvantage for B arises if B wishes to claim that he has an implied Easement over A's land. If A does give B a Lease it is possible for the grant of an Easement to be implied into that Lease by operation of s 62 of the LPA 1925 (see **G5:2.5.4**). However, s 62 does *not* apply if B simply has an Equitable Lease; although there are other means by which B can acquire an implied Equitable Easement (see **G5:6.2.1**).

CHAPTER G2
CO-OWNERSHIP

CO-OWNERSHIP

It is impossible for anyone to hold Ownership of land (see **G1A**). Instead, B can have: (i) a Freehold (an immediate unconditional right to exclusive control of land forever: see **G1A:1**); or (ii) a Lease (an unconditional right to exclusive control of land for a limited period: see **G1B:1**). So, if we say that each of B1 and B2 has co-ownership of land,[1] we really mean that the team comprised of B1 and B2 co-holds a Freehold or a Lease.[2]

In **F2**, we looked at the general principles that apply where B1 and B2 co-hold Ownership. Many of those principles also apply where B1 and B2 co-hold a Freehold or Lease. In this chapter, we will concentrate on the *special rules* that apply where land is concerned.

1 THE CONTENT QUESTION

Co-Ownership can take effect in one of two forms: (i) the joint tenancy; and (ii) the tenancy in common (see **F2:1**). However, if B1 and B2 co-hold a Freehold or Lease they can *only* do so as joint tenants: there is no such thing as a tenancy in common of a Freehold or Lease.

1.1 The joint tenancy

Where B1 and B2 hold a Freehold or Lease as joint tenants, each holds that right as part of *a team*. Individually, each of B1 and B2 has nothing: neither has his own, individual share of the Freehold or Lease (see **F2:1.1.2**).

> EXAMPLE 1
>
> A has a Freehold and transfers that Freehold to B1 and B2. B1 and B2 are registered as joint holders of the Freehold.

In **Example 1**, the rights of B1 and B2 come only from their membership of the team that has the Freehold. If B1 wishes to transfer the Freehold to C, B1 *cannot* do so by himself: he must act together with B2.[3] And if B1 dies, B2 is *solely* entitled to the Freehold. Both before

---

[1] No upper case is used for 'co-ownership' here as the property right co-held by B1 and B2 is not Ownership; it is instead a Freehold or Lease.

[2] Of course, B1 and B2 can also co-hold an Easement: in such a case, B1 and B2 should not be described as having Co-Ownership as the right they co-hold does not give them a right to exclusive control of any land. Similarly, B1 and B2 can also co-hold a Charge. In such a case, B1 and B2 do have a right to exclusive control of land (see LPA 1925, s 87(1)) but, as they hold that right for the purposes of security, they are not generally referred to as having Co-Ownership of land (for the same reason, the Charge is not generally considered as an estate in land: see **E1:1.1**).

[3] Or attempt to obtain a court order forcing B2 to consent to the sale (see **1.4** below).

and after B1's death, the Freehold is held by the team. Before B1's death, the team consists of B1 and B2; after B1's death, the team consists of B2 alone. This feature of the joint tenancy is often known as 'survivorship'.

In **Example 1**, it can be said that the 'four unities' of possession, title, time and interest are present. 'Unity of possession' means that, together, B1 and B2 have a right to exclusive control of the land. The other three unities (title, time and interest) are simply ways of expressing the point that, as B1 and B2 are joint tenants, they do not have independent rights, but rather hold the same right as part of a team (see **F2:1.1.2**).

1.2   The tenancy in common?

1.2.1 No tenancy in common of a Freehold or Lease

In general, it is *only* possible for B1 and B2 to co-hold a right as joint tenants (see **F2:1.2.1**). However, where Ownership is concerned, things are different: B1 and B2 can hold Ownership as tenants in common (see **F2:Example 5**). This occurs where: (i) acting as a team, B1 and B2 have an immediate unconditional right to exclusive control of a thing forever; *and* (ii) *in addition*, each of B1 and B2 has an undivided share of Ownership. So, if A transfers his Ownership of a bike to B1 and B2, with B1 to take a 75 per cent share and B2 to take a 25 per cent share, B1 and B2 co-hold Ownership of the bike as tenants in common.

However, things are different where land is concerned. Section 1(6) of the Law of Property Act 1925 ('the LPA 1925') provides that a Freehold or Lease can *only* be co-held by B1 and B2 as joint tenants. This means that if B1 and B2 co-hold a Freehold or Lease, neither can have his own, undivided share of that right. In effect, then, the general position is restored: like all rights other than Ownership, a Freehold or Lease can *only* be co-held by B1 and B2 as joint tenants.

1.2.2 Justifying the prohibition of tenancies in common

As a result of section 1(6) of the LPA 1925, land is treated differently from other things: B1 and B2 *cannot* hold a right to exclusive control of land as tenants in common. Do the special features of land justify that difference? Well, the limited availability of land may provide a reason for protecting C, a party who wishes to acquire a right in land (see **A:3.1.5**). If transactions in land become complex and expensive, the marketability of land can be severely impeded. This concern is evident, for example, in the special registration system that applies to land (see **C2:5**); it also explains section 1(6) of the LPA 1925.

EXAMPLE 2

It is 1924. C wishes to acquire a Freehold held by B1 and B2. B1 and B2 hold that right as tenants in common.

As B1 and B2 are tenants in common, they have unity of possession: together, B1 and B2 have a right to exclusive control of the land. However, as they are not joint tenants, each of B1 and B2 also has his own, individual share of the Freehold. So, to be sure of acquiring the Freehold held by B1 and B2, C needs to conduct *two* separate investigations. C needs to ensure that *both*: (i) B1 validly acquired B1's individual share; and (ii) B2 validly acquired B2's individual share. Immediately, there is an increase in the time and money C must spend before acquiring his right. The situation will of course be worse if the land is co-owned not by two tenants in common, but by three, four, five or even more tenants in common.[4]

EXAMPLE 3

It is 1926. C wishes to acquire a Freehold held by B1 and B2.

Thanks to section 1(6) of the LPA 1925, C now knows that B1 and B2 hold their Freehold as joint tenants. This means that each of B1 and B2 does *not* have his own, individual share of the Freehold. So C only has to conduct *one* investigation: he needs to ensure that the team validly acquired its Freehold. Hence, acquiring a Freehold from co-owners need not involve any more time or expense than acquiring a Freehold from a single owner.

1.2.3 The consequences of the prohibition of tenancies in common

---

EXAMPLE 4

A has a Freehold. A wants to give: (i) a half share of his Freehold to B1; and (ii) a half share to B2.

In such a case, section 1(6) causes a problem for the parties: B1 and B2 cannot hold the Freehold as tenants in common. So what can A do?

A Freehold is not the only right that cannot be held by tenants in common: in fact, the *general rule* is that it is *only* possible for B1 and B2 to co-hold a right as joint tenants (see F2:1.2.1). So, if B1 and B2 co-hold a personal right against A (eg, an account with A Bank), then neither B1 nor B2 can have his own individual share of the right. If B1 and B2 each wishes to have his own share of the *benefit* of the right against A, the solution is to set up a Trust (see **F2:Example 4**).

A can use exactly the same solution in **Example 4**. A can: (i) transfer the Freehold to B1 and B2 to hold as joint tenants; (ii) impose a duty on each of B1 and B2 to use that Freehold 50 per cent for B1's benefit and 50 per cent for B2's benefit. The beauty of this solution is that it is consistent with section 1(6):

- B1 and B2 hold the Freehold as joint tenants as neither has an individual share of the Freehold itself; *but*
- B1 and B2 do each have a separate, additional right: a right under the Trust to a distinct share of the *benefit* of the Freehold.

This solution means that B1 does have an individual right that he can, for example, pass on in his will to B3. So, if B1 dies, B2 becomes the sole holder of the Freehold (see **F2:1.1.1**). However, B2 will still hold the Freehold on Trust: subject to a duty to use that right 50 per cent for B3's benefit and 50 per cent for his own benefit.

This is a further example of the importance of a Trust in allowing A to respond to a restriction on the content of property rights. Section 1(6) means that A cannot give each of B1 and B2 a *property right* giving him an undivided share of his Freehold. However, by using a Trust, A can give B1 and B2 an undivided share of the *benefit* of the Freehold. This does

---

[4] See eg the extract from Underhill's Fourth Report (1919) (quoted in *Cheshire & Burn's Modern Law of Real Property* (ed Burn and Cartwright, 17th edn, 2006), 464) involving at least 16 tenants in common.

not undermine the purpose of the section 1(6) rule. In **Example 4**, if C wishes to acquire the Freehold held by B1 and B2, he still has only one investigation to make: B1 and B2 hold the Freehold as joint tenants.

EXAMPLE 5

A has a Freehold. A transfers his Freehold to B1 and B2 subject to a duty to use the Freehold: (i) 50 per cent for B1's benefit; and (ii) 50 per cent for B2's benefit. B2 then transfers his persistent right under the Trust to B3. C then buys the Freehold from B1 and B2.

In such a case, it might seem that C faces a problem: as B1 and B2 are joint tenants of the Freehold, C has only one investigation to make when acquiring the Freehold. However, B3 has a pre-existing persistent right under a Trust of that Freehold: that right is prima facie binding on C. Crucially, however, if C pays the purchase price to both B1 and B2, C can rely on the overreaching defence as protection from B3's right (see E2:3.4). That defence thus supports section 1(6) by ensuring that there is no need for C to investigate any persistent rights that might exist under a Trust of B1 and B2's Freehold.[5]

The Trust solution therefore provides a way to: (i) give B1 and B2 an undivided share of the *benefit* of a Freehold or Lease; *and* (ii) to maintain C's protection from the need to investigate more than one claim to that Freehold or Lease. In fact, the Trust solution is so neat that it is imposed by the LPA 1925 even if A is not smart enough to use it.

EXAMPLE 6

A has a Freehold. A transfers that Freehold to B1 and B2, specifying that each is to have a 50 per cent share of the Freehold.

A's intention notwithstanding, section 1(6) means that B1 and B2 acquire the Freehold as joint tenants. However, section 34(2) of the LPA 1925 then steps in to impose a Trust: B1 and B2 hold that Freehold subject to a duty to use it 50 per cent for B1's benefit and 50 per cent for B2's benefit. As in **Example 5**, each of B1 and B2 thus has a persistent right giving him an individual share of the *benefit* of the Freehold. The only difference is that: (i) the Trust in **Example 5** is an Express Trust: it arises as a result of A's exercise of his power to set up a Trust (see Reason 1 in **B:4.3**); and (ii) the Trust in **Example 6** is a Statutory Trust: it arises as a result of a statute imposing a duty on B1 and B2 (see Reason 5 in **B:4.3**).

1.2.4 The extension of the Statutory Trust

EXAMPLE 7

A has a Freehold. A transfers that Freehold to B1 and B2, specifying that they are to hold it as joint tenants.

In **Example 7**, there is no need for a Trust. A's intentions are perfectly consistent with

---

[5] Note that this lends support to the general argument (made by eg Morritt V-C in *National Westminster Bank plc v Malhan* [2004] EWHC 847 at [43]) that C should not have to concern himself with the precise terms of any pre-existing Trust relating to a co-held Freehold or Lease. Land Registration Act 2002, ss 23 and 26 support that principle in a case where the terms of the Trust impose a specific limit on B1 and B2's power to transfer the Freehold or Lease (see E2:3.4.2(i)).

section 1(6): B1 and B2 are to hold the Freehold as joint tenants. It might seem, therefore, that there is no need for a Statutory Trust. Certainly, there is no express statutory provision imposing a Trust: as the Freehold was given to B1 and B2 as joint tenants, section 34(2) does not apply.[6] Nonetheless, there is a very widespread assumption that, in such a case, a Statutory Trust *does* arise: each of B1 and B2 is under a statutory duty to use the Freehold for the benefit of each other. On this analysis, B1 and B2 are joint tenants of *both*: (i) the Freehold; and (ii) a right under a Trust of that Freehold. That Trust arises simply because judges have assumed that, whenever B1 and B2 co-hold a Freehold or Lease, there must also be a Trust.[7]

This extension of the statutory Trust is, on the face of it, surprising: in relation to things other than land, there is no assumption that co-ownership must always give rise to a Trust. The assumption is not based on any doctrinal logic, but it seems to be necessary for two reasons. First, it gives B1 and B2 a joint tenancy not just of the Freehold but also of a right under the Trust of the Freehold. This additional right may seem unnecessary, but it gives each of B1 and B2 the chance, by severing, to acquire his own individual right under the Trust. The crucial point is that the joint tenancy of a right under a Trust, unlike the joint tenancy of a Freehold or Lease, *can*, in effect, be severed (see **2.4** below).

Second, the imposition of a Trust allows a case such as **Example 7** to be regulated by the special statutory regime, imposed by the Trusts of Land and Appointment of Trustees Act 1996, that governs Trusts of land. The rules set out in that Act are designed, in part, to govern disputes between co-owners of land; but, if there were no Trust in **Example 7**, those rules could not apply.

1.2.5 A limit to the Statutory Trust: the Lease and tenancies in common

EXAMPLE 8

A has a Freehold. A enters a contract with B1 and B2 giving B1 and B2 a right to exclusive control of the land for five years. The contract states that B1 and B2 are each to be liable for 50 per cent of the total rent and that each is to have a 50 per cent share of the Lease.

As in **Example 6**, A's intention is that B1 and B2 should each have an undivided share of the Lease. Section 1(6) makes that result impossible but we might expect that, by analogy with **Example 6**, a Statutory Trust would be imposed so that B1 and B2 hold the Lease subject to a duty to use it 50 per cent for B1's benefit and 50 per cent for B2's benefit.

However, in *AG Securities v Vaughan*,[8] the House of Lords took a different approach. It was assumed that, if B1 and B2 wish to co-hold a Lease, they *must* show that they acquired it from A *as joint tenants*. As a result, the section 34(2) 'rescue' does not apply in **Example 8**: no Statutory Trust is imposed. This means that:

---

[6] Equally, s 36(1) of the LPA 1925 does not apply: the Freehold has not been 'beneficially limited to . . . B1 and B2 as joint tenants' as A has not exercised his power to set up a Trust of the Freehold.

[7] See esp *Bull v Bull* [1955] 1 QB 234; *City of London Building Society v Flegg* [1988] AC 54.

[8] [1990] 1 AC 417: the appeal was heard alongside that in *Antoniades v Villiers*. A different result was reached in the *Antoniades* appeal as B1 and B2 were found to have acquired a right to exclusive control as joint tenants. B1 and B2 had signed separate documents, but nonetheless did not acquire separate rights: the mere fact of separate documents being used could not hide the fact that the parties intended the documents to be interdependent and for B1 and B2 to acquire a right to exclusive control together, as a team: see eg *per* Lord Templeman at 460.

- B1 and B2 cannot show that they *together* have a Lease: as they are not joint tenants (as each is intended to have his own individual share) B1 and B2 *do not* co-hold a Lease.
- Neither B1 nor B2 can show that, *individually,* he has a Lease. Each of B1 and B2 has an individual ontractual right against A; and that right is *not* a right to exclusive control of the land as each must share occupation with the other (see **G1B:1.5.4**).

The practical result of the approach taken in *AG Securities v Vaughan* is that it is more difficult for B1 and B2 to acquire a Lease and the statutory protection that may accompany that property right (see **G1B:1.2**): if anything shows that the plan was for each of B1 and B2 to acquire his own, individual share of the Lease, it will be impossible for B1 and B2 to co-hold a Lease. In *AG Securities* itself: (i) the parties claiming to co-hold a Lease (B1, B2, B3 and B4) did not move in together: they each acquired a right from A at different times; so (ii) B1, B2, B3 and B4 were not simply claiming to hold the Lease as a team; instead, each had his own individual right arising from a separate agreement with A; so (iii) B1, B2, B3 and B4 could not show they co-held a Lease as joint tenants; as a result (iv) B1, B2, B3 and B4 each had only an individual, personal right against A.

In *Mikeover v Brady*,[9] B1 and B2, a couple, did move in at the same time and made the same agreement with A. However, when B2 moved out, B1 remained in occupation and paid only half the rent. If B1 and B2 are joint tenants, the team is liable to pay the whole of the rent. B2's moving out makes no difference: B1, as a team member, remains liable to pay A the *whole* of the agreed rent. In *Mikeover*, as B1 in fact paid only half the rent, there was a strong indication that B1 and B2 was each intended to have his own, individual share of the Lease. This is of course consistent with B1 and B2 holding the Lease as tenants in common; but inconsistent with them holding it as joint tenants. As there was no joint tenancy, there was thus no Lease: B1 and B2 each had only a separate personal right against A.

The approach taken by the House of Lords in *AG Securities* has received a great deal of criticism both: (i) on doctrinal grounds—why should section 34(2) apply where B1 and B2 acquire a Freehold but not where they acquire a Lease?;[10] *and* (ii) from the perspective of practical convenience—why should B1 and B2 be denied the often important advantages of a Lease? However, the approach can be defended.

The point is that, in cases such as *AG Securities* and *Mikeover*, B1 and B2 claim that A has entered into a particular sort of contractual agreement. It is *not* possible for B1 and B2 to hold a contractual right against A as tenants in common; such a right can *only* be held by B1 and B2 as joint tenants (see **F2:1.2.1**). Therefore if A does *not* make his contractual promise to B1 and B2 jointly, but instead makes *separate* promises to B1 and B2, each of B1 and B2 can acquire only an individual contractual right against A. And it is clear that B1's right does *not* give him exclusive control: he has to share control of the land with B2. The same is true for B2: he must share with B1. Hence, neither B1 nor B2 has a right to exclusive control of any specific land:[11] each has only a personal right against A (a contractual licence). A has *not* attempted to give B1 and B2 a Lease as A has not attempted to give B1

---

[9] [1989] 3 All ER 618.

[10] See eg Bright (1992) 142 *NLJ* 575; Sparkes (1992) 18 *Anglo-American Law Review* 151.

[11] Of course, things would be different if B1 and B2 could show that each of them was given an individual right to exclusive control of a specific part of the land (eg, a particular room in A's house).

and B2, together, a right to exclusive control of the land. So section 34(2) is irrelevant: no Freehold or Lease has been given to B1 and B2.

Therefore, from a doctrinal point of view at least, the *AG Securities* approach is correct.[12] The distinction between a Freehold and a Lease is based on the fact that, in many cases, the latter depends on a contractual duty of A: and a contractual right cannot be held by B1 and B2 as tenants in common. So, if the Lease claimed by B1 and B2 does *not* depend on a contractual duty of A, it should be possible for section 34(2) to apply: B1 and B2 will then hold a Lease on Trust for themselves as tenants in common.

EXAMPLE 9

A0 has a Freehold. A0 gives A a 99-year Lease. A transfers that Lease to B1 and B2, specifying that B1 and B2 are to hold it as tenants in common.

In such a case, B1 and B2 will be substantively registered as joint tenants of the Lease. Any contractual duties of A0 under the Lease will be owed to B1 and B2 jointly. Section 34(2) will operate to ensure that B1 and B2 hold the Lease on Trust for themselves in the agreed proportions.

EXAMPLE 10

A has a Freehold. In return for a lump sum payment from B1 and B2, A grants B1 and B2 a five-year Lease, as tenants in common. A makes no contractual promises to B1 and B2.

Such cases arise only rarely, but it is possible for A simply to grant a Lease without taking on any contractual duties to B1 and B2 (see **G1B:5.1**).[13] In such a case, there is no reason why B1 and B2 cannot acquire a Lease: section 34(2) will then apply to ensure they hold that Lease as joint tenants on Trust for themselves in the agreed proportions.

SUMMARY of G2:1.2

There are two ways in which B1 and B2 can co-hold Ownership of a thing: as joint tenants or as tenants in common. However, section 1(6) of the LPA 1925 makes it impossible for B1 and B2 to hold a Freehold or Lease as tenants in common. The effect of this is that land can *only* be co-owned by joint tenants. The purpose of the rule is to protect C by ensuring that, when acquiring a Freehold or Lease, he only has to investigate one claim: the claim of B1 and B2, as a team, to have validly acquired the Freehold or Lease. It is therefore impossible for each of B1 and B2 to have an individual, undivided share of a Freehold or Lease. However, each can have an individual right to a share of the *benefit* of a Freehold or Lease. This will occur if B1 and B2 hold a Freehold or Lease subject to a duty to use that right *x* per cent for B1's benefit and *y* per cent for B2's benefit. Indeed, if A attempts to transfer a Freehold to B1 and B2 as tenants in common, such a Trust is automatically imposed by section 34(2) of the LPA 1925. However, if A attempts to give B1 and B2 a Lease as tenants in common, B1 and B2 will

---

[12] The argument from practical convenience is now of less relevance, as the statutory protection available to holders of a Lease has been dramatically reduced (see **G1B:1.2**).

[13] See *per* Millett LJ (dissenting) in *Ingram v IRC* [1997] 4 All ER 395 at 421–2: 'There is no doubt that a lease is property. It is a legal estate in land. It may be created by grant or attornment as well as by contract and need not contain any covenants at all.' There was a successful appeal against the decision of the majority of the Court of Appeal ([2000]1 AC 293) and Lord Hoffmann at 305 and Lord Hutton at 310 expressly agreed with Millett LJ's analysis of the nature of a Lease.

generally only acquire individual personal rights against A. This is because the claimed Lease is likely to be based on a contractual right against A; and it is impossible for B1 and B2 to hold a contractual right against A as tenants in common.

1.3 The rights of co-owners against the rest of the world

The analysis in **F2:1.3** applies in exactly the same way where B1 and B2 are joint tenants of a Freehold or Lease. For example, if X comes onto the land without the consent of one of B1 or B2 or other authority, X commits a wrong against the team of B1 and B2. The team of B1 and B2 thus acquires a personal right against X.

1.4 The rights of one co-owner against another co-owner

1.4.1 The basic principles

The basic principles set out in **F2:1.4** also apply where B1 and B2 are joint tenants of a Freehold or Lease. B1, in his capacity as a member of the co-owning team, *does* have a limited, independent right against B2: B2 is under a duty not to interfere with B1's right, as a member of the team, to have exclusive control of the land. Conversely, of course, B1 is under the same duty to B2.

EXAMPLE 11

B1 and B2 are joint tenants of a Freehold. The land consists of a field of grass. B1 puts a lock on the gate, cuts the grass, turns it into hay and removes it from the field.

In *Jacobs v Seward*,[14] the essential facts of which are identical to **Example 11**, the House of Lords confirmed that B1 has *not* committed any wrong against B2. As a member of the co-owning team, B1 is entitled to use *all* of the land. B1 only commits a wrong if he interferes with B2's matching right by, for example, using the land in a way that excludes B2 from the land or from its profits.[15] And, in **Example 11**, B1 has not excluded B2: the lock may have been put on to keep out third parties;[16] and it is 'perfectly legitimate' to turn the grass into hay and sell it.[17]

   Of course, this does not mean that B1 can keep the hay (and any money made by selling it) solely for his own benefit: (i) the hay (and the proceeds of sale) are the product of the Freehold that is co-owned by B1 and B2; and (ii) B1 is aware of the facts meaning that there is no legal basis for him to have the full benefit of the hay and the proceeds of sale; and so (iii) B1 holds his right to the hay (and the proceeds of sale) on Trust for both B1 and B2 (see **D4:4.4**).

---

[14] (1872) LR 5 HL 464.

[15] The same analysis applies in relation to things other than land: see eg *per* Devlin J in *Baker v Barclays Bank Ltd* [1955] 1 WLR 822 at 527 (**F2:n12**).

[16] See (1872) LR 5 HL 464 at 473.

[17] *Per* Lord Hatherley LC (1872) LR 5 HL 464 at 474. His Lordship made a direct comparison to *Fennings v Lord Grenville* (1808) 1 Taunt 241 (see **F2:n11**).

EXAMPLE 12

B1 and B2 are joint tenants of a Freehold and live together on that land. B1 and B2 fall out and B2 moves out.

The basic position here should be clear: unless B1 can be shown to have taken some positive step to stop B2 occupying (to 'oust' B2), B1 has committed no wrong. It may be that, due to the breakdown in their relationship, B2 finds it intolerable to continue living with B1. However, by simply continuing to occupy the land, B1 commits no wrong against B2. This is confirmed by the decision of the Court of Appeal in *Wiseman v Simpson*, on which **Example 12** is based.[18] Ralph Gibson LJ explained the position of B1 and B2 as follows: 'As joint tenants each has the right to occupy and neither can lawfully exclude the other.'[19]

EXAMPLE 13

B1 and B2 are joint tenants of a Freehold and live together on that land. B1 wants to sell the Freehold and to take his share of the proceeds of sale. B2 instead wants to remain in occupation of the land.

B1 cannot simply go ahead and sell a co-owned right without B2's consent: both B1 and B2 must consent to such a transfer (see **F2:1.4**).[20] If B1 and B2 have a dispute about what use to make of their Freehold, then that dispute is regulated by a *special set of rules*, applying *only* to land. Those rules are set out by the Trusts of Land and Appointment of Trustees Act 1996 ('the 1996 Act'). The special features of land—in particular its social importance and financial value—have again led to land being treated differently.

1.4.2 The effect of the 1996 Act

The rules of the 1996 Act are *not* solely designed to deal with disputes about Co-Ownership of land. Rather, they are designed to regulate *all* cases where a Freehold or Lease is held on Trust. This has a very important consequence: the rules set out in the 1996 Act are necessarily quite broad and often vague as they must be wide enough to deal with *all* the hugely diverse situations in which a Freehold or Lease may be held on Trust (see **E2:1.2.4**).

One of the key advantages of the Trust is its potential to take many different forms and be used for many different purposes (see **D2:1.4**). For example, let us say a board of trustees controls a multi-million-pound pension fund, holding it on a discretionary Trust with a power to make payment to any of thousands of employees (see **D2:1.4.3**). Some of that fund may be invested by acquiring a Freehold: if so that Freehold is held on Trust and the 1996 Act applies. Such a case is clearly a very long way from the standard cases involving co-ownership of land, such as **Examples 11, 12 and 13**; but, like those standard cases, it is regulated by the 1996 Act.

---

[18] [1988] 1 WLR 35.

[19] *Ibid* at 42. The only other judge on the panel, Mustill LJ, agreed with Ralph Gibson LJ.

[20] If B1 and B2 are substantively registered as joint tenants of the Freehold, B1 may attempt to transfer the Freehold by pretending that B2 has consented (eg, by forging B1's signature, as in *Ahmed v Kendrick* (1987) 56 P & CR 120: see **Example 27** below). If C is then substantively registered as the new holder of the Freehold, C will have that right (see s 58 of the LRA 2002); but B2 may ask that the register be rectified to show that B2 and C hold the Freehold as joint tenants.

(i) The right to occupy?[21]

The breadth and vagueness of the rules in the 1996 Act can be a problem when those rules are applied to a standard co-ownership case. For example, the basic position in **Examples 11, 12 and 13**, as noted in *Wiseman v Simpson*, is that 'as joint tenants each [of B1 and B2] has the right to occupy and neither can lawfully exclude the other'.[22] However, things are not so clear cut under the 1996 Act. Sections 12 and 13 determine when a beneficiary of a Trust of land (such as B1 or B2) has a right to occupy that land. Those sections *cannot* simply say that a beneficiary of a Trust of a Freehold or Lease has a right to occupy the land. For example, A0 may set up a Trust, on his death, by leaving his Freehold and £250,000 in his will to be used for the benefit of his grandchildren. If A0 has 10 grandchildren, it cannot make sense for each grandchild to have a right to occupy the land. Similarly, if A invests the £250,000 by buying a Freehold of commercial premises that he plans to rent out, it cannot make sense for each grandchild to have a right to occupy.

As they must apply to *all* cases where a Freehold or Lease is held on Trust, sections 12 and 13 are therefore very qualified. The risk is that those qualifications can then be used, in **Examples 11, 12 and 13**, to deny B1 or B2 his basic right to occupy. For example, section 12(1) gives B1 and B2 a basic right to occupy[23] where:

- the purposes of the trust include making the land available for his occupation; *or*
- the land is held by the trustees so as to be so available.

However, section 12(2) limits this basic right: it states that section 12(1) cannot give B1 or B2 a right to occupy land *if* the land is:

- either unavailable or unsuitable for occupation by him.

This qualification introduces an element of uncertainty: in **Example 12**, could B2 claim that the house is too big to be occupied by one person and so is 'unsuitable for occupation' by B1? And those last two words '*by him*' mean that B1's personal characteristics may be used to limit his right to occupy.[24] For example, if B1's political views lead to B1 falling out with B2, or with their neighbours, does that mean that the land is now unsuitable for occupation by B1? Of course, we would hope that the courts would reject such attempts to limit a co-owner's basic right to occupy. However, the problem for B1 is that, even if a court may eventually find in his favour, B2 can rely on the qualifications in section 12 to place practical obstacles in the way of B1's right to occupy:[25] after all, the prospect of spending time and

---

[21] This section focuses on the question of whether each of B1 and B2 has a right to occupy *in his capacity as a co-owner of land*. It does not consider the question of whether B1 or B2 may have such a right in a different way eg under s 30 of the Family Law Act 1996. As we have seen, that Act may give B a right to occupy even if he has *no* pre-existing property right in the land or persistent right relating to the land (see **B:11.3**).

[22] [1988] 1 WLR 35 at 42.

[23] That basic right is held only by a 'beneficiary who is beneficially entitled to an interest in possession in land'. This means that the s 12 right is not available to a beneficiary if the trustee is not under a duty to use the land for his benefit *at the current time*: so if a Trust is set up in a case such as **E2:Example 2a**, neither B2 nor the National Trust has a s 12 right during the life of B1. However, in standard co-ownership cases such as **Examples 11, 12 and 13**, each of B1 and B2, as soon as they acquire the Freehold or Lease, is clearly under a duty to use the land for the benefit of the other; so, if the further requirements are met, each of B1 and B2 may have a s 12 right.

[24] See eg *per* Jonathan Parker LJ in *Chan v Leung* [2003] 1 FCR 250 at [101].

[25] For example, in *Chan v Leung* [2003] 1 FCR 250 B2 made the argument that a large house, formerly occupied by both B1 and B2 was unsuitable for sole occupation by B1. On the facts of the case, that argument was rejected. However, thanks to s 12(2) both the trial judge and the Court of Appeal had to consider that argument. Jonathan

money in arguing about whether or not the land is 'unsuitable for occupation by him' may well not appeal to B1.

Section 13 can be used to place further limits on a co-owner's basic right to occupy. In a standard co-ownership case, where B1 and B2 each has a section 12 right to occupy, section 13(1) gives the trustees the power to 'exclude or restrict' those rights, provided they do not act 'unreasonably' in doing so. If only one beneficiary has a section 12 right to occupy, section 13(3) still allows the trustees to 'impose reasonable conditions on [B1] in relation to his occupation of land'. Of course, in a co-ownership case, B1 and B2 are *both* the beneficiaries *and* the trustees: they hold the Freehold or Lease as joint tenants on Trust for each other. And given the trustees have to act together in exercising the power to impose restrictions under section 13, there seems to be little risk to B1: in his capacity as a trustee, he can simply refuse to agree to a restriction on his right to occupy.

However, when there is a disagreement between B1 and B2 about how to exercise their rights and powers as trustees, sections 14 and 15 of the 1996 Act come into play. Section 14 allows either B1 or B2 to apply to court; the court then has the power to make an order 'relating to the exercise by the trustees of any of their functions'. Section 15(1) sets out a non-exhaustive list of factors a court must have 'regard' to when deciding what order to make (see **1.4.2(ii)** below). Where the application relates to the trustees' section 13 powers, section 15(2) also makes clear that the court must have 'regard' to the 'circumstances and wishes of each of the beneficiaries' with a section 12 right to occupy.

Certainly, there is nothing in the 1996 Act to make clear that a court will *not* force B1, in his capacity as trustee, to agree to a restriction on his right to occupy proposed by B2. Again, we would hope that a court will not allow such restrictions in a standard co-ownership case. But again, in practice, the thought of spending time and money in opposing a section 14 application by B2 may deter B1 from opposing B2's attempt to restrict his right to occupy.

For example, in **Example 12**, B2 could argue that, as he has now moved out and B1 is occupying the land by himself, B1 should pay B2 an 'occupation rent'. We saw from *Wiseman v Simpson* that, as B1 did not force B2 to leave, B1 has committed no wrong against B2. Further: (i) as B1 is a co-owner of the land; (ii) there *is* a legal basis for B1 to have the benefit of occupation of that land; and so (iii) by occupying the land, B1 is *not* unjustly enriched at B2's expense.[26]

However, a claim for an 'occupation rent' need not be based on the commission of a wrong or unjust enrichment.[27] B2 can say that, under section 13(3), the trustees of land

---

Parker LJ at [102] stated that: 'In any event I would have taken some persuading that a property which was on any footing suitable for occupation by Miss Chan and Mr Leung whilst they lived together should be regarded as unsuitable for occupation by her alone once Mr Leung had left.' This suggests the correct degree of scepticism to B2's argument.

[26] See eg *M'Mahon v Burchell* (1846) 2 Phil 127; *per* Parke B in *Henderson v Eason* (1851) 17 QB 701 at 720: 'For instance, if a dwelling house, or barn, or room, is solely occupied by one tenant in common, without ousting the other, or a chattel is used by one cotenant in common, nothing is received; and it would be most inequitable to hold that he thereby, by the simple act of occupation or use, without any agreement, should be liable to pay a rent or anything in the nature of compensation to his cotenants for that occupation or use to which to the full extent to which he enjoyed it he had a perfect right.' In *Leigh v Dickeson* (1884) 15 QBD 60 a rent was payable; but only because B1 and B2 had reached an agreement under which B1 was to have sole exclusive control in return for paying rent to B2: see *per* Cotton LJ at 66.

[27] A court could impose an occupation rent when, on a sale or partition of the land, applying 'Equitable

have the power to impose 'reasonable conditions' on B1's right to occupy.[28] B2's argument will be that, as (i) B2 no longer enjoys the benefit of occupation; and (ii) B1 gets the benefit of sole occupation, it is 'reasonable' to restore the balance by ordering B1 to pay money to B2. In responding to B2's claim, a court must take into account the factors set out by section 15.

In a standard co-ownership case, the section 15 factors should not alter the basic position: B1 should *not* be ordered to pay an occupation rent if he is simply exercising his right, as a member of the co-owing team, to exclusive control of the land.[29] However, the vagueness of the terms used by the 1996 Act (eg, 'reasonable' conditions) creates a real risk for B1 that the court may find against him.[30] This creates an incentive for B1 to avoid the time and expense of court proceedings and to give in by agreeing to pay B2 some money. So, once again, the qualifications contained in the 1996 Act may *weaken* B1's basic right, as a member of a co-owning team, to have exclusive control of the land without needing to pay for it.[31]

(ii) Applications for a sale of the Freehold or Lease[32]

In **Example 13**, B1 wishes to sell the co-owned Freehold and to take his share of the proceeds of sale; B2 wants to remain in occupation. Section 14 of the 1996 Act allows B1 to apply for a court order forcing B2 to agree to the sale; the court then has to have 'regard' to

accounting' principles to ensure that the sale or partition does not favour one co-owner rather than the other (see **E2:4.4** and **n 30** below). However, it now seems that those 'Equitable accounting' principles have been displaced by the rules set out in the 1996 Act: see *per* Baroness Hale in *Stack v Dowden* [2007] 2 AC 432 at [93]–[95]; *per* Lightman J in *Murphy v Gooch* [2007] EWCA Civ 603 at [11].

[28] S 13(6) specifically refers to the trustees' power to impose an 'occupation rent'; but that section applies only where the trustees have exercised their s 13(1) power to exclude or restrict a beneficiary's right to occupy: that has not occurred in **Example 12**.

[29] The position is, of course, different if B1 forces B2 to leave: see eg *Dennis v McDonald* [1982] 2 WLR 275, where B1's violence forced B2 to leave. In such a case, the money paid by B1 to B2 should not be seen as an 'occupation rent' but instead as payable due to B1's commission of a wrong.

[30] Even before the 1996 Act, the approach advocated by Millett J in *re Pavlou* [1993] 2 FLR 751 at 754 caused problems for B1. Millett J stated that an occupation rent could be ordered 'not only in the case where the co-owner in occupation has ousted the other, but in any other case in which it is necessary in order to do equity between the parties that an occupation rent should be paid. The fact that there has not been an ouster or forceful exclusion therefore is far from conclusive.' That statement seems to be simply incorrect: it should not apply when, as in *re Pavlou*, B1 and B2 are co-holders of a Freehold or Lease. The court should not have an 'equitable' discretion to make B1 pay money simply because B1 has exercised his right, as a member of the co-owning team, to exclusive control of the land (see eg *per* Parke B in *Henderson v Eason* (1851) 17 QB 701 at 720 as set out in **n 26** above). In any case, it is now clear that the 1996 Act governs the question of occupation rents, not the principles of 'Equitable accounting' applied in *re Pavlou* (see **n 27** above).

[31] The difficulties with using the 1996 Act to decide a claim for 'occupation rent' can be seen in *Stack v Dowden* [2007] 2 AC 432. The majority of the House of Lords agreed with Baroness Hale's view ([93]–[95]) that, under the Act, B1 did *not* have to pay any money to B2 after B2 left the land. Lord Neuberger, however, dissented on that point ([151]–[156]). The view of the majority is correct: it seems B1 had not ousted B2 and so should not have to pay any money to B2 (Lord Neuberger's dissent may be based on a view that B1 had in fact ousted B2: at [152] his Lordship states that B1 had 'excluded [B2] against his will'). It is true that, as part of the deal in which B2 agreed to leave, B1 had agreed to pay B2 £900 a month, but that deal was no longer in force. So, provided B1 was not preventing B2 from returning to occupy, B1 should not have to pay any money to B2.

[32] Again, this section focuses on the ability of B1 and B2 to insist on or oppose a sale *in his capacity as a co-owner of land*. Other rules may also be relevant in such a dispute: see eg *Chan v Leung* [2003] 1 FCR 250 (Family Law Act 1996, ss 30–33); *Tee v Tee and Hillman* [1999] 2 FLR 613 (Matrimonial Causes Act 1973, ss 22–5). Therefore, if B1 and B2 are spouses, and their dispute involves no third parties and arises as part of their divorce, it should be determined wholly by the special statutory rules applying to divorce under the Matrimonial Causes Act and not by the general co-ownership rules (see eg *per* Thorpe LJ in *Tee* at 619).

the factors listed in section 15 when making its decision. The court can take other factors into account; but, under section 15(1), it *must* have 'regard' to:

(a) the intentions of the person or persons (if any) who created the trust,
(b) the purposes for which the property subject to the trust is held,
(c) the welfare of any minor who occupies or might reasonably be expected to occupy any land subject to the trust as his home, and
(d) the interests of any secured creditors of any beneficiary.[33]

In **Example 13**, factors (c) and (d) are irrelevant. Factor (a) refers only to a *common* intention of B1 and B2, held *when they acquired the Freehold*.[34] So, the current intentions of B1 and B2 are irrelevant; as is any individual intention B2 may have had that was not shared by B1.[35] However, it will often be the case that, if B1 and B2 are a couple setting up home together, their common intention when acquiring the Freehold was to have a home to live in together. It is unlikely, in such a case, that there will be any other 'purpose' for which B1 and B2 hold the Freehold, so factor (b) will be irrelevant. However, it is worth noting that, unlike factor (a), factor (b) seems to look at any *current* purpose—it refers to the purpose for which the land '*is* held'—and so it is possible for a different purpose to arise after B1 and B2 acquire their Freehold.[36] This may happen, for example, if B1 and B2 acquire a Freehold with the shared intention of living there but then move into a different house and rent out their original home.

In **Example 13**, does section 15(1)(a) help B2 to resist B1's application for sale? In some cases, it can do. For example, if B1 and B2 agreed, when acquiring the Freehold, not to sell it for a fixed period, then a court, as it would have done before the Act,[37] can refuse to order a sale. However, in the standard co-ownership case, where B1 and B2 acquire a Freehold with the shared intention of living there, section 15(1)(a) is very unlikely to assist B2. The problem for B2 is that B1 and B2's initial common intention will be conditional: it will be to use the land as their home *for as long as* their relationship continues. In most cases, a dispute between B1 and B2 as to the use of their co-owned home will only arise where the relationship of B1 and B2 has broken down. In such a case, an order for sale seems inevitable—unless B2 can buy out B1 and become the sole holder of the Freehold.[38]

EXAMPLE 14

B1 and B2 hold a Freehold as joint tenants. It was acquired by B1 and B2 when setting up a home together. B1 and B2 have two young children. Their relationship breaks down. B1 moves out and wants to sell the Freehold and take her share of the proceeds of sale. B2 objects and wants to remain in occupation with the children.

Does the application of section 15(1)(c) make any difference to the outcome? B2 can argue that the children's welfare may be affected if they have to move to different accommodation,

---

[33] See too ss 15(2) and (3).
[34] See eg *per* Arden LJ in *White v White* [2003] EWCA Civ 924 at [23].
[35] Factor (a) includes only the *common* intention of B1 and B2: *per* Arden LJ in *White v White* [2003] EWCA Civ 924 at [22].
[36] See eg *per* Peter Gibson LJ in *Rodway v Landy* [2001] Ch 703 at [26].
[37] See eg *re Buchanan-Wollaston's Conveyance* [1939] Ch 217.
[38] This was also the case before the 1996 Act: see eg *Jones v Challenger* [1961] 1 QB 176.

perhaps in a different area.[39] The problem, however, is that the needs of the children have to be balanced against those of B1. B1, as a member of the team holding the Freehold, is entitled to realise her share of that right. If B2 is unable to buy out B1, why should B1 be prevented from moving on by taking out her share of the value of the Freehold? So, in his capacity as a co-owner, it seems that B2 cannot prevent a sale: the welfare of the children may at most lead to a *postponement* of a sale for a short period, for example, while the children prepare for public exams. This result may seem harsh: we will consider it further, and ask whether it may breach B2's human rights, in **section** 4 below.[40] However, there may be *other* mechanisms, not based on B2's right as a co-owner of the land, that can provide protection to B2 and the children.[41]

SUMMARY of G2:1.4

Whilst the 1996 Act has provided a set of rules to deal with disputes between co-owners of land, those rules are of little value. The problem is that they are designed to deal with *all* cases where a Freehold or Lease is held on Trust; they are not designed to deal with the *specific* case where B1 and B2 are co-holders of a Freehold or Lease. In fact, the 1996 Act has the potential to *weaken* the rights of a co-owner of land. Instead of having a right, as a member of the co-owning team, to exclusive control of the land, B1 now has to surmount the hurdles imposed by sections 12 and 13 in order to show he has a right to occupy. There is also a risk that a court can impose an 'occupation rent' on B1 even in a case where B1 has *not* wrongfully ousted B2. It would therefore be best if the courts, when applying the Act, ensure that they reach the results dictated by the basic rules discussed in 1.4.1. When applied to a dispute about the possible sale of the co-owned Freehold or Lease, the 1996 Act seems to make little difference. The basic position discussed in F2:1.4 will almost always apply: B2 will be forced to consent to a sale, unless he can buy out B1.

1.5 Equitable Co-Ownership?

EXAMPLE 15

A has a Freehold. A is under a duty to use that right for the joint benefit of B1 and B2.

In such a case, the orthodox approach is to refer to B1 and B2 as joint tenants who are 'Equitable Co-Owners' of the land. However, that is incorrect. A can be called an owner in the sense that he has a property right giving him the right to exclusive control of the land forever. B1 and B2 do *not* have a property right and so should not be called co-owners. It is true that B1 and B2 are joint tenants: they each *co-hold*, as joint tenants, a persistent right: a

---

[39] The welfare of children was also a relevant factor before the 1996 Act: see eg *re Evers* [1980] 1 WLR 1327.

[40] In *White v White* [2003] EWCA Civ 924, the Court of Appeal confirmed the order made by the first instance judge: the co-owned land was sold and so B1 and the children had to move into different accommodation.

[41] For example, B1 may apply under the Children Act 1989, s 15 and Sch 1 for financial provision for a child: as well as asking for money to support a child, B1 can ask for a temporary transfer of B2's property right or persistent right so that it can be held for the benefit of the children (eg, so that a child can remain in occupation of the home until he leaves school): such an application had been made in *White v White*: see *per* Thorpe LJ at [4]. If such an application succeeds (the courts are generally circumspect in making such an order: see eg *J v J* [1993] 2 FLR 56), then B2 can no longer insist on a sale as he no longer has the benefit of his property right. Further, just as the Family Law Act 1996 can limit the rights of a spouse or civil partner even if he is a *sole* holder of a Freehold or Lease, so can it limit B2's rights as a co-owner: see esp s 33.

right under the Trust of A's Freehold. However, as there is no such thing as Equitable Ownership, there can be no such thing as Equitable Co-Ownership (see **F2:1.5.2**).

EXAMPLE 16

A has a Freehold. A is under a duty to use that right 50 per cent for the benefit of B1 and 50 per cent for the benefit of B2.

The orthodox approach is to refer to B1 and B2 as tenants in common who are 'Equitable Co-Owners' of the land. However, that is incorrect. B1 and B2 do not have a property right and so should not be called co-owners. In fact, B1 and B2 do not co-hold *any right*. Like a personal right, a persistent right depends on A being under a duty to B1 and B2. It is possible, as in **Example 15**, for A to be under a duty to B1 and B2 *jointly*; but it is not possible for B1 and B2 each to have undivided shares of the same right against A (see **F2:1.2.1**). So, like a personal right, a right under a Trust cannot be co-held by B1 and B2 as tenants in common. In **Example 16**, each of B1 and B2 has an *individual* persistent right under the Trust of A's Freehold.

In **Examples 15 and 16**, as in **Examples 11–14**, the 1996 Act will apply to regulate any disputes about the use of the land. This is because, in all those cases, a Freehold or Lease is held on Trust. However, this should not disguise the fact that, in **Examples 15 and 16**, there is *no* co-ownership: the right to exclusive control is held by only one person (A). In contrast, in **Examples 11–14**, the right to exclusive control is held by B1 and B2 together, as a team.

1.6 Ending co-holding

The general principles set out in **F2:1.6.1** also apply where B1 and B2 are co-owners of land. For example, B1 has the power to make B2 the sole holder of the Freehold or Lease by making a 'release'—ie, by dropping out of the team that co-holds the Freehold or Lease.[42] The co-holding of the Freehold or Lease will also cease whenever its key feature, unity of possession, disappears. B1 and B2's co-holding of a Freehold will therefore cease if they decide that: (i) B1 will have a right to exclusive control of one part of the land; and (ii) B2 will have a right to exclusive control of the other part (as in **F2:Example 3**). Dividing the land in this way is known as partition: B1 and B2's power to partition is regulated by section 7 of the 1996 Act.[43] Partition should be distinguished from a less dramatic course: B1 and B2 can decide that: (i) B1's right to occupy will be limited so that he can only occupy one part of the land; and (ii) B2's right to occupy will be limited so that he can only occupy the other part of it.[44] In such a case, B1 and B2 continue to co-hold their Freehold or Lease: for

---

[42] Where B1 and B2 are substantively registered as joint holders of a Freehold or Lease, the release will only be complete when the register is changed to show B2 as sole holder of that right. Where he makes a release, B1 does *not* transfer any share to B2, as he has no share to give. A release is thus different from a transfer or assignment: see eg *per* Sir John Vinelott in the Court of Appeal in *Burton v Camden LBC* [1998] 1 FLR 681 at 684. However, it seems that, for reasons of practical convenience, the term 'assignment', when used in a particular statute, can be given a special meaning that covers a release: see the House of Lords in *Burton v Camden LBC* [2000] 2 WLR 427. There is an interesting question as to whether the general s 52 formality rule applies to B1's power to make a release.

[43] LPA 1925, s 188(1) (see **F2:1.6.2**) does not apply to land.

[44] See eg *Rodway v Landy* [2001] Ch 703.

example, each of B1 and B2, in his capacity as team member, has a right to the total profits made from the use of the whole of the land.[45]

SUMMARY of G2:1

Due to section 1(6) of the LPA 1925, there is only one way for B1 and B2 to co-hold a Freehold or Lease: as joint tenants. However, B1 and B2 can hold a Freehold or Lease as joint tenants subject to a duty to use that right for the benefit of B1 (to a certain extent, eg, 50 per cent) and for the benefit of B2 (to the remaining extent). This ensures that each of B1 and B2 has his own, individual right: a persistent right under a Trust. The existence of this Trust means that disputes between B1 and B2 can be settled using the rules set out by the Trusts of Land and Appointment of Trustees Act 1996. However, this may cause a problem: those rules apply to *all* cases where a Freehold or Lease is held on Trust and are not specifically designed to deal with co-ownership cases. Indeed, as the Act imposes qualifications on a beneficiary's right to enjoy the land, there is a risk that the imposition of the Trust *reduces* the rights of a co-owner. Those qualifications may be necessary in the wider context of the Act: after all, it has to deal with *all* cases where a Freehold or Lease is held on Trust. But the qualifications may be inappropriate in a case where B1 is *not only* a beneficiary under a Trust but is also a co-holder of a Freehold or Lease.

2   THE ACQUISITION QUESTION

2.1   Independent acquisition

It is possible for B1 and B2 to acquire a Freehold both jointly and independently. If B1 and B2 jointly take physical control of a piece of land, they become joint tenants of a Freehold (see **G1A:2.1.2**). However, a Lease *cannot* be acquired independently, whether by one person or by two or more people acting together (see **G1B:2.1**).

2.2   Dependent acquisition

It is possible for B1 and B2 to jointly acquire a Freehold or Lease from A. Of course, B1 and B2 will need to show that any relevant formality rules have been satisfied (see **E1:2.3**). So, if B1 and B2 claim a Freehold, or a Lease of over seven years, they will need to show that they are substantively registered as joint holders of that right (see **E1:2.3.4**).

2.2.1 Joint tenancy or tenancy in common?

In general, it is crucial to ask whether B1 and B2 have acquired Ownership as joint tenants or tenants in common (see **F2:2.2.1**). In one sense, if B1 and B2 acquire a Freehold or Lease, that question is irrelevant: section 1(6) of the LPA 1925 means that B1 and B2 *must* be joint tenants of the Freehold or Lease. Nonetheless, as we saw in **F2:2.2.1(ii)**, it may still be possible for each of B1 and B2 to acquire his own individual right.

---

[45] So if the Freehold or Lease is sold, B1 and B2 will hold the proceeds of sale as joint tenants (subject to a Trust if they held that Freehold or Lease on Trust for each other in specific proportions).

(i) Proving an intention to hold as tenants in common: express words in the transfer to B1 and B2

EXAMPLE 17

A transfers a Freehold to B1 and B2. The transfer states that each of B1 and B2 is intended to have a 50 per cent share of the Freehold.

Section 1(6) means that A does *not* have the power to transfer that right to B1 and B2 as tenants in common. However, in such a case, section 34(2) of the LPA 1925 steps in to ensure that B1 and B2 *do* each acquire an individual right: they will hold the Freehold on Trust for each other (see **Example 6**).

(ii) Other cases? Circumstances surrounding the transfer to B1 and B2

If A transfers a Freehold or Lease to B and the express words of the transfer do not make clear whether B1 and B2 are intended to hold as joint tenants or tenants in common, the default rule is that: (i) B1 and B2 will simply hold that right as joint tenants; and (ii) neither B1 nor B2 will have an individual right (see **F2:2.2.1**).[46] However, if:

- the surrounding circumstances show that B1 and B2 in fact intended that each would acquire an individual share; then
- a Trust can arise; and
- B1 and B2 will each have an individual right under that Trust to a specific share of the benefit of the Freehold or Lease.

In **F2:2.2.1(ii)**, we noted three prominent situations in which the surrounding circumstances can justify an inference that B1 and B2 intended that each would acquire an individual share, including the case where B1 and B2 make unequal contributions to the price paid when acquiring a right from A.[47] As the Privy Council made clear in *Malayan Credit Ltd v Jack Chia-MPH Ltd*,[48] there is no set list of such circumstances. The question in each case is whether a court can infer that, despite the absence of any express statements, B1 and B2 intended, when acquiring the Freehold or Lease, that each should also acquire his own individual right.

Nowadays, when A transfers a substantively registered Freehold or Lease to B1 and B2, the terms of the transfer itself *should* always reveal the intentions of B1 and B2. They will be asked to tick a box on the relevant registration form indicating whether it is intended that: (i) they will hold that right simply as joint tenants; or (ii) each of them will have his own undivided share of the benefit of the Freehold or Lease.[49] However, this is not a mandatory part of the registration process,[50] and so there may still be situations in which a court has to infer the intentions of B1 and B2 from the surrounding circumstances.

---

[46] This is confirmed by the House of Lords in *Stack v Dowden* [2007] 2 AC 432.

[47] See eg *Robinson v Preston* (1858) 4 K & J 505.

[48] [1986] AC 549.

[49] These boxes have been on the TR1 form since April 1998.

[50] The boxes do not *have* to be filled in: the transfer can go ahead, and B1 and B2 can be substantively registered, even if no box is ticked: see *per* Baroness Hale in *Stack v Dowden* [2007] 2 AC 432 at [52] and (more fully and giving different reasons for the conclusion) Kenny [2007] *Conv* 364.

B1 and B2, lovers, decide to acquire a Freehold so they can live together as a couple. They are registered as joint holders of their Freehold. They make no express statement as to whether they intend that each of them is to have an individual share of the Freehold. The total price of the Freehold is £200,000. B1 earns more than B2. B1 contributes £13,000 of the purchase price; B2 contributes £7,000; the remaining £180,000 is borrowed from C Bank in a 'mortgage' deal. Under that deal, B1 and B2 are each liable to C Bank. B1 and B2 each contributes as much as he can to the repayments to C Bank.[51] In the end B1 contributes 65 per cent to the repayments costs, whilst B2 contributes 35 per cent. B1 and B2 are unmarried and are not in a civil partnership. They split up and the Freehold is to be sold. B2 claims that B1 and B2 acquired the Freehold as joint tenants and so, now severance has occurred, B2 is entitled to 50 per cent of the proceeds of sale of the Freehold.[52] B1 claims that B1 and B2 instead intended that each would have his own individual share of the benefit of the Freehold.

Where should we start in establishing the intentions of B1 and B2 on acquiring the Freehold? In a case of unequal contributions to the costs of paying for the Freehold, the usual starting point is to infer that B1 and B2 *did* intend that each should have his own individual right. After all, given his extra contribution, why should B1 not have his own, individual right to 65 per cent of the benefit of the Freehold? It may be objected that much of B1's contribution was made after the acquisition of the Freehold, through paying mortgage instalments. However, there is no reason why later conduct cannot be taken into account when making an inference as to the parties' initial intentions. In *Stack v Dowden*, the essential facts of which are identical to **Example 18**, Lord Neuberger adopted that starting point. His Lordship took the view that, *even if B1 and B2 acquire a Freehold or Lease in order to live together as a couple*, the starting inference should be that: (i) if each makes a different contribution to the cost of paying for the Freehold or Lease; then (ii) each should have his own, individual share based on the extent of that contribution.[53]

Of course, as in all cases, this is only a starting point: it can be displaced if there is evidence that the parties intended *not* to have such a share. So, in **Example 18**, if there were clear evidence that B1 and B2 intended *only* to act as a team (eg, they merged their financial affairs completely during their relationship), then it would be accurate to say that neither party intended to have his own individual share. However, on the facts of *Stack v Dowden*, that was not the case: B1 and B2 had kept their financial affairs separate. So, Lord Neuberger accepted B1's claim that she should take 65 per cent of the proceeds of sale.

However, in *Stack v Dowden*,[54] the other four members of the panel, whilst reaching the

---

[51] Strictly speaking, only the contributions to the deposit count towards the *acquisition* of the Freehold: mortgage payments instead go to paying off a debt incurred in acquiring that Freehold. This means, for example, that if A steals B's money and uses it to pay some of A's mortgage, the tracing rules (see D4:4.4) do *not* allow B to identify A's Freehold as the product of B's money. This point seems technical but is very important when considering Resulting Trusts of land: see G3:2.2.3. However, here we are looking at the different question of ascertaining the intentions of B1 and B2 when acquiring the Freehold. As the pattern of later mortgage payments may help us ascertain those initial intentions, mortgage payments *can* be considered here.

[52] Of course those proceeds will first be used to pay off any sums due under the mortgage loan.

[53] As suggested by Lord Neuberger at [111], such a Trust is an example of a Resulting Trust: the Type 2 Resulting Trust recognised in *Westdeutsche Landesbank Girozentrale v Islington LBC* [1996] AC 669 *Westdeutsche* (see D4:4.3.2).

[54] [2007] 2 AC 432.

same conclusion as Lord Neuberger,[55] adopted a very different approach. That majority view was:

- where B1 and B2 buy a home together as a couple and have it registered in their joint names; *then*
- the best starting point is to infer that B1 and B2 do *not* intend that each will have his own, individual share of the benefit of the Freehold or Lease;[56] *and*
- that starting point can only be displaced in the 'very unusual'[57] case where one of the parties meets the 'heavy'[58] burden of showing that B1 and B2, despite the absence of any express statements to that effect, did in fact intend that each should have his own individual share.

Hence the starting inference in **Example 18**, even though B1 and B2 made unequal contributions to the cost of paying for the Freehold, is that they did *not* intend that each should have his own individual share of that Freehold. Further, the fact of unequal contributions will not, *by itself*, be enough to displace the starting point that B1 and B2 hold as joint tenants *both*: (i) the Freehold; and (ii) the persistent right under the Trust of that Freehold.[59]

Of course, that is only a starting point: in any individual case, a court has to try to discover B1 and B2's actual intentions when acquiring the Freehold.[60] Indeed, in *Stack* itself, the majority found that B1 *was* able to achieve the difficult task of showing that, although they were a couple, B1 and B2 *did* in fact intend that each of them would have an individual right. Of course, the extent of B1's financial contribution was *a* factor, but B1 was also able to point to the fact that B1 and B2 kept their financial affairs apart:[61] although they had a family together, there was no intention that they should act only as a team when it came to their assets and expenditures.

As a result, in *Stack*, the majority's approach led to the same conclusion as Lord Neuberger's approach: B1 had her own, individual persistent right to 65 per cent of the benefit of the Freehold. On the analysis of the majority, that right under a Trust seems to arise simply because of the intention of B1 and B2 that each would have such a share (see F2:2.2.1(ii)).[62] However, whilst a large number of factors can apparently be taken into

---

[55] At least as to the key issue of the extent of B1's right under the Trust of the Freehold; Lord Neuberger did dissent on the issue of 'occupation rent': see n 31 above.

[56] See eg *per* Lord Walker at [33]; *per* Baroness Hale at [58] and [66] and [86]. Lord Neuberger however took a different approach at [110]–[114].

[57] *Per* Baroness Hale at [69].

[58] *Per* Lord Walker at [33].

[59] Although it is worth noting that Lord Hope at [11] did attach a great deal of importance to the unequal contributions: it may be that his Lordship regarded the burden of showing the starting point does not apply as rather less 'heavy' than Lord Walker and Baroness Hale suggested.

[60] A long list of factors may be relevant when attempting to discern that intention: see esp *per* Baroness Hale at [69].

[61] See *per* Baroness Hale at [90]–[91].

[62] See eg *per* Baroness Hale at [86]. As noted in F2:2.2.1(ii), there is a difficult question as to the *reason* for which that Trust arises: Option 3 as set out in that section seems to be most consistent with the majority's *decision*. In contrast, the majority in *Stack* view the Trust as an example of a 'common intention Constructive Trust': such a Trust is not confined to situations where a Freehold or Lease is transferred to B1 and B2 jointly, and can take into account the parties' intentions *after* they acquired that right. However, there are problems with analysing the Trust in *Stack* in that way: see further G3:2.4.3(v).

account when ascertaining B1 and B2's intentions,[63] the extent of B1's financial contributions was clearly the crucial factor in determining the extent of B1's right under the Trust.

It may be that the contrasting approaches of Lord Neuberger and the majority of the House of Lords are not so far apart. Each adopts a starting point or presumption: this is a reasonable thing to do when trying to establish a past fact. Lord Neuberger's starting point is that, if there are unequal contributions, B1 and B2 each intends to have his own, individual right. The majority's starting point is that, if B1 and B2 acquire a Freehold or Lease in order to live together as a couple, B1 and B2 do *not* intend that each will have his own share: they intend *only* to have a right as part of a co-owning team. But: (i) Lord Neuberger notes that his starting point can be displaced if there is evidence that the parties had a different intention; and (ii) the majority, as shown by the decision in *Stack* itself, is willing to look at a wide range of evidence[64] to see if the parties did intend, after all, that each should have his own, individual share. In addition, it is important to remember that we are here considering the position applying when B1 and B2 *initially* acquire their Freehold or Lease: it may be possible for a later event to cause a change to that position (see eg G3:2.4.3(v)). [65]

Nonetheless, we need to decide which approach is better: (i) that favoured by the majority in *Stack*; or (ii) Lord Neuberger's alternative analysis? To some extent, it depends on what you think B1 and B2 are most likely to intend in a case such as **Example 18**. Is the best guess that, because B1 and B2 are living together as a couple, they intend to have a right *only* as part of a co-owning team? Or is that, because B1 pays more than B2, B1 intends, and B2 accepts, that B1 should have a separate, more valuable right? Lord Neuberger's view is probably the better one: B1 should only be denied a separate persistent right under a Trust if it is *clear* that B1 and B2 do not intend to acquire such a right. But perhaps your view ultimately depends on whether you are a cynic or a romantic.

However, on any view, the approach of the majority causes some important practical problems. First, the general position is that if B1 and B2 each makes unequal contributions to the costs of acquiring a right, the starting inference is that B1 and B2 *do* intend that each will have his own individual share (see F2:2.2.1(ii)).[66] So the approach of the majority must be limited to particular cases: but to which cases? Does it apply *whenever* B1 and B2 acquire a Freehold or a Lease with the plan of living together? Can it apply where friends, work colleagues or relatives choose to live together? Certainly, in those cases, the argument that B1 and B2 intend to act only as a team is much weaker than in a case where B1 and B2 are lovers.[67] Lord Walker also suggests that the approach preferred by Lord Neuberger may be appropriate where B1 and B2 'have lived and worked together in what has amounted to both an emotional and a commercial partnership'.[68] So, even if B1 and B2 are lovers, we may

---

[63] See esp *per* Baroness Hale at [69].

[64] See esp *per* Baroness Hale at [69].

[65] Baroness Hale at [62] and [86] notes that the intentions of B1 and B2 can change over time and states that such a change can alter the extent of their rights. However it is difficult to see how a change in intention, *by itself*, can vary the rights of B1 and B2. Rather, there would have to be a specific reason for imposing a different duty on each of B1 and B2 (eg, a promise by B1 on which B2 relied: see further G3:2.4.3(v)).

[66] See *per* Lord Neuberger at [111].

[67] In *Adekunle v Ritchie* [2007] EW Misc 5 (Leeds County Court, August 2007) HHJ Behrens considered a case where B1 and B2 were mother and son: it was assumed that the *Stack* approach *did* apply; but that, on the facts of the case, B2 met the burden of showing that B1 and B2 did intend that each would have his own individual right.

[68] [2007] 2 AC 432 at [32].

need to ask further questions: eg does the majority's starting point apply if B1 and B2 run a shop and live upstairs?

Second, in a case where the majority's starting point does apply, when can it be displaced? It was emphasised in *Stack* that such displacement can occur only in an 'exceptional' case; but what counts as exceptional? For example, how separate do the financial affairs of B1 and B2 need to be for the starting point to be displaced? Indeed, it may be thought that the facts of *Stack* were not *so* exceptional: if B1 and B2 live together and choose not to marry or become civil partners, is it such a surprise that they organise their financial affairs separately?[69]

The majority's starting point can be displaced whenever it can be shown that B1 and B2 did intend that each should have his own individual right. In considering when B1 and B2 can be said to have had such an intention both Lord Walker and Baroness Hale assume that a court can: (i) make inferences about the parties' intentions; and (ii) *impute* such intentions.[70] There is a vital distinction between those two things. When trying to establish past facts a court almost always has to make inferences: to reach a conclusion from a piece of evidence. So, if it is shown that A hated B and had threatened to harm B, it may be reasonable to infer that, when tripping B up, A did so deliberately rather than accidentally. However, a court is *not* permitted to make imputations: to impute is to add rather than to deduce, to read in something you know not to be present. As Lord Neuberger puts it:[71] 'Imputation involves concluding what the parties would have intended, whereas inference involves concluding what they did intend.' Lord Neuberger is therefore correct when he points out that it would be illegitimate for a court to base its finding that B1 and B2 each has his own individual persistent right on an *imputed* intention.[72]

This rejection of imputed intention is a further point in favour of Lord Neuberger's view as to the correct starting point in a case like **Example 18**. If we: (i) take the preferred starting point of the majority; and (ii) modify their approach to remove the possibility of imputed intention; then (iii) we are left with the risk that there will be many cases in which, despite making a bigger financial contribution than B2, B1 does *not* acquire his own individual right. Whereas if we take Lord Neuberger's starting point, we are left with the reasonable position that B1, because he contributed more than B2, does have his own individual right *unless* there is evidence that B1 and B2 intended that each should have a right *only* as a member of a co-owning team. That approach is consistent with the general rule; so we do not then need to answer the difficult question of just how close B1 and B2 need to be before the majority's starting point can apply.

(iii) Proving a tenancy in common: the needs of practical convenience?
The finding of a joint tenancy may seem to cause injustice in a case where: (i) B1 contributes half (or more) of the costs of acquiring the Freehold or Lease; and then (ii) B1 dies without having first severed that joint tenancy. In such a case, B1 has no individual

---

[69] For example, a study of 1,296 married or unmarried cohabitants found that 21 per cent of childless unmarried cohabitants kept their financial affairs wholly separate (Vogler, Brockmann and Wiggins (2006) 57 *British Journal of Sociology* 455: discussed by George (2008) 29 *Journal of Social Welfare & Family Law* 1).

[70] See *per* Lord Walker at [33] and *per* Baroness Hale at [60].

[71] At [126].

[72] At [127]. Such imputation was also rejected by the House of Lords in *Pettitt v Pettitt* [1970] AC 777. See too Swadling (2007) 123 *LQR* 511 at 516–7

right to pass on in his will: B2 becomes solely entitled to the Freehold or Lease. That perceived injustice can also arise where the co-held right is Ownership of a thing other than land (see **F2:2.2.1(iii)**). However, its effects can be even more dramatic where land is concerned: land is so often a uniquely valuable investment. As a result, we might expect judges to strain to find that, where they co-hold a Freehold or Lease, B1 and B2 are not simply joint tenants but, instead, that each of B1 and B2 also has his own, individual right.[73]

The approach of the majority in *Stack v Dowden* is therefore surprising. It favours the finding that, in a case such as **Example 18**, B1 and B2 do *not* each have an individual right. There are two possible reactions to this. One is to argue that there are three different ways to interpret the starting point applied by the majority in *Stack*:

Interpretation 1   B1 and B2 initially hold both: (i) the Freehold; and (ii) the right under a Trust of that Freehold as joint tenants; *or*

Interpretation 2   B1 and B2 initially hold the Freehold on Trust for each other, with each of B1 and B2 entitled to a 50 per cent share of the benefit of the Freehold; *or*

Interpretation 3   B1 and B2 each initially have an identical right; so *either* **Interpretation 1** or **Interpretation 2** applies, depending on which better fits the intentions of B1 and B2 when acquiring the Freehold or Lease.

It has been assumed in the discussion so far that **Interpretation 1** is correct: it certainly fits the express statements of Lord Walker and Baroness Hale.[74] In *Stack* itself, the majority found that, on the facts, the starting point had been displaced; so there was no need to examine the precise nature of that starting point. In a case where: (i) the starting point is not displaced; and (ii) B1 dies before any act of severance has occurred; then (iii) a court will need to consider whether **Interpretation 1** is correct. There are *some* indications in *Stack* that may favour **Interpretation 2 or 3**;[75] but, overall, it will be very difficult for a judge to depart from **Interpretation 1**. In particular, Baroness Hale emphasises in *Stack* that, when the starting point applies, B1 and B2 hold their Equitable right (the right under the Trust of the Freehold or Lease) in the same way as they hold their Freehold:[76] that analysis is consistent *only* with **Interpretation 1**.

The second possibility involves a less radical reinterpretation of *Stack*. When applying the approach favoured in *Stack*, judges may strain to meet the perceived needs of practical convenience by finding that, even though B1 and B2 acquired a Freehold or Lease in order to live together as a couple, B1 *can* meet the 'heavy' burden of showing that B1 and B2

---

[73] See eg *per* Lord Cowper LC in *York v Stone* (1795) 1 Salk 158 at 158: 'a joint tenancy is an odious thing in equity'; *per* Lord Denning MR in *Burgess v Rawnsley* [1975] 1 Ch 429 at 438: 'The thing to remember today is that equity leans against joint tenants and favours tenancies in common.'

[74] See eg *per* Lord Walker at [33]; *per* Baroness Hale at [58], [66] and [86].

[75] A possible indication of **Interpretation 3** occurs *per* Baroness Hale at [92]. Lord Hope's speech seems to assume that **Interpretation 2** has been adopted as it refers throughout to B1 and B2 having 'equal shares'. Dixon [2007] *Conv* 352 at 354 notes that: 'Indeed, at points in the opinions of the majority, it is as if the tenancy in common in equal shares does not exist at all or as if they take the view that the difference between a tenancy in common and a joint-tenancy is not important.'

[76] See eg at [58]: 'A conveyance into joint names indicates both legal and beneficial joint tenancy'; at [68]: 'The burden will therefore be on the person seeking to show that the parties did not intend their beneficial interests to be different from their legal interests, and in what way'; at [86] 'The starting point is for Ms Dowden to show that the common intention . . . was that they should hold the property otherwise than as beneficial joint tenants.'

intended that each would have his own, individual right.[77] After all, if B1 makes a bigger financial contribution that B2, it may seem harsh that if, B1 dies without first severing, B2 will become solely entitled to the Freehold or Lease. This suggests that, in practice, the presumption favoured by the majority in *Stack* may become so weak as to be of no real value. In particular, it is important to note Lord Hope's approach: whilst nominally agreeing with the majority, his Lordship regarded B1's greater contribution to the costs of paying for the Freehold as a key factor in displacing the majority's starting point.[78] If unequal contributions can have that effect, then we can question if there is really anything to be gained from departing from the general rule applied by Lord Neuberger: unequal contributions suggest that B1 and B2 *do* intend that each will have his own individual right.

2.3 Reform: abolition of the joint tenancy of the right under a Trust?

The majority's approach in *Stack* differs markedly from a particular reform proposed by some commentators: the abolition of the 'beneficial joint tenancy' of a Freehold or Lease.[79] No one argues that the basic section 1(6) rule should change: in order to reduce the time and expense to C of acquiring a right from co-owners of land, B1 and B2 must hold the Freehold or Lease as joint tenants. The suggested reform is that it should be *impossible* for B1 and B2 to hold *the right under a Trust* of a Freehold or Lease as joint tenants.

On this view, the joint tenancy of a right under a Trust of a Freehold or Lease would be eliminated. Hence, even if B1 and B2 *expressly* acquired a Freehold or Lease *only* as members of a co-owning team, each would nonetheless acquire an individual right under a Trust of the Freehold or Lease. Such a reform would have three main advantages:

1. It would avoid the perceived harshness of the doctrine of survivorship: from the outset, each of B1 and B2 would have his own right that he can pass on when he dies.
2. It would avoid a particular pitfall facing B1 if: (i) he contributes more than half of the cost of acquiring a Freehold or Lease; then (ii) chooses not to have his own individual right; but then (iii) severs so as to acquire his own individual right. In such a case, B1's individual right under the Trust will give him only 50 per cent of the benefit of the right; his share of the benefit will *not* reflect his greater contribution to the costs of its acquisition (see **F2:2.3**).
3. It would eliminate the time and expense incurred when B1 and B2 initially hold as joint tenants and an argument then arises about whether or not a severance of that joint tenancy occurred before B1's death.[80]

Of course, these disadvantages of the joint tenancy do not just apply where land is involved. However, reform proposals have been limited to the land context as, due to its social importance and financial value, the disadvantages are deemed to be particularly acute where land is concerned.

---

[77] In *Adekunle v Ritchie* [2007] EW Misc 5 (**n 67** above) B1 had died and B2 claimed to be solely entitled to the Freehold. It was found that the B1's executors were able to displace the starting point and so B1, when she died, did have an individual right to pass on.

[78] [2007] 1 432 at [11]. But note *Fowler v Barron* [2008] EWCA Civ 377 where the *Stack* starting point applied even though B1 had made *all* the payments towards acquiring the Freehold.

[79] See eg Thompson [1987] *Conv* 29 and 275. For a counterargument see Pritchard [1987] *Conv* 273 and R Smith, *Plural Ownership*, ch 5.

[80] See eg *Burgess v Rawnsely* [1975] Ch 429 (see **2.4.3** below).

The downside of such a reform is that parties who *deliberately* opt for a joint tenancy would be deprived of the chance to hold as joint tenants both: (i) a Freehold or Lease; and (ii) a right under a Trust of that Freehold or Lease. Therefore, to evaluate the suggested reform, we need to ask if such parties have a good reason for choosing a joint tenancy. Certainly, some parties, often but not always married couples, choose the joint tenancy as it accords with their notion of owning the land *only* as a team. In fact, in *Stack v Dowden*,[81] the majority of the House of Lords held that, where B1 and B2 acquire a home to live in as a couple, the starting point is to presume that they intend to hold it only as joint tenants. In such a case, the doctrine of survivorship may well hold no fears for B1 and B2: they may both *want* the land to be solely owned by the surviving co-owner. Indeed, the parties may wish to use the joint tenancy as a means to ensure the survivor becomes solely entitled without needing to make a will.[82]

However, it is important to note that the usefulness of the joint tenancy is undermined by the fact that each co-owner can, whenever he pleases, unilaterally sever that joint tenancy and thus ensure that each of B1 and B2 acquires his own, individual right (see F2:2.3.1). This is particularly true in relation to land: if B1 and B2 are co-holders of a Freehold or Lease, B1 can sever simply by giving B2 written notice (see 2.4.1 below). As a result, any protection a co-owner may believe he is gaining by means of a joint tenancy is illusory. In fact, B1 can even foist a new co-owner on B2 by 'an act operating on B1's own share', such as a sale to C or the granting of a Charge to C (see 2.4.2 below).[83]

Where does this leave us? As a matter of doctrine, there is no reason at all why a right under a Trust of a Freehold or Lease, like any other right, should not be co-held by B1 and B2 as joint tenants. And there are also sound practical reasons why B1 and B2 may wish to hold such a right as joint tenants. Yet the advantages of doing so are undermined by the fact that either joint tenant can unilaterally choose to end the joint tenancy. This means the practical advantages of such a joint tenancy are, in the end, *outweighed* by its risks to a party who fails to realise that he has no individual right. The desire to allow well-informed co-owners to opt for the joint tenancy thus seems to be trumped by the desire to protect co-owners from the inadvertent joint tenancy.

So, it may well be that the needs of practical convenience justify a change in the current law. Under such a reform: (i) B1 and B2 would continue to hold a Freehold or Lease itself as joint tenants; and (ii) B1 and B2 would continue to hold that Freehold or Lease on Trust for each other; but (iii) each of B1 and B2 would *always* have an individual right under the Trust to a particular share of the benefit of the Freehold or Lease. The default position is that each of B1 and B2 has a 50 per cent share of the benefit of the Freehold or Lease; that can of course change if B1 and B2 intend otherwise. This conclusion provides a further reason to reject the approach of the majority in *Stack v Dowden*: given the problems of the

---

[81] [2007] 2 AC 432.

[82] As was the case, for example, in *Abbey National v Moss* [1994] 1 FLR 307. For consideration of this and other 'will substitutes', see Langbein (1984) 97 *Harvard Law Review* 1108.

[83] Indeed, it is worth noting that sometimes courts have tried to manipulate the rules precisely to prevent B1 severing unilaterally and hence forcing B2, in effect, to co-own with C: see eg *Thames Guaranty v Campbell* [1985] 1 QB 210; *Penn v Bristol and West BS* [1995] 2 FLR 938. The most dramatic example of that tendency is the judgment of Lord Denning MR in *Bedson v Bedson* [1965] 2 QB 666. His Lordship asserted at 667–8 that, if B1 and B2 are spouses as well as co-owners of land, it is impossible for either of them to sever by a unilateral act operating on his or her own share. That attempt to *restrict* severance was unsuccessful; just as his Lordship's attempt to *extend* severance by allowing a unilateral declaration to sever has also been unsuccessful (see 2.4.5 below).

inadvertent joint tenancy, judges should try to ensure that such a joint tenancy arises *less* often, not more often.

2.4   Severance: the acquisition of an individual right under a Trust

EXAMPLE 19

A transfers a Freehold to B1 and B2 as joint tenants. A year later, B1 and B2 agree that they will each have a 50 per cent share of the Freehold. Two years later, B1 dies.

Mutual agreement is one method by which severance can occur (see **F2:2.3.2**) and there has clearly been such an agreement in **Example 20**. However, as severance is the process by which a joint tenancy is turned into a tenancy in common, its application to co-ownership of land is rather tricky. First, section 1(6) means that a Freehold or Lease *must* be co-held by B1 and B2 as joint tenants. Clearly, such a joint tenancy cannot be severed; if it could be, the whole purpose of section 1(6) would be undermined. So, in **Example 20**, B1 and B2 must continue to hold the Freehold as joint tenants. In such a case, B1 and B2 are also joint tenants of a right under a Trust of the Freehold. However, it is difficult to see how such a joint tenancy can be severed: a right under a Trust *cannot* be held by B1 and B2 as tenants in common (see **1.5** above). Such a right, like a personal right against A, depends on A being under a duty, and B1 and B2 cannot each have a share of a duty owed by A (see **F2:1.2.1**).

Strictly speaking, therefore, the agreement in **Example 20** severs *neither*: (i) the joint tenancy of the Freehold; *nor* (ii) the joint tenancy of the right under the Trust of the Freehold. However, it does have an important effect: it *changes the terms of the Trust*. As B1 and B2 are the only beneficiaries of the Trust, they are of course free to change its terms. And by their agreement, they move from: (i) an initial Trust in which they are joint tenants of a persistent right; to (ii) a *new Trust* in which each has his own, individual right. So, in **Example 20**, as a result of their mutual agreement, B1 and B2 are each under a duty to use the Freehold 50 per cent for B1's benefit and 50 per cent for B2's benefit. As in **Example 17**, there is *no* co-holding of any right under a Trust; instead, each of B1 and B2 has his own, *separate* right under the Trust.

In **Example 20**, B1 *does* have his own, individual right that he can, for example, pass on in his will. Strictly speaking, that change does *not* involve a severance. It does, however, involve the acquisition by B1 of a new right: its effect thus very closely resembles a severance. So, for the sake of convenience, the process by which B1 acquires such a right can be referred to as 'severance': certainly, it is governed by many of the general rules we examined in **F2:2.3**.

EXAMPLE 20

B1, B2 and B3 hold a Freehold as joint tenants. B3 transfers his 'share' of the Freehold to C. B1 then dies.

Initially, B1, B2 and B3 hold the Freehold on Trust for themselves: they are joint tenants both of: (i) the Freehold; and (ii) a right under a Trust of the Freehold. B3's 'act operating on his own share' then causes a severance (see **F2:2.3.1**). B1, B2 and B3 still hold the Freehold as joint tenants, but the terms of the Trust are changed:

- C now has a distinct right under the Trust, giving him one-third of the benefit of the Freehold; *and*
- B1 and B2 are joint tenants of a separate right under the Trust, giving them, as a team, two-thirds of the benefit of the Freehold.

If B1 then dies, there is a change to the holding of the Freehold: B2 and B3 are the remaining joint tenants. B1's death does not change C's position: C still has a right to one-third of the benefit of the Freehold. However, B1's death changes B2's position: B2 is now the sole holder of the right to two-thirds of the benefit of the Freehold.

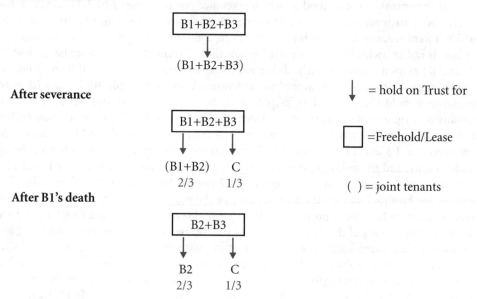

Before severance

B1+B2+B3

(B1+B2+B3)

After severance

$\downarrow$ = hold on Trust for

B1+B2+B3

(B1+B2)   C
2/3   1/3

$\square$ =Freehold/Lease

After B1's death

( ) = joint tenants

B2+B3

B2   C
2/3   1/3

2.4.1 Written notice under section 36(2) of the LPA 1925

(i) Scope

Section 36(2) of the LPA 1925 recognises a special method of severance that applies *only* where B1 and B2 are joint tenants both of: (i) a Freehold or Lease; and (ii) of a right under a Trust of that Freehold or Lease. This additional method consists of B1 simply giving B2 'a notice in writing' of his desire to acquire his own individual right.[84]

EXAMPLE 21

B1 and B2 are joint tenants both of a Freehold and of the right under a Trust of that Freehold. B1 wants to make a will leaving his 'share' of the Freehold to C. B1's solicitor advises B1 to acquire his own individual right by sending a letter to B2 stating that he wishes to end the joint tenancy. B1 sends that letter to B2. B1 dies a week later.

---

[84] In *Burgess v Rawnsley* [1975] Ch 429, the Court of Appeal disapproved of the fact that this useful method of severance is available only where B1 and B2 hold a Freehold or Lease: see eg *per* Lord Denning MR at 440. Nonetheless, it is clear that the method *cannot* apply in other cases.

Thanks to section 36(2), B1 *does* acquire his own individual right under the Trust of the Freehold: that right passes to C when B1 dies. By allowing B1 or B2 unilaterally to 'sever' by means of a written notice, section 36(2) provides the joint tenants with a very useful facility. This is a good example of a formality rule operating as a facility, rather than as a requirement (see C3:2): B1 is given a power, not usually available to joint tenants, to sever by a unilateral declaration to B2. However, B1 can *only* take advantage of that power if he exercises it in the proper form.

There is some confusion about *which* joint tenants can exploit the useful facility of section 36(2) severance. The confusion comes from the wording of the section, which says that it applies where 'a legal estate . . . is vested in joint tenants beneficially'. This seems pretty clear: the section *only* applies where B1 and B2 are joint tenants of *both*: (i) a Freehold or Lease; *and* (ii) a right under a Trust of that Freehold or Lease.

EXAMPLE 22

A holds a Freehold on Trust for B1 and B2. B1 and B2 are joint tenants of the right under the Trust. B1 sends a letter to B2 stating that he wishes to end the joint tenancy. B1 dies a week later.

This time, there is no severance; B1 has no right to pass on when he dies. B1 *cannot* rely on section 36(2) as the Freehold itself was *not* held by B1 and B2: there is no 'legal estate . . . vested in joint tenants beneficially'. The crucial difference is that, in **Example 23**, B1 is *not* a co-owner of land; he is *simply* a co-holder of a right under a Trust.

Can the different results in **Examples 22 and 23** be justified? Many commentators think not.[85] However, it seems the purpose of section 36(2) is to give a co-owner of land, deprived by section 1(6) of the right to sever the joint tenancy of the Freehold or Lease, the compensating option of acquiring his own individual share under a Trust of that Freehold or Lease. That purpose does *not* apply in a case such as **Example 23**: in such a case: (i) B1 and B2 are *not* co-owners of land; so (ii) section 1(6) does *not* deprive B1 or B2 of the opportunity to sever; so (iii) section 36(2) need *not* apply.

There is a further reason for restricting the operation of the section 36(2) method of severance. If it applied in **Example 23**, B1 could sever by simply giving written notice to B2: there is no need for B1 to give such notice to A. This can clearly cause a problem to A:[86] if B1 and B2 each acquire an individual right under the Trust, his duties as trustee would change, yet A would have no means of discovering that change. Moreover, there is a good reason to limit the circumstances in which A's duty can change without A's knowledge (see C3:6.3).[87] However, in **Example 22**, the trustees and beneficiaries are *the same*: by informing B2, B1 ensures that all the trustees know of the change in their duties. This provides a reason for limiting the scope of section 36(2) to cases where the trustees and beneficiaries are the same people.

---

[85] See eg R Smith, *Plural Ownership* (2004), 54; Tee, ch 5 in *Land Law: Issues, Debates, Policy* (Willan, 2002), 141 notes that 'No one has been able to identify any reason at all' for this limit on s 36(2).

[86] As noted by eg R Smith, *Plural Ownership* (2004), 54.

[87] This is not to suggest that, under the current law, A will *always* know if severance has occurred. For example, in a case such as **Example 23**, severance can occur without A's knowledge if B1 and B2 mutually agree that each has his own persistent right under the Trust. However, the argument is that the circumstances in which severance can occur without A's knowledge should not be extended without good reason.

(ii) Satisfaction

If, as in **Example 22**, B1 *chooses* to take advantage of section 36(2) there should be very few problems. B1 simply gives B2 the necessary notice, and each party acquires his individual right under the Trust of the Freehold or Lease.[88] However, difficulties occur in cases where B1's use of the section 36(2) method is *not* deliberate.

EXAMPLE 23

B1 and B2 are joint tenants of both a Freehold and the right under a Trust of that Freehold. B1 dies, leaving all his assets to C.

C will wish to show that, before he died, B1 acquired his own individual right: if B1 did not, B2 will be solely entitled to the Freehold. In such a case, C may well cast around to find *some* piece of writing passing between B1 and B2 that can count as a section 36(2) notice; even if that writing was not produced with the intention of giving B1 his own individual right.

For example, in *re Draper's Conveyance*,[89] B1 and B2 were in the process of divorcing when B1 died. C argued that a document signed by B1 as part of those proceedings could count as a section 36(2) notice.[90] B1 had asked the court to use its powers in the divorce proceedings so that the land 'may be sold and the proceeds of sale thereof may be distributed in accordance with the respective interests of [B1 and B2]'.[91] B1 was hence clearly requesting—in writing that was sent to B2 as well as the court—that B1 and B2 should each have an individual right. The document *did* therefore count as a section 36(2) notice; even though B1 may not have intended it to have that effect. Thus, C succeeded in showing that B1 had his own, individual right under a Trust of the Freehold which could pass on to C through B1's will.

However, section 36(2) should not be seen as a magic wand that allows each party to acquire an individual right *whenever* any writing is sent by B1 to B2. In *Harris v Goddard*,[92] for example, the Court of Appeal made clear that the situation requested by B1 *must necessarily involve* B1 and B2 each acquiring an individual right. It is not enough for B1 simply to ask for the land to be sold: there is nothing to prevent B1 and B2 then holding the proceeds of sale as joint tenants (see **F2:1.6.1**).[93] Nor is it even enough for B1 to ask that the Freehold or Lease be given solely to B1, or solely to B2: such a solution would end the joint tenancy, but it would *not* give each of B1 and B2 an individual right under a Trust of the Freehold or Lease (see **F2:2.3.2**). In *Harris*, the Court of Appeal also insisted that a written request will only satisfy section 36(2) if it asks for an *immediate* severance.[94] Certainly, if the parties are

---

[88] There can be problems with the timing of the notice. For example, if B1 posts the notice to B2, who dies after the notice arrives but before reading it, has severance occurred? Yes, according to *Kinch v Bullard* [1998] 4 All ER 650.

[89] [1969] 1 Ch 486.

[90] C (and C2) were the administrators of B1's estate (B1 had died intestate).

[91] In her supporting affidavit, also given to B2, B1 had asked that the land 'be sold and that the proceeds of sale thereof may be distributed equally; alternatively that the respondent pay me one half of the value of the said property with vacant possession'.

[92] [1983] 1 WLR 1203.

[93] Note eg *per* Dillon LJ in *Harris v Goddard* [1983] 1 WLR 1203 at 1210: 'Severance is, as I understand it, the process of separating off the share of a joint tenant, so that the concurrent ownership will continue but the right of survivorship will no longer apply. The parties will hold separate shares as tenants in common.'

[94] *Per* Lawton LJ at 1209: 'When a notice in writing of a desire to sever is served pursuant to s 36 (2) it takes effect forthwith. It follows that a desire to sever must evince an intention to bring about the wanted result immediately.'

still negotiating, and just discussing possible outcomes, B1 will not be able to rely on section 36(2): there will be no writing showing a definite intention to sever.[95]

2.4.2 'An act operating on a joint tenant's own share'

As well as establishing a new method by which B1 can acquire his own individual right, section 36(2) also confirms that B1 can acquire such a right if he can rely on any of the general methods of severance (see **F2:2.3**).

EXAMPLE 24

B1 and B2 are joint tenants both of a registered Freehold and of the right under a Trust of that Freehold. B1, by forging B2's signature, attempts to transfer the Freehold to C. C is registered as the new holder of the Freehold.

B1's motive is clear: if B1 can fool C into thinking that B2 has also consented to the transfer, B1 can trick C into giving him the full value of the Freehold.[96] Of course, B2 cannot be bound by the forged transfer. C, by virtue of his substantive registration, *does* acquire the Freehold;[97] but B2 can apply to have the register rectified so that B2 and C are registered as joint tenants of the Freehold (see **E5:3.2**). However, as in **F2:Example 12**, C does acquire a valuable right. As a result of the purported transfer of the Freehold, B1 acquires, and transfers to C, his own individual right under the Trust of the Freehold.[98] As a result, when the register is rectified, B2 and C will hold the Freehold subject to a Trust: they are each under a duty to use the Freehold 50 per cent for B2's benefit and 50 per cent for C's benefit.

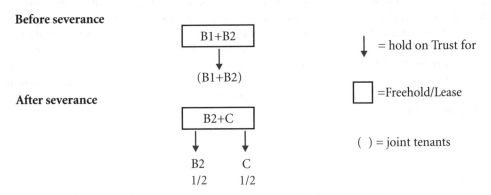

This method of severance is based on a desire to protect C (see **F2:2.3.1**). If B1 did not acquire his own individual right, then C, despite paying B1 the full value of the Freehold, would acquire *nothing*. Given the purpose of this method of severance, if C can acquire a valuable right *without* severance having to occur—ie, without B1 needing to acquire his own right—then severance should *not* occur.

---

[95] See eg *Gore & Snell v Carpenter* (1990) 60 P & CR 456.

[96] The fact that B1 and B2 are registered as co-owners means that it is clear to C that B1 is not the sole holder of the Freehold: that is why, in contrast to **F2:Example 12**, B1 needs to pretend B2 has consented to the transfer.

[97] See s 58 of the LRA 2002: this is an example of the positive operation of substantive registration.

[98] See eg *Ahmed v Kendrick* [1988] 2 FLR 22.

EXAMPLE 25

B1 and B2 are joint tenants both of a registered Freehold and of the right under a Trust of that Freehold. B1, by forging B2's signature, attempts to grant C a five-year Lease of the land.

It seems that severance should not occur (compare **F2:Example 13**). Even without severance, C can still acquire a valuable right. B1, in his capacity as a member of the team holding the Freehold, has a right to exclusive control of the land. B1 can transfer that right to C for five years. C will then have the right to make any use of the land he wishes, provided he does not interfere with B2's same right to exclusive control (see **1.4.1** above). C *can* thus acquire a valuable right *even if* B1 and B2 remain joint tenants of both the Freehold and of the right under the Trust. Although this view is contested,[99] it therefore seems that B1's grant of a Lease to C should *not* lead to a severance.[100]

EXAMPLE 26

B1 and B2 are joint tenants of both a registered Freehold and of the right under a Trust of that Freehold. C agrees to lend B1 £100,000 if B1's duty to repay the money is secured by a Charge over the Freehold. B1, by forging B2's signature, purports to grant C such a Charge.

This is very similar to **F2:Example 14.** The plan again is for C to acquire a security right—a right that: (i) allows C to use the value of the Freehold if B1 does not repay the loan as agreed; *and* (ii) gives C protection if B1 goes into insolvency. Clearly, C cannot acquire a Charge over the land: B2 has not given his consent. And a personal right against B1 cannot give C the security he expects. So, for C to have a useful security right *at all*, he needs to have a persistent right that allows him to get at some of the value of the co-owned Freehold. Although this view is again contested,[101] severance must occur: the desire to protect C means that B1 must have an individual right under a Trust of the Freehold that he can hold as security for C.[102] Similarly, severance must occur if B1: (i) attempts to set up a Trust in C's favour; or (ii) attempts to give C a Purely Equitable Charge: in each case, the protection of C demands that B1 acquire a valuable, individual right against which C can acquire a persistent right.[103]

---

[99] Academic opinions vary: for a survey, see eg L Fox [2000] *Conv* 208; Crown (2001) 117 *LQR* 477 at 484–90. Both authors support the somewhat novel proposal that the joint tenancy of B1 and B2's right under the Trust should be suspended during C's Lease. That solution is consistent with the aim of protecting C as it ensures that C is protected even if B1 dies during C's Lease. It is, however, difficult to see how a joint tenancy can be suspended: Preece (1981) 55 *Law Institute Journal* 115 at 116–7.

[100] The same analysis applies if B1 attempts to give C an Easement, such as a right of way across the co-owned land. There is no need for severance as C can acquire a right of way subject to the limit of not interfering with any use B2 may wish to make of the land (just as B2 is under a duty not to interfere with any use B1 may wish to make of the land, so is B2 under a duty not to interfere with C's right of way).

[101] Nield [2001] *Conv* 462 and Crown (2001) 117 *LQR* 477 at 480–84 both take the opposite view and doubt that severance should occur. Nield at 474 suggests that a suspension of the joint tenancy may be a better solution.

[102] See eg *per* Bingham J in *First National Securities Ltd v Hegerty* [1985] 1 QB 850 at 854; *re Sharer* (1912) 57 SJ 60. *Mortgage Corporation v Shaire* [2000] 3 WLR 639 may also provide evidence: the assumption there seems to have been that B1 and B2 did *not* initially hold the right under the Trust of the Freehold as joint tenants; but that assumption may be incorrect in light of the approach of the majority in *Stack v Dowden* [2007] 2 AC 432.

[103] Crown (2001) 117 *LQR* 477 at 490–92 accepts that B1's attempt to set up a Trust currently leads to a severance.

2.4.3 Agreement between B1 and B2

> **EXAMPLE 27**
>
> B1 and B2 are joint tenants both of a registered Freehold and of the right under a Trust of that Freehold. They agree that each will have an individual right to 50 per cent of the benefit of the Freehold.

Such an agreement causes a severance: B1 and B2 will each acquire an individual right, to have 50 per cent of the benefit of that Freehold (the same result applies in **Example 20**). Where land is involved, the general principles regulating this method of severance still apply (see **F2:2.3.2**). Of particular importance is the principle that the agreement between B1 and B2 does *not* need to be legally binding. Rather, there simply needs to be evidence that the parties agreed that each should have his own, individual right.[104]

> **EXAMPLE 28**
>
> B1 and B2 are joint tenants both of a registered Freehold and of the right under a Trust of that Freehold. In their divorce proceedings, a draft consent order is drawn up: the Freehold is to be sold and the proceeds split between B1 and B2 60:40. B1 dies before that draft order can be approved by the court.

As the draft order has not been approved at the time of B1's death, there is no legally binding agreement between B1 and B2. Nonetheless, as both parties had agreed to the draft order, there is evidence of their mutual intention that each should have his own individual right. As a result, as confirmed by *Hunter v Babbage*,[105] on which **Example 29** is based, severance has occurred. So, at the time of B1's death, each of B1 and B2 has an individual right to 50 per cent of the benefit of the Freehold. B1 did *not* acquire the planned 60 per cent share: that share was agreed as part of a deal that was not legally binding. Instead, B1 acquires the automatic 50 per cent share that arises on severance.

As the agreement does not need to be legally binding, its terms do not need to be as precisely defined as a contract. And section 2 of the Law of Property (Miscellaneous Provisions) Act 1989 (see **E2:2.3.3**) does not apply as severance does *not* require each party to come under a contractual duty to the other. However, severance gives both B1 and B2 a new individual right under the Trust of the Freehold. So, when reaching an agreement, B1 and B2 thus exercise a power to give each other a persistent right relating to land. Section 53(1)(a) of the LPA 1925 imposes the basic formality rule that A's power to give B a persistent right relating to land must be made in writing signed by A (see **E2:2.3.1**). There is a strong argument for applying that basic rule to the case of severance by mutual agreement.[106]

However, the current position, in England at least,[107] is that severance can occur even

---

104 See eg *Burgess v Rawnsley* [1975] Ch 429 *per* Sir John Pennycuick at 446: 'The significance of an agreement is not that it binds the parties; but that it serves as an indication of common intention to sever.'

105 (1994) 2 FLR 806: a decision of John McDonnell QC sitting as a Deputy High Court judge.

106 In which case, *each* of B1 and B2 would have to express his intention in signed writing. For arguments supporting the application of formal requirements, see eg Butt (1982) 9 *Sydney Law Review* 568; McClean (1979) 57 *Canadian Bar Review* 1. R Smith, *Plural Ownership* (2005), 68 considers the arguments, but rejects them, favouring the current approach: however, Smith does not consider the possible application of s 53(1)(a).

107 In the Australian case of *Lyons v Lyons* [1967] VR 169 it was suggested at 171 that formal requirements do apply to this method of severance.

if B1 and B2's agreement *is purely oral.* That result may flow from the wording of section 36(2): that section not only introduces the special method of severance by written notice, it also states that severance will occur if a co-owner of land does such 'other acts or things as would, in the case of a personal estate, have been effectual to sever the tenancy in equity'. This could be taken to mean that as an oral agreement will suffice to sever a joint tenancy of, say, Ownership of a bike, it must also suffice in cases such as **Example 20 and 28**.

In *Burgess v Rawnsley*,[108] for example, the Court of Appeal assumed that an oral agreement can effect a severance. B1 and B2 each provided half of the price of a Freehold. It was expressly conveyed to them as joint tenants: they were thus joint tenants of both: (i) the Freehold; and (ii) a right under a Trust of that Freehold. When B1 died, C (B1's daughter) argued that there had been a severance and that B1's individual right under the Trust of the Freehold had passed to her. The trial judge made a finding of fact that B2 had agreed to sell her 'share' to B1 for a particular price and thus that severance had occurred. On the facts as set out by the Court of Appeal, however, that finding of fact seems very dubious: it seems that: (i) B1 had made an offer to buy B2's 'share'; and (ii) B2 had simply refused that offer. The members of the Court of Appeal nonetheless felt that they were not in a position to interfere with the judge's findings of fact and so concluded that, due to the 'agreement' of the parties, severance had occurred.

Burgess provides a good demonstration of the problems caused by the absence of a formality rule. In particular, there may be a shortage of *evidence*: as a result, judges have to pick through B1 and B2's oral discussions to decide both *if* and *when* an agreement to sever was reached. If a formality rule had applied in *Burgess,* this evidential problem would not have arisen: the absence of signed writing would have made it clear that no severance had occurred.

2.4.4 'Mutual course of dealing'

Severance by a 'mutual course of dealing' protects co-owners who have acted on a shared assumption that each already has his own individual right (see **F2:2.3.3**). The logic of this method of severance depends, in part, on the idea that a co-owner who has failed to sever by another means (as he believed he *already* had his own individual right) should not lose out. This reasoning applies with particular strength where land is concerned: if B1 had known he was a joint tenant, he could very easily have acquired his own individual right by using the section 36(2) method of severance. Further, the doctrine of proprietary estoppel is based on a similar need to protect a party who relies on a belief that he already has, or will acquire, a right in relation to land (see **E4:2**).

That analogy with proprietary estoppel is, of course, not exact. However, it is helpful when considering how formality rules could affect severance by a mutual course of dealing. It was suggested above that there may be good reasons for introducing a formal requirement to severance by agreement. Yet these reasons are trumped, so far as severance by a mutual course of dealing is concerned, by the need to protect a party who relies on a shared assumption that severance has already occurred. For a similar reason, B can acquire a right through proprietary estoppel without having to satisfy any formality rule (see **C3:7.3.1** and **E2:2.3.3(iv)**).[109]

---

[108] [1975] Ch 429.
[109] R Smith, *Plural Ownership* (2005), 68 argues that as severance by a mutual course of conduct clearly does not

2.4.5 Situations where severance is imposed

There are certain situations in which the property law system automatically gives each of B1 and B2 an undivided share of Ownership (see F2:2.3.4). If one of those situations occurs when B1 and B2 hold a Freehold or Lease, each party will automatically acquire his own individual right under a Trust of the Freehold or Lease. So, if B1 goes into insolvency, his trustee in bankruptcy will acquire a persistent right under the Trust, giving him 50 per cent of the benefit of the Freehold or Lease.[110]

2.4.6 Acts which do *not* sever

Severance does *not* occur if B1 simply informs B2 that he wishes to acquire his own individual share of Ownership; or if B1 simply makes a will leaving his 'share' of Ownership to C (see F2:2.3.5). Where B1 and B2 hold a Freehold or Lease, section 36(2) of the LPA 1925 can help B1 in the first case, but only if he gives B2 a *written* notice. And, again, severance by will is *not* possible. However, that rule is often perceived to operate particularly harshly where land is concerned. For example, if: (i) B1 and B2 are joint tenants of both a Freehold and a right under a Trust of that Freehold; and (ii) B1 has paid half or more of the price of the Freehold; and (iii) B1 then makes a will leaving his 'share' of the land to C, then can it really be fair that, if severance has not occurred by any of the recognised methods, C acquires nothing and B2 becomes solely entitled to the Freehold?

It has been suggested that a joint tenant of a right under a Trust of land should be able to sever by will.[111] However, allowing such severance would create a risk that B1 could have the best of both worlds. He could make a will leaving his 'share' to C knowing that:

- if B2 dies *before* B1, B1 can suppress the will and claim that the joint tenancy was intact when B2 died; and
- if B1 dies first, severance will be proved by the production of B1's will, ensuring that C acquires a right and that B2 is not solely entitled to the Freehold or Lease.[112]

To address this risk, it would seem sensible to require that B1 must give *notice* to B2 of his severance by will. Moreover, to avoid disputes, it would be prudent to require that this notice be given in *writing*—not too onerous a requirement as B1 already has to satisfy formal requirements in making his will. Further, B1 is free to revoke or change his will at any time before his death. To avoid the uncertainty this creates, it would be wise to stipulate that if B1 wishes to sever by will, that severance should take effect as soon as the will is made. That leaves us with a suggested reform by which B1 can acquire his own individual right by giving B2 *written notice of his desire for an immediate severance*. But, of course, B1 *already* has the facility, where he is a joint tenant of a Freehold or Lease, thanks to section 36(2) of the LPA 1925. It seems then that there is no need to allow severance by will.[113]

---

require writing 'it would be inexplicable if the factually clearer agreement to sever did require writing'. But such a stance can perhaps be justified: (i) mutual agreement involves each party exercising a power to give the other a persistent right and so falls within the scope of s 53(1)(a); whereas (ii) mutual course of dealing does not involve the exercise of such a power. The persistent right acquired by each of B1 and B2, like a right arising through proprietary estoppel, depends on the 'operation of law' and so the s 53(1)(a) formality rule does not apply.

110 For a consideration of the position where B2 unlawfully kills B1 see *re K* [1985] Ch 85 at 100.
111 See eg Law Com Working Paper No 94 (1985) at 16.14; Pritchard [1987] *Conv* 273.
112 This problem is noted by eg Thompson [1987] *Conv* 275; Tee [1995] *Conv* 105.
113 If instead A holds a Freehold or Lease on Trust for B1 and B2, and B1 and B2 are joint tenants of the right

SUMMARY of G2:2.4

Where B1 and B2 acquire a Freehold or Lease as joint tenants, section 1(6) of the LPA 1925 prevents them from severing that joint tenancy. However, they will also be joint tenants of a right under a Trust of the Freehold or Lease. B1 or B2 can 'sever' that joint tenancy: in such a case, each of B1 and B2 acquires his own individual right, under the Trust, to 50 per cent of the benefit of the Freehold or Lease. To 'sever', B1 or B2 can use any of the three general methods of severance set out in the Summary to F2:2.3. Those general methods operate in essentially the same way whether or not land is involved. This can lead to surprising consequences: for example, B1 and B2's power to sever by agreement, although it allows each party to acquire a new persistent right relating to land, is not currently regulated by a formality rule.

In addition, B1 and B2 can take advantage of the special facility, provided by section 36(2) of the LPA 1925, to sever by giving written notice to the other co-owner. This provides B1 and B2 with a very useful facility, available *only* if B1 and B2 are co-owners of a Freehold or Lease.

3 THE DEFENCES QUESTION

It is very difficult for C to have a defence to B's Freehold or Lease (see G1A:3 and G1B:3). The same is true where a Freehold or Lease is co-held by B1 and B2. Of course, the situation is very different if B1 and B2 are *not* co-owners of a Freehold or Lease but are instead *simply* co-holders of a right under a Trust of a Freehold or Lease.

EXAMPLE 29

B1 and B2 hold a Freehold on Trust for B1, B2, B3 and B4. All four live on the land. In return for receiving a loan from C Bank, B1 and B2 grant C Bank a Charge over the land. C Bank pays the loan money to B1 and B2.

B3 and B4 are *not* co-holders of the Freehold: they have *only* a persistent right under a Trust. Whilst their rights are prima facie binding on C, C can thus rely on any of the defences examined in E2:3. In particular, as the rights of B3 and B4 arise under a Trust of land, C may well be able to rely on the overreaching defence (see E2:3.4). In Example 30, as the House of Lords confirmed in *City of London Building Society v Flegg* (E2:Example 17b),[114] C Bank will be able to use that defence *even though* B3 and B4 are in actual occupation of the land when C Bank commits to acquiring its Charge.

4 THE REMEDIES QUESTION

In general, if B1 and B2, acting as a team, assert their pre-existing Freehold or Lease against C, C is in *exactly the same* position as when B, who is solely entitled to a Freehold or Lease,

---

under the Trust, B1 and B2 cannot rely on the s 36(2) method of severance: see 2.4.1(i) above. In such a case, the argument for severance by will is thus simply an argument for extending the scope of severance by written notice.

[114] [1988] AC 54.

asserts that right against C (see E1:4). However, things are slightly different if C acquires a right from B1 (see too F2:4).

B1 and B2 are joint tenants of both a registered Freehold and of the right under a Trust of that Freehold. C agrees to lend B1 £100,000 if B1's duty to repay the money is secured by a Charge over the Freehold. B1, by forging B2's signature, purports to grant C such a Charge.

In such a case, B2's pre-existing property right will bind C.[115] Nonetheless, as we have seen, B1's 'act operating on his own share' effects a severance: C will thus have an Equitable Charge against B1's persistent right to a 50 per cent share of the benefit of the Freehold. If B1 defaults on the loan, C will want to use that security right by selling the Freehold and taking up to 50 per cent of the proceeds of sale. B2, however, may wish to resist a sale so that he—perhaps with his family—can remain in occupation of the land.

This dispute between B2 and C can be easily resolved if B2 can afford to buy out B1. If not, there may have to be an application to court under section 14 of the 1996 Act. The court will then resolve the dispute by applying the principles discussed in 1.4 above. If the Freehold is not sold, C will be left out of pocket and his security will be of little practical use. So, if B2 is unable to ensure that the duty secured by C's Charge (ie B1's duty to repay the loan made by C) will be performed, a sale seems the only way to ensure that *each* of C and B2 takes some benefit from his right.[116] Certainly, before the 1996 Act was passed, the courts tended to order a sale in situations like Example 27. And, under the Act, section 15(1)(d) instructs the court to have regard to 'the interests of any secured creditors of any beneficiary.'[117] Not surprisingly then, the courts have continued to order a sale—even if it means that both B2 and his children will have to leave their home.[118] B2 is generally forced to settle for receiving the monetary value of his 50 per cent share of the benefit of the Freehold: he is not able to use the land itself.[119]

The result in Example 27 (where B2 has a pre-existing property right as a co-owner of land) is thus the same as in E2:Example 27 (where A is the sole Freehold owner and B has a

---

[115] See eg *Mortgage Corporation v Shaire* [2001] Ch 743. A similar result can occur if B2's apparent consent to the mortgage is procured by B1's undue influence or misrepresentation: see eg *First National Bank v Achampong* [2004] 1 FCR 18, applying the principles discussed in E1:3.2.

[116] In *Edwards v Lloyds TSB* [2004] EWHC 175 sale was postponed for five years (until B2's youngest child reached the age of 18). However, it seems C was adequately protected as, at the end of five years, the sum owed by B1 to C would still be less than the current value of B1's individual right under the Trust of the land. So, assuming no dramatic crash in the housing market in those five years, C's right against B1 would be effectively secured even though the sale was postponed. The decision thus cannot be seen as heralding greater protection for children: see Probert in *New Twists in the Tale: Contemporary Perspectives in Property, Equity and Trusts* (ed Dixon and Griffiths, 2007).

[117] See too s 15(2) and (3).

[118] See eg *Bank of Ireland v Bell* [2001] 2 FLR 809; *First National Bank v Achampong* [2004] 1 FCR 18. It is worth noting that a sale can be ordered even if C initially only has a *personal* right against B1. If C obtains judgment against B1 for a sum of money, C can seek to enforce that judgment by means of a charging order: an order that certain rights held by B1 be sold and their value used to pay C (see B:2.3.1). Moreover, although B2's pre-existing property right and persistent right bind C, such a sale may well be ordered: see eg *Pritchard Englefield v Steinberg* [2004] EWHC 1908.

[119] L Fox, *Conceptualising Home* (2007), 14 notes: 'It is a truism that, in disputes between creditors and occupiers, the creditor almost invariably wins.' See too Probert in *New Twists in the Tale: Contemporary Perspectives in Property, Equity and Trusts* (ed Dixon and Griffiths, 2007).

pre-existing persistent right under a Trust of that Freehold). Once B2's signature has been forged and C is substantively registered as the holder of its Charge, B2 gains no extra protection from the fact that he has an initial *property right*.

In one case,[120] it was suggested that the 1996 Act may allow the courts more scope to resist C's application for sale and instead allow B2 to remain in occupation of the land. After all, section 15 gives the interests of C as *one* of the factors to be taken into account; it does not say it is to be the only, or the dominant, concern. Nonetheless, even if that were true,[121] there is another option open to C. If B1 goes into insolvency, any right he has in relation to the land passes to his trustee in bankruptcy. The trustee in bankruptcy is then under a statutory duty to realise the value of B1's rights and to distribute the money raised to B1's creditors.[122]

In such a situation, there are even stronger arguments in favour of ordering a sale of the co-owned Freehold or Lease. The rules applying are *not* those laid down by section 15; instead, a special regime is applied by the Insolvency Act 1986.[123] The basic rule is that a sale will be ordered.[124] Where: (i) B2 is B1's former or current spouse or civil partner; and (ii) the land in question is or has been the home of B2 or B1, then (iii) the court is directed to take into account the needs of both B2 and any children.[125] However, even in such a case, the Act specifies that, if C applies for a sale of the Freehold or Lease more than one year after B1 goes into insolvency, that Freehold or Lease will be sold, unless there are *exceptional circumstances*.[126]

This means that, even if the section 15 regime were more favourable to B2, C could circumvent those rules by forcing B1 into insolvency: after all, if B1 has defaulted on the loan repayments due to C, the odds are that B1's liabilities exceed his assets.[127] In such a case, B2's only hope is to show that the circumstances are exceptional. It is worth considering what counts as exceptional circumstances: even if B1 is not insolvent, and the general section 15 rules apply, the courts will generally order a sale unless such exceptional circumstances exist.[128] The prevailing approach is not favourable to B2: it may well be that, if the Freehold or Lease is sold, B2 and his children will have to face the disruption that goes with moving to a different area. However, the courts do *not* view that hardship as exceptional: it

---

[120] *Mortgage Corporation v Shaire* [2001] Ch 743. But note that Neuberger J only contemplated refusing a sale on the basis that C would be protected by B2 paying a regular sum of money to C: [2001] Ch 743 at 764.

[121] It is probably not. The Law Commission, whose work led to the 1996 Act, did *not* intend to increase the protection available to B2: s 15 was intended as a restatement of the existing law (see Law Com No 181 at 12.9). And Court of Appeal decisions since *Shaire* confirm that s 15 has made no real difference to B2's position: see eg *Bank of Ireland v Bell* [2001] 2 FLR 809; *First National Bank v Achampong* [2004] 1 FCR 18.

[122] Under s 283A of the Insolvency Act 1986 (introduced by the Enterprise Act 2002), B1 regains his right in relation to the Freehold or Lease if the trustee in bankruptcy has not needed to realise the value of that share within three years of B1's going into insolvency.

[123] Insolvency Act 1986, s 335A.

[124] Under s 313A of the Insolvency Act 1986 (introduced by the Enterprise Act 2002), a sale will not be ordered if the value of B1's right is so low that the proceeds of sale will be of no real benefit to B1's creditors.

[125] Insolvency Act 1986, s 335A(2)(b)(i) and (ii). That specific direction does not apply where there has been no marriage or civil partnership.

[126] Insolvency Act 1986, s 335A(3). The Cork Committee, whose Report had an important influence of the 1986 Act, in fact proposed a scheme giving B2 *more* protection: see (1982) Cmnd 8558 at [1118]–[1123].

[127] This was confirmed by the Court of Appeal in *Alliance & Leicester v Slayford* (2001) 33 HLR 743: despite the amusingly vociferous complaints of the trial judge, C was allowed to rely on the Insolvency Act rules, having forced B1 into insolvency.

[128] See eg *re Citro* [1991] Ch 142: the 'exceptional circumstances' test was used even though B1 was not bankrupt.

is almost bound to occur where a co-held Freehold or Lease is sold.[129] So, B2 will have to point to a factor such as an illness[130] or disability of B2 or of a child[131] occupying the home. Even then, such an exceptional factor will generally lead only to a *postponement* of a sale: after all, if B2 cannot pay back B1's loan, C does need to get access to the financial value of B1's right.

It has been argued that the current approach to resolving such disputes between B2 and C may be contrary to B2's right, under Article 8 of the European Convention of Human Rights, to respect for his home.[132] However, the current approach is simply one way of resolving the **basic tension** between B2 and C. As Article 8 makes clear, B2's right to respect for his home can be restricted where necessary to protect the rights of others, such as C. And in a case such as **Example 27**, C has both: (i) a personal right to recover the agreed payment from B1; and (ii) a security right against B1's share of the benefit of the Freehold. The human rights of C are therefore also at stake: C has a right, under Article 1 of Protocol 1 of the ECHR, to the peaceful enjoyment of his possessions.[133]

Of course, if C can be protected by some other means—eg, by B2 buying out B1's share; or by B2 making periodical payments to ensure B1's loan is paid off—it may be possible to refuse a sale whilst also giving C some protection. However, the current approach *already* allows for the basic tension to be resolved in that way.[134] It therefore seems that the human rights argument adds nothing: it is a way of restating the existence of the basic tension, not of resolving that tension.[135]

---

[129] See eg *per* Nourse LJ in *re Citro* [1991] Ch 142 at 157.

[130] See eg *Claughton v Charalamabous* [1999] 1 FLR 740.

[131] In *re Holliday* [1981] Ch 405 a sale was postponed where the house occupied by B2 and children had been adapted as a result of the disability of one of the children. However, it is worth noting that, as in *Edwards v Lloyds TSB* [2004] EWHC 175 (discussed at **n 116** above) the postponement did *not* prejudice C as, after a later sale, the value of B1's right would still be sufficient to pay the debt owed to C.

[132] See esp *Barca v Mears* [2005] 2 FLR 1 at [39]–[41]. Nicholas Strauss QC, sitting as a Deputy High Court judge, suggested that, in light of Article 8, the court has a duty under s 3 of the Human Rights Act 1998, to interpret the statutory term 'exceptional circumstances' in a way slightly more favourable to B2. A circumstance such as B2 and any children having to move *can* count as exceptional if, on the facts of the case, the *hardship* it causes to B2 and any children is unusually severe. So 'exceptional' has a quantitative as well as a qualitative aspect. There is certainly a good argument for interpreting 'exceptional circumstances', as used in s 336(5) of the Insolvency Act 1986, in that way. But the argument can be made *without* needing to refer to Article 8: for example, s 336(4)(c) and (d) of the Insolvency Act itself list the needs of B2 and any children as relevant factors to be considered. As Dixon has noted [2005] *Conv* 161 at 167 'many might argue that [the interpretation favoured in *Barca*] actually restores the originally Parliamentary intention'. And it is worth noting that, in *Barca* itself, the judge found that adopting the more favourable interpretation of exceptional circumstances would *not* assist B2: a postponement of sale for three years would unduly interfere with C's security right: the same was true in *Donohoe v Ingram* [2006] EWHC 282.

[133] *Wilson v First County* [2004] 1 AC 816 confirms that even a personal right of C against B1 counts as a 'possession' for the purposes of Article 1 of Protocol 1.

[134] See eg *v Lloyds TSB* [2004] EWHC 175 (**n 116** above).

[135] For a discussion of the tension in this area see L Fox, *Conceptualising Home* (2007), 14–5, 23–5.

CHAPTER G3
THE TRUST

THE TRUST

In **F3**, we looked at the *general* principles that apply where A holds a right subject to a Trust. In this chapter, we will concentrate on the *special* rules that apply where A holds a Freehold or Lease on Trust. A number of those special rules come from the Trusts of Land and Appointment of Trustees Act 1996 ('the 1996 Act') which we will evaluate in **section 1A** below.

1 THE CONTENT QUESTION

1.1 The core Trust duty

B's right counts as a right under a Trust if two conditions are met:

- A is under a duty to B to use a specific right, in a particular way, for B's benefit; *and*
- A is, overall, under a duty in relation to the whole of that right.

As long as A is under this core Trust duty, B has a persistent right. This accounts for the incredible *versatility* of the Trust (see **F3:1.1**). For example, in **E2:Example 2a** and **G2:Example 4**, we have seen that a Trust may be used:

- to ensure that B has the protection of a persistent right; *whilst also*
- complying with a restriction on the content of property rights in land.

That use of the Trust is particularly important where land is concerned. For example, by setting up a Trust, A0 can share out the benefits of his Freehold so that: (i) B1 has the benefit of exclusive control of the land for B1's life; then (ii) B2 has that benefit for B2's life; then (iii) the National Trust has that benefit from B2's death onwards (see **E2:Example 2a** and **G1A:1**).

Similarly, we have also seen that a Trust can be used to enable B1 and B2, joint holders of a Freehold or Lease, each to have his own individual right to a share of the benefit of that Freehold or Lease (see **G2:Examples 4, 5 and 6**). Whilst it is impossible for B1 and B2 to have a share of a Freehold or Lease (see **G2:1.2.1**), a Trust can be used to ensure that each of B1 and B2 has a share of the *benefit* of a Freehold or Lease. Indeed, even if A does not set up such a Trust when transferring land to B1 and B2, a Trust may be imposed by statute to ensure that B1 and B2 each acquires a share of the benefit of the Freehold or Lease transferred (see **G2:1.2.3**).

This statutory intervention demonstrates a wider point: the Trust concept can be very important even if no one has expressly chosen to set up a Trust.

EXAMPLE 1

EXAMPLE 1

A and B plan to buy some land together. Each provides half of the purchase price of a Freehold. A is registered as the sole Freehold owner, but B did not make his contribution by way of a gift or a loan to A.

As the only registered party, A is solely entitled to the Freehold (see **E2:2.3.4**). However, B can show that, because of his contribution to the purchase price of the Freehold: (i) A would be unjustly enriched if A were able to use the Freehold entirely for A's benefit; and so (ii) A is under a duty to use that Freehold for B's benefit (to the extent of B's contribution to the purchase price). In such a case, B's right arises under a Resulting Trust (see **D4:4.3**).[1] As a result, whilst A is the sole Freehold owner, *each* of A and B has a right under a Trust of that Freehold.

1.2   Duties arising from the core Trust duty

1.2.1 General duties

Once A is subject to the core Trust duty, A is also subject to a number of additional duties. These duties (eg, not to put himself in a position where his personal interests conflict with his duties as trustee) are not an integral part of the core Trust duty: even if these duties do not exist, B may still have a right under a Trust (see **F3:1.2**). However, they are particularly important: A will be subject to them if they are not expressly excluded when the Trust is set up.

In **F3:1.2**, we saw that, if A is under the core Trust duty, the default position is that A also has a duty to B to take care in managing the right held on Trust. In one way, A is treated with special leniency where the right he holds on Trust is a Freehold or Lease. Section 9 of the 1996 Act gives A special powers of *delegation*: if B is an adult and entitled to current enjoyment of the land, A can delegate any of his functions, as trustee of the land, to B. For example, in **E2:Example 2a**, A holds a Freehold on Trust: (i) for B1 during B1's life; then (ii) for B2 during B2's life; then (iii) for the National Trust. Section 9 permits A to delegate his powers to manage and control the land to B1.

This is in contrast to the normal position whereby a trustee *cannot* delegate any of his functions to a beneficiary.[2] It is not clear why things should be different where A holds a Freehold or Lease on Trust.[3] The thinking behind section 9 seems to be that, as B1 is currently entitled to enjoy the benefits of the land, he may be best placed to decide how to use the land. But that thinking, if it is correct, also applies where land is not involved: it would justify, for example, allowing a trustee to delegate powers to manage and invest shares

---

[1] See eg *per* Lord Neuberger in *Stack v Dowden* [2007] 2 AC 432 at [111]. There is a debate as to whether this form of Resulting Trust can be used where A and B are cohabiting partners (see **2.3.3** below).

[2] The Trustee Act 2000 increased a trustee's ability to delegate. However, the power to delegate under s 11 of that Act *cannot* be exercised in favour of a beneficiary: see s 12(3).

[3] S 9 was *not* recommended by the Law Commission Report No 181 that led to the 1996 Act. It seems to have been introduced in Parliament in order to enable an arrangement similar to one prohibited by the 1996 Act—the 'strict settlement'—to continue. In such a settlement, as in **E2:Example 2a**, A0 would hold land on Trust for B1, then B2, etc; but B1 (the 'tenant for life') would have powers to manage the land. Yet one of the reasons why the 1996 Act prevents the creation of new strict settlements is precisely to prevent the conflict of interest arising when a beneficiary has management powers: see Law Com Working Paper No 94 at 3.16.

to a beneficiary. And a trustee does not have that power as the *risk* introduced by such delegation—that other beneficiaries will lose out as B1 will be tempted to act in his own best interests—outweighs any benefits.[4] The power of delegation given by section 9 is therefore very hard to justify, particularly as the checks on it are quite limited.[5]

The delegation of A's powers can also cause problems for C.[6] For example, after a delegation to B1, C may need to deal with B1 when acquiring a right in relation to the land. However, to qualify for the overreaching defence (see **E2:3.4.2(ii)**), C still needs to ensure that any money he pays in return for acquiring his right is paid to at least two trustees, and not to B1.[7]

1.2.2 Duties imposed by the 1996 Act

Where A holds a Freehold or Lease on Trust for B, the 1996 Act imposes additional duties on A.[8]

(i) A duty to consult
If A wishes to deal with the land in a particular way, section 11 imposes a duty on A, so far as is practicable, to consult any adult beneficiaries with a right to current enjoyment[9] of the land. A then has a duty 'so far as consistent with the general interest of the Trust' to give effect to the wishes of such beneficiaries.[10] Three points are worth noting about this section 11 duty:

1. It is hard to see what difference, if any, section 11 makes. Even if there were no such provision, A would still be under a duty to use his Freehold or Lease for the benefit of the beneficiaries of the Trust: that general duty can lead to a duty to consult the beneficiaries and act accordingly.

2. In practice, the duty to consult may make little difference. If A transfers a Freehold held on Trust to C, without first consulting B, A's failure to comply with section 11 does *not* make it any more difficult for C to have a defence against B's pre-existing persistent right.

---

[4] In our example, B1 is under the same duties as A when exercising the powers delegated to him: see s 9(7). This means, for example, that B1 must take into account the interests of B2 and the National Trust when making decisions about the land. However, the temptation to B1 to prefer his own interests is clear.

[5] Under s 9A(1), A is subject to the statutory duty of care when deciding whether to delegate. Once A has delegated, s 9A(3) then imposes a duty on A to keep the delegation under review. Crucially, s 9A(6) says that A is 'not liable for any act or default of the beneficiary, or beneficiaries, unless [A] fails to comply with the duty of care in deciding to delegate any of [A's] functions under s 9 or in carrying out his [duty to review].' This means that there is little to prevent A, to a large degree, washing his hands off his duties as trustee after delegating.

[6] Particular problems occur where C *reasonably believes* that A has delegated to B1, but that delegation is for some reason invalid. s 9(2) attempts to deal with this problem.

[7] S 9(7) confirms that B1 cannot be regarded as a trustee for the purposes of s 27 of the LPA 1925.

[8] It seems these duties can also apply to A where: (i) A0 holds a Freehold or Lease on Trust for A; and (ii) A holds his persistent right on Trust for B. This is due to the definition of 'land' adopted by the 1996 Act: see in particular the amendment made to s 205(1)(ix) of the Law of Property Act 1925 by s 25(2) and Sch 4 of the 1996 Act. However, it is difficult to see how some of the additional duties imposed by the 1996 Act can apply where A holds only a persistent right: eg, how can s 12 of the Act give B a right to occupy in such a case?

[9] So, in **Example 1**, during B1's life, A is under a statutory duty only to B1: B2 and the National Trust each has a persistent right, but neither has a right to current enjoyment of the land and so, in the phrase used in s 11(1)(a), neither is 'beneficially entitled to an interest in possession in the land'.

[10] If there is a dispute, the relevant wishes are those of the beneficiary or beneficiaries who are entitled to more than a 50 per cent share of the benefit of the Freehold or Lease: see s 11(1)(b).

3.   When setting up a Trust, A0 or A can, if he wishes, exclude the section 11 duty.[11]

(ii) A duty to allow B to occupy the land?

If: (i) A holds a Freehold or Lease on Trust for B; and (ii) B claims that A is under a duty to allow B to occupy that land; then (iii) sections 12 and 13 of the 1996 Act regulate B's claim (see **G2:1.4.2(i)**). Those sections, like the 1996 Act, apply to *all* cases where A holds a Freehold or Lease on Trust. As a result, B's 'right' to occupy is heavily qualified. After all, it cannot make sense for *every* party with a right under such a Trust to have a right to occupy land. For example,

1.   In a case such as **E2:Example 2a** (where a Freehold is held on Trust: (i) for B1's benefit during B1's life; then (ii) for B2's benefit during B2's life; then (iii) for the benefit of the National Trust), it would be odd if B2 or the National Trust had a right to occupy during B1's life.
2.   Similarly, A0 may set up a Trust, on his death, by leaving his Freehold and £250,000 to A to be used for the benefit of A0's grandchildren. If A0 has 10 grandchildren, it cannot make sense for each grandchild to have a right to occupy the land (see **G2:1.4.2(i)**).

The problem is that the qualifications imposed by sections 12 and 13 also apply even if, due to the nature of the Trust, B should have a straightforward right to occupy. The best example of this occurs where A and B jointly hold a Freehold or Lease. In such a case, A and B each: (i) co-holds a property right; and (ii) has a right under a Trust of that property right (see **G2:1.2.4**). We might expect that B, as he co-holds the Freehold or Lease, would have a straightforward right to occupy the land. Indeed, some cases prior to the 1996 Act adopted that position.[12] However, under the Act, A may be able to impose restrictions on B's occupation of the land (see **G2:1.4.2(i)**). Given B faces these obstacles if he is a co-holder of a Freehold or Lease, B necessarily faces them in a case where A is the sole holder of the Freehold or Lease and B has *only* a right under a Trust.

In **Example 1**, A holds his Freehold on Trust for A and B. Under that Trust, each of A and B has his own, separate right to a share of the benefit of A's Freehold. Is A under a duty to allow B to occupy the land? Before the 1996 Act, the position was reasonably clear: A *was* under such a duty and so B *did* have a right to occupy.[13] Although B is not a co-holder of the Freehold, A *is* under a duty to use that Freehold, to a certain extent, for B's benefit. And an obvious way in which B can benefit from the Freehold is by occupying the land.

After the 1996 Act, the qualifications contained in sections 12 and 13 (and discussed in detail in **G2:1.4.2(i)**) seem to make B's position less clear. For example, let us say that, in **Example 1**, A and B bought the Freehold with the intention of using it as a home and sharing occupation. Does B still have a right to occupy if: (i) A and B fall out; and (ii) A chooses to go travelling for a year?

---

[11] See s 11(2)(a).

[12] See eg *per* Parke B in *Henderson v Eason* (1851) 17 QB 701 at 720 (quoted at **G2:n26**); *Wiseman v Simpson* [1988] 1 WLR 35.

[13] See eg *Bull v Bull* [1955] 1 QB 234, esp *per* Lord Denning MR at 238; *Williams and Glyn's Bank v Boland* [1981] AC 487 *per* Lord Scarman at 510; *City of London BS v Flegg* [1988] AC 54 *per* Lord Templeman at 70–71 and Lord Oliver at 81.

1. It is true that section 12(1) gives B a basic right to occupy where 'the purposes of the trust include making the land available for his occupation' *or* 'the land is held by the trustees so as to be so available.'[14] There is a question as to whether the purposes of the Trust include making the land available for B's *sole* occupation.

2. Further, section 12(2) limits B's basic right by stating that section 12(1) cannot give B a right to occupy land if the land is 'either unavailable or unsuitable for occupation by him'. This introduces an element of uncertainty.[15] It could be argued that, as the house was purchased for both A and B to live in, the land is unsuitable for occupation by B alone.[16]

3. Further, even though B has not forced A to move out, A could ask B to pay A money in return for occupying the land (an 'occupation rent': see **G2:1.2.4(i)**). After all, under section 13(3), A has a power to impose 'reasonable conditions' on B's exercise of his section 12 right to occupy.[17] In taking into account whether A can impose such a rent, a court has to consider the factors set out in section 15 of the 1996 Act (see **G2:1.4.2(ii)**).[18]

It may be that a court would find against A if he attempted to exclude or limit B's right to occupy—particularly in a case where B is already in occupation of the land.[19] However, the vagueness of the terms used by the 1996 Act (eg, 'unsuitable for occupation by him'; 'reasonable' conditions) creates a risk for B that a court may find against him. This creates an incentive for B to avoid the time and expense of court proceedings and to give in by, for example, agreeing to pay A an occupation rent. The qualifications contained in the 1996 Act may thus weaken B's basic right, in **Example 1**, to occupy the land without needing to pay.

This analysis supports Barnsley's[20] powerful argument that, in a case such as **Example 1**, B's chances of being able to occupy the land without payment have been *reduced* by the 1996 Act. B would have been better off under the previous law when, instead of being

---

[14] S 12(1) in full states that:

A beneficiary who is beneficially entitled to an interest in possession in land subject to a trust of land is entitled by reason of his interest to occupy the land at any time if at that time—
(a) the purposes of the trust include making the land available for his occupation (or for the occupation of beneficiaries of a class of which he is a member or of beneficiaries in general), or
(b) the land is held by the trustees so as to be so available.'
(2) Subsection (1) does not confer on a beneficiary a right to occupy land if it is either unavailable or unsuitable for occupation by him.
(3) This section is subject to section 13.

[15] As we saw in **G2:1.4.2**, the last two words '*by him*' also mean that B's *personal* characteristics may be used against him in denying him a right to occupy: this is confirmed in *Chan v Leung* [2003] 1 FCR 250 at [101] by Jonathan Parker LJ.

[16] Although note that in *Chan v Leung* [2003] 1 FCR 250 at [102], Jonathan Parker LJ showed some scepticism for that argument in a case where A and B each co-held the Freehold.

[17] It is important to note that s 13(7) means that, as B is already in occupation of the land, A needs the consent of B or of the court to exercise his s 13(3) power in a way which *will* force B to move out or is *likely to result* in B moving out: it is therefore relevant to ask whether B can afford to pay the sum demanded by A. And in any case A can apply to court for permission to charge B.

[18] As confirmed by Lightman J in *Murphy v Gooch* [2007] EWCA Civ 603 at [11], the 1996 Act now provides the exclusive source of principles regulating occupation rents: see *per* Baroness Hale in *Stack v Dowden* [2007] 2 AC 432 at [93]–[95].

[19] S 13(7) recognises that extra protection should be given where B is already in occupation. That section is a little odd, however, as it applies even where B, although occupying the land, does *not* have a section 12 right to occupy.

[20] [1998] *CLJ* 123.

subjected to sections 12 and 13, B could simply rely on A's core Trust duty to show that A had a duty to allow B to occupy the land.

(iii) A duty not to sell the land against B's wishes?

Let us say that, in **Example 1**, A and B fall out: (i) A wants to sell the land and to take the financial value of his share of the benefit of the Freehold; but (ii) B wants to remain in occupation of the land. There is an easy solution if B can afford to buy out A: B becomes sole holder of the Freehold. Otherwise, the dispute between A and B has to be decided according to the principles set out in section 15 of the 1996 Act. Even if B has managed to show that he has a right to occupy under section 12, and A cannot restrict that right under section 13, that does *not* mean that A is under a duty to B not to sell his Freehold.

We examined the section 15 principles in detail in **G2:1.4.2(ii)**: the points made there also apply here. In a case such as **Example 1**, where A also has a right under the Trust, the obvious solution is to permit A to sell the Freehold: after all, if there is no sale, A is prevented from getting at the financial value of his share of the benefit of the Freehold. Certainly, when A and B have fallen out, a court could not plausibly put A in a position where, to get any benefit from the land, A must occupy with B. As we saw in **G2:1.4.2(ii)**, a sale is likely even if B is a co-holder with A of the Freehold or Lease. B's chances of successfully opposing a sale are still smaller in a case, such as **Example 1**, where B has *only* a right under a Trust.

1.3   Further duties

If: (i) A0 transfers a Freehold or Lease to A to hold on Trust for B; *or* (ii) A declares that he holds his Freehold or Lease on Trust for B; then (iii) A may also agree to be under further duties to B, going beyond the duties examined in **1.1** and **1.2** above. For example, A0 can stipulate, when transferring her Freehold to A1 and A2 to hold on Trust for B1 (A0's spouse) and B2 and B3 (A0's children), that B1 is that to have a right to occupy the land for the rest of B1's life. In such a case, there is no need for B1 to rely on sections 12 and 13 of the 1996 Act: the express terms of the Trust give him a right to occupy. However, this does not mean that B1's future occupation of the land is guaranteed: for example, if A1 and A2 apply to the court for permission to sell the Freehold, it is possible for a court, taking into account the factors set out in section 15, to order such a sale.

Similarly, A0 could stipulate that A1 and A2 are not to sell the Freehold without the consent of X. If that limit on A1 and A2's power to sell is recorded by a restriction entered on the register, C should only be registered as the new holder of the Freehold if X's consent has been given (see **E2:3.6.1**) If there is no such restriction, and A1 and A2 then sell to C *without* consulting X, they are in breach of their duties, as trustees, to the beneficiaries of the Trust (ie, B1, B2 and B3). However, in such a case, C can still: (i) acquire the Freehold; *and* (ii) use the overreaching defence against the rights of any beneficiaries of the Trust (see **E2:3.4.2(i)**).

Conversely, A0 could stipulate that A *must* sell the Freehold. This may occur if, for example, A0 wants to ensure that, on his death, each of his 10 grandchildren get a share of the benefit of A0's Freehold. A0 might wish to: (i) transfer that Freehold to A to hold it on Trust for the benefit of A0's grandchildren; (ii) with a duty to sell the Freehold and divide the proceeds of sale amongst A0's grandchildren. Such a Trust is known as a *Trust for Sale*.

Strangely, however, section 4 of the 1996 Act *prevents* A0 from setting up such a Trust: A0 is *not* permitted to impose a duty on A to sell the Freehold or Lease that A holds on Trust. This is very hard to justify: given that any other right can be held by A on Trust for Sale, why should rights relating to land be treated differently?[21] Indeed, prior to the 1996 Act, the land law system had taken the opposite stance: A was given the power to sell land *even if* A0 had attempted to withhold that power from A when setting up a Trust.[22] This was said to be justified by the need to ensure that land, a finite commodity, is not kept out of the market. Given that concern, it is very hard to justify section 4 of the 1996 Act.

1.4 The core Trust duty and C

In **Example 1**, if: (i) A transfers his Freehold to C; and (ii) C has no defence to B's pre-existing right under the Trust; then (iii) B has a power to assert his pre-existing right against C. If B exercises that power (or if C otherwise discovers that A transferred his Freehold to C in breach of his duties as a trustee), then C comes under the core Trust duty to B. C then holds the Freehold on Trust for B and so is also subject to the additional duties set out in **1.2** above. However, C is *not* subject to any of the further duties that the terms of the initial Trust may have imposed on A (see **F3:1.4**).

1A Evaluating the 1996 Act

1A.1 The background and aims of the Act

The 1996 Act is the chief source of the special rules applying where A holds a Freehold or Lease (rather than a different form of right) on Trust. Part I of that Act stems from the Law Commission's Report No 181. It has two main purposes.

First, to *simplify the law relating to Trusts of a Freehold or Lease by subjecting all such Trusts to the same statutory regime*. Before the 1996 Act, there were a number of different forms that such a Trust could take; each was subject to its own particular rules. This was regarded as leading: (i) to unnecessary complexity; and (ii) to practical problems if A0 mistakenly set up the wrong sort of Trust. As a result, the 1996 Act sets out a unitary set of rules that applies to all Trusts of a Freehold or Lease.

Second, to improve the position of a party such as B in **Example 1**—someone who: (i) has a right under a Trust of a Freehold or Lease; but (ii) does not co-hold that Freehold or Lease. In particular, it was felt that: (i) where A and B set up home together; and (ii) B's right in relation to that home arose under Trust; then (iii) B's need to use and occupy that home was given insufficient protection. Before the 1996 Act, B's right was said to arise under a special type of Trust: a *Trust for Sale*. That was the form taken by the statutory Trust imposed in cases where A and B co-hold a Freehold or Lease (see **G2:1.2.3** and **G2:1.2.4**). Oddly, that statutory Trust for Sale was then extended by judges to apply even in cases such as **Example 1**.[23] Despite the absence of any express statutory provision to that effect, the

---

[21] S 4 is doubly odd as it applies with retrospective effect to Trusts for Sale set up *before* the coming into force of the 1996 Act.

[22] See eg Settled Land Act 1925, s 106.

[23] See eg *Bull v Bull* [1955] 1 QB 234.

assumption was that, *whenever* A held a Freehold or Lease on Trust for A and B, that Trust would be a statutory Trust for Sale.

The key feature of any Trust for Sale is that A, the trustee, is under a *duty to sell* the right he holds on Trust. The purpose of such a Trust is to give the beneficiaries of the Trust a right to some or all of the benefit of the proceeds of sale. In some situations, there are good reasons for A0 to set up such a Trust: for example, as we have seen, it may allow all of A0's 10 children and grandchildren to share in the benefit of A0's Freehold or Lease. However, in other situations, a Trust for Sale makes no sense. Certainly, in **Example 1**, it seems very odd to say that there is a Trust for Sale, particularly if A and B intend the land to provide a home for them. Yet, before the 1996 Act, that was the position: a statutory Trust for Sale would exist in **Example 1** and so A was under an *immediate* duty to sell his Freehold.

The 1996 Act removes that odd result. The statutory Trust imposed by the Law of Property Act 1925 ('the LPA 1925') and extended by judges to cases such as **Example 1**, is no longer a Trust for Sale: A is no longer under a duty to sell his Freehold or Lease. Instead, a simple Trust of land arises.[24]

1A.2 Testing the Act

1A.2.1 A unitary scheme
Having one scheme to deal with all Trusts of a Freehold or Lease certainly brings simplicity. However, that simplicity comes at a cost. First, that scheme must cover *all* cases where a Freehold or Lease is held on Trust. Such cases can range from a board of trustees controlling a multi-million-pound pension fund (part of which is invested in land) to a case such as **Example 1**. The desire to create a 'one size fits all' regime for all Trusts of land makes it very difficult to provide tailored solutions appropriate to specific situations. For example, we have seen that sections 12 and 13 of the Act do not give B a simple right to occupy the land: that is the case if B is a co-holder of the Freehold or Lease (see G2:1.4.2(i)); and if B, as in **Example 1**, has only a right under a Trust (see 1.2.2(ii)). This is a product of the fact that the rules of the 1996 Act are *not* solely designed to deal with the rights of a co-holder of a Freehold or Lease; nor with a case such as **Example 1**. Rather, those rules must regulate *all* Trusts of a Freehold or Lease. As a result, the scheme imposed by the 1996 Act necessarily employs vague concepts such as 'suitability' and 'reasonableness'.

Equally, in a unitary scheme, the converse problem can arise: if a provision is inserted into the regime to deal with a specific situation, that provision can then apply to *any* Trust of a Freehold or Lease. For example, the section 9 power of delegation, seemingly introduced to be used in cases such as E2:Example 2a (see 1.2.1 above), can now be used by *any* trustee of a Freehold or Lease.[25]

1A.2.2 The removal of the statutory Trust for Sale
It is very unlikely that a busy Parliament would have found time to pass the 1996 Act if its

---

[24] See 1996 Act, s 1.

[25] Similarly, the prohibition in s 4 on A being under a duty to sell the Freehold or Lease may have been introduced to ensure that A cannot be under such a duty where land is intended to be used as a home. However, the prohibition now applies to *all* Trusts of a Freehold or Lease; even though, in some situations A0 may have perfectly good reasons for wishing to impose such a duty on A (eg, where A0 wishes to ensure that his 10 grandchildren can all take some of the benefit of a Freehold or Lease).

only aim had to been set up a unitary scheme for Trusts of a Freehold or Lease. Such simplification exercises may be appreciated by law students; but they do not excite voters. The political attraction of the 1996 Act lay in its second main aim: to improve the position of B in a case such as **Example 1**. Certainly, it was very hard to defend the position that A was under an immediate duty to sell land acquired as a home for A and B. The removal of the statutory Trust for Sale in such a case therefore seems to be a good use of legislative time. However, put bluntly, B does not care whether his right arises under a Trust for Sale or a standard Trust. B simply wants to know whether, *in practice*, he will be able to use the land *itself*, or whether, instead, he will have to settle for receiving money.

The first point to note is that the Trust for Sale mechanism, in practice, did *not* cause significant problems for B:

1. B had a pre-existing persistent right against A's Freehold or Lease. In *Williams & Glyn's Bank v Boland*,[26] for example, the House of Lords confirmed that, in a case such as **Example 1**, B's right under the Trust of A's Freehold or Lease, even if it arose under a Trust for Sale,[27] was prima facie binding on a third party who acquired a right from A.
2. Whilst A was technically under a duty to sell the Freehold or Lease, A also had a statutory power to postpone that sale.[28] Moreover, if the Freehold or Lease was held for a particular purpose (eg, providing a home for A and B) a court could refuse A's application to sell if that purpose continued.[29]
3. B also had a right to occupy the land.[30] In fact, B may even have had a *stronger* right to occupy before the 1996 Act (see 1.2.2(ii) above). The problem for B is that he must now struggle with the qualifications and restrictions imposed under sections 12 and 13.

Nonetheless, B did face some problems before the 1996 Act: there were situations in which B, despite having a right under a Trust of a Freehold or Lease, was compelled to settle for money and was not able to use the land itself:

1. If A gave C a right in relation to the land without B's consent (eg, if A sold the land to C; or gave C Bank a Charge over that land), then C might be able to use the *overreaching defence* against B's pre-existing right under the Trust (see E2:3.4). If so, B would be unable to assert a right against C and thus would be unable to continue using the land itself. As demonstrated by the decision of the House of Lords in *City of London Building Society v Flegg*,[31] it was possible for C Bank to use that defence even if B was in actual occupation of the land when C Bank committed to acquiring its right (see E2:3.4.2(ii)).

---

[26] [1981] AC 487.

[27] There is an argument that if a right arises under a Trust for Sale, it is better seen as a persistent right against the *proceeds of sale of the right*, and not as a persistent right against the right held on Trust. This argument, said to depend on the doctrine of 'conversion', may be appropriate in some contexts but was not applied to prevent B, even before the 1996 Act, from having a persistent right against A's Freehold or Lease.

[28] LPA 1925, s 25.

[29] That general principle was confirmed in *Jones v Challenger* [1961] 1 QB 176 (although a sale *was* permitted there as the purpose had ended).

[30] See eg *Bull v Bull* [1955] 1 QB 234, esp *per* Lord Denning MR at 238; *Williams and Glyn's Bank v Boland* [1981] AC 487 *per* Lord Scarman at 510; *City of London BS v Flegg* [1988] AC 54 *per* Lord Templeman at 70–71 and Lord Oliver at 81.

[31] [1988] AC 54 (*E2:Example 17b*).

2. Even if C Bank did not have a defence to B's right under the Trust, C Bank could still apply for the land to be sold, so that the proceeds of A's share of the benefit of the Freehold or Lease could be used to pay A's debt to C Bank (see **E2:4.2.2**). In such a case, unless there were exceptional circumstances, a court would order a sale of the land, thus forcing B to leave the land.

3. If A went into insolvency, A's trustee in bankruptcy could apply for a sale of the land, so that the proceeds of A's share of the benefit of the Freehold or Lease could be used to pay A's creditors. In such a case, the provisions of the Insolvency Act 1986 meant that, if a year had passed since A's insolvency, and if there were no exceptional circumstances, a sale would be ordered and B would be forced to leave the land.

4. Even if no third party were involved, if the relationship between A and B broke down and A asked the court for a sale, a sale would generally be ordered (unless B could afford to buy out A's share of the benefit of the Freehold).[32] Again, B would be forced to leave the land.

In each of these cases, B was forced to leave the land and to settle, instead, for receiving money.[33] However, this was *not* a consequence of the Trust for Sale. Rather, in the case of overreaching, it was due to the way in which the land law system solved the **basic tension** between B and C. In other cases, it was due to the need to allow third parties, or A himself, to unlock the financial value of A's right under the Trust of the Freehold or Lease.

The second aim of the 1996 Act was to improve B's position, by allowing B to use the land itself, rather than settling for money. We might therefore expect that, due to the Act, B would no longer face the four problems set out above. Yet those problems remain: the Act has done nothing, in practice, to address them:

1. Despite the Law Commission's suggestion for reform,[34] the overreaching defence operates in the same way (see **E2:3.4**).

2. The interests of a secured creditor (such as C Bank) must still be considered by a court when deciding if the land should be sold; and, in practice, the need to protect C Bank's financial interest is given priority (see **E2:4.2.2** and **G2.4**).[35]

3. The provisions of the Insolvency Act 1986 still apply and were not changed by the 1996 Act.[36]

4. If A applies for a sale of the land, the court has to take into account the factors set out by section 15 of the Act. However, that section did not seek to change the previous law[37] and, where the parties' relationship has broken down, a sale is still the likely

---

[32] See eg *Jones v Challenger* [1961] 1 QB 176.

[33] In the case where B's right was overreached, it may even be that, in practice, no money was available to B: see eg *State Bank of India v Sood* [1997] Ch 276 (**E2:Example 17c**).

[34] The suggestion was that it should not be possible to use the defence against B if B is an adult and is in actual occupation of the land when C commits to acquiring his right (see **E2:3.4.4**). It was made in Law Com No 188 (a separate Report dealing specifically with overreaching) but was not incorporated in the 1996 Act. In fact, the Act *extends* the scope of overreaching: A now has the powers of an 'absolute owner' *whenever* he holds a Freehold or Lease on Trust (see s 6); previously, A's powers arose only where there was a statutory Trust for Sale or strict settlement and so did *not* arise, for example, where A simply held a Freehold or Lease on Trust entirely for B's benefit.

[35] See eg *Bank of Ireland v Bell* [2001] 2 FLR 809; *First National Bank v Achampong* [2004] 1 FCR 18; Probert in *New Twists in the Tale: Contemporary Perspectives in Property, Equity and Trusts* (ed Dixon and Griffiths, 2007).

[36] See eg *Alliance & Leicester plc v Slayford* (2001) 33 HLR 743.

[37] Neuberger J in *Mortgage Corporation v Shaire* [2001] Ch 743 did suggest that s 15 of the 1996 Act gives B a

outcome, even if the home is occupied both by A and B's children as well as B (see G2.1.4.2(ii)).[38]

SUMMARY of G3:1A

The evaluation of the 1996 Act given here is overwhelmingly negative. The Act *has* indeed achieved its first aim of imposing a single scheme to all Trusts of land. But that aim is not, in fact, particularly desirable. It can be achieved only at the cost of applying broad, rather vague rules that attempt to deal with *all* Trusts of a Freehold or Lease and so fail to meet the specific needs of *any* such Trusts. And the Act has clearly *not* achieved its second, more important aim: in practice, the position of B in a case such as **Example 1** has *not* improved. The situations in which B has to settle for receiving money rather than using the land itself remain. The Act has not limited C's ability to use the overreaching defence; it has not made it easier for B to oppose a sale requested by a secured creditor of A; or by A's trustee in bankruptcy; or by A himself. And the Act may even have *weakened* B's basic right to occupy the land.

This is not to say that the Act was necessarily wrong to do these things. Any dispute as to the use of land raises the impossibly difficult **basic tension**; for example, there may be good reasons to give C a defence to B's pre-existing right under a Trust; or to allow the land to be sold despite B's objections. Nonetheless, we can say that the Act has failed in own declared aim of allowing B a greater chance to use the land itself, rather than settling for its monetary value. The mere removal of the Trust for Sale, and thus of A's duty to sell, has done almost nothing, *in practice*, to improve B's position.

---

2   THE ACQUISITION QUESTION

2.1   Consent: Express Trusts

The general rules set out in **F3:2.1** also apply where A0 or A attempts to set up a Trust of a Freehold or Lease. In addition to those general rules, the special formality rule imposed by section 53(1)(b) of the LPA 1925 applies (see **E2:2.3.2**).

2.2   Unjust enrichment: Resulting Trusts

The general rules set out in **D4:4.3** also apply where B claims that A holds a Freehold or Lease on Resulting Trust. However, four specific points are worth noting.

---

better chance of opposing a sale than before the Act (in the context of an application for sale by a secured creditor). However, the Law Commission, whose Report No 181 led to the 1996 Act, did *not* intend to increase the protection available to B: see 12.9 of the Report.

[38] In such a case, B may be able to rely on alternative provisions to remain in occupation: see eg Family Law Act 1996; Children Act 1989 (see **G2:n41**). However, that protection clearly does not come from the Trusts of Land and Appointment of Trustees Act 1996.

2.2.1 Resulting Trusts and section 53(1)(b) of the LPA 1925

EXAMPLE 2

B has a Freehold. B transfers the Freehold to A, who gives nothing in return. B orally tells A that B should still have the benefit of the Freehold, but nothing is put down in writing. A is registered as the new holder of the Freehold. A then transfers the Freehold to C, who is registered as its new holder.

If B had transferred his Ownership of a bike to A, B could argue that A was subject to an Express Trust: B transferred his right to A subject to a duty to use that right for B's benefit. However, as **Example 2** instead involves B's Freehold, the lack of signed writing means that B cannot prove that A consented to hold the Freehold on Trust for B. This formality rule, imposed by section 53(1)(b), means that the Resulting Trust may have an important role to play.

Whilst B's oral statement cannot be used to prove that A has consented to hold the Freehold on Trust, it *can* be used to show that B did not intend A to have the benefit of the Freehold.[39] Therefore, as soon as A acquires the Freehold, a Resulting Trust arises: (i) A acquires the Freehold from B; and (ii) as A knows, B did not intend A to have the benefit of that Freehold; so (iii) A is immediately aware of the facts meaning there is no legal basis for A to have that benefit of the right he received from B (see **D4:4.3**). This means that, in **Example 2**, B *does* have a pre-existing persistent right that is capable of binding C. This analysis is confirmed by the decision of the Court of Appeal in *Hodgson v Marks*,[40] the essential facts of which are identical to **Example 2**.

2.2.2 Resulting Trusts and section 60(3) of the LPA 1925

Section 60(3) of the LPA 1925 states that:

> In a voluntary conveyance a resulting trust for the grantor [B] shall not be implied merely by reason that the property is not expressed to be conveyed for the use or benefit of the grantee [A].

This provision, which is assumed to apply only to a transfer of a property right *in land*,[41] seems to have a fairly obvious effect. In a case such as **Example 2**, where B transfers a Freehold to A without receiving anything in return (and so makes a 'voluntary conveyance' of that right), a court cannot assume that a Resulting Trust arises *simply* because B did not go to the trouble of expressly saying that A should have the benefit of the right. After all, if: (i) the court did make such an assumption; then (ii) B, if he wanted to make a gift of a Freehold or Lease to A, would always have to expressly state that A should get the benefit of

---

[39] See Chambers, *Resulting Trusts* (1997), 34 (see too **F3:n75**).

[40] [1971] Ch 892. An alternative explanation for that decision is based on the idea that 'Equity will not allow a statute to be used as an instrument of fraud': see the first instance decision of Ungoed-Thomas J in *Hodgson v Marks* [1971] Ch 892 at 906 and 908. On that view, the Trust in *Hodgson* is an Express Trust: A is not permitted to rely on section 53(1)(b) as to do so would be to use the statute to assist in a fraud. The problems with that fraud explanation are set out in **E2:2.3.2(iv)**. In fact, there is a further problem on the facts of *Hodgson v Marks*: A had transferred his Freehold to C, who knew nothing about the circumstances in which A acquired the Freehold. It is difficult to see how C would be committing a fraud by relying on section 53(1)(b).

[41] See eg *Hodgson v Marks* [1971] Ch 892 at 933; *Tinsley v Milligan* [1994] 1 AC 340 at 371; *Lohia v Lohia* [2001] EWCA Civ 1691; *Ali v Khan* [2002] EWCA Civ 974; Chambers, *Resulting Trusts* (1997) at 18.

the Freehold or Lease. Such a rule would be tiresome, and could frustrate the parties' expectations if B simply forgot to include the necessary words.

In **Example 2**, and thus in a case such as *Hodgson v Marks*, B's claim is *not* hampered by section 60(3). Of course, B cannot claim a Resulting Trust *simply* by showing that the transfer to A did not include words such as 'for the use and benefit of A'. However, B does not make his claim on those grounds alone.[42] Instead, B can point to the circumstances surrounding the transfer of the Freehold and show that he did *not* intend A to have the benefit of the Freehold. For example, in *Hodgson*, B could show that he had transferred the Freehold to A as a result of A's promise that he would hold that right for B's benefit.

So, section 60(3) does *not* mean that the Resulting Trust operates differently in relation to land. After all, B will *never* be able to acquire a right under a Resulting Trust by *simply* showing that, when he gave a right to A, he did not expressly say that A should have the benefit of the right. For a Resulting Trust to arise, B first needs to convince a court that there was no legal basis for A to have the benefit of the right A received from B; this will *always* require B to do more than simply show the absence of words expressly giving A the benefit of the right transferred. In fact, the purpose of section 60(3) is to *prevent* Resulting Trusts operating differently where land is concerned.[43]

2.2.3 Resulting Trusts, mortgage payments and improvements to the land

EXAMPLE 3a

A and B buy land together. The Freehold is registered in A's sole name. The purchase price of the Freehold is £200,000. A and B each pay £10,000 and the remaining £180,000 is advanced to A by C Bank under a 'mortgage' deal. In return for the loan, A gives C Bank a Charge over the land. B does not make his contribution to the purchase price as a gift or a loan to A, or pursuant to any contractual agreement with A.

Clearly, B cannot claim he has a *property right* in the land: the Freehold is registered in A's sole name (see **E1:2.3.4**). Furthermore, section 53(1)(b) of the LPA 1925 means that B cannot claim that he has a right under an Express Trust: there is no writing signed by A providing evidence that A exercised his power to set up a Trust. However, as there seems to be no legal basis for A to have the benefit of B's £10,000, the standard position (although see **2.2.4** below) is that B can acquire a right under a Resulting Trust. As B's right depends on A's unjust enrichment at B's expense, the extent of B's right depends on the extent of B's contribution: so, in **Example 3**, A will hold his Freehold on Trust for B, with a duty to use that Freehold 5 per cent for B's benefit. The key point is that B can 'trace' from his £10,000 to A's Freehold: A's Freehold can be identified, at least in part, as the product of B's initial right to the £10,000 (see **D4:4.4**).[44]

---

[42] See *per* Mummery LJ in *Lohia v Lohia* [2001] EWCA Civ 1691 at [25].

[43] Its aim is to ensure that an old rule, which applied only to a transfer of a right relating to land, was not revived by the 1925 legislation. That old rule *did* treat land differently, by stating that the absence of express words giving A the benefit of a right relating to land *would*, by itself, allow B to claim a Resulting Trust.

[44] In some cases, A acquires a Freehold or Lease for a reduced price as a result of B's 'sitting tenant discount'. This discount arises where B has a Lease of land held by a local authority: B is allowed to acquire the local authority's Freehold at a reduced price. If A uses that discount, then A is enriched at B's expense and A's enrichment consists in his acquisition of that Freehold: as a result, a Resulting Trust can arise.

EXAMPLE 3b

A and B buy land together. The Freehold is registered in A's sole name. The purchase price of the Freehold is £200,000. A pays £20,000 and the remaining £180,000 is advanced to A by C Bank under a 'mortgage' deal. In return for the loan, A gives C Bank a Charge over the land. A is the only person liable to repay C Bank, but A and B each provide 50 per cent of the monthly mortgage payments. B does not make his contributions to the mortgage payments as a gift or a loan to A, or pursuant to any contractual agreement with A

It is tempting to say that here, as in **Example 3a**, B should be able to acquire a right under a Resulting Trust. However, this depends on whether B can 'trace' from his contribution to the mortgage payments to A's Freehold. Certainly, in substance, we know that B has helped A to meet the costs of paying for A's Freehold. It is therefore tempting to say that A's Freehold is acquired, at least in part, from B. However, as the law currently stands, there is an important problem with that argument. The problem is that, technically, A had *already* acquired the Freehold when B contributed to the mortgage payments. So:

1. In **Example 3a**, B contributes to the *deposit* and hence B can draw a direct link between his payment and A's acquisition of the Freehold.
2. In **Example 3b**, B instead contributes to the *mortgage payments*, and hence B cannot draw such a direct link to A's acquisition of the Freehold. After all, A acquired the Freehold from the vendor *before* any mortgage payments were made.

In **Example 3b**, therefore, A's unjust enrichment at B's expense does not relate directly to A's acquisition of the Freehold; instead, it relates to a reduction in the debt that A owes to C Bank and that is secured on the land.[45] On this view, A's unjust enrichment should *not* lead to B acquiring a right under the Trust of the Freehold; instead, B should be able to rely on 'subrogation' principles to acquire a right equivalent to the reduction in C Bank's right against A (see **D4:3.3**).

However, particularly if the value of A's Freehold has increased, B may prefer to claim a right under a Resulting Trust of the Freehold. Two points can be made. First, it could be said that *whenever* A uses B's money to pay off a loan taken out by A when acquiring a right, B should be able to 'trace' from his money to the right acquired by A. So, if A steals B's money and uses it to pay off a £5,000 loan A took out when buying a car, B should then be able to identify A's Ownership of the car as a product of B's initial right to the money. The argument is that the courts should not blind themselves to the practical reality that the loan was used by A to acquire a specific right.[46]

Second, it could be said that, *where land is concerned*, the courts should not ignore the reality that, by paying off a mortgage loan, B is, in substance, allowing A to acquire his Freehold. An interesting parallel is provided by the decision of the House of Lords in *Abbey National Building Society v Cann*,[47] the essential facts of which were identical to **Example 3a**. The question in that case was whether C Bank was bound by B's right under the Trust. One

---

[45] For example, let us say A takes £100 from B and uses it to pay off a debt A incurred in buying a car. B cannot claim that A is under a duty, arising in unjust enrichment, to use his ownership of the car for B's benefit: see *Bishopsgate v Homan* [1995] Ch 211. B cannot show that A's right to the car is the traceable product of B's £100.

[46] For a strong argument in favour of this 'backwards tracing', see L Smith [1995] *CLJ* 290.

[47] [1991] 1 AC 56.

of the reasons[48] given by the House of Lords for finding in C Bank's favour was that B's right was *not* a pre-existing right. This may seem strange: doctrinally, B's persistent right arose before C Bank's Charge; in fact, it arose *as soon as* A acquired the Freehold. After all, C Bank acquired its Charge over the land from A; and A can only give C Bank such a right once A has his Freehold. So, there must be a very brief moment of time (a 'scintilla temporis') when A has the Freehold free from C Bank's Charge.[49] The House of Lords refused to accept this argument. Instead, it pointed to the practical reality: C Bank's loan was vital in allowing A to acquire the Freehold.[50] The legal position was therefore said to follow the practical position: as C Bank's Charge enabled A to acquire the Freehold, it should be viewed as arising *before* A acquired his Freehold and so *before* B acquired her right under a Trust of the Freehold.

This type of reasoning, considering the effect of a Charge from a practical rather than a doctrinal perspective, can be extended to the case where B makes a contribution to mortgage payments. Doctrinally, such payments cannot give rise to a Resulting Trust of the Freehold, as they are used to pay off a debt, not to acquire A's Freehold. However, practically speaking, such payments *do* go towards allowing A to acquire the Freehold and so *should* give rise to a Resulting Trust of A's Freehold.[51] Certainly, in *Stack v Dowden*,[52] Lord Neuberger (the only member of the panel to base his decision on a Resulting Trust) assumed that contributions to mortgage payments *can* give rise to a Resulting Trust.[53]

EXAMPLE 3c

The basic facts are as in **Example 3b**. This time B does not contribute to the mortgage payments. However, B pays £50,000 for an extension to the house on the land. As a result of that extension, the value of the land immediately increases by £60,000. B does not make that contribution as a gift or a loan to A, or pursuant to any contractual agreement with A.

In such a case, B may again claim a right under a Resulting Trust: (i) there is no legal basis for A to have the full benefit of the improvements paid for by B; and (ii) those improvements have led to an increase in the value of A's Freehold. A comment of Lord Neuberger in *Stack v Dowden* may assist B's claim: his Lordship noted that paying for or carrying out significant and substantial improvements is 'not dissimilar, in financial effect, from the cost

---

[48] For other reasons see E2:3.6.4(i) and G4:4.2.2(ii).

[49] As recognised in eg *Church of England BS v Piskor* [1954] Ch 553.

[50] *Per* Lord Oliver in *Cann* [1991] 1 AC 56 at 92–3 and *per* Lord Jauncey at 102; see too *per* Lord Hoffmann in *Ingram v IRC* [2000] 1 AC 293 at 303: 'For my part, I do not think that a theory based upon the notion of a scintilla temporis can have a very powerful grasp on reality.'

[51] There may be an important distinction between 'interest-only' and 'repayment' loans. In an 'interest only' loan, the payments do not go to reducing the capital sum borrowed by A but they do prevent the debt increasing by paying for the cost of borrowing the money (the interest charged by C Bank). Therefore it is harder to 'trace' interest-only payments into A's acquisition of the Freehold (the special position of interest-only payments is referred to in passing in *Stack v Dowden* [2007] 2 AC 432 at [140] by Lord Neuberger). However, by contributing to interest-only payments, B does allow A to take advantage of any increase in the value of the Freehold that occurs whilst those payments are made. Hence it can be said that B should get a right, under a Resulting Trust, to a proportionate share of the benefit of any *increase in value* of A's Freehold over the period of B's payments.

[52] [2007] 2 AC 432.

[53] *Ibid* at [140]. Lord Neuberger's calculation of the extent of B's right under the Trust also seems to take into account B's mortgage contributions: see [122]. Although note that in *Stack*, there was no need for B to use a Resulting Trust to *establish* a right under a Trust: the Freehold was held by *both* A and B (see G2:Example 18).

of acquiring the home in the first place'.[54] However, as in **Example 3b**, B faces the problem that his payment did not allow A to *acquire* the Freehold. In contrast to **Example 3b**, A's unjust enrichment *does* relate to A's Freehold; however, it relates to its improvement, not its acquisition. So, as in **D1:Example 13** (see **D4:4.5.2**), B's contribution should instead lead to B acquiring a different form of persistent right against A's Freehold: a Purely Equitable Charge. That Purely Equitable Charge can secure A's duty to pay B the benefit A has acquired as a result of B's improvements (£60,000 in **Example 3b**).[55] However, as B does not have a right under a Trust, B will not benefit from any further increase in the value of A's Freehold (eg, due to a boom in the property market); rather, A's duty to B will always be to give B the value of B's improvements.

2.2.4 Resulting Trusts and cohabiting couples

In **Examples 3a, 3b** and **3c**, should our analysis be any different if: (i) A and B happen to be lovers; and (ii) A acquires the Freehold with the intention that A and B should set up their home on the land? It is hard to see why: the Resulting Trust is based on the need to prevent A's unjust enrichment where he acquires a right, in whole or in part, at B's expense; that need may also be present when A and B are lovers. However, with the exception of Lord Neuberger, the members of the panel in *Stack v Dowden* assume that, in such a case, the Resulting Trust has *no* role to play.[56] Of course, the facts of *Stack* are different from those of **Examples 3a, 3b** and **3c**: in *Stack*, A and B were *both* registered as holders of the Freehold. Nonetheless, as confirmed by Baroness Hale when giving the opinion of the Privy Council in *Abbott v Abbott*,[57] the assumption is that the *Stack* approach should also apply where only A is the sole holder of the Freehold or Lease (although that assumption may be questioned: see **2.4.3(v)(b)** below).

This exclusion of the Resulting Trust does not cause a direct problem to B: it seems that, in any case where B would otherwise be able to acquire a right under a Resulting Trust, B will instead simply acquire a right under a common intention Constructive Trust (see **2.4.3(v)(a)** below). However, the approach of the majority in *Stack* does lead to some important practical problems (see **G2:2.2.1(ii)**). In particular, when *precisely* is the Resulting Trust excluded? For example, Lord Walker suggested it may be appropriate where A and B 'have lived and worked together in what has amounted to both an emotional and a commercial partnership'.[58] So, even if A and B are lovers, we may need to ask further questions—eg, is the Resulting Trust excluded if A and B also run a business together?[59] And what about cases where: (i) A acquires a Freehold or Lease for the joint occupation of A and B; but (ii) A and B are not lovers, but are instead friends, work colleagues or relatives?

2.3 Statute: Statutory Trusts

As far as Statutory Trusts are concerned, the acquisition question is straightforward. The

---

[54] At [139]. See too *per* Lord Walker at [36] (although Lord Walker's comment is directed to the 'common intention' Constructive Trust and not to the Resulting Trust).

[55] The same right should arise where B's own work leads to the improvements: in **Example 3c**, the important thing is *not* that B has paid money; rather, it is that B has increased the value of A's Freehold.

[56] See *per* Lord Walker at [31], confirmed by Baroness Hale in *Abbott v Abbott* [2007] UKPC 53 at [4].

[57] [2007] UKPC 53.

[58] [2007] 2 AC 432 at [32].

[59] See eg *James v Thomas* [2007] EWCA Civ 1212.

Trust arises *if* the event set out by the statute has occurred; and the Trust arises *because* Parliament has decided that, where that event occurs, A should be under the core Trust duty. As we saw in **G2:1.2.3** and noted in **1.2.2** above, a special form of Statutory Trust arises, under sections 34(2) and 36(1) of the LPA 1925, where A and B acquire a Freehold or Lease together. That Trust has been extended by the courts so that it now arises *whenever* A and B acquire a Freehold or Lease together, even if they acquire it as joint tenants (see **G2:1.2.4**).

2.4   Contract, wrongs and other events: Constructive Trusts

2.4.1 Contract

The general rules set out in **F3:2.4.1** mean that: (i) if A has a Freehold or Lease; and (ii) A has *either* (a) made a contractual promise to B to set up a Trust of that right in B's favour; *or* (b) made a contractual promise to transfer that right to B; then (iii) B immediately acquires a persistent right under a Constructive Trust of A's Freehold or Lease. That basic principle is true where land is concerned, but three specific points are worth noting.

First, A's promise can only be *contractually* binding if the formality rule set out by section 2 of the Law of Property (Miscellaneous Provisions) Act 1989 is satisfied (see **E2:2.3.3**). If not, A's promise may give rise to a Constructive Trust through some other means (eg, the doctrine of proprietary estoppel), but it cannot impose a contractual duty on A.

Second, if: (i) A has Ownership of a thing; and (ii) A makes a contractual promise to transfer that property right to B; then (iii) A's contractual duty, *by itself*, can lead to B immediately acquiring A's property right (see **D1:2.2.4(iii)**). In such a case, A's contractual promise does not give B a persistent right against A's right: B simply acquires A's right (see **D2:2.1.2(iii)**). However, a contractual promise, by itself, cannot transfer A's Freehold or Lease to B: formality requirements must be satisfied (see **E1:2.3**). As a result, the Constructive Trust arising from a contractual promise to transfer a right is particularly prominent where land is concerned.

Third, this type of Constructive Trust is simply an example of the wider principle we examined in **E2:1.3.1**: B acquires an immediate persistent right *whenever* A has a Freehold or Lease and is under a duty to grant B a property right in that land. For example, if A's duty is to grant B an Easement; B acquires an immediate Equitable Easement. If A's duty is instead to transfer his Freehold or Lease to B, B's right, often said to arise under an 'Estate Contract', is a right under a Constructive Trust (see **E2:Example 2b**).[60]

2.4.2 Wrongs

The general rules set out in **F3:2.1.4(ii)** apply in exactly the same way: if the right that A acquires in breach of his fiduciary duty to B is a Freehold or a Lease, A will therefore hold that right on Trust for B.[61]

---

[60] See esp *per* Sir George Jessel MR in *Lysaght v Edwards* (1876) 2 Ch D 499 at 506.
[61] See eg *Soulos v Korkontzilas* (1997) 146 DLR (4th) 214 (Supreme Court of Canada)

2.4.3 Other events

(i) Rights against a product of B's initial right?
The analysis out in **F3:2.1.4(iii)(a)** applies in exactly the same way: for example, in **Example 3a**, a Resulting Trust of A's Freehold arises as that right can be identified as a product of B's initial right to the £10,000.[62]

(ii) The 'receipt after a promise' principle
If: (i) A, in his will, transfers a right to C on A's death; and (ii) C has promised to hold that right on Trust for B; but (iii) the terms of that Trust are not recorded in the will; then (iv) the formality rule imposed by the Wills Act 1837 prevents B claiming a right under an Express Trust. However, as shown by **D3:Example 2**, the 'receipt after a promise' principle applies and gives rise to a 'secret Trust': a particular form of Constructive Trust (see **F3:2.1.4(iii)(b)**). In such a case, the 'receipt after a promise' principle is important because of a formality rule that prevents B showing that A has exercised his power to set up a Trust.

Similarly, if A0 attempts to set up a Trust by transferring a Freehold or Lease to A to hold on Trust for B, the formality rule set out by section 53(1)(b) of the LPA 1925 means that, if no signed writing is used, B will be unable to show that an Express Trust has been created (see **E2:2.3.2**). This special formality rule, applying only to land, means that the 'receipt after a promise' principle is particularly important where land is concerned (see **E3:2.2.2**).

E2:EXAMPLE 9b

A0 has a Freehold. A0 transfers that Freehold to A. As part of his deal with A0, A orally promises to hold the Freehold on Trust for B.

The absence of signed writing means that B *cannot* show that A0 or A has exercised a power to set up an Express Trust in B's favour. Nonetheless, a Constructive Trust arises: (i) the 'receipt after a promise' principle applies; so (ii) A is under a duty to B to keep his promise to A0; and so (iii) A is under the core Trust duty to B. This analysis is consistent with the result (if not the reasoning) in *Rochefoucauld v Boustead*,[63] the essential facts of which are identical to **E2:Example 9b** (see **E2:2.3.2(i) and (iv)**).

The 'receipt after a promise' principle can also be important if: (i) A makes a promise to B to transfer a Freehold or Lease to B (or to hold such a right on Trust for B);[64] and (ii) due to a failure to comply with the formality rule imposed by section 2 of the Law of Property (Miscellaneous Provisions) Act 1989, that promise is not contractually binding on A (see **E2:2.3.3**). In such a case: (i) if B can show that A, as a result of his promise, acquired an advantage in relation to the acquisition of his Freehold or Lease; then (ii) the 'receipt after a promise' principle means that A is under a duty to B to keep his promise; and so (iii) B

---

[62] See too *Attorney General of Hong Kong v Reid* [1994] 1 AC 324: B's initial persistent right arose under a Constructive Trust of the bribe received by A. When A invested that bribe in land, B then acquired a persistent right against A's right to that land. In fact, A purchased a number of Freeholds, some of which were registered in the names of third parties. In practice this made no difference to B as those third parties had no defence to B's pre-existing right under the Constructive Trust of the bribe.

[63] [1897] 1 Ch 196.

[64] For examples involving a promise to hold on Trust, see *Cox v Jones* [2004] 2 FLR 1010 (see esp *per* Mann J at [45]–[47]) and *Neale v Willis* (1968) 19 P & CR 836 (where A's promise was made to B's mother, who contributed to the purchase price of A's Freehold on the basis that B would acquire a share of its benefit).

acquires a right under a Constructive Trust.[65] The decision of Harman J in *Pallant v Morgan* (see **D3:2.2.2**)[66] provides a good example of the application of the principle in such a case. It also demonstrates that the principle is *not* based on the risk of B suffering a detriment: in that case, B suffered no loss as a result of his reliance on A's promise.[67] Rather, the principle looks to A's benefit and aims to prevent A acquiring an advantage without bearing a correlative burden.

When considering the 'receipt after a promise' principle, we have to bear in mind the risk of *fake Constructive Trusts*: cases in which B's right is *said* by the courts to arise under a Trust even though, in fact, A is *not* under the core Trust duty to B. For example, in *Binions v Evans* (see **E3:Example 6**),[68] Lord Denning MR took the view that: (i) if A0 transfers a Freehold or Lease to A; and (ii) A promises A0 that he will allow B to remain in occupation of the land; then (iii) B acquires a right under a Constructive Trust. In such a case, B should indeed acquire a direct right against A under the 'receipt after a promise' principle; but, as we saw in **E3:2.3.2** and **E6:3.4.2(ii)**, B's right should *not* arise under a Trust. If A's duty is: (i) to keep a promise to hold a Freehold or Lease on Trust for B (as in *Rochefoucauld v Boustead*),[69] or (ii) to keep a promise to transfer such a right to B (as in *Pallant v Morgan*);[70] then (iii) B acquires a right under a Trust. However, if A's duty is simply to allow B to occupy A's land (as in *Binions v Evans*), A is not under the core Trust duty to B.

(iii) Mutual wills: the Contract (Rights of Third Parties) Act 1999?

In **F3:2.1.4(iii)(c)**, we saw that the doctrine of mutual wills can give rise to a Constructive Trust in B's favour where A1 makes a contractual promise to A2 to leave certain rights, on his death, to B. That doctrine is said to be based on A1 and A2 each having made a contractual promise to the other: although developed long before the Contract (Rights of Third Parties) Act 1999, it can be seen to anticipate the principle that lies behind that Act. Where A1's promise relates to land, a problem arises: it can only be contractually binding if it satisfies the formality rule laid down by section 2 of the Law of Property (Miscellaneous Provisions) Act 1989. Hence, if A1 makes an oral promise to A2 to leave his rights to B: (i) the 'receipt after a promise' principle may apply in relation to any rights A1 acquires from A2 as a result of his promise;[71] but (ii) the doctrine of mutual wills should *not* apply to give B a right in relation to any other rights held by A1.[72]

---

[65] This analysis is consistent with the principles set out by Chadwick LJ in *Banner Homes Group plc v Luff Developments Ltd* [2000] Ch 372 at 397–401. The *content* of A's duty is the same as in the situations discussed in **2.4.1** above. The difference is as to the source of that duty: B *acquires* his right as a result of the 'receipt after a promise' principle, not as a result of a contractual promise.

[66] [1953] Ch 43.

[67] As a result of A's promise, B had dropped out of the bidding for a plot of land (see **D3:2.2.2**). B was willing to bid up to £2,000 for the land; A was in any case willing to bid £3,000 so B did not suffer any detriment. However, as a result of B's dropping out, A acquired the land for less than £2,000: A thus gained an advantage as a result of his promise.

[68] [1972] Ch 359.

[69] [1897] 1 Ch 96.

[70] [1953] Ch 43.

[71] See *Healey v Brown* [2002] EWHC Ch 1405 *per* David Donaldson QC sitting as a Deputy High Court judge at [28].

[72] *Ibid* at [17]–[21]. In *Birmingham v Renfrew* (1937) 57 CLR 666, the High Court of Australia took the view that the formality rule applying in Victoria only had effect if A1's promise *expressly* related to land: so if (i) A1's oral promise was to leave 'all my assets' to B; and (ii) those assets, on A1's death, happened to include a Freehold or Lease; then (iii) the formality rule did not apply and so A1's promise could be contractually binding; so (iv) the

(iv) Proprietary estoppel

If: (i) A has a Freehold or Lease; and (ii) A makes a commitment to B to use A's land in a certain way; and (iii) B reasonably relies on that commitment; and (iv) B would suffer a detriment if A does not honour the commitment; then (v) the doctrine of proprietary estoppel can impose a duty on A (see **E4:3**). Although there are strong arguments in favour of extending the doctrine, the prevailing view is that it can apply only where A's commitment relates to the use of A's land (see **E4:3.1.2**). Certainly, the doctrine is particularly important where land is concerned. For example, if section 2 of the 1989 Act means that A's commitment is not contractually binding, B may be able to rely on proprietary estoppel to show that A is under a duty to B. And, in some cases but not all, A's duty will be to keep his commitment to B (see **E4:4**).

If proprietary estoppel imposes a duty on A to: (i) hold his Freehold or Lease on Trust for B; or to (ii) transfer his Freehold or Lease to B; then (iii) A is under the core Trust duty to B: a Constructive Trust thus arises. For example, in *Eves v Eves*,[73] a Constructive Trust arose as A was under a duty to allow B a share of the benefit of A's Freehold (see **E2:Example 9a**). In *Pascoe v Turner*,[74] a Constructive Trust arose as A was under a duty to transfer his Freehold to B (see **C3:Example 3** and **E4:Example 1**).[75]

When considering proprietary estoppel, we have to bear in mind the risk of *fake Constructive Trusts*—cases in which B's right is *said* by the courts to arise under a Trust even though, in fact, A is *not* under the core Trust duty to B. For example, in *Yaxley v Gotts* (see **E4:Example 11**),[76] proprietary estoppel imposed a duty on A to grant B a promised Lease. In such a case, B should acquire a persistent right: an Equitable Lease (see **E2:1.3.1**). A is *not* under the core Trust duty to B: provided A complies with his duty to grant B a Lease, A is otherwise free to use his Freehold as he wishes. Nonetheless, in *Yaxley*, the Court of Appeal held that B's right arose under a Constructive Trust. Similarly, in *Kinane v Mackie-Conteh* (see **E2:Example 11a**),[77] A's duty was to grant B a promised Charge. Again, A is *not* under the core Trust duty; and again, the Court of Appeal nonetheless held that B's right arose under a Constructive Trust.

The fake Constructive Trusts found in *Yaxley* and *Kinane* are misleading and unnecessary. In each case, the Court of Appeal adopted the Constructive Trust label in order to explain why: (i) B could acquire a persistent right as a result of A's promise to give B a property right in land; even though (ii) A's promise was not contractually binding as it did not satisfy the formality rule set out by section 2 of the 1989 Act.[78] The point is that section 2(5) of that Act contains an apparent exception for Resulting Trusts and Constructive Trusts. To rely on that 'exception', the Court of Appeal characterised B's right as a right under a Constructive Trust. However, as we saw in **E3:2.3.3(i) and (iv)**, this tactic is unnecessary. The

---

doctrine of mutual wills could apply. However, it is very difficult to argue that section 2 of the 1989 Act applies only to contracts *expressly* disposing of land rather than to contracts actually disposing of land.

[73] [1975] 1 WLR 1338.

[74] [1979] 1 WLR 431.

[75] Although, as noted in **C3:4.2.3** and **E4:4.5**, it is difficult to defend the Court of Appeal's decision that, on the facts of *Pascoe v Turner*, A was under a duty to transfer his Freehold to B.

[76] [2000] Ch 162.

[77] [2005] EWCA Civ 45.

[78] See eg *per* Robert Walker LJ in *Yaxley* [2000] Ch 162 at 178–80; *per* Neuberger LJ in *Kinane* [2005] EWCA Civ 45 at [45]–[46].

crucial point is that, irrespective of the section 2(5) 'exception', the basic rule imposed by section 2 applies only to regulate the question of whether A is under a *contractual* duty to B. It has no effect on the different question of whether proprietary estoppel imposes a duty on A (see **E3:2.3.3(i)**).[79]

This point may seem pedantic: in cases such as *Yaxley* and *Kinane* (in contrast to *Binions v Evans*) the Constructive Trust label does *not* turn a personal right into a persistent right. However, the misdescription of B's right can have serious consequences for B: it can *weaken* B's position against C. For example, if A is viewed as holding his Freehold or Lease on Trust for B, section 6 of the 1996 Act then applies and A has a power to give C a right free from B's pre-existing persistent right. As a result, C may then be able to rely on the overreaching defence against B's pre-existing persistent right (see **E2:3.4**). In contrast, if B's right is accurately described (ie, as an Equitable Lease in *Yaxley*; as an Equitable Charge in *Kinane*), then: (i) no Constructive Trust arises; so (ii) A does *not* have that power; and so (iii) B is *not* vulnerable to the overreaching defence.

(v) The 'common intention' Constructive Trust

(a) Introduction

The courts recognise a further means by which B can acquire a right under a Constructive Trust of A's Freehold or Lease. It applies *only* where land is concerned and, it seems, *only* where that land is used as a 'family home'. A 'common intention' Constructive Trust is said to arise if:

- A has (or A and B have)[80] a Freehold or Lease of a home that A and B occupy as cohabiting partners; *and*
- A and B have a common intention to share the benefit of that Freehold or Lease; *and*
- B reasonably relies on that common intention and would suffer a detriment if it is not upheld.[81]

EXAMPLE 4a

The facts are as in **Example 3a**. A and B are lovers: A has acquired the Freehold, and B has contributed £10,000 to its acquisition, on the basis that the land will be a home for A and B. However, there are no express discussions between A and B as to whether B will have a share of the benefit of A's Freehold.

In such a case, we might expect B, if his contribution is not intended as a gift or a loan to A, to acquire a right under a Resulting Trust (see **Example 3a** above). However, it seems that, as A and B are cohabiting lovers, the Resulting Trust analysis is excluded (see **2.2.4** above): instead, B's rights depend on the common intention Constructive Trust. So, in a case such as **Example 4a**, B needs to show that A and B had a common intention that B would acquire a

---

[79] See further McFarlane [2005] *Conv* 501.

[80] In *Stack v Dowden* [2007] 2 AC 432 (**G2:Example 18**), a Freehold was co-held by A and B on Trust for each other. The majority of the House of Lords regarded that Trust as a common intention Constructive Trust; Lord Neuberger instead analysed it as a Resulting Trust (see **2.2.4** above).

[81] See eg *per* Lord Diplock in *Gissing v Gissing* [1971] 1 AC 886 at 905; *per* Lord Bridge in *Lloyds Bank v Rosset* [1991] 1 AC 107 at 132–3.

share of the benefit of A's Freehold. As there are no express statements revealing any such intention, B has to persuade a court to *infer* such an intention from the facts of the case.

In **Example 4a**, B will have no difficulty in convincing a court to make the necessary inference: a direct financial contribution to the purchase price, not intended as a gift or a loan, is viewed as a very strong indication of such a common intention.[82] The idea is that, in the absence of that intention, B would have no reason for making such a contribution. This means that B's decision to make the contribution can also be seen as: (i) B's reliance on the common intention; and (ii) sufficient to mean that B would clearly suffer a detriment if the common intention is not upheld.

A common intention Constructive Trust thus arises in **Example 4a**; but what is the extent of A's duty to B? On the Resulting Trust analysis, B's share of the benefit of A's Freehold is based on A's unjust enrichment at B's expense and would thus be 5 per cent (B paid £10,000 of the £200,000 purchase price). However, in a common intention Constructive Trust, things are different: it seems that A is under a duty to uphold the common intention of A and B.[83] So, if B can show that the common intention was that A and B should share the benefit of the Freehold 50–50, B has a 50 per cent share of the benefit of the Freehold. The decision of the Court of Appeal in *Midland Bank v Cooke*[84] provides a very good example. B made a contribution of less than 7 per cent to the purchase price of A's Freehold; but, as it was found that A and B intended to share the benefit of that right equally, B acquired a 50 per cent share of the benefit of the Freehold.

Of course, in **Example 4a**, A and B have made no express statements about the share they intend B to have. So, again, a court has to attempt to infer that intention. This process is carried out in exactly the same way as the initial process of seeing if *any* common intention can be inferred: the size of B's £10,000 contribution will be an important factor; crucially, however, it is not the *only* factor. Other action by B may also be taken into account and may allow B to acquire a larger share of the benefit of the Freehold.[85]

(b) Advantages to B of the common intention Constructive Trust

EXAMPLE 4b

A and B are lovers: A acquires a Freehold on the basis that the land will be a home for A and B. The Freehold costs £200,000: A provides £20,000 and borrows the remainder from C Bank in a 'mortgage' deal. A expressly tells B that B will have a 50 per cent share of the benefit of the Freehold. B relies on that statement by giving up his job, and leaving his current accommodation, in order to live with A. B also assists A in paying the mortgage instalments.

If B relies on A's commitment to give B a right relating to land, the standard approach is for B use proprietary estoppel to show that A is under a duty to B. As we saw in E4:4, the duty imposed on A is not always a duty to keep his commitment to B. A's duty is to ensure that B

---

[82] See eg *per* Lord Bridge in *Lloyds Bank v Rosset* [1991] 1 AC 107 at 132–3; *per* Lord Hope in *Stack v Dowden* at [11]. But note that is not a guarantee that such an intention can be inferred. For example, if B makes such a contribution without A's knowledge or consent, it cannot provide evidence of a common intention: see *Lightfoot v Lightfoot-Brown* [2005] EWCA Civ 201.

[83] See eg *Midland Bank v Cooke* [1995] 2 FLR 915; *Oxley v Hiscock* [2005] Fam 211; *Stack v Dowden* [2007] 2 AC 432; *Abbott v Abbott* [2007] UKPC 53.

[84] [1995] 2 FLR 915.

[85] See *per* Baroness Hale in *Stack v Dowden* [2007] 2 AC 432 at [69] and in *Abbott v Abbott* [2007] UKPC 53 at [6].

does not suffer a detriment as a result of his reasonable reliance on A's commitment; A may be able to meet that duty *without* honouring his commitment to B.[86] However, it seems that things are different under a common intention Constructive Trust: in such a case, A's commitment to B *will* be enforced.[87] In a case such as **Example 4b**, this gives B an important advantage to B: as soon as he reasonably relies on A's commitment, B will acquire a 50 per cent share of the benefit of A's Freehold.

EXAMPLE 4c

The basic facts are as in **Example 4b**. This time B does not contribute to the mortgage payments. However, B pays £50,000 for an extension to the house on the land. As a result of that extension, the value of the land immediately increases by £60,000. B does not make that contribution as a gift or a loan to A, or pursuant to any contractual agreement with A.

We saw above that, in **Example 3c**, standard Resulting Trust principles do not allow B to acquire a right under a Trust of A's Freehold. However, in **Example 4c**, it *is* possible for a common intention Constructive Trust to arise: B may be able to convince a court to infer, from his payment for improvements, that A and B had an intention that B should have a share of the benefit of the Freehold.[88]

In cases such as **Examples 4a and 4c**, the critical question is: when will a court infer, in the absence of any express discussions between A and B, that A and B had a common intention that B would have a share of the benefit of A's Freehold or Lease? In *Lloyds Bank plc v Rosset*,[89] Lord Bridge recommended a restrictive approach: (i) a common intention can be inferred if B makes a direct financial contribution to the purchase price (as in **Example 4a**) or to mortgage payments (as in **Example 4b**); *but* (ii) in the absence of such payments, it is very unlikely that the court will be able to infer the necessary common intention.[90] Under the *Rosset* test, B faces a problem in a case such as **Example 4c**. Indeed, there may be cases where: (i) A and B have lived together for a long time and B has made significant contributions to the parties' relationship and financial affairs (eg, bringing up children, paying utility bills); *but* (ii) as B has not made a direct financial contribution to the purchase price or mortgage payments; then (iii) it is impossible to infer the necessary common intention.

A classic example is provided by *Burns v Burns*,[91] in which A and B had lived together for almost 20 years. When they split up, A simply asked B to leave: B was unable to claim a share of the benefit of the Freehold as: (i) there had been no express discussions between A and B showing a common intention that B should have such a share; and (ii) B had not made a direct financial contribution to the purchase price or mortgage payments. As A and B had not married, B could not appeal to the courts' statutory power to adjust the parties' rights on divorce.[92] As a result, B, despite having made a significant emotional and financial commitment to her relationship with B, was left with no financial protection.

---

[86] See eg *Jennings v Rice* [2003] 1 P & CR 100.
[87] See eg *per* Chadwick LJ in *Oxley v Hiscock* [2005] Fam 211 at [69].
[88] See eg *per* Lord Walker in *Stack v Dowden* [2007] 2 AC 432 at [36].
[89] [1991] 1 AC 107.
[90] *Ibid* at 132.
[91] [1984] Ch 317.
[92] See Matrimonial Causes Act 1973 (as amended): see further (f) below.

In *Stack v Dowden*,[93] the majority[94] of the House of Lords took a different approach and rejected the restrictive *Rosset* test. It was held that a *wide number of different factors* can be taken into account in seeing if the necessary common intention can be inferred.[95] The specific factors set out by Baroness Hale are listed below; but the key point is that the list is *not* exhaustive. Rather, a court can take into account *any factor* that it believes provides a clue as to whether A and B had a common intention that B would have a share of the benefit of A's Freehold or Lease.[96]

The factors specifically mentioned by Baroness Hale are as follows:[97]

- any advice or discussions at the time of A's acquisition of the Freehold or Lease that cast light upon [A and B's] intentions at that point;
- the purpose for which the home was acquired;
- the nature of the parties' relationship;
- whether they had children for whom they both had responsibility to provide a home;
- how the purchase was financed, both initially and subsequently;
- how the parties arranged their finances, whether separately or together or a bit of both; how they discharged the outgoings on the property and their other household expenses;
- the parties' individual characters and personalities.

Baroness Hale also mentions some factors that are relevant only where A and B co-hold a Freehold or Lease (as was the case in *Stack v Dowden* itself): for example, a court can then take into account the reason for which the Freehold or Lease was conveyed to both A and B. This raises the interesting possibility that the wide list of factors set out above is relevant *only* in a case where A and B co-hold a Freehold or Lease. It can be argued that there is an important distinction between two types of case:

Type 1 (eg *Stack v Dowden*)	Where A and B acquire a Freehold or Lease together, the parties' common intention, *by itself*, determines their rights. We simply need to ask how A and B intended to acquire the co-held Freehold or Lease (see **G2:2.2.1(ii)**). If they intended that each would acquire a particular share as tenants in common, that intention must take effect behind a Trust (see **G2:1.2.3**). However, that Trust does not arise as a result of B's reliance on the common intention: it simply reflects the capacity in which A and B intended to acquire their Freehold or Lease.

---

[93] [2007] 2 AC 432.

[94] Lord Neuberger analysed the case differently, applying a Resulting Trust analysis (see **2.2.4** above).

[95] See esp *per* Baroness Hale at [68].

[96] See *per* Baroness Hale at [69]: 'In law, "context is everything" and the domestic context is very different from the commercial world. Each case will turn on its own facts. Many more factors than financial contributions may be relevant to divining the parties' true intentions.'

[97] *Ibid* at [69].

Type 2
(eg *Lloyds Bank v Rosset*;
Burns v Burns;
Examples 4a–4c)

Where A is the sole holder of a Freehold or Lease, it is not simply a question of working out the capacity in which A and B intended they would hold that right: after all, the right is *not* held by B. Rather, B needs to show a positive reason why A should be under a duty to use that Freehold or Lease for B's benefit. One possibility is for B to show he relied on a common intention that he would have a share of the benefit of A's right.

However, it seems that the majority in *Stack* does *not* have this distinction in mind: the wider approach is intended to apply in *both* **Type 1** and **Type 2** cases. This is demonstrated by: (i) the opinion of the Privy Council in *Abbott v Abbott*, [98] where Baroness Hale applied the *Stack* approach to a **Type 2** case; and (ii) the decision of the Court of Appeal in *James v Thomas*,[99] where the *Stack* approach was again applied to a **Type 2** case.

So, the *Stack* approach can assist B in a case where: (i) there have been no express discussions between A and B as to whether B should have a share of the benefit of A's Freehold or Lease; and (ii) B has not made a direct financial contribution to the purchase price or mortgage payments. In **Example 4c**, B can therefore argue that a common intention can be inferred due to his payment for improvements to the land. And, in a case such as *Burns v Burns*,[100] B can point not only to her payment of bills but also, for example, to: (i) the fact that A's Freehold was acquired to provide a home for A and B; and (ii) the nature of A and B's relationship; and (iii) the fact that A and B had children together. If B can convince a court to infer such a common intention, the size of B's share will also depend on that inferred intention: therefore, if a court decides that A and B intended to share everything equally, it will recognise that B has a 50 per cent share of the benefit of A's Freehold or Lease.

(c) Problems with the common intention Constructive Trust

First, there is a problem as to the *scope* of the common intention Constructive Trust. This is the problem we examined in **2.2.4** above, when considering the effect of such a Constructive Trust in excluding a Resulting Trust that might otherwise arise. In particular, the usual context in which the Constructive Trust can arise is where A and B are lovers. Can it also arise where A and B are *both* lovers *and* business partners? In *Stack v Dowden*, Lord Walker seems to suggest that the Constructive Trust may be unsuitable where A and B 'have lived and worked together in what has amounted to both an emotional and a commercial partnership'.[101] However, in *James v Thomas*,[102] a case arising after *Stack* in which A and B were both lovers and business partners, the Court of Appeal were prepared to consider the application of the Constructive Trust.[103] Similarly, as noted in **2.2.4** above,[104] there is a

---

[98] [2007] UKPC 53: *Abbott* shows that the principles set out in *Stack* are intended to apply to a case such as **Example 4a** in which A is the sole holder of the Freehold (of course, in *Stack* itself, the Freehold was co-held by A and B: see **G2:Example 18**).

[99] [2007] EWCA Civ 1212.

[100] [1984] Ch 317.

[101] [2007] 2 AC 432 at [32].

[102] [2007] EWCA Civ 1212.

[103] Although it was found on the facts of that case no Constructive Trust arose: it could not be inferred that A and B had intended B to have a share of the benefit of A's Freehold: see *per* Sir John Chadwick at [27].

[104] See too **G2:2.2.1(ii)**.

question as to whether the common intention Constructive Trust can arise if A and B cohabit not as lovers but as friends, work colleagues or relatives.[105]

Second, there is a problem with *applying* the common intention Constructive Trust. Consider the common case where: (i) A and B, lovers, live together; and (ii) A is the sole holder of a Freehold of that land; and (iii) there is no signed writing that B can use to show he has a right under an Express Trust of A's Freehold or Lease; and (iv) there have been no express discussions between A and B showing a common intention that B should have a share of the benefit of A's Freehold. In such a case, a court, applying the *Stack* approach, can look at a wide list of factors to see if it can infer such a common intention. However, it is very unlikely that A and B have *any* common intention as to whether B should have a share of the benefit of A's Freehold; much less as to the *size* of that share.[106] In fact, A and B may have deliberately avoided forming a common intention about a technical issue that arises only when their relationship ends.[107]

For example, in *Midland Bank v Cooke*,[108] B had made a direct financial contribution to the purchase price of A's Freehold.[109] However, A and B did *not* have any shared intention about whether B should have a share of the benefit of A's Freehold; they simply had not thought about that question. Indeed, when A was asked in court whether he and B had discussed their rights in their home, he poignantly replied 'No. We were just happy, I suppose, you know.'[110] However, Waite LJ went so far as to say that:

> [P]ositive evidence that the parties neither discussed nor intended any agreement as to the proportions of their beneficial interest does not preclude the court, on general equitable principles, from inferring one.[111]

That statement starkly exposes the often fictional nature of the common intention Constructive Trust. It is clearly nonsense for a judge to say that an agreement between A and B can be *inferred* if we *know* that no such agreement was made: if there is really positive evidence that A and B did not reach any express or implied agreement, there should be no common intention Constructive Trust.[112] The danger is that the courts will then *impute* a common intention: instead of finding, from the facts of the case, that A and B genuinely had a common intention, the courts will fill the evidential gap by holding that A and B *should* have had such an intention; or *would* have had such an intention if they had considered the question of whether B should have a share of the benefit of A's Freehold or Lease.[113] Indeed, in *Stack v Dowden*, both Lord Walker and Baroness Hale suggested that a

---

[105] In *Adekunle v Ritchie* [2007] EW Misc 5, (Leeds County Court, August 2007) HHJ Behrens considered that the common intention Constructive Trust applied in a case where A and B were mother and son (although note there A and B were co-holders of the Freehold).

[106] See eg Gardner (1993) 109 *LQR* 263.

[107] As noted by eg Lord Hodson in *Pettitt v Pettitt* [1970] AC 777 at 810: 'The concept of a normal married couple spending the long winter evenings hammering out agreements about their possession appears grotesque.'

[108] [1995] 2 FLR 915.

[109] The contribution took a slightly unusual form: a wedding gift from A's parents.

[110] *Midland Bank v Cooke* [1995] 2 FLR 915 at 920.

[111] *Ibid* at 928.

[112] It may be that Waite LJ meant to make the different and unobjectionable point that positive evidence that there was no *express* bargain between A and B does not prevent a court inferring an *implied* bargain.

[113] See *per* Lord Neuberger in *Stack v Dowden* [2007] 2 AC 432 at [126]: 'Imputation involves concluding what the parties would have intended, whereas inference involves concluding what they did intend.'

court can *impute* A and B's common intention.[114] However, as we noted in **G2:2.2.1(ii)**, and as Lord Neuberger persuasively stated in *Stack v Dowden*,[115] it is illegitimate for judges to manufacture a common intention in this way.

This key point has been made many times before, both by judges[116] and commentators;[117] but it is worth emphasising. The common intention Constructive Trust, along with the special results it produces in cases such as **Examples 4a, 4b and 4c**, is supposedly justified by the existence of A and B's common intention that B should have a share of the benefit of A's Freehold or Lease. Yet, in almost all cases where A is the sole holder of a Freehold or Lease, and no express statement has been made that B is to have a share of the benefit of that right, there will simply be *no* such common intention. From one perspective, this may not be such a problem. It could be argued that common intention is simply used as an artificial mechanism to enable judges to achieve a fair result: it does not matter that it is a fictional concept. However, in *Stack v Dowden*, the House of Lords made very clear that the common intention Constructive Trust *cannot* be used as a vehicle for a judge simply to reach a 'fair' result. Rather, it has to be based on the common intention of the parties.[118] This means that, in many cases, the common intention Constructive Trust rests on fictional foundations.

This leads on to a further problem with *applying* the common intention Constructive Trust. Given that, in practice, there will often be no genuine common intention for a court to discover, how can we predict when such an intention will be found? The former *Lloyds Bank plc v Rosset* approach,[119] whilst quite restrictive, did at least provide a clear guide to the parties and their legal advisers. That clarity is particularly important given the particular context of disputes about the family home. First, as in *Rosset*, B may claim a right under a Trust in order to show that he has a right that is capable of binding C, a party who acquired a right from A. There is a strong argument for giving C, both before and after acquiring his right, a chance to discover any pre-existing persistent right of B. C does, of course, receive important protection through the **defences question**: even if B does have a pre-existing right under a Trust, C may be able to rely on the overreaching defence (see **E2:3.4**) or the lack of registration defence (see **E2:3.6**). However, if the crucial question of whether B has a right under a Trust depends on the outcome of a court's inferences (or even imputations) as to A and B's intentions, C's position is a very difficult one.

Second, even if no third party is involved (as in eg *Burns v Burns*),[120] there is still a need for certainty and predictability. If A and B are lovers who have split up, there may be a good deal of hostility between them. This ill-will can led to time-consuming litigation that may end up costing more than the value of the disputed Freehold or Lease. And if the outcome of a dispute is uncertain, the chances of settlement are reduced. Moreover, if, as the *Stack* approach suggests, B can use *any* evidence to prove his case, he will be able to ask a court to

---

114 [2007] 2 AC 432 at [33] and [60]. This is confirmed, and applied to a case where A was the sole Freehold owner, in *Abbott v Abbott* [2007] UKPC 53: see *per* Baroness Hale at [6].

115 [2007] 2 AC 432 at [126]–[127].

116 See eg *per* Dickson J in *Pettkus v Becker* (1980) 117 DLR (3d) 257 at 269 (Supreme Court of Canada) referring to the hunt for a 'phantom or fugitive common intent'.

117 See esp Gardner (1993) 109 *LQR* 263.

118 See eg *per* Baroness Hale at [61] and *per* Chadwick LJ in *James v Thomas* [2007] EWCA Civ 1212 at [38].

119 [1991] 1 AC 107 *per* Lord Bridge at 132–3.

120 [1984] Ch 317.

pick through the rubble of the parties' relationship to find any shred of evidence of a common intention. The *Rosset* approach, whilst restrictive, had the benefits of simplicity and certainty: if B could not produce bank statements to show a direct financial contribution to the purchase price or mortgage payments, his claim for a inferred common intention Constructive Trust would fail.

A good example of the potential difficulties with the wider *Stack* approach is provided by *James v Thomas*.[121] A and B had cohabited as lovers for almost 15 years: A was the sole Freehold owner. B did not make any direct financial contributions to the purchase price or mortgage payments. However, B made extensive contributions to a business run by A, and eventually became a partner in the business. Profits from the business were used by A to make mortgage payments. B also assisted in improvements that were made to the land. On the *Rosset* approach, it is clear that a court cannot infer a common intention: B made no *direct* financial contribution to the purchase price or mortgage payments. On the *Stack* approach, a court has to look at all the relevant facts and make an inference (or even an imputation) as to the parties' intentions. In *James*, the Court of Appeal found that a common intention could *not* be inferred. Sir John Chadwick stated that, in *some cases*, B's contribution to mortgage payments *could* be used to infer such an intention; but, in *this particular case*, that inference could not be made.[122] A had to use the business profits to make the mortgage payments: it was his only source of income. So the fact that the mortgage had been paid with profits for which B was partly responsible did *not* lead to an inference that B was intended to have a share of the benefit of A's Freehold.

Different views can be taken on the result in *James v Thomas*. On the one hand, it may seem very harsh that, like Mrs Burns, Miss James left a long relationship without any share of the benefit of A's Freehold. On the other, Miss James would at least receive some financial protection in her capacity as a partner in the business: on the dissolution of that business partnership, she would be entitled to a share of the assets (if any) of the partnership. However, the point is *not* whether the result is 'fair': that will depend on your particular views of what fairness demands. Rather, the question here is whether the result is *predictable*: in particular, if the case had been allocated to a different judge, would the result have been the same? In *James*, it is all too plausible that a different judge may: (i) have taken a different view of the significance of B's contributions; and so (ii) have inferred (or even imputed) a common intention. And the land law system is in a bad shape if the key question of whether B has a pre-existing persistent right comes down to the personal views of a particular judge.[123]

Third, there is a problem as to the *doctrinal justification* of the common intention Constructive Trust. This problem has two aspects. First, why should *any* special rules apply in 'family home' cases where A and B live together in land owned by A? In fact, in an important decision,[124] the House of Lords made very clear that B's claim to a share of the

---

[121] [2007] EWCA Civ 1212.

[122] *Ibid* at [27].

[123] It is worth noting that one of the factors identified by Baroness Hale (see *Stack v Dowden* [2007] 2 AC 432 at [69]) as relevant to finding an inferred common intention is 'the parties' individual characters and personalities'. This suggests that A could argue that, even though B made extensive contributions to mortgage payments, as A is a well-known chauvinist, he did not intend that B, his girlfriend, would have a share of the benefit of his Freehold or Lease. Or B could argue that, despite his minimal contributions, A and B did intend that B would have such a share as A is well-known for her liberal views and commitment to fairness in wealth distribution.

[124] *Pettitt v Pettitt* [1970] AC 777 as confirmed by *Gissing v Gissing* [1971] 1 AC 886.

benefit of a family home should *not* be governed by special rules. Rather, B's claim should succeed if, and only if, B can use one of the *generally available* means of showing that A is under the core Trust duty to B.

Further, if the requirements of the common intention Constructive Trust are made out, *why* should B acquire a right under a Constructive Trust?[125] The requirements are very close to those of proprietary estoppel: the Constructive Trust seems to depend on the need to ensure that B does not suffer a detriment as a result of his reasonable reliance on a commitment made by A.[126] On this view, a court, when seeing if a common intention can be inferred, is in effect asking if A made an *implied* commitment to give B a share of the benefit of A's Freehold or Lease. However, if this is the true basis of the common intention Constructive Trust, then it should *not* be the case that A's implied commitment is necessarily enforced, or even that B necessarily acquires a right under a Constructive Trust. Rather, A's duty to B should be limited to ensuring that B does not suffer a detriment as a result of his reasonable reliance on A's commitment (see **E4:4.3**).

(d) A way forward?

First, consider **Example 4b**. In such a case, there is no need to apply the difficult concept of a common intention Constructive Trust. Instead, the doctrine of proprietary estoppel should impose a duty on A. The fact that A and B are cohabiting partners does not mean that any special principle needs to apply.

For example, in *Ottey v Grundy*,[127] A and B were lovers and lived together in a variety of homes all owned by A: a flat in Jamaica; a houseboat moored in London; and a house in Hampshire. A made a very specific commitment, recorded in (unsigned) writing: on his death, B would acquire his Lease of the flat in Jamaica and a life interest in the houseboat. B argued that she had relied on that commitment by caring for A (who had an alcohol problem) and giving up her own career. B's argument was accepted both by the first instance judge and the Court of Appeal. Throughout, B's claim was treated as depending on proprietary estoppel. As a result, there was no assumption that A was automatically under a duty to honour his commitment to B. In fact, instead of being under a duty to give B the flat in Jamaica and a life interest in the houseboat (worth a combined total of £250,000), A was under a duty to pay B £50,000 and to use his best endeavours to transfer the flat in Jamaica to B.[128]

It was easy for the courts to see *Ottey v Grundy* as a proprietary estoppel case: A's commitment was not made when A and B set up home together and did not involve B acquiring an immediate share of the benefit of A's land.[129] If the case had instead been seen

---

[125] See eg Swadling (2007) 123 *LQR* 511.

[126] The common intention Constructive Trust stems from Lord Diplock's speech in *Gissing v Gissing* [1971] 1 AC 886. His Lordship's description of it (at 905) reads very much like the application of proprietary estoppel principles to a case where B has performed his side of an informal bargain with A. This may explain the assumption that A is under a duty to honour his commitment to B (see **E4:4.4**).

[127] [2003] EWCA Civ 1176.

[128] If A (now A's executor as A had died) was unable to procure the transfer of the flat, A had to pay B a further £50,000. This suggests that the flat was valued at £50,000 and that the rights acquired by B through proprietary estoppel were worth £100,000 in total—less than half the combined value of the rights A *promised* B.

[129] See too *Pascoe v Turner* [1979] 1 WLR 431: as A's commitment was made at the end of A and B's relationship, the court applied proprietary estoppel principles. Although the Court of Appeal held that A *was* under a duty to honour his commitment, it is clear that the result was not automatic: the court considered a number of different factors before reaching that conclusion.

as giving rise to a common intention Constructive Trust, the court may have assumed that that A's express commitment would have to be enforced.[130] However, whilst such a result if often assumed, there seems to be no binding authority to that effect.

EXAMPLE 4bi

The facts are as in **Example 4b**. The difference is that A makes a commitment to give B an *unspecified* share of the benefit of A's Freehold.

In such a case, the proprietary estoppel analysis fits perfectly with the common intention Constructive Trust approach. Currently, a court looks at the relevant factors to determine: (i) *if* A and B had a common intention that B should have a share of the benefit of the Freehold; and, if so (ii) *what* share B was intended to have. As B's conduct is vital in determining the extent of B's right, that right, in effect, depends on the need to prevent B suffering a detriment as a result of A's refusal to honour his commitment to B. For example, *Eves v Eves* (**E2:Example 9a**),[131] A and B were cohabiting partners. It was found that A had made an express commitment to give B an unspecified share of the benefit of A's Freehold. Due to her reliance on that commitment, B acquired a 25 per cent share of the benefit of A's Freehold. In quantifying B's right, Brightman J looked at what B had done in reliance on A's commitment (undertaking substantial improvements to the house) and asked what size of share A and B are likely to have regarded as a reasonable reward for that conduct.[132] In such a case, as noted by Chadwick LJ in *Oxley v Hiscock*:[133]

> it seems to me very difficult to avoid the conclusion that an analysis in terms of proprietary estoppel will, necessarily, lead to the same result [as under a common intention Constructive Trust analysis].

The proprietary estoppel analysis may also be useful in cases where A makes *no* express commitment, but the courts find an inferred common intention. Of course, in such cases, the particular factual background is important: it matters that A and B are lovers rather than simply business partners.[134] However, this is not because of any special legal principle; rather, that *factual* difference is relevant to the *factual* question of whether A can be found to have made an implied commitment to give B a share of the benefit of A's Freehold or Lease. It may be unlikely that one business partner would make such a commitment; but, where A's Freehold or Lease is viewed as a joint home for A and B, it may be reasonable for B to believe, despite the lack of an express promise by A, that A is committed to allowing B a share of the benefit of that Freehold or Lease.

Similarly, the proprietary estoppel approach could even be used in a case such as **Example 4a**. If we were to forget about the common intention Constructive Trust, B could

---

[130] See eg *per* Baroness Hale in *Stack v Dowden* [2007] 2 AC 432 at [61]; eg *per* Chadwick LJ in *Oxley v Hiscock* [2005] Fam 211 at [69].

[131] [1975] 1 WLR 1338.

[132] *Ibid* at 1346. Lord Denning MR reached the same conclusion without much in the way of explanation. His Lordship commented in particular (at 1342H–1343B) on the fact that B had since married (presumably reducing her share) and also on the fact that she was looking after children she had had with A (presumably increasing her share). Neither of those factors should be relevant to determining B's pre-existing right: they relate to the future needs of B, not to the past events on which her claim is based.

[133] [2005] Fam 211 at [66].

[134] See eg *per* Baroness Hale in *Stack v Dowden* [2007] 2 AC 432 at [69]: 'context is everything'.

acquire a right under a Resulting Trust (see **2.2.4** above). However, it might also be possible for B to rely on proprietary estoppel, in order to impose a duty on A going beyond the extent of A's unjust enrichment at B's expense. B may be able to show that: (i) A made an implied commitment to B (B can rely at least in part on his £10,000 contribution to the purchase price to do so); and (ii) B reasonably relied on that commitment *not only* through his financial commitment but through other reliance (eg, giving up a job to move in with A). If so, the need to prevent B suffering a detriment may mean that A is under a duty to give B a share of the benefit of A's Freehold *greater than* the 5 per cent contribution made by B's £10,000 payment.

On this view, there is no need for the common intention Constructive Trust. *If* B's proprietary estoppel claim imposes a duty on A to use A's Freehold or Lease, to a certain extent, for B's benefit, B will acquire a right under a Constructive Trust. However, that Constructive Trust will arise because of proprietary estoppel (as in **2.4.3(iv)** above); not because of any special principle applying only to cohabiting partners.

Similarly, there would be no need for the common intention Constructive Trust in a case such as *Stack v Dowden*.[135] If A and B co-hold the Freehold or Lease, the general approach, applying *whenever* A and B co-hold a right, should be applied (see **F2:2.2.1(ii)**). The parties' rights are determined by their shared intention. However, if there are no express discussions showing that intention, the default rule applies: each of A and B is jointly entitled, in his capacity as a member of the co-owning team, to the full benefit of the Freehold or Lease. That default rule is displaced if A and B make unequal contributions to the costs of paying for the right (ie, to the purchase price or mortgage payments): then, following Lord Neuberger's analysis in *Stack v Dowden*,[136] the parties may each acquire his own individual right, based on the extent of his contribution to those payments. The Trust arising in such a case is *not* a common intention Constructive Trust: instead it can be seen either as a Resulting Trust (Lord Neuberger's view in *Stack*); or a Trust arising because of the need to give effect to the fact that A and B intended that each would have an individual right to the benefit of their co-held Freehold or Lease.[137]

(e) Advantages of the proposed new model

The key advantage of the new model lies in its ability to *justify* the results currently reached by using the common intention Constructive Trust. In particular, proprietary estoppel is a recognised means by which A can come under a duty to B, applying throughout the land law system. It does *not* force the courts to make an unprincipled and unstable distinction between: (i) cases where A and B are cohabiting partners; and (ii) other cases. This link between proprietary estoppel and the common intention Constructive Trust has frequently been noted by judges[138] and commentators:[139] there is no reason not to give it full effect.

---

135 [2007] 2 AC 432 (see **G2:Example 18**).

136 *Ibid* at [111]–[122].

137 That intention has to lead to a Trust as it is impossible for either A or B to have an individual share of the Freehold or Lease itself (see **G2:1.2.1**).

138 See eg *per* Browne-Wilkinson V-C in *Grant v Edwards* [1986] Ch 638 at 656; *per* Lord Oliver in *Austin v Keele* [1987] ALJR 605 (PC) at 609; *per* Nourse LJ in *Stokes v Anderson* [1991] 1 FLR 391; *per* Robert Walker LJ in *Yaxley v Gotts* [2000] Ch 162 at 177; *per* Chadwick LJ in *Oxley v Hiscock* [2005] Fam 211 at [66].

139 See eg Hayton [1990] *Conv* 370 and (1993) 109 *LQR* 114. See Ferguson (1993) 109 *LQR* 114 for a different view.

However, in *Stack v Dowden*, Lord Walker expressed the *obiter* view that the common intention Constructive Trust *cannot* be seen as an application of proprietary estoppel principles.[140] His Lordship's doubts seem to be based on two points. First, the fear that, if B's right arises under proprietary estoppel, it may not be capable of binding C, a third party acquiring a right from A before a court order is made in B's favour.[141] This fear is based on the orthodox view that, if B makes a proprietary estoppel claim, he initially acquires only an 'equity by estoppel':[142] he cannot acquire a persistent right, such as a right under a Trust, until a court rules in his favour (see **E4:6.2**). However, as we saw in **E4:6.3**, that view is mistaken. If proprietary estoppel imposes a duty on A, B's right arises before any court order in his favour: it arises as soon as the facts constituting B's claim have occurred. And, in any case, section 116(a) of the Land Registration Act 2002 now confirms that B's 'equity by estoppel' *is* capable of binding C. So, contrary to Lord Walker's fear, reanalysing common intention Constructive Trusts in terms of proprietary estoppel does *not* prevent B acquiring a right under a Trust before any court order in B's favour.

Second, Lord Walker seems to be concerned that, if B's right arises under proprietary estoppel, A may be ordered to pay money to B: in such a case, B cannot acquire a right under a Trust of A's Freehold or Lease. However, this is a *strength* of the proprietary estoppel approach. If it is the case that the payment of money by A to B will prevent B suffering a detriment, there is simply no need for B to acquire a right under a Trust of A's Freehold or Lease. The current assumption that the shared intention of A and B *must* be enforced, whilst it gives an advantage to B, cannot be doctrinally justified: if A's duty arises in order to prevent B suffering a detriment, it would be disproportionate for A's duty to go beyond what is necessary to prevent that detriment (see **E4:4.3**). There is no reason why things should be different simply because A and B happen to be co-habiting partners.

(f) Problems with the proposed new model?

The chief aim of the new model is to deal with the *doctrinal* problems posed by the courts' current approach. However, the common intention Constructive Trust has frequently been attacked from the perspective of *practical convenience* (see **B:9**). In particular, it has been argued that, in a case such as *Burns v Burns*,[143] it is unfair for the courts to refuse to recognise that B has a right under a Trust of A's Freehold or Lease.[144] The new model proposed here does *not* address that concern. On that model, if no Resulting Trust arises (as A has not made a direct financial contribution to the purchase price or, perhaps, the mortgage payments: see **2.3.3** above), A should only come under a duty to B if A has made an implied commitment to give B a share of the benefit of the Freehold or Lease. Many of the factors mentioned by Baroness Hale (eg, the nature of the parties' relationship; whether they had children) are irrelevant to that question.

Of course, it is very difficult to say whether, in cases such as *Burns v Burns*, B *should* have a right under a Trust of A's Freehold or Lease. That depends on the answer to the impossibly difficult questions of: (i) who is entitled to use land? and (ii) how are they entitled to use it?

---

[140] [2007] 2 AC 432 at [37].
[141] This fear was first raised by Ferguson (1993) 109 *LQR* 114.
[142] As Lord Walker put it at [37]: a 'mere equity'.
[143] [1984] Ch 317.
[144] See eg Eekelaar [1987] *Conv* 93; Gardner (1993) 109 *LQR* 263; Rotherham [2004] *Conv* 268; Probert [2005] *Conv* 168. See too Part 4 of the Law Commission's 2006 Consultation Paper No 179.

(See **A:3**.) However, it is important to note that the Law Commission, having considered the issue in great detail, chose *not* to recommend any statutory changes to the existing rules regulating the common intention Constructive Trust.[145] Of course, the Commission was aware of the widespread disapproval of those rules; and it did agree that in, cases such as *Burns v Burns*, B should have some financial protection. However, in its Report No 307 (2007), the Law Commission proposed that B's protection should *not* consist of the courts recognising that B has a pre-existing right under a Trust of A's Freehold or Lease. Rather, it should come from the court having a power to impose a duty on A to provide financial relief to B. A court could thus ensure that, on the breakdown of the relationship, A has a duty to give B financial protection[146] that takes into account: (i) any detriment B has suffered as a result of his contributions to the relationship; or (ii) any benefits A has gained as a result of B's contributions.[147]

Of course, only a statute can give judges such a power to impose a duty on A. The statute would have to answer difficult issues concerning: (i) *when* the court should have a power to impose such a duty on A;[148] and (ii) *what* the extent of A's duty should be.[149] It is worth noting that Parliament has already intervened to give B similar[150] protection in similar contexts. First, in 1970, Parliament gave the judges such a discretion in divorce proceedings.[151] For example, even if B cannot establish that he has a share of his wife's Freehold the court, in setting the spouses' rights for the future, can: (i) divide the benefit of the Freehold between A and B; and/or (ii) order A to pay money to B. Parliament gave judges that power because it obviously felt that the means by which B can acquire a share of the benefit of A's Freehold or Lease—including the common intention Constructive Trust —did not give B enough protection on the breakdown of a marriage.[152] Second, even if A and B are not married, if: (i) the relationship ends due to A's death; and (ii) A's will does not give B adequate financial protection; then (iii) the courts have a statutory power to give B financial support from A's estate.[153]

The Law Commission's proposals should be welcomed. They recognise that the perceived unfairness in cases such as *Burns v Burns* may come *not* from the fact that B has no right under a Trust but, instead, from the fact that B has to leave the relationship empty-handed. The important point is that the law is not unfair in a general sense: it is *inconsistent*. It is difficult to explain why B is not entitled to financial protection when such protection would have been available if: (i) A and B had been married; or (ii) A had died. Parliament, by giving judges a power to impose a duty on A in those cases, has *already* recognised the need

---

[145] See Law Com No 307 at 2.16.

[146] That protection can take the form of A transferring a Freehold or Lease to B, or giving B a share of the benefit of A's Freehold or Lease. In such a case, B does acquire a property right or persistent right; but only after a court order giving B that protection.

[147] Law Com No 307, Part IV esp at 4.32–4.42.

[148] See Law Com No 307, Part III esp at 3.13; 3.31 and 3.45.

[149] See Law Com No 307, Part IV esp at 4.32–4.42.

[150] The Law Commission do *not* propose that the scheme applying to cohabiting partners should be exactly the same as that applying on divorce: see Law Com No 306 at 4.5–4.10.

[151] Under the Matrimonial Proceedings and Property Act 1970. The jurisdiction is now governed by the Matrimonial Causes Act 1973 (as amended). See eg *White v White* [2001] 1 AC 596.

[152] Indeed, the 1970 Act can be seen, in part, as a reaction to the decision in *Pettitt v Pettitt* [1970] 1 AC 777 insisting that, on the breakdown of their marriage, the spouses' rights in relation to marital property were determined by their pre-existing entitlements.

[153] Under the Inheritance (Provision for Family and Dependants) Act 1975.

to protect B where: (i) he has based his life and financial decisions around a relationship with A; and (ii) that relationship ends. Given that need, statutory protection should also be available in cases such as *Burns v Burns*.

The Law Commission's proposals also recognise the point that the land law system cannot meet the need to protect B in such cases. First, that system has to take into account the needs of C: the **basic tension** means that a court cannot simply recognise that B has a pre-existing right under a Trust whenever it might feel it is fair to do so.[154] Second, the need for B to receive financial protection from A may apply even in a case where A does *not* have a valuable Freehold or Lease. For example, if: (i) A and B have lived together for a long period, in a house owned by A's parents; and (ii) B has made significant contributions to that relationship; and (iii) that relationship ends; then (iv) as A does not hold a Freehold or Lease, B cannot claim a right under a Trust. Yet B may still deserve to receive financial relief from A (eg, where B's contributions have allowed A to build up a successful business): only a statutory scheme can enable B to receive such relief.

(g) Consequences of the Law Commission's proposals

If the Law Commission's proposals were adopted, there would still be cases in which B wishes to claim a right under a Trust of a Freehold or Lease held by his cohabiting partner. First, the proposals allow a court to impose a duty on A; they do not mean that A is under a duty to B *before* a court order in B's favour. So, if: (i) A gives C a right in relation to the land *before* any court order (eg, before the end of A and B's relationship); and (ii) B wants to show he has a pre-existing right capable of binding C; then (iii) B may claim he has a right under a Trust of A's Freehold or Lease. This explains why, even if A and B are married and B is thus protected by the current divorce legislation, B may wish to claim a pre-existing right under a Trust.[155] Second, even if no third party is involved, B may claim such a pre-existing right in order to give him a guaranteed share of the benefit of A's Freehold or Lease. Particularly in a case where the land has increased in value, B may believe that he will do better by claiming he has a share of the benefit of A's Freehold or Lease rather than by asking a court to impose a statutory duty on A to give B financial relief.[156]

The Law Commission's proposals, if enacted, could nonetheless have an important impact on the principles regulating B's claim to a right under a Trust. Given the alternative statutory protection available to B, a court would feel less pressure to infer (or even impute) a common intention that B should have a share of the benefit of A's Freehold or Lease. Indeed, given that B would claim such a right: (i) where he wants to show he has a pre-existing right capable of binding C; and (ii) where he wants to take advantage of the value of A's Freehold or Lease; then (iii) the courts would be justified in *limiting* the circumstances in which a common intention could be inferred. To provide certainty for C, and to ensure B only acquires a share of the increased value of A's right where he has contributed to its acquisition, the courts could find that a common intention should only be inferred where B makes a direct financial contribution to the purchase price or mortgage payments. That would of course take us back to the restrictive *Rosset* test and so avoid some of the problems

---

[154] See Law Com No 307 at 2.16; *per* Baroness Hale at [61] and *per* Chadwick LJ in *James v Thomas* [2007] EWCA Civ 1212 at [38].

[155] As was the case in eg *Lloyds Bank v Rosset* [1991] 1 AC 107 and *Midland Bank v Cooke* [1995] 2 FLR 915.

[156] The Law Commission proposed that it should be *impossible* for B both to: (i) claim a pre-existing right under a Trust; *and* (ii) to claim that A should be under a duty to give B financial relief (see Law Com No 307 at 4.132–4.146).

that the wider *Stack* approach may bring (see (c) above). Indeed, it would give the courts a further reason to adopt the model suggested here and to apply standard proprietary estoppel or Resulting Trust principles when assessing whether B has a right under a Trust of A's Freehold or Lease.

There is an irony here. Just as the Law Commission proposed reforms that might justify the restrictive *Rosset* test, the House of Lords in *Stack* rejected that test. However, the latest indication from the Government is that it is *not* currently planning to enact the Law Commission's proposals.[157] Certainly, those proposals are likely to encounter political objections: in particular, they may be seen, in some quarters, to undermine the importance of marriage.[158] The Government's failure to support the Law Commission's proposals is unfortunate. As a result, we are left with the unfortunate sight of judges having to use the common intention Constructive Trust, an ungainly and suspect mechanism, to protect B where he has based his life and financial decisions around a relationship which has ended.

SUMMARY of G3:2.4.3(v)

The common intention Constructive Trust plays an important practical role: according to the majority of the House of Lords in *Stack v Dowden* it seems to be the *only* means by which B can acquire a right under a non-Express Trust of a Freehold or Lease held by A, B's cohabiting partner. However, there are significant problems with this form of Constructive Trust. In theory, there is no obvious reason why: (i) A should come under a duty to B *simply* as a result of A and B's shared intention; or (ii) cases involving cohabiting partners should be treated differently from other cases. And in practice, there are cases, such as *Midland Bank v Cooke*, where A and B do *not* in fact have such a shared intention, but a Constructive Trust arises nonetheless.

It has therefore been argued that the common intention Constructive Trust should be dispensed with: even if A and B are cohabiting lovers, B's claim to have acquired a right under a Trust of A's Freehold or Lease should be judged by applying the same principles that apply in all other cases. In particular: (i) B can acquire a right under a Resulting Trust if he has made a direct financial contribution to the purchase price of A's Freehold or Lease (or, perhaps, to A's mortgage payments: see 2.3.3 above); and (ii) B can acquire a right through proprietary estoppel if he has reasonably relied on an express or implied commitment by A to give B a share of the benefit of A's Freehold or Lease. On this model, there would still be cases, such as *Burns v Burns*, where: (i) B does *not* acquire a right under a Trust of A's Freehold or Lease; but (ii) B may nevertheless deserve some financial protection. In such a case, a statutory scheme, along the lines proposed by the Law Commission, should be introduced so as to give a court the power to impose a duty on A to provide financial relief to B.

SUMMARY of G3:2

If A has a Freehold or Lease, special rules have to be taken into account when considering if A has come under the core Trust duty to B:

---

[157] See http://www.justice.gov.uk/news/announcement060308a.htm for the statement of the Minister for Justice (6 March 2008).

[158] See the comments noted in Law Com No 307 at 2.27. Given the existing provisions under the Inheritance (Provision for Family and Dependants) Act 1975, it is unclear whether the proposals are also regarded as undermining the importance of death.

- To show he has a right under an Express Trust of a Freehold or Lease, B must provide some writing signed by A (or, in a case where A0 has transferred a Freehold or Lease to A, signed by A0): see section 53(1)(b) of the LPA 1925.
- It may be that B can acquire a right under a Resulting Trust of a Freehold or Lease *without* showing that he has contributed to the purchase price of that right. It *may* be enough for B to show that he has contributed to A's mortgage payments.
- To show that a Constructive Trust has arisen as a result of A's contractual promise to set up a Trust of a Freehold or Lease, or to transfer such a right to B, B must show that the formality rule set out by section 2(1) of the Law of Property (Miscellaneous Provisions) Act 1989 has been satisfied.
- However, to show A is under the core Trust duty as a result of the 'receipt after a promise' principle or the doctrine of proprietary estoppel, B does not need to satisfy a formality rule. If, and only if, B can rely on such a principle to impose the core Trust duty on A, a Constructive Trust arises.
- If A and B are cohabiting partners, a Constructive Trust of A's Freehold or Lease also arises if B has relied on a common intention of both B and A that B is to have a share of the benefit of A's right. On the argument made here, any such 'common intention' Constructive Trust can better be seen as based on either: (i) the need to avoid A's unjust enrichment (in which case B should instead acquire a right under a Resulting Trust); or (ii) the doctrine of proprietary estoppel (in which case there should not always be a Constructive Trust in B's favour).

3   THE DEFENCES QUESTION

In **E2:3** we examined the general defences that C may be able to use against a persistent right relating to land. Where B's right arises under a Trust of a Freehold or Lease, C may use *any* of those defences. The most important defences in practice are: (i) the overreaching defence (see **E2:3.4**); and (ii) the lack of registration defence (see **E2:3.6**).

Each defence applies in a special way where B's persistent right arises under a Trust. If A holds a Freehold or Lease on Trust for B:

- *A has a statutory power to give C a right free from B's pre-existing right under a Trust.*[159] Therefore, if C satisfies the provisions of section 27 of the LPA 1925 when acquiring his right, he will be able to use the overreaching defence against B's pre-existing right under the Trust.
- *It is impossible for B to protect his right from the lack of registration defence by entering a notice on the register.*[160] Therefore, if C acquires a property right for value and substantively registers it, B's pre-existing right under a Trust can bind C only if B is in actual occupation of the land when C commits to acquiring his right.

---

[159] S 6 of the Trusts of Land and Appointment of Trustees Act 1996
[160] Land Registration Act 2002, s 33(a)(i). B may be able to enter a restriction on the register (see **E2:3.4.2(i)**).

4   THE REMEDIES QUESTION

4.1   Where A is under a duty to use a Freehold or Lease entirely for B's benefit

If: (i) A is under a duty to use a Freehold or Lease *entirely* for B's benefit; and (ii) A, acting without B's consent or other authority, gives C a right that depends on A's Freehold or Lease (eg, A transfers that Freehold or Lease to C); and (iii) C has no defence to B's pre-existing persistent right; then (iv) B has a power to assert his right under the Trust against C. In such a case, the discussion of the remedies question in **F3:4** applies.

The facts of *Hodgson v Marks*[161] provide an example. B transferred her Freehold to A. As there was no basis for A to have any of the benefit of that right, A held it on Resulting Trust for B. A then transferred his Freehold to C. When B asserted her pre-existing persistent right against C, C came under the core Trust duty to B. As a result, B was (presumably)[162] able to obtain the remedy she had asked for: an order that C must transfer his Freehold directly to B (see **D1:1.4.5(ii)**).[163]

4.2   Where A is under a duty to use a Freehold or Lease partly for B's benefit

E2:EXAMPLE 27

A has a Freehold. A buys that Freehold with the help of money provided by B. As B does not intend a gift of that money, and there is no other legal basis for A to have its benefit, A holds that Freehold on Trust for both A and B. A, in return for a loan from C Bank and without B's consent or other authority, gives C Bank a Charge over the land. A then fails to repay the loan as agreed. C Bank wants to: (i) remove A and B from the land; and (ii) sell the land; and (iii) use the proceeds of sale to meet A's debt.

In such a case, *each* of A and B has a right under the Trust of A's Freehold. Therefore, even though B's pre-existing right under the Trust binds C Bank (as confirmed by *Williams & Glyn's Bank v Boland*,[164] on which **E2:Example 27** is based), the nature of the Trust means that C Bank, like A, is permitted to use a share of the value of the Freehold for its own benefit. C Bank and B are likely to have a dispute about the use of the land: (i) C Bank will wish to sell, so that it can get at the financial value of A's right under the Trust; whereas (ii) B will wish to remain on the land. In resolving that dispute, a court has to take into account the factors set out by section 15 of the 1996 Act.

We considered a very similar dispute in **G2:4**, when looking at the position where B has not only a right under a Trust, but is also a co-holder with A of a Freehold or Lease. We saw there that, even if children are occupying along with B, C Bank's application for sale will succeed *unless* C Bank's financial position can be secured in some other way (eg, by B making regular payments to C Bank).[165] In particular: (i) section 15(1)(d) of the 1996 Act

---

[161] [1971] 1 Ch 892.

[162] The Court of Appeal did not make a specific order. Russell LJ at 935 simply stated that B's appeal should be allowed 'with such order as may be consequential' on B showing that her right under the Resulting Trust bound C.

[163] Before learning of B's right, C had granted C2 a Charge over the land. It seems C was ordered to transfer the Freehold back to B free from that Charge. As each of C and C2 had acquired a right from a registered party, each qualified for an indemnity payment from the Land Registry (see **E5:3.2.3**).

[164] [1981] AC 413.

[165] See eg *Bank of Ireland v Bell* [2001] 2 FLR 809; *First National Bank v Achampong* [2004] 1 FCR 18.

specifically instructs a court to take into account the interests of C Bank: a secured creditor of a beneficiary of the Trust; and (ii) if A goes into bankruptcy, section 335A(3) of the Insolvency Act states that, once a year has passed, a sale will be ordered unless the 'circumstances of the case are exceptional.'

The principles set out in **G2:4**, depressing as they may be to B, apply in exactly the same way to a case such as **E2:Example 27**. Certainly, there is no reason for the courts to be any more favourable to B in a case where, rather than *both* (i) having a right under a Trust; and (ii) co-holding a Freehold or Lease, B has *only* a right under a Trust of A's Freehold or Lease.

CHAPTER G4
SECURITY

G4

SECURITY

---

1 INTRODUCTION

1.1 The special features of land

We can define a security right (see **F4:1.2.1**) as:

- a property right; a persistent right; or a power to acquire a persistent right
- that arises as a means to protect B if a duty owed to B is not performed.

The special features of land (see **A:3:1**) mean that a security right relating to land can be particularly useful to B. Given its capacity for multiple simultaneous use, its social importance and its limited availability, if A has a right to exclusive control of land (ie, a Freehold or Lease) A's right may well be very valuable. Therefore, if A has a Freehold worth £200,000, a security right in relation to A's Freehold can give B useful protection even if he loans A £100,000. The permanence and uniqueness of a piece of land both contribute to its value and enhance B's security right. If B's security right relates to a thing such as a bike, B will face a problem if that bike is destroyed or lost: B's security right in the bike will be of no practical value. If B's security right relates to land, things are different: the land cannot be destroyed (it is permanent); nor can it be lost (it has a unique, fixed location). It is thus clear that a security right relating to land is, from B's point of view, one of the very best forms of security.[1]

1.2 The basic tension

The **basic tension** can be particularly acute where security rights are concerned (see **F4:1.1**), and that tension is already more difficult to resolve where land is concerned (see **A:3.2**). This means that, when those two areas converge in the topic of security rights in land, the tension is *extremely* acute. We can see this by returning to the very first example in this book:

---

[1] Of course, that is not always the case: if land loses its value, B's security right over land may not give it adequate protection should A fail to perform the secured duty. This can be a particular problem where an economic downturn causes A to default on repayments. Such a downturn may also lead to a decline in land values; and if lenders simultaneously start to enforce their security rights by selling off land, its value is likely to drop even further (see further **5.2.2(iii)** below).

A:EXAMPLE 1

A and B, lovers, move in to a home together. The land on which they live is owned by A. A, without telling B, borrows money from C, a bank. It is a 'mortgage' deal: in return for the loan, A gives C, should A fail to repay the loan as agreed, a power to sell the land and use the proceeds to meet A's debt.

The land law system must try to balance three competing needs:

(i)   *The need to protect A.* As in **A:Example 1**, C often takes security when extending credit to A. In such situations there is a risk that C will exploit A's need for money by imposing harsh terms on A. Where A gives C security over land, the consequences to A of failing to perform his duty to C may be particularly severe—A might lose his home or his business premises.

(ii) *The need to protect C:* If the property law system makes it difficult for C to acquire security, there is a risk that the flow of credit will be impeded. This is an important consideration where land is concerned: the vast majority of individuals or companies wishing to buy land can only do so if C agrees to finance the acquisition by providing secured credit.

(iii) *The need to protect B.* If C is allowed to enforce its security by selling A's land, this will affect both A and B. This may seem particularly harsh in a case such as **A:Example 1**, where B did not consent to C's acquisition of the security right.

This means that, when analysing security rights in relation to land, we need to be aware of a tension: (i) between the needs of A and C; and (ii) between the needs of B and C.

1.3   The model adopted in this chapter

The model adopted here is different from the model adopted in F4: in **A:Example 1**, it is C who acquires the security right, *not* B. When examining security rights, there are always three parties to keep in mind: (i) the party giving security (often a borrower); (ii) the party acquiring the security right (often a lender); and (iii) other parties who may be adversely affected by the security right.

When looking at security rights relating to things other than land, the other parties who may be adversely affected by a security right are, chiefly, third parties who acquire a right from A, without realising that another party has *already* acquired a security right in relation to A's thing. In those cases, the parties' rights arise in the following order:

(i)   A, the party giving security, has a right (eg, Ownership of a thing);
(ii) B acquires a security right in relation to A's thing or A's right;
(iii) C then acquires a right that relates to A's thing or A's right.

So, a question can then arise as to whether C has a defence to B's pre-existing security right (see **F4:4**).

In contrast, where land is concerned, the **basic tension** tends to arise where the parties' rights arise in the following order:

(i)   A, the party giving security, has a right (eg, a Freehold);

(ii)   B, a third party, acquires a right that relates to A's land or A's right (eg, B moves in with A); and

(iii)   C acquires a security right in relation to A's land or A's right (eg, A borrows money from C and gives C a security right).

When looking at security rights relating to land, the parties who may be adversely affected by a security right are, chiefly, third parties who acquire a right from A *before* the security right arises. Where land is concerned, it therefore makes sense to call the third party acquiring a right B; and the party acquiring the security right C. This difference comes chiefly from the fact that land has a special capacity for multiple simultaneous use which makes it more likely that a third party *already* has a right in relation to A's land or A's right. In such a case, if B's pre-existing right is a property right or a persistent right, a question can then arise as to whether C (the party with the security right) has a defence to B's pre-existing right (see section 4 below).

In this chapter, we will also assume that A has a property right giving him exclusive control of land: a Freehold or a Lease. Of course, A can use other rights (eg, a right under a Trust of Z's Freehold) as security for a duty owed to C (eg, A could mortgage his right under a Trust of Z's Freehold by transferring that right to C by way of security: see F4:2.2.1). However, we will focus on the central case where C wants to acquire a security right from a party who has a Freehold or Lease.

So, in this chapter:

(i)   A has a Freehold or Lease;

(ii)   B has a pre-existing right to make some use of A's land;

(iii)   C then acquires a security right in relation to A's land or A's right.

1.4   Transactions giving C a security right in relation to land

In general, there are four types of transaction by which A can give another party a security right: (i) mortgage, (ii) pledge, (iii) consensual lien and (iv) charge (see F4:1.2.2). Things are very different if A has a Freehold or Lease and wishes to give C a security right in relation to A's land.

1.4.1 The ban on true mortgages of a Freehold or Lease

A mortgage consists of a *transfer of a right by way of security*. It is *impossible* for A to mortgage a Freehold or Lease as it is impossible for A to transfer such a right to C by way of security.

EXAMPLE 2a

A has a Freehold. To secure A's duty to repay a loan to C, A attempts to transfer his Freehold to C by way of mortgage.

EXAMPLE 2b

A has a Lease. To secure A's duty to repay a loan to C, A attempts to transfer his Lease to C by way of mortgage.

In each case, A's attempt to transfer his right by way of security will *fail*.[2] If A has a registered Freehold or Lease, he will retain that right and C, by substantively registering his right, will instead acquire a Charge: a *new* property right. Hence: (i) A keeps his Freehold or Lease; and (ii) C acquires a Charge over A's land.

This might seem surprising as most people (mistakenly) say that A is taking out a 'mortgage' when he borrows money from C Bank to finance his purchase of a house. As we have seen, a mortgage consists of a *transfer of a right by way of security*, but sections 85 and 86 of the Law of Property Act 1925 ('the LPA 1925') make it clear that it is impossible to transfer a Freehold or a Lease by way of security.[3]

1.4.2 The creation of a Charge over A's land

If A has Ownership of a bike and wants to give C a property right in that bike by way of security, A has only two options: (i) he can transfer his Ownership to C by way of security; or (ii) he can allow C to take or retain physical control of the bike. In either case, C acquires the only property right possible with respect to things other than land: Ownership (see **D1:1.4.2**). The situation is different with land: the Charge exists as a *distinct* property right, designed for the special purpose of giving C a security right.

It is very important to distinguish a Charge over land from the general charge transaction by which A can give C a security right (see **F4:2.2.2**). In such a case, A does *not* give C a property right. Instead, if it is a 'fixed charge' transaction, B acquires a persistent right: a Purely Equitable Charge. And if it is instead a 'floating charge' transaction, B has a power to acquire such a right.

Description	Right Acquired by C	Nature of C's Right	Nature of A's Right
Charge over land	Charge	Property right: a right in land	A must have a Freehold or Lease
Fixed charge	Purely Equitable Charge	Persistent right: a right against A's right	A may have *any* right
Floating charge	Power to acquire a Purely Equitable Charge	Power to acquire a persistent right	A may have *any* right

1.4.3 Charges and the 'Mortgagor's Right to Redeem'

If A transfers a right to C by way of security: (i) C acquires that right; and (ii) C is under a duty to A, if the secured duty is performed, to transfer the right back to A. C's duty relates to the specific right he acquired from A and so A has a persistent right: a Mortgagor's Right to Redeem (see **D2:1.2.3** and **F4:1.4**).

When A has a Freehold or Lease, and gives C a Charge over his land, A does *not* acquire a persistent right: A retains his property right and so the rest of the world remains under a

---

[2] S 85(2) means that, in **Example 2a**, A retains his Freehold and B will acquire a 3,000-year Lease of A's land by way of security. S 86(2) means that, in **Example 2b**, A retains his Lease and B will acquire a sub-Lease (for a term finishing 10 days before the end of A's Lease) by way of security.

[3] See too Land Registration Act 2002 ('LRA 2002'), s 23(1)(a) and (3)(a): that section imposes a further restriction by preventing A from giving B a new Lease by way of security (a 'mortgage by demise or sub-demise'). That form of security right is in any case obsolete (see Law Com No 204 (1991)).

prima facie duty to A—A does not need a persistent right against C's right (the Charge over A's land) and therefore there is no Mortgagor's Right to Redeem.

Judges and commentators often use 'equity of redemption' to refer to the various powers and rights that A may have against C.[4] For example, in **Examples 2a and 2b**, if A performs his duty to repay the loan to C, then C's Charge will disappear. A's power to change C's position in this way can be seen as a power to 'redeem': to free A's land from the Charge. Importantly, if C transfers the Charge to C2, A can also exercise those powers and rights against C2. However, this does *not* mean that A has a distinct, persistent right. It is simply in the nature of C2's security right that the right disappears if the duty it secures is performed.

1.4.4 A pledge or consensual lien of land?

In principle, A can give C a security right over A's land by: (i) allowing C to *take* physical control of A's land until the secured duty is performed (a pledge); or (ii) allowing C to retain physical control of A's land until that point (a consensual lien). However, in practice, these transactions are irrelevant because, in almost all cases, A wants to have or retain physical control of his land. The great advantage of a Charge is that:

(i)   C acquires a property right by way of security; *and*
(ii) A can retain his property right; *and*
(iii) A can have or retain physical control of his land.

Where A's property right is in a thing other than land (eg, where A has Ownership of a bike) it is impossible for these three factors to be present at the same time.[5] In contrast, where land is concerned, A has the convenience of being able to give a lender security *without* losing his Freehold or Lease; and the lender has the convenience of being able to acquire a property right by way of security *without* having to take physical control of A's land.

Transaction	Property Right for C?	A retains his property right?	Can A retain physical control of the thing throughout?
Charge **over land**	Yes	Yes	Yes
Mortgage **of A's Ownership of a bike**	Yes	No	Yes
Pledge **or Consensual Lien of A's bike**	Yes	Yes	No
Fixed/Floating Charge **over A's Ownership of a bike**	No	Yes	Yes

---

[4] L Smith, ch 5 in *English Private Law* (ed Burrows, 2nd edn, 2007), 5.10 notes that: 'The concept of the equity of redemption still performs its traditional function of ensuring that [C's] interest shall be effective only as a security interest, and that the economic benefits of ownership shall remain in [A].'

[5] In theory, A could pledge his land to C by allowing C to take physical control of the land; and then C could allow to retake physical control without destroying the pledge (see **F4:2.1.2**). But the inconvenience in allowing C to acquire physical control and then release it is clear.

1.4.5 A fixed or floating charge transaction

It is also possible for A to give C security over his Freehold or Lease by means of a fixed charge or floating charge transaction.

- In a fixed charge transaction, A makes a binding promise to hold a particular right or rights as security for a duty owed to C. C thus acquires a persistent right: a Purely Equitable Charge (see **F4:2.2.2**).
- In a floating charge transaction, A makes a binding promise to hold a particular right or rights as security for a duty owed to C *if* a particular condition is satisfied (eg, if a specific event, such as A failing to pay a loan instalment, occurs). C thus acquires a power to acquire a Purely Equitable Charge (see **F4:2.3**).

However, the obvious disadvantage to C is that, in either case, C does *not* acquire a property right in land. This means:

(i)   the rest of the world is not under a prima facie duty to C; *and*

(ii)   C has no right to take physical control of A's land; *and*

(iii)   C cannot substantively register his right and so cannot take advantage of the positive operation of registration (see **C2:3.1** and **C2:6**).

SUMMARY of G4:1

In theory, there are four types of transaction by which A, if he has a Freehold or Lease, can give C a security right. The first, and by far the most important in practice, is through the *creation of a Charge*. A Charge is a special form of property right that gives C security over A's land. As the Charge exists *only* in relation to land, we did not come across it in **F4:1.2.2**. In contrast, if A has a Freehold or Lease, he *cannot* transfer that right to C by way of security. As a result, the creation of a Charge is a substitute for the mortgage.

In theory, if A has a Freehold or Lease, A can also give C a security right by allowing C to take, or remain in, physical control of A's land. Therefore, a pledge or consensual lien of land is possible. However, in practice, these transactions are undesirable: in particular, it will usually be the case (as when A borrows money to buy a house) that A wants to keep physical control of the land.

It is also possible for A to give C a persistent right (a Purely Equitable Charge) against A's Freehold or Lease by way of security, through a fixed charge transaction. Equally, by a floating charge transaction, A can give C a power to acquire such a right. As A can give C such a right or power without losing physical control of his land, such a transaction does not have the disadvantage of a pledge or lien. However, if C wants the protection of a substantively registered property right, he needs to acquire a property right (a Charge over A's land); not a persistent right (a Purely Equitable Charge) or a power to acquire a persistent right.

---

2   THE CONTENT QUESTION

2.1   Property rights: the creation of a Charge

It is in theory possible for A to give C a property right in land, by way of security, through a

pledge or a consensual lien. However, given their very limited practical value, we will concentrate here on the creation of a Charge.

2.1.1 Examples

EXAMPLE 3a

A has a Freehold and he wants to borrow money to pay for building work. In return for a
loan from C Bank, A grants C Bank a Charge over the land; C Bank substantively registers its
charge.

EXAMPLE 3b

A wants to buy a Freehold from A0. Acquiring the Freehold will cost A £200,000. A has
£20,000 of his own money and asks C Bank for a loan of £180,000. In return for the loan
from C Bank, A promises to grant C Bank a Charge over the land. C Bank provides the
£180,000 to a solicitor acting for A. When A's solicitor confirms that the money has been
provided, A0 transfers his Freehold to A. When A is registered as the new holder of A0's
Freehold, and A grants C Bank a Charge, A's solicitor release the money to A0's solicitor. C
Bank then substantively registers its Charge.

In each case, C Bank acquires a property right: a Charge. This form of property right was
created by the LPA 1925. It is a special form of property right that exists *only* in relation to
land. The purpose of the Charge is to avoid the complications that may otherwise arise
where: (i) A wants to give C a property right in a particular thing by way of security; *and*
(ii) A wants to keep physical control of that thing. In such a case, where things other than
land are concerned, A has to transfer his property right to C (see F4:2.1.1). This can cause
problems as, although he acquires it by way of security, C thus acquires Ownership of the
thing. In contrast, in land, the possibility of creating a Charge allows A: (i) to keep his
Freehold or Lease; *and* (ii) to retain physical control of his land; *and* (iii) to give C a
property right by way of security (see 1.4.4 above).

It is important to note that, despite its advantages, it is impossible for A to give C a
Charge if A has Ownership of a thing other than land. The fact that a Charge counts as a
property right only in relation to land must depend on the special features of land (see
A:3.1). First, those special features make a property right in land a particularly attractive
form of security for C (see 1.1 above). Second, in a case such as **Example 3b**, it is important
for A to be able to offer C an attractive form of security: given the costs of buying land, A
will often need to borrow a large sum of money from C. Of course, other things (eg, yachts)
or other forms of right (eg, shares) can also be very expensive: but the social importance of
land (its ability to provide a home or business premises) provides a reason why the property
law system should support methods that allow A to raise money to buy land.[6]

2.1.2 The core content of a Charge

The purpose of a Charge is to give C a property right over A's land as security for a duty
owed to C. In practice, that security consists chiefly of C's power, if the secured duty is not

---

[6] Although a balance is needed: if credit is too readily available, this may support existing high prices for land and
thus make land harder still to buy.

performed, to sell the land and use the proceeds to meet that duty. Technically, however, section 87(1) of the LPA 1925 defines the content of B's Charge by reference to the content of a Lease (see **E1:1.1**).

C's rights if A has a Freehold	C's rights if A has a Lease
Section 87(1)(a): C has the 'same protection, powers and remedies' as if he has (by way of security) a 3,000-year Lease	Section 87(1)(b): C has the 'same protection, powers and remedies' as if he has (by way of security) a Lease due to end one day before A's Lease

When adopting the Charge as a new form of property right in land, Parliament took a very dramatic step. No such new right had been recognised since at least the 15th century, when the Lease came to be regarded as a property right in land. Perhaps not surprisingly, Parliament was still influenced by the 'closed list' principle (see **D1:1.2.1**). So, when creating a new form of property right in land, Parliament modelled that right on an existing property right in land: the Lease.[7]

The core content of C's Charge thus depends on the position of a party who acquires a Lease by way of security. As such a party has a Lease, he has a right to exclusive control of A's land for a limited period. It may seem surprising that, in cases such as **Examples 3a and 3b**, it is C Bank, not A, that has such a right. However, that is the clear effect of section 87(1). It should be emphasised that, if C has a Charge, his right to exclusive control of the land does *not* arise only when the secured duty is not performed. Rather, C has that right *as soon as* he acquires his Charge. This point was forcefully made by Harman LJ in *Four Maids Ltd v Dudley Marshall (Properties) Ltd*:[8]

> [C's] right to possession in the absence of some contract has nothing to do with default on the part of the [A]. [C] may go into possession before the ink is dry on the mortgage unless there is something in the contract, express or by implication, whereby he has contracted himself out of that right. [C] has the right because he has a legal term of years in the property or its statutory equivalent.[9]

In practice, C's right to exclusive control only becomes important if the duty secured by the Charge is not performed. For example, in cases such as **Examples 3a and 3b**, the agreement between A and C Bank will *generally* give A a right or liberty, against C Bank, to occupy the land see (**5.3.1** below).[10] After all, if C Bank is in the business of lending money, it will be content if A continues to repay the loan as agreed: there is no need for C Bank to assume the responsibility of taking control of and managing the land. Indeed, if C Bank were to do so, it would come under an onerous duty to account to A for any gains that C Bank had

---

[7] The Law Commission have recommended that the law should be changed so that the content of a Charge is *not* defined by reference to a Lease (Law Com No 204 (1991), eg 3.1 and 3.2). However, that proposal has not been adopted.

[8] [1957] Ch 317 at 320. Although, as C only acquires a Legal property right when he substantively registers his right, the relevant point is when the wet ink is applied (or the keyboard used) on the register.

[9] See too *Paragon Finance plc v Pender* [2005] 1 WLR 3412: even if C2 has a persistent right against C's Charge, C still has a right to exclusive control as C still holds the Charge.

[10] If the agreement gives A a right to occupy after defaulting on loan repayments, it can be inferred that A has such a right before any default: see *per* Russell J in *Birmingham Citizens Permanent BS v Caunt* [1962] Ch 883 at 890.

made, or *should* make, as a result of its control of the land: those actual or notional gains would thus be deducted from the sum owed to C Bank by A.[11]

So, even if A defaults on its repayment to C Bank, C Bank will generally wish to avoid the responsibilities of taking control of the land for a long period. Instead, there are two main options for C Bank. First, C Bank can rely on its right to exclusive control simply as a means to remove any occupiers from the land, so that C Bank can then sell that land with 'vacant possession'. Second, if it wants to delay a sale and instead receive income from the land, C Bank's best course, rather than taking control of the land itself, is to appoint a receiver (see F4:5.2). In each case, C Bank relies on a particular power arising as part of its Charge: in the first case, the power to sell A's Freehold or Lease; in the second case, the power to appoint a receiver. These powers thus form part of the **content** of C's Charge. However, as they arise only when the secured duty is not performed, we will consider them in **section 5** below, when looking at the *enforcement* of C's security right.

2.1.3 The express terms of the charge transaction: additional rights of C

In cases such as **Examples 3a and 3b**, C Bank thus acquires a Charge: a property right giving C Bank a core right to exclusive control of A's land. However, the agreement between A and C Bank will generally give C Bank a number of additional rights. Most obviously, A will usually be under a duty to repay the loan in agreed instalments at an agreed rate of interest. When extending credit to A, it is also possible for C to insist on acquiring other rights. For example, if C Ltd lends money to A Ltd, C Ltd could insist, as part of the deal, that (i) A Ltd grants C Ltd a Charge over its premises; and (ii) A Ltd makes a contractual promise to sell its products to C Ltd, over the next five years, at a 15 per cent discount.

On first principles, it may seem that A and C should be able to reach any agreement they wish: if A makes a contractual promise giving C those additional rights, C clearly acquires those rights. However, as we will see in **2.1.4** and **2.1.5**, there are limits to the possible **content** of C's additional rights. The additional rights that C may gain are often referred to as 'collateral advantages'. The limits discussed in **2.1.4** and **2.1.5** can thus be seen as prohibitions on collateral advantages. However, the crucial question is to ask: what limits are there on *A's power to give C an additional right?*

2.1.4 Additional rights of C: general limits

There are some general limits that affect A's ability to make a binding contractual promise to C. These limits are general in the sense that they apply even where C does *not* acquire a security right as part of his deal with A.

(i) Consumer Credit Act 1974 (as amended by the Consumer Credit Act 2006)

The Consumer Credit Act 1974 (CCA) is *not* limited to cases where A's duty to C is secured; nor is it limited to cases involving land.[12] In general, it applies whenever: (i) A is a consumer; and (ii) C extends credit to A.[13] As well as imposing a number of formality rules,[14]

---

[11] *Robertson v Norris* (1859) 1 Giff 428.

[12] *Wilson v First County Trust Ltd (No 2)* [2004] 1 AC 816: the Act was applied to lower an interest rate charged by C as part of a pledge.

[13] CCA, s 140C(1) (as inserted by Consumer Credit Act 2006, s 19).

[14] See **F4:3.1.1(ii)**.

the Act also gives a court wide powers whenever A and C are in an 'unfair relationship'.[15] In deciding whether A and C's relationship is unfair, a court can take account of *any* factor that seems relevant.[16] For example, if the interest rates imposed by a Charge transaction are very high, a court may decide that the relationship is unfair and use its consequent power to replace the agreed interest rate with a lower rate.

Prior to the amendments made by the Consumer Credit Act 2006, a different test applied. That test allowed a court to 'reopen' an 'extortionate' credit agreement. 'Extortionate' was narrowly defined: for example, an agreed interest rate counted as extortionate only where it was 'grossly exorbitant'.[17] Under the new rule, it seems the courts have a wider power to intervene.[18] Once the term is challenged, it is for the creditor (ie, C) to show that it does not create an unfair relationship.[19] Nonetheless, A will not be able to rely on the Act *whenever* he has to pay a high interest rate: the rate may be justified by, for example, the urgency with which A needs the loan and the difficulty C may have in acquiring the necessary funds within that time.[20]

It is important to note that the Act does *not* apply where the Charge transaction is instead regulated by the Financial Services Authority (FSA).[21] Under the Financial Services and Markets Act 2000, the FSA has responsibility for *regulated mortgage contracts*. Such a contract arises where A gives C a Charge if:

- No other party currently has a Charge over the land; *and*
- At least 40 per cent of A's land is used, or intended to be used, by A 'as or in connection with a dwelling'.

So, in a standard case such as **Examples 3a and 3b**, the rules imposed by the CCA will *not* apply. In such a case, A's protection comes from: (i) his ability to deal with an established institutional lender (eg, a bank); and (ii) the FSA's regulation of the conduct of that lender. The extensive *Mortgage: Conduct of Business* sourcebook (*MCOB*) provided by the FSA gives detailed rules and guidelines to lenders who carry out business by entering regulated mortgage contracts. Thus, A cannot apply to court to have a high rate of interest varied; but he ought to be able to rely on the fact that C Bank, through its compliance with the FSA standards, is not exploiting A's position.[22] Indeed, in some circumstances, A can bring a

---

[15] CCA, ss 140(A)–(C).

[16] CCA, s 140(a)(2).

[17] S 138(1)(a) of the CCA (now repealed): in *Davies v Directloans Ltd* [1986] 1 WLR 823 (Nugee QC) (sitting as a Deputy High Court judge) considered the application of the Act to a case involving a Charge.

[18] The new provisions also seem to take care of a problem noted in *Paragon Finance plc v Nash* [2002] 1 WLR 685 at [83]: before the 2006 Act, rights arising *after* the initial credit bargain (eg, where C exercises a power under the initial bargain to increase interest rates) were *not* caught by the legislation. However, under the 2006 Act, the parties' 'relationship' includes not only the terms of their initial agreement but also the terms of any related agreement; and the way in which C has exercised or enforced any of its rights under an initial or related agreement: see CCA, s 140(A).

[19] CCA, s 140B(9).

[20] Compare eg *A Ketley Ltd v Scott* [1980] CCLR 37: an interest rate of 48 per cent was not 'extortionate' where A had sought a loan at very short notice. The White Paper leading to the 2006 Act (2003, Cmnd 6040) noted the narrow definition the courts had given to 'extortionate' under the 1974 Act and argued in favour of giving the courts a wider power to intervene: see [3.29]–[3.30].

[21] CCA, s 140A(5).

[22] One of the statutory aims of the FSA is the protection of consumers: see Financial Services and Markets Act 2000, s 5(2). This protection comes chiefly through *procedural* safeguards (by ensuring A is given clear information before entering a regulated mortgage contract: see eg *MCOB* sourcebook, chs 4–6) rather than through *substantive* safeguards (eg, there is no set limit on the rate of interest that can be charged in a regulated mortgage contract).

claim for compensation for any loss he suffers as a result of a breach by C Bank of the FSA standards.[23]

As a result, the CCA scheme is left to protect A in cases where A may be particularly in need of protection. For example, it may be that A, when acquiring his home, gave C Bank a Charge over his land. A then runs up further debts (eg, on credit cards) and seeks to consolidate those debts through a *second* loan, secured on A's land. If A, perhaps because of a poor credit record, is unable to obtain a loan from an established bank or building society, he may have to resort to a 'sub-prime' lender. When applying the CCA provisions to such a case, a court will face a tricky balancing act. On the one hand, as A's deal with C is covered by the CCA rather than by the FSA rules, there is already a high risk that A may be exploited. On the other, if A has a poor credit record, it may be justifiable for C to charge a high rate of interest to cover the losses it will incur when other creditors fail to repay their loans.[24]

(ii) Unfair Terms in Consumer Contract Regulations 1999

Like the CCA, the 1999 Regulations are *not* limited to cases where A's duty to C is secured; nor are they limited to cases involving land. Instead, the Regulations apply whenever: (i) A is a consumer; and (ii) C is a seller or supplier. The chief provision of the Regulations is that if a term in a deal between A and C is 'unfair',[25] it will not give C a right against A. However, certain terms are exempt from the unfairness test. For example, if a term has been individually negotiated by A and C, it cannot be challenged under the Regulations. Importantly, certain core parts of A and C's deal are also exempt. Regulation 6(2) states that:

> In so far as it is in plain intelligible language, the assessment of fairness of a term shall not relate
>
> (a)   to the definition of the main subject-matter of the contract, or
> (b)   to the adequacy of the price or remuneration, as against the goods or services supplied
> in exchange.

The Regulations have only a limited impact on a Charge transaction. They *can* apply in such a case,[26] even if C acquires a first Charge that falls under the FSA regime.[27] However, the exclusion of terms relating to the 'adequacy of the price or remuneration' means that agreed interest on the sum borrowed by A *cannot* be challenged under the Regulations:[28] the interest is part of the price paid for the loan.[29]

---

[23] Financial Services and Markets Act 2000, s 150.

[24] C can only make a regulated credit agreement if he is licensed by the Office of Fair Trading so there is already some regulatory control of C's conduct.

[25] A term is unfair if it is *both* (i) contrary to the requirement of good faith; *and* (ii) the cause of a significant imbalance in the parties' rights and obligations arising under the contract to the detriment of the consumer. Sch 2 provides an indicative but non-exhaustive list of terms that *may* be regarded as unfair.

[26] *R (Khatun) v Newnham LBC* [2005] 1 QB 37. There was some initial doubt as to whether their predecessor, the 1994 Regulations, applied to Charges over land: see Bright (1995) 111 *LQR* 655.

[27] In such a case the CCA is excluded, but the 1999 Regulations are not.

[28] *Director General of Fair Trading v First National Bank* [2002] 1 AC 481.

[29] A term giving C the power to vary interest rates could be found to be 'unfair' but such a term cannot be challenged if C can show there is a 'valid reason' for it: Sch 2 para 2 of the Regulations.

(iii) Unconscionable bargains
The courts have a limited jurisdiction (originally recognised by courts of Equity)[30] to refuse to enforce unconscionable bargains.[31] Again, this jurisdiction is *not* limited to cases where A's duty to C is secured; nor is it limited to cases involving land.[32] It is important to note that A cannot escape from a contractual term by simply asserting that the term is 'unconscionable' in the sense of unfair or unreasonable. Nor can A do so by simply saying that there was an 'inequality of bargaining power' between A and C.[33]

The jurisdiction not to enforce unconscionable bargains is best seen as arising only if:

- A has a particular vulnerability (eg, A is unable to understand a particular deal);[34] *and*
- C is aware of and takes advantage of that vulnerability by making a deal with A;[35] *and*
- The deal is clearly disadvantageous to A.

The principle thus seems to be that a contractual promise will not be enforced where C obtained that promise by knowingly exploiting A's vulnerability.[36] If A takes independent advice before making the deal with C, the principle does not apply: presumably because, if A chose to make the deal regardless, it cannot be said that A's promise was made primarily as a result of C's exploitation of A's weakness.[37] If the principle does apply, it seems that A has a power to rescind the contract (see **D1:1.4.5(i)** and **D2:1.6**). By imposing limits on A's exercise of that power, a court can rewrite the terms of the parties' bargain. For example, a court can substitute a different rate of interest for the agreed contractual rate.[38]

The principle *can* apply to a Charge transaction. For example, in *Multiservice Bookbinding Ltd v Marden*,[39] Browne-Wilkinson J considered whether to apply the principle in a case where the interest rate on the loan was set by reference to the value of the Swiss franc and, as a result, A was under a duty to pay a very large sum to C. However, on the facts of that case, the principle did not apply. Browne-Wilkinson J made the very important point that a term cannot be set aside simply because it is unreasonable; instead

a bargain cannot be unfair and unconscionable unless one of the parties to it has imposed the objectionable terms in a morally reprehensible manner, that is to say, in a way which affects his conscience.[40]

---

[30] A similar jurisdiction developed in Admiralty courts where C took advantage of A's circumstances to charge an extravagant price for saving A's ship: see eg *Port Calendonia and the Anna* [1903] P 184.
[31] See eg Peel, *Tretiel's Law of Contract* (12th edn, 2007), 10-039ff.
[32] *Fry v Lane* (1888) 40 Ch D 312 (a sale of B1's persistent right under a Trust to B2 was set aside).
[33] Such a principle was suggested by Lord Denning MR in *Lloyds Bank Ltd v Bundy* [1975] QB 326 but was rejected by the House of Lords in *National Westminster Bank v Morgan* [1985] AC 686.
[34] Cases recognising the principle are sometimes said to depend on A being 'poor and ignorant' (see eg *per* Megarry J in *Cresswell v Potter* [1978] 1 WLR 255n). There is no obvious reason why other vulnerabilities that prevent A fully understanding a particular transaction cannot be relevant. However, the mere fact that A is short of money should not count as a relevant vulnerability: *Alec Lobb Garages Ltd v Total Oil (GB) Ltd* [1985] 1 WLR 173.
[35] This element was emphasised by the Court of Appeal in *Portman Building Society v Dusangh* [2000] 2 All ER (Comm) 221.
[36] See eg the analysis of Burrows, *Casebook on Contact* (2007), 757ff.
[37] *Per* Chadwick LJ in *Jones v Morgan* [2001] EWCA Civ 995 at [42].
[38] *Earl of Aylesford v Morris* (1873) 8 Ch App 484.
[39] [1979] Ch 84.
[40] At 110. The decision in *Multiservice Bookbinding* thus casts doubt on the decision of Goff J in *Cityland and Property (Holdings) Ltd v Dabrah* [1968] Ch 166. Goff J's reasoning in that case seems to be based instead on the distinct 'clogs and fetters' principle that we will examine in **2.1.5** and **2.1.6** below.

(iv) Terms in restraint of trade

A does not have the power to make a contractual promise that operates to restrain A's trade *unless* that restraint is reasonable and not contrary to the public interest. Again, this jurisdiction is not is *not* limited to cases where A's duty to C is secured; nor is it limited to cases involving land. However, it can be important in such cases.

EXAMPLE 4a

A Ltd has a Freehold of a petrol station. A Ltd needs to borrow money to redevelop and improve the facilities. C Ltd, a petrol supplier, agrees to lend A Ltd £150,000 provided that: (i) A Ltd repays the loan in instalments at 5 per cent annual interest; (ii) A Ltd's duty to C Ltd is secured by a Charge over the land; and (iii) for the next 21 years, A Ltd sells only petrol provided by C Ltd and A Ltd keeps the petrol station open, selling C Ltd's petrol, at all reasonable business hours.

In such a case, as confirmed by the House of Lords in *Esso Petroleum Co Ltd v Harper's Garage (Stourport) Ltd*,[41] it may be that clause (iii) is a restraint of trade. If so, that clause does *not* give C Ltd a contractual right against A Ltd. If so, A Ltd of course remains under a duty to repay the loan; and C Ltd retains its Charge as security for that duty. However, A Ltd is free to sell petrol supplied by parties other than C Ltd.

2.1.5 Additional rights of C: a security-specific limit

There is a specific limit that affects A's ability to give C an additional right *as part of a security transaction*. This limit is thus *security-specific* and therefore only applies where C acquires a security right. However, the limit applies *whenever* C acquires a security right: as such, our analysis will consider cases involving security relating to A's Freehold or Lease, as well as relating to A's thing, personal right or persistent right.

(i) The limit: there must be a reasonable prospect of A holding the land free from C's Charge

The limit is based on the idea that: (i) if the transaction between A and C is a security transaction, *then* (ii) that transaction must have certain features; *so* (iii) a promise by A that interferes with one of those features cannot give C a right.

A key feature of any security transaction is that there must be a prospect, if the secured duty is performed, of C's security right disappearing and thus of A holding his initial right free from C's security right. For example, if A transfers his Ownership of a bike to C by way of security (a mortgage), a key feature of the deal is that, if the secured duty is performed, A gets his bike back.

So, *if* the transaction is clearly intended to be a security transaction, a promise by A cannot give C an additional right that *removes* the prospect of A regaining his right. One (not very illuminating) way of explaining this limit is to say that A's additional promise cannot give C a right if it *fetters* the prospect of A holding his right free from C's security right.

---

[41] [1968] AC 269. See the House of Lords' analysis of a similar clause: the period of A's duty is an important factor.

EXAMPLE 4b

It is 1907. A has a Lease of a hotel. The Lease is due to expire in June 1925. In return for a loan from C, A transfers his Lease to C by way of security for A's duty to repay the loan. Under the mortgage deal, the last repayment instalment is due in May 1925. In 1910, A is in a position to repay the entire debt plus the agreed interest. A wants to do so as C will then be under a duty to transfer the Lease back to A. C, however, insists that he has an additional right: A cannot pay off the debt until May 1925.

This example is based on *Fairclough v Swan Brewery*.[42] The mortgage of A's Lease occurred before section 86 of the LPA 1925 prevented such transactions. Lord Macnaghten, giving the advice of the Privy Council, held that A *was* able to pay off the debt early (and therefore place C under a duty to transfer the Lease back to A). Lord Macnaghten's reasoning was that if the additional right were enforceable, the prospect of A regaining his right would, *in effect*, be removed. This was because A would regain his Lease when it only had one month left to run. Technically, of course, there is thus a prospect of A regaining his Lease, but the prospect is clearly not *reasonable*. The principle thus seems to be that A's promise cannot give C an additional right if the additional right would remove the reasonable prospect of A holding his right free from C's security right.

It is important to note that in some circumstances, C acquires an additional right allowing him to keep his security right for a guaranteed period; it is *not* the case that A must *always* have the power to pay off a debt at any point.[43] In fact, in Charge transactions, terms postponing repayment are very common[44] and may be the price paid for certain terms of the Charge—eg, a lender may charge a lower annual rate of interest in return for knowing that he will receive that interest for a fixed number of years.

EXAMPLE 4c

A Ltd has a Freehold. In return for a loan of £180,000 from C Ltd, A Ltd grants C Ltd a Charge over the land to secure A Ltd's duty to repay the loan. Under the Charge transaction, the last repayment instalment is due in 40 years' time. A Ltd is to pay 5.25 per cent annual interest on the loan. Six years later A Ltd is in a position to repay the entire debt plus the agreed interest, but C Ltd insists that A Ltd cannot pay off the debt until the 40 years are up.

This example is based on *Knightsbridge Estates Ltd v Byrne*.[45] In that case, the Court of Appeal confirmed that A could *not* pay off the loan before the agreed date. The situation is clearly different from **Example 4b** because A Ltd *does* have a reasonable prospect of holding its Freehold free from the Charge: it simply has to wait 40 years. Sir Wilfrid Greene MR, giving the judgment of the Court of Appeal, emphasised that the court could not refuse to enforce the term simply because it might be 'unreasonable'.[46] His Lordship noted that a

---

[42] [1912] AC 565.

[43] See eg *Biggs v Hoddinott* [1898] 2 Ch 307 where a term preventing A regaining his mortgaged right within five years was valid.

[44] *Per* Lord Macnaghten in *Bradley v Carritt* [1903] AC 253 at 259–60.

[45] [1939] Ch 441. The decision of the Court of Appeal was affirmed by the House of Lords on different grounds: [1940] AC 613.

[46] [1939] Ch 441 at 456: 'In our opinion the proposition that a postponement of the contractual right of redemption is only permissible for a "reasonable" time is not well-founded.'

court could give relief against a term that is 'oppressive or unconscionable'[47] but that was clearly not the case: A Ltd was a commercial party and C Ltd had not exploited any vulnerability of A Ltd. In going for a long-term deal with a fixed rate of interest, A Ltd had simply gambled that interest rates would go up, whereas C Ltd had gambled that they would go down. A court cannot intervene simply because it seems C Ltd has the better of the bargain.

(ii) Justifying the limit

There is thus a general principle that, in a Charge transaction, A must have a reasonable prospect of holding the land, at some future point, free from C's Charge. That principle can be seen as a limit on the parties' 'freedom to contract'; after all, it cannot be said that the parties should *always* be free to make whatever deal they like. For example,

- A may wish to give B a Lease under which A has a right to install other occupiers on the land. This is simply not possible: *either* (i) A gives B a right to exclusive control of the land for a limited period—in which case B has a Lease and A has no right to insert other occupiers; *or* (ii) A has a right to install other occupiers and B thus has no right to exclusive control of the land—in which case B has a licence, not a Lease.
- Similarly, in a case such as **Example 4b**, A has the power to give C a Charge but does *not* have the power to *both* (i) give C a Charge; *and* (ii) make a binding additional promise that removes the reasonable prospect of A holding his Freehold free from the Charge.

It is therefore clear that the general principle is *not* based on the need to ensure that A genuinely consented when making the additional promise to C; its application does *not* depend on showing that, in a particular case, C's bargaining power is greater than A's. Rather, it is a *general* principle that applies *whenever* A gives C a security right over a thing or right held by A: A cannot *both* (i) give C such a security right; *and* (ii) make a binding additional promise that removes the reasonable prospect of A holding his right free from C's security right. The limit, unlike those examined in **2.1.4** above, is thus security-specific.

(iii) Applying the limit: penalties

EXAMPLE 4d

The basic facts are as in **Example 4c**. There is an additional term in the Charge transaction. Even once the 40 years are up, A is only allowed to remove C Ltd's Charge if it pays a premium of £2,000,000.

In such a case, it is clear that the general principle may apply to prevent A's 'premium' promise giving C a contractual right.[48] If A were under a duty to pay such a large sum, A would not have a reasonable prospect of holding the land, at some future point, free from C's Charge. Of course, the application of the principle must depend on the size of the premium.

For example, it is very common for a bank, when lending money to allow A to acquire a Freehold or Lease, to insert a term that A must pay a penalty if A pays off the loan within a particular period. Let us say C Bank offers a special 'mortgage' deal with a low fixed rate of

---

[47] At 457, see **2.1.4(iii)** above
[48] *Per* Lord Parker in *Kreglinger v New Patagonia Meat and Cold Storage Co Ltd* [1914] 1 AC 25 at 61.

interest for five years. As part of the deal, C Bank may also include an 'early repayment charge'.[49] For example, if A wishes to pay off the loan within the first five years, A may have to pay C Bank a sum equivalent to six months' interests on the initial loan. Such a term attempts to protect C Bank's investment—after all, as noted above, C Bank's profit on the deal comes from the interest payments made by A.[50]

A cannot argue that an 'early repayment charge' promise *never* gives C Bank a contractual right. After all, the decision in *Knightsbridge Estates Ltd v Byrne*[51] shows that it is possible for C Bank to postpone A's right to pay off the loan and thus remove the Charge: it must also be possible for C Bank to charge a premium for early repayment. Again, the crucial question will be the size of the 'early repayment charge'. In a standard 'first mortgage' case, where A believes an 'early repayment charge' is too high, he can complain to C Bank.[52] Under FSA rules, C Bank needs to have an internal complaints procedure; after that procedure is exhausted, A can then complain to the Financial Services Ombudsman. If A then seeks redress through the courts, he can try to appeal to: (i) principles discussed in **2.1.4** above (eg, the CCA rules) or (ii) the general principle that A must have a reasonable prospect of holding his right free from C's security right.

(iv) Applying the limit: can A give C an option to purchase A's right?

EXAMPLE 4e

A has a Freehold. In return for a £150,000 loan from C, A grants C a Charge over the land to secure A Ltd's duty to repay the loan. A promises to repay the loan at 6 per cent annual interest in instalments over 25 years. A is also given a power, with six months' notice, to repay the loan and interest in full at any point. A also makes a contractual promise to allow C to buy A's Freehold, at a fair market price determined by an independent surveyor, at any point in the next 10 years. Five years later, C attempts to exercise his option to buy A's Freehold but A refuses to sell.

In *Jones v Morgan*,[53] the Court of Appeal took the view that, in a Charge transaction, it is *impossible* for A to make a binding promise giving C an option to buy A's Freehold or Lease. Therefore, in **Example 4e**, C has *no* contractual right against A to buy A's Freehold. Lord Phillips MR expressed some concern about that outcome, suggesting that the rule behind it 'no longer serves a useful purpose'.[54] However, his Lordship did agree with Chadwick LJ's

---

[49] This charge could be referred to in other ways (eg, an 'exit fee') but, under FSA rules, a 'regulated mortgage contract' (see **2.1.4(i)** above) *must* refer to such a charge as an 'early repayment charge': see *MCOB* sourcebook, 2.2.3(1).

[50] The risk of early repayment arises not because A is likely to have enough money of his own to pay off the loan; rather, it is because A may find a better 'mortgage' deal with C2 Bank and then borrow money from C2 Bank allowing A to pay off the loan to C Bank.

[51] [1939] Ch 441. The decision of the Court of Appeal was affirmed by the House of Lords on different grounds: [1940] AC 613.

[52] *MCOB* sourcebook, 12.3 states the rule that an early repayment charge must be (i) able to be expressed as a cash value; and (ii) *a reasonable pre-estimate of the costs* suffered by C Bank as a result of A's early repayment. Various rules and guidelines also regulate how C Bank should inform A of the 'early repayment charge' before the parties reach an agreement: eg, C Bank should provide a cash figure of the maximum charge (see *MCOB* 5.6.84 (1)(g))

[53] [2001] EWCA Civ 995.

[54] *Ibid* at [86].

view that previous authorities, in particular the decision of the House of Lords in *Samuel v Jarrah Timber & Wood Paving Corpn Ltd*,[55] demanded the result.

We will examine the House of Lords decision in *Samuel* below (see **2.1.6(iv)**). The facts in that case are clearly different from those in **Example 4e** and as a result, that decision does *not* support a general rule that A has no power to give C, as part of a Charge transaction, an option to purchase A's Freehold or Lease. The instincts of Lord Phillips MR in *Jones v Morgan* are correct: there is *no* general rule preventing A from giving C such an option.

In *Kreglinger v New Patagonia Meat and Cold Storage Co Ltd*,[56] Lord Parker defended the view that A cannot give C such an option to purchase. His Lordship's reasoning was that such an option is inconsistent with A's right, if he performs the secured duty, to hold his right free from C's security right. After all, simply by exercising the option, C can take A's Freehold or Lease away from A. This reasoning cannot be based on simple contractual inter-pretation.[57] Contractual interpretation is about finding the parties' intentions; it cannot be the case that because of A's *implied* right to hold his right free from C's Charge, A and C do not really intend C to have the *expressly* agreed option.

An alternative view explains the case as an application of the general principle that there must be a reasonable prospect of A holding his right free from C's security right. The problem with this view is that C's option to purchase does *not* interfere with A's basic right (ie, the right to hold his right free from C's security right if the secured duty is performed). Hence, in **Example 4e**, if A repays the loan as agreed, he will hold his Freehold free from C's Charge—this can be contrasted with **Examples 4b and 4d**. Whilst C can force A to transfer the Freehold to A (by exercising his option) this does not change the nature of C's security right. This analysis is supported by cases in which A, after giving C a security right, *then* gives C an option to purchase.[58] Logically, the same approach should apply *whenever* C acquires his option to purchase.

It seems, then, that the prevailing approach to options to purchase, applied with some reluctance by the Court of Appeal in *Jones v Morgan*, is misguided. It seems to have arisen as a result of a misunderstanding as to the effect of the decision of the House of Lords in *Samuel v Jarrah Timber & Wood Paving Corpn Ltd*.[59] As we will see below, when examining **Example 5d**, the facts of that case are different in a crucial respect to **Example 4e**. The decision in that case is the product of a principle unrelated to the general principle that there must be a reasonable prospect of A holding his right free from C's security right.

2.1.6 Additional rights of C: a second security-specific limit?

It is often said that there is a second limit on A's ability to make a binding contractual promise to C *as part of a security transaction*. If the first limit can be described as a rule

---

[55] [1904] AC 323.

[56] [1914] AC 25.

[57] This point is forcefully made by G Williams (1944) 60 *LQR* 190 at 191: 'There is no logical contradiction between (a) an option to purchase and (b) a proviso for redemption if the option be not exercised.' Williams's general analysis, however, differs from that adopted in this book: Williams *entirely* rejects the general principle applied in *Fairclough v Swan Brewery Co* [1912] AC 565.

[58] In *Reeve v Lisle* [1902] AC 461 there was only a two-week gap between the security transaction and the option. Yet the option was valid: it did not interfere with A's right, if the secured duty was performed, to hold his right free from C's security right.

[59] [1904] AC 323.

against placing *fetters* on the prospect of A holding his right free from C's security right, the second can be described as a rule against placing '*clogs*' on A's right. The aim of the rule is to ensure that, when the secured duty is performed, A holds his right: (i) free from C's security right; *and* (ii) *in the same condition* as prior to the security transaction. Therefore, if A gives C security over a particular right and also makes an additional promise, as part of the security transaction, that affects A's ability to deal with that secured right, it may be that the additional promise does *not* give C an additional contractual right.

As we will see, this supposed second limit is very difficult to justify. The courts have noted the problems caused by the limit, but regard it as an established part of the law, which only Parliament can change. However, there is in fact *no* compelling authority in favour of the supposed limit.

(i) The supposed limit: A must be able to hold his right in the same condition as he held it prior to the security transaction

EXAMPLE 5a

At a time when holding shares in a tea company includes the opportunity to be a broker for that company, A transfers his tea company shares to C by way of security for a loan. A also promises to ensure that C is always employed by the tea company as a broker. A repays the loan and C returns the shares to A. C loses his job as a broker for the tea company and sues A for breach of contract.

This example is based on *Bradley v Carritt*.[60] In that case, the House of Lords held that A's promise to ensure that C be employed as a broker was *not* enforceable by C. Lord Macnaghten explained this result by stating that A's promise constituted an indirect 'clog' or 'fetter' on A's right to regain the mortgaged shares.[61] His Lordship's reasoning was that, if A was under a duty to ensure that C remained as a broker, this would effectively prevent A from selling the shares once he got them back. If A were to sell his shares to C2, C2 would necessarily displace C as broker, placing A in breach of contract to C: the risk to A of being in breach of contract devalues the shares, and they are therefore not in the same condition as before the security transaction. As a result, A's 'broker' promise could not be allowed to give C a contractual right.

Lord Macnaghten's reasoning is difficult to support. First, A's promise did *not* prevent A from repaying the loan and regaining the shares: the situation in **Example 5a** is clearly different from that in **Example 4b**, and the logic behind the first security-specific limit thus does *not* apply.

Second, A may chose to devalue his assets or rights whenever he makes a bargain with C—the point of contracting is that A values the benefit he receives from C more than the cost of the promise: A's promise may devalue his shares, but why should this be prevented simply because the promise occurs in the context of a security transaction? This point is made clear in Lord Lindley's powerful dissent: 'there being no fraud, undue influence, oppression, or extortion, I can discover no ground whatever for the interference of a Court of Equity with the legal rights of the [C]'.[62]

---

[60] [1903] AC 253.
[61] *Ibid* at 260–61.
[62] *Ibid* at 275.

(ii) Reanalysing the supposed second limit

There is thus a clear problem with the idea that A's promise, because it restricts A's right to use his shares once he regains them, does not give C a contractual right. However, this does not mean that the decision in *Bradley v Carritt* is incorrect. In a case such as **Example 5a** we need to examine A's promise to ensure C is employed as a broker (the 'broker' promise). There are three possible interpretations:

Interpretation 1   A's promise is intended to impose a *second secured duty* on A: ie, a duty that, along with A's duty to repay the loan, will be secured by the mortgage of the shares.

Interpretation 2   A's promise is intended to *support C's security right*: ie, to give C a right, along with the mortgage of the shares, that gives A an incentive to perform his duty to repay the loan (by increasing the cost of not performing that primary duty).

Interpretation 3   A's promise is entirely *unrelated to the mortgage transaction*.

It is important to distinguish between these three interpretations. If **Interpretation 1** applies, then A's 'broker' promise will continue to bind him even if he pays off the loan.[63] Further,[64] C will not be under a duty to return the shares to A until A fully performs the 'broker' duty. If **Interpretation 2** applies, then the duty imposed by A's 'broker' promise will disappear when A pays off the loan: at that point, there is no longer any need for A to be under an incentive to repay the loan. If **Interpretation 3** applies, then, again, A's 'broker' promise will continue to bind him even if he pays off the loan, but C's duty to return the shares to C will arise as soon as A performs that primary duty to repay.

Interpretation	Intentions of A and C as to effect of A's promise	Effect in Example 5a
Interpretation 1	To impose a second secured duty on A	A remains under the duty to C even if A pays off the loan in full; A can only get the shares back if he performs both his duties to C
Interpretation 2	To provide support for C's security right by giving A an incentive to perform his primary duty.	A's duty disappears when A pays off the loan in full
Interpretation 3	The promise is entirely unrelated to the mortgage transaction.	A remains under the duty to C even if A pays off the loan in full

---

[63] In *Santley v Wilde* [1899] 2 Ch 474 A mortgaged a 10-year Lease to C in return for a loan of £2,000; A's additional promise was to pay C one-third of the net rents derived by A from renting out the premises ('net rent' promise). At 476, Lord Lindley MR adopted **Interpretation 1**: 'this lease is granted or assigned by the mortgagor to the mortgagee as security not only for the payment of the £2000 and interest, but also for the payment of the one-third of the net profit rents to the end of the term'.

[64] It is a prima facie duty because A's additional promise may fall foul of the general principle set out in 2.1.5 above: ie, it may remove a reasonable prospect of A holding his right free from C's security right. If that is the case, then the promise *may* still impose a duty on C; but that duty will not be secured. For example, as A's 'broker' promise in *Bradley* was to ensure C was a broker *forever*, A's right to regain the shares could not depend on A fulfilling that promise. And, in *Santley*, A's additional 'net rent' promise related to the *whole* of the 10-year term of A's Lease: as such, it *should* have been possible for A to regain the Lease *before* the end of the 10 years to perform the 'net rent' promise. The House of Lords in *Noakes v Rice* [1902] AC 24 (see *per* Lord Macnagthen at 31 and *per* Lord Davey at 34) was therefore right to doubt the result in *Santley*.

In *Bradley*, when A paid off the loan, C returned the shares to A—as such, **Interpretation 1** cannot be correct: C was not holding the shares as security for *both* promises. If **Interpretation 2** applies, the decision in *Bradley* is correct: A's 'broker' duty disappears when A repays the loan. In contrast, if **Interpretation 3** applies, the decision in *Bradley* is incorrect: there is then no reason why A's performance of his duty to repay the loan should release A from his unrelated 'broker' duty.

So, in a case such as **Example 5a**, contrary to the analysis of Lord Macnaghten in *Bradley v Carritt*, we do *not* need to rely on the principle that 'clogs' are invalid. Instead, the question is simply whether A's 'broker' duty was, in essence, *part of the security* given to C to provide A with an incentive to perform his primary duty to pay off the loan. And, on the facts of the case, that probably is the better view: the promise was given as part of the mortgage transaction and it is unlikely that, given the consequences of such a duty, A intended to be under the 'broker' duty after the loan was paid off and the shares regained.

(iii) The courts' treatment of the supposed second limit

EXAMPLE 5b

A0 has a Lease of a pub: there are 25 years remaining on the Lease. A wishes to acquire that Lease. C Ltd, a brewer, agrees to lend A the £150,000 purchase price provided that: (i) A repays the loan in instalments at 5 per cent annual interest; (ii) A's duty to C Ltd is secured by a Charge over the land; and (iii) both whilst A is paying off the loan, and after that time, A sells only beer provided by C Ltd. A pays off the entire debt plus the agreed interest. C's Charge is removed. A claims that he is no longer bound by his promise to sell only beer provided by C Ltd.

This case is clearly different from **Example 5a**. A cannot argue that his 'beer' duty simply supports C's security right: the contract makes clear that the 'beer' duty is to continue even *after* A has repaid the loan. And the term does not prevent A, as he has in fact done, from paying off the loan and releasing his Freehold from the Charge. Nor can A argue that the term is a restraint of trade (see **2.1.4(iv)** above): A was not trading at all when he made the deal with C.

Yet, in *Noakes v Rice*,[65] on which **Example 5b** is based,[66] the House of Lords held that A's 'beer' promise did *not* give C a contractual right: it was invalid as a 'clog or fetter' on A's right to pay off the debt and have his Freehold free from C's Charge.[67] That decision is impossible to justify. Indeed, in *Kreglinger v New Patagonia Meat and Cold Storage Co Ltd*,[68] the House of Lords retreated from the position taken in *Noakes*.

---

[65] [1902] AC 24.
[66] *Noakes* involved a mortgage of A's Lease (the mortgage took place before 1926), but the discussion there applies equally where C Ltd acquires a Charge: see eg *per* Chadwick LJ in *Jones v Morgan* [2001] EWCA Civ 995 at [64].
[67] [1904] AC 24 *per* Earl of Halsbury LC at 29–30; *per* Lord Macnaghten at 30; and *per* Lord Lindley at 36.
[68] [1914] AC 25.

EXAMPLE 5c

A Ltd, a meat-preserving business, wishes to borrow money from C, a firm of woolbrokers. C agrees to lend A Ltd £100,000 provided that: (i) A Ltd repays the loan at 6 per cent annual interest; (ii) A Ltd's duty to C is secured by giving C a floating charge over all A Ltd's current and future rights; and (iii) for the next five years, A Ltd must give C the chance to buy any of A Ltd's sheepskins at the full market price. Under the floating charge transaction, A Ltd is permitted to repay the loan in full at any point, provided it gives C one month's notice. Two years later, A Ltd repays the loan in full. C then tries to exercise its right to buy the sheepskins: A Ltd argues that C has no such right.

These facts are based on *Kreglinger v New Patagonia Meat and Cold Storage Co Ltd.*[69] The House of Lords rejected the idea that the 'sheepskins' clause was an invalid 'fetter' on A Ltd's right to remove C's floating charge by paying off the loan. That conclusion must be correct: after all, A Ltd has in fact paid off the loan and removed C's floating charge. The crucial question, as in *Bradley v Carritt*, is whether **Interpretation 2** or **Interpretation 3** applies:[70]

> **Interpretation 2**   the 'sheepskins' clause is simply intended to give A Ltd an incentive to repay the loan. In that case, C's right under the clause should stop when the loan is repaid.
>
> **Interpretation 3**   the 'sheepskins' clause is independent of the floating charge transaction and is unrelated to A's duty to repay the loan.

As Viscount Haldane LC noted,[71] that question has to be answered by looking at the facts of the particular case. His Lordship's view of the case fits **Interpretation 3**:

> outside the security and consistently with its terms there was a contemporaneous but collateral contract, contained in the same document as constituted the security, but in substance independent of it.[72]

It makes no difference if C insisted on the 'sheepskins' clause as a condition of making the loan to A Ltd: the clause can still be seen as independent of the floating charge transaction.[73]

(iv) The supposed second limit and options to purchase

EXAMPLE 5d

The facts are as in **Example 4d** above. Five years after giving C his Charge, A attempts to pay off the entire debt plus the agreed interest. C then attempts to exercise his option to buy A's Freehold. A argues that, as he is able to perform the secured duty, C has no right to buy A's land.

---

[69] [1914] AC 25.

[70] On the facts of the case, **Interpretation 1** seems unlikely.

[71] [1914] AC 25, 39.

[72] *Ibid* at 41. Indeed, Viscount Haldane LC explains the dissent of Lord Lindley in *Bradley v Carritt* [1903] AC 253 as based on **Interpretation 3**.

[73] One reason in support of **Interpretation 3** is the fact that, in the type of floating charge transaction entered into in *Kreglinger*, A Ltd has the power to use its rights in the ordinary course of business. So, if A Ltd had given an option to purchase to C2, it would not then have been possible for C to assert its security right against C2 (see F4:4.3.1). As A Ltd's entry into the floating charge transaction with C thus does not prevent A Ltd giving C2 a valuable option to purchase, it is difficult to see why it should prevent A Ltd giving C such an option. I am grateful to Andrew Scott for this observation.

In *Samuel v Jarrah Timber & Wood Paving Corpn Ltd*,[74] the House of Lords considered an essentially identical set of facts. It held that C was *not* able to exercise its option to purchase: as A was able to pay off the entire debt, C had to allow A to keep his Freehold free from *both* the Charge and the option to purchase. That decision has been seen as authority for the proposition that it is simply impossible for A *both* to: (i) give C a security right over a right of A; *and* (ii) to give C an option to purchase A's right (see **2.1.5(iv)** above). However, the result can be explained *without* adopting that unsatisfactory proposition.

In **Example 5d**, as in **Example 5a**, we instead need to examine A's promise to allow C to buy A's Freehold (the 'option' promise). Again, there are three possible interpretations. If **Interpretation 1** applies, the 'option' promise, along with A's duty to repay the loan, is secured by C's Charge. In that case, C should be able to enforce the option. If **Interpretation 2** applies, the 'option' promise is intended to give A an incentive to perform his duty to repay the loan. In that case, as A is willing and able to repay the loan, C should *not* be able to enforce the option. If **Interpretation 3** applies, the 'option' promise is independent of the Charge transaction. In that case, as in *Reeve v Lisle*,[75] C should be able to enforce the option.

It seems that in *Samuel* the House of Lords went for **Interpretation 2**. The 'option' promise was intended to give A an incentive to perform the secured duty: the duty to repay the loan to C. Therefore, as A was willing and able to perform that duty, the 'option' promise *no longer* imposed a duty on A. On the facts of *Samuel*, that interpretation was a reasonable one. **Interpretation 1** is unlikely: C does not need security for A's duty to perform the 'option' promise because if A fails to perform such a promise, C's contractual right will, in any case, be specifically protected. **Interpretation 3** is also unlikely: in a standard Charge transaction, A is not given the power, once C acquires his Charge, to give C2 an option to purchase A's Freehold. So, in attempting to acquire an effective option to purchase, C is clearly taking advantage of his special position as the party acquiring the Charge.[76]

In **Examples 5a and 5d**, and in the House of Lords in *Bradley v Carritt* and *Samuel*, the crucial point therefore is *not* that A's additional promise does not give C a contractual right. Rather, it is that C's initial contractual right *supports C's security right* and thus disappears when A performs his primary, secured duty: his duty to repay the loan. Of course, that reasoning was not adopted by the House of Lords in either *Bradley* or *Samuel*. Yet it provides a way *both* to: (i) justify the *results* in those cases; *and* (ii) to reject the 'clogs' doctrine that, as noted by Lord Phillips MR, serves 'no useful purpose'.[77]

---

[74] [1904] AC 323.

[75] [1902] AC 461.

[76] *Samuel* thus differs from *Kreglinger*: in the latter case, C's security right arose under a floating charge transaction and (see **n 73** above) A Ltd *does* generally have a power, after giving C his floating charge, to give C2 an option to purchase free from C's pre-existing security right.

[77] *Jones v Morgan* [2001] EWCA Civ 955 [86].

SUMMARY of G4:2.1.5 and G4:2.1.6

Lord Parker once stated that an additional promise made by A in a security transaction would *not* give C a contractual right if that promise failed any one of three tests. Such a term must not be: (a) 'unfair and unconscionable'; (b) in the nature of a penalty interfering with the prospect of A holding his right free from C's security right; or (c) 'inconsistent with or repugnant' to that prospect.[78] The unconscionability test is part of the *general* limits on A's power to make a binding additional promise. Lord Parker's second and third points are both part of the *security-specific* limit on A's power to make such a promise. That limit comes simply from the fact that, *whenever* A gives C a security right over a thing or right of A, there must be a reasonable prospect, if the secured duty is performed, of A holding that thing or right free from C's security right. The limit comes from a fundamental feature of security transactions. It explains why, in *Fairclough v Swan Brewery Co*, A's additional promise did not give C a contractual right to prevent A paying off the loan (and thus to retain his security right) until a month before the end of A's Lease.

However, this fundamental limit has been incorrectly extended by the courts. In cases such as *Noakes v Rice* and *Jones v Morgan*, it has been (reluctantly) assumed that, when A gives C security over a thing or a right, it is also impossible for A: (i) to make a binding promise that limits A's ability to deal with the thing or the right; *or* (ii) to give C an option to purchase that thing or right. However, that assumption rests on a misunderstanding of the decisions in cases such as *Bradley v Carritt* and *Samuel v Jarrah Timber*. In those cases A *did* make a binding additional promise to C. That promise thus gave C an additional right. But the additional right was intended simply as a further incentive for A to perform his duty to repay the loan given by C. So, *when* A paid off that loan in full, C's additional right disappeared.

It is thus possible to accept a security-specific limit that A cannot give C an additional right that is a 'fetter': ie, that prevents there being a reasonable prospect of A holding his right free from C's security right. However, it is *not* possible to defend a second security-specific limit that A cannot give C an additional right that is a 'clog': ie that prevents A holding his right free from C's security right *and* in exactly the same condition as he held it before giving C his security right.

3   THE ACQUISITION QUESTION

In this section, we will examine how C can acquire a security right in relation to A's land. It is worth noting that if A Ltd is a company, C's failure to register his security with the Registrar of Companies will mean that C's right will be void against a liquidator, administrator or creditor of A Ltd.[79] Therefore, if C wants to have a *useful* security right against A Ltd he must comply with the rules discussed here *and* register his right with the Registrar of Companies.

3.1   Property rights: the creation of a Charge

It is in theory possible for A to give C a property right in land, by way of security, through a

---

[78] *Kreglinger v New Patagonia Meat and Cold Storage Co Ltd* [1914] 1 AC 25 at 61.
[79] See **F4:n105**.

pledge or a consensual lien. However, given their very limited practical value, we will concentrate here on the creation of a Charge. There are usually two stages: (i) A makes a contractual promise to give C the Charge; (ii) C acquires the Charge itself.

3.1.1. A's power to make a contractual promise to give C a Charge

The Bills of Sale Act 1878 (Amendment) Act 1882 ('the 1882 Act') can regulate A's power to give C a security right where A has Ownership of a thing (see **F4:3.1.1(i)**). That Act does *not* apply where A has a Freehold or Lease and attempts to grant C a Charge. Instead, other formality rules perform the two key functions of protecting A from exploitation, and allowing a third party to discover C's right.

First, section 2 of the Law of Property (Miscellaneous) Provisions Act 1989 regulates A's power to make a contractual promise to grant C a Charge over A's land. A's promise to give C such a right can only be contractually binding if it is made in a document, signed by both A and C, that sets out all the expressly agreed terms of the deal (see **E2:2.3.3**). Like the writing requirement imposed by the 1882 Act, this formality rule can provide A with some protection:[80] it certainly gives A the chance to discover the terms of the Charge transaction.

Second, where A and C enter a *regulated mortgage contract* (see **2.1.4(i)** above), the extensive *MCOB* sourcebook provided by the FSA gives detailed rules and guidelines not only as to the content of that contract but also as to its form. Those formal rules are designed to promote transparency by ensuring that the terms of the deal are made clear to A.[81] Further, the *MCOB* also regulates how such contracts are advertised and sold by lenders. Again the aim is to protect A by ensuring that A is aware of, and freely consents to, the terms of the security transaction.[82] A failure to comply with those rules cannot, by itself, prevent C acquiring a contractual right against A.[83]

Third, where C's Charge does *not* arise under a *regulated mortgage contract*, the CCA 1974 (as amended by the CCA 2006) may apply (see **F4:3.1.1(ii)**).[84]

3.1.2 A's power to grant C a Charge

A binding contractual promise by A cannot, by itself, give C a Charge. A Charge is a property right in land, and so, to acquire that right, C needs to show that: (i) A has used a deed to grant C the right;[85] *and* (ii) C has substantively registered that right (see **E1:2.3**).[86] Once C has registered his Charge, he benefits from the positive operation of registration:[87] C will have that Charge, unless and until the Charge is removed from the register.[88]

---

[80] Although, as it specifically deals with security transactions, the 1882 Act imposes a stricter rule: in contrast to the rule imposed by the 1989 Act, the document must also be signed by a witness: see 1882 Act, ss 9–10.

[81] *MCOB* sourcebook, 6–7.

[82] *Ibid*, 2.2.

[83] As noted above some breaches by C Bank of the FSA standards can allow A (if he is a private person) to bring an action for damages. For example, A can sue to recover loss resulting from C Bank's provision of information in a 'way that is not clear or fair, or that is misleading': see *MCOB* sourcebook, 2.2.

[84] Before the 2006 changes, the formality rules imposed by the Act rarely applied to Charge transactions as agreements giving A £25,000 or more of credit were exempt from those formality rules. The CCA 2006 removed that limit.

[85] LPA 1925, s 52.

[86] LRA 2002, s 27(2)(f).

[87] LRA 2002, s 58(1) (see **C2:6**).

[88] If and when the duty secured by the Charge is performed, A can of course insist on the register being changed so that C's Charge is removed. That change does not count as a 'rectification' as C does not suffer any loss as a result of the change to the register (see **E5:3.2.2**).

3.1.3 Setting aside a Charge transaction

(i) General position

If A apparently exercises his power to transfer Ownership of a thing to C, A may be able to argue that his intention to make that transfer was flawed (see **D1:2.2.2**). The same analysis applies where A apparently exercises his power to give C a new property right in land, such as a Charge. In a Charge transaction, it is very unlikely that A will be able to argue the apparent creation of the Charge was *void*: there is no real chance that A will be mistaken as to either the identity of C or the identity of the land to which the Charge relates.

If the Charge transaction is not void, then it does properly lead to C acquiring a Charge. Nonetheless, A may still have a power to *set aside* the transaction and thus remove C's Charge.[89] For such a power to arise, A needs to show *both* that:

- There was a flaw in A's intention; *and*
- C is in some way responsible for that flaw.

This is clear from the rules relating to duress, fraud, undue influence and misrepresentation and also to unconscionable exploitation of a weakness of A (see **D1:2.2.2** and **2.1.4(iii)** above): in each case, C's conduct is, in some way, the cause of the flaw in A's intention. This does not mean that C must act *wrongfully*: there is no need for C to have breached a duty to A. So, even an entirely *innocent* misrepresentation by C can give A a power to set the transaction aside.[90] This is because, even if the misrepresentation is innocent, it is still C's representation.[91]

In a standard 'regulated mortgage contract', if C Bank follows the rules and guidelines laid down in the *MCOB* sourcebook,[92] it will be very difficult to show that C Bank has procured the Charge transaction by its own misconduct (ie, its own direct duress, fraud, undue influence, misrepresentation or unconscionable exploitation of a weakness of A). However, in some cases, the misconduct of another party may be attributed to C Bank.

(ii) Can A1's misconduct affect C Bank? General position

EXAMPLE 6a

A1 and A2 are married co-holders of a Freehold. A1 runs a business (A Ltd): A2 has no share of that business. A1 wants to convince C Bank to extend A Ltd's overdraft facility. C Bank is only willing to do so if: (i) A1 guarantees the overdraft; and (ii) A1's guarantee is secured by a Charge over A1 and A2's Freehold. A2 is reluctant to agree to the Charge. A1 tells A2 that he has nothing to worry about: A1's maximum liability under the guarantee will be £50,000. That statement is untrue; but as a result of it, A2 signs the necessary documents and A1 and A2 give C Bank the Charge, which C Bank then substantively registers. C Bank does not know about A1's misrepresentation.

---

[89] Such removal will require an application to remove C's Charge from the register (see **n 88** above).
[90] *Redgrave v Hurd* (1881) 20 Ch D 1.
[91] See too *Allcard v Skinner* (1887) 36 Ch D 145. It was emphasised (by eg Bowen LJ) that C had not behaved reprehensibly; but nonetheless, the flaw in A's intention was due to the influence C exercised over A; as noted by Lindley LJ at 183 'the undue influence which Courts of Equity endeavour to defeat is the undue influence of one person over another'.
[92] That is, the FSA's *Mortgage: Conduct of Business* sourcebook.

In such a case, can A2 set aside the Charge transaction by pointing to A1's misrepresentation? To do so, A2 has to show that A1's misrepresentation can be *attributed* to C Bank so that C Bank (*as well as* A1) can be said to be in some way responsible for the flaw in A2's intention.

In *Barclays Bank v O'Brien*,[93] the House of Lords considered a case essentially identical to **Example 6a**. The conclusion reached was that *if*:

- C Bank knew about A1's misrepresentation when acquiring the Charge; *or*
- C Bank *ought to have known* about A1's misrepresentation when acquiring the Charge; then
- A2 has a power to set aside the Charge transaction.

Lord Browne-Wilkinson (with whom the rest of the panel agreed) made clear that the same principles apply if A2 has consented to the Charge as a result of A1's undue influence (or, presumably, as a result of A1's duress, fraud or unconscionable exploitation). Using the language of 'actual and constructive notice',[94] his Lordship described A2 as having an 'equity' to set aside the transaction.[95] However, that description is incorrect.[96] In **Example 6a**, the question is *not* whether C Bank can rely on the 'bona fide purchaser defence' to a pre-existing persistent right of A2. Rather, the question is whether the flaw in A2's intention gives A2 a power to set aside the Charge transaction. And Lord Browne-Wilkinson's test *can* be seen as providing a way to answer that question: A1's misrepresentation can be attributed to C Bank if C Bank: (i) did know about it; *or* (ii) ought to have known about it.

Therefore, if: (i) C Bank *knows* about A1's duress, fraud, undue influence, misrepresentation or unconscionable exploitation of a weakness of A2; but (ii) fails to take steps to address the flaw caused in A2's intention (eg, in **Example 6a**, by telling A2 the true position); then (iii) it is reasonable to say that the flaw in A2's intention can be attributed to C Bank as well as to A1. And the same is true if C Bank *ought to have known* about the flaw: in such a case, C Bank should not be able to use its failure to discover the flaw as an excuse. As a result, Lord Browne-Wilkinson's test can be justified—but *not* by seeing it is an application of the general 'bona fide purchaser' defence. This explains why, in *Barclays Bank plc v Boulter*[97] the House of Lords made clear that the onus is *not* on C Bank to show that, due to his lack of notice, he has a defence to a right of A2. Rather, the onus is on A2 to show that: (i) there was a flaw in A2's intention; *and* (ii) that flaw can be attributed to A1 (as a result of A1's fraud, duress, undue influence, misrepresentation or unconscionable exploitation of a weakness of A); *and* (iii) that flaw can also be attributed to C Bank.

(iii) Can A1's misconduct affect C Bank? Applying the test

In *Royal Bank of Scotland v Etridge (No 2)*[98] the House of Lords considered a whole set of cases very similar to **Example 6a**. In those cases, the flaw in A2's intention came from A1's undue influence, rather than from a misrepresentation. But, as in *O'Brien*, the crucial

---

[93] [1994] 1 AC 180.
[94] *Ibid* at 195–6.
[95] *Ibid* at 195.
[96] As noted, in politer terms by Lord Nicholls in *Royal Bank of Scotland v Etridge* [2002] 2 AC 773 at [39]: 'Lord Browne-Wilkinson would be the first to recognise this is not a conventional use of the equitable concept of constructive notice.'
[97] [1999] 1 WLR 1919.
[98] [2002] 2 AC 773.

question was whether that flaw could be attributed to C Bank as well as to A1. Lord Nicholls (with whom the rest of the panel agreed)[99] emphasised that the general *O'Brien* approach, whilst it is not an application of the 'bona fide purchaser' defence, is correct. However, the difficulty resulting from the *O'Brien* decision was obvious: precisely *when* will a court say that C Bank *ought to have known* about the flaw in A2's intention? This sort of test can cause real problems for a party seeking to acquire a right (see **E2:3.5.1**). In particular, how much time and money must C Bank spend in checking to see if there are any flaws in A2's intention? C Bank may also face some questions of delicacy: how much does it need to know about A1 and A2's relationship; how much about A1's financial position must it reveal to A2? C Bank needs to have a set of clear guidelines that, if followed, can protect it from the risk of suffering as a result of a hidden flaw in A2's intention. To some extent, such guidelines can be provided by the FSA, but of course any guidelines need a court's approval.

In *Etridge*, Lord Nicholls provided guidance for lenders by setting out tests for the two crucial questions: (i) when can it be said that C Bank *ought it to be aware of the risk* that A2's consent may have been procured by A1's misconduct?;[100] *and* (ii) what steps must C Bank take to deal with that risk?

(a) Suspicious transactions: when ought C Bank to be aware of the risk of A1's misconduct?

O'Brien makes clear that C Bank should recognise that risk if: (i) A1 and A2 are married; *and* (ii) A2 gains no direct benefit from the Charge transaction. In **Example 6a**, therefore, C Bank ought to be aware of the risk. However, that cannot be the only situation in which a real risk of misconduct arises.

EXAMPLE 6b

A2 has a 99-year Lease of a flat. A2 is a junior employee of A Ltd, a company run by A1. A2 has no shares in the company. A1 wants to convince C Bank to extend A Ltd's overdraft facility. C Bank is only willing to do so if the overdraft is guaranteed and secured over some land. A2 convinces A1 to: (i) give an unlimited guarantee of A Ltd's duty to pay off its overdraft; and (ii) to give C Bank a Charge over A2's flat in order to secure A2's guarantee. A2 gives C Bank the Charge, which it substantively registers.

Although A2 and A1 are not married, it is clear that C Bank *ought to be aware of the risk* that A2's consent to the Charge has been procured by A1's misconduct: (i) A2 is a junior employee of A1; *and* (ii) A2 gains no direct benefit from the Charge transaction. This was confirmed by the Court of Appeal in *Credit Lyonnais Bank Nederland v Burch*,[101] the essential facts of which are identical to **Example 6b**.

So, it seems there must be a broader principle as to when C Bank ought to be aware of the risk: certainly, the *O'Brien* approach cannot apply only where A1 and A2 are cohabiting; or only where A1 and A2 are lovers. In *Royal Bank of Scotland v Etridge (No 2)*[102] Lord Nicholls suggested a 'general principle' that C Bank ought to be aware of the risk whenever

---

[99] Lord Scott also gave a reasoned speech but the senior Law Lord, Lord Bingham, emphasised at [3] that 'the opinion of Lord Nicholls commands the unqualified support of all members of the House'.

[100] In *Etridge*, Lord Nicholls referred to this as the question of when C Bank should be 'on inquiry' at [87]; but, as his Lordship noted at [44], that term must be used carefully to prevent confusion with the 'bona fide purchaser' defence.

[101] [1997] 1 All ER 144.

[102] [2002] 2 AC 773.

the relationship between A1 and A2 is 'non-commercial'.[103] The general principle therefore seems to be that C ought to be aware of the risk if:

- A2 agrees to give C a right to secure another party's duty (eg, A2 gives C a Charge or a guarantee to secure A Ltd's duty to pay off an overdraft);[104] *and*
- A2 receives no real commercial benefit in return for giving C that right.

Hence, in *Burch*, A2 got no direct commercial benefit from giving C Bank the Charge: the Charge allowed A Ltd to receive more credit, but A2 did not have any shares in A Ltd.[105]

(b) Dealing with the risk: what steps must C Bank take?

In *Etridge*, Lord Nicholls made clear the steps C Bank must take to ensure that A2 will *not* be able to use a hidden flaw in his intention to set aside the Charge transaction:[106]

- C Bank must contact A2 directly and make clear that the Charge transaction cannot go ahead unless A2 receives legal advice;
- C Bank must give to A2 (or her solicitor) details of the financial circumstances relevant to the loan made to A1;
- C Bank must receive written confirmation from a solicitor that A1 has received legal advice and understands the nature of the Charge transaction.

It is important to note that C Bank is protected even if: (i) A2 does *not* receive *independent* legal advice—the advice can given by a solicitor also acting for A1,[107] or (ii) A2 does not receive *competent* legal advice—as long as C Bank is not aware of the defects in the legal advice, it can rely on the solicitor's written confirmation.[108] The rules set out in *Etridge* thus form a compromise: an attempt to balance the need to protect A2 with the need to limit the time and expense involved in a Charge transaction. For example, a requirement of independent advice would have given A2 greater protection, but it was rejected due to the extra expense that would be incurred if, *in every case*, A1 and A2 had to be separately advised.[109]

Conversely, it is also important to remember that the *Etridge* rules will *not* protect C Bank if it *knows* about the flaw in A2's intention. Those rules simply prevent the Charge transaction being set aside due to a *hidden* flaw.

(iv) Can A1's misconduct affect C Bank? Example 6a

In a case such as **Example 6a** C Bank clearly ought to be aware of the risk that A2's consent has been procured by A1's misconduct, because: (i) A2 is providing security for A Ltd's debt; *and* (ii) A2 acquires no real commercial benefit from the overdraft facility of A Ltd. So, as C

---

[103] At [82]–[89], esp at [87].

[104] It is thus important to note that the principle does not apply *only* where A2 gives C a property right or persistent right by way of security right: it can also apply where A2 simply gives C a personal right by way of security (ie, a right to sue A2 if A Ltd fails to perform its duty to pay off an overdraft). For such guarantees, see **F4:1.1**.

[105] That is not to say the result would be different if A2 had *any* shares in A Ltd. If A2 had a very small number of shares the Charge would still fail to give A2 any *real* commercial benefit.

[106] [2002] 2 AC 773, [79]-[80].

[107] *Per* Lord Nicholls at [69]–[74].

[108] *Per* Lord Nicholls at [75]–[78]. At [61]–[67] Lord Nicholls sets out guidelines as to the content of the advice a solicitor should give. A solicitor's failure to follow those guidelines may mean the solicitor has not discharged his contractual duty to A2 to take reasonable care in providing his services.

[109] *Per* Lord Nicholls at [73]–[74]. As Lord Nicholls noted, A2 may often prefer to receive advice from a trusted family solicitor.

Bank has not taken the *Etridge* steps (eg, it has received no written confirmation from a solicitor that A2 understands the Charge transaction), A1's misrepresentation can be attributed to C Bank. A2 thus has a power to set aside the Charge.

It is important to remember that showing that the *Etridge* steps apply and have not been followed is not enough, on its own, to give A2 this power. These steps allow the *attribution* to C Bank of A1's duress, fraud, undue influence, misrepresentation or unconscionable exploitation of a weakness of A; but A2 also needs to show that A1 did in fact procure A2's consent by using such means.

If, as in **Example 6a**, A2 can set aside the Charge transaction, there is a risk that, by exercising that power, A2 may be unjustly enriched at C Bank's expense (by receiving *some* benefit from the money advanced by C Bank). As a result, A2's exercise of his power may be conditional on A2 giving the value of that benefit back to C Bank.[110]

However, this does *not* mean that a court can impose whatever terms it likes on A2's exercise of his power to set aside the transaction: in particular, in **Example 6a**, a court *cannot* say that C Bank's Charge remains valid as security *up to* the £50,000 limit represented by A1.[111] As such, cases where A2's power arises as a result of C's fraud, duress, undue influence or misrepresentation can be contrasted with cases where A2's power arises as a result of A1's unconscionable exploitation of a weakness of A2. In the latter group of cases, but not the former, a court *can* impose general terms on A2's power to set aside the transaction. There is some debate as to whether that distinction can be justified, but the general consensus is in favour of *extending* the courts' power to impose general terms.[112] However, given the court's acceptance of the limits in cases of fraud, duress, undue influence or misrepresentation, it may be better to resolve the inconsistency by *limiting* the courts' powers in 'unconscionable bargain' cases. After all, the courts do not have a general power to rewrite parties' contractual agreements. In a case such as **Example 6a**, any financial limits imposed on A2's power to set aside the Charge transaction should come *only* from the need to ensure A2 is not unjustly enriched at C Bank's expense.

(v) Unconscionable bargains

In a case such as **Example 6b**, it may also be possible for A2 to argue that the Charge transaction should be set aside as an 'unconscionable bargain' (see **2.1.4(iii)** above). That principle can be used not only by a court refusing to enforce *particular* terms of a contract, but also by a party who wants to set aside *all* the terms of a contract. In *Credit Lyonnais Bank Nederland v Burch* the Court of Appeal found that, as A1's undue influence could be attributed to C Bank, A2 could set aside the whole Charge transaction on that basis. However, Nourse LJ suggested that it was 'very well arguable that [A2] could, directly against [C Bank], have had the legal charge set aside as an unconscionable bargain'.[113] It is therefore

---

[110] See eg *Dunbar Bank plc v Nadeem* [1998] 2 FLR 457. In that case, A2 was unable to set aside the Charge, but the Court of Appeal made clear that, if A2 did have such a power, its exercise would be conditional on returning any enrichment received from C: see *per* Millett LJ at 464–6. *Cheese v Thomas* [1994] 1 WLR 129 demonstrates that, where C's advance allows A2 to acquire a right in land, such enrichment can include an increase in the value of A2's right.

[111] *TSB Bank plc v Camfield* [1995] 1 WLR 430; *per* Morritt LJ in *Dunbar Bank plc v Nadeem* [1998] 2 FLR 457 at 468.

[112] See eg Poole and Keyser (2005) 121 *LQR* 273, esp at 298; Ferguson (1995) 111 *LQR* 555; Burrows, *Casebook on Contract* (2007), 549. The High Court of Australia has adopted that wider approach: *Vadasz v Pioneer Concrete (SA) Pty Ltd* (1995) 184 CLR 102.

[113] [1997] 1 All ER 144, 151.

important to distinguish two ways in which A2 may argue that he has a power to set aside the Charge transaction as an unconscionable bargain. A could argue that:

1. As suggested by Nourse LJ, C Bank itself *directly* exploited A2's vulnerability by entering into the Charge transaction. Such a claim depends on showing that C Bank was aware of, and exploited, a vulnerability of A2 (see **2.1.4(iii)**). Or
2. A1 exploited A2's vulnerability by persuading A2 to enter into the Charge transaction; *and* C Bank knew or ought to have known of A1's misconduct. In such a case, the *Etridge* rules will apply to determine if A1's misconduct can be attributed to C Bank.[114]

3.2 Property rights: the transfer of a pre-existing Charge

Let us say A is under a duty to repay a loan to C1; that duty is secured by a Charge over A's land. If C1 decides to assign to C2 his personal right against A (see **C3:5.1.2**), C1 will also wish to transfer his Charge to C2. C1 does have the power to do so.[115] If C1 exercises that power in a deed, and if C2 is substantively registered as the new holder of the Charge, C2 will acquire C1's pre-existing Charge.[116]

It is also worth noting that, if C1 has a Charge, he can also give C2 a *sub-Charge*: ie, C1 can give C2 a security right in relation to C1's Charge.[117] In such a case, there is no transfer of C1's right to C2: instead, C1 keeps his Charge and C2 acquires a new right. The point of C2's right is that, if the duty secured by the sub-Charge is not performed, C2 will be able to use the value of C1's Charge to meet that duty. To acquire his sub-Charge, C2 again needs to substantively register that right.

3.3 Persistent rights: acquiring an Equitable Charge

If A has a Freehold or Lease and is under a duty to grant C a Charge, C has a persistent right: a right against A's power to grant a Charge (see **E2:1.3.1(i)**). That persistent right can be called an Equitable Charge. Hence, if A makes a contractual promise to give C a Charge, C can acquire a persistent right *even before* A performs that promise. It is usually said that C's Equitable Charge arises only if a court would order specific performance of A's contractual promise. However, in practice, that supposed requirement is irrelevant. In general, a court *will* order specific performance of A's promise, not only because A has promised to give C a right in land, but also because A has promised to give C a security right—a mere personal right to receive money from A will inadequately protect C's right.[118] Further, C's ability to acquire a persistent right does *not* depend on the availability of specific performance (see **D2:2.1.2(vi)**).[119]

---

[114] For a case in which A2 unsuccessfully made both arguments, see *Portman Building Society v Dusangh* [2000] 2 All ER Comm 221. The Court of Appeal emphasised that a bargain is only 'unconscionable' if a party can be said to have behaved in a 'morally reprehensible' way by exploiting a known vulnerability of A: see *per* Simon Brown LJ at 229 and *per* Ward LJ at 232.

[115] Such a transfer will generally occur alongside a transfer of the benefit of the secured duty

[116] LRA 2002, s 27(3)(a).

[117] LRA 2002, s 23(2)(b); Law Com No 271 at [7.11].

[118] *Per* Buckley LJ in *Swiss Bank Corpn v Lloyds Bank Ltd* [1982] AC 584 at 595.

[119] It is true, however, that C's Equitable Charge may depend on C advancing money to A. As a Charge is a

EXAMPLE 7a

A has a Freehold. A urgently needs £100,000 to take up a business opportunity. A enters into negotiations with C. C agrees to make the loan if it is given a Charge as security. A writes to C promising to grant C such a Charge. As the money is needed urgently, C advances it to A. A then refuses to grant C the promised Charge.

In such a case, A is *not* under a contractual duty to grant C a Charge. The formality rule imposed by section 2 of the Law of Property (Miscellaneous Provisions) Act 1989 ('the 1989 Act') has *not* been satisfied (see **E2:2.3.3**). The problem is that there is no document, signed by *both* A and C, setting out all the expressly agreed terms of the Charge transaction. Nonetheless, C does have an Equitable Charge, as A is under a *non-contractual* duty to grant C the promised Charge. That duty arises as a result of proprietary estoppel (see **E4:3**): (i) A made a promise to C; (ii) C relied on that promise by advancing the money to A; (iii) C would suffer a detriment if A were allowed to go back on that promise.[120] Further, as C Bank, by advancing the money to A, has performed its side of an agreed bargain, A is under a duty to perform its promise (see **E4:4.4**). Therefore, as proprietary estoppel imposes a duty on A to grant C a Charge, C has an Equitable Charge.

This result was confirmed by the Court of Appeal in *Kinane v Mackie-Conteh*,[121] the essential facts of which are identical to **Example 7a**. However, in that case, the Court of Appeal said that C Bank's right arose under a Constructive Trust.[122] As we saw in **G3:2.4.3(iv)** that is an inaccurate way of describing C's right. A is not under the core Trust duty: he is simply under a duty to grant C a Charge. C's right is therefore better described simply as an Equitable Charge.

Prior to the 1989 Act, an Equitable Charge could also arise if: (i) A made an oral promise to give C a Charge over A's Freehold or Lease; *and* (ii) A deposited his title deeds (ie, the documents evidencing his Freehold or Lease) with C.[123] In *United Bank of Kuwait plc v Sahib* the Court of Appeal considered whether an Equitable Charge could arise in the same way after the 1989 Act. This depends on whether that principle was based on: (i) A being under a *contractual* duty to grant C a Charge; *or* (ii) A being under a *non-contractual* duty to give C a Charge. In *Sahib*, the Court of Appeal held that the principle had an 'essential contractual foundation'.[124] As a result, the formality rule imposed by the 1989 Act must apply to such a case: that Act now regulates how A can exercise his power to come under a contractual duty to C. So, an oral promise can no longer give rise to an Equitable Charge *simply* because it is followed by the deposit of title deeds with C.

---

security right, it has to secure a duty owed to C. So, if the contractual agreement is that (i) C will lend A money; and (ii) C will acquire a Charge as security for A's duty to repay C, then C's Equitable Charge can only arise once C has advanced the money to A: before that point, there is no duty of A that can be secured.

[120] C Bank's detriment would consist of having only a personal right against A and not having a security right to protect A's duty to C Bank.

[121] [2005] EWCA Civ 45. See **E2:Example 11a**.

[122] See eg *per* Neuberger LJ at *Kinane v Mackie-Conteh* at [45].

[123] See eg *Russel v Russel* (1783) 1 Bro CC 269.

[124] See *per* Peter Gibson LJ in *United Bank of Kuwait plc v Sahib* [1997] Ch 107 at 137.

3.4   Persistent rights: acquiring a Purely Equitable Charge

3.4.1 General position

If A has a right, A can give C a persistent right by making a binding promise to hold that right as security for a duty owed to C (see F4:2.2.2). In such a case, there is a fixed charge transaction: C acquires a Purely Equitable Charge. Similarly, if A expects to acquire a right in the future and A makes such a binding promise with respect to that right, C will acquire a Purely Equitable Charge *as soon as* A acquires that right. The same principle applies where A has a Freehold or Lease. The only difference is that, as C's persistent right relates to land, a formality rule regulates A's power to give C that right. That rule is imposed by section 53(1)(a) of the LPA 1925: A must exercise his power to give C the right in signed writing (see E2:2.3.1).

3.4.2 Non-consensual Purely Equitable Charges

C acquires a Purely Equitable Charge *whenever* A is under a duty to hold a particular right as security: A's duty need not arise as a result of a contractual promise by A (see F4:3.2.3). In such a case, the Purely Equitable Charge acquired by C arises 'by operation of law': as a result, the signed writing requirement imposed by section 53(1)(a) does *not* apply. The right B acquires in such a case is often referred to as an 'Equitable Lien'. However, that term is actively unhelpful: an 'Equitable Lien' is simply a Purely Equitable Charge that has arisen for some reason *other* than A's contractual promise to hold a right as security (see F4:3.2.3).

There is no real coherence as to the situations in which A will come under a non-contractual duty to hold a Freehold or Lease as security. One example occurs where: (i) C has a Purely Equitable Charge against a particular right held by A; and (ii) without C's consent or other authority, A uses that right to acquire a Freehold or Lease. In such a case, C can use the tracing rules to identify A's Freehold or Lease as a product of the initial right against which B had a Purely Equitable Charge. To avoid A's unjust enrichment, it seems the new right should also be subject to such a Purely Equitable Charge in C's favour (see D4:4.4).

A further, rather dubious example has occurred in a number of proprietary estoppel cases. In these cases, a court has concluded that: (i) A is under a duty to pay C a sum of money; *and* (ii) A should hold his Freehold or Lease as security for his duty to pay that sum to C.[125] Yet no explanation has been given as to why C should acquire this additional security right.[126] There is a real danger that a security right is given *simply* to protect C against third parties and the risk of A's insolvency.[127] The problem here is that, by protecting C, a court interferes with the claims of other creditors of A. C should acquire the Purely Equitable Charge *only* if that extra right is necessary to prevent C suffering a detriment as a result of A's failure to honour a promise. That could be the case if, for example, A promised

---

[125] See eg *Unity Joint Stock Mutual Banking Association v King* (1858) 25 Beav 72; *Campbell v Griffin* [2001] EWCA Civ 990.

[126] In *Jennings v Rice* [2003] 1 P & CR 100, a Purely Equitable Charge did not arise although Robert Walker LJ at [51] suggested such a right can be justified where C's detriment consists of making improvements to A's land.

[127] For example, in *Campbell v Griffin* [2001] EWCA Civ 990, the court's recognition of the Purely Equitable Charge may have been motivated by the fact that a third party (a council) had since acquired a statutory charge on the house to secure A's duty to pay care home fees.

C that C *already* had a property right or a persistent right in relation to A's land. In such a case, C may able to say that his reliance on A's promise was premised in part on the idea that he had a right that would be protected on A's insolvency.[128] In *Jennings v Rice*[129] Robert Walker LJ suggested that a security right could be justified where C's reliance consisted, at least in part, of making improvements to A's land. The point there may be that A's other creditors should not be entitled to share in benefits conferred by C in reliance on A's promise; but the problem is that some of those other creditors may also have conferred benefits on A (eg, by extending credit to A in reliance on A's contractual promise to pay).[130]

3.4.3 The distinction between an Equitable Charge and a Purely Equitable Charge

It is important to distinguish between: (i) an Equitable Charge; and (ii) a Purely Equitable Charge. First, an Equitable Charge, unlike a Purely Equitable Charge but like a Charge, can exist only in relation to land. Second, even where land is concerned, there is a difference between the two rights. An Equitable Charge arises where A is under a duty to grant C a Charge. A Purely Equitable Charge arises where A is under a duty to hold his Freehold or Lease as security for a duty owed to C. Third, formality rules apply differently to each right:

Equitable Charge	Where A has a Freehold or Lease, his power to come under a *contractual* duty to give C a Charge is regulated by section 2 of the 1989 Act. Therefore, in **Example 7a**, A is *not* under a contractual duty to C as A's promise was not made in writing signed by *both* A and B. However, C can acquire an Equitable Charge in the absence of writing if A is under a *non-contractual* duty to give C a Charge (eg, a duty arising due to proprietary estoppel).
Purely Equitable Charge	Where A has a Freehold or Lease, his power to make a contractual promise to hold his right as security is regulated by section 53(1)(a) of the LPA 1925. That rule requires only writing signed by A. Therefore, in **Example 7a**, C could have argued that he had a Purely Equitable Charge. However, that argument would have failed. A had *not* made a promise to immediately hold his Freehold as security for C—his promise was to grant C a *new* property right (a Charge) in the future.

3.5   Powers to acquire a persistent right: a floating charge transaction

In a floating charge transaction, A can give C a power to acquire a persistent right against particular rights of A (see **F4:Example 11** and **F4:3.3**). The same principle applies where A has a Freehold or Lease. Again, the only difference is that, as C's power to acquire a persistent right relates to land, section 53(1)(a) of the LPA 1925 means that the floating charge transaction must be made in writing signed by A.

---

[128] That argument is harder to make if A has instead promised to give C such a right *in the future*: there C can be said to take the risk (in the absence of a contract) that A will not perform that promise and so C will have only a personal right against A.

[129] [2003] 1 P & CR 100, [51].

[130] Further, there are cases in which C did not acquire a security right even though his reliance did include improving A's land: see eg *Dodsworth v Dodsworth* (1973) 228 EG 1115.

4   THE DEFENCES QUESTION

4.1   Could a later party (D) have a defence to C's security right?

To acquire a Charge over A's land, C must first substantively register that Charge. This registration ensures that no later party, such as D, will be able to use the lack of registration defence against C's Charge. It is very difficult for a party subsequently acquiring a right to have a defence to C's pre-existing property right in land (see **E1:3**).[131] However, in some cases D may be able to rely on the overreaching defence (see **E1:3.4**). For example, if: (i) the terms of the deal between A and C give A a power to grant D a Lease;[132] and (ii) A exercises that power; then (iii) D is not bound by C's pre-existing security right.

> **EXAMPLE 7b**
>
> The facts are as in **Example 7a**. After C advances the money to A: (i) A refuses to grant C the promised Charge; and (ii) A transfers his Freehold, for value, to D.

In such a case, C has only a persistent right: an Equitable Charge. If C has not entered a notice on the register, and so has failed to defensively register his right, then D may be able to rely on the lack of registration defence. As D has acquired his Freehold for value, and substantively registered his right, D will be able to use that defence *unless* C was in actual occupation of A's land when D committed to acquiring his Freehold. This is not the case in **Example 7b** (it is very unlikely that C will take control of A's land if A has not yet defaulted on the loan). Hence, D does have a defence to C's pre-existing Equitable Charge. This example demonstrates why it is so important for C, if he plans to acquire a Charge, to ensure that: (i) A, in a deed, exercises his power to give C that Charge; *and* (ii) C substantively registers his Charge.

4.2   Does C have a defence to a pre-existing right of B?

If C acquires a security right in relation to A's land, it is often vital to know if C has a defence to a pre-existing right of B. In fact, that question can be crucial in the very first example considered in this book: **A:Example 1**. The answer given to that question can thus have a decisive impact on the resolution of the **basic tension** between B and C. As a result, cases where C is allowed a defence are often seen as adopting a 'pro-bank' stance: the property law system promotes commerce by protecting the lender who has acquired a security right. In contrast, cases where C has no defence are often seen as adopting an 'anti-bank' stance: rather than promoting commerce, the property law system protects the home by allowing B to assert a right against C.

That analysis is overly simplistic.[133] If C has a defence to B's pre-existing right, that defence may well *not* depend on C's status as a lender; it may instead result from an application of

---

[131] For an example of the limitation defence being used by A against C Bank's Charge, see *National Westminster Bank v Ashe* [2008] EWCA Civ 55.

[132] Where: (i) A gives C a Charge; and (ii) A remains in physical control of the land; then (iii) A has a statutory power under the LPA 1925, s 99 to grant particular forms of Lease. That statutory power can be, and often is, excluded by the terms of the deal between A and C.

[133] As noted by Conaglen (2006) 69 *MLR* 583.

the *general* principles of the property law system. If so, C's ability to use the defence does *not* prove that the system is taking a 'pro-bank' stance. Evidence for such a stance can come only from cases where C Bank is given *special* treatment *because* it is a lender. Therefore, we need to divide the cases between: (i) those where C Bank simply takes advantage of a general defence, available to any third party; and (ii) those where C Bank is given special protection, available only to lenders with a security right.

4.2.1 C Bank's use of a general defence

(i) The overreaching defence

E2: EXAMPLE 17b

A1, A2 and B live together. A1 and A2 have a Freehold of the land. They acquired the Freehold without needing to take out a 'mortgage loan'. B also contributed to the purchase price of that Freehold, without making a gift or a loan to A1 and A2. Later on, A1 and A2 want to raise money for their business. They accept a loan of £100,000 from C Bank and their duty to repay the loan is secured by giving C Bank a Charge over the land. C Bank pays the loan money to A1 and A2.

Due to his contribution to the purchase price, B has a pre-existing persistent right: a right under a Trust. However, as confirmed by the House of Lords in *City of London Building Society v Flegg*,[134] C Bank can use the overreaching defence against B's right (see **E2:3.4.2**). It is important to note that C can use this defence even though B was in actual occupation of the land when C committed to acquiring its Charge. B's actual occupation may prevent C relying on the lack of registration defence, but it does *not* prevent C relying on the over-reaching defence.

From one point of view, the decision in *Flegg*, along with that in *State Bank of India v Sood*[135] (see **E2: Example 17c**), can be seen as 'pro-bank' decision. Yet the decision does *not* depend on the courts taking a generous attitude to secured lenders; instead, it depends on the *general* principle of overreaching. C had a defence as A1 and A2 had a *power* to give C a right free from B's pre-existing right under the Trust.

(ii) The lack of registration defence

E2: EXAMPLE 17a

A and B live together. A has a Freehold of the land. He acquired the Freehold without needing to take out a 'mortgage loan'. B (A's partner) contributed to the purchase price of that Freehold, without making a gift or a loan to A. Later on, A wants to raise money for his business. He accepts a loan from C Bank and his duty to repay the loan is secured by giving C Bank a Charge over the land.

Due to his contribution to the purchase price, B has a pre-existing persistent right: a right under a Trust. C Bank cannot rely on the overreaching defence as: (i) it paid money in return for its right; and (ii) it did *not* pay that money to a trust corporation or at least two

---

[134] [1988] AC 54.
[135] [1997] Ch 276.

trustees (see **E2:3.4.2(ii)**). C Bank can try to rely on the lack of registration defence as: (i) it has acquired for value and substantively registered its Charge; and (ii) B's pre-existing right under the Trust cannot be defensively registered by entering a notice on the register. However, as confirmed by the House of Lords in *Williams & Glyn's Bank v Boland* (the essential facts of which are identical to **E2:Example 17a**),[136] B's pre-existing right is *immune* from the lack of registration defence: as B was in actual occupation of the land when C Bank committed to acquiring its right, B has an overriding interest (see **E2:3.6.2**).

From one point of view, the decision in *Boland* can be seen as an 'anti-bank' decision. Yet the decision does *not* depend on the courts taking a harsh attitude to secured lenders; instead, it depends on the *general* principle that, *whenever* B is in actual occupation of the land when C commits to acquiring its right, *any* pre-existing persistent right of B is immune from the lack of registration defence. That principle applies whether or not C is a lender with a security right; and whether or not B is occupying land as his home.

4.2.2 Special treatment for C Bank

(i) Acquisition loans: the timing question

EXAMPLE 8

A and B plan to buy a home to live in together. They find a Freehold costing £200,000. A and B each has £10,000 in savings. A approaches C Bank and C Bank agrees to give A a loan of £180,000, secured by a Charge over the land. C Bank is unaware that B is contributing any money to the purchase. Using: (i) the £180,000 advanced by C Bank, (ii) A's £10,000, and (iii) B's £10,000, A acquires the Freehold and becomes the sole registered owner. C Bank substantively registers its Charge.

Due to his contribution to the purchase price, B has a persistent right: a right under a Trust. The crucial question is whether this is a *pre-existing* persistent right: did B acquire it *before* C Bank acquired its Charge? Two analyses are possible: the first is based on doctrine; the second on a practical assessment:

1. B claims a persistent right against A's Freehold; C Bank claims A gave it a Charge over the land. B's right arises *as soon as* A acquires his Freehold: as B contributed to the purchase price, A is under the core Trust duty to B. A can only give C Bank a Charge *once* A has the Freehold. Hence there must be a moment of time (a 'scintilla temporis') in which A holds the Freehold free from C Bank's Charge, but subject to the core Trust duty. So, B's right under the Trust must arise *before* C Bank's Charge.
2. In practice, C Bank's loan was crucial in allowing A to acquire the Freehold. It would therefore be overly technical to say that B's persistent right arose before C Bank's Charge: if C Bank had not given A the loan, B could not have a right against that Freehold.

The first analysis is doctrinally correct and traditionally found favour with the courts.[137] On that analysis, in **Example 8**, B does have a *pre-existing* persistent right and so has a prima

---

[136] [1981] AC 487.
[137] See eg *Church of England BS v Piskor* [1954] Ch 553.

facie power to assert that right against C Bank. However, in *Abbey National v Cann*[138] the House of Lords adopted the second analysis. As noted in **G3:2.2.3**, that analysis is based on the practical effect of C Bank's loan in allowing A to acquire his Freehold. It thus departs from the general doctrinal position and, in doing so, favours a secured lender. In practice, the analysis adopted in *Cann* provides very important protection for such lenders. It means that, *whenever* C Bank provides a loan used by A to *acquire* a Freehold or Lease, C Bank does *not* risk being bound by B's right under a Trust of that Freehold.

Can this special treatment of secured lenders be justified? The answer seems to be 'Yes'. First, as C Bank's loan allows B to acquire his right under the Trust, it does not seem un-reasonable to reflect this practical 'reality'[139] by giving priority to the Charge acquired in return for the loan. Second, as noted in **A:3.2**, there are arguments in favour of giving such protection to lenders. If C Bank knows that, when lending money to allow A to acquire land, its Charge will take priority to any possible right under a Trust, C Bank does not need to concern itself with checking to see if B has such a right. As a result, there is a reduction in the cost to C Bank of the 'mortgage' deal. This means that C Bank can lend to A at a lower rate and still make a profit. In turn, this may help to make loans more accessible to parties who hope to buy some land. This is an important consideration, given the costs of purchasing land.

(ii) A special application of 'defensive estoppel'

EXAMPLE 9

A and B plan to buy some empty land and build a home on it. They purchase a Freehold for £20,000. The Freehold is registered in A's sole name but B contributes £10,000, without making a gift or a loan to A. A and B know that the building they plan will cost £180,000. B knows that, between them, A and B have only £150,000 of further assets. A arranges a loan of £180,000 from C Bank, secured by a Charge over A's Freehold (as well as by a Purely Equitable Charge over other rights held by A). A and B pay for the building work using: (i) their combined assets of £150,000; and (ii) £30,000 of the money advanced by C Bank. A then runs off with the remaining £150,000 from C Bank. A fails to repay the loan from C Bank, and C Bank cannot recover the money owed by A by enforcing its Purely Equitable Charge over A's other assets.

In such a case, it may seem that B should be able to assert its right under a Trust against C Bank:

1. The loan provided by C Bank is *not* an acquisition loan. It is clear that B's right under the Trust of A's Freehold arose *before* C Bank acquired its Charge.
2. As C Bank: (i) paid money in return for its Charge; and (ii) did *not* pay that money to a trust corporation or at least two trustees, then (iii) C Bank *cannot* use the over-reaching defence.

---

[138] [1991] 1 AC 56.

[139] *Ibid per* Lord Oliver at 92–3; *per* Lord Jauncey at 102. See too *per* Lord Hoffmann in *Ingram v IRC* [2000] 1 AC 293 at 303: 'For my part, I do not think that a theory based upon the notion of a scintilla temporis can have a very powerful grasp on reality.'

3. As B was in actual occupation of the land when C Bank committed to acquiring its Charge, C Bank *cannot* use the lack of registration defence.[140]

However, in *Abbey National v Cann*, the House of Lords stated that, in a case such as **Example 9**, C Bank *will* have a defence to B's pre-existing right.[141] This defence is based on the idea that: (i) B knew that A and B did not have enough assets to pay for the building work; *so* (ii) B knew that A would need to take a loan to cover the extra costs; *so* (iii) B knew that A would have to give that lender a security right over A's Freehold; *so* (iv) B cannot now assert his pre-existing persistent right against C Bank.

From a doctrinal perspective, it is very hard to justify this defence.[142] It seems to be linked to the 'apparent power' defences (see **section 3.3 of D1, D2 and E1, E2**). It could be argued that C Bank has a defence as: (i) it had a reasonable expectation that A had a power to give C Bank a Charge free from B's pre-existing persistent right; *and* (ii) C Bank relied on that expectation by making the loan to A. The defence may thus be linked to the *general* defensive estoppel defence (see **D1:3.3.1(ii)**). However, the problem is that B did *not* make a commitment to C Bank (either by his words or by his conduct) that B would not assert his pre-existing right against C Bank.

As there have been no direct dealings between B and C Bank, the defensive estoppel defence can apply only if we can say that: (i) A, acting as an agent for B, made an implied commitment to C Bank on behalf of B; *or* (ii) B was under a *duty* to inform C Bank of his right. Yet neither (i) nor (ii) is persuasive. As to (i), in **Example 9**, it is *at most* tenable to say that B allowed A to give C Bank a Charge in order to raise the extra £30,000 necessary for the building work. B certainly did not give A any authority to borrow £180,000. And yet, in *Cann*, the House of Lords stated that C Bank has a defence *irrespective* of the fact that A borrowed more than was necessary to achieve A and B's plan. As to (ii), it is very odd to say that B, who has a pre-existing persistent right, is under any duty to inform others of that right: such an idea is entirely absent from the property law system. Rather, if anything, the opposite approach is adopted: C's failure to check for a pre-existing persistent right of B may be important in denying C a defence to that right.[143]

As a matter of doctrine, therefore, the position adopted in *Cann* cannot be defended: in **Example 9** C Bank should *not* have a defence to B's pre-existing persistent right. The *Cann* position thus gives *special* protection to a secured lender. Can that special treatment be justified by the needs of practical convenience? Probably not. The *Cann* position is *not* a simple rule that C Bank always wins; rather, it is based on B's knowledge of the shortfall in A and B's funds. To defend the *Cann* position, we therefore need to show why that knowledge should affect C Bank's position. And it is hard to find a convincing practical reason why that knowledge should make any difference.

In practice, this particular aspect of the *Cann* decision is not too important: the real impact of that decision is in protecting C Bank whenever it makes a secured loan used by A to *acquire* a Freehold or Lease. In fact, cases before *Cann* adopting the modified 'defensive

---

[140] For a consideration of how B may be in actual occupation of derelict land, see *Lloyds Bank v Rossett* [1989] Ch 350, 375–9, 393–9, 403–7 and **E2:3.6.4**.

[141] *Bristol & West BS v Henning* [1985] 1 WLR 778; *Paddington BC v Mendelsohn* (1985) 50 P & CR 244; *Equity & Law Home Loans Ltd v Prestidge* [1992] 1 WLR 137.

[142] R Smith (1990) 109 *LQR* 545.

[143] As occurs, for example, where B's actual occupation of land makes B's pre-existing persistent right immune from the lack of registration defence; or when, in relation to things other than land, C's failure to check for B's right means that C has 'constructive notice' of that right and so cannot use the 'bona fide purchaser' defence (see **D2:3.5**).

estoppel' defence may well have done so precisely because, at that time, it was *not* possible for C Bank to argue that its Charge arose before B's persistent right.[144] So, when changing the approach to the timing question in *Cann*, the House of Lords should also have taken the opportunity to change the approach to 'defensive estoppel' by stating that C Bank cannot use that defence if, as in **Example 9**, B has made no commitment to C Bank.

4.3   What happens where C is bound by a pre-existing right of B?

EXAMPLE 10

A and B are registered as the co-holders of a Freehold. A and B acquired the Freehold without needing to take out a 'mortgage loan': each contributed 50 per cent of the purchase price. Later on, A wants to raise money for his business. C Bank agrees to give A a loan of £180,000 *if* it is secured by a Charge over the land. B knows nothing about this deal and A forges B's signature on the necessary forms. C Bank is substantively registered as holding a Charge over A and B's Freehold; A defaults on his monthly payments. C Bank tries to enforce its security right by selling A and B's Freehold. B objects to this. A's Freehold is now worth £200,000.

In such a case, it is clear that C Bank has no defence to B's pre-existing *property* right as co-holder of a Freehold. B can have the register rectified: as B did not give consent to the creation of the Charge, it is clearly a 'mistake' for C Bank to have a Charge over the land (see **E5:3.2**). However, A's attempt to give C Bank such a Charge does have an important effect. As A and B are co-holders of the Freehold, each has a right under a Trust of that Freehold (see **G2:1.2.3** and **G2:1.2.4**): A is entitled to deal unilaterally with his right under that Trust.[145] So A's attempt to give C Bank a Charge over the land will result in C Bank having an Equitable Charge: a security right against A's right under the Trust of the Freehold. A's continued failure to pay the instalments gives C Bank a prima facie power to enforce that security right by selling A's right under the Trust (see **5.1** below): in practice, this will mean selling the land.

As a secured creditor of A, C Bank can apply to court for a sale of A and B's Freehold (see **G2:4**).[146] And, to allow such a sale to take place smoothly, C Bank may also ask the court to order A and B to vacate the land.[147] Of course, a court must take into account B's

---

[144] So, after *Cann*, *Bristol & West BS v Henning* [1985] 1 WLR 778 and *Paddington BC v Mendelsohn* (1985) 50 P & CR 244 could each be decided simply on the basis that, as C Bank's loan was used to acquire A's Freehold, B had no pre-existing right. In *Equity & Law Home Loans Ltd v Prestidge* [1992] 1 WLR 137, A acquired his Freehold with a secured loan from C1 Bank and then paid off that loan with a second secured loan from C2 Bank. *Prestidge* was decided after *Cann* but did not refer to the earlier case and adopted the 'defensive estoppel' reasoning. As C1 Bank's loan was used to acquire A's Freehold, B's right under a Trust could not bind C1 Bank. As the loan from C2 Bank was used to pay off that first loan, C2 Bank could then take over C1 Bank's security right (through a doctrine often known as 'reviving subrogation' and described by eg May LJ in *Filby v Mortgage Express (No 2) Ltd* [2004] EWCA Civ 759 at [63]: see **D4:3.3**). That would give C2 priority over B to the extent of the initial loan made by C1. That was the very result reached by the Court of Appeal in *Prestidge* using the modified 'defensive estoppel' defence. See further Dixon, *Modern Studies in Property Law* (ed Cooke, 2001), 193–8.

[145] If A and B were initially joint tenants of the right under the Trust, A's unilateral act in attempting to give C a Charge will sever that joint tenancy, giving each of A and B a 50 per cent share of the right under the Trust: see **G2:2.4.2**.

[146] Trusts of Land and Appointment of Trustees Act 1996 ('the 1996 Act'), s 14.

[147] *Re McCarthy* [1975] 1 WLR 807: that case concerned the court's powers under s 30 of the LPA 1925 but the same result must apply under the 1996 Act. See Conaglen (2006) 69 *MLR* 583 at 597–8.

desire to resist the sale;[148] but it must also take into account the needs of C Bank, a secured creditor.[149] As we saw in **G2.4**, if B is unable to remedy A's default by offering to repay A's loan or give C Bank some other financial protection, a court will generally order a sale of the land—even if B is occupying the land with children.[150] So, *even if* B does have a power to assert a pre-existing *property* right against C Bank, that does *not* mean that B will have a guaranteed right to remain in occupation of his home.

Exactly the same result arises where (in cases such as **E2: Example 17a**) B is able to assert a pre-existing *persistent* right against C Bank (see **G3:1A.2.2** and **G3:4.2**). This provides a further reason why cases where B's right binds C cannot simply be viewed as adopting an 'anti-commerce' and 'pro-home' approach. In fact, if his right binds C, the practical advantage gained by B is that he will acquire *money*: a share of the proceeds of the sale of the Freehold. In **Example 10**, if the Freehold is sold for £200,000, B and C Bank will each take £100,000 of the proceeds and C Bank will be left to sue A for any sum A owes beyond that £100,000: if A goes into insolvency, C Bank will not recover the full sum due.

In contrast, if C Bank (as in **E2: Example 17b** and **Example 8**) is *not* bound by B's right, C Bank could use *all* the proceeds of sale to meet any outstanding debt of A. In such a case, B's right under a Trust gives B only a share of the proceeds left after A's debt is paid off.

EXAMPLE 11

A and B live together. A has a Freehold of the land acquired without needing to take out a 'mortgage loan'. B (A's partner) contributed 50 per cent of the purchase price of that Freehold, without making a gift or a loan to A. A is an electrician and enters a contract with C to rewire C's house. A acts carelessly when carrying out the job, causing a fire that destroys the contents of C's house. A thus commits a wrong against C. C sues A: A is ordered to pay C £200,000.

If A is unable to pay the £200,000, C may enforce his judgment by applying for a *charging order* (see **B:2.3.1**). If a court grants such an order over A's Freehold, C, in effect, has a Purely Equitable Charge: a right securing A's duty to pay C. If A does not perform that duty, C has a power to sell A's Freehold. However, B may well oppose such a sale; B's pre-existing persistent right certainly binds C. Nonetheless, if there is no means by which A or B can pay the money due to A, a court will generally allow C to sell A's Freehold.[151] And, to allow such a sale to take place smoothly, a court will, if necessary, order B to vacate the land. Once again, B has to settle for money.

SUMMARY of G4:4

If C has a Charge over A's land, it will be very difficult for D (a party later acquiring a right from A) to have a defence to C's pre-existing property right. If C instead has an Equitable Charge or a Purely Equitable Charge, D may be able to rely on the lack of registration defence against C's pre-existing persistent right.

---

[148] 1996 Act, s 15(1)(a) and (b).
[149] 1996 Act, s 15(1)(d).
[150] *Ahmed v Kendrick* (1987) 56 P & CR 120 (that case involved a sale to C rather than a Charge, but the same principles apply); *First National Bank v Achampong* [2003] EWCA 487 (in that case, B had given her consent to the Charge, but was able to set aside that consent under the *Etridge* test: see **3.1.3(iii)** above).
[151] See eg *Pritchard Englefield v Steinberg* [2004] EWHC 1908.

Where C has a security right in relation to A's land, the **defences question** usually arises not between C and D but between C and B, a party claiming a pre-existing right in relation to A's land. If B has a pre-existing property right, such a right will almost always bind C; however, such cases are relatively rare. The important question in practice is whether a pre-existing *persistent* right of B, in particular a right under a Trust, will bind C.

As we would expect, that question is primarily determined by simply applying the *general* principles of the land law system. C Bank may therefore be able to use the overreaching defence or the lack of registration defence, but that protection is not available to C Bank simply because it is a secured lender. However, it seems secured lenders do receive some special, favourable treatment. First, the *Cann* decision protects C Bank from B's right *if* C Bank's loan was used by A to acquire the land. Second, it is also stated in *Cann* that C Bank can rely on what seems to be a modified version of defensive estoppel *if* B knew that some money would have to be borrowed by A. The first part of this special protection simply reflects practical reality and is easily justified; the second part is, however, impossible to justify either on doctrinal or practical grounds.

Even if C Bank has no defence to B's pre-existing property right or persistent right, that does *not* necessarily mean that B will, for example, be able to continue occupying A's land. After all, C Bank's security right exists to protect it from the risk that a secured duty is not performed. C Bank may need the protection provided by: (i) selling A's Freehold and Lease; and (ii) using part of those proceeds to meet the secured duty. So it may well be that B's ability to bind C simply means that B is entitled to a share of the proceeds of a sale of A's Freehold or Lease.

5   THE REMEDIES QUESTION: ENFORCEMENT OF B'S SECURITY RIGHT

There are four ways in which C may be able to enforce a security right: (i) sale; (ii) appointment of a receiver; (iii) taking physical control of A's land; and (iv) foreclosure (see **F4:5**). In practice, sale is the most important method of enforcement. To get a reasonable price for A's Freehold or Lease, C will need to sell the land with 'vacant possession': a third party will be very reluctant to buy the land if A or B is still living there and refusing to leave.[152] Therefore, C will, in practice, need to take physical control of A's land in order to exercise his power of sale.[153]

If a sale is not possible, C may want to take and *retain* physical control of the land. As we saw in **F4:5.3.2**, the disadvantage of taking physical control is that C is under a strict duty to account to A for any profits C *should* make as a result of his control of the land. Nonetheless, if he currently has no power of sale, taking physical control may be an important way for C to preserve the value of his security right (as, for example, if A is failing to look after the land properly).[154] As we saw in **F4:5.2**, the appointment of a receiver

---

[152] Technically, if C has a power of sale, his sale to C2 will overreach A's right even if A is in actual occupation of the land at the time of the sale. However, C2 will not want the inconvenience of having to remove A: C2 wants to buy the land; not the land and a lawsuit.

[153] See *per* Harman J in *Hughes v Waite* [1957] 1 WLR 713 at 715.

[154] See eg *Western Bank v Schindler* [1977] Ch 1 *per* Buckley LJ at 9–10 and *per* Scarman LJ at 17.

may be a useful option for C if A's land can be used to generate income (eg, by being rented out).

The general rules discussed in **F4:5** also apply where B's security right relates to A's land: in fact some of the cases discussed there involved land.[155] In this section we will therefore look only at the *special* principles that apply where land is concerned. A key question arises where C wants to take physical control of the land, whether: (i) as a preliminary to a sale; or (ii) in order to preserve the value of his security right by looking after the land. Clearly, being forced to leave the land may have a dramatic effect on A and anyone occupying the land along with A. So, do the special features of land (in particular its social importance: see **A:3.1.4**) justify giving A special protection where C, in order to enforce his security right, attempts to remove A from the land?

Before looking at the special rules of the land law system, it is important to bear in mind the regulation provided by the FSA and set out in the *MCOB* sourcebook (see **2.1.4(i)** and **3.1.1** above). Chapter 13 of the *MCOB* sourcebook deals with the action a lender should take where A, by defaulting on repayments, is in breach of the secured duty. It emphasises that taking action to remove A from the land ('repossession') is a last resort.[156] C Bank must 'deal fairly' with A and attempt to resolve the problem by using 'reasonable efforts' to agree a repayment plan that will allow A to catch up on arrears, adopting a 'reasonable approach' to the time over which A can make up the shortfall.[157] Further, it is often in C Bank's best interests to reach such an agreement with A. If C Bank's business depends on secured loans, it has an interest in avoiding a slump in the housing market. If, because of an economic downturn, a large number of people are facing problems in making their repayments, then C Bank may be reluctant simply to sell off all their houses: such a response would only depress the housing market.[158]

5.1 Sale

The principles set out in **F4:5.1** also apply where land is concerned. One point to note is that, if C has a Charge, a deed will necessarily have been used to give C that right: as a result, C may have access to the statutory power of sale under section 101(1)(i). That power applies only where the 'mortgage money is due'. So, if C lends a large sum of money (eg, to allow A to acquire a Freehold or Lease), and A's duty is to repay that sum in instalments, C may well include a term in the security transaction that, for the purposes of section 101(1)(i), A's duty to repay the entire sum arises a very short time (eg, one month) after B lends A the money (see **F4:5.1.1(iii)**).[159]

One possible difference where land is concerned comes from section 52 of the LRA 2002:

---

[155] *Cuckmere Brick Co v Mutual Finance Ltd* [1971] 1 Ch 949; *Silven Properties Ltd v Royal Bank of Scotland plc* [2004] 1 WLR 997; *Medforth v Blake* [2000] Ch 86; *Four-Maids Ltd v Dudley Marshall (Properties) Ltd* [1957] Ch 317.

[156] *MCOB* sourcebook, 13.3.2.1(f): C Bank should remove A from the land 'only where all other reasonable attempts to resolve the position have failed'. It is also stated at 13.3.2.1(e) that, where a sale is necessary, C Bank must 'give consideration' to allowing A to remain in possession and make the sale; however, C Bank may well have legitimate concerns about allowing A to conduct the sale: see eg *Bristol & West BS v Ellis* (1996) 73 P & CR 158.

[157] *MCOB* sourcebook, 13.3.2.

[158] See further **5.2.2(iii)** below.

[159] See *West Bromwich BS v Wilkinson* [2005] 1 WLR 2303 at [25] for an example of such a clause. Alternatively, those terms can provide that *if* A misses an instalment payment, the whole sum is due.

it applies where C has a substantively registered Charge and purports to exercise a power to sell A's Freehold or Lease to C2. The Law Commission[160] intended section 52 to give C2 complete protection against the risk that C might not have a power of sale.[161] On that view: (i) *even if C had no power of sale*, C2 would still acquire A's Freehold or Lease; and (ii) A would not be able to seek rectification of the register. Section 52 seems most likely to be useful to C2 if an express term of the initial security transaction between A and C places limits on C's power of sale but C sells to C2 contrary to one of those limits. However, section 52 can only assist C2 *if* C has a statutory power of sale under section 101(1)(i): as a result of his substantive registration, C has the power of sale 'conferred by law on the owner of a legal mortgage':[162] as such, 'mortgage money' must be due.[163]

5.2   Taking physical control of A's land prior to a sale

C's power of sale is of practical importance only if C can also remove A from the land and then sell with vacant possession. This is why a court deciding to permit a sale of A's land by C Bank may also order B (a party with a pre-existing right that binds C Bank) to vacate the land. In F4:5.3.1 we considered the general rules applying where C seeks physical control of A's thing prior to a sale. However, where land is concerned special rules apply. First, in practice, C cannot simply take physical control of A's land: if A, or someone in occupation of A's land, opposes C's entry onto the land, it is a criminal offence for C to use or threaten violence in order to gain entry.[164] Second, if C instead applies for a court order allowing him to remove A from the land, C must contend with section 36 of the Administration of Justice Act 1970 ('the 1970 Act'). The 1970 Act does not apply *whenever* land is concerned. Instead, it recognises the social importance of A's home and so applies only where C seeks physical control of a 'dwelling house' or land that includes such a house.

5.2.1 A general judicial discretion?

It is important to note that where A fails to perform a duty secured by a Charge[165] and C seeks physical control of A's land in order to sell it, a court has *no* general discretion to prevent C removing A.[166] After all, if C has a Charge, C has an immediate right to such control: *as soon as* C acquires his Charge he acquires the 'same protection, powers and remedies' as a party with a Lease.[167] Whilst the Charge transaction will generally give A a

---

[160] Law Com No 271, [7.7] and [7.8].

[161] It is important to note that the section only protects C2, and *not* C: s 52(2).

[162] The section states: '(1) Subject to any entry in the register to the contrary, the proprietor of a registered charge is to be taken to have, in relation to the property subject to the legal charge, the powers of disposition conferred by law on the owner of a legal mortgage.'

[163] R Smith, *Property Law* (5th edn, 2006), 590.

[164] Criminal Law Act 1977, s 6.

[165] Or an Equitable Charge; if C has an Equitable Charge, A is under a duty to grant C a Charge (see **3.3** above) and so must allow C to exercise the same rights as a party with a Charge: see Wade (1955) 72 *LQR* 204. However, C does not necessarily have a right to physical control of A's land if he has only a Purely Equitable Charge: see F4:5.3.

[166] This point was emphasised in *Birmingham Citizens PBS v Caunt* [1962] Ch 883. Before then, it had suggested that such a discretion existed: Ball (1961) 77 *LQR* 331, 351, reporting on the practice of Chancery masters when hearing C's claim for physical control of A's land.

[167] LPA 1925, s 87(1). See *per* Harman J in *Four-Maids Ltd v Dudley Marshall (Properties) Ltd* [1957] Ch 317 at 320: C has his right to exclusive control 'before the ink is dry on the mortgage'. That statement needs to be updated: C's right arises as soon as his Charge is substantively registered; if that occurs electronically, C's right arises as soon as his solicitor presses 'Enter': see E5:4.

right to retain control of the land,[168] it will usually provide that A's right ceases when A fails to perform the secured duty (of course, if A is able to 'redeem' by fully performing the secured duty, C's right to physical control of A's land will cease).

This orthodox position was challenged by Lord Denning MR in *Quennell v Maltby*.[169] In that very unusual case, C did *not* seek physical control of the land in order to enforce its security right. A gave C a Charge in return for a loan, and then granted a Lease to B. A was unable to remove B from the land (although the Lease had ended, B could use the statutory protection then available to tenants: see **G1B:1.2**). However, because B was bound by C's charge, C could remove B. C had no reason to remove B from the land and so A2 (A's wife) decided to pay off the money owing to C[170] in return for which C transferred its Charge to A2. A2 then attempted to remove B from the land.

As pointed out by Bridge and Templeman LJJ, the case was straightforward. A's wife, acting on behalf of A, should not be permitted to undermine the statutory protection enjoyed by B.[171] Lord Denning noted this point[172] but also took a wider approach, stating that a party with a Charge

> will be restrained from getting possession except when it is: (i) sought *bona fide* and reasonably for the purpose of enforcing the security, and then (ii) only subject to such conditions as the court thinks fit to impose.[173]

The first part of this principle is entirely consistent with the general approach to security rights (see **F4:1.3**)[174] although it has little impact in practice because C will only rarely seek physical control of A's land for a purpose unrelated to enforcing its security.[175] In contrast, the second part of Lord Denning's principle is unsupported by authority: the court's only discretion comes from section 36 of the 1970 Act.

---

[168] Such a provision may also be implied: eg, in a standard Charge transaction, if C lends money to A and A promises to repay in instalments over a long period, it is reasonable to infer that A and C intended that A should have a right to occupy the land whilst paying off the loan: see *per* Walton J in *Esso Petroleum Co Ltd v Alstonbridge Properties Ltd* [1975] 1 WLR 1474 at 1484 'I accept that the court will be ready to find an implied term in an installment mortgage that the mortgagor is to be entitled to remain in possession against the mortgagee until he makes default in payment of one of the instalments. But there must be something upon which to hang such a conclusion in the mortgage other than the mere fact that it is an installment mortgage.' In a standard case, the additional factor (missing in *Alstonbridge*) may be A's occupation of land as a home.

[169] [1979] 1 WLR 318.

[170] The Court of Appeal assumed (see *per* Templeman LJ at 324) that, as a result of A2's payment, A then came under a duty to pay A2 the secured sum. However, that assumption is questionable: as A2 made the payment willingly, it is difficult to see why A should come under a liability to A2 as a result. So another basis for the result in *Quennell* is that C's Charge ceased when A2 made the payment and therefore B was no longer bound by a Charge.

[171] *Ibid per* Bridge LJ at 323 and *per* Templeman LJ at 324.

[172] *Ibid* at 322: finding in A2's favour would lead to 'widespread evasion of the Rent Acts'.

[173] *Ibid* at 322.

[174] It was also supported by Templeman LJ at 324: 'The estate, rights and powers of a mortgagee, however, are only vested in a mortgagee to protect his position as a mortgagee and to enable him to obtain repayment. Subject to this, the property belongs in equity to the mortgagor.' See too *per* Chadwick LJ in *Abbey National v Tufts* [1999] 2 FLR 399 at 407.

[175] Lord Denning MR's principle was also referred to in *Albany Home Loan Ltd v Massey* [1997] 2 All ER 609. However, the decision in that case is more obviously based on the fact that it is pointless to give C a possession order against A when A2 (A's partner) is also in occupation and possession proceedings against A2 are ongoing: see *per* Chadwick LJ in *Abbey National v Tufts* [1999] 2 FLR 399 at 406–7.

5.2.2 The special statutory discretion under the 1970 Act

(i) When the discretion arises

Parliament reacted to the absence of a general judicial discretion by giving judges a special statutory discretion under section 36 of the 1970 Act when C seeks physical control of a 'dwelling house' or land that includes such a house.

The basic scheme is that, when C applies for a possession order (ie, an order allowing C to remove A and take physical control of A's land), the court can: (i) adjourn the proceedings; or (ii) give C a suspended possession order *if* it is likely that A, within a reasonable period, will be able to remedy his breach of the secured duty.

We have seen that, in a standard Charge transaction, even if A is due to repay a loan in instalments, there may well be a provision that: (i) the *whole* sum is due a short time (eg, one month) after C advances the money; *or* (ii) if A misses an instalment, the whole sum then becomes due. In such a case, C can argue that the court does *not* have a section 36 discretion as there is no reasonable prospect of A performing the secured duty. Section 8 of the Administration of Justice Act 1973 deals with this point:[176] in such circumstances, a court may regard A as owing 'only such amounts as [A] would have expected to be required to pay if there had been no such provision for earlier payment'.

(ii) Gaps in the discretion?

(a) A's duty to repay a bank overdraft

The key to section 8, and hence to the section 36 discretion, is *deferral*. For example, if A's duty is to make instalment payments spread out over time, A can resist C's application for possession by convincing a court that, within a reasonable period, A can make up the shortfall and get back on track with making future payments.[177] This means that the section 36 discretion does *not* apply if, *as soon as* A comes under a duty to C, A has to pay C the *whole sum owed by A*. For example, let us say A gives C Bank a Charge to secure A's overdraft with C Bank. Under a standard overdraft, A's duty to pay the bank arises only when the bank demands repayment. At that point, A is under a duty immediately to pay the bank the whole sum represented by the overdraft. There is thus no point at which: (i) A is under a duty to pay C Bank; *and* (ii) that duty is deferred. Therefore, if C's Charge secures A's duty to repay an overdraft, A *cannot* rely on the section 36 discretion.[178]

(b) C taking physical control of A's land without a court order

The section 36 discretion applies only where C 'brings an action in which he claims possession of the mortgaged property'. In practice, this 'gap' is not too important: as we have seen, if A refuses to leave, C will need to obtain a court order. However, if C is fortunate enough to be able to take control of A's land without needing to remove any occupiers (eg, when the occupiers are temporarily away), the section 36 discretion does *not* apply.[179]

---

[176] Until that provision was enacted, C's argument was correct and had to be accepted (see *Halifax BS v Clark* [1973] Ch 307): the courts have no general discretion to refuse C's claim for physical control.

[177] As long as deferral is contemplated, the Act applies even if there is no express term in the Charge transaction calling for instalment payments (see *Centrax Trustees Ltd v Ross* [1979] 2 All ER 952). The Act also applies to 'endowment mortgages' where the future maturing of an endowment policy is used to pay off the capital sum lent by C (see *Bank of Scotland v Grimes* [1985] QB 1179).

[178] See eg *Habib Bank Ltd v Taylor* [1982] 1 WLR 1218.

[179] As confirmed by the Court of Appeal in *Ropaigealach v Barclays Bank plc* [2000] QB 263. C Bank did *not* take

(iii) Exercising the discretion

The court can exercise its section 36 discretion when A is 'likely to be able within a reasonable period' to remedy his failure to perform the secured duty: eg, to make up any existing arrears and to get back on track with making future payments. Clearly, this is primarily a factual question. It is worth noting that the 'reasonable period' will usually be the *entire repayment period*.

EXAMPLE 12

A has a Freehold. In 2005, A borrows £90,000 from C Bank. A is under a duty to repay that sum with 6 per cent interest in monthly instalments spread over 25 years. The duty is secured by a Charge over A's land. Five years later, A has missed a number of monthly payments and is £7,500 in arrears. C Bank applies for a possession order: by the time of the hearing A is £15,000 in arrears and the rate for each monthly instalment is £1,250.

In general, the correct starting point for a judge exercising the section 36 discretion is to consider whether, *over the remaining 20 years* of the agreed repayment period, A is likely to be able to make up the current arrears and pay the future instalments.[180] This means that, in a case such as **Example 12**, a judge will need to: (i) estimate the future monthly instalments A will need to pay; (ii) work out the current arrears; (iii) work out the sum A would have to pay, on top of future instalments, to pay off those arrears over the next 20 years; (iv) examine a detailed 'budget' from A setting out A's means of payment;[181] and (v) see if A (or someone acting on A's behalf)[182] is likely to be able to make those payments as required over the next 20 years.[183]

If the judge, as is likely, then allows A to retain physical control of the land on that basis and A then later fails to keep up with the new monthly payments, C Bank can again apply for a possession order. In such a case, because of A's second default, it is likely that C Bank *will* be allowed to take physical control of the land.[184]

One useful aspect of that approach is that it begins by being as generous as possible to A, but attempts to limit A's chances of resisting a possession application in the future. Of course, if a future application is made by C Bank, a court may still use its section 36 discretion; but it is important to limit, as far as possible, the time and expense incurred by repeated applications to court.[185]

---

physical control in that case: rather it took advantage of A's absence to sell the land to C2 with vacant possession. If A had then returned before C2 took physical control of the land, the court *would* have the s 36 discretion if C2 then brought proceedings to remove A: see the 1970 Act, s 39(1).

180 See *Cheltenham & Gloucester BS v Norgan* [1996] 1 WLR 343.

181 It may be possible for A to raise the necessary money by selling the house: see *National & Provincial BS v Lloyd* [1996] 1 All ER 630.

182 In general, C Bank will not be too concerned as to where its money comes from. The Family Law Act 1996 s 30(3) states that if a payment is made by A's spouse or civil partner then, if that party has a statutory right of occupation under the Act, the payment is as 'good as if made' by A.

183 For a summary of some of the considerations a court may take into account when exercising its discretion, see *per* Evans LJ in *Cheltenham & Gloucester BS v Norgan* [1996] 1 WLR 343 at 357.

184 *Ibid per* Waite LJ at 354.

185 *Ibid per* Waite LJ at 354: 'The parties have been before the court with depressing frequency over the years on applications to enforce, or further to suspend, the warrant of possession, while [A] and her husband have struggled, sometimes with success and sometimes without, to meet whatever commitment was currently approved by the court. [C Bank] has (in exercise of its power to do so under the terms of the mortgage) added to its security the costs it has incurred in connection with all these attendances.'

The general approach may need to be departed from if C Bank has valid concerns that a delay may jeopardise the usefulness of its security right. So if, in **Example 12**: (i) the current value of A's land is close to the sum owed to C Bank; and (ii) that value is likely to decrease in the future; then C Bank may have a stronger case that it should not have to wait before removing A and selling the land. This means that, in practice, C Bank's application may be more likely to succeed where the housing market is in decline. We noted above that, in periods of such decline, C Bank may be initially reluctant to depress the market further by attempting to sell a large number of houses. However, at some point, C Bank may decide to cut its losses. This may cause the housing market to decline further, thus making other repossessions and sales more likely. As a result, there can be periods where there is a sharp rise in successful repossession actions.[186]

5.3   Taking physical control of A's land for purposes other than sale

We noted above that, if a sale is not possible, C may want to take and *retain* physical control of the land in order to preserve its value until the point when a sale is possible. In this way, taking physical control can be seen as a way of protecting C's security right. In *Western Bank v Schindler*[187] the Court of Appeal considered A's ability to resist such an application for a possession order. The case was unusual. C Bank made a loan to A to enable A to buy a house. It seems a standard 'endowment' mortgage was intended. A was under a duty: (i) to repay the sum, with interest, in 10 years' time and (ii) to make monthly premium payments on a policy that would mature at that point and could be used to pay off the debt. However, due to an unusual (and presumably unintended) arrangement, A's duty to make the monthly premiums was *not* part of the secured duty: C Bank's Charge secured *only* A's duty to repay the loan plus interest at the end of the 10-year period. A then missed a number of the monthly premiums. This did *not* give C Bank a statutory power of sale: no money was yet due from A. C Bank instead applied for a possession order, presumably as a way to put pressure on A to make the monthly premiums.

    Western Bank v Schindler thus raised the issue of whether C Bank can exercise its right to exclusive control of A's land *even though* A has not failed to perform the secured duty. There are two questions to ask in such a case.

5.3.1 Does A have a contractual right to occupy the land?

The usual answer is to say that, as part of the Charge transaction, A has an express or implied contractual right to remain in occupation of the land until he defaults on the secured duty. However, that answer was *not* given in *Schindler*. A had no express right to remain in occupation; and the court decided that it could not infer that A and B had intended A to have such a right. This may well be a result of the unusual form of the Charge transaction used. As A's duty to pay the monthly premiums was not secured by the Charge,

---

[186] 1990–92 was one such period: according to figures supplied by the Council of Mortgage Lenders, the annual number of properties taken into possession by lenders rose from 16,000 in 1989 to 44,000 in 1990; 76,000 in 1991; before falling back slightly to 69,000 in 1992. The figure then declined fairly steadily to 8,000 in 2004. There is then evidence of another rise: 15,000 in 2005; 22,000 in 2006; 27,000 in 2007 (see Council of Mortgage Lenders, Table AP4: http://www.cml.org.uk/cml/statistics).

[187] [1977] Ch 1.

the Charge transaction was simply that: (i) A had a duty to C Bank to repay the loan plus interest in 10 years' time and (ii) that duty was secured by a Charge over A's land. In such a transaction, C Bank is clearly at risk if A abandons or otherwise fails to maintain the land: C Bank cannot be expected to sit by and watch the value of its security deteriorate for 10 years. It was therefore impossible to say A had an implied right to occupy.

So, given the unusual Charge transaction in *Schindler*, the Court of Appeal reached the correct result. However, this does not alter the point that in a *standard* Charge transaction, where C Bank *will* have a power of sale if A misses monthly repayments, it is easy to infer that A is intended to have a right to occupy unless and until he defaults on those repayments.

5.3.2 Does the court have a discretion under section 36 of the 1970 Act?

In *Schindler*, given A had no contractual right to remain in occupation, the question was whether A could instead resist C Bank using section 36 of the 1970 Act. The problem for A is that the section 36 discretion is clearly premised on the basis that C is seeking a possession order *as a result of A's failure to perform the secured duty*. However, if C has a Charge, C has a prima facie right to exclusive control of A's land *whether or not* A is in default. Therefore, if: (i) the Charge transaction does not give A an express or implied right to occupy until default; and (ii) C applies for an order to remove A when no default has occurred; then on its express wording, the section 36 discretion is *not* available to the court. Such cases must be rare: as we noted above, it is generally possible to find that A has at least an implied right to occupy his home until default. However, in those cases, the wording of section 36 seems clear: the court has no discretion to refuse C Bank's claim for physical control of the land.

From one point of view, that result, even if it occurs only rarely, seems absurd: why should A have *less* protection in a case when A has *not* failed to perform a secured duty? So, in *Schindler*, Scarman and Buckley LJJ both held that, despite its wording, the section 36 discretion could be extended to cover such a case.[188] In fact, this made little difference in *Schindler* itself: C Bank was given a possession order to take effect in one month's time. Nonetheless, the *Schindler* decision is often seen as providing a welcome remedy to a seeming absurdity in the scope of section 36.

However, from a different point of view, the express words of section 36 *do* make sense: where A does *not* have a right of occupation under the terms of the Charge, there is no reason why C Bank should not be able to exercise its right to exclusive control:[189] (i) if C Bank has a Charge, it has all the 'protection, powers and remedies (including the right to take proceedings to obtain possession from the occupiers)' of a prty with a Lease;[190] (ii) C Bank may need to take physical control in order to protect the value of its security right;[191]

---

[188] In *Schindler*, A was found to have no implied right to occupy the land until default. In that case, the Charge transaction, unusually, gave C Bank no right to receive any money from A until the end of 10 years. So C Bank had to be able to take physical control of the land to protect its security if, for example, A was failing to properly maintain the land: see *per* Scarman LJ at 17.

[189] This is the argument made by Goff J in *Western Bank*, doubting the approach of Scarman and Buckley LJJ. Goff J's approach is persuasively championed by Harpum (1977) 40 *MLR* 356.

[190] LPA 1925, s 87(1).

[191] *Western Bank v Schindler* [1977] Ch 1 *per* Buckley LJ at 9–10 and *per* Scarman LJ at [17].

and (iii) C Bank will be under a duty to account to A for any income it should receive whilst in physical control of the land (see **F4:5.3.2**).

> ### SUMMARY of G4:5 and THE IMPACT OF HUMAN RIGHTS
>
> If C has a security right in relation to A's land, the primary means by which C can enforce that right is through a sale of A's Freehold or Lease. In practice, such a sale can only occur if C first removes A and any other occupiers from the land. If C's security right takes the form of a Charge, C immediately acquires a right to exclusive control of A's land.[192] However, there are checks on C's ability to exercise that right.
>
> The first check on C's right to exclusive control is the likelihood of A having an express or implied right to remain in occupation of the land until he fails to perform the secured duty (eg, by missing an instalment payment). The second check, which may apply even where A has no such right, is that C can exercise his right to exclusive control only in order to enforce his security right (eg, by taking possession and then selling the land) or to protect his security right[193] (eg, by taking possession to improve and maintain the condition of the land).[194] The third check, applying only where A's land is (or includes) a dwelling house, is provided by the section 36 discretion; that discretion does not apply where A's secured duty is to repay an overdraft; or where C can take physical control of A's land without a court order.
>
> It has been argued that, taken together, these checks give insufficient protection to A's human rights under: (i) Article 1 of Protocol 1 to the European Convention on Human Rights (ECHR) (see **B:8.3.1**); and (ii) Article 8 of the ECHR (see **B:8.3.2**).[195] However, this is a very difficult argument to make. The European Court of Human Rights has confirmed that, if A is in default, the 'public interest in ensuring the payment of contractual debts' justifies the effect that C's enforcement of his security right may have on A.[196] Further, if A is in occupation of the land, his right to his home is given procedural protection via section 6 of the Criminal Law Act 1977: to avoid committing a criminal offence, C Bank needs to apply for a court order to remove A.[197]
>
> The human rights argument is strongest in two very unusual cases.
>
> 1. Where (as in *Western Bank v Schindler*) *C Bank applies for a possession order even though A is not in default.* However, in such cases the property law system already protects A by insisting that C Bank can only use its right to exclusive control where it is necessary to enforce or protect its security right. Further, in the rare case where the transaction between A and C Bank does not give A an express or implied right to occupy the land, it is hard to see why C Bank should be prevented from using its security right, as intended, to protect the secured duty.

---

[192] LPA 1925, s 87(1).

[193] *Western Bank Ltd v Schindler* [1977] Ch 1.

[194] *Quennell v Maltby* [1979] 1 WLR 318.

[195] See eg Rook, *Property Law and Human Rights* (2001), 199ff; the suggestion by Dixon (1999) 58 *CLJ* 281 at 283; Nield in *Modern Studies in Property Law* (vol 3, ed Cooke, 2005), 155ff.

[196] *Wood v UK* (1997) 24 EHRR CD 69; *per* Mance LJ in *Michalak v London Borough of Wandsworth* [2003] 1 WLR 617 at [64]: the ECHR, in *Wood*, gave 'short shrift' to the claim that enforcement of a security right on A's default was a breach of A's human rights.

[197] The importance of such procedural protection was emphasised by the ECHR: *Connors v UK* (2004) 40 EHRR 189.

2. Where (as in *Ropaigealach v Barclays Bank plc*) *C Bank is able to take physical control of A's land without a court order, as A is temporarily absent from the land.* The fact that C Bank can thus enter A's home without the procedural protection provided by a court order strengthens the argument that A's Article 8 right is breached. Yet it is important to remember that A, by choosing to give C Bank a Charge, has given it a right to exclusive control of A's land. It is true that C Bank has that right only by way of security; but this is recognised by the principle that C Bank can only use its right to exclusive control where it is necessary to enforce or protect its security right.

After all, C Bank also has a human right, under Article 1 of Protocol 1, in relation to the enjoyment of both: (i) its security right (ie, his Charge); and (ii) the secured duty (ie, A's duty to repay a loan to C).

So, in a case such as **A:Example 1**, a dispute arises because: (i) C Bank wishes to enforce its Charge by selling the land with vacant possession; and (ii) A and B wish to remain in occupation of the land. In resolving such a dispute about the use of a thing, the **basic structure** provides us with a clear set of questions to ask. In developing that structure, the property law system grapples with exactly the same issues as the ECHR: it attempts to resolve the impossibly difficult basic tension between B and C; or, in this case, between A and B on one hand and C Bank on the other. It is always possible to disagree with the result the property law system reaches in a particular case; as we noted in **A:1**, disputes about things—and in particular about the use of the land—are inherently controversial. Yet that should not reduce our respect for the success and subtlety of the basic structure.

CHAPTER G5
THE EASEMENT

G5

THE EASEMENT

Like the Lease and the Charge, the Easement is a property right that exists only in relation to land. An Easement allows B, a party who has a Freehold or Lease, to make a *specific, limited* use of some nearby land that is owned by A.[1] The Easement thus supplements B's ownership of B's land by detracting from A's ownership of A's land.[2]

EXAMPLE 1

A and B are neighbours; each has a Freehold. A new road is built and A's land lies between B's land and the road. In return for payment from B, A (using a deed) grants B a right of way, allowing B to get to his land from the road by walking along a path on A's land. B substantively registers his right of way.

B's right of way counts as an Easement. It supplements B's Freehold, by making it more convenient for B to reach his land. At the same time, the Easement detracts from A's Freehold: for example, it prevents A from building on his land in a way that would interfere with B's right of way. Moreover, as B's Easement is a property right, it not only prevents A from acting in that way: the *rest of the world* is also under a prima facie duty to B not to interfere with B's right of way.

If B wishes to make some limited use of A's land, it may be possible for B to do so *without* relying on an Easement.

1. B may be able to rely on a right available to *every member of the public*. For example, if A's land is crossed by a public footpath, B, like any member of the public, will be able to use that path.

2. B may be able to rely on a right available to *every member of a particular local community*. For example, if A's land is subject to an ancient 'customary' set of rules, B, like any member of the local community included in the custom, may have a customary right to make a particular use of A's land.[3]

---

[1] There is another type of property right in land, known as a Profit, that is linked to, but distinct from an Easement. It consists of a right to use A's land by taking something from A's land (eg, timber, fish, wild animals, turf, minerals). Unlike an Easement, a Profit does not have to enhance a Freehold or Lease of B: it can be free-standing. The most important rules governing Profits apply equally to Easements, so we will not specifically discuss Profits in this book. For more on Profits, see eg Law Com Consultation Paper No 186 (2008) Part 6.

[2] Law Com Consultation Paper No 186 (2008), 3.66 suggests that the law should be changed so that: (i) if B holds two separate registered estates (eg, two registered Freeholds); then (ii) B can create an Easement for the benefit of Freehold No 1 taking effect over Freehold No 2. This would necessarily require legislation: as a matter of doctrine, it is impossible for B to give himself a right.

[3] See eg *Brocklebank v Thompson* [1903] 2 Ch 344: B had a customary right to walk across C's land to get to a parish church. For a discussion of the nature of customary rights, see Lord Hoffmann in *R v Oxfordshire CC, ex p Sunningwell PC* [2000] 1 AC 335.

3. B may be able to rely on a right arising *as part of his Freehold or Lease*. B has a basic level of protection by virtue of his Freehold or Lease. For example, if A's land physically supports B's adjacent land, A may commit a wrong against B if A removes that support (see **G1A:4.1.3**).[4] B is often said to have a 'natural right' to support for his land—a right which arises simply because B has a property right in land, without B needing to show that he has an Easement.

4. B may of course have a direct right against A (see **E3:2**). For example, if A has made a contractual promise to allow B to walk across A's land, B can rely on that contractual right against A.

The rights enjoyed by B in the absence of a direct right or an Easement are quite limited. For example, if A's building supports a building on B's land, A does not necessarily commit a wrong by pulling down A's building: A's basic duty is to support B's land, not to support a building on B's land.[5]

1 THE CONTENT QUESTION

The simplest way for B to satisfy the content question is to show that the courts have already recognised that the type of right he claims can count as an Easement. For example, if B claims that he has: (i) a right of way over A's land; or (ii) a right to store goods on A's land, he will simply be able to point to previous cases in which such rights have been recognised as Easements.[6] However, the list of Easements is not closed: even if B's right has not been previously recognised as an Easement, that is not fatal to his claim. In such a case, B's right counts as an Easement if:

- It allows B to make a specific, limited use of A's land; *and*
- It enhances B's Freehold or Lease (ie it benefits B's land); *and*
- It lasts for forever (like a Freehold) or for a limited period (like a Lease); *and*
- It is not a right to exclusive control of A's land; *and*
- It does not impose a positive duty on A; *and*
- When created, it was not intended to be only a personal right against A.

1.1 A right to make a specific, limited use of A's land

1.1.1 A right relating to A's land

It is impossible to have an Easement in relation to a thing other than land. First, land's capacity for multiple, simultaneous use makes it possible for A to give B a right to use A's land that is both limited and valuable. Second, the permanent, fixed location of a piece of land means that a right to use neighbouring land may be vital in allowing B to get the full

---

[4] See eg *Redland Bricks Ltd v Morris* [1970] AC 652.

[5] See eg *Wyatt v Harrison* (1832) 3 B & Ad 871; *per* Lord Penzance in *Dalton v Angus & Co* (1881) 6 App Cas 740 at 804.

[6] Other examples of accepted Easements include: (i) the right to park on A's land; (ii) the right to receive water flowing through pipes on A's land; (iii) the right to receive air passing from A's land through a defined channel; (iv) the right to receive light passing from A's land to a window; (v) the right to have a building supported by a building on A's land.

benefit of his own land. In contrast, it is difficult even to think of a situation in which B can claim that his ownership of land or of a thing other than land is enhanced by a right to make some limited use of A's thing.

1.1.2 A right to make use of A's land

Any Easement will, indirectly, impose a negative duty: not just on A, but also on anyone who does not have a defence to the Easement. For example, if B has a right of way over A's land, B will, prima facie, be able to prevent anyone from putting up a building that obstructs the right of way. As a result, B's Easement can severely restrict A's ability to make use of his own land.[7]

However, to count as an Easement, B's right must do *more* than simply impose a negative duty. In *Phipps v Pears*,[8] for example, A demolished a building on A's land. This left the wall of B's adjoining house exposed to the weather. B suffered damage as a result. B claimed compensation from A by alleging that A had interfered with an Easement: B's right to have his house protected by A's building. The Court of Appeal rejected B's claim: such a right, as it imposes *only* a negative duty, cannot count as an Easement. Lord Denning MR did, however, acknowledge that certain well-established Easements are permitted despite being 'negative' in nature.[9] His Lordship's approach, therefore, was not to prohibit all 'negative' Easements, but rather to say that the land law system should be very careful before recognising any 'new' negative Easements.[10]

However, we have to be very careful in describing particular Easements as 'negative'. Every Easement is negative, in the sense that it restricts the uses that can be made of A's land. Lord Denning MR identified a right to receive light as a negative Easement: unlike, for example, a right of way, it does not involve B 'doing something on or to his neighbour's land'.[11] Similar rights recognised as Easements include a right to receive air; and a right to support of a building. There are two possible ways to explain these Easements. One is to see them as exceptional, as their *principal* effect is to stop an owner of A's land from using his land as he wishes. However, we still need to ask why the right claimed by B in *Phipps* cannot fit in this exceptional category: for example, like a right to light, air or support from a building, it was clearly defined and was claimed only against an immediate neighbour.[12]

An alternative way to explain Easements of light, air and support of a building is to see each of them as doing *more* than simply imposing a negative duty. In each case, B can be said to be making some use of A's land: not by physically going on to that land, but rather by benefiting from light or air passing over A's land; or from the physical support of a building on A's land. In *Phipps*, the right claimed by B was different: (i) B did not wish to receive anything passing over A's land;[13] (ii) B did not want to benefit from any physical

---

[7] See eg *per* Lord Scott in *Moncrieff v Jamieson* [2007] 1 WLR 2620 at [54]: 'Every servitude or easement will bar some ordinary use of the servient land. For example, a right of way prevents all manner of ordinary uses of the land over which the road passes. The servient owner [A] cannot plough up the road. He cannot grow cabbages on it or use it for basketball practice.'

[8] [1965] 1 QB 76.

[9] *Ibid* at 82.

[10] In *Phipps*, C did not choose to demolish the building on its land. Rather, he was ordered to do so by the local authority. As a result, finding in B's favour and forcing C to pay money to B would have seemed particularly harsh in *Phipps* (unless, of course, C could have claimed some form of statutory indemnity from the local authority).

[11] [1965] 1 QB 76 at 82.

[12] See *per* Lord Hoffmann in *Hunter v Canary Wharf* [1997] 1 AC 655 at 709.

[13] In fact, B specifically did *not* want to receive the rain and wind passing over A's land to his own.

pressure provided by the building on A's land. Instead, B wished to benefit from the simple *presence* of a building on A's land; that building was not providing any direct physical benefit to B's land but was simply preventing rain and wind reaching B's land. The Court of Appeal was therefore right to see B's claimed right as different from a right to support.[14] B's right cannot count as an Easement as it would impose a purely negative duty: a duty not to demolish the building on A's land.

This may seem pedantic. It is possible for A, and future owners of A's land, to be under a negative duty to B and future owners of B's land: A simply needs to give B a Restrictive Covenant. However, there is a good reason for distinguishing between the content of an Easement and the content of a Restrictive Covenant. A Restrictive Covenant can only be acquired by A expressly exercising his power to give B such a right. In contrast, as we will see in **section 2** below, an Easement can be acquired through long enjoyment (prescription) or by an *implied* exercise of A's power to give B an Easement. Indeed, in *Phipps* itself, A had not expressly given B a right to protection from the elements. Rather, B claimed that he had acquired the right through an *implied* grant;[15] hence, once it was established that B's right could not count as an Easement, B was unable to argue that he had instead acquired a Restrictive Covenant.

In some cases, B's claimed Easement may include: (i) a right allowing B to make some use of A's land; *and* (ii) a right that merely imposes a negative duty. In such a case, it may be possible to say that: (i) B does have a valid Easement as regards the right to use A's land, but (ii) only A is bound by the negative duty to B. For example, in *Hill v Tupper*,[16] A promised to allow B an 'exclusive' right to run pleasure boats on A's canal (see **E1:Example 1**). This promise had both positive and negative aspects: positively, B was allowed to make a use of A's land. That right, if it benefited some land of B, could count as an Easement. Negatively, the promise attempted to allow B to prevent anyone else from operating such trips. That right, even if it benefited some land of B, could not count as an Easement: it is a negative right. Hence, when C began to compete with B by also renting out pleasure boats, B could not show that C had committed a wrong against B: B had no right imposing the purely negative duty on C not to put boats on the canal. A's promise to give B 'exclusive' use thus gave B only a *personal* right to sue A if A allowed others to run boats on the canal.[17]

1.1.3 A right to make a specific, limited use of A's land

This limit is often linked to the requirement that B's right must not be a right to exclusive control of A's land.[18] However, it is an independent rule. It explains, for example, that whilst B can have an Easement that allows him to receive air passing from A's land to his through a defined channel, a *general* right to receive air flowing over A's land cannot count as an Easement.[19] Similarly, B can have an Easement allowing him to receive light passing from A's

[14] See *per* Lord Denning MR [1965] 1 QB 76 at 83.

[15] That seems to have been B's principal argument. B may also have relied on prescription as it seems he enjoyed the claimed right for a total of 31 years before C demolished his building.

[16] (1863) 2 H&C 121.

[17] It was therefore possible for B to use that right against A to pressure A into asserting his right, as a Freehold owner of the canal, to prevent C running boats on the canal.

[18] For example, in *Copeland v Greenhalf* [1952] Ch 488 the apparently unlimited scope of B's right meant that it was incompatible with the limited nature of an Easement.

[19] See eg *Webb v Bird* (1861) 10 CBNS 268; (1862) 13 CBNS 841; *Chastey v Ackland* [1895] 2 Ch 389. In the latter

land to his via a particular window,[20] but a *general* right to light or to the enjoyment of a view cannot count as an Easement. For example, in *Burrows v Lang*,[21] B claimed a right to let his cattle drink at A's pond, taking whatever water was remaining once A's animals had taken their fill. That right could not count as an Easement: its scope was too uncertain.

1.2   A right that enhances B's Freehold or Lease

EXAMPLE 2a

A has a Freehold that includes a garden with a swimming pool.[22] B, a friend of A, lives in a town 20 miles away, but works in an office near A's land. B regularly drops in, before or after work, for a swim. A plans to sell his Freehold to C, but wants to ensure that, even after the sale, B will still be able to use the pool. A therefore attempts to give B an Easement allowing him to use the pool.

A's attempt to give B a property right will fail. To show that his right counts as an Easement, B needs to show that it enhances his Freehold or Lease of some other land. It is not enough that B's use of the pool benefits *him*; it needs to benefit *his land*.[23] And, as B lives 20 miles away, he cannot claim that the right to use A's pool confers a benefit on his land. This restriction on the content of an Easement is important.[24] A general argument against recognising property rights in land is that such rights limit the future use of A's land: given the limited stock of land, this is an unwelcome result. However, whilst the value of A's land may be reduced by the burden of an Easement, the value of B's land may be greatly increased. In this way, any harm to the marketability of A's land can be more than compensated by an increase in the value of B's land. It is therefore no surprise that, in its recent review of the law of Easements, the Law Commission rejected the idea that it should be possible for B to have an Easement 'in gross':[25] ie, a property right to make some use of A's land that does *not* enhance a Freehold or Lease of B.[26]

---

case, C put up a building on his land that cut off the flow of air to B's land. This had a particularly unpleasant effect, as it meant the smell emanating from an adjoining drill-hall urinal was no longer carried away on the air. Indeed, a judge who often lodged in B's house complained of a headache when he returned there after C had put up his building. But B could not claim that he had an Easement preventing C interfering with the general flow of air.

[20] See eg *Levet v Gas Light & Coke Co* [1919] 1 Ch 24. The area through which B receives the light must be clearly defined: in *Allen v Greenwood* [1980] Ch 119 an Easement to receive light into a greenhouse was permitted.

[21] [1901] 2 Ch 502: see *per* Farwell J at 510–12.

[22] The swimming pool example comes from a discussion by R Smith, *Property Law* (5th edn, 2006), 489. See too *per* Lord Scott in *Moncrieff v Jamieson* [2007] 1 WLR 2620 at [47].

[23] For this reason, it is not possible for A to give B an Easement which is personal in the sense of benefiting B but not benefiting future owners of B's land.

[24] Although it has been suggested that it is based on an illegitimate importation of Roman law principles into English law, encouraged by the work of Gale (the first edition of his *Treatise on the Law of Easements* was published in 1839): see eg Hackney, in *The Classification of Obligations* (ed Birks, 1997), 141. In **D1:2.1**, we noted that part of Pollock's analysis of the role of possession could be seen as an example of such an illegitimate importation of Roman law principles (see esp **D1:n94**).

[25] For such a proposal, see eg Sturley (1980) 96 *LQR* 557.

[26] See Law Com Consultation Paper No 186 (2008), 3.16.

EXAMPLE 2b

The facts are as in **Example 2a** with the difference that B has a Freehold of the land neighbouring A's land.

It may still be difficult for B to show that his right to use the pool benefits his land. Of course, the right may make B's land more valuable; but this does not suffice. For example, in *re Ellenborough Park*,[27] Lord Evershed MR accepted counsel's suggestion that a right to 'use the Zoological gardens free of charge or to attend Lord's cricket ground without payment', even if given to a party who owns land near such an attraction, *cannot* count as an Easement.[28] Whilst of value to its holder, such a right does not satisfy the **content question**: there is 'no sufficient nexus between the enjoyment of the right and the use of the house . . . it would be wholly extraneous to, and independent of, the use of a house as a house'.[29]

This raises a difficult question: how can we tell if B's right does benefit his land? In *re Ellenborough* itself, a right to use a nearby communal garden *was* allowed to count as an Easement. The court took the view that this right 'undoubtedly enhances, and is connected with, the normal enjoyment of the house to which it belongs'.[30] The assumption here seems to be that use of a garden is something commonly regarded as a natural supplement to a Freehold or Lease of a house. It is difficult to know whether the same view could be taken of a swimming pool.[31] Certainly, judgements can change over time: as we will see, it has been accepted that a right to park a car can count as an Easement. One reasonably clear point is that a right can count as an Easement if it benefits a business carried out on B's land. For example, the right to fix, on the wall of A's house, a sign drawing attention to B's pub has been recognised as an Easement;[32] and the right to fix a ventilation duct on A's land can count as an Easement where that duct enables B to use his land as a restaurant.[33]

1.3 A right that lasts forever or for a limited period

When giving B a right to make some use of his neighbouring land, A may put a time limit on B's right. For example, rather than simply giving B a permanent right of way, A may give B such a right for a period of seven years. This will often occur if A gives B an Easement at the same time as giving B a Lease of adjoining land; the Easement and the Lease will last for the same limited period. It is perfectly possible for A to do this: B's right of way over A's land, like his right to exclusive possession of the adjoining land, can count as property right if it lasts for a limited period.

However, section 1(2)(a) of the Law of Property Act 1925 ('the LPA 1925') ensures that B's right can only be an Easement if it exists for an unlimited period (like a Freehold) or for

---

[27] [1956] 1 Ch 131.

[28] *Ibid* at 174.

[29] *Per* Lord Evershed MR at 174.

[30] *Ibid*. It had been argued, in reliance on Roman law (Paul, Digest, 8.1.8) that a right to use a garden was too uncertain to count as an Easement (see **1.1.3** above) but that argument was rejected in *re Ellenborough Park*: *per* Lord Evershed MR[1956] 1 Ch 131 at 163, 177–87.

[31] The point is discussed by R Smith, *Property Law* (5th edn, 2006), 489. As Gray and Gray have noted, 'the definition of qualifying rights in the law of easements is heavily coloured by an element of value judgment' (*Elements of Land Law* (4th edn, 2005), 628–9).

[32] *Moody v Steggles* (1879) 12 Ch D 261.

[33] *Wong v Beaumont Property Trust Ltd* [1965] 1 QB 173.

a limited period (like a Lease).[34] So, for example, A cannot give B1 an Easement for B1's life;[35] or give B2 an Easement to take effect after B1's death; nor can A give B an Easement for an uncertain period, such as until England win the football World Cup (see **G1B:1.7.1**)

1.4   A right that is not a right to exclusive control of A's land

An Easement, in contrast to a Freehold or a Lease, simply allows B to make a limited use of A's land. If the right claimed by B instead amounts to a right to exclusive control of A's land, it cannot count as an Easement.

> **EXAMPLE 3a**
>
> A has a Freehold that includes a narrow strip of land adjoining a road. Over a long period, and without A's permission, B stores and repairs large motor vehicles on that strip of land. B claims that, by means of his long use of A's land, he has acquired an Easement.

The doctrine of prescription allows an Easement to be acquired by B's long use of A's land (see **2.8** and **2.9** below). However, that doctrine can apply only if the right claimed by B counts as an Easement. In *Copeland v Greenhalf*,[36] the essential facts of which are identical to **Example 3a**, Upjohn J decided that the right claimed by B could *not* count as an Easement. Instead, as B could leave as many vehicles as he pleased, and come onto the land when he wished to repair them,[37] B's right amounted to a right to exclusive control of the strip of land. On this view, in a case such as **Example 3a**, B cannot rely on the doctrine of prescription to prevent A removing B's vehicles from the land. Instead, B will have to apply, on the basis of his 'adverse possession' of the land, to be registered as the new holder of A's Freehold of the strip. The problem for B is that, in most cases, A can simply object to B's application for rectification and then remove B's vehicles (see **G1A:3** and **E5:3.2.5**).

This decision should not, however, be taken to mean that a right to park a vehicle on A's land can never amount to an Easement. In *Moncrieff v Jamieson*,[38] the House of Lords confirmed that, as long as B's right does not amount to a right to exclusive control of A's land, it can count as an Easement.[39] Hence, a right to park a car on a particular part of A's land can be an Easement. It does not matter if B's parking prevents A from making an effective or reasonable use of A's land: as long as B's right is to make a *limited* use of A's land (eg, to use that land for the specific purpose of parking), it can be an Easement.[40] There is thus an important link between: (i) this part of the **content** test for an Easement; and (ii) the **content** of a Lease. To show he has a Lease, B needs to show he has, for a limited period, a right to 'exclusive possession': ie, a right to exclusive control of A's land (see **G1B:1.4**). So, for the period of the Lease, the right to exclusive control of A's land must have passed from

---

[34] If it is for an 'interest equivalent to an estate in fee simple absolute in possession [a Freehold] or a term of years absolute [a Lease]', an Easement can count as an 'interest in or over land [that is] capable of subsisting or of being conveyed or created at law'.

[35] See *per* Lord Denning MR in *ER Ives Investments Ltd v High* [1967] 2 QB 379 at 395. Such a right may count as an Equitable Easement: see **section 5** below.

[36] [1952] 1 Ch 488.

[37] *Ibid* at 498.

[38] [2007] 1 WLR 2620.

[39] Scottish law governed that particular case; but on the points discussed here English law was viewed as identical.

[40] See *per* Lord Scott in *Moncrieff v Jamieson* [2007] 1 WLR 2620 at [59].

A to B. In contrast, to show he has an Easement, B needs to show that he does *not* have a right to exclusive control of A's land. So, for the period of the Easement, the right to exclusive control of A's land must remain with A; B acquires only a specific, limited right to use A's land.

EXAMPLE 3b

A and B have neighbouring Freeholds. B's land is surrounded by the sea and a steep cliff. A's land lies between B's land and a road. To allow B access to the road, A grants B a right of way, for access both on foot and by a vehicle, across A's land. B cannot drive onto his land: he must park on A's land, at the foot of the cliff, and climb stairs up to B's land. A and B informally agree that B can park on a particular part of A's land: it is close to the stairs and big enough for one or two vehicles.

In such a case, as a necessary corollary of the right of way, B must have a right to park on A's land. The question is whether that right can count as an Easement. In *Moncrieff v Jamieson*,[41] the essential facts of which are identical to **Example 3b**, A argued that such a right to park cannot count as an Easement, as it deprives A of any reasonable use of part of A's land. The House of Lords rejected that argument. It is true that, when exercising his right to park, B may take up all of a particular part of A's land. Crucially, however, B's right is simply a right to use that part of A's land for a *specific, limited* purpose: it is not a right to exclusive control. After all, A is still free to use that part of the land as he wishes, *provided* only that A does not interfere with the reasonable exercise by B of his right to park on the land.[42] So, the right to exclusive control of the land remains in A and has not passed to B.

This part of the content test for an Easement, like the analogous part of the content test for a Lease, is: (i) easy to state; but (ii) can be difficult to apply in practice (see **G1B:1.4.1**).[43] In any particular case, it may be that the 'essential question is one of degree'.[44] Nonetheless, it does seem clear that if B's right is expressed to be only for a limited purpose, such as a right to park, it *will* satisfy this part of the content test.[45]

1.5   A right that does not impose a positive duty on A

There is a general reluctance within English law to impose a general duty on the rest of the world, owed to B, to do a positive act for B's benefit. This is clear in the law of wrongs: whilst B's right to physical integrity imposes a general *negative* duty on the rest of the world, it does not impose a general *positive* duty. Hence, C commits a wrong against B if he deliberately pushes B down some steps; but C2 does not commit a wrong against B if he walks

---

[41] [2007] 1 WLR 2620.

[42] *Ibid per* Lord Scott at [53].

[43] Note too Lord Scott at [56] queried whether the facts of *Copeland v Greenhalf* [1952] Ch 488 (ie, **Example 3a**) justified Upjohn J's conclusion that B was claiming a right to exclusive control of A's land.

[44] *Per* Judge Paul Baker QC in *London & Blenheim Estates v Ladbroke Retail Parks* [1992] 1 WLR 1278 at 1288. In that case, B's right to park did count as an Easement: on the terms of the agreement between A and B, B's right applied only: (i) as long as there was an area of A's land set aside for parking; and (ii) as long as 'space is available' on A's land.

[45] As noted by Lord Scott in *Moncrieff v Jamieson* [2007] 1 WLR 2026 at [59]–[60] and by Lord Neuberger at [143], this analysis casts serious doubt on the decision of the Court of Appeal in *Batchelor v Marlow* [2003] 1 WLR 764. See too Hill-Smith [2007] *Conv* 223 (an article expressly relied on by Lord Scott).

past and refuses to help B to his feet, even though it would be very easy for C2 to do so.[46] This reluctance has important implications for the **content** of property rights. If B's right counts as a property right, it imposes a prima facie duty on the rest of the world. It is therefore no surprise to find that property rights cannot impose general positive duties.

EXAMPLE 4

A and B have neighbouring Freeholds. B claims he has an Easement to receive water from pipes that run over A's land.

In such a case, A can claim that B's right does not count as an Easement: it appears to impose a positive duty on A to maintain the flow of water by paying for the water entering his pipes. In *Rance v Elvin*,[47] on which **Example 4** is based, the Court of Appeal rejected that argument: B can have an Easement that: (i) allows B to receive water *as long as* A chooses to keep his pipes connected to the water supply; *but* (ii) does *not* impose a positive duty on A to continue to keep his pipes connected; *and* (iii) does *not* impose a positive duty on A to pay for the water used by B. Such a right can count as an Easement as it does *not* impose a positive duty on A: A has a liberty, if he wishes, not to keep his pipes connected to the water supply.

The approach in *Rance v Elvin* may be useful when considering **Examples 2a and 2b**. Those cases raise the issue of whether a right to use a swimming pool can count as an Easement. In *Moncrieff v Jamieson*, Lord Scott (in an *obiter dictum*) suggested that such a right *cannot* count an Easement as it imposes a positive duty on A—a duty to maintain the pool.[48] However, it may be possible to say that B can have an Easement that: (i) allows B to use the pool *as long as* A chooses to keep and maintain it; *but* (ii) does *not* impose a positive duty on A to keep and maintain the pool.

There is commonly said to be one exception to the rule that an Easement cannot impose a positive duty. In *Crow v Wood*,[49] the Court of Appeal seemed to accept that B's right to have A repair and maintain a fence on A's land can count as an Easement. That description of B's right is very surprising. A property right imposes a prima facie duty on the rest of the world. So, if there really is an 'Easement of fencing' then not only A, but also the *whole world*, must be under a duty to maintain the fence on A's land. That clearly cannot be right. The better explanation of the so-called 'Easement of fencing' is that, due to an ancient local custom, it may be that each owner of land adjoining a common area may be under a duty, owed to other users of that common area, to maintain a fence separating his land from the common area. In *Crow v Wood*, for example, A and B both owned farms that adjoined a large sheep moor. Like the other owners of such farms, A and B each had a right to graze a certain number of sheep on the moor. In return for that benefit, each had a duty to fence. In most cases, this duty can be explained as arising because of an *ancient local custom*—an unwritten law applying to a particular area.

If such a custom exists, it is not accurate to describe B's right as an Easement.[50] The rest

---

[46] For a general discussion of this reluctance to impose positive duties, see eg *per* Lord Hoffmann in *Stovin v Wise* [1996] AC 923 at 943–4.

[47] [1985] 50 P & CR 9.

[48] [2007] 1 WLR 2026 at [47].

[49] [1971] 1 QB 77.

[50] In *Crow v Wood*, the Court of Appeal wrongly assumed that a right to fence cannot arise by custom, and so did

of the world is not under a duty to B; rather, the neighbouring landowners bound by the customary 'local law' are under a duty to B. This means that A does *not* have the power to give B an Easement of fencing. For example, if A and B own neighbouring land in a town, A cannot impose a duty on himself and future owners of his land to maintain, for the benefit of B and future owners of B's land, a fence between A's land and B's land.

1.6   A right that is not intended to be only a personal right against A

EXAMPLE 5a

A and B have neighbouring Freeholds. In return for payment from B, A grants B a right to walk across a path on A's land. A and B intend that B's right will bind not only A but also future owners of A's land.

EXAMPLE 5b

A and B have neighbouring Freeholds. In return for payment from B, A promises B that, as long as A continues to his land, he will allow B to walk across a path on A's land. However, A makes clear that he does not intend B to have a right against future owners of A's land.

In **Example 5a**, B has a property right in A's land: an Easement; in **Example 5b**, B has only a personal right against A: a contractual licence. In each case, B has a right to walk across A's land; but, in **Example 5b**, B's right cannot count as an Easement as: (i) it arose as a result of A and B's intention; and (ii) it was intended to bind only A.

So, if A gives B a right that is capable of counting as an Easement, we need to ask if that right was intended to bind only A. In some cases, such as **Example 5b**, A's express intention will provide the answer. In other cases, the intention of the parties must be inferred from the surrounding circumstances. For example, let us say A, who has a Lease of a ground-floor flat with a garden, allows B, a friend who has a Lease of the flat above, to use A's garden. It may be that, as the use of the right involves co-operation between the two friends, A does *not* intend B's right to be capable of binding other parties, such as future parties who acquire A's Lease of the ground-floor flat.[51]

This requirement may seem to be inconsistent with the role of A's intention in defining the content of a Lease. After all, if A gives B a right to exclusive control of A's land for a limited period, B's right counts as a Lease *even if* A only intends to give B a purely personal right (see **G1B:1.5.1**).[52] The requirement that A must intend to give B more than a purely

---

not consider this explanation (see eg *per* Lord Denning MR [1971] 1 QB 77 at 84, relying on *Bolus v Hinstocke* (1670) 2 Keb 686). However, in *Egerton v Harding* [1975] QB 62, after a more thorough review of the cases, the Court of Appeal held that a duty to fence *can* arise as a result of an ancient local custom. It is not clear whether the decision in *Crow v Wood* could be explained on these grounds. The first instance judge found that there was a custom by which tenants of farms adjoining the moor were obliged to maintain fences; but it is unclear whether that custom was of ancient origin. In any case, the local custom was crucial to the result in *Crow v Wood*, as it was used as the basis for finding that A had impliedly granted B an Easement when giving him his Freehold. A second possible explanation for some duties to fence is that B may have a direct right arising as a result of the 'benefit and burden' principle (see **E3:2.3.3**): a duty to fence may be the price paid by those who own land adjacent to the moor, in return for a right to graze sheep on that ancient common land. That explanation cannot apply in *Crow v Wood*, however, as C did not *choose* to exercise his right to graze sheep on the moor.

[51] See too *IDC Group Ltd v Clark* (1992) 65 P & CR 179: A's intention was the crucial factor in determining that B's right to go across A's land was a licence and not an Easement.
[52] See eg *Street v Mountford* [1985] AC 809.

personal right thus applies to Easements but *not* to Leases; it has been suggested that this difference cannot be justified.[53]

However, the difference is quite easily explained. An Easement, like a licence, consists of B making a *specific, limited* use of A's land. Therefore, if A gives B a right to walk across A's land, that right may be *either*: (i) a licence; or (ii) an Easement. In order to distinguish the two, we need to look at A's intention and see if B's right is intended to bind parties other than A. In contrast, a Lease consists of B having a right to exclusive control of land for a limited period: it gives B temporary ownership of land. If B has such a right to exclusive control, that right *cannot* be a purely personal right. It is an inherent part of a right to exclusive control that it is prima facie binding on the rest of the world. Therefore, if B has such a right, we do *not* need to ask the question of whether B was intended to have a right that can bind parties other than A; we have *already* answered that question by finding that A has given B a right to exclusive control of A's land.

1.7   Regulating the use of an Easement: excessive user

As an Easement consists of a right to make a *limited* use of A's land, it is clear that B cannot exceed the limits imposed on that use. It is important to realise that this point is independent of the requirement that a right to exclusive control cannot count as an Easement. It is possible for B's use to be *both*: (i) not so extensive as to amount to exclusive control of A's land; *and* (ii) beyond the limits of B's particular Easement.

EXAMPLE 6

A has a Freehold of a large plot of farm land. A sells part of that Freehold to B and also gives B a right of way to get to that land by using a private road on A's retained land. B initially uses his land as a farm, and takes advantage of his right of way by driving his car and the occasional tractor on A's road. B then gets planning permission to turn his land into a caravan park, with up to 200 plots for caravans and/or tents.

In such a case, can B, by virtue of his right of way, permit all the users of the caravan park to use A's road? The Court of Appeal considered this question in *Jelbert v Davis*,[54] the essential facts of which are identical to **Example 6**. It was held that B was *not* permitted to make this increased and 'excessive use' of his Easement: it would be 'far beyond anything contemplated at the time of the grant'.[55] In that case, A had granted B the right to use his road 'at all times and for all purposes . . . in common with all persons having the like right'. The concluding phrase was important: the use of the road by parties using the caravan park would make it inconvenient for other parties, such as A himself, to use the road. Therefore, B's planned use of the Easement was excessive in the particular sense that it interfered with the express provision that B had to use his right in common with other parties.

However, in a case such as **Example 6**, although there is no such express limit on B's Easement, the result is very likely to be the same. There is a general assumption that, when granting B a right, A will intend there to be some limit on the extent of B's use.[56] Of course,

---

[53] See Hill (1996) 16 *LS* 200.
[54] [1968] 1 WLR 589.
[55] *Ibid per* Lord Denning MR at 596.
[56] This general assumption applies whether the Easement was acquired through an express or implied grant.

where such a limit is implied in this way there may be some doubts as to just when B's use becomes excessive: that will be a matter to be determined on the facts of the particular case.[57] It is important to remember that, even once the scope of B's Easement has been determined, B must 'exercise the right reasonably and without undue interference with [A's] enjoyment of his own land'.[58] If B's use is excessive, then B, like anyone interfering with A's enjoyment of land without authority, commits the wrong of nuisance.[59]

1.8   Regulating the use of an Easement: suspension and termination

We saw above that the duration of an Easement can be inherently limited as when, for example, A gives B an Easement for a period of seven years. It is also possible for an Easement to come to an end *before* any such limit has expired.

First, as an Easement consists of a right to make a specific, limited use of land owned by *another*, an Easement will end if B acquires the Freehold of A's land.[60] If B acquires a Lease of A's land, the Easement will be suspended for the period of the Lease; it will revive when B's Lease ends.

Second, as an Easement consists of a right that enhances B's Freehold or Lease, an Easement ought to be suspended if a change in circumstances means that the right *no longer* benefits B's land.[61] However, unless that change in circumstances is irreversible, so that the right will *never* again enhance B's Freehold or Lease,[62] it will be not be possible to say that B's Easement has been permanently lost. For example, if B stops using his land as a restaurant, a right to use a ventilation duct on A's land may cease to benefit B's land. However, it is not impossible that the land may again be used as a restaurant.

Finally, it seems that an Easement can be suspended, or even terminated,[63] if there is: (i) a radical change in the character of B's land; that (ii) substantially increases the impact of B's Easement on A's land.[64]

---

[57] And note too the general principle that any reasonable doubts about the scope of an Easement granted by A to B will be resolved in B's favour (see **2.2** below).

[58] *Per* Lord Scott in *Moncrieff v Jamieson* [2007] 1 WLR 2026 at [45]. This principle is also found in the Scottish law concept of 'civiliter'. That concept does not determine the *scope* of an Easement; it instead regulates how the Easement may be used: *per* Lord Rodger at [95].

[59] As noted in *McAdams Homes Ltd v Robinson* [2005] 1 P & CR 30 at [27] *per* Neuberger LJ: 'excessive use of an easement by the dominant land will render the dominant owner liable in nuisance'.

[60] As noted in **n 2** above, Law Com Consultation Paper No 186 (2008), 3.66 suggests that the law should be changed so that: (i) if B holds two separate registered estates (eg, two registered Freeholds); then (ii) B can hold an Easement for the benefit of Freehold No 1 taking effect over Freehold No 2. On that view, B's acquisition of A's Freehold will only end B's Easement if the two plots of land are registered under one title.

[61] This seems to be the approach in Scotland, Canada and the United States (see P Jackson [1981] *CLP* 133). It has not, however, been accepted in England.

[62] In *Huckvale v Aegean Hotels Ltd* (1989) 58 P & CR 163 at 173, Slade LJ contemplates that 'in a very clear case', such a change of circumstances will end an Easement; Nourse LJ at 170 is however more sceptical. Davis [1995] *Conv* 291 at 296 suggests that *Midland Railway Co Ltd v Gribble* [1895] 2 Ch 827 may be an example of a change in circumstances ending an Easement.

[63] Termination will presumably occur only where the change of circumstances is irreversible: see eg *per* Neuberger LJ in *McAdams Homes Ltd v Robinson* [2005] 1 P & CR 30 at [12].

[64] See *per* Neuberger LJ in *McAdams Homes Ltd v Robinson* [2005] 1 P & CR 30 at [50].

EXAMPLE 7

A and B have neighbouring Freeholds. B has an Easement allowing him to use a drainage pipe running across A's land. That Easement was acquired when B's land was used as a bakery. The bakery has been demolished and replaced by two houses, each with four bedrooms.

This change from a commercial to a residential use of B's land will lead to a (potentially large) increase in the volume of water passing from B's land through the drains on A's land. In *McAdams Homes Ltd v Robinson*,[65] the essential facts of which are identical to **Example 7**, it was argued that the change in use led to the termination of B's Easement. That argument was accepted by the first instance judge. The Court of Appeal considered that the judge's finding should not be disturbed: it could reasonably be said that: (i) there had been a radical change in the use of B's land; (ii) as a result, there had been a substantial increase in the burden of the Easement on A's land.[66]

The Court of Appeal emphasised, however, that the case was not clear-cut. Certainly, an Easement would *not* be lost where: (i) B used his land in the same way as when the Easement was acquired, but did so more intensively;[67] or (ii) if the change in the character of B's land did not impose extra burdens on A.[68] Again, it is helpful to remember that B must 'exercise [his Easement] reasonably and without undue interference with [A's] enjoyment of his own land'.[69]

The Law Commission have suggested a further means by which an Easement can be terminated or modified.[70] Section 84 of the LPA 1925 currently gives the Lands Tribunal the power, in certain circumstances, to discharge or modify a Restrictive Covenant held by B (see **G6:1.5**). The suggestion is that a similar power should exist where B has an Easement. So, for example, if: (i) B has a right of way over A's land; and (ii) as a result, A is unable to build on A's land; and (iii) A's planned building is in the public interest and could not reasonably be built elsewhere; and (iv) money would adequately compensate B for the loss of his Easement; then (v) A could apply to the Lands Tribunal to have B's right of way modified or removed so that it does not prevent A's building.[71]

The Law Commission's general point seems sound: (i) *as* the Lands Tribunal has a power to discharge or modify a Restrictive Covenant; then (ii) there is no obvious reason why it should not have the same power in respect of an Easement. However, given that an Easement can be very important in allowing B to derive the full benefit from his land, it would be reasonable to hope that the Lands Tribunal would be reluctant to find that money alone would be an adequate substitute for B's right to make some positive use of A's land.

---

[65] [2005] 1 P & CR 30.

[66] The Law Commission have supported that test: see Law Com Consultation Paper No 186 at 5.51.

[67] See eg *British Railways Board v Glass* [1965] Ch 538 (no loss of the Easement where an existing caravan park on B's land was expanded); *Cargill v Gotts* [1981] 1 WLR 441 (no loss of the Easement where an existing agricultural use was replaced by a more intensive agricultural use).

[68] See eg *Harvey v Walton* (1873) LR 8 CP 162; *Atwood v Bovis Homes Limited* [2001] Ch 371.

[69] *Per* Lord Scott in *Moncrieff v Jamieson* [2007] 1 WLR 2026 at [45].

[70] Law Com Consultation Paper No 186 (2008), 14.25ff.

[71] *Ibid* at 14.71.

SUMMARY of G5:1

An Easement, a special form of property right that exists only in land, consists of a specific, limited right to use land owned by another. Positively, the right must do more than simply prevent a particular use of A's land; it must enhance a Freehold or Lease held by B; and it must be capable of lasting forever (like a Freehold) or be given for a limited period (like a Lease). Negatively, the right cannot amount to a right to exclusive control of A's land; it cannot impose a positive duty on A; and it cannot be a right that is intended to bind only A.

It is of course possible for B to have a persistent right that simply prevents a particular use of A's land (a Restrictive Covenant); or for B to have a property right that amounts to exclusive control of land (a Freehold or Lease). Those two limits on the scope of an Easement may therefore seem to be no more than an exercise in labelling. However, labelling is crucial. As we will see in **section 2** below, once a right counts as an Easement, it becomes easier for B to satisfy the **acquisition question**. The doctrine of prescription allows B to rely on his long enjoyment of the claimed right; B can also rely on an implied, rather than an express, exercise by A of his power to give B an Easement. These additional methods of acquisition ensure that, when looking at the **content question**, we must be very careful in asking whether B's right can count as an Easement.

2 THE ACQUISITION QUESTION

2.1 Two key distinctions

2.1.1 Initial acquisition and later acquisition

When looking at how an Easement can be acquired, we need to examine two separate questions:

(i) How can B initially acquire an Easement?
(ii) Once B has an Easement, how can that Easement be acquired by B2, a future owner of B's land?

(i) Initial acquisition

Like any property right, an Easement can be acquired through a dependent acquisition: by A exercising his power to give B an Easement over A's land. A distinctive feature of Easements is that there are a number of factual situations in which a court will *infer*, even if there is no formal record, that A has exercised his power to give B an Easement. In such cases, B is said to have an *implied* Easement. The possibility of such 'implication' is not unique: in certain situations, a court will infer, even if there is no formal record, that A has exercised his power to give B a Lease (see **G1B:2.2.1(ii)**). However, there is a much wider range of situations in which the grant of an Easement will be inferred.

The orthodox position is that an Easement, like a Lease or a Charge, cannot be acquired independently. However, when B acquires an Easement by prescription (ie, by long use of the claimed right) that assumption is highly questionable: the acquisition of an Easement by prescription seems to be a form of independent acquisition. Nonetheless, there may be a reason why the courts have developed the fiction that an Easement arising by prescription was in fact granted, at some point in the past, by an owner of A's land (see **2.8.1** below).

(ii) Later acquisition

Like any property right, an Easement can be transferred by B to B2. However, unlike a Freehold, Lease or Charge, an Easement can only be held by B2 if B2 also has a Freehold or Lease that benefits from the Easement. This means that B cannot transfer his Easement to just anyone: he can only transfer it to B2 if the Easement will enhance B2's enjoyment of a Freehold or Lease. So, if B has an Easement over A's land, B cannot transfer that Easement to a friend who lives 20 miles away.

The transfer of an Easement will usually occur when B transfers his Freehold or Lease to B2. In such a case, there is no reason for B to retain his Easement; and every reason for B2 to acquire it. As a result, in such a case, there is no need for B *expressly* to exercise his power to give B2 the Easement. Instead, section 62 of the LPA 1925 means that: (i) if B transfers his Freehold or Lease to B2; then (ii) that transfer will (unless B expressly provides otherwise) operate to transfer to B2 any Easement benefiting B's Freehold or Lease.

EXAMPLE 8

A and B have neighbouring Freeholds. A exercises his power to give B a right of way, enabling B to walk across A's land to B's house. B then builds a cottage on his land and sells the Freehold of that part of the land to B2.

If *both* B's retained land *and* B2's land benefit from the right of way over A's land, B will want: (i) to keep his right of way over A's land; *and* (ii) to give B2 the benefit of that right as well. The land law system gives B that power to *duplicate* his Easement: in a case such as **Example 8**, it is therefore possible for B both: (i) to keep his Easement; *and* (ii) to give B2 the benefit of that Easement. In such a case, there is no transfer of the Easement from B to B2; instead, *both* B and B2 have a right of way over A's land.

We encountered the possibility of duplication when considering the annexation of a direct right to B's Freehold or Lease (see **E3:2.1.3**). There we saw that B's contractual right against A (or C) can be annexed to B's land *if* certain conditions are met. However, where B acquires an Easement, that right is *automatically* annexed to B's land. And it is automatically annexed to *each and every part* of B's land. This means that, in a case such as **Example 8**, unless B expressly provides otherwise, section 62 of the LPA 1925 ensures that B2 automatically acquires an Easement.

When B2 acquires a pre-existing Easement in this way, formality rules do not present a problem. By satisfying the formality rules regulating his acquisition of a Freehold or Lease from B, B2 *necessarily* satisfies the formality rule applying to the transfer or duplication of the Easement. So, in **Example 8**, once B2 substantively registers his Freehold, B2 also acquires an Easement over A's land. There are only two possible problems for B2:

1. It may be that B's Easement does not benefit the part of B's land acquired by B2. In such a case, B2's claimed right cannot count as an Easement as it does not satisfy the **content** test: it does not benefit a Freehold or Lease held by B2.
2. It may be that the change of circumstances involved in B2's acquisition of a right counts as: (i) a radical change in the character of B's land; that (ii) substantially increases the impact of B's Easement on A's land (see **1.8** above). In such a case, B's Easement cannot be duplicated.

As a result, the transfer or duplication of a pre-existing Easement is very straightforward, and so we will concentrate here on the *initial* acquisition of an Easement by B.

2.1.2 Grant and reservation

When looking at the initial acquisition of Easements, it is important to distinguish between: (i) the *grant* and (ii) the *reservation* of Easements.

EXAMPLE 9a

A has a Freehold of a large plot of land. A sells part of that Freehold to B. B claims that A has also given B a right of way to get to B's land by using a private road on A's retained land.

EXAMPLE 9b

A has a Freehold of a large plot of land. A sells part of that Freehold to B. On the part of the land sold to B, there is a drainage pipe running to A's land. B threatens to remove the pipe and A claims that he has a right to keep that pipe on B's land.

In **Example 9a**, B claims that A has *granted* him an Easement: that A, when selling part of his land to B, also exercised his power to give B an Easement over A's retained land. In **Example 9b**, A claims that he has *reserved* an Easement: that A insisted, as part of the terms of the sale to B, that A will have an Easement over B's newly acquired land. Technically, a reservation operates as a 're-grant': A grants a Freehold or Lease to B; and B then grants A an Easement over B's land. In practice, the process does not have two stages: A insists, as part of the terms of the sale to B, that A will have an Easement over B's land. Section 65(1) of the LPA 1925 simplifies things by allowing A *directly* to reserve the Easement when giving the Freehold or Lease to B.

The distinction between grant and reservation is particularly important when considering *implied* Easements. The basic point is that it will be very difficult for A to infer that he has reserved an Easement. The effect of this is that, if A wishes to reserve an Easement, he will generally have to do so expressly. In contrast, it is easier for B to acquire an implied Easement: a court is more willing to infer that, when giving B a Freehold or Lease, A also exercised his power to give B an Easement. This means that, in **Example 9a**, B may well be able to show that A has granted him an Easement, even if A did not do so expressly. In contrast, in **Example 9b**, it will be much harder for A to show that he has impliedly reserved an Easement over B's land.

2.2   Express grant

A's power to expressly give B a new Easement is regulated by formality rules (see **E1:2.3**).

1. A must exercise his power in a deed: see section 52 of the LPA 1925;
2. B must substantively register his Easement: see section 27(2)(d) of the Land Registration Act 2002 ('the LRA 2002').

EXAMPLE 9c

A has a Freehold of a large plot of land. A sells part of that Freehold to B. A expressly grants B a right of way allowing B to get to B's land by using a private road on A's retained land. B then offers rooms in his house to bed and breakfast guests. A claims that B cannot permit guests to use the right of way as A granted B the right of way simply for the purpose of allowing B to get to his house.

Where A expressly gives B an Easement, questions can arise as to the *scope* of the right given to B. The basic principle is that, in case of doubt, the terms of the grant are to be interpreted in favour of B. A, the party choosing to exercise his power to give B a right, is in control of the grant. If A fails to set clear limits on B's right, any reasonable doubt as to the scope of the right will be resolved in B's favour. This rule of interpretation is often said to depend on the principle that a party granting a right cannot '*derogate from his grant*'—ie, A cannot later attempt to cut down the right he seemingly gave to B. So, in **Example 9c**, A's argument will only succeed if: (i) A *expressly* limited the right of way when granting it to B;[72] or (ii) B's use of the Easement infringes the principle that B must 'exercise the right reasonably and without undue interference with [A's] enjoyment of his own land'.[73]

2.3 Express reservation

Formality rules also govern A's power, when granting B a Freehold or Lease, to reserve an Easement over B's land. Again:

1. A must reserve the right in a deed: see section 52 of the LPA 1925;
2. A must substantively register his Easement: see section 27(2)(d) of the LRA 2002.

When considering the interpretation of an expressly reserved Easement, it is vital to bear in mind that, technically, a reservation by A actually consists of B exercising his power to grant A an Easement. As B is thus the party granting the Easement, any reasonable doubts as to its scope will be resolved in *A's* favour. It has been pointed out that this technical approach may be harsh on B;[74] the Law Commission has recommended its reversal.[75] After all, the logic of the rule is that the grantor is in charge of the situation. And when a reservation occurs, whilst B *technically* grants A a right, it is, in practice, A who is more likely to be in charge of the transaction. However, whilst noting that argument, the Court of Appeal has confirmed that an Easement reserved by A, as it is technically granted by B, must be interpreted in A's favour.[76] This reflects the important principle that any dependent acquisition of a property right depends on a grant: an exercise by a party (in this case B) of his power to give another party a property right.

---

[72] See eg *White v Grand Hotel, Eastbourne Ltd* [1913] 1 Ch 113.
[73] *Per* Lord Scott in *Moncrieff v Jamieson* [2007] 1 WLR 2026 at [45]: see **1.7** above.
[74] See eg Megarry and Wade, *The Law of Real Property* (ed Harpum, 6th edn, 2000), 1104–5.
[75] See Law Com Consultation Paper No 186 (2008), 4.21–4.24.
[76] See *St Edmundsbury and Ipswich Diocesan Board of Finance v Clark (No 2)* [1975] 1 WLR 468.

2.4 Implied grant: general rules

2.4.1 No need for substantive registration

To acquire an implied Easement, B needs to show that a court can *infer*, from the surrounding circumstances, that A has in fact exercised his power to grant B an Easement. To acquire an Easement, B also needs to show that A exercised that power in a *deed*. In a case such as **Example 9a**, that formality rule presents no problem for B. As A has transferred his Freehold to B, a deed must have been used: any implied Easement can be implied into that deed. Importantly, an implied Easement, unlike an express Easement, does *not* need to be substantively registered: section 27(2)(d) of the LRA 2002 applies only to the 'express grant or reservation' of an Easement.

EXAMPLE 9d

The facts are as in **Example 9a**. B argues that he has an implied right of way to use a private road on A's retained land as A's land entirely surrounds B's land and there is no other means for B to reach his land. A then sells his Freehold to C.

In such a case, B will acquire an implied Easement (see **2.5.1** below). B does not need to substantively register his right. This seems as though it may cause a problem for C: because B acquired his Easement as a result of an implied grant, the publicity provided by registration is absent. However, where the surrounding circumstances allow B to acquire an implied Easement, those very circumstances can provide the publicity registration otherwise brings. So, in **Example 9d**, the fact that B's land is entirely surrounded by A's land makes it obvious that B may well have a right of way over A's land.

2.4.2 The basis of implied grant

Two requirements have to be satisfied for an implied grant to occur:

1. A must grant B a Freehold or Lease. B's failure to substantively register a Freehold or Lease will generally prevent B acquiring that right (see **E1:2.3.4**) and so can prevent B acquiring an implied Easement; and
2. The circumstances surrounding the grant of B's Freehold or Lease must justify the inference that A, when giving B the Freehold or Lease, also exercised his power to give B an Easement.

Where B acquires an implied Easement, the land law system protects B's *reasonable expectation* that, when granting B a Freehold or Lease, A also granted B an Easement. In developing specific rules about implied grant, the land law system is therefore effectively defining *when it is reasonable* for B to believe that A has exercised his power to give B an Easement. There is thus a close similarity to the implication of terms, from surrounding circumstances, into a contract between A and B.[77] Terms can be implied into a contract when the background to the bargain makes it reasonable for B to believe that A intends to give him a particular right. For example, if A promises B that he will not *sell* certain land

---

[77] As noted by eg Lord Neuberger in *Moncrieff v Jamieson* [2007] 1 WLR 2620 at [113]; see too Law Com Consultation Paper No 186 (2008), 4.122ff.

without giving B the chance to buy it, a term will be implied preventing A from giving the land to X as a gift without first giving B the chance to buy the land.[78]

An important tension informs the rules relating to implied grant. On the one hand, those rules seek to express an underlying idea: B should acquire an Easement when, due to the circumstances at the time when B acquired his Freehold or Lease, it is reasonable for B to believe that A also gave B an Easement. On the other hand, those rules seek to provide *specific rules* that express that idea in a precise form, allowing the parties (and in particular a third party such as C) to discover if B has acquired an implied Easement. As we will see, there may be points at which the courts, in developing specific rules, have strayed too far from the underlying rationale of an implied grant.[79]

2.5 Implied grant: specific examples

2.5.1 Necessity

It is reasonable for B to believe that A has granted him an Easement if such a right is *necessary* for B to have access to the land given by A to B (see **Example 9d**). It is clear that, in such a case, B has a reasonable expectation of acquiring an Easement.

It could be argued that, when implying a grant on grounds of necessity, a court is advancing a *public policy*: to promote the use of land, a limited resource, by ensuring that all land is accessible. However, the real concern is instead to ensure that B's reasonable expectation, arising from the surrounding circumstances, is protected.[80] This means, for example, that if A makes clear that he does not intend to grant B an Easement, B will *not* acquire that right, even if, as a result, his land is inaccessible.[81]

2.5.2 Necessary to achieve a common purpose

It is reasonable for B to believe that A has granted him an Easement if such a right is *necessary to achieve a common purpose of A and B* that lies behind the grant of the Freehold or Lease to B. For example, A may give B a Lease of commercial premises, stipulating that it must be used as a restaurant. If that use requires B to have an Easement over A's neighbouring land (eg, a right to use a ventilation duct on A's land), it is clear that B has a reasonable expectation of acquiring an Easement.[82]

It is important to appreciate the limits of the principle, as was made clear by the House of Lords in *Pwllbach Colliery Co Ltd v Woodman*.[83] First, it does *not* apply if the Easement claimed by B merely facilitates, and is not necessary for, the planned use of the land.[84]

---

[78] *Gardner v Coutts & Co* [1968] 1 WLR 173.

[79] The reasoning of Chadwick LJ in *Kent v Kavanagh* [2006] EWCA Civ 162 esp at [45] may provide an example.

[80] See esp *per* Buckley LJ in *Nickerson v Barraclough* [1981] Ch 426 at 447 (approved by Carnwath LJ in *Adealon International Corpn Pty Ltd v Merton LBC* [2007] 1 WLR 1898 at 1903–4).

[81] See esp *per* Megarry V-C in *Nickerson v Barraclough* [1980] Ch 325 at 334: 'I do not think it can be said that, whatever the circumstances, a way of necessity will always be implied whenever a close of land is made landlocked.'

[82] This example is based on *Wong v Beaumont Property Trust Ltd* [1965] 1 QB 173. In that case, a public health inspector had said that the restaurant would have to close down if such ventilation were not provided: see *per* Lord Denning MR at 179–80.

[83] [1915] AC 634.

[84] *Ibid per* Lord Atkinson at 643: 'it is, I think, clear that what must be implied is, not a grant of what is convenient, or what is usual, or what is common in the district, or what is simply reasonable, but what is necessary for the use and enjoyment, in the way contemplated by the parties, of the thing or right granted'.

Second, it does *not* apply if there is no common intention, between A and B, that B will use the land for a particular purpose. So, in *Pwllbach* itself, the principle did not apply to give B2 a right supporting his coal mining: there was no evidence that, at the time of the original grant, A and B had a common intention that B's land would be used for that purpose.

2.5.3 Transfer by A of part of his land to B: the *Wheeldon v Burrows* principle

EXAMPLE 10a

A has a Freehold. A sells part of that land, including a house, to B. A's retained land includes a strip of land near a busy road. When getting to the house, A used to drive across that strip of land. B can drive from the road to his land without driving on that strip, but only by taking a longer route involving a difficult and somewhat dangerous turn.

B cannot rely on the first two methods of acquiring an implied Easement: (i) a right to drive over A's strip of land is not necessary to allow B to get to his land; and (ii) A and B had no common plan as to the use of B's land. Nonetheless, as a result of A's previous use of the strip to get to the house that is now on B's land, it may be reasonable for B to expect an Easement. In fact, in *Millman v Ellis*,[85] the essential facts of which are identical to **Example 10a**, the Court of Appeal *did* allow B to acquire an implied Easement. The Easement arose because:

- A granted B a Freehold or Lease of part of A's land; *and*
- Prior to that grant, A made a particular, regular use of his land; *and*
- A's use of the land was apparent from the layout of A's land, or a feature of A's land; *and*
- A right for B to make that same use of A's retained land was necessary for the reasonable enjoyment of B's land.

This principle was recognised by the Court of Appeal in *Wheeldon v Burrows*,[86] and is often named for that case. There, it was said that A's prior use of the land must be 'continuous and apparent'.[87] If the right claimed by B is indicated by a feature of A's land (such as, in **Example 10a**, the physical layout of A's land) B's right is 'apparent'.[88] The term 'continuous' has an unusual meaning: it does not mean that A must have been making an uninterrupted use of the right. Rather, it means that A must have been using his land in that way as and when required. In **Example 10a**, the fact that A may not *always* have driven across the strip of land to reach his house is *not* fatal to B's claim, provided A did so regularly.

In *Wheeldon v Burrows*, it is suggested that an Easement can be implied if it is 'continuous and apparent' *or* 'necessary to the reasonable enjoyment [of B's Freehold or Lease]'.[89] However, it has since been confirmed that these are two *separate* requirements.[90] It is important to realise that B does not need to show that the Easement he claims is necessary to give him access to his land. After all, if B could do so, he would simply rely on an implied

---

[85] [1995] 71 P & CR 158.
[86] (1879) 12 Ch D 31.
[87] *Ibid per* Thesiger LJ at 49.
[88] See eg *per* Ungoed Thomas J in *Ward v Kirkland* [1967] Ch 194 at 225 (the right claimed by B in that case failed the test: there was no feature on A's land indicating the existence of the right).
[89] *Per* Thesiger LJ (1879) 12 Ch D 31 at 49.
[90] See eg *Millman v Ellis* (1995) 71 P & CR 158.

grant by necessity. Here, as B has already shown that something about the use of A's land can lead B to believe that he would acquire an Easement (ie, he has passed the 'continuous and apparent' requirement), B does not need to go so far as passing the necessity test set out above in **3.5.1** above. However, B does need to do more than simply show that the right he claims enhances his Freehold or Lease.

Example 10a provides a useful demonstration of these points. B cannot show that his claimed right is vital: he can access his land by other means. However, those other means are difficult and dangerous (particularly for visitors to B's land). So, as the Court of Appeal confirmed in *Millman v Ellis*,[91] B can show that the right does more than simply enhance his Freehold: it is necessary for the reasonable enjoyment of B's land.

EXAMPLE 10b

The facts are as in **Example 10a**, with the difference that, before selling that part of his Freehold to B, A rents out the house on his land. So A's tenants, rather than A himself, used to drive across the strip of A's retained land to get to the house that now stands on B's land.

In *Kent v Kavanagh*,[92] Chadwick LJ suggested that the principle discussed here *cannot* apply in **Example 10b**: it applies only where A himself makes a particular use of A's land before dividing up that land and transferring part to B. That restriction on the principle is very difficult to justify: after all, it is just as reasonable for B to expect that he will acquire an Easement in **Example 10b** as in **Example 10a**.[93] Indeed, it may even be *more* reasonable for B to expect an Easement in such a case: prior to his dealings with B, A was allowing other people to make a particular use of A's land. The restriction thus seems to be the result of an undue concentration on the minutiae of the specific rules relating to implied Easements, rather than on the general principle underlying all implied Easements: the need to protect a reasonable expectation of B.

2.5.4 Section 62 of the LPA 1925

(i) General position
We have already seen that section 62 plays a useful and uncontroversial role in allowing B2, when acquiring a Freehold or Lease of all or part of B's land, also to acquire B's *pre-existing* Easement over A's land (see **2.1.1(ii)** above). Where B deals directly with A, it can also be used to allow B to acquire a *new* Easement.

EXAMPLE 11a

A has a Freehold. A grants B a five-year Lease of part of A's land. There is a garage on the part of A's land *not* covered by B's Lease. As part of that Lease, A expressly gives B an Easement (for five years) to park his motorbike in that garage. At the end of the five years, A grants B a new five-year Lease: that Lease does *not* give B an express right to continue parking his motorbike in A's garage.

---

[91] (1995) 71 P & CR 158.
[92] [2007] Ch 1 at [45].
[93] In a case such as **Example 10b**, B will instead be able to acquire an implied Easement by relying on the LPA 1925, s 62 (see **2.5.4** below). However, s 62 cannot help B if A has not yet transferred his Freehold to B, but has instead only made a contractual promise to do so (see **5.2.1** below).

In such a case, section 62 operates to give B an *implied* Easement, as part of the new Lease, to park his motorbike in A's garage for the next five years. If A wishes to stop B continuing to enjoy his right to park, the onus is on A, when granting B the new Lease, to *expressly* state that B does *no longer* has that Easement. If A fails to do so, it is reasonable for B to expect that his previous Easement, like his previous Lease, has been renewed.

EXAMPLE 11b

A has a Freehold. A grants B a five-year Lease of part of A's land. There is a garage on the part of A's land *not* covered by B's Lease. A does *not* give B an express Easement to park his motorbike in that garage. However, in practice, A allows B to park his motorbike in A's garage. At the end of the five years, A grants B a new five-year Lease: that Lease does *not* give B an express right to continue parking his motorbike in A's garage.

There is a clear difference between **Example 11a** and **Example 11b**. In the latter case, B's previous Lease did *not* include a right to park his motorbike in A's garage. As a result, before the new Lease, B had only a licence: a *liberty* to park (see **D2:1.1.3** and **E6:1**). That liberty arose as a result of A's permission; and A could revoke that permission whenever he pleased (see **E6:2.2**). It seems that the most B can reasonably expect is for the previous liberty to continue as part of the new Lease: so, just as A could have revoked that liberty before the new Lease, so should A be able to revoke the liberty *after* granting B the new Lease.

However, surprisingly, section 62 *does* give B an implied Easement in **Example 11b**. This is confirmed by the decision of the Court of Appeal in *Wright v Macadam*.[94] This means that B's liberty to park is turned into a *right* to park: it is no longer possible for A to revoke B's permission. This 'metamorphic' effect of section 62 has been criticised,[95] and the Law Commission have recommended its removal.[96] As a matter of principle, it is impossible to defend. Implied Easements should be based on the need to protect B's reasonable expectations; and, in **Example 11b**, it is *not* reasonable for B to expect to acquire an Easement as part of the new Lease.

Nonetheless, as a pure matter of statutory interpretation, the result in **Example 11b** can be defended. Section 62 duplicates an older provision: section 6 of the Conveyancing Act 1881. Before 1925, that provision had been interpreted by the courts as allowing an implied Easement to arise in a case such as **Example 11b**.[97] As Parliament chose to duplicate the wording of that provision when passing section 62, it must be assumed that Parliament intended section 62 to have the same effect: to allow a liberty to turn into an Easement. Certainly, that effect is consistent with the wording of section 62. It states that: (i) if A makes a 'conveyance of land' to B (ie, in this context, where A gives B a Freehold or Lease); then (ii) A is also deemed to 'convey, with the land' all 'liberties, privileges, easements, rights and advantages whatsoever, appertaining or reputed to appertain to the land or any part

---

[94] [1949] 2 KB 744. That case involved B storing coal in a coal shed on A's land. **Example 11b** is an attempt at a more modern version of the case.

[95] The term 'metamorphic' is used by Tee in her criticism of this effect: (1998) *Conv* 115. For further disapproval see too Lawson in *Land Law: Issues, Debates, Policy* (ed Tee, 2002), 95. Judges too have expressed doubts (see eg *per* Cross J in *Green v Ashco Horticulturist Ltd* [1966] 1 WLR 889 at 897); even when deciding in B's favour (see eg *per* Tucker LJ in *Wright v Macadam* [1949] 2 KB 744 at 755).

[96] Law Com Consultation Paper No 186 (2008), 4.73, 4.74.

[97] *International Tea Stores Co v Hobbs* [1903] 2 Ch 247.

thereof'. Crucially, it is impossible for A to *convey* a liberty to B: a conveyance, in this context, consists of the grant of a property right. So, in **Example 11b**: (i) prior to A's grant of the new Lease, B has a liberty; (ii) section 62 means that, when A grants B the new Lease, A also 'conveys' to B (ie, gives B a property right); (iii) so B must have a property right with the same content as his previous liberty: an Easement to park his motorbike in A's garage.

(ii) *Limits to section 62*

The result in **Example 11b** may seem harsh on A, but it is easily avoided. The effect of section 62 is simply to impose an onus on A, when granting B the new Lease, to tell B that he will *not* have a right to continue parking his motorbike in A's garage.

There are further limits on the operation of section 62:

1. The principal limit comes from the **content question**: obviously, B cannot use section 62 to acquire an Easement if the right B claims cannot count as an Easement.
2. Section 62 can apply only if there is a 'conveyance' from A to B. This means that B can only rely on the section if A has granted B a Freehold or Lease. So, section 62 is no use to B if A has simply entered a *contract* to give B such a right (see **5.2.1** below).
3. Section 62 cannot apply if it is clear that the liberty or right enjoyed prior to the conveyance was purely personal[98] *or* purely temporary[99] and so cannot be said to be linked to B's land (ie, in the words of section 62, it does not 'appertain' nor is 're-puted to appertain' to B's land).
4. Section 62 can only apply where, before the grant of the Freehold or Lease to B, *someone other than* A made a particular use of A's land: so, in **Example 11b**, it is important that, before A granted the new Lease to B, *B* parked his motorbike in A's garage. Section 62 therefore may be used in a case such as **Example 10b**, but *not* in a case such as **Example 10a**.

The fourth limit comes from the wording of section 62. In a case such as **Example 10a**, it is impossible for B to say that, before he acquired his Freehold from A, there was an apparent 'liberty, privilege, easement, right or advantage' to drive across the strip of A's land. True, A did drive across that strip to get to the house that is now on B's land; *but* A did so simply in his capacity as a Freehold owner of that strip.[100] A's action thus has a very simple explanation: *by itself*, it cannot give B a reasonable expectation that, as a result of acquiring the land that includes the house, he will also acquire a right to drive over the strip on A's land. To show that such a reasonable expectation exists, B will need to do more: he will have to satisfy the *Wheeldon* criteria by showing that: (i) A regularly drove on that strip to get to the house now on B's land; *and* (ii) A's use of that strip is indicated by the layout of the land; *and* (iii) a right to drive on that strip is necessary for the reasonable enjoyment of B's land (see **2.5.3** above).

---

[98] See eg *per* Lord Evershed MR in *Goldberg v Edwards* [1950] Ch 247 at 257. In that case, A allowed B to reach a rear annex via the front door of A's house. It was held that right was *not* purely personal: A gave B that liberty in B's capacity as a tenant, not in B's capacity as a friend of A.

[99] See eg *Birmingham, Dudley & District Banking Co v Ross* (1888) 38 Ch D 295: B's liberty of receiving light was clearly temporary as A was in the process of putting up a building that would soon block that light.

[100] See *per* Lord Wilberforce in *Sovmots Investments Ltd v Secretary of State for the Environment* [1979] 1 AC 144 at 169; see too *per* Lord Edmund-Davies at 176 and *per* Lord Keith at 184.

The fourth limit thus seems to be justified. However, it has been challenged. It has been suggested that there are two situations in which section 62 can apply *even* where it is A himself who has been making a particular use of A's land. The first exception is for a right to light.[101] It has been suggested that section 62 can apply to give B a right to light over A's remaining land if A has built a house on his land and then sold that house to B.[102] This exception is said to come from the Court of Appeal's decision in *Broomfield v Williams*.[103] However, that case can be explained on a different ground. Whilst Lindley and Rigby LJJ did both rely on the statutory rule,[104] AL Smith LJ did not, instead pointing out that A cannot: (i) sell a house to B; and then (ii) block out light reaching the windows of B's house; as (iii) this would 'frustrate the very object of the grant—namely, that [B] should be able to use his house as a house'. On this view, the decision depends on an implied grant of an Easement necessary to achieve a common purpose of A and B (see **2.5.2** above). Alternatively, the decision can perhaps be seen as an application of the *Wheeldon* principle (see **2.5.3** above): the right to light was regularly used by A before the sale to B; was apparent from the layout of the land; and was necessary for the reasonable enjoyment of B's land.[105]

The second supposed exception is more significant and was accepted by the Court of Appeal in *Platt v Crouch*.[106] The Court of Appeal held that, where the right claimed by B is 'continuous and apparent' (ie, indicated by the layout of A's land, or a feature of A's land), section 62 *can* apply, even if the right claimed by B comes from A's prior use of the land. It seems that counsel for A did *not* raise the objection that section 62 could not apply. Certainly, the approach in *Platt* has some support.[107] However, it suffers from some serious problems.[108] The fact that A's prior use of his land involved a visible feature on that land cannot change the key point: A's use of his own land can readily be explained and does not provide evidence of any special right appertaining, or reputed to appertain, to the land acquired by B. There is a 19th-century case[109] which may seem to support the Court of Appeal's reasoning. However, that case is best seen as part of the development of the rule in *Wheeldon* principle; it should not therefore be used as a means to bypass the extra requirement imposed by that principle, namely that where land is divided and part given to B, an Easement will be implied only where: (i) it is indicated by the layout of A's land, or a feature of A's land; *and* (ii) it is necessary for the reasonable enjoyment of B's land.

---

[101] Lord Edmund-Davies recognised this exception in *Sovmots* at 176. However, it was not mentioned by any of the other Lordships.

[102] In such a case, the specific rule set out in section 62(2) applies: that rule is based on the same principle as the general section 62 rule.

[103] [1897] 1 Ch 202.

[104] Then contained in the Conveyancing Act 1881, s 6(2).

[105] It is perhaps not too surprising that the court in *Broomfield v Williams* (1897) did not explicitly rely on the *Wheeldon v Burrows* (1879) principle as that rule was still in the early stages of its development.

[106] [2004] 1 P & CR 242.

[107] It was based on the analysis set out in Megarry and Wade, *The Law of Real Property* (ed Harpum, 6th edn, 2000), 1114–5.

[108] Not least the fact that the House of Lords decision in *Sovmots Investments Ltd v Secretary of State for the Environment* [1979] 1 AC 144 is not mentioned in any of the judgments given by the Court of Appeal.

[109] *Watts v Kelson* (1870) 6 Ch App 166: it is relied on by Megarry and Wade, *The Law of Real Property* (ed Harpum, 6th edn, 2000), 1115, where two further 19th-century cases approving of *Watts* are also noted.

SUMMARY of G5:2.5.4

B can rely on section 62 to acquire an implied Easement if:

- A grants B a Freehold or Lease of all or part of A's land; *and*
- Prior to that grant, *someone other than A* (eg, B) made a particular, regular use of A's land that was not intended to be purely personal or purely temporary.

One application of section 62 is controversial and difficult to defend as a matter of principle. It can be used to give B an Easement even if the prior use of A's land arose as a result of a *liberty*, rather than a right (see **Example 11b**). In such a case, it is hard to say that B can reasonably expect to have acquired an Easement along with his Freehold or Lease. Nonetheless, this certainly does not mean that section 62, as a whole, should be repealed. Section 62 performs a crucial and entirely uncontroversial role in allowing: (i) B2 to acquire an Easement where B has an Easement and then gives a Freehold or Lease to B2 (see **Example 8**); and (ii) B to acquire an Easement where B had such a right before A's grant of a Freehold or new Lease to B (see **Example 11a**). Rather, the argument is that section 62 should perhaps be amended to mean that, in a case such as **Example 11b**, it cannot be used to promote a pre-existing liberty into an Easement.

2.5.5 Other situations?

We have seen four specific situations in which it may be reasonable for B, when acquiring a Freehold or Lease from A, also to expect an Easement over A's land. In those cases, B can acquire an Easement by means of an implied grant. Can there be other situations, *not* falling within any of those four categories, in which it is nonetheless reasonable for B to expect to acquire an Easement?

This raises a difficult question. The need to protect B's reasonable expectation lies behind the rules on the implied grant of an Easement. Yet that principle may well be too vague to be applied directly. Instead, B must bring his claim within one of the four specific situations that both: (i) give effect to; and (ii) *define the limits of* the need to protect B's reasonable expectation. After all, it should be remembered that, if B does acquire an implied Easement, this has an important effect on the **basic tension** between B and C. C, a party later dealing with A's land, is also entitled to expect something: that the rules regulating when B can acquire a property right will be defined with certainty. That need for certainty is particularly important when dealing with an implied Easement: B can acquire such a right without needing to substantively register it. So, whilst it is not impossible that the courts may develop a further specific situation in which it is reasonable for B to expect an Easement,[110] it seems that B cannot acquire an implied Easement by simply relying *directly* on that general principle.

---

[110] The decision in *Platt v Crouch* [2004] 1 P & CR 242 could be seen as an attempt to develop such an additional situation: ie, one where: (i) A has used his land in a particular way before dividing it; and (ii) there is a feature on A's land that indicates that use.

SUMMARY of G5:2.4 and G5:2.5

If A has given B a Freehold or Lease, whilst retaining a Freehold or Lease of some neighbouring land, B may be able to claim that, in addition to giving B that Freehold or Lease, A also gave B an implied Easement over A's retained land. To do so, B needs to show that the surrounding circumstances allow the court to infer that, even though he did not expressly give B an Easement, A nonetheless exercised his power to give B such a right. The surrounding circumstances must allow B to say that it would have been reasonable for him to expect to acquire that Easement. If B can do so, he can acquire the implied Easement without needing to substantively register it.

However, it is impossible for B to rely *directly* on the need to protect a reasonable expectation. Instead, an implied Easement can arise only in four specific situations:

- Where such a right is necessary to allow B to use his land.
- Where such a right is necessary to allow B to make a particular use of his land, planned by both A and B.
- Where A transfers some of his land to B and, before that transfer: (i) A (or, perhaps, someone other than A)[111] regularly used A's land in a particular way; *and* (ii) that use is apparent from the layout of A's land or a feature on A's land; *and* (iii) that use is necessary for the reasonable enjoyment of the land transferred to B. In such a case, B will acquire an Easement allowing him to use A's retained land in that way.
- Where A transfers some of his land to B and, before that transfer, *someone other than A* used A's land in a particular way. In such a case, B will acquire an Easement allowing him to use A's retained land in that way.

The Law Commission has stated that these rules are unclear and in need of general reform.[112] However, it is hard to see the problem. There may be specific difficulties with individual rules, but the purpose of each rule, and its relationship to the other rules, seems clear.

2.6   Implied reservation: general rules

2.6.1 No need for substantive registration

Where a court assumes from surrounding circumstances that A has exercised his power to grant B an Easement, B can acquire that right without needing to substantively register it. The same is true where surrounding circumstances lead a court to assume that A has exercised the very similar power, when giving a Freehold or Lease to B, to *reserve* an Easement over the land given to B.

2.6.2 The basis of implied reservation

Two requirements have to be satisfied for an implied reservation to occur:

---

[111] This depends on whether the restriction suggested in *Kent v Kavanagh* [2007] Ch 1 at [45] is to be accepted: see **2.5.3** above.
[112] Law Com Consultation Paper No 186 (2008), 4.99.

1. A must grant B a Freehold or Lease, whilst retaining a Freehold or Lease of some neighbouring land; and
2. the circumstances surrounding the grant of B's Freehold or Lease must justify the inference that A, when giving B the Freehold or Lease, also exercised his power to reserve an Easement over B's newly acquired land.

Where A acquires an implied Easement, the land law system protects A's *reasonable expectation* that, when granting B a Freehold or Lease, A also reserved an Easement. In effect, then the question is whether it is reasonable for A to believe that B exercised his power to grant A an Easement over B's newly acquired land.

It is clear that A will face a significant problem when claiming that he has impliedly reserved an Easement. When looking at implied grant, we saw that the underlying principle was based on the idea that A cannot 'derogate from his grant'. However, B has not made *any* express grant to A: he has not given A a Freehold or Lease. The assumption is that it is A, the party granting a Freehold or Lease to B, who is in charge of the transaction. The starting point is thus that, if A wants to reserve an Easement, he must do so *expressly*; otherwise, B is entitled to assume that he has his new Freehold or Lease *free from* any Easement in A's favour.[113] As a result, there are only two, narrowly defined situations in which A can claim that he has impliedly reserved an Easement. Certainly, A *cannot* rely on: (i) the *Wheeldon* principle; or (ii) section 62 of the LPA 1925.

2.7 Implied reservation: specific examples

2.7.1 Necessity

EXAMPLE 12

A has a Freehold, including a house entirely surrounded by fields. A sells his Freehold of the fields to B, but keeps the part of the land on which the house stands.

In such a case, it is reasonable for A to expect that B, as part of the deal in which he acquired his land, would allow A a right of way over B's land. After all, without such a right, it would be impossible for A to get to his retained house. So, if B wants to deny A such an Easement, the onus is on B expressly to say so when acquiring his land from A. Necessity can thus be used as the basis of an implied reservation as well as an implied grant.

2.7.2 Necessary to achieve a common purpose

EXAMPLE 13

A has a Freehold of business premises. A gives B a Lease of some of the upper floors. Throughout the duration of the Lease, A keeps advertising boards on the exterior walls of those upper floors. The terms of B's Lease do not give A an express right to do this, but B does not complain. After ten years, A renews B's Lease. The new Lease does not give A an express right to keep the advertising boards up.

---

[113] See eg *per* Thesiger LJ in *Wheeldon v Burrows* (1879) 12 Ch D 31 at 49: 'if the grantor intends to reserve any right over the tenement granted, it is his duty to reserve it expressly in the grant'; *per* Carnwath LJ in *Adealon International Corpn Pty Ltd v Merton LBC* [2007] 1 WLR 1898 at [16].

In such a case, A may argue that, in the new Lease, he impliedly reserved an Easement. However, it will be very difficult for A to succeed. In *Re Webb's Lease*,[114] the essential facts of which are identical to **Example 13**, the Court of Appeal held that, despite the fact that B had never complained about the advertising boards, A had no right to keep them up. If A wanted such a right, the onus was on him to *expressly* reserve the right when renewing the Lease. The Court of Appeal did accept that an implied reservation can occur on grounds other than necessity, but only if the circumstances surrounding A's grant of a right to B are consistent *only* with the inference that A and B both intended A to have an Easement over B's newly acquired land.[115]

The reasoning in *Re Webb's Lease* thus shows that there may be *some* circumstances in which an implied reservation occurs in order to allow A to make a particular use of his retained land, intended by both A and B.[116] However, the decision equally makes clear that, where reservation is concerned, this principle will be very narrowly interpreted.

SUMMARY of G5:2.6 and G5:2.7

It would be foolish to expect the rules that apply to implied grant also to apply to implied reservation. The rules about implied grant rest on the basic idea that, if A gives B a Freehold or Lease, whilst retaining a Freehold or Lease of some neighbouring land, it may possible to infer that A has also given B an Easement over A's retained land. That principle is of no relevance where A claims that he has impliedly *reserved* an Easement over land that he has given to B.

Instead, A has to show that the surrounding circumstances mean that B must have realised that, when acquiring his Freehold or Lease from A, he was also expected to give A an Easement over that land. A will only be able to do this if the Easement is: (i) necessary to allow A to use his retained land; or (ii) absolutely necessary to allow A to make a particular use of his retained land planned by both A and B. The lesson for A is clear: if he wants to reserve an Easement, he should do so expressly.

2.8 Prescription: general rules

2.8.1 Independent acquisition?

It is possible for B to acquire an Easement simply through the *consistent exercise, over a long period, of a right to use A's land*. This method of acquisition, referred to as *prescription*, looks very much like a form of independent acquisition:

1. B acquires the right through his own, independent conduct, without needing to show that A has exercised his power to give B an Easement.
2. Once B has behaved, for a long period, *as though* he has the right, it is no longer possible for A to deny B that right.

---

[114] [1951] Ch 808.

[115] *Ibid per* Jenkins LJ at 829.

[116] For a possible example see *Peckham v Ellison* (1998) 79 P & CR 276. Note too Lord Parker's statement in *Pwllbach Colliery Co Ltd v Woodman* [1915] AC 634 at 646–7 (italics added): 'The law will readily imply the grant *or reservation* of such easements as may be necessary to give effect to the common intention of the parties to a grant of real property, with reference to the manner or purposes in and for which the land granted or some land retained by the grantor is to be used.'

However, the courts do *not* currently treat prescription as an example of independent acquisition. Instead, when B acquires an Easement through long use, it is assumed that A, or a former owner of A's land, exercised his power to give B an Easement.[117] Strictly speaking then, prescription is simply another type of implied grant. This approach seems puzzling: why should we rely on an (almost certainly incorrect)[118] assumption that the claimed Easement was once granted by an owner of A's land to an owner of B's land? It would seem simpler to say that prescription is an example of an independent acquisition.

EXAMPLE 14a

A and B have neighbouring Freeholds. A acquires his Freehold in 1980; B acquires his in 1985. Between 1985 and 2005, B walked across a path on A's land to get to a road. B did so openly; without using force; and without permission from A. In 2006, A attempts to stop B walking across the path. B relies on the doctrine of prescription to show he has an Easement allowing him to walk across A's land.

In such a case, B *can* acquire an Easement through prescription. The orthodox analysis is that B's long use of the claimed right allows us to assume that, at some point, A (or a former owner of A's land) must have given B (or a former owner of B's land) that Easement. This explains why B's Easement binds A; but it forces us to rely on an inconvenient untruth: the fiction that there was, in the past, a grant of the Easement.

A different approach to **Example 14a** would be to say that: (i) B's right arises independently, *as soon as* B begins exercising that right. So, at that point, B already has an Easement. However, A has his pre-existing Freehold and so can clearly prevent B exercising that right. Then (ii) once B has exercised that right for 20 years, B has a defence against A's pre-existing Freehold. At that point, it is no longer possible for A to stop B exercising his right. To fully protect B's long use of the land, we also need to ensure that B has a defence not only against A, but also against *anyone* later acquiring a right from A.

Certainly, that is the model applying to the independent acquisition of a Freehold (see **G1A:2.1** and **G1A:3**). First, by taking physical control of A's land, B *immediately* acquires a Freehold. Second, if the lapse of time allows B the adverse possession defence as set out by Schedule 6 of the Land Registration Act 2002, B can register as the new holder of A's Freehold. This ensures that B is protected not only against A but also against anyone later acquiring a right from A. However, there is no similar possibility here: it would be wholly disproportionate to say that A should lose his Freehold simply because B has acquired an Easement by prescription. So, the land law system currently gives B a defence against A, and anyone later acquiring a right from A, by pretending that A (or a former owner of A's land) granted the Easement to B (or a former owner of B's land). A more transparent approach would be to state directly that the lapse of time gives B a defence *not* only against A but also against parties later acquiring a right from A.

2.8.2 No need for substantive registration

Formality rules do *not* regulate the acquisition of an Easement by prescription: B can hence

---

[117] See eg *per* Lord Lindley in *Gardner v Hodgson's Kingston Brewery Co* [1903] AC 229 at 239.
[118] In *Tehidy Minerals Ltd v Norman* [1971] QB 528, Buckley LJ at 552 noted that the doctrine of prescription may depend on a 'legal fiction'.

acquire an Easement by prescription without needing to substantively register his right. This rule is consistent with the view that the Easement arises independently. On the orthodox view, B's Easement arises through an implied grant: the consistent exercise of the right leads to an assumption, not requiring any formal proof, that A (or an owner of A's land) granted B (or an owner of B's land) the Easement. On that view, an Easement acquired by prescription is thus similar to a Lease arising under an 'implied periodic tenancy' (see **G1B:2.2.1(ii)**).

2.8.3 The limits of prescription

In the discussion here, we will, for convenience, talk about B's consistent exercise of a right. Of course, this does not mean that B himself must have exercised the right for the whole, or indeed any, of the prescription period. The crucial question is whether, for that period, the claimed right has been exercised by: (i) B; and/or (ii) former owners of B's land. Equally, it does not matter if A has not had his Freehold or Lease for all, or any, of the prescription period.

B's claim depends on the consistent exercise of a right. Therefore, prescription cannot apply where B has used A's land by permission. Similarly, if B uses A's land through force, or in secret, B is not asserting a right: if B were claiming a right, he would not need to resort to such underhand tactics. These points are often summed up by saying that B's use of A's land cannot be by force, stealth or permission:[119] each is simply an aspect of the rule that B must be consistently exercising a *right* to use A's land.[120] As for consistent exercise, it is clear that B does not need to be constantly using the claimed right. For example, B would not have to use a right of way over A's land every time he wants to get to his own land.[121] However, if B fails to use the right for a number of years,[122] or only uses the right sporadically,[123] his claim is likely to fail.

EXAMPLE 14b

The facts are as in **Example 14a**, with the difference that B does not have a Freehold of the neighbouring land; instead, he has a 99-year Lease of that land, given to him by B0.

As B has a 99-year Lease, B can, at most, claim a 99-year Easement. The obvious outcome thus seems to be that: (i) B acquires an Easement by prescription; but (ii) that Easement, like the Lease it enhances, is limited to a 99-year period. However, the courts have consistently held that only a *permanent* Easement can be acquired by prescription. In the abstract, that principle seems correct: by consistently exercising a right over A's land, B is effectively claiming a permanent right to make that use of A's land: there is no inherent limit to the right claimed by B. For the very same reason, it is (or at least should be) impossible for B to independently acquire a Lease (see **G1B: 2.1**).

---

[119] In the Latin, B's use must be 'nec vi, nec clam, nec precario'.

[120] A cannot deny B an Easement by prescription by showing that he 'tolerated' B's use of his land: as long as A has not given B permission for that use, prescription can still operate: *Mills v Silver* [1991] Ch 271.

[121] See eg *Dare v Heathcote* (1856) 25 LJ Ex 245.

[122] See eg *Parker v Mitchell* (1840) 11 A & E 788: the right had been used for 50 years, but not at all in the four years immediately preceding B's claim. See too *per* Lindley LJ in *Hollins v Verney* (1884) 13 QBD 304 at 315.

[123] See eg *Hollins v Verney* (1884) 13 QBD 304: B had exercised a right of way only three times in the space of 24 years.

However, in practice, as in **Example 14b**, B may claim an Easement to support an existing Lease. In such a case, it seems odd to deny B *any* chance of acquiring an Easement by prescription. Yet that is exactly what the courts have done: the basic position is that, if B has a Lease, he *cannot* acquire an Easement by prescription.[124]

In a case such as **Example 14b**, the courts' analysis is that B is asserting a permanent Easement, *on behalf of a Freehold owner of B's land*. This means that the Easement B acquires by prescription does *not* enhance his Lease; instead, it enhances the Freehold of B0 (eg, the party who granted B his Lease). This solution is obviously artificial, and moreover cannot work if A is the Freehold owner who gave B a Lease.[125] So, in the reasonably common case where: (i) A has a Freehold; and (ii) A gives B a Lease of part of that land; then (iii) B *cannot* acquire an Easement by prescription over the part of the land retained by A. This odd limit on prescription would not arise if the courts took the easier route of: (i) allowing B to acquire an Easement by prescription *on his own behalf*; and (ii) limiting the duration of that Easement to the duration of B's Lease.

EXAMPLE 14c

The facts are as in **Example 14a**, with the difference that A does not have a Freehold; instead, he has a 99-year Lease of that land, given to him by A0.

As far as B is concerned, it is irrelevant that A has a Lease: by the consistent exercise of his right of way, B should acquire a permanent Easement over A's land. After all, if B takes physical control of land subject to a Lease, B acquires a Freehold of the land (see **G1A:2.1**). However, it would be very harsh to say that A0 should be bound by B's Easement: after all, A0, unlike A, cannot be said to have failed to object to B's right. The best solution is to: (i) allow B to acquire a permanent Easement; and (ii) to give B a defence against A's pre-existing Lease but *not* against A0's pre-existing Freehold. This could be done by giving B an Easement for the duration of A's Lease. This would mirror the operation of the adverse possession defence (see **G1B:2.1**).

However, in a case such as **Example 14c**, the courts have *not* adopted this solution. Instead, it has simply been assumed that B cannot acquire *any* Easement by prescription.[126] This result has, not surprisingly, been subject to much disapproval.[127] The Law Commission has suggested that a more 'nuanced' scheme would allow B to acquire, through prescription, an Easement of a limited duration.[128]

2.8.4 The basis of prescription

On the orthodox analysis, it is assumed that B does *not* acquire his Easement as soon as he begins, as of right, to use A's land. Rather, B must wait for the prescription period to run: only then will it be inferred that A has granted B the Easement. And, because of that

---

[124] See eg *per* Lindley LJ in *Wheaton v Maple & Co* [1893] 3 Ch 48 at 63: 'A right claimed by prescription must be claimed as appendant or appurtenant to land, and not as annexed to it for a term of years.' For arguments against this approach, see eg Delany (1958) 74 *LQR* 82. The position in Ireland is different: B, even if he has a Lease, can acquire an Easement (for the duration of the Lease) by prescription (see eg *Tallon v Ennis* [1937] IR 549).

[125] See eg *Kilgour v Gaddes* [1904] 1 KB 457; *Simmons v Dobson* [1991] 1 WLR 720.

[126] See eg *Roberts v James* (1903) 89 LT 282.

[127] See eg Delany (1958) 74 *LQR* 82; Sparkes [1992] *Conv* 107; Harpum [1992] *CLJ* 220 at 222–3.

[128] Law Com Consultation Paper No 186 (2008), 4.244.

assumption, B will have not only the Easement, but also a defence to A's pre-existing right. As a result, it is often said that the acquisition of an Easement by prescription is based on the *acquiescence* of A (or the former owners of A's land): their failure to object to B's use of A's land allows the court to assume that an Easement must, at some point, have been granted to B.[129]

However, there are a number of problems with this analysis. Most importantly, simply allowing B to believe he has a right, or even allowing B to exercise a right for a long period does *not*, in general, allow B to acquire that right. For example, an 'adverse possessor' of land does *not* acquire a right because of A's failure to remove B. Rather, B acquires his Freehold *as soon as* he takes control of the land; A's failure to remove B then gives B a chance of a defence against A's pre-existing property right (see **G1A:2.1**). Further, whilst A's acquiescence may allow B to bring a proprietary estoppel claim against A, such a claim: (i) depends on showing he would suffer a detriment if A denied him the claimed right; and (ii) at most, only imposes a duty on A to give B a right (see **E4**). In contrast, the acquiescence involved in prescription has a wholly different function: without showing any detriment, B acquires a property right in A's land. The second problem with the 'acquiescence' analysis is that B can acquire an Easement by prescription where, during the prescription period, A's land has been in the hands of a number of different owners. In such a case, it may be implausible to say that A, who may only have had his Freehold for a month or so, has acquiesced in B's use of the land.

A better, but novel view, is the one set out in **2.8.1** above: B independently acquires an Easement *as soon as* he exercises a right to use A's land. After all, B can acquire a Freehold as soon as he takes physical control of A's land.[130] This means that, as soon as B begins to exercise the right to use A's land, he will have a property right that is capable of binding a stranger, such as X. However, B's Easement cannot yet bind A, or anyone who later acquires a right from A. The passage of time is then crucial in giving B a *defence* against A's prior property right and other rights dependent on A's right. Such a defence is necessary because, as Lord Hoffmann noted in *R v Oxfordshire County Council, ex p Sunningwell Parish Council*: 'Any legal system must have rules of prescription which prevent the disturbance of long-established de facto enjoyment.'[131]

2.9 Prescription: specific examples

2.9.1 Common Law

There are three specific ways in which B can acquire an Easement by prescription. The first

---

[129] See eg *Sturges v Bridgman* (1879) 11 Ch D 852 at 863 *per* Thesiger LJ: 'Consent or acquiescence of the owner of [A's land] lies at the root of prescription, and of the fiction of a lost grant.' See too *Dalton v Angus* (1881) 6 App Cas 740: in his advice to the House of Lords in that case, Fry LJ stated at 773 that: 'the whole-law of prescription and the whole law which governs the presumption or inference of a grant or covenant rest upon acquiescence. The courts and the judges have had recourse to various expedients for quieting the possession of persons in the exercise of rights which have not been resisted by the persons against whom they are exercised, but in all cases it appears to me that acquiescence and nothing else is the principle upon which these expedients rest.'

[130] This analogy is strengthened by the fact that an Easement, like a Freehold (and unlike a Lease) is an 'incorporeal hereditament'. That antiquated term essentially means that, for some purposes at least, an Easement *counts as land*. So, as A can immediately acquire a Freehold by taking physical control of land, it seems only logical that A should immediately acquire an Easement by exercising a right to make a limited use of A's land.

[131] [2000] 1 AC 335 at 349. Law Com Consultation Paper No 186 (2008), 4.205 rejects the view that an Easement arising by prescription is based on acquiescence, preferring to see it as arising as a result of B's long use of the land.

is often known as 'prescription at common law'. It depends, in theory, on the odd idea that an Easement was granted by a former owner of A's land to a former owner of B's land *before 1189*. The idea is that, as the grant was presumed to have been made so long ago, B can be released from the usual task of having to bring evidence of that grant. This fiction is supplemented by a further presumption: if B can show that the right he claims was exercised for at least 20 years, then it will be inferred that the right was granted before 1189. However, it is possible for A to rebut this presumption. And in some case it is very simple for A to rebut it. For example, if B claims an Easement to support the use of a building on his land (such as a right to receive light through windows of that building) A will be able to point out that, if that building did not exist in 1189, B's right cannot have been acquired before then.

2.9.2 Lost modern grant

This form of prescription is a development of prescription at common law. It replaced an awkward fiction that A could sometimes disprove, with an equally bizarre fiction that is harder for A to disprove. It is based on an inference that, if the right B claims was consistently exercised for over 20 years, that Easement must have been granted in a deed made *after* 1189 that has subsequently been lost. Again, A can try to disprove this presumption, by seeking to prove that the grant could not, in fact, have been made. It was decided, in the end, that A *cannot* disprove the presumption in this way. As a result, courts accepted the entirely fictional nature of the 'lost' grant.[132]

2.9.3 Prescription Act 1832

The two methods of prescription discussed so far sound like the crudest forms of legal parody, mixing fictions with ancient dates. The Prescription Act 1832 brought some improvements. It does not replace those two methods, but introduces a third, supposedly clearer form of prescription. The basic principle is that: (i) if B can show continued exercise of the right for 20 years; then (ii) he can acquire an Easement *without* needing to rely on the presumptions of a grant before 1189 or of a lost modern grant.

However, the Act is not as clear as it might have been. It is in fact very complex,[133] and we have no space to go into its details here.[134] It is worth noting the major limit on this method of prescription: B needs to show that the right has been consistently exercised during the 20 years *immediately before* he makes his claim to the Easement.[135] This limit does not apply to either of the other two methods of prescription.

---

[132] However, A can disprove the presumption by showing that *no one* had the power to give B the alleged Easement. For example, if all former owners of A's land only had the power to grant an Easement with the consent of a particular body, and A can show that such consent had not been given, B cannot acquire an Easement by lost modern grant.

[133] For example, there are special rules dealing with the right to light: see s 3 of the Prescription Act 1832. There are also rules dealing with situations where an owner of A's land is under a 'disability' which prevents him from granting a right: see s 7.

[134] For detail, see eg *Gale on Easements* (ed Gaunt and Morgan, 17th edn, 2002), 179–98 (4-17 to 4-50).

[135] This does not mean that A can prevent B from using the 1832 Act by simply preventing B from exercising the right—eg, by locking a gate through which B entered A's land. This form of interruption will be disregarded, unless B has allowed it to occur for over a year. Even if B waits for longer before making his claim, he will be protected provided that he makes clear to A that he objects to A's attempt to prevent him using the right: see eg *Davies v Du Paver* [1953] 1 QB 184.

2.9.4 The impact of human rights?

The clear link between prescription and the adverse possession defence leads to an important question: is the doctrine of prescription compatible with A's human rights under Article 1 of Protocol 1 to the European Convention on Human Rights (ECHR)? The main point is that its effect on A is much less severe than the effect of the adverse possession defence: A does not lose his land without compensation; rather, he keeps the land but his land is subject to a new burden. Further, the fact that B's use has to be as of right, and hence cannot be carried out in secret, does increase A's chances of being able to discover and object to B's use. Finally, to return to Lord Hoffmann's point: 'Any legal system must have rules of prescription which prevent the disturbance of long-established de facto enjoyment.'[136] So, even if those rules interfere with A's right to the peaceful enjoyment of his possession, it seems that the interference should be seen as a proportionate means of protecting that important goal of protecting the factual enjoyment of a claimed right.[137]

2.9.5 The Law Commission's proposals

The Law Commission has sensibly proposed that there should be only one, statutory method by which long use of A's land can give B an Easement.[138] It would be based on use by B (or former owners of B's land) for 20 years; that period of use would have to be ongoing; or to have ended no more than 12 months before B makes his claim.[139] B would not actually acquire his Easement until he is registered as holding it; but if B applies for registration and can show the necessary long use, A will be unable to object to that registration. The Law Commission recognised both: (i) the analogy between prescription and adverse possession;[140] and (ii) the undesirability of basing an Easement arising by prescription on a fictional 'grant' by A or a former owner of A's land.[141] Its proposals are thus different from, but consistent with, the view taken here: an Easement arising by prescription is independently acquired.

SUMMARY of G5:2.8 and 2.9

It is possible for B to acquire an Easement as a result of the consistent exercise, by B (or former owners of B's land) of a right to make a particular use of A's land. A's land must have been used *as of right:* use by force, secretly or with A's permission is inconsistent with B's claim to an Easement. Anomalously, B *cannot* rely on this method of acquisition if he only has a Lease; nor can B use it to acquire an Easement if A has a Lease.

---

[136] *R v Oxfordshire CC, ex p Sunningwell PC* [2000] 1 AC 335 at 349.

[137] The interference could thus be seen as within one of the permitted exceptions to Art 1 of Protocol 1: as either 'in the public interest' or as part of a State's right to 'enforce such laws as it deems necessary to control the use of property in accordance with the general interest'. Compare the decision of the Grand Chamber of the European Court of Human Rights in *JA Pye (Oxford) Ltd v UK* [2007] ECHR 44302/02 (30 August 2007 (see **B:8.3.1(iii)**).

[138] Law Com Consultation Paper No 186 (2008), 4.168, 4.174.

[139] *Ibid* at 4.211ff.

[140] *Ibid* at 4.224.

[141] *Ibid* at 4.171.

There are three specific forms of prescription. Prescription at *common law* depends on an inference that the Easement was granted before 1189. This assumption will be made if B can show that the consistent exercise of the right lasted for at least 20 years. However, A can disprove the assumption by pointing to a fact that means the Easement cannot have been granted before 1189. In such a case, B can instead try to rely on prescription by a *lost modern grant*. Here, the 20-year user leads a court to assume that a former owner of A's land must have granted B an Easement. B is released from having to prove this grant through the fiction that the deed of grant has been lost. However, A can again disprove this fiction if he can show that no relevant former owner of his land had the power to give B that Easement. Finally, B can turn to the Prescription Act 1832. The basic principle of the Act is that B can acquire an Easement through continued exercise of the right during the 20 years immediately preceding B's claim.

It is clear that the rules relating to prescription are comically inappropriate. The Law Commission have recommended that a single, statutory scheme should take their place. But it is also important to address the underlying problem: the insistence that an Easement arising through prescription must have been created by an owner of A's land exercising his power to give an Easement to B, or a former owner of B's land. This need to find a grant has forced the courts into the fictions inherent in doctrines such as the lost modern grant; the use of such fictions always leads to confusion. A better, but novel, approach would depend on recognising that prescription is an example of the independent acquisition of a property right. On that approach, the prescription rules would be modelled on, and consistent with, the rules regulating the independent acquisition of a Freehold.

3   THE DEFENCES QUESTION

An Easement is a property right: it imposes a prima facie duty on the rest of the world not to interfere with B's right to make a specific, limited use of A's land. For example, if B has a right of way over A's land, B will be able to bring a claim against *anyone* who interferes with that right of way. In theory, it is possible for a third party such as C to have a defence to B's Easement. However, it is very difficult for C to have a defence to B's pre-existing property right in land (see **E1:3**).

3.1   The lack of registration defence

If B has an Easement, it will be *almost impossible* for C to use the lack of registration defence provided by the LRA 2002. First, if B has an express Easement, B will by necessity have substantively registered that right (see **2.2** above): in such a case, C clearly cannot rely on the lack of registration defence. So, C's protection against the risk of being bound by an expressly granted Easement does not come from the **defences question**; instead, it comes from the **acquisition question**: an expressly granted Easement can only exist if it is substantively registered.

Second, if B has an implied Easement, B may not have registered that right. However, in such a case, B's Easement will *almost always* count as an overriding interest: as a result, it will be immune from the lack of registration defence. Under Schedule 3, paragraph 3 of the

LRA 2002, B's implied Easement is an overriding interest *if* B can prove *any* of the following three factors:

- B has used the Easement in the year before C acquired his right; *or*
- B's Easement would have been obvious to C on a reasonably careful inspection of A's land; *or*
- C knew about B's Easement.

It is important to remember that these rules deal with implied Easements. The grant of an Easement will only be implied if the circumstances surrounding the grant of B's Freehold or Lease justify the inference that A must also have granted B an Easement (see **2.4** and **2.5** above). Those surrounding circumstances will generally ensure that B's Easement *will* be obvious to C if he makes a reasonably careful inspection of A's land. Similarly, as an implied Easement will often be crucial to allowing B to make a particular use of his own land, it is very likely that B *will* have used the Easement in the last year.

It is therefore reasonably safe to assume that, in practice, any implied Easement will be immune from the lack of registration defence. As a result, Easements fit into the general scheme of the LRA 2002: if B has a property right, C will not be able to use the lack of regis-tration defence. C's protection comes not from the **defences question** but rather from the limits imposed on B by the **content** and **acquisition questions**.

3.2   Consent: release of an Easement

An Easement can end for good if B, the current holder of the Easement, exercises his power to 'release' (ie, to terminate) that Easement. Strictly speaking, such a release does not give C a defence to B's Easement: instead, it destroys the Easement. B's power to release an Easement can only be validly exercised by means of a deed.[142] Moreover, if B's Easement has been substantively registered, B will, strictly speaking, retain the Easement unless and until the register is changed and B's Easement is removed.[143]

3.3   Apparent consent: 'abandonment' or estoppel

A problem may arise if C incorrectly believes that B has released an Easement. C may act on the assumption that B's Easement no longer exists: for example, in the belief that B has released a right to light, C may build on his land. If B then attempts to assert the Easement against C, C will have to rely on a form of *estoppel*. First, C can rely on *defensive estoppel* if: (i) B made a commitment to C that he would no longer use the Easement; and (ii) C reasonably relied on that commitment; and (iii) C will suffer a detriment if B is allowed to go back on his commitment (see **D1:3.3.1(ii)**). This defensive estoppel can be used by C to show that B should be prevented (at least for a time) from asserting his Easement against C.

Second, C could appeal to the doctrine of proprietary estoppel (see **E4**). That doctrine is currently used where one party makes a commitment to give another a right relating to land; however, it ought logically to be extended to cases where B makes a commitment to

---

[142] Co. Litt 264b.

[143] Such a change would be an example of an alteration, not a rectification (see **E5:3.2.3**). No indemnity would be payable to B as, given that he has already terminated the Easement, he does not lose anything by the change to the register.

give up such a right. Under that doctrine, the extent of C's right should be governed by the need to prevent C suffering a detriment as a result of his reliance on B's commitment (see **E4:4**). If C has, for example, put up a new building on his land, it may be that the only way to protect C is to impose a duty on B to release the Easement.

Cases which seem to involve C using estoppel are often said to depend on B having 'abandoned' his Easement, through the conduct that leads to C's reasonable belief that B's Easement no longer exists.[144] However, the concept of abandonment is very problematic. In general, a party with a property right does *not* have the power simply to give up that right: if he wishes to dispose of the right, he needs to transfer it to another. B can of course release an Easement; but only if a deed is used. Cases of so-called informal 'abandonment' are hence better seen as examples either of: (i) C having a defence to B's Easement as a result of defensive estoppel; or (ii) C relying on proprietary estoppel to show that B is under a duty to release his Easement.[145]

The Law Commission has adopted the view that: (i) it is possible for B to 'abandon' an Easement; and (ii) B should be presumed to have done so if he fails to use an Easement for a period of 20 years.[146] However, the Law Commission: (i) simply assumed that abandonment is possible; and (ii) stated that as B's long use of a claimed right can lead to B's acquisition of an Easement by prescription, B's long failure to use an Easement should also lead to B losing that right. Yet that simply does not follow: (i) there is clearly a difference between gaining a new right and losing an existing right; and (ii) even on the Law Commission's view, the effect of time passing is different in each case. Where B acquires an Easement through prescription, B's long use, by itself, gives B that right.[147] Where B fails to use his Easement, that leads to a presumption about B's intention: that B intended to give up that right. Further, on the Law Commission's view, no such presumption would arise where B fails, for no matter how long, to use a *registered* Easement.[148] Yet it is hard to see why the fact of registration makes any difference to the question of B's intention which, according to the Law Commission at least, provides the basis of abandonment.

3.4 Limitation

The basic rule is that the lapse of time, by itself, cannot give C a defence against B's pre-existing Easement. However, three points are worth noting.

1. *The limitation period in nuisance is six years.* If C interferes with B's Easement, he commits the wrong of nuisance. B then has six years to bring a claim against C in relation to that particular interference.[149]

2. *B's delay in asserting his Easement may be taken into account in deciding whether to specifically protect B's right.* For example, B may ask for an injunction requiring C to

---

[144] See eg *Moore v Rawson* (1824) 3 B & C 332. B had a right to light through certain windows on a wall. B pulled down that wall and replaced it with a windowless wall. Over 10 years later, A put up a building on his land, in front of B's now windowless wall. Three years later, B installed windows in that wall and claimed his right to light: B's claim failed.

[145] This point is persuasively made by Davis [1995] *Conv* 291.

[146] Law Com Consultation Paper No 186 (2008), 5.14, 5.27.

[147] Or, on the Law Commission's proposals, that long use entitles B to register and thus gain an Easement: see Law Com Consultation Paper No 186 (2008), 4.222.

[148] *Ibid* at 5.29.

[149] Limitation Act 1980, s 2.

remove an obstruction to B's right of way. Where B delays in bringing his claim, the court may take that delay into account in deciding whether to give B such specific protection. B's delay may thus be relevant to the **remedies question** even if it does not give C a defence to B's pre-existing Easement.

3. *B's inaction may count as an implied representation to C that B does not have an Easement; or an implied promise to C that B will not enforce his Easement.* If B allows C, over a long period, to act in a way that is inconsistent with B's Easement, this may allow C to rely on an estoppel defence (see **3.3** above).

4   THE REMEDIES QUESTION

4.1   Preface: the protection of B's Easement

Like all property rights, the Easement is protected through the law of wrongs. If B has an Easement, the rest of the world is under a prima facie duty to B not to interfere with B's right to make a specific, limited use of A's land. It is important to bear in mind that C only commits a wrong if he interferes with B's *reasonable* use of the Easement. So it seems that a trivial interference by C (eg, building foundations that take up one foot of a ten-foot driveway over which B has a right of way)[150] does not count as a wrong.

If C's interference with B's Easement is more than merely trivial, C commits the wrong of nuisance.[151] So, when looking at the remedies available where C interferes with B's Easement, we need to look at the remedies a court can give where the defendant commits the wrong of nuisance.[152] The crucial issue, as usual, is whether B's right will be *specifically protected*.

4.2   Specific protection

4.2.1 The risk of future interference with B's Easement

If B can show that there is a risk of C's future conduct interfering with B's Easement, B's right will, in general, be specifically protected. The starting point is that a court will grant an injunction ordering C not to interfere with B's Easement.[153] As we have come to expect where property rights in land are concerned, B is not forced to settle for money.

---

[150] That example is given by Lord Scott in *Moncrieff v Jamieson* [2007] 1 WLR 2620 at [45].

[151] See eg *Paine & Co v St Neots Gas & Coke Co* [1939] 3 All ER 812 at 853. If C instead interferes with B's Profit, he commits the wrong of trespass: see eg *Fitzgerald v Firbank* [1897] 2 Ch 96.

[152] In theory, B can bypass court proceedings and deal with the defendant's interference himself—eg, by physically removing an obstacle blocking B's right of way: see eg *Raikes v Townsend* (1804) 2 Smith 9. This form of 'self-help' measure is known as 'abatement'. It is permissible in certain circumstances, but the courts are understandably not keen to encourage B in taking the law into his own hands in this way: see *per* Lord Atkinson in *Lagan Navigation Co v Lambeg Bleaching, Dyeing and Finishing Co* [1927] AC 226 at 244. So if B does try to abate the nuisance himself, he runs a serious risk that he might himself be committing a wrong against C. It is hence more prudent for B to ask the court for a remedy.

[153] *Pugh v Howells* (1984) 48 P & CR 298 provides a good example: C was ordered to knock down a building interfering with B's Easement. Compare however *Snell & Prideax Ltd v Dutton Mirrors Ltd* [1995] 1 EGLR 259: the Court of Appeal refused to award an injunction requiring C to demolish a building where C built in the honest belief that B did not have an Easement and only after inviting B to apply for an injunction.

However, we have seen that, in relatively rare cases, a court may decline to order an injunction, even where C's nuisance will continue (see **E1:4.2** and **G1A:4.2**). The principles discussed there apply in exactly the same way where B has an Easement.[154]

EXAMPLE 15

A and B have neighbouring Freeholds. A grants B an Easement allowing B a right to drive on a road on A's land. B substantively registers that Easement. A sells his Freehold to C. The road is in disrepair so B cannot safely drive on it.

In such a case, it may seem that B has a problem. We have seen that an Easement cannot impose a positive duty (see **1.5** above). So C may argue that, although he is bound by B's Easement, he does not have to spend money in repairing the road. It seems that a court will accept that argument.[155] B may instead: (i) offer to pay a third party to carry out the necessary works on C's land; or (ii) offer to carry out such works himself. The problem then is that C may simply refuse to allow anyone on to his land to do the work. So, B may ask the court for an order forcing C to allow B or another to repair the road (at B's expense). It seems that a court is likely to grant such an order:[156] it does not breach the principle that an Easement cannot impose a positive duty on C, as C's duty is simply *not* to prevent the work being done.

4.2.2 Past interference with B's Easement

Where C has already interfered with B's Easement and that interference is not continuing, ordering C to pay money is the primary way of protecting B's right: after all, it is generally too late for B's right to be specifically protected. However, in rare cases, B may be able to obtain an injunction ordering C to reverse his past act. For example, let us say: (i) B has a right to receive light through a window on his land; and (ii) C has interfered with this right by constructing a new building on C's land. In such a case, it is possible for a court to order C to reverse his interference by pulling down the building.[157]

Not surprisingly, the courts have indicated that care must be taken before ordering such a drastic remedy.[158] The payment of money is the primary remedy; specific protection will be reserved for special cases in which, for example, C has acted at his own risk by continuing to build despite objections from B.[159] The court will also take into account the waste, and harm to third parties, that could be caused by ordering C to reverse his wrong. So if the

---

[154] Note *per* Stamp LJ in *Saint v Jenner* [1973] Ch 275 at 280: 'We see no reason in principle why there should be any relevant distinction in point of remedy between an ordinary case of nuisance and disturbance of an easement, frequently referred to as a nuisance.'

[155] See eg *per* Parker J in *Jones v Pritchard* [1908] 1 Ch 630 at 637.

[156] *Per* Lord Scott in *Moncrieff v Jamieson* [2007] 1 WLR 2620 at [47]: '[B] would be entitled, although not obliged, as a right ancillary to his right of way to do such repairs to the driveway as were necessary or desirable.' Where the work that B wishes to carry out is 'reasonably necessary for the preservation' of all or part of his land, a court can make an 'access order' under the Access to Neighbouring Land Act 1992 (see **G1A:n52**).

[157] See eg *Lawrence v Horton* (1890) 59 LJ Ch 440.

[158] See eg *ibid* at 441; *Redland Bricks v Morris* [1970] AC 652; *Shepherd Homes Ltd v Sandham* [1971] Ch 340 (the last is a Restrictive Covenant case, but the same principles should apply to an Easement).

[159] This was the case in *Lawrence v Horton* (1890) 59 LJ Ch 440: C continued to build even after receiving a written complaint from B.

building constructed by C was sold and is now occupied by a family, it is unlikely that the court will order the house to be pulled down.[160]

4.3 Money awards

4.3.1 Money as a substitute for B's right

If C has interfered with B's Easement, C has committed the wrong of nuisance. C can be ordered to pay money to B even if C's interference has not caused B any consequential loss.[161] As soon as B shows that his right has been infringed, B is entitled to money as a substitute for that right (see **D1:4.3.1**).

4.3.2 Money as compensation for B's consequential loss

If C's interference has also caused B relevant consequential loss, C will also be ordered to pay B money as compensation for that loss (see **D1:4.3.2**).[162]

4.3.3 Money to remove C's gain?

Where C commits a wrong against B, there may be rare cases in which C can be ordered to pay B money based on the gain C has made by committing that wrong (see **D1:4.3.3**). For example, B could argue for an award of exemplary or punitive damages against C where : (i) C has deliberately interfered with B's Easement; and (ii) C has made a profit by doing so; and (iii) due to the intervention of third parties, a court will not order C to reverse his wrong.

5 THE EQUITABLE EASEMENT

B has an Equitable Easement if, and only if, A is under a duty to grant B an Easement (see **E2:1.3.1(i)**). In such a case, B does not yet have a property right in A's land; rather, he has a persistent right: a right against A's power to grant B an Easement. As a result, B will be unable to assert his Equitable Easement against a third party who does not acquire a right from A. Therefore, if: (i) A is under a duty to grant B a right of way across A's land; and (ii) X obstructs that right of way, then (iii) X does *not* commit a wrong against B.[163] B's only recourse is to ask or, if necessary, force A to take action against X.

---

[160] See eg *Wrotham Park Estate Co Ltd v Parkside Homes Ltd* [1974] 1 WLR 798 (**E2:Example 26**: a Restrictive Covenant case, but, again, the same principles should apply).

[161] See eg *Nicholls v Eky Beet Sugar Factory Ltd* [1936] Ch 343; *per* Lord Hoffmann in *Hunter v Canary Wharf Ltd* [1997] AC 665 at 706.

[162] To claim damages for consequential loss, B will need to show some 'substantial interference' by C: see eg *Weston v Lawrence Weaver Ltd* [1961] 1 QB 402.

[163] *Gale on Easements* (ed Gaunt and Morgan, 17th edn, 2002), 14–45 suggests that B *could* bring a claim against X in such a case, but cites no authority for this proposition.

5.1   The content question

B can have an Equitable Easement only if A is under a duty to grant B a right that counts as an Easement. So, if: (i) A is under a duty to give B a right; but (ii) that right does not pass the **content** criteria set out in **section 1** above, then (iii) B does *not* have an Equitable Easement.

5.2   The acquisition question

No persistent right can be substantively registered (see **C2:6**). If B has an Equitable Easement, B cannot take advantage of the protection provided by substantive registration. Equally, however, B can acquire an Equitable Easement without needing to substantively register that right. Further, B can acquire such a right without needing to show that a deed has been used.

5.2.1 Contract

If B claims that A is under a *contractual* duty to grant B an Easement, B needs to show that the formality rule imposed by section 2 of the Law of Property (Miscellaneous Provisions) Act 1989 has been satisfied (see **E2:2.3.3**). For example, an oral promise by A to give B an Easement *cannot* impose a contractual duty on A.

If the section 2 formality rule has been met, then, even if A has not made an *express* contractual promise to give B an Easement, it may be possible for B to show that A has made an *implied* contractual promise. The crucial question is whether it is reasonable for B to expect that, as part of his contract with B, A has also made a promise to give B an Easement. In general, any of the methods of implied grant (or implied reservation) set out in section 2 above are relevant when considering the acquisition of Equitable Easements. The exception is section 62 of the LPA 1925: that provision allows for an Easement to be implied into a *conveyance*: ie, into the grant or transfer of a property right. It cannot assist a party where he has only a *contract* for the grant or transfer of such a right.

EXAMPLE 16

A has a Freehold. A rents out a house on his land. The land not rented out by A includes a strip of land near a busy road. To get from that road to the house, A's tenants regularly drive across that strip of land. The tenants' Lease ends. A and B enter a contract under which A promises to transfer part of his Freehold including the house, but not including the strip of land near the road. It is possible to drive from the road to the house without driving on that strip; but only by taking a longer route involving a difficult and somewhat dangerous turn.

Example 16 is based on **Example 10b**: the difference is that A has not yet transferred a Freehold to B. This causes a problem for B: it means that B cannot rely on section 62 of the LPA 1925 to acquire an implied Easement. Instead, B may try to rely on the *Wheeldon* principle (see **2.5.3** above) to show that a promise to grant B a right to drive over the strip of land can be implied into A's contract with B. However, according to Chadwick LJ in *Kent v Kavanagh*,[164] that principle *cannot* apply in a case where, prior to A's dealings with B,

---

[164] [2007] Ch 1 at [45].

someone other than A has made a particular use of A's land. If that limit on the *Wheeldon* principle is correct, it is impossible for B to acquire an implied Equitable Easement in a case such as **Example 16**. The limit certainly seems arbitrary: B would have been able to acquire an implied Equitable Easement if A had been driving over the strip of land to get to the house; [165] why should things be different where A's tenants have been doing so?

5.2.2 Non-contractual means of imposing a duty on A

If B can show that A is under a non-contractual duty to grant B an Easement, the section 2 formality rule does not apply (see **E2:2.3.3(i)**).

(i) Proprietary estoppel

E4: EXAMPLE 5

A and B have neighbouring Freeholds. A and B enter negotiations about A possibly giving B an Easement over A's land. The negotiations have not led to a final contract, but A and B reach an agreement in principle as to the route B would take over A's land. A then builds a fence, separating his land from B's land. A leaves a gap in the fence to allow B access to A's land. In reliance on his expectation that A will grant B the planned Easement, B sells off part of his land without reserving a right of way over that land to his retained land.

In such a case, the doctrine of proprietary estoppel imposes a duty on A to B (see **E4:3.1.1**) In *Crabb v Arun DC*,[166] the essential facts of which are identical to **E4:Example 5**, the Court of Appeal found that A was under a duty to grant B an Easement. It made no difference that A had made no final contractual promise to B: A's duty arose as a result of proprietary estoppel. A's duty (and hence B's Equitable Easement) arose *as soon as* B's reliance led to A being under a duty to give B an Easement.[167] A was therefore under a duty: (i) to grant B the promised Easement; *and* (ii) to compensate B for the loss B suffered as a result of A's failure to grant that Easement. As a result, B acquired the Equitable Easement without needing to pay for it.[168]

It should be noted that the detriment suffered by B in *Crabb v Arun DC* was particularly significant: it could only be addressed by imposing a duty on A to give B an Easement.[169] If: (i) A has promised to give B an Easement; and (ii) the doctrine of proprietary estoppel imposes a duty on A; then (iii) there is no guarantee that A will be under a duty to perform his promise (see **E4:4**). A court may instead decide, for example, that the need to prevent B suffering a detriment can be adequately addressed by ordering A to pay B a sum of money.

---

[165] For an example of B relying on the rule in *Wheeldon* principle to acquire an implied Equitable Easement, see *Borman v Griffith* [1930] 1 Ch 493.

[166] [1976] Ch 179.

[167] In *Sweet v Sommer* [2004] EWHC 1504 at [44], Hart J (obiter) took the view that B's Equitable Easement arises only after a court order in his favour: that orthodox view of the operation of proprietary estoppel is challenged in **E4:6**.

[168] The original plan was that B would pay A for the Easement (a price of £3,000 had been suggested).

[169] B had sold off part of his land without reserving a right of way over that land to allow him to access his retained land. B did so as he believed he would be able to access the retained land by using the expected right of way over A's land. So, if B were denied that right of way over A's land, he would be unable to access his retained land.

(ii) 'Benefit and burden' principle

EXAMPLE 17

A and B have neighbouring Freeholds. A wants to put up a building that will encroach slightly onto B's land. B allows A to do so, provided A allows B to walk across A's land to get to a side road. A then sells his land to A2. A2 allows B to use the right of way across A2's land. In reliance on that right of way, B builds a garage on his land that can be reached only by using that right of way. A2 then sells his land to C.

In *ER Ives Investments Ltd v High*,[170] the essential facts of which are identical to **Example 17**, the Court of Appeal found that B had acquired an Equitable Easement. The reasoning of the judges is quite unclear;[171] but there are two ways to justify their conclusion.[172] First, B may be able to rely on the 'benefit and burden' principle to show that A was under a duty to give B an Easement: A and B made an agreement under which A was to have a right to encroach on B's land *if* A allowed B a right of way across A's land. If that right of way was intended to bind future owners of A's land, B can then say that: (i) as A has chosen to exercise his right to encroach on B's land; then (ii) A comes under a duty to give B the agreed Easement. Second, B may be able to rely on proprietary estoppel to show that A2 was under a separate duty to give B an Easement: A2 allowed B to build the garage, knowing that B did so in the belief that he had a right of way over A2's land (see eg **E4:Example 6**).

However, B cannot use either principle to acquire a direct right against C. The 'benefit and burden' principle does not apply as C has not *chosen* to encroach on B's land: he has no choice in the matter as he has simply acquired the building put up by A. And proprietary estoppel is irrelevant as C has made no commitment to B. Therefore, B needs to show that C is bound by B's pre-existing Equitable Easement (arising as a result of either A or A2's duty to B). This brings us to the **defences question**.

5.3 The defences question

5.3.1 The lack of registration defence: unregistered land

In *ER Ives Investments Ltd v High*,[173] the Freehold acquired by C was *not* registered. However, a registration scheme does apply to unregistered land (see **C2:7**). Under the Land Charges Act 1972 an Equitable Easement counts as a 'Class D land charge':[174] as such, if not noted on the Land Charges Register, it is 'void' against a purchaser for money or money's worth of the burdened land.[175] So, in *Ives*, C should have been able to use that lack of registration defence against any pre-existing Equitable Easement of B. It is true that C was aware that B might have such a right; however, as later confirmed by the House of Lords in *Midland Bank Trust Co Ltd v Green*,[176] C's knowledge of B's unregistered right cannot prevent C

---

[170] [1967] 2 QB 379.
[171] For a thorough analysis of the decision see Battersby [1995] *MLR* 637.
[172] See esp *per* Lord Denning MR [1967] 2 QB 379 at 394–5.
[173] [1967] 2 QB 379.
[174] See Land Charges Act 1972, s 2(5)(iii).
[175] In *ER Ives* itself the relevant statute was the Land Charges Act 1925, s 13(2); see now Land Charges Act 1972, s 4.
[176] [1981] AC 513.

using that lack of registration defence (see **C2:Example 5**). However, through some unconvincing interpretation of that Act, the Court of Appeal in *Ives* held that C could *not* use the lack of registration defence given by the LCA 1925.[177]

5.3.2 The lack of registration defence: registered land

If a case such as **Example 17** occurs where C acquires a registered Freehold from A2, C will be able to use the lack of registration defence against B's Equitable Easement *unless*: (i) prior to C's acquisition of his Freehold, B has defensively registered his Equitable Easement by entering a notice on the register; *or* (ii) when C committed to acquiring his right, B was in actual occupation of A2's land. Crucially, an Equitable Easement does not qualify, in its own right, as an overriding interest: Schedule 3, paragraph 3 of the LRA 2002 applies only to Easements (ie, to 'legal easements').[178] This means that, in practice, B needs to defensively register his Equitable Easement if he hopes to assert it against a third party: in general, if B has an Equitable Easement over A's land it is very unlikely that B will be in actual occupation of that land.

Actual occupation may be more likely where B's Easement, in its **content**, allows B to make a reasonably continuous use of part of A's land: eg, if B has a right to store things on A's land; or to park on A's land. The question then arises of whether such storage or parking can count as actual occupation for the purpose of Schedule 3, paragraph 2 of the LRA 2002. This may well be possible: after all, the definition of actual occupation varies according to the nature of A's land (see **E2:Example 23**). Hence, it seems that a garage (or defined parking space) can be occupied by parking a car there.[179] However, it seems that simply parking a car on unenclosed land does *not* count as actual occupation of that land.[180]

5.3.3 Consent or apparent consent

We saw above that, if B has an Easement, he has a power to release that right. If B has an Equitable Easement, B equally has a power to waive that right. B does *not* need to use a deed to exercise that power: as an Equitable Easement depends on C being under a duty to B, B simply needs to waive that duty. If: (i) B makes a commitment to waive the duty; and (ii) C relies on that commitment; then (iii) C will be able to rely on defensive estoppel, as discussed in 3.3 above.

5.4   The remedies question

5.4.1 B's position against A

If B has an Equitable Easement, A is under a duty to grant B an Easement. If A fails to

---

[177] See eg *per* Lord Denning MR [1967] 2 QB 379 at 395–6, adopting a very unusual definition of the term 'Equitable Easement'. Winn LJ at 405 assumes, without any authority, that an Equitable Easement does not count as a land charge if it arises by estoppel. Danckwerts LJ at 400 seems to base his decision on B having a direct right against C based on the 'benefit and burden' principle: but C had not *chosen* to exercise any right conditional on allowing B a right.

[178] The equivalent section of the Land Registration Act 1925 (s 70(1)(a)) had, rather surprisingly, been interpreted as applying to Equitable Easements as well as to Easements: see *Celsteel Ltd v Alton House Holdings Ltd* [1985] 1 WLR 204.

[179] *Kling v Keston Properties Ltd* (1983) 49 P & CR 212.

[180] *Epps v Esso Petroleum Co Ltd* [1973] 1 WLR 1071.

comply with that duty, B can: (i) seek specific protection by asking for an order that A must grant B the Easement; and (ii) seek money as a substitute for A's failure to grant B an Easement and as compensation for any relevant loss that failure has caused B. So, in *Crabb v Arun DC*,[181] for example, A was ordered: (i) to grant B the promised Easement; and (ii) to give B that Easement *for free*. The parties' plan had been that B would pay for the Easement; but B was released from that duty in order to compensate B for the loss he had already suffered as a result of A's failure to give B the Easement. It seems in general that B's right against A will be specifically protected: as we have seen, that is usually the case where B's right relates to land.

5.4.2 B's position against C

If B has an Equitable Easement, he has a *power* to assert that right against C. This means that if: (i) B exercises that power; or (ii) C is independently aware of B's pre-existing Equitable Easement; then (iii) C is under a duty to B to grant B an Easement. It is important to note that, if B has an Equitable Easement, he *cannot* use the wrong of nuisance to assert that right against C. As B has a persistent right rather than a property right, the rest of the world is *not* under a prima facie duty to B (see **B4.4.4.3**). However, *once* C is under a duty to grant B an Easement, B can again: (i) seek specific protection by asking for an order that C must grant B the Easement;[182] and (ii) seek money as a substitute for C's failure to grant B an Easement and as compensation for any relevant loss that failure has caused B.

SUMMARY of G5:5

As it is a persistent right rather than a property right, an Equitable Easement clearly differs from an Easement. It does *not* impose a duty on the rest of the world; it is impossible for X to commit the wrong of nuisance by interfering with an Equitable Easement. However, if B has an Equitable Easement, then: (i) A is under a duty to grant B an Easement; and (ii) B has a prima facie power to impose the same duty on C, a party who later acquires a right that depends on A's right. However, if B fails to defensively register his Equitable Easement, it is almost certain that C, if he later acquires for value a property right in A's land, will be able to rely on the lack of registration defence against B's pre-existing Equitable Easement.

---

[181] [1976] Ch 179.
[182] See eg *McManus v Cooke* (1887) 35 Ch D 681; *per* Ungoed-Thomas J in *Ward v Kirkland* [1967] Ch 194 at 242–3.

CHAPTER G6
THE RESTRICTIVE COVENANT

THE RESTRICTIVE COVENANT

Like an Easement, a Restrictive Covenant can exist only if it enhances a Freehold or Lease held by B. An Easement is: (i) a property right in A's land; and (ii) allows B to make a specific, limited use of A's land. In contrast, a Restrictive Covenant is: (i) a persistent right against A's Freehold or Lease; and (ii) allows B to *prevent A from making a particular use of A's land*.

We have seen that, even in the absence of a Restrictive Covenant, B can prevent A (a neighbouring landowner) from making particular uses of A's land. For example, it may be unlawful for A to build a nuclear power station on his land without planning permission (see **B:Example 10**). Further, if B has a Freehold or Lease, A is under a duty to B not to unreasonably interfere with B's enjoyment of that right; A commits the wrong of nuisance if he breaches that duty (see **G1A:4.1.1**). However, a Restrictive Covenant can provide B with important *additional* protection.

EXAMPLE 1

B has a Freehold. B decides to split up his land: he keeps half of it (No 32B) and sells a Freehold of the other half to A (No 32A). B insists that A promises, as part of his contractual deal with B, that: (a) A and all future owners of all or any part of A's land will *not* use that land for any commercial purpose; and (b) A and all future owners of A's land will ensure that the house on A's land is properly repaired and maintained.

In such a case, contractual promise (a) gives B a Restrictive Covenant. It supplements B's Freehold by ensuring that the neighbouring land is used only for residential purposes. At the same time, the Restrictive Covenant detracts from A's Freehold: for example, it prevents A from using that land to run a shop or business. As B's Restrictive Covenant is a persistent right, B also has a prima facie power to impose the same duty on C, a party later acquiring a right from A. It has also been held that, uniquely amongst persistent rights, B also has a prima facie power to impose the same duty on C if C *independently* acquires a Freehold of A's land—as when C acquires such a right by simply taking physical control of A's land.[1]

However, in **Example 1**, promise (b) does *not* give B a Restrictive Covenant. Unlike promise (a), it imposes a *positive* duty on A: a duty that cannot be satisfied by doing nothing. Such a promise cannot give B a persistent right (see **1.1.2** below). Nonetheless: (i) promise (b) naturally gives B a direct contractual right against A; (ii) it may also be possible for it to give B2 (a later owner of B's land) a direct right against A (see eg **E3:2.1.1** and **E3:2.2.1**) and (iii) it may even be possible for it to give B or B2 a direct right against C, a

---

[1] See *re Nisbet & Potts' Contract* [1906] 1 Ch 386 (see **1.6** below). In general, it is impossible for a persistent right to bind a party whose right does not depend on A's right (see **B:4.4.3**).

later owner of A's land (see eg **E3:2.3.3**). Further, if C makes a promise to A when acquiring his land, C's promise may also give B or B2 a direct right against C (see eg **E3:2.1.1** and **E3:2.2.1**).

There is thus an important link between the Restrictive Covenant and the direct rights we examined in **E3**. If B (or B2) wants to impose a duty on A (or C) in relation to the use of A's land, we need to remember that, as well as trying to assert a Restrictive Covenant, it may also be possible for B to rely on a direct right.

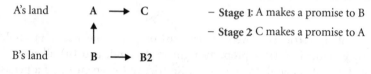

A's land　　A ⟶ C　　　　– **Stage 1**: A makes a promise to B

　　　　　　　↑　　　　　　– **Stage 2**: C makes a promise to A

B's land　　B ⟶ B2

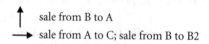

↑　　sale from B to A

⟶　　sale from A to C; sale from B to B2

The table below examines the disputes that may arise (in the left-hand column) and how B (or B2) *may* be able to use a particular promise to acquire a right. For further detail on the direct rights discussed, see **E3:2**. For further details on the methods (assignment, annexation or scheme of development) that B2 can use to get the benefit of B's Restrictive Covenant, see **2.3** below.

	A's promise to B (imposing a negative duty)	A's promise to B (imposing a positive duty)	C's promise to A (whether negative or positive)
B v A	Direct right (contract)	Direct right (contract)	
B v C	**Restrictive Covenant**	Direct right (benefit and burden)	Direct right (1999 Act;[2] 'receipt after a promise' principle)[3]
B2 v A	Direct right (passing to B2 by assignment; or by annexation)	Direct right (passing to B2 by assignment; or by annexation)	
B2 v C	**Restrictive Covenant** (passing to B2 by assignment; annexation; or scheme of development)	Direct right (benefit and burden)	Direct right (1999 Act; 'receipt after a promise' principle)

It is important to realise that a Restrictive Covenant is just *one* means by which B may be able to prevent a neighbour (A or C) from making a particular use of neighbouring land. In addition, B may be able to: (i) show that A (or C)'s action is unlawful; (ii) show that A (or C's) action is a wrongful interference with B's Freehold or Lease; (iii) show that he has a direct right against A (or C).

[2] The Contract (Rights of Third Parties) Act 1999 (see **E3:2.2.1** and **E3:2.3.1**).
[3] See **E3:2.2.2** and **E3:2.3.2**

1 THE CONTENT QUESTION

B's right can only count as a Restrictive Covenant if A is under a duty to B *and* the following criteria are satisfied:

- A's duty is a duty not to make a particular use of A's land; *and*
- A's duty enhances B's Freehold or Lease (ie it benefits B's land); *and*
- A's duty, when created, is *not* intended to impose only a personal duty on A.[4]

1.1 A duty not to make a particular use of A's land

1.1.1 A duty relating to A's land

> **EXAMPLE 2**
>
> B has a Freehold including both No 32A and 32B Acacia Gardens. B runs a newsagents from No 32B. When selling his Freehold of No 32A to A, B makes A promise that neither A nor future owners of all or any part of A's land will run a newsagents within a two-mile radius of No 32B. A then transfers his Freehold of No 32A to C. C happens to have a Freehold of some other land, a mile from Acacia Gardens, and intends to run a newsagents from that land.

A's promise gives B a direct right against A, preventing A from running a newsagents not just from No 32A but also from any other land within the two-mile exclusion zone.[5] A's promise may also give B a Restrictive Covenant: a right to prevent C running a newsagents business on No 32A. However, B *cannot* stop C from doing so on C's *other* land. The point is that A's initial promise to B cannot give B a right against C's Freehold of that other land. A Restrictive Covenant cannot assist B: a persistent right is capable of binding parties who acquire a right that depends on A's right. C's Freehold of the other land was not acquired from A; and so cannot be subject to any pre-existing persistent right B may have as a result of A's promise to B.

The land benefiting from A's duty must be clearly defined. This does not mean that, in a case such as **Example 2**, A's promise to B must be expressly stated to be for the benefit of B's retained land (No 32B). Rather, the courts are prepared to look at the surrounding circumstances and see if it is possible to make an inference as to the land that is intended to benefit from A's promise. Therefore, given the nature of A's promise in **Example 2**, it is clear that the promise is intended to benefit No 32B.[6]

The Restrictive Covenant is an anomalous right: it is an exception to the general rule that, if A is under a duty to B in relation to a liberty, B does not have a persistent right (see **D2:1.1.3** and **E2:1.3.1(ii)**). It also exists only in relation to land, yet does not depend on A being under a duty to give B a property right in land.[7] It seems that the special features of

---

[4] These seem to be the 'three basic conditions' for a right to count as a Restrictive Covenant, referred to by Robert Walker LJ in *Morrells of Oxford Ltd v Oxford United Football Club* [2001] 1 Ch 459 at [39].

[5] Subject to any possible challenge A may make under the 'restraint of trade' doctrine (see **G4:2.1.4(iv)**). It may even be that a Restrictive Covenant is part of an anticompetitive agreement prohibited by European law: see the discussion in *Inntrepeneur Estates (GL) Ltd v Boyes* [1993] 2 EGLR 112.

[6] See *Newton Abbot Co-operative Society v Williamson & Treadgold Ltd* [1952] Ch 286 and *Marten v Flight Refuelling Ltd* [1962] Ch 115

[7] It is thus different from the Equitable Lease, Equitable Charge and Equitable Easement.

land (in particular its fixed location) mean that it is important for B, when transferring part of his land to A, to retain some control over the land transferred (see **E2:1.3.2**). So, whilst B *cannot* acquire a persistent right against A's Ownership of a thing if B sells that thing to A subject to a duty not to sell it on for less than a certain price (see **D1:Example 1**), B can, exceptionally, acquire a persistent right when giving A a Freehold or Lease subject to a duty not to make a particular use of that land.

1.1.2 A duty *not* to make a particular use of A's land

(i) The requirement

The clue is in the title: a Restrictive Covenant must be restrictive and so must depend on A being under a duty to B *not* to use his land in a particular way. This rule, established towards the end of the 19th century,[8] was confirmed by the House of Lords in *Rhone v Stephens.*[9] In that case, the essential facts of which are identical to **E3:Example 7b**, it was held that A's promise to keep the roof of his cottage in good repair could *not* give B a persistent right against A's Freehold. As a result, B attempted to show that he had a direct right against C: however, that claim also failed (see **E3:2.3.3**).

In practice, this requirement is fairly easy to apply. A's duty can count as a Restrictive Covenant *only* if A can satisfy it by doing nothing. It is important to remember that 'the question is not whether a covenant is negative in wording, but whether it is negative in substance'.[10] So, if A promises to 'maintain a garden' on A's land, that promise may seem to impose a positive duty. However, in substance, the promise is negative: A can satisfy it by simply leaving his land as it is.[11]

(ii) Justifying the requirement: doctrine

The House of Lords' confirmation, in *Rhone v Stephens*, that B *cannot* acquire a persistent right where A is under a positive duty to B has attracted criticism on doctrinal grounds.[12] However, from the doctrinal perspective, the decision is perfectly correct. First, there is the general point that, in English law, there is a reluctance to impose a positive duty on a party, such as C, who has not in some way consented to that duty (see **G5:1.5**). Second, if B wants to show he has a persistent right, he must identify a *specific* right of A against which B has a right. In *Rhone*, if B were attempting to identify such a right, it would have to be A's liberty *not* to maintain the roof. To assert his pre-existing persistent right against C, B would then need to show that: (i) when acquiring A's Freehold, C also acquired A's liberty not to maintain the roof; and (ii) A's liberty was subject to B's pre-existing persistent right. However, in a case such as *Rhone*, C does *not* acquire A's liberty not to maintain the roof. C had that liberty *before* he acquired A's Freehold: after all, everyone in the world has a prima facie liberty, against B, not to maintain the roof of the cottage. The only way C can lose that liberty is to come under a *direct* duty to B.

---

[8] See *Haywood v Brunswick PBBS* (1881) 8 QBD 403; *Austerberry v Oldham Corporation* (1885) 29 Ch D 750.
[9] [1994] 2 AC 310.
[10] Per Megarry J in *Shepherd Homes Ltd v Sandham (No 2)* [1971] 1 WLR 1062 at 1067.
[11] In *Tulk v Moxhay* (1848) 2 Ph 774, A made such a promise. However, in that case, the court was not concerned about the distinction between positive and negative duties; instead, its reasoning is based on the idea that B had a *direct right* against C (see **1.7** below).
[12] See eg Gardner [1995] *CLJ* 60 and *Introduction to Land Law* (2007), 183–4; Cooke, *Land Law* (2007), 193.

This analysis is reflected in Lord Templeman's reasoning in *Rhone*. His Lordship's conclusion is certainly consistent with the doctrinal analysis set out here:

> Enforcement of a positive covenant lies in contract; a positive covenant compels an owner to exercise his rights. Enforcement of a negative covenant lies in property; a negative covenant deprives the owner of a right over property.[13]

The distinction between a Restrictive Covenant and a positive duty of A therefore depends on the fact that the former, unlike the latter, imposes a duty on A in relation to a specific liberty (eg, the liberty to build on A's land) that A acquires *as a result* of having a Freehold or Lease of the land. When C later acquires a right that depends on A's Freehold or Lease, C acquires that liberty from A and can hence be subject to B's pre-existing persistent right.

(iii) Justifying the requirement: practical convenience

The Restrictive Covenant is an anomalous form of persistent right: uniquely, it allows B to acquire a persistent right where A's duty relates to a *liberty* held by A. It seems that the needs of practical convenience led the courts to ignore, in this limited context, the doctrinal limit on the content of persistent rights (see **E2:1.3.2**). It is therefore possible to argue that the needs of practical convenience could justify a further breach of doctrine: allowing a positive duty of A to give B a persistent right. Such a dramatic change would have to come from Parliament (see **E2:1.4**).

Nonetheless, it is worth noting that parties seem to have adapted reasonably well to the existing position. The inability of positive covenants to bind third parties has been a particular problem where flats are concerned: if you own a flat, you will want: (i) the current and future owners of the flat below to be under a duty to keep their ceiling in good repair; and (ii) the current and future owners of the flat above to be under a duty to keep their floor in good repair. One common method of solving this problem is for each flat to be held under a Lease.

EXAMPLE 3

A has a Freehold of a large house. A decides to develop the house into three flats. A transfers his Freehold to A Co. A Co then grants long Leases (eg, 199 years) to each purchaser (B1, B2 and B3) of an individual flat. When acquiring his Lease, each of B1, B2 and B3 acquires shares in A Co. The Leases impose a duty on each of B1, B2 and B3 to keep his flat in good repair. B1 then sells his flat by transferring his Lease to C.

When C acquires his Lease, he enters into a landlord–tenant relationship with A Co. By doing so, C is subject to any duties, even positive duties, that count as leasehold covenants (see **G1B:1.8**). C therefore owes a duty to A Co to keep his flat in good repair. B2 and B3, as shareholders of A Co, can each ensure that A Co enforces its right against C. Further, as shareholders, C, B2 and B3 each has the security of knowing that, even if the period of his current Lease is coming to an end, he will be able to ensure that A Co renews the Lease.

---

[13] [1994] 2 AC 310 at 318. See too *per* Farwell J in the first instance decision in *re Nisbet & Potts Contract* [1905] 1 Ch 391 at 397: 'Effect is to be given to the negative covenant by means of the land itself. But the land cannot spend money on improving itself and there is no personal liability on [C] . . . because there is no contract on which he can be sued.'

This offsets the general disadvantage of a Lease: that it provides only a temporary right to exclusive control.

This solution does of course involve some artificiality and some unwelcome side-effects. For example, A Co, like any company, will have to file annual accounts, even though it is generally unlikely to have received or spent any money. It is not uncommon for the party (eg, B2) who has the misfortune to be the nominated company secretary to incur a fixed penalty by forgetting to file these accounts.

A different solution was introduced by the Commonhold and Leasehold Reform Act 2002 (CLRA). That Act introduced a further method of allowing positive duties to bind future owners of neighbouring land: the establishment of a Commonhold scheme.[14] The key advantage of such a scheme is that each owner of an individual unit within the scheme can: (i) have a permanent right to exclusive control (effectively a Freehold) of that unit; *and* (ii) benefit from the fact that, under the scheme, other holders of a unit can be under positive duties, such as a duty to keep a unit in good repair.

So, in a case such as **Example 3**, A now also has the option of setting up a Commonhold scheme, in which each of the three flats counts as a unit. However, such a scheme also has its disadvantages. It consists essentially of a management structure for a particular area of land and can be (or at least seem to be) administratively complex.[15] It seems that, in practice, the apparent complexity of Commonhold schemes, as well as their novelty, has scared people off. In particular, the adoption of such schemes has been impaired by banks' initial doubts as to whether to lend money to those participating in such schemes.[16] Further, if flats in a house or block of flats are already held under Leases, as in **Example 3**, the consent of *all* the current unit owners (assuming each has a Lease of over 21 years) is needed to convert that existing arrangement into a Commonhold scheme: in practice, that consent can be very difficult to achieve.[17]

It can be argued that the mechanisms employed in response to the existing rule (eg, Leases, Commonhold schemes) are clumsy and unnecessary.[18] However, it can equally be said that their supposedly clumsy features are, in fact, important safeguards for C. For example, in both a Lease and a Commonhold scheme there is some degree of *mutuality*. C may have to bear the burden of a positive duty he has not consented to; but, in return, C will acquire particular benefits either against his landlord or against other unit-owners and the commonhold association. In contrast, if positive covenants, like Restrictive Covenants, were simply allowed to count as a persistent right, C could be bound by a positive duty he has not consented to without receiving any benefit in return: there would be no guarantee of mutuality.[19]

---

[14] See eg Clarke [2002] *Conv* 349; Clarke, *Commonhold* (2004); van der Merwe and Smith [2005] *Conv* 53.

[15] There must be: (i) a commonhold association—ie, a company that will own any common areas in the scheme; and (ii) a commonhold community statement setting out the rights and duties of the commonhold association and the owners of the individual units. The CLRA, coupled with usual company law rules, regulates the commonhold association, the powers of the unit owners and the scope of the community statement.

[16] See Clarke [2002] *Conv* 349. However, there are now some signs of commonhold schemes being adopted more frequently by developers: see eg [2006] 09 EG 173.

[17] Clarke [2002] *Conv* 349 at 353–7 and 385.

[18] See eg Law Com Consultation Paper No 186 (2008), 7.46, 7.60ff.

[19] A further mechanism is to give B a Rentcharge—a relatively rare form of property right in land consisting of a duty, owed by a Freehold owner of land, to make periodic payments to B (see Rentcharges Act 1977). As it counts as a property right, a Rentcharge over A's land, granted by A to B, is prima facie binding on C (although it cannot bind

1.1.3 A specific duty in relation to a specific right

First, if B claims that A is under a contractual duty to B (as in **Examples 1 and 2**) there is the general point that a promise can only be contractually binding if there is sufficient certainty as to its scope.[20] Nonetheless, it is worth noting that the courts have allowed a Restrictive Covenant to arise where A is under a seemingly vague duty, such as a duty not to cause any 'nuisance or annoyance' to B.[21] As a result, the courts are faced with the task of applying these terms to grey areas. On occasion, seemingly surprising decisions have been made: for example, the use by C of land as a hospital,[22] or even as a finishing school,[23] has been found to constitute an 'annoyance'. Of course, each particular case must be evaluated on its particular facts.

Second, there is the particular point that, to give B a persistent right, it must be clear that A is under a duty in relation to a specific right. So, if A's duty is intended to relate only to a particular part of A's land, that part must be: (i) expressly defined by the parties; or (ii) clear from the surrounding circumstances. After all, if C later acquires a Freehold or Lease of part of A's land, C needs to know whether his right is subject to B's Restrictive Covenant.

1.2   A duty that enhances B's Freehold or Lease

To count as a Restrictive Covenant, it is not enough that A's duty benefits *B*; it needs to benefit *land owned by B*.[24] For example, let us say that: (i) B sells *all* his land to A; and (ii) makes A promise not to build on that land. As B does not retain any land that benefits from A's promise, B does *not* acquire a Restrictive Covenant: A's promise will simply give B a personal right against A.[25]

As we saw when examining Easements, the requirement can raise a difficult practical question (see **G5:1.2**). As with Easements, it is reasonably clear that a right can count as a Restrictive Covenant if it benefits a business carried out on B's land.[26] In some cases, difficult value judgments, involving the consideration of expert evidence,[27] may need to be

---

C if C acquires a Lease from A: *re Herbage Rents, Greenwich* [1896] 2 Ch 811). A Rentcharge can be used to impose a duty to pay for a service provided by B: in such a case, mutuality is again present as C gets the benefit of the service (see eg *Orchard Trading Estate Management Ltd v Johnson Security Ltd* [2002] EWCA Civ 406). A Rentcharge can also be used to secure a positive duty owed to B (as noted by Lindley LJ in *Austerberry v Corpn of Oldham* (1885) 29 Ch D 750 at 783): if C fails to perform that duty B has a right to take physical control of C's land (see eg Bright [2002] *Conv* 507). With that form of Rentcharge, mutuality is *not* guaranteed, but, in practice, this type of Rentcharge tends to be used to allow Freehold owners of individual plots within a development to have the benefit of mutually enforceable positive covenants.

[20] See eg *Walford v Miles* [1992] 2 AC 128 in relation to contractual promises.

[21] See eg *Tod-Heatley v Benham* (1888) 40 Ch D 80; *Hampstead Suburban Properties Ltd v Diomedous* [1969] 1 Ch 248.

[22] See eg *Bramwell v Lacy* (1879) 10 Ch D 691; *Tod-Heatley v Benham* (1888) 40 Ch D 80.

[23] *Kemp v Sober* (1851) 1 Sim (NS) 517. Cranworth V-C stated at 520 that 'neighbours will suffer annoyance not only from their practising music and dancing, but from their relations and friends continually calling on them'.

[24] Of course, the Restrictive Covenant need not benefit *all* the land retained by B; it is enough that it benefits *some* of that land.

[25] See eg *London County Council v Allen* [1914] 3 KB 642.

[26] See eg *Newton Abbot Co-operative Society v Williamson & Treadgold Ltd* [1952] Ch 286. Newsom in *Preston & Newsom's Restrictive Covenants Affecting Freehold Land* (9th edn, 1998), 3–20, however, expresses some doubt, arguing that the courts should draw a distinction between truly benefiting B's land and simply benefiting a business which is run from B's land.

[27] Such evidence was considered, for example, in *Marten v Flight Refuelling* [1962] Ch 1115.

made. It is worth noting that the courts, in general, have been fairly lenient in applying this requirement.[28] In particular, if A's promise is stated to be for the benefit of B's land, the court will assume that the promise does indeed benefit B's land: 'so long as [B] may reasonably take the view that the restriction remains of value to his estate'.[29] In such a case, the onus is on C to show why A's promise cannot reasonably be regarded as benefiting B's land.

1.3   A duty that is not intended to impose only a personal duty on A

In **Example 1**, A made a contractual promise relating to the conduct of both (i) A and (ii) all future owners of all or any part of A's land. In such a case, it is clear that A's promise is not intended to give B a purely personal right against A. As a result, it is possible for that promise to give B a persistent right: a right capable of binding parties other than A. However, it may be that, when acquiring his land from B, A is: (i) willing to impose a duty on himself not to make a particular use of his land; *but* (ii) is *not* willing to give B a right that can bind future owners of that land. For example, it may be that A has no plans to make a commercial use of his land; but wants to reserve the option of selling that land to a developer who will pay A a premium if he is free to build shops on the land. In such a case, A can make clear that he does not intend his promise to bind future owners of A's land: A can expressly make a promise that A, *and only A*, will not make a commercial use of A's land. If A does so, that promise cannot give B a Restrictive Covenant.

It is thus possible for A's intention to turn a right that could otherwise count as a Restrictive Covenant into a purely personal right against A: we saw a similar point when examining Easements (see **G5:1.6**). The point is that if B has a right to stop A making a particular use of A's land, this right may be *either*: (i) a personal right against A; or (ii) a Restrictive Covenant. Where B's right arises as a result of A's promise, we can distinguish between those two possibilities by looking at the intentions of A and B.

EXAMPLE 4a

B has a Freehold. B decides to split up his land: he keeps half of it and sells a Freehold of the other half (No 32A) to A. As part of his contractual deal with B, A makes a promise that 'for the benefit of B and future owners of B's land, No 32A will not be used for commercial purposes'. A then transfers his Freehold to C.

On the one hand, A's promise does not expressly refer to future owners of A's land: C may therefore argue that it does not give B a Restrictive Covenant. On the other hand, A's promise does not expressly state that *only* A will be bound by the promise. To resolve such ambiguities, section 79 of the Law of Property Act 1925 ('the LPA 1925') sets out a default rule: if A makes a promise 'relating to any land of [A]',[30] then, unless A expresses a contrary intention, that promise is deemed:

---

[28] See eg *Lord Northbourne v Johnston & Son* [1922] 2 Ch 309; *Marten v Flight Refuelling* [1962] Ch 1115; *Earl of Leicester v Wells UDC* [1973] Ch 110.

[29] *Per* Brightman J in *Wrotham Park Estate Co v Parkside Homes Ltd* [1974] 1 WLR 798 at 808.

[30] The section also applies to any covenant made by A relating to land which is 'capable of being bound by [A]' and so covers a situation where A does not own land, but has the authority to make a binding promise in relation to that land.

to be made by [A] on behalf of himself his successors in title and the persons deriving title under him or them and . . . shall have effect as if such successors and other persons were expressed.

Hence, as a result of section 79, A's promise, in **Example 4a**, must be read as a promise made by A *on behalf of A and future owners of all or any part of A's land*. This means that the promise is *not* seen as imposing only a personal duty on A; and so it *can* lead to B acquiring a Restrictive Covenant.[31] This seems to be a sensible way to resolve the ambiguity. If A makes a promise 'relating to his land' it may be reasonable for B to expect that the promise is not just intended to bind A. Of course, the section 79 solution only applies in cases of doubt: therefore, if A wishes to make a promise that: (i) relates to his land; but (ii) only binds him; then (iii) A can do so by making a promise that refers only to his own conduct.[32]

1.4   The duration of a Restrictive Covenant

An Easement must be intended to be either permanent like a Freehold or to last for a limited period like a Lease (see **G5:1.3**). However, as a Restrictive Covenant is a persistent right rather than a property right, that restriction on duration, imposed by section 1(2)(a) of the LPA 1925, does *not* apply. Thus, it is possible, albeit unusual, for B to acquire a Restrictive Covenant where A makes a promise that is binding only until the occurrence of a future event. For example, A can promise that, until England win the football World Cup, neither he nor a future owner of all or any part of A's land will use that land for commercial purposes.

1.5   Regulating the Restrictive Covenant: suspension and termination

If B has an Easement, it is possible for that right to be suspended; or to terminate (see **G5:1.8**). The same is true where B has a Restrictive Covenant:

1.   Like an Easement, a Restrictive Covenant will end if B acquires A's Freehold or Lease: it is not possible for B to have a right against his own Freehold or Lease.[33] If B acquires

---

[31] In *Sefton v Tophams* [1967] 1 AC 50 at 81, Lord Wilberforce pointed out that s 79, by itself, does *not* give B a persistent right: that is correct, as the other aspects of the **content** test must also be satisfied (they could not be in that case, as B had no land that benefited from A's promise). However, Lord Wilberforce's suggestion, given as part of his dissent, that s 79 has the effect, and *only* the effect, of extending A's duty (ie, making A liable for the acts of later owners of A's land) seems incorrect. Certainly, in *Morrells of Oxford Ltd v Oxford United Football Club* [2001] Ch 459, the Court of Appeal proceeded on the view that s 79, if applicable, would have the effect of allowing A's promise, if it met the other tests, to give B a Restrictive Covenant: see esp *per* Robert Walker LJ at [35] and [39]–[40].

[32] See eg *re Royal Victoria Pavilion, Ramsgate* [1961] Ch 581: A made a promise that he would not make a particular use of his land and also that he would 'procure' that future owners of the land would not use the land in that way. As this promise focused on A's conduct, imposing a duty on A to control future owners, rather than a duty on the future owners themselves, it was interpreted as intended to bind A alone. See too *Morrells of Oxford Ltd v Oxford United Football Club* [2001] Ch 459: B argued, relying on s 79, that clause 3 of A's contract was intended to bind future owners of A's land. However, clause 2 of the same contract had clear words showing such an intention; the omission of those words from clause 3 showed an intention that clause 3 was *not* intended to bind future owners of A's land and so s 79 could not apply: see *per* Robert Walker LJ at [28].

[33] This basic point is recognised in *Preston & Newsom's Restrictive Covenants Affecting Freehold Land* (ed Newsom, 9th edn, 1998), 3–15 and seems to have been accepted by the Privy Council in *Texaco Antilles Ltd v Kernochan* [1973] AC 609, 626. However, things are different where a scheme of development applies: see **2.3.3(iii)** below.

a Lease of A's land, it seems B's Restrictive Covenant will be suspended for the period of the Lease, but will revive when B's Lease ends.

2. Like an Easement, a Restrictive Covenant enhances B's Freehold or Lease. As a result, a Restrictive Covenant ought to be suspended if a change in circumstances means that it no longer enhances B's land. Unless that change in circumstances is irreversible, the Restrictive Covenant should not be terminated.

3. An Easement can be released by B; a Restrictive Covenant can be waived by B. To be on the safe side, B will generally be advised to use a deed to do so.[34] Strictly speaking, however, if A or C gives something in return for the waiver, there is no need for a deed to be used:[35] writing signed by B should suffice.[36] It is important to note that if B simply decides to allow a particular person (eg, C) to act contrary to the duty imposed by a Restrictive Covenant, this does not amount to a waiver: a waiver consists of B giving up his Restrictive Covenant for good.

An Easement can also be suspended or terminated by a change in circumstances that radically increases the burden of the Easement on A's land (see **G5:1.8**). This principle does *not* apply to a Restrictive Covenant: the burden it imposes is negative and hence constant. However, there is a different method that C may use in an attempt to change, or wholly remove, B's Restrictive Covenant. C can make an application to the Lands Tribunal.[37] Under section 84 of the LPA 1925, that body has the power to modify or terminate a Restrictive Covenant[38] in the following situations:

- the Restrictive Covenant is 'obsolete'; *or*
- the modification/ termination of the Restrictive Covenant will not 'injure' B; *or*
- B has expressly or impliedly agreed to the modification/ termination; *or*
- (i) the Restrictive Covenant impedes some 'reasonable user of [C's] land for public or private purposes'; *and* (ii) B can be compensated in money for any loss caused by the modification/discharge; *and* (iii) the Restrictive Covenant is *either* contrary to the public interest *or* does not 'secure to [B] any practical benefits of substantial value or advantage to [B]'.

In any case where the Lands Tribunal does decide to modify or terminate B's Restrictive Covenant, it may also order the party who made the application to pay money to: (i) compensate B for any loss caused by the change; *or* (ii) to give B the extra money he could have received from A if he had sold his land to A *without* requiring A to enter into the Restrictive Covenant.

Section 84 is very difficult to explain as a matter of doctrine. It is highly unusual for any body, even a court, to be given the power to limit or even eliminate a persistent right of B.

---

[34] The leading practitioners' work *Preston & Newsom's Restrictive Covenants Affecting Freehold Land* (ed Newson, 9th edn, 1998), 5–4 advises using a deed to release a Restrictive Covenant.

[35] S 52 of the LPA 1925 does not apply as B is not giving up a property right.

[36] Signed writing is necessary to satisfy s 53(1)(a) and (c) of the LPA 1925.

[37] The Lands Tribunal is a court with a limited jurisdiction (see *per* Diplock LJ in *re Purkiss* (1962) 1 WLR 902 at 914). When considering an application, the Lands Tribunal may refer certain questions to the High Court: see s 84(2) of the LPA 1925 and Rule 22 of the Lands Tribunals Rules 1975.

[38] S 84(12) also gives the Tribunal the power to modify or discharge a leasehold covenant, if it is in a Lease granted for more than 40 years, of which at least 25 years have run. However, this power will only rarely be exercised: see eg *per* Harman LJ in *Ridley v Taylor* [1965] 1 WLR 611 at 617–8.

Indeed, any change made without B's consent is, prima facie, an infringement of B's right, under Article 1 of the First Protocol to the European Convention on Human Rights (ECHR), to the peaceful enjoyment of his possessions. However, that Article does allow interference where it is in 'the public interest'. That Article, when applied to disputes involving things, simply restates the **basic tension**, evident throughout the property law system, between protecting B and protecting C (see **B:8.3.1**).[39]

That **basic tension** also lies behind section 84. On the one hand, B can argue that if: (i) he has a Restrictive Covenant; and (ii) if C has no defence to that right, then (iii) it is wrong for the Lands Tribunal to have the power to interfere with B's right. On the other, C can argue that section 84 is a necessary part of balancing the needs of B with those of C. After all, we have seen throughout this chapter that the Restrictive Covenant depends, essentially, on the needs of practical convenience. And those needs, rather than any doctrinal concerns, are very clear in section 84: a section that allows a change to occur if, in a particular case, the practical advantages of B's Restrictive Covenant are outweighed by the burden it imposes.

The Law Commission have proposed changes to the operation of section 84.[40] As well as an extension to its scope (so that the Lands Tribunal also has a power to discharge or modify, for example, B's Easement: see **G5:1.8**), the Law Commission has also suggested an extension to the grounds on which discharge or modification is available. Although the recommended change is said simply to reflect existing practice,[41] the reform, if enacted, would increase the powers of the Lands Tribunal and make it easier for B's Restrictive Covenant to be discharged or modified.[42] Such changes may clearly benefit some parties (eg, developers who are keen to build new homes and can show that providing such housing is in the 'public benefit'); but in doing so they necessarily undermine the protection that a Restrictive Covenant can give to B's land.

1.6 The anomalous nature of the Restrictive Covenant

EXAMPLE 4b

The facts are as in **Example 4a**. C2, a squatter, comes onto C's land and begins to use that land for commercial purposes.

In such a case, B may face a problem. As a Restrictive Covenant is a persistent right, it is not a right against A's land; instead it is a right against A's Freehold. B thus has a prima facie power to impose a duty on C when C acquires A's Freehold. However, C2 has *not* acquired a right that depends on A or C's Freehold; instead, C2 has *independently acquired* his right. As a matter of doctrine, it should therefore be impossible for B to assert any pre-existing persistent right against C2 (see **B:4.4.3**). However, if that is the case, B faces a real problem when deciding whether to sell part of his land to A. The possibility of imposing a Restrictive

---

[39] You might expect that s 84 cannot be used by A, the party who made the original promise to B, to escape from that promise, as B can simply assert a direct contractual right against A. However, surprisingly, the Lands Tribunal has held that A *can* apply under s 84 (see *Ridley v Taylor* [1965] 1 WLR 611) and such applications have, in some cases, been successful.

[40] Law Com Consultation Paper No 186 (2008), Part 14.

[41] *Ibid* at 14.43.

[42] For the suggested test see Law Com Consultation Paper No 186 (2008), 14.70, 14.71.

Covenant may be decisive in convincing B to sell part of his land: it gives B a way to deal with the risk that A, or a future owner of A's land, might use that land in an unwelcome way (see **E1:1.3.2**). But if, in **Example 4b**, B is unable to control C2's use of the land, the protection given by a Restrictive Covenant can become an illusion: if A's land falls into the hands of a party independently acquiring a Freehold, B will be unable to control that party's use of the land.

Thus, the needs of practical convenience triumphed once again. In *re Nisbet & Potts' Contract*,[43] the Court of Appeal decided that, in a case such as **Example 4a**, B *does* have the power to assert his Restrictive Covenant against C2. So, alone amongst persistent rights, a Restrictive Covenant can bind a party who *independently acquires* a right in the land to which the Restrictive Covenant relates. The practical basis for that conclusion is clear in part of the reasoning of Cozens-Hardy LJ:[44]

> The value of estates in the neighbourhood of London and all large towns, and the amenity of those estates, depend almost entirely upon the continuance of the mutual restrictive covenants affecting the user and enjoyment of the land.

Whilst the decision in *re Nisbet & Potts* is impossible to justify as a matter of doctrine,[45] it comes as no surprise. After all, the *very existence* of the Restrictive Covenant as a persistent right is a departure from doctrine, based on the needs of practical convenience. The existence of the Restrictive Covenant, as well as its ability to bind C2 in **Example 4b**, is a result of the need to promote the availability of land by assuring B that he can both: (i) transfer some land to A; and (ii) control future use of that land.

Despite these anomalies, it is still important to recognise that the Restrictive Covenant is a persistent right, not a property right. First, it does *not* impose a prima facie duty on the rest of the world; the decision in *re Nisbet & Potts* does not go that far as it simply allows B's Restrictive Covenant to bind a further, but limited class of third parties: those independently acquiring a Freehold of A's land. Second, the duty imposed by a Restrictive Covenant must relate to a liberty A holds *as a result* of his Freehold or Lease. This explains why a positive duty of A cannot give rise to a Restrictive Covenant (see **1.1.2** above). It also explains why a promise by A not to shop at Tesco's cannot give B a Restrictive Covenant (even if it benefits B's land): A's duty does not relate to a liberty A has by virtue of his Freehold or Lease.

1.7   The development of the Restrictive Covenant as a persistent right

It can be argued that, due to the needs of practical convenience, at least some contractual licences of land should be recognised as persistent rights (see **E6:3.4.2**). The history of the Restrictive Covenant provides a useful comparison: it shows how a particular type of right relating to land may develop into a persistent right.[46] However, a warning is necessary: the Restrictive Covenant was developed by judges before 1926. Nowadays, section 4(1) of the LPA 1925 makes clear that only Parliament can recognise a new persistent right relating to land (see **E2:1.4**).

---

[43] [1906] 1 Ch 386.
[44] *Ibid* at 409.
[45] Maitland, *Lectures on Equity*, (1929), ch 12, 169–70 rightly sees the result as doctrinally unjustified.
[46] See further McFarlane [2003] *Conv* 473.

EXAMPLE 5

B has a Freehold. B decides to split up his land: he keeps half of it and sells a Freehold of the other half to A. As part of his contractual deal with B, A makes a promise 'to maintain [part of A's land] as a garden'. A then sells his Freehold to C: when doing so: (i) A tells C that the land must be maintained as a garden; and (ii) C pays a lower price as a result. C then begins to build on the land.

Nowadays, we would concentrate on the question of whether A's promise gives rise to a Restrictive Covenant. However, things were different in 1848 when the Court of Appeal considered (in *Tulk v Moxhay*)[47] the facts set out in **Example 5**: the Restrictive Covenant had not yet been recognised as a persistent right. So, counsel for C argued that A's promise did not 'run with the land': it did not give B a right capable of binding C. However, the court rejected that argument as irrelevant: without even asking for the arguments of B's counsel, the Lord Chancellor, Lord Cottenham, found in favour of B. His Lordship stated that:

> the question is, not whether the covenant runs with the land, but whether a party shall be per-mitted to use the land in a manner inconsistent with the contract entered into by his vendor, and with notice of which he purchased.[48]

It is therefore clear that, contrary to the orthodox view,[49] the result in *Tulk v Moxhay* is *not* based on B asserting a pre-existing persistent right against C; rather, it is based on B having a new, *direct* right against C. This explains why C's argument that A's promise could not bind C was irrelevant. It also explains why the Court of Appeal did not concern itself with the question of whether A's promise to B imposed a negative or positive duty: that question is irrelevant where B claims a direct right (see **E3:Overview**).

Nonetheless, *Tulk v Moxhay* is a key case in the gradual evolution of the Restrictive Covenant from a personal right into a persistent right. It can be seen as a case that, albeit indirectly, recognises the importance of A's original promise to B, by making it easy for B to acquire a direct right that prevents C from breaching that promise. By relaxing the requirement for a direct right, *Tulk* thus indirectly acknowledges that B's original right against A may be worthy of special protection. By building on that idea, later courts could then go further and find that B's right was so important that it gave B a prima facie power to impose a duty on C. At this point, B's original right crossed the boundary separating personal rights from persistent rights: it was no longer the case that *B* needed to show that C's conduct justified the acquisition by B of a new, direct right against C; instead C needed to show why he is not bound by B's original, persistent right.

Once the Restrictive Covenant came to be recognised as a right capable of binding C, the decision in *Tulk* was *reinterpreted* as depending on the fact that A's promise gave B a persistent right (see **E3:2.3.5**). This reinterpretation had two consequences. First, it helped later courts to reject the controversial idea, clearly present in Lord Cottenham's judgment, that B can acquire a direct right against C *simply* because: (i) B has a personal right against A; and (ii) C knows about, or should have known about that right.[50] That idea had some

---

[47] (1848) 2 Ph 774.
[48] *Ibid* at 777–8.
[49] That orthodox view is adopted in eg Law Com Consultation Paper No 186 (2008), 2.10, 2.11.
[50] See esp *per* Scrutton LJ in *London County Council v Allen* [1914] 3 KB 642 at 647: *Tulk* cannot be used as

currency in the mid-19th century: it is also, for example, expressed in the famous dictum of Knight Bruce LJ in *de Mattos v Gibson*.[51] However, the courts have since rejected it (see **D3:2.3.5** and **E3:2.3.5**). To acquire a direct right against C, B must do more than simply show that C knew about A's promise to B.

Second, the reinterpretation of *Tulk* forced the courts to focus more carefully on the content of A's promise and to ask precisely *when* that promise should give B a persistent right.[52] As a result, the courts developed the special requirements of the Restrictive Covenant that we have examined in this section. For example, the courts soon made clear that A's promise cannot count as a Restrictive Covenant if it imposes a positive duty on A.[53] It was also held that, to count as a Restrictive Covenant, A's promise had to benefit some land of B.[54]

1.8   The Law Commission's proposals: the Land Obligation

The Law Commission has proposed that it should no longer be possible for B to acquire a Restrictive Covenant in relation to registered land.[55] Instead, Parliament should introduce a new form of property right: a 'Land Obligation'. In a case such as **Example 1**, therefore, B would need to ensure that his sale to A includes the creation of such a right. This change would certainly remove (in relation to registered land at least) the doctrinal anomalies brought about by the current recognition of the Restrictive Covenant as a persistent right. First, there would no longer be an exception to the general rule that, if B has only a right against a *liberty* of A, B does *not* have a persistent right (see **1.1.1** above). Second, there would no longer be an exception to the general rule that, if B has a persistent right against A's right, B can only assert that right against a third party who acquires a right that depends on A's right (see **1.6** above).

On the Law Commission's proposals, the **content** of the new Land Obligation would have much in common with the content of the Restrictive Covenant. In particular, a Land Obligation must: (i) benefit some land of B; and (ii) be intended to bind A and future owners of A's land.[56] However, a *positive* duty of A could also count as a Land Obligation.[57] As a Land Obligation is to be a property right, not a persistent right, the doctrinal problem of a positive duty counting as a Restrictive Covenant disappears: B no longer has to identify a right of A in relation to which B has a right (see **1.1.2(ii)** above). However, as noted in **E1:1.3.1**, allowing a positive duty of A to count as a property right raises a different doctrinal problem. A property right imposes a prima facie duty on the rest of the world: yet it cannot be the case that if, for example, A enters a Land Obligation to repair the roof of A's cottage, the *rest of the world* is then under that positive duty to B. Therefore, a positive Land

---

evidence that B acquires a direct right whenever C knowingly breaches A's promise to B as 'the question of notice to the purchaser has nothing whatever to do with the question whether the covenant binds him, except in so far as the absence of notice may enable him to raise the plea of purchaser for valuable consideration without notice'.

[51] (1858) 4 De G & J 276.
[52] See Gardner (1982) 98 *LQR* 279 at 317–20.
[53] See eg *Haywood v Brunswick PBBS* (1881) 8 QBD 403; *Austerberry v Oldham Corporation* (1885) 29 Ch D 750.
[54] See eg *Formby v Barker* [1903] 2 Ch 539; *London County Council v Allen* [1914] 3 KB 642.
[55] Law Com Consultation Paper No 186 (2008), 8.98ff.
[56] *Ibid* at 8.63–8.65, 8.25–8.28.
[57] *Ibid* at 7.67ff, 8.23.

Obligation has to be an anomalous form of property right: one that binds (at least some) future owners of A's land,[58] but is *not* prima facie binding on the rest of the world.

A reinterpretation of the Restrictive Covenant as a property right also raises another problem. Currently, B needs to show that A's promise relates to a specific liberty A has *by virtue of A's Freehold or Lease* (see **1.6** above). However, on the Law Commission's current proposals, a Land Obligation would not be so restricted. If: (i) B can show that A's duty benefits B's land; then (ii) it seems A's duty can count as a Land Obligation even if it does not relate to any liberty A has by virtue of his Freehold or Lease.[59] So, perhaps surprisingly, A's duty not to shop at Tesco's could count as a Land Obligation (and so bind future owners of A's land) if it benefits B's neighbouring grocery.

SUMMARY of G6:1

The Restrictive Covenant, a special form of persistent right existing only in relation to land, can arise where A is under a duty to B not to make a particular use of A's land. If that duty enhances B's Freehold or Lease; and is not intended to bind only A, it gives B a persistent right: a right against A's Freehold or Lease. It is no surprise that the Restrictive Covenant has been viewed as a kind of 'negative Easement'. There are of course some important differences: for example, as it is not a property right, the Restrictive Covenant does not impose a prima facie duty on the rest of the world and it can exist for an uncertain period. However, as far as content is concerned, the characterisation of the Restrictive Covenant as a 'negative Easement' is broadly correct. Why, then, do we bother to distinguish the Restrictive Covenant from the Easement: is it just an exercise in labelling? Well, we have already seen one key reason: the Restrictive Covenant is a persistent right, not a property right. Further, once a right counts as an Easement, it becomes easier for B to satisfy the **acquisition question**. In contrast, as we will see now see, acquiring a Restrictive Covenant is a far more demanding task.

2 THE ACQUISITION QUESTION

2.1 The key distinction: initial acquisition and later acquisition

When we looked at how an Easement is acquired, we distinguished between two separate questions (see **G5:2.1.1**):

1. How can B initially acquire his right?
2. Once B has that right, how can the benefit of that right be acquired by B2, a future owner of all or part of B's land?

Those same two questions apply to the acquisition of a Restrictive Covenant. However, where a Restrictive Covenant is concerned, the answers are very different. As to the first

---

[58] See *ibid* at 9.11–9.21, 9.37, 10.11–10.27 for consideration of which particular parties should be prima facie bound by a positive Land Obligation.

[59] *Ibid* at 8.71ff. There is an ambiguity in the Law Commission's approach: it emphasises the need for a Land Obligation to 'relate to land'; but interprets that requirement as meaning *only* that A's duty should benefit B's land (see eg at 8.73). It thus seems to overlook the current requirement of a Restrictive Covenant that A's duty must relate to a liberty A has by virtue of his Freehold or Lease.

question, different rules apply: the Restrictive Covenant is a persistent right rather than a property right. As to the second question, if B has a Restrictive Covenant there is *no* general rule that, when B gives B2 a Freehold or Lease of all or part of B's land, B2 also gets the benefit of B's Restrictive Covenant.

2.2   Initial acquisition by B

No persistent right can be substantively registered (see **C2:6**): if B has a Restrictive Covenant, B cannot take advantage of the protection provided by substantive registration. Equally, however, B can acquire a Restrictive Covenant without needing to substantively register that right. Like any persistent right, a Restrictive Covenant exists only if A is under a duty to B. This means that, like any persistent right, a Restrictive Covenant *cannot* be acquired independently: B's unilateral conduct cannot impose a duty on A.[60]

2.2.1 Contract

In the examples we have considered in this chapter, A's duty to B has arisen as a result of A's contractual promise to B. And that promise has been made as part of a deal under which A is to acquire a Freehold or Lease from B. In such a case, A's promise can only be contractually binding if the formality rule imposed by section 2 of the Law of Property (Miscellaneous Provisions) Act 1989 has been satisfied (see **E2:2.3.3**). So if, in **Example 1**, A's promise (a) is made *orally*, it cannot impose a contractual duty on A.

  A's contractual promise to B can give B a Restrictive Covenant even if that promise is not made as part of a contract to transfer a Freehold or Lease to A. For example, if A and B have neighbouring Freeholds, A could, in return for payment from B, make a promise that neither A nor future owners of all or any of A's land will make a commercial use of A's land. To be contractually binding, such a promise does *not* need to comply with section 2 of the 1989 Act. However, it can only give B a persistent right if the general formality rule imposed by section 53(1)(a) of the LPA 1925 is satisfied: to give B a persistent right against A's Freehold, A's promise must be made in writing and signed by A (see **E2:2.3.1**).

  It is worth noting that the term 'Restrictive Covenant' is slightly misleading. A covenant is generally thought of as a promise made *in a deed*. In the examples we have examined so far, A's promise may well be made in a deed, executed as part of the sale of land from B to A. However, as we have seen, A's promise can give B the persistent right known as a Restrictive Covenant even if it is not made in a deed.[61] After all, the formality rule requiring the use of a deed (imposed by section 52 of the LPA 1925) applies only where B claims that A has given B a *property right* in land.

2.2.2 Non-contractual means of imposing a duty on A

In practice, a Restrictive Covenant almost always arises from a contractual promise of A. However, in theory, it can arise if A is under a non-contractual duty to B—provided of course that the content of A's duty passes the tests set out in **section 1** above.

---

[60] In contrast, an Easement can be acquired through prescription: on the orthodox view that is a form of dependent acquisition, but, as we saw in **G5:2.8.1**, it may perhaps better be seen as a form of independent acquisition.

[61] As noted by eg Law Com Consultation Paper No 186 (2008), 7.9.

EXAMPLE 6a

A and B have neighbouring Freeholds. B wants to put up a new building on his land, but is worried that, if A were to build on A's land, the view from B's new building would be completely blocked out. A, knowing of B's plan, assures B that, due to an earlier promise by a former owner of A's land, A and future owners of A's land are already under a duty to B not to build on A's land. As a result, B puts up the building. It then turns out that the earlier promise made by a former owner of A's land does *not* in fact impose a duty not to build on A and future owners of A's land.

In such a case, the doctrine of proprietary estoppel should impose a duty on A to B. And if the only way to prevent B suffering a detriment as a result of his reliance is to hold A to his assurance, then: (i) A is under a duty to B; and (ii) that duty passes the content test for a Restrictive Covenant; so (iii) B has acquired a Restrictive Covenant through proprietary estoppel. In such a case, it does not matter that no signed writing has been used: B's right arises by 'operation of law' and so is exempt from the formality requirement imposed by section 53(1)(a) (see **E2:2.3.1**).

2.2.3 Implied Restrictive Covenants?

In some situations, a court will infer that A has exercised his power to give B an Easement: in such cases, B is said to have an *implied* Easement (see **G5:2.4** and **G5:2.6**). In contrast, it seems there are *no* specific sets of situations in which a court will infer that A has made a promise to B not to make a particular use of A's land. This reflects an important difference between the Easement and the Restrictive Covenant. In some situations, a right to make some use of a neighbour's land will be essential, or at least very important, in allowing B to make full use of his own land. In contrast, it is very difficult to see define any specific situations in which: (i) a right to *prevent* a neighbour from making a particular use of his land can ever be essential, or even very important, in allowing B to make full use of his own land; and (ii) B does not already have that right simply through holding a Freehold or a Lease (see **G1A:4.1.1**).

Of course, the general principles allowing for a contractual promise to be inferred can apply and may, in a particular case, justify a finding that A has made an implied promise not to make a particular use of his land.

EXAMPLE 6b

A has a Freehold of a large block of flats. A gives B a Lease of one of the flats and B promises not to use that flat for commercial purposes. As B knows, parties acquiring Leases of the other flats in the block also have to make such a promise. A then gives a Lease of the whole of the rest of the building to C, who proceeds to use the building for commercial purposes.

In such a case, B may argue that A had breached an *implied* promise not to allow others to make a commercial use of the block of flats. A had made no such express promise to B: A and B's agreement simply imposed a duty on *B* not to make such a use. Yet, in *Newman v Real Estate Debenture Corporation Ltd*,[62] on which **Example 6b** is based, Atkinson J found in

---

[62] [1940] 1 All ER 131.

B's favour. Given the surrounding circumstances, it was reasonable for B to expect that A was under a duty not to allow a commercial use to be made of any of the flats.[63]

2.3   Later acquisition by B2 of B's Restrictive Covenant

If B has an Easement in A's land, that right will *automatically* pass to B2 whenever B gives B2 a Freehold or Lease of all or any part of, B's land (see **G5:2.1.1(ii)**). It is assumed that: (i) if the Easement would benefit B2's Freehold or Lease; then (ii) B, when giving B2 that Freehold or Lease, must also have exercised his power to give B2 the Easement.

However, that assumption does *not* apply if B has a Restrictive Covenant. Rather, the starting point is that B2 has to show that, on the particular facts of the case, B2 has *in fact* acquired the Restrictive Covenant. As a result, the later acquisition of a Restrictive Covenant is far more complicated than the later acquisition of an Easement.

2.3.1 Assignment

(i) The effect of an assignment

EXAMPLE 1a

The facts are as in **Example 1** above. B then transfers his Freehold of No 32B to B2.

In such a case, there is no obvious reason for B to keep his rights against A, arising as a result of A's promises (a) and (b). However, as those rights benefit No 32B, they may be very useful to B2. As a result, B may well exercise his power to transfer ('assign') those rights to B2. If such assignment occurs, B2 then acquires B's direct rights against A: so B2 can enforce *both* promises (a) and (b) against A. This is simply an example of the principle we examined in **E3:2.1.2**.

EXAMPLE 1b

The facts are as in **Example 1** above. B then transfers his Freehold of No 32B to B2. When doing so, B also transfers his rights against A to B2. A then transfers his Freehold of No 32A to C.

In such a case, we need to distinguish between A's promises (a) and (b). Promise (a) gives rise to a Restrictive Covenant: so, when B transferred that right to B2, B2 acquired a persistent right.[64] As a result, B2 now has a prima facie power to impose a duty on C to comply with promise (a): if C has no defence to B2's pre-existing Restrictive Covenant, C can thus come under a duty to B2 not to use No 32A for a commercial purpose.

In contrast, promise (b) *cannot* give rise to a Restrictive Covenant, as it imposes a positive duty. So, whilst B's transfer of that right to B2 did give B2 a direct, personal right against A, it *cannot* give B2 a pre-existing persistent right. Thus, if B2 wants to show that C

---

[63] Atkinson J's decision was instead based on the idea that: (i) there was a 'scheme of development'; and (ii) in such a scheme, A must be under a mutual duty to B. However, that reasoning is dubious: as we will see in **2.3.3(i)** below, a 'scheme of development' is simply one method in which B2 can later acquire B's initial Restrictive Covenant.

[64] It is important to note that B2 acquires that persistent right because B2 has a Freehold or Lease that benefits from A's duty. B cannot transfer a Restrictive Covenant to someone with no such right.

is under a positive duty to keep C's house in good repair, B2 must show he has a new, direct right against C (see **E3:Example 7b**).

We considered the general rules relating to assignment in **E3:2.1.2**. Those rules are modified in one respect where B assigns a Restrictive Covenant to B2. As well as having the power to transfer that right to B2, B has another, slightly different power. If: (i) B gives B2 a Freehold or Lease of only part of B's land; and (ii) *both* B2's land *and* the land kept by B benefit from the Restrictive Covenant; then (iii) B has the power to duplicate his Restrictive Covenant: ie, *both* to: (i) keep that right for himself; *and* (ii) to give B2 the same right.

(ii) The requirements of an assignment

An assignment of B's Restrictive Covenant to B2 can occur if:

- B expresses his intention to immediately transfer his right to B2, or to duplicate it in favour of B2; *and*
- B expresses that intention in signed writing; *and*
- B2 acquires a Freehold or Lease of land that benefits from A's duty.

The signed writing requirement is imposed by section 53(1)(a) (see **E3:2.3.1**) and section 53(1)(c) of the LPA 1925 (see **F3:2.2**): B's assignment leads to B2 acquiring a persistent right relating to land; and it involves the disposition of a pre-existing persistent right. This requirement for signed writing causes few problems in practice: B's power to assign is almost always exercised as part of a formal transaction in which B gives B2 a Freehold or Lease of all or part of B's land.[65]

Where he relies on an assignment, B2 is still subject to the general rule that, to have a Restrictive Covenant, he must have land that benefits from A's duty (see **1.2** above). Therefore, B2 will have to show that the Restrictive Covenant benefits specific, identifiable land of which B2 now has a Freehold or Lease.[66] This means that B cannot: (i) sell all of his land; and *then* (ii) attempt to assign his Restrictive Covenant.[67] As a Restrictive Covenant must benefit some land of B, that right ends when B loses all his land.[68]

(iii) Implied assignment? Section 62 of the LPA 1925

We have seen that, in a case such as **Example 1a**, there is every reason for B to assign his Restrictive Covenant to B2. This raises the question of whether we can assume that *whenever*: (i) B gives B2 a Freehold or Lease of all or part of B's land; and (ii) the land acquired by B2 benefits from the Restrictive Covenant; then (iii) B also intends to exercise his power to assign his Restrictive Covenant to B2. Certainly, such an inference is made where B has an Easement (see **G5:2.1.1(ii)**).

---

[65] It was argued in **C3:6.3** that the transfer of a pre-existing persistent right, like the transfer of a pre-existing personal right (see **C3:5.1.2**), should also require notice to be given to A. Such a requirement would cause no problem in this context: B2 will necessarily give notice to A or C when attempting to enforce his right.

[66] See eg *Miles v Easter* [1933] Ch 611 (the official name of that case is *Re Union of London and Smith's Bank Ltd's Conveyance* but it is usually referred to as *Miles v Easter* and that name will be used here); *Newton Abbot Co-operative Society Ltd v Williamson & Treadgold Ltd* [1952] Ch 286.

[67] See eg *Chambers v Randall* [1923] 1 Ch 149. See too *Miles v Easter* [1933] Ch 611.

[68] If B sells only part of his land to B2, then B can retain the Restrictive Covenant if it benefits B's remaining land. B could then later try to assign that Restrictive Covenant to B2. However, it seems that this is impossible as, once B has sold part of his land, the Restrictive Covenant is regarded as a right benefiting B's remaining land and so can only be assigned to B3, a party acquiring all or a part of B's remaining land.

In the case of an Easement, that assumption is reflected in section 62 of the LPA 1925:

A conveyance of land shall be deemed to include and by virtue of this Act operate to convey all . . . liberties, privileges, easements, rights and advantages whatsoever, appertaining or reputed to appertain to [the Freehold or Lease given to B2].

Can this section apply to the Restrictive Covenant as well as the Easement? The former, unlike the latter, is not expressly mentioned. However, it can be argued that a Restrictive Covenant counts as a right 'appertaining or reputed to appertain' to land transferred by B to B2. After all, as a Restrictive Covenant must enhance B's original Freehold or Lease, it seems fair to say that such a right does 'appertain' to B's land.

However, the courts have rejected this interpretation of section 62, holding that it *cannot* be used to infer an assignment of a Restrictive Covenant. Some fairly unconvincing explanations have been given, but the key point is that section 62 cannot apply where B2 claims a persistent right: it is impossible to say that a Restrictive Covenant can ever be *conveyed* by B to B2. The verb 'convey' refers to the exercise by B of a power to give B2 a *property right* (see **E3:n7**). This is why, for section 62 to apply at all, B2 needs to show that B has exercised his power to give B2 a property right, such as a Freehold or Lease: if B has not done so, there is no 'conveyance' into which a right can be implied (see **G5:5.2.1**).

(iv) Problems with assignment?

In **E3:2.1.2(iii)**, we saw some of the problems a party may have if he wants to rely on an assignment. The first problem also applies here: assignment can be difficult to prove if B's land changes hands a number of times. For example, B3 will need to show both that: (i) B assigned his Restrictive Covenant to B2; *and* (ii) B2 then assigned that right to B3. In contrast, the second and third problems do *not* arise here: exceptionally, B does have the power to assign a Restrictive Covenant even when keeping part of his land; and it seems B2 *can* claim money based on the loss caused to him by any breach of the Restrictive Covenant.

SUMMARY of G6:2.3.1

It is possible for B to assign a Restrictive Covenant to B2. In **E3:2.1.2**, we saw that if B has a direct personal right, he generally has the power to transfer that right to B2. However, special rules apply to the assignment of a Restrictive Covenant. First, as well as transferring that right to B2, B can also duplicate the right. If: (i) B gives B2 only part of B's land; *and* (ii) each of B's retained land and B2's land benefits from the Restrictive Covenant; then B can *both* (i) retain his Restrictive Covenant; and (ii) give that right to B2. The weakness of assignment comes from the facts that: (i) if B's land changes hands a number of times, a Restrictive Covenant must be assigned on each transfer: there must be a 'chain of assignments'; and (ii) each such assignment must be proved—section 62 of the LPA 1925 does *not* allow a court to assume that an assignment has occurred.

2.3.2 Annexation

(i) The effect of annexation

> **EXAMPLE 1c**
>
> The facts are as in **Example 1** above. When A makes promises (a) and (b), A and B make clear that the promises are made 'to, and for the benefit of, B and all future owners of all or any part of B's land'. B then transfers his Freehold of No 32B to B2.

If B has a right against A, that right can be *annexed* to B's Freehold or Lease (see **E3:2.1.3**). This has occurred in **Example 1c**: B's rights against A, arising as a result of promises (a) and (b) have thus become part and parcel of B's Freehold. Hence, when B transfers that Freehold to B2, B2 *automatically* acquires B's rights against A. There is no need for B2 to show that B assigned those rights to B2.

> **EXAMPLE 1d**
>
> The facts are as in **Example 1c** above. B transfers his Freehold of No 32B to B2. A then transfers his Freehold of No 32A to C.

In such a case, we need to distinguish between A's promises (a) and (b). Promise (a) gives rise to a Restrictive Covenant. That persistent right has been annexed to B's Freehold, and so when B transfers his Freehold to B2, B2 also acquires a persistent right. As a result, B2 now has a prima facie power to impose a duty on C to comply with promise (a): if C has no defence to B2's pre-existing Restrictive Covenant, C can thus come under a duty to B2 not to use No 32A for a commercial purpose.

In contrast, promise (b) *cannot* give rise to a Restrictive Covenant, as it imposes a positive duty. So, whilst the annexation of that right did give B2 a direct, personal right against A,[69] it *cannot* give B2 a pre-existing persistent right. If B2 wants to show that C is under a positive duty to keep C's house in good repair, B2 must show he has a new, direct right against C.

We considered the general rules relating to annexation in **E3:2.1.3**. Those rules apply in exactly the same way to a Restrictive Covenant. There is a clear difference between assignment and annexation. When B2 claims to have acquired a Restrictive Covenant by assignment, B2 focuses on his dealings with B: he argues that, when giving B2 a Freehold or Lease, B also exercised his power to assign the Restrictive Covenant to B2. Annexation, in contrast, focuses on the *initial* creation of the Restrictive Covenant. B2 argues that, when A made the original promise to B, A and B also exercised their power to annex the Restrictive Covenant to B's Freehold. If that annexation has occurred, *all* future holders of that Freehold will acquire the Restrictive Covenant: there is no longer any need for a party such as B3 to prove a 'chain of assignments'

(ii) The requirements of annexation

As we saw in **E3:2.1.3(ii)**, there are four requirements for annexation:

- A is under a duty to B; *and*

---

[69] See eg *Smith & Snipes Hall Farm Ltd v River Douglas Catchment Board* [1949] 2 KB 500 (**E3:Example 3**).

- A's duty benefits B's land; *and*
- A and B intend, when creating A's duty, that future owners of B's land will automatically acquire B's right;[70] *and*
- The land to which B's right is annexed can be easily ascertained by looking at the agreement between A and B.[71]

As we are assuming that A's promise to B counts as a Restrictive Covenant, we know that the first and second requirements have been satisfied. In practice, then, there are two requirements for the annexation of a Restrictive Covenant:

- *Intention*—A and B must intend that future owners of B's land will automatically acquire B's Restrictive Covenant; *and*
- *Identification*—by looking at the agreement between A and B, it must be possible to easily ascertain the land to which B's Restrictive Covenant is annexed.

(iii) The intention requirement: section 78 of the LPA 1925

As we noted in E3:2.1.3(ii), section 78 of the LPA 1925 can be important in establishing that *one particular* requirement of annexation (the intention requirement) has been satisfied. The section states that:

> (1) A covenant relating to any land of [B] shall be deemed to be made with [B] and his successors in title and the persons deriving title under [B], and shall have effect as if such successors and other persons were expressed.
>
> For the purposes of this subsection in connection with covenants restrictive of the user of land 'successors in title' shall be deemed to include the owners and occupiers for the time being of the land of [B] intended to be benefited.[72]

The crucial point about section 78 is that: (i) where A makes a promise relating to B's land (such as a Restrictive Covenant); then (ii) that promise is assumed to be made not just with B but also with *future owners* of B's land. Therefore, even if A and B do not make clear that A's initial promise is for the benefit of B *and* future owners of B's land, the intention requirement of annexation can still be satisfied.

Surprisingly, the significance of section 78 remained hidden for a long time. Its effect in allowing a court to assume that A and B intended to annex was only spotted in 1979: in the judgment of Brightman LJ in *Federated Homes Ltd v Mill Lodge Properties Ltd*.[73] That judgment proved controversial,[74] not least because it meant that, for over 50 years, lawyers had held a mistaken view of the effect of section 78.[75] Nonetheless, it seems clear that section 78 *does* allow a court to assume that A and B intended to exercise their power to annex: section 78 reads into A's promise words which, if expressly used by the parties, would

---

[70] The promise thus cannot be one that is intended to be purely personal to B.

[71] See eg *Marquess of Zetland v Driver* [1939] Ch 1 at 8; *per* Chadwick LJ in *Crest Nicholson Residential (South) Ltd v McAllister* [2004] 1 WLR 2409 at [30]–[34].

[72] S 78(2) goes on to state that s 78 applies to covenants made after 1 January 1926; and that the repeal of s 58 of the Conveyancing Act 1881 does not affect the operation of covenants to which that section applied, ie, covenants made before 1 January 1926.

[73] [1980] 1 WLR 594.

[74] See eg Newsom (1981) 97 *LQR* 32; (1982) 98 *LQR* 202; and [1982] *JPL* 295.

[75] Although that point should not be decisive: as we noted in section G5:2.5.4(i), when considering the effect of s 62 of the LPA 1925, the fact that a mistake has been made in the past is no excuse for, and much less a justification for, repeating the mistake in the future.

clearly show an intention that future owners of B's land will automatically acquire B's Restrictive Covenant.

However, it would be very dangerous to assume that section 78 makes *annexation itself* automatic. It merely allows a court to assume that the intention requirement has been satisfied. Section 78 provides no help as to the *identification* requirement: to prove annexation, B2 must also show that: (i) the Restrictive Covenant has been annexed to *particular land*; and that (ii) that land can be easily ascertained by looking at the agreement between A and B.

(iv) The identification requirement: annexation to particular land

EXAMPLE 7a

B has a Freehold. B decides to split up his land: he keeps half of it (No 32B) and sells a Freehold of the other half to A (No 32A). B runs a newsagents on No 32 B. The contract of sale between A and B states that 'A promises B that neither A nor future owners of A's land will run a newsagents business from the land sold by B to A.' B then sells his Freehold of No 32B to B2. A then sells his Freehold of No 32A to C. C tells B2 that he plans to set up a newsagents on No 32A.

Does B2 have a pre-existing Restrictive Covenant that he can assert against C? As there has been no assignment from B to B2, B may try to rely on annexation. The intention requirement has been met. The express terms of A's promise to B do not show an intention to annex; but section 78 can be used to assume that A and B had that intention. However, the identification requirement causes a problem for B2. Can B2 show that, by looking at the agreement between A and B, a court can easily ascertain the land to which B's Restrictive Covenant is annexed?

This promise is made to B and makes no express mention of future owners of B's land. It can count as a Restrictive Covenant if, by looking at the surrounding circumstances, we can say that the promise benefits, and that A and B intended the promise to benefit, some land of B (see **1.2** above). So, if B runs a newsagents from his land, it will be easy to say that B has land that benefits, and was intended to benefit, from A's promise. However, the Restrictive Covenant can only be annexed to land if A's promise *identifies* the particular piece of land to which the Restrictive Covenant is to be annexed. And there is no such identification here. There is nothing *in A's promise* to tell us what land, if any, the Restrictive Covenant is annexed to.[76]

It is therefore important to distinguish two separate issues:

1. To count as a Restrictive Covenant, A's duty must benefit, and be intended to benefit, some land of B. In resolving this issue, the courts are happy to look at the surrounding circumstances: there is no need for A and B expressly to identify the particular land that is intended to benefit from A's promise (see **1.2** above).[77] This test is part of the **content question**.

---

[76] See eg *per* Chadwick LJ in *Crest Nicholson Residential (South) Ltd v McAllister* [2004] 1 WLR 2409 at [45]–[54].
[77] See eg *Newton Abbot Co-operative Society v Williamson & Treadgold Ltd* [1952] Ch 286.

2. To be annexed, B's Restrictive Covenant must be annexed to a particular piece of land. In resolving this issue, the courts have refused to rely *solely* on surrounding circumstances: A and B must ensure that A's promise contains enough *express information* to enable a court easily to identify the land to which the Restrictive Covenant is annexed. This test is part of the **acquisition question**: if annexation occurs, B2 can acquire B's pre-existing Restrictive Covenant.

It should be emphasised that, for annexation to occur, A's promise does not need to give a completely unambiguous definition of the land to which B's Restrictive Covenant is annexed. Rather, the key thing is that, for annexation to occur, the land to which the Restrictive Covenant is annexed must be 'defined so as to be easily ascertainable'.[78] For example, if A's promise is said to be for the benefit of 'B's land at Croydon' a court will look at other evidence, including the surrounding circumstances, to pin down the definition of that land.[79] The point is that, in doing so, the court is not going *solely* on the surrounding circumstances; rather, it is using, and taking its lead from, the definition set out in A's promise.

To return to **Example 7**, B2 seems to face a clear problem. There is nothing in the *express* terms of A initial promise that can define the land to which B's Restrictive Covenant is to be annexed. Therefore, annexation *cannot* occur in **Example 7**.

That result may seem harsh on B2 and, perhaps, overly technical. This point is addressed by Chadwick LJ in *Crest Nicholson Residential (South) Ltd v McAllister*.[80] His Lordship justified the requirement by pointing out that C needs to be able to discover *who*, if anyone, has a Restrictive Covenant relating to his land. So, if A initially gave B a Restrictive Covenant, C needs to be able to discover *what particular land, if any*, the Restrictive Covenant was annexed to. This will be particularly important if B has since split up his land and sold it to a number of different purchasers: C will need to know if: (i) the Restrictive Covenant was annexed to *every part* of B's land (and so has passed to all the new purchasers of parts of B's land); *or* (ii) it was instead only annexed to *particular parts* of B's land (so that only some of the new purchasers have acquired the Restrictive Covenant). And, if (ii) is the case, C will need to know *which* particular parts of B's land the Restrictive Covenant was annexed to. This will be particularly important if, for example, C wants to use his land in a way *contrary* to the Restrictive Covenant: C then needs to: (i) discover any parties who can enforce that Restrictive Covenant; and (ii) negotiate with each of those parties to see if each is willing (perhaps in return for payment) to allow C to act contrary to the Restrictive Covenant.

C's task will be much easier if the initial promise between A and B allows C easily to ascertain the land to which the Restrictive Covenant was annexed.[81] In contrast, if A's promise does *not* identify the land to which the Restrictive Covenant is annexed, C will face problems: he will have to try to discover, from surrounding circumstances, the land to which A and B presumably intended to annex B's Restrictive Covenant. And, in *Crest*

---

[78] See *Marquess of Zetland v Driver* [1939] Ch 1 at 8, approved by Chadwick LJ in *Crest Nicholson Residential (South) Ltd v McAllister* [2004] 1 WLR 2409 at [32]–[34].

[79] See *Whitgift Homes Ltd v Stocks* [2001] EWCA Civ 1732, approved by Chadwick LJ in *Crest Nicholson Residential (South) Ltd v McAllister* [2004] 1 WLR 2409 at [49].

[80] [2004] 1 WLR 2409 at [34].

[81] C will have a copy of this promise either because: (i) it was given to him by A when C acquired the land; or (ii) because it was filed with the Land Registry when B defensively registered his Restrictive Covenant.

Nicholson, Chadwick LJ thought that it would be unfair and 'oppressive' to impose that guessing game on C.[82]

It thus seems then that the courts' approach to the identification requirement of annexation is designed to provide *certainty* and *publicity* to C. This makes the requirement quite easy to justify: after all, the need for such certainty and publicity is recognised throughout the land law system.[83] Indeed, the requirement has a very similar role to a formality rule: it regulates A and B's exercise of their power to annex. As that power can impose a burden on C (by increasing the number of parties that can enforce B's Restrictive Covenant) it seems right that it should be limited by a rule that allows C more easily to discover the identity of anyone acquiring a right as a result of the annexation.[84] Once again, the **basic tension** of the property law system is apparent. On the one hand, annexation helps protect a future owner of B's land: his Freehold or Lease is enhanced by a right to prevent A or C from making a particular use of nearby land. On the other hand, annexation imposes a greater burden on A or C: it makes it easier for parties other than B to acquire the Restrictive Covenant.

(v) The identification requirement in practice

It is clear that annexation does not take place in the abstract: a Restrictive Covenant must be annexed to *particular land*. Moreover, annexation can take different forms, depending on which land the Restrictive Covenant is annexed to. In fact, there are four main forms of annexation:

Option 1   A and B can annex the Restrictive Covenant to *each and every part* of some land of B (eg, to each and every part of all of the land retained by B). So, if B2 acquires a Freehold or Lease of *any* part of B's land, B2 will acquire the Restrictive Covenant.

Option 2   A and B can annex the Restrictive Covenant to the *entirety* of some land of B (eg, to the entirety of all of the land retained by B). So, B2 can rely on the annexation *only* if he acquires a Freehold or Lease of *all* of that land; or of *substantially* all of that land.

Option 3   A and B can annex the Restrictive Covenant to *land of B continuing to remain unsold by B and any land sold by B with the benefit of the Restrictive Covenant*. So, B2 will only acquire the Restrictive Covenant if B chooses to give B2 that right. However, if B does choose to do so, the Restrictive Covenant will become annexed to B2's land and hence will pass automatically to B3.[85]

Option 4   A and B can annex the Restrictive Covenant to *land of B continuing to remain unsold by B*. This is similar to **Option 3**: B2 will only acquire the Restrictive Covenant if B chooses to give B2 that right. The difference is that, if B does

---

[82] [2004] 1 WLR 2409 at [34].

[83] Law Com Consultation Paper No 186 (2008), 7.36 also recognises the need for the benefiting land to be clearly identified.

[84] A and B's exercise of their power to annex is not regulated by any specific formality rule; but annexation can only occur as part of A's original promise, and s 53(1)(a) of the LPA 1925 means that promise must be made in signed writing.

[85] In theory, A and B could annex the Restrictive Covenant to land of B continuing to remain unsold by B and *the entirety* of any land sold by B with the benefit of the Restrictive Covenant. If B then sold land to B2 with the benefit of the Restrictive Covenant, annexation to the entirety of B2's land would occur. In that case, B3 would automatically acquire the Restrictive Covenant only if he acquired a Freehold or Lease of *all* or substantially all of B2's land.

choose to do so, the Restrictive Covenant will *not* become annexed to B2's land, and so B3 will have to rely on a further assignment from B2.

Option 4 seems, in effect, to deny annexation: B2 and B3 each need to rely on assignment to acquire B's Restrictive Covenant. Technically, however, it does count as a form of annexation: it seems that if B2 acquires his right from B by a means *other* than a sale (eg, in B's will) B2 will automatically acquire the Restrictive Covenant.

EXAMPLE 8a

B has a Freehold. In 1930, B decides to split up his land: he keeps half of it (the 'Blandings Estate') and sells a Freehold of the other half to A. In the contract of sale A promises not to make a commercial use of A's land. B's retained land is then divided up and sold a number of times: by 2008, B7 has a Freehold of a small part of the initial Blandings Estate (No 32B), bordering the land sold to A back in 1930. A's Freehold is now held by C, who plans to build a large retail centre on that land.

In such a case, it may be very difficult for B7 to rely on a chain of assignments of B's initial Restrictive Covenant. So, B7 may turn to annexation:

> **Option 1** If B7 can show that A's initial promise was annexed to *each and every part* of the 'Blandings Estate', B7 will have that Restrictive Covenant: he does have part of B's land.
>
> **Option 2** If B7 can show (this is quite unlikely in practice) that A and B annexed the Restrictive Covenant to the *entirety* of the particular part of the land now owned by B7 (No 32B), B7 will have the Restrictive Covenant: he does have the entirety of that particular part.
>
> **Option 3** If A and B annexed the Restrictive Covenant to *land of B remaining unsold by B and to land sold by B with the benefit of the Restrictive Covenant*, B7 will need to find someone (eg, B2) who, in the past: (i) bought land from B that includes the land currently held by B7 (or part of that land); *and* (ii) was given the benefit of the Restrictive Covenant by B when buying that land. That earlier sale to B2 with the benefit of the Restrictive Covenant will mean that the Restrictive Covenant is annexed to each and every part of B2's land, so that it automatically passes to anyone, such as B7, who now has all or part of B2's land.

However, if A and B adopted **Option 2** and annexed the Restrictive Covenant to the entirety of *all* of B's retained land[86] (ie, to the entirety of the Blandings Estate), then B7, as he only has *part* of that land, cannot rely on annexation. Similarly, if A and B annexed the Restrictive Covenant only to *land of B remaining unsold by B* (**Option 4**), annexation will not assist B7.

(vi) Annexation in practice

(a) Avoiding or limiting annexation

It is therefore clear that, when A makes an initial promise giving B a Restrictive

---

[86] Or to the entirety of any piece of B's land not now owned by B7.

Covenant, A and B have some important choices to make. First, there is the question of whether annexation should take place *at all*. If the answer to that question is 'Yes', there is the question of *what land* the Restrictive Covenant should be annexed to. It may seem that, from B's point of view, the preferable option is for the Restrictive Covenant to be annexed to *each and every part* of B's land. This would seem to increase the value of B's land, by ensuring that a purchaser of *any* part of that land benefiting from the Restrictive Covenant will also acquire that right. However, B may have sound financial reasons for not wishing to annex a Restrictive Covenant to each and every part of his land.

EXAMPLE 9

B has a Freehold of a large piece of land. He decides to divide it up and sell a Freehold of half of his land to A. As part of the contract of sale A makes a promise that neither A nor future owners of A's land will use that land for a commercial purpose. B then divides up his remaining land: he keeps part of it but sells other parts to B2, B3 and B4. A's Freehold is now held by C, who plans to build a large retail centre on that land.

C may well be prepared to pay a substantial sum of money (let us say up to £500,000) to release any Restrictive Covenant that prevents the development. If A's Restrictive Covenant is *not* annexed to each and every part of B's land, B may be the *only* person with that Restrictive Covenant. Therefore, if C is prepared to pay £500,000 to be able to proceed, he may well pay that entire sum to B. In contrast, if A's Restrictive Covenant *is* annexed to each and every part of B's land, each of B2, B3 and B4 will *also* be able to demand money from C for the release of the Restrictive Covenant. As a result, each owner will only be able to demand a smaller sum from C. B may thus end up receiving only £125,000 from C; and, if just one of B2, B3 or B4 refuses to release the Restrictive Covenant, B will get nothing.

So, in a case such as **Example 9**, B may wish to avoid annexation to each and every part of his land, preferring instead to retain control over the Restrictive Covenant. There are two ways in which B may keep that control. First, B can ensure that *no annexation* occurs. Following the Court of Appeal's decision in *Federated Homes*, some concern was expressed that annexation might be compulsory: section 78 of the LPA 1925, unlike section 79, contain no 'contrary intention' provision.[87] However, that fear is misplaced. It must be remembered that section 78 deals with only *one* of the requirements for annexation. If A and B do not intend to annex, then A's promise to B will *not* identify any particular land to which B's Restrictive Covenant can be annexed: as a result, the identification requirement of annexation will not be satisfied.

In *Roake v Chada*,[88] for example, A's promise was made with B

but so that this covenant shall not enure for the benefit of any owner or subsequent purchaser of any part of [B's] Sudbury Court Estate at Wembley unless the benefit of this covenant shall be expressly assigned.

In such a case, no annexation can occur: there is no identified land to which B's Restrictive Covenant can be annexed.[89] In fact, in *Roake*, B's Restrictive Covenant did prevent A from

---

[87] This was one of the arguments made by Newsom against the *Federated Homes* decision: (1981) 97 *LQR* 32; (1982) 98 *LQR* 202

[88] [1984] 1 WLR 40.

[89] The reasoning adopted by Judge Paul Baker QC at 46 differs from the analysis set out here. The judge stated

developing the land, and so B may have had financial reasons for wishing to keep exclusive control of that Restrictive Covenant.

Alternatively, A and B can limit the impact of annexation by defining the land to which the Restrictive Covenant is annexed in a narrow way. For example, in *Crest Nicholson Residential (South) Ltd v McAllister*,[90] a number of the promises considered by the Court of Appeal were based on **Option 3**: B's Restrictive Covenant was annexed only to 'land of B remaining unsold by B and to land sold by B with the benefit of the Restrictive Covenant'. Technically, annexation has occurred; but, the Restrictive Covenant is not automatically annexed to land sold by B.[91] Crucially, B thus retains exclusive control of the Restrictive Covenant: B2 only acquires its benefit if B *chooses* to pass it on.

(b) Annexation and ambiguity

EXAMPLE 8b

The facts are as in **Example 8a**. In the contract of sale to A, A's promise that neither A nor future owners of A's land will make a commercial use of A's land is made 'for the benefit of the Blandings Estate'.

In such a case, we need to know if A and B have gone for **Option 1** or **Option 2**. If the former: (i) B's Restrictive Covenant is annexed to *each and every part* of the Blandings Estate; and so (ii) B7, as a Freehold owner of part of B's land, acquires that Restrictive Covenant. If the latter: (i) B's Restrictive Covenant may be annexed only to the *entirety* of the Blandings Estate; and so (ii) B7, as he has only *part* of that land, cannot acquire that Restrictive Covenant through annexation. The problem is that the express content of A's promise is ambiguous: it is consistent with both **Option 1** and **Option 2**.

In some cases, the surrounding circumstances will assist in resolving the ambiguity. For example if, in **Example 8b**, it was clear when A made his promise that B intended soon to sell off parts off the Blandings Estate, it would make no sense for the Restrictive Covenant to be annexed only to the entirety of that land: so **Option 1** must be more plausible.[92] In

---

that even if s 78 means that A's promise is deemed to be with B and future owners of B's land, that promise still has to be interpreted in its context: 'one has to consider the covenant as a whole to determine its true effect'. The problem with that reasoning is that it reads into s 78 something that is clearly not there: a contrary intention provision. The entirely sensible result in *Roake* can instead be achieved by different means: by concentrating on the failure to fulfil the identification requirement.

[90] [2004] 1 WLR 2409.

[91] The reasoning adopted by Chadwick LJ differs from the analysis set out here and focuses instead on the second sentence of s 78: 'For the purposes of this subsection in connection with covenants restrictive of the user of land "successors in title" shall be deemed to include the owners and occupiers for the time being of the land of [B] intended to be benefited.' The argument is that, in a case such as *Roake*, B2 is not an owner of any land *intended to be benefited* by the Restrictive Covenant and so does *not* count as a 'successor in title' who can acquire B's Restrictive Covenant by annexation. That reasoning is unconvincing and unnecessarily complex. S 78 states that the term 'successor in title' *shall be deemed to include* a later owner or occupier of the land intended to be benefited. Yet Chadwick LJ seems to interpret that as meaning that B2 cannot be a 'successor in title' *unless* he is a later owner or occupier of the land intended to be benefited. The logic of this is dubious: for example, if a statute says that the term 'motor vehicles' includes electric scooters, that does not mean that only electric scooters can count as motor vehicles.

[92] See eg *Page v King's Parade Properties Ltd* (1967) 20 P & CR 710. On this basis, the decision in *re Jeff's Transfer (No 2)* [1966] 1 WLR 841 is probably incorrect: the court held that A's promise for the benefit of the 'Chorleywood Estate' caused an annexation only to the entirety of B's land; but, as is pointed out by Newsom in *Preston & Newsom's Restrictive Covenants Affecting Freehold Land* (9th edn, 1998), 2-24, B's development plans meant that A's promise probably should have been interpreted as causing annexation to *each and every* part of B's land.

other cases, where those circumstances provide no assistance, we simply need a default rule to deal with the ambiguity. In the past, that rule seems to have been in favour of **Option 2**: if A's promise refers only to the 'Blandings Estate', then B's Restrictive Covenant is annexed only to the *entirety* of that land. However, the more modern rule is the opposite one.[93] **Option 1** is to be favoured: it was adopted by Brightman LJ in *Federated Homes*, stating that, *once* a Restrictive Covenant is annexed to land, 'prima facie it is annexed to every part thereof, unless the contrary clearly appear'.[94]

SUMMARY of G6:2.3.2

As we saw in **E3:2.1.3**, annexation applies only in relation to land: it allows A and B to make a particular right part and parcel of B's Freehold or Lease of particular land. This anomalous power to annex responds to the needs of practical convenience: it provides a simple way for a future owner of B's land to acquire a right without needing to rely on a chain of assignments. The general annexation requirements apply to a Restrictive Covenant just as they apply to other rights. Where a Restrictive Covenant is concerned, the two crucial questions concern *intention* and *identification*: (i) did A and B *intend* at least some future owners of all or part of B's land to automatically acquire B's Restrictive Covenant; and (ii) does A's promise to B adequately *identify* the particular land to which the Restrictive Covenant is annexed. The first requirement is simple to satisfy: section 78 of the LPA 1925 means that A and B will, in effect, be deemed to have the necessary intention to annex. The second requirement is more difficult: A's promise must allow the court and, more importantly, C, to easily ascertain the land to which the Restrictive Covenant is annexed. If annexation does occur, it is vital to ask to what particular land the Restrictive Covenant has been annexed. For example, if the Restrictive Covenant is annexed only to: (i) the entirety of B's land; or (ii) only to land remaining unsold by B; then (iii) a later purchaser of *part* of B's land will not be able to rely on annexation.

2.3.3 Schemes of development

(i) The effect of a scheme of development

EXAMPLE 10a

B has a Freehold of a large plot of land. B divides that land into three smaller plots and builds a house on each: Nos 2, 3 and 4 Acacia Gardens. B sells a Freehold of plot No 2 to B2. As part of the contract of sale, B2 promises not to use that land for commercial purposes. B then sells a Freehold of plot No 3 to B3, ensuring that B3 makes the same promise. B then sells a Freehold of plot No 4 to B4, ensuring that B4 makes the same promise.

It is clear that B's goal, in effect, is to set up a 'local law' governing all three plots and guaranteeing the residential character of that area. To achieve this goal, B wants to give B2, B3 and B4, and all future owners of those plots, a Restrictive Covenant in relation to each of the neighbouring plots. However, B faces a problem. Assignment and annexation both deal with the *later* acquisition of a Restrictive Covenant: so either method can give B3 a

---

[93] For example, see s 79A of the Property Law Act 1958 (Victoria), which, in that Australian jurisdiction, establishes a presumption of annexation to each and every part of the benefited land.

[94] [1980] 1 WLR 594 at 606.

Restrictive Covenant against B2; and B4 a Restrictive Covenant against both B2 and B3. But B also wants to give B2 the benefit of the Restrictive Covenants arising from the promises of B3 and B4; and B3 the benefit of the Restrictive Covenant arising as a result of B4's promise. The problem is that those promises were made *after* B2 (or B3) acquired his land from B. Second, there is a more severe problem with B4's final promise. When B sells to B4, he sells his last plot and so no longer has any land that can benefit from B4's promise. It seems then that B4's promise may not pass the **content question**: it cannot give rise to a Restrictive Covenant as it does not benefit any land of B.

It is just about possible for B, using assignment and annexation, to get around these two problems. However, once again, the rules relating to the Restrictive Covenant have been adapted to the needs of practical convenience. This has occurred through the recognition of a *scheme of development*. Where such a scheme arises (as in **Example 10a**), each party acquiring a Freehold or Lease within the scheme (i) acquires the benefit of one or more Restrictive Covenants against all the other plots within the scheme; and (ii) is subject to those Restrictive Covenants in favour of all other plots within the scheme.

(ii) The requirements of a scheme of development

At one point, the requirements for a scheme of development were fairly strict.[95] For example, the land within the scheme had to be sold by the same person. There would thus be a problem if B began the sales, but then died and was replaced by B2 (eg, the person to whom B left his land in his will). Further, before beginning the sales, B had to have an explicit plan to divide the land within the scheme into distinct lots and to sell subject to specific Restrictive Covenants. Those restrictive rules recognised that a scheme of development is an anomalous concept, and should arise only where clearly intended. However, it is doubtful that those rules really allowed the scheme of development to do its job in promoting practical convenience. After all, if B had doubts as to whether his plans counted as a scheme of development, he could well resort to more complex and artificial means of achieving his goal of establishing a 'local law'.[96]

As a result of these concerns, the requirements of a scheme of development have been relaxed. A scheme of development will now arise if:

- A number of Freeholds or Leases are acquired with the common intention that each party will take the benefit and burden of a set of mutual Restrictive Covenants; *and*
- The land covered by the scheme is clearly identified.

The focus of the courts is thus where it always should have been: on the question of whether each purchaser intended to take the benefit and burden of a mutual set of Restrictive Covenants.[97] The mere fact of B's selling off his land to a number of purchasers, each of whom make identical promises not to use their land in a particular way, will not, *by itself*, give rise to a scheme of development.[98] For the parties may simply intend that *B* (and

---

[95] See eg *Elliston v Reacher* [1908] 2 Ch 374 (confirmed by the Court of Appeal [1908] 2 Ch 665).

[96] For example, by giving the Freehold over the plots to a company, selling long Leases of each plot, and then giving each purchaser shares in the company (cf **Example 3** above).

[97] See *per* Stamp J in *re Dolphin's Conveyance* [1970] Ch 654 at 661–4.

[98] In *Jamaica Mutual Life Assurance Society v Hillsborough Ltd* [1989] 1 WLR 1101 at 1108, the Privy Council approved Goff J's comment in *Re Wembley Park Estate Co Ltd's Transfer* [1968] Ch 491 at 502–3, that to imply 'a building scheme from no more than a common vendor and the existence of common covenants' would be going much too far.

possibly future owners of B's land) will acquire the Restrictive Covenant. For a scheme of development to arise, B and each purchaser must intend that: (i) the purchaser's promise will give rise to a Restrictive Covenant *not just* for B *but also* for owners of other land in the scheme; and (ii) that each purchaser will acquire a Restrictive Covenant over all the other land in the scheme.

If such intention *is* present, then a scheme of development can arise even if the plots have not all been sold by B;[99] and even if B did not divide all the land into plots before beginning to sell.[100] It is also worth noting that a scheme of development can exist even if one or more of the plots is subject to a different Restrictive Covenant: within the local law, a plot can be subject to a different burden as long as an owner of the plot has the benefit of a Restrictive Covenant over other land in the scheme.[101]

The concept of a scheme of development, like annexation, is an anomalous one. It imposes an additional burden on B4: B4's promise, when buying his land from B, will allow a Restrictive Covenant to be acquired not just by B and future owners of B's land, but also by any pre-existing owner of land within the scheme of development (eg, B2 and B3). It is therefore crucial that B4 should be able to tell what he is getting into when making his promise. In particular, B4 (as well as C, a future owner of B4's land) must be able to identify the *scope* of the scheme, so that he can discover *who* has a Restrictive Covenant in relation to B4's land. Therefore, the land covered by the scheme must be clearly defined.[102] If the boundaries of the scheme are unclear, then B4 (as well as C, a future owner of B4's land) may be unsure as to who has a right to prevent him making a particular use of his land. This would cause the very 'oppression' noted by Chadwick LJ in *Crest Nicholson*.[103] Hence, just as annexation can occur only if A's promise to B identifies the land to which the Restrictive Covenant is annexed, so a scheme of development can exist only if the agreement between B and each of the purchasers identifies the land covered by the scheme.[104]

(iii) Special consequences of a scheme of development?

EXAMPLE 10b

The facts are as in **Example 10a**. After B2, B3 and B4 has each bought his plot, B2 then buys B3's Freehold.

---

[99] See *re Dolphin's Conveyance* [1970] Ch 654.

[100] See *Baxter v Four Oaks Properties Ltd* [1965] Ch 816.

[101] See eg *Elliston v Reacher* [1908] 2 Ch 374 at 384, where Parker J notes that the restrictions imposed on each plot of land can vary in detail as to particular lots; in *Emile Elias & Co Ltd v Pine Groves Ltd* [1993] 1 WLR 305 at 311 the Privy Council also noted that there is no requirement for all the lots in the scheme to be subject to identical Restrictive Covenants.

[102] See *per* Lord Jauncey in *Jamaica Mutual Life Assurance Society v Hillsborough Ltd* [1989] 1 WLR 1101 at 1106: 'It is now well established that there are two prerequisites of a building scheme namely: (1) the identification of the land to which the scheme relates, and (2) an acceptance by each purchaser of part of the lands from the common vendor that the benefit of the covenants into which he has entered will enure to the vendor and to others deriving title from him and that he correspondingly will enjoy the benefit of covenants entered into by other purchasers of part of the land.' See too *per* Buckley LJ in *Reid v Bickerstaff* [1909] 2 Ch 305 at 323.

[103] [2004] 1 WLR 2409 at [34].

[104] See eg *Reid v Bickerstaff* [1909] 2 Ch 305 at 319 and, more recently, *Emile Elias & Co Ltd v Pine Groves Ltd* [1993] 1 WLR 305 at 310–11. On this view, a court should adopt the same test as applies to annexation: it is not enough for the scope of the scheme to be established *simply* by reference to the surrounding circumstances.

Of course, B2 cannot have a Restrictive Covenant over his own land. The normal rule is that if: (i) B2 has a Restrictive Covenant against a Freehold of B3; and (ii) B2 acquires B3's Freehold; then (iii) B2's Restrictive Covenant is terminated (see **1.5** above).[105] So, if B2 later splits up the land again, by, for example, selling off No 3 to C, B2's Restrictive Covenant over plot No 3 will *not* revive. However, a special rule applies to a scheme of development. It seems that, if B2 does redivide the land, the Restrictive Covenant *will* reappear: B2 will thus have a Restrictive Covenant in relation to No 3; and C will have a Restrictive Covenant in relation to No 2.[106]

There are two possible explanations for this special feature. One is to say that it depends on the 'local law' set up by a scheme of development: each piece of land within the scheme is to have the benefit and burden of the relevant Restrictive Covenants; that result should endure even if parts of the land come into common ownership.[107] However, this is not terribly convincing: a scheme of development (like assignment or annexation) is really no more than a way to allow a party to acquire a Restrictive Covenant, and it is hard to see why the standard rules regulating the Restrictive Covenant should not apply. For example, although a scheme of development can be seen as a form of 'local law', it cannot be used as a means for a *positive* duty to count as a persistent right.

The second explanation is based on practical convenience. If the Restrictive Covenants did not reappear, we would be left with a seemingly odd position. Let us say C plans to use No 3 for a commercial purpose. If the Restrictive Covenant has *not* reappeared, then B2 cannot prevent C from using his land in this way. However, any other owner of land in the scheme of development (eg, B4) *can* intervene to stop C: B4 has a Restrictive Covenant over plot No 3. That Restrictive Covenant existed as soon as B4 acquired his land and cannot be affected by the temporary amalgamation of plot No 2 and plot No 3. It may seem strange that: (i) an owner of another plot, such as B4, can enforce the Restrictive Covenant against C; whereas (ii) B2, the owner of a neighbouring plot cannot. To avoid this supposedly strange result, the courts have allowed B2 to enforce the Restrictive Covenant against C, despite the previous amalgamation of plot No 2 and plot No 3.[108]

It is no surprise to find that, again, practical convenience is used to justify an odd feature of the rules regulating the Restrictive Covenant. However, this particular feature is specific to a scheme of development and is anomalous even when compared to the general rule for Restrictive Covenants: amalgamation of plot No 2 and plot No 3 should terminate any Restrictive Covenants between those two pieces of land. It is debatable that the prospect of B4 having a Restrictive Covenant in relation to plot No 3, whilst B2 does not have such a right, is really so odd as to justify departing from this general rule. It can therefore be argued that courts' current stance is incorrect, as it attaches too much weight to the 'special' nature of a scheme of development.[109]

---

[105] Under the Law Commission's proposals, a 'Land Obligation' can be held by B for the benefit of one plot of land owned by B *and* impose a burden on other land owned by B *provided* each plot has a separate registered title: see Law Com Consultation Paper No 186 (2008), 8.84.

[106] See the Privy Council's decision in *Texaco Antilles Ltd v Kernochan* [1973] AC 609, building on earlier comments of Megarry J in *Brunner v Greenslade* [1971] Ch 993 at 1003.

[107] Presumably, if *all* of the plots were amalgamated in the hands of one owner, the scheme would cease and would not revive simply as a result of the plots again being sold off individually.

[108] See eg *per* Megarry J in *Brunner v Greenslade* [1971] Ch 993 at 1003.

[109] Although note that the view adopted in *Texaco Antilles Ltd v Kernochan* [1973] AC 609 is widely supported: see eg Brooke-Taylor [1977] *Conv* 107 at 116–23.

> **SUMMARY of G6:2.3.3**
>
> The power for parties to enter into a scheme of development is unique. Where such a scheme exists, the parties are subject to a local law, consisting of a set of mutually enforceable Restrictive Covenants. A party acquiring a Freehold or Lease of land within the scheme thus acquires the benefit of a Restrictive Covenant *without* needing to show an assignment or an annexation.
>
> There are two requirements for a scheme of development. First, the original parties to such a scheme must intend to benefit from, and be bound by, the local law. Second, the promises made by each of the original parties to the scheme must identify the land that falls within the scheme. This is essentially the same as the identification requirement of annexation: it fulfils the same function of allowing an owner of land to discover who has a Restrictive Covenant in relation to his land.
>
> Whilst there are said to be further special consequences of a scheme of development, resting on the fact that such a scheme constitutes a 'local law', it is important not to get carried away by the special nature of a scheme of development. For example, a scheme of development does *not* allow a positive duty to be imposed on a party who has not consented to such a duty. A scheme of development, like assignment or annexation, is simply a means of allowing a party to acquire a Restrictive Covenant.

2.4 Simplification? The 'Land Obligation'

The Law Commission has proposed that it should no longer be possible for B to acquire a Restrictive Covenant in relation to registered land; instead, Parliament should introduce a new form of property right: a 'Land Obligation' (see **1.8** above). The formality rules currently applying to property rights in land would therefore regulate the initial acquisition of a Land Obligation (see **E1:2.3**). To initially acquire such a right, B would therefore need to show: (i) that A, by means of a deed, has exercised his power to grant such a right to B; and (ii) that B has substantively registered his Land Obligation.[110] That registration would include both: (i) inclusion of the Land Obligation on the record of B's registered title;[111] and (ii) inclusion of the Land Obligation on the record of A's registered title.[112]

Once registered, B's Land Obligation would *automatically* pass to anyone later acquiring all or any of B's land; provided that: (i) B2's land does in fact benefit from the Land Obligation; and (ii) B has not exercised his power to 'hold back' the Land Obligation by making clear, when giving B2 his right, that he does *not* intend B2 to have the benefit of the Land Obligation.[113] In effect, B's Land Obligation is automatically annexed to each and every part of B's land. However, as under the current law, this can occur only if the land to which B's right is annexed is *clearly identified*. Under the Land Obligation scheme, that identification comes through: (i) the provision of a plan identifying the benefiting land;[114] and (ii) the fact that B's Land Obligation must be included in the registered title of a particular piece of land. This meets the need, discussed in **2.3.2(iv)** and **2.3.3(ii)** above, to ensure that C, a

---

110 See Law Com Consultation Paper No 186 (2008), 8.43, 8.45.
111 This would occur on the proprietorship register of B's registered title (see **E1:n44**).
112 This would occur on the charges register of A's registered title (see **E1:n44**).
113 Law Com Consultation Paper No 186 (2008), 9.8.
114 *Ibid* at 8.40.

party later acquiring all or some of A's land, can discover which parties have a right to control the use of C's land. The ability for B to 'hold back' a Land Obligation also allows B, as in **Example 9** above, to retain exclusive control over A's land by ensuring that B2, despite acquiring some of B's land, does *not* acquire the same right to control the use of A's land.

In a case such as **Example 10a**, the Land Obligation scheme cannot directly assist B2 or B3 to acquire a right as a result of a *later* promise made by B4. However, that scheme would allow B to achieve the same result as currently reached through a scheme of development. Under the scheme, it would be possible for B to have a Land Obligation over his *own land*, provided that there is a separate registered title for each of: (i) the land benefiting from the Land Obligation; and (ii) the land burdened by that right. So, prior to selling to B2, B3 and B4, B could: (i) divide up his land into three plots and separately register each plot; and then (ii) create a mutual scheme of Land Obligations benefiting and burdening each plot.[115]

The scheme proposed by the Law Commission can be seen, from one perspective, as simplifying the law. Where Land Obligations are concerned, there would be no need for separate rules about assignment, annexation or schemes of development. However, B bears the cost of that simplification: he has to make sure, when creating the initial Land Obligation, that he meets a number of formal requirements that do *not* currently apply to the Restrictive Covenant. The right granted by A to B must be *expressly* labelled by the parties as a 'Land Obligation';[116] A and B must provide a plan clearly setting out the land benefiting from the right *and* the land burdened by that right;[117] and B's right must also be substantively registered.[118] This means that if the parties' intention is that the Land Obligation will benefit only a specific part of B's land, B must first separately register that part of the land, so that the Land Obligation can then be included on that registered title. In a case where a scheme of development can currently be used, B must instead divide his land into separate plots and register each of them. In some ways, the Land Obligation scheme is thus *more* technical than the current law. The justification for imposing such extra burdens on B is that the current law is needlessly complex; however, as the **Summary of G6:2** below shows, that assumption is dubious.

SUMMARY of G6:2

To initially acquire a Restrictive Covenant from A, B must show that A is under a duty to B. If that duty arises as a result of A's exercise of his power to make a contractual promise to B, A must exercise that power in signed writing (see section 53(1)(a) of the LPA 1925). Once B has a Restrictive Covenant, there are three methods by which B2 can acquire that right. Assignment is most likely to occur when B gives B2 his Freehold or Lease: B2 simply needs to show that B exercised his power to transfer or duplicate the Restrictive Covenant. Annexation occurs when A makes the original promise giving rise to the Restrictive Covenant. Two requirements must be satisfied: intention and identification. As for intention, A and B must intend that the Restrictive Covenant will pass automatically to later owners of B's land; as for

---

[115] *Ibid* at 8.85.
[116] *Ibid* at 8.25–8.28.
[117] *Ibid* at 8.40.
[118] If B fails to substantively register, he will have an Equitable Land Obligation if he can show that A is under a duty to grant him that right (see Law Com Consultation Paper No 186 (2008), 8.45–8.47). This accords with the principle discussed in **E2:1.3.1**.

identification, A's promise must allow the land to which the Restrictive Covenant is annexed to be easily ascertained. A scheme of development arises between two or more neighbours, each of whom participates in a set of mutual Restrictive Covenants. Two requirements must be satisfied: intention and identification. As for intention, the vendors and purchasers must intend that each owner of land within the scheme will get the benefit of a Restrictive Covenant over other land in the scheme, whilst also accepting the burden of a Restrictive Covenant over his land, held by owners of the other land in the scheme. As for identification, the terms of each sale must allow the land falling within the scheme to be easily ascertained. In contrast to assignment and annexation, a scheme of development can also be used by B2 to acquire a Restrictive Covenant arising from a promise made *after* B2 acquired his Freehold or Lease.

These rules, regulating the acquisition of a Restrictive Covenant by B2, are widely regarded as unduly complex and uncertain.[119] First, it is said that confusion is caused by the fact that there are three different methods. Second, it is said that the rules regulating each of these three methods are themselves overly technical. Finally, and underlying both those complaints, is the unflattering contrast with the rules relating to Easements. The later acquisition by B2 of an Easement initially acquired by B is simplicity itself: B2 simply needs to show that: (i) he has acquired a Freehold or Lease from B of all or any part of the land benefiting from B's Easement; and (ii) that B2's Freehold or Lease itself benefits from that Easement (see **G5:2.1.1(ii)**).

However, it is easy to overstate these criticisms. There is no need for the mere existence of three separate methods, each with its own distinct role, to cause confusion. Nor are the rules regulating each method unduly technical or complex. Assignment is based on the general principle that B can transfer a persistent right to B2, coupled with B's special power to duplicate a Restrictive Covenant. As for a scheme of development, there are just two key requirements: intention and identification. Those two requirements are also crucial to annexation. Thanks to section 78, there is already an assumption that the intention requirement has been met. And, as acknowledged by the Law Commission in its Land Obligations proposal,[120] the identification requirement is necessary as it provides certainty and publicity to C: it enables him easily to discover who has a Restrictive Covenant over his land.

Finally, the current differences with the Easement can be justified. There is a clear difference between the **content** of each right; it is no surprise that the **acquisition** rules also differ. And the current law depends on the key distinction between property rights and persistent rights. As the Restrictive Covenant is a persistent right (albeit an anomalous one), it depends on A being under a duty to B. Prima facie, that duty is owed to B alone: special factors (eg, assignment, annexation or a scheme of development) must be present before B2 can also take the benefit of that duty. As recognised by the Law Commission, any change to the current rules must therefore involve the bold step of preventing the Restrictive Covenant from existing as a persistent right and instead recognising a new form of property right in land.

[119] See eg Law Com Consultation Paper No 186 (2008), 7.37, 9.1.
[120] *Ibid*, 8.39, 8.40.

3 THE DEFENCES QUESTION

If B (or B2) has a Restrictive Covenant in relation to A's land, he has a persistent right: a right against A's Freehold or Lease. B will therefore have a prima facie power to assert that right against C, a party who later acquires a right that depends on A's Freehold or Lease.[121] However, C may have a defence to B's pre-existing Restrictive Covenant.

3.1 The lack of registration defence

If C: (i) acquires a property right for value; then (ii) C has a defence to any pre-existing persistent right of B *unless* (a) that right has been defensively registered *or* (b) B is in actual occupation of A's land when C commits to acquiring his right. In practice, it is very unlikely that B will be in actual occupation of A's land. So, to protect his Restrictive Covenant, B needs to ensure that he defensively registers that right by entering a notice on the register. That notice will allow C to discover the Restrictive Covenant before deciding to acquire a right from A.

3.2 Consent: waiver of a restrictive covenant

A Restrictive Covenant can end for good if B, the current holder of that right, exercises his power to waive the right (see 1.5 above). Strictly speaking, such a waiver does not give C a defence to B's Restrictive Covenant; instead, it destroys B's right.

3.3 Apparent consent: estoppel

If C incorrectly, but reasonably, believes that B has waived his Restrictive Covenant, C is in a similar position to a party who incorrectly, but reasonably, believes that B has released an Easement. In such a case, C may be able to rely on *defensive estoppel* (or, perhaps, proprietary estoppel) if B attempts to assert his right against C (see G5:3.3). It is clear that C does not have a defence because of the *mere fact* that B does not immediately object to C's breach of the Restrictive Covenant.[122] However, C can have a defence if, for example: (i) B, to C's knowledge, does not complain when C, in a breach of a Restrictive Covenant, begins to build on C's land; and (ii) C relies on B's acquiescence by continuing to build; and (iii) C would suffer a detriment if B were now able to assert his Restrictive Covenant: B may then be prevented from asserting that right against C.[123]

3.4 The limitation defence

The Limitation Act 1980 does not provide any specific rules where B wishes to assert a Restrictive Covenant against C. The lapse of time alone therefore cannot give C a defence to B's pre-existing Restrictive Covenant, although it may be relevant when considering the remedies question (see too G5:3.4).

---

[121] Anomalously, B also has a prima facie power to assert his right against a party who later *independently* acquires a Freehold of A's land: see *re Nisbet & Potts Contract* [1906] 1 Ch 386 (see Example 4b above).

[122] See eg *per* Aldous LJ in *Jones v Stones* [1999] 1 WLR 1739 at 1745–6 (that case did not involve a Restrictive Covenant, but did consider the general principles of defensive estoppel).

[123] See eg *Gafford v Graham* (1998) 77 P & CR 73.

First, the doctrine of 'laches' may be relevant: it may be that, due to the lapse of time, C can show he would suffer an unfair prejudice were B allowed to assert his right against C (see **D2:3.7**). Second, a court may also take into account the lapse of time when deciding whether to specifically protect B's right. For example, if C, in breach of a Restrictive Covenant, has built a number of houses, which are now occupied by third parties, the court is extremely unlikely to order C to demolish those houses.[124] In contrast, if B had applied for an injunction as soon as C began building, a court may have ordered C to cease.

The lapse of time may also be relevant in rendering B's Restrictive Covenant obsolete. For example, it may be that a Restrictive Covenant preventing C building on his land no longer serves any purpose, as the character of the surrounding neighbourhood has radically changed. In such a case, C can apply to the Lands Tribunal, a body that has a statutory power under section 84 of the LPA 1925 to discharge or modify Restrictive Covenants (see **1.5** above).[125]

3.5   The 'Land Obligation'

Under the Law Commission's proposed scheme, a Land Obligation counts as a property right rather than as a persistent right. We would therefore expect it to be very difficult for C to have a defence against such a right. Certainly, to acquire his Land Obligation in the first place, B must ensure that it is registered: this will include registration of the right on the charges register relating to A's land. As a result, *if* B has a Land Obligation,[126] it will be impossible for C to rely on the lack of registration defence. However, under the Law Commission's proposals, C may be able to benefit from the Lands Tribunal's extended power to modify or discharge a Land Obligation (see **1.5** above).

4   THE REMEDIES QUESTION

4.1   Preface: the protection of B's Restrictive Covenant

Like all persistent rights, the Restrictive Covenant is protected through B's exercise of his power to impose a duty on C. Once that duty is imposed either because of: (i) B's exercise of his power; or (ii) C's independent awareness of B's pre-existing Restrictive Covenant, the remedies question arises: how will a court protect B's right against C? The crucial issue, as usual, is whether B's right will be *specifically protected*.

4.2   Specific protection

4.2.1 The risk of future interference with B's Restrictive Covenant

If B can show that there is a risk of C breaching the duty imposed by the Restrictive

---

[124] See eg *Wrotham Park Estate Co v Parkside Homes Ltd* [1974] 1 WLR 798.

[125] A change in the character of a neighbourhood can also be taken account by a court in declining to specifically protect B's Restrictive Covenant: see eg *Duke of Bedford v Trustees of British Museum* (1822) My & K 552.

[126] If B has failed to register his right and has only an Equitable Land Obligation (see **n 118** above), that right will be vulnerable to the lack of registration defence: like any persistent right, it will be immune from that defence only if B is in actual occupation of A's land when C commits to acquiring his right (see **E2:3.6.2**).

Covenant (eg, a duty not to use C's land for a commercial purpose), B's right will, in general, be specifically protected. The starting point is that a court will grant an injunction ordering C not to breach his duty to B. As we have come to expect where C's duty relates to land, B is not forced to settle for receiving money from C. However, we have seen that, in relatively rare cases, a court may decline to order an injunction, even where C's action interferes with B's *property right* in land (see **G1A:4.2** and **G5:4.2**). The principles discussed there apply in exactly the same way where B has a Restrictive Covenant.

4.2.2 Past interference with B's Restrictive Covenant

Where C has already interfered with B's Restrictive Covenant and that interference is not continuing, ordering C to pay money is the primary way of protecting B's right: after all, it is generally too late for B's right to be specifically protected. However, in rare cases, B may be able to obtain an injunction ordering C to reverse his past act. For example, let us say: (i) B's Restrictive Covenant imposes a duty on C not to build on C's land; and (ii) C breaches that duty by constructing a new building on C's land. In such a case, it is possible for a court to order C to reverse his interference by pulling down the building.[127]

Not surprisingly, the courts have indicated that care must be taken before ordering such a dramatic remedy.[128] The payment of money is the primary remedy, and specific protection will be reserved for special cases in which, for example, C has acted at his own risk by continuing to build despite objections from the B or B2.[129] The court will also take into account the waste, and harm to third parties, that could be caused by ordering C to reverse his wrong.

E2:EXAMPLE 26

B and C have neighbouring Freeholds. C is bound by B's pre-existing Restrictive Covenant: as a result, C is under a duty to B not to build more than 60 houses on C's land. C breaches that duty by building and selling 90 houses.

In such a case, as confirmed by the Court of Appeal in *Wrotham Park Estate Co Ltd v Parkside Homes Ltd*,[130] a court will *not* order C to pull down 30 houses: after all, this would have a drastic effect on the residents of those houses.

4.3   Money awards

4.3.1 Money as a substitute for B's right

In **E2:Example 26** B has to settle for receiving money from C. But how should a court calculate the sum to be paid by C? In *Wrotham Park*, C pointed out that B had suffered no real consequential loss as a result of C's breach of his duty to B. In particular, B could not show that the value of his land was affected by the fact that B lived near an estate with 90

---

[127] See eg *Lawrence v Horton* (1890) 59 LJ Ch 440 (an Easement case, but the same principles should apply); *Wakeham v Wood* (1981) 43 P & CR 40.

[128] See eg *Shepherd Homes Ltd v Sandham* [1971] Ch 340.

[129] This was the case in *Lawrence v Horton* (1890) 59 LJ Ch 440: C continued to build even after receiving a written complaint from B.

[130] [1974] 1 WLR 798.

houses, rather than 60 houses. However, this does not mean that C should have to pay *nothing* to B. Compensating B for consequential loss is only *one* of the purposes served when ordering C, as a result of his wrong, to pay money to B. B should also receive money as a substitute for the right C has interfered with. This can explain why, in *Wrotham Park*, the Court of Appeal ordered C to pay a sum of money to B: that money can be seen as a substitute for B's right (see **E2:4.3.1**).

4.3.2 Money as compensation for B's consequential loss

In some cases, in contrast to **E2:Example 26**, C's breach of a Restrictive Covenant can cause B relevant consequential loss. For example, if C breaches a duty not to run a rival business from his land, that may cause a drop in the profits of B's business. Such loss is a reasonably foreseeable consequence of C's breach of duty: B can therefore recover compensation in respect of it.

4.3.3 Money to remove C's gain?

Where C commits a wrong against B, there may be rare cases in which C can be ordered to pay B exemplary or punitive damages based in part on the gain C has made by committing that wrong (see **D1:4.3.3**). A possible example may be where: (i) C has deliberately interfered with B's Restrictive Covenant; and (ii) C has made a profit by doing so; and (iii) due to the intervention of third parties, a court will not order C to reverse his wrong.

The decision in *Wrotham Park* is often seen as providing evidence that, if C breaches a Restrictive Covenant, C will be more readily ordered to pay B money based on C's gain.[131] It is often suggested that the decision depends on a *special rule* that gain-based damages are available if C interferes with a property right or persistent right of B.[132] However, to understand *Wrotham Park*, there is no need to engage with the difficult and controversial question of when, if at all, gain-based damages should be available. The award in that case is best understood as based on the general principle that C can be ordered to pay B money as a substitute for B's right (see **E2:4.3.1**). On that view, the *Wrotham Park* result does *not* depend on the fact that B had a persistent right: the same principles should apply whether C's duty to B not to build more than 60 houses comes from: (i) a Restrictive Covenant; or (ii) a direct personal right of B.[133]

---

[131] In *Attorney-General v Blake* [2001] 1 AC 268 at 283, Lord Nicholls referred to the decision in *Wrotham Park* as a very rare example (a 'solitary beacon') of restitutionary damages being awarded for a breach of a contractual duty. See too *per* Steyn LJ in *Surrey CC v Bredero Homes Ltd* [1993] 1 WLR 1361 at 1369.

[132] See eg *per* Megarry V-C in *Tito v Waddell (No 2)* [1977] Ch 106 at 335–6; *per* Steyn LJ in *Surrey CC v Bredero Homes Ltd* [1993] 1 WLR 1361 at 1369–70; Burrows, *Remedies for Torts and Breach of Contract* (3rd edn, 2004), 398.

[133] See Lord Nicholls in *Attorney-General v Blake* [2001] 1 AC 268 at 283: 'It is not easy to see why, as between the parties to a contract, a violation of a party's contractual rights should attract a lesser degree of remedy than a violation of his property rights.' However, if B has only a personal right against C, the value of that right must be lower than the value of a Restrictive Covenant: after all, B has no protection if C sells his land to C2. This may explain the otherwise puzzling decision of the Court of Appeal in *Surrey CC v Bredero Homes Ltd* [1993] 1 WLR 1361. That case was very similar to *Wrotham Park*, but B was awarded only nominal damages. The best explanation may be that B's right, as it was only a *personal right*, was simply less valuable than that of the claimant in *Wrotham Park*.

4.4 The 'Land Obligation'

Under the Law Commission's proposed scheme, a new cause of action would be introduced where A or C interferes with B's Land Obligation.[134] The principles set out here could also be used by a court deciding how to enforce B's Land Obligation. In cases where B's Land Obligation imposes a *positive* duty on C, special considerations would arise: those factors are already taken into account where B has a direct right that imposes a positive duty on C (see G1A:4.2).

5 COMPARING THE RESTRICTIVE COVENANT AND THE EASEMENT

5.1 Introduction

There are many good reasons for comparing the Restrictive Covenant with the Easement. Conceptually, a comparison can help us to understand the essential nature of each right. As we have seen, the analogy to the Easement was very important in the development of the Restrictive Covenant. The latter right has often been seen, from an early stage of its life as a persistent right, as an 'an extension in equity of the doctrine of negative easements'.[135] And some of the more recent changes in the rules regulating the Restrictive Covenant also have the effect, and possibly the purpose, of aligning the Restrictive Covenant with the Easement.[136] Practically, a comparison can help us to evaluate proposals that the Restrictive Covenant and the Easement should be treated together, under one unitary scheme regulating the means by which B can assert some control over land neighbouring his own. This is a very topical task: the Law Commission's Consultation Paper No 186 (2008), whilst resiling from an earlier plan to unify Easements and Restrictive Covenants in a single structure,[137] does propose the creation of a 'Land Obligation'—essentially a new form of Restrictive Covenant that is, in important ways, modelled on the Easement.

5.2 The starting point

The basic conceptual starting point is that the Restrictive Covenant and the Easement are two quite different rights. First, we can look at the **content question**. The crucial point here is that the Easement counts as a property right; the Restrictive Covenant as a persistent right. The Easement, like other forms of property right, allows B to make a particular use of a thing (A's land). As a result of that right, the rest of the world is under a prima facie duty to B. The Restrictive Covenant, like other forms of persistent right, is instead *based* on a

---

[134] Law Com Consultation Paper No 186 (2008), 8.90.

[135] *Per* Sir George Jessel MR in *London & South Western Railway Co v Gomm* (1882) 20 Ch D 562 at 583; approved by Vaughan Williams LJ in *Formby v Barker* [1903] 2 Ch 539 at 552–3; and by Cozens-Hardy LJ in *re Nisbet & Potts Contract* [1906] 1 Ch 386 at 402.

[136] For example, see the discussion in 5.3 below of the decision in *Federated Homes v Mill Lodge Properties Ltd* [1980] 1 WLR 594.

[137] Law Com Consultation Paper No 186 (2008), 15.2ff. The earlier plan was put forward in Law Com No 127 (1984): it was not acted on by Parliament.

duty of A: in this case, a duty not to make a particular use of A's land. Hence in order to count as an Easement a right must do more than simply impose a negative burden on A's land (see G5:1.1.2);[138] in contrast, a Restrictive Covenant arises precisely because A is under a duty *not* to act in a particular way.

Second, we can look at the **acquisition question**. An Easement can be acquired both dependently (where A exercises his power to give B an Easement) and, it seems, independently (as a result of prescription).[139] A Restrictive Covenant, like all persistent rights, can only be acquired dependently: A needs to act in such a way as to come under a duty to B. And dependent acquisition seems to operate differently for each of the two rights. There are a number of situations in which the courts can *infer*, from the surrounding circumstances, that A exercised his power to give B an Easement. In such a case, A does not need expressly to give B an Easement; B can instead acquire an implied Easement (see G5:2.4 and G5:2.6). In contrast, whilst it may be possible for the courts to assume, from the surrounding circumstances, that A made a particular promise to B not to use his land in a particular way (see **Example 6b** above) there is no set of recognised circumstances in which such an inference is made. So, the *specific* methods of acquiring an implied Easement (see G5:2.5 and G5:2.7) cannot be used to acquire an implied Restrictive Covenant.

In addition, A's power to give B an Easement, and his power to make a promise to B that counts as a Restrictive Covenant, are regulated by different formality rules. Where A expressly attempts to give B an Easement, B can only acquire that right if: (i) a deed has been used (see section 52 of the LPA 1925); *and* (ii) B substantively registers his right (see section 27(2)(d) of the LRA 2002). Where B claims an implied Easement, (ii) is not necessary, but (i) still applies. In contrast, a Restrictive Covenant, like all other persistent rights, can be acquired without registration, and without a deed. The basic rule is that B instead needs to show that A's promise was made in writing signed by A (see section 53(1)(a) of the LPA 1925).

Third, we can look at the **defences question**. An Easement counts as a property right and it is therefore very difficult for C to have a defence to it. In fact, as we saw in G5:3.1 , it is almost impossible for C to use the lack of registration defence against an Easement. In contrast, if B does not protect his Restrictive Covenant by defensively registering it, his right will be vulnerable to the lack of registration defence: unlike an Easement, a Restrictive Covenant can only count as an overriding interest if B is in actual occupation of A's land.

Finally, we can look at the **remedies question**. It does seem possible to say that, as far as remedies are concerned, the Easement and the Restrictive Covenant can be governed by a unitary regime. The same basic principles apply to each type of right. However, those principles also apply where B has a *direct* personal right against C that relates to C's land. So this apparent similarity may tell us little about the nature of the Easement and the Restrictive Covenant, other than the fact that each applies in the same context: a dispute about the use of a neighbour's land.

It is worth noting that the Equitable Easement does share some of the important features

---

[138] Law Com Consultation Paper No 186 (2008) adopts (eg at 15.32ff) the orthodox view that there is a category of 'negative' Easements (see G5:1.1.2). It then asks whether such Easements should be abolished in order to avoid an overlap with the proposed Land Obligation (at 15.42). On the view taken here, there is *already* no such overlap between Easements and the duties not to act that can be imposed by a Restrictive Covenant.

[139] Although, as noted in G5:2.8.1 , this is a novel analysis of prescription.

of a Restrictive Covenant. It is a persistent right; it can be acquired without registration or a deed; and it is equally vulnerable to the lack of registration defence. However, the crucial difference is that an Equitable Easement arises only where A is under a duty to grant B an Easement. The Equitable Easement is therefore dependent on the content of the Easement: if A is under a duty to give B a right that does *not* count as an Easement, B *cannot* acquire an Equitable Easement. In contrast, a Restrictive Covenant simply depends on A being under a duty not to make a particular use of A's land. As a result, it would be wrong to think that a Restrictive Covenant is somehow equivalent to an Equitable Easement.

5.3 Convergence?

The starting point is that, with the exception of the **remedies question**, there are clear differences between the Easement and the Restrictive Covenant. On this view, there would be no point in adopting a unitary regime for the two rights—unless of course, the aim is to effect a radical change in the law. However, there are some suggestions of a more gradual, and limited, convergence between the two rights. These changes have involved the Restrictive Covenant departing from its basis as a persistent right and instead acquiring *some* of the characteristics of a property right. For example, the decision that a Restrictive Covenant can bind C even if C *independently* acquires a right in A's land[140] narrows one gap between the Restrictive Covenant and the Easement. Nonetheless, it is still clear that a Restrictive Covenant is not a property right: unlike an Easement, it is *not* prima facie binding on third parties who have not acquired any right in relation to A's land.

More recently, the decision in *Federated Homes v Mill Lodge Properties Ltd*[141] narrowed another gap between the Restrictive Covenant and the Easement. It did so by making it easier for a court to find that A and B exercised their power to annex a Restrictive Covenant to each and every part of B's land so that B's Restrictive Covenant, like an Easement, will automatically pass to B2, a later owner of all or part of B's land (see **2.3.2(iii)** above). Nonetheless, there is still a clear difference between a Restrictive Covenant and an Easement: the latter automatically becomes part and parcel of each and every part of B's land; a Restrictive Covenant has the same effect only *if* A and B *choose* to exercise their power to annex B's Restrictive Covenant to each and every part of B's land. And, as shown by the Court of Appeal's decision in *Crest Nicholson Residential (South) Ltd v McAllister*,[142] there may well be situations in which A and B choose *not* to exercise that power.

The steps taken towards convergence have, so far, been very small. A genuinely unitary scheme would have to go much further. However, it is doubtful that such a scheme is needed. The differences between the Easement and the Restrictive Covenant are readily understandable, given that the former is a property right and the latter a persistent right. The rules that the Law Commission proposes for the regulation of Land Obligations do more closely resemble those applying to Easements; but that is no surprise given the Law Commission's proposal that a Land Obligation should count as a property right rather than as an 'Equitable property right' (ie, as a persistent right).

---

[140] *In re Nisbet & Potts Contract* [1906] 1 Ch 386.
[141] [1980] 1 WLR 594.
[142] [2004] 1 WLR 2409 at [34].

SUMMARY of G6:5

Calls for a unification, and simplification, of the Easement and the Restrictive Covenant are frequently made, and rarely opposed. However, the analysis set out here suggests that those calls should be resisted. At a very general level, the Easement and the Restrictive Covenant play a similar role, in regulating the positions of neighbouring landowners. However, there are many other rights that can perform the same function: for example (i) B's Freehold or Lease imposes certain duties on his neighbours (see **G1A:4.1.2** and **G1A:4.1.3**); and (ii) B may have a direct right against a neighbour (see **E3**). And there is no suggestion that all these different rights should be unified, just because they can apply between neighbours. Context is not everything; instead, we need to look more closely at the true nature of the Easement and the Restrictive Covenant. And, when we look at the **content, acquisition** and **defences questions**, it becomes clear that the two rights are, in fact, quite different. It is crucial not to overlook the distinction between: (i) property rights; and (ii) persistent rights.

SELECT BIBLIOGRAPHY

H Beale et al, *The Law of Personal Property Security* (Oxford, Oxford University Press, 2007).

J Beatson, *The Use and Abuse of Unjust Enrichment* (Oxford, Clarendon Press, 1991).

J Bentham, *Rationale of Judicial Evidence* (London, 1827).

P Birks, *An Introduction to the Law of Restitution* (Oxford, Clarendon Press, 1985).

——, (ed), *Laundering and Tracing* (Oxford, Clarendon Press, 1995).

——, (ed) *The Classification of Obligations* (Oxford, Oxford University Press, 1997) .

——, *Unjust Enrichment* (2nd edn, Oxford, Oxford University Press, 2005).

P Birks and G McLeod (trs), *Justinian's Institutes* (London, Duckworth, 1987).

P Birks and A Pretto, *Breach of Trust* (Oxford, Hart Publishing, 2002).

P Birks and FD Rose, (eds), *Restitution and Equity,* vol 1: *Resulting Trusts and Equitable Compensation* (London, Mansfield Press, 2000).

Lord Blackburn, *A Treatise on the Effect of the Contract of Sale* (London, W Benning, 1845).

M Bridge, *The Sale of Goods* (Oxford, Oxford University Press, 1997).

——, *Personal Property* (3rd edn, Oxford, Oxford University Press, 2002).

S Bright (ed), *Landlord and Tenant Law: Past, Present and Future* (Oxford, Hart Publishing, 2006).

——, *Landlord and Tenant Law in Context* (Oxford, Hart Publishing, 2007).

S Bright and J Dewar (eds), *Land Law: Themes and Perspectives* (Oxford, Oxford University Press, 1998).

E Burn and J Cartwright, *Cheshire & Burn's Modern Law of Real Property,* 17th edn (Oxford, Oxford University Press, 2006).

A Burrows (ed), *Essays on the Law of Restitution* (Oxford, Clarendon Press, 1991).

——, *The Law of Restitution* (2nd edn, Oxford, Oxford University Press, 2004).

——, *Remedies for Torts and Breach of Contract* 3rd edn (London, LexisNexis UK, 2004).

——, *A Casebook on Contract* (Oxford, Hart Publishing, 2007).

—— (ed), *English Private Law* (2nd edn, Oxford, Oxford University Press, 2007).

A Burrows, E McKendrick and J Edelman, *Cases and Materials on the Law of Restitution* (2nd edn, Oxford, Oxford University Press, 2006).

A Burrows and A Rodger (ed), *Mapping the Law: Essays in Memory of Peter Birks* (Oxford, Oxford University Press, 2006).

R Chambers, *Resulting Trusts* (Oxford, Clarendon Press, 1997).

——, *An Introduction to Property Law in Australia* (2nd edn, Pyrmont, New South Wales, LawBook Co, 2008).

A Clarke and P Kohler, *Property Law: Commentary and Materials* (Cambridge, Cambridge University Press,2005).

E Coke, *Commentaries on Littleton* (reissued, London, Brooke, 1809).

E Cooke (eds), *Modern Studies in Property Law,* vol 1 (Oxford, Hart Publishing, 2001) and vol 3 (Oxford, Hart Publishing, 2005) .

——, *Land Law* (Oxford, Clarendon Press, 2006).

W Cornish et al (eds), *Restitution: Past, Present & Future: Essays in Honour of Gareth Jones* (Oxford, Hart Publishing, 1998).

S Degeling and J Edelman, *Equity and Commercial Law* (Sydney, Lawbook Co, 2005) .

Department of Trade and Industry, *A Review of Security Interests in Property* (London, Stationary Office Books, 1989).

M Dixon et al (eds), *Ruoff and Roper's Law and Practice of Registered Conveyancing* (London, Sweet and Maxwell, 2003).

M Dixon and G Griffiths (eds), *New Twists in the Tale: Contemporary Perspectives in Property, Equity and Trusts* (Oxford, Oxford University Press, 2007).

A Dugdale, M Jones and M Simpson, *Clerk and Lindsell on Torts* (19th edn, London, Sweet & Maxwell,2006).

J Edelman, *Gain-Based Damages: Contract, Tort, Equity and Intellectual Property* (Oxford, Hart Publishing, 2002).

J Eekelaar and J Bell (eds), *Oxford Essays in Jurisprudence* (3rd Series, Oxford, Oxford University Press, 1987) .

L Fox, *Conceptualising Home: Theories, Law and Policies* (Oxford, Hart Publishing, 2007).

S Gardner, *Introduction to the Law of Trusts* (2nd edn, Oxford, Clarendon Press, 2003).

——, *Introduction to Land Law* (Oxford, Hart Publishing, 2007) .

J Gaunt and P Morgan (eds), *Gale on Easements* (18th edn, London, Sweet & Maxwell, 2002).

J Getzler et al (eds), *Rationalizing Property, Equity and Trusts: Essays in Honour of Edward Burn* (London, LexisNexis UK, 2003) .

J Getzler and J Payne (eds), *Company Charges: Spectrum and Beyond* (Oxford, Oxford University Press, 2006) .

R Goode, *Hire-Purchase Law and Practice* (2nd edn, London, Butterworth, 1970).

——, *Legal Problems of Credit and Security* (3rd edn, London, Sweet & Maxwell, 2003).

——, *Commercial Law* (3rd edn, London, Penguin, 2004).

A Goodhart, *Essays in Jurisprudence and the Common Law* (Cambridge, Cambridge University Press, 1931).

A Guest et al, *Benjamin's Sale of Goods* (7th edn, London, Sweet & Maxwell, 2007).

K Gray and S Gray, *Elements of Land Law* (4th edn, London, LexisNexis UK, 2005).

J Hackney, *Understanding Equity and Trusts* (London, Fontana, 1987) .

K Handley, *Estoppel by Conduct & Election* (London, Sweet & Maxwell,2006).

C Harpum et al, *Megarry and Wade: The Law of Real Property* (6th edn, London, Sweet & Maxwell, 2000).

C Harpum and J Bignell, *Registered Land: Law and Practice under the Land Registration Act 2002* (Bristol, Jordans, 2004).

J Harris, *Property and Justice* (Oxford, Clarendon Press, 1996).

—— (ed), *Property Problems: From Genes to Pension Funds* (London, Kluwer Law International, 1993).

H Hart, *The Concept of Law* (2nd edn, Oxford, Clarendon Press, 1994).

D Hayton, P Matthews, C Mitchell, *Underhill & Hayton's Law Relating to Trustees* (17th edn, Butterworths, London, 2006).

A Hudson, *New Perspectives on Property Law, Obligations and Restitution* (London, Cavendish, 2004) .

J Johnson and F Miller, *The Man Who Sold the Eiffel Tower* (London, W H Allen, 1962).

G Jones, *Goff & Jones' The Law of Restitution* (7th edn, London, Sweet and Maxwell, 2007).

G Jones and W Swadling (eds), *The Search for Principle: Essays in Honour of Lord Goff of Chieveley* (Oxford, Oxford University Press, 1999).

H Kotz and T Weir (trs), *European Contract Law: Formation, Validity, and Content of Contract—Contract and Third Parties* vol 1 *European Contract Law* (Oxford, Clarendon Press, 1997).

F Lawson and B Rudden, *The Law of Property* (3rd edn, Oxford, Clarendon Press, 2002).

M Lupoi, *Trusts Laws of the World: A Collection of Original Texts* (Rome, ETI Editore, 1996).

M Lupoi and S Dix, *Trusts: A Comparative Study* (Cambridge, Cambridge University Press, 2000).

F Maitland, *Equity, Also the Forms of Action at Common Law: Two Courses of Lectures* (Cambridge, Cambridge University Press, 1909).

N McBride and R Bagshaw, *Tort Law* (2nd edn, Harlow, Longman, 2005).

J McGhee (ed), *Snell's Equity* (31st edn, London, Sweet and Maxwell, 2005).

R Meagher, W Gummow and JRF Lehane, *Equity: Doctrine and Remedies* (4th edn, Sydney, Butterworths LexisNexis, 2002).

C Mitchell and P Mitchell (eds), *Landmark Cases in the Law of Restitution* (Oxford, Hart Publishing, 2006).

C Mitchell and S Watterson, *Subrogation: Law and Practice* (2nd edn, Oxford University Press, Oxford 2007).

A Mowbray, *The Development of Positive Obligations under the European Convention on Human Rights by the European Court of Human Rights* (Oxford, Hart Publishing, 2004).

J Mowbray et al, *Lewin on Trusts* (18th edn, London, Sweet & Maxwell, 2008).

B Nicholas, *An Introduction to Roman Law* (Oxford, Clarendon Press, 1962).

D O'Sullivan, S Elliott and R Zakrzewski, *The Law of Rescission* (Oxford, Oxford University Press, 2008).

A Oakley, *Parker & Mellows' Modern Law of Trusts* (8th edn, London, Sweet & Maxwell, 2003).

N Palmer and E McKendrick (eds), *Interests in Goods* (2nd edn, London, LLP Professional Publishing, 1998).

E Peel, *Treitel's Law of Contract* (12th edn, Sweet and Maxwell, 2007).

J Penner, *The Idea of Property in Law* (Oxford, Oxford University Press, 1997).

F Pollock and R Wright, *Possession in the Common Law* (Oxford, Clarendon Press, 1888).

F Pollock and F Maitland, *History of English Law before the time of Edward I* (2nd edn reissue, Cambridge, Cambridge University Press, 1968).

C Preston and G Newson, *Restrictive Covenants Affecting Freehold Land* (9th edn, London, Sweet & Maxwell, 1998).

A Pretto-Sakmann, *Boundaries of Personal Property Law: Shares and Sub-Shares* (Oxford, Hart Publishing, 2005).

C Proctor (ed), *Mann on the Legal Aspect of Money* (6th edn, Oxford, Oxford University Press, 2005).

C Rickett and R Grantham (eds), *Structure and Justification in Private Law: Essays for Peter Birks* (Oxford, Hart Publishing, 2008).

D Rook, *Property Law and Human Rights* (Oxford, Blackstone Press, 2001).

C Rotherham, *Proprietary Remedies in Context* (Oxford, Hart Publishing, 2002).

A Simpson, *A History of the Land Law* (2nd edn, Oxford, Oxford University Press, 1986).

L Smith, *The Law of Tracing* (Oxford, Clarendon Press, 1997).

M Smith, *The Law of Assignment: The Creation and Transfer of Choses in Action* (Oxford, Oxford University Press, 2007).

R Smith, *Plural Ownership* (Oxford, Oxford University Press, 2005).

——, *Property Law* (5th edn, Harlow, Longman, 2006).

M Spence, *Protecting Reliance: The Emerging Doctrine of Equitable Estoppel* (Oxford, Hart Publishing, 1999).

——, *Intellectual Property* (Oxford, Clarendon Press, 2007).

R Stevens, *Torts and Rights* (Oxford, Oxford University Press, 2007).

W Swadling (ed), *The Limits of Restitutionary Claims: A Comparative Analysis* (Edinburgh, United Kingdom National Committee of Comparative Law, 1997).

—— (ed), *The Quistclose Trust: Critical Essays* (Oxford, Hart Publishing, 2004).

L Tee (ed) *Land Law: Issues, Debates, Policy* (Cullompton, Willan, 2002).

E Tyler & N Palmer, *Crossely Vaines' Personal Property* (5th edn, Butterworths, London, 1973).

G Virgo, *The Principles of the Law of Restitution* (2nd edn, Oxford, Oxford University Press, 2006).

T Weir, *Tort Law* (Oxford, Clarendon Press, 2002).

G Woodbine and S Thorne (eds), *Bracton de Legibus et Consuetudinibus Angliae* (London, Publications of the Selden Society, 1968–77).

S Worthington, *Proprietary Interests in Commercial Transactions* (Oxford, Clarendon Press, 1997).

——, *Personal Property: Cases and Materials* (Oxford, Hart Publishing, 2000).

——, *Equity* (2nd edn, Oxford, Clarendon Press, 2006).

F De Zulueta (trs), *The Institutes of Gaius: Text with Critical Notes and Translation* (Oxford, Clarendon Press, 1946).

INDEX

Introductory note

References such as '178–9' indicate (not necessarily continuous) discussion of a topic across a range of pages. Where a topic has more than one reference, page numbers in bold indicate particularly significant discussions of that topic. References to the definition of a specific term are also highlighted in bold. Some topics (eg, Co-Ownership; direct rights) are divided into a general entry and an entry for references specific to land.